The SAGE
Handbook *of*

Special
Education

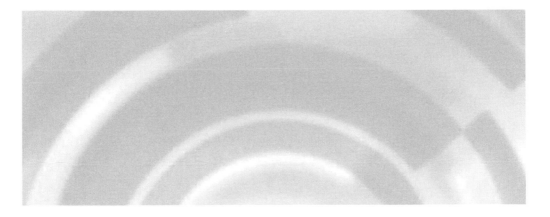

The SAGE
Handbook *of*
Special
Education

Edited by

Lani Florian

SAGE Publications
London • Thousand Oaks • New Delhi

SAGE Publications Ltd
1 Oliver's Yard
55 City Road
London EC1Y 1SP

SAGE Publications Inc.
2455 Teller Road
Thousand Oaks, California 91320

SAGE Publications India Pvt Ltd
B-42, Panchsheel Enclave
Post Box 4109
New Delhi 110 017

British Library Cataloguing in Publication data

A catalogue record for this book is available from
the British Library

ISBN 10 1 4129 0728 4   ISBN 13 978 1 4129 0728 6
ISBN 10 1 4129 0729 2   ISBN 13 978 1 4129 0729 3 (pbk)

Library of Congress Control Number: 2006922307

Typeset by Dorwyn, Wells, Somerset
Printed in Great Britain by The Cromwell Press Ltd, Trowbridge, Wiltshire
Printed on paper from sustainable resources

Contents

List of figures

List of tables

Contributors

Anupam Ahuja is an international consultant on inclusion and the development and review of educational programmes. She works with the National Council of Educational Research and Training in Delhi and is a founding member of EENET Asia. Over the past 20 years she has initiated, led and evaluated inclusive programmes in Africa, Asia and eastern Europe for UNESCO, UNICEF, World Bank, Braillo Norway, Save the Children and other international organizations, and has contributed to many international publications on education and school improvement.

Mel Ainscow is Professor of Education and co-director of the Centre for Equity in Education at the University of Manchester, UK. His work attempts to explore connections between inclusion, teacher development and school improvement. Mel was director of a UNESCO Teacher Education project on inclusive education which involved research and development in over 80 countries, and is co-director of the school improvement network Improving the Quality of Education for All (IQEA). He was until recently a member of the National Curriculum and Assessment Committee; he is consultant to UNESCO, UNICEF and Save the Children; and is Marden Visiting Professor at the Hong Kong Institute of Education.

Julie Alonzo is a PhD candidate in Educational Leadership at the University of Oregon, specializing in Learning Assessments/Systems Performance. Prior to beginning her doctoral studies, she spent 12 years as a high school English teacher in California. In 2002, Julie received her National Board for Professional Teaching Standards certification in Adolescence and Young Adulthood English Language Arts. Her primary research interests include teacher professional development and instruction geared towards helping all students achieve high standards. She represents the University of Oregon as a Stafford Scholar with the National Institute on Leadership, Disability, and Students Placed at Risk.

Colin Barnes teaches disability studies at the University of Leeds, England, and is founder and Director of the University's Centre for Disability Studies, an independent publisher: The Disability Press, and the electronic Disability Archive UK. He is an executive editor and regular contributor to the international journal *Disability and Society*. He is a member of several organizations controlled and run by disabled people and Chair of the British Council of Disabled People (BCODP) and National Centre for Independent Living's (NCIL) Research Committee. He has an international reputation as a disability activist and has spoken before the House of Commons, the European Parliament and the World Health Organization.

Roseanna Bourke is the Director of the Centre for Educational Development at Massey University, New Zealand. Her experiences in learning and teaching have been as a classroom teacher, an educational psychologist, senior lecturer and for three years as manager, professional practice at the Ministry of Education, New Zealand. While a Senior Lecturer at Massey University Roseanna taught post-graduate and doctorate programmes in inclusive education, teaching strategies and assessment. Her work at the university and the Ministry involved developing and implementing an evidence-based model of practice through research programmes and practice-related initiatives. Roseanna's PhD explored students' conceptions of learning and self-assessment in a range of school and out-of-school contexts and her current research interests are in learning, assessment and professional learning.

Ann Cranston-Gingras, PhD, is a Professor of Special Education and Director of the Center for Migrant Education at the University of South Florida. She directs the federally funded High School Equivalency Program for Youth from Migrant Farmworker Families and the College Assistance Migrant Program. Dr Cranston-Gingras conducts research and publishes in the areas of migrant education and special education. She is the co-author of the texts, *Teaching Learners with Diverse Abilities* and *Rethinking Professional Issues in Special Education*.

Lesley Dee is a Senior Lecturer at the University of Cambridge Faculty of Education. She has taught both in schools and colleges and worked as a local authority inspector until 1991. Since that time she has researched and taught in the field of young people and adults with learning difficulties and/or disabilities in post-compulsory education.

Carolyn A. Denton is an Assistant Professor in the Department of Special Education at the University of Texas at Austin and serves on the Board of Directors of the Vaughn Gross Center for Reading and Language Arts at the University of Texas. Dr Denton is the author of articles, books, and book chapters in the areas of reading intervention, reading disabilities, response to intervention as an indicator of learning disability, supporting teacher development through coaching and consultation, and the process of bringing research-validated educational practices to scale. She is currently leading several large-scale research projects investigating reading intervention and instructional coaching at the primary and middle school levels.

Cristina Devecchi is a Research Assistant and PhD candidate at the University of Cambridge. Her research interests focus on theoretical developments in learning theory and their practical applications. Her PhD dissertation is an ethnographic study of teachers and teaching assistants' collaboration for the inclusion of children with difficulties in learning. Previously she taught English Communication Studies at the American University of Beirut, and Italian at the Lebanese University. Since moving to the UK she has taught Italian to adults and children for the Italian Vice Consulate and worked as a teaching assistant in an English secondary school.

Eric Dion is Assistant Professor at the Department of Special Education and Vocational Training at the Université du Québec à Montréal, Québec, Canada. He conducts research on the prevention of attentional problems and reading disabilities using classwide regular education classroom strategies, including peer-mediated activities. He has published in journals such as *Exceptionality, Behavioral Disorders, Education and Training in Mental Retardation*.

Mary Beth Doyle, PhD, is an Associate Professor of Education at St Michael's College in Colchester, Vermont, USA. Her research has focused on teacher–paraprofessional collaboration, curriculum modification for inclusive communities and teacher preparation. At St Michael's College she prepares graduate and undergraduate secondary education students to welcome, support and teach students with disabilities who will be members of their classes. She is the author of *The Paraprofessional's Guide to the Inclusive Classroom: Working as a Team* (2nd edition, Brookes, 2002) as well as several other professional publications.

Mary Jane Drummond is an experienced teacher, lecturer, writer and researcher, specialising in early childhood education. Her most recent publication, *First Hand Experience: What Matters to Children* (published by Rich Learning Opportunities, 2005), was stimulated by her research into the quality of the educational experiences offered to 4 and 5 year olds, and her findings that there were few opportunities for authentic, engaging, first-hand experiences of the real world. Her abiding interest is in children's learning, and a new edition of her book, *Assessing Children's Learning*, was published in 2003 by David Fulton.

Jennifer Evans is currently Senior Lecturer in Education at the Institute of Education, London University. She is currently working on a DfES-funded project on collaboration between schools. She has also worked as a specialist adviser to the Education Select Committee and as an expert consultant to the OECD. Her main interests are in education policy and management, focusing on policy and provision for pupils with special educational needs.

Ralph Ferretti is a Professor of Education and Psychology at the University of Delaware. His research focuses on the design of technology-supported learning environments that promote the effectiveness of children's academic problem-solving, including children with disabilities. This work has often been done in inclusive classrooms and has targeted the solution of ill-defined problems involving historical analysis and persuasive writing. He is currently co-editor of *The Journal of Special Education*.

Lani Florian is Senior Lecturer in Inclusive and Special Education in the Faculty of Education at the University of Cambridge, and Fellow of St Edmund's College, Cambridge. She has worked at universities in the USA and the UK and she was a Legislative Assistant to the US Senate Subcommittee on the Handicapped during the 99th Congress. Her co-edited book, *Promoting Inclusive Practice*, won the 1999 NASEN/TES academic book award and was translated into Spanish and Portuguese. She has worked as a consultant for UNICEF in a number of CEE and CIS countries. Research interests include categorization of children, models of provision for meeting special educational needs, and teaching practice in inclusive schools.

Kathleen Fowler is an advanced Doctoral Student of Special Education and Coordinator of the Families as Faculty Project at the University of South Florida. Her research interests include the areas of emotional and behaviour disorders and philosophies of research. She is the co-author of *Perspectivism and Critique of Research: An Overview*.

Susan A. Fowler, PhD, is a Professor of Special Education at the University of Illinois at Urbana-Champaign. Her research has focused on issues of early intervention and early childhood special education. In particular, she has investigated issues surrounding the transition of young children and their families through service systems. Her recent research has looked at cultural and linguistic factors in the design and delivery of early intervention services.

Douglas Fuchs is the Nicholas Hobbs Professor of Special Education and Human Development at Vanderbilt University, Nashville, Tennessee, where he also directs the Kennedy Center Reading Clinic. He has conducted programmatic research on response-to-intervention as a method for preventing and identifying children with learning disabilities and on reading instructional methods for improving outcomes for students with learning disabilities. He has published more than 200 empirical studies in peer-review journals. He sits on the editorial boards of 10 journals including the *American Educational Research Journal*, *Journal of Educational Psychology*, *Elementary School Journal*, *Journal of Learning Disabilities* and *Exceptional Children*.

Lynn S. Fuchs is the Nicholas Hobbs Professor of Special Education and Human Development at Vanderbilt University, Nashville, Tennessee, where she also co-directs the Kennedy Center Reading Clinic. She has conducted programmatic research on assessment methods for enhancing instructional planning and on instructional methods for improving reading and maths outcomes for students with learning disabilities. She has published more than 200 empirical studies in peer-review journals. She sits on the editorial boards of 10 journals including the *Journal of Educational Psychology*, *Scientific Studies of Reading*, *Elementary School Journal*, *Journal of Learning Disabilities* and *Exceptional Children*.

Deborah J. Gallagher is Professor of Education at the University of Northern Iowa. Her research interests centre on the philosophy of science as it pertains to research, pedagogy and policy in education and special education. Among other recent publications, she is the lead author of a book entitled *Challenging Orthodoxy in Special Education: Dissenting Voices* (Love Publishing Company, 2004) with co-authors Lous Heshusius, Richard Iano and Thomas Skrtic.

Russell Gersten is Executive Director of Instructional Research Group, a non-profit educational research institute in Long Beach, California. He is also Professor Emeritus in the College for Education at the University of Oregon. Dr Gersten is a nationally recognized expert in both quantitative and qualitative research and evaluation methodologies. He is currently principal investigator on several large studies and has written extensively on translation of research into practice, issues facing English language learners, reading comprehension and early intervention in mathematics. He recently won the AERA Award for Distinguished Special Education Researcher.

Michael F. Giangreco, PhD, is a Professor at the University of Vermont's Center on Disability and Community Inclusion. His work focuses on various aspects of educating students with disabilities in inclusive classrooms such as curriculum planning, related services coordination, and paraprofessional issues. Dr Giangreco is the author or co-author of numerous professional publications including *Choosing Outcomes and Accommodations for Children: A Guide to Educational Planning for Students with Disabilities* (2nd edition, Brookes, 1998). He has created over 300 cartoons depicting educational issues and research findings, most recently, *Absurdities and Realities of Special Education* (Peytral, 2002).

Michael L. Hardman is Professor and Chair of the Department of Special Education at the University of Utah. In 2004–05, he served as the Matthew J. Guglielmo Endowed Chair at California State University, Los Angeles. He is also Senior Education Advisor to the Joseph P. Kennedy Jr. Foundation in Washington, DC, a member of the California Advisory Commission on Special Education, and was recently elected to the Board of Directors for the Council for Exceptional Children. Dr Hardman has authored numerous publications including several college textbooks. He is the recipient of the 2000 National Distinguished Service Award from the Council for Exceptional Children, Division on Teacher Education.

Beth Harry is a Professor of Special Education in the Department of Teaching and Learning at the University of Miami, Florida. Her research and teaching focus on the impact of special education on culturally and linguistically diverse families and children. She served as a member of the National Academy of Sciences' (2002) panel to study ethnic disproportionality in special education, and is first author of *Why are so many minority students in special education? Understanding race and disability in schools*. In 2003 she received a Fulbright award to do research on Moroccan children's schooling in Spain, where she was based at the University of Seville. Dr. Harry, a native of Jamaica, entered the field of special education as a parent of a child with cerebral palsy. She earned her Bachelors and Masters degrees at the University of Toronto, Canada, and her PhD at Syracuse University.

Susan Hart has been a teacher and researcher in schools and universities for more than 30 years. Her specific area of interest has always been the dynamics of classroom life and how they impact upon young people experiencing difficulties in learning. Her publications include *Beyond Special Needs* (Paul Chapman), *Thinking Through Teaching* (David Fulton) and, most recently, *Learning Without Limits* (Open University Press), with a team of colleagues and teachers based at the University of Cambridge Faculty of Education. She is currently working as a specialist teacher in a support service committed to fostering access and inclusion.

Susan Brody Hasazi, EdD, is the Stafford Distinguished Professor of Leadership and Special Education in the Department of Education and Director of the Doctoral Program in Educational Leadership and Policy Studies at the University of Vermont. Dr Hasazi has conducted a variety of research studies related to inclusive education, educational change and collaboration between educational and human services organizations serving children and youth. She recently initiated the National Institute on Leadership, Disability and Students Placed at Risk.

Seamus Hegarty is Chairman of the International Association for the Evaluation of Educational Achievement (IEA) and visiting professor at five universities. He served as Director of the National Foundation for Educational Research for 12 years until his retirement in 2005. He is founder editor of the *European Journal of Special Needs Education*, now in its twenty-first year. He has written or co-authored more than 20 books and numerous papers. He has advised UNESCO and other international bodies on special needs issues for over 20 years and served as Principal Academic Adviser for the Salamanca World Conference.

Christopher J. Johnstone, PhD, is Research Associate at the National Center on Educational Outcomes, University of Minnesota. His areas of concentration include accessible assessments for students with disabilities and English language learners. Recent projects include studies on Universal Design, accommodations, accessible reading assessments, and state special education reporting. Dr Johnstone has 15 years of experience in disability-related occupations, including research, teaching, and consulting work that has taken place in Africa, Asia and North America. In 2005, he concluded two years of service as a Scholar at the National Leadership Institute on Disability and Students Placed at Risk.

Kenneth A. Kavale is Distinguished Professor of Special Education at Regent University in Virginia Beach, Virginia. He holds a doctoral degree from the University of Minnesota and has held faculty positions at the Universities of Georgia, Colorado, California, Riverside and Iowa. His research interests focus on definitional, assessment and intervention issues for students with specific learning disability and emotional and behavioural disorders.

Ruth Kershner is a Lecturer in the psychology of education at the University of Cambridge, Faculty of Education. She has particular interests in children's learning difficulties, special educational needs and inclusion, and in the development of teachers' pedagogical knowledge through participation in school-based research. Her current research relates to teachers' knowledge about pupils' special educational needs, the use of combinations of teaching strategies for pupils with learning difficulties, and the impact of new information and communication technologies on pupils' learning in the primary classroom environment.

Leanne R. Ketterlin-Geller, PhD, is an Assistant Professor at the University of Oregon, where she teaches a variety of courses on issues relating to theoretical and practical applications of measurement theory. She is also the Director of Research Projects for Behavioral Research and Teaching at the University of Oregon, where she manages several federally funded research projects that address issues relating to the measurement of academic achievement. Her research interests include universal design for assessment and instruction, large-scale and classroom-based assessment, curriculum-assessment alignment, and teacher/administrator preparation and use of data for decision-making.

Judy W. Kugelmass is Bartel Professor at Binghamton University, New York (SUNY). Her understanding of the significance of socio-cultural contexts in the development of inclusive schools reflects her research in the USA, Western and Eastern Europe, and South East Asia. Her two recent books, *Curriculum and Instruction for ALL Learners: Blending Systematic and*

Constructivist Practices in Inclusive Elementary Schools (co-edited with Beverly Rainforth) and *The Inclusive School: Sustaining Equity and Standards*, explore the development of inclusive schools and provide in-depth examples of effective practices.

Ann Lewis is Professor of Special Education and Educational Psychology in the School of Education (University of Birmingham, UK) where she heads a unique research group of around 35 academics specializing in children with disabilities or special educational needs. She has published widely internationally; her books include *Special Teaching for Special Children, Pedagogies for Inclusion?* (edited with Brahm Norwich, 2005), *Researching Children's Perspectives* (edited with Geoff Lindsay, 2000) and *Children's Understanding of Disability* (1995, 1999). Her current main research, funded by the Disability Rights Commission, focuses on the experiences of disabled children and their families across England, Scotland and Wales.

John W. Maag is a Professor at the University of Nebraska-Lincoln where he specializes in the education and treatment of children and adolescents with emotional and behavioural disorders. He is a nationally recognized behavioural consultant on best practices for managing resistance and improving relationships with others. Dr Maag has published over 90 articles and book chapters as well as authoring four books – one of which, *Parenting without Punishment*, won a Parent's Choice award. He was also the recipient of the University of Nebraska-Lincoln Distinguished Teaching Award. A licensed psychotherapist, Dr Maag is a frequent public speaker and consulting editor to numerous journals.

Dawn B. Male is a Senior Lecturer in the School of Psychology and Human Development at the Institute of Education, University of London. Her areas of particular expertise are moderate, severe and profound and multiple learning disabilities and autistic spectrum disorders. Her research interests include friendships among and between children and young people with and without learning disabilities, challenging behaviour, and mnemonic functioning of children and young people with moderate and severe learning disabilities. Dawn is also a consultant educational psychologist and previously was a teacher of children and young people with moderate, severe and profound and multiple learning disabilities.

John McDonnell is currently a Professor and the Program Coordinator in Severe Disabilities in the Department of Special Education at the University of Utah. He received his PhD from the University of Oregon in 1984. His research has focused on the validation of effective instructional practices and programme models for students with developmental disabilities. He has published numerous articles, chapters and textbooks on these topics.

Jayne McGuire is a doctoral candidate in the Department of Special Education at the University of Utah. Her research has focused on self-determination and the impact of recreation programming on people with disabilities. She is currently a research coordinator on a project investigating the impact of the Special Olympics on its athletes and its community. Ms McGuire enjoys skiing, snowboarding, running and travelling with her family.

Donald McIntyre has worked as a teacher, educator and educational researcher for over 40 years, with a particular interest in classroom teaching and in teachers' learning. After working previously at Stirling and Oxford universities, he has been a Professor of Education at Cambridge University since 1996, semi-retired since 2004. His publications include *Making Sense of Teaching* (1993, with Sally Brown), *Effective Teaching and Learning: Teachers' and Pupils' Perspectives* (1996, with Paul Cooper), *Learning Without Limits* (2004, with Susan Hart, Annabelle Dixon and Mary Jane Drummond) and *Learning Teaching from Teachers* (2006, with Hazel Hagger), all published by the Open University Press.

Margaret J. McLaughlin is Associate Director of the Institute for the Study of Exceptional Children and Youth, University of Maryland. Her research has focused on the areas of disability and special education policy. She has published extensively in areas related to special education and general education policy, systems change and inclusion and has an international reputation as a scholar in these areas. She recently co-chaired a National Academy of Sciences Committee on Goals 2000 and students with disabilities, and served as a member of a National Academy of Sciences Special Committee on Education Finance and the Committee on Over-representation of Minority Students in Special Education.

Mandia Mentis is a Senior Lecturer in the Department of Learning and Teaching at Massey University, Auckland, New Zealand. She co-ordinates the Post-Graduate Special Education programmes. She has taught at primary, secondary and tertiary levels and has worked as an educational psychologist in a variety of inclusive education settings. Her teaching and research interests include assessment, teaching methods, cognitive education and e-learning. Her doctoral research focuses on developing an e-learning Community of Practice model for teaching practitioners, such as educational psychologists and teachers.

Susie Miles is the Programme Director of the MEd in Special and Inclusive Education in the University of Manchester's School of Education. She was the founding Coordinator of the Enabling Education Network (EENET) from 1997-2006 and has worked as a consultant for the International Deaf Children's Society, Save the Children-UK and Leonard Cheshire International. Prior to taking up her position at the University of Manchester, she worked for 12 years as a teacher of the deaf and as Save the Children's Regional Disability Adviser in seven countries in southern and East Africa.

Ann I. Nevin is Professor Emerita at Arizona State University and Visiting Professor at Florida International University. She has a PhD from the University of Minnesota. Her doctoral research focused on how teachers and administrators can integrate students with special learning needs. She also earned advanced degrees in special education and educational administration and has participated in the development of innovative teacher education programmes since the 1970s. Her writing, advocacy, research and teaching spans more than 30 years of working with a diverse array of people to create environments where students with disabilities and those without disabilities can work together towards their mutual success.

Brahm Norwich is Professor of Educational Psychology and Special Educational Needs at the School of Education and Lifelong Learning, University of Exeter. His recent research and publications have been in the areas of student perspectives, self-perceptions, pedagogy for students with SEN, policy and practice for SEN and inclusion and the nature of moderate learning difficulties. Recent books have been *Special Pedagogy for Special Children: Pedagogies for Inclusion* (Open University Press, edited with Ann Lewis, 2004), and *Moderate Learning Difficulties and the Future of Inclusion* (RoutledgeFalmer, with Narcie Kelly, 2005).

Michaelene M. Ostrosky, PhD, is an Associate Professor of Early Childhood Special Education at the University of Illinois at Urbana-Champaign. Professor Ostrosky's research interests focus on young children's social-emotional and communication skills, transitions, and personnel preparation. She is extremely committed to translating research into practice, and helped create the Division for Early Childhood's practitioner journal, *Young Exceptional Children*.

James L. Paul, EdD, is a Professor of Special Education at the University of South Florida. Prior to joining the faculty at USF as Chair of the Department of Special Education, he was a Professor of Special Education at the University of North Carolina in Chapel Hill. Dr Paul has authored, co-authored or edited 26 books and numerous articles in special education and related areas. The current focus of his scholarship is on ethics and philosophies of research.

Susan Peters is an Associate Professor at Michigan State University, College of Education. She has travelled extensively, and taught at primary school level in Japan as well as university level courses in Zimbabwe. She is currently a core faculty member of the African Studies Center at MSU and served as their Chairperson from 2002 to 2004. As a Fulbright Scholar to Zimbabwe in 1994, she undertook extensive fieldwork there as well as in South Africa. Her work in Africa has centred on Inclusive Education. She co-edited *Education and Disability in an African Context: Different Voices*. As a consultant for the World Bank, Disability Group, she authored *Inclusive Education: Achieving Education for All by Including those with Disabilities and Special Needs* (2004). Susan has been an advocate of disability rights for over 25 years and has held various leadership positions in disability rights organizations.

Jill Porter is a Senior Lecturer in Research Methods and Special Education at the University of Bath where she is Programme Director for the cross-faculty Master's in Research. She has a particular interest in services for children and young people with severe, profound and multiple learning difficulties and in collecting the views of young people to inform the evaluation and development of provision and co-authored *Researching Learning Difficulties*. Her research interests include provision for young people with challenging behaviour and complex needs, self-assessment and personalisation. Her most recent research includes a review of the research literature on the role of special schools, and the use of ICT to promote community participation.

Sheila Riddell taught for seven years in a secondary school in the southwest of England before doing a PhD in sociology of education at Bristol University. She is currently Professor of Inclusion and Diversity at Edinburgh University, where she is Director of the Centre for Research in Education Inclusion and Diversity. She was previously Director of the Strathclyde Centre for Disability Research, and has published extensively in the field of disability and gender, particularly in relation to education.

Marcia Rioux is a Professor at York University, Canada. She is Graduate Programme Director, M.A. (Critical Disability Studies), and Director, York Institute for Health Research. Her research addresses a broad range of public policy issues dealing with human rights, disability and discrimination, education for all, globalization, social welfare and social justice. Dr Rioux has advised on policy issues in numerous countries including the Americas, Europe, Africa and India as well as government commissions, parliamentary committees, international NGOs and UN agencies. Currently she is heading an international disability rights monitoring project, Disability Rights Promotion International, and is finishing an edited book on law and disability. She holds a PhD in Jurisprudence and Social Policy.

Richard Rose is Professor of Special and Inclusive Education and Director of the Centre for Special Needs Education and Research at the University of Northampton, UK. Before taking up his present post he taught in schools in several parts of England. His current research interests are in the use of mentoring support for inclusion, and the development of research partnerships with young people with special educational needs. Richard's recent publications include *Encouraging Voices: Listening to the Voices of Young People Who Have Been Marginalised*, with Michael Shevlin, and *Strategies to Promote Inclusive Practice*, with Christina Tilstone.

Martyn Rouse is Professor of Social and Educational Inclusion at the University of Aberdeen. Previously he was a senior lecturer in special educational needs and inclusion at the University of Cambridge. He has undertaken research and development work on special needs and inclusion for a number of international agencies, including UNICEF, the British Council and the UK

Department for International Development (DFID). Current projects include work with the Kenyan Ministry of Education and Kenyatta University to build educational capacity at the local level and work on issues of inclusion and achievement in English schools.

Lana Edwards Santoro is a Research Associate with the Instructional Research Group, Long Beach, California. She was a faculty member in the College of Education at Lehigh University, Bethlehem, Pennsylvania, for four years. She has written about reading instruction, specifically spelling, vocabulary, and reading in the content areas. She received awards from the Council for Exceptional Children (Division of Learning Disabilities) and the American Educational Research Association in recognition of her research on reading and spelling instruction for young children at risk of early reading difficulties.

Stan F. Shaw is Co-Director of the University of Connecticut's (UConn) Center on Post-secondary Education and Disability. He is also a Professor and Coordinator of the Special Education Program at UConn. Dr Shaw is the current President of the Higher Education Consortium for Special Education (HECSE). His primary areas of interest are transition assessment and documentation, professional development for post-secondary disability personnel, services for college students with disabilities, and the implementation of Section 504. Recent articles have been published in *Remedial and Special Education, Journal of Postsecondary Education and Disability, Teacher Education and Special Education, Intervention in School and Clinic* and *Journal of Special Education Leadership*.

Alison Sheldon is a Teaching Fellow in disability studies at the Centre for Disability Studies, School of Sociology and Social Policy, University of Leeds. She is committed to disability politics and her specific research interests include disability and development, disability and information technology, and disability and feminism.

Katharine Shepherd, EdD, is an Assistant Professor in the Department of Education at the University of Vermont. Her research includes a series of policy implementation studies exploring the role of principals in developing inclusive schools and support systems for students with disabilities and those placed at risk. Dr Shepherd is co-Principal Investigator of a project designed to develop collaborative leadership skills among parents of children with disabilities. She is also a Faculty Fellow with the National Institute for Leadership, Disability and Students Placed at Risk, where she contributes to the development of web-based learning modules for aspiring school administrators.

Roger Slee is the founding Editor of the *International Journal of Inclusive Education* and Dean of the Faculty of Education at McGill University in Montreal, Canada. Formerly a school teacher, Roger has been Dean of Education at Goldsmiths College, University of London and at The University of Western Australia. He was also Deputy Director General of the Queensland Department of Education.

Gary Thomas is Chair of Inclusion and Diversity at the University of Birmingham's School of Education in the UK. His interests are principally in research method, particularly in special and inclusive education, and the changing political and social contexts of inclusion. He is co-author of *Deconstructing Special Education and Constructing Inclusion*, along with a range of other books and papers, and is editor of the *International Journal of Research and Method in Education*.

Sandra J. Thompson, PhD, was Research Associate at the National Center on Educational Outcomes, University of Minnesota, when she completed her chapter. She passed away in December 2005 after a career of improving outcomes for students with disabilities. Dr Thompson assisted states in the design of inclusive assessment systems, developing tools for determining inclusive assessment practices in the areas of accommodations, alternate assessment and universal design. She published a number of book chapters, journal articles, technical reports, and training materials, and presented at numerous state, regional and national conferences.

Jacqueline S. Thousand is a Professor in the special education teacher preparation and graduate programmes in the College of Education at Cal State San Marcos in California. Jacqueline has an international reputation as a teacher and disability rights and inclusive education advocate. She has published widely on issues related to co-teaching, inclusive schooling, organizational change, differentiated instruction and universal design, cooperative teaching and learning, collaborative teaming processes, creative problem-solving, and discipline with dignity. She is involved in international teacher education and inclusive education endeavours, and serves on the editorial and advisory boards of several national and international journals and professional organizations.

Martha L. Thurlow, PhD, is Director of the National Center on Educational Outcomes, University of Minnesota, where she addresses the implications of contemporary US policy and practice for students with disabilities, including national and state-wide assessment policies and practices, accommodations, alternate assessments and graduation requirements. She has published extensively on these topics, presented at numerous state, regional, national and international conferences, testified before Congress on the inclusion of students with disabilities in accountability systems, and is often called upon by individuals at all levels of the educational system to provide input on challenging issues surrounding the inclusion of special needs students.

Gerald Tindal joined the University of Oregon in 1984 and recently became the Castle-McIntosh-Knight Endowed Professor in the College of Education at the University of Oregon. He also serves as the Area Head of Educational Leadership and is the Director of Behavioral Research and Teaching (BRT). He teaches courses on measurement systems for general and special education teachers and administrators. His work includes using curriculum-based measurement of basic skills and concept-based instruction and problem-solving in secondary content classrooms to integrate students with disabilities in general education classrooms.

J. S. de Valenzuela is an Associate Professor of Special Education at the University of New Mexico. Professor de Valenzuela's research interests include alternative assessment/evaluation, bilingual special education, and language socialization and communication development among culturally and linguistically diverse populations. She has contributed to assessment development efforts at the state and national levels. Her recent publications include contributions to *The Bilingual Special Education Interface*, a well-recognized textbook in the area of bilingual special education.

Sharon Vaughn is the H. E. Hartfelder/Southland Corp Regents Chair at the University of Texas. She has served as editor-in-chief of the *Journal of Learning Disabilities* and co-editor of *Learning Disabilities Research and Practice*. She is currently directing several research grants investigating the effectiveness of interventions of various intensity through a response to intervention model. She is also working with Sylvia Linan-Thompson and other colleagues investigating the effectiveness of interventions with English language learners. She is the author of several textbooks on learning difficulties and disabilities and numerous research articles.

Richard A. Villa is President of Bayridge Consortium, Inc., and adjunct faculty at California State University San Marcos. He has worked with tens of thousands of teachers, administrators, families, universities and state departments of education throughout the USA and the world to develop and implement organizational and instructional support systems for educating all students within general education. Rich has been a classroom teacher, a special educator, a special education director, pupil personnel services director and director of instructional services. He has authored over 90 book chapters and articles regarding inclusive education, co-teaching, organizational change and universal design.

Jeanne Wanzek, PhD, is a Research Associate at The University of Texas at Austin. She is currently coordinating research projects examining student response to intervention at the elementary and middle school levels. Her research interests include effective instructional design and beginning reading instruction.

Margret A. Winzer is a Professor at the University of Lethbridge in Alberta, Canada where she teaches courses in special education and early childhood education. She has written widely in the field of special education on various facets that include history, comparative studies, multicultural special education, and early childhood special education.

John Woodward is currently Distinguished Professor in the School of Education at the University of Puget Sound in Tacoma, Washington. He has conducted technology and mathematics research for the US Department of Education, Office of Special Education Programs for over 25 years. Woodward has published over 80 articles in professional journals and one book on technology and professional development in special education. In addition, he has co-authored four technology-based instructional programmes and two mathematics curricular programmes. His areas of interest include ICT, mathematics education and professional development.

Tweety J. Yates, PhD, is a Visiting Assistant Professor in the Department of Special Education at the University of Illinois at Urbana-Champaign. Dr Yates has been involved in a number of research, training and technical assistance grants related to issues around preparation and credentialling of early intervention personnel, literacy, parent–child interaction, social and emotional development and the prevention of challenging behaviour. She provides training and technical assistance throughout the USA on these topics. She is currently President-Elect for the Division of Early Childhood (DEC) of the Council for Exceptional Children.

Editorial Advisors

Sam Odom
Indiana University
School of Education
201 North Rose Avenue
Bloomington Indiana 47405–1006
USA

David Rodrigues
Faculdade de Motricidade Humana
Estrada da Costa
1499–688 Cruz Quebrada
Portugal

Mike Rosenberg
Johns Hopkins University
School of Professional Studies in Business
and Education
Homewood Campus
Baltimore Maryland
USA

Martyn Rouse
School of Education
MacRobert Building
King's College
Aberdeen AB24 5UA
Scotland

Michael Shevlin
Trinity College
Department of Education
College Green
Dublin 2
Ireland

Tom Skrtic
University of Kansas
1122 W. Campus Rd.
Joseph R. Pearson Hall
Room 525
Lawrence Kansas 66045–3101
USA

Gary Thomas
The University of Birmingham
Professor of Inclusion and Diversity
School of Education
Edgbaston
Birmingham B15 2 TT
England

Martha Thurlow
University of Minnesota
Director of the National Centre on
Educational Outcomes
College of Education and Human
Development
350 Elliott Hall, Room 350
Minneapolis MN 55455
USA

Vianne Timmons
University of Prince Edward Island
550 University Avenue
Charlottetown
Prince Edward Island
C1AA 4P3 Canada

Jane West
American Association of Colleges for
Teacher Education
1307 New York Avenue NW
Suite 300
Washington DC 20005
USA

Preface

To organize scholarship within the field of special education in order to produce a one-volume handbook that speaks to a broad and international professional audience is to negotiate a vast area. An account of the field is a complicated task that carries a heavy responsibility. As Roger Slee has argued, a handbook of special education can both advance and undermine the progress of disability rights in education. The challenge has been to develop an account of the field that combines a retrospective view of it with new ways of thinking about the issues that it faces.

This *Handbook* is intended as a source book of information and ideas about special education. It is concerned with the educational responses that are made when students experience difficulties in learning and to those who have or are considered to have disabilities. This concern has traditionally found expression in the form of special education, and thus the book focuses on special education as a form of provision and an area of research, rather than on categories of learning difficulties. Reviewers pointed out that a book on special education might limit the audience, as many professionals concerned with disability rights in education reject a concept of special education and other educators do not consider special education knowledge relevant to their own work. However, as the *Handbook* argues, much research generated within the field of special education has a great deal to offer education more generally and my hope is that the book will reach a wide audience despite a title that will lead some to think it has nothing to offer them.

A kind of philosophical pragmatism guided decisions about the content and this was underpinned by three principles that are discussed within the various chapters. These were: a rejection of medical categories of disability as educationally relevant; an anti-determinist view of learning; and a commitment to social justice in education. A five-section structure allowed an exploration of how special educational needs are understood, the challenge of inclusion, the production of knowledge, teaching strategies and approaches, and future directions for research and practice. Within this framework, what might appear to be unrelated or incompatible views were brought together in order to summarize recent work in and about special education.

The account of special education provided in the *Handbook* makes a number of demands on the reader as the scholars contributing to it view their central task from different national and theoretical perspectives. As a result, the text contains a range of terms reflecting these different national contexts, competing ideological stances and varying epistemological positions. A decision was taken not to attempt to reconcile the tensions associated with these differences but to make a virtue of them by exploring what they have to say to those who are committed to education for all. The terms special education and special needs education are used interchangeably to mean 'educational intervention and support designed to address special educational needs' (UNESCO, 1997). In addition, a glossary has been included to help readers who may be unfamiliar with particular terminology or various national policies and organizations.

The book brings together a range of scholars from across the English-speaking world in an attempt to move beyond particular national views of disability and special educational needs. Although one aim was to bring together scholarship on an international level and cover topics that transcend national boundaries, decisions also had to be made about what could be achieved coherently in one volume. The *Handbook* does not attempt to provide a comparative analysis, however it is characterized by several different national perspectives, particularly from the countries of North America and the United Kingdom. Contributors from other English-speaking countries are also included though there are fewer of them, reflecting population density rather than lack of interest in the work that goes on there. The focus on the English-speaking world is also more a reflection of my own experience as an American living in England than a belief in the superiority of one way of thinking over another. Indeed, I have learned much from my international experiences and I hope this learning is reflected in the *Handbook*. The emphasis on an English-speaking perspective is not to say that developments elsewhere are unimportant, but they do deserve fuller treatment than could have been achieved in this volume. Other handbooks that explore education and notions of disability from non-Western and non-English perspectives would be welcome additions to the literature.

Ideally this *Handbook* will draw attention to the challenges of providing education for all in ways that are just and equitable. The contributors to this volume all share a commitment to improving educational outcomes for those who experience difficulties in learning. Implicit in their contributions are a range of views and a theoretical diversity that collectively map what is currently known as special education, or special needs education, and illuminate the inherent problems facing all who are concerned with educational access and equity.

REFERENCE

United Nations Educational, Scientific and Cultural Organization (UNESCO). (1997). *International Standard Classification of Education, ISCED*. Paris: Author.

Lani Florian
University of Cambridge
January 2006

Acknowledgements

Marianne Lagrange of Sage Publications first approached me with her idea for a handbook of special education at the 2003 European Conference on Educational Research in Hamburg, Germany. Since that time this book has been my constant companion. I am thankful to have had the support of the Faculty of Education at the University of Cambridge, as well as access to the University of Cambridge libraries, the Folger Library at the University of Maine in Orno, and the Special Education Resource Center in Middletown, Connecticut. The public library in Blue Hill, Maine, provided an unparalleled summer work setting.

A book such as this is not possible without the support and involvement of many people and I am obliged to them all. I am thankful to Professor Donald McIntyre of the University of Cambridge for encouraging me to undertake the project. As I have ruminated about the book, I have been inspired and sustained by memories of the students I taught over the years as well as the teachers and colleagues who taught me. Professor A. J. Pappanikou of the University of Connecticut stands out as a model of teacherly love and professional guidance.

The team at Sage provided outstanding support. Publisher Marianne Lagrange and her editorial assistant Lauren Allsop, production editors Rebecca de Luca Wilson and Jeanette Graham, copy editor Carol Lucas, and cover designers Jennifer Crisp and Chris Rychter all worked tirelessly to the high standards for which Sage is renowned. It has been a privilege to work with such an excellent team.

From the beginning of this project colleagues have been incredibly generous in sharing their expertise and working to deadlines. Anonymous field reviewers provided helpful feedback on the original proposal for the *Handbook*. Editorial advisors not only commented on chapter outlines and draft chapters, but also were available to discuss issues when I felt stuck. I have no doubt that the generosity of so many colleagues has strengthened the book. To the extent that it accurately and adequately reflects the state of the field, the credit is due to their contributions, although the responsibility for any omissions or errors is mine alone.

Acknowledgements are due to the publishers who granted permission to use material or quote from the following: *Minority Students in Special and Gifted Education* (© 2002 by the National Academy of Sciences, courtesy of the National Academies Press, Washington, DC); *The Mismeasure of Man* (revised and expanded edition) by Stephen Jay Gould (© 1996, 1981 by Stephen Jay Gould and used with the permission of W. W. Norton & Co, Inc); and *Hiding from Humanity: Disgust, Shame, and the Law* by Martha C. Nussbaum (© 2004 by Martha C. Nussbaum and used with the permission of Princeton University Press).

I am indebted to my colleagues in Cambridge, Kristine Black-Hawkins, Richard Byers, Lesley Dee, Martyn Rouse and Nidhi Singal who patiently overlooked my preoccupation with the details of the manuscript during busy academic terms. Editorial assistants Alison Craig and Anne Chippindale were meticulous in their attention to detail. Cristina Devecchi read the entire manuscript in draft form and prepared the glossary. Rosie Snajdr joined in when needed to keep me organized and on schedule.

Finally, I am thankful for cherished friends who not only take an interest in my work, but also provide respite from it. I am indebted to my family for the enduring love that enables me to take risks in life, and I am deeply grateful to my partner Martyn Rouse, who with sagacious tact, wit, grace and good humour remained devoted to me while I was devoted to this book.

Introduction

Lani Florian

There are many stories that could be told about special education and the account in this *Handbook* is but one. This story explores special education as a response to notions of human difference. In addition it explores the contribution that different understandings of this response make, not only to theory, but also to practical knowledge. In other words, how do we know when, why and how to respond when students experience difficulties in learning? For many years scholarship in the field of special education has sought to develop this knowledge, and it has been influenced by competing ideas about what constitutes a special educational need and how pupils who experience difficulty in learning might be taught. The *Handbook* attempts to present a range of perspectives about the nature and purpose of special education as well as what might be considered an appropriate response to disability or other difficulties, and the extent to which research reproduces or addresses problems in the field. The overall aim is to provide a coherent account of the state of the field and consider where it might usefully go in the future. To this end, the book is organized in five sections as discussed briefly below.

HOW SPECIAL EDUCATIONAL NEEDS ARE UNDERSTOOD

This section covers theoretical foundations of the field and related policy areas. The opening chapters explore the dilemmas of access and equity that have characterized special education to date. They 'problematize' special education and locate it firmly in a mainstream context of education for all. A chapter on the history of special education tells a particular story but, as the author notes, much of it remains an 'unexplored cul de sac in the history of education'.

Other contributors to this section bring different perspectives to bear on what is known about the history of the field. Riddell points out that special education and its related constructs have been construed differently at different points in time. She argues that professional language and terminology also tell stories about underlying assumptions, values and beliefs. Though different terminology is used in different national contexts there is a continuing struggle to find an acceptable language for special education. From 'handicapped child', to 'child with a disability', to 'child with a learning difficulty', to 'child who experiences difficulty in learning' or 'child who is considered to experience difficulty in learning', there is a constant struggle to articulate more adequately the nature of what is meant and who is considered to have 'special needs'. This theme is developed from a psychological perspective by Norwich.

Clearly, understanding what constitutes a special educational need is not straightforward. Nor are the responses to it. As pointed out in Chapter 1, a response to the difficulties students experience in learning is often defined as provision that is different or additional. In other words, it is largely defined by what is not generally available to all. The effects of policy decisions that are made about general and special education, whether they are to do with eligibility, funding, forms of provision or outcomes, are considered in other chapters in this section. Evans argues that funding mechanisms set parameters on forms of provision. Rouse and McLaughlin consider special education in the broader international context of education reform, and Harry shows how institutional racism reverberates in educational placement of ethnic minorities in special education provision.

THE CHALLENGE OF INCLUSION

The second section of the *Handbook* considers notions of disability rights in education, inclusion and inclusive education as a model for meeting educational needs. Rioux takes up the issue of rights in education. Through an analysis of the *Eaton* case from the Canadian Supreme Court she critiques the arguments in support of segregating children in education and identifies what she calls the myths that deny inclusion.

Inclusive education can be understood in the context of 'Education for All', an international policy intended to provide universal access to primary school education. Peters gives an account of this and other international policies designed to protect and promote the rights of disabled people. Miles and Ahuja provide examples of how these policies are being implemented in different regions of the world. They argue that studying developments elsewhere, particularly in poor countries, can generate valuable insights and have implications for practice in other countries.

Slee considers inclusive schooling a precondition of democratic education but finds that much of what is offered in the name of inclusion fails to live up to the name. He theorizes that much of what is done in the name of inclusive education maintains a status quo of unequal power relationships among groups. Like other contributors he calls for changes in thinking about educational practice. Ainscow goes one step further and describes how he has attempted to apply this shift of thinking in practice.

KNOWLEDGE PRODUCTION

Much has been made of the so-called 'paradigm wars' in research into the social sciences, and special education has not been exempt from these disputes or the battle scars that have accompanied them. Indeed, many of the contributors to the *Handbook* are clearly associated with particular world views, for example, logical positivism, post-positivism, constructivism, and so on. As Tashakkori and Teddlie (1998) have summarized, some take the view that these paradigms are irreconcilable and adherence to one precludes not only the values and beliefs associated with another but a rejection of the methods associated with it and the knowledge that has been produced by it. Others disagree, arguing that the emphasis on epistemological differences is misplaced and overstated.

The association of particular methods of teaching and/or research with particular paradigms has reinforced the idea that they are incompatible. Behaviourism is rejected because some claim logical positivism has been discredited, experimental designs are rejected because they control rather than capture variation. Yet one does not have to believe in logical positivism in order to conduct an experiment or use a behavioural technique. Similarly, it is not necessary to reject the view that there is a single reality or universal truth in order to appreciate the role of language in the construction meaning. One need not agree on a particular philosophy of science to share the view that all children can learn.

This section of the *Handbook* contains a range of arguments about paradigms, methodology and method, on the grounds that these differences in perspective, and the arguments that arise from them, have coexisted for many years and a great deal has been learned from all of them. It also contains three chapters covering contrasting theoretical perspectives (Maag, Kugelmass and de Valenzuela). Each was chosen because of its implicit rejection of determinist views of ability, and because the theoretical perspective does not rely on medical categories of disability for coherence. While readers will form their own views about the value of each of these perspectives, all make important contributions to understanding the difficulties learners encounter and, as such, deserve careful consideration.

TEACHING STRATEGIES AND APPROACHES

The section on teaching strategies and approaches contains several subsections exploring issues of curriculum and assessment, the phases of education, and cross-phase issues of teaching and learning. Rose notes how two major international developments, inclusion and standards-based reform are influencing decisions about curriculum, but these developments are also influencing assessment policy and practice, as the chapters in this subsection discuss.

Although many aspects of teaching and learning cross the various phases of education, chapters specific to each of the four main phases (early years, elementary, secondary and post-secondary) are included. Although these chapters are all located in the same national context, they are not intended to be read as an endorsement of any one model of provision. However, as so much research in special education is generated in the USA and exported elsewhere, it is useful to foreground this work in an understanding of special education as it is organized in this country.

The chapters on phases of education are followed by Dee's discussion of lifelong learning and quality of life for people who experienced difficulties in learning at school. Issues of transition are located in the tension between national policies that foster citizenship and those that emphasize education for employment. Here it can be seen how analysis of a policy from one national context can illuminate issues related to post-school experience that are relevant in other countries.

A range of teaching approaches and strategies used to teach pupils identified as having the full range of special educational need are reviewed. Thousand, Villa and Nevin examine the knowledge base on collaborative teaching; Giangreco and Doyle provide an international review on teaching assistants, while Woodward and Ferretti address the contribution of assistive technologies. Dion, Fuchs and Fuchs review peer-mediated strategies and Male contextualizes this with a discussion of the importance of friendship.

As much of the research reported in this section was conducted in the USA it is difficult to avoid medical-categorical descriptions of the difficulties children experience in learning. However, it can be argued that the use of these descriptions does not invalidate the outcomes of the research. If, as Ysseldyke (2001) has argued, medical categories are irrelevant to instruction, it is possible to read research based on these designs as tests of particular strategies rather than tests of strategies for particular sub-groups of learners. As such, effective practice is construed as both informing and being informed by general education.

FUTURE DIRECTIONS FOR RESEARCH AND PRACTICE

The final section of the *Handbook* considers the issues raised at the end of Chapter 1. These are issues of rights to and in education, the challenge of adopting anti-determinist views of ability, and the need for a shift in focus from studying differences between learners to learning for all. Chapter 1 sets an agenda but the concluding section details how it is being articulated at present. Gallagher's analysis of the debates within the field is set alongside Kershner's reflection on teacher knowledge and expertise, and how that knowledge develops through teaching. This theme is also taken up by Hart, Drummond and McIntyre who explore the work of teachers who reject ability labelling.

Furney and Hasazi argue that the demands of social justice require school leaders to take responsibility for promoting the success of *all* students, and in the concluding chapter

Hegarty considers the contribution of special education to the broader education community. He extends his reflections on the contents of the book as a whole by considering the knowledge that underpins educational action and the relationships between the different kinds of knowledge that underpin educational progress. He concludes that special education knowledge offers a great deal to education more generally. The argument advanced in this *Handbook* is that it is time to reflect on what special education consists of currently, and how it might be different in the future.

REFERENCES

Tashakkori, A. & Teddlie, C. (1998). *Mixed methodology: Combining qualitative and quantitative approaches.* London: Sage.

Ysseldyke, J. E. (2001). Reflections on a research career: Generalizations from 25 years of research on assessment and instructional decision making. *Exceptional Children, 67*(3), 295–309.

How special educational needs are understood

Reimagining special education

Lani Florian

INTRODUCTION

Positioned as it is, as both the problem of and the solution to injustice in education, the field of special education occupies contested terrain. Throughout its history, advocates and critics have simultaneously hailed and condemned it as both a means of achieving equal educational opportunity and a perpetrator of injustice in education. The historian of education, Martin Lazerson (1983), articulated the issue well:

> From its inception, some have condemned special education for not being available to enough children, and some, especially parents of handicapped children, have demanded more as well as better programs. Yet others have condemned special education for too readily identifying children as handicapped, and too readily placing them in segregated classes. All, from within and outside the educational system, have acknowledged that special education has been the least accepted of our public school programs. To paraphrase John Dewey, if a society ought to provide for its children that which the best parent would provide, special education stands out as a measure of the failure of public responsibility. (p. 16)

Though Lazerson was writing before the full implementation of the human and civil rights laws and policies that were adopted in many countries since the 1970s, the dilemmas of access and equity that he articulated have continued, despite the hope and the promise of national rights-based policies intended to resolve them, such as P.L. 94–142 (now part of the Individuals with Disabilities Education Act – IDEA) in the United States, National Law 118/71 in Italy, or P.L. 10/2002, Ley Orgánica de Calidad de la Educación (LOCE) in Spain.

This chapter considers dilemmas of access and equity by examining the role of special education in the context of the larger education system. It explores the right to education, the power of the human need to mark some people as deviant, the corresponding concept of normal, and the conundrum this creates for special education. It argues that future progress in addressing the dilemmas of access and equity will require a reimagining of what special education is and can become. The chapter calls for changes in thinking about provision and practice, and suggests what some of these changes might entail.

THE PROMISE OF EDUCATION

Education is defined as a universal right by Article 26 of the United Nations Universal Declaration of Human Rights (1948). As such, it is commonly invoked for the purposes of establishing standards for the right to education (access) and for human rights in education (equity). Thus education is both a human right and a means of achieving human rights. As the concept of human rights has evolved, education has also come to be seen as a development right (Gearon, 2003), and as an economic, social and cultural right (Tomasevski, 2001). Though there is great philosophical promise in a rights concept of education, support for it is often based on a belief in its power to transform society (Grubb & Lazerson, 2004). Over the past century, education has been seen as a remedy to many forms of social injustice. Where compulsory schooling exists, it has helped to eliminate child labour (Tomasevski, 2003), and more schooling for more people is considered the solution to social and economic problems in many countries (Grubb & Lazerson, 2004). As a result, support for education is justified throughout the world, not simply as a human right but as an investment in the 'development' of individuals and societies to meet the demands of a market economy and as a requirement of a democratic society. World Bank policy makes this position clear:

> Education is central to development. It empowers people, strengthens nations, and is key to the attainment of the Millennium Development Goals. Already the world's largest external financier of education, the World Bank is today more committed than ever to helping countries develop holistic education systems aimed both at achieving Education For All (EFA) and building dynamic knowledge societies that are key to competing in global markets through Education for the Knowledge Economy (EKE). (World Bank, n.d.)

Here support for education is seen not as a remedy for injustice or a human right but as a way to strengthen economic competitiveness. The co-mingling of rhetoric about human rights, nation building and compet-

tive markets is difficult to unravel. Linking the human right to education with education for the purpose of economic independence for individuals and prosperity for nations makes it difficult to see them as two distinct policies. Yet this is what we must do if we are to understand the role of special education in contemporary society.

THE ROLE OF SPECIAL EDUCATION

When access to education is widened it puts pressure on education systems and schools to accommodate increasingly diverse student populations. Indeed, as many have documented, special education is one of the mechanisms by which such diversity has been accommodated. For many years special education was seen as a fulfilment of the right to education for children with disabilities and there were expectations that the implementation of rights-based special education laws would promote social and economic acceptance and enable disabled children to participate in community life as adults. As one of the congressional reports that accompanied P.L. 94–142 in the United States noted: 'With proper educational services many of these handicapped children would be able to become productive citizens contributing to society instead of being left to remain burdens on society' (United States Congress, 1976, p. 11).

Yet these outcomes did not follow. A series of national surveys in the United States found that disabled people were less well educated, less likely to be employed and less likely to participate in social activities than non-disabled groups (Harris and Associates, 1986, 1987, 1989). Special education, it seemed, was not preparing children identified as having disabilities for life after school. Moreover, there were difficulties with the identification and classification of disabilities for educational purposes (Dunn, 1968; Mercer, 1973), and these created additional problems of access and equity, generating controversies that persist to this day (see, for example, Keogh & MacMillan, 1996; MacMillan &

Reschly, 1998;Ysseldyke, 2001; Florian et al., 2006). Experience in many other countries followed a similar pattern (CERI, 1994).

Sociologists of education (for example, Tomlinson, 1982) and others (for example, Skrtic, 1986, 1991) presented a critique of special education, not as a fulfilment of the right to education, but as a denial of that right by virtue of its exclusionary practices. Such analyses locate the problem of special education in the structures of mainstream education systems. Here the co-mingling of the right to education as a human right and the right to education as a mechanism of economic prosperity become conflated and confused. Legislation guaranteeing the right to education does not exist in a vacuum and rights-based legislation in and of itself has not proved sufficient for achieving access to education or preventing discrimination. Many children and young people continue to be marginalized within, or excluded from, education systems around the world, including those who live in countries with policy frameworks that appear supportive.

It has been argued that too much faith was placed in the law to overcome the deeply entrenched biases against and prejudices towards disabled people as judicial systems themselves are also influenced by problems of bias and prejudice (Hahn, 2001). In a provocative analysis, the philosopher Martha Nussbaum (2004) suggests how this dynamic operates. She asks why stigmatization is ubiquitous, why all societies view some people as normal and consider those who deviate shameful. In a detailed review of theoretical and empirical psychoanalytic work on shame and stigma she arrives at the following:

> Human beings are deeply troubled about being human – about being highly intelligent and resourceful, on the one hand, but weak and vulnerable, helpless against death, on the other. We are ashamed of this awkward condition and, in manifold ways, we try to hide from it. In the process we develop and teach both shame at human frailty and disgust at the signs of our animality and mortality ... In the case of disgust, properties pertinent to the subject's own fear of animality and mortality are projected onto a less

> powerful group, and that group then becomes a vehicle for the dominant group's anxiety about itself ... In the case of shame, a more general anxiety about helplessness and lack of control inspires the pursuit of invulnerability ... An appearance of control is then frequently purchased by the creation of stigmatized groups. (pp. 336–7)

If such an insight is correct then it is little wonder that those who believed that the law could provide a complete remedy to the problem of discrimination were disappointed. What Nussbaum is arguing is that an understanding of the dynamics of shame, disgust and stigma and the ways they function in human social life helps us to understand why people with disabilities are marked as deviant or different in all societies. After all, what is 'normal' is generally decided by groups and it changes from place to place and over time. Nussbaum points out that the idea of normal is linked to two very different ideas: statistical frequency (usual and unusual) and a normative conception of the good (proper and improper, or appropriate and inappropriate). She questions why this connection should be drawn:

> For, obviously enough, what is typical may or may not be very good. Bad backs, bad eyes and bad judgement are all very typical ... [while] much progress in human affairs comes from people who are unusual ... So why, in more or less all societies, has the notion of the normal as the usual also served as a normative function, setting up the different for stigmatizing treatment? (p. 218)

Her answer is that normal is a construction that permits us to protect ourselves from disruption, to hide from the imperfections about which we feel the deepest shame in ourselves. Little wonder then that special education is marked out as a measure of the failure of public responsibility. For no matter what educational rights it protects or what it achieves for individuals, it still permits others to hide from the shame of imperfection because it reinforces the notion of normal as usual and good. In this analysis, special education can never really be a good thing. So long as it remains focused on difference or what is unusual, normal can be defended as an appropriate standard.

Interestingly, Nussbaum argues that it is essential that an individual rights approach serves as a first response to the problem of stigma. She is in favour of laws that protect individual rights such as the IDEA because she sees their focus on human rights as a strategy for challenging stigma. However such an approach is not without its own difficulties for, as Minow (1990) observes, the laws and policies that are created to protect vulnerable groups also serve to marginalize them. Thus we are caught in a vicious cycle where efforts to grant or protect rights to equal opportunity and treatment also mark and stigmatize.

Indeed, the history of special education can be seen as the effort to meet the dual purpose of providing for all children while protecting 'normals' from 'deviants' (Lazerson, 1983). Special education thus embodies what Minow calls the 'dilemma of difference' as it occupies the space between the inclusionary and exclusionary forces which operate simultaneously at all times in service of society's dual purpose of providing and controlling civic life. Consider the work of teachers of children who are designated as having 'special needs'. They aim to include children who have been excluded from what Booth and Ainscow (2002) call the culture, curriculum and community of school, but in so doing collude with an educational system that is underpinned by complex and subtle deterministic assumptions about difference, deviance and ability that produced the exclusion in the first instance.

Nearly half a century ago, Burton Blatt exposed the hazards involved in doing this work. *Christmas in Purgatory* (Blatt & Kaplan, 1966), *Exodus from Pandemonium* (Blatt, 1970) and *Souls in Extremis* (Blatt, 1973), highlighted the legally sanctioned forms of abuse that were part of 'caring' for disabled people in institutions. He showed how those who do the 'care-giving' as well as who are 'cared for' can also be victims of unjust social structures.

Teaching, it can be argued, is different from social care but the practices of special education have been subject to the same kind of critical analysis (Tomlinson, 1982; Skrtic, 1986,

1988, 1991; Brantlinger, 1997) provoking a heated debate about whether the effects of special education are beneficial or detrimental. There is concern about the nature and purpose of special education as well as what might be considered an appropriate response to disability and other difficulties. The idea of special education as a parallel or separate system of education to that which is provided to the majority of children has been challenged by notions of inclusion in which all children are part of one education system. The problem, of course, is that inclusive education is not a denial of individual difference, but an accommodation of it, within the structures and processes that are available to all learners. The process of accommodating difference as a mechanism of equal opportunity, and as a fulfilment of the right to education for all, is not generally disputed by educationalists. But the means to this end, whether through 'special' or 'inclusive' education, continues to be forcefully debated.

'SPECIAL' OR 'INCLUSIVE' EDUCATION?

Fuchs and Fuchs (1992) have labelled those who undertake a critical analysis of special education as 'abolitionists' and those who do not as 'conservationists'. They noted:

> By the early 1980s [abolitionists] had developed a trenchant critique of the field, encompassing all aspects of service delivery. But their plans for rehauling special education tended toward extremism, and the accompanying rhetoric was often unremittingly negative, if not downright hostile and threatening. By the late 1980s, conservationists had fixed on their adversaries' unrealistic remedies and intemperate rhetoric to portray them as out-of-touch ideologues. To some extent, they succeeded. Simultaneously, and often inadvertently, they discredited, or at least muffled, the truthful ring of the abolitionist critique. (p. 413)

As a result, it could be argued that the discourse of special education was changed. Now, one was either in favour of special education or against it. To be in favour of special education was to be against the 'extremism' and the 'intemperate rhetoric' of advocates for change. To support the reform of the 'cascade of services model' of special education provision was to be against special education itself. Brantlinger (1997) called those in favour of special education 'traditionalists' and those who advocated for systemic change (for example, models of inclusive education to replace the cascade of services model), 'inclusionists'. Traditionalists called those who advocated for inclusive education 'radicals'. More recently the camps have been described as 'incremental reformers' and 'substantial reconceptualists' (Andrews et al., 2000). There is the beginning of a recognition that a 'with us or against us' type of debate has polarized the field in ways that have made it difficult to move practice forward. In an attempt to find common ground in the widely shared commitment of acting in children's best interests, a group of scholars representing a range of divergent perspectives has come to the following position:

> We believe that special education can shape public opinion about disability in ways that help schools see all children as important stakeholders, while promoting the development of methods that enhance capacity for successful postschool adjustments among individuals with disabilities ... We believe that a division of labour makes sense, wherein the incremental reformers focus on what to do on behalf of children, and the substantial reconceptualists focus on achieving the conditions necessary for promoting optimal methods. We believe the field needs to work simultaneously with the children and on the system (Andrews et al., 2000, p. 260).

While this is a refreshing departure from what had become a very polarized debate, there is a need to recognize that a call to work *simultaneously with the children and on the system* does not simply call a truce between those who hold different perspectives, but that new ways of conceptualizing the work are required.

THE PROBLEM OF DIFFERENCE DISCOURSE

Sociological critiques (Tomlinson, 1982), legal analyses (Minow, 1990) and philosophical explorations of disability (Nussbaum, 2004) all show how assumptions about difference, deviance, ability and what is considered normal, interact in ways that produce, sustain and reproduce the dilemmas of access and equity in education that special education was intended to address. As one of the mechanisms by which schools accommodate diversity, special education, as currently construed, reinforces the exclusionary practices of general education, in part because it relies on a 'difference discourse' that essentially, though not entirely, agrees with the mainstream view that some children are qualitatively different from others and therefore require something different from that which is available to the majority.

Difference discourse is a term used by Ford (2005) to describe what he calls a set of interconnected beliefs conversations and practices that are mutually reinforcing and socially pervasive. Though he uses the term in an analysis of the concept of racial culture he is careful to point out that the concept applies to other social classifications and identities. Many disabled activists and scholars argue for a concept of disability culture, a kind of identity politics that seeks to challenge representations of disability as deviant, grotesque or otherwise impoverished (for example, Mitchell & Snyder, 2000). This is important work that serves to uncover and expose the deeply held belief that disability is tragic because it is abnormal. Although this begs any number of questions about what is normal, it also unwittingly affirms the concept of normalcy. Disability studies scholars do not want to abandon difference discourse; they seek to change it in favour of a concept of disability culture that is vibrant, beautiful and alive. But until that day arrives, disabled people in general and children with disabilities in particular will rightly continue to require and demand protection from discrimination within the larger society and its institutions. What Ford cautions is an awareness that difference discourse itself is problematic and limited. It might alter, but will not alone solve, the problem of discrimination. So long as there is discrimination, dilemmas of access and equity remain.

Thus far, this analysis suggests two interdependent problems facing the field of special education. The first is the concept of normal as usual and good, the second is the dilemma of difference. Clearly there is a need for understanding and challenging the roles that notions of deviance, difference, disability and special educational need play in all aspects of social life, but particularly in education. There is also a need to confront the paradoxical nature of special education as it currently operates within the larger education system. Should it be acceptable that dilemmas of difference are seen as an inevitable feature of special education, a necessary evil that must be endured for the sake of providing special education? Or is it time to reimagine the work of educating children who experience difficulties in learning, not as a Faustian pact whereby in exchange for access the field is eternally condemned *as a measure of the failure of public responsibility* to children with disabilities and 'special needs', but as an integral part of a school's response when students experience difficulties?

REIMAGINING SPECIAL EDUCATION

Changing the difference discourse is necessary and urgent work for the future of special education (whatever name it calls itself). The task of reimagining special education suggests that current assumptions, systems and procedures might be replaced by new ways of thinking and working, and many of the contributors to this book point in such directions. In the remainder of this chapter three areas of particular importance to the task of reimagination are discussed: issues of definition (what is special education?) deterministic assumptions (what is ability?) and the practices they have given rise to (what is special about special education?).

Special education, special needs education, or something else?

In 1997 the International Standard Classification of Education replaced the term special education with *special needs education* in order to differentiate it from the earlier international definitions of special education as that which took place in special schools or institutions (OECD, 2005). This change in terminology distinguished the provision of special education, meaning intervention, from placement in special education schools or classrooms. It is an important distinction because the concept of place had long been associated with provision, as placement in special schools and classes was often assumed necessary for provision. Special needs education, meaning provision, is defined as 'educational intervention and support designed to address special educational needs', wherever that intervention takes place.

The concept of special educational needs is broad, extending beyond categories of disability, to include all children who are in need of additional support. However, many countries still use categorical descriptions of disability for the purpose of special educational provision though the precise nature of the categories varies. In the United States, the Code of Federal Regulations defines special education as 'specially designed instruction … to meet the unique needs of a child with a disability' (34 C.F.R. § 300.14). Currently there are 13 categories of disability covered by the American special education legislation.

Identifying children as having special educational needs (needing special treatment) or needing special education (requiring additional resources) has never been a straightforward process within education. First, children rarely fit categorical descriptions of difficulty. Second, not all disabilities give rise to special educational needs, nor are all special educational needs a result of a disability. A child with spina bifida may or may not experience difficulties in learning. A child who experiences difficulty with literacy may or may not have dyslexia. Categorical descriptions of difficulty may or may not have educational relevance. It was for these reasons that they were abolished in England and Wales in 1981 as a result of the recommendations of the Warnock Report (DES, 1978).

Though a number of countries have tried to leave the notion of discrete categories behind, some process of classification remains in place. England abandoned the use of medical categories in favour of a classification of 'special educational need' (SEN). Special education provision is that 'which is additional to, or otherwise different from, the educational provision made generally for children of their age in schools maintained by the LEA, other than special schools, in the area' (Department for Education and Employment, 1996, § 312). In Scotland, the non-categorical nature of special educational needs is also recognized. Recent education legislation specifies that 'a child or young person has additional support needs (ASN) where, for whatever reason, the child or young person is, or is likely to be, unable without the provision of additional support to benefit from school education provided or to be provided for the child or young person' (Scottish Parliament, 2004).

Whether the term special education, SEN provision or additional support is used, there is a common understanding that special needs education involves something 'different from' or 'additional to' that which is generally available in schools. When students are classified as needing something different or additional they become categorically distinct from other children and are often assumed, by virtue of needing something different or additional, to be qualitatively different as learners. This is the central dilemma. To further complicate the picture there is evidence that in countries without a system of special needs education, little educational provision is available to disabled children (see Peters, this volume). The shame and stigma associated with disability in many countries without a system of special needs education often acts as a barrier to the development of any kind of educational provision, as children are hidden at home or in institutions (UNICEF, 2005). The challenge is how to make educational provision available to all children without the shame of marking some as different or deviant.

Deterministic assumptions about ability, difference and deviance

Since its inception, special education has been bound by deterministic notions of ability. The idea of one's 'intelligence' or 'ability' as a single fixed entity that is normally distributed throughout a population is so deeply entrenched and pervasive in Western human thought that it generally goes unquestioned even by those who have studied this controversial topic as part of their professional training. The debates about intelligence and IQ (whether it exists, in what form, how to measure it, under what conditions and when) are well known in education and psychology, and yet it is a widely used construct for sorting learners and in attempting to understand the difficulties they encounter in school. The belief in intelligence as something an individual is born with, though it may be stimulated or stunted, is foundational in education despite professional acknowledgement that it is a problematic concept. As a result, there is a deep professional ambivalence about the notion of intelligence that reflects both the discomfort and the usefulness in using the construct.

Gould (1996) attributes the belief in fixed ability to the pervasive influence of biological determinism, the recurrent view that we are primarily determined by biological rather than social or environmental factors. Though most contemporary accounts of this position claim that biological, environmental and social factors are not isolated from each other but *interact* in reciprocal ways that influence each other and produce individual differences, Gould asserts that these complex insights have been misunderstood:

> Errors of reductionism and biodeterminism take over in such silly statements as 'Intelligence is 60 percent genetic and 40 percent environmental.' A 60 percent (or whatever) 'heritability' for intelligence means no such thing. We shall not get this issue straight until we realize that the 'interactionism' we all accept does not permit such statements as 'Trait x is 29 percent environmental and 71 percent genetic.' When causative factors (more than two, by the way) interact so complexly, and throughout growth, to produce an intricate adult

being, we cannot, in principle, parse that being's behaviour in to quantitative percentages of remote root causes. The adult being is an emergent entity who must be understood at his own level and in his own totality. The truly salient issues are malleabity and flexibility, not fallacious parsing by percentages. A trait may be 90 percent heritable, yet entirely malleable. A twenty-dollar pair of eyeglasses from the local pharmacy may fully correct a defect of vision that is 100 percent heritable. (p. 34)

The Mismeasure of Man, Gould's 1981 masterpiece (revised in 1996), presents a critique of biodeterminsm not as a rejection of science but using the tools of science and philosophy to reveal the fallacious reasoning that underlie the theory of a unitary, innate, linearly rankable IQ. His analysis of the history of mental testing and measurement shows that the notion of fixed intelligence is based on some fundamental errors of science, notably reductionism, dichotomization, hierarchy and reification. As Gould explains it, the drive to understand intelligence resulted in the parsing of complex phenomena by subdividing and ranking it into grades of intelligence, for example, normal or retarded, average or above average, smart or stupid, and so on. This in turn led to the reification of intelligence as an entity rather than an abstract concept. Gould's central argument does not reject a concept of intelligence or deny individual differences but points out that, contrary to popular belief, intelligence, expressed as IQ, has not been verified as a single entity let alone one that can be expressed numerically. He disagrees with IQ as an expression of the concept of intelligence

because the two most contradictory hypotheses are both fully consistent with it: 1) that it reflects an inherited level of mental acuity (some people do well on most tests because they are born smarter); or 2) that it records environmental advantages and deficits (some people do well on most tests because they are well schooled, grew up with enough to eat, books in the home, and loving parents. (p. 282)

It is important to remember that there are many definitions of intelligence and a number of views about its development, measurement and assessment. Though scholarly reviews of the concept remind us that intelligence is an

attribute that reflects what a person has learned (for example, Sattler, 2001), the popularity of IQ as a meaningful expression of a person's ability persists. Many educational practices are based on a tacit assumption of fixed ability and the belief that it is normally distributed within the population. Moreover, in many parts of the world, identification of disabilities and/or special educational needs depends, at least in part, on some form of ability test scores, and again this tends to reinforce the notion that groups of learners can be sorted into students with and without special educational needs, who become those in special and those in mainstream or general education.

Hart (1998) has argued that much educational practice, including special education policy, standards-based reforms and classroom practice serves to reaffirm the legitimacy of the notion of fixed ability. Schools use 'cognitive abilities tests' to group pupils and target additional support, but this serves to confirm judgements about ability rather than raise questions about intervention. In commenting on the resilience of the concept of fixed ability, she cites Brown and McIntyre (1993), and Cooper and McIntyre's (1996) suggestion that the concept of fixed ability serves a practical purpose in that it enables teachers to reduce vast amounts 'of information about their pupils to a manageable form that can inform and guide their teaching' (p. 161). But is there another way to serve such a purpose? Hart and her colleagues (this volume) suggest what might *replace* the notion of fixed, differential ability in practice. Their notion of transformability offers an alternative way of thinking about the difficulties children experience in learning.

Reimagining special education beyond special needs education

Many of those who have attempted to articulate what is 'special' about special education begin with a defence of teaching practices that have been shown to work with students identified as having disabilities. However, contrary to definitions of special education as something 'different from' or 'additional to' that which is available to other pupils, the strategies they identify also work with students who are not identified as having special educational needs. There is a similar situation in the field of psychopharmacology where the drugs used to treat presumed neurological disorders such as attention deficit hyperactivity disorder also improve the functioning of those who are not so identified (Farah et al., 2004). Tenner (2005) describes hypermotivational syndrome, a condition where students who have not experienced difficulty in learning use prescription drugs to attain a competitive advantage by chemically enhancing their performance. As they note, this begs a number of questions about who should have access to drugs that enhance neurocognitive enhancement, when and why. It also suggests that those whose neurocognitve functioning is considered to be impaired or deficient may not be qualitatively different physiologically to those who are considered to have normal functioning. The same can be said about teaching strategies. If strategies work with children who experience difficulty in learning *and* they work with other children, then who should have access to them and under what conditions should this access be available?

Critics of special education have questioned the terms and conditions of this access and they have questioned the high price that is paid by the unintended consequences of a dual system of special and regular education. To argue that sound teaching practices have been developed by special educators does not refute the criticisms that are levelled at the field. Placement in special education does have unintended side effects. It can and often does stigmatize those who are singled out for the 'extra help'. Thus, to justify placement in special education on the grounds that it is better than the alternatives is to close off the possibility of thinking differently about alternative ways of working.

It is the process of providing something 'additional to' or 'different from' that which is 'otherwise available' in school that defines special education provision. The task is not to defend what is 'special' about this kind of provision but to challenge complacency about what is not 'otherwise available'. Reimagining special education involves rejecting the questionable construct of normal as biologically determined, usual and good in favour of a more nuanced understanding of difference. As Minow (1990) reminds us, it is not difference, but the difference we make of it, that matters. Responding to individual difference is important but *how* this is done is equally important. Much has been learned about the processes of education. Our understanding of the relationship between teachers, learners, schools as communities and their relationship to society has deepened, creating an opportunity to think differently about the nature of special needs education, what it is called and how it is provided. Palinscar (1997) suggested that the sheer number of students served by special education programmes in the US – approximately 11.5 per cent of all school aged students – renders it a part of general education rather than one branch of a dual system of 'general' and 'special' education as it has been seen historically. The problem is that the history of a dual system has become part of the field's view of itself rather than a history of the struggle to achieve education for all.

The impact of this version of history can be clearly seen in the attempts to articulate what is special about special education. In examining the research evidence, Cook and Schirmer (2003) found that there was 'substantial and compelling evidence of effective practices developed by special educators for students with disabilities' though the 'techniques that are effective for students with disabilities are generally effective for all students' (p. 202). They went on to conclude that 'there is little inherent, [then,] in the content of the particular effective practices that make special education special'. What is unique is what Vaughn and Linan-Thompson (2003) called 'the delivery of instruction'. In their review of notions of specialist pedagogy, Lewis and Norwich (2005) came to a similar conclusion and suggested that rather than thinking of particular teaching strategies as differentially effective, they might be arranged along a continuum from high to low intensity. Here again the emphasis is on application rather than technique. If it is true that practices that are effective for students with disabilities are effective for all students, then it cannot be concluded, as it often is, that mainstream classroom teachers do not recognize or know to implement effective teaching practices for pupils with special needs. A cursory look at the content of many teacher education and educational psychology textbooks will recommend virtually the same teaching practices to those identified as empirically validated procedures in special education.

Arguing that the notion of a distinct special pedagogy is unhelpful, Davis and Florian (2004) pointed out that sound practices in teaching and learning in both mainstream and special education literatures are often informed by the same basic research, and that certain teaching strategies developed for one purpose could be effectively applied to other groups of children with different patterns of educational need. In fact, attempts to define what is special about special education generally acknowledge that effective practices in special education often originate in general education (for example, Kavale, this volume). Cook and Schirmer (2003) list direct instruction, self-monitoring, mnemonic instruction, strategy training, curriculum-based measurement, applied behaviour analysis and functional assessment as effective special education techniques. However, these are all well-known mainstream educational practices discussed in many mainstream educational psychology and teacher education texts (see, for example, Lefrancois, 2000; Pollard, 2002; Whitebread, 2000) though, as Cook and Schirmer point out, little is known about their uptake in special or general education classes.

This is not to say that all learners are the same or that there is no need to differentiate or otherwise be concerned with the delivery of instruction. On the contrary, it is the interest in how learners differ and the ways in which they can be helped to over-

come the difficulties they experience in learning that is what drives much research in special education. But when the work is done in collusion with the exclusionary force that dichotomizes learners on the basis of 'ability' it cannot help us to resolve the dilemma of difference. Nor can it help with improving what is generally available in schools.

CONCLUSION

Seymour Sarason, in his foreword to Blatt's (1973) *Souls in Extremis*, noted that in between values and actions are our knowledge theories and conceptions. He suggested that 'the road to hell is not only paved with good intentions, it is often coated with a thick layer of what is thought to be the best thinking'. It is important therefore to reconsider what is thought to be best thinking, not because it is necessarily wrong, but because what may have seemed logical, just or right, no longer serves these aims, or when the cost of unintended consequences becomes too high. In this chapter, I have argued that the paradox of unintended consequences, of perpetuating exclusionary practices in the name of equity, that has defined the nature of special education to date, need not do so in the future. To move forward, however, will require some new thinking and a fuller level of engagement with the complex processes of education in general, than scholars have undertaken to date. Three areas of work deserve particular attention.

The right to education. Many educators accept the right to education as a human right and align themselves with the Deweyan idea of education for democracy. However, the right to education is situated within the purposes of education. In recent times the concept of democracy and the principles of a market economy have been combined, resulting in an emphasis in education on high standards and competition (see, for example, Rouse and McLaughlin, this volume). The curriculum is driven by international competition that places a premium on the skills thought to produce economic advantage. In such a situation there are winners and losers. As Nussbaum's examination of the role of shame in social life suggests (Nussbaum, 2004), those who lose in the educational marketplace are stigmatized by being considered to have 'special educational needs'. Nussbaum argues that:

> modern liberal societies can make an adequate response to the phenomena of shame only if they shift away from a very common intuitive idea of the normal citizen that has been bequeathed to us by the social-contract tradition so influential in the history of European thought: the image of the citizen as productive worker, able to pay for the benefits he receives by the contributions he makes. (pp. 176–7)

Reimagining special education requires differentiating education as a human right from education as a means of achieving human rights, for example, economic and development rights. Such differentiation shows how designations of special educational need or placement in special education can be unjust, a barrier to, rather than a fulfilment of, human rights. But as Nussbaum's analysis points out, deeply rooted feelings of shame about human frailty make it difficult to change accounts of difference.

In her 2002 Tanner Lecture on Human Values, Nussbaum (2006) suggests that the idea of the normal citizen bequeathed by the social-contract tradition itself is fundamentally flawed because it is underpinned by a notion of reciprocity that assumes some level of equality among those who enter into it. She argues that theories of justice based on the social contract treat those with severe disabilities and long-term care needs as an afterthought rather than as full citizens. So, although rights-based policies are essential in combating stigma, they cannot be adequate if our theories of justice do not take account of human difference. Failure to take difference into account perpetuates the cycle of marginalizing and protecting vulnerable groups. However, accounting for difference as part of the human condition renders obsolete the

notion of normal as the appropriate educational standard.

Challenging deterministic beliefs. In addition, deeper consideration needs to be given to the power of the beliefs that teachers hold about human ability, teaching, learning and specialist knowledge. Rethinking the concept of normalcy requires a consideration of how it is conveyed in teacher education and reinforced when working with pupils in schools. This is essential. It may not be possible to win the battle to change the structure of schools, as so-called 'radical reformers' advocate, but efforts to challenge and confront biological determinism in all it various guises must continue. As Skrtic (1991) reminds us, though professional work is inextricably bound by the organizational context in which it is performed, professions set their own standards. While it may not be possible to change the organizational context of schools, the field can determine the standards by which it aspires be held to account. To adopt an anti-determinist stance as a professional standard sets a new agenda for research and practice that requires, as I have tried to argue, a reimagining of what special education is and can become.

Researching teaching practice. Many who have attempted to articulate what is special about special education cite the lack of evidence that classroom teachers use 'validated' strategies when 'including' pupils with special educational needs (for example, Cook & Schirmer, 2003). Based on the logic of the evidence-based practice movement in medicine, the demand for more 'scientific' educational research is seen as the way to improve both practice and outcomes (Howe, 2005). Yet the scientific research base in education has been 'stubbornly indeterminate' (Huberman, 1993, p. 26) limiting its usefulness to improve practice. Studies of how teachers do their work (for example, Brown & McIntyre, 1993; Little & McLaughlin, 1993) suggest that its complexity and demands have not been fully appreciated or captured by many experimental or quasi-experimental research designs. As Huberman (1992) notes:

Essentially teachers are artisans working primarily alone, with a variety of new and cobbled together materials in a personally designed work environment. They gradually develop a repertoire of instructional skills and strategies ... through a somewhat haphazard process of trial and error, usually when one or other segment of the repertoire does not work repeatedly ... Teachers spontaneously go about tinkering with their classrooms. (p. 136)

Though some would say that such a seemingly haphazard process is insufficient and inadequate for teaching pupils who experience difficulties in learning, it has been shown that teachers who are adept at embedding responsiveness to individual need within the process of whole-class teaching are able to sustain inclusive practice (Jordan & Stanovich, 1998). In other words, it is when teachers persist in tinkering that they expand their repertoire of responses to the difficulties students encounter in learning. Perhaps it is a mistake to deride teachers' practice as unsystematic and lacking in rigour (Hammersley, 2001). McIntyre (2005) has argued that the kind of knowledge that is produced by research is different from that which classroom teachers need. He outlines a series of steps for bridging the gap between research and practice that calls on teachers to articulate fully their craft knowledge and researchers to understand better the indirect influence of the knowledge they generate. The question is not why teachers do not make better use of research but how to develop research strategies that more fully capture the complexity of classroom practice when teaching diverse groups of learners. Such strategies can help to generate new understandings about how to respond when pupils experience difficulty that do not continue to depend on designations of special educational need.

These three things, clearer thinking about the fulfilment of the right to education, the challenge to deterministic beliefs about ability, and a shift in focus from differences among learners, to learning for all, set an agenda for special needs education that can change the nature of what special education is and might become in the future. In time it may also help change the organization of educational provision and prevailing concepts of schooling so that the reimagining of special education becomes a reimagining diversity in education. Then research on the difficulties students experience in learning might lead to pedagogical practices that are inclusive of all learners.

REFERENCES

Andrews, J. E., Carnine, D. W., Coutinho, M. J., Edgar, E. B., Forness, S. R., Fuchs, L., et al. (2000). Bridging the special education divide, *Remedial and Special Education, 21*(5), 258–260, 268.

Blatt, B. (1970). *Exodus from pandemonium: Human abuse and a reformation of public policy.* Boston, MA: Allyn and Bacon.

Blatt, B. (1973). *Souls in extremis: An anthology on victims and victimizers.* Boston, MA: Allyn and Bacon.

Blatt, B., & Kaplan, F. (1966). *Christmas in purgatory: A photographic essay on mental retardation.* Boston, MA: Allyn and Bacon.

Booth, T., & Ainscow, M. (2002). *Index for Inclusion* (2nd ed.). Bristol: Centre for Studies in Inclusive Education.

Brantlinger, E. (1997). Using ideology: Cases of non-recognition of the politics of research and practice in special education. *Review of Educational Research, 67*(4), 425–460.

Brown, S., & McIntyre, D. (1993). *Making sense of teaching.* Buckingham: Open University Press.

Centre for Educational Research and Innovation (CERI). (1994). *Disabled youth and employment.* Paris: Organisation for Economic Co-operation and Development (OECD).

Cook, B. G., & Schirmer, B. R. (2003). What is special about special education? Overview and analysis. *The Journal of Special Education, 37*(3), 200–204.

Cooper, P., & McIntyre, D. (1996). *Effective teaching and learning: Teachers' and students' perspectives.* Buckingham: Open University Press.

Davis, P., & Florian, L. (2004). *Teaching Strategies and Approaches for Pupils with Special Educational Needs: A Scoping Study* (Research Report 516). London: DfES. Available via the 'publications' section of the DfES research website: http://www.dfes.gov.uk/research

Department for Education and Employment (DfEE). (1996). *Education Act 1996.* London: HMSO.

Department of Education and Science (DES). (1978). *Special educational needs: Report of the Committee of Enquiry into the education of handicapped children and young people* (The Warnock Report). London: HMSO.

Dunn, L. M. (1968). Special education for the mentally retarded – is much of it justifiable? *Exceptional Children, 35*(1), 5–22.

Farah, M. J., Illes, J., Cook-Degan, R., Gardner, H., Kandel, E., King, P., et al. (2004). Neurocognitive enhancement: What can we do and what should we do? *Nature, 5,* 421–425.

Florian, L., Hollenweger, J., Simeonsson, R. J., Wedell, K., Riddell, S., Terzi, L., & Holland, A. (2006). Futures of children revisited: issues in the classification of children with disabilities. *The Journal of Special Education, 40*(1) 36–45.

Ford, R. T. (2005). *Racial culture: A critique.* Princeton, NJ: Princeton University Press.

Fuchs, L. S., & Fuchs, D. (1992). Special education's wake-up call, *The Journal of Special Education, 25*(4), 413–414.

Gearon, L. (2003). *The human rights handbook: A global perspective for education.* Stoke-on-Trent: Trentham Books.

Gould, S. J. (1996). *The mismeasure of man.* London: Penguin Books.

Grubb, N., & Lazerson, M. (2004). *The education gospel: The economic power of schooling.* Cambridge, MA: Harvard University Press.

Hahn, H. (2001). Adjudication or empowerment: contrasting experiences with a social model of disability. In L. Barton (Ed.), *Disability politics and the struggle for change* (pp. 59–78). London: David Fulton.

Hammersley, M. (2001). Some questions about evidence-based practice in education. Paper presented to the British Educational Research Association Annual Meeting, University of Leeds, September.

Harris, L. and Associates. (1986). *The ICD survey of disabled Americans: Bringing disabled Americans into the mainstream.* New York: Louis Harris and Associates.

Harris, L. and Associates. (1987). *The ICD survey II: Employing disabled Americans.* New York: Louis Harris and Associates.

Harris, L. and Associates. (1989). *The ICD survey III: A report card on special education.* New York: Louis Harris and Associates.

Hart, S. (1998). A sorry tail: Ability, pedagogy and educational reform. *British Journal of Educational Studies, 46*(12), 153–168.

Howe, K. R. (2005). The education science question: A symposium. *Educational Theory, 55*(3), 235–243.

Huberman, M. (1992). Teacher development and instructional mastery. In A. Hargreaves & M. Fullan (Eds.), *Understanding teacher development* (pp. 122–142). London: Cassell.

Huberman, M. (1993). The model of the independent artisan in teachers' professional relations. In J. W. Lit-

tle & M. W. McLaughlin (Eds.), *Teachers Work* (pp. 11–50). New York: Teachers College Press.

Jordan, A., & Stanovich, P. (1998). Exemplary teaching in inclusive classrooms. Paper presented at the Annual Meeting of the American Educational Research Association, San Diego, CA, April.

Keogh, B. K., & MacMillan, D. L. (1996). Exceptionality. In D. C. Berliner & R. C. Calfee (Eds.), *Handbook of Educational Psychology* (pp. 311–330). New York: Simon Schuster Macmillan.

Lazerson, M. (1983). The origins of special education. In J. G. Chambers & W. T. Hartman (Eds.), *Special education policies: Their history, implementation and finance* (pp. 3–47). Philadelphia, PA: Temple University Press.

Lefrancois, G. R. (2000). *Psychology for teaching* (10th ed.). Belmont, CA: Wadsworth/Thompson Learning.

Lewis, A., & Norwich, B. (Eds.). (2005). *Special teaching for special children? Pedagogies for inclusion.* Maidenhead: Open University Press.

Little, J. W., & McLaughlin, M. W. (Eds.). (1993). *Teachers Work.* New York: Teachers College Press.

MacMillan, D. L., & Reschly, D. J. (1998). Overrepresentation of minority students: The case for greater specificity or reconsideration of the variables examined. *The Journal of Special Education, 32*(1), 15–24.

McIntyre, D. (2005). Bridging the gap between research and practice. *Cambridge Journal of Education, 35*(3), 357–382.

Mercer, J. (1973). *Labeling the mentally retarded: Clinical and social system perspectives on mental retardation.* Berkeley, CA: University of California Press.

Minow, M. (1990). *Making all the difference: Inclusion. exclusion and American law.* Ithaca, NY: Cornell University Press.

Mitchell, D. T., & Snyder, S. L. (2000). *Narrative prosthesis: Disability and the dependencies of discourse.* Ann Arbor, MI: University of Michigan Press.

Nussbaum, M. C. (2004). *Hiding from humanity: Disgust, shame and the law.* Princeton, NJ: Princeton University Press.

Nussbaum, M. C. (2006). *Frontiers of justice: disability, nationality, species membership.* Cambridge, MA: Harvard University Press.

Organisation for Economic Co-operation and Development (OECD). (2005). *Students with disabilities, learning difficulties and disadvantages: Statistics and indicators.* Paris: Author.

Palinscar, A. S. (1997). Introduction. *Review of Educational Research, 67*(4), 373–376.

Pollard, A. (2002). *Reflective teaching: Effective and evidence-informed professional practice.* London: Continuum.

Sattler, J. M. (2001). *Assessment of children: Cognitive applications.* San Diego, CA: Jerome M. Sattler.

Scottish Parliament, Education Committee (2004). *Official report*, 25.2.04. Available at: http://www.scottish.parliament.uk/education/or/ed04–0602.htm #Col919 (Accessed August 11, 2004.)

Skrtic, T. M. (1986). The crisis in special education knowledge: A perspective on perspective. *Focus on exceptional children, 18*(7), 1–16.

Skrtic, T. M. (1988). The organizational context of special education. In E. Meyen & T. Skrtic (Eds.), *Exceptional children and youth: An introduction* (pp. 479–517). Denver, CO: Love Publishing.

Skrtic, T. M. (1991). *Behind special education: A critical analysis of professional culture and school organisation.* Denver, CO: Love Publishing.

Tenner, E. (2005). Hypermotivational syndrome. *Technology Review, 108*(8), 82.

Tomasevski, K. (2001). *Human rights obligations: Making education available, accessible, acceptable and adaptable* (Right to education primers no. 3). Lund: Raoul Wallenberg Institute of Lund University.

Tomasevski, K. (2003). *Human rights in education: A global challenge.* London: Zed Books.

Tomlinson, S. (1982). *A sociology of special education.* London: Routledge & Kegan Paul.

United Nations. (1948). *Universal Declaration of Human Rights.* New York: Author.

United Nations Children's Fund (UNICEF). (2005). *Children and Disability in Transition.* Florence: United Nations Children's Fund Innocenti Research Centre.

United States Congress. (1976). *Education for all handicapped children Act,* Report No. H.R. 94–332. Washington, DC: US Government Printing Office.

Vaughn, S., & Linan-Thompson, S. (2003). What is special about special education for students with learning disabilities? *The Journal of Special Education, 37*(3), 140–147.

Whitebread, D. (Ed.). (2000). *The psychology of teaching and learning in the primary school.* London: RoutledgeFalmer.

World Bank. (n.d.) *Education and the World Bank.* Available at: http://web.worldbank.org/WEBSITE/EXTERNAL/TOPICS/EXTEDUCATION/ (Accessed September 15, 2005).

Ysseldyke, J. E. (2001). Reflections on a research career: Generalizations from 25 years of research on assessment and instructional decision making. *Exceptional Children, 67*(3), 295–309.

2

Confronting difference: an excursion through the history of special education

M a r g r e t   A .   W i n z e r

Across the range of human behaviour, there is some point at which different societies and cultures make a judgement as to whether an individual is normal or abnormal. Those considered abnormal are variously labelled exceptional, different, disabled, or deviant. While all societies have faced the fact of individuals who differed physically, intellectually, or socially, how these differences have been addressed mirrors the vibrant and shifting gestalt of societal dynamics and forms one critical indicator of a society's humanity. However, because the markers for the moral correctness of a position stand in their own time and space, difference and disability have been conceptualized and addressed differently from era to era. It is the interweaving of many complex threads – social, political, economic, and religious which create a propitious climate – one that respects the rights of all individuals in a particular society at a given time. It also establishes the climate in which models of schooling and schools evolve in a particular society.

It was not until the middle decades of the eighteenth century that Europe turned, for the first time, towards the education of persons with disabilities. The spirit of reform, crystallized in the philosophy and precepts of the European Enlightenment, created new vistas for disabled persons and the pioneers who ventured to teach them. Although special education emerged in a number of national contexts, France was the crucible where innovative pedagogies to assist those deaf, blind, and intellectually disabled emerged and flourished (Winzer, 1986). Following the French initiatives, movements to provide services for those in the normative categories of deaf, blind, and intellectually disabled were contemporaneous in continental Europe, Britain, and North America. And, taking into account national idiosyncrasies, the broad outlines of intervention were similar. For example, following a progression that has become a constant pattern in the development of special education provision, deaf persons were the first to be served, followed by services to assist those who are blind, followed by services for persons with intellectual disabilities (Winzer, 1998). In addition, much education for people with disabilities has been inspired by evangelical commitment; early pioneers and teachers often arose from the clergy.

From the outset, special education has been subject to reforms. In fact, more than in general education, reform movements directed at curriculum, at specific groups, at discrete settings, or at the entire enterprise, have redounded. The complex history and cycles of special education show a field always vulnerable to the caprice of changing fashions, politics, and fads, and characterized by fervent appeals to new philosophies and paradigm shifts. Quests for reform come from within the profession; just as often from without. The field can catalogue a long series of reforms constructed in particular eras in response to political rhetoric, social perceptions, and fiscal conditions.

The emotional appeal of school location – where students designated as having special needs should receive services – has made school addresses central to all reform in special education. As reforms are continuous and reflect a society's view of what is important at a given time, a gradual humanizing stance from society in general has been accompanied with significant thrusts for general school environments, currently encapsulated as inclusive education, inclusive schooling or, occasionally, progressive inclusion.

Given the critical nature of location in the history of special education, this chapter uses locational developments as stepping stones through its history to provide an overview of historical developments. The history of special education is complex and the debates, issues, and controversies that have always characterized the enterprise so interwoven that a quick review cannot capture the reforms and detours in development nor the subtle ways in which particular contentions have been woven together to generate arguments for a particular ideological stance. More detailed accounts of these issues can be found in Cole (1989), Lazerson (1983), Tomlinson (1982), and Winzer (1993).

ADDRESSING THE HISTORY OF SPECIAL EDUCATION

The history of special education cannot be described as extensive; the historical literature tends to be scattered and specialized. Save perhaps for the history of deaf education, there is so little comprehensive research that the historical development remains a relatively unexplored cul-de-sac within the history of education.

Indeed, many special educators seem curiously disinterested in the foundations of the field; historical knowledge is learned incidentally and unintentionally (Mostert & Crockett, 1999–2000; Winzer, 2004). To some, history becomes increasingly selective, with the past made over to suit present intentions; others speak to the 'lack of history' (Renzaglia, Hutchins & Lee, 1997, p. 361). At the same time, some contemporary writers disparage earlier events, programmes, and pioneers in favour of contemporary models. Some point to fossilized traditions; others hold that if today's inclusive movement embodies the best ideals of social justice then the past, by extension, had to be unjust (Winzer, 2004). Implicit to this position is a steadfast unwillingness to learn from the wisdom of the accumulated past.

In 1975, Blatt observed that 'in this field we call special education, history has not served us well. We have not learned from it' (p. 404). Yet, the complex dilemmas of contemporary special education did not emerge in a vacuum; rather, they arose from almost two centuries of social, legal, and educational changes that have left a storehouse of unresolved issues.

Historical inquiry is a vital component of the struggle to understand our ideologies and practices. Complex issues seldom yield to broad generalizations and a historical tool enables us to examine theoretical stances in different ways and challenge the inadequacies of single explanations for complex educational movements. Certainly, a consideration of the historical background of current issues is no guarantee that special education will not repeat its mistakes, but an examination of the past illuminates both past endeavours and the underpinnings of current dilemmas. Distinguished pioneers have provided a legacy and a 'heritage rich with lessons abundantly able to inform contemporary issues in special education, particularly those related to intervention' (Mostert & Crockett, 1999–2000, p. 134).

While some detours cannot be erased from our professional history, special educators do not need to assuage some collective guilt. Rather, we should celebrate the contributions of the brilliant, innovative, often controversial and erratic philosophers, physicians, pedagogues and many others of a philanthropic bent who laboured in their own societies and eras to improve the lives of persons with disabilities. Among the venerable list are those who created opportunities for deaf persons such as John Wallis, John Bulwer, John Comad Amman, Samuel Heinicke, Michael Charles de l'Epée, and Thomas Hopkins Gallaudet. For those blind stand Edward Ruston, Valentin Häuy, and Samuel Gridley Howe. Phillippe Pinel, Jean Etienne Esquirol, Benjamin Rush, and William Tuke improved the lives of those mentally ill; Itard, Seguin, Belhomme, Ferrus, Falret, Voisin, Vallee, and Saugert intervened with people who were mentally retarded.

PIONEERING EFFORTS

Prior to the mid-eighteenth century, individual deviations were rarely tolerated and little was done for those who in some way disrupted the norms of a society. Disability was not an innocuous boundary; rather, it was a liability in social and economic participation. People perceived as disabled – whatever the type or degree – were lumped together under the broad categorization of *idiot*, scorned as inferior beings and deprived of rights and privileges.

This early period is replete with innumerable stories of healing, many imbued with an aura of the miraculous. By the close of the fifteenth century, the uncertain recitation of miracle and legend conceded to the more or less stable compilation of authenticated records. By the end of the next century, there was a growing literature, a spawning of ideas, and innovative individual interventions, particularly with deaf persons (see Winzer, 1993).

The middle decades of the eighteenth century witnessed the pervasive influence of the European Enlightenment. While the intellectual project of the Enlightenment was to build a sound body of knowledge about the world, its humanitarian philosophy prompted ideas about the equality of all people and the human responsibility to take care of others, particularly individuals outside the private circle of the home and the family. Reform movements sprang up, aimed at the improvement of the well-being of groups of individuals, varying from poor people and slaves to prisoners, the insane, and disabled people.

In France, the Abbé Michel Charles de l'Epée assimilated Enlightenment ideals of equality, as well as novel concepts about language and its development. He joined these to the sensationalist philosophy of John Locke and the French *philosophes* to promote innovative approaches to the education of deaf persons. If de l'Epée's doctrine promoting a silent language of the hands was not unprecedented, it was nevertheless revolutionary in the context of the times. In devising and instructing through a language of signs, the Abbé gave notice that speech was no longer the apex of instruction in the education of deaf persons. Simultaneously, he influenced and guided innovations for other groups with disabilities, specifically those blind, deaf blind, and intellectually disabled.

Following de l'Epée's successful mission with deaf students, Valentin Häuy in 1782 initiated the instruction of blind persons using a raised print method. Somewhat later, in 1810, Edouard Seguin devised pedagogy for those considered to be mentally retarded.

The French educational initiatives travelled the Atlantic to be adopted by pioneer educators in the United States and Canada.

The influence in Britain was less pervasive. In that turbulent period, religious zealotry and political conservatism held sway, while one dominant mode in British thought was animosity to all things French. Although the British social climate promoted education of some disabled persons largely as an extension of schemes for managing the impecunious, the dependent, orphans, and 'vicious' children, the French advances were largely denounced. For example, the sign language system developed by de l'Epée was characterized as 'altogether useless' and 'an absurd and inexcusable waste of time' (cited by Seigel, 1969, p. 115).

Rejection of French innovations did not imply that British advances were minor. On the contrary. Building on the prerogatives of earlier pioneers, teachers and clergy such as Thomas Braidwood and John Townsend promoted education for deaf persons. Schemes to assist other groups soon followed.

By the close of the eighteenth century in Europe and Britain, the instruction of disabled persons was no longer confined to isolated cases or regarded merely as a subject of philosophic curiosity. Permanent facilities were established, staffed by a cadre of teachers experimenting with novel and innovative pedagogical methods. The French endeavours formed the core of systems and methods adopted in the United States and much of British North America (Canada). In the latter, however, the Maritime provinces of Nova Scotia and New Brunswick initially adopted British pedagogy (see Winzer, 1993).

INSTITUTIONAL MODELS

Prompted by Enlightenment thought, early-nineteenth century Americans found a common level of sympathy to improve the lives of people who were weak, dependent, or disabled. Founded on a humanitarian philosophy, evangelical commitment, and unbounded philanthropy, they established from 1817 onwards a complex of institutions designed to cater to the unique needs of exceptional individuals.

As social philosophy, special education was reformist but not radical. Institutional openings coincided with a period of wide social reform and embodied the three major principles of nineteenth-century child rescue – protection, separation, and dependence. Development was built on the recognition of the need for organized social responsibility and intrinsically associated with changing social, economic, political, and religious determinants of early-nineteenth century American society. As well as being urged on the grounds of expediency, charity, and imperative duty, institutional formation represented rapidly changing perceptions of the role of disabled persons in an industrializing society.

This early special education, under the aegis of the clergy and philanthropy, and presented in an expanding complex of institutional settings, had two faces. On the one hand, it was the protector of vulnerable children. Pioneer reformers, not uncertain in their piety and concerned with humane treatment for the disabled and disenfranchised, set out to provide for those perceived as being in need of assistance. Institutional settings would protect children and youth from a callous world, while at the same time providing examples of the evangelical belief that all people were capable of being saved. For examples, Thomas Hopkins Gallaudet, reflecting his views of upper-class Protestant New England society, defined his role within a missionary context. He viewed himself as responsible for the character formation of pupils, and entrusted by God as a private steward of their welfare (Valentine, 1991). Deaf people to Gallaudet (1836) were 'Long-neglected heathens,' (p. 217), excluded from the hopes and knowledge of Christianity and dwelling in a 'moral desert' (in Barnard, 1852, p. 102).

On the other hand, the activities had the effect of limiting opportunities for the very pupils they set out to serve. Child-saving was sanctioned in the interests of social control: special schooling served the interests of advantaged members of society by maintaining and rationalizing the further marginalization of those it purported to help. It also served to turn consumers into producers. Schooling for blind children would remove from society 'so many dead weights' and prevent them from becoming 'taxes on the community' (Dunscombe, 1836, p. 97). Education would emancipate deaf children from 'the fetters ... imposed by their deafness' (Ontario Institution, 1895, p. 12) so that 'the old ignorance, the old animism, the old brutishness are passed away' (Turner, 1858). For the mentally retarded, 'Being consumers and not producers they are a pecuniary burden to the state. Educate them and they will become producers' (Knight, 1860, cited in Trent, 1994, p. 25).

Reformers held that students with disabilities required different forms of organization. The system that emerged reflected the perception of disabled persons as different, deviant, and charity recipients. The nature of services was educational, but the context in which they were presented fell wholly within the confines of public charities. Hence, the common designations of institution, asylum, colony, or training school reflected a fact – students were public beneficiaries, dependent on official charity.

Institutionalization, as an idealistic reform, sought to concentrate persons with disabilities in rural environments where the daily regimes were typical of rural life. For persons with mental retardation, the rural institutions soon evolved into farm colonies consisting of a custodial department, a training school, an industrial department, and a farm. Inmates laboured on the farm, worked the heavy machinery in the laundry, print shop or boiler room, and tended the animals and farm. Females performed domestic chores, did the sewing and mending, and the hand laundry. For custodial clients, even rudimentary optimism was soon abandoned. Samuel Gridley Howe ([1848A], 1972) described idiots – at that time the lowest category of feeble mindedness – as 'mere organisms, masses of flesh and none in human shape' (p. 7). Seen as incurable and totally unteachable, the even-

tual release of custodial inmates grew increasingly doubtful.

Throughout the nineteenth century, institutions formed the chief setting for training and instruction. By the close of the century, a complex of institutions was in place and the social, educational, and psychological philosophies that propelled the institutional movement were well developed. However, these institutional settings were not developed within the framework of a stable school system. Permanent facilities predated the common school movement by four decades and birthed the dual system of special and general education that, despite reform efforts, remains prevalent today.

COMMON SCHOOLS

Robert Osgood (1997) points out that 'The common school movement has long constituted one of the defining themes and primary focal points of scholarship in the history of American education' (p. 375). Not only did the movement stamp indelibly the historical and cultural fabric of America and other countries with similar movements, but it changed the course of educational intervention for students with special needs. North American special education drew heavily on British and European experience, particularly in philosophy and pedagogy. Therefore, although this and the following sections address chiefly the North American experience, other nations were, in the broadest way, similar in their development of pedagogies and settings that allows for some generalizations to be made.

Under Horace Mann's reorganization, American public education became, for the first time, a state vehicle. With the primary object the socialization of all children, the common schools represented the unique means to instil American values into students with diverse ethnic, cultural, linguistic, and religious backgrounds and therefore provided a bulwark against the radical social, economic, and demographic changes that threatened to destabilize American society in the post-Civil War period.

The initial vision of the common schools embraced all students, from the docile and tractable to the deviant and the intractable. But almost from the outset, the reformist and optimistic impulses that characterized the common school ideal faltered when confronted with disobedient, rambunctious, and nonconforming students. Issues of classroom behaviour touched upon basic notions of child normalcy (or deviance), and the authority of both adults and social institutions such as schools. The school system was little willing to tolerate students who violated social mores, failed to conform to the expectations of teachers, and mounted threats to the placidity of general classrooms.

Adopting models developed in Halle, Germany in 1859, jurisdictions in the eastern United States established ungraded classes in the 1870s. Those sent to ungraded classes tended to show the unholy trinity of academic retardation, low intelligence, and undesirable behaviour. They were the trouble-makers, depicted in contemporary reports, as the 'morally as well as intellectually weak,' and the 'troublesome and obnoxious' (see Osgood, 1997). The majority of students were male. As Baker (1949/50) later pointed out, 'Boys of all ages bully, fight, and act smart aleck much more frequently than girls' (p. 203). Joining the disabled group were children of immigrant backgrounds. In ungraded classes, the Americanization of immigrant children and English language instruction were fundamental activities (Osgood, 1997).

Leading educators articulated the philosophical and pedagogical bases for the establishment of special segregated classes within the public schools. Bolstering arguments about class size, teacher time, and declining standards were the voices of prominent special educators such as Alexander Graham Bell and Samuel Gridley Howe who disputed institutional landscapes and the congregating of persons with disabilities together. Edward Johnstone, superintendent of the Vineland

Institution for Feeble Minded Boys and Girls took a more modern stance. 'The blind, the deaf, the crippled, and the incorrigibles must some day take their place in the life of the commonwealth with normal people,' he said. Therefore, 'they at least must have training in the public schools to keep them from becoming institutionalized and thus losing touch with normal community life' (Vineland, 1912, p. 22).

Many of the special classes that were formed before 1900 faltered. Classes which sought to raise the pupils' standards to those of regular class members failed in their efforts at remediation; others suffered from a lack of trained teachers, materials, official commitment, and funding. Many schools' systems operated only one type of special class, which were often used merely to dispose of children who did not conform to a school's behavioral standards. Little distinction existed between obstreperous and recalcitrant pupils and defective learners. Only small numbers attended, a condition preserved by attrition. As one administrator pointed out in 1909, these students 'tend to drop out, or be forced out, of school and the problem of the exceptional child disappeared with him' (in Tropea, 1987a, p. 31).

By the close of the nineteenth century, many European jurisdictions provided both free and compulsory education for exceptional students. Denmark, for example, mandated compulsory education for children with sensory impairments in 1817. France passed legislation in 1882 enforcing primary instruction for disabled children. The British Elementary Education Act (Deaf and Blind Children) of 1893 placed the financial responsibility of compulsory education with departments of education. The movement from supplicant to school child emerged more tardily in North America. Although many of the early state constitutions of the United States spoke freely and somewhat loosely about guaranteeing free public education to all children, compulsory schooling became a reality only in the 1890s. Even then, most state's earliest requirements were lax, with exemptions for poor families, families involved in agriculture, and families with sick or disabled children (Trent, 1994).

Thus the majority of children with disabilities remained unserved. Yet, the tightening of compulsory attendance laws meant that schools could no longer ignore part of the clientele; once the state assured the right to compel attendance, then the state also had the responsibility to provide an education congruent with students' needs. Hence, special education, still largely confined to institutional settings and nascent segregated classes, was established as a permanent enterprise. It was, however, a fairly well-kept secret in the entire education establishment. The system was separate from general education with different settings and classes, and the beginning of specialized training for teachers and the development of a cadre of specialists from allied disciplines that bolstered school efforts. Special, segregated classes, which were destined to become both the backbone and the chief bone of contention in special education for all of the next century, arrived largely unheralded.

SPECIAL CLASSES

From about 1890, the movement for special classes gathered strength. By the turn of the century, the schools' responses to student heterogeneity became more organized and the new century ushered in a massive expansion of special, segregated classes. By 1913, 108 cities had special classes and special schools (Trent, 1994). By 1927, 218 US cities had special or ungraded classes for about 52,000 children labelled 'mentally handicapped' (Osgood, 1997).

A matrix of reasons accounted for the mounting numbers of special classes and the students in them. These included rapidly increasing numbers of immigrant children entering neighbourhood schools; the lessened participation of youth in the labour market; greater state involvement in the hitherto sacrosanct domain of the family; legislation affecting women, families, and children; new concepts about child normalcy; the birth of compulsory attendance laws; the testing movement; the development of the fields of psychiatry, psychology, and the mental hygiene movement; slowly changing conceptions of exceptional persons which generated altered ways of viewing the institutionalized population; and complaints about the custodial and retrogressive nature of public residential institutions. Child mortality and child morbidity decreased and faced schools with large numbers of students with mild disabilities to learning. As well, constructs of disability had shifted and evolved during the latter half of the nineteenth century as new knowledge and beliefs about the nature of various conditions and the educability of those identified as having them emerged. The child study movement and new psychological and medical findings made professionals, parents, and the public more alert to the educational implications of physical and mental disabilities.

Medical models prevailed, although deeply influenced by the religious and moral preoccupations of the times. Medical models assumed both quantitative and qualitative difference between normal and abnormal. By the 1880s, socially constructed categories that included emotional and behavioural indices truly emerged. It was believed that 'Minor mental defections were fertile ground that allowed ineradicably evil mental attitudes to take ready root' (Vineland, 1894, p. 37). Contributing further to a medical stance was the popularity of evolutionary explanations for social problems, manifested as Social Darwinism and the eugenics movement.

As biology became destiny, evolutionary analogies, explanations, and ways of thinking rapidly became ubiquitous in North America. The public gravitated towards uncomplicated interpretations and explanations of human differences. Many interpreted the ideas of Darwinism and natural selection to mean that procreation was a social, not an individual, issue. Moreover, individuals could be scientifically shaped and controlled to fulfil the nation's destiny.

Civilized society, threatened by genetically defective strains from both immigration and at home, became hostile and repressive and developed an enthusiasm for sterilization. The first state sterilization law, passed by the Indiana legislature in 1907, provided for the 'prevention of the procreation of "confirmed criminals, idiots, imbeciles, and rapists"' (Landman, 1932, p. 55). Special educators joined the new breed of moral entrepreneurs in their crusade for a genetically and socially pure America. By the mid-1930s, more than 20,000 people with mental retardation and epilepsy had been sterilized (see Winzer, 1993).

Educators operationalized the medical model in various modes. For example, with the emphasis on biology and medical orientations, mental abnormality was propelled to prominence to become the major category of disability by the late 1800s. In the institutions for the mentally retarded, a great reliance developed on medical practice, medical institutional structure, and medical leadership. In the school milieu, educators assumed that disorders had distinct patterns of symptoms and signs that resulted from different disease entities and causes, and responded to different treatments. Children were classified within medical knowledge, labelled with a particular disability designation, viewed as deviant, and propelled toward certain institutions, special classes, and pedagogical practices.

The period that matched the growth of scientific racism – from about 1880 to 1925 – was also the most critical for the development of special classes. Special class promoters in the early twentieth century built cogent and persuasive arguments on an already existing body of sentiment and experience. They argued that special education was a logical extension of regular education and the sole effective means of turning handicapped people into producers, and a means of protecting society from 'the threat of the feeble-minded'.

Within the confines of the school system, segregated classrooms effectively removed what Wallin (1914) called the 'flotsam and jetsam', the 'hold backs and the drags' (p. 390). Thus removed from the mainstream, problem children could not disrupt classrooms or contaminate the learning of others. As well, educators could 'ensure diagnosis and treatment at an early age' and use the classes or 'clearing houses for personnel segregation before adult life is reached' (Fernald, 1912, p. 9). Moreover, said a later writer, 'The special school or class has many advantages in that the various resources of the school system can be centered upon traditional and certain desirable routines in behavior can be more easily established' (Notes ..., 1946/47, p. 49).

From 1910 to 1930 there occurred a huge spurt in the enrolments in and types of special classes. Special settings and specially trained teachers served children variously described as deaf, blind, hard of hearing, near blind, undernourished, crippled, academically maladjusted, mentally retarded, speech defective, tubercular, and so on (Palen, 1923). The most heavily funded programmes in Canada and the United States were in mental retardation, followed by speech and hearing disorders.

As the special classes expanded and the fields of psychology, mental testing, social work, and health care developed, a corps of special personnel emerged. Special services provided by psychologists, public health nurses, school workers, and clinics supplemented the work of the schools.

Increased financial support for special classes and schools after World War I ushered in a period of rapid growth in services for mildly handicapped students (Johnson, 1962). Classes, pupils, the teaching force, teacher training facilities, and allied specialists expanded even further. By 1949, there were 175 institutions offering preparation programmes for special educators. The curricula designed for segregated classrooms were refined and structured.

Traditionally, those considered abnormal were seen as not only valueless but generally harmful to society; besides being non-producers, they absorbed the energies and the productive power of others. During the 1920s, special educators flirted with the concepts of Progressive education. They embraced the notion that schools should assume leadership in initiating social change and accept responsibility for the present and future needs of students. To many practitioners, the ultimate goal of special classes was 'to provide as many as possible with the means of living as normally as possible and of procuring independent livelihood' (Percival, 1946/47, p. 237).

In special classrooms, teachers constructed and then reaffirmed the belief that their students were both capable of and deserving of an education. They abandoned the inflexible curricula that proved the undoing of children who did not conform to the common notion of normal. Rather, practical instruction in trades and agriculture for the boys and in domestic skills for the girls took precedence over the academic programme. About half the time was spent on academics. The remainder was on practical handwork – sewing, weaving, knitting, and cooking for the girls; woodwork for the boys (Percival, 1946/47).

Percival observed in 1946 that 'The immediate purpose of most of these special classes is, of course, to enable the pupils to mingle in due course with normal children' (p. 237). This rarely happened. Right into the 1960s, the segregated class was the unchallenged leader as the preferred setting for students with special needs. In fact, special classes expanded even more during the late 1960s, in part due to the creation of the category of learning disabilities in 1963.

At the same time, the expansion of special classes confirmed for general teachers the parameters of acceptable achievement and behaviour in their own classrooms. Social rejection and stigmatization of pupils and perceptions of the field as unique and different widened into a chasm separating both sets of players within a dual system. Special education remained different and separate from the general stream, with alternate guidelines for programme planning and service provisions.

CREATING A PROFESSION

At the time of the founding institutions, schooling was a charitable enterprise; worthy, but unimportant to the national interest. Early administrators arose from the clergy; it was not until mid-century that private philanthropy ceded to bureaucratic social welfare and school leaders introduced an ethic of disinterested public service. As they developed, the institutions came to share two basic qualities: a highly progressive and reformist zeal among the leaders, and an increasing reliance on the expertise of a scientific and professionalized teaching corps.

Teachers of the deaf came early to asserting a sense of unique professional identity; the process of professionalization began during the 1840s when various organizations such as the Convention of American Educators of the Deaf and Dumb emerged. Associations for teachers, administrators, and workers in the fields of blindness and mental retardation developed a little later.

In concert with the burgeoning special classes that grew so rapidly in the opening decades of the twentieth century, the professional paradigm that guided special education shifted and expanded. As teachers of students with special needs assiduously established their own sense of professionalism and authority, they increasingly developed a belief about their mission, how it should be carried out, and the credentials that qualified a person to enter the profession. In doing so, they generated new beliefs about educators' status and power in relation to the clients, to parents, to allied disciplines, and to the world at large (see Osgood, 1999).

New visions of teacher training emerged. College and university programmes paralleled the growth of day schools and day classes. By 1930, ten states set forth legal requirements for teacher certification, usually an elementary degree plus supplemental training (Scheier, 1931).

New and more encompassing professional associations flourished. These not only validated a sense of separateness and uniqueness among special educators as they struggled for recognition and acceptance in the world of public education, but also distanced special educators from their general education peers, setting them apart in terms of what they knew and how they saw themselves (see Osgood, 1999).

Because 'Pupils with dull minds, crippled bodies, speech defects, deafness, or twisted emotions came to school' (Laycock, 1937/38, p. 108), teachers had to respond to the complex interrelationships of social, emotional, and intellectual traits. It is not surprising that unique attributes quickly attached to special education teachers and expectations regarding their superior teaching skills and personal characters were set high. Writers pointed out that teachers should be selected on the basis of personality qualifications (Font, 1944/45). Samuel Laycock (1940/41) warned that the teacher of special classes should be 'emotionally mature and have a wholesome emotional life of her own' (p. 5). She could not be irritable or bad tempered, fussy or coddling, a self-pitier, not starved in her emotional life; rather, grown up in her sex life and free from frustration and conflict in her own life.

CHANGING SCHOOL ADDRESSES

The 1960s, which marked large-scale political, social, and economic change in the context of many disenfranchised and marginalized groups, saw the modern rewriting of the special education script and the beginning of a genuine movement towards integration and desegregation. Parents, consumers, and advocates used the period's increased sensitivity to human and civil rights to promote the normalization philosophy, the 'handicappism' movement, and to mount a case against special education as it was practised at that time.

The United States has a long history of relying on legislative and judicial remedies for social issues, including special education. By 1930, 16 US states had passed legislation authorizing special education. By 1946, there were well over a hundred laws directed toward the education of exceptional students (Martens, 1946). The 1960s witnessed a boom in legislation and generous funding provided for training personnel and implementing separate programmes. There was an upsurge of funding federally and by the states in the 1960s, as well as critical initiatives such as the President's Panel on Mental Retardation. However, critics chided still that 'One-half of the estimated 7,000,000 handicapped children in our nation are still not receiving special education services in our schools' (Gallagher, 1970, p. 712).

As the fervent egalitarianism and humanism of the 1960s created a new climate, the educational integration of students with disabilities became the central theme of special education. Vexatious questions about segregated instruction mounted, chiefly on the basis of efficacy studies on pupil outcomes. The reasoning of the Supreme Court in the 1954 *Brown* vs *Board of Education* decisions was widely cited in arguments against segregated classes. Calls by persons with disabilities and their advocates for increased participation grew more strident during the 1970s. The next decade introduced overarching and prescriptive federal legislation with the comprehensive enabling legislation (PL 94–142, the Education for All Handicapped Children Act) and the concept of the least restrictive environment, interpreted as mainstreaming.

Beginning in the early 1980s, waves of reform surged across the educational systems of many nations. One of the strongest and most basic of the reform efforts in general education revolved around ensuring educational equity and opportunity for all students. Special education quickly co-opted the voice of reform. Now the rallying cry of greater access to the mainstream was replaced by a much more complex note, that of full access to a restructured mainstream, encapsulated as inclusive schooling.

In its philosophical guise, inclusive schooling for students with special needs is grounded in quite specific conceptions of social justice, ethics, and rights. These are an outgrowth of a liberal-democratic social philosophy focusing on individual civil rights, mobilizing the discourse of equity, and guided by axiomatic moral imperatives. Ultimately, as Barton (1999) observes, inclusion 'is about the transformation of a society and its formal institutional arrangements, such as education. This means changes in the values, priorities and policies that support and perpetuate practices of exclusion and discrimination' (p. 58). Operationalized, inclusive schooling aims to rid education of stubborn, long-standing inequalities through a revisualization of the organizational structures of schools.

Because location – a student's school address – has become a central motif of the inclusion movement in North America, inclusive schooling has become a code phrase for school restructuring. When inclusion was adapted from general school reforms, the basic constructs of individual rights and equity translated into 'sameness of treatment' which immediately mutated to 'sameness of experience'. Because sameness of experience has been interpreted by many as physical place, the question of location has become the hub of controversy and the podium for much emotional moralizing and value-laden stances.

In the early-1990s, the clarion call was for full inclusion. Advocates contended that it was more enlightened to alter the classroom and school structure to allow all children to gain an education there than to segregate some students in special settings. The area is complex and fluid. Today, full inclusion in general classrooms is not blanket policy; rather, there exist selective and pragmatic policies based on student needs and the capacity-building of school systems.

Certainly, inclusive schooling has moved from an idea to a conviction to become the dominant ideology in contemporary special education. But despite ideological and philosophical convictions, inclusion remains better accepted in the concept than in the practice. The undergirding philosophy is resilient and can be advocated unequivocally. When the ideology is transferred to the lived worlds of teachers and the hard realities of general classrooms, problems abound. Efforts to forge a fundamentally different educational framework for students with special needs are ambitious but school restructuring and reform efforts have failed to have the necessary impact on traditional school structures.

POSTSCRIPT

As a complex and challenging area, special education is often shaped by emotional responses and historical and cultural beliefs. This brief survey of the major stepping stones in its development shows that over the decades as society has confronted difference, there has been a gradual humanizing attitude toward persons with disabilities manifested both as societal attitudes and as school addresses. It also points out that there are significant patterns of change, as well as patterns of continuity, in the history of special education.

Special education was established formally and permanently in the United States in 1818. The complex of institutions that rapidly arose predated education for normally developing students by decades and grew as essentially a dual system, quite separate from the general stream. However, the systems of service delivery produced by special education from 1817 onwards were not short-lived or static; they evolved and changed, producing new events and actions.

Almost from the time of Horace Mann's creation of the common schools, the public system was tested by student differences and the concern for bureaucratic efficiency. Educators embarked on sustained efforts to address the obstacles that student diversity meant to the organizational structures of the system. Rapidly, the troublesome matters of difference, deviance, and delinquency were addressed not through the general classrooms' assumption of the process, but through the mechanisms of ungraded and unruly class.

At the dawn of the twentieth century, new medical and scientific knowledge, increasing social fears and a climate of interventionist social reform provided the historical context within which the end result was steadily increasing numbers of children identified as in need of special schooling. The growth of segregated settings in both numbers and importance provides vivid portraits of societal and educational perceptions of students with exceptionalities. Not only did the establishment of special classes illustrate how changing societal and educational conditions and priorities eroded the underpinnings of the common school movement, but also how those considered deviant and different were viewed by society.

Right into the 1960s, institutional settings and segregated classes remained the primary mechanisms for educating students with disabilities. However, in light of increasing concerns about social justice, equity, and individual civil rights within education, there occurred a massive remodelling of special education beginning in that decade. Agents of change challenged the persistence of traditional attitudes. Still, the intensification of the trend away from special classes answered not the education decision-making process but, rather, non-educational influences such as civil rights concerns.

In the current climate, special education is no longer viewed as a distant and not too respectable cousin of general education. Inclusive education makes children and youth with exceptionalities the concern of all involved in the school system. Today's inclusive schooling movement may be viewed as one more resolution to the matter of difference. For the moment, inclusion seems set to remain at the forefront of special education reform. Nevertheless, it must be recognized that for students with special needs, the ethic of universal provision remains an elusive dream and many issues remain unresolved. While it is almost universally conceded that people with disabilities have a natural and rightful place in society and that schools should mirror this broader commitment, the dilemma that emerges is not just what such a commitment should mean but how to operationalize it and make it happen.

Special educators are perhaps more adept at advocacy than prophecy. While the concepts and practices we strive towards today may appear sophisticated and socially just, this may not be a permanent status. Solutions to the dilemma of difference and the resolutions of special education do not emerge out of a social vacuum. Today's reforms may indeed appear primitive to historians in another hundred years.

REFERENCES

Baker, H. J. (1949/50). Significance of individual items in case work. *Journal of Exceptional Children*, 16, 203–206.

Barnard, H. (1852). Eulogy: Thomas Hopkins Gallaudet. *American Annals of the Deaf and Dumb, 4*, 81–136.

Barton, L. (1999). Market ideologies, education and the challenge. In H. Daniels & P. Garner (Eds.), *World yearbook of education: Inclusive education* (pp. 54–62). London: Kogan Page.

Blatt, B. (1975). Toward an understanding of people with special needs. In J. M. Kauffman & J. S. Payne (Eds.), *Mental retardation: Introduction and personal perspectives* (pp. 388–427). Columbus, OH: Merrill.

Cole, T. (1989). *Apart or a part? Integration and the growth of British special education.* Milton Keynes, UK: Open University Press.

Dunscombe, C. (1836). *Report upon the subject of education made to the Parliament of Upper Canada, 25 February 1836, through the Commissioners, Doctors Morrison and Bruce, appointed by a resolution of the House of Assembly in 1835 to obtain information upon the subject of education, etc.* Upper Canada: M. C. Reynolds.

Fernald, W. (1912). *History of the treatment of the feebleminded.* Boston, MA: Geo. H. Ellis.

Font, M. M. (1944/45). Who is the exceptional child? *Journal of Exceptional Children*, 11, 19–20.

Gallagher, J. J. (1970). Unfinished educational tasks: Thoughts on leaving government service. *Exceptional Children*, 37, 709–716.

Gallaudet, T. H. (1836). The duty and advantages of affording instruction to the deaf and dumb. In E. J. Mann, *The deaf and dumb: Or, a collection of articles relating to the condition of deaf mutes, and the principal asylums devoted to their instruction* (pp. 217–231). Boston, MA: D. K. Hitchcock.

Howe, S. G. [1848A] (1972). *On the causes of idiocy: being the supplement to the report of Dr. S. G. Howe and the other commissioners appointed by the governor of Massachusetts to inquire into the condition of idiots of the Commonwealth, dated February 26, 1848, with an appendix.* New York: Arno Press and New York Times reprint.

Johnson, G. O. (1962). Special education for the mentally handicapped – a paradox. *Exceptional Children, 29,* 62–69.

Landman, J. H. (1932). *Human sterilization: The history of the sexual sterilization movement.* New York: Macmillan.

Laycock, S. R. (1937/38). The whole child comes to school. *Journal of Exceptional Children, 4,* 97–100, 108–109.

Laycock, S. R. (1940/41). Mental health qualifications for special class teachers. *Journal of Exceptional Children, 7,* 4–8, 23.

Lazerson, M. (1983). Educational institutions and mental subnormality: Notes on writing a history. In M. Begab & S. Richardson (Eds.) *Mental subnormality and society: Social science perspectives.* Baltimore, MD: University Park Press.

Martens, E. H. (1946). State legislation for the education of exceptional children – some basic principles. *Exceptional Children, 13,* 225–230.

Mostert, M. P., & Crockett, J. B. (1999–2000). Reclaiming the history of special education for more effective practice. *Exceptionality, 8,* 133–143.

Notes from the twenty-second annual meeting (1946/47). *Journal of Exceptional Children, 13,* 49–57.

Ontario Institution for the Education and Instruction of the Deaf and Dumb (1895). *Annual Report.* Toronto: Queen's Printer.

Osgood, R. L. (1997). Undermining the common school ideal: Intermediate schools and ungraded classes in Boston, 1838–1900. *History of Education Quarterly, 37,* 375–398.

Osgood, R. (1999). Becoming a special educator: Specialized professional training for teachers of children with disabilities in Boston, 1870–1930. *Teachers College Record, 161,* 82–105.

Palen, I. (1923). Ears that hear not. *Social Welfare, 5.*

Percival, W. P. (1946/47). Special education in Quebec and Maritime provinces. *Exceptional Children, 13,* 237–241.

Renzaglia, A., Hutchins, M., & Lee, S. (1997). The impact of teacher education on the beliefs, attitudes, and dispositions of preservice special educators. *Teacher Education and Special Education, 20,* 360–377.

Scheier, S. (1931). *Problems in the training of certain special-class teachers.* New York: Columbia University.

Seigel, J. P. (1969). The Enlightenment and the evolution of the language of signs in France and England. *Journal of the History of Ideas, 30,* 96–115.

Tomlinson, R. (1982). Special needs in education. ERIC Doc. No. 235 614.

Trent, J. W. (1994). *Inventing the feeble mind: A history of mental retardation in the United States.* Los Angeles: University of California Press.

Tropea, J. L. (1987). Bureaucratic order and special children: Urban schools, 1950s–1960s. *History of Education Quarterly, 27,* 341–361.

Tropea, J. L. (1987a). Bureaucratic order and special children: Urban schools, 1890s–1940s. *History of Education Quarterly, 27,* 29–53.

Turner, W. W. (1858). A contrast. *American Annals of the Deaf and Dumb, 7,* 12–15.

Valentine, P. (1991, June). Thomas Hopkins Gallaudet: Benevolent paternalism and the origins of the American Asylum. Paper presented at the First International Conference on the History of Deafness, Washington, DC.

Vineland, New Jersey Training School for Feeble-Minded Boys and Girls (1894). *Annual report.* Vineland, NJ: Author.

Vineland, New Jersey Training School for Feeble-Minded Boys and Girls (1912). *Annual report.* Vineland, NJ: Author.

Wallin, J. E. W. (1914). *The mental health of the school child: The psycho-educational clinic in relation to child welfare.* New Haven, CT: Yale University Press.

Winzer, M. A. (1986). Early development in special education: Some aspects of Enlightenment thought. *Remedial and Special Education, 7,* 42–49.

Winzer, M. A. (1993). *The history of special education: From isolation to integration.* Washington, DC: Gallaudet University Press.

Winzer, M. A. (1998). A tale often told: The early progression of special education. *Remedial and Special Education, 19,* 212–218.

Winzer, M. A. (2004). The history of special education: The past confronts new paradigms. In *In service of school and science* (pp. 65–71). Krakow: Polish Academy of Pedagogical Sciences.

3

A sociology of special education

Sheila Riddell

INTRODUCTION

This chapter identifies social theories currently in play in the field of special education, drawing on literature from Scotland, the wider UK, Europe, North America and Australia. Particular reference is made to the Scottish policy context, placed within a wider UK and national context. An underlying assumption is that theories of special/additional support needs and disability are crucial in terms of understanding policy responses in school and the wider society. As Kirp (1982) noted, the way in which a 'social problem' is constructed says a great deal about how it will be resolved. In an earlier paper (Riddell, 1996), I suggested that the following sociological perspectives were in evidence: essentialist, social constructionist, materialist, postmodern and disability rights. Here, I argue that these perspectives are still evident, but can be grouped under the broad headings of functionalist and critical paradigms. As noted by Fulcher (1989), discourses are malleable and words such as inclusion can be used by different interest groups to refer to almost diametrically opposed concepts. A theme running throughout the chapter is that language and taxonomies, far from being innocent descriptors, are deployed tactically by different actors for a range of strategic purposes. It is therefore always important to consider who benefits from the dominance of particular discourses. The overall aim of the chapter is not simply to discuss the epistemological underpinning of particular approaches to research and theory in the field of special education, but also to illuminate their role in shaping the policy and practice agenda.

It should be noted that whilst reference is made to the US literature and policy context, the major focus is on UK research and scholarship, with a particular emphasis on the Scottish context.

WHAT IS SPECIAL EDUCATION?

Booth (1996) noted that there is often a reluctance to be clear about what is meant by special education and special/additional support needs, with the result that commentators may be operating with different concepts. It is evident that special education, and those considered to be in need of it, are shifting rather than fixed constructs. For example, in the developed world it is evident that separate institutions still exist for those at the social margins, including children with behavioural problems and those with severe mental health or learning difficulties. The term special education has often been used to refer to these types of segregated institutions. At the same time, there is a trend for disabled children, and those with special/additional support needs, to be accommodated within mainstream schools. Following the Salamanca statement (UNESCO, 1994) inclusion has been accepted as the policy orthodoxy of the European Union and member states. However, this does not mean that segregation is a dying concept, but rather that its form is changing, with far more emphasis on placement in special units within mainstream schools. This can be an invisible form of segregation, since the child's name may appear on the mainstream roll, whilst spending virtually all of his or her time in a separate location removed from the wider school community. Munn, Lloyd & Cullen (2000) noted that, whilst the stated aim is to reintegrate children placed in special units back into the mainstream, this goal is scarcely ever achieved as the child increasingly drifts away from their peer group.

It is important, therefore, to be sensitive to the shifting construction of special education, and to the fact that segregation increasingly takes place within mainstream settings. At the same time, there are shifting patterns in the construction of which pupils are deemed to require special or additional education. There is growing evidence from social attitudes research in Scotland and the wider UK that the population is sympathetic to the inclusion of people with physical or sensory impairments or learning difficulties (see, for example, Scottish Executive, 2003a), and placement in mainstream schools for these groups is generally non-contentious. However, teachers, backed up by their unions, are expressing growing concern in relation to a perceived increase in the number of disruptive and violent pupils

(Tomlinson, 2001). Including these children in mainstream classes is claimed by teachers to run counter to the UK government's desire to raise attainment, particularly for socially disadvantaged groups.

To summarise, special education and the child with additional/special educational needs are construed differently at different points in history and within different cultures. Following Bogdan and Knoll's (1995) distinction between special education sociology, which applies existing constructs uncritically, and the sociology of special education, which deconstructs theories and practices, this chapter problematises the core assumptions, categories and practices underlying constructions of special education. In the following sections, I review the sociological theories which underpin the construction of disability and special/additional support needs, the proponents of particular theoretical positions and the type of special education policy supported by particular theories, whether implicitly or explicitly.

FUNCTIONALIST AND CRITICAL PARADIGMS

As noted above, for the purposes of this chapter I have divided theories of special education into two broad camps, functionalist and critical. Functionalist thinking is rooted in the ideas of the French sociologist Emile Durkheim, which were set out a hundred years ago. Durkheim developed the view that social cohesion was a natural and desirable state, and conflicts which threatened this social stability were to be repressed. The aim of the healthy society was to include as many people as possible, and neutralise or reform those at the margins. Exclusion was thus seen as residual rather than endemic (Levitas, 1998). Within the current UK context, with a Labour-controlled UK government and a Labour–Liberal coalition in Scotland, the problem of social and school exclusion and inclusion have been high on the political agenda, and different discourses have emerged as ways of tackling exclusion. These have ranged from radical attempts to tackle poverty through wealth distribution, through to more conservative ideas associated with reforming or punishing the excluded. Finally, in all developed countries, there is an emphasis on active labour market policies, with the aim of hooking those at the margins into mainstream society through the redeeming properties of vocational education and work. As explained below, individualist and managerialist theories of special education, and the policies and practices which flow from them, fall under the broad heading of functionalist accounts since they are driven by the desire to define normal behaviour which will contribute to social stability.

Critical paradigms, on the other hand, rather than seeing conflict and challenge as abnormal, regard these as manifestations of unequal power relations or social interactions. Accounts located within critical social policy and socio-cultural theory tend to be more common in the academic rather than the policy literature, and often serve as challenges to common sense notions of how the world should be organised.

FUNCTIONALIST PARADIGMS

Essentialist or individual needs approaches

Early approaches to special education were informed by eugenic ideas which were in the ascendancy in Europe and the US in the late nineteenth and early twentieth centuries (Kerr & Shakespeare, 2002). Francis Galton distinguished between 'positive eugenics', which focused on encouraging good stock to breed, and 'negative eugenics', which focused on discouraging the mentally and morally unfit from reproducing. Those exhibiting mental or physical deficiency should be isolated from the rest of the population to avoid contamination. IQ tests, developed in the early twentieth century, provided educational psychologists with an additional tool to use in determining whose

intelligence fell outwith the normal range. Lubeck and Garrett (1990), describing the construction of the 'at risk' child in the USA, noted that American pioneers of mental testing believed that intelligence was inherited and fixed rather than malleable, and was linked to racial origin. Henry Goddard, an early proponent of mental testing, was invited by the government to administer the Binet Simon scale and other performance tests to recent immigrants at the Ellis Island receiving station. Data gathered by means of these early psychometric tests was reported as showing that a very high proportion of new immigrants, specifically Jews, Hungarians, Italians and Russians were 'feeble-minded' (Laosa, 1973).

Translated into practice, eugenic thinking was sometimes brutal in its insistence on incarceration, but could sometimes adopt a more benevolent face, suggesting that identifying the weak and feeble-minded was essential in order to provide appropriate treatment. Tomlinson (1982) noted that the Egerton Commission of 1889 recommended access to basic vocational education for the blind to prevent them becoming a burden on the state.

Early eugenic social theories played a pivotal role in shaping the development of special education in the US and Europe. In Scotland, individualised assessment leading to specialised and special education has been the traditional approach, although the focus has shifted from categorising handicaps to assessing individual educational needs (see Riddell, 2001, for a detailed account of the development of special education in Scotland). Prior to 1980, Scotland operated with nine legal categories of handicap (deafness, partial deafness, blindness, partial sightedness, mental handicap, epilepsy, speech defects, maladjustment and physical handicap). If a child was suspected of having one of these conditions, parents were legally obliged to present the child at a clinic for medical assessment with a view to ascertaining whether 'special educational treatment' was required. In urban areas, special schools were set up to deal with each of these conditions, whilst in rural areas children were either educated within local schools or sent to residential establishments at some distance form their homes. Until 1974, a certain proportion of children were deemed 'ineducable and untrainable', and the health board rather than the local authority had responsibility for their care.

Following the Warnock Report (DES, 1978), legislation in England and Scotland replaced the legal categories of handicap with the overarching category of 'special educational needs' (SEN) whose definition was somewhat circular: 'A child or young person has "special educational needs" if the child or young person has a "learning difficulty" which calls for provision for special educational needs to be made.' This new category was intended to emphasise that special educational needs were not solely located in the child, but were due to the relationship between the child and the school. Control of the special education terrain shifted from medical practitioners to educational psychologists, who orchestrated the process of assessment and recording. Teachers were accorded only a subordinate role in assessment and diagnosis.

Despite the official rejection of the idea that special education should be reserved for those identified as having medical deficits, categorical thinking proved to be highly resistant to change. For example, Scottish official statistics continued to gather information on children with special educational needs based on impairment categories. Indeed, the number of categories continue to expand, so that language and speech disorder and autistic spectrum disorders are now reported separately. Complex and multiple difficulties are now subdivided into a number of different categories. This is in marked contrast to the Warnock Report's ambition of replacing multiple (medical) categories with one over-arching category. Attention deficit (hyperactive) disorder (AD(H)D) is an example of a 'new' disability which is currently enjoying a surge of popularity, seen by parents as a 'label of forgiveness' (Slee, 1995) and by drug companies as a money-making opportunity (Lloyd & Norris, 1999).

To summarise, the individualised, or essentialist approach, which regards mental or physical deficits as being rooted in the individual, is the traditional approach to special education throughout the developed world. Challenged in the late 1970s and early 1980s, it is currently enjoying something of a resurgence. Parents and voluntary organisations, supported by allies in medicine and psychiatry, have campaigned for the re-adoption of particular labels, often with a view to accessing resources or avoiding more stigmatising categories. The individual needs approach also creates a triangular tension for resource allocation, with parents, professionals and bureaucrats pulling in different directions. In practice, professionals may be co-opted into the work of the bureaucracy, ensuring that their assessments do not conflict with budgetary controls (Riddell, Baron & Wilson, 2002).

At the time of writing, new legislation is being implemented in Scotland which, whilst still located within an individualised approach, recasts the categories. The Education (Additional Support for Learning) (Scotland) Act 2004 scraps the category of special educational needs, replacing it with a wider category of additional support needs, encompassing not only disabled children, but also socially disadvantaged children, the children of travellers, refugees, asylum seekers and migrant workers, and children looked after by the local authority. Proponents of the legislation maintain that its purpose is to ensure that a wider group of children receive detailed assessments and have programmes in place to meet their needs. On the other hand, it could be seen as an effort by the state to spread the special educational net wider, justifying the social exclusion of growing numbers of people, whilst passing to schools the responsibility for the management of competing resource claims. This point is discussed further below in the section on materialist approaches.

Managerialist or systems-based approaches

A particular branch of sociology of special education draws on a range of approaches to management, based on the fundamental assumption that if organisational systems are correctly aligned, public sector institutions will operate smoothly and effectively. In the UK, the new focus on the management of special education was driven in large measure by the emphasis on 'integration' within the Warnock Report (DES, 1978). The abandonment of the special remedial class and the inclusion of more children with learning difficulties in mainstream classes required a reformulation of the curriculum, pedagogy and classroom organisation. In Scotland, a report published by HM Inspectorate (SED, 1978) argued that children with learning difficulties should be educated alongside their peers, but should not be subjected to a curriculum which might be too difficult or to teaching methods geared to the average child. Rather, the onus should be on the mainstream teacher, assisted by the newly styled learning support teacher, to accommodate the needs of each child through the use of differentiated teaching materials and appropriate pedagogy. The use of standardised assessment tests was discouraged, and classroom observation was seen as a better method of gaining information about pupil strengths and weaknesses.

The role of the learning support teacher or 'special educator' in comprehensive schools has dominated discussion in the professional literature. For example, Dyson and Gains (1995) point out that the emergence of the 'whole school approach' resulted in problems of 'uncertainty, ambiguity and conflict', as learning support teachers, known as Special Educational Needs Co-ordinators in England, were expected to adopt significant management and legal responsibilities for which they often lacked training and institutional back-up.

Management discourses within special education became even more dominant with the advent of new public management from the 1980s onwards. Informed by the ideas of economists such as von Hayek, and drawing on behaviourist psychology, the central thesis of new public management is that everything associated with the workplace can and should be measured. Targets are essential to human motivation and effective management, and external regimes of accountability are necessary to discipline the actions of otherwise self-serving professionals (Pollitt, 1993; Clarke & Newman, 1997). Within the field of special education, questions were increasingly asked about the performance of children with special educational needs and the extent to which the funds allocated to this area of education were delivering improved results.

In Scotland, Individualised Educational Programmes (IEPs) were seen as the vehicle for raising standards and improving accountability for children with special educational needs, and were couched in terms of the Scottish Executive's raising standards programme. Guidance issued in 1999 indicated to schools that IEPs should be formulated for all children in special schools and units, children with Records of Needs in mainstream and those receiving 'significant planned intervention'. The IEPs were to include long- and short-term targets, and a level of 80 per cent success in achieving targets should be aimed for. Research on the implementation of IEPs suggested that teachers welcomed the opportunity to chart the progress of individual children against personal goals, but were hostile to the idea of accountability at the level of the institution or the individual teacher (Banks et al., 2001).

In the US, there is a longstanding commitment to the use of IEPs as a means of accountability. Instituted under the terms of the Education for All Handicapped Children Act 1975 (PL 94–142), about 12 per cent of the pupil population in US schools has an IEP, compared with about 4 per cent of the Scottish school population. Gallagher (1972) argued that legal contracts should be established, 'with parents as equal partners in the plan, using objective measures of goal attainments, and developing punitive consequences of failure to deliver' (Goodman & Bond, 1993, p. 411). Legal sanctions for failure to achieve objectives were necessary, according to Gallagher, because 'bureaucracies such as educational systems will move institutionally only under threat or duress' (Gallagher, 1972, p. 531).

More recently, there has been concern that the expansion in the use of IEPs may lower expectations, and the No Child Left Behind Act, 2002, makes it obligatory to include students with disabilities in states' wider target-setting programmes. Evidence from small-scale studies continues to suggest that students with disabilities may be excluded from the general curriculum:

> Teachers often ... provide extensive modifications, particularly to performance expectations, believing that they were just accommodating a student's disability. Administrators questioned accommodations that were so extensive that they effectively changed the content and the expected student performance. Lack of guidance and assistance to teachers resulted in lowered expectations and created haphazard performance goals for students under the guise of full participation in standards. (McLaughlin & Tilstone, 2000, p. 57)

The Labour–Liberal coalition administration in Scotland continues to channel considerable monies towards local authorities and their schools to promote inclusion. For example, funds have been put aside for Alternatives to Exclusion, to raise standards in Scotland's schools (the Excellence Fund), and SEN Innovation Grants. A major educational initiative in 1998 was to pilot New Community Schools, which sought to provide integrated services to children, and was directly linked to the social justice agenda. Finally, the Discipline Task Group in its report Better Behaviour – Better Learning (Scottish Executive, 2001) recommended that funds be allocated to local authorities to enable the employment of additional staff, such as classroom assistants and home–school link workers, to support positive behaviour.

Along with these 'carrots' have been the 'sticks' associated with new public management, including targets and national standards, which local authorities and schools have been asked to meet on threat of their funding being reduced, negative inspections and even potential enforcement by the Scottish Executive. Within special education, there have been two particular performance measures of note: reducing absences due to school exclusion; and timing to produce a Record of Needs. However, as is the case in the US, the Scottish Executive has been fairly reluctant to hold local authorities to account with regard to their provision for children with SEN. Targets for reductions in the number of exclusions were dropped in 2004, and figures for 2002/03 (Scottish Executive, 2004b) show a higher number of exclusions (36,946) than the target baseline set by the social justice agenda of 34,831 in 1998/99. Records of Needs have been abolished and no timescales apply to the production of IEPs. In many ways, schools and local authorities are being given considerable freedom to self-regulate in this area, but the trade-off here is weaker public accountability.

To summarise, it is evident that functionalist approaches have been dominant in the field of special education, particularly in areas of social research most closely tied to practice. Both individualist and managerialist approaches rest on the assumption that it is necessary for educators to identify which children require adapted curricula, without paying a great deal of attention to the underlying social forces constructing particular individuals and groups as different. In the following section, I consider critical paradigms in the field of special education, which regard the unpacking of taken for granted assumptions about the nature of special needs as their prime focus.

CRITICAL PARADIGMS

Materialist or critical social policy approaches

Materialist approaches in the sociology of education have sought to understand the link between education, the reproduction of social relations within capitalism and the way this relationship is regulated by the state. In the 1970s, neo-Marxist writers such Bowles and Gintis (1976) suggested that social and curricular divisions in school corresponded directly to those in the labour market. Children in vocational programmes were prepared for their future role in blue collar jobs, whilst the academic elite were groomed for their future place in the professions. The label 'learning difficulties' might be applied to some of these children, but academic excellence was not expected of those destined for manual work and therefore poor literacy and numeracy skills were regarded as less of a problem.

Willis (1977), in his classic text *Learning to Labour: How Working Class Kids Get Working Class Jobs*, presented a slightly more complex picture. Working-class boys who understood that their future lay in hard manual labour responded by celebrating a particular version of masculinity. School was to be treated as a 'laff', since it had very little relevance to their future lives. Studious boys were labelled the 'ear 'oles' and were treated with the derision suggested by their name. Girls who conformed to the role of the supportive home-maker were dubbed 'good as gold'. Willis characterised the lads' rejection of schooling as a form of heroic resistance, since it allowed them to assert a degree of agency, whilst forcing them into a life of exploitation. Were the same group of lads to be observed in a contemporary classroom, the label of behavioural difficulties, learning difficulties or ADHD might well be attached to them.

Over recent years, behavioural difficulties have been regarded as classroom management problems and there has been less analysis of competing sub-cultures and their relationship to the capitalist social relations. This, of course, reflects the fact that government funders of research want to know what behaviour management strategies work in school, and are unsympathetic to the message that behavioural difficulties are an unwelcome by-product of unequal social relations. The implicit social determinism underlying

neo-Marxist accounts is difficult to incorporate into New Labour approaches to social inclusion which regard social cohesion, rather than conflict, as a natural and desirable state.

A body of literature has sought to apply a materialist analysis to the construction of special education. For example, Tomlinson (1985) argued that special education was expanding to embrace an increasing number of children, most of whom were male and from socially disadvantaged backgrounds, reflecting the collapse of the youth labour market particularly in the field of manufacturing. The following three reasons were advanced for this deliberate restructuring of the education system: professional vested interest, comprehensive school dilemmas and the declining youth labour. As a proportion of the population, she noted that in 1946 it was thought that 2 per cent of the population had a 'disability of body or mind', whilst a further 8–9 per cent of children were thought to be likely to make inadequate progress in schools. By the time of the Warnock Report (DES, 1978), the proportion of school children estimated to have learning difficulties had increased to 20 per cent. As Armstrong (2003) pointed out, the expansion of special education was accompanied by an increasing tendency to pathologise the behaviour of black pupils. 'Special educational needs', he noted, 'is a convenient tool for legitimising discrimination, racism and the lack of opportunities generally for young people' (Armstrong, 2003, p. 121).

In Scotland, it is clear that, in accordance with Tomlinson's argument, the official recognition of the SEN category has expanded. Since 2003, the Scottish Executive has collected and published data on children with SEN who do not have Records but have IEPs, as well as children who are recorded. Whilst a greater proportion of children with special educational needs are now being educated in mainstream schools, almost one in five such children are not always in mainstream classes (Scottish Executive, 2004a). The numbers of children in special schools has remained remarkably consistent for at least 20 years and continues to account for about 1 per cent of the total school population (Scottish Executive, 2004a). Spatial exclusion is therefore experienced by a good number of children with special educational needs.

The social class differentials noted by Tomlinson are also evident in Scotland. Tisdall and Riddell (forthcoming) noted that a disproportionately high number of children eligible for free school meals[1] are excluded from school (Scottish Executive, 2004b). There have been concerns that children who are looked after by the state are not having their special educational needs recognised, perhaps because local authorities are not acting as 'good parents' in taking forward the assessment procedures (Borland, Pearson, Hill, Tisdall & Bloomfield, 1998). A disproportionate number of looked after children are excluded from school (Scottish Executive, 2004b). Boys are also more likely than girls to be identified as having SEN, excluded from school and placed in special schools and units. In 2003, 70 per cent of pupils with SEN, 67 per cent of pupils attending special schools and 80 per cent of those excluded from schools were male (Scottish Executive, 2004a, 2004b).

Social constructionist approaches

Thus far, we have reviewed social accounts of special education which locate difficulties in learning within the individual child, within the management structures of the organisation or within wider social structures rooted in economic relations. In this section, we explore the use of interactionist ideas in the sociology of special education. Goffman (1968) challenged the thinking of Durkheim and Parsons by questioning the extent to which behaviour is an expression of a rigid system of defined status and roles. For example, in his work *Asylums* (1968), Goffman examined the 'career' of mental patients and prisoners in their respective closed institutions. His aim was to understand the way in which individuals make sense of the world

and negotiate their social identity, often in very difficult circumstances. This may well involve resisting unwelcome labels imposed by others in establishing their own definition of the situation. The familiar criticism of interactionist work is that, in emphasising the power of individual agency, it may underplay the power of wider social forces, such as those associated with gender or class. Mehan (1992) noted the criticisms of 'ultra-relativism' and 'sentimental egalitarianism' which have been levelled against the interpretive paradigm. Nonetheless, he argues that this approach may contribute usefully to the study of educational inequality by introducing cultural elements into highly deterministic macrotheories, injecting human agency into theories accounting for social inequality and opening the black box of schooling to examine the reflexive relations between the institutional practices and students' careers.

The socio-cultural approach advocated by Mehan is particularly evident in a number of recent Swedish studies which seek to understand the reification of labels in the field of special education. For example, Hjorne and Saljo (2004) explore the use of the term ADHD/DAMP in Swedish schools in the context of 'the politics of representation' (Mehan, 1993). They comment:

ADHD/DAMP as a category, thus, has established itself within schooling, and in this sense is both a social fact and a resource that is actively used for dealing with problems. It has implications for the manner in which teaching is organised and for the use of limited resources. It will also have consequences for the student's educational career, and obviously, a neuropsychiatric diagnosis, indicative of a brain injury, will play a critical role identity formation of young people. (Hjorne & Saljo, 2004, p. 7)

Their analysis of verbal exchanges in pupil-student welfare team meetings illustrates the way in which professionals focus on evidence which supports the emerging idea that particular pupils have a specific form of neural deficit, seeking only confirming rather than disconfirming data. Virtually no attention was paid to the classroom environment, the approaches or actions of the teacher or the curriculum, which might provide alternative explanatory accounts for individual children's failure to learn. Many parents accepted the professionals' diagnosis quiescently, and only one example is given of a parent offering a counter-narrative which challenges the teacher's version of events. However, they do not deny the salience of the wider social context in which the school is located, suggesting that the use of categories such as ADHD/DAMP must be understood in terms of changes in public schooling in Sweden, as the principle of universal education provided in comprehensive schools is increasingly challenged. As noted by Lloyd and Norris (1999), disputes over the label ADHD have been taking place in many parts of the world.

A further example of the exploration of the establishment and contestation of labels in special education may be found in the Scottish study of dyslexia conducted by Riddell, Duffield and Brown (1994). Drawing on interviews, surveys and observation, the researchers noted the different understandings of dyslexia promoted by different groups. Voluntary organisations and some doctors tended to believe that dyslexia was inherently different from other forms of learning difficulty. They believed that the condition was physiological in origin, favoured forms of psychometric assessment designed to identify discrepancies in ability and promoted particular teaching methods which were best delivered by specially trained teachers. Educational psychologists, education officers and teachers, on the other hand, believed that children with specific learning difficulties (their preferred term), did not represent a discrete group but were part of a continuum, with a diverse array of abilities and difficulties attributable to environmental and individual factors operating interactively. According to this perspective, there was no absolute dividing line between children with 'common or garden' learning difficulties and others. The preferred form of assessment was classroom observation of difficulties in order to devise a range of teaching strategies, to be implemented by the class or learning support teacher, without the need for intervention by an educational psychologist. Faced with a refusal to acknowledge dyslexic children as a discrete group with specific problems and teaching needs, parents often became extremely frustrated, and adopted a range of strategies including engaging independent psychologists to conduct assessments and, in England, taking appeals to the Special Educational Needs Tribunal.

To summarise, struggles over the creation and negotiation of categories within the field of special education are still taking place and social interactionist theories have a great deal to offer in terms of understanding the material consequences which ensue. In the final section, we consider the impact of the sociology of disability, a relatively new influence in the field of special education.

Civil rights approaches

A very different type of social theory and action has developed via the adult-dominated disability movement. According to early social model theorists such as Oliver (1990) and Barnes (1991), within capitalist societies disabled people are systematically excluded or marginalised. Whilst impairments may have real effects, these are not automatically disabling. Rather, disability is always experienced within a specific social context and it is always political, cultural and economic arrangements, rather than impairments, which exclude. Recently, the sociology of disability has diversified. For example, some of the literature on learning difficulties adopts a strong social constructionist position (Goodley, 2001). Shakespeare and Corker have emphasised the historical contingency of disability, describing it as 'the ultimate postmodern category' because of its mutability. Abberley (1987) has drawn attention to the fact that many impairments arise as a result of war, disease and global economic oppression.

The social model of disability has had a major impact on everyday thought and action, and has led to significant political progress for disabled people. As we noted above, the Disability Discrimination Act 1995 (DDA) reflects a view of impairment as being located in the individual, but at the same time requires providers of goods and services and education to make anticipatory adjustments. Employers are also obliged to make reasonable adjustments to ensure that discrimination does not occur in the workplace. The GB Disability Rights Commission has rights of formal investigation, which are likely to be strengthened by forthcoming legislation which places a duty on public bodies to positively promote equality for disabled people.

We noted above some of the shortcomings of the DDA and other anti-discrimination legislation. In particular, the fact that the onus lies on the complainant to demonstrate that they are covered by the legislation has been a drawback, although in the future it will no longer be essential to demonstrate that a mental impairment is a result of a 'clinically well-recognised condition'. The new public sector duty is also likely to be significant, forcing public bodies, including those responsible for education, to demonstrate that they are taking action to redress former injustice and achieve progress towards a fairer distribution of social goods. This suggests that the initial medical model underpinning is weakening, and the legislation is moving much reflecting social model thinking more closely.

Taking a case to court is still dependent on individual parents (and children) deciding to do so, and knowledge of the DDA is therefore of paramount importance. Early baseline research on the DDA in Scotland showed that, whilst local authorities were well informed and had undertaken a risk analysis to ensure that they complied with the law, parents and schools had little knowledge and understanding of the legislation (Cogan et al., 2003). Subsequent research (Edson, 2005) demonstrates that knowledge and understanding is slowly growing, but a third of parents and half of schools still reported that they knew little about the provisions.

Despite the power of the social model as an analytical tool and a driver of social change, only a small number of studies have explicitly adopted this approach in ethnography (Riddell et al., 2001) and in life story accounts (Armstrong, 2003).

CONCLUSION

It is evident that many social theories jostle for position in making sense of the field of special education. This chapter grouped theories under two broad headings, functionalist and critical paradigms. The former are based on the idea that stability and cohesion are natural and desirable social states, whilst the latter see tension and conflict as an inevitable product of capitalist social relations. Functionalist accounts have traditionally reflected the view that the role of special education is to identify those children who should be excluded or marginalized because of the threat which they seemed to pose for the social order. Over recent years within developed countries, a growing emphasis has been placed on inclusion as a key ingredient in the creation of a modern knowledge economy. However, debates continue with regard to which children should be excluded from the mainstream classroom and what sort of provision should be made for them. These struggles were often over the allocation of scarce educational resources, as government insisted that more attention should be placed on recognising the needs of individual children, whilst targeting resources on improved educational output. Efforts to commandeer additional resources, or justify exclusion, often hinged on claiming particular labels of forgiveness or justification.

Whilst functionalist accounts tended to be favoured by parents, practitioners and policymakers because of their focus on how to achieve social improvement, critical paradigms provided important insights into the forces of change and challenge. Given the array of social forces operating in the field of special education, each perspective contributed distinctive understandings into the ways in which the field of special education had developed thus far, and the tensions and challenges which continue to shape its future direction.

The framework which I have described above should be regarded as only one way of understanding the range of theories which currently exist in the field of special education. It should be recognised that these concepts are not discrete, but may overlap with each other or be categorised differently. It is always important to recognise that abstract concepts should not be reified, and there are also dangers in arguing that one way of viewing the world is intrinsically superior to another. All have their strengths and limitations, and may be used in different ways and for different purposes. Pragmatic approaches, which are likely to have functionalist underpinnings, may be useful when the main object is to address the tricky question of what is to be done on Monday morning, whilst critical approaches serve as a helpful corrective to easy assumptions that the current organisation of the world is the only possibility.

NOTE

1 A proxy for socio-economic disadvantage.

REFERENCES

Abberley, P. (1987). The concept of oppression and the development of a social theory of disability. *Disability Handicap and Society*, 2, 5–19.

Armstrong, D. (2003). *Experiences of special education*. London: RoutledgeFalmer.

Banks, P., Baynes, A., Dyson, A., Kane, J., Millward, A., Riddell, S., & Wilson, A. (2001). *Raising the Attainment of Pupils with Special Educational Needs*. Report to the Scottish Executive Education Department Strathclyde Centre for Disability Research, University of Glasgow, Glasgow.

Barnes, C. (1991). *Disabled people in Britain and discrimination: A case for anti-discrimination legislation*. London: Hurst.

Bogdan, R., & Knoll, J. (1995). The sociology of disability. In E. L. Meyen & T. Skrtic (Eds.), *Special Education and Student Disability* (4th ed.) (pp. 675–911). Denver, CO: Love.

Booth, T. (1996). The poverty of special education: Theories to the rescue? In C. Clark, A. Dyson, & A. Millward (Eds.), *Theorising special education* (pp. 79–90). London: Routledge.

Borland, M., Pearson, C., Hill, M., Tisdall, K., & Bloomfield, I. (1998). *The education of children looked after away from home*. Edinburgh: SCRE.

Bowles, S., & Gintis, H. (1976). *Schooling in capitalist America*. New York: Basic Books.

Clarke, J., & Newman, J. (1997). *The managerial state*. London: Sage.

Cogan, N., Riddell, S., & Tisdall, K. (2003). *Knowledge and awareness of Part 4 of the Disability Discrimination Act 1995 (as amended) in Scotland*. Edinburgh: Disability Rights Commission.

Corker, M. and Shakespeare, T. (Eds.). (2001). *Disability/Postmodernity: Embodying Disability Theory*. London: Continuum.

Department for Education and Science (DES). (1978). *Special educational needs: Report of the Committee of Enquiry into the education of handicapped children and young people* (The Warnock Report). London: HMSO.

Dyson, A., & Gains, C. (1995). The special educational needs co-ordinator: Poisoned chalice or crock of gold? *Support for Learning*, 10(2), 50–56.

Edson, J. (2005). *Making legislation accessible: The impact of the Disability Discrimination Act Part4 4 on Scottish schools*. Paper presented to the Nordic Conference on Disability Research.

Fulcher, G. (1989). *Disabling policies? A comparative approach to education policy and disability*. Lewes: Falmer Press.

Gallagher, J. (1972). The special education contract for mildly handicapped children. *Exceptional children*, 38, 527–535.

Goffman, E. (1968). *Asylums*. Harmondsworth: Penguin.

Goodley, D. (2001). 'Learning difficulties', the social model of disability and impairment: challenging epistemologies. *Disability and Society*, 16(2), 207–232.

Goodman, J. F., & Bond, L. (1993). The individualised educational programme: A retrospective critique. *Journal of Special Education*, 26(4), 408–422.

Hjorne, E., & Saljo, R. (2004). 'There is something about Julia': Symptoms, categories and the process of invoking attention deficit hyperactivity disorder in the Swedish school: a case study. *Journal of Language, Identity and Society*, 3(1), 1–24.

Kerr, A., & Shakespeare, T. (2002). *Genetic politics: From eugenics to genome*. Cheltenham: New Clarion Press.

Kirp, D. L. (1982). Professionalism as a policy choice: British special education in comparative perspective. *World Politics*, 34(2), 137–74.

Laosa, L. M. (1973). Reform in educational and psychological assessment: cultural and linguistic issues.

Journal of Mexican-American Education, 1, 19–24.

Levitas, R. (1998). *The inclusive society? Social exclusion and New Labour.* Basingstoke: Macmillan.

Lloyd, G. & Norris, C. (1999). Including ADHD? *Disability and Society, 14*(4), 505–517.

Lubeck, S., & Garrett, P. (1990). The social construction of the 'at risk' child. *British Journal of Sociology of Education, 11*(3), 327–341.

McLaughlin, M. & Tilstone, C. (2000). Standards and curriculum: the core of educational reform. In M. McLaughlin & M. Rouse (Eds.), *Special education and school reform in the United States and Britain* (pp. 38–66). London: Routledge.

Mehan, H. (1992). Understanding inequality in schools: the contribution of interpretive studies. *Sociology of Education, 65*(January), 1–20.

Mehan, H. (1993). Beneath the skin and between the ears: A case study in the politics of representation. In S. Chaiklin & J. Lave (Eds.), *Understanding practice: Perspectives on activity and context* (pp. 241–269). Cambridge MA: Cambridge University Press.

Munn, P., Lloyd, G., & Cullen, M. A. (2000). *Exclusion from school and alternatives.* London: Paul Chapman Publishing.

Oliver, M. (1990). *The politics of disablement.* Basingstoke: Macmillan.

Pollitt, C. (1993), *Managerialism and the Public Services.* Oxford: Blackwell.

Riddell, S. (1996). Theorising special educational needs in a changing political climate. In L. Barton (Ed.), *Disability & society: Some emerging issues and insights* (pp. 83–107). London: Longman.

Riddell, S. (2001). Special education needs and procedural justice in England and Scotland. In C. Vincent (Ed.), *Social justice, education and identity* (pp. 185–209). London: RoutledgeFalmer.

Riddell, S. (2002). *Policy and practice in special education: Special educational needs.* Edinburgh: Dunedin Academic Press.

Riddell, S., Baron, S., & Wilson, A. (2001). *The learning society and people with learning difficulties.* Bristol: Policy Press.

Riddell, S., Duffield, J., & Brown, S. (1994). Parental power and special educational needs: the case of specific learning difficulties. *British Educational Research Journal, 20*(3), 327–344.

Scottish Education Department (SED). (1978). *The education of pupils with learning difficulties in primary and secondary schools in Scotland: A progress report by HM Inspector of Schools.* Edinburgh: HMSO.

Scottish Executive. (2001). *Better behaviour – better learning: The report of the Discipline Task Group.* Edinburgh: Scottish Executive Education Department.

Scottish Executive. (2003a). *Report of the first round of accessibility strategies.* Edinburgh: Scottish Executive.

Scottish Executive. (2003b). *Pupils with a record of needs, September 2002.* Retrieved December 4, 2003 from http://www.scotland.gov.uk/

Scottish Executive. (2004a). *Pupils in Scotland, 2003.* Retrieved August 11, 2004 from http://www.scotland.gov.uk/

Scottish Executive. (2004b). *Exclusions from schools 2002/03.* Retrieved August 11, 2004 from http://www.scotland.gov.uk/

Slee, R. (1995). *Changing theories and practices of discipline.* London: Falmer.

Tisdall, E. K. M. & Riddell, S. (Forthcoming). Policies on special needs education: competing strategies and discourses. *European Journal of Special Needs Education.*

Tomlinson, S. (1982). *A sociology of special education.* London: Routledge.

Tomlinson, S. (1985). The expansion of special education. *Oxford Review of Education, 11*(2), 157–165.

Tomlinson, S. (2001). *Education in a post-welfare society.* Buckingham: Open University Press.

United Nations Educational, Scientific, and Cultural Organization (UNESCO). (1994). *The Salamanca Statement and Framework on Special Needs Education.* Paris: UNESCO.

Willis, P. (1977). *Learning to labour: How working class kids get working class jobs.* Aldershot: Gower Publishing.

4

Forms of provision and models of service delivery

Jennifer Evans

This chapter will argue that the ways in which special education is funded are a key parameter in the development of provision and the delivery of services. It will provide a historical overview of developments in funding provision and delivery of services, looking briefly at developments in the second half of the twentieth century, but focusing more on recent and current debates about inclusion. Examples will be drawn from the UK experience with reference to developments in other European countries, the US, India and South Africa. The chapter will cover the following areas:

- Historical overview – the development of specialist and separate provision.
- The moves from the 1970s onwards, towards a more flexible approach – termed 'integration' or 'mainstreaming'. The development of specialist services to support mainstream placements.
- The emergence of 'inclusive education' as a rights issue and subsequent development and reorganisation of services.
- The role of funding and funding mechanisms to support special education in promoting or preventing inclusion.
- Some examples of contrasting responses to the

organisation of provision and services in the UK.
- Evaluating the effectiveness of the different models of provision.

INTRODUCTION

The basis of provision for special educational needs in the UK is the 1981 Education Act, which represented the culmination of a series of changes in the dominant conceptualisation of special educational needs and provision which had taken place during the 1960s and 1970s. Prior to the implementation of the Act in March 1983, special education had been organised around a number of categories of handicap and provided, for the most part, in separate segregated institutions, which were themselves categorised in terms of distinct disabilities. The development of the use of these categories and the system of education, which grew up around them has been documented by, *inter alia*, Tomlinson (1982) and Norwich (1990). Their creation had been part of the 1944 Education Act, the underlying premise of which was that children should be classified and differentiated according to their 'age, ability and aptitude' (Heward & Lloyd-Smith, 1990) and which had established 12 categories of handicap (or 'defects of body or mind') for which provision had to be made. One group, the 'severely sub-normal', were deemed to be the responsibility of the health rather than the education authorities, but, for the rest, provision was to be made in special schools, provided either by local education authorities or charitable institutions. Funding and placement were dependent upon children being identified and categorised. The categories corresponded to sensory and physical handicaps and intellectual and emotional difficulties. The emphasis in assessment was on deficits within the individual child and a medical model of diagnosis and treatment reflected the dominance of the medical profession in decision-making about this group of children. At this time (the 1940s and 1950s), the education system of England and Wales was highly differentiated in terms of measured intellectual ability, with an examination, for children in ordinary schools, at the age of 11, to classify them into groups suitable for one of three main types of secondary school: academic, technical or modern. It is not surprising, then, that the special education system reflected the dominance of selection, categorisation and segregation on the basis of ability and disability, which had implications for the future employability and career development of individuals.

During the 1960s and 1970s, parents and others interested in the education and welfare of children with disabilities, campaigned for a change in approach (Peter, 1995) . There was concern that a significant proportion of children (those deemed to be severely sub-normal) were the responsibility of the health authorities rather than the education authorities and were being provided for in 'junior training centres' rather than in schools. This was felt to be unacceptable, and, in 1971, after a long campaign, the responsibility for the education of 'educationally sub-normal (severe)' children was transferred to local education authorities. Thus, the right of all children to some form of education was established. This was part of a wider movement in education towards 'comprehensivisation', and the abolition of selection at eleven years old in many local education authorities (LEAs). There had been a sustained critique of the rigid categorisation of children into 'academic' and 'non-academic' at this early age, and a concern that many children were not realising their potential. The work of educational sociologists in the 1960s and 1970s had drawn attention to the social class bias within the system (for example, Jackson & Marsden, 1962; Jackson, 1964; Bernstein, 1977; Willis, 1977) and it was argued that the abolition of selection at 11 would eliminate the worst effects of this, although later experience has shown this to be an over-optimistic aspiration (Hargreaves, 1989).

A second concern of many parents, educators and other professionals was the system of categorisation which appeared to be both rigid and arbitrary, and relied upon a medical model in which the emphasis was on a child's deficits and did not take into account compensating strengths or the interaction between the child and his or her environment in creating or ameliorating educational difficulties. It was also seen as simplistic, because it did not acknowledge the complexity of children's problems and that a child might have a number of areas of difficulty, some of which might be ignored if he or she were categorised by a single handicap. During the 1970s, increasing numbers of children were being placed in special schools, and 'ascertainment' of a child as 'handicapped' became increasingly seen as having the consequence of marginalisation in respect of a child's peers and opportunities within the labour market (Coard, 1971; Tomlinson, 1982).

The 1981 Education Act was part of a shift in ideas and policies about special education which was taking place in many other Western states, including the United States of America, which passed similar legislation in 1975, and Italy which brought about a radical change, requiring the integration of all but the most severely handicapped children, by legislation passed in 1971. Many of these legislative changes resulted from a wider political and societal emancipation, which embodied ideas about democracy, equity and human rights. Similar moves are now taking place in some developing countries, such as South Africa, which has dismantled a system of education based on race and colour, and moved towards a more inclusive system, where students with special needs will be educated in mainstream schools (Ntombela, 2004). In India, where children with disabilities still come under the remit of the Ministry of Welfare, and not of Education, the government is under pressure to provide education for disabled students, 90 per cent of whom do not, at present, receive any education. The educational provision for disabled children that is available is provided by charities and non-governmental organisations (NGOs) (Alur, 2002).

A key component of the definition of special educational needs in the British legislation was that children 'had' special educational needs if they required provision additional to or otherwise different from that which was 'normally' available in schools. Thus, the population of children with special educational needs was no longer defined in terms of categories of need (and provision made according to category), but was now inextricably linked to resourcing. This freed up providers to be more flexible in response to needs, and opened the way to greater inclusion, but at the same time placed the emphasis on funding, rather than educational issues.

DEFINING INCLUSION

The inclusion of pupils with special educational needs within mainstream education was said to be a growing feature of a more comprehensive conceptualisation of education current in the late 1970s (Cole, 1989; Booth & Ainscow, 1998). This conceptualisation has been under threat since the 1980s, with the introduction of specialist schools in England, and moves to select some pupils on the basis of 'aptitude'. Furthermore, the inclusion of pupils

with special educational needs has not shown a marked increase since the implementation of the 1981 Act (Swann, 1991; Norwich, 1994, 1997). The 1981 Act was seen by many as promoting inclusion, since it stipulated that LEAs had a duty to ensure that children with special educational needs, including those with statements, were educated in ordinary schools, if this is what their parents wanted. There were three provisos attached to this: that the child received the special education he or she required; that it was compatible with the efficient education of other children in the school; and, that it was an efficient use of resources. In practice, this meant that the proportion of children being educated in special schools dropped by only 12.5 per cent, from around 1.7 per cent to just under 1.5 per cent, between 1983 and 1991 (Audit Commission, 1992). In some LEAs, the proportion of pupils in special schools had increased (Swann, 1991; Norwich, 1994, 1997). The proportion of children with statements in mainstream schools had also increased, but this was due, in most LEAs, to the overall increase in children with statements in the school population (Evans & Lunt, 1992). So, despite the hopes of parents and educators, the 1981 Act did not provide the basis for a revolution in the ways in which children with special educational needs were educated.

Although the placement of children with special educational needs in mainstream settings is an essential precursor to inclusion, the practice of inclusion is a contested arena and one that needs to be explored. There are both 'radical' and 'pragmatic' perspectives on the issue, one emanating from a 'rights' perspective and the other from a 'professional' perspective. Those who take a rights perspective argue that to be included in the local mainstream school is the right of every child and that schools and LEAs should be actively working towards bringing this about. Thus the Centre for Studies in Integration in Education (CSIE) has produced league tables of local authorities showing how much, if at all, they have moved towards this ideal (Norwich, 1994). However, a cautionary note has been struck by a number of writers who feel that the issue of inclusion is a complex one and that the ways in which inclusion (or integration) are defined in terms of its aims and objectives and ultimate goals for individuals, have to be explored (see, for example, Hornby, Atkinson & Howard, 1997). The broader issue of inclusion as a social goal for all members of society has also influenced the debate on the inclusion of children with special educational needs in mainstream schools (Christensen & Rizvi, 1996). Thus the issues of the inclusion of marginalised groups, such as refugees, people in poverty, the unemployed, and disaffected young people, have become part of the debate about the educational inclusion of pupils with special educational needs. Social inclusion was one of the professed goals of the current Labour government in the UK.

In England and Wales, the government's stance on special educational needs, in the form of a Green Paper, was published in 1997. The paper, entitled *Excellence for All Children*, stated that the government would 'promote the inclusion of children with SEN in mainstream *wherever possible*' (GB. DfEE, 1997, my emphasis). The section on 'Increasing Inclusion', begins with the statement:

> The ultimate purpose of SEN provision is to enable young people to flourish in adult life. There are therefore strong educational, as well as social and moral, grounds for educating children with SEN with their peers. We aim to increase the level and quality of inclusion within mainstream schools, while protecting and enhancing specialist provision for those who need it. We will redefine the role of special schools to bring out their contribution in working with mainstream schools to support greater inclusion. (GB. DfEE, 1997, p. 43)

It appears that the government has espoused a pragmatic rather than a radical inclusion policy, taking account of the views of teachers, that becoming more inclusive presents schools with real challenges. Nevertheless, the foundation of their policy is based upon a philosophy of social justice. This is evidenced in the document that gives policy guidance to LEAs and schools about how to implement the government's programme – *Meeting Spe-cial Educational Needs: A Programme of Action* (GB. DfEE, 1998). This document states that resources will be available to support inclusion, from funds allocated under the Social Exclusion: Pupil Support Standards Fund programme, for projects that aim to improve provision and raise achievements for children with emotional and behavioural problems. There is also to be funding for pupils with disabilities from the Schools Access Initiative (for making adaptations to buildings) and through the SEN Standards Fund to promote inclusion. Thus the link between the ways in which resources are allocated and deployed and the process of inclusion are acknowledged at government level. These links will be explored further in the next section of this chapter.

THE FUNDING FRAMEWORK IN THE UK

The issue of resources is one that continues to feature prominently in discussions about policy, provision and practice for special educational needs. During the 1980s, a series of reforms in school funding in England and Wales took place, which gave delegated budgets to schools to enable them to manage their own finances. The aim of these reforms was to place the responsibility for decisions about the use of resources as close to the point of service delivery as possible. These reforms have been subject to commentary by a number of authors (Ball, 1990; Bines, 1995; Bowe & Ball, 1992; Fish & Evans, 1995). In particular, Lawton (1992) has pointed out that the restructuring of education systems to give more managerial responsibility to schools was a phenomenon common to a number of countries in the developed world, including the UK, the USA, Australia and New Zealand.

In England and Wales, responsibility for managing schools, including budgetary decisions, was given to head teachers and school governors. Governing bodies, which consist of representatives from parents, the local authority, the school and the community (and from the Church in schools with religious affiliation), are ultimately responsible for the management of the school, but, in practice, are guided quite substantially by the head teacher (Scanlon, Earley & Evans, 1998).

The school funding system introduced in 1999 built upon local management of schools (LMS) by increasing the level of financial delegation to schools. Its key aspects are formula funding and the delegation of financial responsibility to schools. It is used by local education authorities to calculate the budgets of all schools maintained by them. It also sets the framework for the financial relationship that operates between schools and their LEAs. Local authorities in England and Wales are currently required by law to delegate the major proportion of their budget for funding schools to the schools, holding some funding centrally to support central administration and services to support schools, such as psychological services, advisors to support school improvement, and funding for making provision for pupils with statements of special educational needs. This two-tier system of special needs funding (that is, resources given to schools and resources provided by the LEA from central funds) has set up a dichotomy, which leads to a wide range of practice across England and Wales (Lee, 1996; Heward & Lloyd Smith, 1990; Evans & Lunt, 1994; Marsh, 1995).

THE SPECIAL NEEDS POPULATION

Briefly, the current context for funding special educational needs in England and Wales is as follows:

- Around 3 per cent of the student population in England and Wales has a statement of special educational needs (GB. DfES, 2004a). These pupils will receive an individual allocation of resources in a mainstream school, through funding held centrally by the LEA or delegated to schools, or they will be placed in a special school or unit.
- Around 17.6 per cent of pupils in primary schools in England are registered as having special educational needs of whom 1.6 per cent will

have statements. The remainder (16.0 per cent) will be supported through the schools' delegated formula budget.
- Around 15.9 per cent of pupils in secondary schools in England are registered as having special educational needs, of whom 2.4 per cent will have statements. The remaining 13.5 per cent will be supported through the schools' delegated formula budget.
- The proportion of pupils educated in special schools is currently 1.2 per cent in England, with a range of 0.2–2.3 per cent across local authorities. Most of these pupils will have statements.

Thus, the major proportion of the special needs population, with and without statements, is being educated in mainstream schools. There is, however, a huge variation across schools in the proportion of pupils with special educational needs that they identify – from none to over 60 per cent of the total school roll. The median figure is 30 per cent, compared to the mean, which is around 19 per cent. There may also be an element of over- or under-reporting from schools, so that the special needs funding from the LEA might not necessarily reflect the level of need perceived by the schools. However, the figures indicate that the education system of England and Wales is moving towards a more inclusive pattern (Meijer, Pijl & Hegarty, 1994; OECD, 1995; Norwich, 1994). Nevertheless, some students, for example those with social, emotional and behavioural difficulties, are more likely to experience exclusion in some form, either through being excluded from school or by being placed in a Pupil Referral Unit (PRU). These forms of exclusion are not captured in the official statistics quoted here.

APPROACHES TO FUNDING PROVISION IN ENGLAND AND WALES

Research on patterns of funding carried out by the National Foundation for Educational Research (Evans, Castle & Cullen, 2002) shows that the mechanism through which such funding was allocated varied widely between LEAs. The elements included by LEAs in calculating 'pupil-led' funding for special needs included:

- pupil entitlement to free school meals
- pupil mobility
- an audit of special educational needs in the school
- specific groups of pupils (such as children being looked after by the local authority)
- pupil entitlement to clothing grant
- scores on standardised tests.

Each of these elements might have different weightings within the formula in different LEAs.

Some LEAs used a number of factors in combination to produce the amount allocated to schools. It is clear that the underlying rationale for allocating funding is dependent on a perception, in a large proportion of the LEAs, that social deprivation, measured by entitlement to free school meals or clothing grant, was closely associated with special educational needs. Over half the LEAs in the study (29 out of 56) used social deprivation indicators as part of their formula to allocate special needs funding.

Almost half (26 out of 56 LEAs) used some kind of audit or measure of pupil ability to allocate funding. Some used placement of children on stages of the Code of Practice[1] as the basis for funding. Others used more standardised measures, such as National Curriculum test results, reading tests or cognitive ability tests.

These formula mechanisms relate to pupils without statements of special educational needs, but some LEAs were also delegating funding for statements to schools. Almost half the LEAs (27 out of 56) did not delegate funding for statements. Those who did so used a variety of methods, ranging from funding on a *per capita* basis or according to the amount of individual support tuition required (that is, not according to a formula, but at cost) to funding based on bands or categories of difficulty within the formula.

There are indications from this analysis, that LEAs approach funding special educa-

tional needs in mainstream schools in a wide variety of ways and within a wide variety of conceptual and policy frameworks about special education. One could argue that the most inclusive authorities would be those that delegate substantial proportions of the SEN budget to mainstream schools and where the SEN budget makes up a significant proportion of LEA spending on schools. However, the retention of a significant proportion of funding for SEN centrally might indicate that a large support service is available for schools to support special educational needs in mainstream. The delegation of money for statements might indicate that an LEA has a policy of making schools take responsibility for meeting special educational needs, or it might indicate that a high proportion of children with special educational needs in that authority have statements and that pupils with similar needs in another authority might have those needs met by schools through their non-statemented SEN budgets.

THE INFLUENCE OF FUNDING MECHANISMS ON FORMS OF PROVISION

The issue of whether free school meals (or other measures of social deprivation) are a good proxy indicator of special needs and whether the use of this measure is an indicator of an LEA's view about the causation and amelioration of special needs is another question thrown up by this analysis. Do LEAs who have complex and sophisticated audit systems have policies and aims for special education that are different from those LEAs which use free school meals as their indicator of special needs?

A major question for the research was: 'What policy goals in relation to special education are LEAs hoping they achieve by the ways in which they allocate resources to schools and the balance they set up between delegated and centrally retained funding?' The analysis of funding mechanisms revealed a number of themes and issues arising from the ways in which local authorities chose to allocate funding, and their spending priorities and the implications that these have for the process of inclusion.

There has been much critical analysis of the link between special educational needs and social deprivation. The former Secretary of State for Education, David Blunkett, has stated that 'poverty is no excuse for failure'. However, many analysts (for example, Kumar, 1993; Mortimore & Whitty, 1997) have demonstrated a link between poverty and low educational attainment. This link is acknowledged by LEAs, in directing resources through their formula for both special educational needs and social deprivation. The contentious issue, however, is whether measures of social deprivation can stand as a proxy measure for special educational needs. As demonstrated above, many LEAs include a measure of social deprivation in their formula to target funding to schools as part of the special educational needs budget. Sharp (2000) has argued that although special educational needs which are cognitive in nature (that is, learning difficulties) are closely associated at the school level with social deprivation, this association does not necessarily hold at the individual level. In other words, schools with high levels of social deprivation are likely to have high levels of special educational needs, but not all socially deprived children will have special educational needs, and conversely, not all children with special educational needs will be socially deprived. Thus, Sharp argues, an audit is a more useful measure for directing resources into schools. There is also a high level of correspondence between social deprivation and emotional and behavioural difficulties, but again Sharp argues that some more direct measure would be preferable to a proxy measure. Marsh (1995, 2003) is equally dismissive of the use of free school meals as a proxy indicator. Writing at a time when a Common Funding Formula was being developed at national level he suggested that:

> FSME (free school meals entitlement) has been shown to be a poor indicator of SEN at a pupil level and the use of a single unit cost does nothing to address the continuum of SEN. LEAs who are currently revising their formulae to follow the current policy thrust of differential funding for individual SEN, will not be impressed by having their own attempts replaced by the worn and toothless proxy indicator of SEN. (1995, p. 114)

However, one could argue that having an audit system, which individually identifies and places children on a series of levels of SEN, has a number of consequences for inclusive education.

First, it raises the profile of those children and places a premium on identification of special needs and difference. Thus children with SEN will be actively sought out, assessed and labelled.

Secondly, it provides a perverse incentive whereby children are of more monetary value to a school while their special educational needs continue to be a problem, and the more severe the needs, the more money will be available to support them.

It could be argued that free school meals, which both Marsh and Sharp concede is an effective proxy indicator at the school level of both learning and behaviour difficulties, is less stigmatising for individual children and provides a school with resources to deploy as effectively as possible to meet the needs of all children in the school. This is not to say that identification of individual children's needs is not vital in order to assess what support they need to be able to make progress. This is clearly highly important. However, an audit system, based on school identification of SEN requires moderation to ensure consistency, which is highly resource intensive (although it may be useful for purposes of monitoring by the school and the LEA) and, however good the moderation, may not lead to a fair allocation of resources to schools because of the issue of perverse incentives. An audit based on scores on standardised tests does not present these problems, but can lead to setting and streaming in schools, which could be problematic for inclusion.

This analysis seems to indicate that LEAs are attempting to promote their special education policies through the ways in which they fund schools and services. The funding of services to support pupils with special educational needs in mainstream schools is hampered by the government's drive to force LEAs to delegate more of their education budget to schools. This leads LEAs to set up service level agreements, whereby they delegate funds to schools and expect them to buy back support from the LEA. However, research has shown that this may lead to a discontinuation of some services, if schools decide not to buy back (Bowers, 1991).

Support for pupils with statements is protected in that, even if it is delegated, schools are legally obliged to provide the support detailed on the statement. Our research indicates that schools can be quite creative with this support, using it to provide for a number of children, some with and some without statements. This practice could be said to lead to more inclusive education, since pupils with statements are more likely, in this situation, to be part of a class group, rather than be isolated with one-to-one support.

Recent policy developments in English education indicate that there is to be more emphasis in future on 'personalised learning' and on expanding the criteria by which schools are judged as effective to include elements such as physical and mental health, personal safety and the ability to make a positive contribution to society, as well as academic achievement (GB. DfES, 2004b). These developments are supported by the requirement to bring education and social welfare departments under one management system and to link this much more closely with health services. Such developments indicate that a more holistic approach to children's needs is to be developed and this may help to resolve some of the dilemmas highlighted above. If all children are to be entitled to 'personalised learning', which was described by an education minister in these terms:

High expectations of every child, given practical form by high quality teaching based on a sound knowledge and understanding of each child's needs. It is not individualised learning where pupils sit alone. Nor is it pupils left to their own devices – which too often reinforces low aspirations. It means shaping teaching around the way different youngsters learn; it means taking the care to nurture the unique talents of every pupil. (Miliband, 2004)

then children whose needs are 'special', may not be stigmatised when they have an individualised curriculum or different learning needs. School budgets will have to be used in flexible ways to ensure the most effective approach for each child, and the issue of funding will be less focused on individuals and more on curriculum delivery across teaching groups. However, it remains to be seen whether this huge shift in the culture of funding and provision for special needs will be achieved.

NOTE

1 The Code of Practice on the Identification and Assessment of Special Educational Needs (revised in 2002) proposed five stages of intervention, which indicated five levels of need: the first three stages would be school-based (that is, from within the schools' own resources). Stages 4 and 5 were those at which a statement (and therefore extra funding to provide support) was being considered.

REFERENCES

Alur, M. (2002). Special needs policy in India. In S. Hegarty & M. Alur, *Education and children with special needs: from segregation to inclusion.* London: Sage.

Audit Commission (1992). *Getting in on the Act.* London: HMSO.

Ball, S. (1990). *Politics and policy making in education.* London: Routledge.

Bernstein, B. (1977). *Class, codes and control: Towards a theory of educational transmissions.* London: Routledge.

Bines, H. (1995). Special educational needs in the market place. *Journal of Education Policy, 10*(2), 157–171.

Booth, T., & Ainscow, M. (Eds.). (1998). *From them to us.* London: Routledge.

Bowe, R. & Ball, S. (with Gold, A.). (1992). *Reforming education and changing schools.* London: Routledge.

Bowers, T. (Ed.). (1991). *Schools, services and special educational needs.* Milton Keynes: Open University Press.

Christensen, C. & Rizvi, F. (Eds.) (1996). *Disability and the dilemmas of education and justice.* Buckingham: Open University Press.

Coard, B. (1971). *How the West Indian child is made educationally subnormal in the British school system: The scandal of the black child in schools in Britain.* London: Beacon Press.

Cole, T. (1989). *Apart or a part? Integration and the growth of British special education.* Milton Keynes: Open University Press.

Evans, J. & Lunt, I. (1992). *Developments in special education under LMS.* London: Institute of Education.

Evans, J. & Lunt, I. (1994). *Markets, competition and vulnerability: Some effects of recent legislation on children with special educational needs.* London: Tufnell Press.

Evans, J., Castle, F., & Cullen, M. A. (2002). *Fair funding? LEA policies and methods for funding additional and special needs and schools' responses* (LGA research report 27). Slough: NFER.

Fish, J. & Evans, J. (1995). *Managing special education: Codes, charters and competition.* Buckingham: Open University Press.

Great Britain. Department for Education and Employment (GB. DfEE). (1997). *Excellence for all Children: Meeting special educational needs* (Cm.3785). London: The Stationery Office.

Great Britain. Department for Education and Employment (GB. DfEE). (1998). *Meeting special educational needs: A programme of action.* London: DfEE.

Great Britain. Department for Education and Skills (GB. DfES). (2004a). *Special educational needs in England, January 2004.* London: DFES.

Great Britain. Department for Education and Skills (GB. DfES). (2004b). *Every child matters: Next steps.* London: DFES.

Hargreaves, A. (1989). The crisis of motivation and assessment. In A. Hargreaves & D. Reynolds, *Education policies: Controversies and critiques* (pp. 41–63). London: Falmer Press.

Heward, C. & Lloyd-Smith, M. (1990). Assessing the impact of legislation on special education policy. *Journal of Education Policy, 5*(1), 21–36.

Hornby, G., Atkinson, M., & Howard, J. (1997). *Controversial issues in special education.* London: David Fulton.

Jackson, B. (1964). *Streaming: An education system in miniature.* London: Routledge & Kegan Paul.

Jackson, B. & Marsden, D. (1962). *Education and the working class.* London: Routledge & Kegan Paul.

Kumar, V. (1993). *Poverty and inequality in the UK: The effects on children.* London: National Children's Bureau.

Lawton, S. (1992). Why restructure? An international survey of the roots of reform. *Journal of Education Policy, 7*(2), 139–54.

Lee, T. (1996). *The search for equity: Funding additional educational needs under LMS.* Aldershot: Avebury.

Marsh, A. (1995). The effect on budgets of different non-statemented special educational needs indicators within a common funding formula, *British Educational Research Journal, 21*(1), 99–115.

Marsh, A. (2003). *Funding inclusive education: The economic realities.* Aldershot: Ashgate.

Meijer, C., Pijl, S. J. & Hegarty, S. (1994). *New perspectives in special education: A six-country study of integration.* London: Routledge.

Miliband, D. (2004). *Personalised learning: Building a new relationship with schools.* Speech delivered at North Of England Education Conference, Belfast, January 2004.

Mortimore, P. & Whitty, J. (1997). *Can school improvement overcome the effects of disadvantage?* London: University of London, Institute of Education.

Norwich, B. (1990). *Reappraising special needs education.* London: Cassell.

Norwich, B. (1994). *Segregation and inclusion: English LEA statistics 1988–92.* Bristol: Centre for Studies on Inclusive Education.

Norwich, B. (1997). *A trend towards inclusion: Statistics on special school placements and pupils with statements in ordinary schools, England 1992–1996.* Bristol: Centre for Studies in Inclusive Education.

Ntombela, T. (2004). *From policy to practice? Teachers' perceptions of inclusive education in South Africa: three case studies.* Paper given at Doctoral School Conference, Institute of Education, London, July 2004.

Organisation for Economic Co-operation and Development (OECD). (1995). *Integrating students with special needs into mainstream schools.* Paris: OECD.

Peter, M. (1995). Lobbying for special education. In I. Lunt, B. Norwich, & V. Varma. *Psychology and Education for special needs* (193–210). Aldershot: Arena Ashgate.

Scanlon, M., Earley, P. & Evans, J. (1998). *Improving the effectiveness of school governing bodies* (DfEE Research Report 111). London: DfEE.

Sharp, S. (2000). Allocating resources for learning support: A case study, *Educational Management & Administration, 28*(2), 211–21.

Swann, W. (1991). *Variations between LEAs in levels of segregation in special schools, 1982–90.* Centre for Studies in Inclusive Education. Preliminary report.

Tomlinson, S. (1982). *A sociology of special education.* London: Routledge & Kegan Paul.

Willis, P. (1977). *Learning to labour.* Farnborough: Saxon House.

5

Categories of special educational needs

Brahm Norwich

INTRODUCTION

The classification of children's difficulties in learning into categories has played a key role in the history of special educational provision. Categories have been at the root of the endeavour to identify and provide for a group of children and young people identified as being exceptional. Categories are the basis for parents who group themselves into specific voluntary organisations to promote the interests of a specific group of children. Researchers use categories to sort and describe the groups of children they study. Service administrators and managers use categories to monitor and plan additional educational provision, while teachers are prepared professionally and have their professional identities in terms of categories. Without some system of categories or a position about the place and function of categories, there would be no system of special or additional education, as we know it. Yet, it is very difficult to find a systematic, coherent and evidence-based position about classification that commands wide support. This is a situation which has not improved much over the last 18 years, since Ysseldyke (1987) drew

attention to these issues. The aim of this chapter is to examine the issues associated with categories and consider some of the options which face us.

When examining classification schemes we need to consider the various aspects of categories in these schemes. The first is what is being categorised. Categories have been used to determine the:

1   patterns of exceptional child functioning relevant to education,
2   underlying disorders, disabilities or impairments relevant to child functioning in education,
3   kinds of exceptional placement and general provision (by location, kinds of resources allocated),
4   kinds of curriculum design and content, and teaching strategy.

The traditional focus of special education categories, one which is still dominant internationally (OECD, 2000), is a mixture of exceptional child functioning and underlying disorders, disabilities or impairments. A second aspect concerns the nature of the system for differentiating; whether difference is represented in terms of kind or degree. Where classification systems represent differences of kind these can be either in terms of single or multiple axes. By contrast, differences of degree are represented by dimensional systems in which the child is placed along a continuum or set of continua. However, regions within these continua are often defined to identify groups of children. In this way, differences of degree become difference of kind, but more finely defined categories.

PURPOSES OF CATEGORIES

The historic basis for special education and the function of categories has been to delineate a group for different or additional educational provision of some form. The purpose of categories, in this sense, is an administrative one of additional resource allocation. These additional resources, compared to what is allocated for children not identified with additional needs, are often justified in terms of compensating for disadvantages, a kind of affirmative action. Several points can be made about what could be called the political-administrative reason for needing categories. One is that there are different areas where 'additional needs' have been recognised in addition to the traditional special education focus on difficulties and disabilities. There are children whose first language is different from the language medium of the school they attend. In the UK they might be called children with English as an additional language. Another is the area of 'gifted and talented' for very high attaining and able children and those with specific talents. A fourth area concerns children who are identified as 'at risk' of school difficulties, but without clear-cut disabilities, what is sometimes referred to in the UK, as children 'at risk of educational exclusion'.[1] The prominence of these three allied areas of additional need varies with the priorities of government educational policy, as shown recently in the UK, for example. There are similar issues about the definition of categories to specify eligibility for and the limits to the additional provision in these three allied areas as there

are for educational disability. There are also issues about the overlap between these areas.

As regards the disability area of additional needs, it is possible to use only a single broad category, like 'educational disability', a kind of super-category for political-administrative purposes. An example of this was the introduction of the term 'special educational needs' in the UK with the 1981 education legislation based on the Warnock Report (DES, 1978). Though the Report has been interpreted as abandoning categories, it actually replaced a set of disability-specific categories with a more general category. This move avoided the issue of overlapping disability categories and enabled a focus on the individual needs of children in curriculum and teaching terms rather than membership of a category group. Categories for political-administrative purposes are therefore about additional resource allocation and do not in themselves imply that distinct curricula, teaching or placement are required. The eligibility criteria for additional resources are by their nature general and not necessarily about specific education needs at the level of face-to-face teaching.

Another main purpose for categories in education has been concerned with curriculum and teaching. This has taken the form of using categories to inform decisions and sometimes to determine decisions about curriculum, teaching and placement for children. Associated with this has been the use of categories to determine teacher preparation and training. Though the historic role of categories for curriculum and placement decisions has declined, their role in teaching has continued and for some categories increased. Categories for these teaching purposes have their historic origins in the use of medical classifications and categories of disorder and impairments in the diagnostic assessment of children with learning difficulties. Several points can be made about the role of categories with medical origins for teaching purposes. The first point is that these categories are meant to be diagnostic in the sense that they aim to identify causal factors (aetiology) that underlie the presenting difficulties and have implications for future outcomes (prognosis) (Cromwell, Blashfield & Strauss, 1975). The validity of the category depends on identifying interventions (or treatments) with known outcomes. However, this idealised diagnostic-intervention aspect of medical categories does not apply to many developmental conditions either in the curative or the rehabilitative senses of intervention. This is because the historic medical categories used in special education (for example, intellectual retardation) do not approach the criteria for adequate classification. Some medical categories are only constellations of loosely associated symptoms and signs (syndromes); as such they are inclusive and cannot even be defined in terms of clear-cut presenting difficulties. If the diagnostic-intervention assumptions cannot be made, then this kind of category cannot be expected to have relevance for the specific planning of curriculum and teaching. Children identified as having needs associated with a particular special education category (for example, mild mental retardation in the USA, or moderate learning difficulties in the UK) might require different teaching approaches; as children in different categories might require the same teaching approach.

A second point about the role of the medical categories used in special education is that they have reinforced some particular false assumptions and ways of thinking that have undermined educational assessment as the basis for planning teaching. One assumption is that diagnosis is in terms of general child difficulties or deficits rather than in terms of the child's strengths and difficulties in interaction with learning environmental supports and obstacles (Wedell & Lindsay, 1980; Adelman & Taylor,[2] 1993). Another assumption is that specifying differential characteristics is seen to be enough to justify category use and validity. These false assumptions arise from the lack of understanding of the incomplete nature of the medical categories imported into and used in special education. Ysseldyke (1987) summarised this situation in special education as

the use of 'inappropriate and invalid diagnostic-intervention paradigm' (p. 256) and classification practice not being treated theoretically. However, none of this discussion implies that medical categories cannot and do not have some relevance to special education, as the chapter will illustrate in what follows.

CURRENT CATEGORY SYSTEMS

Despite the fact that the broad category 'special educational needs' was used in legislation and sub-categories were widely used in service delivery in the UK system for a quarter of a century, the UK system has been represented from an international perspective as having a non-categorical system (OECD, 2000). The reason for this view was the official focus on need and the abandonment of sub-categories in the 1981 legislation. From the Organisation for Economic Co-operation and Development (OECD) perspective, the UK was similar to Denmark, which also distinguished between significant SEN and less significant SEN – in UK terms SEN with and without Statements – within a philosophy which responds to exceptionalities rather than defining student categories. In the OECD analysis, the definitions used in 23 countries were presented as fitting four basic patterns:

1 use of disability categories only (for example, France, Germany)
2 use of disability categories + disadvantaged students (for example, Greece, New Zealand)
3 use of disability categories + disadvantaged students + gifted students (for example, Spain, Turkey)
4 base provision on the need to respond to exceptionalities rather than defining students (for example, New Brunswick, Canada, UK, Denmark).

Though this is an interesting and useful set of international distinctions, it does not explain the detailed aspects of the definitions of need in the fourth pattern, such as the degrees of need and how what is needed is conceptualised in provision terms. The OECD only defines special educational needs as: 'those with special educational needs are defined by the additional public and/or private resources provided to support their education' (OECD, 2000, p. 8). The reference to 'additional resources' shifts the focus away from child characteristics to the available educational provision, its flexibility and appropriateness, but does not advance the provision-focused approach. It is in even less detail than the analysis presented in the introduction to this chapter, in terms of patterns of child functioning, disorder and disabilities, on the one hand, and kinds of exceptional placement, curriculum and teaching, on the other. But, what the OECD needs focus does offer is a way of bringing together the four areas of exceptional need into a common framework. Though this kind of thinking probably has its origins in the UK Warnock critique of child-focused categories, the OECD position highlights the anomaly in the UK system between adopting a provision focus while still separating provision for disabilities from that for 'gifted and talented', for English as a second language and for social disadvantage.

The UK government has introduced a national English system for monitoring individual school children which includes details of their kind of special educational needs (DfES, 2003). However, SEN is not defined in terms of provision but child categories; 11 areas of SEN[3] similar in principle to the 11 categories of education handicap used until 1980, which formed the basis for the pre-Warnock system of special education. This new classification system applies to children at only two of the three levels of SEN, those with Statements (about 3 per cent) and those at School Action plus (about 4 per cent), not to the larger groups of children with SEN at School Action (about 10 per cent). This move brings the English system into line with other countries, like the USA, where federal regulations under the IDEA legislation prescribed 12 separate disabling conditions, covering similar areas to the UK one, but using different terms (OECD, 2000). Though the different states making up the USA may vary in their classification poli-

cies, most use the federal one with some changes in terminology. Since 1997 states and school districts in the USA have the option of eliminating disability classification for children aged 3–9, a practice also found in other countries, such as South Korea, for example. However, this classification practice is not like the UK focus on needed provision, as the focus is still on the child's difficulties and developmental delays.

The OECD study also provided an interesting higher-order system of cross-country categories for comparing the categories of 22 countries. These were represented as:

1 category A – where there is substantial normative agreement about the categories, for example, sensory, motor, severe, profound intellectual disabilities
2 category B – difficulties which do not appear to be attributable to factors which lead to categories A and C; what could be called 'contested' disabilities (Dyson, 2002)
3 category C – difficulties that arise from socio-economic, cultural, and/or linguistic factors; some disadvantaged or atypical background which education seeks to compensate for.

When the national panels classified their national SEN classification system in terms of this scheme, it showed very wide variations between countries. For example, the USA was reported to have between 5.6 per cent of all primary and lower secondary aged children in category A (normative agreement about disabilities) and almost 70 per cent of these children in regular classrooms; whereas Holland, which only had 1.8 per cent in category A, had 87 per cent of them in special schools.

THE PROBLEMS UNDERLYING CATEGORIES

During the consultations over the proposed English SEN classification in 2002, the arguments about categories re-surfaced, especially over those areas identified as contested disabilities, category B in OECD terms. Over the last two decades there has been persistent criticism of the concept of special educational needs from a critical sociological perspective as part of a wider critique of the special education system, (Tomlinson, 1982, 1985; Barton & Tomlinson, 1984). Tomlinson (1985) argued that the concept of special needs was ambiguous and that it had become part of a rhetoric that served little educational purpose. It was tautological because needs were defined in terms of additional provision without specifying who was to have this additional provision, other than that it was for those with special needs. Tomlinson's point was that while the identification problem had not been resolved, the SEN concept was expanded by the 1981 educational legislation.

However, it has been and still remains unclear whether the normatively agreed versus contested disabilities distinction is one of causation, severity of disability, the setting and use of norms or some combination of these aspects. If it were one of causation, then it parallels one made traditionally in medicine between organically and functionally or psycho-socially caused conditions. However, this is currently not a clear medical distinction as even organically based conditions might also be associated with psycho-social causal and maintenance conditions. Also, all medical disorders, whatever their causation, are initially identified in terms of social norms and values (Kennedy, 1980). To use a current example, whether over-activity and attention difficulties are interpreted either as an attention deficit hyperactivity disorder (ADHD), or as a reactive difficulty to social-emotional conditions or as adult intolerance of child energy, is initially a matter of setting norms. If a child's 'problem' is identified, then this is judged in terms of a deviation from the norms, whether it is identified as a disorder or reactive difficulty.

Following the OECD scheme, in some 'problem' areas there is more agreement and in others less agreement over the norms. One interpretation of this difference is that more normative agreement is found where there are identifiable biologically based impairments,

and where there are greater deviations from the norms and a lower frequency of identification. By contrast, contested categories are found more in those areas where functioning cannot be attributed clearly and mainly to biological impairments and where the degree of deviation is less from the norm or average and identification rates more frequent. There is some evidence for this interpretation of the difference between category A and category B areas in the data from the OECD study. For 9 of the 11 countries (82 per cent) for which there was incidence data, there were higher national percentages of children in the contested category B areas than normatively agreed category A areas, even though there were many more categories in category A than category B. Also, in the 14 of the 22 countries (64 per cent) where national panels identified contested disabilities, the most frequent areas were:

1   learning disabilities (50 per cent of countries), as understood in the USA, or specific learning difficulties, as understood in the UK
2   learning difficulties (43 per cent of countries), with reference to social origins, slow learning and remedial needs
3   social-emotional difficulties and/or behaviour disturbance or difficulties (50 per cent of countries).

These are the SEN areas where there is less deviation from the norms and/or biological causation is more uncertain.

HAVE GENERAL CATEGORIES OUTLIVED THEIR USEFULNESS?

The recent UK system is interesting internationally in view of the earlier policy of 'abandoning' and then re-introducing categories. The Warnock position of rejecting child categories because there was no clear dividing line between disability and no disability, conflicted with the recommendation for more positive sounding categories. Attention was distracted from this contradiction by its other proposals, by the distancing of medical categories through concentrating on educational needs and provision, and by highlighting the individuality of needs that could not be captured by crude general categories. That the Warnock position was based on traditional categories was clear from its dependence on well known epidemiological studies, like the Isle of Wight study (Rutter, Tizard & Whitmore, 1970).

There have been several challenges to the Warnock philosophy in the UK. One has been the resurgence of interest in the causal role of within-child causal factors in the interaction with the role of the social and learning environment. This has been especially from interest groups defining themselves in terms of medical categories, such as, dyslexia, dyspraxia, autism and attention deficit hyperactivity disorder. A different challenge has also come from members of a rights-based disability movement, who reject the term 'needs' as implying paternalistic and professional control. A third challenge to the Warnock orthodoxy has come from a financial management perspective, best exemplified in the recent case for common national definitions of need by the UK government funded Audit Commission (Audit Commission, 2002).

The contemporary case for defining national common categories of SEN, as expressed by the government Department for Education and Skills (DfES, 2003), is based on the need for planning and monitoring provision. Strategic planning of the education services is possible, it is argued, only if there are clear and consistent definitions of need; comparison with health planning is made here. This is presented as an equal opportunities issue; consistency of service requires common definitions across schools and local education authorities. One major criticism of the re-introduction of categories is that the government refers to kinds of special educational needs and only presents a mix of definitions of areas of difficulties, impairments and disorders; and so loses the benefits of the Warnock switch to educational needs and provision.

Recent criticism of the new SEN classification in England and Wales has questioned its validity, desirability and necessity (Gray, 2003). The validity issue, as discussed above, is about whether the categories have implications for specific provision or interventions for those in a category compared to those not in the category and those not having SEN. Ysseldyke (1987) concluded in the US context that, with the exception of children with sensory impairments, there were no teaching strategies and techniques that were uniquely effective for certain categories of children. Mercer and Mercer (2001) and McDonnell, McLaughlin and Morison (1997) have come to similar conclusions about the validity of categories for teaching and curriculum more recently in the USA. In the UK, Lewis and Norwich (2004) concluded that the traditional SEN categories, used in the UK and internationally, have limited usefulness in the context of planning, monitoring, teaching and learning in most areas. Where they are judged to be useful, the categories operate as orienting concepts and inform decision-making about teaching as one of several other important elements.

The criticism about the desirability of the new categories connects with the political-administrative reasons for categories, discussed in the introduction as related to additional resource allocation decisions. One criticism has been that they create pressure and incentives to increase the rate of identification of children with SEN, what are called 'perverse incentives'. The problem of 'perverse incentives' can be dealt with in two broad ways. One is to counter the pressures to over-identify by using systems of external checking of assessment judgements by external professionals, such as psychologists, or external teachers to moderate audits of a school's identification of SEN. The other way is not to use categories at all, but this will undermine the basis of a system of additional educational resourcing for children with SEN and disabilities. This raises the question of the necessity of categories. One position is that services can respond to individual variations if they focus on what is to be achieved, on outcomes (Gray, 2003). It is argued that additional resources can be funded at a school level, based on aggregate baseline attainment levels and measures of social disadvantage. However, like others advocating this alternative in the UK (Dyson, 2002), nobody is advocating the full replacement of child-level resourcing and planning, only a reduction in the numbers involved in child-level resourcing. In this situation, some decisions are needed about which children are to be covered by the SEN categories and the individual identification and planning SEN framework. So, the category question does not go away with more school-level resourcing, just the number of children covered by it is reduced. Also, even if all additional resourcing was based on school-level aggregate baseline attainment and social disadvantage indicators, decisions within schools about resource allocation would most likely call for some child-level allocations and thus some classification system of child difficulties.

HARD DECISIONS AND FUTURE OPTIONS

It is possible to conclude that SEN categories have limited validity in terms of specific curriculum and teaching needs, while justifying the continued use of some child-focused categories for compensatory additional resource allocation. The differentiation in SEN classification marks the threshold at which some children would get more educational resources than others, between more and less resource worthy groups. However, disability is the not the only area in receipt of additional resourcing. There are also doubts about the children who come into the OECD category B – contested disabilities – would they receive additional resourcing in terms of disabilities, as at present, or in terms of social disadvantage? Whether additional resourcing is in terms of disability or disadvantage, there are hard decisions or dilemmas both ways about difference and differentiation – to identify or to not identify differences such as difficulties in learning (Norwich, 1993, 1996).

These dilemmas arise from the positive and negative conceptions in our society about human differences and what we call differentiation in education. The negative perspective is that 'difference' reflects lower status and value and so perpetuates inequalities and unfair treatment. The positive perspective is that 'difference' reflects the recognition of individuality, individual needs and interests. It is the tension between these conceptions of difference which leads us to address *dilemmas of difference*. The dilemma is that both options, to recognise or not to recognise difference, have negative risks. Recognising difference can lead to different provision, which might be stigmatised and devalued; but not recognising difference can lead to overlooking and ignoring individuality. The tension is between the values of inclusion and individuality. From an inclusive perspective, SEN categories can be seen as a form of terminological separation and exclusion. From this dilemmatic perspective, the challenge is to provide appropriate and individually relevant provision, while minimising stigma and devaluation. One way of doing this is to adopt a three-dimensional model of educational needs which sets special or specific group-based educational needs within the context of general needs common to all, on the one hand, and individual needs, on the other (Norwich, 1996). Individual educational needs are considered at the same time in this framework in terms of:

1 general needs common to all
2 specific needs associated with group membership
3 unique needs.

Disability categories, as with other general categories, do not therefore fully define a child's educational needs. Children coming within a broad category will share some needs in common with those not in that category. Also different children within a category will have some needs that are unique to them.

If categories are useful for political-administrative purposes, then there is still the need to determine which groups or areas of educational need require additional resources and what the relationships are between these areas. This is important in policy terms as the additional resourcing can come under different legislative and administrative systems. In the UK, for example, additional resourcing for disability (called SEN) operates differently from additional resourcing for social disadvantage (under the heading of social exclusion). It is also important in terms of the quality of services, the assurances and controls available to parents about appropriate additional provision and the social identities of children who receive additional provision and their parents. Is it justifiable that the areas of moderate learning difficulties, specific learning difficulties and social, emotional and behaviour difficulties, to use the UK SEN classification, continue to be regarded as areas of SEN with the implication that they are disabilities? In international terms, using the OECD scheme, what is the future for category B areas, the contested disability areas of special educational needs? These are some options:

1   Keep them with disabilities, as in the UK.
2   Treat them like difficulties associated with social disadvantage.
3   Separate them into two areas: the more severe, complex and pervasive problems, which will be treated as disabilities, will be differentiated from the milder and less pervasive problems, which will be treated like social disadvantage.

In a North American context it has been argued that the equivalent of the UK categories of moderate learning difficulties (MLD) (mild mental retardation), specific learning difficulties (SpLD) (learning disabilities) and social, emotional and behaviour difficulties (SEBD) (behaviour disorders) cannot be distinguished from each other. Johnson (1998) exemplifies this position, in using the generic term 'mild educational disabilities'. It is interesting that this generic approach is widely used in preparing and licensing special education teachers for teaching children with mild disabilities in the USA (Hardman & McDonnell, 2004). Johnson

argues for the merging of the mild educational disabilities category with the wider group of children at risk of educational failure on the grounds that the student-based risk factors are very similar in the at-risk and the mild disability groups. The benefits of merger are that the at-risk framework includes a range of environmental at-risk factors (class, school, neighbourhood, family, societal) that enables more and broader systemic interventions that connect educational needs in schools with other social and personal needs. In the UK context, Norwich and Kelly (2004) in a review of the field of moderate learning difficulties identify three options about the future of the MLD category, based on the assumption of a dilemma about identification:

1   Retain and specify operational criteria for a revised tighter MLD category as an area of disability.
2   Abandon MLD as a disability category and merge with a non-disability low-attainment group with educational provision under a social inclusion framework
3   Abandon MLD for the majority of children currently identified (as in the second option), while redefining a new tighter category of mild mixed difficulties as a new disability category for a minority of the children currently identified.

It is argued that empirical research is needed to examine whether there is a justification for the MLD category as distinct from allied disability categories (SpLD and BESD) and the at-risk or low-attaining group (Norwich and Kelly, 2004). It is clear that a similar set of considerations would apply to examining the other two allied SEN areas, SpLD and BESD. This is especially relevant in the UK context in which the 2003 SEN classification was introduced without empirically based research and development work.

OTHER BROAD CLASSIFICATION OPTIONS

Though it has been argued that some system of categories can be justified in terms of political administrative reasons of additional resource allocation, it does not follow that the traditional classification like the recent UK 11 categories, and other similar systems, best serves this purpose. It has also been noted that most SEN category systems are still child-focused categories and have limited validity in terms of specific curriculum and teaching provision. A third position taken in this chapter has been the adoption of an interactive causal model of child difficulties in learning. Putting these assumptions together calls for a model of child functioning across a range of life contexts, that takes account of social factors and does not focus exclusively on impairments and disorders. Such a system has begun to be constructed and evaluated by the World Health Organization (WHO) as its International Classification for Functioning, Disability and Health (ICF: WHO, 2002). It is designed to act as a planning and policy tool for decision-makers, by shifting the focus from causes (as in the International Classification of Diseases (ICD) and the Diagnostic and Statistical Manual (DSM) medical classification systems) to impacts and functioning. It is based on a broader concept of disability that goes beyond impairments to include activity limitations and social participation restrictions. It also assumes an integrated model that rejects the polarisation between the 'medical' and the 'social' model, and espouses what has come to be called a bio-psycho-social model.

The ICF model represents disability in terms of the interaction of (1) bodily functions/structures, (2) activities (tasks and activities that can be executed) and (3) participation (what the person can do in current environment). These interrelated dimensions are seen as being influenced by health conditions (disorders/diseases), on the one hand, and contextual factors (environmental and personal factors), on the other. The ICF therefore identifies a person within four dimensions:

1   body function (covering physical and psychological function)
2   body structure

3   activity and participation
4   environmental factors.

The ICF has been adapted in a child and youth version, the ICF-CY (Simeonsson et al., 2003) using the same model and assumptions as above, but for four age groups (0–1, 3–6, 7–12 and 13–18 years). What is particularly interesting about the ICF system is that it is designed to monitor change over the lifespan. It does this through its multidimensional structure and by focusing at a level of detail about activities and participation that can capture change. Though the system includes the effects of health conditions, activity limitations are not necessarily specific to any disorder whether physical or mental. However, the ICF system has been designed as a classification to cover functions, activities and participation in general across a range of life contexts, and therefore goes well beyond those aspects that relate specifically to educational functions, needs and specific contexts. This is evident in the main areas identified for activities and participation.[4] Though the ICF-CY has potential for use in planning and monitoring change in an inter-service context that considers function, activity and participation in terms of broader health, care and educational needs, its usefulness for specific educational planning and decision-making may turn out to be limited. It could therefore be argued that there is a need for an ICF-type classification of function, activity and participation specifically relevant to curriculum and teaching decisions and practices.

This kind of classification could be based on the same assumptions as the ICF and ICF-CY (see Figure 5.1), but would be confined to educationally relevant functional impairments (for example, phonological difficulties) and learning activity limitations, with a curriculum basis, (for example, early word reading difficulties) and participation restrictions in educational settings (for example, inadequate numeracy support programme in mainstream class) (see Table 5.1).

Table 5.1   Dimensions of a possible classification of educational disability

1. Educationally relevant functional impairments	– covering range of functional areas
2. Health conditions (disease, disorder)	– current conditions, conditions treated/remedied condition or uncertain conditions
3. Environmental factors	– facilitators and barriers in current home and school situations
4. Personal factors	– abilities, skills, dispositions that are educationally relevant
5. Learning activity limitations	– activity limitations in range of curriculum areas
6. Learning participation restrictions	– learning participation restrictions in class, wider school, home and community

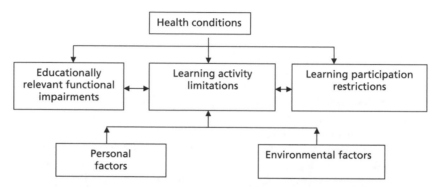

Figure 5.1   Representation of a model of educational disability

CONCLUDING COMMENTS

This chapter has come to similar conclusions as Ysseldyke (1987), some 18 years ago, though from a different national context and in a changed international educational context. Classification has not been addressed in theoretical terms and despite some positive moves in the UK after the Warnock Report to consider classification from an educational perspective, the current situation is characterised by inappropriate models and a lack of theoretical analysis.

The chapter has been based on the distinction between categories for political-administrative purposes and for curriculum, teaching and provision purposes. Some system of categories for resource allocation is necessary, but this does not require the traditional 11–13 special education categories. Research reviews and analyses have consistently indicated the limited usefulness of these categories in many areas, especially in the contested disabilities (for a child coming under the OECD contested disabilities – cate-

gory B). Even when categories have some educational significance, their general nature means that they inform rather than determine specific education planning and provision.

The chapter has also explained the hard decisions about identification that need to be addressed in this field in terms of dilemmas of difference. The identification dilemma arises from positive and negative conceptions about differences in education and society generally, of which disabilities are the most notable. Categories may be justified in positive compensatory terms, for disability and other areas of additional need, but at the risk of negative outcomes such as stigma, devaluation and exclusion. Recognising the tension is the first step to finding classifications which best support compensatory provision while minimising the negative risks and consequences.

Two broad areas for future classificatory development were considered as well. One was about the boundaries between disabilities and social disadvantage for the large proportion of children identified as having mild educational disabilities – in the area of the OECD category B. The other was the development of sophisticated multidimensional category systems based on the ICF assumptions and model, but geared to educational contexts and purposes. Both areas depend on national and international commitment to research and development work about classification systems. The criteria by which we should evaluate classification systems were outlined many years ago: they should be reliable, have coverage, be consistent, useful, acceptable to users, reviewed periodically, and evaluated in terms of the balance of gains to losses to those affected by them (Cromwell et al., 1975). It is time to take them more seriously.

NOTES

1   Boys and girls, minority ethnic groups, travellers, asylum seekers, refugees, English as additional language, SEN, gifted and talented, looked after by the local authority, sick children, young carers, children where families under stress, pregnant schoolgirls, at risk of disaffection and exclusion (at risk of educational exclusion: Office for Standards in Education).

2   Transactional model of causation: a continuum of person – environment transactions – at one pole type I problems where causation mainly environmental, type II problems where causation equally caused by person and environment, and type II problems where causation mainly in the person.

3   A. Cognition and Learning Needs: Specific Learning Difficulty (SpLD), Moderate Learning Difficulty (MLD), Severe Learning Difficulty (SLD), Profound and Multiple Learning Difficulty (PMLD). B. Behaviour, Emotional and Social Development Needs: Behaviour, Emotional and Social Difficulty (BESD). C. Communication and Interaction Needs: Speech, Language and Communication Needs (SLCN), Autistic Spectrum Disorder (ASD). D. Sensory and/or Physical Needs: Visual Impairment (VI), Hearing Impairment (HI), Multi-Sensory Impairment (MSI), Physical Disability (PD).

4   ICF activity and participation areas: learning and applying knowledge, general tasks and demands, communication, mobility, self-care, domestic life, interpersonal interactions and relationships, major life areas, community, social and civic life.

REFERENCES

Adelman, H. S., & Taylor, L. (1993). *Learning problems and learning disabilities.* Pacific Grove, CA: Brooks/Cole.

Audit Commission. (2002). *Statutory assessment and statements of SEN: in need of review?* London: Audit Commission.

Barton, L., & Tomlinson, S. (1984). The politics of integration. In L. Barton & S. Tomlinson (Eds.), *Special education and social interests.* Beckenham: Croom Helm.

Cromwell, R. I., Blashfield, R. K., & Strauss, J. S. (1975). Criteria for classification systems. In N. Hobbs (Ed.), *Issues in the classification of children* (Vol. 1, pp. 4–25). San Francisco, CA: Jossey-Bass.

Department for Education and Science (DES). (1978) *Special educational needs: Report of the Committee of Enquiry into the education of handicapped children and young people* (The Warnock Committee Report. London: HMSO.

Department for Education and Skills (DfES). (2003). *Data collection by type of special educational needs.* London: DfES.

Dyson, A. (2002). Special needs, disability and social inclusion – the end of a beautiful friendship? In SEN Policy Options Steering Group (Ed.), *Disability, disadvantage, inclusion and social inclusion* (pp. 12–17). Tamworth: NASEN.

Gray, P. (2003). Categories revisited: the emergence of a new epidemiology of SEN. In SEN Policy Options Steering Group (Ed.), *Examining key issues underlying the Audit Commission Reports on SEN* (pp. 23–34). Tamworth: NASEN.

Hardman, M. L., & McDonnell, J. (2004). *Perspectives and purposes of disability classification systems in research and clinical practice: Implications for teachers, pedagogy and curriculum.* Paper presented at Perspectives and Purposes of Disability Classification Systems conference, University of Cambridge.

Johnson, G. M. (1998). Students at risk: toward a new paradigm of mild educational disabilities. *School Psychology International, 19*(3): 221–37.

Kennedy, I. (1980, November 6). Unmasking medicine. *Listener.*

Lewis, A., & Norwich, B. (Eds.). (2004). *Special teaching for special children? Pedagogies for inclusion.* Maidenhead: Open University Press.

McDonnell, L. M., McLaughlin, M. J., & Morison, P. (Eds.). (1997). *Educating one and all: Students with disabilities and standards based reform.* Washington, DC: National Research Council, National Academic Press.

Mercer, C. D., & Mercer, A. R. (2001). *Teaching students with learning problems.* Upper Saddle River, NJ: Merrill Publishing Company.

Norwich, B. (1993). Ideological dilemmas in special needs education: practitioners' views. *Oxford Review of Education, 19*(4), 527–546.

Norwich, B. (1996). *Special needs education, inclusive education or just education for all?* Inaugural Lecture. Institute of Education, London University.

Norwich, B., & Kelly, N. (2004). *Moderate learning difficulties and the future of inclusion.* London: RoutledgeFalmer.

Organisation for Economic Co-operation and Development (OECD). (2000). *Special needs education: statistics and indicators.* Paris: OECD.

Rutter, M., Tizard, J., & Whitmore, K. (1970). *Education, health and behaviour.* London: Longman.

Simeonsson, R. J., Leonardi, M., Bjorck-Akesson, E., Hollenweger, J., Lollar, D. J., & Matinuzzi, A. (2003). Measurement of disability in children and youth: implications of the ICF. *Rehabilitation & Disability, 25*(11), 3–17.

Tomlinson, S. (1982). *A sociology of special education.* London: Routledge & Kegan Paul.

Tomlinson, S. (1985). The expansion of special education. *Oxford Review of Education, 11*(2), 157–165

Wedell, K., & Lindsay, G. (1980). Early identification procedures: What we have learned. *Remedial Education, 15,* 130–135.

World Health Organization (WHO). (2002). *International classification of functioning, disability and health: Towards a common language for functioning, disability and health.* Geneva: WHO.

Ysseldyke, J. E. (1987). Classification of handicapped students. In N. C. Wang, M. C. Reynolds, & H. J. Walberg (Eds.). *Handbook of special education: Research and practice* (Vol. 1, pp. 230–254). Oxford: Pergamon Press.

6

The disproportionate placement of ethnic minorities in special education

Beth Harry

Ethnic disproportionality in special education refers to the fact that students from certain historically excluded minority groups have been placed in special education programs at rates that are disproportionate to their presence in the student population as a whole.

For a variety of reasons that will be explained in this chapter, this pattern, noted in the US since the inception of the Education of All Handicapped Children's Act (EHA) in 1975, has been the source of controversy regarding whether disporportionality represents discriminatory decisions that result in the excluding or stigmatizing of historically oppressed minorities. The EHA was re-authorized in 1990 under the name of The Individuals with Disabilities Education Improvement Act (IDEIA, 2004).

While the term disproportionality includes both over and underrepresentation, the focus of this chapter will be on overrepresentation, since this continues to be the main issue of concern to educators. Further, the concern with disproportionate placements is confined to the 'high incidence' disability categories, which are determined by clinical judgment, rather than the 'low incidence' categories, which rely on evidence of biological or organic anomalies. Of the 13 disability categories identified by the IDEIA, consistent evidence of minority disproportionality has been found only in Specific Learning Disability (more commonly known as LD), Mild Mental Retardation (MMR), and Emotional Disturbance (ED). According to Donovan and Cross (2002), in the low incidence categories, 'few would question the professional judgment or accuracy of a diagnosis' (p. 54). In contrast, the lack of proof in the high incidence categories challenges the veracity of the clinical judgments leading to disproportionality, and points to the elusive nature of the dividing line between low achievement and 'disability'.

Although the focus of this chapter is on the situation in the US, low achievement and/or special education placement of certain ethnic minority groups are of concern in many countries. An international view provides us with a key insight: first, it is not race, as a biological construct, which accounts for low educational achievement, but rather the historical status of a given 'minority' group within a society. Thus, 'race' is really a proxy not just for low socioeconomic status as some have argued (MacMillan & Reschly, 1998), but for an enduring history of discrimination and exclusion. A second insight essential to the argument of this chapter is that the high incidence disabilities represent social constructions by which relatively arbitrary points on the continuum of achievement are designated as 'disabilities'. When both race and disability are viewed as socially constructed categories, it is easy to see how the educational difficulties of minorities are statements about societies rather than about children. In brief, the argument of this chapter is that the main reason the overrepresentation of ethnic minorities in programs for students with 'high incidence' disabilities is problematic is that it is rooted in a paradigm of categorization and classification which, despite good intentions, tends to perpetuate inequities historically ingrained in the society.

THE IMPACT OF ETHNIC MINORITY STATUS ON EDUCATIONAL ACHIEVEMENT: CROSS-CULTURAL VIEWS

Cross-cultural studies of the educational performance of minorities indicate that the lowest achievers are typically those minority groups who have experienced a history of exclusion and stigmatization within a society. Integral to this pattern are education systems with a history of having provided inferior schooling for these groups and having excluded their cultures or languages from the curriculum. It is clear that, while these minority groups may or may not be racially different from the mainstream, their relegation to the lowest rungs of the society reflects their history as outsiders or dominated peoples within the society. In discussing the 'social construction of difference', Gillborn and Youdell (2000) observed that groups defined socially by gender, ethnicity, race, or class are 'defined by social convention, not by inherent, fixed, or "natural" differences' (p. 4). Hence, there can be no assumption of intrinsic differences in group members' capacity to participate successfully in the educational arena.

Collections of studies by Skutnabb-Kangas and Cummins (1988) and Gibson and Ogbu (1991) exemplify the global pattern of minority underachievement. For example, 'outsiders' include Koreans in Japan, Finns in Sweden, West Indians, Pakistanis, and Bangladeshis in Britain (Gillborn & Youdell, 2000; Office of Standards for Education, 2002), and Moroccans in Spain (Escandell, 2002). These studies and others show that indigenous minorities fare even worse than immigrant groups: To name but a few – the Burakumin in Japan (De Vos & Wagatsuma, 1966), the Sami in Finland, Aboriginal natives in Australia (Jordan, 1988), the Maori in New Zealand (Barrington, 1991), and Gitanos ('gypsies') in Spain (Enguita, 1999).

The point at which low achievement comes to be interpreted as 'disability' represents the intersection of general and special education. Besides the US, only a few countries have so far explicitly noted that disproportionately low minority achievement leads to disproportionately high placement in special programs for the 'disabled'. These cases support the view that historically oppressed minorities are particularly vulnerable to inappropriate use of the construct of 'disability', with the intentional or unintentional result of further discrimination. Most notably, in the Czech Republic, the charge that special classes were being used for the purpose of discrimination was brought to public attention in 1999. The Roma, a formerly nomadic people commonly known as 'gypsies', whose history is marked by exclusion and discrimination across Europe, charged that their children were grossly overrepresented in special schools for the disabled. While the court ruled that discrimination could not be proven, there was no dispute that 50 per cent of Romani students were in special schools as compared with 1.80 per cent of non-Roma students (European Roma Rights Center, 2005). Similar charges were made in Slovenia, where the government has set up a commission to investigate the overrepresentation of Roma children in classes for children with 'special needs' (Petricusic, 2004).

A review of information on discrimination in education against immigrant and non-migrant ethnic minorities in 15 member states of the European Union (Luciak, 2004) pointed to the socially constructed nature of the identity of minorities. Noting the difficulties of gaining accurate comparative data, Luciak cited differences in data collection, terminology and classification of ethnic groups, different types of ethnic groups, and different educational systems. For example within the European Union, nine of the 12 member states identify students by their national origin, so that children born in the country of immigrant parents 'disappear' from the statistics on minority groups. In the UK, by contrast, school records distinguish students on the basis of a mixture of skin color and nationality, such as White (with many subcategories based on national origin), mixed, Asian or Asian British, Black or Black British. Further, it is notable that the Roma are identified in Europe as an ethnic rather than a racial group but, in Britain, they are among the groups identified as 'White' (Luciak, 2004). Despite these differences in data collection, Luciak's study revealed that several member states evidenced an overrepresentation of migrant and ethnic minority groups in 'educational institutions with lower academic demands, an overrepresentation in special education, as well as disproportional early dropout and expulsion rates' (p. 2). As in the studies of indigenous groups cited earlier, these difficulties were evidenced more intensely by students from non-migrant ethnic groups, a pattern that Luciak linked to the distrust in the educational system engendered by 'a history of social exclusion, assimilationist tendencies, and a monocultural orientation in education' (p. 3)

In the US, the concern with race as the main marker of minority status has resulted in a categorization system that simultaneously reflects the nation's over-simplification of race, yet also its increasing racial heterogeneity and complexity. For example, the five official 'racial' categories represent a mixture of skin color and ethnic designations, namely, 'White', 'Hispanic (regardless of race)', 'Black (not of Hispanic origin)', 'Asian/ Pacific Islander', and 'American Indian/ Alaskan Native'. It is clear that Hispanic and Asian/Pacific Islander are broadly generalized categories that include a wide variety of racial, ethnic and linguistic features, while White, Black and American Indian/Alaskan Native presumably represent recognizably discrete racial, and possibly, ethnic groups. It seems the US classification system does not consider color an important dimension in identifying its 'Asian' and 'Hispanic' citizens, but does care to distinguish between citizens who are White, Black, or American Indian. This approach is not as nonsensical as it appears. Rather, it is a reflection of America's historical and continuing preoccupation with a presumed Black/White binary and with the history of exclusion and oppression of what Ogbu (1987) referred to as America's involuntary minorities – those of African origin who were brought to the North American continent through enslavement and the native peoples of the continent who were conquered by the European invasion.

As Ogbu (1987) argued, a history of oppression also includes peoples whose nations, through historical annexation or colonization, stand in a subservient relation to the dominant society. Thus, a look at the performance of Hispanics in the US, for example, shows those of Mexican and Puerto Rican origin to be less successful in schools than those who came to the US with a history relatively free of US domination.

Similarly, an intriguing example of this trend exists within the 'Asian/Pacific Islander' sub-group known as Native Hawaiians, who are known to be disproportionately represented in programs for MMR (US Department of Education, 1999). This is the only group of Americans of 'Asian' origin whose culture, language, and religion were outlawed by virtue of conquest by the US, and who therefore fit Ogbu's categorization as an 'involuntary' minority group. Whether or not one agrees with Ogbu's theory, the trends within sub-groups of minorities indicate that historical oppression in the US has left a legacy of structural discrimination that is hard to undo and that continues to have the most negative impact on those ethnic groups who experienced intense historical exclusion.

The concept of the social construction of categories, which was first explicated by Berger and Luckman (1966), is now a well-known framework for understanding how social decisions come to be reified through institutionalization. As with race and minority status, the high incidence disability categories, as defined in the US, are socially constructed categories that have little to do with disability and everything to do with the effects of the society's historical cultural agenda on the education system. I will begin with an overview of the extent of ethnic over-representation in the three categories of concern, LD, MMR, and ED. I will then discuss the implications of these patterns, placing the discussion in the context of historical educational structures in the United States.

RATES OF ETHNIC DISPROPORTIONALITY IN THE HIGH INCIDENCE CATEGORIES

The continuing pattern of ethnic disproportionality in the US has been so troubling that the Office for Civil Rights (OCR) has collected data on the high incidence categories since the early 1980s, and the Office of Special Education Programs (OSEP) has done so since 1997. In addition, two panels of the National Academy of Sciences (NAS) have studied the issue (Heller, Holtzman, & Messick, 1982; Donovan & Cross, 2002). In outlining the extent of the problem I will rely on data from the latter report, which offers a synthesis of current knowledge on the topic.

In studying the extent of ethnic disproportion in special education, scholars have determined two main ways of describing the data – a composition index and a risk index; an odds ratio can also be calculated, comparing the risk rates among groups (Donovan & Cross, 2002). The composition index examines ethnic composition in a program: that is, it compares the ethnic group's composition in the student population to their composition in the special education program. For example, the OCR data for 1998 revealed that African Americans constituted approximately 17 per cent of the school population but 33 per cent of the mentally retarded (MR) population, indicating that they were placed in MR programs at almost double their rate in the school population as a whole. The risk index examines the rate of placement within an ethnic group and compares it to the rate within other ethnic groups. For example, OCR data for 1998 indicated that 2.64 per cent of all African American students were placed in MR programs, as compared with 1.28 per cent of American Indian/Alaskan Natives, 1.18 per cent of Whites, 0.92 per cent of Hispanics, and 0.64 per cent of Asian/Pacific Islanders. While there are advantages and disadvantages to either perspective, the finding of relative disporportionality obtains with both methods. However, the risk ratio is more economical for purposes of reporting since it does not require noting percentages in both the program and the school population.

Since we know that the 'high incidence' and 'low incidence' categories have distinctly different profiles, it is not helpful to aggregate data across these categories. Differential patterns of disproportionate placement occur across the high incidence disability categories, over time, across geographical regions, and even across school districts. Looking first at the general pattern of disproportionality that currently exists, Figure 6.1 displays the risk indices for all ethnic groups in the categories of LD, MMR and ED as reported by Donovan and Cross (2002). In MMR, the predominant pattern of overrepresentation is for African American students, who are more than twice as likely as Whites to be so designated. In LD, American Indian/Alaskan Native students are at the greatest risk of placement, although the rates are high for all but Asians. In ED, African Americans are one and a half times as likely as Whites to be so identified. Overall, despite many regional variations on the pattern of overrepresentation, Donovan and Cross (2002) concluded that, 'both black and American Indian/Alaskan Native children are at heightened risk for identification as having mental retardation and emotional disturbance' (p. 82).

Figure 6.1 OSEP data by disability and ethnic group: risk index

(Source: adapted from Donovan & Cross, 2002, p. 57. Reprinted with permission from Minority Students in Special and Gifted Education ©(2002) by the National Academy of Sciences, courtesy of the National Academies Press, Washington, DC)

Mental Retardation	Risk Index
AI/AN	1.20%
A/PI	0.57%
Black	2.63%
Hispanic	0.98%
White	1.12%
Total	1.33%

Learning Disability	
AI/AN	7.30%
A/PI	2.25%
B	6.58%
H	6.81%
W	6.08%
Total	6.14%

Emotional Disturbance	
AI/AN	1.00%
A/PI	0.27%
B	1.56%
H	0.68%
W	0.98%
Total	1.10%

(AI/AN: American Indian/Alaskan Native; A/PI: Asian/Pacific Islander)

Beyond these general patterns there are many contradictory trends. First, we note the dramatic changes in these figures over time. According to Donovan and Cross (2002), between 1974 and 1998, the following trends obtained in the student population as a whole: a reduction in the use of MMR from 1.58 per cent to 1.37 per cent; an 'epidemic' (p. 47) increase in the use of LD, from 1.21 per cent to 6.02 per cent; and an increase in the use of ED, from just over 1 per cent to just over 5 per cent.

Second, when examined by geographical region, the issue of variable categorization intensifies. Zhang and Katsiyannis (2002), analyzing nation-wide data from the 22nd Annual Report to Congress on the Implementation of the Individuals with Disabilities Education Act (IDEA) and the National Center for Education Statistics (NCES), found extensive variability in LD, MMR, and ED placement rates among Hispanics and African American students according to five geographic regions of the nation. Specifically, rates of placement of Hispanics for all disabilities were significantly higher in the North East than in the other five regions, while rates for African Americans in all three categories varied widely by region. On the other hand, research by Artiles, Rueda, Salazar and Higareda (2002) arguing for a more discriminating examination of subgroups within the population of English Language Learners (ELL's), reported that secondary age ELLs in 11 urban school districts in California were twice as likely as English-proficient students to be placed in special education programs. Overall, Donovan & Cross (2002) indicated that, while nation-wide figures show African Americans and Hispanics to be not overrepresented in LD, the rates differ widely across states:

> The nationally aggregated data have been interpreted to suggest no overrepresentation of either black or Hispanic students in LD. But state-level data tell a more complex story. For black students, for example, the risk index ranges from 2.33 percent in Georgia to 12.19 percent in Delaware. For Hispanic students, the risk index ranges from 2.43 in Georgia to 8.93 in Delaware. Clearly there is overrepresentation for these two minorities in the LD category in some states. (p. 67)

The third dimension of variability is at the level of the school district. One line of work has examined the relationship between sociodemographic features of school districts and patterns of placement by each of the high incidence disability categories as well as by gender (Coutinho, Oswald, & Best, 2002; Coutinho, Oswald, Best, & Forness, 2002; Oswald, Coutinho, Best, & Nguyen, 2001). Focusing on two competing hypotheses – either that there is bias in the placement process, or that ethnic groups are differentially susceptible to disabilities – these researchers found such complexity in the data that they concluded that disproportionality is 'multiply determined' (Coutinho, Oswald, & Best, 2002, p. 55). For example, just taking the variable of the relative presence of White and non-White students in the school population, the researchers found exactly opposite effects for Black as compared with American Indian students. In the ED category, placement of Black students increased in the presence of *high White enrolment* while, conversely, ED placement of American Indian students increased in the presence of *high non-White enrolment*. Moreover, although these researchers' findings indicated that poverty increases the likelihood of special education placement, even poverty worked in opposite directions for Blacks as compared to Whites, with White students more likely to be labeled LD in higher income neighborhoods, and Black students more likely to be so placed in low income neighborhoods. With relation to the EMR category, the opposite was true – that Black students were more likely to be so labeled if they were in higher income neighborhoods with a higher proportion of White peers.

Eitle (2002) found similar, though even more complex patterns. Based on national survey data of 1,203 school districts, she examined the relationships between disproportionality and variables representing school district structural factors, local racial and political-economic structures, and school desegregation politics. Similar to Oswald et al. (2001), Eitle found increased Black overrepresentation in EMR programs in the presence of high White economic resources, but also in districts where there was court ordered school desegregation and in southern regions with a history of de jure segregation. Eitle interpreted these patterns of overrepresentation as 'alternative forms of segregation' (p. 599) and called for research that could delineate the social processes by which placement decisions are made.

Overall, the variability across categories, time, and place strongly contest the belief that the high incidence disability categories represent meaningful interpretations of children's difficulties in schooling. Rather, much evidence points to the enduring impact of America's social history on the educational sorting of its students.

THE SORTING AND CLASSIFYING PARADIGM: THE CONVERGENCE OF RACE AND DISABILITY

Race and ability are inextricably woven into the history of American public education. The society's project of racial exclusion was reinforced by the eugenics movement, in which presumed inherited deficits became inseparable from beliefs regarding the racial inferiority of non-White peoples. The nineteenth-century common school movement represented the society's main tool for accomplishing a cultural program of 'Americanization' or assimilation of immigrant Whites and the marginalization of both immigrant and native non-Whites. In contrast to mandatory schooling for White students, policies such as separate schooling for Native Americans and anti-literacy laws regarding slaves reflected the fact that 'White supremacy defined people of color as nonassimilable, ineradically different, and therefore not full citizens' (Tyack, 1993, p. 20).

Until the middle of the twentieth century, discrimination on the basis of ability and race represented two parallel streams of exclusion within the educational system. The Civil Rights movement of the 1950s–1960s, however, with its premise that separate cannot be equal, constituted the point on which these excluded streams would converge. The school desegregation ordered by the *Brown* (1954) decision represented the first official step towards the vision of education as a vehicle of equity. While the moral power of this decision remains unquestionable, it is also true that it resulted in at least two unintended consequences: first, racial desegregation, despite representing the beginnings of equal access to education, meant a loss of solidarity and a re-framing of identity for many African American children who had to struggle with the experience of being rejected and viewed as deficient in integrated schools (Ferri & Connor, 2005; Irvine & Irvine, 1983; Morris & Morris, 2000; Siddle-Walker, 1996). Second, the reluctance of many states to comply with the *Brown* ruling resulted in the use of classes for 'slow' or 'mildly retarded' students as a means of continuing the marginalization of African American and other traditionally devalued groups.

This covert form of racial segregation was officially recognized by the courts in the 1971 case of *Johnson v. San Francisco Unified School District* (Prasse & Reschly, 1986). Of several subsequent cases charging racial discrimination in IQ testing and tracking, the most famous, *Larry P. v. Riles* (1979) and *Marshall et al. v. Georgia* (1984), resulted in opposite judgments. The court in the *Larry P.* case concluded that IQ tests were culturally biased against African Americans while the courts in the *Marshall* case disagreed. Despite different outcomes of these cases, however, the continuing salience of race was underscored by the fact that in neither case did the school districts deny the existence of significant overrepresentation of African Americans in low tracks and programs for the mildly retarded. Even if, as Reschly, Kicklighter, and McKee (1988) suggested, the discrepant placements were a result of poverty rather than race per se, this in itself points to the enduring intertwining of racism, economic inequity, and educational outcomes. The issue of overrepresentation in MMR programs was also brought to the courts on behalf of Mexican American and Native American children, the focus of these cases being language of testing (*Diana v. State Board of Education*, 1970; *Guadalupe v. Tempe*, 1972). The consent decrees in these two cases had immediate and lasting repercussions on educational policy and practice in the form of the requirement that, wherever feasible, testing be done in the native language.

THE CATEGORICAL FRAMING OF DISABILITY UNDER THE EHA/IDEIA

This history of classification and exclusion by race and disability left an indelible mark on the special education system. Essentially, the provisions of the EHA superimposed one more layer of categorization upon a system already built on a sorting and classifying paradigm, into which racial and socioeconomic inequities were tightly interwoven. In the words of Skrtic (1991), special education represents 'the institutional practice that emerged in the 20th century to contain the failure of public education to realize its democratic ideals' (p. 46). The categorical framing of the high incidence categories of LD, MMR, and ED purported to construct them as distinctly different conditions, but this effort has been confounded by definitional dilemmas that reflect close ties to issues of race and socioeconomic status.

Mental retardation or learning disability?

The construct of MMR is defined as 'substantially sub-average' development over a range of developmental tasks, to be determined by a score of 70 or less on a standardized IQ test. Prior to 1969, the cut-off point was 85, underscoring the socially constructed nature of the definition. The construct of Specific Learning Disability (LD) purports to represent an entirely different population, and was proposed in the 1960s as a category that would encompass children who were having serious difficulties in acquiring academic and/or communication skills, but whose overall intelligence appeared to be within the normal range.

The LD construct, first defined by Kirk (1962), grew out of the early work of researchers such as Strauss and Werner (1942) whose discovery of certain deficits in reading, writing, and/or communication among war veterans with known brain injury led to speculation that the presence of such deficits in otherwise normally developing children might also indicate brain injury. Despite the leap in logic in making this inference, the field of special education quickly became enamored of the notion that normally developing children who demonstrated deficits in school learning had probably suffered 'minimal brain injury'. Although that original concept has since been discredited, research has continued in search of an organic cause for the symptoms of LD. In a series of studies, Shaywitz et al. (2003), using brain imaging technology during the performance of a reading task, noted differential patterns of brain activity between good readers and poor readers. Up to this time, however, these studies have not provided evidence of the direction of these effects, that is, of whether differential brain activity is a result or a cause of deficits in reading skills. Moreover, their finding that the brain activity of poor readers changed after intensive instruction in reading strongly suggests that the brain patterns are the result of reading and not the other way around.

The notion of an intrinsic cause remains a central tenet of both MMR and LD constructs. In the case of MMR, it was sufficient to require that developmental delays be manifested before the age of 18, with measures of deficit on tests of both intellectual and adaptive functioning. For LD, however, the tenet of intrinsic deficit resulted in a convoluted set of criteria for diagnosis, much of which revolved around the exclusion of competing explanations. Thus, the definition relied upon the logic of default, by which the clinician should determine that the child's difficulties were caused *neither* by other disabilities, such as mental retardation or sensory impairments, *nor* by social and environmental disadvantages such as poverty or family stress. Another central criterion was that there be evidence of a discrepancy between a child's intellectual potential as measured on an IQ test and his/her actual achievement. Thus, the element of *unexpected underachievement* was essential to a diagnosis of LD.

Keeping in mind the history of racist beliefs that were only just being challenged at

the time of the emergence of the LD construct, it is not hard to see how the foregoing definitions would come to work, in a paradoxical way, against ethnically diverse students, by making it less likely that low achievers within these groups would be assigned an LD label. First, LD was clearly a more desirable diagnosis than MMR, since it is less stigmatizing to be seen as having accidental damage to specific areas of the brain, than as having global deficits that affect one's total development. Sleeter (1986) argued that the differential social power of Whites was the driving force behind the pattern that quickly emerged in the years just preceding the EHA – a pattern of disproportionate incidence of White students in the LD category, as contrasted with the disproportionate incidence of non-White students in the MMR category. Updating this argument, Ferri (2004) noted that, as the placement of Black and Hispanic students in LD programs becomes more common, there is a concomitant and increasing focus on 'dyslexia and research aimed at identifying subgroups of students labeled as having LD' (p. 512). Ferri queried whether this development might 'serve the unanticipated function of resegregating the category of LD in ways that mirror earlier racial hierarchies' (p. 512).

In addition to the relationship between social desirability and social power, there was the fact that the LD definition itself would exclude many children whose environments could be construed to account for their learning difficulties – that is, children living in poverty, a disproportionate number of whom continued to be non-White. Further, as Collins and Camblin (1983) cogently argued, the cultural bias inherent in IQ tests meant that ethnically diverse students would be likely to earn scores that were too low to allow for the required discrepancy between IQ and achievement. In the absence of this discrepancy, minority children were more likely to be diagnosed as MMR than LD.

The result of these definitional and social discrepancies between the MMR and LD categories was that, from the time of the emergence of the LD category in the 1960s until close to the end of the century, the overrepresentation of African American students in special education occurred in the MMR category. Over the past decade, however, an increase in representation of Black students in the LD category has been noted. For example, research by Gottlieb, Alter, Gottlieb, and Wishner (1994) found that 1 in 6 students classified as LD in urban New York schools met criteria for MMR. MacMillan and Reschly (1998) and MacMillan, Gresham, and Bocian (1998) reported similar findings in California, and interpreted this trend as a reluctance on the part of school personnel to use the MMR category and to use the LD category to serve 'an undifferentiated and nonspecific group of children' (p. 324).

Coutinho, Oswald, and Best (2002), noting that increasing poverty was associated with higher rates of Black, Hispanic, and Asian male placement in LD programs, concluded that the clause excluding environmental effects was not being applied, and pointed out that this could be construed as a biased process that could result in disproportionately large minority placements in LD. These authors observed, however, that the converse to this argument could also be true – that if we believe that poverty and other environmental detriments do in fact contribute to LD, then to exclude them would mean excluding many minority students from services they need. Indeed, the conundrum of the LD category's desirability/undesirability was reflected in the case of *Crawford v. Honig* (1994), in which African American parents charged that their children were being excluded from needed LD services by virtue of the California courts ruling (*Larry P. v. Riles*, 1979), against the use of IQ tests for any purpose.

The debate around the IQ achievement discrepancy model has resulted in recent developments in research on LD, which propose an approach that seeks to rule out the possibility that poor achievement may simply be the result of poor instruction. Thus, identification of LD would be made only after intensive, tiered instruction has been implemented (for example, Vaughn & Fuchs, 2003). The strength of this 'response to instruction' (RTI) movement was marked by a symposium of researchers organized collaboratively by Vanderbilt University and the University of Kansas (National Research Center on Learning Disabilities, 2003) and was acknowledged by the 2004 reauthorized IDEA as one alternative to the IQ-discrepancy model.

Emotional Disturbance, the third high incidence category with which we are concerned, is equally problematic in terms of definition and equally susceptible to social influences and to co-morbidity with cognitive difficulties such as LD or MMR (Montague & Rinaldi, 2001). The federal regulations for ED require that a child consistently, and in different settings, exhibits mood and relationship difficulties that cannot be explained by other disabilities. While the more extreme end of the spectrum includes mental illnesses such as schizophrenia, at the milder end it is evident that professional judgments will vary according to personal tolerance of non-compliance as well as to the social and cultural norms of different groups. Several authors have pointed to the many ways in which culturally conditioned behaviors may be interpreted depending on the cultural lens with which they are viewed (Cartledge, Kea, & Simmons-Reed, 2002; Obiakor et al., 2002; Townsend, 2000). Further, an increasing body of literature notes the disproportionate use of punitive disciplinary practices against African American youth (Leone, Walter, & Wolford, 1990; Maag, 2001; Skiba, Michael, Nardo, & Peterson, 2000).

In sum, the ambiguities and contradictions outlined above, and the historical ties of the categorizing paradigm to racism and classism in the US, undermine the validity of the high incidence disability categories. The NAS report (Donovan & Cross, 2002) was clear in its assessment of these ambiguities:

> In terms of cognitive and behavioral competence, students fall along a continuum … there is no black and White distinction between those who have disabilities or gifts and those who do not. At the far ends of the continuum there is little dispute about

a child's need for something different ... But as one moves away from the extremes, where the line should be drawn between students who do and do not require special supports is unclear. A variety of forces push on the lines from opposing directions

We have argued that where along the continuum of achievement the lines are drawn for specialized education is artificial and variable. Perhaps of greater concern, however, are factors that affect where a student falls along the continuum. For students having difficulty in school who do not have a medically diagnosed disability, key aspects of the context of schooling itself, including administrative, curricular/instructional, and interpersonal factors, may contribute to their identification as having a disability and may contribute to the disproportionately high or low placements of minorities. (pp. 25–27)

Coming as it does from the most influential and comprehensive publication on the topic of overrepresentation, this statement reveals the essential fallacy of the notion of high incidence 'disabilities'. If it is impossible to say where low achievement ends and disability begins, why should the field continue to use the frame of disability for the provision of services to students in the 'high incidence' categories? In the absence of 'a medically diagnosed disability', is the term 'disability' in fact a misleading misnomer that inappropriately implicates the abilities of minority children and youth? It is evident that these categories are social constructions that fall far short of science.

DISPROPORTIONALITY AND SOCIETAL INEQUITY

Along with many others (Artiles, 2003; Hilliard, 1995; Patton, 1998; Skiba, Knesting & Bush, 2002), I contend that minorities' disproportionately large share of difficulties in schooling represents an extension of the societal inequities to which historically oppressed minorities continue to be disproportionately subjected. As Wilson (1998) emphasized, 'the impact of the structure of inequality' (p. 508) must be understood as the context in which inequitable outcomes occur for individual members of minority groups in all areas of

society. To name but a few from Wilson's list – education, residential patterns, labor market, financial markets, government policies and corporate decisions. Special education, as a discrete arm of the education system, cannot be the sole answer to this mountain of inequity, especially because it perpetuates the deficit view of minority children.

The uniqueness of special education: the criterion of intrinsic deficit

Arguing that ethnic disproportionality in special education represents inequity reflects a painful paradox: why should a program that provides costly and specialized services be construed as inequitable? In the words of MacMillan and Reschly (1998), '*Something weighs so heavily on the minds of critics that it more than offsets these apparently desirable features*' (p. 22). These authors concluded that disproportionality is seen as problematic because of minority stakeholders' suspicion that it is tied to beliefs about inferior genetic endowment, and because special education programs are not seen to be effective. These are, indeed, two powerful concerns. But there is yet another, which is the simple fact that special education is unique in the educational system in its focus on intrinsic deficit. This alone is enough to render it suspect, except in the case of clear-cut (low incidence) disabilities, where performance deficits are incontrovertible, and where, in fact, ethnic disproportionality in placement *has not* been noted. Thus, for example, while Head Start, Chapter I and other compensatory programs for the poor are perceived as additions to children's educational opportunities, special education's unique focus on deficit in the high incidence disabilities is marked by four concerns: placement usually means removal of the child from the general education program; it is often, though not always, imposed rather than freely chosen by parents; there is a requirement for testing to confirm a 'disability'; and there is a societal stigma attached to the concept of disability. Against the context of historical and continuing discrimination, why should minorities trust this process?

Inequity and risk in families and communities

The second NAS report, by Donovan and Cross (2002), in its search for causes of disproportionality, pointed to both home and school environments. In considering the former, the report focused on biological and environmental conditions typically occasioned by poverty, such as high lead content in urban homes, iron deficiency in the diets of infants, and poor access to health care. These were linked to problems such as developmental delay and hyperactivity. The social conditions identified implicated both socioeconomic status and ethnicity or cultural behaviors in matters such as drug or alcohol abuse, child rearing practices, and early educational activities such as introducing children to print or to basic numeracy.

These arguments gave rise to two concerns by critics. First, by not discussing the policy context that allows for such environmental inequities, the report gave the impression of a 'blaming the victim' argument by which minority groups' choices and behaviors were seen as the sources of their children's difficulties (Harry, Klingner, & Hart, 2005). As an example of the effects of policy contexts, the NAS itself, within the same year as its Donovan and Cross report (2002), published a separate report (NAS, 2002) presenting resounding evidence of active discrimination against minorities in health care. The second objection to the NAS's focus on environmental effects was that the report's analysis did not succeed in linking the detrimental practices and influences to actual special education placement rates (Losen & Orfield, 2002).

The notion of lasting effects of detrimental family and community environments has both an intuitive and research based appeal. For example, the work of Sameroff, Seifer, Baldwin, and Baldwin (1993) analyzed the effects of poverty in terms of a group of risk factors, which, when combined, can have devastating effects on children's mental and physical health. These researchers argued that, since the IQ scores of children in poverty were found to remain stable when tested at early childhood and again in early puberty, this indicates the lasting power of early negative influences. In a similar argument, Blair and Scott (2000) concluded that neonatal factors such as low birth weight and mother's education accounted for low IQ scores in adolescence. There is, however, an important missing piece in these powerful correlational studies: namely, the effects of schooling in the years that intervened between the early measures and IQ testing at puberty.

Inequity and risk in schooling

In the case of the foregoing studies, which point to the lasting effects of pre-natal and neo-natal factors, the lack of attention to the mediating power of 'school risk' (Keogh, 2000) is a serious omission. The reason schooling itself cannot be excluded from a list of risk factors in a study based on IQ scores is that IQ scores represent knowledge and skills that children have had the opportunity to learn both in their homes and schools. A look at the popular Weschler Intelligence Scale for Children (WISC) (Weschler, 1974) test, for example, makes it clear that much of the verbal content represents information that can be learned at the dinner table, from the media and/or in the classroom. The NAS report described these tests as 'measures of what individuals have learned ... reflecting broad, culturally rooted ways of thinking and problem solving' (p. 284). Thus, while a 4-year-old child's home may not have prepared him/her well for the kinds of information valued on IQ tests, it would be reasonable to expect that six or seven years of effective schooling could make a difference to the same child's scores at age 14. When children's scores remain stable on a test that places high value on school learning, it should not be assumed that innate limitations account for this pattern. It is possible that the child has not received adequate schooling. As

Skiba et al. (2002) have argued, the reliability of standardized test scores may be an accurate summary of 'the tragic history of limited cultural and educational opportunity that led to those depressed capacities' (p. 70).

Numerous studies of the quality of curriculum, instruction, and human as well as material resources in schools verify that children living in poverty and many English language learners receive distinctly inferior schooling (Anyon, 1997; Darling-Hammond & Post, 2000; Kozol, 2005). Funding patterns account for the most important variables in the quality of education: teacher quality, class size, physical surroundings, and material resources. Funding structures that rely on property taxes obviously place students living in poverty at risk of inferior schooling. Moreover, Harry and Klingner's (2006) ethnographic study of 12 urban schools noted that decisions regarding hiring, assignment of principals, assignment of teachers to classes, and funding for paraprofessionals worked in favor of students from higher income backgrounds.

Inequity and risk in the special education placement process

Beyond the provision of inferior opportunities to learn, the process that leads to special education placement is often another contributor to the overrepresentation of minorities in special education. The first NAS panel on disproportionality (Heller et al., 1982) argued that disproportionality should be considered problematic if either the precursors to, or the outcomes of, placement are biased or inadequate. This perspective includes poor quality of instruction prior to referral, bias in the referral process, inappropriate or biased assessment, and ineffective instruction in the special education program. The discussion in the previous section focused on the provision of poor schooling prior to referral. In this section I reflect on the subsequent steps that lead to special education placement.

Efforts to determine bias in the placement process have focused on the process and outcomes of referrals. It is well established that the vast majority of students who are referred for special education evaluation will be tested and the vast majority of those tested will be placed (Gerber & Semmel, 1984; Ysseldyke & Algozzine, 1983). According to Donovan and Cross's (2002), review of this topic, referred children, regardless of ethnicity, typically do exhibit severe academic and behavioral deficiencies for their age. The literature is not clear, however, on whether these children differ significantly from many of their peers who are not referred. Harry and Klingner's (2006) ethnographic investigation of referral processes found wide variability across 12 schools in the same school district, and concluded that although referrals for academic reasons were based on more objective criteria than were referrals for behavioral issues, even academic referrals were seriously influenced by local norms and by concerns about state-wide testing. Similarly, Mehan, Hartwick and Meihls (1986) found that referral and placement decisions were more driven by organizational concerns than by children's needs.

Another thorn in the side of the special education process has been the long standing debate about potential bias in testing. While it is beyond the scope of this review to detail this debate, the highlights must be mentioned. I have already alluded to the contradictory findings of the courts on this issue (see Reschly et al., 1988). Scholars, also, have come to differing conclusions about the possibility of bias (for a comprehensive summary of these studies see Harry, 1994). According to Travers (1982) key interpretations of this issue have turned on a contrast between technical and holistic interpretations of bias, the former focusing on bias in specific test items, as contrasted with the latter, which examine the possibility of an overall depressive effect on a group's scores as a result of cultural dissonance both in the process and content of testing.

Skiba et al. (2002) place the issue in the larger context of societal inequity, which is also the central argument of this chapter. These researchers contend that the historical and continuing inequities that place minorities at a disadvantage in schools must be considered an essential part of the equation. They state: 'Neglecting the contribution of educational opportunity when interpreting minority test scores may in fact introduce statistical error, regardless of whether a specific test can be shown to be "unbiased" ... Failure to take into account issues of limited educational opportunity for disadvantaged students thus increases measurement error' (p. 71).

In Harry and Klingner's (2006) qualitative study, although school personnel believed that the psychological evaluation provides a scientific gateway to special education placement, the researchers' observation of assessments, examination of documents, and interviews with psychologists, contradicted this belief. These data identified six sources of influence on the assessment: the influence of teachers' informal diagnoses of children's problems; school personnel's negative perceptions of children's families; external pressures for placement, such as the desire to remove low achievers from state-wide testing; the exclusion of information on classroom ecology; variable choice and implementation of assessment instruments; and psychologists' varying philosophical orientations. The researchers concluded that the power of 'unofficial practices and influences' undermined the belief that the assessment is either scientific or objective.

Overall, regardless of proofs of the technical adequacy of IQ tests, the logic of the holistic argument is easy to see. In Hilliard's (1995) words: 'Item content is simply a matter of the arbitrary choices of an in-group of item writers. Certainly the Afro Americans are poorly represented, if at all. To many Afro-Americans the "norm" is abnormal' (p. 197).

Inequity and risk in special education programs

As many have observed (for example, Heller et al., 1982; MacMillan & Reschly, 1998), the problematic nature of ethnic disproportionality in special education cannot be discussed without asking whether its outcomes are positive and equitable. This means not only whether special education overall has proven efficacious, but also whether minorities' treatment and outcomes are equal to those of their White peers. Key dimensions of concern are, the law's requirement that children be placed in the Least Restrictive Environment (LRE), relative drop-out rates, relative rates of return to the general education program, and overall program quality.

Restrictive programming appears to be the most detrimental effect of the high rates of overrepresentation of Black students in MMR and ED programs (Fierros & Conroy, 2002). While the case of *Corey H.* v. *Chicago* (1992) resulted in stringent requirements that the school district and the state of Illinois correct its pervasive use of restrictive placements for students with MMR (Soltman & Moore, 2002), the disproportionate segregation of minorities through restrictive programs continues to be evidenced across the country. The Twenty Second Annual Report to Congress (US Department of Education, 2000) indicated that, in 1999–2000, while 47.3 per cent of all students with disabilities were served outside of the regular classroom for less than 21 per cent of the day, when this is disaggregated by ethnicity, only 35.3 per cent of Black students met this criterion as compared with 52.9 per cent of Whites. Moreover, 31 per cent of Blacks spent more than 60 per cent of the day outside of the regular class as compared with only 15.3 per cent of Whites.

Parrish (2002) reported that disaggregated data on specific placements by ethnicity are not readily available in most school districts. However, in examining California data, Parrish found glaring disparities on several dimensions related both to the cost and the quality of services. For example, of all the children served in the ED category in California, Hispanic students represented 47 per cent of those placed under the jurisdiction of the California Youth Authority, compared to 15 per cent of White children. The situation was reversed in costly private special education residential schools, where Hispanics represented only 15 per cent of the students, as compared with 58 per cent of Whites. This meant that Hispanic students were roughly three times more likely to experience what Parrish described as the 'more punishing than remedial' (p. 27) services of the California Youth Authority than were their White peers. The California data also showed that Black students were more likely to be placed in the most restrictive settings than were Whites, who generally were only so placed when their need for intensive services was high.

With regard to the comparability of program quality by ethnicity of students, Donovan and Cross (2002) found no statistical evidence, but reported that studies of low parental empowerment and poor instructional quality in general education in schools serving the poor suggest that the situation would not be expected to be very different for special education. This was borne out by Harry and Klingner's (2006) ethnographic study of 12 urban schools, which found that special education class sizes for students with LD and/or mixed high incidence disabilities ranged from 6 to 24, the lowest numbers being noted in the schools serving the highest income populations. This study also noted that curriculum and instruction in most of the ED programs studied displayed a narrow focus on behavior management rather than academic learning and that punitive strategies were particularly common in these classrooms.

With regard to post-special education placement outcomes, accurate rates of exit from special education are difficult to find. OSEP data on exit are framed in terms of just about all means of exit except return to general education (US Department of Education, 2000). Graduation and drop-out rates for students in special education are further cause for lack of confidence in the efficacy of special education. The Twenty Second Annual Report to Congress (US Department of Education, 2000) indicated that almost a third of students with LD and ED failed to graduate from high school. Post-school outcomes are equally unsatisfactory: as reported by the National Longitudinal Transition Study of Students in Special Education (SRI International, 1995),

only 73 per cent of students with LD were engaged in employment or post-secondary education or training, and only 50 per cent of students with ED were employed.

CONCLUSION: SPECIAL EDUCATION AS A POINT ON THE CONTINUUM OF INSTRUCTION

In conclusion, there is no question that the disproportionate placement of minorities in special education reflects deep societal inequities embedded in the educational system. These inequities need to be addressed in all the society's systems. Clearly, recommendations regarding these systems are beyond the scope of this reviewer and this text. Thus, while calling for increased collaboration among researchers in these various fields, I conclude this limited discussion with suggestions for the field of education.

Notwithstanding the historical importance of the disabilities movement and its culmination in the 1975 EHA, the direction of special education is now in need of revision. What were once two parallel streams – exclusion by race and by disability – have converged in the special education system. Further, special education's categorical framing of the high incidence disabilities has resulted in decision-making that can be described, at best, as arbitrary, at worst, as discriminatory. The resulting placement patterns are so variable and contradictory as to defy accurate analysis and to produce outcomes that are seriously questionable. Overall, the ambiguities of the high incidence categories indicate that it is not worth while to continue using the construct of disability to provide services to children at the low end of the achievement spectrum. Rather, special education needs to be reconceptualized as a point on the continuum of instruction, rather than requiring a redefinition of struggling learners as 'disabled' and an arbitrary placement into categories of deficit.

To reconceptualize special education will require a restructuring of the funding, hiring, and resource provisions that perpetuate inferior general education schooling for minorities. As recommended by a comprehensive report by Rouse, Brookes-Gunn, and McLanahan (2005), universal preschool opportunities should be a sine qua non in this wealthiest of nations. Incentives for teachers in the form of additional stipends, decreased class size, administrative and material supports, and ongoing professional development are essentials if the neediest children are to receive equitable schooling. Referral for special services should be reconceptualized to mean referral for specialized assistance, not for removal from the mainstream of general education. Assessment of children's learning and behavioral difficulties should be educational assessment, whose purpose is to determine instructional practices that will assist the struggling student. Instructional support should be offered by specialists trained in remediation, with no need for categorical labeling or placement.

Central to this entire argument is the need for the field to recognize that the obsession with categorization further entrenches the hegemony of a norm based on the achievement levels of the mainstream of the society. Those levels are the result of home, community, and school preparation, not of intrinsic capability. Thus, the criterion for special education services should be, simply, a specified level of achievement, rather than ambiguous 'proof' of some innate deficit.

REFERENCES

Anyon, J. (1997). *Ghetto schooling: A political economy of urban educational reform.* New York: Teachers College Press.

Artiles, A. J. (2003). Special education's changing identity: Paradoxes and dilemmas in views of culture and space. *Harvard Educational Review, 73,* 164–202.

Artiles, A. J., Rueda, R., Salazar, J., & Higareda, I. (2002). English-language learner representation in special education in California urban school districts. In D. J. Losen & G. Orfield (Eds.), *Racial inequity in special education* (pp. 117–136). Cambridge, MA: Harvard Education Press.

Barrington, J. M. (1991). The New Zealand experience: Maoris. In M. A. Gibson, & J. U. Ogbu (Eds.), *Minority status and schooling: A comparative study of immigrant and involuntary minorities* (pp. 309–326). New York: Garland Publishing.

Berger, P., & Luckman, T. (1966). *The social construction of reality: A treatise in the sociology of knowledge.* Garden City, NJ: Doubleday.

Blair, C., & Scott, K. G. (2000). Proportion of LD placements associated with low socioeconomic status: Evidence for a gradient? *The Journal of Special Education, 36,* 14–22.

Brown v. Board of Education. (1954). 349 US 294, at 300.

Cartledge, G., Kea, C., & Simmons-Reed, E. (2002). Serving culturally diverse children with Serious Emotional Disturbance and their families. *Journal of Child and Family Studies, 11*(1), 113–127.

Collins, R., & Camblin, L. D. (1983). The politics and science of learning disability classification: Implications for Black children. *Contemporary Education, 54*(2), 113–118.

Corey H. et al. v. Board of Education of the City of Chicago et al., and the Illinois Stated Board of Education et al. (1992). No. 92 C 3409 (N.D. Ill. 1992).

Coutinho, M. J., Oswald, D. P., & Best, A. M. (2002). The influence of sociodemographics and gender on the disproportionate identification of minority students as having learning disabilities. *Remedial and Special Education, 23*(1), 49–60.

Coutinho, M. J., Oswald, D. P., Best, A. M., & Forness, S. R. (2002). Gender and sociodemographic factors and the disproportionate identification of minority students as emotionally disturbed. *Behavior Disorders, 27,* 109–125.

Crawford v. Honig. (1994). 37 F.3d 485 (9th Circuit. 1994).

Darling-Hammond, L., & Post, L. (2000). Inequality in teaching and schooling: supporting high quality teaching and leadership in low income schools. In R. D. Kahlenberg (Ed.), *A notion at risk: Preserving public education as an engine for social mobility* (pp. 127–168). New York: The Century Foundation Press.

De Vos, G., & H. Wagatsuma (Eds.). (1966). *Japan's invisible race.* Berkeley, CA: University of California Press.

Diana v. State Board of Education. (1970). Civil Action No. C-70–37 RFP US District Court, Northern District of California, Consent Decree.

Donovan, S., & Cross, C. (2002). *Minority students in special and gifted education.* Washington, DC: National Academy Press.

Eitle, T.M. (2002). Special education or racial segregation: Understanding variation in the representation of Black students in Educable Mentally Handicapped programs. *Sociological Quarterly, 43*(4), 575–605.

Enguita, M. F. (1999). *Alumnos gitanos en la escuela paya: Un estudio sobre las relaciones etnicas en el sistema educativo.* Barcelona: Ariel.

Escandell, J. R. V. (2002). *Inmigracion y escuela: La escolarizacion en Espana de los hijos de los inmigrantes Africanos.* Alicante: Universidad de Alicante.

European Roma Rights Center. (2005). *The ERRC legal strategy to challenge racial segregation and discrimination in Czech schools.* Retrieved April 3, 2005 from http://www.tolerance.cz/english/sem2000/ecmi07.htm

Ferri, B. A. (2004). Interrupting the discourse: A response to Reid and Valle. *Journal of Learning Disabilities, 37*(6), 509–515.

Ferri, B. A., & Connor, D. J. (2005). In the shadow of Brown: Special education and overrepresentation of students of color. *Remedial and Special Education, 26*(2), 93–100.

Fierros, E.G., & Conroy, J.W. (2002). Double jeopardy: An exploration of restrictiveness and race in special education. In D. J. Losen & G. Orfield (Eds.), *Racial inequity in special education* (pp. 39–70). Cambridge, MA: Harvard Education Press.

Gerber, M., & Semmel, M. (1984). Teacher as imperfect test: Reconceptualizing the referral process. *Educational Psychologist, 19*, 137–148.

Gibson, M. A., & Ogbu, J. U. (1991). *Minority status and schooling: A comparative study of immigrant and involuntary minorities.* New York: Garland Publishing.

Gillborn, D., & Youdell, D. (2000). *Rationing education: Policy, practice, reform and equity.* Buckingham: Open University Press.

Gottleib, J., Alter, M., Gottlieb, B. W., Wishner, J. (1994). Special education in urban America: It's not justifiable for many. *The Journal of Special Education, 27*(4), 453–465.

Guadalupe Organization *v.* Tempe Elementary School District No. 3. (1972). No. 71–435 (D. AZ, Consent decree).

Harry, B. (1994). *The overrepresentation of minority students in special education: Theories and recommendations.* Paper commissioned by the National Association of State Directors of Special Education, Alexandria, VA.

Harry, B., & Klingner, J. (2006). *Why are so many minority students in special education? Understanding race and disability in schools.* New York: Teachers College Press.

Harry, B., Klingner, J., & Hart, J. (2005). African American families under fire: Ethnographic views of family strengths. *Remedial and Special Education, 26*(2), 101–112.

Heller, K.A., Holtzman, W.H., & Messick, S. (1982). *Placing children in special education: A strategy for equity.* Washington, DC: National Academy Press.

Hilliard, A. G. (1995). Either a paradigm shift or not mental measurement. *Psych Discourse, 26*(10), 6–20.

Irvine, R. W., & Irvine, J. J. (1983). The impact of the desegregation process on the education of Black students. *Journal of Negro Education, 52*(4), 410–422.

Jordan, D. F. (1988). Rights and claims of indigenous people: Education and the reclaiming of identity. The case of the Canadian Natives, the Sami and Australian Aborigenes. In T. Skutnabb-Kangas & J. Cummins (Eds.), *Minority education: From shame to struggle* (pp. 251–276). Clevedon, UK: Multilingual Matters.

Keogh, B. K. (2000). Risk, families, and schools. *Focus on Exceptional Children, 33*(4), 1–10.

Kirk, S. (1962). *Educating exceptional children.* Boston, MA: Houghton Mifflin.

Kozol, J. (2005). *The shame of the nation: The restoration of apartheid schooling in America.* New York: Crown.

Larry P. v. *Riles.* (1979). C -71-2270, RFP. Dis. Ct.

Leone, P. E., Walter, M. B., & Wolford, B. I. (1990). Toward integrated responses to troubling behavior. In P. E. Leone (Ed.), *Understanding troubled and troubling youth* (pp. 290–298). Thousand Oaks, CA: Sage.

Losen, D., & Orfield, G. (2002). Introduction. In D. Losen & G. Orfield (Eds.), *Racial inequity in special education* (pp. xiii–xxxvii). Cambridge, MA: Harvard University Press.

Luciak, M. (2004, August). *The educational situation of migrants and ethnic minorities in 15 EU member states in comparative perspective.* University of Vienna, Austria. Retrieved April 3, 2005 from *http://www.inst.at/trans/15Nr/08_1/luciak15.htm* .

Maag, J. W. (2001). Rewarded by punishment: Reflections on the disuse of positive reinforcement in education. *Exceptional Children, 67*(2), 173–186.

MacMillan, D. L., & Reschly, D. J. (1998). Overrepresentation of minority students: The case for greater specificity or reconsideration of the variables examined. *The Journal of Special Education, 32*(1), 15–24.

MacMillan, D. L., Gresham, F. M., & Bocian, K. M. (1998). Discrepancy between definitions of learning disabilities and school practices: An empirical investigation. *Journal of Learning Disabilities, 31*, 314–326.

Marshall et al. v. Georgia. (1984). US District Court for the Southern District of Georgia, CV482–233.

Mehan, H., Hartwick, A., & Meihls, J.L. (1986). *Handicapping the handicapped: Decision making in students' educational careers.* Stanford, CA: Stanford University Press.

Montague, M., & Rinaldi, C. (2001). Classroom dynamics and children at risk: A follow up. *Learning Disabilities Quarterly, 24*, 73–84.

Morris, V. G., & Morris, C. L. (2000). *Creating caring and nurturing educational environments for African American children.* Westport, CT: Bergin & Garvey.

National Academy of Sciences (NAS) (2002). *Unequal treatment: Confronting racial and ethnic disparities in health care.* Washington, DC: National Academy of Sciences.

National Research Center on Learning Disabilities. (2003, December). Responsiveness to Intervention Symposium, Kansas City, MO.

Obiakor, F., Algozzine, B., Thurlow, M., Gwalla-Ogisi, N., Enwefa, S., Enwefa, R., & McIntosh, A. (2002). *Addressing the issue of disproportionate representation: Identification and assessment of culturally diverse students with emotional or behavioral disorders* (ERIC Document No. Emotional Disturbance 458779). Arlington, VA: Council for Exceptional Children.

Office of Standards for Education. (2002, June). *Ofsted News.* Unacceptably wide variation in standards achieved in post-16 education and training in Leeds. NR 2002–117. Retrieved April 17, 2005 from http://www.ofsted.gov.uk/news/index.cfm?fuseaction=news.details&id=1304

Ogbu, J. U. (1987). Variability in minority school performance: A problem in search of an explanation. *Anthropology and Education Quarterly, 18,* 312–334.

Oswald, D. P., Coutinho, M. J., Best, A., & Nguyen, N. (2001). The impact of sociodemographic characteristics on the identification rates of minority students as mentally retarded. *Mental Retardation, 39,* 351–367.

Parrish, T. (2002). Racial disparities in the identification, funding, and provision of special education. In D. Losen & G. Orfield, (Eds.), *Racial inequity in special education* (pp. 15–38). Cambridge, MA: Harvard Education Press.

Patton, J.M. (1998). The disproportionate representation of African Americans in special education: Looking behind the curtain for understanding and solutions. *The Journal of Special Education, 32,* 25–31.

Petricusic, A. (2004, Autumn). *NOVES SL.* Slovenian legislative system for minority protection: different rights for old and new minorities. Retrieved April 17, 2005 from http://www6.gencat.net/llengcat/noves/hm04tardor/petricusic2–2.htm

Prasse, D. P., & Reschly, D.J. (1986). Larry P.: A case of segregation, testing, or program efficacy? *Exceptional Children, 52,* 333–346.

Reschly, D.J., Kicklighter, R.H., & McKee, P. (1988). Recent placement litigation, Part III: Analysis of differences in Larry P., Marshall, and S-1 and implications for future practices. *School Psychology Review, 17,* 37–48.

Rouse, C., Brooks-Gunn, J., & McLanahan, S. (2005). School readiness: Closing racial and ethnic gaps. Introducing the issue. *The Future of Children, 15*(1), 5–14. Princeton, NJ: Princeton University, Brookings Institution.

Sameroff, A. J., Seifer, R., Baldwin, A., & Baldwin, C. (1993). Stability of intelligence from preschool to adolescence: The influence of social and family risk factors. *Child Development, 64,* 80–97.

Shaywitz, B. A., Shaywitz, S. E., Pugh, K. R., Mencl, W. E., Fulbright, R. K., Skudlarski, P., et al. (2003). Disruption of posterior brain systems for reading in children with developmental dyslexia. *Biological Psychiatry, 52*(2), 101–110.

Siddle-Walker, V. (1996). *Their highest potential: An African American school community in the segregated South.* Chapel Hill, NC: University of North Carolina Press.

Skiba, R. J., Knesting, K., and Bush, L. D. (2002). Culturally competent assessment: More than nonbiased tests. *Journal of Child and Family Studies, 11*(1), 61–78.

Skiba, R. J., Michael, R. S., Nardo, A. C., & Peterson, R. (2000). The color of discipline: Sources of racial and gender disproportionality in school punishment. *The Urban Review, 34*(4), 317–342.

Skrtic, T. M. (1991). The special education paradox: Equity as the way to excellence. *Harvard Educational Review, 61*(2), 148–206.

Skutnabb-Kangas, T., & Cummins, J. (Eds.). (1988). *Minority education: From shame to struggle.* Clevedon, UK: Multilingual Matters.

Sleeter, C. (1986). Learning disabilities: The social construction of a special education category. *Exceptional Children, 53,* 46–54.

Soltman, S.W., & Moore, D.R. (2002). Ending segregation of Chicago's students with disabilities: Implications of the Corey H. lawsuit. In D. Losen & G. Orfield, (Eds.), *Racial inequity in special education* (pp. 239–272). Cambridge, MA: Harvard Education Press.

SRI International. (1995). *National Longitudinal Transition Study of Students in Special Education.* Menlo Park, CA: SRI.

Strauss, A., & Werner, H. (1942). Disorders of conceptual thinking in the brain injured child. *Journal of Nervous and Mental Disease, 96,* 153–172.

Townsend, B. L. (2000). The disproportionate discipline of African American learners: Reducing school suspensions and expulsions. *Exceptional Children, 66*(3), 381–391.

Travers, J. R. (1982). Testing in educational placement: Issues and evidence. In K. A. Heller, W. H. Holtzman, & S. Messick (Eds.), *Placing children in special education: A strategy for equity* (pp. 230–261). Washington, DC: National Academy Press.

Tyack, D. B. (1993). Constructing difference: Historical reflections on schooling and diversity. *Teachers College Record, 95*(1), 8–34.

US Department of Education. (1999). 1997 Elementary and secondary school civil rights compliance report: National and state projections. Washington, DC: DBS Corporation, Office for Civil Rights.

US Department of Education. (2000). Twenty Second Annual Report to Congress on the Implementation of the Individuals with Disabilities Education Act. Washington, DC.

Vaughn, S., & Fuchs, L. (2003). Redefining learning disabilities as inadequate response to instruction: The promise and potential problems. *Learning disabilities: research & practice*, *18*, 137–146.

Weschler, D. (1974). *Weschler Intelligence Scale for Children – Revised Manual*. New York: Psychological Corp.

Wilson, W.J. (1998). The role of the environment in the Black-White test score gap. In C. Jencks & M. Phillips (Eds.), *The Black-White test score gap* (pp. 501–510). Washington, DC: Brookings Institution Press.

Ysseldyke, J. E., & Algozzine, B. (1983). LD or not LD: That's not the question! *Journal of Learning Disabilities*, *16*, 29–31.

Zhang, D., & Katsiyannis, A. (2002). Minority representation in special education. *Remedial and Special Education*, *23*(3), 180–187.

7

Changing perspectives of special education in the evolving context of educational reform

Martyn Rouse and Margaret J. McLaughlin

INTRODUCTION

In many post-industrial societies there is a growing interest of central government in defining and shaping educational reform. In both the United Kingdom (UK) and the United States (US), this interest arose from concerns by politicians and the media about poor results on international comparisons of achievement and the implications of these poor results for long-term economic competitiveness. There were also concerns about the causes and consequences of the persistent under-achievement of particular groups of students, notably those living in poverty and those from certain minority ethnic groups. In the UK these concerns first found expression in the so-called 'great debate' beginning in the late 1970s, and in the US the 'educational call-to-arms' that occurred during the 1980s with publication of *A Nation at Risk* (National Commission on Excellence in Education, 1983).

Current reforms are designed to address these long-standing frustrations about the poor performance of some schools and the perceived lack of accountability in education. The reforms are grounded in the belief that schools serve particular functions in society as producers of strong human capital, including an educated workforce capable of competing internationally in a knowledge-based economy. As such, schools are expected to raise educational expectations and increase the performance of every student (McLaughlin & Shepard, 1995). Policymakers in the UK and the US have embarked on a reform agenda characterized by increasingly standardized curricula and greater accountability that are intended to close the achievement gap between high-performing, often white middle-class students, and students from low-income working class and ethnic minority groups. The central elements of this reform agenda, referred to as 'standards-driven reform' are common curriculum content, high achievement standards, a system of assessment that is aligned with or measures progress against content standards and systems of accountability for the performance of all students. There was little mention of students with disabilities and special educational needs in the first wave of educational reforms in the 1980s and 1990s when these reforms were first initiated, but more recently, both the UK and the US have introduced reforms designed to include such students and to raise standards for all children.

Although the motivating forces behind the educational reforms under way in the UK and US are similar, the ways in which they have been enacted differ. For the purpose of education policy in the UK, England and Wales share a broadly similar framework, while Scotland and Northern Ireland have their own systems. For the remainder of this chapter only the English reforms will be discussed. The US with its federalist system of government has both federal educational reform laws and individual state reform regulations which together create the context for what happens in schools. However, in both England and the US, the reforms have major implications for special education.

While the evolution of reform in England and the US differs in time and circumstance, the central tensions and implications for the provision of special education in publicly funded schools are similar. As a consequence, the long struggle to provide public education to students with disabilities is undergoing a transformation in England and the US from a largely separate and highly specialized endeavour into a more inclusive educational system based on policies that endorse universal access to common standards, and transparent accountability.

This chapter considers the impact of standards-driven educational reform policies on the provision of education to students with disabilities and special educational needs (SEN) in the US and in England. It will consider whether universal content standards and achievement expectations are appropriate for all students. It will also explore the challenges inherent in having one assessment and accountability system for all students.

Current reforms in England

In England, the education of students with special educational needs has been influenced by two parallel but in many ways opposing sets of reform. On one hand there has been a push towards greater inclusion starting with the Warnock Report (DES, 1978) and the associated 1981 Education Act. The latter legislation stressed the non-categorical nature of disability and embraced an ecological or interactive view of special educational need (SEN). However, attempts to leave behind categories of handicap were not without problems because many forms of provision, especially special schools, were themselves categorical. Nevertheless, in 1993 new legislation introduced guidelines for mainstream schools in the form of the *Code of Practice on the Identification and Assessment of Special Educational Needs* (DfE, 1994) suggesting that every school should have a special educational needs co-ordinator (SENCO). After the election of the Labour government in 1997 new policies of social inclusion were introduced. The Special Educational Needs and Disability Act 2001 (SENDA) strengthened the right to a mainstream school placement for students with disabilities and SEN. These and other developments such as the Department for Education and Skills (DfES, 2001a) statutory guidance *Inclusive Schooling: Children with SEN*, the revised *Special Educational Needs Code of Practice* (DfES, 2001b)*,* and the requirements of the National Curriculum (QCA, 1999) all provide a firm legislative context for developing inclusive education nationally. In addition, the Office for Standards in Education (Ofsted, 2003) now inspects and judges schools on the extent to which they are inclusive of pupils with SEN. More recently, the government's strategy for special educational needs, *Removing Barriers to Achievement* (DfES, 2004b) reaffirms a commitment to inclusive education as a model for meeting special needs.

The government has also introduced a major new initiative *Every Child Matters* (DfES, 2003), an ambitious approach for improving the well-being of children and young people from birth to age 19. Its aim is for every child, whatever their circumstances, to have the support they need to be healthy, stay safe, enjoy and achieve, make a positive contribution and achieve economic well-being. The initiative entails greater coordination of human services, such as education, health, social care and youth justice that involves sharing information and working together in new ways to protect children and young people from harm and help them achieve what they want in life (DfES, 2003). As can be seen, since 1997 there has been a range of socially progressive legislation designed to promote a more inclusive educational system and to reduce social exclusion among students with SEN.

However, much of the existing educational reform legislation in England has a very different policy intent. The key principles underlying the first round of educational reforms in England and Wales, the Education Reform Act 1988, included privatization, increased accountability, greater scrutiny, more choice for parents and competition between schools. As a result, many decision-making powers were delegated from local authorities to schools as part of the process of decentralization while other important decisions were shifted from local education authorities to central government. The Education Reform Act introduced a national curriculum, which specified content, together with national assessment, which specified achievement standards, and a series of other changes designed to bring the rigour of the market place to bear on schools. Today in England there is a prescribed national curriculum, the publication of results from national assessments, target setting at the individual and institutional (school and local authority) level based on the notion of continuous improvement, and very clear expectations about how schools will teach literacy and numeracy. Together, these changes are intended to raise standards and improve national competitiveness.

National framework for assessment

At the heart of the reforms is a national framework for assessment which involves testing at ages 7, 11, 14 and 16 that is designed to ensure that all publicly funded schools comply with the national curriculum.

The National Curriculum is constructed as a series of eight progressive levels of achievement (level one to level eight) to cover the age range 5–16. For example at the end of primary school, at age 11, children are expected to have reached at least level 4 and the percentage of students who achieve the expected levels are incorporated into school and local authority targets. However, the steps from one achievement level to the next represent more than one year's progress for many children and are too big for other students to demonstrate their learning. In addition, the starting point of the National Curriculum and its associated system of assessment is too high for many who have SEN. Although the National Curriculum was intended as an 'entitlement curriculum' for all, it was in reality not attainable for some children. In response to these difficulties, the Qualifications and Curriculum Authority (QCA, 2001) issued guidance to help overcome such problems, specifically for students with profound and multiple learning difficulties who are operating below general expectations for children of their age.

The concept of a national assessment was one of the most controversial aspects of the Education Reform Act (1988). The government at the time saw the accountability function of assessment as the means by which it could raise standards in schools and control the curriculum. Not surprisingly, given that the intent was to raise standards, the involvement of students who experience the difficulties in learning was not considered when the original proposals were announced and some commentators foresaw difficulties ahead (Wedell, 1988). Although the reforms re-emphasized the Warnock (DES, 1978) principle that educational aims of schooling are the same for all students, it became clear that the reforms were having a major impact on many aspects of education for those who experience difficulties (Gilborn & Youdell, 2000; Rouse & Florian, 1997). However, the idea of a common curriculum and national standards was central to the Education Reform Act which stressed the *entitlement* of pupils to a broad, balanced and relevant curriculum (Dearing, 1994). The Act further challenged schools with the duty of providing *all* students with access to the national curriculum.

Accountability

In England, accountability goes beyond high stakes assessment and publishing results. A system of inspection covers all ages, including pre- and post-school provision, in both the publicly funded and independent sectors. All educational institutions and local authorities are subjected to external scrutiny through a process of inspection carried out by the Office for Standards in Education (Ofsted) under the direction of Her Majesty's Chief Inspector of Schools (HMCI). Reports of these inspections are published and schools that do not meet the criteria are subjected to 'special measures'. This policy of 'name and shame' has been criticized by many commentators but its preoccupation with academic standards and its failure to understand the specific issues relating to the education of students with SEN in mainstream schools were seen by many as causing particular problems for schools. In response, new guidance on the inspection of inclusive practice was issued and all inspectors were required to undergo training on special needs (Ofsted, 2000).

The inspection process has been further revised by *The Framework for the Inspection of Schools* (Ofsted, 2005). Under these new arrangements, the Chief Inspector of Schools has the responsibility to keep the Secretary of State for Education informed about a range of matters including the:

- quality of education provided by schools
- educational standards achieved in those schools
- quality of leadership in and management of those schools
- spiritual, moral, social and cultural development of pupils at those schools
- extent to which the education provided by schools meets the needs of the range of pupils
- contribution made by schools in England to the well-being of their pupils.

The last two items have recently been added to the list in light of *Every Child Matters* and government concern about the education of vulnerable children, including those with SEN.

School inspection now takes place at least every three years and schools can expect only two days' notice of a forthcoming inspection. The new inspection regime has a 'lighter touch' than its predecessor but it still goes beyond compliance monitoring and includes observations of classroom practice and judgments about the quality of teaching and learning. Reports of these inspections are published within three weeks of the completion of the inspection. A school judged not to have met the criteria specified in the *Framework* is described as 'causing concern'. This may be in one of two categories, 'in need of significant improvement' or 'special measures'. Section 44 of the Education Act 2005 provides definitions of schools that require special measures or significant improvement and specifies what action must be taken by the school and/or the local authority. If the situation does not improve the school may be closed down.

Within the English context, therefore, there are two main strands within the reforms. On one hand, there are those aspects of legislation designed to protect vulnerable children, to encourage their inclusion, to reduce their social exclusion and to improve the quality of the services they receive. On the other hand, there are the standards-based reforms which stress academic excellence and high-stakes accountability for individuals, schools and local authorities. Often these reforms are in conflict and lead to a series of tensions and confusion in schools.

Reform policies in the US

The education of students with disabilities in US schools is currently being shaped by two very powerful laws: the 2004 Individuals with Disabilities Education Improvement Act (*IDEA*, PL 108–446) and the 2001 Elementary and Secondary Education Act (*No Child Left Behind Act*, PL 107–110). While neither law is entirely new, recent changes to both have solidified standards-driven educational policies in schools across the country.

The Elementary and Secondary Education Act (ESEA)

As noted in the introduction to this chapter, current reform policies being enacted in the US schools can be traced to major policy changes begun during the 1980s, initially within individual states. These changes were characterized by the adoption of universal content and performance standards, mandatory pupil assessments and high-stakes accountability for schools and students. This model of reform represented a significant departure from traditional US educational policymaking which left most educational decisions related to curriculum, assessment and accountability to local education agencies in conjunction with states. The notion of a strong federal presence in local schools has long been resisted within the US. Thus, as the first federal-level policies began to be constructed, they required specific actions on the parts of states, such as establishing core content and performance standards and developing a single accountability system. This model of reform was taken from those already enacted within many individual states.

The first major federal level policy directive that endorsed the concept of standards-driven reform came in 1994 through changes made to Title I of the Elementary Secondary Education Act. This Act is the major federal law governing k-12 education in the US and Title I of the Act currently provides about $13 billion to US school districts. Title I has been in place since the ESEA was first passed in 1965 and has as its central policy goal closing the achievement gap between students who live in poverty and middle-class white students. The 1994 amendments to ESEA required that each state develop challenging content and performance standards in at least reading and math and adopt yearly assessments to determine how well all students were meeting the states' performance standards. The 1994 amendments further mandated that, as a condition of receiving federal

funds, states develop and implement one state-wide assessment and accountability system that applied to all schools, and stipulated that all students should participate in the state assessments, and that the results for all students must be publicly reported. Furthermore, individual states were to develop plans for holding schools accountable for student achievement, including setting performance targets and imposing mandatory consequences for failing schools. These requirements represented a major departure in US federal educational policy. In defining 'all students' the Act specifically referred to students with disabilities as well as students with limited English proficiency (*Improving America's Schools Act*, 1994). By the late 1990s, an educational accountability model was put in place across the US through a combination of state and federal educational laws and regulations. These were characterized by the following: (1) a single system of assessment; (2) a system of accountability that relied on student assessment data and focused on the school as a unit of improvement; (3) the use of specific school and district sanctions or rewards based on student progress on assessments; and (4) the use of achievement data to allocate resources and school improvement initiatives.

The No Child Left Behind Act

In 2001 the ESEA was again amended and a number of significant changes were made to Title I. The amended act, renamed the No Child Left Behind Act (NCLB), continued to require that states establish challenging content and achievement standards. However, NCLB expanded the assessment requirement to include annual testing of all students in reading/language arts, math, and science in grades 3–8 and at least once during secondary school. States were also required to set, at minimum, three levels of performance on their assessments: 'Basic', 'Proficient', and 'Advanced.' Perhaps most dramatic and controversial were the new accountability requirements.

Critical new provisions focused on strengthening the accountability provisions.

The key accountability tool that is used in NCLB is Adequate Yearly Progress (AYP), which is focused on closing the achievement gap among specific subgroups of students. The goal of AYP is to ensure that 100 per cent of all students and each of five specific subgroups reach the state standard of 'proficient' by 2014. This requires that states set annual goals or targets that increase the percentage of students in each subgroup who attain the 'Proficient' and 'Advanced' level of performance. In addition, for a school to make AYP it first must have assessed 95 per cent of all its students in each grade. Assessment results must be calculated and reported by grade and by each of five racial/ethnic groups, low-income students, English language learners, and students with disabilities in each content area. Schools that do not meet their annual goals for any subgroup are subject to a mandatory sequence of increasingly serious consequences including offering parents school choice and requiring that states take over failing schools and either convert them to charter schools and/or engage in other restructuring activities. How students with disabilities are to be included in these provisions is addressed in both the IDEA and regulations that accompany NCLB.

No Child Left Behind and students with disabilities

The NCLB contains an explicit policy commitment to ensure that all students, including those with disabilities, have a fair and equal opportunity to meet state standards. The policy clearly intends that students with disabilities share in the opportunities created by education reform and has included provisions in NCLB requiring that the content standards, achievement standards, and assessments as defined by the Act include students with disabilities to the maximum extent possible.

The NCLB requires that students with disabilities be included in general state-wide and district-wide assessment programs and that they should be provided with appropriate testing accommodations as specified in their Individual Education Plan (IEP). Results are to be reported both as part of and separate from the total population and all accountability procedures apply to these students. However, NCLB has some unique provisions concerning students with significant cognitive disabilities. Policymakers recognized that another method of assessing the progress and achievement of the students was necessary.

In 2003, the US Department of Education issued regulations for NCLB that build on requirements specified in 1997 amendments to the IDEA stating that states or districts must develop guidelines that allow 'for the participation of students with disabilities in alternate assessments for those students who cannot participate in state and district-wide assessment programs' (§612(a)(17)(A)(i)). These alternate assessments were to be developed and conducted beginning not later than July 1, 2000. The NCLB regulations require students with the most significant cognitive disabilities to be assessed using alternate assessments based on alternate achievement standards if they cannot participate in the general education assessments even with appropriate accommodations. However, under the IDEA, the rules established that the general education academic content standards must apply to these students. Alternate achievements standards are defined as 'an expectation of performance that differs in complexity from a grade-level achievement standard' (34 C.F.R. §200 I(c)(1)(i)). Individual states are allowed to define alternate achievement standards provided the standards meet four conditions. First, alternate achievement standards must be aligned with the state's academic content standards, although they may reflect prerequisite skills rather than grade-level skills. Second, they must describe at least three levels of attainment (that is, Basic, Proficient, and Advanced). Third, they must include descriptions of the competencies associated with each level of attainment and finally, they must include assessment scores (cut scores) that differentiate among the levels and a description of the rationale and procedures used to determine each achievement level (US Department of Education, 2005).

The NCLB regulations make clear that alternate achievement standards are appropriate for only a small percentage of students with disabilities and that proficiency for all other students with disabilities must be measured against grade-level achievement standards. To prevent states and districts from assigning too many students with disabilities to alternate performance standards the number of proficient scores included in district and state level AYP may not exceed 1 per cent of all students in the grades tested, totaling about 9 per cent of students with disabilities. However, if states can demonstrate that they have a larger population of students with the most significant cognitive disabilities, they could apply for an exception. Most recently, the Department has signaled its intent to make another change to the NCLB rules that would permit an additional group of students with disabilities, those with 'persistent academic difficulties', to be held to 'modified' achievement standards and to be assessed using modified assessments (US Department of Education, 2005). Up to 2 per cent of the school-age population may be considered 'Proficient' using modified achievement standards if a state wished to establish these. Similar to alternate achievement standards the academic content standards assessed are to be the same as those used for all students.

The IDEA and reform policies

In the US, the education of children with disabilities is defined by the federal IDEA. The basic elements of this law have been in place since 1975 and guarantee each eligible child with a disability a free and appropriate public education (FAPE) in the least restrictive environment (LRE). Under the IDEA students become eligible to receive special education if they are determined to have a disability to include one of 13 disabilities defined in the Act and if the disability has an adverse impact on the students' ability to learn. The primary accountability instrument used in IDEA is the Individual Education Plan which is crafted by a team, including the child's parent, according to very prescriptive timelines and proce-

dures. The IEP is to be based on individualized assessment of a student with a disability and defines specific annual educational goals to be addressed.

In 1997 a number of significant changes were made to the IDEA to align special education policies with the model of standards-driven reform articulated in the 1994 ESEA as well as various state-level reforms. Specific provisions were added to the IDEA in 1997 requiring that students with disabilities have access to the general education curriculum and participate in the state and local assessments with accommodations and/or alternate assessments if needed. Although the 1997 IDEA amendments implied that students with disabilities should participate in accountability by requiring their participation in assessments and reporting of scores, the IDEA did not specifically mandate their inclusion in accountability systems (Thurlow, 2004). The IDEA referred to the student's IEP as the method for ensuring accountability and did not require that any agency or person be held accountable if a child does not achieve the goals and objectives listed on the IEP. The IDEA also did not require states to reward or sanction schools based on the outcomes for students with disabilities.

This lack of public accountability was cited as a significant problem by a National Academy of Sciences committee (McDonnell, McLaughlin, & Morison, 1997) which noted that the IEP was a form of 'private' (p. 151) accountability and inconsistent with the move toward transparent reporting of student achievement and of holding schools and school systems accountable for that achievement. In fact, as states developed their own assessment and accountability systems during the decades of the 1980s and early 1990s, students with disabilities were erratically and inconsistently included (McLaughlin & Thurlow, 2003). For example, in some states the scores of students with disabilities who received an assessment accommodation were not reported at all or were not included in any statistical measures of accountability. Few states reported the assessment results of all of their students with disabilities and even fewer states had implemented and reported student performance on alternate assessments (McLaughlin & Thurlow, 2003).

In 2004 Congress again reauthorized the IDEA and even more explicitly aligned the educational provisions of the Act with the requirements of NCLB. Changes to the IEP provisions once again stressed access to the general education curriculum and specifically referenced the NCLB in citing how students with disabilities were to be included in assessments and accountability systems. The IEP remains the mechanism for determining which, if any, individual accommodations will be necessary to measure the academic achievement of the child on state and district wide assessments. The IEP also specifies if the child will participate in an alternate assessment rather than a state or district assessment and the document must explain why the child cannot participate in the regular assessment and indicate why the particular alternate assessment selected is appropriate for the child. It is important to note that, in addition to the IDEA, students with disabilities are also entitled to reasonable accommodations under Section 504 of the Rehabilitation Act and the Americans with Disabilities Act (ADA). These accommodations apply to physical and instructional environments as well as assessments.

In the previous sections we have discussed the current policy frameworks in England and Wales and the US that govern how students with disabilities are to be included in standards-driven reforms. The following sections discuss some of the more pressing challenges associated with implementing these reforms with students with disabilities.

IMPACTS AND CHALLENGES OF REFORMS AND STUDENTS WITH DISABILITIES

The standards-driven reform policies currently being implemented in both England and the US pose a number of challenges for the education of students with disabilities. These challenges may be categorized as conceptual, which contest some of the core assumptions underlying special education policies and those that are more technical and which might be addressed through research and development or through intensive professional development. In this section we consider some of the more immediate challenges that are emerging from early implementation of standards driven reform and students with disabilities and SEN. For example, a report issued by the National Center on Educational Outcomes (Thurlow & Wiley, 2004) indicated that the performance gap between students with disabilities and all students can vary from state to state but is as wide as 43 points at the elementary school level, 56 points at the middle school level, and 67 points at the secondary level.

Equity and fair measures of improvement

A core tenet of the reforms in both England and the US is the requirement that schools, school districts, and in the US states, demonstrate continual gains in student performance. Yet, research has emphasized the particularly negative consequences of such high stakes accountability when educators feel that the competition is not fair (Firestone, Mayrowetz, & Fairman, 1998). When it comes to considering students with disabilities, a question of fairness arises concerning holding all students to the same achievement standards on the same subject matter content when the level of achievement may be unattainable.

Research in the US that has focused on the achievement of students with disabilities on large-scale assessments is limited but seems to suggest that as a group these students are achieving at higher levels on state assessments (Thompson et al., 2005) but are not closing the achievement gap (Quality Counts, 2004). The use of cut scores that set absolute thresholds for performance (for example, 'Proficient' and 'Advanced') in conjunction with establishing performance targets for schools attempts to establish one expectation for all students. However, when professionals recognize this standard is not attainable by some students the response from schools can be counterproductive to improvement. For example, school staff may become demoralized and 'helpless' or they decide simply to focus efforts on students who are perceived to be able to make achievement gains and ignore the students they consider to be too low (Darling-Hammond, 2004). School professionals might also conclude that it is not fair to hold students with disabilities to the same standards because the standards are not relevant or meaningful to long-term educational goals which might be more vocational and not as academically oriented (McLaughlin & Henderson, 2001). Nonetheless, a central policy goal of the reforms in both England and the US is to promote equity in educational outcomes thus requiring that all students be held to the same expectations, assessed in the same manner and that schools be held accountable in the same way. To establish different standards or separate assessment and accountability systems is viewed as counter to the goal of educational equity. Furthermore, accountability requires uniform approaches to measuring the progress of students.

Nonetheless, maintaining uniform performance and progress goals for all students is complex. In part, the complexity stems from how we define performance and progress, which can be understood in at least three ways. Performance can be measured in relation to standardized scores, which are underpinned by assumptions about the normal distribution of abilities within a population. Performance can also be criterion referenced in relation to attainment of specific knowledge, skills or competences. Alternatively, performance and progress can be personally referenced, in other words the child knows and can do things today that they could not do in the past.

Attempts have been made by the government in England (DfES, 2004a) not only to extend the range of students for whom 'reasonable progress' is considered important through the use of more fine-grained measures such as 'P-scales', but also to widen learning beyond the core academic areas of the curriculum (English, math and science) to include 'broader achievements in terms of personal and social development' (para. 3.22).

These developments are part of a gradual evolution of policies and practices in England that attempt to include all students in broader reform initiatives. But unresolved tensions remain between the need for policies that are responsive to the needs of individual student and the demand for higher standards and greater accountably. A recent Ofsted report on inclusion (Ofsted, 2004), notes that 'many schools have difficulty in setting targets and knowing what represents reasonable progress' (para. 35). Wedell (2005) points out that 'reasonableness' is not a straightforward concept. He suggests that there are least four distinct contexts in which questions about the 'reasonable progress' of students with special needs are asked:

- Teachers need to know whether the method chosen to help a pupil is effective, or whether alternative methods might improve progress.
- Teachers and parents want to know whether teaching is helping their students to make optimum progress.
- Staff performance review procedures for teachers involve them in setting targets for the effectiveness of the help they give pupils.
- League tables and other comparisons between schools ask questions about the 'value added' they offer (Wedell, 2005, p. 105).

Similar issues related to measuring progress exist in the US. One issue facing schools is sustaining progress on assessments from year to year. Fluctuations in test results at the school level often occur for reasons that have very little to do with the quality of teaching and effectiveness of the school (Linn, Baker, & Betenbenner, 2002; Malmgren, McLaughlin, & Nolet, 2005; McLaughlin & Embler, 2005). For example, changes in both the number and characteristics of students being tested due to student mobility can produce significant year to year variations in average test scores. There are also difficulties involved when trying to compare schools' performance over time because different cohorts of students within any given school will have different strengths and weaknesses.

Judgments about the progress of students with disabilities is affected by the relatively small number of these students who are enrolled in most public schools. Section 1111(b)(2)(C) (v)(II) of NCLB provides that the dissagregation of data by subgroup for the purposes of calculating AYP 'shall not be required in a case in which the number of students in a category is insufficient to yield statistically reliable information or the results would reveal personally identifiable information about an individual student'. What states define as statistically reliable varies but a typical number is 40, with some states having set a minimum subgroup size as high as 200.

Kane and Staiger (2002) point out that although reliability is greater when sample sizes increase there is no magical sample size above which subgroup results are statistically reliable. An interpretation of the minimum threshold differs from state to state based on the technical qualities of the assessment. However, although increasing the minimum subgroup size could help school systems reach more defensible conclusions about school quality, it can also mean that many schools will not be held accountable at all for some students or they may be held accountable one year but not the next because certain subgroups become invisible. Clearly, judging a school on the basis of two or three students is not valid, but setting minimum group size at such a high level excludes many schools and even smaller districts from being accountable for the progress of small subgroups, most notably students with disabilities. In fact, a recent study of five states (Simpson, Gong, & Marion, 2005) indicated that 80 per cent of the schools that met AYP in these states for the 2003–04 school year did so without having to report the performance for the subgroup of students with disabilities.

One response to the issue of how to measure progress more fairly is to consider 'value-added' systems of accountability that are based upon students' progress in learning.

These are seen by some as providing a more meaningful and fairer measure of a school's academic effectiveness (Sammons, Mortimore, & Thomas, 1996) and have recently been introduced in England. These arrangements are intended to demonstrate the achievement of individual students and schools over time. Thus the assessments of individual pupils are personally referenced and do not depend on comparisons with other students or to externally impose criteria. Value-added measures are now also being used at the school level in order to make more nuanced judgments about the effectiveness of schools (for details see http://www.dfes.gov.uk/performancetables).

The US Department of Education has created a task force to examine the feasibility of these approaches to be used in conjunction with the current method of accountability under the No Child Left Behind Act. However, advocates for children who are most likely to be in the lowest scoring groups are concerned that such 'value-added' methods in effect set lower standards and expectations for their children. That the net effect is to help schools avoid the reality that poor and minority children and children with disabilities are indeed achieving significantly below their middle-class peers and to give up trying to close the achievement gap.

Instruction and assessment

The extent to which a single assessment can provide all the necessary data for both formative and summative (that is, evaluative) purposes is debatable. Assessment experts in both the UK and the US have noted the problems associated with using only one type of assessment (Cline, 1992; Koretz & Barton, 2004; Pellegrino, 2001). Cline states categorically that, 'All too often a variety of outcomes is anticipated from the same procedure that does not work. The assessment arrangements associated with the National Curriculum assessment in the UK offer a vivid example of the difficulties that can arise' (p. 122).

Although the introduction of systems of assessment that support rather than inhibit learning has been slow, there are encouraging signs in England that initiatives such a 'assessment for learning' (Black & Wiliam, 1998) and the work of the Assessment Reform Group (2002) are beginning to have a positive impact in schools because these approaches stress formative assessment that improves learning in ways that assessment for accountability do not. Such approaches stress the involvement of students in self-assessment as well as encouraging teachers to give regular, explicit feedback to students in relation to their curriculum objectives and targets. It is argued that such approaches to assessment are a powerful tool for learning (Black & Wiliam, 1998).

Within the US, the notion of developing more formative or instructionally supportive systems of assessment that are aligned with the large-scale state accountability assessments is also catching on (Fuchs & Fuchs, in press; Nolet & McLaughlin, 2005). Through the use of curriculum-based assessments teachers are able to better target specific instructional needs, but these needs are defined by the state content and achievement standards.

Universal standards and the ideology of individualization

The legal entitlements of students with disabilities and special educational needs in both England and the US involve a process of individualized educational decision-making designed to meet each student's unique educational needs. Individually referenced systems of accountability, such as IEPs and annual reviews, are a largely private exercise involving the professionals, the student and his or her parents. Rarely is the wider educational community involved and for the most part there has been little transparency or public accountability in this process. The recently imposed accountability systems have opened up special education to greater scrutiny. However, special education has also exposed a series of tensions in the standards-

driven reform policy framework.

The focus on student achievement as well as other critical outcomes such as graduation is shifting the goal of special education policy from equal access to education to ensuring equal opportunity to achieve a meaningful education, defined in terms of specific levels of performance. Professionals, families and advocates generally applaud this focus on student achievement and the concept of enhanced system accountability for students with disabilities, but there is significant tension between the concept of an 'individualized' education and the notion of common standards. As interpreted under standards-driven accountability, individualization defines how a student will access and learn universal subject matter content and achievement standards. Thus, professionals and families are struggling with how to reconcile the goals of the reforms while maintaining effective and meaningful instruction for students who may require more functional skills.

In the US, research related to the IEPs have demonstrated that individualized planning has been only loosely coupled to the general education curriculum and has resulted in IEPs that set low expectations for students and separate their instruction from the core curriculum (for example, Pugach & Warger, 1996; Shriner & DeStefano, 2003). Under standards-driven reform, IEP teams are finding that they are operating in an environment in which a state's academic content and achievement standards define the ultimate goals of education for all students. Traditional special education content such as functional or independent living skills and vocational and career skills are expected to somehow be integrated into academic content instruction posing challenges for all but the most skilled teachers (Kohl, McLaughlin, & Nagle, 2005; McLaughlin, Nolet, Rhim, & Henderson, 1999).

It is interesting to note that the term 'individualized learning' has been replaced in government guidance in England with the term 'personalized learning'. It was felt that individualization led to too much separation and isolation, and to teachers feeling overwhelmed as they tried to offer individual instruction to pupils in their classes. However, it is too early to determine the effects of these changes on teachers and schools.

Definitional issues

As a result of the pressure on schools to attain specific performance targets, a new functional classification system seems to be emerging in both England and the US. That is, we observe schools conducting a form of 'triage' by sorting students into those who are performing at or above 'Proficient', those who are just below the 'Proficient' level and those who are scoring at the bottom of the distribution (Booher-Jenning, 2005; Gilborn & Youdell, 2000; Nagle, 2004). Schools and teachers are focusing resources and attention on those students who are most likely to jump into the 'Proficient' category. What this means for students, both with and without special education needs, who continually perform well below the 'Basic' level of achievement is not yet clear. With little incentive to improve the performance of such students, schools may well provide palliative education not intensive specialized education. Furthermore, one must question whether it is in the best interests of students who are making only the most basic progress in the general education content standards to continue instruction in these areas. Responses to this reality include the aforementioned pending policy change in the US that will permit another group of students with disabilities to be held to modified achievement standards. Yet, questions about which students might be held to modified standards are a chief concern in the US and England, but for different reasons. England faces a particular dilemma concerning who is classified as eligible to receive special educational provision.

As mentioned earlier, during the 1980s England and Wales moved towards a non-categorical notion of special educational needs (SEN). It was argued that medical categories of handicap and labels were not helpful in planning educational provision because labels persist and are associated with low expectations. Recognizing that difficulties in learning could only be understood in the context in which they occurred, SEN was seen as covering an array of difficulties and 'does not assume that there are hard and fast categories of special educational need ... [and] recognizes that there is a wide spectrum of special educational needs that are frequently inter-related, although there are also specific needs that usually relate directly to particular types of impairment' (DfES, 2001b, p. 85, §7.52). Further, special education is defined as 'education that is additional to, or different from, what is normally available in schools' (DfES, 2001b). What is normally available in some schools is not normally available in others. Thus the statutory assessment process leading to a Statement of SEN is subject to variation. In reality, variations in local context produce different ideas about who has special educational needs and who should get a Statement.

Patterns of provision to meet special educational needs are variable across England and Wales. Different local histories and traditions mean that the implementation of a national policy varies between LEAs. Indeed, there are sizeable variations between LEAs in terms of who gets special education services, where and how they are provided, and these variations have been consistently reported since the implementation of the 1981 Education Act (see, for example, Audit Commission, 1992; Lunt & Evans, 1994; Norwich, 1997). In England and Wales the variation in the numbers of students who receive Statements is fivefold (Audit Commission, 2002) and the variation in the percentage of students attending special schools is eightfold (Norwich, 1997). The implications of such variation for accountability and research purposes will be clear, as comparisons across schools and local authorities are fraught with difficulty.

Somewhat similar issues exist in the US, which has demonstrated variances across states, LEAs and schools in the percentage of students who have IEPs (Donovan & Cross, 2002). However, given that, in the US, both the identification procedures as well as definitional criteria are somewhat bounded by the IDEA and corresponding state policy, one might assume a narrower range of learner characteristics. This is, however, open to question.

Assessment accommodations and modifications

The involvement of students with disabilities and SEN in the assessments administered in both England and the US raises a number of technical and professional dilemmas. In a review of the National Curriculum in England carried out by Dearing (1994), it was reiterated that the national curriculum was an entitlement for all students and therefore to the maximum extent possible, students with special needs must participate in this national educational and assessment framework. The Schools Curriculum and Assessment Agency claimed that national assessment should 'provide a standard, summative assessment of attainment … which can properly be assessed under controlled conditions' (SCAA, 1996). Rouse and Agbenu (1998) reviewed the use of national assessment and reported that the standard assessment tasks (that is, tests) present particular difficulties for pupils with special educational needs.

Modification of the standard assessment tests is possible for students with SEN by using permitted special arrangements, such as additional time, a reader or alternative modes of response. However, there is considerable uncertainty about the validity and reliability of these adapted tests because they have to be modified to such an extent that they no longer constitute a standard means of assessment. The modifications are often so substantial that the tests become a form of teacher assessment, but one that is separate from the ongoing process of teaching and learning. Furthermore, it is difficult for the modified tests to be carried out under controlled conditions. Attempts to provide controlled assessment conditions for the modified tests create circumstances which prevent an accurate reflection of student's level of attainment.

Similar problems with assessing students with disabilities have been noted in US research since states began their large-scale assessment programs (Koretz & Barton, 2004; McLaughlin & Thurlow, 2003; Pullin, 2005). An assumption underlying accountability for student performance is that student performance can be accurately and authentically measured by state assessments (Fuhrman, 2003). This assumption is challenged by some of the policies concerning assessment of students with disabilities. Students with disabilities participate in these assessments in the following ways: (1) assessments may be taken in the same way as other students take them; (2) assessments may be taken with accommodations; and (3) students take an alternate assessment based on alternate or modified achievement standards (Thompson, Thurlow, & Moore, 2003). As noted earlier, students with disabilities have a legal entitlement to test accommodations under three federal laws, the IDEA, Section 504 of the Rehabilitation Act, and the Americans with Disabilities Act. Assessment accommodations are defined as changes in testing materials or procedures designed to offset the impact of a student's disability on performance and allow him or her to participate in an assessment. An assessment accommodation should not alter either the content being measured or the achievement standard. If students with disabilities cannot participate in a general assessment even with accommodations, they may be tested using an alternate assessment.

There is no set of universally approved assessment accommodations, and state policies on accommodations vary tremendously (Thompson et al., 2003). Some accommodations are believed to change what is being tested, yielding scores that are considered invalid. These kinds of accommodations may be referred to as 'nonstandard' or 'invalid'. It is not uncommon to find an accommodation that is permitted in one state but considered invalid in another. Such variations in state accommodation policies reflect a lack of agreement in the field regarding which accommodations pose a genuine threat to validity (National Research Council, 2004).

Research on the impact of accommodations on score validity (Sireci, Li, & Scarpati, 2003) indicates that an accommodation uniquely interacts with an individual student's disability and support needs, such that it is impossible to generalize about the effects on validity. In addition, accommodations are often 'bundled' such that an individual student rarely receives one accommodation, but rather a set (Rhode Island Department of Education, 2003). For example, a student who receives extended time may automatically be assessed in a separate setting within a small group, and perhaps have instructions read aloud. Because a nonstandard accommodation may affect scores, states may remove these scores from summary reports and/or report them differently. Under NCLB scores obtained as a result of a nonstandard administration are scored but are included as 'Basic' with the AYP accountability calculations.

Alternate assessments

Another assessment issue that impacts the validity of information about students with disabilities is that of alternate assessments. In the US both the IDEA and NCLB permit the use of alternate assessments for students with disabilities who cannot participate in the regular state assessment even with accommodations. These alternate assessments can measure progress toward grade-level, modified, or alternate achievement standards. The latter are intended for students with more significant cognitive disabilities and not more than 1 per cent of these students may be counted as 'Proficient' using the alternate achievement standards. States have or are developing alternate assessments based on grade level standards for students with other disabilities. Kohl et al. (2005) in a study of 16 randomly selected states found that nine had more than one alternate assessment and four included a broader group of students beyond those with significant cognitive disabilities. Browder, Spooner, Ahlgrim-Delzell, Flowers, and Karvonen (2003) found participation to

vary widely, with up to 2.5 per cent of the total student population in some states taking an alternate assessment.

Participation rates on alternate assessments also varied by disability, ranging from 6.2 per cent for students with learning disabilities to 32.0 per cent for students with autism, and 32.6 per cent for students with mental retardation (Browder et al., 2003). The number of states using out-of-level tests as alternate assessments rose from five states in 1997 to 17 states in 2003 (Quenemoen, Thompson, & Thurlow, 2003). However, the use of these is declining as they are expressly forbidden under NCLB regulations due in part to fears that too many students with disabilities will be assigned to an off-level assessment that is not appropriately challenging in order to avoid accountability consequences (Browder et al., 2003). Additionally, in some states alternate high school exit assessments are being offered to a broader group of students, beyond those with significant cognitive disabilities, because of the significant consequences attached to these exams (see Karger & Pullin, 2002).

The Department of Education as well as individual states provide guidance to IEP teams to help them determine which assessment is most appropriate for each student (Kohl et al., 2005). For the students held to alternate achievement standards, the most common variables are the instructional level of the student and whether the student is considered to have a significant cognitive disability as required by NCLB regulations. However, despite extensive guidelines and procedures, the determination and actual alternate assessment process is highly individualized and ultimately leaves a great deal of discretion to individual teachers in terms of with what and how to assess students, at least those with significant cognitive disabilities (Kohl et al., 2005; Zatta & Pullin, 2004).

In England recording progress of students with severe cognitive difficulties involves the use of an alternative set of objectives that forms the foundation of the National Curriculum. These are known as 'P-scales', a series of graded assessment criteria against which progress below level one in the National Curriculum can be measured. The scales were developed to support the process of planning and individual target setting and to enable these pupils to be connected with the National Curriculum (QCA, 2001). Their use involves summative assessment at the end of each key stage of education (ages 7, 11, 14 and 16) and for those pupils making more rapid progress, possibly once a year. But they were never intended to be part of an institutional accountability process. In a review of 'P-scales' carried out for the DfES, Byers (2002) suggested that, 'There are persistent and unhelpful suspicions that P-scale data will be used to make judgments about school effectiveness. P-scale data should not be used in order to try to "drive up standards" for pupils with SEN or to generate "league tables" of special and inclusive schools' (p. 17).

SUMMARY AND IMPLICATIONS FOR PRACTICE

For all of their difficulties, the reforms enacted in England and Wales and the US offer opportunities for parents and families, the community, taxpayers and educators to know something about the performance of students whose achievements were largely hidden in the past. While we welcome the transparency offered by these reforms, we are cognizant of the numerous caveats regarding the types of inferences we may currently be able to make about schools based on performance data of students with disabilities. As the reforms are implemented we are learning how they are changing practices in schools. McLaughlin and her colleagues (McLaughlin & Henderson, 2001; Malmgren et al., 2005) in the US, and researchers in the UK (Dyson, Farrell, Polat, Hutcheson, & Gallannaugh, 2004; Rouse & Florian, in press), have researched how standards and high-stakes accountability are being implemented with students with disabilities and SEN.

Interestingly, when the concept of including students with disabilities in standards, assessments and accountability first emerged in the 1990s, schools often interpreted this as synonymous with physical inclusion, meaning educating students with disabilities in general education classrooms. What content standards were taught and how well students performed were determined by a child's teacher and/or in some cases an instructional assistant without regard for standards of performance. With the imposition of accountability systems requiring disaggregated assessment results and attainment of established performance targets, the demand to ensure that all students are being taught the same subject matter content has become the dominant discourse in schools.

Yet, this notion of universal content and achievement standards is likely the most controversial and most difficult of all of the reform requirements. Fundamental to achieving educational equity, common standards can promote higher expectations and create a focus for instruction in the schools. Nonetheless, special education teachers in both England and the US struggle to reconcile the competing priorities of state or national curricula with what they considered more relevant skills and their traditional practice (McLaughlin, Henderson, & Rhim, 1997). Permitting special educators to decide which skills are important and which can be ignored results in what Tomlinson (1982) referred to as a 'curriculum of academic non-knowledge'. Clearly a standards-based curriculum provides a short- and long-term scope and sequence for what teachers need to teach (Nolet & McLaughlin, 2005).

As we have noted, a fundamental tension arises from the way in which content and achievement standards are currently defined. Decisions about what students should know and be able to do at any given age arise from expectations about what 'normal' students should be able to do at that age. To that extent they are norm-referenced, governed by the 'laws' of normal distribution even when the standards are described as criterion referenced. Fixed grade or age achievement norms are problematic in that they ignore the realities of human difference. The levels of attainment within the National Curriculum assessed through national tests in England and Wales and the grade level assessments and AYP requirements in the US assume that all students must reach the same level of performance in the same amount of time. Only recently have both England and Wales and the US begun to permit achievement to be defined as the progress learners make over time. The former makes it is possible for students to have achieved well (given their starting point) but not to have reached the standard as pre-specified by the performance criteria. Then again, we cannot ignore the fact that for some students with disabilities and SEN, advancing toward proficiency or making progress in academic subject matter, especially at the upper grades or levels, may not only be unattainable but also not relevant to our most ambitious goals for them. In some part, increasing the percentage of students with disabilities who can be held to alternate and modified standards may solve part of the problem. However, discussions of what we should be teaching as well as how schools should be accountable for student progress should be central to the current debate about students with disabilities.

Judgments about learning require value-added measures in addition to absolute indicators of performance. Defining achievement in this way offers the potential of a fairer, more meaningful accountability measure for individuals and a better indication of school effectiveness than do measures of absolute standards. This is particularly true of schools that include a high proportion of pupils designated as having SEN or have higher proportions of students from low socio-economic status (SES), which by their very definition are working with students whose starting points are often lower than those of other pupils who do not have SEN or low SES. Yet, outcome-based accountability cannot be rejected outright as there is an urgent need to close the achievement gap. But if this goal is to be achieved, the reforms need to incorporate curriculum content and measures of achievement that are more meaningful and more likely to motivate students and teachers.

Notwithstanding the various issues constraining policymakers at they attempt to include all students in new accountability schemes, one thing is certain, both England and the US are now collecting data on the learning of students with disabilities and SEN over time and there is a growing interest in the development of 'data-driven decision-making'. Looking at student performance outcome can help in resource allocation as well as understanding what works and what does not. In England it is now possible for researchers and policymakers to examine the performance of individuals within particular schools over time. As part of the development of a national pupil data-set (NPD), every child in England has been allocated a unique pupil number (UPN). This means that individual pupils can be tracked over their whole school careers. In addition, it is now possible to combine 'value-added' information about pupil progress from one key stage of education to the next key stage from the NPD, with demographic data (such as age, gender, ethnicity, first language spoken, socio-economic status and disability) from the pupil-level annual schools census (PLASC). Merging these data-sets makes it theoretically possible to explore, for the first time, relationships between individuals' characteristics, forms of provision and attainment. In addition, school management and local authorities are using the data to raise standards in schools (Demie, 2003). These developments are part of a broader initiative to introduce the *National Performance Framework for Special Educational Needs* (NPF; DfES, 2004a). The aim of the NPF is to give local authorities and government easy access to a variety of datasets and indicators to support monitoring, self-review and development. The indicators include data on contextual information, levels of inclusion, pupil outcomes and service delivery. The emphasis throughout is on 'outputs' and 'outcomes' as well as 'inputs'. While these developments have potential to improve data-driven decision-making, they also have major technical and conceptual problems associated with the quality of the data and difficulties with validity and reliability (Florian, Rouse, Black-Hawkins, & Jull, 2004). Similar analyses of pupil performance trends are available within individual states in the US, albeit data relative to students with disabilities have only been available over the past few years.

In conclusion, in the current context of schools, special education is in the spotlight and its practices and outcomes are being subjected to healthy scrutiny. But, if the reforms are to lead to higher standards and better opportunities for all students, then it is essential that systems of assessment be developed that are capable of demonstrating the learning and progress of all students. In addition, the content of the curriculum needs to be sufficiently flexible for it to be meaningful for all learners. Surely it is not beyond the creativity of policymakers and educators to design a standards-driven accountability system that is truly inclusive and which reflects the needs of individuals and society better than current efforts? Such a system will enable schools to celebrate the progress that individuals are making towards achieving meaningful standards that will be of benefit to themselves and society.

REFERENCES

Assessment Reform Group. (2002). *Assessment for learning: 10 principles.* London: Author.

Audit Commission. (1992). *Getting in on the act.* London: HMSO.

Audit Commission. (2002). *Statutory assessment and statements of SEN: In need of review?* London: Author.

Black, P., & Wiliam, D. (1998). *Inside the black box.* London: King's College Press.

Booher-Jenning, J. (2005). Below the bubble: 'educational triage' and the Texas accountability system. *American Educational Research Journal, 42*(2), 252–268.

Browder, D., Spooner, F., Ahlgrim-Delzell, L., Flowers, C., & Karvonen, M. (2003). What we know and need to know about alternate assessment. *Exceptional Children, 70*(1), 45–61.

Byers, R. (2002). *Developing the P-scales: A Report.* London: DfES.

Cline, T. (1992). Assessment of special educational needs: Meeting reasonable expectations? In T. Cline (Ed.), *The assessment of special educational needs: International perspectives.* London: Routledge.

Darling-Hammond, L. (2004). From 'separate but equal' to 'No Child Left Behind': The collision of new standards and old inequalities. In D. Meier & G. Wood (Eds.), *Many children left behind: How the No Child Left Behind Act is damaging our children and our schools* (pp. 3–32). Boston, MA: Beacon Press.

Dearing, R. (1994). *The national curriculum and its assessment. Final Report.* London: School Curriculum and Assessment Authority.

Demie, F. (2003). Using value-added data for school self evaluation: A case study of practice in inner-city schools. *School leadership and management, 23*(4) pp. 445–467.

Department for Education (DfE). (1994). *Code of practice on the identification and assessment of special educational needs.* London: HMSO.

Department of Education and Science (DES). (1978). *Special educational needs: Report of the Committee of Enquiry into the education of handicapped children and young people (The Warnock Report).* London: HMSO.

Department for Education and Skills (DfES). (2001a). *Inclusive schooling: Children with SEN.* London: DfES.

Department for Education and Skills (DfES). (2001b). *Special educational needs code of practice* (revised). London: DfES.

Department for Education and Skills (DfES). (2003). *Every Child Matters. Cm.5860.* London: The Stationery Office

Department for Education and Skills (DfES). (2004a) *National performance framework for special educational needs.* London: DfES.

Department for Education and Skills (DfES). (2004b). *Removing barriers to achievement.* London: DfES.

DfES (2006) http//www.dfes.gov.uk/performancetables/nscoringsys.shtml Retrieved 12 April 2006.

Donovan, M. S., & Cross, C. T. (Eds.). (2002). *Minority students in special education and gifted education.* Washington, DC: National Academy of Sciences.

Dyson, A., Farrell, P., Polat, F., Hutcheson, G., & Gallannaugh, F. (2004). *Inclusion and pupil achievement.* London: DfES.

Firestone, W. A., Mayrowetz, D., & Fairman, J. (1998). Performance-based assessment and instructional change: The effects of testing in Maine and Maryland. *Educational Evaluation and Policy Analysis, 20*(2), 95–113.

Florian, L., Rouse, M., Black-Hawkins, K., & Jull, S. (2004). What can national datasets tell us about inclusion and pupil achievement? *British Journal of Special Educa-*

tion, 31(3), 115–121.

Fuchs, L.S., and Fuchs, D. (In press). Determining annual yearly progress from Kindergarten through Grade 6 with curriculum-based measurement. *Assessment for Effective Intervention.*

Fuhrman, S. H. (2003). *Redesigning accountability systems for education* (Policy Brief). Philadelphia, PA: Consortium for Policy Research in Education.

Gilborn, D., & Youdell, D. (2000) *Rationing education: policy, practice, reform and equity.* Buckingham: Open University Press

Improving America's Schools Act (1994), 34 C.F.R §111(b) (3) (F).

Individuals with Disabilities Education Act 1997, 105–17, 611 et seq.

Individuals with Disabilities Education Improvement Act 2004, 108–446, Part A, Sec. 601(c).

Kane, T. J., & Staiger, D. O. (2002). Validity in school test scores: Implications for test-based accountability scores. In D. Ravitch (Ed.), *Brookings papers on education policy.* Washington, DC: Brookings Institution.

Karger, J., & Pullin, D. (2002). *Exit documents and students with disabilities: Legal issues* (Issue Brief 2). College Park, MD: University of Maryland, Educational Policy Research Reform Institute, Institute for the Study of Exceptional Children and Youth.

Kohl, F.L., McLaughlin, M.J., & Nagle, K. (2005). *Alternate achievement standards and assessments: A descriptive investigation of 16 states* (Technical Report). College Park, MD: University of Maryland, Institute for the Study of Exceptional Children and Youth.

Koretz, D., & Barton, K. (2004) Assessing students with disabilities: Issues and evidence. *Educational Assessment, 9*(1&2), 29–60.

Linn, R. L., Baker, E. L., & Betenbenner, D. W. (2002). Accountability systems: Implications of requirements of the No Child Left Behind Act of 2001. *Educational Researcher, 31*(6), 3–6.

Lunt, I., & Evans, J. (1994). Dilemmas in special educational needs: Some effects of local management of schools. In S. Riddell & S. Brown (Eds.), *Special needs and policies in the 1990s.* London: Routledge.

Malmgren, K., McLaughlin, M.J., & Nolet, V. (2005). Accounting for the performance of students with disabilities on statewide assessments. *Journal of Special Education, 39*(2), pp. 86–96.

McDonnell, L. M., McLaughlin, M. J., & Morison, P. (Eds.). (1997). *Educating one and all: Students with disabilities and standards-based reform.* Washington, DC: National Academy Press.

McLaughlin, M.J. & Embler, S. D. (2005). Educational reform and high stakes testing. In P. Wehman (Ed.), *Life beyond the classroom* (4th ed.). Baltimore, MD: Paul H. Brookes.

McLaughlin, M. J., & Henderson, K. (2001). Foundations of special education in the US. In K. Mazurek & M.

Winzer (Eds.), *Defining special education into the 21st century* (pp. 41–61). Washington, DC: Gallaudet University Press.

McLaughlin, M. J., & Thurlow, M. (2003). Educational accountability and students with disabilities: Issues and challenges. *Journal of Educational Policy, 17*(4), 431–451.

McLaughlin, M. J., Henderson, K., & Rhim, L. M. (1997). *Snapshots of reform: A report of reform in 5 local school districts.* Alexandria, VA: Center for Policy Research on the Impact of General and Special Education Reform, National Association of State Boards of Education.

McLaughlin, M. J., Nolet, V., Rhim, L.M., & Henderson, K. (1999). Integrating standards including all students. *Teaching Exceptional Children, 31*(3), 66–71.

McLaughlin, M. W., & Shepard, L. A. (1995). *Improving education through standards-based reform: A report of the National Academy of Education panel on standards-based reform.* Stanford, CA: National Academy of Education.

Nagle, M. (2004). *Emerging state-level themes: Strengths and stressors in educational accountability reform* (Topical Review No. 4). College Park, MD: University of Maryland, Educational Policy Reform Research Institute. Available from www.eprri.org

National Commission on Excellence in Education. (1983). *A nation at risk: The imperative for educational reform.* Washington, DC: U.S. Department of Education.

National Research Council. (2004). *Keeping score for all: The effects of inclusion and accommodation policies on large-scale educational assessments.* Washington, DC: National Academy Press.

No Child Left Behind Act 2001, 107–110, § 1001 et seq.

Nolet, V., & McLaughlin, M. J. (2005). *Accessing the general curriculum: Including students with disabilities in standards-based reform* (2nd ed.). Thousand Oaks, CA: Corwin Press.

Norwich, B. (1997). *A trend towards inclusion: Statistics on special school placements and pupils with statements in ordinary schools.* Bristol: Centre for Studies on Inclusive Education.

Office for Standards in Education (Ofsted). (2000). *Evaluating educational inclusion.* London: Author.

Office for Standards in Education (Ofsted). (2003). *Inspecting schools: Framework for inspecting schools* (No. HMI 1525). London: Author.

Office for Standards in Education (Ofsted). (2004). *Special educational needs and disability: Towards inclusive schools* (No. HMI 2276). London: Author.

Office for Standards in Education (Ofsted). (2005) *The framework for the inspection of schools.* London: Author.

Pellegrino, J. W. (2001). *Rethinking and redesigning education assessment.* 17. Washington, DC: Education Commission of the States.

Pugach, M. C., & Warger, C. L. (Eds.). (1996). *Curriculum trends, special education, and reform: Refocusing the conversation.* New York: Teachers College Press.

Pullin, D. (2005). When one size does not fit all: The special challenges of accountability testing for students with disabilities. *Yearbook of the National Society for the Study of Education, 104*(2), 199–222.

Qualifications and Curriculum Authority (QCA). (1999). *The National Curriculum: Handbook for primary teachers in England.* London: Author.

Qualifications and Curriculum Authority (QCA). (2001). *Planning, teaching and assessing the curriculum for pupils with learning difficulties.* London: Author.

Quality Counts. (2004). Quality Counts 2004: Count me in: Special education in an era of standards. *Education Week, 23*(7).

Quenemoen, R., Thompson, S., & Thurlow, M. (2003). *Measuring academic achievement of students with significant cognitive disabilities: Building understanding of alternate assessment scoring criteria* (Synthesis No. 50). Minneapolis, MN: University of Minnesota, National Center on Educational Outcomes. Available from http://education.umn.edu/NCEO/OnlinePubs/Synthesis50.html

Rhode Island Department of Education. (2003). *Rhode Island assessment accommodation study: Research summary.* Minneapolis, MN: University of Minnesota, National Center on Educational Outcomes. Available from http://education.umn.edu/NCEO/TopicAreas/Accommodations/RhodeIsland.htm

Rouse, M., & Agbenu, R. (1998). Assessment and special educational needs: Teachers' dilemmas. *British Journal of Special Education, 25*(2), 81–87.

Rouse, M., & Florian, L. (In press). Inclusion and achievement: student achievement in secondary schools with higher and lower proportions of pupils designated as having special educational needs. *International Journal of Inclusive Education.*

Rouse, M., & Florian, L. (1997). Inclusive education in the marketplace. *International Journal of Inclusive Education, 1*(4), 323–336.

Sammons, P., Mortimore, P., & Thomas, S. (1996). Do schools perform consistently across outcomes and areas? In J. Gray, D. Reynolds, C. Fitz-Gibbon & D. Jesson (Eds.), *Merging traditions: The future of school effectiveness and school improvement.* London: Cassell.

School Curriculum and Assessment Authority (SCAA). (1996). *Planning the curriculum for pupils with profound and multiple learning difficulties.* London: SCAA.

Shriner, J. G., & DeStefano, L. (2003). Participation and accommodation in state assessment: The role of Individualized Education Programs. *Exceptional Children, 26*(2), 9–16.

Simpson, M. A., Gong, B., & Marion, S. (2005, November 7–8). *Effect of minimum cell sizes and confidence interval sizes for special education subgroups on school-level AYP determinations.* Paper presented at the Longitudinal Modeling of Student Achievement Conference, College Park, MD.

Sireci, S. G., Li, S., & Scarpati, S. (2003). *The effects of test accommodation on test performance: A review of the literature* (Research Report No. 485). Washington, DC: Board on Testing and Assessment, National Academy of Sciences.

Thompson, S., Johnstone, C., Thurlow, M., & Altmen, J. (2005) *2005 State special education outcomes: Steps forward in a decade of change.* Minneapolis, MN: University of Minnesota, National Centre on Educational Outcomes. retrieved April 12, 2006, from http://education.umn.edu/nceo/OnlinePubs/2005Statereport.htm

Thompson, S. J., Thurlow, M., & Moore, M. (2003). *Putting it all together: Including students with disabilities in assessment and accountability systems* (Policy Directions No. 16). Minneapolis, MN: University of Minnesota, National Center on Educational Outcomes. Available from http://education.umn.edu/NCEO/OnlinePubs/olicy16.htm

Thurlow, M. L. (2004). Biting the bullet: Including special-needs students in accountability systems. In S. Fuhrman & R. Elmore (Eds.), *Redesigning accountability systems for education.* New York: Columbia Teachers College Press.

Thurlow, M.L., & Wiley, H.I. (2004). Almost there in public reporting of assessment results for students with disabilities (Technical Report 39). Minneapolis, MN: University of Minnesota, National Center on Educational Outcomes.

Tomlinson, S. (1982). *A sociology of special education.* London: Routledge & Kegan Paul.

U.S. Department of Education. (2005). *US Department of Education's fiscal year 2005 performance and accountability report,* Washington, DC: Author.

Wedell, K. (1988). The new act: A special need for vigilance. *British Journal of Special Education, 15*(3), 98–101.

Wedell, K. (2005). What is reasonable progress for pupils? *British Journal of Special Education, 32*(2), 105–106.

Ysseldyke, J., & Bielinski, J. (2002). Effect of different methods of reporting and reclassification on trends in test scores for students with disabilities. *Exceptional Children, 68*(2), 189–200.

Zatta, M., and Pullin, D. (2004, April 10). Education and alternate assessment for students with significant cognitive disabilities: Implications for educators. *Education Policy Analysis Archives, 12*(16). Retrieved April 5, 2005 from http://epaa.asu.edu/epaa/v12n16/

The challenge of inclusion

8

Disability rights in education

Marcia Rioux

The best reparation for the suffering of victims and communities – and the highest recognition of their efforts – is the transformation of our society into one that makes a living reality of the human rights for which they struggled. (Mandela, 1999)

It then occurred to me that the right to be the same … and the right to be different … were not opposed to each other. On the contrary, the right to be the same in terms of fundamental civil, political, legal, economic and social rights provided the foundation for the expression of difference through choice in the sphere of culture, lifestyle and personal priorities. In other words, provided that difference was not used to maintain inequality, subordination, injustice and marginalisation. (Sachs, 1997, p. 15)

A recent development in understanding education is to contextualize it from the perspective of human rights, that is, to put it in the framework of social justice. However, it is by no means certain that the entitlement to education as a human right will be able to defeat the overbearing technology and pedagogical theory that have become the evidence base on which to judge the capacity of children to learn and the ability of people to participate in our current education systems. Added to this are the public attitudes that reflect a hegemonic economic analysis favouring the idea that the economic well-being of nations is dependent on schools training a productive labour force. This is furthered by the privatization of schools in many countries, which has in some cases, resulted in class-based and race-based segregation in those schools. These are powerful inhibitors to the right to education for those who are 'different'. Difference has been used to marginalize many in the school industry.

Education is influenced by a variety of social, economic and environmental factors, and not just by access to school. Equity in education is a commitment of the pubic education system to social justice. To implement a rights-based approach to education requires using human rights as a framework for pedagogical theory, for access to places of learning, for testing of capacity and for measuring success. It makes principles of human rights integral to the design, implementation and evaluation of policies and programmes, and it means assessing the human rights implications of education policy, programmes and legislation.

A human rights and social justice approach enables the use of various categories of rights and recognizes how rights have to be a concern in thinking about approaches to education and social policy that enhance, rather than diminish, the well-being of all people. These include political and civil rights, such as the right to life, freedom of opinion, a fair trial, and protection from torture and violence. These are the rights that are the most common concern of nations, particularly in countries of the North and West. Human rights also, however, include economic, social and cultural rights such as the right to work, social protection, an adequate standard of living, the highest possible standards of physical and mental health, education, enjoyment of the benefits of cultural freedom and scientific progress. Finally, human rights include the right of nations to development, economic autonomy and the security of their citizens.

Education, law and rights are inextricably intertwined. The surprise is how little attention has been paid to putting a human rights lens on education despite the obvious importance of this to ensuring that people have access to it. As Amartya Sen (2000) has suggested, we need radical reform to overcome barriers of social and economic disadvantage. He advocates tolerance of diversity, equal freedoms and allowing for people's direct participation in decisions affecting their lives. 'Since participation requires basic educational skills, denying the opportunity to schooling to any group, for example, female children, is immediately contrary to the basic conditions to participatory freedom' (Sen, 2000, p. 32). Recognizing that, Sen suggests that there is a need for social action in removing deprivation, gender inequality, illiteracy and barriers to schooling. He sees communal or social benefits of basic education that are more than simply the gains of the person being educated. He maintains that a general expansion of education and literacy in a region can facilitate social change, including the reduction of fertility and mortality as well as helping to enhance economic progress from which everyone benefits. In other words, education is not just about reading and writing, it is about population control, environment, health and well-being.

The questions that we are left with are: how far down the road we are to ensuring that all children have access to rights-based education? What is the opposition to the evident benefit that can be claimed by inclusion and the entrenchment of the right to education? What is the international context of this right as a matter of social justice? What have the courts been able to provide? What are the prevailing attitudes towards a right to education and the opposition that blocks its entrenchment?

Despite international recognition of the importance of education as a fundamental right (UN General Assembly, 1989), it is not uniformly provided. Estimates report that there are 113 million children worldwide with no access to primary education and 880 million illiterate adults (UNESCO & Peppler Barry, 2000). Universal access to education and knowledge is still a distant goal. The chance of being denied schooling is much greater for some children than for others, with girls and those with disabilities having much less chance than others, even within the same economic class.

The United Nations High Commission has recognized the importance of universal education, calling on states 'to give full effect to the right to education and to guarantee that this right is fully recognized and exercised without discrimination … [and] to take all appropriate measures to eliminate obstacles limiting effective access to education, notably by girls … children with disabilities' (UN General Assembly, High Commissioner for Human Rights, 2004). Just as education is an issue of human rights, so too is disability.

> As a human rights issue, disability is not about the medical condition of people, it is about social justice, about fairness, and about opportunities to participate in everyday life. It is to be a part of society not to be apart from society. To understand disability in a human rights context means to recognize the inequalities that are inherent to our institutional structure. (Wills, 2000)

Moreover, 'It is to understand the international community has an obligation to all people, including those with disabilities, to address those conditions that result in social and legal exclusion and maltreatment'(Walter Eigner, in Wills, 2000). The onus is most often on the individual to fit within the system, not on the system to fit the individual. Professionals retain the power and expertise and, though they may be well intentioned, they are compelled to make decisions about what is in a person's 'best interests' that may contradict the person's own goals and desires. Interventions based on ideas about disability as an individual pathology, which are intended to be beneficial, can at times compromise an individual's rights and equality (Rioux, 2001, 2003).

We are then challenged to think about education as education, not as special education and not as benevolence. Within the framework of the disabled persons' movement for human rights, equal opportunity, citizenship and development, the first priority is access to basic essentials including income, housing, public transportation and education. School is a place for children to learn to reach their full potential. Education is arguably 'both an end in itself, that is, a process through which personal development and respect are obtained and a means to an end, that is, an integral part of the achievement of social citizenship' (Basser, 2005, p. 534). The responsibility of the school system is to develop and sustain a place of learning that enables every child to exercise their fundamental right to education and learning. It is about the right of children to an equal place in society. And to exercise all those other rights that are dependent on that learning: to vote, to work, to participate in activities in the community and society and so on. Taking a social determinants approach to disability means examining the physical and pedagogical accessibility of schools. There is a presumption that public policy and programmes will reflect a social responsibility to reduce civic inequalities and address social and economic disadvantage that results from educational disadvantage.

The policy of labelling children based on their perceived capacity to learn often results in exclusion from school which is unjust and unjustifiable. The common practices of segregating children leads to the creation of vast numbers of children who are denied ordinary childhood experiences and the potential to live ordinary adult lives (Barnes, Mercer, & Shakespeare, 1999; Barton, 1995; Oliver, 1996). These are the children who are segregated, not just physically, but because a school or a curriculum does not take into account the very diverse and unique learning patterns of every child.

HOW THE LAW DEALS WITH EXCLUSION

A legal case in Canada, as well as one from Australia, provide some perspective on how the complicated issues related to inclusion are framed in law and in policy.

The *Eaton* case from the Canadian Supreme Court (*Eaton v. Brant County Board of Education*, 1997) is a case study of the inherent tensions and contradictions of the arguments about segregating children in education. It raises the fundamental presumptions that lurk behind arguments for exclusion. It exposes charity cloaked as technical expertise. And it unveils how easily fundamental infringements of rights can be explained away as being in the best interests of the student and the school. This is important because the *Eaton* case is often hailed as an important example of entrenching rights, of using technical expertise and pedagogical tools to find ways to give a child the greatest opportunity to learn. As with many rights issues, it is sometimes the subtleties, rather than the blatant discrimination, which tells the most.

In 1997, the Supreme Court of Canada heard an appeal in the case of Emily Eaton, a 10 year old with cerebral palsy (*Eaton v. Brant County Board of Education*, 1995). Her parents asserted an entitlement to being educated in a regular classroom in a regular public school. While Emily started school and went to her local public school for kindergarten and grade one, the School Board and the Identification, Placement and Review

Committee (IPRC[1]) decided that she should be placed in a special class for disabled students in grade 2.

As with many education systems, the system in Ontario, Canada allows the School Board to decide who is an 'exceptional student' – that is, a student whose 'behavioural, communicational, intellectual, physical or multiple exceptionalities are such that s/he is considered to need placement in a special education programme by a committee established by the board.' The school remains responsible for the education of the child in providing special education programmes and special education services without cost to the families. This has to be done with due process of early and ongoing identification of the learning abilities and needs and with an appeal process for parents. Every board of education therefore has to have an IPRC for this purpose.

Students who are identified as exceptional, either because they have disabilities, or because their educational needs are outside the range of what is offered in a regular age-appropriate programme, are provided with either remedial or enriched instruction appropriate to their needs. Each student is required to have an individual education plan.

At the Special Education Appeal Board the decision was that it was in Emily's best interests, based on expert evidence, to receive her education in a special school. Emily Eaton's parents appealed the decision to the Courts, believing it was Emily's constitutional right under the equality clause of the Canadian Constitution for Emily to be educated along with her peers (*Canadian Charter of Rights and Freedoms, Part I of the Constitution Act, 1982*).[2] In the ruling from the Ontario Court of Appeal (*Eaton v. Brant County Board of Education*, 1995), the Court found that the Ontario Education Act 1990 and subsequent regulations to the Act were unconstitutional under the equality rights provisions of the Canadian Charter of Rights and Freedoms, because they did not provide the equality rights of children with disabilities to be educated with their peers. Justice Arbour (now the United Nations High Commissioner for

Human Rights), writing for the Court found that: 'Inclusion into the main school population is a benefit to Emily because without it, she would have fewer opportunities to learn how other children work and how they live. And they will not learn that she can live with them and they with her' (*Eaton v. Brant County Board of Education*, 1995). Arguing as well that pedagogical theories can be inherently exclusionary and on that basis questionable, she found that: 'In short, the *Charter* requires that, regardless of its perceived pedagogical merit, a non-consensual exclusionary placement be recognised as discriminatory and not resorted to unless alternatives are proven inadequate' (*Eaton v. Brant County Board of Education*, 1995).

On appeal to the Supreme Court of Canada, however, the decision that was rendered did not enable Emily to go to school with her peers. Despite making clear that inclusion of children in the regular schools should be considered to be the norm, the Court fell back onto the presumptive premises which suggest that selective, evidence-based exclusion is an appropriate model for organizing learning.

The arguments were relatively straightforward and reinforced the inequity that is masked by expert evidence about pedagogical theory that is discriminatory – evidence-based discrimination that appeals to an argument that children with disabilities fall outside the range of what is offered in a regular age-appropriate programme. 'Conflicting opinions from expert witnesses have become a consistent feature of similar court or tribunal hearings in both the United States and Australia. Experts provide evidence according to their own informed educational philosophies about inclusion or in some cases according to their own stereotypical attitudes, values and beliefs' (Keeffe-Martin, 2001, p. 30).

The *Purvis* case in Australia (2003) also illustrates the underlying contradictions that arise in the decisions by school authorities when they determine that a disabled child cannot be in the regular school system. The case involved a disabled student who was suspended and later expelled from school because of violent and disruptive behaviour. In 1998, Mr Purvis, the foster father of Daniel Hogan, complained to the Human Rights and Equal Opportunity Commission (HREOC) that the State of New South Wales discriminated against Daniel on the ground of his disability. The Commissioner appointed by HREOC found that the school had treated Mr Hogan less favourably than it would have treated another student in similar circumstances because it did not adjust the policy to his needs; it did not provide teachers with the skills to deal with his behavioural problems and it did not get expert expertise on how to deal with the problems that were manifested. This decision was subsequently overturned in the Federal Court, a decision that was upheld by the High Court. The majority of the Court accepted that less favourable treatment because of behaviour that is the result of disability can be less favourable treatment because of the disability. However, in considering whether there was a duty to accommodate that would have required the school to make adjustments to ameliorate Daniel's behaviour, the Court found that under the terms of the Act a positive duty of that nature could not be implied. In a dissenting decision by Justices McHugh and Kirby, they argued that the case should have turned on 'the failure of an educational authority to treat Mr. Hogan equally with other students by taking steps that would have eliminated or substantially reduced his disruptive behaviour and allowed him to enjoy the same quality education as his fellow students enjoyed ... To avoid a finding of discrimination against a disabled person, a person may have to take steps that cause expense and inconvenience to that person' (*Purvis v New South Wales (Department of Education and Training)*, 2003, p. 6). The ruling of the Court suggests that it is not possible to require that the education system provide the accommodations necessary to enable a student to gain equal benefit from a school.

The recognition that a student's behaviour is the result of the complex and unpredictable interaction of the student, the school environment and the pedagogy in the school is left unexamined in deciding that the school cannot cope with the student and the student cannot cope with school. Far from identifying the student's difference as a means of providing the student with additional support, it identifies the student's behaviour as an individual characteristic that is the cause of his behaviour without any consideration of the part that the school system itself plays in that behaviour. It justifies discrimination without consideration of the environmental factors that may be the source of the behaviour.

The use of these cases is illustrative and is not to suggest that Canada and Australia are somehow in the backwaters of inclusive education. Both countries have, in fact, been reasonably progressive in initiating and furthering inclusive education. Their courts have tried to struggle with equality and rights in the context of education, without being overshadowed and trumped by the notion of the least restrictive alternative. What is clear, however, is that even in jurisdictions where inclusion is held to be the desired norm, that right is circumscribed by conventional notions of education, of the place of difference within that system and of the capacity to learn in a conventional manner. What the student has a right to is to show that he or she can conform to the pedagogical methods and the policies and procedures of the local school board. The right to equal and non-segregated education would require a significantly different set of standards – where the onus of changing would fall on the school authority rather than on the individual student.

MYTHS THAT DENY INCLUSION

Both *Eaton* and *Purvis* are exemplars of the complicated issues raised by inclusive education and they suggest a number of presumptive and prevalent ideas which underpin the idea that selective exclusion is the best model for organizing learning. These premises have become fundamental to the justification used by courts and policy-makers to maintain segregated education for people with disabilities in the face of disability discrimination laws, constitutional equality provisions and disability and education policies that have a contrary intent. The principle of 'separate but equal', the principle that was defeated as the basis for desegregating race-based education in the United States, in *Brown v Board of Education* (1954)[3], is precisely the principle that is relied upon in many arguments to segregate.[4] It is argued that separate and segregated, is both equal, preferable, and in the best interests of the student who is different (MacMillan & Hendrick, 1993). This assumption is often held as fact and underpins many of the policies and programmes that are in place.

The underlying myths of the arguments for the benefit of separate but equal are found in twenty-first-century education philosophy and practice. First, most countries stand by the assertion that education is universal and is universally available, independent of personal characteristics. Education has been held as both a right and a necessity in democratic society. Consequently, in most northern countries it is compulsory; thereby ensuring that a basic set of social values will be learned by all children. Historically, disability has been viewed as a matter of deviance, deficiency or disease – a failure to achieve a standard of normalcy. It is the standard of normalcy that has been the dividing line between those who go to regular schools and those who are not given the choice of attending regular state-funded schools. Schools (or school boards) are generally presumed to have the ability to distinguish those individual students who will be able to benefit from their pedagogical skills and those who will not; those who, in other words, can meet the standard of normalcy on which they base their teaching methodology. The error underlying this thinking is the inference that disability is a condition inherent to an individual, to a student, rather than the structural conditions and in particular, the pedagogical practices of the school (Underwood, McGhie-Richmond, & Jordan, 2005). The supposition that there is no necessity to investigate how the structural conditions of schooling affect a

child's ability to benefit from regular education is a significant underpinning of the type of reasoning that results in the segregation of children while maintaining that there is universal education.

The second myth is that the education that is available is equitable. It is argued that a supposedly fair spectrum of qualities is targeted in education – that is, that there is a normative student to whom curriculum content and pedagogical methods can be directed (Kauffman, 1999; Sasso, 2001). If this is done well, the argument goes, then students will rise to the expectations and people who fail are legitimate failures. The structure of the process of targeting, however, makes it difficult to question whether the narrow spectrum of intellectual properties targeted is the entire range of properties on which education ought to focus. Another central part of the educational experience is the way in which students adapt to the learning environment. Even if a student meets the norms expected of the student body, there is no guarantee that he or she will succeed in meeting the standards that are imposed. How well a student does is substantially impacted by the skills of the teacher (Jordan & Stanovich, 2003; Kagan, 1992). The more homogeneous the students and the more the teacher is like the students in class, culture and intellectual ability, the greater the chance the student will achieve high grades. Arguments that rely on the equity of education then provide an easy rationale for excluding students because they cannot make it, a finding that is then proved by the student's lack of success.

The third idea that contributes to the argument that selective exclusion is the best model for organizing learning is the myth of meritocracy. There is a widespread belief in education, in government and in the public, that the way in which the current education system operates is necessary for the social and economic system to function. The public school system is upheld as an objective, dispassionate, impartial, rational mechanism for ensuring that children learn and for differentiating the abilities of students to determine who will have access to higher levels of education, credentials and jobs. Arguments in favour of school exit exams in the United States (and other jurisdictions) generally include the case that they allow the state to remain competitive in the market economy (Karumanchery & Portelli, 2005; Vinson, Gibson, & Ross, 2001). The school system then is an important pillar of the meritocracy,[5] which is not only justified but is necessary for the economic efficiency of any society. A presupposition of inequality is essential to that notion.

Notions of meritocracy include the essentialist argument that the structure of the current education system is necessary for social and economic growth and that it ensures equality based on ability. When grounded in the notion of meritocracy, equality is based on a narrowly defined and measurable set of abilities that contribute to the social and economic order rather than on human characteristics or attributes. This slips quickly into the argument that the economic and social distributions in society are a reflection of biological capacity. So it is fair that some people have more and some less because it simply reflects their contribution to society. Education is the linchpin to the argument because it is the school system which is responsible for knowing and judging intellectual ability and thus justifying the social and economic place of individuals. The school system is structured then to act as a sorting system for the long-term social and economic order rather than to equalize opportunities. Those who fail, or are filtered out, are, for the most part, denied the desirable social outcomes and benefits.

The outcome of these ideas and arguments for selective exclusion, far from being benign, fundamentally denies the ability of people who are different, from being able to exercise their right to education. The dilemma of difference[6] is not then about, as it should be, being identified as a way of being privileged for additional attention. It is instead about being identified for justifying disadvantage (Minow, 1985, 1990). It reverts to the argument of separate but equal, a fundamentally flawed principle that was discredited 50 years ago.

INTERNATIONAL RECOGNITION OF DISABILITY RIGHTS IN EDUCATION

It seems clear that the right to education is a universal right. Significantly, international initiatives from the United Nations, UNESCO, the World Bank and non-governmental organizations jointly contribute to a growing consensus that all children have the right to be educated together, independent of disability or learning difficulty (Quinn, Degener, & Bruce, 2002). Thus the human right to education is expressed in education systems that are inclusive of all learners.

In the 1982 UN *World Programme of Action Concerning Disabled Persons* there was a statement of the importance of the preference of inclusive practices in education.

> Member states should adopt policies, which recognize the rights of disabled persons to equal educational opportunities with others. The education of disabled persons should as far as possible take place in the general school system. Responsibility for their education should be placed upon the educational authorities and laws regarding compulsory education should include children with all ranges of disabilities, including the most severely disabled. (UN General Assembly, 1982)

In 1993, the United Nations (UN) General Assembly adopted the *Standard Rules on the Equalization of Opportunities for Persons with Disabilities*[7] (UN General Assembly & High Commissioner for Human Rights, 1993) which sets an agenda for promoting inclusive and equal education for children with disabilities. The Rules specifically mandate inclusive education with attention to disability issues forming an integral part of national educational planning, curriculum development and school organization. Supports and services needed to ensure accessibility of mainstream education are also addressed. Specific attention is paid to structural or systemic strategies, widely communicated policy, flexible curriculum, and the provision of quality materials, ongoing teacher training and support for teachers. Special education is considered only in those cases where the mainstream school system does not yet adequately address the needs of students with disabilities, and the Rules specify that it should be aimed at preparing students for full inclusion.

The *Convention on the Rights of the Child* (UN General Assembly, 1989), an authoritative international standard, sets a framework for education for all, which has been taken up internationally as a goal in policy and practice, although how far that includes children with disabilities when it is interpreted is unclear. In addition, a number of important international conferences have also addressed standards that ought to guide national priorities in issues of the education of children with disabilities. This includes the World Conference on Education for All in Jomtien, Thailand in 1990 (UN Development Programme, UNESCO, UNICEF, & World Bank, 1990), *The World Declaration on Education for All (WDEA)*, adopted at that meeting, reaffirms the principle of integrated education for all children with learning or educational needs (UNESCO, 1990). The Salamanca *Statement and Framework for Action* (UNESCO & Ministry of Education and Science Spain, 1994) has the clearest support to date recognizing inclusive education. Nearly 125 countries have signed this declaration which proclaims that every child is unique and has a fundamental right to education. The conference participants agreed to a Framework of Action which stipulated the inclusion of all children with disabilities in regular schools, under the rubric of Education for All. Article 2 pointed to inclusion as a model of best practice: '[R]egular schools with inclusive orientation are the most effective means of combating discriminatory attitudes, creating welcoming communities, building inclusive society and achieving education for all' (UNESCO & Ministry of Education and Science Spain, 1994). Inclusion and participation are framed as 'essential to human dignity and to the enjoyment and exercise of human rights' (UNESCO & Ministry of Education and Science Spain, 1994, section 1, para. 6, p. 11). Its guiding principle is that ordinary schools should accommodate all children,

regardless of their physical, intellectual, emotional, social, linguistic and other differences. The Framework directs that all educational policies should stipulate that disabled children attend whatever school they would have attended if they did not have a disability. Governments are called upon to make improving education a priority and to adopt the principle of inclusive education as a matter of law and policy. This was followed in April 2000 with the World Education Forum in Dakar, Senegal, sponsored by UNESCO (see UNESCO & Peppler Barry, 2000).[8] In response to the concern that education for all applied to children with disabilities created some difficulties, the frameworks for action adopted at these conferences laid out plans of action to work towards full inclusion.

National and bilateral aid agencies, UNESCO, UNICEF, and non-governmental organizations such as Save the Children Fund, have all had demonstration programmes of inclusive education in developing economies. While these have been inconsistent in terms of their commitments to full inclusion, they have established that it is a goal towards which education has to work.

EDUCATION FOR ALL

Education for all is not education for some children some of the time. There is no evidence base that shows who deserves to enter school. The labelling of children as less able to learn or as not needing an education is evidence about pedagogy and about teaching capacity, not about children's capacity to learn. It is about curricula that are inflexible and that undermine effective learning and it is about disrespect for the child who is different – because of race, poverty, disability or some other characteristic. Children are a heterogeneous group making teaching each child in the unique manner that their individual strengths and weaknesses demand an essential underlying premise of education for all. The barriers that exist for learning come from many sources including curricula, laws, segregating policies, technical jargon, specialist expertise and the foreign aid that builds segregated schools in some countries. They are also found in the redefinition of education as primarily an economic activity and in the development of schools for particular elite groups.

The negative attitudes and the lack of knowledge and understanding of difference and diversity are not solved by dividing and excluding. The challenges that children present because of their differences, should not provide an excuse for inaction and exclusion. The key to social tolerance is to educate and empower children through learning and development.

NOTES

1 The legislative process for special education is based on an identification process which relies on an assessment by a doctor or a psychologist. After the student is assessed their name is put forward for identification to the IPRC. These meetings are held on an annual basis for each exceptional student. If a parent does not agree with the decision of the IPRC they can appeal through a Special Educational Tribunal, which reviews decisions.

2 See also Rioux, H. M., & Frazee, C. (1999).

3 'In the field of public education, the doctrine of "separate but equal" has no place. Separate education facilities are inherently unequal' (*Brown v. Board of Education*, 1954).

4 That children with disability will face the same type of stigma from segregated educational settings was recognized by the US Court in *Mills v. Board of Education of the District of Columbia* (1972) which quoted *Brown* extensively.

5 The meritocracy has been justified because it has been presumed that social and economic efficiency and progress are necessary. These are dependent on identifying and rewarding people whose natural capacity sustains the social well-being, the culture and the progress of society.

6 Martha Minow refers to the following question as the difference: 'when does treating people differently emphasize their difference and stigmatize or hinder them on that basis? and when does treating people the same become insensitive to their difference and likely to stigmatize or hinder them on that basis?' (Minow, 1990, p. 20).

7 Rule 6 of the *Standard Rules* states: 'States should recognize the principle of equal primary, secondary and tertiary educational opportunities for children, youth and adults with disabilities, in integrated settings. They should ensure that education of persons with disabilities is an integral part of the educational system' (UN General Assembly & High Commissioner for Human Rights, 1993).

8 This Forum, sponsored by UNESCO, was a follow-up to the World Declaration on Education for All in Jomtien, Thailand in 1990.

REFERENCES

Barnes, C., Mercer, G., & Shakespeare, T. (1999). *Exploring Disability: A Sociological Introduction*. Malden, MA: Polity Press.

Barton, L. (1995). Segregated special education: Some critical observations. In G. Zarb (Ed.), *Removing disabling barriers* (pp. 27–37). London: Policy Studies Institute.

Basser, L. A. (2005). Justice for all? The challenge of realizing the right to education for children with disabilities. *The Journal of Gender, Race and Justice, 8*, 531–559.

Brown v. Board of Education (1954). 347 U.S. 483.

Canadian Charter of Rights and Freedoms, Part I of the Constitution Act (1982) being schedule B to the Canada Act 1982 (U.K.), 1982, c. 11, s. 15 (1) (2).

Eaton v. Brant County Board of Education (1995) 22 O.R. (3d) 1, at 21 (C.A.).

Eaton v. Brant County Board of Education (1997) 1 S.C.R. 241.

Education Act, R.S.O. (1990) c. E.2.

Jordan, A., & Stanovich, P. (2003). Teachers' personal epistemological beliefs about students with disabilities as indicators of effective teaching practices. *Journal of Research in Special Educational Needs, 3*(1), 1–14.

Kagan, D. M. (1992). Implications of research on teacher belief. *Educational Psychologist, 27*, 65–90.

Karumanchery, L. L., & Portelli, J. P. (2005). Democratic values in bureaucratic structures: Interrogating the essential tensions. In N. Bascia, A. Cumming, A. Datnow, K. Leithwood & D. Livingstone (Eds.), *International Handbook of Educational Policy* (pp. 329–349). Dordrecht, Netherlands: Springer.

Kauffman, J. M. (1999). Commentary: Today's special education and its message for tomorrow. *Journal of Special Education, 32*(4), 244–254.

Keefe-Martin, M. (2001). Legislation, case law and current issues in inclusion: An analysis of trends in the United States and Australia. *Australia and New Zealand Journal of Law and Education, 6*(1–2), 25–46.

MacMillan, D. L., & Hendrick, I. G. (1993). Evolution and legacies. In J. I. Goodlad & T. C. Lovitt (Eds.), *Inte-*

grating general and special education (pp. 23–48). New York: Merrill, an imprint of Macmillan Publishing Company.

Mandela, N. (1999). *Opening address by President Nelson Mandela in the special debate on the report of the Truth and Reconciliation Commission (TRC), 25 February.* Retrieved from http://www.info.gov.za/speeches/1999/99225_trc-ma99_10201.htm

Mills v. Board of Education of the District of Columbia, D.D.C. (1972) 348 F. Supp. 866.

Minow, M. (1985). Learning to live with the dilemma of difference: Bilingual and special education. *Law and Contemporary Problems, 48*(2), 157–211.

Minow, M. (1990). *Making all the difference: Inclusion, exclusion, and American law.* Ithaca, NY: Cornell University Press.

Oliver, M. (1996). *Understanding disability: From theory to practice.* New York: St. Martin's Press.

Purvis v New South Wales (Department of Education and Training) (2003) HCA 62 (11 November 2003).

Quinn, G., Degener, T., & Bruce, A. (2002). *Human rights and disability: The current use and future potential of United Nations human rights instruments in the context of disability.* New York: United Nations, Office of the High Commissioner for Human Rights.

Rioux, H. M. (2001). Bending towards justice. In L. Barton (Ed.), *Disability, politics and the struggle for change* (pp. 34–48). London: David Fulton.

Rioux, H. M. (2003). On second thought: Constructing knowledge, law, disability and inequality. In S. S. Herr, H. H. Koh & O. L. Gostin (Eds.), *The human rights of persons with intellectual disabilities: Different but equal* (pp. 287–317). Oxford: Oxford University Press.

Rioux, H. M., & Frazee, C. (1999). The Canadian framework for disability equality rights. In M. Jones & L. A. Basser Marks (Eds.), *Disability, divers-ability, and legal change* (pp. 171–187). The Hague & Boston, MA: M. Nijhoff Publishers.

Sachs, A. (1997). Human rights in the twenty first century: Real dichotomies, false antagonisms. In T. Cromwell, A. D. Pinard & H. Dumont (Eds.), *Human Rights in the 21st Century: Prospects, Institutions and Processes = Les Droits de la Personne au 21ème Siecle: Perspectives et Modes de Protection* (pp. 7–19). Montreal: Editions Themis/Canadian Institute for the Administration of Justice.

Sasso, G. M. (2001). The retreat from inquiry and knowledge in special education. *Journal of Special Education, 34*(4), 178–193.

Sen, A. K. (2000). *Development as Freedom.* New York: Anchor Books.

United Nations (UN) Development Programme, UNESCO, UNICEF, & World Bank. (1990). *Final report: World Conference on Education for All, Meeting Basic Learning Needs, 5–9 March 1990, Jomtien, Thailand.* New York: Inter-Agency Commission, WCEFA.

United Nations (UN) General Assembly. (1982). *The world programme of action concerning disabled persons, 37th regular session, December 3rd, resolution 37/52.* UN Doc. A/RES/37/52. Retrieved from http://www.un.org/esa/socdev/enable/wpa.doc

United Nations (UN) General Assembly. (1989). *Convention on the rights of the child (CRC), 61st plenary meeting, 20 November, resolution 44/25.* UN Doc. A/RES/44/25. Retrieved from http://www.un.org/documents/ga/res/44/a44r025.htm

United Nations (UN) General Assembly, High Commissioner for Human Rights. (2004). *60th session, resolution 2004/25.* UN Doc. E/CN.4/RES/2004/25.

United Nations (UN) General Assembly & High Commissioner for Human Rights. (1993). *Standard rules on the equalization of opportunities for persons with disabilities, 48th session, 85th mtg., resolution 48/96.* UN Document A/RES/48/96.

Underwood, K., McGhie-Richmond, D. R., & Jordan, A. (2005). The acquisition of effective instructional practices for students with disabilities in inclusive classrooms. *Inclusive and Supportive Education Congress, 1–4 August, Glasgow, Scotland.*

United Nations Educational, Scientific, and Cultural Organization (UNESCO). (1990). *The World Declaration on Education for All (WDEA), adopted by the World Conference on Education for All, Meeting Basic Learning Needs, 5–9 March, Jomtien, Thailand.* Retrieved from http://www.unesco.ru/files/docs/educ/wdefa.pdf

United Nations Educational, Scientific, and Cultural Organization (UNESCO) & Ministry of Education and Science Spain. (1994). *The Salamanca Statement and Framework for Action on special needs education, adopted by the World Conference on Special Needs Education: Access and Quality, 7–10 June, Salamanca, Spain.* UNESCO. retrieved from: http://www.unesco.org/education/pdf/SALAMA_E.PDF

United Nations Educational, Scientific, and Cultural Organization (UNESCO) & Peppler Barry, U. (2000). *The Dakar Framework for Action: Education for All: Meeting our collective commitments, including six regional frameworks for action, adopted by the World Education Forum, 26–28 April, Dakar, Senegal.* UNESCO, Paris. Retrieved from http://unesdoc.unesco.org/images/0012/001211/121147e.pdf

Vinson, K. D., Gibson, R., & Ross, E. W. (2001). High-stakes testing and standardization: The threat to authenticity. *Progressive Perspectives [Monograph Series], 3*(2).

Wills, D. G. (2000). Embedding a human rights culture: Starting with education for all. *International Special Education Congress (ISEC), 24–28 July, University of Manchester, England.*

9

Inclusion as a strategy for achieving education for all

Susan Peters

FRAMING THE ISSUE: OVERVIEW AND SIGNIFICANCE

In a report for the United Nations Children's Fund (UNICEF), Bengt Lindqvist, the United Nations Special Rapporteur on Human Rights and Disability, provided the following challenge:

> A dominant problem in the disability field is the lack of access to education for both children and adults with disabilities. As education is a fundamental right for all, enshrined in the Universal Declaration of Human Rights, and protected through various international conventions, this is a very serious problem. In a majority of countries, there is a dramatic difference in the educational opportunities provided for disabled children and those provided for non-disabled children. It will simply not be possible to realize the goal of Education for All if we do not achieve a complete change in the situation. (Lindqvist, 1999, p. 7)

Following the 1990 World Congress on Education for All (EFA) in Jomtien, the Dakar Framework for Action adopted a World Declaration on Education for All in 2000 which established the goal of universal access to primary school education for every girl and boy by 2015. Education for All also clearly iden-

tified inclusive education as one of the key strategies to address issues of marginalization and exclusion for vulnerable children, notably girls and disabled children. 'Inclusion was seen as the fundamental philosophy throughout UNESCO's programmes and the guiding principle for the development of EFA' (UNESCO, 2002, p. 17).

Inclusive education in the context of the goals of Education for All is a complex issue. Unlike health and labour markets, disability includes an array of issues crossing health, education, social welfare, and employment sectors (Cameron & Valentine, 2001). As a result, the development of policy faces challenges if it is to avoid fragmented, uneven, and difficult to access services. Inclusive education may also be implemented at different levels, embrace different goals, be based on different motives, reflect different classifications of special education needs, and provide services in different contexts. For example, Kobi identified six levels of inclusive education: physical, terminological, administrative, social, curricular and psychological (Meijer, Pijl, & Hegarty, 1994). Goals may include integration of 'special education needs'

(SEN) students in classrooms or changing societal attitudes to promote societal integration. Specific objectives may focus either on improved educational performance and quality of education, or on autonomy, self-determination, proportionality, consumer satisfaction or parental choice. Some of these goals may conflict and produce tensions. Similarly, motives for inclusive education may derive from dissatisfaction with existing systems, from economic or resource allocation concerns, or from a vision of educational reform. Finally, SEN services may be viewed as a continuum of placement options (multi-track approach), as a distinct education system (two-track approach) or as a continuum of services within one placement – the general education school and classroom (one-track approach) (EADSNE, 2003).

A further layer of complexity involves the definition of special educational need. Classification systems vary to a great extent from country to country, and even within countries. Some countries have adopted a definition based on need for special education services, and do not count or label students. In England and Wales, for example, the *Warnock Report* (DES, 1978) defined a special educational need on this basis. Other countries apply a two-tier definition based on extent and type of disability. These countries base entitlement to special education on two conditions: under-educational performance (observed or predicted), and 'objective cause'. For those countries that use traditional 'objective cause' labels to determine special education need, categories vary. For example, Denmark uses two categories, while Poland and the United States have more than 10 categories of disability. Most countries use the categorical approach with a range of 4–10 types of special needs. In countries of the South,[1] four categories/types of disability are usually recognized: physical disability, blindness, deafness, and cognitive impairment (sometimes referred to as mental retardation). Further, countries may also include non-disabled individuals in special education needs categories; for example, refugee children, gifted and tal-ented children (who may also have impairments), and those with various learning difficulties and disadvantages that result in educational underperformance (for example, street and working children, children from nomadic populations, children who have lost their parents through AIDS or civil strife, children from linguistic, ethnic or cultural minorities).

In an attempt to standardize classifications, ISCED-97 (International Standard Classification of Education) has been adopted by Organisation for Economic Co-operation and Development (OECD) member countries. This definition uses a supply-side approach based on resources; that is, the definition recognizes 'those with SEN are defined by additional public and/or private resources provided to support their education' (OECD, 2000, p. 8). Additional resources can be personnel (for example, student/pupil ratios in classrooms or teacher training), material (for example, curriculum adaptations), or financial (for example, formulas that set aside money for SEN within the regular budget allocation). This resource approach to defining SEN brings together students with a wide variety of learning difficulties, based on perceived causes of educational failure. The tripartite system below is being used in a growing number of countries participating in an OECD cross-national comparative study.

> Category A: students whose disabilities have clear biological causes
> Category B: students who are experiencing learning difficulties for no particular reason
> Category C: students who have difficulties arising from disadvantages

This tripartite categorization system places students with different disabilities in the same category. This 'cross-categorical' approach represents a growing trend. For example, a 2002 US report of the President's Commission on Excellence in Special Education (PCESE) questions the 'proliferation of categories' and 'could not identify firm practical or scientific reasons supporting the current classification of disabilities in IDEA' (PCESE, 2002, p. 22). This report noted that 90 per cent of all students served under the Individuals with Disabilities Education Act (IDEA) included 'high-incidence' disabilities: that is, those with specific learning disabilities, speech and language impairments, emotional disturbance and mild mental retardation. For these students, the Commission expressed concern that classification systems 'waste valuable special education resources in determining which category a child fits into rather than providing the instructional interventions the child requires' (p. 22).

Variance in identification and classification of school-aged children and youth with disabilities and SEN makes it difficult to estimate potential demand (that is, incidence and prevalence rates) for education to meet their needs. However, a 1993 report prepared by the Special Rapporteur on Human Rights and Disability found that at least 1 out of 10 persons in the majority of countries has a physical, mental or sensory impairment (Despouy, 1993). Because these persons reside within families, it is estimated that at least 25 per cent of the entire population is affected by the presence of disability (Lansdown, 2001). Of 500 million disabled people worldwide, 120–150 million are children. Eighty per cent reside in developing countries. Further, there is every indication that this number is growing due to global conditions of increasing poverty, armed conflict, child labour practices, violence and abuse, and HIV/AIDS. For example, the International Labor Organization (ILO) reports that of the 250 million children working, more than two-thirds (69 per cent) are affected by injury or illness. Almost a third of all people living with HIV/AIDS are between 15 and 24 years of age, or 10 million children and youth of whom 2.2 million live in sub-Saharan Africa (Lansdown, 2001, p. 9).

Poverty and EFA

A significant number of impairments are caused by factors related to poverty: malnutrition is the leading cause, followed by infectious diseases, non-infectious diseases, and congenital diseases. In addition, an estimated 15.6 per cent (78 million) impairments are caused by accidents, trauma, and/or war (Lansdown, 2001). In developing countries, 50 per cent of all disabilities are acquired before the age of 15, so that the estimated prevalence of school-aged children and youth with disabilities may be higher than the estimated incidence rate of 10 per cent. When the number of children with 'objective cause' disabilities is added to the total number of children identified with special education needs, OECD estimates that between 15–20 per cent of all students will require special needs education during their primary and secondary school years (OECD, 1999). These figures may also vary widely in urban and rural populations. Coleridge (1996) reports a probable urban bias in prevalence due to greater risk of injury, the attraction of possible services and institutions, better medical care, and the possibility of begging. However, Coleridge points out that some rural areas may have higher than average prevalence rates, citing as an example some villages in Zaire where more than 30 per cent of the population may be affected by river blindness (Coleridge, 1996, p. 106). Finally, estimates of the percentage of disabled children and youth who attend school in developing countries range from fewer than 1 per cent (*Salamanca Statement and Framework for Action*, para. 10, UNESCO, 1994a) to 5 per cent (Habibi 1999).

Gender differences and EFA

The OECD (2000) reports a consistent gender imbalance in the identification of SEN. An approximate 60:40 ratio of males to females appeared across all cross-national categories in special education systems. The report concludes, 'This robust finding is not easy to interpret, but its ubiquity makes it tempting to suggest that it reflects a systematic difference in the extent to which males and females are perceived to have special education needs'

(OECD, 2000, p. 102). This consistent gender difference raises important policy issues related to identification and treatment of girls and boys (Evans, 2000).

In short, there are problems in defining and providing for the significant numbers of disabled children and youth many of whom are excluded from educational opportunities for primary and secondary schooling. The usefulness of categorical classifications of disability is being questioned in terms of their cost-effectiveness and their ability to identify needed services. Environmental factors play a significant role in disabling the vast majority of students. Exclusion, poverty and disability are linked. Education is widely recognized as a means to develop human capital, to improve economic performance, and to enhance people's capabilities and choices so that exclusion from education can result in a staggering loss of freedom and productivity in the labour market (Metts, 2000, p. 71). The international community (at least at the policy level) has recognized education as a fundamental child right and has committed to a framework for action to address this right, and to redress exclusion as directed by EFA 2000.

HISTORICAL BACKGROUND: BEFORE AND AFTER SALAMANCA

In order to understand exclusion and strategies for working toward inclusion, it is necessary to examine the historical context in which they are located. The philosophy of inclusion and its operating principles originate from several key international declarations that specifically address those designated as having 'special educational needs' (SEN). The United Nations *Declaration on the Rights of Disabled Pesons* (1975) was the first of its kind to explicitly recognize the rights and needs of people with disabilities. However, the declaration defined a disabled person as one who is 'unable to ensure the necessities of normal social life due to deficiency' (UN, 1975, p. 1). Further, the goal was to 'promote inte-

gration in normal life' (UN, 1975, p. 1).

In 1982, the developers of the World Programme of Action (WPA) concerning disabled persons focused on more specific goals of prevention, rehabilitation, and equalization of opportunity. In terms of education, the WPA stated: 'Whenever possible education should take place in the ordinary school system' (UN, 1982, p. 3). The document further states that 'social attitudes ... may be the greatest barrier to participation and equality ... What is required is to focus on the ability, not on the disability of disabled persons' (p. 4). The caveat, 'whenever pedagogically possible' was to be repeated in 1990 in the Convention on the Rights of the Child (CRC). In Article 23, the CRC declared that disabled children have a right to access and integration, however these rights should be 'subject to available resources and appropriate to the child's condition' (UN, 1989).

The UN Standard Rules (1993) moved definitively towards a social model of inclusive education, and away from caveats, in Rule 6 on Education. However, the focus is still on access and equality of opportunity without addressing the question of quality.

Following closely on the heels of the UN Standard Rules, the Salamanca Statement and Framework for Action was endorsed by 92 governments and 25 international organizations at the World Conference on Special Needs Education, June 1994 in Salamanca, Spain. This key document identifies inclusive education as the means by which Education for All may be achieved. The Salamanca Statement proclaims that every child has unique characteristics, interests, abilities, and learning needs and that 'those with special education needs must have access to regular schools which should accommodate them with a child-centred pedagogy capable of meeting those needs' (UNESCO, 1994, para. 2). The Salamanca Statement also asserts that educational systems that take into account the wide diversity of children's characteristics and needs 'are the most effective means of combating discriminatory attitudes, creating welcoming communities, building an inclusive society and achieving education for all; moreover, they provide an effective education to the majority of children and improve the efficiency and ultimately the cost-effectiveness of the entire education system' (UNESCO, 1994, para. 2).

Because of the high level of global participation in its development, the Salamanca Framework for Action provides perhaps the best cross-cultural definition of inclusive education in action.

The Inclusive School
The fundamental principle of the inclusive school is that all children should learn together, wherever possible, regardless of any difficulties or differences they may have. Inclusive schools must recognize and respond to the diverse needs of their students, accommodating both different styles and rates of learning and ensuring quality education to all through appropriate curricula, organizational arrangements, teaching strategies, resource use and partnerships with their communities. There should be a continuum of support and services to match the continuum of special needs encountered in every school. (Salamanca Framework for Action, 1994, para. 7)

A growing body of research supports the Salamanca Statement and its principles (Ferguson, 1992; Baker, Wang, & Walberg, 1994; Lipsky & Gartner, 1997; Allan, 1999; Armstrong, Armstrong, & Barton, 2000; Sailor, 2002; Thomas & Glenny, 2002; Vinneau, 2002). Metts' (2000) report is typical of the evidence in support of inclusive education. Specifically, Metts cites a 1993 World Bank study of Special Education in Asia which concluded that (1) there are personal, social and economic dividends to educating primary school aged children with special education needs in mainstream schools; (2) most special education needs can be successfully and less expensively accommodated in integrated schools than in segregated institutional settings and; (3) the vast majority of children with special education needs can be cost-effectively accommodated in regular primary schools.

In assessing progress towards EFA since Jomtien, UNESCO's Final Report – Part II (2000) contains a sub-section entitled 'meeting special and diverse education needs: mak-

ing inclusive education a reality.' This sub-section contains the statement:

Concern about inclusion has evolved from a struggle in behalf of children 'having special needs' into one that challenges all exclusionary policies and practices in education as they relate to curriculum, culture and local centres of learning. Instead of focusing on preparing children to fit into existing schools, the new emphasis focuses on *preparing schools* [emphasis added] so that they can deliberately reach out to all children. It also recognizes that gains in access have not always been accompanied by increases in quality. (UNESCO, 2000, p. 18)

PARADIGMS, PROMISES AND PARADOXES

The above historical overview points to a growing realization that the environment plays a significant role in disabling many students. The new International Classification of Functioning and Disability (ICF) developed by the World Health Organization (WHO) supports this concept. Under concerted pressure from international disability rights organizations, the WHO adopted this new classification system in 2001. The ICF replaces the ICIDH-2 and organizes disability along two dimensions: functioning and disability (including body functions/structures and activities/participation in society), and contextual factors (environmental and personal). This ICF definition shifts the focus from disability as an innate deficit to disability as constructed through the interaction between the individual and the environment. This conceptual model of disability encourages focus on kinds and levels of interventions appropriate to the disablement needs of individuals within specific contexts, and is consistent with the social model of disability that is upheld by disability rights organizations and many disabled people (Dudzik & McLeod, 2000). Ingstad (2001) reports that this ICF classification system was developed using a process of consensus involving both developed and developing countries. Ingstad argues that the ICF distinctions are particularly important in many developing countries, where personhood depends more on social identity and the fulfilment of family obligations than on individual ability.

It is important to recognize the distinction between impairment and disablement. Disabled Persons International promotes the following distinction: 'Impairment is the loss or limitation of physical, mental or sensory function on a long term or permanent basis. Disablement is the loss or limitation of opportunities to take part in the normal life of the community on an equal level with others due to physical and social barriers' (Rieser, 2000). Specifically, the *social model of disablement* focuses on environment. The *medical model of disability* focuses on an individual who needs fixing – either by therapy, medicine, surgery or special treatment. The distinction between impairment and disablement is also an important one for inclusive education. Focus on the environment means schools and teachers must accommodate to individual learners. A focus on individual students means that students must either be 'cured' or fit in if they do not want to be denied access to 'regular' education.

Ballard (1999), observed:

> There is general agreement from those who support and oppose inclusive education that there is nothing about special education that is not already part of practice in regular schools. Rather, special education is supported as a political strategy for ensuring that some students, those who fit predetermined categories, receive additional services and are not ignored or neglected. (p. 169)

The terms 'special education' and students with 'special education needs' are widely used. However, as Ballard points out, 'special' makes an unnecessary distinction. Lynch (2001) supports this point and warns that the term SEN should be used with caution. Lynch argues that the term may perpetuate the binary divide between 'ordinary' and 'special' students and systems. Second, the label may present a barrier to the development of inclusive practice, and it is not very helpful in pinpointing the educational difficulties of the learner. Third, the label tends to put the burden on the learner and a focus on individual

deficits, rather than the characteristics of the school and environment, and therefore excuses schools from change (Lynch, 2001).

These two paradigms (social and medical models of disability), and their correlative suppositions perpetuate the paradox of recognizing differences, while promising equality.

PATTERNS AND TRENDS OF INCLUSIVE EDUCATION

Having presented a background in terms of the complexity of the issues involving inclusive education and their historical underpinnings, this section reviews patterns and trends in inclusive practice. The first wave originated with countries of the North, so a brief review of patterns and trends in these countries follows. This review is followed by a discussion of a second wave of practice in countries of the South. For, as Stubbs (1996) and others report, in this second wave, countries of the South have taken the best from international 'solutions' found in Western contexts, and built on the strengths in indigenous practice to produce culturally appropriate sustainable inclusive education programmes.

Countries of the 'North'

Provision of SEN services began with residential schools for blind and deaf students. First established in the eighteenth century in Europe, these schools grew rapidly during the nineteenth century. Special schools for those with mobility impairments came later around the turn of the twentieth century. North America followed a similar route, although beginning later than in Europe. At the same time, those with intellectual impairments were largely institutionalized as uneducable in both Europe and North America. These beginnings of SEN provision in the North were driven by professionals who developed diagnoses, interventions and treatment focused on specific impairments. As a result, the medical model of disability became thoroughly accepted and entrenched. Charitable and religious organizations played a major role during these early years in the provision of services, leading to what became known as the 'charity' model of services; that is, education of disabled children and youth was not viewed as a right, but as a charitable means of providing *for* them.

World War II and its aftermath witnessed the emergence of family, community and consumer models of service delivery for SEN students. The social model began to be developed and parents pressured for deinstitutionalization in both Europe (for example, the concept of normalization promoted by Wolfensberger) and in North America (for example, the landmark decision of *PARC v. The Board of Education* in the US). A growing number of disabled people, parents and coalitions of advocates began to organize for political action to redress discrimination and inequities in society and in education. By the 1970s, the Independent Living Movement and principles of self-advocacy gathered strength. One result was the landmark US education law, PL-94-142, Part B of the Education of the Handicapped Act (EHA). Passed in 1975, PL 94-142 mandated access to education for students with all types and degrees of disability. The Education of the Handicapped Act is reauthorized periodically (for example, every five years). The 1990 reauthorization renamed the EHA the Individuals with Disabilities Education Act. The IDEA raised the level of expectations, requiring maximum access to the general education curriculum for students with disabilities and mandating new accountability measures to assure their progress and success. In Europe, Italy's National Law 118 (1971) and National Law 517 (1977) established inclusive education as national policy. Other major disability rights laws in Canada, Britain (the Disability Discrimination Act of 1995) and the US (Americans with Disabilities Act of 1990) mandated an end to discrimination in all aspects of life and required the elimination of all types of barriers to participation in society. As a result, the end of the twentieth century saw the establishment of a new era based on civil rights, social participation, and an emerging cross-disability perspective.

In the United States inclusive education programs have grown exponentially since the passage of PL94-142 in 1975. Lipsky and Gartner (1997) report that between 1994 and 1995 the number of school districts reporting inclusive education programs in the US tripled (Lipsky & Gartner, 1997, p. 100). A 1994 report of National Centre on Educational Restructuring and Inclusion (NCERI) documented inclusion programs in every state, at all grade levels, involving students across the entire range of disabilities.

A 30-country study (EADSNE, 2003) focused on five areas of inclusive education: (1) inclusive education policies and practice; (2) funding of special needs education; (3) teachers and special needs education; (4) information and communication technology in special needs education; and (5) early intervention. In terms of inclusive education practices, the findings of this study reinforce findings of earlier OECD studies in some areas. Specifically, a policy towards inclusive education is a general trend. However, special schools still enrol between 1 and 6 per cent of all pupils in segregated schools and classes. A high correlation exists between the percentage of pupils in segregated educational provision and population density. There appears to be clear disadvantages to segregation in countries with low population density related to cost-effectiveness factors.

In light of the development of inclusive education a number of trends can be discerned. These include:

1 *Transforming special schools into resource centres* continues to be a common trend. These centres typically provide the following cost-effective supports:
   - provide training and courses for teachers and other professionals
   - develop and disseminate materials and methods
   - support mainstream schools and parents
   - provide short-term or part-time help for individual students
   - support students in entering the labour market.

2 *Individualized education plans* continue to play a major role in programming to determine the degree and type of adaptations needed and to evaluate students' progress.

A significant portion of this report focuses on *barriers and challenges* experienced by European countries, as follows:

1 Secondary level education: countries report 'serious problems' at this level as compared to primary schooling. Countries attribute these problems to insufficient teacher training, less positive teacher attitudes, an increasing achievement gap between SEN students and their peers, increased academic subject specialization and different school organization.
2 Role of parents: most countries reported positive attitudes toward inclusive education on the part of parents, and that parental pressure towards inclusive education is increasing. However, those families that have students with severe disabilities sometimes prefer segregated settings. Also, the trend toward decentralization has led to increased parental power over decision-making.
3 Funding: this is cited as a major barrier of inclusive education and training. Countries are undergoing major funding reforms.
4 Legislation: progress has been achieved, but problems still remain.
5 Decentralization: there is a clear and widespread trend toward decentralization that plays a key role in inclusive education. The shift of resources and decision-making to local authority is seen to increase flexibility, and allow better adaptation to local circumstances. However, disadvantages include wide variations in quality and level of service.

Accountability has become a predominant issue across all countries of the North, fuelled by public pressure, lower than expected student achievement, and scarce resources. The shift in focus has moved from access and quality issues to outcomes. In many countries, new standards-based curricula and new laws requiring improved achievement outcomes on standards-based tests are being used as measures of school performance (McLaughlin and Rouse, 2000). In England, league tables which rank schools by achievement data are published, and in the US, The No Child Left Behind Act (NCLB, 2002) mandates severe economic sanctions for schools that 'fail' to perform on the certain achievement measures. These policies and legislation exert enormous pressures on schools, with adverse effects on students identified as SEN. Reports indicate that these policies have led to a reluctance on the part of some to accept students with SEN because they may depress test scores, or to omit children with learning difficulties from testing programmes. Schools may also be encouraged to expel students whom they find difficult to teach (OECD, 1999, p. 34).

EURYDICE (2003) also reports the trend toward accountability as having an adverse effect on inclusive education and students with SEN. For example, they report a recent slight increase in segregated placements. This report also emphasizes a general need in all European countries for better monitoring and evaluation procedures. Complicating evaluation efforts, however, is the argument that the development of more inclusive education requires reduction of labelling and assessment procedures.

In summary, although there is a definite trend toward inclusive practice in all countries of the North, considerable variation exists, most notably in the areas of classification and placement decisions. In addition, all countries face several challenges. The most significant of these are meeting the needs of SEN students in secondary schools, funding, and resource constraints. Special issues of accountability are exerting enormous pressures on schools to document effectiveness in terms of outcomes. This emphasis on accountability represents a significant shift from issues of access and quality of services. Systems of evaluation and documentation of effectiveness in terms of outcomes are lacking and need attention. While the studies provide some evidence of positive inclusive education effects, gaps in the research are most noticeable in this area. Finally, significant gender differences exist that reveal boys more likely to be identified as having SEN than girls. This is a significant area of concern that has been largely omitted in studies of inclusive education.

Countries of the 'South'

Much of the literature in this area is recent and focuses mainly on in-country reports, making definitive patterns and trends difficult to discern. However, the current picture that emerges from country reports is one of a focus on increasing access, on teacher training, and on maximizing system efficiency and resource capacity through improved multi-sector coordination and community-based collaboration. As a result, inclusion emerges as a dynamic process of participation within a net of relationships. While the South faces major challenges in terms of resources and access within the Dakar Framework, creative in-country strategies to meet EFA goals have emerged that distinguish them from the first wave of well-resourced countries. An examination of these strategies provides glimpses of emerging patterns and trends in terms of inputs, processes and outputs related to inclusive education.

Inputs to Inclusive education

1 *Demand issues* provide arguably predominant challenges to inclusive education in countries of the South. In contrast to countries of the North where access to education is virtually universal, access to education in Southern countries remains dramatically lower. For example, it has been estimated that as few as 1–5 per cent of students with disabilities have access to education (Habibi, 1999) in the South. Difficulties with *access, retention, and drop-out rates* have plagued efforts in this area. *Access issues* in particular are affected by factors at all levels: student, school, family/ community and national. Probably most influential are socio-economic and cultural factors within the family: family economic survival needs (for example, mothers' choices between sending children to school or having children work to generate income needed for family survival), traditional societal attitudes towards disability that may involve shame, guilt, under-expectations, sheltering/patronization. These factors often combine with distance to school, mobility, school-building accessibility, discrimination, shortage of trained teachers and resource supports to address teachers' working conditions, and shortage of school places. Typical responses to difficulties with access have been modifying buildings, knowledge dissemination and awareness campaigns, teacher and parent training on special needs.

2 *Finding, identifying and encouraging children to go to school* have been other critical challenges. Some programmes have combined parent education and community awareness with 'child-find' strategies. In Guyana, volunteers in a local community based rehabilitation (CBR) programme formed a Village Health Committee and conducted a joint survey of 4,500 people in the village. The survey identified children needing services, and parents conducting the survey helped to encourage parents to send their children for services (O'Toole, 1994). At Kabale primary school in Mpika, Zambia, a Child-to-Child programme conducted a community survey that identified 30 children with special needs staying at home, and succeeded in gaining their access to school (Miles, 2000).

Ingstad (2001) argues that surveys are 'highly cherished tools by planners and politicians who usually see this type of information as mandatory' before initiating projects. However, surveys tend to be costly. For this reason, voices have been raised, especially from disabled people's organizations (DPOs), to limit (or drop) the surveys and to 'start to give help, on a small scale, to those in need and to expand help as needs arise' (Ingstad, 2001, p. 774).

3 *Student characteristics* are another critical input consideration. Most countries of the South have concentrated their inclusive education efforts on moderately and severely disabled children in four categories: physical/mobility impairments, blindness, deafness and cognitive impairments. This focus is understandable for several reasons: (a) these children have easily identifiable characteristics; (b) providing services is politically high profile; (c) they are the most disadvantaged and marginalized. However, the vast majority of children with disabilities have mild impairments. These children most likely constitute a significant percentage of drop-outs and grade-level repeaters. The Mozambique Federation of Disabled Peoples Organization (FAMOD), for example, assert that the majority of out-of-school students in Mozambique are either disabled or have learning difficulties which require special education (Lehtomaki, 2002). Reports from Vietnam indicate that many students with mild disabilities tend to drop out due to 'lack of attention' (EENET, 1998). These students are also more likely to engage in illegal activities and socially deviant

behaviour than their moderate/severely impaired peers. A number of countries in the South report growing numbers of these children; for example, street children (many of whom have impairments), but also orphans of HIV/AIDS parents, or children who suffer from various forms of abuse and neglect (UNESCO, 2001a).

To address these issues, some programmes have opened up special schools to disadvantaged poor children (UNESCO, 2001a, p. 85). Others have considered economic needs of students as well, including government stipends for subsidized school fees and costs of school uniforms. Flexible curriculum approaches are also being adopted that allow children to be at home at times when they are needed for household chores (and/or to work in order to generate family income) (UNESCO, 2001b).

4   *Attitudes* constitute a critical challenge. Traditional approaches to attitudes focus on teacher attitudes in classrooms. However, root problems have been associated with lack of political will based on attitudes of government officials. Training programmes are beginning to target these groups prior to implementing programmes. For example, a study funded by the Economic and Social Commission of Asia and the Pacific (ESCAP) trained disabled people to organize national training workshops for government officials in Malaysia. The impetus for the training arose from the realization that even though legislation on accessibility and building codes/standards existed, they were not being implemented. These experiences in Malaysia led to a recommendation for specific disability training targeted at 'people who make and implement decisions, people in local government, and particularly technical personnel with responsibility for designing the built environment [for example, schools]' (ESCAP, 2001).

5   *Conditions of teachers' work* is another critical input in inclusive education programmes. Most implementation efforts focus on training teachers in effective instructional strategies and ignore the conditions within which teachers must carry these out. Many projects do not meet goals due to teacher/staff turnover and transfers. Education for All Monitoring Report 2002 (UNESCO, 2002) reports that donor agencies, which countries of the South rely on for teacher training, are reluctant to pay for the recurring costs of teacher salaries. However, teacher salaries account for the large proportion of school budgets, and

some countries cannot afford to pay teachers a living wage. Other conditions of teachers' work reported to have a significant impact on their ability to provide effective education are class size, classroom physical layout, administrative support and supervision, incentives for participation, and release time for preparation and evaluation (Jangira & Ahuja, 1994). For example, the Teacher Development Initiative in India suffered from failing to attend to these factors, noting that: 'The most serious barrier to the project has been the attitude of administrators who have insufficient time and patience to learn about and understand its [the programme's] objectives' (Jangira & Ahuja, 1994, p. 38). As a consequence, lack of support, as well as a prescriptive and examination-oriented curriculum, discouraged teachers from trying innovations and 'made it difficult for them to implement the new approaches they were learning' (Jangira & Ahuja 1994, p. 38).

6   *Retention and drop-out rates* have been linked to curriculum and instruction. Typically the focus has been on adapted curriculum and upgrading teachers' skills by providing training in child-centred, active pedagogy/instruction. Less often, the curriculum content itself is challenged. The lesson that has been learned is that adapting a curriculum that is not relevant or is not teaching functional life skills in the first place, does little to motivate students to stay in school. In India, for example, UNESCO reports that many parents cite the irrelevance of the curriculum as a reason for not sending their children to school. They feel the curriculum is not geared to real life, and fruitful years of income generation will be lost even if the child receives only a primary education (UNESCO, 2001a).

Bernard (2001) provides a comprehensive documentation of patterns of exclusion, causes, and conditions at school, administrative and national levels that affect exclusion and drop-out rates. This report identifies the excluded learners as those who: (a) are not considered to 'fit' into majority-based classrooms; (b) contradict accepted norms of who can or should learn; (c) cannot afford the cost of the time for schooling; (d) are not free or available to participate (for example, geographically isolated children, child soldiers or unregistered migrants); (e) are living in the context of disaster (Bernard, 2001, p. 11).

Schools contribute to excluding children when they: (a) apply narrow paradigms and are unable to cope with diversity; (b) fail to concern themselves with children who do not turn up and do not track the non-attender; (c) do not reach out proactively to the families of children who are the most vulnerable (Bernard, 2001, pp. 5–6). With regard to this last factor, the Convention on the Rights of the Child (CRC) stresses that families and parents should be the first line of intervention in and support for children. 'Families are the key in keeping children out of exploitative working conditions and in school; the opposite is equally true' (Bernard, 2001, p. 6).

A UNESCO report (2001c) summarizing work in several countries suggests key elements of inclusive curriculum that are linked to retention: (a) broad common goals defined for all, including the knowledge, skills and values to be acquired
(b) a flexible structure to facilitate responding to the diversity and providing diverse opportunities for practice and performance in terms of content, methods and level of participation
(c) assessment based on individual progress
(d) cultural, religious and linguistic diversity of learners acknowledged and
(e) content, knowledge and skills relevant to learners' context (UNESCO, 2001c, p. 9).

Processes of inclusive education

School climate, and teaching and learning are two broad domains concerned with process. A whole-school approach to inclusive education is emerging, as in the North. Basic principles of whole-school approaches include participation and collaboration. A personal change process appears to be important for changing attitudes as part of the process of teaching and learning. In Uganda, teachers reported that ignorance, fear, and a lack of confidence were the causes of their attitudes towards children with disabilities before these children entered their classrooms. As they 'got used to' these children, they reported increased confidence, coping strategies, and positive attitude change (Arbetter & Hartley, 2002).

Outcomes of inclusive education

Programme evaluation appears to be under-developed in the South as well as in the North. Evaluations have traditionally focused on summative data, to interpret effects of pro-grammes. Currently, inclusive education programmes are beginning to place more emphasis on continuous evaluations as inputs (for example, assessments of needs and feasibility studies), process (both formative and summative evaluations of the implementation activities) and outcomes/impacts of inclusive education programmes. As an example of *input assessment*, prior to implementing an inclusive education project in Nicaragua, four data instruments were used to carry out a situation analysis in each school (UNESCO, 2001d). These input assessments have been used to promote sustainability. Another project in Guyana actively involved parents, who established a village health committee and conducted a needs assessment. As a result of the needs assessment, they set up a resource centre in the village near the elder leaders' compound. From this, they converted the centre into a regional school, and now conduct a regional programme (O'Toole, 1994, pp. 25–31).

Process assessments are emerging in the form of action research projects conducted by teachers, with technical support and training. The UNESCO supported 'Inclusive Schools' project in Nicaragua used this model with teachers who were involved in action research projects. Regular meetings were scheduled for them to share experiences and deepen the action research process (UNESCO, 2001d). However, the project experienced several barriers to effective implementation of the model: a lack of a coordinating plan to guide implementation was cited as a key weakness.

The Committee on the Rights of the Child (UNICEF, 2002) expressed concern about disabled children's basic right to education (article 28) and about the low proportion of disabled children enrolled in schools, particularly in the South. The new reporting guidelines for 2002/03 require countries to document their progress on several specific activities, including: (a) the disabled child's access to education and the consideration given to their inclusion within the general education system; (b) measures taken to ensure an effective evaluation of the situation of disabled children, including the development of a system of identification and tracking of disabled children, the assessment of progress, difficulties encountered and targets set for the future; (c) measures taken to ensure adequate training of those responsible for educating disabled children (UNICEF, 2002, p. 321). With this information, a more accurate and definitive picture of patterns and trends in the South should emerge in the future.

MAJOR EPISTEMOLOGICAL ISSUES

We are not the sources of problems. We are the resources that are needed to solve them. We are not expenses, we are investments. We are the children of the world and despite our different backgrounds we share a common reality. We are united in our struggle to make the world a better place for all. (Opening address at the UN Special Session on Children, May 2002. Ms Gabriela Arrieta (Bolivia) and Ms Audrey Cheynut (Monaco))

Inclusive education practice in all countries occurs within economic and political contexts underpinned by cultural values. The fundamental principle of EFA is that all children should have the opportunity to learn. The fundamental principle of inclusive education is that all children should have the opportunity to learn – together. Diversity is a characteristic that all children and youth have in common – both within each individual child and across individual children. There is strength in diversity, and all children have strengths. It is the fundamental responsibility of all those who teach and of all those who support teachers to build on children's strength, believe in all children's capacity to learn, and uphold their right to learn. Children are our future. As Ms Gabriela Arrieta and Ms Audrey Cheynut put it in their opening address at the UN Special Session on Children (May 2002): 'We are not the sources of problems. We are the resources that are needed to solve them. We are not expenses, we are investments.'

The educational community must collectively invest beliefs, resources, and intellectual problem-solving abilities in inclusive education. A growing body of research provides evidence of what works. Every country in the world today has at least one teacher, one school, one inclusive education programme committed to inclusive education. Some countries have a great deal more. These 'islands of excellence' must help the rest of the world cross the artificial divide between 'special' and 'regular' education. Arguments of excess costs no longer justify exclusion. Compared to segregated programmes, inclusive education is cost-effective. Moreover, the costs of exclusion are high in terms of lost productivity, lost human potential, and lost health and well-being.

Some children start school with more advantages than others – advantages of wealth and health among the most influential. Children in poverty and children with impairments, and all marginalized children (whether due to language, religion, race, ethnicity, gender) do not have to be disadvantaged by their treatment in schools or by exclusion from schools. 'If you deny disabled people educational opportunities, then it is the lack of education and not their disabilities that limit their opportunities.'[2] Lack of opportunities is a reflection of the ways in which resources are allocated as well as of beliefs about the value of education for all children, and for particular children. National priorities say more about values and philosophical commitment to education than they do about capacities to provide education. Conditions of marginalized children at the edge of a society reveal more about the state and progress of a society than conditions at the middle. These children, as a radically marginalized sector of society, reflect the unadorned aims of education and society in general.

The current state of progress toward EFA provides both challenges and opportunities. If the world is to meet the Millennium Development Goals – ratified by 152 countries – then countries are challenged to commit to the frameworks for action. Opportunities will manifest themselves in day-to-day tasks undertaken with individual children, in classrooms, in schools and in society. Universal primary education and Education for All are worthy goals. It is hoped that this chapter has made a contribution to them.

ACKNOWLEDGMENTS

This chapter is revised and adapted with permission from a 150-page report prepared by the author for the World Bank Disability Group, April 2003. The findings, interpretations and conclusions expressed in the report as well as in this chapter are entirely those of the author and should not be attributed in any manner to the World Bank, to its affiliated agencies, to members of its Board of Executive Directors, or to the countries they represent. The author wishes to thank Judith Heumann and the Disability Group staff at the World Bank for the opportunity to undertake the original review.

NOTES

1 The terms Countries of the North and South, rather than the terms developed and developing countries are used in this chapter. This choice conforms to the trend in the literature. 'North' and 'South' in this review are used as a short-hand to describe the rich, industrialized countries, and those countries that are still in the process of economic development. (Definition adopted from UNESCO Thematic Study, 2001: *Inclusion in Education: The Participation of Disabled Learners.*)

2 Quote is taken from a 2003 press release of the World Bank and is attributed to Judith Heumann, the Senior Advisor to the Disability Group, The World Bank.

REFERENCES

Allan, J. (1999). *Actively seeking inclusion: Pupils with special needs in mainstream schools.* London: Falmer Press.

Arbetter, S., & Hartley, S. (2002). Teachers' and pupils' experiences of integrated education in Uganda. *International Journal of Disability, Development and Education, 49*(1), 61–78.

Armstrong, F., Armstrong, D., & Barton, L. (Eds.). (2000). *Inclusive education: Policy, contexts and comparative perspectives.* London: David Fulton.

Baker, E. T., Wang, M. C., & Walberg, H. J. (1994). The effects of inclusion on learning. *Educational Leadership, 52*(4), 33–35.

Ballard, K. (Ed.). (1999). *Inclusive education: International voices on disability and justice.* London: Falmer Press.

Bernard, A. K. (2001). *Education for All and children who are excluded.* Paris: UNESCO.

Cameron, D., & Valentine, F. (2001). *Disability and federalism: Comparing different approaches to full participation.* Montreal: McGill-Queens University Press.

Coleridge, P. (1996). *Disability, liberation and development.* London: OXFAM.

Department of Education and Science (DES). (1978). *Special educational needs: Report of the Committee of Enquiry into the education of handicapped children and young people* (The Warnock Report). London: HMSO.

Despouy, L. (1993). *Human rights and disability.* New York: United Nations.

Dudzik, P., & McLeod, D. (2000). *Including the most vulnerable: Social funds and people with disabilities.* Washington, DC: World Bank.

Economic and Social Commission for Asia and the Pacific (ESCAP). (2001). *Pathfinders: Towards full participation and equality of persons with disabilities in the ESCAP region.* New York: United Nations.

Enabling Education Network (EENET). (1998). Focusing on community support for inclusive education. *EENET, October 1998,* 5.

European Agency for Development in Special Needs Education (EADSNE). (2003). *Special needs education in Europe.* Brussels: EADSNE.

EURYDICE (2003) Special Needs Education in Europe: Thematic Publication. Brussels: EURYDICE.

Evans, P. (2000). *Developing equity indicators based on additional resources supplied for disabled and disadvantaged students.* Paris: OECD.

Ferguson, D. (1992). *Regular class participation system.* Eugene, OR: University of Oregon.

Habibi, G. (1999). UNICEF and children with disabilities. *Education Update, 2*(4), 2.

Ingstad, B. (2001). Disability in the developing world. In K. S. G. Albrecht & M. Bury (Eds.), *Handbook of disability studies* (pp. 772–792). London: Sage.

Jangira, N., & Ahuja, A. (1994). Teacher development initiative (TDI) to meet special needs in the classroom. In UNESCO (Ed.), *Making it happen: Examples of good practice in special needs education & community-based programmes* (pp. 43–54). Paris: UNESCO.

Lansdown, G. (2001). *It is our world too! A report on the lives of disabled children.* London: Disability Awareness in Action.

Lehtomaki, E. (2002). Inclusive schools in Mozambique. *EENET, 6,* 4.

Lindqvist, B. (1999). Education as a fundamental right. *Education Update, 2*(4), 7.

Lipsky, D. K., & Gartner, A. (1997). *Inclusion and school reform: Transforming America's classrooms.* Baltimore, MD: Paul Prookes.

Lynch, J. (2001). *Inclusion in education: The participation of disabled learners.* Paris: UNESCO.

McLaughlin, M., & Rouse, M. (Eds.). (2000). *Special education and school reform in the United States and Britain.* London: Routledge.

Meijer, C. J., Pijl, S. J., & Hegarty, S. (1994). *New perspectives in special education: A six country study of integration.* London: Routledge.

Metts, R. (2000). *Disability, issues, trends, and recommendations for the World Bank.* Washington, DC: World Bank.

Miles, S. (2000). *Enabling inclusive education: Challenges and dilemmas.* Paper presented at the Children with Disabilities and the Convention on the Rights of the Child Conference, Bonn.

No Child Left Behind, 20 U.S.C. §16301 *et seq.*

O'Toole, B. (1994). Involvement of volunteer, parents and community members with children with special needs. In UNESCO (Ed.), *Making it happen: Examples of good practice in special needs education & community-based programmes* (pp. 25–31). Paris: UNESCO.

Organisation for Economic Co-operation and Development (OECD). (1999). *Inclusive education at work: Students with disabilities in mainstream schools.* Paris: OECD.

Organisation for Economic Co-operation and Development (OECD). (2000). *Special needs education statistics and indicators.* Paris: OECD.

Pennsylvania Association of Retarded Citizens (PARC) v. Commonwealth of Pennsylvania, 343 F. Supp. 279 (E.D. Pa. 1972).

President's Commission on Excellence in Special Education (PCESE). (2002). *A new era: Revitalizing special education for children and their families.* Washington, DC: U.S. Dept. of Education.

Rieser, R. (2000). *History of our oppression. Why the social model in education is inclusive education.* Paper presented at the International Special Education Congress, Manchester, England.

Sailor, W. (Ed.). (2002). *Whole-school success and inclusive education: Building partnerships for learning, achievement, and accountability.* New York: Teachers College Press.

Stubbs, S. (1996). *Poverty and membership of the mainstream: Lessons learned from the South.* Retrieved February 24, 2003 from www.eenet.org.uk/theory_practice/poverty..shtml

Thomas, G., & Glenny, G. (2002). Thinking about inclusion: Whose reason? What evidence? *International Journal of Inclusive Education, 6*(4), 345–370.

United Nations (UN). (1975). *Declaration on the rights of disabled persons.* Retrieved February 23, 2003 from www.ohchr.org/english/law/res3447.htm

United Nations (UN) (1982) *World programme of action concerning disabled persons.* Adopted by the UN General Assembly on 3 December 1982. Resolution 37/52. Accessed from the web on 5 May, 2006 at: http//www.un.org/socdev/enable/diswpa01.htm

United Nations (UN) (1989). *Convention on the Rights of the Child.* Adopted by the UN General Assembly on 20 November 1989, Resolution 44/25.

United Nations (UN) (1993). *The Standard Rules on the Equalization of Opportunities for Persons with Disabilities.* Adopted by the UN General Assembly, 48th session, resolution 48/96, annex of 20 December 1993. Downloaded on May 5, 2006 at: http//www.un.org/esa/socdev/enable/dissre00.htm

United Nations Children's Fund (UNICEF). (2002). *Implementation handbook for the Convention on the Rights of the Child: Fully revised edition.* New York: UNICEF.

United Nations Educational, Scientific, and Cultural Organization (UNESCO). (1994). *The Salamanca statement on principles, policy and practice in special needs education.* Paris: UNESCO.

United Nations Educational, Scientific, and Cultural Organization (UNESCO) (1994a). *The Salamanca statement and framework for action on special needs education.* Paris: UNESCO.

United Nations Educational, Scientific, and Cultural Organization (UNESCO). (2000). *World Education Forum final report. Part II: Improving the quality and equity of education for all.* Paris: UNESCO.

United Nations Educational, Scientific, and Cultural Organization (UNESCO). (2001a). *Developing sustainable inclusion policies and practices.* Paris: UNESCO.

United Nations Educational, Scientific, and Cultural Organization (UNESCO). (2001b). *Including the excluded: Meeting diversity in education. Example from Uganda.* Paris: UNESCO.

United Nations Educational, Scientific, and Cultural Organization (UNESCO). (2001c). *Overcoming exclusion through inclusive approaches in education: A challenge and a vision.* Paris: UNESCO.

United Nations Educational, Scientific, and Cultural Organization (UNESCO). (2001d). *Inclusive schools & community support programmes: Phase II.* Paris: UNESCO.

United Nations Educational, Scientific, and Cultural Organization (UNESCO). (2002). *Education for All: Is the world on track?* Paris: UNESCO.

Vienneau, R. (2002). Pédagogie de l'inclusion: fondements, définition, défis, et perspectives. *Education et francophonie, 30*(2), 10–33.

10

Learning from difference: sharing international experiences of developments in inclusive education

Susie Miles and Anupam Ahuja

This chapter considers ideas about how inclusive education can be shared across national borders. We argue that important lessons can be learned from international experiences, including from countries facing considerable economic constraints, but that this is a complex process because cultural and linguistic differences sometimes create barriers such that accounts of developments in a particular context can easily be misinterpreted and misconstrued, therefore making it difficult to learn from each other.

Building on our experience of cross-cultural learning within the Enabling Education Network (EENET), an international, information-sharing network, we explore ways of overcoming such difficulties. We set this argument in the wider context of current debates about the nature of inclusive education and Education for All (EFA) in Southern contexts. We also consider the way knowledge about inclusive education is constructed in such contexts, given the pressures and opportunities of globalisation and knowledge networking.

Bearing in mind that published literature on inclusive education in Southern contexts is relatively scarce, we go on to discuss some of the challenges of documenting experience in a way that it can be widely shared between Southern contexts and, indeed, between countries of the South and the North. More specifically, we illustrate what this involves by reflecting on a recent action research project in which practitioners were supported in articulating their own knowledge about attempts to support and promote inclusive education.

LEARNING FROM DIFFERENCE

Our own interest in educational inclusion stems from our earlier work as teachers, but more recently from our work as researchers, networkers and external consultants (for example, Abiroux & Ahuja, 2004; Ahuja, 2003; Ahuja & Ibrahim, 2004; Miles, 2002a, 2005; Save the Children, 2002). We share a concern that the term 'inclusive education' is too often exclusively associated with children identified as having a special educational need or a disability. At the same time we appreciate that in some contexts children with particular impairments may face considerable hardship, discrimination and exclusion from education, not only because of their disability, but also because of their gender, ethnicity, health status, or the extreme poverty in which they live (Jones, 2001).

Translating research and practitioner knowledge into forms that teachers can use to improve their practice is inherently difficult, even in rich countries (Hiebert, Gallimore & Stigler, 2002). How, then, can we advocate for information sharing between stakeholders in inclusive education in countries of the South, where access to information and technology is limited, and the provision of quality education an enormous challenge?

In recent years we have been involved in supporting the process of knowledge creation within Southern countries and the cautious 'transfer' of knowledge across cultural borders. These experiences lead us to believe that the sharing of examples of innovative inclusive practice can inspire practitioners. However, they also lead us to be sensitive to the nature of the knowledge that can be moved from place to place, and the sorts of barriers that make this difficult. Here it is helpful to make a distinction between 'generalisations' that attempt to determine patterns that are assumed to be relevant to any country, and 'transferability', where there is an emphasis on the importance of understanding contextual factors in shaping how ideas are interpreted (Heshusius, 1989; Iano, 1986; Lincoln & Guba, 1984).

This distinction leads Fuller and Clarke (1994) to caution that local meanings have to be taken into account by researchers when working internationally to improve schools, in other words, we ignore local culture at our peril. Similarly, in her influential book, *Education and Disability in Cross-Cultural Perspective*, Peters (1993) argues that the assumption that a country is a homogeneous unit should be avoided and that a historical perspective is vital to a deeper analysis of an educational context.

With these warnings in mind, we have found it helpful in our work to explore forms of knowledge transfer that take account of the way local circumstances, histories and cultures shape ideas that are introduced from elsewhere. This leads us to argue that accounts of practice from elsewhere, and ideas that emerge from reflection on such accounts, can help people to think more analytically and, perhaps, in new ways about their own contexts. The argument we develop illustrates how this can be helpful in moving thinking and practice forward by pointing to possibilities that extend ideas about what might be possible; by providing explanations of practice that might be adapted for use in different contexts; and, most important of all, by challenging the unstated assumptions that inform existing ways of working. This is what we mean when we say, 'learning from difference'.

PROMOTING EDUCATION FOR ALL

Considering how we might 'learn from difference' begins with an understanding of international developments towards inclusive education, efforts to promote Education for All (EFA), and the impact of the *Salamanca Statement and Framework for Action* (UNESCO, 1994).

The first 'World Conference on Education for All', held in Jomtien, Thailand, in 1990, was particularly significant because it acknowledged that large numbers of vulnerable and marginalized groups of learners were excluded from education systems worldwide. It also provided a vision of education which was much broader than schooling, indeed the right of all citizens to receive an education and to achieve a basic level of literacy was upheld at Jomtien. However it is important not to underestimate the challenges facing education systems in some of the world's economically poorest countries. Although 652 million children worldwide are enrolled in primary education, the out-of-school population still stands at over 100 million children, 80 per cent of whom live in South Asia and Sub-Saharan Africa (DFID, 2005). In India alone, it is estimated that at least 35 million children are not in school (DFID, 2001). Families trapped in multidimensional poverty are excluded from educational opportunities and health facilities (Chronic Poverty Research Centre, 2005). Urgent economic solutions are clearly needed to eradicate poverty and ensure that all children have equal access to appropriate and affordable education.

The key challenge identified at the Forum in Dakar, Senegal, in 2000, when progress was reviewed in the 10 years since Jomtien, was 'to ensure that the broad vision of Education for All as an inclusive concept is reflected in national government and funding agency policies' (UNESCO, 2000, para. 19). Following Dakar, a set of international development targets was developed to help governments and international development agencies to focus their efforts on eliminating poverty. These targets, collectively known as the Millennium Development Goals, provide countries with an opportunity to work together on a set of measurable objectives, the second of which is to achieve universal primary education, by ensuring that all boys and girls *complete* a full course of primary schooling by 2015. This is unlikely to be achieved, however, unless the necessary financial support is put in place (Global Campaign for Education, 2005).

The Right to Education of Persons with Disabilities: Towards Inclusion is one of nine EFA Flagship initiatives. Flagship members work in partnership with the United Nations and other international agencies on the development of inclusive national EFA action plans, in order to ensure that learners with disabilities are included in EFA plans (UNESCO, 2004). However, the Flagship initiative is facilitative. It does not have the authority to ensure that these plans are clearly conceptualised or that countries are supported to develop their own contextually appropriate inclusive practices. A recent analysis of 17 EFA plans from the South and South-East Asia region concluded that inclusive education does not appear as a theme; special

schools and residential hostels are suggested as a strategy for meeting the needs of disadvantaged students; non-formal education is seen as the solution to marginalised groups; issues of equity are not addressed in the education sector as a whole; and the increasing role of private education is not discussed (Ahuja, 2005).

Providing education for the most disenfranchised and marginalised groups in the poorest countries in the world remains an enormous challenge. Disabled children, though not a homogeneous group, tend to be identified internationally as a group of children who are excluded from education in countries of the South in disproportionately large numbers (Mittler, 2005). In the previous chapter, Peters noted that it will be impossible to realise the goals of EFA if the majority of disabled children continue to be excluded from education. Moreover, as Stubbs (1995) points out, definitions and perceptions of disability and special needs are culturally and contextually determined. This is highlighted in the inconsistency in the numbers of children being reported as disabled or having special educational needs in Southern countries. Stubbs further argues that a focus on demographic data and accurate statistics obscures problems associated with negative attitudes, policies and institutions which exclude children, leading us to emphasise the importance of analysing indigenous understandings of fundamental concepts such as 'play', 'children' and 'teaching and learning', which can carry very different meanings in different contexts (Miles, 1999).

It is easy to be overwhelmed by the apparent enormity of the challenges in countries of the South and to adopt a negative deficit approach to an analysis of educational activities in such environments. Most of the literature paints a negative picture of education systems struggling to cope with poorly trained teachers, inadequate budgets, large class sizes and, more recently, the HIV/AIDS crisis. Access to the latest technological developments in special education, for example, is unlikely to be an option for children in

Southern countries who tend to be perceived by visiting experts as being in need of such interventions. While we do not wish to romanticise resource-poor environments, we believe that education practitioners in resource-rich countries can learn some very useful lessons for their own practice if they engage with experience of efforts to promote inclusion in the South. Our intention, therefore, is to highlight some of these possibilities, while drawing attention to the complexities of such cross-cultural information sharing. In so doing, we set out to show how innovative programmes in the South have a great deal to teach the economically wealthy countries of the North, where public services are increasingly faced with diminishing resources, and where access to resources is sometimes a cause of conflict. There are lessons to be learned from the experience of overcoming seemingly insurmountable resource barriers. These lessons are essentially about long-term social processes, in which stakeholders work together to address barriers to participation and learning, rather than about resource-intensive and specialised technological solutions.

MAKING SENSE OF INTERNATIONAL DEVELOPMENTS

In this volume, Susan Peters notes that most of the literature from Southern countries is recent and is mainly focused on in-country reports. She notes that such literature rarely takes account of how local circumstances have shaped what happened (Peters, 1993). Similarly, in the search for generalised explanations that will be of value to readers in different countries, reports published by international agencies tend to provide relatively superficial and oversimplified accounts of developments in countries and in regions (UNESCO, 1995, 2001a, 2001b). At the same time they tend to be written by authors from Northern countries whose experience of the countries they analyse may be limited.

The dangers of such an approach are vividly illustrated by the work of a Tanzanian academic and special educator, Joseph Kisanji – one of the few African scholars to challenge the relevance of Northern concepts of inclusion and to provide evidence of indigenous educational responses to disabled children. Kisanji documents his experience of growing up partially sighted in a Tanzanian village in the 1960s where he was exposed to a form of education which he describes as 'customary' or 'indigenous', both prior to and during the period of his 'Western' schooling. He reports that 'children with severe and profound physical and intellectual impairments were involved [in the customary education] to the best of their abilities' (Kisanji, 1998, p. 59), and so challenges the widely quoted, yet unsubstantiated assertion by UNESCO, that less than 2 per cent of disabled children attend any form of school in Southern countries (Mittler, 2005). Kisanji goes on to argue that 'the customary education principles of universality, relevance, functionality and community localization are central to the success of an inclusive education system' because 'inclusive education is a "return to the basics" in a technologically advanced world' (Kisanji, 1998, p. 54). Consequently, he proposes the development of a research base which reflects cross-cultural realities.

In a similar way, accounts by South African scholars illustrate their distinctive approach to inclusive education, which arises from the need to equalise educational opportunities following a long history of racial segregation (Engelbrecht, Green, Naicker, & Engelbrecht, 1999; Porteus, 2003). A report produced jointly by the South African National Commission on Special Needs in Education and Training and the National Committee on Education Support Services (Department of Education, 1997) argued that a range of needs exists among *all* learners. The education system is expected to address those factors that lead to the failure of the system to accommodate diversity, or which lead to learning breakdown (Muthukrishna, 2000). Naicker (1999) has suggested that mainstream educators, rather than specialists, should take ownership of the management of diversity in the South African education system. The policy development process which has taken place since the end of apartheid in 1994, as reflected in the Education White Paper 6 (Department of Education, 2001), has been both progressive and inspiring, since difference and diversity are central to the transformation of the education system, rather than marginal issues championed by specialists.

Singal (2005) describes how the ongoing influence of Western discourses on special education in India has resulted in a narrow interpretation of the term 'inclusive education'. In her review of Indian literature she asserts that, 'the field of inclusive education continues to be driven by a narrow and limiting perspective that does not critically engage with the system as a whole' (p. 346). She highlights the discrepancies in the use of language and the fact that most of the published literature in India is highly theoretical. She explains how, alongside increased discussion of imported ideas about inclusive education, there has been an increase in the number of special schools from approximately 1,035 in the early 1990s to about 2,500 at the turn of the century.

In her critical review of the literature related to the education of disabled children in developing countries, Stubbs (1995) provides further arguments as to why attention has to be focused on how ideas about inclusion are constructed socially within particular contexts. In so doing, she notes two striking features: the paucity of accessible published literature and the dominance of a small elite of Northern writers. Reflecting on the process of carrying out a literature review a few years later, she raises some important doubts about the authenticity of published literature focusing on Southern contexts: it lacks references to indigenous knowledge (which tends to be communicated orally), and where written accounts do exist, they tend not to be accessible to a wider audience (Stubbs, 1999).

Despite these concerns, published literature in the field is still heavily influenced by Northern perspectives. For example, in her introduction to a special issue of the South African journal, *Perspectives in Education*, Muthukrishna (2003) notes that the inclusion/exclusion debate has been dominated by Northern countries. She goes on to assert that this has led to attempts to generalise paradigms, theories and policies and practices which have been developed in the very different contexts of Northern countries to countries of the South.

This situation has been further encouraged by other policy and technological developments. In 1996, for example, the World Bank announced its intention to become the world's 'Knowledge Bank' (King, 2002), in recognition of the increased role of knowledge in economic and institutional development evident in the industrialised countries of the North. The relatively new ability to move information around the world at the 'click of a button' has enormous advantages, of course, but it creates an illusion that access to knowledge has increased globally. Yet the 'digital divide' between North and South, and the broader 'communication divide', which includes access to telephones, are enormous. Although the situation is changing rapidly, the distribution of internet hosts in July 1999, for example, was heavily weighted towards the North: Canada and the US had 65.3 per cent, developing Asia-Pacific 3.7 per cent and Africa just 0.3 per cent (DFID, 2000).

Although globalisation and the emergence of the knowledge economy could provide opportunities for learning to be shared between Southern countries, and even for Northern countries to learn from experience in the South, in practice this tends not to be the case. Practitioners in Southern countries still tend to look to the literature and higher education institutions in English-speaking industrial nations, primarily, for knowledge and information about inclusive education. However, Northern countries clearly do not have all the answers. For example, in England, despite considerable efforts to promote inclusive education, school attendance and drop-out rates are a matter of considerable concern, and although the proportion of children placed in separate special education provision has steadily declined over the last 20 years, there are disturbing variations between education authorities (Norwich, 2002; Rustemier & Vaughan, 2005).

Reflecting on such evidence, Dyson (2004) warns of the danger of any one country being perceived to have 'discovered the secret of inclusion' (p. 615). This leads him to stress the importance of understanding policy and practice within particular contexts. He goes on to warn against the imposing of solutions that may not work in different contexts, and instead suggests that countries should be vigilant about the many different threats to equity which can arise in education systems.

Nevertheless, the World Bank remains committed to global knowledge networking because of 'powerful examples of how specific local needs could be met by relevant local experience elsewhere' (King, 2002, p. 316). King highlights the tension, however, between in-context knowledge and 'best practice' as approved, in most cases, by an outside expert. Artiles and Dyson (2005, p. 43) share similar concerns in relation to understanding the global phenomenon of inclusive education by suggesting that: 'If the common language of inclusion is not simply to over-ride local concerns and conditions, the global inclusion "movement" must engage in dialogue with – and be engaged in dialogue by – the local and specific context.'

The argument we draw from these sources is perhaps best summarised by Booth and Ainscow (1998) who warn against two pitfalls of comparative research: 'the idea that there is a single national perspective on inclusion or exclusion and the notion that practice can be generalised across countries without attention to local contexts and meanings' (p. 4). Their study of developments in eight countries looked at inclusive education in the context of highly resourced schools and well-developed policies in a range of countries, each with its own literature. Comparisons could therefore have been made, but the authors argued against doing so, partly because they do not consider

the search for 'good practice' to be a worthwhile exercise. They argue that it is likely to distort reality, and, in order to learn from the practice of others, it is essential to 'uncover' the way in which perspectives are politically and culturally constrained.

ENABLING EDUCATION

In order to explore some of the complexities of cross-cultural learning, we draw on our own experience as initiators of, and participants in, the Enabling Education Network (EENET). EENET was established in 1997 with the technical and financial support of a group of concerned international non-governmental organisations and with the support of the United Nations Educational, Scientific, and Cultural Organization (UNESCO). Its mission is to support and promote the inclusion of marginalized groups in education worldwide (Miles, 2002b) by sharing information between similar contexts in Southern countries, primarily through an annual publication, *Enabling Education*, and through its website. The EENET website has been visited by people in 186 countries, with about 9,000 visits to the site per month.

The word 'enabling' was chosen as a deliberate strategy to encourage a broad vision of inclusion. It was felt that the words 'special', 'integrated' and 'inclusive' were too often associated with the education of children identified as having special educational needs and that the words would prove to be problematic in the long term, especially in the context of global poverty and international efforts to promote EFA. Indeed, Slee has recently argued that the idea of inclusive education is showing signs of jetlag, losing its freshness and increasingly used to mean too many different things, though when the term was first used it was a radical idea, which rebelled against medical and psychological explanations of educational difficulties (Slee, 2004).

Unfortunately, some efforts to promote inclusion have involved new forms of segregation, albeit within the mainstream settings, through the use of what Slee (1996) calls 'dividing practices'. For example, in some of the richer countries we have seen the proliferation of largely untrained classroom assistants working with the most vulnerable children who tend to follow individual programmes in mainstream schools. When such support is withdrawn, teachers feel that they can no longer cope. Meanwhile, the legal requirement for individualised education plans has encouraged colleagues in some schools to believe that even more children will require such responses, and so putting school budgets under considerable strain in some countries (Ainscow, 1999).

Conscious of these dangers and guided by a clear set of values and principles developed by its steering group, EENET shares information about inclusive education written and generated by, and for, a wide range of stakeholders including children, parents and consumer groups, as well as policy-makers, academics, teacher trainers and teachers themselves. Although the network is located at the University of Manchester's School of Education, it adopts a non-academic style to ensure wide accessiblity to readers who use English as an additional language. Documents posted on the website are not necessarily representative of inclusive education practice, nor are they peer-reviewed. Practitioners are simply encouraged to share their experience, their ideas and their training materials. Nevertheless the EENET website is regarded by many as an important emerging database and a unique international resource on inclusive and enabling education. Most of the evidence for this has so far been anecdotal. However, a detailed analysis was recently carried out of all correspondence received and the final report contains many examples of the way EENET information is used, by whom and in which countries (Lewis, 2003).

Owing to the inequities of access to digital technology, EENET prioritises the dissemination of materials in 'hard copy'. Its annual paper publication, *Enabling Education*, is disseminated annually to almost 2,000 individuals and organisations in around 150 countries. Though many network users have access to computers and can send emails, few have affordable access to the Internet to search for information. Increasingly, CD-ROMs containing key documents are compiled for EENET readers, as this saves the relatively high cost involved in downloading big email attachments or documents from the Internet in countries where telephone charges and printing costs are simply unaffordable. The world is further divided by language, and there is a tendency for experiences in English-speaking countries to be disseminated more widely than experiences in other parts of the world. In response to this imbalance EENET has made some of the most well-used documents available on its website in Spanish, French, Portuguese, Arabic and Russian. However, correspondence in these, and other languages, remains limited.

EENET also compiles information and has organised international seminars to promote debate about the specific issues and challenges related to deafness and inclusion in the South. For example, accounts of sustainable and innovative approaches to community-based education for deaf children in countries as diverse as Afghanistan, Mozambique, Democratic Republic of Congo and Papua New Guinea can be found on EENET website. This is particularly important as the communication needs of deaf children, and their right to use sign language, are highlighted in Article 21 of the Salamanca Framework for Action (UNESCO, 1994) which suggests that education in special schools or special classes attached to mainstream schools may be more suitable for deaf children.

In recent years we have moved towards more regionalised activities. For example, Anupam Ahuja is a member of the South, South-East and Central Asia editorial team that produces the EENET Asia newsletter. This was launched in June 2005 and published in both English and Bahasa (a language spoken by approximately 300 million people in South-East Asia). EENET's activities have increasingly been regionalised in order to promote wider dissemination of information. Committed individuals and organizations in Brazil, Hong Kong, Kenya and Egypt have been promoting EENET as a resource and translating key documents into relevant languages.

More recently, discussions have taken place with a team of practitioners committed to adapting the *Index for Inclusion* for use in countries of the North and South (Booth & Black-Hawkins, 2005). Influenced by the educational discourse in South Africa, the Index is a set of materials devised in England for supporting the learning and participation of all learners, not only those categorized as having special educational needs or disabilities. It contains four main elements: key concepts; a planning framework; indicators and questions; and an emphasis on an inclusive process (Booth, Ainscow, Black-Hawkins, Vaughan, and Shaw, 2002). Key documents related to the use of the Index internationally are now available from the EENET website, and it is hoped that this will enable users of the Index to share their experience with a wider audience.

CREATING CONVERSATIONS

The main approach taken by EENET is one of 'creating conversations' between practitioners and others within local communities who are attempting to develop more inclusive forms of education. This approach starts from the assumption that there is more knowledge available than is currently being used. Furthermore, it is assumed that some of the most relevant and interesting knowledge tends to remain within individuals whose voices are rarely heard. The challenge, therefore, is to find ways of getting such people to share their stories.

Many of the stories that we have been able to collect and disseminate focus on small-scale community-based projects in countries facing economic hardship, where class sizes are large (sometimes more than 100) and where material resources are scarce. These stories demonstrate the way 'insider' practitioners can engage with 'outsiders' as critical

friends, and how this can lead to mutual learning and a greater appreciation of the meaning of inclusion in different contexts. The following brief examples illustrate some of the shared learning taking place:

- A lecturer in psychology in Namibia wrote to say that her colleague was convinced that the idea of inclusion was born in England and would only work there. She revised her opinion after reading examples from Mozambique and Zambia.
- A Zambian head teacher had paid little attention to the four children being educated in a special unit for children with learning difficulties. After reading *Enabling Education* he assessed them and placed them in regular classes where they achieved high grades.
- A group of Ethiopian teacher trainers and district officials visited Mpika, Zambia, to observe the way a set of action research guidelines were used to promote teacher reflection on inclusive education. All 89 teachers involved in the training in Ethiopia have subsequently agreed to teach disabled children in their classes for the first time.

In a study of inclusive education for the World Bank, Peters (2003) referred to examples of inclusive education in the South as 'islands of excellence', implying that the practitioners involved in these 'islands' are cut off from each other. This is certainly true in many cases and it was with the aim of reducing such isolation that EENET was established. As the examples of what we have come to call innovation and instructive practice above demonstrate, it is necessary to be mindful that the context in which these short accounts have been produced, and the knowledge developed, is crucial to the understanding and use of that knowledge, and that, 'knowledge without context is in fact not knowledge at all' (Denning, 2001, p. 135).

The following vignettes illustrate some of the ways in which barriers to the learning and participation of disabled children have been overcome in Southern Africa and Central Asian countries with minimal financial resources. It is difficult in such short examples to do justice to the richness of each example and there is a great danger that generalisations may be made without appreciating the complexity of each cultural and political context. However we offer these examples not for export to a different situation, but as 'interruptions' (Ainscow, this volume) to thinking about inclusion, and to perhaps encourage us to look at more familiar contexts in different ways.

FOCUSING ON PARENTS IN LESOTHO, SOUTHERN AFRICA

Following the adoption of a progressive national policy on integrated education in Lesotho in the late 1980s, a parents' organisation, the Lesotho Society of Mentally Handicapped Persons, was formed with support from the Ministry of Education and a Norwegian parents' organisation. All the teachers in each of the 10 pilot schools, one in each of Lesotho's 10 districts, received in-service training on inclusion (Khatleli, Mariga, Phachaka, and Stubbs, 1995). This was a deliberate strategy to avoid the situation that tends to arise in England, for example, where one teacher tends to be appointed as the school's Special Educational Needs Coordinator. There were only two centrally based advisers in the Ministry when this national programme began. The parents' organisation took the following initiatives to support the advisers and develop a knowledge base among parents of children with learning difficulties:

- A group of 'resource parents' were trained to pass on their knowledge and skills to the other branch members of the organisation (Mphohle, 2000).
- Meetings were organised in the parents' communities for chiefs, health workers, parents and school children to raise awareness of the needs of disabled children, and of their right to attend school.
- The parents adopted a problem-based approach to the development of expertise in schools and provided advice to teachers.
- Parents became involved in pre-service teacher education through occasional lectures and by accompanying the student teachers on home visits.

The teachers soon began to use their new knowledge in responding to all children in their classes who experienced difficulties in learning and who were considered to be in 'difficult circumstances', such as children affected by HIV/AIDS, although they expressed uncertainty about the definition of inclusive education and whether it included all vulnerable children.

FOCUSING ON COMMUNITIES IN CENTRAL ASIA

Alleviating poverty and challenging the segregation and discrimination of disabled children and their families are the two main objectives of the Save the Children UK supported inclusive education programme in Uzbekistan, Kyrgystan and Tajikistan. Disability is sometimes seen as a punishment, yet the importance of helping those who are weaker is underpinned by strong religious beliefs. The perception that disability needs to be cured, and that disabled children need specialist treatment and are unable to learn alongside their peers, is reflected in the current educational legislation, as was the case under the Soviet system. (See Ainscow and Haile-Giorgis, 1998, for more information about the particular challenges of promoting inclusive education in the countries of southeast Europe.) Government is highly centralized in all three countries, and much of the education system was destroyed by civil war in Tajikistan. Despite this difficult context, the inclusive education programme mobilised civil society to participate in the management and monitoring of educational services, using the following strategies:

- Community Education Committees and Parent Associations were formed.
- Community assessments included the mapping of all 'out of school' children.
- The information collected was entered into a database and used for planning purposes (in Uzbekistan).
- Children's Clubs were established – their members conduct home visits, encourage parents to send their children to school, raise awareness in schools, and lead extra-curricular activities.

The process revealed that children excluded from the education system were child drug users, street-based children, working children, children in conflict with the law and child sex workers, as well as disabled children.

Some of the practices highlighted by these examples may not prove to be sustainable in the long term due to their reliance on external agencies for funding and technical support. Nevertheless they are instructive of what is possible in extremely difficult circumstances. We understand that the parents' organisation in Lesotho has faced many challenges recently and so cannot guarantee that the activities are continuing with such high levels of commitment. However, the national inclusive education programme is still supported by the government, and a video-based training package based on the work in Lesotho has been widely disseminated by EENET.

AN ACTION RESEARCH STUDY

The many accounts of practice from economically poor and isolated contexts that have been disseminated by EENET over the last eight years give encouragement to the idea that we can find ways of learning from difference. At the same time, we feel that we have still only scratched the surface of the rich vein of expertise and experience that exists internationally. With this challenge in mind, EENET embarked upon an action research study in collaboration with practitioners in Zambia and Tanzania in 2001 funded by the UK Department for International Development (Miles et al., 2003). The main purpose was to develop ways of helping practitioners within particular contexts to analyse and document their experience of promoting more inclusive practices in education. The study was based on the assumptions that it is more relevant and useful for ideas about practice to be exchanged between similar cultures and contexts, than to continue to export inappropriate models from the richer countries of the North; and that the process of developing analytical and writing skills within a commu-

nity will promote moves towards more inclusive practice. Teachers were involved in identifying exclusionary factors in schools and communities, which both exclude learners from attending school, and from activities once they are in school. Having identified the barriers to inclusion, they were encouraged to develop strategies to overcome these barriers.

The methodology for the study was developed by teams of facilitators in Tanzania and Zambia, with support from the EENET team in the UK. It was based on the principles of 'collaborative inquiry' (Reason, 1988; Reason & Rowan, 1981) which emphasise the value of group processes and varied methods of recording. The study was also informed by Participatory Learning and Action, as developed by Chambers (1994) and refined by Stubbs (1995) and Ainscow (1999) for use in educational contexts. Gosling and Edwards (1995) argue that such approaches involve a particular form of qualitative research that can be used to gain an in-depth understanding of a community or situation. This methodology was unusual, as it was both an intervention, carried out in partnership with colleagues in the field, and the main strategy for collecting and analysing evidence in relation to the overall research agenda.

The writing of accounts by teachers was one of the significant outcomes of the study and some of these were published by EENET (2003). However, the appropriateness of collecting text-based data in the context of an oral tradition was a major tension in the study. The lead researcher in Zambia, for example, described the role of the school-based teams set up to monitor the action research as one of coordinating, supporting, communicating and sharing ideas in the school. The words 'writing, recording, and documenting' were noticeably absent.

The teachers found writing extremely difficult, as can be the case even in literacy-based societies. Towards the end of the study, the research team began to explore the potential of photo elicitation (Harper, 2002) as a more appropriate way of promoting reflection and analysis in an oral culture (Miles & Kaplan,

2005). Participatory photography, and other image-based approaches, can offer a more engaging and relevant alternative to traditional text-based research approaches and can help overcome linguistic and cultural barriers, as Wang (1996, p. 1392) has stated, 'The visual image is a communication tool that can educate, inspire and influence decisions'. At the same time images can enable the views of students to be presented to teachers in unusual and striking ways (Ainscow & Kaplan, 2005; Lewis, 2005).

Writing proved difficult, but the teachers were highly motivated by the prospect of their work being published and disseminated through EENET and wanted their names to appear in the publication. In the wider context of international networking, and publicity within Tanzania and Zambia, anonymity and confidentiality would have denied the teachers the recognition they deserved. This raised inevitable dilemmas for the UK-based research team who were accustomed to anonymising children's identities. As EENET engages with education practitioners, it assumes some responsibility for raising awareness about child protection issues, which relate directly to the ethical considerations associated with carrying out such practitioner-led research.

Facilitating the documentation of experience in one district, Mpika, involved a process of knowledge generation and construction about inclusive education in the context of Northern Zambia. Mpika is a small provincial town situated 600 kilometres from the capital. Schools in the Mpika area range from government-funded institutions which are well established, to those that are still in the process of being built by community members in more remote rural areas, and which receive very little government funding.

Although the teachers in some of the Mpika schools already used the language of child rights, democracy, participation and social justice, they regarded the teaching of children identified as having special needs or disabilities as a specialist activity, for which they were not qualified. Yet only two of the 17 schools taking part had specialist 'units' in which specialist teachers were based: one for deaf children and one for children with learning difficulties. The teacher responsible for facilitating the action research study had no specialist training, either as a researcher or as a special educator, but he had experience of including children with a wide range of educational needs in his class, and of documenting his experience over many years (Mumba, 2000).

The language of special education and inclusion proved to be a barrier in the developments that occurred. The lead researcher in Zambia led a process of de-constructing the teachers' understanding of terms such as 'special education' and supported them in constructing their own knowledge and understanding of 'inclusion' in the context of Mpika. The teachers began to realise that they already included a wide range of children in their classes, some of whom had disabilities, while others experienced discrimination because they had become pregnant, were affected by HIV/AIDS, could not afford to buy uniforms, or had exhausting domestic responsibilities and chaotic home lives.

Defining inclusive education in the context of Mpika was a slow process requiring skilled facilitation, but it was a more sustainable way of promoting inclusive education than the more usual approach of 'transferring knowledge' from more 'developed' settings. It was also consistent with the move away from the individual focus of a special education approach towards an examination of the many other exclusionary pressures within society and its schools (Ahuja, 2002), as advocated by UNESCO in its *Teacher Education Resource Pack: Special Needs in the Classroom* (UNESCO, 1993). The key to progress, it seems, is to start from where people are and assist them to be more skilful at analysing their own context.

CONCLUSION

Providing practitioners with an opportunity to reflect on the way inclusive education is interpreted and implemented in other contexts can help to shed new light on their own practice which can lead to change and development. At the same time, the accounts of practice disseminated by the EENET open up a further interesting possibility – that those who live and work in the economically richer countries of the world can also learn from experiences in the South.

However, as we have seen, encouraging practitioners to document and share their experience is not an easy task. The majority of EENET network users come from a strong oral tradition, where stories are told rather than published, and most use English as an additional language. Approaching the development of inclusive education by encouraging documentation is a slow process and tends to be less high profile than some of the 'quick fix' examples where donors want to see rapid results for their money. Yet we believe that reflection and documentation can lead to a more sustainable set of social processes in communities, which are more likely to make an impact on practice in the long term.

In their work in the UK, Ainscow, Booth and Dyson (in press) have highlighted the importance of 'interrupting' the thinking of teachers and other practitioners, in order to stimulate them to think differently about their own situations by making the familiar unfamiliar. This echoes the idea of Delamont (1992, p. 45) who argues that familiarity can be a problem and suggests devising strategies for 'making the familiar bizarre, unusual and novel' so that 'the familiarity is thus thrown into relief by the unfamiliar'.

Often it is assumed that inclusive education can only be implemented in contexts which have a minimum level of resources. Indeed, in the well-resourced classrooms of Northern countries, resistance to inclusion on the grounds that 'there are insufficient resources' is very common. As we have attempted to demonstrate in this chapter, some pioneering education practitioners in the South are embracing the philosophy of inclusion in their classrooms and communities, and are working within available resources to include all children in education.

Ainscow (1999) reports that in the richer industrialised nations there is worrying evidence of a significant increase in the proportions of children being categorised in order that their schools can earn additional resources. This is a continuation of the important analysis provided earlier by Fulcher (1989), who suggested that the increased bureaucracy that is often associated with special education legislation, and the struggles that take place for additional resources, have the effect of escalating the proportion of children who come to be labelled as disabled.

Initiatives to enable all children to gain access to, and complete, primary education have stimulated a more complex debate about the changing role of special education in the context of Education for All. The current trend to move towards more inclusive education within the context of Education for All has major implications for the future development of both general and special education in the South. Practitioners in the South have the potential to 'leapfrog' over some of the expensive and exclusionary practices developed in special education over recent decades. Networking and information sharing can help practitioners to avoid some of the mistakes and pitfalls, while constructing their own knowledge base and response to difference and discrimination in education. Difference, it can be argued, is in itself our greatest available resource, rather than a problem to be solved – regardless of the level of material and financial resources in a particular context.

REFERENCES

Abiroux, E., & Ahuja, A. (2004). *Final Evaluation of the Community Based Care and Inclusive Education for Disabled Children in Central Asia Programme.* Save the Children UK Office for South and Central Asia Region.

Ahuja, A. (2002). Teacher training for inclusive education in developing countries: The UNESCO experience. In S. Hegarty & M. Alur (Eds.), *Education and children with special needs. From segregation to inclusion* (pp. 77–96). New Delhi: Sage Publications.

Ahuja, A. (2003). *Inclusive Education Pilot Project in*

Bandung Indonesia (Consultant Report). Bangkok: UNESCO.

Ahuja, A. (2005). *EFA national action plans review study: Key findings.* Bangkok: UNESCO.

Ahuja, A., & Ibrahim, M. D. (2004). *An assessment of inclusive education in Bangladesh* (Consultant Report). Dhaka: UNESCO.

Ainscow, M. (1999). *Understanding the development of inclusive schools.* London: Falmer Press.

Ainscow, M., & Haile-Giorgis, M. (1998). *The education of children with special needs: Barriers and opportunities in Central and Eastern Europe.* Economic and Social Policy Series, EPS 67. International Child Development Centre. Florence: UNICEF.

Ainscow, M., & Kaplan, I. (2005). Using evidence to encourage inclusive school development: possibilities and challenges. *The Australasian Journal of Special Education, 29*(2), 106–116.

Ainscow, M., Booth, T., & Dyson, A. (In press). *Improving schools, developing inclusion.* London: Routledge.

Artiles, A., & Dyson, A. (2005) Inclusive education in the age of globalisation. The promise of comparative cultural-historical analysis. In D. Mitchell (Ed.), *Contextualising inclusive education* (pp. 37–62). London: Routledge/Falmer.

Booth, T., & Ainscow, M. (Eds.). (1998). *From them to us: An international study of inclusion in education.* London: Routledge.

Booth, T. & Black-Hawkins, K. (2005). *Developing learning and participation in countries of the South. The role of an Index for Inclusion* (revd ed.) Paris: UNESCO. Retrieved December 22, 2005, from www.eenet.org.uk/theory_practice/develop_learning_participation.doc

Booth, T., Ainscow, M., Black-Hawkins, K., Vaughan, M., & Shaw, L. (2002). *Index for Inclusion: Developing learning and participation in schools* (revd ed.).Bristol: Centre for Studies on Inclusive Education.

Chambers, R. (1994, September). The origins and practice of participatory rural appraisal. *World Development, 22*(9), 1253–1268.

Chronic Poverty Research Centre. (2005). *The Chronic Poverty Report 2004–5.* Manchester: Chronic Poverty Research Centre.

Delamont, S. (1992). *Fieldwork in educational settings: Methods, pitfalls and perspectives.* London: Falmer Press.

Denning, S. (2001). Knowledge sharing in the North and South. In W. Gmelin, K. King & S. McGrath (Eds.), *Development, knowledge, national research and international cooperation* (pp. 131–152). Edinburgh: Centre for African Studies.

Department of Education. (2001). *Education White Paper 6. Special Needs Education: Building an Inclusive Education and Training System.* Pretoria: Government printer.

Department for International Development (DfID). (2000). *Eliminating world poverty: Making globalisation work for the poor. White paper on international development.* London: DfID.

Department for International Development (DfID). (2001). *Children out of School.* London: DfID.

Department for International Development (DfID). (2005). *MDG Goal 2 education factsheet.* London: DfID. Retrieved November 5, 2005, from www.dfid.gov.uk/mdg/education.asp

Department of Education. (1997). *Quality education for all: Overcoming barriers to development.* Pretoria: National Commission on Special Needs in Education and Training/National Committee on Education Support Services, Department of Education.

Dyson, A. (2004). Inclusive education: a global agenda? *Japanese Journal of Special Education, 41*(6), 613–625.

Enabling Education Network (EENET). (2003). *Researching our experience: Teachers stories from Mpika, Zambia.* Manchester: EENET. Retrieved November 24, 2005, from www.eenet.org.uk/action/rsrching_experience.pdf

Engelbrecht, P., Green, L., Naicker, S., & Engelbrecht, L. (1999). *Inclusive education in action in South Africa.* Pretoria: JL van Schaik.

Fulcher, G. (1989). *Disabling policies? A comparative approach to education, policy and disability.* London: Falmer Press.

Fuller, B., & Clarke, P. (1994). Raising school effects while ignoring culture? Local conditions and the influence of classroom tools, rules, and pedagogy. *Review of Educational Research, 64*(1), 119–157.

Global Campaign for Education. (2005, September). *UN Millennium Summit delivers rhetoric without commitment.* (A report by the Global Campaign for Education.) Retrieved October 2, 2005, from http://www.campaignforeducation.org/resources/resources_latest.php

Gosling, L., & Edwards, M. (1995). *Toolkits: A practical guide to assessment, monitoring and evaluation.* London: Save the Children.

Harper, D. (2002). Talking about pictures: A case for photo elicitation. *Visual Studies, 17*(1), 13–26.

Heshusius, L. (1989). The Newtonian mechanistic paradigm, special education and contours of alternatives. *Journal of Learning Disabilities, 22*(7), 403–421.

Hiebert, J., Gallimore, R., & Stigler, J. W. (2002). A knowledge base for the teaching profession: What would it look like and how can we get one? *Educational Researcher, 31*(5), 3–15.

Iano, R. P. (1986). The study and development of teaching: With implications for the advancement of special education. *Remedial and Special Education, 7*(5), 50–61.

Jones, H. (2001). *Disabled children's rights – a practical guide.* Stockholm: Save the Children Sweden.

Khatleli, P., Mariga, L., Phachaka, L., & Stubbs, S.

(1995). Schools for all: national planning in Lesotho. In B. O'Toole & R. McConkey (Eds.), *Innovations in developing countries for people with disabilities* (pp. 135–160). Chorley: Lisieux Hall Publications. Retrieved November 24, 2005, from www. eenet.org.uk/parents/book/bookcontents.shtml

King, K. (2002). Banking on knowledge: The new knowledge projects of the World Bank. *Compare, 32*(3), 311–326.

Kisanji, J. (1998). The march towards inclusive education in non-Western countries: retracing the steps. *International Journal of Inclusive Education, 2*(1), 55–72.

Lewis, I. (2003). *Seven years of conversations. An analysis of EENET's correspondence records, 1997–2004.* Manchester: EENET. Retrieved November 24, 2005, from www.eenet.org.uk/about/sevenyears.pdf

Lewis, I. (2005). *Inclusive classrooms: The use of images in active learning and action research, May 2005, Mpika, Zambia.* Retrieved November 25, 2005, from: www.eenet.org.uk/action/ mpika_report.pdf

Lincoln, Y. S., & Guba, E. G. (1984). *Naturalistic Inquiry.* Beverley Hills, CA: Sage.

Miles, M. (1999). Can formal disability services be developed with South Asian historical and conceptual foundations? In E. Stone (Ed.), *Disability and development. Learning from action and research on disability in the majority world* (pp. 228–256). Leeds: The Disability Press.

Miles, S. (2002a). *Family action for inclusion in education.* Manchester: EENET. Retrieved December 1, 2005, from http://www.eenet.org.uk/parents/family_action.pdf

Miles, S (2002b). Learning about inclusive education: The role of EENET in promoting international dialogue. In P. Farrell & M. Ainscow (Eds.), *Making special education inclusive* (pp. 51–62). London: David Fulton.

Miles, S. (2005). Inclusive education. A discussion paper. In P. Amerena and S. Mavillapalli (Eds.), *Inclusive development* (pp. 59–96). London: Leonard Cheshire International.

Miles, S., & Kaplan, I. (2005). Using images to promote reflection: an action research study in Zambia and Tanzania. *Journal of Research in Special Educational Needs, 5*(2), 77–83.

Miles, S., Ainscow, M., Kangwa, P., Kisanji, J., Lewis, I., Mmbaga, D., & Mumba, P. (2003). *Learning from difference: Understanding community initiatives to improve access to education.* (Research report to the UK Department for International Education.) Manchester: EENET. Retrieved November 24, 2005, from www.eenet.org.uk/action/learning-from_diff.no.pdf

Mittler, P. (2005). The global context of inclusive education: the role of the United Nations. In D. Mitchell (Ed.), *Contextualising inclusive education* (pp. 22–36). London: Routledge/Falmer.

Mphohle, P. (2000). Contribution of parents in inclusive education. In M. Ainscow & P. Mittler, *Including the excluded.* Proceedings of 5th International Special Education Congress, University of Manchester. Delph: Inclusive Technology Ltd.

Mumba, P (2000). Democratisation of primary classrooms in Zambia: A case study of its implementation in a rural primary school in Mpika. In M. Ainscow & P. Mittler, *Including the excluded.* Proceedings of 5th International Special Education Congress, University of Manchester. Delph: Inclusive Technology Ltd.

Muthukrishna, N. (2000). Transforming the education system: The development of sustainable education policy and practice in South Africa. Keynote speech. In M. Ainscow & P. Mittler, *Including the excluded.* Proceedings of 5th International Special Education Congress, University of Manchester. Delph: Inclusive Technology Ltd.

Muthukrishna, N. (2003, September). The inclusion/exclusion debate in South Africa and developing countries. *Perspectives in Education, 21*(3), vii.

Naicker, S.M. (1999). *Curriculum 2005. A space for all: An introduction to inclusive education.* Cape Town: Renaissance.

Norwich, B. (2002). *LEA inclusion trends in England 1997–2001. Statistics on special school placements & pupils with statements in special schools.* Bristol: Centre for Studies in Inclusive Education.

Peters, S. (Ed.). (1993). *Education and disability in cross-cultural perspective.* London: Garland.

Peters, S. (2003). *Inclusive education: Achieving education for all by including those with disabilities and special education needs.* Washington, DC: World Bank.

Porteus, K. (2003, September). Decolonising inclusion: Constructing an analytic framework for inclusion/exclusion for the decolonising context. *Perspectives in Education, 21*(3), 13–24.

Reason, P. (1988). *Human inquiry in action: Developments in new paradigm research.* London: Sage.

Reason, P., & Rowan, J. (1981). *Human inquiry: A sourcebook for new paradigm research.* Chichester: Wiley.

Rustemier, S., & Vaughan, M. (2005). *Segregation trends – LEAs in England 2002–2004. Placement of pupils with statements in special schools and other segregated settings.* Bristol: Centre for Studies in Inclusive Education.

Save the Children. (2002). *Schools for all: Including disabled children in education.* London: Save the Children. Retrieved December 1, 2005, from http://www.eenet.org.uk/bibliog/scuk/schools_for_all.shtml

Singal, N. (2005). Mapping the field of inclusive education: a review of the Indian literature. *International Journal of Inclusive Education, 9*(4) 331–350.

Slee, R. (1996). Inclusive schooling in Australia? Not yet. *Cambridge Journal of Education, 26*(1), 19–32.

Slee, R. (2004). Inclusive education: a framework for reform? In V. Heung & M. Ainscow (Eds.), *Inclusive education: A framework for reform* (pp. 58–66). Hong Kong: Hong Kong Institute of Education.

Stubbs, S. (1995). *The Lesotho National Integrated Education Programme: A case study on implementation.* Unpublished MEd thesis, Faculty of Education, University of Cambridge. Retrieved November 24, 2005, from www.eenet.org.uk/action/sthesis/contents.shtml

Stubbs, S. (1999). Engaging with difference. In E. Stone (Ed.), *Disability and development. Learning from action and research on disability in the majority world* (pp. 257–279). Leeds: The Disability Press.

United Nations Educational, Scientific, and Cultural Organization (UNESCO). (1993). *Teacher education resource pack: Special needs in the classroom.* Paris: UNESCO.

United Nations Educational, Scientific, and Cultural Organization (UNESCO). (1994). *The Salamanca statement and framework for action on special needs education.* Paris: UNESCO.

United Nations Educational, Scientific, and Cultural Organization (UNESCO). (1995). *Review of the present situation in special needs education.* Paris: UNESCO.

United Nations Educational, Scientific, and Cultural Organization (UNESCO). (2000). *Education for all: Meeting our collective commitments. Notes on the Dakar Framework for Action.* Paris: UNESCO.

United Nations Educational, Scientific, and Cultural Organization (UNESCO). (2001a). *Including the excluded: Meeting diversity in education. Example from Romania.* Paris: UNESCO.

United Nations Educational, Scientific, and Cultural Organization (UNESCO). (2001b). *Including the excluded: Meeting diversity in education. Example from Uganda.* Paris: UNESCO.

United Nations Educational, Scientific, and Cultural Organization (UNESCO). (2004). *The right to education for persons with disabilities: Towards inclusion.* A conceptual paper, December 2004. ED/BAS/EIE/2004/1 REV. Paris: UNESCO. Retrieved November 27, 2005, from http://unescodoc.unesco.org/images/0013/001378/137873e.pdf

Wang, C. (1996). Chinese village women as visual anthropologists: A participatory approach to reaching policymakers. *Social Science and Medicine*, 42(10), 1391–1400.

11

From special education to effective schools for all: a review of progress so far[1]

Mel Ainscow

Since the late 1980s a growing number of international scholars have provided a critical commentary on the field of special education. In so doing they have argued that progress towards more inclusive education systems requires a move away from practices based on the traditional perspectives of special education, towards approaches that focus on the development of schools for all.

This shift in thinking has been characterised by some scholars as the 'organisational paradigm' (Dyson & Millward, 2000). In general terms it involves moves away from explanations of educational failure that concentrate on the characteristics of individual children and their families, towards an analysis of the barriers to participation and learning experienced by students within school systems (Ainscow, 1994; Booth & Ainscow, 2002). In this way, those students who do not respond to existing arrangements come to be regarded as 'hidden voices' who, under certain conditions, can encourage the improvement of schools.

In 1991 I edited a book entitled *Effective Schools for All*, which included contributions from scholars, such as Tom Skrtic, Roger Slee and Margaret Wang, who were at that time arguing for a change of perspective (Ainscow, 1991). In that book I concluded that this new thinking had had limited impact upon policy and practice in the field. I went on to suggest that progress would depend upon a new culture in schools that encouraged teacher reflection and collaborative problem-solving. I also argued that this required 'those of us who have made our careers in special education to reconsider our perspectives once more and act accordingly' (p. 227).

In this chapter I reflect on developments since the publication of that book in a way that is intended to challenge readers to think critically about their own thinking and practice. In particular, I review research carried out within an organisational frame of reference in order to map progress and point to areas that would warrant further attention. More specifically, I examine the findings of research that focuses on: classroom practice and teacher development; school development and leadership; and systemic change. Building on this analysis, the chapter goes on to focus attention on possible levers that can help to move education systems in a more inclusive direction.

RETHINKING SPECIAL NEEDS

The field that has been known as special education or, more recently, special needs education, is involved in a period of considerable uncertainty. In particular, the emphasis on inclusive education that is now evident in many countries challenges special needs practitioners to reconsider their own thinking and practice. My own view is that this context of uncertainty provides the special education field with new opportunities for continuing its historical purpose of addressing the needs of those learners who become marginalised within existing educational arrangements.

A brief look at history reminds us that in the nineteenth century special educators in many countries argued for and helped develop provision for children and young people who were excluded from educational plans (Reynolds & Ainscow, 1994). Only much later did this provision become adopted by national governments. It is worth noting, for example, that in my own country it was only as recent as 1970 that one group of learners, those categorised as 'having severe learning difficulties', was deemed to be even worthy of education.

Similarly, provision for children experiencing difficulties within mainstream schools grew as a result of a gradual recognition that some students were marginalised within and, in some instances, excluded from existing arrangements for providing education. As this provision developed during the latter part of the twentieth century, there was also increased emphasis on notions of integration, as special educators explored ways of supporting previously segregated groups in order that they could find a place in local community schools.

It can be argued, therefore, that the current emphasis on inclusive education is but a further step along this historical road. It is, however, a major step, in that the aim is to transform the mainstream in ways that will

increase its capacity for responding to all learners (Ainscow, 1999). And, of course, such a project requires the participation of many stakeholders in ways that challenge much of the status quo.

In some countries, inclusive education is thought of as an approach to serving children with disabilities within general education settings (Mittler, 2000; Pijl, Meijer, & Hegarty, 1997). Internationally, however, it is increasingly seen more broadly as a reform that responds to diversity amongst all learners (UNESCO, 2001). The argument developed in this chapter adopts this broader formulation. It presumes that the aim of inclusive school improvement is to eliminate exclusionary processes from education that are a consequence of attitudes and responses to diversity in race, social class, ethnicity, religion, gender and attainment (Vitello & Mithaug, 1998). As such, it starts from the belief that education is a basic human right and the foundation for a more just society (Thomas & Vaughn, 2004).

This approach was endorsed just over 10 years ago by the Salamanca World Conference on Special Needs Education (UNESCO, 1994). Arguably the most significant international document that has ever appeared in the field of special education, the Salamanca Statement argues that regular schools with an inclusive orientation are 'the most effective means of combating discriminatory attitudes, building an inclusive society and achieving education for all'. Furthermore, it suggests that such schools can 'provide an effective education for the majority of children and improve the efficiency and ultimately the cost-effectiveness of the entire education system' (UNESCO, 1994).

Such arguments have led to proposals for a re-conceptualisation of the 'special needs' task. This revised thinking suggests that progress will be much more likely if we recognise that difficulties experienced by students result from the ways in which schools are currently organised and from the forms of teaching that are provided. Consequently, it is argued, schools need to be reformed and pedagogy needs to be improved in ways that will lead them to respond positively to pupil diversity – seeing individual differences not as problems to be fixed, but as opportunities for enriching learning (Ainscow, 1999). Within such a conceptualisation, a consideration of difficulties experienced by students can provide an agenda for reforms and insights as to how such reforms might be brought about. However, it has been argued that this kind of approach is more likely to be successful in contexts where there is a culture of collaboration that encourages and supports problem-solving (Tilstone, Florian, & Rose, 1998; Skrtic, 1991). According to this view, the development of inclusive practices is seen as involving those within a particular context in working together to address barriers to education experienced by some learners.

Given the confusion and uncertainties that exist, advancing towards the implementation of inclusive education is far from easy and evidence of progress is limited in most countries. Moreover, it must not be assumed that there is full acceptance of the inclusive philosophy (Brantlinger, 1997; Fuchs & Fuchs, 1994; Sebba & Sachdev, 1997). Not only are many educationalists resistant to the idea, but some disability-focused organisations argue for separate, 'specialist' services. For example, some organisations of deaf people argue that children with hearing impairments have to be educated separately in order to guarantee their right to education in the medium of sign language and access to deaf culture. Also, there are those who believe that small units located in the standard school environment can provide the specialist knowledge, equipment and support for which the mainstream classroom and teacher can never provide a full substitute.

Consequently, as we consider the way forward for developing educational systems that encourage and support the development of schools that are effective in reaching all children, it is necessary to recognise that the field itself is riddled with uncertainties, disputes and contradictions. However, what can be said is that throughout the world attempts are being made to provide more effective educational responses for all children, whatever their characteristics, and that, encouraged by the Salamanca Statement, the overall trend is towards making these responses within the context of general educational provision. As a consequence, this is leading to a reconsideration of the future roles and purposes of practitioners throughout the education system, including those who work in specialist provision.

IMPROVING THE QUALITY OF EDUCATION FOR ALL

My own research is concerned with the development of effective strategies for making policies and practices inclusive. Much of this work has been set in the context of a school improvement initiative known as Improving the Quality of Education for All (IQEA) that involves university academics working in partnership with networks of schools, in the UK and other countries (see Ainscow, 1999; Hopkins, Ainscow, & West, 1994; and Hopkins, 2001, for more detailed accounts).

The IQEA approach to school improvement emphasises the following features:

- Developments in teaching and learning, through the creation of conditions within schools for managing change successfully;
- School improvement led from within schools, focusing on areas that are seen to be matters of priority;
- Collecting and engaging with evidence in order to move thinking and practice forward, and to evaluate progress; and
- Collaboration amongst colleagues in partner schools, and with IQEA consultants, so that a wider range of expertise and resources is available to support improvements in all of the participating schools.

The overall framework used to guide these activities is shown in Figure 11.1.

Groups of staff are encouraged to examine the realities of their schools in relation to the four areas outlined within this framework. As can be seen, this emphasises the centrality of the quality of experience provided for students. Engaging with evidence about this,

Figure 11.1 *IQEA framework*

school groups go on to develop areas of focus that will guide their improvement efforts. They then look more specifically at ways in which teaching and leadership practices can be developed within their schools in order to bring about improvements.

The analysis of the experience of IQEA over 15 years provides strong evidence of how inclusive school improvement can be achieved. More than anything this points to the importance of developing a school culture that fosters positive attitudes towards the study and development of practice. This is based on the assumption that teachers are the key to the development of more inclusive education systems. As Fulcher (1989) implies, as far as children are concerned, teachers are the key policy-makers: once the classroom door is closed, it is their decisions that determine what the class experiences. This being the case, our aim must be find effective ways of supporting teachers in developing their capacity for reaching out to all of their learners.

DEVELOPING INCLUSIVE TEACHING

Much of the early work of IQEA involved attempts to introduce particular policy changes and, in so doing, to strengthen the schools' capacity to handle change. Gradually we recognised that even where such initiatives were successful they did not necessarily lead to changes in classroom practice. Our experience is that developments of practice are unlikely to occur without some exposure to what teaching actually looks like when it is being done differently, and exposure to someone who can help teachers understand the difference between what they are doing and what they aspire to do. It also seems that this sort of problem has to be solved at the individual level before it can be solved at the organisational level (for example, Elmore, Peterson, & McCarthy, 1996). Indeed, there is evidence that increasing collaboration without some more specific attention to change at the individual level can simply result in teachers coming together to reinforce existing practices rather than confronting the difficulties they face in new ways (Lipman, 1997).

At the heart of the processes in schools where changes in practice do occur is the development of a common language with which colleagues can talk to one another and, indeed, to themselves about detailed aspects of their practice (Huberman, 1993). Without such a language teachers find it very difficult to experiment with new possibilities. Frequently, when observers report to teachers what they have seen during their lessons they express surprise (Ainscow, 1999). It seems that much of what teachers do during the intensive encounters that occur is carried out at an automatic, intuitive level. Furthermore, there is little time to stop and think. This is why having the opportunity to see colleagues at work is so crucial to the success of attempts to develop practice. It is through shared experiences that colleagues can help one another to articulate what they currently do and define what they might like to do (Hiebert, Gallimore, & Stigler, 2002). It is also the means whereby taken-for-granted assumptions about particular groups of students can be subjected to mutual critique.

In this respect, student diversity has the potential to provide an important stimulus for teachers to think about their practices in new ways. We have also seen how various forms of evidence can be helpful in stimulating discussion and reflection amongst teachers (Ainscow, 1999, 2000; Ainscow & Brown, 1999; Ainscow, Howes, Farrell, & Frankham, 2003). Specifically, evidence can help to create space for reappraisal and rethinking by interrupting existing discourses, and by focusing attention on overlooked possibilities for moving practice forward. Particularly powerful techniques in this respect involve the use of mutual observation of lessons (Ainscow, Barrs, & Martin, 1998) and evidence collected from students about teaching and learning arrangements within a school (Ainscow & Kaplan, 2005). Under certain conditions these approaches provide *interruptions* that help to make the familiar unfamiliar in ways that can stimulate self-questioning, creativity and action.

However, such approaches are also likely to be disturbing. Consequently, their successful use depends on forms of leadership that foster a willingness to address the challenges that emerge as a result of listening to the voices of different people about existing classroom arrangements. Lambert and her colleagues seem to be talking about a similar process in their discussion of what they call

'the constructivist leader'. They stress the importance of leaders gathering, generating and interpreting information within a school in order to create an 'inquiring stance'. They argue that such information causes 'disequilibrium' in thinking and, as a result, provides a challenge to existing assumptions about teaching and learning (Lambert et al., 1995).

We have found, however, that whilst an engagement with evidence can create space for reviewing thinking and practice, it is not in itself a straightforward mechanism for the development of more inclusive practices. The space that is created may be filled according to conflicting agendas. In this way, deeply held beliefs within a school may prevent the experimentation that is necessary in order to foster the development of more inclusive ways of working. So, for example, at the end of a lesson in a secondary school during which there was a very low level of participation amongst the class, the teacher explained what had happened with reference to the fact that most of the class were listed on the school's special educational needs register.

Such explanations make us acutely aware that the relationship between the recognition of anomalies in school practices and the presence of students presenting difficulties as the occasions for such recognition is deeply ambiguous. It is very easy for educational difficulties to be pathologised as difficulties inherent *within* students. This is true not only of students with disabilities and those defined as 'having special educational needs', but also of those whose socioeconomic status, race, language and gender render them problematic to particular teachers in particular schools. Consequently, it is necessary to develop the capacity of those within schools to reveal and challenge deeply entrenched deficit views of 'difference', which define certain types of students as 'lacking something' (Trent, Artiles, & Englert, 1998).

Specifically, it is necessary to be vigilant in scrutinising how deficit assumptions may be influencing perceptions of certain students. As Bartolome (1994) explains, teaching methods are neither devised nor implemented in a vacuum. Design, selection and use of particular teaching approaches and strategies arise from perceptions about learning and learners. In this respect even the most pedagogically advanced methods are likely to be ineffective in the hands of those who implicitly or explicitly subscribe to a belief system that regards some students, at best, as disadvantaged and in need of fixing, or, worse, as deficient and, therefore, beyond fixing.

Writing about similar processes, Timperley and Robinson (2001) explain how teachers' existing understandings influence the way evidence is interpreted, such that they perceive what they expect to perceive. Consequently, new meanings are only likely to emerge when evidence creates 'surprises'. Usually it is helpful to have an external perspective that can use moments of surprise to challenge accepted meanings and take teachers beyond their existing understandings.

The work of many IQEA schools has demonstrated how a close scrutiny of the processes involved in teaching can challenge teachers to review their thinking and, as a result, to experiment with new practices. This has caused us to reflect carefully on how best to introduce such approaches. Clearly, there are many possibilities and each school has to decide on an approach that fits with its circumstances and traditions. In general, we favour the use of 'lesson study', a systematic procedure for the development of teaching that is well established in Japan and some other Asian countries (Hiebert, et al., 2002; Lo, Yan, & Pakey, 2005; Stigler & Hiebert, 1999). Recently some IQEA schools in Hong Kong and the United Kingdom have used the approach to great effect.

The goal of lesson study is to improve the effectiveness of the experiences that the teachers provide for all of their students. The core activity is collaboration on a shared area of focus that is generated through discussion. The content of this focus is the planned lesson, which is then used as the basis of gathering data on the quality of experience that students receive. These lessons are called 'study lessons' and are used to examine the teachers' practices and the responsiveness of the students to the planned activities. Members of the group work together to design the lesson plan, which is then implemented by each teacher. Observations and post-lesson conferences are arranged to facilitate the improvement of the research lesson between each trial.

Lesson study can be conducted in many ways. It may, for example, involve a small sub-group of volunteer staff, or be carried out through departmental or special interest groupings. It can also happen 'across schools', and is then part of a wider, managed network of teachers working together. Within IQEA the local school network offers the scope for such dissemination and sharing events to occur. The collection of evidence is a key factor in the lesson study approach. This usually involves the use of video recordings of the study lessons. Emphasis is also placed on listening to the views of students in a way that tends to introduce a critical edge to the discussions that take place.

DEVELOPING INCLUSIVE LEADERSHIP

Research in IQEA schools suggests that using strategies such as lesson study to move practice forward often leads to periods of 'turbulence' (Hopkins et al., 1994). This may take a number of different forms, involving organisational, psychological, technical or micropolitical dimensions. At its heart, however, it is usually about the dissonance that occurs as people struggle to make sense of new ideas. It reminds us, of course, that change often requires 'old dogs to learn new tricks'.

There is evidence to suggest that without a period of turbulence, successful, long-lasting change is unlikely to occur (Hopkins et al., 1994). In this sense, turbulence can be seen as a useful indication that the school is on the move. So, how can teachers be supported in coping with such periods of difficulty? What organisational arrangements are helpful in encouraging the development of practice?

From our experience of many schools that have made tangible progress we note the existence of certain arrangements that seem to be helpful. These provide structures for supporting teachers in exploring their ideas and ways of working, whilst, at the same time, ensuring that maintenance arrangements are not sacrificed. More specifically, they seek to support the creation of a climate of risk-taking within which these explorations can take place.

In attempting to make sense of such arrangements we have formulated a typology of six inter-connected organisational 'conditions' that seem to be a feature of inclusive school development (Hopkins, 2001). These are attention to the potential benefits of *enquiry and reflection*; a commitment to *collaborative planning*; the *involvement* of staff, students and community in school policies and decisions; *staff development* activities that focuses on classroom practice; *coordination* strategies, particularly in relation to the use of time; and effective *leadership roles*, not only by senior staff but spread throughout the school. In working with schools on their improvement initiatives we ask them to carry out a review of these organisational conditions to see whether it might be helpful to make adjustments in ways that will provide greater support to staff as they face the inevitable periods of turbulence. This has led us to focus particular attention on the development of forms of leadership that will challenge existing beliefs and assumptions within a school (Kugelmass & Ainscow, 2005).

Helpful theoretical and empirical leads in respect to this challenge are provided by Riehl (2000). As a result of a detailed review of relevant literature, she concludes that school leaders need to attend to three broad tasks: fostering new meanings about diversity; promoting inclusive practices within schools; and building connections between schools and communities. This analysis leads the author to offer a positive view of the potential for school leaders to engage in inclusive, transformative developments. She concludes: 'When wedded to a relentless commitment to equity, voice, and social justice, administrators' efforts in the tasks of sensemaking, promoting inclusive cultural practices in schools, and building positive relationships outside of the school may indeed foster a new form of practice' (Riehl, 2000, p. 71).

Bearing these ideas in mind, we have recently been working with a 'think-tank' of school principals in England to address the question: '*What forms of leadership practice encourage behaviour that facilitates the learning of all students within a school?*' (Fox & Ainscow, 2006) Like Spillane, Halverson and Diamond (2001), the practitioners and researchers involved assumed that school leadership has to be understood as a distributed practice, stretched over a school's social and situational contexts. We saw this as a transformational perspective on leadership that sets out to empower others to bring about change, particularly in relation to the ways in which social relationships influence teaching and learning. Consequently, we took *leadership practice* as our unit of analysis, rather than focusing on the work of individual leaders.

It was also assumed that the development of leadership practice starts from personal experience and involves forms of social learning, as those within a given workplace explore ways of solving the practical problems they face in carrying out their duties (Copland, 2003). Much of this professional learning goes on at a largely intuitive level and the knowledge that it creates is mainly unarticulated. In other words, those who develop leadership skills find it difficult to describe the ways in which they do what they do. This led us to assume that the most effective form of leadership development is likely to be based within the workplace, using social learning processes that influence thinking and action in a particular context.

The experience of working with the think-tank principals revealed some important ideas about the nature of leadership practice and how it can be developed. In particular, it showed how, under certain conditions, written accounts of leadership practice in different schools can be used to stimulate a form of reflection that makes use of the experience and knowledge that exists within a group of educational leaders. It also showed how joint visits to schools in order to produce such accounts can have similar effects.

The approach used within the think-tank emphasised the value of group processes and the use of varied methods of recording information. In this way, the action learning process experienced by this group of principals became the process by which their own leadership practices were challenged. The written accounts were seen as a tool for stimulating a process that brought about changes in the behaviour of staff and, as a result, students.

As a result of this project, a set of leadership development materials was produced in order to guide other groups of leaders who wish to use the accounts as the basis for leadership development (Ainscow & Fox, 2003). These materials focus on ten 'accounts of practice'. They also include selected readings that are used to: *further stimulate reflection*, by enabling readers to compare what they do with accounts of leadership practice elsewhere; *challenge and reframe existing thinking*, by reading evidence about leadership practices that have proved to be successful in other contexts; and *conceptualise learning*, through engagement with texts that provide deeper theoretical explanations of what is involved in leadership practice. These three approaches throw light on how ideas from the literature can be helpful in generating different types of knowledge that are relevant to the development of leadership practice in schools (West, Ainscow, & Notman, 2003).

The project materials are intended to be used by groups of leaders within schools, or from a group of schools, in order to foster yet further action learning activities of the sort that took place within the think-tank. The central aim is to encourage groups of colleagues to work together in order to move thinking and practice forward within their organisations. The starting point for the work of such an action learning group is the existing experience and knowledge of its members. Those taking part must, therefore, be helped to take responsibility for their own learning. Their colleagues in the group are seen as sources of challenge and support, bringing their experiences and perspectives to the discussions that take place. Within such contexts, written accounts of practice, plus the additional readings, are used to stimulate reflection and creativity.

Four other networks (26 schools in total) have subsequently used the materials and processes in order to review and develop their leadership practices. School leaders from these schools formed local action learning groups and each was facilitated and supported by a school principal from the original group. At the same time, the participants used the materials to facilitate a similar review and development process with leadership teams in their own schools. There was also a programme of school-to-school visits within the groups, leading to the writing of further accounts of practice. These experiences indicate that the process can lead to significant changes in thinking and practice within schools, and that these have a positive influence on the behaviour of students and staff.

SUSTAINABLE DEVELOPMENT

So far I have explained how inquiry-based approaches can foster the study and development of inclusive teaching and leadership. Our experience is that schools using such approaches are likely to have considerable success in bringing about changes in thinking and practice. As Copland (2003) suggests, inquiry can be the 'engine' to enable the distribution of leadership, and the 'glue' that can bind a school community together around a common purpose. Turning these successes into processes that make a deeper and more sustainable impact on the culture of schools is, however, much more difficult. This necessitates longer-term, persistent strategies for capacity building at the school level (Dyson, Howes, & Roberts, 2002; Kugelmass, 2001, 2004; Rouse & Florian, 1997). It also requires new thinking and, indeed, new relationships at the systems level. In other words, efforts to foster inclusive school development are more likely to be effective when they are part of a wider strategy.

My own country, England, is particularly instructive in this respect. Recent years have seen fundamental changes in structures and relationships within its education service. These changes have been reflected most significantly in the evolving relationships between schools and their local education authorities (LEAs). This movement, from 'dependency' towards greater 'independence', has been consistently orchestrated through legislation and associated guidance. At the same time, the relationship between schools has also changed. In particular, competition between schools has come to be seen as one of the keys to driving up standards. This is encouraged by open enrolment, supported by the publication of league tables of school examination results. All of this is intended to 'liberate' schools from the bureaucracy of local government and establish what has been described as 'school quasi-markets' (Thrupp, 2001), in which effective schools will have an 'arms-length' relationship with the LEA and, indeed, with each other.

This is arguably the most troubling aspect of our own research. It has revealed how a competitive context that values narrowly conceived criteria for determining success creates barriers to the development of a more inclusive education system (Ainscow, Howes, & Tweddle, 2006; Ainscow et al., 2006). Giroux and Schmidt (2004) explain how similar reforms in the United States have turned some schools into 'test-prep centres'. As a result, they tend to be increasingly ruthless in their disregard of those students who pose a threat to success, as determined by measured forms of assessment.

Bearing this in mind, I suggest that progress towards a more equitable system will require negotiations about values and principles, and a much greater emphasis on the sharing of expertise and resources between schools. Such an approach is consis-

tent with what Stoker (2003) calls 'public value management', with its emphasis on network governance. Stoker argues that the origins of this approach can be traced to criticisms of the current use of strategies drawn from private sector experience which emphasise performance targets and incentives. He goes on to suggest that 'the formulation of what constitutes public value can only be achieved through deliberation involving the key stakeholders and actions that depend on mixing in a reflexive manner a range of intervention options'. Consequently, 'networks of deliberation and delivery' are seen as key strategies. In the education service, this would imply the negotiation of new, inter-dependent relationships between schools, LEAs and their wider communities (Hargreaves, 2003).

Our recent work suggests that Wenger's (1998) notion of a community of practice, defined as a social group engaged in the sustained pursuit of a shared enterprise, is helpful in explaining the networking processes that can occur within groups of schools (Ainscow et al., 2006). Wenger himself notes the particular value of interconnected communities of practice. He uses the term 'constellation' to describe a grouping of discrete communities of practice that are related by some form of common meaning. At the same time, common meanings between those in different schools are, in our experience, more partial, more temporary and not as fully shared as those within a more discrete community. Indeed, we have found that this very partiality and lack of commonality can be provocative, providing opportunities to learn from difference through processes of school-to-school collaboration.

I argue, then, that strategies have to be developed that will encourage inter-dependence between schools, whilst, at the same time, easing those involved in a more inclusive direction. Indeed, a series of recent studies provides strong evidence that school-to-school collaboration has an enormous potential for fostering system-wide improvement, particularly in challenging urban contexts (Ainscow & West, 2006, provides detailed accounts of this research). These studies show how collaboration between schools can often provide an effective means of solving immediate problems, such as staffing shortages; how it can have a positive impact in periods of crisis, such as during the closure of a school; and, how, in the longer run, schools working together can contribute to the raising of expectations and attainment in schools that have had a record of low achievement. There is also some evidence that collaboration can help to reduce the polarisation of schools, to the particular benefit of those students who have been marginalised at the edges of the system and whose performance and attitudes are a cause for concern.

We have also tried to 'map' factors at the district level that have the potential to either facilitate or inhibit such forms of collaboration (Ainscow & Tweddle, 2003). This research suggests that two factors, particularly when they are closely linked, seem to be potentially very powerful. These are *clarity of purpose*, and *the forms of evidence* that are used to measure educational performance.

Our experience has been that a well-orchestrated debate about the values that inform policy development can lead to a wider understanding of the principle of inclusion within a network of schools and the local communities it serves. We are also finding that such a debate, though by its nature slow and, possibly, never ending, can have leverage in respect to fostering the conditions within which schools can feel encouraged to move in a more inclusive direction (Ainscow, 2005). Such a debate must involve all stakeholders within the local community, including political and religious leaders, and the media. It must also involve those within the local education district office.

In England, as in many other countries, there is still considerable confusion about what 'inclusion' means (Ainscow, Farrell, & Tweddle, 2000). To some extent, this lack of clarity might be tracked back to central government policy statements. For example, the use of the term 'social inclusion' has been associated mainly with improving attendance and reducing the incidence of exclusions from schools. At the same time, the idea of 'inclusive education' has appeared in most national guidance in connection with the rights of individual children and young people categorised as having special educational needs to be educated in mainstream schools, whenever possible. Most recently, Ofsted, the national inspection agency, has introduced the term 'educational inclusion', noting that 'effective schools are inclusive schools'. The subtle differences between these concepts adds to the sense of uncertainty as to what is intended and, of course, it is now well established that educational reform is particularly difficult in contexts where there is a lack of common understanding amongst stakeholders (for example, Fullan, 1991).

This being the case, in our own work we have supported a number of English LEAs as they have attempted to develop a definition of inclusion that can be used to guide policy development. Predictably, the exact detail of each LEA's definition is unique, because of the need to take account of local circumstances, cultures and history. Nevertheless, four key elements have tended to feature strongly, and these are commended to those in any education system who are intending to review their own working definition. The four elements are as follows:

- *Inclusion is a process.* That is to say, inclusion has to be seen as a never-ending search to find better ways of responding to diversity. It is about learning how to live with difference, and learning how to learn from difference. In this way differences come to be seen more positively as a stimulus for fostering learning, amongst children and adults.
- *Inclusion is concerned with the identification and removal of barriers.* Consequently, it involves collecting, collating and evaluating information from a wide variety of sources in order to plan for improvements in policy and practice. It is about using evidence of various kinds to stimulate creativity and problem-solving,

- *Inclusion is about the presence, participation and achievement of all students.* Here 'presence' is concerned with where children are educated, and how reliably and punctually they attend; 'participation' relates to the quality of their experiences whilst they are there and, therefore, must incorporate the views of the learners themselves; and 'achievement' is about the outcomes of learning across the curriculum, not merely test or examination results.
- *Inclusion involves a particular emphasis on those groups of learners who may be at risk of marginalisation, exclusion or underachievement.* This indicates the moral responsibility to ensure that those groups that are statistically most at risk are carefully monitored, and that, where necessary, steps are taken to ensure their presence, participation and achievement in the education system.

Our search for 'levers' has also led us to acknowledge the importance of data. In essence, it leads us to conclude that, within education systems, 'what gets measured gets done'. So, for example, English LEAs are required to collect far more statistical data than ever before. This is widely recognised as a double-edged sword precisely because it is such a potent lever for change. On the one hand, data are required in order to monitor the progress of children, evaluate the impact of interventions, review the effectiveness of policies and processes, plan new initiatives, and so on. In these senses, data can, justifiably, be seen as the life-blood of continuous improvement. On the other hand, if effectiveness is evaluated on the basis of narrow, even inappropriate, performance indicators, then the impact can be deeply damaging. Whilst appearing to promote the causes of accountability and transparency, the use of data can, in practice, conceal more than they reveal, invite misinterpretation and, worst of all, have a perverse effect on the behaviour of professionals not least in terms of their attitude to students who are seen to be challenging. This has led the current 'audit culture' to be described as a 'tyranny of transparency' (Strathern, 2000). This suggests that great care needs to be exercised in deciding what evidence is collected and, indeed, how it is

used. The challenge is, therefore, to harness the potential of data as a lever for change. In other words, we must learn to 'measure what we value', rather than is often the case, 'valuing what we can measure'.

In one English LEA, for example, we are currently collaborating with officers and school principals on the development and dissemination of its 'Inclusion Standard', an instrument for evaluating the progress of schools on 'their journey to becoming more inclusive' (Moore, Jackson, Fox, & Ainscow, 2004). The Standard focuses directly on student outcomes, rather than on organisational processes, and uses statistical data and the views of students as the main sources of evidence. So, for example, it does not require a review of the quality of leadership in a school. Rather, it focuses on the presence, participation and achievements of students, on the assumption that this is what good leadership sets out to secure. Similarly, the Standard does not examine whether or not students are given the opportunity to take part in school activities. Rather, it sets out to assess whether students, particularly those at risk of marginalisation or exclusion, actually take part and benefit as a result. In these ways, the aims are to increase understanding within schools of inclusion as an ongoing process, to foster inclusion (in terms of presence, participation and achievement) and to use the student voice as a stimulus for school and staff development. The intention of the LEA involved is that the Standard will become an integral part of schools' self-review and development processes.

CONCLUSION

The arguments presented in this chapter are a major challenge to the current orthodoxy in the field of special education. At the same time, they imply deep changes in mainstream schools and across education services.

Some of the practical implications of what I am proposing are well illustrated in the *Index for Inclusion* (Booth & Ainscow, 2002).

Developed originally for use in England, the Index is a set of school review materials that is being used in an increasing number of countries (see *The International Journal of Inclusive Education*, 8(2), for articles about some of these developments). It enables schools to draw on the knowledge and views of staff, students, parents/carers, and community representatives about barriers to learning and participation that exist within their existing 'cultures, policies and practices' in order to identify priorities for change. In connecting inclusion with the detail of policy and practice, the Index encourages those who use it, to build up their own view of inclusion, related to their experience and values, as they work out what policies and practices they wish to promote or discourage.

Such an approach is based upon the idea that inclusion is essentially about attempts to embody particular values in particular contexts. In other words, it is *school improvement with attitude*. That is to say, unlike mechanistic views of school improvement, it acknowledges that decisions about how to improve schools always involve moral and political reasoning, as well as technical considerations.

The Index approach also involves an emphasis on collaboration and inquiry, and, as we have seen, leadership practices are central to these ways of working. In particular, there is a need to encourage coordinated and sustained efforts by whole staff groups around the idea that changing outcomes for all students is unlikely to be achieved unless there are changes in the behaviours of adults. Consequently, the starting point for inclusive school development must be with teachers: in effect, enlarging their capacity to imagine what might be achieved, and increasing their sense of accountability for bringing this about. This may also involve tackling taken for granted assumptions, most often relating to expectations about certain groups of students, their capabilities, behaviour and patterns of attendance.

This requires groups of stakeholders within a particular context to engage in a search for a common agenda to guide their efforts and,

at much the same time, a series of struggles to establish ways of working that enable them to collect and find meaning in different forms of evidence. In so doing the members of the group are exposed to manifestations of one another's perspectives and assumptions. At its best, this provides endless opportunities for developing new understandings as to how schools can become more inclusive.

My experience is that *schools know more than they use* and that the logical starting point for development is, therefore, with a detailed analysis of existing practices (Ainscow, 1999). This allows good practices to be identified and shared, whilst, at the same time, drawing attention to ways of working that may be creating barriers to the participation and learning of some students. However, as I have stressed, the focus of these approaches is not just on practice. It is also on the thinking behind these ways of working. Collecting and engaging with evidence within a school provides a means of surfacing taken for granted assumptions that may be the source of the barriers that some learners experience.

NOTE

1 An earlier version of this paper was presented as a keynote lecture presentation at the International Conference of School Effectiveness and Improvement, Barcelona, January 2005.

REFERENCES

Ainscow, M. (Ed.). (1991). *Effective schools for all.* London: Fulton.

Ainscow, M. (1994). *Special needs in the classroom: A teacher education guide.* London: Jessica Kingsley/UNESCO.

Ainscow, M. (1999). *Understanding the development of inclusive schools.* London: Falmer Press.

Ainscow, M. (2000). Reaching out to all learners: some lessons from international experience. *School Effectiveness and School Improvement, 11*(1), 1–9.

Ainscow, M. (2005). Developing inclusive education systems: What are the levers for change? *Journal of Educational Change, 6*(2), 109–124.

Ainscow, M., & Brown, D. (Eds.). (1999). *Guidance on*

improving teaching. Lewisham: LEA.

Ainscow, M., & Fox, S. (2003). *Linking behaviour, learning and leadership (pilot version)*. Nottingham: National College for School Leadership with the University of Manchester .

Ainscow, M., & Kaplan, I. (2005). Using evidence to encourage inclusive school development: possibilities and challenges. *Australasian Journal of Special Education, 29*(2), 106–116.

Ainscow, M., & Tweddle, D. (2003). Understanding the changing role of English local education authorities in promoting inclusion. In J. Allan (Ed.), *Inclusion, Participation and democracy: What is the purpose?* (pp. 165–177). Amsterdam: Kluwer Academic.

Ainscow, M., & West, M. (Eds). (2006). *Improving urban schools: Leadership and collaboration*. Maidenhead: Open University Press .

Ainscow, M., Barrs, D., & Martin. J. (1998). Taking school improvement into the classroom. *Improving Schools, 1*(3), 43–48.

Ainscow, M., Beresford, J., Harris, A., Hopkins, D., Southworth, G., & West, M. (2000). *Creating the Conditions for School Improvement* (2nd ed.). London: David Fulton.

Ainscow, M., Booth, T., & Dyson, A., with Farrell, P., Frankham, J., Gallannaugh, F., Howes, A., & Smith, R. (2006). *Improving schools, developing inclusion*. London: Routledge.

Ainscow, M., Farrell, P., & Tweddle, D. (2000). Developing policies for inclusive education: A study of the role of local education authorities. *International Journal of Inclusive Education, 4*(3), 211–229.

Ainscow, M., Howes, A., Farrell, P., & Frankham, J. (2003). Making sense of the development of inclusive practices. *European Journal of Special Needs Education, 18*(2), 227–242.

Ainscow, M., Howes, A., & Tweddle, D. (2006). Making sense of the impact of recent education policies: A study of practice. In M. Ainscow & M. West (Eds.), *Improving urban schools: Leadership and collaboration*. Maidenhead: Open University Press .

Bartolome, L. I. (1994). Beyond the methods fetish: towards a humanising pedagogy. *Harvard Education Review, 54*(2), 173–194.

Booth, T., & Ainscow, M. (2002). *The Index for Inclusion*. Bristol: Centre for Studies on Inclusive Education.

Brantlinger, E. (1997). Using ideology: cases of non-recognition of the politics of research and practice in special education. *Review of Educational Research, 67*(4), 425–459.

Copland, M. A. (2003). Leadership of inquiry: Building and sustaining capacity for school improvement. *Educational Evaluation and Policy Analysis, 25*(4), 375–395.

Dyson, A. & Millward, A. (2000). *Schools and special needs: Issues of innovation and inclusion*. London: Paul Chapman Publishing.

Dyson, A., Howes, A., & Roberts, B. (2002). *A systematic review of the effectiveness of school-level actions for promoting participation by all students*. (Inclusive Education Review Group for the EPPI Centre, Institute of Education, London.) Retrieved from http://eppi.ioe.ac.uk/EPPIWeb/home.aspx?page=/reel/review_groups/inclusion/review_one.htm

Elmore, R. F., Peterson, P. L., & McCarthy, S. J. (1996). *Restructuring in the classroom: Teaching, learning and school organisation*. San Francisco, CA: Jossey-Bass.

Fox, S., & Ainscow, M. (In press). Moving leadership practice in schools forward. In M. Ainscow & M. West (Eds), *Improving urban schools: Leadership and collaboration*. Maidenhead: Open University Press.

Fuchs, D. & Fuchs, L. S. (1994). Inclusive schools movement and the radicalisation of special education reform. *Exceptional Children, 60*(4), 294–309.

Fulcher, G. (1989). *Disabling policies? A comparative approach to education policy and disability*. London: Falmer.

Fullan, M. (1991). *The new meaning of educational change*. London: Cassell.

Giroux, H. A., & Schmidt, M. (2004). Closing the achievement gap: A metaphor for children left behind. *Journal of Educational Change, 5*, 213–228.

Hargreaves, D. H. (2003). *Education epidemic: Transforming secondary schools through innovation networks*. London: Demos.

Hiebert, J., Gallimore, R., & Stigler, J. W. (2002). A knowledge base for the teaching profession: What would it look like and how can we get one? *Educational Researcher, 31*(5), 3–15.

Hopkins, D. (2001). *School Improvement for real*. Lewes: Falmer Press.

Hopkins, D., Ainscow, M., & West, M. (1994). *School improvement in an era of change*. London: Cassell.

Huberman, M. (1993). The model of the independent artisan in teachers' professional relationships. In J. W. Little & M. W. McLaughlin (Eds.), *Teachers' work: Individuals, colleagues and contexts*. New York: Teachers College Press.

Kugelmass, J. W. (2001). Collaboration and compromise in creating and sustaining an inclusive school. *Journal of Inclusive Education, 5*(1): 47–65.

Kugelmass, J. W. (2004). *The inclusive school: Sustaining equity and standards*. New York: Teachers College Press.

Kugelmass, J., & Ainscow, M. (2005). Leading inclusive schools: a comparison of practices in three countries. *Journal of Research in Special Needs Education, 4*(3), 3–12.

Lambert, L., Walker, D., Zimmerman, D. P., Cooper, J. E., Lambert, M. D., Gardner, M. E. (1995). *The constructivist leader*. New York: Teachers College Press.

Lipman, P. (1997). Restructuring in context: a case study

of teacher participation and the dynamics of ideology, race and power. *American Educational Research Journal, 34*(1), 3–37.

Lo, M. L., Yan, P. W., & Pakey, C. P. M. (Eds.). (2005). *For each and everyone: Catering for individual differences through learning studies.* Hong Kong: Hong Kong University Press.

Mittler, P. (2000). *Working towards inclusive education.* London: Fulton.

Moore, M., Jackson, M., Fox, S., & Ainscow, M. (2004). *The Manchester inclusion standard.* Manchester: City Council.

Pijl, S. J., Meijer, C. J. W., & Hegarty, S. (Eds.). (1997). *Inclusive education: A global agenda.* London: Routledge.

Reynolds, M. C., & Ainscow, M. (1994). Education of children and youth with special needs: An international perspective. In T. Husen & T. N. Postlethwaite (Eds.), *The International Encyclopedia of Education* (2nd edn.) Oxford: Pergamon.

Riehl, C. J. (2000). The principal's role in creating inclusive schools for diverse students: A review of normative, empirical, and critical literature on the practice of educational administration. *Review of Educational Research, 70*(1), 55–81.

Rouse, M., & Florian, L. (1997). Inclusive education in the market-place. *International Journal of Inclusive Education, 1*(4), 323–336.

Sebba, J., & Sachdev, D. (1997). *What works in inclusive education.* Ilford: Barnardos.

Skrtic, T.M. (1991). Students with special educational needs: Artifacts of the traditional curriculum. In M. Ainscow (Ed.), *Effective schools for all.* London: Fulton.

Spillane, J. P., Halverson, R., & Diamond, J. B. (2001). Investigating school leadership practice. *Educational Researcher, 30*(3), 23–28.

Stigler, J. W., & Hiebert, J. (1999). *The teaching gap.* New York: The Free Press.

Stoker, G. (2003). *Public value management: a new resolution of the democracy/efficency trade off.* Retrieved from www.ipeg.org.uk/publications.htm

Strathern, M. (2000). The tyranny of transparency. *British Educational Research Journal, 26*(3), 309–321.

Thomas, G., & Vaughn, M. (2004). *Inclusive education: Readings and reflections.* Maidenhead: Open University Press.

Thrupp, M. (2001). School quasi-markets in England and Wales: Best understood as a class strategy? Paper presented at the conference of the British Education Research Association, Leeds, September 2001.

Tilstone, C., Florian, L., & Rose, R. (Eds.). (1998). *Promoting inclusive practice.* London: Routledge.

Timperley, S. H., & Robinson, V. M. J. (2001). Achieving school improvement through challenging and changing teachers' schema. *Journal of Educational Change, 2*, 281–300.

Trent, S. C., Artiles, A. J., & Englert, C. S. (1998). From deficit thinking to social constructivism: A review of theory, research and practice in special education. *Review of Research in Education, 23*, 277–307.

United Nations Educational, Scientific, and Cultural Organization (UNESCO). (1994). *The Salamanca statement and framework for action on special needs education.* Paris: UNESCO.

United Nations Educational, Scientific, and Cultural Organization (UNESCO). (2001). *The open file on inclusive education.* Paris: UNESCO.

Vitello, S. J., & Mithaug, D. E. (Eds.). (1998). *Inclusive schooling: National and international perspectives.* Mahwah, NJ: Lawrence Erlbaum.

Wenger, E. (1998). *Communities of practice: Learning, meaning and identity.* Cambridge: Cambridge University Press.

West, M., Ainscow, M., & Notman, H. (2003). *What leaders read 2: Key texts from education and beyond.* Nottingham: National College for School Leadership.

12

Inclusive schooling as a means and end of education?

Roger Slee

INTRODUCTION

In his book *Meditations of a Broomstick*, the celebrated scientist Baron Rothschild (Rothschild, 1977) muses on the 'promises and panaceas that gleam like false teeth in the party manifestoes'. Working in government I came to observe myself as being incorporated into a disingenuous inclusive educational dental practice where too many of the patients, attracted by the allure of the promise of cosmetic orthodontics, awoke from the procedure to find the promise unfulfilled. Worse still, their own teeth were missing, having been replaced by a set of 'false choppers' that looked nothing like the smile on display in the government brochure (Slee, 2003).

In this brief discussion I will contend that inclusive schooling is a precondition of democratic education (Bernstein, 1996; Knight, 2000), that it is theoretically contested and as a consequence passed off in many guises. Ultimately, inclusive education is an inherently troubled and troubling educational and social project. Allan (2003, p. 229) enlists Derrida to depict the interrogation of inclusion, participation and democracy as an 'epic gesture' to unravel our misunderstanding by 'refusing to dodge the confusion, contradictions and ambiguities and indeed the silences that exist in the discourses of inclusion' (Allan, 2003, p. 225). Notwithstanding this stipulation of inclusive education as a prerequisite for democratic schooling it saddens me to report that much of what is offered as inclusive education is less than democratic, less than inclusive.

To impose some order in my argument, I will organize this chapter into three sections. 'Part 1: Meaningful ends?' will take up the challenge of means and ends in the public policy arena to suggest that ends are too seldom explicated allowing the allure of the immediate, of the political or 'educational' fix, to attenuate schooling as a reconstructive social project in a troubled world. 'Part 2: The trouble with inclusion' will examine the epistemological tensions, exemplified and amplified within a handbook such as this, that simultaneously advance and undermine the progress of disability rights in education. 'Part 3: Putting the public in policy – promises with teeth' proposes an agenda for the pursuit of democratic education within which inclusion and reciprocity are writ large (Bernstein, 1996; Touraine, 2000).

PART 1: MEANINGFUL ENDS?

When Maggie X died, the [aged care] home decided that her savings of 450 pounds was insufficient to pay for the funeral and asked the council to pay. It refused and the owner of the home appealed to the Local Ombudsman. In his comments to the latter, the council Chief Executive wrote that 'without wishing to appear insensitive, one could argue that from a commercial viewpoint residents of a home are its income producing raw material. Ergo, from a purely commercial view, deceased residents, may then may be regarded as being the waste produced by their business'. Since, he continued, the resident's body was 'controlled waste likely to cause pollution of the environment or harm to human health' the home had, under the definition of controlled waste as defined by the Environmental Protection Act, 'a specific duty' to dispose of the remains. Disposal, under the definitions of the Act, was 'a business cost'. (Doig & Wilson, 1999, p. 26)

Readers' sensibilities will no doubt be offended by the crass reductionism of the Chief Executive who, while wishing not to appear insensitive, still found it possible to identify deceased elderly residents as *business waste* for the purpose of financial reporting and cost recovery. Needless to say technocratic reductionism is not confined to aged care, nor indeed to the United Kingdom. Apple (2001) meticulously tracks the way that a coalition of conservative forces in the US, having declared 'open season on education', has effectively reduced schooling, teaching and learning to a 'business to be treated no differently than any other business'. Mobilized within an international trope of choice and standards (Apple, 2001; Gewirtz, Ball, & Bowe, 1995; Gillborn & Youdell, 2000; Lauder and Hughes, 1999; Tomlinson, 1997) the distribution of educational opportunity is played out according to the logic and inequity of a Hayekian marketplace. In Australia as elsewhere the grammar of the marketplace insinuated itself and created the discursive terrain for education

policy decision making. Simon Marginson observes that:

> Under the sign of the New Right, and within the space created by its initial political breakthrough in the mid-1970s, market-liberalism constituted a new political rationality, supported by a new language of markets, competition and enterprise, in which the objective of government was not so much the welfare of its citizens per se as the formation of a competitive economy within a Hayekian order ... this new political rationality was associated with new kinds of programmes that, over time, grew out of or displaced those of the welfare state era. These new programmes operated with new technologies of government, new strategies, techniques and procedures for securing governmental objectives. The conception of citizenship was changing, from the citizen of the welfare state, bound by solidarity and mutual interdependence, to a market-active and entrepreneurial citizen whose objective was personal fulfillment. (Marginson, 1997, p. 64)

For education, they were

> conceived as competitive system-markets, although no less subject to government for that. The norms of public service were replaced by those of competition, efficiency and customer demand. Relations between the state and educational professionals were reworked, so that accountability was rerouted through client relations. Here the individualization of costs signified more than a decline in the benefit-tax ratio. It signified a change in the subject-object of education, in the governmental construction of students themselves. Market liberal government was characterized by the privatization of opportunity and risk management. (Marginson, 1997, pp. 64–65)

Addressing the Fifteenth Conference of Commonwealth Education Ministers in Edinburgh (October, 2003), the eminent development economist Amartya Sen, paradoxically for some, drew inspiration from the philosopher Adam Smith to highlight risk and folly in trusting education to the marketplace. It seems, after all, that Smith was not so sanguine about a less than benign invisible hand to conduct public education: 'why it would be wrong to leave this to the market: for a very small expense the public can facilitate, can encourage, and can even impose upon almost the whole body of people, the necessity of acquiring those most essential parts of education' (Smith, 1976, p. 27). For Sen, the marketization of schooling exacerbates material inequalities, and in doing so represents a key threat to the communitarian aspirations espoused by neo-liberal governments. In the UK and the US there are numerous accounts of how the competitive schooling marketplace has instigated a white flight from inner urban – not yet gentrified – community schools (Gewirtz et al., 1995). The comprehensive school project has lapsed through the reassertion of traditional grammar schools and the proliferation of Charter schools. Public schooling, having 'lost its civic imagination' (Rose, 1995), is tiered and residualized. Gillborn and Youdell (2000, p. 133) present compelling case studies of schools in Britain and the way that they allocate grades in the 'A-to-C economy' 'to further target resources on a limited number of pupils in one last push to maximize their scores in the nationally published school performance league tables'. The role of teacher as gatekeeper, through the regressive impact of the league tables and the narrow adjudication of standards, has intensified. Enlisting the powerful metaphor of educational triage, the application of grade management in the schools' strategies to scale the league table becomes abundantly clear.

at a deeper level the strategies share similar characteristics and can be understood as a form of educational triage – a means by which scarce resources are rationed, leaving some to perish while others survive … like medics in a crisis, teachers are increasingly seeking to identify those individuals who will benefit most from access to limited resources. In a medical emergency triage is the name used to describe attempts to direct attention to those people who might survive (with help), leaving other (less hopeful) cases to die. In school, educational triage is acting systematically to neglect certain pupils while directing additional resources to those deemed most likely to benefit (in terms of the externally judged standards). These strategies seek to maximize the effectiveness of scarce resources but their effect, in practice, is to privilege particular groups of pupils marked especially by social class and 'race'. (Gillborn & Youdell, 2000, pp. 133–134)

The marketization of schooling has generated perverse and deleterious effects. Eschewing established findings from the corpus of educational assessment and evaluation research (Black, 1998; Gipps & Murphy, 1994), education jurisdictions have alighted on high stakes standardized testing (Sacks, 1999) to provide a simple set of ratings against which to argue raising standards (Meier, Sizer, Nathan, and Thernstrom, 2000). Combined with the drive for a 'national curriculum' based variously on Eurocentric cultural artifacts that effectively excludes the cultures of the increasingly diverse student populations of these countries and schedules of performance standards against which to inspect teachers and schools, education jurisdictions construct competitive tables to demonstrate the raising of standards through competition and accountability. The reality is that students are privileged or marginalized according to class, geographic location, ethnicity, and perceived notions of 'ability'. In other words, the architecture of schooling becomes more distinctly tiered – sponsored schools for achievers and residualized schools for the less deserving (Gillborn & Youdell, 2000).

My argument is not with standards as such. The critique is advanced against reductive public discourse, the Death Sentences (Watson, 2003) that conflate equity with 'back to the basics' (Lingard, 1998), that substitute high stakes mono-lingual minimum standards testing for richer assessment and evaluation schedules (Luke, 2003) and pretend that inclusive education can be pursued without tackling institutional reconstruction and economic redistribution in highly stratified societies (Anyon, 2005; Kozol, 1991). Bob Chase, then President of the National Education Association in North America is unequivocal:

we must pursue higher academic standards with our eyes wide open. The objective of the standards movement – to successfully educate all children, rich and poor, to the same high standards – is truly revolutionary. We must match our revolutionary intentions with commensurably revolutionary intententerventions to ensure that all students, especially underprivileged students, succeed. (Chase, in Meier et al., 2000, p. 41)

Schooling is not the benign allotment of prizes according to merit as conservative philosophers like Nozick (1974) would have it.

> Education is not … a mirror of social or cultural inequalities. That is all too still an image. Education systems are busy institutions. They are vibrantly involved in the production of social hierarchies. They select and exclude their own clients; they expand credentialed labour markets; they produce and disseminate particular kinds of knowledge to particular users. (Connell, 1993, p. 27)

Schools include some and they exclude others. All this is pursued within rhetorical flourishes of 'building social capital', 'excellence for all', 'raising standards' and, perhaps most cruelly, through the increasingly popular public policy descriptor, 'inclusive schooling'.

Elsewhere I have observed that under these conditions of *performativity* (Ball, 1998), schools become more risk averse, more selective, more exclusive. Simply put, they are more choosey about who's in and who's out (Slee, 1998). Apprehensive schooling has replaced comprehensive schooling. Ultimately there has been a confusion of means and ends, a confusion of aims and strategies. More particularly the political and educational rhetoric is little more than distractive noise at odds with the divisive reality of schooling. A survey of inclusive education policy documents across education authorities reveals a sheer screen that barely conceals traditional assumptions and approaches developed through the complimentary interests of traditional segregated special and regular education. For government (*sic* Treasury), inclusive education becomes a complex set of algorithms for allocating finite *additional* resources to disabled children. It is worth noting that the provision of resources essential for the education of disabled children is construed as additional, contingent, or provisional; they are an afterthought. Consequently, in some quarters, inclusive education paradoxically has become a rhetorical exercise to revise the categories of special need, to call in the actuaries to set the levels of distribution according to *severity of disability*, stave off the need to radically alter the structure of school-ing and parade our liberal credentials. Central to the problem of regular and special education is the issue of an ever narrowing tolerance of who is to be counted as the deserving or regular student. The efficient governance of difference drives greater calibration and categorization. In this way the therapeutic or scientific pursuit is essentially political (Furedi, 2004; Rose, 1996), inclusive education becoming a form of governance.

Perhaps it is time to insert two caveats. Though I am strident in my critique of the dividing practices (Foucault, 1979) embraced by public policy and manifest in schools I am also deeply respectful of hopeful exceptions where communities have engaged in the struggle to interrogate new social ends and set out on divergent means for securing them (Carrington & Robinson, 2004). The second caveat is an acknowledgement that the operation of education policy decision-making is far messier than the preceding discussion suggests (Ball, 1994). Education is an intensely political activity. The politics relate to competing views of the good society and how to secure it through schooling. Conflict also speaks to struggles for authority in bureaucracy driven by ideology, personality and ambition.

PART 2: THE TROUBLE WITH INCLUSION

I turn once more to Watson who enlists Donald Rumsfeld to impose clarity:

> As we know, there are no known knowns. There are things we know we know. We also know there are known unknowns. That is to say we know there are some things we do not know. But there are also unknown unknowns, the ones we don't know we don't know. (Watson, 2003, p. 45)

What conclusions do we draw from Rumsfeld? Let me suggest that he serves to remind us that language simultaneously serves to reveal and conceal meaning. Inclusive education is in Watson's terms approaching the status of a *death sentence*. Notwithstanding its insurrectionary heritage, it has been appropriated and is most frequently a default vocabulary (Slee, 1996) to connote the fitting of disabled kids into regular schools or classrooms. We run the risk of inclusion becoming a front for assimilation. Increasingly, people gather to discuss inclusive education only to find that they are describing very different worlds. Special education conferences frequently select inclusion as their organizing theme. Special educational textbooks, the 'big glossies' as Brantlinger (2004) refers to them, have acquired an additional chapter on inclusion. There is a need to take issue with this state of affairs and systematically dissect it. The following paragraphs are pointers in this direction.

Mindful of our discussion of means and ends, we could commence with an interrogation of whether inclusive education is a programme of sponsored immigration where we take an excluded population from segregated settings and place them in regular schools. Within such a proposition resides a range of subsidiary issues. The binary of the special and the regular school privileges both as an acceptable set of institutional arrangements. There is ample evidence to suggest the deeply irregular practices of schooling. Schools are formed through a range of institutional practices, pedagogic, curricular and organizational, that continues to erect barriers to the participation of students on the basis of the diverse characteristics of the student population. Such institutional arrangements will continue to disable students wherever they might be. The drive through the state to order and standardize schooling is an acknowledgement of the social condition of irregularity. As DSM-IV-TR (American Psychiatric Association, 2000) expands exponentially it may be that the special is regular, the regular special.

The *regular school/special school (regular student/special student)* binaries deflect from the epistemic weight of normality and abnormality. Epistemology distributes status and power unevenly; some are in, some others will always be others. 'All societies produce strangers; but each kind of society produces

its own kind of strangers, and produces them in its own inimitable way … *These strangers are by definition an anomaly to be rectified'* (Bauman, 1997, p. 17, own emphasis). Inclusive education is not about the relocation of people into the mainstream. A further concern is the assumption that the regular is something to be sought after. Given the rates of exclusion from regular schooling and its differentiated dispensation of the prizes, the quest is not the movement of population into regular schools but the movement of regular schools into new times. Inclusive education presses us to consider the ontology of special and regular; presses us to resist such a bifurcation as redundant in democratic education.

I choose the term 'assisted immigration' as it was a common way of describing the sponsorship of immigrants from Europe to Australia after World War II. People of carefully selected national origins (*sic* not 'coloured', for Australia had a White Australia Immigration Policy policed through a language dictation test) were encouraged to come to Australia to satisfy the burgeoning requirements of the labour market. The passage was heavily subsidized. In return for the opportunities on offer complete assimilation was expected. The analogy holds for many in education who conceptualize inclusive education as a normalizing project. Liberals will of course *celebrate* difference and diversity on occasions, but the objective remains conservative. A parallel was elegantly argued some time ago now by Troyna (1993, p. 26) when he proposed anti-racist education as a counter to the soft liberalism of multiculturalism embodied in schools hosting 'samosas, saris and steelbands' days to increase tolerance for ethnic difference.

Particularly troubling is the fact that while the immigration is being conditionally encouraged for some, others are being shown the educational backdoor as the surge in special educational needs categories advances, generating a proliferation of off-site centres for the disturbed and disturbing children. That most referred and deferred children are working class, Aboriginal or from minority ethnic groups is seldom confronted substantively. Sally Tomlinson stepped forward to suggest that special education was a racialized social construct (Tomlinson, 1981). At issue then is the way in which education jurisdictions around the world have appropriated a once rebellious call for inclusive education to describe an essentially conservative normalizing function of schooling. More astonishing is their failure to acknowledge the deeply exclusionary practices endorsed through the standards and choice agenda.

Accordingly we might suggest that for schooling to be inclusive there is a reconstructive project ahead of us. Placing kids with *appropriate support* in schools and classrooms that retain all the cultural hallmarks of exclusion ought not to be described as inclusive education. Just as segregation is unacceptable to communities that describe themselves as democratic, assimilation is reprehensible and speaks not to an educated citizenry. Inclusive education as I am construing it here is not simply a matter of matching children with support to legitimize their seat at a desk. However, it is about location and it is about the resources to enable all children to learn. But these are contingencies for the larger cultural work of building communities that embrace and represent. In other words the political question, who's in and who's out?, precedes the technical question of repatriation: how and with what resources?

Since it continues to trouble folk, we need to confront ideology (Brantlinger, 1997, 2004; Kauffman & Hallahan, 1995; Kavale, 2004). Zizek (1994, p. 17) captures the essence of the debate observing that ideology 'is at work in everything we experience as reality'. In summary, the charge is that inclusive education has forfeited its claim to validity as scientific research activity, given its ideological transparency and affiliations. Dismissing this charge is somewhat repetitious. Troyna dealt effectively with critiques from Hammersley, Gomm and White along similar lines when he rightfully declared the partisan nature of his anti-racist research project (Troyna, 1994). First, science is a branch of the knowledge tree that is socially constructed and ideologically charged. Objectivity is a fallacious claim. The crux of the debate more correctly should centre on questions of rigor. There should be a reflexivity that puts all of our assumptions (and mine too) on the table for interrogation and analysis.

Inclusive education as a claim against exclusionary political arrangements through education must play host to research that identifies and analyses the structure and operation of exclusion. It is therefore a very broad research programme that sponsors the research of diverse communities of researchers as they work across a number of research issues through a range of methodologies. Clearly the division between qualitative and quantitative methods becomes redundant as we judiciously enlist all tools to build a more complete analysis of the conditions for exclusion and inclusion. Identity politics research is at the heart of this project. This will inform the methodological choices as we design the evaluation of curriculum, pedagogy and school organization.

Underlying this discussion is a call for epistemic transparency – who are we, what do we stand for, for whom do we claim to speak? Special education cannot pass itself off as an unproblematic ally or as a branch member in the inclusive education fraternity. Attention to disability studies is a precondition for a more productive exchange. The popularity of inclusive education as a rhetorical device for governments that do not acknowledge their role in the pervasiveness of exclusion is also problematic. As Said observed, travelling theories born of a political context and purpose to change unequal power relations are domesticated and tamed as they become popular and frequently cited catechisms (Said, 2000). While Said highlights Lukacs' theory of reification to demonstrate the erosion of analytic and revolutionary force through the transposition of theory across time and place, I believe that there is a case for plotting the travels of inclusive education from its beginnings as a protest against traditional special education to its present academic and governmental popularity. Perhaps we could intervene and reset its path in order that it does not lapse into liberal shibboleth.

PART 3: PUTTING THE PUBLIC IN POLICY – PROMISES WITH TEETH

> Democracy is hard to love. Perhaps some people enjoy making speeches, or confronting those with whom they disagree, or standing up to privileged and powerful people with claims and demands. Activities like these, however, make many people anxious. Perhaps some people like to go to meetings after a hard day's work and try to focus discussion on the issue, to haggle over the language of a resolution, or gather signatures for a petition, or call long lists of strangers on the telephone. But most people would rather watch television, read poetry or make love. To be sure democratic politics has some joys … Defeat, co-optation, or ambiguous results are more common experiences than political victory, however. Citizens must often put in a great deal of time to gain a small reform. Because in a democracy nearly everything is revisable, and because unpredictable public opinion counts for something, uncertainty shadows democracy. (Young, 2000, p. 16)

The central argument that inclusive education is an important but fragile educational project in this chapter proceeds from a number of propositions. First is a view that inclusive education is not an end in itself. It ought to be conceptualized and pursued tactically as a means for achieving an education in and for democratic citizenship. Inclusive schooling is a requirement of this apprenticeship in democracy (Pearl & Tony, 1999). This is not new; others such as Bernstein (1996) *announced* the requirement for a democratic education and the conditions necessary for it. For Bernstein (1996, pp. 6–7) inclusiveness was not absorption, it connoted authentic reciprocity. Through his provocatively entitled *Can We Live Together?* Alain Touraine concluded that this could only be achieved 'through a school that democratizes' (2000, p. 283). 'In a world of intense cultural exchanges', he argues, 'there can be no democracy unless we recognise the diversity of cultures and relations of domination that

exist between them' (Touraine, 2000, p. 195). For both Bernstein and Touraine the question of voice, of who speaks for who, is fundamental. Inclusive education has yet to seriously interrogate the role of disabled researchers and advocates in the production of knowledge about disability and disablement.

The second undergirding proposition is that just as inclusive schooling is a precondition for democratic education, it is simultaneously deployed counter-democratically to maintain institutional equilibrium. Inclusive education is appropriated to maintain unequal power relations and disenfranchise vulnerable people. As Young observes, this invites vigilance to ensure greater possibilities for participation in decision-making:

> Our democratic policy discussions do not occur under conditions free of coercion and threat, and free of the distorting influence of unequal power and control over resources. In actually existing democracies there tends to be a reinforcing circle between social and economic inequality and political inequality that enables the powerful to use formally democratic processes to perpetuate injustice and preserve privilege. One means of breaking this circle, I argue, is to widen democratic inclusion. (Young, 2000, p. 17)

A *deliberative democracy* (Gutmann & Thompson, 2004) capable of confronting complex social issues demands extensive and inclusive participation in decision-making. The third proposition is perhaps the most difficult for public policy-making in education. Public policy making is not so public. Policy decision-making is a professional enterprise that structures the terms and conditions of representation. The professional is privileged over community. Bureaucracies are often large and chaotic intersections for competing interests and contest over the nature and form of schooling. Textbook models of policy-making in public administration (Davis & Bridgman, 2004; Dye, 1984) often ascribe greater rationality to government decision-making than is warranted. Where a very public forum selected as a broadly representative body was created in Queensland to provide advice to the Minister for Education on inclusive education, decision-making was advanced through the budget process with a very different set of objectives than those advanced in published policy documents.

Notwithstanding attempts to engage and mobilize greater levels of participation and to invite deliberation over education for disabled students, there remains a tendency for this to collapse in the wake of government and industrial relations interplay (Slee, 2003). Dissent is gathered and circumscribed; often ground down through the rituals of representation. How do we safeguard the publics in policy? In particular, how do we honour disabled people through the processes of decision-making that will deliver an enabling schooling? Let me attempt to suggest some elements for an agenda for change.

First is a call for an epistemological shove. Here I refer to the need for us to move our gaze from describing individual *defective* pathologies to understanding the more pervasive and complex pathology of schooling. The discussion of the marketization of education and its ineluctable drive to differentiate students as projections of measurable outcome is central to the recognition of exclusionary practices. How do education practices, that is, pedagogy, curriculum, assessment, banding and coding, placement and enrolment policy, and classroom organization, affect the gravitational push and pull? In other words, does the grammar of schooling bring students to the centre of institutional life or launch them in marginal trajectories. Here I am reminded of McLuhan's dictum that the medium is the message:

> In a culture like ours, long accustomed to splitting and dividing all things as a means of control, it is sometimes a bit of a shock to be reminded that, in operational and practical fact, the medium is the message. This is merely to say that the personal and social consequences of any medium – that is, of any extension of ourselves – result from the new scale that is introduced into our affairs by each extension of ourselves, or by any new technology. (McLuhan, in McLuhan & Zingrone, 1995, p. 151)

It seems then that inclusive schooling is not the adaptation or refinement of special education. It is a fundamental rejection of special education's and regular education's claims to be inclusive. Inclusion demands that we address the politics of exclusion and representation. Different kinds of research present themselves as requirements for the kind of educational reconstruction required for democratic schooling. Investigations of the distribution of poverty and privilege, impacts of pedagogic approaches and educational measurement and assessment, the relationship between curriculum and the politics of representation, school reform that changes outcomes for formerly excluded children, all push toward the front of the research queue in the new educational laboratory.

I have suggested a need to put the public into public policy. In reality I am thinking of those publics that have been excluded by the prevailing conditions of policy-making. Policy is written at all levels as people receive, interpret and enact education policy in their sphere of activity and influence. Consequently, the agenda change must simultaneously advance itself across a number of sites. I will comment on two of these.

The academy is simultaneously enormously influential and irrelevant to the determination of practice in schools. Focus and accessible language are essential elements in constructing a platform to speak to government. Pursuant to this there is a need to demonstrate the deleterious impacts that our research has had upon the subjects of our research. Here, education has tended to ignore disabled researchers while priding itself on lessons learned through discussions around gender and 'race'. Mike Oliver confronts the reality of exploitative research of disabled people.

> the research act is not an attempt to change the world through the process of investigation but an attempt to change the world by producing ourselves and others in differing ways from those we have produced before, intentionally or not. Increasingly as oppressed groups such as disabled people continue the political process of collectively empowering themselves, research practice based upon the investigatory discourse and utilizing 'tourist' approaches by 'tarmac' professors and

researchers will find it increasingly difficult to find sites and experiences ripe for colonization. Disabled people and other oppressed groups will no longer be prepared to tolerate exploitative investigatory research based upon exclusionary social relations of research production. (Oliver, 2002)

Preparation of inclusive education is not well served by returning to Departments of Special Education to perpetuate monistic research designs. New coalitions of researchers should be enlisted to produce nuanced research capable of interrogating the complexity of exclusion as it is advanced through the matrix of education's activities. Disabled people, disabled researchers and their allies should be sought as leaders in this endeavour. This research programme for new times should reflect a determination to take up the big questions about the redistribution of privilege and advantage.

For the civil service to respond to this reconfiguration, academics have to consider the medium and message system and how it is made useful to government. In this respect I would argue that engagement in the field to highlight thinking and teaching initiatives at the school and classroom levels that introduce discomfort to old practices is a good point of embarkation. This must form a basis of credibility for the consideration of the large-scale curriculum reconstruction. There exist practitioner-friendly while not reductive examples manifest in the New Basics research in Queensland and the refinement of this in the Essential Learnings work in Tasmania (www.Itag.education.tas.gov.au/reference. html/#ELsresources). Inclusive education warrants nothing short of the interrogation and reconstruction of curriculum to ensure that it engages with the world of students and their futures in order to re-engage them with authentic learning (Newmann and Associates, 1996). Critiques of special education and inclusive education need to be advanced through street-level operation in order to establish credibility (Ainscow, 1999).

The second site for intervention is the most complex. The education bureaucracy, schools being the local branches, is most challenging.

It is here where centre and periphery are in a state of constant tension and where this tension may be used productively. Suzanne Carrington and Robyn Robinson's (2004) work, building on the excursions into school reform by Ainscow and Booth (Booth, Ainscow, Black-Hawkins, Vaughan, & Shaw, 2000), demonstrates the gravitational pull that school-based reconstruction of educational practices can have on large education bureaucracies and, in turn, on the academy. The establishment of a Staff College for Inclusive Education in Queensland provided for a focus on school-based development of professional learning communities. Authentic initiatives in inclusive education were funded and broadcast as prompts for similar approaches to thinking about community reconstruction in schools. This is not of itself sufficient to produce the changes required that speak to the redistribution of the material resources required to impact upon the exclusions borne of poverty, disadvantage and Aboriginality, and then concealed through the redefinition of fundamental social issues as behaviour, intelligence and language problems encased within clinically deflective medical aetiologies.

Inclusive education invites the application of a new imagination to consider the impact of different forms of schooling and its constituent elements of curriculum, pedagogy, assessment and organization upon different groups of students. The implication is that inclusive education warrants more than the application of modes of thinking associated with the construction of exclusion: regular and special education. This is, of course, a big ask. Inclusive education asks us to jettison linearity in our thinking, to invite new coalitions to the table to establish the parameters of the issues we are dealing with and directions for educational reconstructions.

REFERENCES

Ainscow, M. (1999). *Understanding the development of inclusive schools.* London: Falmer Press.

Allan, J. (Ed.) (2003). *Inclusion, participation and*

democracy: What is the purpose? Dordrecht: Kluwer Academic.

American Psychiatric Association. (2000). *Diagnostic and statistical manual of mental disorders. DSM-IV-TR* (4th ed.). Arlington, VA: American Psychiatric Association.

Anyon, J. (2005). *Radical possibilities. Public policy, urban education and a new social movement.* New York: Routledge.

Apple, M. (2001). *Educating the 'right' way. Markets, standards, god and inequality.* New York: Routledge-Falmer.

Ball, S. J. (1994). *Education reform. A critical and post-structural approach.* Buckingham: Open University Press.

Ball, S. J. (1998). Educational studies, policy entrepreneurship and social theory. In R. Slee, G. Weiner, & S. Tomlinson (Eds.), *School effectiveness for whom?* (pp. 70–83). London: Falmer Press.

Bauman, Z. (1997). *Postmodernity and its discontents.* Cambridge: Polity Press.

Bernstein, B. (1996). *Pedagogy, symbolic control and identity. Theory, research, critique.* London: Taylor & Francis.

Black, P. (1998). *Testing: Friend or foe?* London: Falmer Press.

Booth, T., Ainscow, M., Black-Hawkins, K., Vaughan, M., & Shaw, L. (2000). *Index for Inclusion.* Bristol: Centre for Studies on Inclusive Education.

Brantlinger, E. (1997). Using ideology: Cases of non-recognition of the politics of research and practice in special education, *Review of Educational Research, 67*(4), 425–459.

Brantlinger, E. (2004). The big glossies: How textbooks structure (special) education. In D. Biklen (Ed.), *Common solutions: Inclusion and diversity at the center.* Syracuse, NY: University of Syracuse.

Carrington, S., & Robinson, R. (2004). A case study of inclusive school development: a journey of learning. *International Journal of Inclusive Education, 8*(2), 141–153.

Connell, R. W. (1993). *Education and social justice.* Philadelphia, PA: Temple University Press.

Davis, G., & Bridgman, P. (2004). *Australian Policy Handbook* (3rd ed.). Crows Nest, Australia: Allen & Unwin.

Doig, A., & Wilson, J. (1999). Ethics, integrity, compliance and accountability in contemporary UK government business relations. Till death do us part. *Australian Journal of Public Administration, 58*(4), 26–31.

Dye, T. R. (1984). *Understanding Public Policy* (5th ed.). Englewood Cliffs, NJ: Prentice-Hall.

Foucault, M. (1979). *Discipline and punish: The birth of the prison.* Harmondsworth: Penguin Books.

Furedi, F. (2004). *Therapy culture: Cultivating vulnerabil-ity in an uncertain age.* London: Routledge.

Gewirtz, S., Ball, S. J., & Bowe, R. (1995). *Markets, choice and equity in education.* Buckingham: Open University Press.

Gillborn, D., & Youdell, D. (2000). *Rationing education: Policy, practice, reform and equity.* Buckingham: Open University Press.

Gipps, C., & Murphy, P. (1994). *A fair test?* London: Falmer.

Gutmann, A., & Thompson, D. (2004). *Why deliberative democracy?* Princeton, NJ: Princeton University Press.

Kauffman, J. M., & Hallahan, D. P. (1995). *The illusion of full inclusion: A comprehensive critique of a current special education bandwagon.* Austin, TX: Pro-Ed.

Kavale, K. A. M. (2004). *The positive side of special education.* Oxford: Scarecrow Education.

Knight, T. (2000). Inclusive education and educational theory: inclusive for what? *Melbourne Studies in Education, 41*, 17–43.

Kozol, J. (1991). *Savage inequalities. Children in America's schools.* New York: Harper Perennial.

Lauder, H., & Hughes, D. (1999). *Trading in futures: Why markets in education don't work.* Philadelphia, PA: Open University Press.

Lingard, R. (1998). The Disadvantaged Schools Programme: caught between literacy and local management. *International Journal of Inclusive Education, 2*(1), 87–107.

Luke, A. (2003). Literacy and the other: A sociological approach to literacy research and policy in multilingual societies. *Reading Research Quarterly, 38*(1), 132–141.

Marginson, S. (1997). *Markets in Education.* St Leonards, Australia: Allen & Unwin.

McLuhan, E., & Zingrone, F. (1995). *Essential McLuhan.* Toronto: Anansi.

Meier, D., Sizer, T., Nathan, L., & Thernstrom, A. (2000). *Will standards save public education?* Boston, MA: Beacon Press.

Newmann, F. & Associates. (1996). *Authentic achievement. Restructuring schools for intellectual quality.* San Francisco, CA: Jossey-Bass.

Nozick, R. (1974). *Anarchy, state, and utopia.* New York: Basic Books.

Oliver, M. (2002). *Emancipatory research: A vehicle or policy development.* Paper presented to 1st Annual Disability Research Seminar: Using Emancipatory Methodologies in Disability Research. The National Disability Authority and The Centre for Disability Studies, University College Dublin, Dublin.

Pearl, A., & Tony, K. (1999). *The democratic classroom. Theory to inform practice.* Cresskill, NJ: Hampton Press.

Rose, M. (1995). *Possible lives.* New York: Penguin Books.

Rose, N. (1996). Psychiatry as a political science:

advanced liberalism and the administration of risk, *History of the Human Sciences, 9*(2): 1–23.

Rothschild, N. M. V. R. (1977). *Meditations of a broomstick.* London: Collins.

Sacks, P. (1999). *Standardized minds: The high price of America's testing culture and what we can do to change it.* Cambridge, MA: Perseus Books.

Said, E. W. (2000). Travelling theory reconsidered. In E. W. Said (Ed.), *Reflections on exile and other literary and cultural essays* (pp. 436–452). London: Granta Books.

Slee, R. (1996). Clauses of conditionality. In L. Barton (Ed.), *Disability and society: Emerging issues and insights* (pp. 436–452). London: Longman.

Slee, R. (1998). High reliability organisations and liability students – the politics of recognition. In R. Slee, G. Weiner, & S. Tomlinson (Ed.), *School effectiveness for whom?* (pp. 101–114). London: Falmer.

Slee, R. (2003). Teacher education, government and inclusive schooling: The politics of the Faustian waltz. In J. Allan (Ed.), *Inclusion, participation and democracy: What is the purpose?* (pp. 207–223). Dordrecht: Kluwer Academic Publishers.

Smith, A. (1976). *An inquiry into the nature and causes of the wealth of nations.* Oxford: Clarendon Press.

Tomlinson, S. (1981). *Educational sub-normality: A study in decision-making.* London: Routledge & Kegan Paul.

Tomlinson, S. (1997). Diversity, choice and ethnicity: The effects of educational markets on ethnic minorities. *Oxford Review of Education, 23*(1), 63–76.

Touraine, A. (2000). *Can we live together? Equality and difference.* Cambridge: Polity Press.

Troyna, B. (1993). *Racism and education.* Buckingham: Open University Press.

Troyna, B. (1994). Critical social research and education policy. *British Journal of Educational Studies, 42*(1), 70–84.

Watson, D. (2003). *Death sentence. The decay of public language.* Sydney: Knopf.

Young, I. M. (2000). *Inclusion and democracy.* Oxford: Oxford University Press.

Zizek, S. (1994). Introduction: The spectre of ideology. In S. Zizek (Ed.), *Mapping ideology* (pp. 1–33). New York: Verso.

Knowledge production

Research Method and Methodology

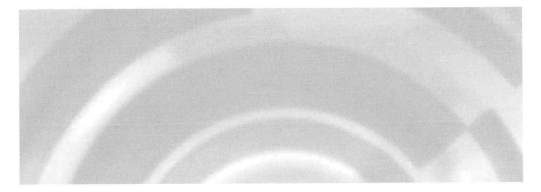

13

Perspectives shaping and challenging research approaches in special education

James L. Paul, Kathleen Fowler and Ann Cranston-Gingras

Special education as a modern professional area of research and practice developed and expanded in the last half of the twentieth century. During that period, dramatic changes occurred across disciplines in the social sciences with respect to what was considered legitimate research. Logical positivism, the traditional epistemology of research, was defeated around the middle of the century and several worldviews emerged that provided alternative understandings of knowledge and logics for doing science (Popper, 1959: Quine, 1961; Phillips, 1987). Social scientists were deeply divided in their views and there were no shared rules for adjudicating differences. These differences also existed among special education researchers who struggled to develop a well-reasoned and relevant epistemology for doing social science in a political environment that enacted strong vested interests in supporting particular policies and approaches to intervention. These researchers were charged with developing knowledge bases for interventions even as opinions were divided about what children with disabilities needed and where they could best be served. Research philosophy in special education,

then, reflects an accommodation of the political force of professional opinion about the nature of the work as well as philosophical challenges about the nature of research. Although many of the professional issues in special education changed during the last half of the twentieth century, the current political environment continues to shape the discourse about philosophical preferences and the research approaches being funded and published.

This chapter examines cultural, political, and professional forces that have shaped research perspectives in special education and changes in approaches to research published in special education journals. After discussing changes in views of knowledge and knowing, we consider the evolution of research perspectives in special education and influences of public policy on the nature of research. We then examine the history of research perspectives as reflected in publications in special education journals. Finally, we share some concluding observations about changes that have occurred in the perspectives guiding special education research and the current forces influencing that research.

SHIFTS IN PERSPECTIVES ON KNOWLEDGE AND KNOWING

Substantial changes in perspectives regarding both knowledge and knowing in philosophy of science, the social sciences, and the humanities greatly impacted the development of special education. One of the most dramatic changes was a shift from logical positivism, as the normative philosophy of science, to postpositivism and other nonpositivist perspectives. Led by philosophers and historians of science, the shift changed the assumptions about the nature of knowledge and how it is acquired.

Logical positivism was the intellectual product of the Vienna Circle that met during the 1920s and 1930s. Comprised mostly of mathematicians and philosophers, the Vienna Circle articulated principles of knowledge that became the gold standard for the physical sciences. Challenging Kantian philosophy and Hegelian metaphysics, they believed an objectively knowable world exists independent of mind, that is, an observer, and that it can be known with certainty. They argued that, for purposes of science, the truth of a statement must rely exclusively either in the ability to verify it empirically or in the logic of the statement itself. Further, they asserted that the grammar of sentences describing objective reality must be perfected. This worldview and philosophy of knowledge was adopted by the social sciences that were developing early in the twentieth century.

During the last four decades, the worldview and the principles of logical positivism have been challenged by philosophers and a wide range of critics in the social sciences and humanities. The idea of value-free and theory-free observations that are objectively independent of observers has been defeated on both logical and empirical grounds. Quantum physics set aside the mechanistic worldview of Descartes that had prevailed for more than two centuries. The verification principle was defeated on logical grounds by Popper (1959) and the empirical position by Quine (1961). Philosophers of science for more than three decades have considered logical positivism to be dead as a philosophy of science. This has led to new and interesting scholarship in rethinking assumptions about knowledge and the worldview within which research is framed. Kuhn (1970), Lyotard (1984), and Rorty (1991) have been among the strongest and most articulate voices in this regard.

This change in thinking about knowledge and knowing has profound implications for educational research. Borrowing, as it does, on substantive and epistemological traditions of several different disciplines, research in education has been challenged to interpret a complex and dynamic intellectual landscape and to define standards for research. Some of the leading educators and psychologists in reframing the discourse about research have been Koch (1964), Rist, (1977), Lincoln and Guba (1985), Howe (1985, 1988), Phillips (1987, 1992), Lagemann (1988), Gage, (1989), Lyons (1990), Gross and Levitt (1994), Donmoyer et al. (1996), Scheurich and Young (1997), Constas (1998), Creswell (1998), Gieryn (1999), Lagemann and Shulman (1999), Gergen (2001), and Garrison and Kobor (2002).

The process of negotiating new understandings about research has been contentious, sometimes involving heated debates in what some referred to as 'paradigm wars.' During the late 1980s and 1990s there appeared to be much more intellectual diversity in the education research community and less consensus about basic topics such as what counts as research. This was reflected in many ways, as will be illustrated in a later section of this chapter, including the publication of perspective pieces and different kinds of research in refereed journals. (Since 2000, however, there has been shift back to more positivist-oriented research and less valuing of diverse approaches to research.)

During the 1990s, researchers in special education responded to the perspectival shifts in the larger social science and education research community with considerable vigor and, at times, rancorous debates that have been published in special education research journals for over two decades The focus of the debates has ranged from quantitative *vs* qualitative research (Stainback & Stainback, 1984, 1985; Simpson & Eaves, 1985; Iano, 1987; Forness & Kavale, 1987) to challenges of the positivist paradigm and either voicing support for or registering serious objection to postmodern philosophies (Smith & Heshusius, 1986; Skrtic, 1986; Heshusius, 1994; Biklen and Cardinal, 1997; Gallagher, 1998; Kauffman, 1998, 1999; Danforth, 1999, 2004; Brantlinger, 1997; Crockett, 2001; Sasso, 2001). Some have focused more on the value of informed respect for different perspectives in creating a more diverse intellectual discourse about research and different kinds of knowledge to inform the ways we understand and respond to the needs of exceptional students (Smith, 1983; Howe, 1985, 1988; Paul, 2002; Sailor & Paul, 2004).

These debates have centered on issues ranging from methods to values and epistemology, with researchers divided in their views, for example, of the standards for rigor, the possibility and desirability of objectivity, the necessity of generalization, and relevance of findings for interventions. The contrasts of positions on these issues are most starkly drawn between positivists who emphasize objectivity, generalizability of findings, and rigor in designs that control for competing hypotheses such as one finds in experiments, and interpretivists who place more emphasis on subjectivity, local knowledge, individual experience, and meaning such as one finds in narrative and arts based research.

THE EVOLUTION OF RESEARCH PERSPECTIVES IN SPECIAL EDUCATION

The cultural context of the 1960s

The 1960s provided a dynamic context within which all knowledge in the social sciences was challenged. For example, the civil rights movement focusing on the disenfranchisement of minorities, women, children, and persons with disabilities challenged all aspects of society, including values, laws, and public policy that had been accepted in the past. Deep and widespread distrust of public institutions fueled the debate about research which focused on the nature of knowledge. Professional educators, psychologists, and other social scientists were challenged by the spirit of fundamental social and institutional reform. Ethical as well as epistemological questions were raised about research bias. For example, could women and minorities possibly fare well in a white male-dominated understanding of knowledge and knowing? This kind of question was in stark contrast to the claim that credible research was unbiased, a basic principle of logical positivism. This concern over the conflation of scholarship and science with social and political values in the 1960s set the stage for substantive challenges for the rest of the century.

The cultural context shaping debates about the intersection of research with social and political values was particularly relevant for special education where public support had been predicated in part on arguments of fairness and antidiscrimination in education practices and policies. The political and philosophical 'space' connecting science and culture during the 1960s and 1970s was volatile. Consequently, researchers charged with developing a knowledge base during the formative years of what we now know as special education for children were faced with a complex philosophical challenge. Perhaps the signature issue in this context was fitting a moral mission of a field, characterized by race-biased tests and placement practices, with an objective research mission. Challenges to the culture fairness of tests of intelligence and achievement and the bias in placement procedures raised questions about the nature of the data researchers gathered (Williams, 1974; Dent, 1976; Flaugher, 1978; Reschly, 1980). A related thread of bias has run through special education into the present time in terms of issues associated with disproportionate placement of minority children in special education (Dunn, 1968; Heller, Holtzman, & Messick,

1982; Chinn & Hughes, 1987; Cooper, Upton, & Smith, 1991; Artiles & Trent, 1994; Harry & Anderson, 1994; Russo & Talbert-Johnson, 1997; Coutinho & Oswald, 2000; Townsend & Patton, 2000). The disjunctive ethical arguments about serving the needs of all children in a culturally pluralistic society and the epistemological arguments about an objective science framed much of the philosophical debates about research approaches in special education during the last half of the twentieth century.

As the arguments about knowledge expanded and the usefulness of existing educational research to support the work of special educators came increasingly under attack, some researchers turned their attention to alternative approaches that incorporated more explicit cultural perspectives such as those in anthropology. Many, however, moved more aggressively to a more carefully defined science of behavior, especially single subject designs. The latter researchers focused less on cultural, interpersonal, and ethical issues and more on discrete behavioral outcomes associated with specific interventions.

The divergence of research perspectives in special education is in large part attributable to the powerful cultural context of the 1960s in which modern special education policies and practices developed. This context provided the values and substance for a cultural research agenda, contributed to the ethical as well as epistemological complexity of arguments about objective social science, and created the environment within which research communities in special education came to value and approach research from different perspectives.

Conflation of advocacy values and research

The logical positivist tradition of science, well established in the social sciences during the first half of the twentieth century, was clear in separating values from objective data. Within this view, it was expected that one should not approach a question of what is true with a prior set of convictions about the truth one hoped to find. Complete objectivity in collecting, analyzing, and drawing conclusions about data was a primary standard.

The vested interests of professional special educators in understanding and providing a credible education for children with disabilities made the objective work of researchers difficult, especially in the 1960s. Some professional special educators argued, for example, that 'trainable' mentally retarded children did not belong in schools because they, by definition, were not educable. The overwhelming response to that argument was captured in slogans such as, 'all children can learn' or 'all children can be taught.' This kind of rhetoric and ethical debate focused the mainstreaming agenda of special education policies and, therefore, the work of researchers in the 1960s and the decades that followed (Kauffman, Gotlieb, Agard, & Kukic, 1975; Sailor et al., 1989).

The civil rights movement helped focus on the rights of all children to an appropriate education and to due process in procedures that had kept some out of the educational mainstream. Section 504 of the Vocational Rehabilitation Amendments in 1972 advanced the legal principle that all barriers, including but not limited to architectural barriers, that limited the participation of individuals with disabilities in public life must be removed. The passage of the Education for All Handicapped Children Act (PL 94–142) in 1975 clearly established the ethic of inclusion in public education policy. However, researchers were not prepared to teach all children, curriculum theory had not been developed to accommodate them, theories of learning had not been moved much beyond animal studies, and theories of child development had provided limited understandings of atypically developing children that were useful to teachers.

A major challenge facing educators was the lack of a research base for understanding children with disabilities and for theorizing about curricular and behavioral interventions. The emergence of special education policies and practices, then, created the need for new research programs focused on the education of children with disabilities. Although educational researchers are not laboratory scientists, most of them value objectivity and standard protocols, or rigor, for research to insure trustworthiness of findings.

Research philosophy adopted from psychology

Research on child development and learning had been primarily the province of psychology; furthermore, there was already a well-established relationship between education and psychology. It was expectable, therefore, that educators would turn to knowledge bases in psychology and to psychologists to provide leadership in new research programs. Education researchers had adopted the philosophy of science and the methods of psychology at the beginning of the twentieth century when educators needed a way to group children for instruction and to evaluate the effectiveness of programs. Tests and program evaluation protocols were developed and the field of educational psychology emerged to address the technical research and research preparation needs in education. Departments of educational psychology, statistics, and measurements – in some universities they are combined in one department and in others they are separate – continue to be the standard bearers and gatekeepers of research philosophy and practices. Educational psychologists have provided leadership in defining research, in specifying the canons of rigor, and in teaching research and measurement courses in academic and professional education preparation programs.

Basic categories that have formed the clinical structure of special education, such as developmental disabilities, behavior disorders, and learning disabilities, were defined and given direction by psychologists, some of whom were working in the field of special education at the time. The imprint of positivist philosophy of science guiding research in psychology during the twentieth century indelibly marked the tradition in special education that evolved during the last half century.

The debates about research in psychology in the 1970s influenced debates in education and special education in the 1980s and 1990s. There was a general reductive argument that distinguished between quantitative and qualitative methods, and researchers were inclined to identify with one or the other. Most identified with quantitative methods because they were normative and most fundable. Although the debates often centered on the differences between these broad categories of methods, the fundamental problem was with the different epistemologies that provided the justifying reasons for the methods. At this level, the differences were paradigmatic, including fundamental assumptions about what is true and how it can be known.

There was some rapprochement between many quantitative and qualitative researchers in psychology and education during the late 1970s and early 1980s when quantitative researchers explicitly valued 'qualitative data' in generating informed hypotheses and better discussions of findings. The 'real research', however, was in the positivist science, that is, quantitative methods. While it is true that qualitative data can be used to improve quantitative research, the epistemological differences remained unaddressed.

More sophisticated bridges have been built with mixed method approaches during the past 10 years. More researchers are valuing quantitative and qualitative methods as complementary and, unlike the limited use of qualitative observations to improve quantitative approaches, more qualitative methods are used to study different phenomena in a study employing quantitative approaches. The clear value of mixed methods is that the studies are more inclusive of questions that could not be addressed by either approach alone. This provides a much broader perspective for research. Although research in special education, following the well-established tradition in psychology, continues to be strongly anchored in positivist epistemology, courses in qualitative and mixed methods have been added to the research preparation curriculum in many programs.

Epistemological perspectives

Notwithstanding the power of positivist science in discovering what is considered to be objectively true and the cache of political interests and privilege accompanying the positivist paradigm, positivism became the focus of extensive critiques during the last quarter of the twentieth century (Rorty, 1991; Gieryn, 1999; Gergen, 2001). These critiques focused on the modern worldview within which positivism gained conceptual footing as well as its methods.

Epistemological perspectives are systems of thought that articulate specific beliefs about knowledge that lead to methods for knowing. Some of the fundamental differences among the perspectives include considerations of whether knowledge is local or can be generalized, whether knowledge is independent of a knower or a product of mind, and the nature and role of language in knowing.

Although many researchers in special education continue to accept logical positivism as a philosophy of science, alternative epistemological perspectives were advanced and gained primacy in different scholarly communities during the last three decades. These communities of scholars now include many researchers in special education. Postpositivism, the perspective widely supported by researchers in education, accepts many of the assumptions of logical positivism but explicitly rejects the view that complete objectivity is possible. Constructivism, which regards reality as a creative product of mind interacting with the external world, is another perspective with wide and growing support among researchers in education and special education. Critical theory, which critiques knowledge and knowing from particular perspectives such as race, gender, and disability, has become a primary epistemological lens for an increasing number of researchers in special education. Other communities of scholars in special education are guided by different perspective such as prag-

matism, narrative, aesthetics, ethics, and poststructuralism.[1]

PUBLIC POLICY INFLUENCES ON RESEARCH PERSPECTIVES

The role of social values in policy development is relatively clear: the rules we make and the understandings we negotiate in order to conduct the affairs of institutions should reflect the values we wish to enact and the kind of society we want. One hopes that policies are informed by relevant research but, in the main, policies tend more to guide than to be the product of research. The plethora of research on the efficacy of educating children in the least restrictive educational environment following the passage of PL 94-142 is an example. Special education policies have been fashioned as a reflection of society's wish to include children with disabilities in schools, not as a reflection of what we have known about these children and how to teach them.

Public policy also influences the perspectives used in determining the nature of knowledge and research methods. The passage of the *No Child Left Behind Act* (NCLB) of 2001 and the publication of *Scientific Research in Education* (NRC, 2002) by the National Research Council of the National Academy of Sciences are compelling examples.

The NCLB has strong accountability provisions, including high stakes tests in reading, science, and mathematics. Funding is provided only to programs that use 'scientifically proven' approaches in teaching children to read. Further, Section 1208 of the Act defines 'scientifically based reading research' as research that applies rigorous, systematic, and objective procedures to obtain valid knowledge relevant to reading development, reading instruction, and reading difficulties. It specifies that research will:

1 employ systematic, empirical methods that draw on observations or experiments;
2 involve rigorous data analyses that are adequate to test the stated hypotheses and justify the general conclusions drawn;

3 rely on measurements or observational methods that provide valid data across evaluators and observers and across multiple measurements and observations; and

4 be accepted by a peer-reviewed journal or a panel of independent experts through a comparably rigorous, objective, and scientific review.

These provisions clearly indicate a rather strong positivist view of research and are consistent with the evidence-based practices movement that is so strong in special education.

Scientific Research in Education (NRC, 2002) described the work of a distinguished panel of scholars convened by the National Research Council (NRC), the research arm of the National Academy of Sciences (NAS). The panel was charged with responding to a bill proposed by Representative Mike Castle, (R:Del), that would have considered only 'scientifically based quantitative research' and 'scientifically based qualitative research.' The qualifier 'scientifically based' included only experiments in quantitative research and was incomprehensible as applied to qualitative research (Eisenhart & Towne, 2003, p. 32). The panel advanced a much more acceptable view of research as a 'continual process of rigorous reasoning supported by a dynamic interplay among methods, theories, and findings. It builds understandings in the form of models or theories that can be tested' (NRC, 2002, p. 2). It further described six principles that should guide researchers and underlie all scientific inquiry, including education research. These principles provide that researchers should:

1 pose significant questions that can be investigated empirically;
2 link research to relevant theory;
3 use methods that permit direct investigation of the questions;
4 provide a coherent and explicit chain of reasoning;
5 replicate and generalize across studies; and
6 disclose research to encourage professional scrutiny and critique.

The publication has been widely discussed and there is general acknowledgement of its value in helping clarify fundamental issues with respect to the nature of research. Although the report is largely a postpositivist view of research, the panel did attempt to position its report as inclusive of some of the more common epistemological positions. Eisenhart (personal communication, 2003), a member of the panel, has pointed out that the report does not advance a view that promotes the tenets of logical positivism, for example, that research is neutral or value free, that knowledge is necessarily cumulative, or that methods are infallible.

Of interest here, however, is the role of the panel in defining research in a way that has implications for the work of researchers. Research is defined within the context of a perspective. Some perspectives such as narrative, critical theory, ethics, and aesthetics, were not included, even by implication, in the panel's definition. A significant concern is that the political voice of the panel – the work of an expert panel appointed by the NRC – will silence the vigorous debates about alternative epistemologies at the end of the 20th century.

In the following section we will consider how epistemological perspectives have framed research in special education as reflected in selected periodical literature during the last half of the twentieth century.

RESEARCH PUBLICATIONS IN SPECIAL EDUCATION

In order to examine changes in research perspectives as reflected in special education publications, we reviewed the following journals: *Journal of Learning Disabilities* (JLD), *Behavioral Disorders* (BD), *Mental Retardation* (MR), *Journal of Special Education* (JSE), *Exceptional Children* (EC), *Remedial and Special Education* (RASE) and *Teacher Education and Special Education* (TESE). All issues of each journal were reviewed for the years 1965, 1975, 1985, 1995 and 2003 except in a case where a journal began publishing at a later date. The abstracts and first two pages of every article were photocopied. Two of this chapter's authors, a special education faculty member and an advanced doctoral student, read the copied material. Articles were categorized as Quantitative, Qualitative or Not Applicable. The category of Not Applicable was used for articles that did not have a research focus such as opinion pieces or descriptions of programs. We generated subcategories for both quantitative and qualitative research. To maximize consistency between raters, articles published during one year in *Teacher Education and Special Education* (TESE), were reviewed by both raters independently. Identical ratings were made for all but a few of the articles. For articles on which there was disagreement, the raters discussed how their decisions were made and reached consensus regarding how to rate similar articles.

The quantitative, that is, positivist, perspective was well established before the development of the modern field of special education after the middle of the twentieth century. Since it was to be expected that this normative perspective would guide research in special education, our interest in research publications is primarily the evolution of non-quantitative perspectives. Of course, the philosophical bases or justifying reasons for quantitative and qualitative research cannot be reduced simply to these two broad categories. Although quantitative research methods are justified logically in positivist terms, nonquantitative methods vary widely and so do the logics that support them. They range from qualitative research such as Robert Yin's Case Study Method that relies on positivist assumptions to autoethnography that is understood in narrative and interpretive terms. For purposes here, therefore, we were interested in the kinds of qualitative research published and when they were published. We found case studies, biographies, narratives, studies using grounded theory, and others that used qualitative methods but could not be specifically categorized.

As expected, the number of studies published increased after 1965 as more research funding became available. As with most education research journals that do not specifi-

cally focus on qualitative research, research published in special education journals has been and continues to be predominantly quantitative. In 1975, 91 per cent of the studies published were quantitative, 83 per cent in 1985, 67 per cent in 1995, and 76 per cent in 2003. The drop during the 1980s appears to be the result of an increase in the percentage of position papers. Research perspective was one of the major issues addressed in those papers, with researchers taking a stand for or against qualitative research. A great deal was written about how qualitative research lacked rigor and could be a dangerous trend and, by others, how quantitative researchers were controlling publications and research funding and not valuing other ways of knowing. Although quantitative studies continued throughout the latter part of the twentieth century to account for the largest percentage of research publications, there was a corresponding increase in the percentage of qualitative studies published.

Current perspectives in special education journals vary as reflected in the kinds of research they publish. MR and TESE, for example, published 10 qualitative studies each in 2003 while EC and RASE published five each and JSE (three), BD (one) and JLD (one) published even fewer.

Qualitative research has been a part of the tradition in special education since the 1960s when the modern field of research and practice began. For example, there were 14 qualitative studies published in 1965 and that number increased to 30 in 1985 and 59 in 1995. It declined, however, to 39 in 2003. This is an interesting shift in that it corresponds with the change in research perspectives in education since 2000 as discussed in the previous sections. That is, changes in the kinds of studies published in special education journals correspond to the research perspectives described in the NCLB legislation and the NRC report on the definition of educational research.

Case study is the most common qualitative research published in the special education journals examined. There were 10 case studies published in 1965, 10 in 1985, and 24 in 1995 but the number dropped to 12 in 2003. Three grounded theory studies were published in 1985, four in 1995, and four in 2003. Very few ethnographic and interpretive studies have been published in special education journals. One ethnography was published in 1985, three in 1995, and none in 2003. Four narrative studies were published in 1995 and two in 2003. Two biographical studies were published in 1995 and two in 2003. We included in the category of 'other' all research that used qualitative methods such as interviewing, focus groups, and observations that did not describe a specific research design such as ethnography or case study. There were four of these types of studies in 1965, six in 1975, 16 in 1985, 21 in 1995, and 19 in 2003. These are relatively small numbers when one considers the publications in all of the seven journals reviewed. Clearly, some journals are more open to publishing non-quantitative research than others. MR, for example, appears to have more interest in a wider range of studies, including those conducted from an interpretive perspective.

So what can be concluded from these observations about research publications? First, by far most research published in special education journals throughout the modern history of the field has been quantitative. In view of the normative philosophy of science, that is, positivism, during the first half of the twentieth century and considering the strong influence of psychology on the development of the modern field of special education during the last half, it is not surprising that most research published in special education journals would be quantitative. Second, only a small number of the special education journals publish interpretive research. This, too, may be expected in a relatively new and growing field of education with professionals, armed with a positivist legacy and responding to the current political zeitgeist, devoting most of their attention to conducting intervention studies to improve specific outcomes for children with disabilities. Interpretive research continues to evolve

as an area of inquiry in education and special education. It has growing support among some scholarly communities but also many critics who focus on what they consider to be its lack of specific applications to practice. Third, the proportion of quantitative to qualitative publications varies over time and among the seven journals reviewed but the overall trend appears to be clearly in line with federal initiatives emphasizing objective, outcome-focused research.

CONCLUSION

There are three general arguments advanced in this chapter. First, researchers were deeply steeped in logical positivism from the beginning of the modern field of special education because it began in the 1960s when there were no competing philosophies of science in the social sciences, especially psychology. Second, although debates about the philosophy of special education research during the last half of the twentieth century reflected perspectival differences and shifts in the social sciences, the field has, in general, remained primarily grounded in positivism as reflected in an analysis of research publications and journal policies. Third, the current forces influencing educational research, especially the NCLB Act and the policy position described in the publication by the National Academy of Sciences defining research, suggest that the positivist leaning of special education research has broad support at the present time. Although we have acknowledged the role and force of politics influencing research perspectives, we have raised some questions and expressed serious concerns about an apparent retrenchment in thinking about research methods and the philosophical arguments that support or justify their use. We need vigorous and respectful debates informing diverse discourses on knowledge and knowing in order to develop deeper knowledge about practice and to inform policy.

The threats to the development of more productive and relevant educational research programs in the future may not be, as often assumed, the unyielding retrenchment of positivist researchers or, as also often assumed, the forceful entrenchment of those advocating radical nonpositivist epistemologies that challenge the traditional canons of educational research. The deeper threat is more likely the possibility that the dynamics of intellectual battle, where political advantage is used to leverage outcomes of arguments about truth and value, will prevail over thoughtful and respectful argument. The most desirable future is most likely to be realized if researchers, working within different epistemological perspectives, are committed to creating a valued space for different epistemological perspectives rather than making their own more dominant.

NOTE

1 For an extended discussion of all of these perspectives see Paul (2005).

REFERENCES

Artiles, A. J., & Trent, S.C. (1994). Overrepresentation of minority students in special education: A continuing debate. *The Journal of Special Education, 27,* 410–437.

Biklen, D., & Cardinal, D. N. (Eds.). (1997). *Contested words, contested science: Unraveling the facilitated communication controversy.* New York: Teachers College Press.

Brantlinger, E. (1997). Using ideology: Cases of non-recognition of the politics of research and practice in special education. Review of educational research. 67(4), 425–461.

Chinn, P. C., & Hughes, S. (1987). Representation of minority students in special education classes. *Remedial and Special Education, 8,* 41–46.

Constas, M. (1998). The changing nature of educational research and a critique of Postmodernism. *Educational Researcher,* 27(2), 26–33.

Cooper, P., Upton, G., & Smith, C. (1991). Ethnic minority and gender distribution among staff and pupils in facilities for pupils with emotional and behavioral difficulties in England and Wales. *British Journal of Sociology of Education,* 12(1), 77–94.

Coutinho, M. J., & Oswald, D. P. (2000). Disproportion-

ate representation in special education: A synthesis and recommendations. *Journal of Child and Family Studies, 9,* 135–156.

Creswell, J. W. (1998). *Qualitative inquiry and research design: Choosing among five traditions.* Thousand Oaks, CA: Sage.

Crockett, J. B. (2001). Prologue. Exploring the meaning of science and defining rigor in the social sciences. *Behavioral Disorders,* 27(1), 7–11.

Danforth, S. (1999). Pragmatism and the scientific validation of professional practices in American special education. *Disability and Society,* 14(6), 733–751.

Danforth S. (2004). The 'postmodern' heresy in special education: a sociological analysis. *Mental Retardation,* 42(6): 445–458.

Dent, H. (1976). Assessing black children for mainstream placement. In R. L. Jones (Ed.), *Mainstreaming and the minority child* (pp. 77–92). Minneapolis, MN: Leadership Training Institute.

Donmoyer, R., Eisner, E., Gardner, H., Stotsky, S., Wasley, P., Tillman, L., Cizek, G., & Gough, N. (1996). Viewpoints: Should novels count as dissertations in education? *Research in Teaching of English, 30,* 403–427.

Dunn, L. (1968). Special education for the mildly retarded: Is much of it justifiable? *Exceptional Children, 23,* 5–21.

Eisenhart, M., & Towne, L. (2003). Contestation and change in national policy on 'scientifically based' education research. *Educational Researcher,* 32(7), 31–38.

Flaugher, R. (1978). The many definitions of test bias. *American Psychologist, 33,* 671–679.

Forness, S., & Kavale, K. (1987). Holistic inquiry and the scientific challenge in special education: A reply to Iano. *Remedial and Special Education,* 8(1), 47–51.

Gage, N. L. (1989). The paradigm wars and their aftermath: A historical sketch of research on teaching since 1989. *Educational Researcher,* 18(7), 4–10.

Gallagher, D. J. (1998). The scientific knowledge base of special education: Do we know what we think we know? *Exceptional Children,* 64(4), 493–502.

Garrison, E. G., & Kobor, P. C. (2002). Weathering a political storm: A contextual perspective on a psychological research controversy. *American Psychologist,* 57(3), 165.

Gergen, K. J. (2001). Psychological science in a postmodern context. *American Psychologist,* 56(10), 803–813.

Gieryn, T. F. (1999). *Cultural boundaries of science: Credibility on the line.* Chicago, IL: University of Chicago Press.

Gross, P., & Levitt, N. (1994). *Higher superstition: The academic left and its quarrels with science.* Baltimore, MD: Johns Hopkins University Press.

Harry, B., & Anderson, M. (1994). The disproportionate placement of African American males in special education programs: a critique of the process. *The Journal of Negro Education, 63*, 602–619.

Heller, K. A., Holtzman, W. H., & Messick, S. (Eds.). (1982). *Placing children in education; A strategy for equity.* Washington, DC: National Academy Press.

Heshusius, L. (1994). Freeing ourselves from objectivity: Managing subjectivity or turning towards a participatory mode of consciousness? *Educational Researcher, 23*(3), 15–21.

Howe, K. (1985). Two dogmas of educational research. *Educational Researcher, 14*(8), 10–18.

Howe, K. (1988). Against the quantitative-qualitative incompatibility thesis (or dogmas die hard). *Educational Researcher, 17*(8), 10–16.

Iano, R. P. (1987). Neither the absolute certainty of prescriptive law nor a surrender to mysticism. *Remedial and Special Education, 8*(1), 52–61.

Kaufman, M. J., Gotlieb, J., Agard , J. A. & Kukic , M. B. (1975). Mainstreaming: Toward an explication of the concept. In E. L. Meyen, G. A. Vergason, & R. J. Whelan (Eds.), *Alternatives for teaching exceptional children.* Denver, CO: Love.

Kauffman, J. M. (1998). Are we all postmodernists now? *Behavioral Disorders, 23*(3), 149–152.

Kauffman, J. M. (1999). The role of science in behavioral disorders. *Behavioral Disorders, 24*(4), 265–272.

Koch, S. (1964). Psychology and emerging conceptions of knowledge as unitary. In T. W. Wann (Ed.), *Behaviorism and phenomenology: Contrasting bases for modern psychology* (pp. 1–42). Chicago, IL: University of Chicago Press.

Kuhn, T. S. (1970). *The structure of scientific revolutions.* Chicago: University of Chicago Press.

Lagemann, E. (1988). The plural worlds of educational research. *History of Education Quarterly, 29*(2), 184–214.

Lagemann, E. C., & Shulman, L. S. (Eds.). (1999). *Issues in education research: Problems and possibilities.* San Francisco, CA: Jossey-Bass.

Lincoln, Y. S., & Guba, E. G. (1985). *Naturalistic inquiry.* Newbury Park, CA: Sage.

Lyons, N. (1990). Dilemmas of knowing: Ethical and epistemological dimensions of teachers' work and development. *Harvard Educational Review, 60*(2), 159–180.

Lyotard, J. F. (1984). *The postmodern condition: A report on knowledge.* Minneapolis, MN: University of Minnesota Press.

National Research Council (NCR). (2002). Scientific research in education. R. J. Shavelson & L. Towne (Eds.). Washington, DC: National Academy Press.

No Child Left Behind Act 2001, Pub. L., 107–110, 20 U.S.C. 6301 et seq. (2002).

Paul, J. (2002). Perspectival and discursive discontinuities in special education research. *Disability, Culture, and Education, 1*(2), 73–95.

Paul, J. (2005). *Introduction to the philosophies of research and criticism in education and the social sciences.* Columbus, OH: Merrill/Prentice Hall.

Phillips, D. C. (1987). *Philosophy, science and social inquiry: Contemporary methodological controversies in social science and related applied fields of research.* New York: Pergamon Press.

Phillips, D. C. (1992). *The social scientists' bestiary: A guide to fabled threats to, and defenses of naturalistic social science.* New York: Pergamon Press.

Popper, K. R. (1959). *The logic of scientific discovery.* New York: Harper.

Quine, W. V. O. (1961). *From a logical point of view.* Cambridge, MA: Harvard University Press.

Reschly, D. J. (1980). *Nonbiased assessment.* Ames, IA: Iowa State University. ERIC Reproduction # ED 209810.

Rist, R. (1977). Overview on the relations among educational research paradigms: From disdain to détente. *Anthropology & Educational Quarterly, 8*, 42–49.

Rorty, R. (1991). *Objectivity, relativism, and truth: Philosophical papers* (Vol. 1). Cambridge, & New York: Cambridge University Press.

Russo, C., & Talbert-Johnson. (1997). The overrepresentation of African American children in special education: The resegregation of educational programming? *Education and Urban Society, 29*(2), 136–148.

Sailor, W., & Paul, J. (Winter 2004). Disjunction of positivist science and postmodern social theory in special education discourses: Positioning positive behavior support in the debates. *Journal of Positive Behavior Interventions,. 6*(1), 37–49.

Sailor, W., Anderson, J., Halvorsen, A., Doering, K., Filler, J., & Goetz, L. (1989). *The comprehensive local school.* Baltimore, MD: Paul H. Brookes.

Sasso, G. M. (2001). The retreat from inquiry and knowledge in special education. *The Journal of Special Education, 34*(4), 178–193.

Scheurich, J. J., & Young, M. D. (1997). Coloring epistemologies: Are our research epistemologies racially biased? *Educational Researcher, 26*(4), 4–17.

Simpson, R., & Eaves, R. (1985). Do we need more qualitative research or more good research? A reaction to Stainback and Stainback. *Exceptional Children, 51*(4), 325–329.

Skrtic, T. M. (1986). The crisis in special education knowledge: A perspective on perspective. *Focus on Exceptional Children, 18*(7), 1–16.

Smith, J. (1983). Quantitative versus qualitative research: An attempt to clarify the issues. *Educational Researcher, 12*, 6–13.

Smith, J., & Heshusius, L. (1986). Closing down the conversation: The end of the quantitative-qualitative debate among educational inquirers. *Educational Researcher, 15*(1), 4–12.

Stainback, S., & Stainback, W. (1984). Broadening the research perspective in special education. *Exceptional Children*, *50*, 400–408.

Stainback, S., & Stainback, W. (1985). Quantitative and qualitative methodologies: Competitive or complementary? A response to Simpson and Eaves. *Exceptional Children*, *51*(4), 330–334.

Townsend, B. L., & Patton, J. M. (2000). Reflecting on ethics, power and privilege. *Teacher Education and Special Education*, *23*, 32–33.

Williams, R. L. (1974). The problem of match and mismatch in testing black children. In L.P. Miller (Ed.), *The testing of black students: A symposium* (pp. 17–30). Englewood Cliffs, NJ: Prentice Hall.

14

Advances in research on teaching students who experience difficulties in learning: grappling with the issue of access to the general curriculum[1]

Russell Gersten and Lana Edwards Santoro

The field of special education seems to lurch forward on waves of humanistic impulses, legal initiatives, and impressive technical advances. The speed of these advances has been extraordinary. Findings and speculations from research have often played a pivotal role in many of the changes in the field of special education. For example, the term *functional analysis*, originally a term used exclusively by researchers in the field of behavior analysis, is mandated now by American law. In particular, advances in research in instructional research have shaped recent reauthorizations of special education legislation in the US, in part, for students with disabilities. Legislation has also been influenced by the aspirations, hopes, dreams and theoretical conceptions of researchers.

In this chapter, we discuss some of the major advances in instructional methodology that have emanated from this body of research in the United States. We link this body of research to several key concepts in recent special education legislation in the US, specifically the 2004 reauthorization of IDEA (the Individuals with Disabilities Education Act; hereafter IDEA 2004) and to trends in research methods and methodology.

Current legislation reflects the increasingly high expectations for achievement of students with disabilities and they must be included in district and state accountability systems. Special education teachers must also be 'highly qualified' instructors with expertise and knowledge about the content they teach as well as about methods for teaching students with disabilities. Current legislation reinforces and amplifies that all students with disabilities are provided with instruction aligned to age-appropriate curriculum standards, regardless of the nature and severity of the disability. In other words, students must receive *meaningful access* to the general curriculum. This goes beyond earlier concepts of inclusion, which tended to focus on *where* students were taught. As with earlier legislative mandates on issues such as least restrictive environment, main-streaming and inclusion, the intent is admirable: the supportive research, however, is minimal. A major impetus for this continued emphasis on meaningful access to the age-appropriate general curriculum is a small body of research demonstrating that, given appropriate support, many students with disabilities can participate in cognitively challenging activities well beyond what one would predict from their actual reading abilities (Vaughn, Gersten, & Chard, 2000; Graham & Harris, in press).

In addition to IDEA 2004, there is much recent discussion about how students who experience difficulties in learning respond to typical classroom instruction, and how the use of ongoing academic performance data could be used as the primary determinant for whether or not the student requires additional, specialized instructional services (Vaughn & Fuchs, 2003). Responsiveness to typical classroom instruction as an approach to identifying students for special education requires that special education is *only* considered when a student performs below the level of classroom peers and demonstrates a substantially lower rate of learning (Fuchs, Fuchs, & Speece, 2002). This approach is an attempt to operationalize the concept of *dynamic assessment* (Campione & Brown, 1987; Baker, Santoro, & Gersten, in press). Dynamic assessment is predicated on the belief that students' need for intensive individualized instruction should be based not on their current skill level in reading or mathematics, but on their ability to benefit from evidence-based instruction. This idea has been appealing to special educators since the 1970s, in part because it seems a much more valid means for assessing English learners and other students who may have had limited early exposure to information essential for becoming a fluent reader or proficient in mathematics. However, dynamic assessment has proven difficult to operationalize (for example, Irvine, Gersten, & Heiry, 1984).

Response to intervention (RTI) is a serious large-scale attempt to operationalize this concept. This responsiveness to treatment intervention model is based on four phases. During the first phase, some type of brief, but reliable, assessment is used to determine the overall rate of learning by all students in a given classroom, school, or district. In the second phase, these assessments are used to determine if there are any target students whose level of performance and rate of learning are significantly below their peers. In Phase III, teachers or other school personnel provide extra assistance to students in small groups. Typically, these sessions involve intensive review of critical skills such as phonemic awareness in reading or fluency-building in reading, and counting strategies and quantity discrimination in mathematics. Students are then reassessed after a period of six to ten weeks to determine whether the intensive instruction or adaptations used within the classroom have helped improve the performance of target students. If students *respond to the intervention* provided, they do *not* require additional services and thus do not qualify for special education (although their progress is still monitored to ensure they remain at or above average). However, if assessment data indicates that the interventions used in the general education classroom are not contributing to improved student performance, an 'extended assessment plan' is developed to understand the nature of the problems and provide guidance for possible special education service (Fuchs et al., 2002).

Recent research on the response to treatment intervention (RTI) model emphasizes two critical components: (a) assessing the performance of a classroom of students to determine the overall student learning within a classroom and whether there are any students that differ significantly from their peers and (b) determining the rate or actual progress in learning over time (Speece, Case, & Molloy, 2003). There is an intrinsic link between assessment and instruction, which has always been the goal of special education assessment (for example, Fuchs & Deno, 1991; Gersten, Keating, & Irvin, 1995).

Given current emphasis in both research and legislation (IDEA 2004) on responsiveness to instruction, as well as increased use of assessment to both inform and reflect instructional accountability, it is essential to consider evidence-based interventions. Evidence-based interventions that have proven to be successful for students with disabilities are essential for the RTI model to be valid. A critical aspect of research methodology involves evaluating the instructional impact of interventions on student performance and providing workable answers to problems identified by practitioners, policymakers, and consumers. To be considered as 'an evidence-based instructional approach' as emphasized in US Federal policy, rigorous experimental research with randomized controlled trials must be conducted. Historically, rigorous research design and methodology have been conducted for interventions that are scripted or that are behavioral in nature. Although quasi-experimental designs are invariably easier to implement in school settings, the various research syntheses we conducted at the time (for example, Gersten & Baker, 2000b, 2001; Gersten, Fuchs, Williams, & Baker, 2001) convinced us that many of the quasi-experiments conducted in our field were compromised by uncertainty as to whether the experimental and comparison groups were truly comparable. Many of the quasi-experimental designs we reviewed were so flawed that their findings were not interpretable.

A new trend in educational research is the use of design experiments (Brown, 1992; Gersten, Baker, & Lloyd, 2000) to evaluate instructional interventions and assessments before implementing more large-scale, experimental research. When using design experiments, researchers begin with specifying the desired instructional goal and then, based on student performance data, direct observation, and responses from teachers implementing the intervention, the intervention is continually adjusted to reach the goal (Newman, 1990). Rather than to continue implementing flawed quasi-experimental designs, the hope is that an increased use of systematic design experiments will promote later implementation of more rigorous studies. The need for design experiments before conducting more rigorous research was captured eloquently, in a self-deprecating fashion by Reinking and Pickle (1993):

> As the school year progressed, we found ourselves in a seemingly endless cycle of compromises that threatened the control required in a true experiment … Each compromise seemed like a defeat in a war we were quickly losing … Our need to maintain control of extraneous variation was a barrier to finding and understanding the most relevant aspects of implementing the intervention and the effects it might have on the educational environment. (pp. 266–267)

Some proponents of design experiments stress that seriously trying out various ideas over an extended period of time will help researchers later design high-quality research studies based on the findings from their design experiments (for example, Newman, 1990). Therefore, before conducting a rigorous experiment, a series of design experiments can help pilot, or test, observation systems of classroom instruction, perceptions of student work products, and the perceptions of classroom teachers. In other words, by not needing to develop valid and reliable measures, and not having to create randomly assigned control groups, for example, researchers can focus energy on things like developing a curriculum to use in an instructional intervention, assessing whether heterogeneous pairings of students would be a successful grouping strategy, and obtaining information about the best approach to review information.

In addition to recognizing the importance of rigorous experimental research when discussing evidence-based instructional interventions, criteria for evaluating knowledge claims have also been developed (National Research Council and Committee on Minority Representation in Special Education, 2002). There have been dramatic shifts in paradigms and conceptions of what is valid research on teaching (including special education teaching) since the 1990s.

In that decade, many prominent researchers (for example, Richardson, 1990; 1994) argued, often eloquently, that quantitative methodologies for studying research on teaching (such as randomized controlled trials or correlation studies) rarely led to findings that were significant or worthwhile for practising teachers. This led to a decade-long wave of qualitative research studies, and of collaborative research studies involving teachers as active participants, and attempts to understand the perspectives and belief systems of teachers.

However, after a decade, there was a growing sense that this approach to research had failed to present much knowledge that was relevant for teachers, and provided little guidance in helping them teach students who were struggling in learning to read, write or understand key concepts in mathematics and history. Many of us (these authors included) concluded that much of the qualitative research was subjective, and potential for bias was high. In addition, a good deal of the research suffered from reliance on teacher self-reports, and the tendency to let theories override more objective analyses of the data. As a result, it was unclear how much useful, generalizable knowledge was developed.

As often happens, an equally strong countermovement developed arguing that research on teaching and instruction should follow the canons of science. In fact, a prestigious panel convened by the National Research Council (2002) concluded that there was nothing about the field of education that precluded the type of scientific research that is conducted in disciplines as diverse as medicine, agriculture, electronics, and sociology.

Scientific criteria for evaluating knowledge claims include the publication of findings in peer reviewed journals, the replication of results by other researchers, and a general consensus in the research community on whether there is a group of studies with converging emphasis (Stanovich, 1997). In our review of evidence-based instructional interventions related to accessing the general education curriculum, we have summarized studies and converging findings with immediate implications for students identified as having high incidence disabilities (learning disabilities, attention deficit disorders, behavior disorders). The organizational framework used to encompass this broad range of instructional studies involves:

- the importance of early intervention to reduce inappropriate placements in special education
- the fall and rise of direct instruction
- procedural facilitators and cognitive strategies as a

means to teach complex cognitive skills
- content enhancement strategies and meaningful access to the general curriculum.

THE IMPORTANCE OF EARLY INTERVENTION FOR STUDENTS WITH POTENTIAL DIFFICULTIES IN READING AND MATHEMATICS

National and state education standards recognize the importance of preventing academic difficulties in the early grades, and converging evidence documents the impact of early intervention on the prevention of early academic disabilities, particularly in reading (National Research Council, 1998; Texas Department of Education, 1998). Moreover, research recognizes that students at risk of academic failure require instruction that is quantitatively and qualitatively superior to instruction received by students who are already facile with early skills like phonological awareness and letter-sound identification in reading (Adams, 1990; Carnine, Silbert, & Kame'enui, 1997; Foorman, Francis, Shaywitz, Shaywitz, & Fletcher, 1997; Foorman, Francis, Fletcher, Schatschnedier, & Mehta, 1998). Carefully designed instruction, instruction that may be considered as more intensive than traditional regular kindergarten or first-grade reading curricula, is required to help students at risk of academic failure attain grade-level expectations.

Perhaps of all the academic domains, reading has received the most attention and discussion. As Stanovich (1999) asserted, we now know more about reading disabilities than about all the other learning disabilities put together. National commissions, such as the National Reading Panel (2000) were instructed to synthesize the results from empirical studies conducted on the effectiveness of instructional interventions on the reading achievement of at-risk learners. A common theme throughout empirical research is that quality instruction makes the symbolic alphabetic writing system of the English language explicit to students through instructional activities emphasizing skills in phonological awareness and alphabetic understanding. *Phonological awareness*, the ability to perceive spoken words as a sequence of sounds, and *alphabetic understanding*, the understanding that letters represent sounds and that whole words embody a sound structure of individual letters and sound patterns, are recognized as essential for the development of proficient reading (for example, Adams, 1990; Foorman et al., 1998).

Reading First

Recent large-scale education reform legislation has also focused on early intervention in reading. The national *Reading First* initiative, part of the 2001 *No Child Left Behind* Act, emphasizes how to address the reading achievement gap between higher and lower performing students. As important as reducing the achievement gap is *Reading First*'s primary goal 'to ensure that every student can read at grade level or above not later than the end of grade 3' (NCLB, 2001, Title I, Part B, Sec. 1201). *Reading First* legislation outlines what K-3 reading programs would look like if they were based on scientifically based reading research. Precise specifications are given for organizing beginning reading instruction around five essential features: phonological awareness, phonics, reading fluency, vocabulary, and comprehension. *Reading First* also requires that daily reading instruction in K-3 classrooms must explicitly target some combination of these five areas for no less than 90 minutes per day.

Reading First incorporates an RTI component. The reasoning behind this requirement is that we do have valid, reliable screening measures to detect potential reading problems in young children, so beginning early intervention in Kindergarten, first and second grades make sense. If students cannot benefit from extra help in their regular classroom, providing special education in reading while they are young may enable them to benefit from subsequent classroom instruction, which increasingly relies on silent independent reading of textbooks and other materials.

Recent research (Chiappe, Siegel, & Wade-Wooley, 2002; Gersten, & Geva, 2003; Baker, Gersten, Haager, Goldenberg, & Dingle, in press) demonstrates that the same screening measures are valid indicators for second language learners and that these students can benefit from clear explicit instruction in building reading and pre-reading skills. In fact, English language learners often surpass native English speakers in acquiring both phonological processing skills and word level reading. However, there remains a paucity of research on early intervention in the development of comprehension and vocabulary for second language learners, and for those who enter school with limited vocabularies.

Early intervention in comprehension and vocabulary

While much of the research in early intervention has focused on beginning reading instruction, there is growing attention to the need for increased emphasis on comprehension in the earliest elementary grades (Scarborough, 2001; National Research Council, 2002). The National Research Council states that the 'successful development of beginning reading skills does not ensure that the child will automatically become a skilled reader' (p. 6). We also need to direct attention towards individual differences in children's oral language and vocabulary and the influence of these differences on comprehension development (Hart & Risley, 1995; Biemiller, 2001; Scarborough, 2001), though more research needs to be conducted on comprehension and vocabulary instruction in the early grades. The following components appear to have potential impact on student comprehension gains: (a) dialogic interactions among students and teachers aimed at extending discussions using decontextualized language, (b) visual representations of text elements that facilitate intertextual connections, and (c) strategic vocabulary instruction (Snow & Dickinson, 1991; Beck & McKeown, 2001; Baker, Gersten, & Grossen, 2002).

Number sense

Another growing area of research in early intervention is in the area of mathematics and number sense. Gersten and Chard (1999) present an analogy comparing number sense in the development of mathematics skills as phonological awareness in the development of beginning reading skills. Number sense is the ability to think fluidly and flexibly about numbers, sense what numbers mean, make comparisons between numbers, and perform mental mathematics. Emerging research suggests that activities that build number sense can inform and significantly enhance the quality of mathematical interventions for students with disabilities (Griffin, Case, & Siegler, 1994; Fuchs, Fuchs, & Karns, 2001). Some early skills related to number sense include obtaining an informal concept of numerical equivalence, performing informal addition and subtraction, understanding how a whole relates to its parts, understanding equal partitioning, and obtaining an information understanding of addition and subtraction of fractions. Often number sense can be emphasized in regular, everyday routines such as counting the front steps of a building and matching plates, napkins, and cups during table setting. A small body of intervention research suggests that number sense should serve as a basis for early intervention (Griffin et al, 1994; Fuchs et al., 2001).

BROAD ISSUES IN RESEARCH ON SPECIAL EDUCATION TEACHING

A remaining issue is how to teach these key skills and proficiencies in reading, language and mathematics to struggling students. The National Reading Panel (2000) is clear that, in order to be effective with all students, instruction needs to be clear and explicit. Yet, this term has multiple interpretations. In the remainder of this chapter, we discuss two complementary approaches towards explicit instruction: direct instruction and procedural facilitators/cognitive strategies.

Direct instruction: its fall and rise

Greta Garbo, the great movie star of the 1930s, made one movie whose title is invariably garbled. The film is actually called *Susan Lennox: Her Fall and Rise*, though many reverse the order of 'rise' and 'fall.' The story of direct instruction over the past 15 years reminds one of the story of Susan Lennox.

Beginning in the late 1970s, direct instruction became a popular method for special education teaching practice in the US, and several events stimulated its use. The first was the 1977 release of the findings from the evaluation of Project Follow Through, a study of the effectiveness of various instructional models for teaching students at risk for school failure. These results (Stebbins, St Pierre, Proper, Anderson, & Cerva, 1977) indicated that direct instruction was an effective means for teaching at-risk learners, and that in most instances, these students from low-income communities were reading at or near grade level and performing equally well in mathematics. Implications for special education seemed clear to many. In addition, the major direct instruction developers released a reading series meant for students with reading disabilities in grades 4 and beyond, the *SRA Corrective Reading Series*. Several research studies demonstrated significant positive effects for this program (Lloyd, Cullinan, Heins, & Epstein, 1980; Lovett et al., 1994).

In addition, the first major wave of empirical research on teaching (summarized in Brophy & Good, 1986; Rosenshine & Stevens, 1986) seemed to indicate that teachers who implemented direct instruction teaching practices had classes where students made the most growth in reading and mathematics, at least in the elementary grades. Several attempts to link direct instruction practice to growth in outcomes for special education students (Christenson, Ysseldyke, & Thurlow, 1989) also tended to support the use of direct instruction. By far its main use has been to teach foundational academic skills to students with disabilities. In particular, it has been used to teach students how to read. Our recent observational research in special education settings in three states indicates that it remains in wide use as a means to teach reading to special education students (Brownell et al., 2005). One of the most lucid definitions of direct instruction comes from a researcher who, until recently, has been one of direct instruction's staunchest critics, Courtney Cazden. Cazden (1992) noted that the key feature of direct instruction is 'Explicitness. Direct instruction means being explicit about what needs to be done, or said, or written – rather than leaving it to learners to make inferences from experience' (p. 111). Direct instruction is a structured approach to teaching – with a minimal emphasis on 'hands-on,' inductive, experiential learning and relatively few opportunities for freewheeling, informal open-ended discussion.

No two authors often mean precisely the same thing by the term *direct instruction.* To Rosenshine or Brophy and Good, for example, it was a series of observed teaching practices that were often linked to superior student outcomes. To Carnine et al. (1997), it was a theory of both curriculum design and teaching practices, an approach that included, clear teaching and explanation of strategies, and ample review of previously learned concepts. In 1982, Gersten, White, Falco, and Carnine (1982) noted that the overarching principle in direct instruction is to promote learning for all students with a clear and unambiguous presentation of the curriculum. An associated feature of this instructional clarity is to ensure high rates of student success and increase students' self-confidence and willingness to take risks and persist in academic problem-solving activities. With direct instruction, high rates of success are partly ensured by designing instruction so that students learn how to solve each step of a particular strategy or concept.

Direct instruction was extremely controversial at the time of its inception. It remains so to this day. Its use – or what some see as its overuse – in special education has been steadily questioned (Heshusius, 1991; Palincsar, David, Winn, & Stevens, 1991; Pugach & Warger, 1993; Woodward & Montague, 2002).

In preparing this chapter, we reviewed several of the seminal works on direct instruction. In fact, the seminal research was quite rich. For example, Brophy and Good (1986) describe the indicators of effective teaching in the following fashion: 'The more successful teachers taught more actively, spending more time lecturing, demonstrating, or leading recitation or discussion lessons. They devoted less time to seatwork, but were more instructionally active during the seatwork time ... more likely to monitor and assist students ... The more successful teachers asked many more questions' (p. 343). Many of these questions were focused on *product* rather than *process questions.* For example, instead of asking students *how* they might approach a problem, teachers using product questions asked questions with clear right or wrong answers. For example, 'What is 197? What is the difference between an island and a peninsula?' In addition, the high-achieving teachers provided immediate, non-evaluative feedback. They also maintained a brisk instructional pace by integrating explanations and questions into their presentation of content.

The researchers did note, however, that instruction was modulated in many ways. For one thing, the more successful teachers incorporated ideas from students into the lesson. Those with strongest gains did balance *product* questions with more complex *process* questions. Thus, Brophy and Good (1986) concluded that effective teaching is actually a blend of direct and indirect instruction, in part dependent on the content being taught and the age level of students. However, their research and the various syntheses by Rosenshine were typically simplified and categorized as support for consistent direct instruction.

The fall from grace

By the late 1980s, instructional researchers realized that systematic, 'step by step,' explicit instruction is inappropriate for cognitive activities like expressive writing, where flexibility is always important, where revising and refining (that is, self-monitoring) are critical, and where no two people engage in the process the same way. All researchers were aware that algorithmic or 'lock step strategies' that were effective in teaching many students how to decode or compute were not appropriate for complex, cognitive activities, such as comprehension, expressive writing, and problem-solving. We discuss this body of research in the next section of the chapter. However, the emphasis on teaching flexible cognitive and metacognitive strategies, along with the emphasis on social constructivism (for example, Palincsar & Klenk, 1993), led to a backlash against direct instruction (for example, Pugach & Warger, 1993). In addition, this was the period of the whole language movement, and the unfortunate decision made by many states and districts to use whole language as a means to teach beginning reading to young children. Whole language typically defined itself as being vehemently opposed to direct instruction in foundational skills, and argued that students would only learn and remember new skills if they were exposed to them in 'meaningful' contexts (Stahl, 1999). Teacher spontaneity and intuition were stressed (for example, Routman, 1988); the precision and careful structuring and organizing of classroom interactions that Brophy and Good (1986) articulated was largely ignored.

The following is an example of some of the concerns raised about direct instruction. In this case, the authors focus on mathematics, and discuss implications of the various mathematics reform movements for special education. Woodward and Montague (2002) noted, quite aptly, that

> special education research has a history of placing a considerable emphasis on rote learning and mastery of mathematics facts and algorithms for basic operations. Even though traditional methods, such as direct instruction, may be effective for teaching factual content, 'there is less evidence that this instruction transfers to higher order cognitive skills such as reasoning and problem solving … Given the long-standing need to provide general education curriculum for students with disabilities, special educators must reconsider traditional approaches and provide instruction that is more consistent with the reform agenda (p. 91)

Woodward and Montague present several important concepts from the mathematics reform movement. In particular, they note that 'making common mathematics topics such as two-digit addition or subtraction, problematic and treating them as "ill-defined" are … discussed … as a means to get students to "think mathematically"' (2002, p. 90). Similar analyses appeared during this time period in the area of reading comprehension (for example, Palincsar et al., 1991). These essays, while often erudite and thoughtful, typically pitted direct instruction against reform or constructivist approaches, thus creating false dichotomies. In addition, direct instruction was often considered a traditional approach, as in the Woodward and Montague (2002) material, above. In reality, direct instruction most assuredly has its limitations, but it never should be considered as traditional drill or recitation. In fact, the nuanced research of Good, Brophy, Stallings, and others clearly demonstrates the profound differences between direct instruction and traditional recitation.

The view that direct instruction or explicit instruction in foundational skills was failing to provide students with high-incidence disabilities with access to the general curriculum, and thus should be abandoned, or minimized, was a common motif in the 1990s and even the beginning of this decade.

The rising

Despite the controversy often surrounding direct instruction, recent legislation in the US, such as the 2004 *No Child Left Behind* Act, and the corresponding *Reading First* initiative, has contributed to a resurgence in the use of curricula based on principles of direct, systematic instruction. Classroom observational research (Foorman et al., 1998) indicated that explicit instruction in phonemic awareness and decoding in the primary grades leads to higher growth in reading. An extensive research base, including a wide range of well-controlled, experimental studies, indicates that explicit, focused instruction leads to higher growth and significantly higher success rates in teaching young children to read (for example, Lovett et al., 1994; O'Connor, 1999; Vaughn et al., in press).

In the next section, we include a brief overview of a recent study on explicit instruction as a means of teaching young students critical reading (and reading-related) skills. While we know the fundamental components of beginning reading instruction that address the learning needs of at-risk students, we still do not have definitive answers regarding which combination of approaches, and which levels of explicitness, integration, emphasis, and review, promote greater acquisition of reading skills (Lyon & Moats, 1997). To examine the added benefits of explicit spelling and writing as an extension of core reading instruction for kindergarten students at risk of reading disabilities, Edwards, Simmons, Coyne, Kame'enui, and Harn (2004), designed an instructional intervention to strategically use spelling skills to teach beginning reading. Students participating in the instructional intervention received approximately 15 minutes of core beginning reading instruction with emphasis on phonological awareness and alphabetic understanding skills, followed by 15 minutes of spelling and writing.

The spelling and writing instructional component was designed to explicitly reinforce and strategically integrate the skills taught during core reading instruction. This 'enhanced' instructional component provided: (a) additional emphasis on phonemic segmentation skills (saying the sounds in the word 'mat' —/m//a//t/), (b) additional instruction involving an explicit connection between letters in print and sounds (spelling the word 'mat'), (c) the use of writing to practise letters and spell words (writing the letter that makes the first sound in 'mat,' or writing the word 'mat'), and (d) activities targeting the fluent recall of letters (writing dictated letters as quickly as possible from memory).

An implied hypothesis of this study was that the integrated and intentional linkage of phonological awareness, spelling, handwriting, and reading would result in students' improved and differential ability to read words. This hypothesis was supported. After participating in a November through mid-May intervention, students who received core reading instruction and the spelling instructional component performed reliably better on a range of reading measures compared to students who received the same core reading instruction with an added 15 minutes of storybook reading with language-based comprehension and vocabulary activities.

But, what aspect, emphasis, or components of the spelling component contributed to the differences observed in student outcomes? One possible explanation is the spelling component's combined emphasis on phonemic segmentation with explicit use of alphabet letters to represent sounds. In other words, students who received spelling instruction received additional phonemic segmentation practice with a clear and consistent use of letters to represent sounds. In other words, the use of letters to represent sounds through the process of spelling provided a more concrete representation of the alphabetic writing system that subsequently fostered word reading. Spelling essentially was a more tangible way to help students learn the sounds in spoken words.

In addition, students who received the spelling component spelled words through writing. In a review of spelling instruction, Treiman (1998) noted that 'through writing, children learn to see spellings as maps of phonemic content rather than as arbitrary sequences of letters. Practice in using the alphabetic strategy to spell [by writing] helps children transfer this strategy to reading' (p. 296). Overall, the explicit instruction used in the Edwards et al. spelling intervention represents several features of direct instruction discussed earlier, such as systematic instructional design, clear and unambiguous presentation of content, and review and mastery of skills through spelling's enhanced, instructional emphasis.

Recent research on teaching students foundational skills in mathematics, reading and handwriting continues to support the efficacy of direct, systematic, intense instruction in building these skills in struggling learners (Lovett et al., 1994; Foorman et al., 1998; Swanson & Hoskyn, 1998; Gersten & Vaughn, 2001).

The need for explicit instruction for students who experience difficulties in learning

Stein, Leinhardt, and Bickel (1989, p. 164) once remarked that real learning does 'not materialize from brief encounters' with new material, but rather develops with the type of systematic guidance and structure provided by an approach such as direct instruction. Research by Zigmond et al. (1994) on the impact of traditional social studies instruction on students with learning disabilities demonstrates this point. Observational data in general education classrooms by Zigmond et al. revealed, 'students with learning disabilities in these classes were selectively attentive, often focusing on an extraneous part of a lesson or explanation. (They were) easily confused and (overly) concrete in their understandings' (p. 14). Concepts that were discussed only incidentally *were rarely even remembered.*

Direct instruction strives to provide a structure or framework so that students can make sense of new concepts, relationships, and learning experiences. With this approach, students are provided with: (a) explicit models of reasonable ways to solve problems, such as converting letter sounds in meaningful words, (b) ample support during the stages of the learning process, (c) frequent opportunities to respond, and (d) extensive practice and review (Gersten, Woodward, & Darch, 1986).

The frequent student responding that is a core component of direct instruction also gives teachers a chance to 'see' one dimension of what students are learning or not learning during a lesson. For many teachers who work with students with disabilities, the frequent and easily observable feedback on how well their students are learning how to read is crucial. This may well explain why, in his meta-analysis, Swanson (in press) concluded that of all academic domains, the ability to read words was the area of the strongest, most consistent effectiveness for direct instruction with students with learning disabilities.

Extended conceptions of explicit instruction

Carnine, Caros, Crawford, Hollenbeck, and Harniss (1996) provide an example; their focus was on teaching US history to middle school students. In the words of Leinhardt (1994), history instruction needs to move away from the idea that 'students ... need to learn the facts first and then start to do the interesting "good" stuff'. Instruction, instead, should focus on 'helping the student learn to reason about and with history' (p. 253). This was a major goal of this line of research. The entire course was based on the problem–solution–effect text structure. In other words, the text consistently articulated problems for a group of people (for example, colonists, American Indians, British), described attempts by the group to resolve the problem, and then described effects. Students were taught to see events from two different perspectives, how a solution for one group (for example, the colonists) might be perceived as a major problem for another.

The problem–solution–effect text structure is very flexible in the way it can be applied to a wide array of situations (Kinder, Bursuck, & Epstein, 1992; Harniss, Hollenbeck, Crawford, & Carnine, 1994). In general, students are taught that historical events or *problems* can typically be organized according to whether they involve the rights of people, have an economic focus, or include aspects of both dimensions. The way people or groups respond to these problems can be organized according to five broad categories of responses or *solutions*. In turn, these solutions have *effects* that can be tied to the original problem: the problem is either solved, the problem continues, or a new problem is created.

For students with learning disabilities, this framework helps them understand historical events in a way that de-emphasizes the memorization of names, dates, and places, and emphasizes the meaning-based aspects of history. It was also possible with this framework to help students understand the human dimension of history and to grapple with the idea that multiple perspectives on key events do exist.

A variety of graphic organizers and semantic maps were employed by Carnine et al. (1996) within the direct instruction framework because of the *clarity* with which information could be conveyed, the vividness with which students could see contrasts, and the fact that students with reading difficulties could still easily access the key information.

Middle school students with learning disabilities and behavior disorders were taught using this approach and their performance was contrasted with similar students taught using conventional texts, texts that did not rely on an underlying conceptual framework. The resultant effect size difference was .68 standard deviation units (Harniss, 1996). Similar results were reported by Kinder and Bursuck (1993) for students with emotional and behavioral disorders. This study helps elucidate how increasingly principles and findings from cognitive psychology and curriculum reformers have been woven into the direct or explicit instruction research tradition. The findings also demonstrate a means of providing students with disabilities access to the general curriculum in a meaningful fashion, as current Federal policy requires.

What the meta-analyses reveal about direct and explicit instruction

Swanson and Hoskyn (1998) performed an extensive meta-analysis of the impact of various instructional models and approaches on students with learning disabilities. In analyzing 180 studies, Swanson concluded that two approaches were effective in enhancing learning. Both direct instruction and strategy instruction had consistent, moderately strong effects, with virtually identical magnitudes (.68 for direct instruction and .72 for strategy instruction). (The strategy approaches are essentially the approaches we discussed in the preceding section, involving procedural facilitators or cognitive strategies.) When the two were used in combination, the effect was significantly stronger (.84). Note how the type of

artful blending that Brophy, Good and Rosenshine struggled to articulate in the 1970s and 1980s remains a critical framework for conceptualizing special education teaching.

Procedural facilitators and cognitive strategies: tools for unraveling the mysteries of reading comprehension and the writing process

As researchers tackled issues relating to teaching comprehension and expressive writing to students with learning disabilities, they were aware that flexibility, and the ability to evaluate one's own progress on a task, needed to be taught. Instruction needed to include ways to decipher the meaning of paragraphs in which there was more than one main idea, ways to identify and integrate the range of character clues that may support valid inferences about the reasons characters in novels take action, and ways to communicate to students that literature and historical events can be interpreted from multiple perspectives. Overall, academic improvement in reading comprehension and written expression is related to the use of interventions with several integrated instructional components (Isaacson, 1994).

Thus, the dilemma was posed: how was it possible to 'teach' something as mysterious as the process of writing (Graham & Harris, in press), or discerning themes in a short story (Williams, 2005)? The field of special education has made extraordinary progress in tackling this dilemma by studying methods such as procedural facilitators (Bereiter & Scardamalia, 1987; Englert, Raphael, Anderson, Anthony, & Stevens, 1991), cognitive strategies (Harris & Pressley, 1991), learning strategies (Deshler, Ellis, & Lenz, 1996), coached elaborations, or scaffolds. Some rely heavily on graphic organizers (Idol, 1987; Englert et al., 1991). Most involve intensive modeling and monitoring by the teacher (Graham & Harris, 1989; Wong, Butler, Ficzere, & Kuperis, 1997). Many rely heavily on peer interaction (Englert et al., 1991; Palincsar et al., 1991). All are multifaceted. In this section, we use the term procedural facilitators to refer to the whole set of instructional approaches described by these various terms.

Procedural facilitators to guide students toward expert performance

Procedural facilitators are questions, prompts, or simple outlines of important structures that teachers use on a daily basis to help students emulate the performance of more expert learners (Scardamalia & Bereiter, 1986), and to provide a common language for discussing the cognitive task or activity. Despite the different terminologies, the goal is the same – to provide a 'plan of action' and a system for providing ongoing feedback and support. This 'plan of action' is derived from the learners' need for help with organization and structure (Kolligian & Sternberg, 1987), and their need for a road map or guide to move through the process. A rich empirical base has established the effectiveness of procedural facilitators in scaffolding learning for students with disabilities.

Helping students effectively use a 'plan of action' is accomplished by having competent adults or peers verbalize the processes they go through when they read or write. These procedural facilitators assist the teacher (or peer) in the unfamiliar task of verbalizing how they actually compose a piece of narrative writing, or know when they need to re-read a troubling portion of a textbook, or how they glean the central concept from a page of text or infer character motives. They typically help to provide a shared language between teachers and students, and provide students with a permanent reminder of the steps and strategies used by highly proficient readers or writers.

Story grammar and story mapping as a tool to enhance reading comprehension

One of the seminal studies on the use of procedural facilitators was conducted by Idol (1987), who used a story mapping technique to enhance the reading comprehension of students with and without learning disabilities.

In particular, the study was important because Idol wanted to try out the technique in an inclusive setting with heterogeneous groups of students. Her earlier research had established the efficacy of the story mapping procedure with a small group of students with learning disabilities (Idol & Croll, 1987).

Idol's goal was to use a procedural facilitator that would 'draw the readers' attention to the common elements among stories,' which she hoped would enhance the 'possibility of the reader searching his or her mind for possible information' related to the text (that is, activating background knowledge in contemporary terminology) (Idol, 1987, p. 197). In other words, the story map was to serve as a framework for integrating story elements from the text with the reader's own experiences.

The procedural facilitator was a story map. This map had room for students to record information directly related to nine or 10 story grammar questions. The map helped students record as they were reading – or after they finished reading – important elements of the story, including descriptions of the setting, the problem, the actions taken to solve problems, and final outcomes. Examples of the questions used throughout the intervention include: where did the story take place? When did the story take place? How did [*main character*] try to solve the problem? Was it hard to solve the problem? (*Explain in your own words*).

Numerous studies that followed Idol's confirmed that explicitly teaching text structures such as the story map enhances reading comprehension for students with learning disabilities (Dimino, Gersten, Carnine, & Blake, 1990; Gurney, Gersten, Dimino, & Carnine, 1990; Williams, Brown, Silverstein, & deCani, 1994).

Using text structures to enhance the quality of students' writing

Writing instruction has become a major thrust of instructional research and an area for which the use of procedural facilitators has clear benefits. Wong et al. (1997) enumerated several barriers to effective writing documented by research from the last two decades. Specifically, they noted that students with learning disabilities have trouble both with mechanical aspects of writing (for example, spelling, grammar) as well as with knowledge of – or comfort with – procedures utilized by skilled writers. Empirical findings over the decades have consistently shown that these barriers result in writing by students with disabilities that is very short, poorly organized, and lifeless (Isaacson, 1995).

While there are writing conventions specific to certain genres, there is no 'correct' way to construct text. In narrative writing, for example, some writers like to begin with the climax of a story and proceed outward; others like to develop their characters before developing the plot. The approach used to construct a narrative is not what makes the story more or less engaging.

Moreover, different types of writing are based on different inherent structures. For example, a persuasive argument contains elements (for example, thesis with supporting points) that differ considerably from those found in narrative writing (for example, characters and plot). This variability makes it difficult if not impossible to teach writing explicitly. Rather, good writing instruction involves teaching what Englert et al. (1991) call 'overlapping and recursive processes'. These processes do not proceed in a particular order and one process may inform another in such a way that the author returns to previous steps to update or revise on a regular basis. Teaching learners to write requires showing students how to develop and use 'plans of action' or procedural facilitators that help them organize what they want to say and guide them in how to get it down on paper.

Thinking aloud and together: interactive dialogue as a means of teaching

Almost from the beginning, researchers seemed to be implicitly aware that all of the

procedural facilitators or cognitive strategies could really accomplish was encouraging students to think aloud – and that often, groups of peers were essential for promoting this process, since it easily becomes contrived between an adult and a child. Researchers have begun to make more explicit the primarily supportive role strategies and facilitators play in helping students develop interesting ideas to write about and to discuss with their peers ways to express those ideas effectively in their writing. Kucan and Beck (1997) are explicit in noting 'the shift from identifying and teaching discrete strategies to focusing on students' efforts to make sense of ideas or build their own understanding of them' (p. 285).

Frequently, procedural facilitator and learning strategy researchers have drawn on the social nature of learning to help students arrive at greater degrees of independence and resultant flexibility (Palinscar & Brown, 1989; Englert & Mariage, 1996; Scanlon, Deshler, & Schumaker, 1996; Wong et al., 1997). The vehicle most commonly used today for maximizing the social nature of learning is elaborated dialogue.

Elaborated dialogue is also known as interactive dialogue, think-alouds, and collaborative processes. It is a verbal exchange about a complex cognitive activity among a teacher and students or students with each other. The dialogue can include explicit modeling of strategies, critical evaluation of verbal or written student responses, questioning and elaborated responses. During these exchanges, students are apprenticed into higher, more detailed, and richer forms of expression and processes for higher order activities (Englert & Mariage, 1996; Wong et al., 1997).

Contemporary research recognizes the importance of interactive dialogue between students and teachers as a means of 'teaching' students reading comprehension and writing. Procedural facilitators are essentially tools providing a common language between teachers and students to help guide dialogue on these elusive topics. The fact that the procedural facilitators (think sheets, story maps, and so on) are visible to the students with disabilities helps demystify the process. In other words, it seems to be less important to teach all steps in a strategy to a student than to use a strategy or procedural facilitator to initiate and focus dialogue, which leads to higher levels of performance. In these interactions, teachers model ways of thinking and students display their current ways of thinking, either with the teacher or with their peers. They also respond to students' attempts at organization, originality, and unique interpretation. Then, as part of the dialogical process of revisiting aspects of expert ways of thinking, questioning, answering, and elaborating dialogue, new ways of thinking are constructed and practiced. We believe this recurring theme of thoughtfully integrating a variety of instructional approaches and techniques is critical if students with disabilities are going to be successful in today's classrooms.

Attempts to understand why students, regardless of educational disability, failed to transfer skills across classroom settings contributed to the insight that each academic discipline has its own unique ways of reasoning and its own structure. Transfer of knowledge and strategies across academic domains is often limited for students with disabilities (Brown, Collins, & Duguid, 1989). For example, Palincsar, Anderson, and David (1993) quickly learned that the reciprocal teaching approach they had used so successfully to teach reading comprehension was fundamentally different from teaching the language of science – the nature of discourse in science, and the methods of science. Thus, new approaches needed to be developed for science learning.

Historically, in both elementary and secondary settings, early attempts to teach cognitive strategies focused on generic skills without sufficient attention to how they are executed in specific academic domains (Wong, 1994). We now know that much of strategy use is domain specific, and generalization of strategy learning to learning content in other academic domains is extremely

difficult (Brown et al., 1989). Teaching generic learning strategies divorced from teaching academic content in science or math or history tends to result in students' failure to apply these strategies when it really counts, in learning academic content or in daily living.

Other researchers have written about teaching in a way that conveys this domain-specific perspective. Cobb (1994), for example, called for a conception of teaching in which the classroom teacher's role is to both convey the content of a lesson as well as to teach students the processes of learning required for reasoning, analysis, and problem-solving in a particular academic domain. The goal is that the two be truly integrated. As we mentioned, this is a significant shift from conceptions of strategy instruction developed in the 1980s.

The importance of multiple teaching strategies

Throughout this chapter, we have stressed the importance of using multiple approaches to teaching to reach the complex goals of special education, and attempted to delineate occasions where intentional use of multiple teaching strategies leads to greater learning and greater transfer. Given recent emphasis on high academic expectations and standards, instructional accountability, and student responsiveness to instructional interventions, it is even more critical to rely on a variety of research-based instructional strategies for students with disabilities. We conclude with examples that combine these principles.

Santoro, Baker, and Chard (2005) focused on designing and evaluating a framework for teaching comprehension of complex narrative and information texts to first-grade students in general education classrooms. Because students were just acquiring beginning reading skills, comprehension skills and vocabulary knowledge were taught in a listening comprehension context through teacher read alouds. A total of 42 first-grade teachers participated in an intervention study to investigate the effects of a read aloud curriculum on the comprehension and vocabulary achievement of 210 at-risk and average achieving first-grade students. Teachers were randomly assigned to experimental and comparison conditions. The experimental classrooms' read aloud curriculum consisted of a 15 week intervention focusing on topics related to animals, famous people, and holidays and addressed in the first-grade general education curriculum. Each week, the social studies or science unit included a narrative storybook and expository book used in a teacher's read aloud.

The lessons used during the read alouds in the experimental classrooms were designed to incorporate multiple instructional strategies. For example, lessons included before, during, and after reading components, and emphasized strategies for setting a purpose for reading (for example, determining whether the read aloud book was a story or information text), building vocabulary knowledge, making text-to-text and text-to-life connections, and proving predictions. Explicit instruction was used to model text retells through teacher think alouds, and children worked with partners to practise story or expository retells, with story or 'information' maps as prompt sheets. In addition to strategy instruction and regular retell practice, text read alouds included active dialogic interactions and elaborated discussion between the teacher and students, as discussed earlier in the context of procedural facilitators. Overall, the instructional intervention used during classroom read alouds relied on multiple strategies to help students access the complex narrative and information text used in the general education classroom reading program.

Results from the Santoro, Baker, and Chard study suggest that optimizing instructional opportunities during read alouds improves comprehension for first-grade students when compared to the performance of students from comparison classrooms, classrooms where teachers had access to the read aloud texts, but not to the curriculum lessons with the instructional strategies described above. Specific differences between children in the experimental and comparison classrooms were observed for accuracy and quality of narrative and expository retells, vocabulary knowledge, and metacognitive understanding of differences between narrative and expository text.

Gersten, Baker, Smith-Johnson, Peterson, and Dimino (in press) also incorporated multiple instructional strategies into a study of teaching key concepts and content about the American Civil Rights Movement to seventh and eight graders with learning disabilities in inclusive settings. Our working hypothesis was that these students could learn the content and concepts of grade-level history courses if: (a) instruction included comprehensible and accessible materials (rather than sole reliance on traditional textbooks) and (b) incorporated instructional delivery strategies that provided numerous opportunities for students to interact with peers and the teacher during the lesson (rather than heavy reliance on lectures and whole-class discussions).

Our goal was to develop and then rigorously evaluate an instructional intervention that:

- provided students with explicit structures to help them organize information
- incorporated structured peer interactions involving heterogeneous pairs of students
- used a curriculum that provided meaningful access to the content in such a way that weak readers could still learn the material.

The documentary *Eyes on the prize* (DeVinney, 1991) was the primary 'text.' We showed excerpts from this video disc documentary for about 5–12 minutes a day. These selections were broken into 2–4-minute segments; teachers stopped the video and asked questions to assess understanding and clarified difficult points. Students also read (in heterogeneous pairs of one student with learning disabilities and one non-disabled student) articles from magazines of that era and selections from texts. Students worked in heterogeneous pairs on a range of activities. They compared and contrasted important figures in the movement such as Rosa Parks with Minnijean Brown, one of the teenagers who integrated Central High school in Little Rock, Arkansas. They were presented with questions to answer including questions with no clear right or wrong answers, for example, 'How would you feel going through training in nonviolence as Andrew Goodman (one of the Voting Registration volunteers who was murdered in Philadelphia, Mississippi) did?' We used a Think–Pair–Share technique, so that students first thought about an answer and then discussed the answer with their partner. They then wrote down a response they agreed on, and only then debriefed with the whole class.

The intervention was evaluated using randomized trials. Students in the comparison group used the same materials, but did not work in dyads and saw full 5–12 minute segments of the video without pauses for discussion. Results indicated superior learning by the students with learning disabilities in the experimental condition. In fact, these students performed as well as the average-ability students in the comparison group.

Finally, classrooms can be organized to optimize the impact of instructional strategies and help students access the general education curriculum. A good example of a research program that has gone beyond the evaluation of the effects of a single strategy to the design of a comprehensive 'classroom package' is PALS (Peer-Assisted Learning Strategies). PALS is described by Fuchs, Fuchs, Mathes, and Simmons (1997) as a classwide one-to-one peer-tutoring program involving partner reading, paragraph summarizing, predictions, and other such activities to encourage students to practise strategies that have been shown to strengthen reading comprehension. The program is a result of extensive earlier work on classwide peer tutoring (Simmons, Fuchs, Fuchs, Hodge, & Mathes, 1994; Simmons, Fuchs, Fuchs, Mathes, & Hodge, 1995). For example, in Fuchs et al. (1997) 20 teachers implemented PALS for 15 weeks, and another 20 teachers did not implement PALS. Students in the PALS classrooms demonstrated greater read-

ing progress on all three measures or reading achievement used: words read correctly during a read aloud, comprehension questions answered correctly, and missing words identified correctly in a cloze (maze) task. The program was effective not only for students with learning disabilities but also for non-disabled students, both low achievers and average achievers.

We believe the type of research that examines multiple strategies within 'organized' classrooms demonstrates an orchestration of some of the instructional strategies that research on effective teaching consistently demonstrates is most effective. We do envision research on special education teaching to continue to integrate these various traditions, including advances from the research on peer-assisted learning (for example, Fuchs, Fuchs, & Burish, 2000), socially mediated instruction (for example, Beck, McKeown, Sandora, Kucan, and Worthy 1996), and cognitive science (for example, Williams, 2005), with what we know about effective, explicit instruction.

NOTE

1 Sections of this chapter are adapted from Gersten, Baker, Pugach, Scanlon, & Chard (2001).

REFERENCES

Adams, M. J. (1990). *Beginning to read: Thinking and learning about print.* Cambridge, MA: MIT Press.

Baker, S., Gersten, R., & Grossen, B. (2002). Remedial interventions for students with reading comprehension problems. In M. R. Shinn, G. Stoner, & H. M. Walker (Eds.), *Interventions for academic and behavior problems II: Preventive and remedial approaches* (pp. 731–754). Bethesda, MD: National Association of School Psychologists.

Baker, S., Gersten, R., Haager, D., Goldenberg, C., & Dingle, M. (In press). The relationship between observed teaching practice and growth in reading in first graders who are English learners. *Elementary School Journal.*

Baker, S., Santoro, L., & Gersten, R. (In press). Assessment of content knowledge for students with LD. *Elementary School Journal.*

Beck, I. L., & McKeown, M. G. (2001). Text talk: Capturing the benefits of read-aloud experiences for young children. *The Reading Teacher, 55*, 10–20.

Beck, I. L., McKeown, M. G., Sandora, C., Kucan, L., & Worthy, J. (1996). Questioning the author: A year-long classroom implementation to engage students with text. *Elementary School Journal, 96*, 385–414.

Bereiter, C., & Scardamalia, M. (1987). *The psychology of written composition.* New York: Erlbaum.

Biemiller, A. (2001). Estimating root word vocabulary growth in normative and advantaged populations: Evidence for a common sequence of vocabulary acquisition. *Journal of Educational Psychology, 93*, 498–520.

Brophy, J., & Good, T. L. (1986). Teacher behavior and student achievement. In M. Wittrock (Ed.), *The third handbook of research on teaching* (pp. 328–375). New York: Macmillan.

Brown, A. L. (1992). Design experiments: Theoretical and methodological challenges in creating complex interventions in classroom settings. *The Journal of Learning Sciences, 2*, 141–178.

Brown, J. S., Collins, A., & Duguid, P. (1989). Situated cognition and the culture of learning. *Educational Researcher, 18*. 32–41.

Brownell, M., Bishop, A., Gersten, R., Klingner, J., Dimino, J., Haager, D., Penfield, R. & Sindelar, P. (2005). *Defining and Assessing the Quality of Beginning Special Education Teachers: First Steps, Conclusions Drawn, and Challenges Encountered.* Gainesville, FL: University of Florida.

Campione, J., & Brown, A. (1987). Linking dynamic assessment with school achievement. In C. S. Lidz (Ed.), *Dynamic assessment* (pp. 82–116). New York: Guilford.

Carnine, D., Caros, J., Crawford, D., Hollenbeck, K., & Harniss, M. (1996). Designing effective United States history curricula for all students. In J. Brophy (Ed.), *Advances in research on teaching*, Vol. 6, history teaching and learning (pp. 207–256). Greenwich, CT: JAI Press.

Carnine, D., Silbert, J., & Kame'enui, E. J. (1997). *Direct instruction reading* (3rd ed.). Upper Saddle River, NJ: Prentice-Hall.

Cazden, C. B. (1992). *Whole language plus: Essays on literacy in the United States and New Zealand.* New York: Teachers College Press.

Chiappe, P., Siegel, L., & Wade-Wooley, L. (2002). Linguistic diversity and the development of reading skills: A longitudinal study. *Scientific Studies of Reading, 6*, 369–400.

Christenson, S. L., Ysseldyke, J. E., & Thurlow, M. L. (1989). Critical instructional factors for students with mild handicaps: An integrative review. *Remedial and Special Education, 10*, 21–31.

Cobb, P. (1994). Constructivism in mathematics and science education. *Educational Researcher, 23*, 4.

Deshler, D. D., Ellis, E. S., & Lenz, B. K. (1996). *Teaching adolescents with learning disabilities: Strategies and methods* (2nd ed.). Denver, CO: Love Publishing Company.

DeVinney, J. A. (1991). *Eyes on the prize – America's civil rights years, 1954–1965* [video]. Blackside Inc, special feature length.

Dimino, J., Gersten, R., Carnine, D., & Blake, G. (1990). Story grammar: An approach for promoting at-risk secondary students' comprehension of literature. *Elementary School Journal, 91*, 19–32.

Edwards, L., Simmons, D. C., Coyne, M., Kame'enui, E. J., & Harn, B. (2004, submitted for publication). Does spelling intensify beginning reading instruction?: The effects of two beginning reading interventions on the reading and spelling achievement of kindergarten students at-risk of reading disabilities.

Englert, C. S., & Mariage, T. V. (1996). A sociocultural perspective: Teaching ways-of-thinking and ways-of-talking in a literacy community. *Learning Disabilities Research and Practice, 11*, 157–167.

Englert, C. S., Raphael, T. E., Anderson, L. M., Anthony, H. M., & Stevens, D. D. (1991). Making writing strategies and self-talk visible: Cognitive strategy instruction in regular and special education classrooms. *American Educational Research Journal, 28*, 337–372.

Foorman, B. R., Francis, D. J., Shaywitz, S. E., Shaywitz, B., & Fletcher, J. M. (1997). The case for early reading intervention. In B. Blachman, *Foundations of reading acquisition: Implications for intervention and dyslexia.* Hillsdale, NJ: Erlbaum.

Foorman, B.R., Francis, D. J., Fletcher, J. M., Schatschnedier, C., & Mehta, P. (1998). The role of instruction in learning to read: Preventing reading failure in at-risk children. *Journal of Educational Psychology, 90*, 37–55.

Fuchs, D., Fuchs, L. S., & Burish, P. (2000). Peer-assisted learning strategies: An evidence-based practice to promote reading achievement. *Learning Disabilities Research & Practice, 15*, 85–91.

Fuchs, D., Fuchs, L. S., Mathes, P. H., & Simmons, D. C. (1997). Peer-assisted learning strategies: Making classrooms more responsive to diversity. *American Educational Research Journal, 34*, 174–206.

Fuchs, L. S., & Deno, S. L. (1991). Paradigmatic distinctions between instructionally relevant measurement models. *Exceptional Children, 57*, 488–500.

Fuchs, L. S., Fuchs, D., & Karns, K. (2001). Enhancing kindergartners' mathematical development: Effects of peer-assisted learning strategies. *Elementary School Journal, 101*, 495.

Fuchs, L. S., Fuchs, D., & Speece, D. L. (2002). Treatment validity as a unifying construct for identifying learning disabilities. *Learning Disability Quarterly, 25*, 33–45.

Gersten, R., & Baker, S. (2000a). The professional knowledge base on instructional interventions that support cognitive growth for English-language learners. In R. Gersten, E. Schiller, & S. Vaughan (Eds.), *Contemporary special education research: Syntheses of the knowledge base on critical instructional issues.* Mahwah, NJ: Lawrence Erlbaum.

Gersten, R., & Baker, S. (2000b). What we know about effective instructional practices for English-language learners. *Exceptional Children, 66,* 454–470.

Gersten, R., & Baker, S. (2001). Teaching expressive writing to students with learning disabilities: A meta-analysis. *The Elementary School Journal, 101,* 251–272.

Gersten, R., & Chard, D. (1999). Number sense: Rethinking arithmetic instruction for students with mathematical disabilities. *Journal of Special Education, 33,* 18–28.

Gersten, R., & Geva, E. (2003). Teaching reading to early language learners. *Educational Leadership, 60,* 44–49.

Gersten, R., & Vaughn, S. (2001). Meta-analyses in learning disabilities: Introduction to the special issue. *Elementary School Journal, 101,* 247–249.

Gersten, R., Baker, S., & Lloyd, J. W. (2000). Designing high quality research in special education: Group experimental design. *Journal of Special Education, 34,* 2–18.

Gersten, R., Baker, S. K., Pagach, M., Scanion, D., and Chard, D. (2001) Contemporary research on special education teaching. In V. Richardson's (Ed.), *Handbook for research on teaching* (pp. 695–722). Washington, D.C.: American Educational Research Association.

Gersten, R., Baker, S., Smith-Johnson, J., Peterson, A., & Dimino, J. (In press). Eyes on the prize: Teaching history to students with learning disabilities in inclusive settings.

Gersten, R., Fuchs, D., Williams, J., & Baker, S. (2001). Teaching reading comprehension strategies to students with learning disabilities. *Review of Educational Research, 71,* 279–320.

Gersten, R., Keating T. J., & Irvin, L. K. (1995). The burden of proof: Validity as improvement of instructional practice. *Exceptional Children, 61,* 510–519.

Gersten, R., White, W. A., Falco, R., & Carnine, D. (1982). Teaching basic discriminations to handicapped and non-handicapped individuals through a dynamic presentation of instructional stimuli. *Analysis and Intervention in Developmental Disabilities, 2,* 305–317.

Gersten, R., Woodward, J., & Darch, C. (1986). Direct instruction: A research-based approach for curriculum design and teaching. *Exceptional Children, 53,* 17–36.

Graham, S., & Harris, K. R. (1989). Components analysis of cognitive strategy instruction: Effects on learning disabled students' compositions and self-efficacy. *Journal of Educational Psychology, 81,* 353–361.

Graham, S., & Harris, K. R. (In press). Literacy: Writing. In S. Graham & K. R. Harris (Eds.), *Encyclopedia of cognitive sciences.* London: Wiley.

Griffin, S. A., Case, R., & Siegler, R. S. (1994). Rightstart: Providing the central conceptual prerequisites for first formal learning of arithmetic to students at risk for school failure. In K. McGilly (Ed.), *Classroom lessons: Integrating cognitive theory and classroom practice* (pp. 24–49). Cambridge, MA: MIT Press.

Gurney, D., Gersten, R., Dimino, J., & Carnine, D. (1990). Story grammar: Effective literature instruction for high school students with learning disabilities. *Journal of Learning Disabilities, 23,* 335–342.

Harniss, M. (1996). *The instructional design of United States history texts: Student and teacher effect.* Unpublished doctoral dissertation, University of Oregon, Eugene.

Harniss, M., Hollenbeck, K. L., Crawford, D. B., & Carnine, D. (1994). Content organization and instructional design issues in the development of history texts. *Learning Disability Quarterly, 17,* 235–248.

Harris, K., & Pressley, M. (1991). The nature of cognitive strategy instruction: Interactive strategy construction. *Exceptional Children, 57,* 392–404.

Hart, B., & Risley, T. R. (1995). *Meaningful differences in the everyday experiences of young American children.* Baltimore, MD: Paul H. Brookes.

Heshusius, L. (1991). Curriculum-based assessment and direct instruction: Critical reflections on fundamental assumptions. *Exceptional Children, 57,* 315–328.

Idol, L. (1987). Group story mapping: A comprehension strategy for both skilled and unskilled readers. *Journal of Learning Disabilities, 20,* 196–205.

Idol, L., & Croll, V. J. (1987). Story-mapping training as a means of improving reading comprehension. *Learning Disability Quarterly, 10,* 214–229.

Irvine, L.K., Gersten, R.M., & Heiry, T.J. (1984). Validating vocational assessment of severely mentally retarded persons: Issues and an application. *American Journal of Mental Deficiency, 88,* 411–417.

Isaacson, S. (1995). A comparison of alternative procedures for evaluating written expression. Paper presented at annual meeting of Pacific Coast Research Conference, Laguna Beach, CA.

Isaacson, S. L. (1994). Integrating process, product, and purpose: The role of instruction. *Reading and Writing Quarterly, 10,* 39–62.

Kinder, D., & Bursuck, W. (1993). History strategy instruction: Problem-solution-effect analysis, timeline, and vocabulary instruction. *Exceptional Children, 59,* 324–335.

Kinder, D., Bursuck, W., & Epstein, M. (1992). An evaluation of history textbooks. *Journal of Special Education, 25,* 472–491.

Kolligian, J., & Sternberg, R. J. (1987). Intelligence, information processing, and specific learning disabilities: A triarchic synthesis. *Journal of Learning Disabilities, 20*, 8–17.

Kucan, L., & Beck, I. L. (1997). Thinking aloud and reading comprehension research: Inquiry, instruction, and social interaction. *Review of Educational Research, 67*, 271–299.

Leinhardt, G. (1994). History: A time to be mindful. In G. Leinhardt, I. L. Beck & C. Stainton (Eds.), *Teaching and learning in history* (pp. 206–255). Hillsdale, NJ: Erlbaum.

Lloyd, J., Cullinan, D., Heins, E., & Epstein, M. (1980). Direct instruction: Effects on oral and written language comprehension. *Learning Disabilities Quarterly, 3*, 70–76.

Lovett, M. H., Borden, S. H., DeLuca, T., Lacerenza, L., Benson, N. J., & Brackstone, D. (1994). Treating the core deficits of developmental dyslexia: Evidence of transfer of learning after phonologically and strategy based reading training programs. *Developmental Psychology, 30*, 805–822.

Lyon, G. R., & Moats, L.C. (1997). Critical conceptual and methodological considerations in reading intervention research. *Journal of Learning Disabilities, 30*, 578–588.

National Reading Panel (2000). *Teaching children to read: An evidence-based assessment of the scientific research literature on reading and its implications for reading instruction.* Retrieved in 2000 from http://www.nichd.nih.gov/publications/nrp/smallbook.html

National Reading Panel (2000a). *Evidence-based assessment of the scientific research literature on reading and its implications for reading instruction.* Washington, D.C.: National Institute of Child Health and Human Development.

National Research Council (1998). *Preventing reading difficulties in young children.* Washington, DC: National Academy Press.

National Research Council, & Committee on Minority Representation in Special Education. (2002). *Minority students in special and gifted education* (M. S. Donovan & C. T. Cross, Eds.). Washington, DC: National Academy Press.

Newman, D. (1990). Opportunities for research on the organizational impact of school computers. *Educational Researcher, 19*, 8–13.

O'Connor, R. E. (1999). Teachers learning ladders to literacy. *Learning Disabilities Research & Practice, 14*, 203–214.

Palinscar, A. S., & Brown, A. L. (1989). Classroom dialogues to promote self-regulated comprehension. In J. Brophy (Ed.), *Advances in research on teaching* (pp. 35–72). Greenwich, CT: JAI Press.

Palinscar, A.S., & Klenk, L. (1993). Third invited response: Broader visions encompassing literacy, learners, and contexts. *Remedial and Special Education, 14*, 19–25.

Palincsar, A. S., Anderson, C., & David, Y. M. (1993). Pursuing scientific literacy in the middle grades through collaborative problem solving. *Elementary School Journal, 93*, 643–658.

Palincsar, A. S., David, Y. M., Winn, J. A., & Stevens, D. D. (1991). Examining the context of strategy instruction. *Remedial and Special Education, 12*, 43–53.

Pugach, M. C., & Warger, C. L. (1993). Curriculum considerations. In J. Goodland & T. Lovitt (Eds.), *Integrating general and special education* (pp. 125–148). New York: Merrill.

Reinking, D., & Pickle, J. M. (1993). Using a formative experiment to study how computers affect reading and writing in classrooms. In C. Z. Kinzer & D. J. Leu (Eds.), *Examining central issues in literacy research, theory, and practice* (pp. 263–270). Chicago: National Reading Conference.

Richardson, V. (1990). Significant and worthwhile change in teaching practice. *Educational Researcher, 19*, 10–18.

Richardson, V. (1994). Conducting research on practice. *Educational Researcher, 23*, 5–10.

Rosenshine, B., & Stevens, R. (1986). Teaching functions. In M. C. Wittrock (Ed.), *Handbook of research on teaching.* New York: Macmillan.

Routman, R. (1988). *Transitions: From literature to literacy.* Portsmouth, NH: Heinemann.

Santoro, L. E., Baker, S., & Chard, D. (2005). *The Read Aloud Project: Optimizing First Grade Read Aloud Instruction to Promote Comprehension and Vocabulary.* Paper presented at the American Educational Research Association Annual Meeting, April, Montreal Canada.

Scanlon, D., Deshler, D. D., & Schumaker, J. B. (1996). Can a strategy be taught and learned in secondary inclusive classrooms? *Learning Disabilities Research & Practice, 11*, 41–57.

Scarborough, H. (2001). Connecting early language and literacy to later reading (dis)abilities. In S. B. Neuman & D. K. Dickinson (Eds.), *Handbook of early literacy research.* New York: Guilford Publications.

Scardamalia, M., & Bereiter, C. (1986). Research on written composition. In M. C. Wittrock (Ed.), *Handbook on research on teaching* (pp. 778–803). New York: Macmillan.

Simmons, D. C., Fuchs, D., Fuchs, L. S., Hodge, J. P., & Mathes, P. G. (1994). Importance of instructional complexity and role reciprocity to classwide peer tutoring. *Learning Disabilities Research and Practice, 9*, 203–212.

Simmons, D. C., Fuchs, L., Fuchs, D., Mathes, P., & Hodge, J. P. (1995). Effects of explicit teaching and peer tutoring on the reading achievement of learning-disabled and low-performing students in regular classrooms. *Elementary School Journal*, *95*, 387–408.

Snow, C. E., & Dickinson, D. K. (1991). Some skills that aren't basic in a new conception of literacy. In A. Purves & T. Jennings (Eds.), *Literate systems and individual lives: Perspectives on literacy and schooling* (pp. 175–213). Albany, NY: SUNY Press.

Speece, D. L., Case, L. P., & Molloy, D. E. (2003). Responsiveness to general education instruction as the first gate to learning disabilities identification. *Learning Disabilities Research and Practice*, *18*, 147–156.

Stahl, S. (1999). Why innovations come and go (and mostly go): The case of whole language. *Educational Researcher*, *28*, 13–22.

Stanovich, K. E. (1997, December). *Twenty-five years of research on the reading process: the grand synthesis and what it means for our field*. Oscar S. Causey Research Award Address presented at the National Reading Conference, Scottsdale, AZ.

Stanovich, K. E. (1999). The sociopsychometrics of learning disabilities. *Journal of Learning Disabilities*, *32*, 350–361.

Stebbins, L., St Pierre, R. G., Proper, E. L., Anderson, R. B., & Cerva, T. R. (1977). *Education as experimentation: A planned variation model* (Vol. IV A–D). Cambridge, MA: Abt Associates.

Stein, M. K., Leinhardt, G., & Bickel, W. (1989). Instructional issues for teaching students at risk. In R. E. Slavin, N. L. Karweit & N. A. Madden (Eds.), *Effective programs for students at risk* (pp. 145–194). Boston, MA: Allyn & Bacon.

Swanson, H. L. (2003). Reading research for students with learning disabilities: A Meta-analysis of intervention outcomes. In E. Schiller & S. Vaughn (Eds.), *Research syntheses in special education*. Mahwah, NJ: Erlbaum.

Swanson, H. L., & Hoskyn, M. (1998). Experimental intervention research on students with learning disabilities: A meta-analysis of treatment outcomes. *Review of Educational Research*, *68*, 277–321.

Texas Department of Education. (1998). *Essential knowledge and skills*. Dallas, TX: Author.

Treiman, R. (1998). Why spelling? The benefits of incorporating spelling into beginning reading instruction. In J. L. Metsala & L. C. Ehri (Eds.), *Word recognition in beginning literacy* (pp. 289–313). Mahwah, NJ: Erlbaum.

Vaughn, S., & Fuchs, L. S. (2003). Redefining learning disabilities as inadequate response to instruction: The promise and potential problems. *Learning Disabilities Research & Practice*, *18*, 137–146.

Vaughn, S., Gersten, R., & Chard, D. (2000). The underlying message in LD intervention research. *Exceptional Children*, *67*, 99–114.

Vaughn, S., Mathes, P., Linan-Thompson, S., Cirino, P., Carlson, C., Francis, D., et al. (In press). First-grade English language learners at-risk for reading problems: Effectiveness of an English intervention. *Elementary School Journal*.

Williams, J. (2005). Instruction in reading comprehension for primary-grade students: A focus on text structure. *The Journal of Special Education*, *39*, 6–18.

Williams, J. P., Brown, L. G., Silverstein, A. K., & deCani, J. S. (1994). An instructional program in comprehension of narrative themes for adolescents with learning disabilities. *Learning Disability Quarterly*, *17*, 205–221.

Wong, B. Y. L. (1994). Instructional parameters promoting transfer of learned strategies in students with learning disabilities. *Learning Disability Quarterly*, *17*, 110–120.

Wong, B. Y. L., Butler, D. L., Ficzere, S. A., & Kuperis, S. (1997). Teaching adolescents with learning disabilities and low achievers to plan, write, and revise compare-contrast essays. *Learning Disabilities Research and Practice*, *12*(1), 2–15.

Woodward, J., & Montague, M. (2002). Meeting the challenge of mathematics reform for students with learning disabilities. *Journal of Special Education*, *36*, 89.

Zigmond, N., Woolery, R., Meng, Y., Flumer, D., & Bean, R. (1994). Students with learning disabilities in elementary-level mainstream history classes: What gets taught? What gets learned? New Orleans, L.A. Annual meeting of the American Educational Research Association.

15

Quantitative research synthesis: meta-analysis of research on meeting special educational needs

Kenneth A. Kavale

INTRODUCTION

Since the passage of landmark federal law (now IDEA) in 1975, special education in the United States has witnessed significant change but not necessarily real progress. The consequences are found in attitudes that oscillate between optimism and pessimism about the prospects for special education (see Zigler & Hodapp, 1986). For example, there is optimism about the law's success in providing access to special education but pessimism about whether or not the appropriate education provision is achieving the desired outcomes (Finn, Rotherham, & Hakanson, 2001). Such pessimism is not new; the innovative program developed by Jean-Marc-Gaspard Itard for Victor, the 'wild boy of Aveyron' (Itard, 1806/1962) was perceived as a 'failure' (for example, Kirk & Johnson, 1951) because of Victor's modest attainments. In reality, the gains were meaningful and demonstrated the potential of special education (Gaynor, 1973).

Questions about the efficacy of special education are thus long-standing (for example, Milofsky, 1974) and typically take the form of asking: is special education special? Answers may become confounded because the *special* in special education possesses two meanings: (a) teaching students designated as having special educational needs, and (b) using special instruction. Too often, however, the desire to enhance education experiences for students identified as having special educational needs means that teaching may be based on uncritical decisions about the efficacy of techniques used for *special* instruction. The fact that the most effective teaching is predicated on scientific ground may be ignored when a teacher is faced with the challenge of teaching students with special needs (see Gage, 1978). Without a scientific foundation for practice, special education is likely to become a variable enterprise that may be effective or not effective.

To determine whether methods for special instruction are effective (that is, do they work?), special education has long-endorsed the scientific method where decisions about efficacy are based on empirical evidence (Kauffman, 1987). The empirical evidence is available but too often remains isolated when individual study findings do not agree. Which findings are to be believed? Differences among studies are not a problem if individual findings are combined to produce 'usable knowledge' (Lindblom & Cohen, 1979) that may be used to judge the efficacy of special instruction.

Traditional methods for combining individual study findings (for example, narrative review) are too subjective and may produce biased findings (see Jackson, 1980). In an effort to reduce the subjectivity associated with traditional methods of reviewing research findings (see Cooper & Rosenthal, 1980), quantitative methods, usually termed 'meta-analysis' (Glass, 1976), have become an accepted means of combining empirical findings. Meta-analysis is the application of statistical procedures to collections of empirical findings from individual studies for the purpose of integrating, synthesizing, and making sense of them (Glass, McGaw, & Smith, 1981).

As a research methodology, meta-analysis uses rigorous and systematic procedures that parallel primary research activities including: (1) problem formulation (Is intervention X effective?), (2) sampling (a comprehensive and representative set of studies from the domain under investigation), (3) study classification (organizing and coding study information), (4) data analysis (calculation of the 'effect size' [ES] statistic that permits quantification and standardization of individual study findings), and (5) ES interpretation (Kavale, 2001b).

An ES is most often interpreted as a z-score indicating level of improvement on an outcome assessment for students initially at the 50th percentile. To gain greater insight, two additional ES interpretations are provided. The 'common language effect size' (CLES) (McGraw & Wong, 1992) converts ES into a probability that a score sampled from one distribution will be greater than a score sampled from another. For example, in a sample of studies investigating the use of intervention Y with a CLES of .83, 83 out of 100 would show that a subject using intervention Y would improve when compared to subjects not using intervention Y. The 'binomial effect size display' (BESD) (Rosenthal & Rubin, 1982) addresses the question: what is the percentage increase in the number of successful responses when using a new instructional practice? Based on converting an ES to r, the BESD for the use of intervention Z (ES = 1.16, for example) would show an increase in success rate from 25 per cent to 75 per cent. The 50-per-centage-point spread between treatment (75 per cent) and comparison (25 per cent) success rate shows that the use of intervention Z possesses, not only statistical significance, but also *practical* significance (Kirk, 1996). Finally, Cohen (1988), based on notions of statistical power, offered 'rules of thumb' for classifying ES as small (.20), medium (.50), or large (.80). Thus, the ES metric imparts a clarity and explicitness to empirical findings that make synthesized evidence more objective and verifiable (Kavale, 1984).

This chapter reviews meta-analyses investigating the effectiveness of special education in order to make decisions about 'what works' (see Kavale, 2001a).

The nature of special education

The definition of special education as 'specially designed instruction ... to meet the unique needs of a child with a disability' (US Department of Education, 1999, p. 124–25) emphasizes individualized instruction but does not stipulate the nature of the special instruction to be delivered. Special education, in an effort to differentiate itself from general education, has historically opted for developing unique and exclusive methods. Although 'special' methods provided a distinct identity, they also introduced a separateness from general education that produced a skepticism about their benefits on the part of general education. Because of its higher costs, special education was being held increasingly accountable: could special education substantiate its benefits?

Special education has historically assumed a goal of correcting or reversing the altered learning functions of students. Beginning with Itard, special education has focused on enhancing cognitive *processes* so students in special education may then be able to learn in the same way as general education students. Consequently, process training has long been a primary form of special education (see Mann, 1979). Although intuitively appealing, does research support the theoretical assumption that training processes enhance learning ability?

A large body of empirical research has investigated the efficacy of process training but the difficulties in deciding 'what the research says' were illustrated in the case of psycholinguistic training, a prominent form of process training during the 1960s and 1970s. Psycholinguistic training was developed by Samuel A. Kirk and embodied in the Illinois Test of Psycholinguistic Abilities (ITPA). The model was based on the assumption that psycholinguistic ability is comprised of discrete components and that these components can be improved with training. By the mid-1970s, empirical research summaries revealed very different interpretations about the efficacy of psycholinguistic training.

A review of 39 studies by Hammill and Larsen (1974) concluded that, 'the idea that psycholinguistic constructs, as measured by the ITPA, can, in fact, be trained by existing techniques remains nonvalidated' (p. 11). In response, Minskoff (1975) offered a more positive evaluation and concluded that psycholinguistic deficits can be remediated. The Minskoff review was immediately challenged by Newcomer, Larsen, and Hammill (1975) who concluded that, 'the reported literature raises doubts regarding the efficacy of presently available Kirk-Osgood psycholinguistic training programs' (p. 147). The divergent interpretations made it increasingly difficult to determine 'what the research says' about the efficacy of psycholinguistic training.

Several years later, Lund, Foster, and McCall-Perez (1978) re-evaluated the original 39 studies, and concluded that, 'It is, therefore, not logical to conclude either that all studies in psycholinguistic training are effective or that all studies in psycholinguistic training are not effective' (p. 319). Hammill and Larsen (1978) contested the Lund et al. analysis and concluded that, 'the cumulative results ... failed to demonstrate that psycholinguistic training has value' (p. 413). Although polemics abounded, a primary question remained unanswered: What is really known about the efficacy of psycholinguistic training?

META-ANALYSIS AND THE EFFICACY OF SPECIAL EDUCATION

Psycholinguistic training

The traditional methods of research integration used to evaluate psycholinguistic training failed to accumulate knowledge in an objective manner. To provide verifiable and replicable conclusions, Kavale (1981) conducted a meta-analysis on 34 studies that yielded an average ES of .39. In a statistical sense, an ES shows outcomes in standard deviation (SD) units that can be interpreted in terms of overlapping distributions (treatment vs control). The ES of .39 indicates that the average treated subject would gain 15 percentile ranks on the ITPA and would be better off than 65 per cent of control (no treatment) subjects. Using Cohen's (1988) rules of thumb, an ES of .39 approaches a 'medium' level but does not represent an unequivocal endorsement of psycholinguistic training.

To gain insight, ES data were aggregated by ITPA subtest and five of nine ITPA subtests revealed 'small', albeit positive, effects. Such a modest response suggests that training would not be warranted in these five cases. For four subtests (Auditory and Visual Association, Verbal and Manual Expression), however, training improves performance from 15 to 24 percentile ranks and makes the average trained subject better off than approximately 63 per cent to 74 per cent of untrained subjects.

The findings regarding the Associative and Expressive constructs appear to belie the conclusion of Hammill and Larsen (1974) that, 'neither the ITPA subtests nor their theoretical constructs are particularly ameliorative'

Table 15.1   Effectiveness of Process Training

Method	Mean effect size	Percentile rank	Power rating equivalent
Irlen lenses (34)	.02	49	Negative
Perceptual-motor training (33)	.08	53	Negligible
Diet modification (Feingold) (31)	.12	55	Small
Modality-matched instruction (32)	.14	56	Small
Social skills training (17, 42, 44)	.23	64	Small
Psycholinguistic training (27, 29)	.39	65	Small-medium
Frostig visual perceptual training (30)	.10	54	Negligible-small

( )=ES source listed in Appendix A

(p. 12). The meta-analytic findings should *not*, however, be interpreted as approval for psycholinguistic training. In the case of Auditory Association, for example, there are difficulties in defining the skill: What is Auditory Association? Additionally, it is important to determine whether improvement in Auditory Association provides enhanced functioning in other than that discrete ability. In contrast, the case for Expressive constructs particularly Verbal Expression presents a different scenario because it represents the tangible process of productive language behavior whose improvement is critical for school success. In fact, the Verbal Expression ES (.63) exceeds what would be expected from six months of general education language instruction (ES = .50). Thus, the Kavale (1981) meta-analysis showed where psycholinguistic training might be effective and might be initiated when deemed an appropriate part of an intervention program.

Process training

Mann (1979) suggested that, 'process training is, in fact, one of the oldest forms of education and that, despite periodic discontinuities in its practice, it has continued unabated into our own day'. Table 15.1 reveals that popular forms of process training demonstrate limited efficacy. (Note: The ES reported for each intervention was obtained from the numbered primary sources listed in Appendix A. In cases with more than one meta-analysis, the ES rep-

resents a weighted mean. Appendix B lists general sources where ES data are reported.) For example perceptual-motor training, the embodiment of 1960s special education, had practically no effect on improving educational performance; famous programs such as those developed by Kephart (ES = .06) and Barsch (ES = .16) revealed very modest effectiveness. The limited efficacy of process training may be related to difficulties in attempting to ameliorate unobservable (hypothetical) constructs. The outcomes of training (products) are the only observable component while the means by which those products were achieved (process) are not observable. Although these difficulties are evident for constructs like perception, the same problems can be identified for, as an example, social skills training where the actual skills (that is, behaviors) represent products that are presumed related to the hypothetical construct of social competence.

Although attacks on process training have been vigorous (for example, Mann, 1971), its historical, clinical, and philosophical foundation creates a resistance to accepting negative evidence (for example, Hallahan & Cruickskank, 1973) because, 'the tension between belief and reality provides a continuing sense of justification for process training' (Kavale & Forness, 1999, p. 35). The failure to change beliefs about efficacy was found for modality-matched instruction (ES = .14) which has received a number of previous negative evaluations (for example, Arter & Jenkins, 1979; Larrivee, 1981; Tarver & Dawson, 1978). The negative evidence is resisted because teachers have maintained a strong belief that students learn best when instruction is modified to match individual modality patterns (Kavale & Reese, 1991). The beliefs, however, must be modulated by the empirical evidence indicating that interventions developed to define the uniqueness of special education (for example, process training methods not likely to be used in general education) are not effective. Such evidence needs to be heeded because, 'schools must view the time, money,

and other resources devoted to [process training] as wasteful [and] as an obstruction to provision of appropriate services' (Council for Learning Disabilities, 1986, p. 247).

Creating effective special education

The long dominant tradition of process training in special education reflected a pathology model; academic problems were regarded as a 'disease' and interventions were aimed at 'curing' the disease (that is, removing the

Table 15.2 Effective Instructional Practices

Practice	Mean Effect Size	Common Language Effect Size	Binomial Effect Size Display Success Rate Increase	
			From (%)	To (%)
Mnemonic instruction (39)	1.62	.87	18	82
Self-monitoring (55, 58, 59)	1.36	.83	22	78
Reinforcement (58, 59, 64)	1.17	.80	25	75
Self-questioning (55, 57)	1.16	.79	25	75
Drill & practice (4, 58, 64)	.99	.76	28	72
Strategy instruction (55, 56, 57, 58)	.98	.75	28	72
Feedback (58, 59, 64)	.97	.75	28	72
Direct instruction (1, 2, 65)	.93	.75	29	71
Visual displays (58)	.90	.74	29	71
Computer-assisted instruction (47, 58)	.87	.73	30	70
Repeated reading (59, 61)	.76	.71	32	68
Error correction (58, 64)	.72	.70	33	67
Early intervention (8, 23, 24, 49, 50, 51, 65)	.71	.70	33	60
Formative evaluation (18, 52)	.70	.69	33	67
Peer mediation (58, 59)	.64	.67	35	65
Diagnostic-prescriptive teaching (58)	.64	.67	35	65
Peer tutoring (10, 41, 59)	.62	.67	35	65
Positive class morale (64)	.60	.66	36	64
Grouping (13, 14, 48)	.43	.62	40	60
Cooperative learning (7, 26, 53)	.40	.61	40	60
Increased time (64)	.38	.61	41	59

( ) = ES source listed in Appendix A

pathology) (Kauffman & Hallahan, 1974). By about 1975, the realization that process training was not producing desired outcomes shifted attention to an 'instructional imbalance' model where school failure was viewed as the result of a mismatch between instructional methods and student developmental level (Hagin, 1973). The 'effective schools' research (see Bickel & Bickel, 1986) was a major influence that stressed, for example, the importance of teachers believing that *all* students can achieve, that basic skill instruction should be emphasized, and that clear instructional objectives should be used to monitor student performance.

At the same time, a 'learning process' model emerged that viewed teaching within a 'process-product' paradigm where variables depicting what occurs during teaching are correlated with products (that is, student outcomes) (Needels & Gage, 1991). Research revealed the importance of a number of principles such as, for example, encouraging students' active engagement in learning, exploring innovative approaches to grouping and organizing classroom instruction, and making learning meaningful by keeping it enjoyable, interesting, student-centered, and goal-oriented (see Brophy & Good, 1986). These principles became 'best practice' and were interpreted for special education (for example, Christenson, Ysseldyke, & Thurlow, 1989; Reith & Evertson, 1988; Reynolds, Wang, & Walberg, 1992).

Effective special educational practice

Research investigating the teaching-learning process has identified a number of effective instructional practices. Table 15.2 shows a sample of effective instructional practices and reveals that substantial positive influence on learning is possible by modifying the way instruction is delivered.

The use of effective instructional practices moves special education toward the general education teaching-learning model and away from a reliance on 'special' interventions (for example, process training). For example,

mnemonic instruction (MI) is a strategy that transforms difficult-to-remember facts into a more memorable form through recording, relating, and retrieving information (Mastropieri & Scruggs, 1991). A student receiving MI would be better off than 95 per cent of students not receiving MI and would show a 45 percentile rank gain on an outcome assessment. In a sample of studies investigating MI, 87 out of 100 would show that students receiving MI would demonstrate improvement when compared to students in the control condition (CLES = .87). The BESD shows a 64 per cent increase in success rate which indicates substantial practical significance. Compare the success rate of MI to, for example, perceptual-motor training (ES = .08) where the modest 4 per cent increase in success rate indicates a negligible statistical effect and almost no practical significance.

Effective special education instruction

The ultimate purpose of implementing effective instruction is to enhance academic performance. Achievement outcomes are shown in Table 15.3 and indicate the potential for substantial gains across subject areas. All achievement domains show 'large' ES with gains ranging from 29 to 41 percentile ranks on academic achievement measures. On average, almost eight out of 10 investigations of effective special education instruction will likely show improvement (CLES = .77). The success rate increases from 27 per cent to 73 per cent indicating an average 46 per cent improvement for students showing a positive response to instruction.

The example of reading comprehension demonstrates how meta-analysis can be useful for judging the magnitude of 'real' effects. Two meta-analyses contributed almost all ES measurements and produced ESs of 1.13 and .98, a modest three percentile rank difference in outcomes (87 vs 84). When specific methods for improving reading comprehension are compared, the two meta-analyses revealed a similar pattern of findings. The largest effects (ES = 1.60 and 1.33) were found for metacog-

Table 15.3 Effective special education instruction

Subject area	Mean effect size	Percentile rank equivalent	Common language effect size	Binomial effect size display Success rate increase	
				From (%)	To (%)
Handwriting (21, 56, 58)	1.32	91	.82	22	78
Oral reading (9, 54, 59)	1.31	90	.82	22	78
Language (36, 43, 50)	1.27	90	.82	23	77
Reading comprehension (40, 54, 60)	1.04	85	.77	27	73
Word recognition (3, 54, 56)	.98	84	.75	28	72
Narrative writing (19, 21, 22)	.97	83	.75	28	72
Math (35, 37, 67)	.96	83	.75	28	72
Spelling (56, 58)	.87	81	.73	30	70
Vocabulary (25, 54, 58)	.85	80	.73	30	70

( ) = ES source listed in Appendix A

nitive techniques (for example, self-questioning, self-monitoring). Text enhancement procedures (for example, advanced organizers, mnemonics) produced ES of 1.09 and .92. The least powerful (but nevertheless effective) techniques involved skill training procedures (for example, vocabulary, repeated reading) with ES of .79 and .62. The consistency of findings across these two meta-analyses provides confidence in concluding that it is possible to enhance reading comprehension.

The meta-analytic evidence suggests that, on average, the 'real' effect of reading comprehension instruction is 1.05, a level comparable to one year's worth of reading comprehension instruction in general educa-

tion (ES = 1.00). Thus, methods adapted for the purposes of special education produced the same effect as one year of general education instruction but did so in approximately 20 hours. Clearly, special education students can significantly improve their ability to better understand what they read.

Effective special education related services

A hallmark of special education is the provision for related services to be provided when deemed appropriate in augmenting the instruction program. Table 15.4 shows a sample of adjunct activities and most demon-

Table 15.4 Effective special education related services and activities

Subject area	Mean effect size	Common language effect size	Binomial effect size display Success rate increase	
			From (%)	To (%)
Memory training (16, 58)	1.12	.79	25	75
Prereferral (5)	1.10	.78	26	74
Cognitive behavior modification (12, 46)	.74	.70	32	68
Stimulant medication (11, 28, 62)	.62	.67	35	65
Counseling (58)	.60	.66	35	65
Consultation (45, 58)	.55	.65	36	64
Rational-emotive therapy (15, 20)	.50	.64	38	62
Attribution training (56, 58)	.43	.62	39	61
Placement (6, 57, 63)	.12	.53	47	53

( ) = ES source listed in Appendix A

strate, at least, 'medium' ES. On average (ES = .65), related services produced a 24 percentile rank gain on an outcome assessment. In 68 out of 100 cases, a positive response to the related service was achieved (CLES = .68). Thus, related services appear to be useful supplements to the instructional program.

Placement has often been viewed as having a positive influence on student performance (see Kavale & Forness, 2000). The ES magnitude (.12) negates such a view and indicates that the success rate associated with placement increases only 6 per cent from 47 per cent to 53 per cent (BESD). The 'small' ES suggests that 'what' (that is, the nature of the instruction) is a more important influence on student outcomes than 'where' (that is, placement). In contrast, prereferral activities revealed significant positive effects. The CLES (.78) indicates that in 78 of 100 cases prereferral activities produce positive outcomes. Prereferral 'works' because it is predicated in modification of *instructional* activities, and its 48 per cent success rate means that almost half of students given preferential activities will *not* need to enter special education.

Drug treatment is often an integral part of the treatment regimen for some students in special education. Stimulant medication (usually Ritalin) is the most popular and produces significance positive changes in behavior. In two out of three cases (CLES = .67), positive outcomes were found in gains averaging 23 percentile ranks on behavior ratings and checklists. The ES (.62) was obtained primarily from a meta-analysis done in 1982 (ES = .58) and a replication completed in 1997 (ES = .64). The consistency of the obtained ES (that is, .58 and .64) provides confirmation for the positive influence of stimulant medication. Special education, however, has long criticized the use of stimulant medication and has sought more natural and unobtrusive treatments. One such alternative, popularized during the 1970s, was the Feingold diet designed to eliminate all foods containing artificial additives from the diet. The ES (.12) obtained for the Feingold diet (see Table

15.1) clearly indicates that it has limited influence on modifying behavior. A comparison of the two treatments shows stimulant medication to be better than five times more effective than the Feingold diet; the debate about the efficacy of stimulant medication appears unequivocal.

Evaluating special education

Special education has demonstrated increased efficacy that may be attributable to a change in instructional emphasis. Until about 25 years ago, special education emphasized its 'special' nature by developing singular and different methods not found in general education. The goal was to enhance hypothetical constructs (for example, 'processes') that were presumed to be the cause of learning deficits. Basic skill instruction was a secondary consideration until processes were remediated and learning became more efficient. When intervention activities emphasize, for example, process training and that basic skill instruction is subordinate, the nature of special education can be conceptualized as *SPECIAL education*, with a focus on unique and exclusive 'special' interventions. The limited efficacy of *SPECIAL education* (see Table 15.1) suggests that process deficits are difficult to 'fix' and such an intervention focus produces little benefit.

The recognition that 'special' interventions did not produce desired outcomes moved special education to emphasize 'education' in an effort to enhance academic outcomes. When intervention activities emphasize alternative *instructional* techniques, the nature of special education can be conceptualized as *special EDUCATION*. Such instructional techniques usually originate in general education and are adapted to assist students with disabilities in acquiring and assimilating new knowledge; *special EDUCATION* demonstrates significant success (see Table 15.2) and produces improved *achievement* outcomes (see Table 15.3).

The difference between the two forms of special education is seen in the mega ES (mean of means) for 'special' (.15) versus 'education' (.89) techniques. The comparison reveals *special EDUCATION* to be six times more effective than *SPECIAL education*; it produces achievement outcomes (mega ES = 1.04) that exceed one year's worth of general education instruction (ES = 1.00). On average, *SPECIAL education* provides only a 6 per cent advantage meaning that the students in special education receiving primarily 'special' interventions exceeds only about 56 per cent of the group not receiving such interventions; this level of improvement is only slightly above chance (50 per cent). Additionally, across meta-analyses investigating *SPECIAL education*, about 25 per cent of the calculated ES were negative indicating that in one out of four cases the student *not* receiving the 'special' intervention performed better. Clearly, there is little reason to include *SPECIAL education* in most intervention programs.

In contrast, the methods associated with *special EDUCATION* provide an efficacious foundation for designing an academic instructional program. The use of effective techniques is likely to move the average student in special education from the 50th to the 81st percentile. The 31-percentile-rank gain is better than five times the gain found with the use of 'special' interventions, and indicates students are better off than 81 per cent of those not receiving the preferred *special EDUCATION*. For example, Direct Instruction (DI), a behaviorally oriented teaching procedure based on an explicit step-by-step strategy (ES = .93) is 6.5 times more effective than the intuitively appealing modality-matched instruction that attempts to enhance learning by capitalizing on learning style differences (ES = .14). Students in special education taught with DI would be better off than 87 per cent of students not receiving DI and would gain over 11 months' credit on an achievement measure compared to about one month for modality-matched instruction. With its grounding in effective instructional methodology, *special EDUCATION* can sometimes be up to 20 times more effective than *SPECIAL education*.

Effective special education

The meta-analyses synthesized provide insight into the indications and contra-indications of special education interventions (Lipsey & Wilson, 2001). The interventions associated with *special EDUCATION* may be considered a form of 'evidenced-based practice' (EBP) (Odom et al., 2005) where intervention decisions are based on empirical findings demonstrating that the actions produce efficacious and beneficial outcomes. The use of EBP promotes *instructional validity* where changes can be attributed to the specific activities and can be used to produce similar results with other students in special education (generalization).

Although EBP is desirable, the implementation of EBP is often limited by extraneous factors. For example, tradition ('We have always used it') and history ('It has worked before') are powerful barriers. Additionally, the *bandwagon effect*, where an intervention suddenly becomes popular and gains momentum rapidly, may have a significant influence. As pointed out by Mostert (1999–2000), 'Bandwagons are used to champion a cause, engage in sweeping yet attractive rhetoric, and generally to promise far more than they ever have hope of delivering' (p. 124). Finally, *belief*, a strong conviction about the truth, although a legitimate consideration in making intervention decisions, is only appropriate when the belief is grounded in empirical evidence.

The negative influence of these extraneous factors is one reason why research findings in special education 'are embraced by some, ignored by others, and modified to suit the routines and preferences of still others' (Gersten, Vaughn, Deshler, & Schiller, 1997, p. 466). Regardless of how exciting teachers may find new proven techniques, they often resist implementing them in favor of more comfortable existing practices (Swanson, 1984). Heward (2003) identified 10 faulty notions that may hinder the effective delivery of special education. All told, the obstacles that interfere with making sound instructional decisions are a primary reason why there is a continuing research-to-practice gap in special education (Greenwood & Abbott, 2001). The failure to use EBP is a major contributor to the problem of *sustainability*, the maintained use of an instructional practice supported by evidence of improved outcomes for students in special education (Gersten, Vaughn, & Kim, 2004).

Because students in special education, by definition, possess unique learning needs, instructional decisions are critically important in the design of *individualized* programs. The complexities surrounding instructional decision making introduce a degree of 'uncertainty' (that is, the program may not work) (Glass, 1979). Besides uncertainty, there is also the possibility of 'risk' (that is, negative outcomes) that can be described in meta-analysis by the standard deviation (SD), a measure of dispersion around the mean ES that represents an index of variability. Taken together, the ES and SD provide a theoretical expectation about intervention efficacy (that is, ES ± SD). For example, psycholinguistic training (.39 ± .54) spans a theoretical range (−.15 to .93) from negative ES to 'large' ES; the difficulty is the inability to predict the outcome (that is, ES) for a particular student. The mega ES for *SPECIAL education* (.15) is associated with a larger mega SD (.48) making 'special' interventions actually more variable than effective (.15 ± .48). The theoretical range for *SPECIAL education* (−.33 to .63), although possibly producing 'medium' effects, also includes significant risk (that is, a negative ES indicating that those *not* receiving the intervention perform better). In contrast, *special EDUCATION* (.89 ± .87) reveals itself to be more effective than variable and, although the theoretical range shows that it may not 'work' in some cases (ES = .02), there also exists the theoretical possibility of being almost twice as effective (ES = 1.76).

Although the use of *special EDUCATION* can reduce risk (that is, no negative ES), the special education teaching-learning process remains a capricious enterprise (that is, variable, unpredictable, and indeterminate). To create more certainty, instructional decisions should not be prescriptive (that is, do A in circumstance X or Y, and do B in circumstance Z) but rather based on an assortment of effective options (that is, practices with large ES). This means that teachers are central characters in the special education decision-making process who must replace dogmatic beliefs with rational choices about 'what works'. Instructional decisions thus include elements of science (theoretical and empirical knowledge) and art (interpretation necessary to initiate action) (see Gage, 1978). The teacher's goal is to narrow the gap between the state of the art (what has been demonstrated to be possible) and the state of practice (current ways of providing instruction). Consequently, the actions of 'special education practitioners will need to go beyond the scientific basis of their work ... and must be mediated through the teacher's own creative rendering of best practice ... because quality education for special education students will always be based on the artful application of science' (Kavale & Forness, 1999, p. 93).

REFERENCES

Arter, J. A., & Jenkins, J. R. (1977). Examining the benefits and prevalence of modality considerations in special education. *Journal of Special Education*, *11*, 281–298.

Bickel, W. E., & Bickel, D. D. (1986). Effective schools, classrooms, and instruction: Implications for special education. *Exceptional Children*, *52*, 489–500.

Brophy, J., & Good, T. (1986). Teacher behavior and student achievement. In M. C. Wittrock (Ed.), *Handbook of research on teaching* (Vol. 3, pp. 328–375). New York: Macmillan.

Christenson, S. L., Ysseldyke, J. E., & Thurlow, M. L. (1989). Critical instructional factors for students with mild handicaps: An integrative review. *Remedial and Special Education*, *10*, 21–31.

Cohen, J. (1988). *Statistical power analysis for the behavioral sciences* (2nd ed.). Hillsdale, NJ: Erlbaum.

Cooper, H. M., & Rosenthal, R. (1980). Statistical versus traditional procedures for summarizing research findings. *Psychological Bulletin*, *87*, 442–449.

Council for Learning Disabilities. (1986). Measurement and training of perceptual and perceptual-motor functions: A position statement. *Learning Disability Quarterly*, *9*, 247.

Finn, Jr., C. E., Rotherham, A. J., & Hakanson, Jr., C. R. (Eds.). (2001). *Rethinking special education for a new century*. Washington, DC: Thomas B. Fordham Foundation.

Gage, N. L. (1978). *The scientific basis of the art of teaching*. New York: Teachers College Press.

Gaynor, J. F. (1973). The 'failure' of J. M. G. Itard. *Journal of Special Education, 7*, 439–445.

Gersten, R., Vaughn, S., & Kim, A. E. (2004). Special issue on sustainability. *Remedial and Special Education, 25*, 3–4.

Gersten, R., Vaughn, S., Deshler, D., & Schiller, E. (1997). What we know about using research findings: Implications for improving special education practice. *Journal of Learning Disabilities, 30*, 466–476.

Glass, G. V. (1976). Primary, secondary, and meta-analysis of research. *Educational Researcher, 5*, 3–8.

Glass, G. V. (1979). Policy for the unpredictable (uncertainty research and policy). *Educational Researcher, 8*, 12–14.

Glass, G. V., McGaw, B., & Smith, M. L. (1981). *Meta-analysis in social research*. Beverly Hills, CA: Sage.

Greenwood, C. R., & Abbott, M. (2001). The research to practice gap in special education. *Teacher Education and Special Education, 24*, 276–289.

Hagin, R.A. (1973). Models of intervention with learning disabilities: Ephemeral and otherwise. *School Psychology Monograph, 1*, 1–24.

Hallahan, D. P., & Cruickshank, W. M. (1973). *Psychoeducational foundations of learning disabilities*. Englewood Cliffs, NJ: Prentice-Hall.

Hammill, D. D., & Larsen, S. C. (1974). The effectiveness of psycholinguistic training. *Exceptional Children, 41*, 5–14.

Hammill, D. D., & Larsen, S. C. (1978). The effectiveness of psycholinguistic training: A reaffirmation of position. *Exceptional Children, 44*, 402–414.

Heward, W. L. (2003). Ten faulty notions about teaching and learning that hinder the effectiveness of special education. *Journal of Special Education, 36*, 186–205.

Itard, J. M. G. (1806/1962). *The wild boy of Areyron*. (G. Humphrey & M. Humphrey, trans). New York: Appleton-Century-Crafts. (Original work published 1806.)

Jackson, G. B. (1980). Methods of integrative reviews. *Review of Educational Research, 50*, 438–460.

Kauffman, J. M. (1987). Research in special education: A commentary. *Remedial and Special Education, 8*, 57–62.

Kauffman, J. M., & Hallahan, D. P. (1974). The medical model and the science of special education. *Exceptional Children, 41*, 97–102.

Kavale, K. A. (1981). Functions of the Illinois Test of Psycholinguistic Abilities (ITPA): Are they trainable? *Exceptional Children, 47*, 496–510.

Kavale, K. A. (1984). Potential advantages of the meta-analysis technique for research in special education. *The Journal of Special Education, 18*, 61–72.

Kavale, K. A. (2001a). Meta-analysis: A primer. *Exceptionality, 9*, 177–183.

Kavale, K. A. (2001b). Decision making in special education: The function of meta-analysis. *Exceptionality, 9*, 245–268.

Kavale, K. A., & Forness, S. R. (1999). *Efficacy of special education and related services*. Washington, DC: American Association on Mental Retardation.

Kavale, K. A., & Forness, S. R. (2000). History, rhetoric, and reality: Analysis of the inclusion debate. *Remedial and special education, 21*, 279–296.

Kavale, K. A., & Reese, J. H. (1991). Teacher beliefs and perceptions about learning disabilities: A survey of Iowa practitioners. *Learning Disability Quarterly, 14*, 141–160.

Kirk, R. E. (1996). Practical significance: A concept whose time has come. *Educational and Psychological Measurement, 36*, 746–759.

Kirk, S. A., & Johnson, G. O. (1951). *Educating the retarded child*. Cambridge, MA: Riverside Press.

Larrivee, B. (1981). Modality preference as a model for differentiating beginning reading instruction: A review of the issues. *Learning Disability Quarterly, 4*, 180–188.

Lindblom, C. E., & Cohen, D. K. (1979). *Usable knowledge: Social science and social problem solving*. New Haven, CT: Yale University Press.

Lipsey, M. W., & Wilson, D. B. (2001). *Practical meta-analysis* (Vol. 49). Thousand Oaks, CA: Sage.

Lund, K. A., Foster, G. E., & McCall-Perez, G. C. (1978). The effectiveness of psycholinguistic training: A reevaluation. *Exceptional Children, 44*, 310–319.

Mann, L. (1971). Psychometric phrenology and the new faculty psychology: The case against ability assessment and training. *Journal of Special Education, 5*, 3–14.

Mann, L. (1979). *On the trail of process: A historical perspective on cognitive processes and their training*. New York: Grune & Stratton.

Mastropieri, M. A., & Scruggs, T. E. (1991). *Teaching students ways to remember: Strategies for learning mnemonically*. Cambridge, MA: Brookline Books.

McGraw, K. O., & Wong, S. P. (1992). A common language effect size. *Psychological Bulletin, 111*, 361–365.

Milofsky, C. D. (1974). Why special education isn't special. *Harvard Educational Review, 44*, 437–458.

Minskoff, E. (1975). Research on psycholinguistic training: Critique and guidelines. *Exceptional Children, 42*, 136–144.

Mostert, M. P. (1999–2000). A partial etiology and sequelae of discriminative disability: Bandwagons and beliefs. *Exceptionality, 8*, 117–132.

Needels, M. C., & Gage, N. L. (1991). Essence and accident in process-product research on teaching. In H. C. Waxman & H. J. Walberg (Eds.), *Effective teaching: Current research* (pp. 3–31). Berkeley, CA: McCuthan.

Newcomer, P., Larsen, S., & Hammill, D. (1975). A response. *Exceptional Children, 42,* 144–148.

Odom, S. L., Brantlinger, E., Gersten, R., Horner, R. H., Thompson, B., & Harris, K. R. (2005). Research in special education: Scientific methods and evidence-based practices. *Exceptional Children, 71,* 137–148.

Reith, H. J., & Evertson, C. (1988). Variables related to the effective instruction of difficult-to-teach children. *Focus on Exceptional Children, 20,* 1–8.

Reynolds, M. C., Wang, M. C., & Walberg, H. J. (1992). The knowledge bases for special and general education. *Remedial and Special Education, 13,* 6–10, 33.

Rosenthal, R., & Rubin, D. B. (1982). A simple, general purpose display of magnitude of experimental effect. *Journal of Educational Psychology, 74,* 166–169.

Swanson, H. L. (1984). Does theory guide practice? *Remedial and Special Education, 5*(5), 7–16.

Tarver, S. G., & Dawson, M. M. (1978). Modality preference and the teaching of reading: A review. *Journal of Learning Disabilities, 11,* 5–17.

U.S. Department of Education (1999). Assistance to states for the education of children with disabilities program and the early intervention program for infants and toddlers with disabilities: final regulations. *Federal Register, 64* (48), CFR Parts 300 and 303.

Ziglar, E., & Hodapp, R. M. (1986). *Understanding mental retardation.* New York: Cambridge University Press.

APPENDIX A: PRIMARY EFFECT SIZE SOURCES

(1) Adams, G. L, & Carnine, D. (2003). Direct instruction. In H. L. Swanson, K. R. Harris, & S. Graham (Eds.), *Handbook of learning disabilities* (pp. 403–416). New York: Guilford Press.

(2) Adams, G. L., & Englemann, S. (1996). *Research on direct instruction: 25 years beyond DISTAR.* Seattle, WA: Educational Achievement Systems.

(3) Browder, D. M., & Xin, Y. P. (1998). A meta-analysis and review of sight word research and its implications for teaching functional reading to individuals with moderate and severe disabilities. *Journal of Special Education, 32,* 130–153.

(4) Burns, M. K. (2004). Empirical analysis of drill ratio research: Refining the instructional level for drill tasks. *Remedial and Special Education, 25,* 167–173.

(5) Burns, M. K., & Symington, T. (2002). A meta-analy-sis of prereferral intervention teams: Student and systemic outcomes. *Journal of School Psychology, 40,* 437–447.

(6) Carlberg, C., & Kavale, K. (1980). The efficacy of special versus regular class placement for exceptional children: A meta-analysis. *Journal of Special Education, 14,* 296–309.

(7) Carlson, M. (1987). *Social and academic outcomes of cooperative learning in the mainstreamed classroom: A meta-analysis.* Unpublished manuscript, Claremont Graduate School, CA.

(8) Casto, G., & Mastropieri, M. A. (1986). The efficacy of early intervention programs: A meta-analysis. *Exceptional Children, 52,* 417–424.

(9) Conners, F. A. (1992). Reading instruction for students with moderate mental retardation: Review and analysis of research. *American Journal on Mental Retardation, 96,* 577–597.

(10) Cook, S. B., Scruggs, T. E., Mastropieri, M. A., & Casto, G. C. (1985–86). Handicapped students as tutors. *Journal of Special Education, 19,* 483–492.

(11) Crenshaw, T. M., Kavale, K. A., Forness, S. R., & Reeve, R. E. (1999). Attention deficit hyperactivity disorder and the efficacy of stimulant medication: A meta-analysis. In T. E. Scruggs & M. A. Mastropieri (Eds.), *Advances in learning and behavioral disabilities* (Vol. 13, pp. 135–165). Stamford, CT: JAI Press.

(12) Durlak, J. A., Fuhrman, J., & Lampman, C. (1991). Effectiveness of cognitive-behavior therapy for maladapting children: A meta-analysis. *Psychological Bulletin, 110,* 204–214.

(13) Elbaum, B., Vaughn, S., Hughes, M., & Moody, S. W. (1999). Grouping practices and reading outcomes for students with disabilities. *Exceptional Children, 65,* 399–415.

(14) Elbaum, B., Vaughn, S., Hughes, M., Moody, S. W., & Schumm, J. S. (2000). How reading outcomes of students with disabilities are related to instructional grouping formats: A meta-analytic review. In R. Gersten, E. Schiller, & S. Vaughn (Eds.), *Contemporary special education research* (pp. 105–135). Mahwah, NJ: Erlbaum.

(15) Engles, G. I., Garnefski, N., & Diekstra, R. F. W. (1993). Efficacy of rational emotive therapy: Aquantitive analysis. *Journal of Consulting and Clinical Psychology, 61,* 1083–1090.

(16) Forness, S. R., & Kavale, K. A. (1993). Strategies to improve basic learning and memory deficits in mental retardation: A meta-analysis of experimental studies. *Education and Training in Mental Retardation, 28,* 99–110.

(17) Forness, S. R., & Kavale, K. A. (1996). Treating social skill deficits in children with learning disabilities: A meta-analysis of the research. *Learning Disability Quarterly, 19,* 1–13.

(18) Fuchs, L. S., & Fuchs, D. (1986b). Effects of system-

atic evaluation. A meta-analysis. *Exceptional Children, 53*, 199–208.

(19) Gersten, R., & Baker, S. (2001). Teaching expressive writing to students with learning disabilities: A meta-analysis. *Elementary School Journal, 101*, 251–272.

(20) Gonzalez, J. E., Nelson, J. R., Gutkin, T. B., Saunders, A., Galloway, A., & Shwery, G. S. (2004). Rational emotive therapy with children and adolescents: A meta-analysis. *Journal of Emotional and Behavioral Disorders, 12*, 222–235.

(21) Graham, S., & Harris, K. R. (2003). Students with learning disabilities and the process of writing: A meta-analysis of SRSD studies. In H. L. Swanson, K. R. Harris, & S. Graham (Eds.), *Handbook of learning disabilities* (pp. 323–344). New York: Guilford Press.

(22) Hillocks, G. (1984). What works in teaching composition: A meta-analysis of experimental treatment studies. *American Journal of Education, 93*, 133–170.

(23) Horn, W. F., & Packard, T. (1985). Early identification of learning problems: A meta-analysis. *Journal of Educational Psychology, 77*, 597–607.

(24) Innocenti, M. S., & White, K. R. (1993). Are more intensive early intervention programs more effective? A review of the literature. *Exceptionality, 4*, 31–50.

(25) Jitendra, A. K., Edwards, L. L., Sacks, G., & Jacobson, L. A. (2004). What research says about vocabulary instruction for students with learning disabilities. *Exceptional Children, 70*, 299–322.

(26) Johnson, D.W., Johnson, R. T., & Maruyama, G. (1983). Interdependence and interpersonal attraction among heterogeneous and homogeneous individuals: A theoretical formulation and meta-analysis of the research. *Review of Education Research, 53*, 5–54.

(27) Kavale, K. (1981). Function of the Illinois Test of Psycholinguistic Abilities (ITPA). Are they trainable? *Exceptional Children, 47*, 496–510.

(28) Kavale, K. (1982a). The efficacy of stimulant drug treatment for hyperactivity: A meta-analysis. *Journal of Learning Disabilities, 15*, 280–289.

(29) Kavale, K. (1982b). Psycholinguistic training programs: Are there differential treatment effects? *The Exceptional Child, 29*, 21–30.

(30) Kavale, K. A. (1984). A meta-analytic evaluation of the Frostig test and training program. *The Exceptional Child, 31*, 134–141.

(31) Kavale, K. A., & Forness, S. R. (1983). Hyperactivity and diet treatment: A meta-analysis of the Feingold hypothesis. *Journal of Learning Disabilities, 16*, 324–330.

(32) Kavale, K. A., & Forness, S. R. (1987). Substance over style: Assessing the efficacy of modality testing and teaching. *Exceptional Children, 54*, 228–239.

(33) Kavale, K. A., & Mattson, P. D. (1983). 'One jumped off the balance beam': Meta-analysis of perceptual-

motor training. *Journal of Learning Disabilities, 16*, 165–173.

(34) Kavale, K. A., & Mostert, M. P. (2005). *Somewhere over the rainbow: A meta-analysis of Irlen lenses/color overlays for improving reading.* Unpublished manuscript, Regent University, Virginia Beach, VA.

(35) Kroesbergen, E. H., & VanLuit, J. E. H. (2003). Mathematics interventions for children with special educational needs: A meta-analysis. *Remedial and Special Education, 24*, 97–114.

(36) Lapadat, J. C. (1991). Pragmatic language skills of students with language and/or learning disabilities: A quantitative synthesis. *Journal of Learning Disabilities, 24*, 147–158.

(37) Mastropieri, M. A., Bakken, J. P., & Scruggs, T. E. (1991). Mathematics instruction for individuals with mental retardation: A perspective and research synthesis. *Education and Training in Mental Retardation, 26*, 115–129.

(38) Mastropieri, M. A., & Scruggs, T. E. (1985–86). Early intervention for socially withdrawn children. *Journal of Special Education, 19*, 429–441.

(39) Mastropieri, M.A., & Scruggs, T. E. (1989). Constructing more meaningful relationships: Mnemonic instruction for special populations. *Educational Psychology Review, 1*, 83–111.

(40) Mastropieri, M. A., Scruggs, T. E., Bakken, J.P., & Whedon, C. (1996). Reading comprehension: A synthesis of research in learning disabilities. In T. E. Scruggs & M. A. Mastropieri (Eds.), *Advances in learning and behavioral disabilities* (Vol. 10, pp. 227–303). Greenwich, CT: JAI Press.

(41) Mastropieri, M. A., Spencer, V., Scruggs, T. E., & Talbott, E. (2000). Students with disabilities as tutors: An updated research synthesis. In T. E. Scruggs & M. A. Mastropieri (Eds.), *Advances in learning and behavioral disabilities: Educational interventions* (Vol. 14, pp. 247–279). Stamford, CT: JAI Press.

(42) Mathur, S. R., Kavale, K. A., Quinn, M. M., Forness, S. R., & Rutherford, R. B. (1998). Social skills interventions with students with emotional and behavioral problems: A quantitative synthesis of single-subject research. *Behavioral Disorders, 23*, 193–201.

(43) Nye, C., Foster, S. H., & Seaman, D. (1987). Effectiveness of language intervention with the language/learning disabled. *Journal of Speech and Hearing Disorders, 52*, 348–357.

(44) Quinn, M. M., Kavale, K. A., Mathur, S., Rutherford, R. B., & Forness, S. R. (1999). A meta-analysis of social skill interventions for students with emotional or behavioral disorders. *Journal of Emotional and Behavioral Disorders, 7*, 54–64.

(45) Reddy, L., Barboza-Whitehead, S., Files, T., & Rubel, E. (2000). Clinical focus of consultation outcome

research with children and adolescents. *Journal of Applied School Psychology, 16,* 1–22.

(46) Robinson, T. R., Smith, S. W., Miller, M. D., & Brownell, M. T. (1999). Cognitive behavior modification of hyperactivity-impulsivity and aggression: A meta-analysis of school-based studies. *Journal of Educational Psychology, 91,* 195–203.

(47) Schmidt, M., Weinstein, T., Niemic, R., & Walberg, H. J. (1985–86). Computer-assisted instruction with exceptional children. *Journal of Special Education, 19,* 494–501.

(48) Schumm, J. S., Moody, S. W., & Vaughn, S. (2000). Grouping for reading instruction: Does one size fit all? *Journal of Learning Disabilities, 33,* 477–488.

(49) Scruggs, T. E., Mastropieri, M. A., Cook, S., & Escobar, C. (1986). Early intervention for children with conduct disorders: A quantitative synthesis of single-subject research. *Behavioral Disorders, 11,* 260–271.

(50) Scruggs, T. E., Mastropieri, M. A., Forness, S. R., & Kavale, K. A. (1988). Early language intervention: A quantitative synthesis of single-subject research. *Journal of Special Education, 22,* 259–283.

(51) Shonkoff, J. P., & Hauser-Cram, P. (1987). Early intervention for disabled infants and their families: A quantitative analysis. *Pediatrics, 80,* 650–658.

(52) Skiba, R. J., & Casey, A. (1985). Interventions for behaviorally disordered students: A quantitative review and methodological critique. *Behavioral Disorders, 10,* 239–252.

(53) Stevens, R. J., & Slavin, R. E. (1991). When cooperative learning improves the achievement of students with mild disabilities: A response to Tateyama-Sniezck. *Exceptional Children, 57,* 276–280.

(54) Swanson, H. L. (1999). Reading research for students with LD: A meta-analysis of intervention outcomes. *Journal of Learning Disabilities, 32,* 504–532.

(55) Swanson, H. L. (2001). Research on interventions for adolescents with learning disabilities: A meta-analysis of outcomes related to higher-order processing. *Elementary School Journal, 101,* 331–348.

(56) Swanson, H. L., Carson, C., & Sachsee-Lee, C. M. (1996). A selective synthesis of intervention research for students with learning disabilities. *School Psychology Review, 25,* 370–391.

(57) Swanson, H. L., & Hoskyn, M. (1998). Experimental intervention research on students with learning disabilities: A meta-analysis of treatment outcomes. *Review of Educational Research, 68,* 277–321.

(58) Swanson, H. L., & Hoskyn, M. (2000). Intervention research for students with learning disabilities: A comprehensive meta-analysis of group design studies. In T. E. Scruggs & M. A. Mastropieri (Eds.), *Advances in learning and behavioral disabilities* (Vol. 14, pp. 1–153). Stamford, CT: JAI Press.

(59) Swanson, H. L., O'Shaughnessy, T. E., McMahon, C. M., Hoskyn, M., & Sachsee-Lee, C. M. (1998). A selective synthesis of single subject design intervention research on students with learning disabilities. In T. E. Scruggs & M. A. Mastropieri (Eds.), *Advances in learning and behavioral disabilities* (Vol. 12, pp. 79–126). Greenwich, CT: JAI Press.

(60) Talbott, E., Lloyd, J. W., & Tankersley, M. (1994). Effects of reading comprehension interventions for students with learning disabilities. *Learning Disability Quarterly, 17,* 223–232.

(61) Therrien, W. J. (2004). Fluency and comprehension gains as a result of repeated readings: A meta-analysis. *Remedial and Special Education, 25,* 252–261.

(62) Thurber, S., & Walker, C. E. (1983). Medication and hyperactivity: A meta-analysis. *Journal of General Psychology, 108,* 79–86.

(63) Wang, M. C., & Baker, E. T. (1985–86), Mainstreaming programs: design features and effects, *Journal of Special Education, 19,* 503–521.

(64) Waxman, H. C., Wang, M. C., Anderson, K. A., & Walberg, H. J. (1985). Adaptive education and student outcomes: A quantitative synthesis. *Journal of Educational Research, 78,* 228–236.

(65) White, K. R. (1985–86). Efficacy of early interventions. *Journal of Special Education, 19,* 401–416.

(66) White, W. A. T. (1988). A meta-analysis of the effects of direct instruction in special education, *Education and Treatment of Children, 11,* 364–374.

(67) Xin, Y. P., & Jitendra, A. K. (1999). The effects of instruction in solving mathematical word problems for students with learning problems: A meta-analysis. *Journal of Special Education, 32,* 207–225.

APPENDIX B: SECONDARY EFFECT SIZE SOURCES

Forness, S. R. (2001). Special education and related services: What have we learned from meta-analysis? *Exceptionality, 9,* 185–198.

Forness, S. R., Kavale, K. A., Blum, I. M., & Lloyd, J. W. (1997). Mega-analysis of meta-analysis: What works in special education and related services. *Teaching Exceptional Children, 29,* 4–9.

Kavale, K. A. (1990). Variances and verities in learning disability interventions. In T. E. Scruggs & B. Y. L. Wong (Eds.), *Intervention research in learning disabilities* (pp. 3–33). New York: Springer-Verlag.

Kavale, K. A., & Dobbins, D. A. (1993). The equivocal nature of special education interventions. *Early Child Development and Care, 86,* 23–37.

Kavale, K. A., & Forness, S. R. (2000). Policy decisions in special education: The role of analysis. In R. Gersten, E. Schiller, & S. Vaughn (Eds.), *Contemporary special edu-*

cation research (pp. 281–326). Mahwah, NJ: Erlbaum.

Kavale, K. A., & Glass, G. V. (1982). The efficacy of special education interventions and practices: A compendium of meta-analysis findings. *Focus on Exceptional Children, 15*(4), 1–14.

Kavale, K. A., & Glass, G. V. (1984). Meta-analysis and policy decisions in special education. In B. K. Keogh (Ed.), *Advances in special education* (Vol. IV, pp. 195–247). Greenwich, CT: JAI.

Lipsey, M. W., & Wilson, D. B. (1993). The efficacy of psychological, educational, and behavioral treatment. *American Psychologist, 48*, 1181–1209.

Swanson, H. L. (1999). *Interventions for students with learning disabilities: A meta-analysis of treatment outcomes.* New York: Guilford.

Vaughn, S., Gersten, R., & Chard, D. J. (2000). The underlying message in LD intervention research: Findings from research syntheses. *Exceptional Children, 67*, 99–114.

Walberg, H. J. (1984). Improving the productivity of America's schools. *Educational Leadership, 41*, 19–30.

16

Research and pupil voice

Ann Lewis and Jill Porter

INTRODUCTION

There are many reasons for involving children and young people in the process of research (Kirby, Lanyon, Kronin, & Sinclair, 2003). We may for example believe that the research will be better or more meaningful, and have greater validity in revealing children's views and experiences. Additionally we may believe in the importance of democratic participation, and that children should contribute to the decision-making process in the development of aspects of their lives that particularly concern them. We may also as educators recognize that contributing to the research process provides an important vehicle for personal development. There is therefore a growing body of interest in developing research that might be described as participatory, whether this involves ensuring that the voices of all children are included, extends to the active engagement of children in the research process, or (as in emancipatory research traditions) involves children explicitly leading the research process.

A key theme in this chapter will be what we term 'flexing the boundaries' – that is, exploring where the limits to engagement of pupil voice come and how those limits ebb and flow both with different methodological perspectives and in the course of evolving methods. This has clear implications for the very way in which research is understood in two ways; first, in relation to researchers' different epistemological and ontological stances and, second, to questions about whether research is uncritically 'a good thing'. A continuing challenge for researchers is to work in a critical and self-reflective way including testing the boundaries. Research in the field of disability has been both innovative and radical in its attempt to flex the boundaries of what is possible, drawing on the creativity of practitioners and researchers to develop their own skills as well as those of their co-researchers (Porter & Lacey, 2005). This has provided an important body of research that documents many of the challenges that are shared by those eliciting the voice of children and young people.

We start the chapter by recognizing the extensive influence of the rights agenda before exploring the assumptions underpinning different research positions. A number of broad tensions are raised prior to looking at some of the ethical issues raised by participatory research. We look specifically at the challenge of developing research tools that meet the needs of children with limited communication skills and the ways in which researchers are pushing out the boundaries of conventional approaches and conclude by reviewing the implications of these practices for research and researchers.

BACKGROUND

The United Nations *Convention on the Rights of the Child* (UNCRC) calls for state parties to: 'assure to the child who is capable of forming his or her own views the right to express those views freely in all matters affecting the child, the views of the child being given due weight in accordance with the age and maturity of the child' (Article 12).

Following from this, there has been a torrent of initiatives worldwide involving hearing children's views in matters that concern them. These range from formal procedures, often taking a rights emphasis (UNICEF, 2004), through the development of children as participant or co-researchers and their involvement in national and local evaluations of their provision (for example, NECF in the UK). All these are found worldwide and many have included hearing the views of children with learning difficulties and disabilities. The United Nations Children's Fund (UNICEF, 2004) reported on the proliferation of one aspect – independent national institutions for children's rights, such as a commissioner or ombudsman offices for children. However there is a danger that such mechanisms over-formalize the hearing of children's views and interestingly UNICEF notes: 'Now it (the movement towards having spokespersons for children) can only gain from rigorous evaluation – by children and young people among others – to inform the strengthening of existing institutions and the continuing development of new ones' (UNICEF, 2004, p. 10).

EPISTEMOLOGICAL ISSUES – CONTRASTING STANCES

Interest in pupil voice is not only fuelled by the rights agenda. As researchers, a situation may be seen as not fully understood without representation of the views of all stakeholders. The validity of research must be immeasurably strengthened where not only have we collected information on the views of all our participant group, but we have also ensured that the topics we have addressed and the questions we have asked are meaningful. This is well illustrated with reference to the clinical interview. This approach (a long-established method in much cognitive and developmental work) places the power emphasis with the researcher, and even in this context there has been increasing recognition of the multidimensional child perspective. The viewpoint of the child is essential to investigating and therefore understanding a given context. So, for example, in post-/neo-Piagetian work the cluster of expectations engendered in the child by the interview situation has been recognized. As a result of the classic 'naughty teddy' studies (Donaldson, 1987), experimenters have had to reappraise young children's apparent failure to conserve, and emphasize the importance of basing research around an assumed shared meaning.

A further point concerning work in this tradition is that it has tended typically to focus on developing children. It is important to involve a wide range of children in such developmental studies for several reasons. First, any theory of development needs to be based on a diverse group of children (covering variables of gender, age, social background and ability, and so on) if it is to be generally applicable. Second, evidence concerning children who are not typically developing can shed light on typical processes (see work by Lewis, 2004).

These points relate to the conclusions of such studies but there are also methodological reasons for including children who are not typically developing in such studies. Where disabled children have been the specific focus of interest (as in Theory of Mind and autism) the clinical interview has also prompted developments in method. Thus, contrary to what may at first appear to be the case, the clinical interview, like participatory research, can contribute to our understanding and methods for giving all children a voice.

We have, in this chapter, used the term participatory research to refer to approaches that are best characterized as 'research with' rather than 'research on' (such as the clinical interview). This distinction emphasizes the social relations between researcher and researched, a key aspect of emancipatory research. Although there is dispute about the use of the term 'emancipatory' (Oliver, 1997; Zarb, 1997; Barnes, 2002) there is an underlying recognition of the role of research in bringing about change that is empowering, that uncovers the barriers placed by society and reveals how lives are constrained by systems that are oppressive. Emancipatory research is explicitly underpinned by a social model of disability (French & Swain, 1997) although this may not be apparent in all participatory approaches (Chappell, 2000).

Collaborative research can involve a number of participatory practices: at a fundamental level it strives to ensure that the voice of all those with special educational needs (SEN) are represented, not simply those whose views are more readily captured. Further along the participatory continuum, it can include collaboration in all or some of the following: establishing the research agenda, applying for research funding, designing and carrying out the research including analysing the data, and disseminating the research findings.

CHALLENGING THE BOUNDARIES

Hearing children's views in research and policy contexts presents us with several significant challenges. First, there are indications that commentators and professionals are beginning to express some disquiet about what is possible and reasonable in this context (Hart, 2002). Richard Dawkins has written that 'with so many mindbytes to be downloaded, so many mental codons to be replicated, it is no wonder that child brains are gullible, open to almost any suggestion, vulnerable to subversion' (cited in Mills & Keil, 2005). Felce (2002), with reference to people with learning disabilities, has also raised concerns: 'Obtaining the views of people with learning difficulties – even those with severe or profound intellectual impairment – is becoming a ubiquitous imperative'. We should, he suggested, be much more cautious than we usually are about assuming the validity of views passed on via proxies or facilitators (Ware, 2004, see below).

The UNCRC assumes, broadly, that there are no boundaries, that is, that (ultimately) pupil/children's voice as users and as research participants is a reasonable goal for all children. The UNCRC does include, in passing, reference to recognition of the impact of developmental level. This point has not generally been taken up (but see Hart, 2002) as it has been obscured by the much stronger reference to, and interpretation of, the UNCRC as essentially a rights-based document. However, in contrast to this position, scepticism is still voiced about the feasibility of (any) children expressing 'reliable' views.

Second, there is a danger that the pressure arising from the welter of policy initiatives leads to an over-formalizing and/or an over-pressurizing of the process of hearing the views of children, perhaps particularly those with learning disabilities. The presence of assigned support workers, signers or translators may (despite good intentions) be, or be seen by the child, as making obligatory a response of some kind (see further below). The position of governments, as well as that of children's charities and even the groups run by children themselves, invariably understates or ignores the possible choice by a child for silence, privacy and a non-response. Some children may genuinely and freely prefer silence to voicing their views. Silence is a very powerful statement if others, particularly those in authority, expect one's voice to be loud. In line with this, the philosopher Roger

Homan (2001) has argued that children are particularly susceptible to intrusions of private space and so the urge to hear children's views needs to be tempered with respect for their choices even (especially) if this is for silence. (See Lewis & Lindsay, 2000; Alderson & Morrow, 2004; Clegg, 2004; and Porter & Lewis, 2004, for reviews of ethics and consulting with children in a research context.)

Third, the emphasis in policy-making has been on giving individual children a voice. How do we move from hearing individual children's views, to helping children to present a collective 'choir' which always, and routinely, includes those with disabilities and difficulties? For example, if physically able children make vociferous calls for better play areas and those calls are acted upon, do the resultant facilities reflect the views and needs of all children or only those of the physically able? This would represent a second-order representation of the views of disabled children, that is, obtained second hand through other children's perceptions.

Finally, how do we explain to all children (including those with difficulties or disabilities) how and why, having heard their views, we are making (or not making) a particular response? This will test whether adults are serious about the process of not just hearing, but also responding to, children's views (which, as implied in the above UN comment about the balancing of rights, does not necessarily mean acting on them); that is, creating a 'radical collegiality' (Fielding, 2004).

ETHICAL ISSUES

In this section we shall discuss three key aspects of ethical issues in this context. Given the potential breadth of this section we shall consider in particular:

- the impact on the child of being given a voice in the research context
- issues about adult response/actions to that voice in the research context
- a re-evaluation of child voice drawing on

debates (see, for example, Fielding, 2004) about the ways in which adults may, perhaps unwittingly, subordinate the child's voice in the research context.

Education has been slower to respond to ethical issues, in sharp contrast to the formal and often lengthy procedures for research approval characteristic of other disciplines. There has been a tacit assumption that the gatekeepers are the arbiters of the research, so that local education authority (LEA) or school-level agreement together with parental consent determine the inclusion of children in the research process. In this way children's views can be collected without their explicit consent and often without a clear understanding of the purpose of the research. This highlights the power relations in much child-based research. As others have highlighted, consent should be seen as an ongoing process with children consulted at each step along the way rather than a single hurdle through which the researcher has to pass (Rodgers, 1999; Knox, Mok, & Permenter, 2000). Even when the child is unable to give informed consent, there should be opportunities for assent and dissent to ensure that their inclusion in the study is voluntary and not as a result of coercion. Tozer (2003) provided children with autistic spectrum disorder (ASD) with a stop symbol alongside reminders that they could use it to control whether the interview continued. In our research (Parsons, Daniels, Porter, & Robertson, 2004; Porter et al., 2005) participants with learning disabilities were given control over the video recorder thereby being able to terminate the interview at any point if they so wished. One of the outcomes of this shift in power is that some groups of pupils are more likely to actively dissent than others and we need to reflect on the implications of this both for the format content of research.

As we shall see in the following section, research has focused more readily on examining linguistic and cognitive influences than on recognizing the emotional aspects of giving one's views. There has to be an element of self-belief on the part of the child; that their view is worth listening to and, moreover, that people will hear their voice and that it will make a difference. If the researcher does not actively gain the consent from the child then they are reinforcing a notion (often unwittingly) that the child does not have a voice or that only certain views are worth listening to.

Fielding (2004) poses a number of questions and dilemmas:

- Do we recognize the plurality of voices?
- Do we downplay the voices that seem too strident and foreground those that most readily make sense to us? Are we genuinely attentive to criticism?
- How does our professional and adult status frame our perspective?
- How confident can we be that our research does not perpetuate the status quo? Can we be sure that our data will not be ultimately used for the purposes of control?

He argues that what is needed is a transformation of roles – we need to rethink what it means to be a pupil and therefore our own professional position and responsibilities. We need to establish a dialogic process in which the research is collaborative at each of the key points and 'avoid the equally mistaken polar opposites of, on the one hand, ignoring or excluding the speech of the marginalized group, and, on the other hand, treating its inclusion as unproblemmatically insightful and liberating' (Fielding, 2004, p. 305). Walmsley, in a recent article on the role of the (non-disabled) researcher, argues for the importance of 'honest reflection' in order to avoid being 'trapped in a cycle of sentimental biography or individual anecdotes' (2004, p. 65). We therefore need to be self-critical about the way that we collect children's views and recognize how the methods we use can subordinate the child's voice.

The difficulties inherent in this process are well illustrated in the following case study in which a facilitator acted as intermediary conveying the views of Lucy, a 9-year-old girl with profound hearing loss (from Lewis, Robertson, & Parsons, 2005). In this exam-

ple, the facilitator interpreted Makaton signs for the researcher and also translated the child's signing back to the researcher. However, the filter of the facilitator can distort the views held by the child in several ways. First, the facilitator may unwittingly introduce bias in the way a comment or question is phrased (as discussed further below). Second the signed language (for example, Makaton or British/American sign language) will have different nuances from spoken language (and from one another) and so shift emphasis or meaning and differences between what disabled, compared with non-disabled, children are being asked. Some expressions may be difficult to sign, as in the following extract in which sense of autonomy was the focus of discussion with Lucy. (Note: throughout the signer was signing and speaking, as given.)

Interviewer	Can you tell me something where you have lots of choice in school?
Signer	Lots of choices. Lots of things (). Lots of things that you like to do or friends. You've got lots of friends
Interviewer	Where you decide.
Signer	You decide. Lucy says. Lucy decides what. What do you decide?
L	[signing]
Signer	Decide. Idea. Lucy's idea. When does Lucy have an idea?
L	Idea.
Signer	When? When do you have an idea? Outside? What?
L	[signing]
Signer	Do you have an idea when you're playing? What do you choose?
L	[signing]
Signer	Skipping.
Interviewer	You choose skipping?
Signer	(?)
Interviewer	Choose skipping. So that's lots of choice.
Signer	That's lots of things to choose and have your own ideas.

Interviewer	Now here. No choice. When does Lucy have no choice?
Signer	Lucy must do. Not Lucy's idea but Lucy must do when? In school. Lucy must what?
L	School.
Interviewer	Yes. That's right. Good. To come to school. No choice. What else?
Signer	What else do you choose?
L	[signing]
Signer	To play with ball.
Interviewer	Playing with a ball. Is that more or less choice?
Signer	I don't think she really understands the concept.

Lucy was very able but her communication difficulties seem to have prevented her from, in this context, conveying her views about degree of autonomy and the choices she was able to exercise in various contexts. The signer, perhaps inevitably, gave leads and the interviewer was totally dependent on the signer to present and interpret to/from Lucy. Lucy's deafness makes more transparent a process that may well be occurring with other children but is less noticeable there.

We turn now to consider in more detail the challenges in collecting and representing the views of children who are less articulate including those who do not communicate through speech.

SPECIFIC CHALLENGES: COMMUNICATION SKILLS

Much of the research methodology literature has focused on those who make verbal responses in interview situations and has, particularly, investigated different question forms. Three aspects of these have been highlighted: the vocabulary, the syntax and the pragmatic demands (Dockrell, 2004) in the search for reliable and valid methods. It can be difficult to distinguish between cognitive and linguistic aspects of communication. Studies that make a fine-grained analysis of

typically developing children, in addition to those with special educational needs, contribute to our understanding. Dockrell (2004) reviews research on studies of memory as well as language. As she points out, we are often specifically interested in children's feelings and their emotional response to an event or situation. Research suggests, however, that their recall is tempered by how well they coped with the situation, with those who fared well later reported as having more intense emotional states than those who did not. She also highlights the impact of repeated questioning which can negatively impact on children's recall of events. Research with people with learning difficulties has highlighted the increased likelihood of acquiescence (or 'yea-saying') (Sigelman, Budd, Spanhel, & Schoenrock, 1981; Finlay & Lyons, 2002), and, as with young children, this tendency has often been seen to reflect increased suggestibility rather than being a product of the interview situation. We need to consider whether such agreement is an artefact of the interrogative force of a question, or one that involves an abstract concept or a judgement that is too difficult, or whether we are demanding an opinion about something that has never been considered in detail before. Lewis (2004) draws our attention to the importance of children feeling that they can ask for clarification or say simply that they do not know. Some interviewers use a device, such as a squeaky toy, which the child pushes to signal 'don't know'. Equally it is important that the setting does not suggest that the adult knows the answer or indeed that there is a right response. Research suggests that a yes/no answer format encourages those who do not know to respond. Dockrell (2004) suggests that we use open-ended and 'wh' questions and Lewis (2004) that we use statements rather than questions; however, both these recommendations suggest that the child has the vocabulary to respond to these.

If we turn now to consider children with only limited independent ability to use a formal linguistic code, we are likely to rely on others to make inferences about meaning and to distinguish between intentional and non-intentional communicative acts. This group of children is not well placed to contradict an interpretation (Grove, Porter, Bunning, & Olsson, 1999). Clearly researchers who do not know the child personally are disadvantaged, not only in understanding the child, but when liaising with others and being certain about the ownership of the message. Research with adults with learning difficulties has debated the veracity of data collected through a third party (Hatton & Ager, 2002; Schalock et al., 2002; Schwartz & Rabinovitz, 2003) and has recognized that surrogates may consider the standpoint of the individual including their interests, preferences, values and past experiences (Freedman, 2001) or make a response that reflects their own position. If facilitators or proxies are used then any report needs to acknowledge how views were collected so that the reader/listener can make a judgement about whether the conduit for views may have distorted the evidence. Rigorous and systematic checking of the data, including a search for contradictory evidence, are important parts of the validation process (Porter, 2003). There are also implications for work in schools when school-based facilitators, although well-meaning, may unwittingly lead a child or, if not well briefed, may be uncertain and possibly anxious about the degree to which they can do so.

Research on the use of advocates gives us some important further suggestions for the characteristics needed by someone who supports people with learning disabilities. These include being seen as independent and willing to put forward views that they do not share, having time for them and treating them with respect, and lastly someone who will give them confidence (Dalrymple, 2005). Facilitators who are well known to the child may be reassuring but may also inhibit the child from expressing negative views about, for example, experiences in school. Clearly, it is crucial that such facilitators liaise with researchers/interviewers beforehand about the purpose of the interview and how much to lead. They also need

ample time before the interview to consider how best to sign a point/question so that it is more likely to be understood/interpreted appropriately by the child.

These potential difficulties may lead researchers or professionals to conclude that it is preferable to use indirect methods (such as observation of the child in particular contexts) in order to gauge children's views, particularly of those with profound or multiple learning difficulties (Ware, 2004). The debate around such issues shows how far opinion has moved in formally recognizing the importance and feasibility of trying to ascertain the views of those children.

POSSIBLE METHODS – WAYS IN WHICH THE BOUNDARIES CAN BE PUSHED OUT

Materials about how to explore children's views are widely available and encompass general guidelines, accounts of projects and specific materials (for example, Kirby, 1999; Clark and Moss, 2001; Kirby et al., 2003). These materials vary widely in how far they incorporate approaches applicable to children and young people with learning difficulties. Materials to use in exploring the views of children with learning difficulties have come from the larger children's charities, often working in collaboration with academic researchers. These materials include general accounts and guidelines (for example, Aitken & Millar, 2004); materials (for example, Marchant & Cross, 2002) and accounts of projects (for example, Whittles, 1998).

The range of potential methods varies on at least four dimensions:

1   Degree of support offered (for example, facilitator, puppet, information and communications technology (ICT)-linked, friend, peer group).
2   Mode of communication to and from the child (for example, varying degrees of reliance on linguistic, receptive and/or expressive skills; pictorial; symbolic; dramatic; ICT-linked; enactive).
3   Use of concrete referents (for example, materials to manipulate).

4 Degree to which the child sets the agenda and/or pace (for example, those in which the child has a comparatively free rein such as using observation, mapping, photos, drawing; contrasted with those in which the child is primarily responsive to the interviewer/researcher such as prompted interviews). Note: children, including those with learning difficulties, have been involved as co-researchers and this has considerable potential, although such work should not place expectations on children that are not applied to adults in comparable situations.

Researchers from differing epistemological backgrounds will differ in what they regard as an appropriate method of data collection, whether, for example, they use a method which predetermines the outcomes (perhaps by the choice of available vocabulary or symbols) or whether a more open-ended approach is adopted that allows for the possibility of serendipity. Choices about methods will in turn prompt particular approaches to data analysis. It is beyond the scope of this chapter to explore methods of data analyses more fully. Whatever the epistemological position, implementing diverse methods effectively can be fostered by building on insights and findings derived from more formal, developmental approaches. This recognizes that exploring children's views does need to take into account differing developmental levels.

Methods suited to exploring the views of children with learning difficulties include (outline typology based on Greene and Hogan, 2005):

• Observation. Naturalistic observations of children have a long tradition in this field, particularly with children with multiple or profound difficulties, and may supplement more child-derived approaches. The dangers in making unwarranted assumptions about the wishes of children through observation have been explored by Ware (2004). Observational approaches encompass various degrees of structure depending on the area of interest and the researcher's epistemological stance (for example, structured observations of specific behaviours or more open, ethnographic, observations).

• Individual interviews (possibly supported through a facilitator or signer, see above, or supported through the structure, for example using cue card prompts; Lewis, 2004).

• Small group interviews (possibly supported, as for individual interviews).

• Creative methods (such as cameras, video, drawings, drama). These are a growing area of researcher interest in this context and have considerable potential to gain insights into a child's construction of the world that does not rest on their facility with language (see Tozer, 2003; Brewster, 2004; Germain, 2004). Motor-assisted cameras can be used if children have difficulty winding on the film. Researchers will be aware that there are ethical issues in possibly photographing children in, for example, school contexts and fully informed consent from parents, teachers and children is needed first.

• Elicited and spontaneous narrative accounts (such as questionnaires, e-surveys, life stories).

• Prompted (via material or visual cues) approaches (for example, using mapping, puppets or photographs). For example, the PATH approach (Pearpoint, 2002) is being used in several areas for self- and project-evaluation. 'Talking mats' is used to elicit the views of people with learning difficulties (Cameron & Murphy, 2002).

• Projective techniques (for example, specific projective tests).

Some of these approaches can start to address qualms about researcher–researched power relationships but they raise issues about how best to interpret and analyse resultant data in ways which are convincing to research communities. It is usually necessary to validate the meaning through the collection of other data (Porter & Lacey, 2005). The recurrent message from workers in the field is of the importance of exploring children's views flexibly, collaboratively and variously. Researchers may endeavour to present the child or young person with a portfolio of methods from which they can choose, and so realize their preferences across these dimensions (Lewis et al., 2005). If children are given a choice of methods, including cameras, then all these permissions (and the materials) need to be obtained in advance.

CONCLUSION

One of the key drivers behind eliciting pupil voice has been the rights movement whereby children are seen to be vital contributors to decision-making around the provision of services. In the fields of SEN and disability this drive for more participatory forms of research is paralleled in the disability rights movement. Both are underpinned by the assumption that change will result from the collection of views. The channelling of much research to contribute to evidence-informed policy and practice suggests that children should have an expectation that their views will indeed contribute to the shape of provision. It is not, however, simply a process of acting on pupil views. Such power comes with responsibilities, and perhaps we need to be more honest with the child in our recognition of the tensions this raises.

If we accept the importance of pupil voice then it is vital that we include all children. Challenges have led to the innovation of new methods. There is a need to view methods of communication in flexible and imaginative ways in order to circumvent possible problems including memory, emotion, social skills, linguistic pragmatics, receptive language, expressive language. Using proxies is increasingly seen as inappropriate, so the emphasis has shifted to finding better ways of communicating directly. This may in itself lead to both more caution (because it is difficult) and more optimism (because with trial and error it is likely to be found to be possible) about boundaries. New methods include technological solutions as well as creative ones – but we must be aware that the medium may distort the message. New methods need developing as research tools and evaluating. We need to recognize the choice of a child to be silent but also recognize that silence gives a message of its own that we should hear.

More than ever, we need to recognize that there are no universal solutions, nor a perfect methodology (Northway, 2000; Nind, Benjamin, Sheeny, Collins, & Hall, 2005) waiting out there to be discovered. As others have argued, there is a need for transparency around the difficulties and a fuller sharing of the methods used, including those which were not successful. This calls for a willingness to be flexible in using more innovative approaches and developing new skills, and to be thorough and systematic in validating our analysis. It is likely that such research will take longer and require a much greater level of commitment than that of a 'hit and run' researcher (Vincent & Warren, 2005).

Fielding has argued that we need to rethink what it means to be a pupil and the implications for our own role. This will mean that we rethink not only our role as researcher but the many assumptions that underpin our thinking about the nature of research.

REFERENCES

Aitken, S., & Millar, S. (2004). *Listening to children.* Edinburgh: CALL Centre, University of Edinburgh/SENSE Scotland.

Alderson, P., & Morrow, V. (2004). *Ethics, social research and consulting with children and young people.* London: Barnardos.

Barnes, C. (2002). 'Emancipatory disability research': Project or process? *Journal of Research in Special Educational Needs, 2,* 1.

Brewster, S. (2004). Putting words into their mouths? Interviewing people with learning disabilities and little/no speech. *British Journal of Learning Disabilities, 32*(4), 166–169.

Cameron, L., & Murphy J. (2002). Enabling young people with a learning disability to make choices at a time of transition. *British Journal of Learning Disabilities, 30*(3), 105–112.

Chappell, A. L. (2000). Emergence of participatory methodology in learning difficulty research: Understanding the context. *British Journal of Learning Disabilities, 28*(1), 38–43.

Clark, A., & Moss, P. (2001). *Listening to young children. The mosaic approach.* London: Joseph Rowntree Foundation/National Children's Bureau.

Clegg, J. (2004). Practice in focus: A hermeneutic approach to research ethics. *British Journal of Learning Disabilities, 32*(4), 186–190.

Dalrymple, J. (2005). Constructions of child and youth advocacy: Emerging issues in advocacy practice. *Children and Society,* 19(1), 3–15.

Dockrell, J. (2004). How can studies of memory and language enhance the authenticity, validity and reliability of interviews? *British Journal of Learning Disabilities, 32*(4), 161–165.

Donaldson, M. (1987). *Children's minds*. London: Fontana.

Felce, D. (2002). *Gaining views from people with learning disabilities: Authenticity, validity and reliability*. Paper presented at the seminar series: Methodological issues in interviewing children and young people with learning difficulties. Funded by ESRC 2001–3, School of Education, University of Birmingham.

Fielding, M. (2004). Transformative approaches to student voice: Theoretical underpinnings, recalcitrant realities. *British Educational Research Journal, 30*(2), 295–311.

Finlay, W., & Lyons, E. (2002). Acquiescence in interviews with people who have mental retardation. *Mental retardation, 40*, 14–29.

Freedman, R. I. (2001). Ethical challenges in the conduct of research involving persons with mental retardation. *Mental retardation, 39*(2), 130–141.

French, S., & Swain, J. (1997). Changing disability research: Participating and emancipatory research with disabled people. *Physiotherapy, 83*(1), 26–32.

Germain, R. (2004). An exploratory study using cameras and talking mats to access the views of young people with learning disabilities on their out of school activities. *British Journal of Learning Disabilities, 32*(4), 170–174.

Greene, S., & Hogan, D. (Eds.) (2005). *Researching children's experience: Approaches and methods*. London: Sage.

Grove, N., Porter, J., Bunning, K., & Olsson, C. (1999), See what I mean: Interpreting the meaning of communication by people with severe and profound learning difficulties: Theoretical and methodological issues. *Journal of Applied Research in Intellectual Disabilities, 12*(3), 190–203.

Hart, S. N. (2002.) Making sure the child's voice is heard. *International Review of Education, 48*(3–4), 251–258.

Hatton, C., & Ager, A. (2002). Quality of life measurement and people with intellectual disabilities: A reply to Cummins. *Journal of Applied Research in Intellectual Disabilities, 15*, 254–260.

Homan, R. (2001). The principle of assumed consent: The ethics of gatekeeping. *Journal of Philosophy of Education, 35*(3), 329–343.

Kirby, P. (1999). *Involving young researchers: How to enable young people to design and conduct research*. Plymouth: Save the Children.

Kirby, P., Lanyon, C., Kronin, K., & Sinclair, R. (2003). *Building a culture of participation*. London: CYPU.

Knox, M., Mok, M., & Permenter, T. R. (2000). Working with the experts: Collaborative research with people with an intellectual disability. *Disability and Society, 15*(1), 49–61.

Lewis, A. (2004). And when did you last see your father? Exploring the views of children with learning difficulties/disabilities. *British Journal of Special Education, 31*(1), 4–10.

Lewis, A., & Lindsay, G. E. (Eds.). (2000). *Researching children's perspectives*. Buckingham: Open University Press.

Lewis, A., & Porter, J. (2004). Interviewing children and young people with learning disabilities: Guidelines for researchers and multi-professional practice. *British Journal of Learning Disabilities, 32*, 1–7.

Lewis, A., Robertson, C., & Parsons, S. (2005). *Experiences of disabled students and their families. Phase 1*. Birmingham: Disability Rights Commission/University of Birmingham, School of Education. Retrieved from http://www.drc.org.uk/publicationsandreports/reseducation.asp?cats2show=6&section=resed&sectionid=5

Marchant, R., & Cross, M. (2002). *How it is*. London: NSPCC.

Mills, C., & Keil, F. (2005). The development of cynicism. *Psychological Science, 16*, 385–390.

Nind, M., Benjamin S., Sheeny K., Collins, J., & Hall, K. (2005). Methodological challenges in researching inclusive school cultures. In K. Sheeny, M. Nind, J. Rix, & K. Simmons (Eds.), *Ethics and research in inclusive education. Values into practice* (ch. 15). London: RoutledgeFalmer.

Northway, R. (2000). Ending participatory research? *Journal of Learning Disabilities, 4*(1), 27–36.

Oliver, M. (1997). Emancipatory research: realist goal or impossible dream? In C. Barnes,. & G. Mercer, (Eds.), *Doing disability research* (15–31). Leeds: Disability Press.

Parsons, S., Daniels, H., Porter, J., & Robertson, C. (2004). *Developing the use of ICT to enhance community participation with people with learning disabilities*. Final report for Home Farm Trust, Bristol. School of Education, University of Birmingham.

Pearpoint, J. (2002). *Hints for graphic facilitators*. Toronto: Inclusion Press.

Porter, J. (2003). *Interviewing children and young people with learning disabilities*. SLD Experience, Summer 2003.

Porter, J., & Lacey, P. (2005). *Researching learning difficulties*. London: Sage

Porter, J., & Lewis, A. (2004). Interviewing children and young people with learning disabilities: Guidelines for researchers and multi professional practice. *British Journal of Learning Disabilities, 32*(4), 191–197.

Porter, J., Aspinall, A., Parsons, S., Simmonds, L., Wood, M., Culley, G., & Holroyd, A. (2005). Time to listen. *Disability and Society, 20*(5), 575–585.

Rodgers, J. (1999). Trying to get it right: Undertaking research involving people with learning difficulties. *Disability and Society, 14*(4), 421–433.

Schalock, R.L., Brown, I., Brown, R., Cummins, R.A., Felce, D., Matikka, L., Keith, K.D., & Permenter, T. (2002). Conceptualization, measurement, and application of quality of life for persons with intellectual disabilities: Report of an international panel of experts. *Mental Retardation, 40*(6), 457–470.

Schwartz, C., & Rabinovitz, S. (2003). Life satisfaction of people with intellectual disability living in community residences: Perceptions of the residents, their parents and staff members. *Journal of Intellectual Disability Research, 47*(2) 75–84.

Sigelman, C., Budd, E. C., Spanhel, C. L., & Schoenrock, C. J. (1981). When in doubt say yes: Acquiescence in interviews with mentally retarded persons. *Mental Retardation, 19*, 53–58.

Tozer, R. (2003). *Involving children with ASD in research about their lives.* Paper presented at the seminar series: Methodological issues in interviewing children and young people with learning difficulties. Funded by ESRC 2001–3, School of Education, University of Birmingham.

United Nations Children's Fund (UNICEF) (2004). *Summary report: Study on the impact of the implementation of the Convention on the Rights of the Child.* Florence: UNICEF Innocenti Research Centre.

Vincent, C., & Warren, S. (2005). 'This won't take long … ' Interviewing, ethics and diversity. In K. Sheeny, M. Nind, J. Rix, & K. Simmons (Eds.), *Ethics and research in inclusive education Values into practice* (ch. 9). London: RoutledgeFalmer.

Walmsley, J. (2004). Inclusive learning disability research: The (non disabled) researcher's role. *British Journal of Learning Disabilities, 32*, 65–71.

Ware, J. (2004). Ascertaining the views of people with profound and multiple learning disabilities. *British Journal of Learning Disabilities, 32*(4), 175–179.

Whittles, S. (1998). *Can you hear us? Including the views of disabled children and young people.* London: Save the Children.

Zarb, G. (1997). Researching disabling barriers. In C. Barnes, & G. Mercer (Ed.), *Doing disability research* (ch. 4). Leeds: Disability Press.

17

'Emancipatory' disability research and special educational needs

Colin Barnes and Alison Sheldon

INTRODUCTION

Disability Studies is a relatively new and rapidly expanding field that offers radical challenges to conventional thinking about the education of disabled children, and thus often appears at odds with more traditional approaches to the study of 'special education' and 'special educational needs' (SEN). In the UK, Disability Studies examines 'inclusive education' not 'special education', unmet educational needs not 'special educational needs' and disabled children not children with 'SEN'. The disabled people's movement has organised around the premise that no one aspect of the disablement of people with impairments should be treated in isolation (UPIAS, 1976). Disability scholars then would argue that the inferior education received by disabled people cannot be separated from their inferior status in society and cannot therefore be examined in isolation. Despite these differences, this chapter will argue that the emerging discipline has much to offer the field of special education (Conway, 2004) – not least in its ongoing critique of 'disability' research.

It is over ten years since British researcher and disability activist Mike Oliver coined the term 'emancipatory disability research' to refer to a radical new approach to researching disability (Oliver, 1992). Since then there has been much discussion in the UK about whether such an approach is a 'realistic goal' or an 'impossible dream' (Oliver, 1997). This chapter is a reflection on key issues and concerns associated with the 'emancipatory' research model, and a consideration of its potential in the arena of 'SEN' research.

The chapter is divided into two main sections; the first provides a brief introduction to the reconceptualisation of disability by disabled activists in the UK and to the notion of 'emancipatory' disability research. The second focuses on some core principles associated with this perspective, and the challenges it presents for those conducting research in the area of 'special' education. These core principles – were they enacted fully – might increase the chance that research would indeed be emancipatory, producing significant gains for disabled people at both micro and macro levels. In conclusion, it will be suggested that whilst the practice of 'emancipatory' disability research may remain an 'impossible dream', the process is something towards which all those involved in researching disability and 'SEN' could and should be striving.

THE EMERGENCE OF 'EMANCIPATORY' DISABILITY RESEARCH

Here the social model of disability will be briefly described before the emergence and ethos of 'emancipatory' disability research are considered.

The social model of disability

Whilst the predominant view of disability was once informed by religion, since the rise of scientific medicine in the eighteenth century, disability in industrialised countries has largely been understood in terms of health and illness, and viewed as a problem of individuals. The individual or medical model of disability – elaborated by non-disabled professionals and medical sociologists – focuses on disability as functional limitation, with disability commonly referring to any 'restriction or lack (resulting from an impairment) of ability to perform an activity in the manner or within the range considered normal for a human being' (Wood, 1981, pp. 27–29). According to the individual model then, people are disabled by their impairments, and it is the role of medicine and psychology to restore them to 'normality'. The problem of disability is thus located within the impaired individual.

These assumptions began to be questioned in the latter part of the twentieth century, with the politicisation of disability by disabled people in America, Britain and elsewhere. In Britain, the disabled people's movement redefined disability as a form of oppression on a par with racism and sexism. The social model of disability thus emerged from disabled people's own critiques of the individual model, including its view of causality, its assumptions about the existence and nature of

'normality', and its failure to recognise disabled people as the experts on their own situation (Oliver, 1996). A twofold definition of impairment and disability, analogous to the sex/gender distinction, was elaborated by the Union of the Physically Impaired against Segregation (UPIAS), a collective of disabled people. Here, impairment is defined as 'lacking part of or all of a limb, or having a defective limb, organ or mechanism of the body', whilst disability denotes 'the disadvantage or restriction of activity caused by a contemporary social organisation which takes no or little account of people who have … impairments and thus excludes them from participation in the mainstream of social activities' (UPIAS, 1976, pp. 3–4). No causal link is assumed between impairment and disadvantage; rather, disability is viewed purely as a social construction.

The insights of the social model of disability have been vitally important for disabled people, both personally and politically. They have instigated the development of Disability Studies as an academic discipline and prompted the elaboration of the 'emancipatory' research paradigm as an alternative to traditional ways of conducting disability research.

The emergence and ethos of 'emancipatory' disability research

It has long been argued that traditional research in the social sciences has mirrored and perpetuated the power relationships experienced by oppressed people in their day-to-day lives (Bourne, 1980; Stanley & Wise, 1993). Following in this tradition, research is often said to be an alienating experience for disabled research participants – it is something that is done to them over which they have little or no control (Oliver, 1992). The main benefit of research into disability is often to the researcher and their academic record – it does little to improve the position of disabled people and may even compound their problems (Oliver, 1990).

The shift away from the unquestioned dominance of the individual, medical model of disability has been accompanied by a shift in the way disability research is carried out. Disabled people have taken a lead from critical social science, feminism, and majority world writers like Freire (1972), and have produced critiques of both positivist and interpretative research methodologies (Oliver, 1990, 1992; Ward & Flynn, 1994). The new 'emancipatory' research paradigm now serves as an ideal towards which researchers working within a social model of disability can aspire – its aim – 'to make disability research more relevant to the lives of disabled people' (Oliver, 1992, p. 109) and thus to make research part of the solution not part of the problem. The 'emancipatory' paradigm then is concerned with: 'the systematic demystification of the structures and processes which create disability and the establishment of a workable dialogue between the research community and disabled people in order to facilitate the latter's empowerment' (Barnes, 1992, p. 122).

The emergence of the 'emancipatory' research model has stimulated considerable debate within the disability research community both in Britain and the rest of the world (see, for example, Albrecht, Seelman, & Bury, 2001; Barnes & Mercer, 1997; Rioux & Bach, 1994; Stone & Priestley, 1996). Above all, the 'emancipatory' research agenda warrants the transformation of the material and social relations of research production. In short, this means that disabled people and their organisations, rather than professional academics and researchers, should have control of the research process. This control should include both funding and the research agenda. Both areas will now be briefly considered.

Controlling funding

A decade ago, the bulk of disability research in Britain was financed by large government-sponsored agencies such as the Department of Health (DoH), the Medical Research Council (MRC) and the Economic and Social Research Council (ESRC). These bodies were dominated by traditional medical and academic concerns; and conventional assumptions about disability and disability-

related research. Today, however, the situation is somewhat different. A large number of recent research projects, focusing exclusively on disability and related issues, are funded by charitable agencies and trusts such as the Joseph Rowntree Foundation (JRF) and the National Lottery's Community Fund. Both these organisations prioritise user-led initiatives and concerns over those of the academy and professional researchers.

As a consequence in recent years there have been several pieces of research which arguably conform to an 'emancipatory' research model – albeit implicitly rather than explicitly. Perhaps most significantly, in 1989 the British Council of Disabled People (BCODP) – Britain's national umbrella for organisations controlled and run by disabled people – commissioned a large-scale study of the discrimination encountered by disabled people in the United Kingdom in support of their campaign for anti-discrimination legislation (Barnes, 1991). Other notable examples include Michael Oliver and Gerry Zarb's (1992) analysis of personal assistance schemes in Greenwich and subsequent BCODP research on direct payments (Zarb and Nadash, 1994).

Controlling the research agenda

Although the rhetoric has yet to be matched with meaningful outcomes, there is a growing emphasis on user participation, if not control, within the research programmes of the various research councils including the ESRC. Whilst these changes might not go as far as some might wish, and certainly their impact has yet to be comprehensively evaluated, they do mark something of a shift in the right direction. Whether this move towards user control will be extended to disabled children and young people remains to be seen however.

Recent innovative work has called for the incorporation of the social model into educational research, and its insights have begun to inform research into the barriers faced by children and young people categorised as possessing 'SEN' (for example, Clough &

Barton, 1995a, 1998; Morris, 2003). As yet however, the potential of the 'emancipatory' disability research model is largely untested in the context of 'SEN'. Indeed it is unlikely in today's world that disabled children – the 'users' of 'special' education – would ever be in a position to control both research funding and its agenda.

Transforming the relations of research production so that control lies with disabled people and their organisations is no easy task. Hence many researchers committed to emancipatory ideals settle instead for doing participatory or action research (Zarb, 1992). Both of these have a concern with praxis – 'purposive action (including political action) to alter the material and social world' (Jary and Jary, 1995, p. 517) – such that 'the intention to effect social practice stands shoulder to shoulder with the intention to understand it' (Kemmis, 1982, p. 17). Control of the research does not however lie completely with the research participants.

Beyond the crucial issue of control, this new paradigm is more a set of loosely defined principles than a set of rules for doing disability research (Zarb, 1992). The six core principles which are said to characterise the model centre on the role of the social model of disability, accountability, the question of objectivity, choice of methodology, the place of experience in the research process, and research outcomes (Stone & Priestley, 1996). These core principles will now be examined, and the particular challenges they may present for those researching 'special' education considered.

CORE PRINCIPLES OF AN 'EMANCIPATORY' DISABILITY RESEARCH MODEL

The role of the social model of disability

… research itself creates – rather than merely studies – the phenomenon of special education/disability, and hence the constructs which researchers themselves bring to the work are important determinants not only of the success of the study itself but indeed also of the nature and direction of the field itself. (Clough & Barton, 1995b, p. 3)

The initial question which any social researcher should ask themselves deals with ontological position: 'What is the nature of the phenomena or entities, or social "reality" that I wish to investigate?' (Mason, 1996, p. 11). Thus, a core principle of an 'emancipatory' research model is said to be: 'the adoption of a social model of disability as the ontological … basis for research production' (Priestley, 1997, p. 91). As described above, much disability research has assumed an individual model of disability as its ontological base. Disability is equated with lack of 'normal' functioning and its social and political realities are thus elided. Research that begins from such a premise cannot hope to further disabled people's self-emancipation. Instead, 'emancipatory' research *must* adhere to the social model of disability.

A decade ago adopting an overtly social model perspective may have been something of a novelty. This is no longer the case however. In Britain, for example, social model thinking underpins the work of the government-initiated Disability Rights Commission (DRC). Internationally, it has been incorporated into the World Health Organization's recently developed *International Classification of Functioning, Disability and Health* (WHO, 1999), which replaces its overtly individualistic and discredited predecessor the *International Classification of Impairment, Disability and Handicap* (Wood, 1981). As yet, however, the social model has made little impact on governmental thinking in the area of 'special educational needs'. Whilst lip service is now paid to the benefits of 'inclusive education' (for example, DfEE, 1997), it is doubtful how far this is carried through in practice. Whilst one of the features of such an approach is said to be the questioning of 'existing categories and language, including the validity of the discourse of "special needs" and "special educational needs"' (Barton, 2005, p. 3), such a critical stance is not, as yet, forthcoming from the UK government.

The research community too needs to question its assumptions about 'SEN', since 'what we as researchers think and, importantly, where we are coming from, inevitably influences how we construct things' (Clough & Barton, 1995b, p. 5). Sally Tomlinson (1982, p. 72) argues that uses of the term 'special needs' are 'more ideological than educational'. Hence, the ontology underpinning this social categorisation merits further consideration if research in this area is ever to conform to an 'emancipatory' paradigm. Like traditional notions of disability, hegemonic notions of 'SEN' as 'real (that is, observable and objectively describable) phenomena in the world' (Dyson, 1998, p. 2) must also be rigorously questioned (Barton, 2005).

In the UK, the term 'special educational needs' first received official recognition in the 1978 Warnock Report. The report advocated the abolition of previous medical categories of 'handicap' – still in use in many parts of the world – in favour of the broader concept of 'SEN'. Arguably though, this apparent demedicalisation was little more than a 'cosmetic exercise'. Indeed, the very concept of 'SEN' 'retains the assumption that people categorised in this way are somehow "less than human". The emphasis is still on the inadequacy of the individual: it is s/he who is different; it is s/he who is at fault; and, most importantly, it is s/he who must change' (Barnes, 1991, p. 33).

In reality then, little has changed with this shift from a categorical to non-categorical system. Take the 2001 *Special Educational Needs Code of Practice* definition for example. Here, we are told, children have 'special educational needs' 'if they have a *learning difficulty* which calls for *special educational provision* to be made for them' (DfES, 2001, p. 6, original emphasis). A learning difficulty, in turn 'may be the result of a physical or sensory disability, an emotional or behavioural problem, or developmental delay' (Cabinet Office, 2005, p. 26). Disability here is clearly defined *not* according to a social model perspective, but as individual functional limitation. The failure of the education system to provide for disabled children's needs is not

questioned. This does not provide a sound starting point for research which strives to be emancipatory.

Furthermore, the ontological assumption that disabled people's needs are in some way 'special' is seen to be intensely problematic (Corbett, 1996), and, indeed, to serve professional interest first and foremost. As Tomlinson argues:

> Needs are relative, historically, socially and politically. The important point is that some groups have the power to define the needs of others, and to decide what provision shall be made for these predetermined needs. The unproblematic acceptance of 'special need' in education rests upon the acceptance that there are foolproof assessment processes which will correctly diagnose and define the needs of children. But the rhetoric of special needs may have become more of a rationalisation by which people who have power to define and shape the system of special education and who have vested interests in the assessment of, and provision of, more and more children as special, maintain their influence and interests. The rhetoric of special needs may be humanitarian, the practice is control and vested interests. (Tomlinson, 1982, p. 75)

Researchers and other professionals, then, determine inclusion in the category 'children with special educational needs'. It is not an objective category, but a category based on 'unacceptable assumptions that legitimate and maintain existing exclusionary, discriminatory policies and practices' (Barton, 2005, p. 3). Clearly then, the notion of 'SEN' does not sit comfortably alongside a social model perspective. 'Emancipatory' disability research *cannot* be built upon ontological foundations that construct disabled children and young people as having needs that are 'special'. Instead, it must be recognised that they are children like any others, but their needs are not currently met by our education system. Research might then seek to facilitate a 'fundamental restructuring' of that system (Triano, 2000, p. 13).

Accountability

Accountability to the disabled community is a key component of the 'emancipatory' research model. This poses particular problems for all researchers working within a market-led environment where continued employment and future career prospects are all too often determined by the ability to secure lucrative and long-term research contracts. Most of the organisations led by disabled people are local, hand-to-mouth operations with very limited resources (Barnes, Mercer, & Morgan, 2000). In such organisations funding for research is usually accorded a low priority and, when it is needed, the demand is usually for small-scale, locally based projects that are relatively short term in character.

The standard for accountability was set, however, with the BCODP discrimination project (Barnes, 1991). The research was conceived by representatives of the BCODP, with funding from the JRF and charity projects. It began in 1990 and was coordinated throughout by a research advisory group of five people, only one of whom was non-disabled. The group met on a bi-monthly basis to comment on and review progress. The first five months of 1990 were spent discussing the aims and objectives of the research with key figures in Britain's disabled people's movement. Data analyses and drafts of chapters were circulated to the advisory group and representatives of disabled people's organisations, along with requests for comments and recommendations which were then discussed at advisory group meetings. When the final report was completed a protracted process of dissemination was undertaken (see below). Similar levels of accountability have been achieved by other BCODP research projects including the work on direct payments (Zarb & Nadash, 1994) and the more recent *Creating Independent Futures* project (Barnes et al., 2000).

Ensuring accountability becomes a particular challenge when the views and participation of disabled children and young people are sought. Children are assumed incapable of finding solutions to their own problems. Instead, adults are deemed to be the 'experts', who 'know what is best for children' (Davis, 2004, p. 144) and frequently make decisions about children's lives without consulting

them. However, participatory research with disabled children and young adults has successfully challenged stereotypical assumptions of 'disabled childhood as static, vulnerable and dependent, and disabled children as lacking agency, imagination and creativity' (Davis & Hogan, 2004, p. 185).

Jenny Morris (2003) for example, documents her involvement in three research projects, all of which set out to involve disabled children and young people. Each project had a reference group comprising disabled young people who had similar experiences to the research participants. These reference groups had an input into the research at various points: deciding what information should be gathered, designing the information schedule and advising on how best to elicit information from disabled children and young people; commenting on a preliminary analysis of the data generated and identifying key themes; and making suggestions for disseminating the research findings.

Whilst young disabled people are without doubt 'critical social actors' (Davis & Watson, 2001, p. 672), they face various barriers to attending meetings and having meaningful involvement in such reference groups. This necessitates incredible attention to detail on the behalf of researchers, including the physical environment of meeting venues, the quality of assistance provided and the way in which meetings are run. It also involves negotiating with adult gatekeepers, who frequently act to disempower young people, yet may need to consent to their participation (Morris, 2003). There are enormous challenges then in making research accountable to disabled children, which further work in this area may help to highlight. As Jenny Morris (2003, p. 23) suggests, it is vitally important that details of what does and does not work are shared, and that 'we are brave enough to share our experiences of not getting it right'.

The problem of objectivity

Historically, disability research has been dominated by medical and academic interests. These have generally been seen as *objective* whilst alternate views, such as a social model perspective, have been viewed as politically biased and/or subjective. As indicated above in many ways this is no longer the case. Nonetheless, all social scientists, particularly those who endorse a politically sensitive or minority group perspective, are vulnerable to accusations of bias. Disability activist Paul Hunt (1981, p. 42) suggests that research can never be detached and impartial:

> Faced with any socially oppressed group, social scientists have a choice of only two alternatives: either a firm commitment to serve the interests of the oppressed group to end their oppression, or a commitment to serve the interests of the oppressors to continue their oppressive practices ... There is no middle way.

It is vital then for researchers to overtly serve the interests of disabled people in challenging their oppression. Hence, a core principle of 'emancipatory' research is said to be: 'the surrender of claims to objectivity through overt political commitment to the struggles of disabled people for self emancipation' (Stone & Priestley, 1996, p. 706). As disabled researchers and activists, the authors of this chapter make no claims to be detached or impartial. Disablist oppression however exists not just in 'the thoughts and actions of individuals or groups', but is 'objectively structured by the social and material relations of capitalism' (Oliver, 1999, p. 184). It can be examined then as an objective reality, and 'science can be placed at the service of the oppressed group to help them free themselves' (Hunt, 1981, p. 42). It is thus difficult to support the notion that those involved in disability research should put aside any claims to objectivity. One *can* be objective about oppression, even whilst experiencing it oneself. Indeed, as Hunt (1981, p. 43) suggests, it is 'precisely those who try to take a detached view of oppression who *cannot be objective*' (original emphasis).

In response, all that researchers can do is make their position clear at the outset. This means stating clearly their ontological and epistemological positions and ensuring that their choice of research methodology and data collection strategies are logical, rigorous and open to scrutiny. Information such as this is vitally important in helping disabled children make a decision about whether they want to participate in research (Morris, 2003).

The choice of methods

Since its inception the 'emancipatory' disability research model has generally been associated with qualitative rather than quantitative data collection strategies, in part because such strategies allow more scope for participants to take control over their words and thus affect the direction of the research (Shakespeare, 1996). In contrast, 'special' educational needs research has traditionally relied on positivist research strategies. Whilst educational researchers have also recognised the benefits of qualitative research, there are as yet 'relatively few published qualitative research studies on the theme of special educational needs' (Vulliamy and Webb, 1995, p. 265). Perhaps such studies pose a particular challenge when disabled children/young people are involved as research participants. Traditional methods such as face-to-face interviews may not be appropriate, and more creativity may be needed on behalf of researchers. A wide variety of innovative alternative methods have been utilised when working with children, including drawing, role play, using toys to tell a story and participating in children's games (Davis, 1998). It is important then to look beyond tried and tested orthodoxies. As one researcher has suggested:

> There are no rules for research with children! When apparent 'formal methods' do not work, it is important to acknowledge 'just hanging out' time with groups of children as valuable data in itself. It's OK to bin the questionnaires or work-sheets and follow your instinct, or the children's lead ... (Smith, in Gallagher, 2005, p. 5)

Quantitative research methods have been somewhat discredited within Disability Studies in the wake of various large-scale surveys conducted in Britain. The infamous Office of Population Censuses and Surveys (OPCS) disability surveys for example (Martin, Meltzer, & Elliot, 1988) adhered to an individual model of disability and were used to count and classify disabled individuals. Whilst their findings are still cited by those working in the field of Disability Studies, they stand accused of disempowering their disabled research participants and producing little in the way of positive change (Abberley, 1992). Politicians and policy-makers, however, make use of figures and statistics to add weight to their arguments and to justify particular actions or policy developments. Surely then quantitative research must also have some potential?

The disabled people's movement has used quantitative data not to research individual disabled people, but to highlight the various deprivations encountered by people with accredited impairments, and to research disabling barriers in society. The BCODP research on discrimination mentioned above, for example, was heavily reliant on government figures to underline the case for anti-discrimination legislation. Gerry Zarb and Pamela Nadash (1994) utilised both quantitative and qualitative research methods to substantiate their argument. The *Creating Independent Futures* project (Barnes et al., 2000) employed a similar array of research strategies. Similarly, Vulliamy and Webb (1995, p. 265) have outlined recent calls for a 'judicious blending of quantitative and qualitative approaches' when conducting research in 'special' education. All data collection strategies then may have their strengths and weaknesses when researching disability/ 'SEN'. What is most important is that the choice of research methods be determined by the needs of the research participants and/or disabled people generally.

The role of experience

The place of individual experience within 'emancipatory' disability research, and Disability Studies generally, is hotly contested.

On the one hand, it is argued that disabled people are the experts on their own situations and should have their long-silenced voices heard. On the other, it is argued that disabled individuals should not be the subjects of research – rather it is the disabling society that should be examined.

Within Disability Studies it is widely acknowledged that an 'essential element in the politicisation of disability has been the recognition that the personal is political' (Barton & Oliver, 1997: xii). For disabled feminists particularly, an engagement with personal experience is viewed as 'an essential part of developing an understanding of disability' (Thomas, 2001, p. 54). Others argue compellingly that: 'Seeking out the constructions of the oppressed ... is a political act which critiques the constructions of the oppressors and makes possible emancipatory action which will transform the oppressive relationships of the groups involved' (Dyson, 1998, p. 6).

The question of 'voice' is also said to be crucial in relation to educational research that strives to be non-oppressive (see, for example, Clifton, 2004; Gwynn, 2004). Children's voices are seldom sought or heard, let alone taken seriously. This is particularly the case with disabled children and young people, to whom multiple assumptions of incompetency are ascribed. According to the UN Convention on the Rights of the Child however: 'Disabled children have the human right to express their views and for these to be taken into account' (Morris, 1999, p. 1). It is said to be *essential* then that these views are not discounted. Giving priority to the voices of disabled children in the research process not only upholds their human rights, it also provides a 'more accurate evidence base for informing improvements in policy' (Garth & Aroni, 2003, p. 573). Arguably then, there is 'considerable urgency attached to the agenda of raising the voices of young disabled people' (Gwynn, 2004, p. 107).

This, of course, presents enormous challenges for researchers, especially when children have communication or cognitive impairments (Morris, 2003). It must be assumed however that *all* children and young people are capable of expressing their views. Furthermore, they must be enabled to 'challenge the structural, cultural and individual conditions which create disability' (Davis & Watson, 2001, p. 671). Researchers simply have to make the effort to learn the different ways in which they communicate and find ways of understanding their experiences (Davis, 2004; Morris, 2003).

However, as stated above, the place of 'experience' is much debated amongst disability activists and researchers (Finkelstein, 1996; Sheldon, 1999). We are warned about extolling the virtues of 'giving voice', and urged to beware of the 'sloppy and sentimental view that what is often described as "giving disabled people a voice", suggesting an act of generosity, automatically improves the quality of their lives' (Riddell, Wilkinson, & Baron, 1998, p. 79). As with disabled adults, by focusing on the individual experiences of children labelled as having SEN, we may undermine or ignore the significance of the environment in which those experiences are shaped – both inside and outside the educational context. In so doing, we may run the risk of reverting to an individual model framework. As Jenny Bourne (1980, p. 339) famously argued of research into black people's disadvantage: 'It was not Black people who should be examined, but White society'. Similarly it could be argued that it is not those deemed to have 'special educational needs' that should be examined, but the system that creates and sustains the SEN category.

There, is indeed, a very real danger that the use of personal experience as the only analytical tool 'can obscure the collective nature of disablement as a form of social oppression' (Stone & Priestley, 1996, p. 705). Whilst experience may be 'a necessary starting point', it should not be viewed as 'an end in itself' (Kelly, Burton, & Regan, 1994, p. 29). Instead, it is vital that researchers 'locate individual's narratives in the wider socio-cultural context, and explore narratives principally, though not exclusively, for what they tell us about disablism and other sources of oppres-

sion' (Thomas, 1999, p. 151).

If is suggested that in order to facilitate the removal of inequality in education, solutions must be sought at various levels – at the macro level 'through legislation, policy and guidance'; and at the micro level, because 'individuals, both staff and pupils can make significant differences to young people's lives' (Clifton, 2004, p. 89). It is at this micro level that listening to the insider perspective becomes most important. At the macro level, however, it may be that such accounts have little or no value. By no means *all* research which incorporates 'emancipatory' principles is concerned with disabled people's individual experiences. Barnes (1991), for example, did not set out to 'give voice' to disabled people. They were not the focus of study. Instead the attention was turned on the oppressive society in which disabled people are forced to live their lives. If disabled people's experiences *are* discussed, it is vital that they are couched firmly within an environmental and cultural context in order to highlight the disabling consequences of a society that is increasingly organised around the needs of a mythical, affluent, non-disabled majority. This is equally true in relation to research in SEN. As Sally Tomlinson (1982, p. 73) has argued, the rhetoric of 'special needs' involves 'seeing children outside a social context'. Thus, 'It is essential when considering the question of "voice" in relation to educational research that we are aware of, and seek to learn from, the struggles disabled people have been and still are involved in outside the educational context' (Barton, 1998, p. 29).

Practical outcomes

Much research involving disabled participants has been criticised for failing to have 'any serious effect on services for disabled people and their quality of life'. Instead, the chief beneficiaries are said to be the researchers themselves (Oliver, 1992, p. 109). Similarly, critiques of educational research often centre on its 'lack of relevance to schools and classrooms' (Barton, 1998, p. 32). Here at least the two disciplines are in accord: 'There are clear parallels between the criticisms leveled at disability research and those made of educational research by classteachers regarding its irrelevance to those researched, the distorted representation of their experience and the failure to bring about change' (Vulliamy and Webb, 1995, p. 269).

Within Disability Studies, then, we are urged 'only to undertake research where it will be of some practical benefit to the self empowerment of disabled people and/or the removal of disabling barriers' (Stone and Priestley, 1996, p. 706). The same is argued of research and consultation with children and young people: 'don't involve them unless there is really something in it for them' (Duffy, in Gallagher, 2005, p. 4).

A disabled woman interviewed by Kitchin (2000, p. 29) is quoted as saying: 'I would be cynical about what actually happens with research. The majority of times it just sits on a desk'. Research which seeks to make changes cannot simply sit on a desk. It must share knowledge and ideas with disabled people. It must influence policy-makers. It must also highlight the inherent contradictions of such short-term reformist solutions. It is vital then that research findings are disseminated appropriately, in a variety of formats, since 'even good research is wasted if it does not reach those who need to be reached' (Ward & Flynn, 1994, p. 44). It is not enough simply to write academic journal articles or book chapters to be read by fellow academics and researchers. Findings must not only be read by fellow researchers, they must also be disseminated widely, in accessible ways throughout the disabled community. As Penny Germon argues, it makes little sense to promote an 'emancipatory' research model 'when the findings are inevitably inaccessible to an audience of disabled activists' (Germon, 1998, p. 251).

The data from the BCODP research on institutional discrimination were disseminated in a variety of formats. This included presentations by those involved in the research project at various locations; the pro-duction of various articles in journals, magazines and the popular press; a book; and an eight-page summary leaflet. Two thousand leaflets were produced and distributed free of charge to all BCODP member groups, so that the research made an important contribution to the further politicisation of disabled people both in the UK and across Europe (Hurst, 1995). The research played a crucial role in getting anti-discrimination legislation onto the statute books in the UK. Similarly, the production and dissemination of the projects on direct payments and personal assistance schemes made a significant contribution to the argument for the introduction of the 1996 Community Care (Direct Payments) Act. This is not to suggest that these projects in themselves are responsible for these outcomes. They are not. They did, however, provide some substance to the arguments for changes in policy put forward by disabled activists and their allies. In so doing they also contributed to the further mobilisation of the disabled people's movement.

Dissemination of research findings to disabled children and young people requires innovative approaches. Dan Goodley and Michelle Moore (2000, p. 876) have successfully used cartoons and pictures to disseminate research findings to people with the label of learning difficulties, a strategy that might be equally useful for disabled young people. Ideally though, those young people with a direct interest in the research should be consulted about how the findings would best be disseminated (Morris, 2003). Goodley and Moore (2000, p. 876) caution however that: 'academic researchers find their careers obstructed if they attach greater precedence to research outputs valued by disabled people than to the blueprint laid down within academic departments. This turns out to be especially true when it comes to dissemination'. Whilst there have been definitive moves forward, then, it is clear that the 'emancipatory' research paradigm is still not fully supported in the current market-led academic environment. This perhaps presents the greatest challenge of all.

CONCLUSION

This chapter has described the emergence of a radical new approach to researching disability, and highlighted both its potential and the challenges it poses for research in 'special' education. By definition 'emancipatory' disability research should be judged by its ability to empower disabled people – both inside and outside the actual research process. Whether this is achievable is highly debatable however. The 'emancipatory' research paradigm, then, must be seen not in terms of one single project or projects but as a process. This process is still in its early stages, especially in the context of 'special' education where the principles of user-led 'emancipatory' research have yet to be fully explored. Each piece of research must build on and develop what has gone before. It must seek to make a further contribution to our understanding and our ability to erode the various forces – economic, political and cultural – which continue to create and sustain disability at both the macro and micro levels. This is not an easy task. Neither, however, is it an 'impossible dream'. It is a goal for which everyone involved in doing disability research – both within and without the 'special' educational setting – should be aiming. If we aren't, then what's the point in doing it?

REFERENCES

Abberley, P. (1992). Counting us out: a discussion of the OPCS disability surveys, *Disability, Handicap and Society*, 7(2), 139–155.

Albrecht, G. L., Seelman, K., & Bury, M. (Eds.). (2001). *Handbook of disability studies*. London: Sage.

Barnes, C. (1991). *Disabled people in Britain and discrimination: A case for anti-discrimination legislation*. London: Hurst and Co. Available at: http://www.leeds.ac.uk/disability-studies/archiveuk/index.html

Barnes, C. (1992). Qualitative research: valuable or irrelevant? *Disability, Handicap and Society*, 7(2), 115–124.

Barnes, C., & Mercer, G. (Eds.). (1997). *Doing disability research*. Leeds: The Disability Press. Available at: http://www.leeds.ac.uk/disability-studies/archiveuk/index.html

Barnes, C., Mercer, G., & Morgan, H. (2000). *Creating independent futures, Stage one report*. Leeds: Disability Press.

Barton, L. (1998). Developing an emancipatory research agenda: Possibilities and dilemmas. In P. Clough & L. Barton (Eds.), *Articulating with difficulty: Research voices in inclusive education* (pp. 29–39). London: Paul Chapman Publishing.

Barton, L. (2005). *Special educational needs: an alternative look*. Available at: http://www.leeds.ac.uk/disability-studies/archiveuk/index.html

Barton, L., & Oliver, M. (Eds.) (1997). *Disability studies: Past, present and future*. Leeds: The Disability Press. Available at: http://www.leeds.ac.uk/disability-studies/archiveuk/index.html

Bourne, J. (1980). Cheerleaders and ombudsmen: The sociology of race relations in Britain. *Race and Class*, 21(4), 331–352.

Cabinet Office. (2005). *Improving the life chances of disabled people*. London: HMSO.

Clifton, M. (2004). 'We like to talk and we like someone to listen': Cultural difference and minority voices as agents of change. In F. Armstrong & M. Moore (Eds.), *Action research for inclusive education: Changing places, changing practices, changing minds* (pp. 77–91). London: RoutledgeFalmer.

Clough, P., & Barton, L. (Eds.). (1995a). *Making difficulties: Research and the construction of SEN*. London: Paul Chapman Publishing.

Clough, P., & Barton, L. (1995b). Introduction: Self and the research act. In P. Clough & L. Barton (Eds.), *Making difficulties: Research and the construction of SEN* (pp. 1–5). London: Paul Chapman Publishing.

Clough, P., & Barton, L. (Eds.). (1998). *Articulating with difficulty: Research voices in inclusive education*. London: Paul Chapman Publishing.

Conway, M. A. (2004). Introduction: Disability studies meets special education, *Review of Disability Studies*, 1(3), 3–9.

Corbett, J. (1996). *Bad-mouthing: The language of special needs*. London: Falmer Press.

Davis, J. M. (1998). Understanding the reflexive meanings of children: A reflexive process. *Children and Society*, 12, 325–335.

Davis, J. M. (2004). Disability and childhood: Deconstructing the stereotypes. In J. Swain, S. French, C. Barnes, and C. Thomas. (Eds.), *Disabling barriers – enabling environments* (2nd ed.) (pp. 142–148). London: Sage.

Davis, J. M., & Hogan, J. (2004). Research with children: Ethnography, participation, disability and self-empowerment. In C. Barnes & G. Mercer (Eds.), *Implementing the social model of disability: Theory and practice* (pp. 172–190). Leeds: Disability Press.

Davis, J. M., & Watson, N. (2001). Where are the children's voices? Analysing social and cultural exclusion in 'special' and 'mainstream' schools. *Disability and Society, 16*(5): 671–687.

Department for Education and Employment (DfEE). (1977). *Excellence for all children: Meeting special educational needs.* London: Department for Education and Employment.

Department for Education and Skills (DfES). (2001). *Special educational needs code of practice.* Nottingham: Department for Education and Skills.

Dyson, A. (1998). Professional intellectuals from powerful groups: wrong from the start? In P. Clough & L. Barton (Eds.), *Articulating with difficulty: Research voices in inclusive education* (pp. 1–15). London: Paul Chapman Publishing.

Finkelstein, V. (1996, April). Outside, 'inside out'. *Coalition*, 30–36.

Freire, P. (1972). *Pedagogy of the oppressed.* Harmondsworth: Penguin.

Gallagher, M. (2005). Top tips for research and consultation with children and young people. Available at: http://www.crfr.ac.uk/cpd/listeningtochildren/

Garth, B., & Aroni, R. (2003). 'I value what you have to say': Seeking the perspective of children with a disability, not just their parents. *Disability and Society, 18*(5), 561–576.

Germon, P. (1998). Activists and academics: part of the same or a world apart? In T. Shakespeare (Ed.), *The disability reader: Social science perspectives* (pp. 245–255). London: Cassell.

Goodley, D., & Moore, M. (2000). Doing disability research: Activist lives and the academy. *Disability and Society, 15*(6): 861–882.

Gwynn, J. (2004). 'What about me? I live here too!' Raising voices and changing minds. In F. Armstrong & M. Moore (Eds.), *Action research for inclusive education: Changing places, changing practices, changing minds* (pp. 105–122). London: RoutledgeFalmer.

Hunt, P. (1981). Settling accounts with the parasite people: A critique of 'A Life Apart' by E. J. Miller & G. V. Gwynne, *Disability Challenge, 1*, 37–50. Available at: http://www.leeds.ac.uk/disability-studies/archiveuk/ index.html

Hurst, R. (1995). International perspectives and solutions. In G. Zarb (Ed.), *Removing disabling barriers* (89–95). London: Policy Studies Institute.

Jary, D., & Jary, J. (Eds.). (1995). *Collins dictionary of sociology: Second edition.* Glasgow: HarperCollins.

Kelly, L., Burton, S., & Regan, L. (1994) Researching women's lives or studying women's oppression? Reflections on what constitutes feminist research. In M. Maynard & J. Purvis (Eds.), *Researching women's lives from a feminist perspective* (pp. 27–48). London: Taylor & Francis.

Kemmis, S. (1982). Introduction: Action research in retrospect and prospect. In S. Kemmis (Ed.), *The action research reader* (pp. 11–31). Waurn Ponds, Australia: Deakin University.

Kitchin, R. (2000). The researched opinions on research: disabled people and disability research. *Disability & Society, 15*(1), 25–47.

Martin, J., Meltzer, H., & Elliot, D. (1988). *The prevalence of disability among adults.* London: HMSO.

Mason, J. (1996). *Qualitative researching.* London: Sage.

Morris, J. (1999). *Disabled children, the Children's Act and human rights.* Paper presented at Young and Powerful conference, May 26, Disability North. Available at: http://www.leeds.ac.uk/disability-studies/ archiveuk/index.html

Morris, J. (2003). *Including all children: finding out about the experiences of disabled children.* Presentation at Childhood Disability Research Forum. Available at: http://www.leeds.ac.uk/disability-studies/archiveuk/ index.html

Oliver, M. (1990). *The politics of disablement.* Tavistock: Macmillan. Available at: http://www.leeds.ac.uk/ disability-studies/archiveuk/index.html

Oliver, M. (1992). Changing the social relations of research production. *Disability, Handicap and Society, 7*(2), 101–114.

Oliver, M. (1996). Defining impairment and disability: Issues at stake. In C. Barnes & G. Mercer (Eds.), *Exploring the divide: Illness and disability* (pp. 39–54). Leeds: Disability Press.

Oliver, M. (1997). Emancipatory research: Realistic goal or impossible dream? In C. Barnes & G. Mercer (Eds.), *Doing disability research.* Leeds: Disability Press. Available at: http://www.leeds.ac.uk/disability-studies/archiveuk/index.html

Oliver, M. (1999). Final accounts and the parasite people. In M. Corker & S. French (Eds.), *Disability discourse* (pp. 183–192). Milton Keynes: Open University Press.

Oliver, M., & Zarb, G. (1992). *Personal assistance schemes in Greenwich: An evaluation.* London: University of Greenwich.

Priestley, M. (1997). Who's research? A personal audit. In C. Barnes & G. Mercer (Eds.), *Doing disability research* (pp. 88–107). Leeds: Disability Press. Available at: http://www.leeds.ac.uk/disability-studies/ archiveuk/index.html

Riddell, S., Wilkinson, H., & Baron, S. (1998). From emancipatory research to focus group: People with learning difficulties and the research process. In P. Clough & L. Barton (Eds.), *Articulating with difficulty: Research voices in inclusive education* (pp. 78–95). London: Paul Chapman Publishing.

Rioux, M. H., & Bach, M. (Eds.). (1994). *Disability is not measles: New research paradigms in disability.* Toronto: Roeher Institute.

Shakespeare, T. (1996). Rules of engagement: Doing disability research. *Disability and Society, 11*(2), 115–119

Sheldon, A. (1999). Personal and perplexing: Feminist

disability politics evaluated, *Disability and Society*, *14*(5), 645–659.

Stanley, L., & Wise, S. (1993). *Breaking out again: Feminist ontology and epistemology* (2nd ed.). London: Routledge.

Stone, E., & Priestley, M. (1996). Parasites, pawns and partners: Disability research and the role of non-disabled researchers. *British Journal of Sociology, 47*(4), 699–716.

Thomas, C. (1999). *Female forms: Experiencing and understanding disability*. Buckingham: Open University Press.

Thomas, C. (2001). Feminism and disability: The theoretical and political significance of the personal and experiential. In L. Barton (Ed.), *Disability, politics and the struggle for change* (pp. 48–58). London: David Fulton.

Tomlinson, S. (1982). *A sociology of special education*. London: Routledge & Kegan Paul.

Triano, S. L. (2000). Categorical eligibility for special education: The enshrinement of the medical model in disability policy. *Disability Studies Quarterly, 20*(4): 1–16. Retrieved October 20, 2005 from www.cds.hawaii.edu

Union of Physically Impaired Against Segregation (UPIAS) (1976). *Fundamental principles of disability*. London: Union of Physically Impaired Against Segregation. Available at: http://www.leeds.ac.uk/disability-studies/archiveuk/index.html

Vulliamy, G. & Webb, R. (1995). Special educational needs: From disciplinary to pedagogic research, in P. Potts, F. Armstrong & M. Masterton (Eds.), *Equality and diversity in education 2: National and international contexts* (pp. 261–278). London: Routledge/The Open University.

Ward, L., & Flynn, M. (1994). What matters most: Disability, research and empowerment. In M. H. Rioux & M. Bach (Eds.). *Disability is not measles: New research paradigms in disability* (pp. 29–48). Toronto: Roeher Institute.

Warnock Report. (1978). *Special educational needs: Report of the Committee of Enquiry into the education of children and young people*. London: HMSO.

World Health Organization (WHO). (1999). *International classification of functioning, disability and health*. Geneva: World Health Organization. Available at: http://www.who.int/icidh/

Wood, P. (1981). *International classification of impairment, disability and handicap*. Geneva: WHO.

Zarb, G. (1992). On the road to Damascus: First steps towards changing the relations of disability research production. *Disability, Handicap and Society, 7*(2), 125–138.

Zarb, G., & Nadash, P. (1994). *Cashing in on independence*. Derby: British Council of Disabled People. Available at: http://www.leeds.ac.uk/disability-studies/archiveuk/index.html

18

An epistemology of special education

Gary Thomas

KNOWING

In February 2002, Donald Rumsfeld, the US Secretary for Defense, gave a notorious news briefing in which he said: 'There are known knowns. These are things we know that we know. There are known unknowns. That is to say, there are things that we know we don't know. But there are also unknown unknowns. There are things we don't know we don't know' (12 February 2002, Department of Defense news briefing). Rumsfeld's analysis does not tell the whole story about the problems of knowledge and how we come by it and professional epistemologists would probably have difficulty accepting the simplicity of Rumsfeld's 'known knowns'. Epistemology takes as problematic the whole subject of knowledge, and the bald ascription of knowledge into categories such as this would not impress them. Epistemologists investigate questions of the variety:

- What is knowledge?
- Are there different kinds of knowledge?
- Are there good procedures for discovering knowledge?
- How can you know if you are wrong?

This chapter will examine some of these questions in the context of special education. There have been assumptions in the empirical evidence and rational arguments behind special education almost of a kind of special, privileged knowledge, and trust in the knowledge of special education has secured special education's reputation as a rational, sensible way of educating a portion of the population. But if one takes a questioning disposition to this knowledge, challenges to the legitimacy of special education can begin to emerge.

KNOWING IN EDUCATION AND SPECIAL EDUCATION

The knowledge that educators seek ranges across individual and social behaviour, economics, linguistics, the study of teaching subjects, and much more. Arguably, special education is even more complex: special educators have especially needed to confront issues concerning difference, measurement, assessment, special pedagogy and a range of other themes. The way that the community of inquiry in education, and special education, has reacted to this complexity differs. Inquirers in one tradition have tried to make education's inquiry similar to that of scientists studying chemistry or physics or biology, asking very precise questions and experimenting to discover the answers. Those in another, more recent, tradition suggest that we should behave more like anthropologists, infiltrating ourselves into educational cultures to observe in intricate detail what happens there. Yet others propose that we might behave more like historians, listening to the accounts and narratives of the people with whom we are concerned: students, parents, teachers. Still others contend that we might be eclectic and do all of these, depending on the kinds of questions that we want to pose.

The last point, about eclecticism, perhaps throws into sharper relief the real issue about the complexity of education – education is about a range of different issues and if we want to ask questions about these different issues we have to think seriously about the best ways of answering them. The basic questions are about what we are studying, and about knowledge, what it is, and how we come by it. Some people seem to have felt not only that they are sure about what there is to be studied in educational research, but also that they have cornered the market on finding the sunlit path to true knowledge about this subject. Other people are not so sure, and it is this lack of certainty that has led to such interest in questions about what we are studying and how we come by knowledge in education.

My aim in this chapter is briefly to examine the epistemology of special and inclusive education. First, I shall examine how epistemology can be thought about in this area. I shall then go on to look at the kind of knowledge traditionally held and promulgated by some special educators and the means by which this knowledge is secured.

It is as well to begin this examination by trying to unpack 'epistemology' in the context of special education. When philosophers talk about epistemology, they take a particularly structured view, framing the study of knowledge around ontology (the study of what there is to be known), and methodology (the study of the methods by which we discover knowledge). Recently, though, this focused view has broadened in the social sciences and the humanities. Here, the philosopher-historian Michel Foucault has had a significant influence on the way that epistemology is considered. Indeed, it could be argued that his work has been the principal stimulus in the questioning disposition of which I spoke at the beginning of this chapter. In two of Foucault's works, *The Archaeology of Knowledge* (Foucault, 1972) and *The Order of Things* (Foucault, 1970), he makes it clear that knowledge is never constituted in objective terms but rather is defined in a particular place and in a particular era by sets of habits, rules and expectations about what can and cannot be said. The ways we think, and the things we know (or think we know) are, for Foucault, products of our cultural, institutional, professional and personal histories and the intellectual environments that those histories have framed. Foucault uses the words *episteme* and *archive* to describe these intellectual environments. McNay (1994, p. 66) puts it thus: 'Like the episteme, the archive is defined as the general condition of possibility – the system of discursive regularities – which determines what can and cannot be spoken in a given historical era'.

The key words here are not only 'episteme' and 'archive', but perhaps more importantly 'discursive regularities'. For Foucault, much of what defines ways of knowing lies in *discourse* – patterns of contact and communication – and the *discursive* is central for Foucault's analysis of knowledge. Discourse, in other words, defines what counts as knowledge, and epistemology – the study of what we know and how we know it – centres in the human sciences around cultural, institutional and personal communications, all of these being constructed in an historical context. The foregrounding of discourse thus suggests that knowledge is *located* socially and historically.

Foucault's analyses help one to understand that social structures – in our case special schools, special assessments and special pedagogy – far from being God-given are made by people acting intentionally. The interesting insight which Foucault provides is that the intellectual apparatus which has emerged ostensibly to add objectivity, humanity and disinterested 'science' to an analysis of social structures in fact does nothing of the kind. In the highly complex world of human beings and human relations, this intellectual apparatus does little other than provide in new words and garb what we already recognise and know. The real knowledge, in other words, lies in the discourses permitted by the cultures that we live in, albeit that these are given added legitimacy by being reframed in the context of special education in the language of science and in the 'officialese' of professionals. Philp (1990, p. 67) puts it thus: 'The normal child, the healthy body, the stable mind … such concepts haunt our ideas about ourselves, and are reproduced and legitimated through the practices of teachers, social workers, doctors, judges, policemen and administrators'.

This is all relevant for our examination of special education and its knowledge, for this knowledge displays particular characteristics that have changed according to the predominant discourses of the time (see also Reid & Valle, 2004; Thomas & Loxley, 2005). It is important to remember that special education is a product of social and political frameworks – the ways people think at a particular time frame their views about what is good for children and how education should be made to happen. It is a product of Foucault's 'archive'. Remember that at one time, at the beginning of the twentieth century, young children were separated from their communities and expatriated from Britain to Australia for a 'better life' (see Newman & Roberts, 1996). The people who made the decision to do this acted not out of spite or malice, but out of a genuine belief that this was the best thing to do for these children. Their knowledge, ideas and beliefs were constructed by the discourses of the time.

So, in examining the knowledge of special education, it is worth looking briefly at the history of the subject and at the intellectual currents that appear to have shaped its development since its institutional beginnings. It is worth looking also at the discourses that have moulded the field as it exists today.

The beginnings of organised special education occurred in the eighteenth and nineteenth centuries, when schools for blind and deaf children were established, usually by philanthropists. But around the end of the nineteenth century a sea change occurred in thinking. Assumptions about what education might be for and about what might make a child worthy of special education shifted. Around this time, a cluster of ideas was emerging which gave strength to the notion that not simply those with conspicuous disabilities – the blind and the deaf – should be educated separately, but that those who were less able could and should be educated separately, for their own benefit and for the benefit of the majority. Thus, although a philanthropic impulse had stimulated the establishment of the first special schools, an entirely different kind of thinking – and a different kind of knowledge – was behind the growth that occurred from the beginning of the twentieth century.

There was a new world-view, a new episteme in Foucault's terms, constructed out of some streams of thought that were developing at the time. Three movements dominated the thinking that might be said to have given rise to the knowledge that led to the expansion of special education in the twentieth century. These were Social Darwinism, psychometrics and scientism, and I shall explore these, their consequences and their limitations.

Social Darwinism

If one is considering the knowledge of special education one cannot underestimate the importance of Darwinism for the thinking of ordinary people at the end of the nineteenth century. Darwin's ideas were new and exciting and, after some resistance from the ecclesiastical establishment, had acquired respectability and status. The new status, however, gave credence also to some biological fictions, most notably the idea that for society it was important that the 'weakest' should be prevented from infiltrating the genetic stock. If degenerates and ne'er-do-wells were to mix and interbreed unhindered with others, the argument went, the inevitable result would be the degeneration of the stock of the race. Social Darwinism, as this school of thought came to be called, was responsible for much of the mindset that at that time promoted interest in special schools – promoted interest in different kinds of teaching for supposedly different kinds of children.

One should remember how powerful these ideas were at the time. They led to the popularity of eugenics, a school of thought about the improvement of the stock of the race through selective breeding. Eugenics was part of mainstream thinking – part of the archive – that had influenced even those who claimed to be part of the new Socialist movement. Even prominent socialist intellectuals such as Sidney and Beatrice Webb (see McBriar, 1966) were persuaded by eugenic arguments. It was received knowledge that there should be constraints on the fertility of elements of the population, and the natural extension of the argument was that boundaries should be more firmly drawn around those elements that might disadvantage the majority. The consensus about the good sense embodied in eugenics in this climate of opinion is evidenced by the fact that at the end of the 1920s 24 American states had passed laws enabling sterilisation of elements of the population.

As a corollary, it is worth noting that Social Darwinism had its effects in a more general way upon popular thinking and popular knowledge. It was promulgated enthusiastically in Britain by the influential scientific polymath Sir Francis Galton, who in *Hereditary Genius, its Laws and Consequences* (1869), proclaimed that it would be perfectly possible to 'produce a highly gifted race of men by judicious marriages during several consecutive generations'. The futility ascribed to education in counteracting the effects of heredity in accounts such as this amounts almost to contempt. If education was not

entirely useless, it was certainly of no benefit for the purpose of raising the achievement of the least able. The feeling of the intellectual establishment of the time is summed up by one of Galton's protégés, Karl Pearson, who at the beginning of the twentieth century was able to claim that 'No training or education can create [intelligence] … You must breed it' (in Kevles, 1985). Clearly, such thought encouraged a view that intellectual strata should be separated and segregated for the purpose of such breeding. As a logical sequel, different kinds of education should be provided for the most and the least intelligent.

Psychometrics and the notion of intelligence

Roughly concurrent with all of this, psychology was establishing itself as a discipline, and a new branch of psychological 'science' was developing: psychometrics. If intelligence could be accurately measured, it would be possible to sort and sift among children to determine how they should be placed according to the segregative thinking propagated by a eugenic mindset.

At the turn of the century, Alfred Binet had developed the first mental tests in France, and in 1916 the American psychologist Lewis M. Terman developed what he called the 'intelligence quotient', or IQ, as a usable heuristic – a technology – for the explication of the mental age that Binet had been examining. This measuring technology, psychometrics, gave the promise of effectively calibrating levels of ability and sorting the population for the most and least intelligent. If this was possible, of course, it was possible also to separate out and educate differently children of differing levels of ability. Terman (1924, p. 336) had asserted that 'The first task of the school would be to establish the native quality of every pupil; second, to supply the kind of instruction suited to each grade of ability'.

It is important to note in parenthesis, though, that the feeling was not all one way, even at that time, about the benefits of psychometrics and the efficient separation according to strata of intelligence that it promised. The political scientist Walter Lippmann (1922) had published a series of articles in the USA in which he argued that intelligence testers cleaved to an erroneous dogma about the heritability of intelligence, and that 'Intelligence testing in the hands of men who hold this dogma could not but lead to an intellectual caste system'. The foresight of Lippmann was borne out by later events in the acceleration of special education provision. In the selective and segregative systems enabled by psychometrics were to be found precisely the caste system predicted and feared by Lippmann.

In the UK, much of this psychometric (and eugenic) thinking was crystallised in the writing of Cyril Burt, who was appointed the first psychologist for London in 1911. Burt had great faith in the new science of psychometrics, and this faith together with an arrogant confidence in the idea that intellectual functioning showed a fixedness determined by inherited potential, gave stimulus in Britain to a segregative education system based on the categorisation of the child. This was especially so as Burt was one of the principal architects of the 1944 Education Act insofar as it related to special education in Britain. Burt had officially advised the government thus: 'it is possible at a very early age to predict with some accuracy the ultimate level of a child's individual power' (cited in Hearnshaw, 1979, p. 115), and the 1944 Act subsequently constructed a highly segregative post-war education system with its 10 categories of handicap for which special schools would cater. The fact that Burt's work represented, as it was after his death discovered, a gross scientific fraud (see Hearnshaw, 1979) itself provides an interesting glimpse into the power of the discursive in influencing thought, and indeed distorting the processes used to arrive at knowledge.

Psychometrics lived (and still lives) in symbiosis with the notion of intelligence. Together, they gave credence from the early part of the twentieth century onwards to assertions about the significance of intelligence in children's failure at school. Not only could natively endowed intelligence explain difference and failure, its method of assessment – IQ tests – could, it was asserted, accurately separate out those who would benefit from certain kinds of education. Intelligence, and the way it was studied and measured, provides a powerful case study for the dangers which inhere in a certain kind of epistemology – one which elevates certain kinds of supposedly empirical analysis and rational theorisation – about teaching and learning.

Scientism

A great deal of the success of the new discourse, with a faith in psychometrics and a confidence in the correctness of Social Darwinism, was related to the success of natural science as a powerful new force in inquiry. Then, at the turn of the century, the successes of science meant that the methods of the natural sciences were looked upon increasingly favourably by the intelligent layperson. The influential philosopher-sociologist Herbert Spencer was able to promote the notion, in a reification of science's methods that has come to be known as 'scientism', that the only reliable knowledge of the universe was that found in the sciences. (It is important to distinguish here between scientism and science. While the word 'science' is generally taken to mean the wholly legitimate use of particular methods for studying particular subjects, 'scientism' describes the more questionable use of the same methods for studying or thinking about a far wider range of subjects.)

And this has continued. For the best part of the twentieth century, there has been the optimistic assumption that the path of progress in scientific knowledge would be a smooth one – that progress would follow naturally out of scientific advance, and science would broaden its virtuous ambit to advance and enrich study in fields other than the natural sciences. It was assumed that the methods of investigation that had been so successful for physics and chemistry would be appropriately used not just in those sciences but also in social inquiry. For many years, therefore, 'social scientists' emulated their peers in the natural sciences, in presumptions about the nature of knowledge, theoretical advance, research design and the use of inference. Psychologists and sociologists adopted the epistemological and methodological clothes of physicists and chemists – and educators, in turn, copied psychologists and sociologists. The agglomerations of putatively scientific knowledge and technique represented in psychology and sociology came to assume an enormous importance in the growth of educational institutions, and in particular in the growth of special education.

Inquiry in education – and in special education the phenomenon has occurred to an exaggerated degree – has tended to follow the methods of science, or at least what has been taken to be those methods (see Chambers, 1992, for a critique). At the heart of these methods has been experimental study used to advance theory. It was assumed that theory would, refined and improved, go on to explain and predict more effectively, that theory would stimulate research, and theory and research hand in hand would inform practice. The model is deeply flawed for education generally, as I have tried to indicate elsewhere (see Thomas, 1997), and in special education it has had particularly unfortunate effects (Thomas & Loxley, 2001). Academic special educators during the twentieth century regarded the theoretical products of the social sciences – Piagetian, psychoanalytic, psychometric and behavioural theoretical models – almost as a kind of pick'n'mix. The result has been, in the field of special education, an epistemic jumble, an agglomeration of bits and pieces from many and varied theoretical provenances, often contradictory in their tenets and widely different in their recommendations.

It is only of late that there has been recognition of the limits of supposedly scientific inquiry in determining the ways in which we should examine education. It has come to be recognised that in education, and in special education in particular, foci for analysis do not usually lend themselves to the analytical instruments borrowed from the major disciplines. A position increasingly taken of late is that far too much has been made of the potential contribution of these schools of thought and that they have exercised a disproportionate influence on special education, on our understanding of why children fail at school, and on our prescriptions for action when they do. Too much has been invested in their significance. Their status as frameworks within which thinking can be usefully constructed has been overplayed and the extent to which practice can usefully follow from research generated within their parameters has been exaggerated.

Indeed, a theme of late twentieth-century epistemology is that there are no certainties – and, more important, there are no special means of getting to knowledge about the human world. (This issue is also examined in Gallagher's Chapter 39 in this volume.) Special education forms a particularly interesting case study of this change of view. In the set of epistemological and ontological assumptions that are often summed up by the word 'paradigm', the traditional paradigm of special education – characterised, as I noted above, by scientism and separation – has had few notable successes. There is no body of research showing special education to have been more successful than mainstream education, despite the greatly increased resources directed to it (see OECD, 1994; Wang, Reynolds, & Walberg, 1995). Children with similar difficulties educated in mainstream or special schools leave school with similar results. The knowledge that this is the case has been available since the early 1960s. As Johnson put it then:

> It is indeed paradoxical that mentally handicapped children having teachers especially trained, having more money (per capita) spent on their education, and being enrolled in classes with fewer children and a program designed to provide for their unique needs, should be accomplishing the objectives of their education at the same or lower level than similar mentally handicapped children who have not had these advantages and have been forced to remain in the regular grades. (Johnson, 1962, p. 66)

Indeed, most of the assessments and pedagogies developed by special education have failed on mature evaluation to live up to the hopes their early use excited (see Thomas & Loxley, 2001). Despite the disappointing record, though, faith remains in the 'fix-its' of special education. Partly, this is because the discourse underpinning this faith – a discourse of diagnosis and supposed cure – has an enduring allure, an allure enriched by the epistemological lustre provided by association with the methods of science.

NEW METHOD: VALUING DIFFERENT KINDS OF KNOWLEDGE

Questioning has come both from inside special education and from the research community generally about the paucity of outcome from the knowledge produced by the traditional procedures of special education inquiry (see Gallagher, 2004). New methods have therefore come to be sought and tried. Qualitative methods have gained credibility as valid research tools in education and psychology and there are excellent examples of the use of such methods in critical analysis of special education (see, for example, Ferguson, Ferguson, & Taylor, 1992; Benjamin, 2002). While the genealogy of these methods is usually attributed in the methodological literature to the anthropologists and their emphasis on participant observation, it may be helpful to look more widely at their intellectual history.

The legacy of positivistic science when transplanted to a focus on human beings was that we should deny what we know, as people, and put faith in a certain kind of disinterested knowledge. Calls for recognition of the validity of other kinds of knowledge, resting in self report (on the part of respondents) and self-knowledge (on the part of the researcher and practitioner) are novel in social science but not recent in philosophical terms, stemming from philosophical thought in the early twentieth century. Hans-Georg Gadamer is credited with transforming the idea of inquiry from one in which an inquirer

aimed to understand something in as disinterested and unprejudiced a way as possible to one where 'preconceptions or prejudices are what makes understanding possible' (Outhwaite, 1990, p. 25). These preconceptions and prejudices, these 'sentiments, imaginings and fancies', as Oakeshott (1989, p. 65) put it, are what go to construct our understanding of others. To deny their significance in making sense of other people – their utterances, feelings, fears and failings – is to ignore the most important research tool at our disposal. Until recently the knowledge-base of special education self-consciously disavowed the sentiments, imaginings and fancies, rejecting as valid data anything that could not be judged to be at least notionally objective – anything that could not be counted.

Out of these changes has come a resurgence of interest in personal knowledge. More recently, the argument has been that we should trust in our own knowledge as people – trust in our own experiences and understanding of our emotions and our human experience. We have self-knowledge, and this is our principal tool in helping us to understand others. As the psychologist Joynson (1974, p. 2) put it: 'Human nature is not an unknown country, a *terra incognita* on the map of knowledge. It is our home ground. Human beings are not, like the objects of natural science, things which do not understand themselves'.

When trying to understand why students might not be succeeding at school, we each have to use our own humanity, recognising our 'failings', our frailties, misunderstandings and prejudices. These 'failings', it increasingly seems to have been realised in the last 20 years or so, have to be used in our understandings of the predicament of others, and not 'controlled out' in our investigative procedures. There is not likely to be discovered some special method for unearthing data about people nor some rational calculus for interpreting their trials and tribulations. The methods of a 'scientific' psychology or sociology have encouraged not only an illusory vision of a set of certain answers regarding human existence. They have led also to a garbled, two-dimensional discourse which has stripped from our study of people any of the recognition that we, as people, have ourselves of the plight of others.

It is perhaps too kind a judgement on twentieth-century psychology to say merely that it has failed to take stock of and use such knowledge. For it is not as though psychologists have merely mislaid this kind of understanding. The process has been far more conscious and deliberate than that. It has involved an intentional casting-off of certain kinds of knowledge – the knowledge we have of other human beings which comes by virtue of our own membership of the human species – in the assumption that these kinds of knowledge would contaminate a dispassionate, disinterested understanding of others. And in doing this, a strange kind of professional and academic language has been encouraged. Straightforward understandings have often been puffed up into something to look impressive and 'scientific'.

The trouble is that this apparatus does not merely re-name and smarten-up old ideas. The real trouble is that the shining instruments of the social sciences add legitimacy to common-or-garden ideas and prejudices. The notion of a gradient of cleverness, for example, was given a shot of adrenaline by the scientific paraphernalia of assessment testing, converting it to the far more impressive-sounding intelligence quotient. Mental infrastructures have emerged to support these social structures – paradigms, theories, research methods, research findings – but it is increasingly recognised that these are less disinterested and less informative than was once assumed.

The changing mindsets of which I have spoken have led all in education – practitioners, planners, parents, students, academics, researchers – to place less faith in the kind of knowledge once revered. The secure epistemic base that led to the segregative and pedagogic systems of the past has begun to give way. As the certainties associated with that epistemic base evaporate, new ideas have filled the void, and these have concerned less

the deficit and needs-based thinking of the past, and more an agenda of rights. Ideals about equity, social justice and opportunity for all have come to be taken as a valid knowledge-base for special education. This is the new inclusive discourse – the new epistemology – within which changes to special education are being framed.

NEW DISCOURSES; NEW KNOWLEDGE

What then can be said in general terms about the knowledge of special education? First, one can remind oneself of the Foucauldian principle that such knowledge is located – located in the discourses of the time, and that these have been concerned with processes of institutional education designed to benefit the majority. A Foucauldian perspective also discourages a specifically methodological view of epistemology. In other words, we are encouraged to look beyond the 'usual culprits' of paradigm and research method, important though these are, in our understanding of knowledge and its production. In special education, a field that straddles the academic and the practical, much stress has been laid on the integration of the theoretical and the practical, and the ways in which the theoretical – and in turn the way that this theoretical knowledge has been constructed out of particular methods – has informed practice. This influence has certainly been profound, as I have tried to indicate. However, a Foucauldian perspective reminds us that knowledge production occupies a far broader canvass, encompassing that which is constructed out of social, institutional and cultural discourse.

In the last third of the twentieth century this social, institutional and cultural discourse began to take a sharp turn away from the direction it had followed, certainly until the Second World War. After the war, the exposure of the horrific events to which eugenic thinking had led put paid to any resurgence of Social Darwinism. Simultaneously, there was a drift away from respect for authority, of whatever kind, and this included a more questioning disposition about the certainties provided by science. Greater openness in public life exposed the frailties of academics, doctors and others in positions of authority. The authority of the law, the church, the medical establishment, science and the state began to be freely interrogated, and with such interrogation came an attenuation in the validity attributed to the knowledge of these authorities.

The political scene reflected these changes and one of the most visible manifestations of the more questioning approach to authority occurred in the USA in the civil rights movement of the 1960s. Discriminatory laws, traditions and customs came to be attacked as black people demanded the same rights as those enjoyed by whites. The stress on rights encouraged a similar set of rights-based demands among ex-special school students. Why, they asked, should a minority of students whom the mainstream finds it difficult to educate be forced to accept a different and more limiting education? It was the right of everyone to have an education in the mainstream, with all the opportunities that this conferred.

Decline in respect for authority showed itself particularly markedly in a falling-off in the automatic deference to the power exercised by professionals and other experts. It has given rise to an increase in parental voice and power in education. More assertive parents have asked what benefits accrue from many of the diagnoses proffered by professionals. They have questioned the wisdom of segregated education for their children. In particular, the definitive statements that were sometimes made by medics about the prognosis for particular children in countless cases proved to be inaccurate. The exposure given to these in an open and litigious society has dented the authority of the professional source, and this too has resulted in a reduced confidence in the putative knowledge of professionals and experts.

Latterly an opening up of knowledge has occurred that would have been unheard of even in the 1980s, culminating in calls for a

hearing of the child's voice. As these various new voices have been heard, and as their speakers have gained in confidence, the equation of power in the construction of knowledge has shifted from expert to user. The culture of doctor knows best (or psychologist or teacher knows best) has diminished substantially as new discourses – valuing openness and the knowledge that comes from everyday experience – have begun to be valued more.

CONCLUSION

The underpinning principles on which special education and special pedagogy are built rely for their status on kinds of knowledge and reasoning that have in the past three or four decades come under close scrutiny. They rely on notions that have been elevated by 'scientific' methodology and theory to something more than they really are. The great thinkers of disciplines from which special education has drawn (usually psychology) have built impressive theory that gave credibility and stature to particular, and often mistaken, ways of viewing learning, viewing children and viewing the difficulties that they experience at school. Often, the 'knowledge' that has been constructed has distracted attention from more straightforward explanations for children's failure to thrive at school. More recently there has been a renewal of confidence in the knowledge of practitioners in understanding the failure of children at school. Simultaneously, as errors of the past have been recognised, the legitimacy of a discourse based in rights, equity and social justice has been accepted, and has provided the way for a new epistemology, an inclusive epistemology, to guide education.

REFERENCES

Benjamin, S. (2002). *The micropolitics of inclusive education.* Buckingham: Open University Press.

Chambers, J. H. (1992). *Empiricist research on teaching: A philosophical and practical critique of its scientific pretensions*. Dordrecht: Kluwer Academic.

Ferguson, P. M., Ferguson, D. L., & Taylor, S. J. (Eds.). (1992). *Interpreting disability: A qualitative reader.* New York: Teachers College Press.

Foucault, M. (1970). *The order of things: An archaeology of the human sciences.* London: Tavistock.

Foucault, M. (1972). *The archaeology of knowledge.* London: Tavistock.

Gallagher, D. (2004). Educational research, philosophical orthodoxy, and unfulfilled promises. In G. Thomas & R. Pring (Eds.), *Evidence-based practice in education.* Maidenhead: Open University Press.

Galton, F. (1869). *Hereditary genius, its laws and consequences.* London: Macmillan.

Hearnshaw, L. S. (1979). *Cyril Burt: psychologist.* London: Hodder & Stoughton.

Johnson, O. G. (1962). Special education for the mentally handicapped – a paradox. *Exceptional Children, 29,* 62–69.

Joynson, R. B. (1974). *Psychology and common sense.* London: Routledge & Kegan Paul.

Kevles, D. J. (1985). *In the name of eugenics: Genetics and the uses of human heredity.* New York: Alfred A. Knopf.

Lippmann, W. (1922, October 25). The mental age of Americans. *The New Republic,* 213–215.

McBriar, A. M. (1966). *Fabian socialism and English politics 1884–1918.* Cambridge: Cambridge University Press.

McNay, L. (1994). *Foucault: A critical introduction.* Cambridge: Polity Press.

Newman, T., & Roberts, H. (1996). Meaning well and doing good: Interventions in children's lives. In P. Alderson, S. Brill, I. Chalmers, R. Fuller, P. Hinkley-Smith, G. Macdonald, T. Newman, A. Oakley, H. Roberts and H. Ward, *What works? Effective social interventions in child welfare.* London: Barnardos.

Oakeshott, M. (1989). Education: The engagement and the frustration. In T. Fuller (Ed.), *The voice of liberal learning: Michael Oakeshott on education.* London: Yale University Press.

Organisation for Economic Co-operation and Development (OECD). (1994). *The integration of disabled children into mainstream education: Ambitions, theories and practices.* Paris: Organisation for Economic Co-operation and Development.

Outhwaite, W. (1990). Hans-Georg Gadamer. In Q. Skinner (Ed.), *The return of grand theory in the human sciences.* Cambridge: Canto.

Philp, M. (1990). Michel Foucault. In Q. Skinner (Ed.), *The return of grand theory in the human sciences.* Cambridge: Canto.

Reid, D. K., & Valle, J. W. (2004). The discursive practice of learning disability: Implications for instruction and parent-school relations. *Journal of Learning Disabilities, 37,* 4.

Terman, L. M. (1924). The possibilities and limitations of training. *Journal of Educational Research, 10,* 335–343.

Thomas, G. (1997). What's the use of theory? *Harvard Educational Review, 67*(1) 75–105.

Thomas, G., & Loxley, A. (2001). *Deconstructing special education and constructing inclusion.* Buckingham: Open University Press.

Thomas, G., & Loxley, A. (2005). Discourses on bad children and bad schools. *Journal of Learning Disabilities, 38*(2), 175–182.

Wang, M. C., Reynolds, M., & Walberg, H. (1995). Serving students at the margins. *Educational Leadership, 52*(4), 12–17.

Theoretical Perspectives

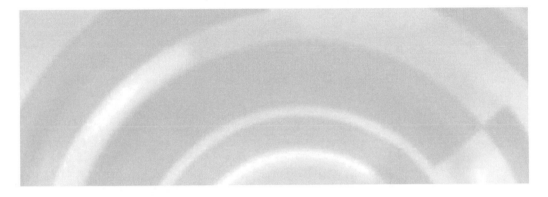

19

Behavioral theory and practice: current and future issues

John W. Maag

Behavioral theories are based on the underlying epistemological model known as *logical positivism*. Positivism asserts that the only valid knowledge is that which is objectively observed. It is from this model that scientific theories of behavior are generated which, in turn, are used to develop and apply technology whose primary goal is cost-effective, useful, and ethical behavior change (Fishman, Rotgers, & Franks, 1988). Behavioral theory has its roots in two orientations: Skinner's (1938) operant conditioning and Pavlov's (1927) respondent (classical) conditioning. Hull (1943), an early contemporary of Skinner, developed a systematic behavior theory that meshed together operant and respondent conditioning.

Behavior modification – a term believed to have first appeared in a chapter written by R. I. Watson (1962) – is the systematic application of learning principles and techniques to assess and improve individuals' behaviors. Two closely related terms are *behavior therapy* and *applied behavior analysis*. Behavior therapy is closely aligned with respondent conditioning and Wolpe's (1958) construct of reciprocal inhibition which formed the basis

for systematic desensitization. It tended to be used by behavioral psychologists and psychiatrists who were concerned primarily with treatment in traditional clinical settings, such as a therapist's office, by means of verbal interaction (that is, 'talk therapy'). Applied behavior analysis (ABA) tends to follow an operant orientation and was popularized in 1968 with the founding of the *Journal of Applied Behavior Analysis*. Applied behavior analysis has been defined as a systematic, performance-based, self-evaluative method for changing behaviors. Although the three terms have been used interchangeably, Martin and Pear (2003) preferred the term behavior modification because it subsumes both behavior therapy and ABA.

The science of behavior modification has, arguably, made its most valuable contributions to education (for example, Heward, Heron, Hill, & Trap-Porter, 1984; Sulzer-Azaroff, & Meyer, 1986). Skinner (1984) suggested that the most effective instructional practices are based on behavioral theory. Nevertheless, it still elicits strong reactions from educators who continue to savagely castigate and extravagantly praise its use. General educators tend to condemn behavior modification as being coercive and stifling internal motivation – a view expounded by Kohn (1993) in his book *Punished by Rewards*. Conversely, most special educators embrace behavior modification – perhaps since Itard's work with Victor, the wild boy of Aveyron – as an essential foundation of classroom management (Haring & Kennedy, 1996).

Ishaq (1996) suggested that the social relevance of behavior modification can only be acknowledged when the issues facing its use have been addressed. Some issues have been successfully resolved (for example, guidelines for using schedules of reinforcement) while others continue to pose reoccurring and vexing problems (for example, social validity, promoting generalization). It is impractical to address – even summarize – every issue related to behavior modification in education in a single book chapter. It would even be a daunting task to untangle the complex issues within an entire book. Therefore, the purpose of this chapter takes a different tack. It begins with a brief overview of behavior modification in special education – the faction within education that has embraced its use the most. This synopsis is followed by a discussion of four current issues that have particular relevance to special educators in today's schools. The chapter concludes with a discussion of two issues that pose future challenges to behaviorists in education.

OVERVIEW OF BEHAVIOR MODIFICATION IN SPECIAL EDUCATION

The education of youngsters with disabilities has changed considerably throughout the years – ranging from neglect and ridicule to compassionate concern and integration (Winzer, 1993). Concomitant with these changes in social attitudes and emerging legislation (for example, P.L. 94–142), new programs for children with disabilities, based on empirically validated behavior modification techniques, were established in public schools.

Origins of behavioral approaches

Kauffman (2001) traced the use of behavior modification by educators back to the late 1950s and 1960s. William Cruickshank and his colleagues developed a highly structured experimental public school program for brain-injured and hyperactive children in Montgomery County, Maryland. Norris Haring and E. Lakin Phillips developed a similar program to work with students with emotional disturbances in Arlington, Virginia, public schools. Haring later collaborated with Richard Whelan who had previously developed a structured approach to teaching at the Southard School of the Menninger Clinic in Topeka, Kansas. Together, they developed a program at the University of Kansas Medical Center that included the direct daily measurement of behaviors.

Early applications of the behavioral approach were being reported by others in the literature. For example, Zimmerman and Zimmerman's (1962) study of how the use of systematic consequences reduced students' temper tantrums and refusal to write spelling words ushered in a plethora of behavior modification research. Perhaps the most extensive use of behavioral theory was by Frank Hewett who, in the middle 1960s, developed the engineered classroom that was based on the use of a token economy and special curricula as exemplified in the Santa Monica Project. Hewitt also had an interest in using operant conditioning techniques to teach children with autism. Perhaps the most notable person to use behavioral approaches in the treatment of autism was O. Ivar Lovaas. His research focused on teaching children with autism language and daily living skills. His Early Intervention Program has generated much recent attention and some controversy.

Applications of behavioral theory

A large body of research accumulated during the 1970s and early 1980s that focused on developing and validating the efficacy of various techniques based on operant learning principles. These techniques could be categorized as those designed to increase or decrease youngsters' behaviors. So much research has accumulated on these technique that new empirical reports on their application have become more rare and even reviews of each technique have become dated. In essence, their effectiveness has become established fact.

Three of the most researched techniques for increasing behaviors have been behavioral contracting (Rutherford & Polsgrove, 1981), token economies (Kazdin & Bootzin, 1972; O'Leary & Drabman, 1971), and group-oriented contingencies (Hayes, 1976; Litow & Pumroy, 1975). Several techniques for decreasing behaviors have been the subject of extensive research: time out (Brantner & Doherty, 1983; Rutherford & Nelson, 1982), response cost (Walker, 1983), overcorrection (Foxx & Bechtel, 1983), and various schedules of differential reinforcement (Jones & Baker, 1990; Lancioni & Hoogeveen, 1990; O'Brien & Repp, 1990; Whitaker, 1996).

SOME CURRENT ISSUES IN BEHAVIORAL THEORY

A conundrum is created when selecting current issues in the use of behavior modification. The reason is that many 'current' issues have been around for decades. For example, over 35 years ago, Baer, Wolf, and Risley (1968) first discussed the notion that generalization must be specifically planned and rarely occurs spontaneously. In their seminal article nine years later, Stokes and Baer (1977) described a technology for programming generalization. Almost a decade later, Stokes and Osnes (1986) were reiterating those techniques. Around the same time, Rutherford and Nelson (1988) reviewed 5,300 behavioral treatment studies with children and adolescents and reached the conclusion that less than 2 per cent addressed generalization and maintenance of educational treatment effects and less than 1 per cent programmed for stimulus and response generalization.

The point is that the list of potential past issues, many of which are still current, as well as more recent ones, is enormous. For this chapter, four issues were included based on their relevance to the increasingly challenging behaviors displayed by children who attend public school: functional assessment, social validity, improving natural reinforcement, and momentum of compliance. Each of these issues have been the topic of articles, chapters, and in some cases, entire books (for example, functional assessment). The goal was to extract one or two unique aspects of each issue to present here.

Functional assessment

Functional assessment involves describing a problem behavior, identifying setting events that predict when it will and will not occur, identifying consequences that maintain it, developing hypotheses that describe the behavior, when it occurs, what reinforcers (positive or negative) maintain it, and collecting observational data that supports the hypotheses (O'Neill et al., 1997). The results are used to develop a behavior support plan. Functional assessment has been used extensively to develop situationally appropriate interventions for students with developmental disabilities in special education settings (Dunlap, Kern-Dunlap, Clarke, & Robbins, 1991; Dunlap et al., 1993; Kern, Childs, Dunlap, Clarke, & Falk, 1994; Lalli, Browder, Mace, & Brown, 1993; Northrup et al., 1994; Repp & Karsh, 1994; Sasso et al., 1992). It has also been used with students with mild disabilities (cf. Reid & Nelson, 2002). Its use with this population in the era of full inclusion raises the issue of whether it can feasibly be implemented by general educators in mainstreamed settings.

Applications in general education classrooms

Functional assessment has not been widely used by general educators because it has been perceived as time-consuming, complicated, and multi-faceted (Larson & Maag, 1998). However, the issue may not be the ability of general education teachers to learn and implement functional assessments but rather if they can implement it in their classrooms and still manage the many tasks their profession demands. Preliminary results are encouraging. For example, Moore et al. (2002) trained three general education teachers to correctly implement functional assessments. However, no data were collected on the students' behaviors, nor were measures of treatment acceptability collected. Packenham, Shute, and Reid (2004) obtained similar results while also obtaining positive changes in the target students' behaviors. Admittedly, their approach was a truncated version of functional assessment. But that raises the question as to how streamlined can functional assessment be made while still retaining its fidelity?

Larson and Maag (1998) developed the Functional Assessment Hypotheses Formulation Protocol (FAHFP) to address this very question. Combining elements of other checklists, interviews, and observation forms, the FAHFP directs a teacher to independently operationally define a behavior, identify setting events, consequences, and functions associated with the occurrence of the behavior, and conduct a systematic observation of the behavior. The protocol culminates with a teacher generating hypothesis statements and formulating a functional analysis plan. Maag and Larson (2004) found that a general educator could independently use the FAHFP, collect direct observations of students' behaviors, and implement contextual and curricular modifications. In addition, treatment acceptability was quite high. Although these results are promising, this area of inquiry is still in its infancy and requires considerably more research.

Overruling results of functional analysis

Functional analysis is the second stage of functional assessment and involves testing a hypothesis by recording the target behavior during baseline and intervention (that is, contextual or curricular modifications) phases and graphing the results. Behavior support plans flow directly from functional analyses (Maag, 2004). It is a straightforward empiri-cally validated practice. However, Leslie (1997) questioned whether certain ethical principles would overrule the results of a functional analysis. His question was framed within the context of the least restrictive environment (LRE) in which treatments for individuals with disabilities should not be unduly restrictive. His concern is germane to educators given the inclusion zeitgeist.

Typically, a hierarchy of options – beginning with the least restrictive – guides the use of behavioral interventions. For instance, in the case of punishment, a response cost should be used first, followed by mild forms of time-out, and culminating in the use of seclusion, restraint, and overcorrection, respectively (Maag, 2004). However, Johnston and Sherman (1993) argued that a hierarchy of methods does not always exist for all individuals. Rather, it is assumed that results of functional analysis will be the most empirically valid and, consequently, an ethically acceptable guide to implementing interventions.

Is this assumption valid? What if functional analysis reveals that an individual's self-injurious behavior (SIB) is maintained by attention and, therefore, its withdrawal (that is, extinction) becomes a centerpiece of the behavior support plan? Extinction typically results in a temporary increase in the target behavior (that is, extinction curve). So wherein does the restriction lie? During the initial stages of extinction, the individual theoretically could suffer more from the therapeutic restrictions of the functionally derived intervention than more restrictive punitive approaches that would eliminate SIB quickly.

Are experts in behavior modification the best individuals to develop and implement an intervention? Although functional assessment is empirically based, it is not perfect and results vary, in part, based on the training and expertise of the individual using it. Therefore, should the wider community be involved to impose restraints on treatment decisions? Perhaps it would be a valuable exercise to bring the ideas of functional analysis to a wider audience – a proposal related to social validity.

Social validity

Issues surrounding social validity were first addressed over 25 years ago in a seminar article written by Wolf (1978). At its most basic level, social validity addresses whether a relevant audience (for example, educators, mental health providers) finds interventions in real-life settings to be acceptable in terms of their goals, methods, personnel, outcomes, and ease of integration into the consumer's current environment and responsibilities (Schwartz & Baer, 1991). This information is then immediately used to modify the current intervention, future applications, and outcome evaluation. Therefore, social validity evaluations, in this larger context, are not dependent measures but rather meant to supplement them.

A misapplication of this concept is illustrated by outcome evaluation in social skills training that had been characterized as an exercise in social validation (Elliott, Gresham, & Heffer, 1987). Namely, changes in targeted behaviors should predict a student's status on socially important outcomes using such measures as sociometric techniques, teacher ratings, and measures of academic performance (Gresham, 1983; Hughes & Sullivan, 1988). However, Schwartz and Baer (1991) suggested that social validity assessment is a defensive technique because it is oriented toward detecting unacceptability in any of three major areas: the goals of intervention, its methods, and its personnel. Therefore, social validity assesses the viability of an intervention and not its effectiveness.

The ongoing challenge in social validity is predicting why certain interventions are liked and others disliked by educators rather than simply being an early warning or endorsement (Schwartz & Baer, 1991). To accomplish this goal, educators in a position to use interventions based on behavior modification need to be identified and reliably assessed. At issue here is not what to ask but *whom* to ask. There are other passive, but important consumers besides educators. For example, peers can be participants in enhancing entrapment for a student receiving social skills training or sabotage it as soon as school personnel are absent

(McConnell, 1987). The point is that many people may be consumers of interventions other than the target child and that there are very little data indicating what turns them into either supporters or critics.

A related concern is how to collect information in a valid, reliable, and cost-efficient manner. The subjective nature of the assessments (for example, interviews, questionnaires) and intrusion of the experimenter make this type of data difficult to interpret. What does it mean, for example, if a teacher circles 'pretty much' for the level of satisfaction he or she had for an intervention? Instead, a wider range of observable behaviors should be sampled. For example, instead of an item that asks a respondent to rate how much a child 'fidgets', it may ask to rate how many times in a day a child handles materials not related to the lesson.

Improving natural reinforcement

For all the hundreds of empirically sound research reports validating the efficacy and scope of behavior modification, this technology has largely been ignored, or at least seriously questioned, by many educators (Axelrod, Moyer, & Berry, 1990). Maag (2001a) described how many teachers resist using positive reinforcement because they erroneously view it as an artificial device tantamount to bribery rather than the naturally occurring phenomenon it is that exists in every classroom. He then posed the following question to these teachers: what would you prefer, to ignore the effects of reinforcement and run the risk of it haphazardly maintaining inappropriate behaviors or program its use to increase appropriate behaviors? Teachers will not be able to consider seriously the implications of this question until behaviorists proffer strategies that teachers will accept – those that are socially valid (Fantuzzo & Atkins, 1992).

Perhaps the most socially valid behavioral approach for teachers is through the use of natural reinforcement. The goal is to identify reinforcers that students can receive without the mediation of teachers and that contribute to making the natural consequences of behavior

reinforcing (Horcones, 1992). Natural reinforcement has also been called intrinsic consequences because they originate in the behavior
itself and are the natural or automatic results of
responding (Vaughan & Michael, 1982). Conversely, extrinsic consequences originate in
sources other than the behavior itself such as
when a teacher verbally praises a student.

The irony is that because natural reinforcers
are intrinsic consequences, they cannot be
deliberately manipulated and, therefore, would
appear meaningless to teachers. However,
appearances can be misleading. It is possible
for teachers to establish or eliminate the reinforcing function of natural consequences and
make them more or less conspicuous (Horcones, 1992). Extrinsic reinforcement is still an
important tool to shape, increase, and condition natural consequences as reinforcers.

Horcones (1992) recommended the following sequence in conditioning a natural consequence as a reinforcer. First, teachers should
select a target behavior and identify the natural
consequences of the selected behavior through
the use of an A-B-C analysis (Maag, 2004).
Second, an intrinsic consequence should be selected to be conditioned as a natural reinforcer.
For example, the intrinsic consequences of
typing could be the noise made by the keys on
the board or the accumulating words appearing
on the monitor. The latter consequence is the
most educationally salient and, consequently,
should be the one conditioned as the natural
reinforcer. Third, intrinsic consequences
should be identified that are easily observed by
a student. For example, the intrinsic consequences for a student singing in a chorus are
hearing herself singing the same words in the
same volume and key as the rest of the group.
Therefore, a teacher may first condition, as a
natural reinforcer, the consequences of singing
the same words because it is the easiest for the
student to observe followed by singing at the
right volume and finally in the right key – the
latter being the most difficult to discriminate.
Fourth, the teacher should arrange the conditions so that the intrinsic consequences are easily observable. For example, a teacher could
point out and describe the correct sequence a

student used to arrive at the solution to a division problem. The final step is for a teacher to
select appropriate back-up reinforcers.

There are several features of natural reinforcement that teachers should find appealing. First, it may be easier to shape students'
behaviors because this type of reinforcement
occurs immediately and is simultaneously
available to all students. It is impossible for
even the most devoted behaviorally oriented
teacher to match the frequency and breadth
that intrinsic contingencies offer. Second,
intrinsic consequences may bring a student's
behavior under the control of natural discriminative stimuli. This type of entrapment is an
essential ingredient for promoting generalization. Third, natural reinforcement is always
individual-specific. It is an oxymoron when
teachers say 'I've tried reinforcement and it
doesn't work.' They are actually lamenting
the difficulty finding consequences that students find reinforcing. The time used in trying
to accumulate a large variety of external reinforcers can be better spent promoting natural
reinforcement.

Momentum of compliance

The metaphor of behavioral compliance is a
way to describe two independent dimensions
of behavior: (a) rate of responding established
and maintained by contingencies of reinforcement and (b) resistance to change when
responding is in some way challenged or disrupted. The goal is to establish desirable
behaviors that persist through changes in contingencies from external to natural reinforcement. The process begins with 'momentum'
being a type of *discriminated operant* that
follows a fairly classic A-B-C model (A =
antecedent, B = identified response class, C =
contingencies of reinforcement). It proceeds
when a teacher uses a multiple schedule of
reinforcement to present two or more distinctive stimuli successively – in regular or irregular alteration – for predetermined durations.

Maag (2001b) described how behavioral
momentum can be used as an intervention for
managing students' resistance. The process

begins by instructing a student to engage in behaviors that she wants to perform (that is, high probability requests). Once the student is compliant, an instruction is given to perform an unfavorable behavior (that is, low probability requests). For example, a teacher may follow a request to have a student tack pictures on a bulletin board (high probability behavior) with the instruction to throw away trash (low probability behavior). The idea is to build momentum toward compliance by first getting the student to perform a series of desired behaviors. Rhode, Jenson, and Reavis (1995) developed easy-to-follow teacher guidelines for implementing behavioral momentum.

Nevin (1992a, 1992b) conducted two laboratory studies in order to refine the stimulus-reinforcer relation that characterizes behavioral momentum. He concluded that resistance to change depended on the relative, rather than the absolute, reinforcer rate in the presence of a stimulus. The implication of his studies for educators is that student resistance to following directions depends on the reinforcer rate not only within the classroom but also outside it. Therefore, educators should identify both proximal and distal reinforcement contingencies to use behavioral momentum effectively.

SOME FUTURE ISSUES IN BEHAVIORAL THEORY

The same conundrum exists when selecting future issues as that previously raised for current issues. Issues are updated and contextually relevant to other factors being discussed in education and psychology – both in and outside behavioral theory. Two issues are presented in this section: studying emotions and behavioral cusps. These topics are timely and less has been written about them than other issues. The purpose of only presenting two issues here was to give them each a more detailed account than what had appeared for the current issues which have received more attention elsewhere.

Studying emotions

The topic of emotions cannot be discussed without including cognitions. The relation between emotions and cognitions has been debated since Aristotle and continues to the present. There are two main opposing positions in this debate: cognitively oriented emotion theorists who hold that cognitions (that is, cognitive appraisals) are necessary for emotions (Lazarus, 1984) and independent systems theorists who hold that cognitive appraisals are not causally necessary for emotions and that they are independent of each other (Zajonc, 1984). The argument is not so much dichotomous – few would deny that cognition and emotion function conjointly – as it is programmatic (that is, understanding how the two interact).

It has not been easy to behaviorally study emotion because it tends to be an ambiguous and subjective term that cannot be reliably observed until the specific behaviors within the category are operationally defined. At its simplest level, Skinner (1989) believed that the meaning of an emotional term (for example, anxiety) resided in the functional relation between antecedents and consequences. For example, a student who said 'I feel anxious' would require identifying setting events (for example, giving a speech in front of the class) and consequences (for example, peers yawning, drawing pictures, writing notes, or talking amongst themselves).

Although Skinner's approach has been commended as providing a needed opening for the behavioral study of emotion, it has also been criticized as being limited and unproductive (Friman, Hayes, & Wilson, 1998). For example, knowing that an antecedent (giving a speech) elicits a verbal behavior ('I feel anxious') or that a consequence (peers yawning) exists does not help with prediction and control of the phenomenon called emotion – two of the fundamental goals of behaviorists.

An expanded view of emotion
Friman et al. (1998) provided a conceptualization of emotion (using the example of anxiety)

that – unlike Skinner who believed its study was theoretically and practically unnecessary – helps understand emotional problems characteristic of several anxiety disorders (for example, obsessive-compulsive disorder, panic disorder with agoraphobia, post-traumatic stress disorder). They discussed four points that make the study of emotion relevant.

First, language-able humans have the ability to draw relations between events and that it is straightforward to demonstrate that neutral stimuli can acquire discriminative functions indirectly with no direct training. That is, a child, in the presence of one stimulus, taking out a piece of paper, learns to select an arbitrarily related stimulus, grabbing a pencil, then this trained unidirectional relation will lead to a derived bidirectional relation in which grabbing a pencil leads to taking out a piece of paper without any direct training. This simple process can be observed in children as young as 16 months (Lipkens, Hayes, & Hayes, 1993). Many other relations can be learned, applied arbitrarily to stimulus events, combined, and transferred into networks of stimulus relations of incredible complexity (Dymond & Barnes, 1996). Transformation of stimulus functions provides a behavioral approach for studying emotion and other private events (Friman et al., 1998).

Second, private events can readily acquire discriminative functions. There is some research indicating that generalized responding to stimuli with discriminative function spread via stimulus generalization to novel stimuli resulting in large relational nebulous categories of responses (Fields, Reeve, Adams, & Verhave, 1991). In addition, events in relational classes spread with these stimulus generalization effects. Emotions may become part of the same relational class (DeGrandpre, Bickel, & Higgins, 1992).

Third, anxiety disorders seem to occur with little apparent direct learning or that the amount of direct learning is extraordinarily out of proportion with the amount of responding. It is difficult to examine emotions because they are influenced by indirect relations between events and public and private responses to public and private events (Friman et al., 1998). For example, high levels of anxiety may be experienced by a person because of repeated public and private events involving the process of stimulus generalization, derived relational responding, and transformation of stimulus function.

Fourth, the primary function of anxious behavior is experiential avoidance. Early in life, humans learn a myriad of strategies (for example, vigilance, withdrawal) for avoiding events (for example, pain, danger) (Friman et al., 1998). As verbal skills develop, their responses to aversive events become more verbal. For example, a child at an amusement park who sees the speed at which a rollercoaster travels (event) may say 'I'm afraid' (response). Through a transformation of function, the response (fear) may become aversive, resulting in two instances of negative reinforcement: the event (rollercoaster) and the response to it (fear). Therefore, humans, unlike animals, can exhibit experiential avoidance whose primary function is to reduce or eliminate private events such as anxiety or fear (Hayes, Wilson, Gifford, Follette, & Strosahl, 1996).

Implications for practice

The typical treatment for emotional related problems such as anxiety disorders is to repeatedly expose the person to the feared stimulus while engaging in incompatible behaviors (for example, relaxation) to extinguish the maladaptive avoidance response class. The belief is that extinguishing overt reactions to the feared event or object causes a reduction in private responses such as negative self-talk and emotional overreaction. However, taking into account an expanded view of emotion, treatment would necessarily involve exposure to the private events as well as the external stimuli. The goal would be not only to have a person master being in the presence of a feared event or object but also to be free of thinking about or feeling fear. Acceptance and commitment therapy (ACT) is a behaviorally based approach that focuses on exposing a person to their private verbal events as a way of weakening them (Hayes & Wilson, 1994).

Behavior cusps as an alternative to developmental theories

Numerous theories have been put forth to describe, explain, predict, and guide human development: Freud's psychosexual stages, Piaget's cognitive-developmental stages, Kohlberg's stages of moral reasoning, and Maslow's hierarchy of needs are some of the most well known. Each of these theorists hypothesized an invariable set of emerging stages which reflect a progression of various intellectual abilities, discriminations, conflicts to be resolved, or products. Children are believed to traverse through these stages to adulthood somewhat analogous to a train beginning, stopping at various stations, and eventually ending its journey on a relatively linear path.

Almost every field of psychology endorses, or at least accepts, developmental theories except behavior modification. The closest behavioral theorists come to developmental theory is their basic analytical and empirically validated behavior-shaping contingencies that are irrespective of any theoretical lifespan patterning (Maag, 2005). The issue for behaviorists is whether there is any systematic pattern to these contingencies. Authors of some college textbooks believe it is possible to discern these types of patterns across the lifespan (for example, Novak, 1996; Schlinger, 1995). The question is whether these conceptualizations have meaningful implications for behavior analysts. Rosales-Ruiz and Baer (1997) believed they did and coined the term *behavioral cusps* to explain them in an analytic fashion.

A pragmatic concept of behavioral cusps

A behavioral cusp refers to any behavior change that results in a child's behavior coming into contact with new contingencies that have more far-reaching consequences than the initial ones. The previous discussion on emotion provides an extreme example of the complexity and variety of this process. But within the current context, a cusp is a special instance of behavior change in which the next stimulus in a chain portents a shift in the entire sequence. In other words, a cusp (that is, behavior change) has an important consequence for a child beyond the initial change it produces (Rosales-Ruiz & Baer, 1997). Granted, every behavior change results from antecedent changes in interaction between a child and his environment. What makes a behavior change a cusp is that it exposes a child's repertoire to new environmental contingencies (that is, antecedents and consequences) that either maintain or destroy those contingencies.

Rosales-Ruiz and Baer (1997) used the context of a baby learning to crawl to illustrate this process. A baby in motion will have increased access to the environment and its contingencies. She can increasingly acquire reinforcing objects, activities, and interactions with family members, but still encounter stumbling blocks (that is, punitive consequences) – all of which potentiate subsequent stimulus–response chains that shape the scope and breadth of future interactions. Any turning point in the sequence, such as the child walking (that is, becoming mobile), would be considered a behavioral cusp.

The previous example does not deny the development of many small sequential skills culminating in crawling. Task analysis has long been a mechanism with which behaviorists operationalize shaping (Maag, 2005). The point is that, unlike traditional stage theorists who assume new challenges will suddenly appear, behaviorists observe that each subtask opens the child's world only to the next subtask in a perpetually changing environment. A cusp can be created either by changing one behavior or an entire response class.

Consequences and behavior change

Similar to stimulus control, the concept of cusps emphasize how consequences of behavior shape whether certain individuals find stimuli salient. Cusps can be either simple such as asking a question to get access to information or complex such as reading. However, if reading had little relevance (that is, consequence) beyond the act of reading it would not be a cusp. The goal would then be to bring reading under the control of contingencies so it leads to broader changes such as the ability to access a dictionary to look up the definition of a word.

Children without disabilities get through many cusps when interacting with their environments, usually through widespread fundamental processes such as imitation and spoken language. They acquire self-regulation skills through prior cusps. Children with developmental disabilities do not get through as many cusps and become problems that attract special education services. The point is that cusps can vary in size, particularly in the length or intensity of their teaching programs, yet have similarly important consequences for what can happen next. The importance of cusps is defined by the degree of behavior change outcomes behaviors produce rather than their complexity. Therefore, teachers may begin to make a list of cusps, chunk them together, and teach the behaviors that produce them. Teaching reading to see its consequences fits the cusp concept whereas awaiting mature skeletal growth does not.

CONCLUSION

There are numerous issues facing behaviorally oriented educators. Some of those issues – both current and future – were described in this chapter. They provide central challenges for effective behavior modification with students with disabilities who are educated in a wide range of settings. Students with disabilities who are fully included in general education classrooms require unique interventions that can be tailored to this setting. Acceptance of behavioral techniques for these students requires an increasing emphasis on making functional assessment easy to use, educating teachers on the use of natural contingencies, and how behavioral momentum can increase compliance. None of these approaches will be accepted in the absence of social validity. In essence, behaviorists need to enlist the support of educators and show them the practical value of such principles and techniques. Behaviorists

have also provided a working model for dealing with emotions and developmental transitions – both of which are salient to educators.

One of the trends in special education has been to move away from traditional behavior modification and blend it with more constructivist approaches. This eclecticism, although popular, diverts attention away from empirically based interventions for which behaviorism is at its core. As a result, some of the great strides behavior modification has made, as typified in the issues described in this chapter, are largely ignored or sidetracked into rhetorical debates between positivists and postmodernists. Behaviorists need to go beyond this distraction and present principles and techniques to teachers in an easy-to-understand user-friendly manner. Once teachers experience the effectiveness of behavioral techniques first hand, they are more likely to use them in the future. In essence, their successful use becomes a positive reinforcer for their subsequent use, thereby expanding educators' foundational understanding and willingness to address current and future issues.

REFERENCES

Axelrod, S., Moyer, L., & Berry, B. (1990). Why teachers do not use behavior modification procedures. *Journal of Educational and Psychological Consultation, 1,* 309–320.

Baer, D. M., Wolf, M. M., & Risley, T. (1968). Current dimensions of applied behavior analysis. *Journal of Applied Behavior Analysis, 1,* 91–97.

Brantner, J. P., & Doherty, M. A. (1983). A review of timeout: A conceptual and methodological analysis. In S. Axelrod & J. Apsche (Eds.), *The effects of punishment on human behavior* (pp. 87–132). New York: Academic Press.

DeGrandpre, R. J., Bickel, W. K., & Higgins, S. T. (1992). Emergent equivalence relations between interoceptive (drug) and exteroceptive (visual) stimuli. *Journal of the Experimental Analysis of Behavior, 58,* 9–18.

Dunlap, G., Kern, L., dePerczel, M., Clarke, S., Wilson, D., Childs, K. E., White, R., & Falk, G. D. (1993). Functional analysis of classroom variables for students with emotional and behavioral disorders. *Behavioral Disorders, 18,* 275–291.

Dunlap, G., Kern-Dunlap, L., Clarke, S., & Robbins, F. R. (1991). Functional assessment, curricular revision, and severe behavior problems. *Journal of Applied Behavior Analysis, 24,* 387–397.

Dymond, S., & Barnes, D. (1996). A transformation of self-discrimination response functions in accordance with the arbitrarily applicable relations of sameness and opposition. *Psychological Record, 46,* 271–300.

Elliott, S. N., Gresham, F. M., & Heffer, R. W. (1987). Social-skills interventions: Research findings and training techniques. In C. A. Maher & J. E. Zins (Eds.), *Psychoeducational interventions in the schools* (pp. 141–159). New York: Pergamon.

Fantuzzo, J., & Atkins, M. (1992). Applied behavior analysis for educators: Teacher centered and classroom based. *Journal of Applied Behavior Analysis, 25,* 37–42.

Fields, L., Reeve, K. E., Adams, B. J., & Verhave, T. (1991). Stimulus generalization and equivalence classes: A model for natural categories. *Journal of the Experimental Analysis of Behavior, 55,* 305–312.

Fishman, D. B., Rotgers, F., & Franks, C. M. (1988). Paradigms in wonderland: Fundamental issues in behavior therapy. In D. B. Fishman & F. Rotgers (Eds.), *Paradigms in behavior therapy: Present and promise* (pp. 7–19). New York: Springer.

Foxx, R. M., & Bechtel, D. R. (1983). Overcorrection: A review and analysis. In S. Axelrod & J. Apsche (Eds.), *The effects of punishment on human behavior* (pp. 133–220). New York: Academic Press.

Friman, P. C., Hayes, S. C., & Wilson, K. G. (1998). Why behavior analysts should study emotion: The example of anxiety. *Journal of Applied Behavior Analysis, 31,* 137–156.

Gresham, F. M. (1983). Social validity in the assessment of children's social skills: Establishing standards for social competency. *Journal of Psychoeducational Assessment, 1,* 299–307.

Haring, T. G., & Kennedy, C. H. (1996). Behavior-analytic foundations of classroom management. In W. Stainback & S. Stainback (Eds.), *Controversial issues confronting special education: Divergent perspectives* (2nd ed., pp. 184–194). Boston, MA: Allyn & Bacon.

Hayes, L. A. (1976). The use of group contingencies for behavioral control: A review. *Psychological Bulletin, 83,* 528–643.

Hayes, S. C., & Wilson, K. G. (1994). Acceptance and commitment therapy: Undermining the verbal support for experiential avoidance. *The Behavior Analyst, 17,* 289–303.

Hayes, S. C., Wilson, K. G., Gifford, E. V., Follette, V. M., & Strosahl, K. (1996). Experiential avoidance and behavior disorders: A functional dimensional approach to diagnosis and treatment. *Journal of Consulting and Clinical Psychology, 64,* 1152–1168.

Heward, W. L., Heron, T. E., Hill, D. S., & Trap-Porter, J. (1984). *Focus on behavior analysis in education.* Columbus, OH: Bell & Howell.

Horcones. (1992). Natural reinforcement: A way to improve education. *Journal of Applied Behavior Analysis, 25,* 71–75.

Hughes, J. N., & Sullivan, K. A. (1988). Outcome assessment in social skills training with children. *Journal of School Psychology, 26,* 167–183.

Hull, C. L. (1943). *Principles of behavior.* New York: Appleton-Century-Crofts.

Ishaq, W. (1996). The social relevance of applied behavior analysis and psychological intervention strategies. In J. R. Cautela & W. Ishaq (Eds.), *Contemporary issues in behavior therapy: Improving the human condition* (pp. 235–259). New York: Plenum.

Johnston, J. M., & Sherman, R. A. (1993). Applying the least restrictive alternative principle to treatment decisions: A legal and behavioral analysis. *The Behavior Analyst, 16,* 103–116.

Jones, R. S., & Baker, L. J. (1990). Differential reinforcement and challenging behaviour: A critical review of the DRI schedule. *Behavioural Psychopathology, 18,* 35–47.

Kauffman, J. M. (2001). *Characteristics of emotional and behavioral disorders of children and youth* (7th ed.). Upper Saddle River, NJ: Prentice Hall.

Kazdin, A. E., & Bootzin, R. R. (1972). The token economy: An evaluative review. *Journal of Applied Behavior Analysis, 5,* 343–372.

Kern, L., Childs, K. E., Dunlap, G., Clarke, S., & Falk, G. D. (1994). Using assessment-based curricular intervention to improve the classroom behavior of a student with emotional and behavioral challenges. *Journal of Applied Behavior Analysis, 27,* 7–9.

Kohn, A. (1993). *Punished by rewards: The trouble with gold stars, incentive plans, A's, praise, and other bribes.* Boston, MA: Houghton-Mifflin.

Lancioni, G. E. & Hoogeveen, F. R. (1990). Non-aversive and mildly aversive procedures for reducing problem behaviours in people with developmental disorders: A review. *Mental Handicap Research, 3,* 137–160.

Lalli, J. S., Browder, D. M., Mace, F. C., & Brown D. K. (1993). Teacher use of descriptive analysis data to implement interventions to decrease students' problem behavior. *Journal of Applied Behavior Analysis, 26,* 227–238.

Larson, P. J., & Maag, J. W. (1998). Applying functional assessment in general education classrooms: Issues and recommendations. *Remedial and Special Education, 19,* 338–349.

Lazarus, R. S. (1984). On the primacy of cognition. *American Psychologist, 39,* 124–129.

Leslie, J. C. (1997). Ethical implications of behavior modification: Historical and current issues. *Psychological Record, 97,* 637–649.

Lipkens, G., Hayes, S. C., & Hayes, L. (1993). Longitudinal study of derived stimulus relations in an infant.

Journal of Experimental Child Psychology, 56, 201–239.

Litow, L., & Pumroy, D. K. (1975). A brief review of classroom group-oriented contingencies. *Journal of Applied Behavior Analysis, 3,* 341–347.

Maag, J. W. (2001a). Rewarded by punishment: Reflections on the disuse of positive reinforcement in schools. *Exceptional Children, 67,* 173–186.

Maag, J. W. (2001b). *Powerful struggles: Managing resistance, building rapport.* Longmont, CO: Sopris West.

Maag, J. W. (2004). *Behavior management: From theoretical implications to practical applications* (2nd ed.). Belmont, CA: Wadsworth/Thomson Learning.

Maag, J. W. (2005). Shaping to teach new behaviors. In G. Sugai & R. H. Horner (Eds.), *Encyclopedia of behavior modification and cognitive behavior therapy: Vol. 3 Educational applications* (pp. 1516–1519). Thousand Oaks, CA: Sage.

Maag, J. W., & Larson, P. J. (2004). Training a general education teacher to apply functional assessment. *Education and Treatment of Children, 27,* 26–36.

Martin, G., & Pear, J. (2003). *Behavior modification: What it is and how to do it* (7th ed.). Upper Saddle River, NJ: Prentice Hall.

McConnell, S. R. (1987). Entrapment effects and the generalization and maintenance of social skills training for elementary school students with behavioral disorders. *Behavioral Disorders, 12,* 252–263.

Moore, J. W., Edwards, R. P., Sterling-Turner, H. E., Riley, J., DuBard, M., & McGeorge, A. (2002). Teacher acquisition of functional analysis methodology. *Journal of Applied Behavior Analysis, 35,* 73–77.

Nevin, J. A. (1992a). Behavioral contrast and behavioral momentum. *Journal of Experimental Psychology: Animal Behavior Processes, 18,* 126–133.

Nevin, J. A. (1992b). An integrative model for the study of behavioral momentum. *Journal of the Experimental Analysis of Behavior, 57,* 301–316.

Northrup, J., Wacker, D. P., Berg, W. K., Kelly, L., Sasso, G., & DeRaad, A. (1994). The treatment of severe behavior problems in school settings using a technical assistance model. *Journal of Applied Behavior Analysis, 27,* 33–47.

Novak, G. (1996). *Developmental psychology: Dynamical systems and behavior analysis.* Reno, NV: Context Press.

O'Brien, S. & Repp, A. C. (1990). Reinforcement-based reductive procedures: A review of 20 years of their use with persons with severe or profound retardation. *Journal of the Association for Persons with Severe Handicaps, 15,* 148–159.

O'Leary, K.D., & Drabman, R. (1971). Token reinforcement programs in the classroom: A review. *Psychological Bulletin, 75,* 379–398.

O'Neill, R. E., Horner, R. H., Albin, R. W., Sprague, J. R., Storey, K., & Newton, J. S. (1997). *Functional assessment and program development for problem behavior: A practical handbook* (2nd ed.). Pacific Grove, CA: Brooks/Cole.

Packenham, M., Shute, R., & Reid, R. (2004). A truncated functional behavioral assessment procedure for children with disruptive classroom behaviors. *Education and Treatment of Children, 27,* 9–25.

Pavlov, I. P. (1927). *Conditioned reflexes: An investigation of the physiological activity of the cerebral cortex* (G. V. Anrep, Trans.). London: Oxford University Press.

Reid, R., & Nelson, J. R. (2002). The utility, acceptability, and practicality of functional behavioral assessment for students with high-incidence problem behaviors. *Remedial and Special Education, 23,* 15–23.

Repp, A. C., & Karsh, K. G. (1994). Hypothesis-based interventions for tantrum behaviors of persons with developmental disabilities in school settings. *Journal of Applied Behavior Analysis, 27,* 21–31.

Rhode, G., Jenson, W. R., & Reavis, H. K. (1995) *The tough kid book: Practical classroom management strategies* (5th ed.). Longmont, CO: Sopris West.

Rosales-Ruiz, J., & Baer, D. M. (1997). Behavioral cusps: A developmental and pragmatic concept for behavior analysis. *Journal of Applied Behavior Analysis, 30,* 533–544.

Rutherford, R.B., Jr., & Nelson, C.M. (1982). Analysis of the response contingent time-out literature with behaviorally disordered students in classroom settings. In R.B. Rutherford, Jr. (Ed.), *Severe behavior disorders of children and youth* (Vol. 5, pp. 79–105). Reston, VA: Council for Children with Behavioral Disorders.

Rutherford, R. B., Jr., & Nelson, C. M. (1988). Generalization and maintenance of treatment effects. In J. C. Witt, S. W. Elliott, & F. M. Gresham (Eds.), *Handbook of behavior therapy in education* (pp. 277–324). New York: Plenum.

Rutherford, R. B., Jr., & Polsgrove, L. J. (1981). Behavioral contracting with behaviorally disordered and delinquent children and youth: An analysis of the clinical and experimental literature. In R. B. Rutherford, Jr., A. G. Prieto, & J. E. McGlothlin (Eds.), *Severe behavior disorders of children and youth* (Vol. 4, pp. 49–69). Reston, VA: Council for Children with Behavioral Disorders.

Sasso, G. M., Reimers, T. M., Cooper, J. J., Wacker, D., Berg, W., Steege, M., Kelly, L., & Allaire, A. (1992). Use of descriptive and experimental analyses to identify properties of aberrant behavior in school settings. *Journal of Applied Behavior Analysis, 25,* 809–821.

Schlinger, H. (1995). *A behavior analytic view of child development.* New York: Plenum.

Schwartz, I. S., & Baer, D. M. (1991). Social validity assessments: Is current practice state of the art? *Journal of Applied Behavior Analysis, 24,* 189–204.

Skinner, B. F. (1938). *The behavior of organisms.* New York: Appleton-Century-Crofts.

Skinner, B. F. (1984). The shame of American education. *The American Psychologist, 39,* 947–954.

Skinner, B. F. (1989). *Recent issues in the analysis of behavior.* Columbus, OH: Merrill.

Stokes, T. F., & Baer, D. M. (1977). An implicit technology of generalization. *Journal of Applied Behavior Analysis, 10,* 349–367.

Stokes, T. F., & Osnes, P. G. (1986). Programming the generalization of children's social behavior. In P. S. Strain, M. J. Guralnick, & H. M. Walker (Eds.), *Children's social behavior: Development, assessment, and modification* (pp. 407–443). Orlando, FL: Academic Press.

Sulzer-Azaroff, B., & Mayer, R. G. (1986). *Achieving educational excellence using behavioral strategies.* New York: Holt, Rinehart, & Winston.

Vaughan, M. E., & Michael, J. (1982). Automatic reinforcement: An important but ignored concept. *Behaviorism, 10,* 217–227.

Walker, H.M. (1983). Application of response cost in school settings: Outcomes, issues, and recommendations. *Exceptional Education Quarterly, 3*(4), 46–55.

Watson, R. I. (1962). The experimental tradition and clinical psychology. In A. J. Bachrach (Ed.), *Experimental foundations of clinical psychology* (pp. 3–25). New York: Basic Books.

Whitaker, S. (1996). A review of DRO: The influence of the degree of intellectual disability and the frequency of the target behaviour. *Journal of Applied Research in Intellectual Disabilities, 9,* 61–79.

Winzer, M. A. (1993). *The history of special education: From isolation to integration.* Washington, DC: Gallaudet University Press.

Wolf, M. M. (1978). Social validity: The case for subjective measurements, or how behavior analysis is finding its heart. *Journal of Applied Behavior Analysis, 11,* 203–214.

Wolpe, J. (1958). *Psychotherapy by reciprocal inhibition.* Stanford, CA: Stanford University Press.

Zajonc, R. B. (1984). On the primacy of affect. *American Psychologist, 39,* 117–123.

Zimmerman, J., & Zimmerman, E. (1962). The alteration of behavior in a special class situation. *Journal of the Experimental Analysis of Behavior, 5,* 59–60.

20

Constructivist views of learning: implications for inclusive education

Judy W. Kugelmass

This chapter explores the strengths and limitations of educational approaches emerging from two major streams of constructivism – cognitive and social constructivism. Although both acknowledge the significance of physical and social interactions to development and agree that learning is a meaning-making process, they differ in the attention given to the impact of contexts to these processes (Brooks & Brooks, 1994; Fosnot, 1996; Perkins, 1999; Poplin, 1988; von Glaserfeld, 1995, 1998). Educators whose practice reflects cognitive constructivism attend to experiences that support the sequential development of the internal 'schema' they believe to be essential for psychological development of an individual, while social constructivists focus on the impact of the meaning given to interactions within the sociocultural context of families, classrooms, schools and surrounding communities. Although both stand in opposition to behaviorist claims that direct instruction of discreet knowledge and skills can, by themselves, lead to independent mastery of complex ideas and tasks, their difference in emphasis regarding the significance of sociocultural contexts will be seen to have significant implications for the inclusion of all children in general education settings.

PIAGET AND COGNITIVE CONSTRUCTIVISM

Piaget's work in cognitive psychology in the mid-twentieth century (Piaget, 1963; Piaget & Inhelder, 1969) provided theoretical support for the earlier work of Sequin and Itard (Lane, 1976) in the eighteenth and nineteenth centuries, and Montessori (1964) in the early twentieth century. These pioneer 'special educators' were unique among their contemporaries in developing educational approaches designed to demonstrate that children previously believed to be 'uneducable' could learn. Their teaching methods reflected Piaget's subsequent understanding that learning occurred when children were actively engaged in meaningful interactions with people and objects. Piaget did not, however, attend to the social/contextual features of learning that limited or promoted learning as did these early educators but, rather, focused on understanding the internal nature of 'normal' cognitive development. Piagetian theories and the educational approaches that followed reflect that focus.

Piaget demonstrated that development occurred through a process whereby new experiences were integrated with previous ones (assimilation), shaping the development of cognitive structures (schema) within the child (accommodation) through a process called 'equilibration'. Through his observations, he theorized that infants and children were self-regulating learners, intrinsically motivated to construct deeper and richer understandings by building new cognitive structures through the integration of prior with new sensori-motor and linguistic experiences. This 'natural' process required no external rewards or structures, but unfolded as a child interacted with the world. These ideas provided the framework for educational approaches later identified as 'constructivist.' Their emphasis would be on the child's construction of new knowledge through child-determined explorations and guided discovery rather than guided teaching.

In 1987, the National Association for the Education of Young Children (NAEYC) codified this approach as 'Developmentally Appropriate Practice' (DAP) (Bredekamp & Copple, 1987). Developmentally Appropriate Practice called for the preparation of what were assumed to be stimulating, age-appropriate, child-centered environments. Teachers in these settings were to stand back and allow children to make choices regarding when and how to 'construct' their own learning. Because it was assumed that children with special educational needs were unable to benefit from this kind of approach without active intervention from adults, they were generally excluded (Mallory & New, 1996). The exclusion of those children considered to have special education needs was based on the assumption that normal cognitive and psychological development unfolded by itself and followed predetermined and biologically structured sequential patterns. This belief pathologized children from non-middle class families and/or non-dominant cultures, and

others whose learning was at variance with developmental expectations.

This application of cognitive constructivism reflected white, middle-class child-rearing practices and was supported by middle- and upper-class ideologies (Burman, 1994; Walkerdine, 1984). This mismatch between teachers' non-directive interactions with children and the more directive approaches of many parents from lower socio-economic and/or non-European American backgrounds, disadvantaged non-dominant culture children as well as some children with disabilities (Delpit, 1995, 1998; Ladson-Billings, 1994; Mallory & New, 1996). A growing recognition of these limitations of DAP led to NAEYC's 1997 revisions of its definition and suggestions for applications in early childhood classrooms. These proposed changes did not reject the basic premise that children needed to be actively involved in their learning but, rather, acknowledged the importance of modifying instructional practices to address the needs of students with developmental differences as well as those from diverse cultural backgrounds, and included the need for more active mediation by adults and direct instruction within contexts that were individually and culturally appropriate (Bredekamp & Copple, 1997). This alteration, in turn, opened the doors of typical early childhood classrooms to a wider range of children.

In spite of a normative maturationist perspective that limited appreciation for diverse paths towards competency found in individuals with disabilities (Fraiberg, 1977; Gallagher, 2004), cognitive constructivism has played an important role in the creation of educational programs for children with sensory and physical impairments. The demonstration of the importance of early sensori-motor experiences to cognitive and linguistic development was instrumental in the creation of early intervention and infant stimulation programs. Although designed to remediate what were believed to be developmental 'deficits,' these programs led to major advances in understanding and appreciating variance in development. Recognition of the importance of children's active participation in social and physical environments to cognitive development was also central to the creation of special education and related services for children previously believed to be, at best, 'trainable'.

VYGOTSKY AND SOCIAL CONSTRUCTIVISM

Social constructivism provides the framework for instructional approaches that emerged from the sociocultural theory of Lev Vygotsky and his colleagues in Russia during the 1920s (Moll, 1990; van der Veer & Valsiner, 1991; Vygotsky, 1962, 1978; Wertsch, 1985a, 1985b). Although attaching 'constructivism' to Vygotsky's theories has been criticized as confounding his ideas with those of Piaget (see de Valenzuela, this volume, for a discussion of this issue and in-depth examination of sociocultural theory), the term provides a useful label to distinguish both cognitive and social constructivism from the behavioral approaches typically associated with special education. There are, however, significant differences between social constructivist applications of sociocultural theory and cognitive constructivism that should not be overlooked. Cognitive constructivism supports the belief that children must first achieve competence in tasks believed to represent developmental milestones before engaging in more complex tasks. For children with disabilities, this can mean never being exposed to social and cognitive experiences assumed to be beyond their capacity.

Sociocultural theory offers an alternative view, proposing that significant learning takes place before developmental competency can be achieved. Rather than assuming development unfolds from within, social constructivists focus on the need for intentional mediation and interactions within meaningful physical, social and cultural contexts. Learning and development take place as individuals operate within their 'zone of proximal development' (ZPD). This hypothetical place lies just beyond what can be achieved independently but can be approximated with assistance (Moll, 1990). Adults and more competent peers are called upon to provide guided opportunities for engagement at higher levels of learning than students may be able to accomplish on their own.

This understanding emerged, in part, from Vygotsky's experiences with institutionalized and orphaned children, many of whom had physical disabilities, sensory impairments and/or were identified as 'mentally retarded' (Knox & Stevens, 1993, p. 19). He proposed that the degree of cognitive and linguistic deficits seen in institutionalized children was a function of two related aspects of 'special education':

1 A focus on remediation of deficits rather than promotion of children's abilities.
2 The social isolation and negative meaning attached to being placed in a 'special' school or institution.

Both reflected the negative meaning attributed to impairments and the devaluing of individuals with disabilities in Russian society during the early twentieth century (Vygotsky, 1993).

To address these concerns, Vygotsky proposed two related strategies that remain relevant for special education a century later. First, there needed to be a shift in focus from children's deficits to their strengths and abilities. This required the identification of assets from which compensatory skills could be developed to support the learning of culturally appropriate social and academic competencies. To this end, Vygotsky advocated for individualized educational practices that incorporated 'the use of a different symbolic system which maintains the same content as any other instructional or educational process' (Vygotsky, 1993, p. 85). These alternative 'symbolic' systems would be determined by individual children's cognitive and sociocultural needs and abilities, and be directed toward teaching the same content as taught to all other children. This would increase their access to socially and intellectually stimulating social contexts, thereby addressing the second problem facing children with disabilities: social isolation. Vygotsky believed that their inclusion in ordinary schools would reduce negative valuation and the social isolation experienced by individuals in social contexts designed to serve devalued populations.

APPLICATIONS OF SOCIAL CONSTRUCTIVIST THEORY IN INCLUSIVE CLASSROOMS

Social constructivism's focus on the significance of context to learning provides the theoretical rationale for the inclusion of students with disabilities and other special educational needs in general education settings. The creation of these settings requires appropriate supports, adaptations, modifications and differentiation of the general education curriculum. The instructional approaches described in the following sections are those that require students' active involvement and are adaptable to the abilities and needs of all children. Their successful application requires the creation of a social, cultural and physical context that supports and promotes a 'constructivist sociomoral atmosphere' (DeVries & Zan, 1994). This kind of classroom organization addresses children's physiological, emotional, and intellectual needs through mediated interactions among peers, and promotes self-regulation and responsibility for individual and group learning. The 'Responsive Classroom' (Northeast Foundation for Children, n.d.) offers one model of classroom management practices that support this kind of inclusive, social constructivist classroom.

Following from sociocultural theory, social constructivist practices reflect the understanding that learning is a meaning-making process (von Glaserfield, 1995). Unlike the more traditional assumption that learning occurs by adding pieces of information to one another, social constructivism attends to the processes through which learning occurs. Moll (1990) points out that although the 'zone of proximal development' (ZPD) is the primary concept connecting Vygotsky's ideas to one another and their educational applica-

tions, identifying and working with a child within his/her ZPD, although essential, is not all that is required for optimal learning. Reciprocal social interactions in contexts that support problem solving are also essential. Teaching skills or subjects (even those that fall within the child's ZPD) through decontextualized drills and other forms of passive lessons employs 'hidden processes', creating contexts that interfere with cognitive development and social competence.

There is no formula or any one technique that defines either social constructivist instruction or the role of the teacher in a social constructivist classroom. Drawing from several theorists, Gallagher (2004) has instead identified guidelines that best reflect these kinds of teaching practices:

- Instruction starts with a problem.
- Skills are taught within a conceptual context.
- Errors are treated as useful information.
- Students seek solutions to problems.
- Information and knowledge are linked to students' interests and experiences.

Specific instructional approaches that apply these guidelines include: strategy instruction; reciprocal teaching and cooperative learning; project-based and other forms of integrated and thematic teaching; modeling, guided discovery and apprenticeships. These examples reflect social constructivist theory and have been applied and validated in inclusive classrooms serving a wide range of students (Berres et al., 1996; Collins, 2003; Kugelmass, 2005; Palinscar & Brown, 1984; Palinscar et al., 2000; Rainforth & Kugelmass, 2003; Stainback & Stainback, 1992; Trent et al., 1998).

The teacher in a social constructivist classrooms shifts from being the conveyor of information to an active mediator of children's learning. Berk and Winsler (1995) offer the following as examples of teachers' roles in social constructivist classrooms. The teacher:

- Engages in joint problem solving with students.
- Creates common ground for communication through verbal reflection and dialogue.

- Maintains a warm, responsive and supportive emotional tone.
- Provides clues and other supports in response to children's abilities and needs.
- Breaks tasks into smaller components.
- Arranges and adapts materials and activities.
- Relinquishes external control as soon as a child demonstrates independence.

Social constructivist approaches to literacy instruction

'Whole Language' instruction reflects a philosophy of literacy development most often associated with constructivism (Goodman & Goodman, 1990). Not represented by any one teaching method, Whole Language focuses on the importance of developing a literate environment, the use of themes to organize instruction, authentic learning tasks and student ownership of learning (Rankin-Erickson, 2000). Although they state that its underlying philosophy reflects Vygotsky's theories, Goodman and Goodman's (1990) statement that 'learning in school and learning out of school are not different' (p. 229) illustrates a lack of consideration for the significance of context to learning and the need for teacher mediation. The guiding belief that learning to read and write is a 'natural' process, unfolding much in the same way as learning to speak, reflects a cognitive constructivist perspective that has frequently failed to reach children from non-mainstream cultures and those who require direct instruction and/or teacher mediation. The failure to include more active mediation and direct instruction, as originally intended by the developers of Whole Language approaches in New Zealand, has lead to an unfortunate swing of the educational pendulum in the United States toward total reliance on de-contextualized skill instruction (Bromley, 2003).

Social constructivism supports a balanced approach to literacy that requires explicit, systematic, mindful and contextualized instruction (Cambourne, 1999). Reading Recovery (Clay, 1985; Clay & Cazden, 1990) represents an application of these elements that has been successfully applied to literacy development among young children whose rate of progress does not match that of their peers. This approach recognizes the need for teacher mediation, guiding children through the literacy strategies needed to become independent readers and writers. The 'Early Literacy Project' (Englert et al., 1995) is another related approach. Incorporating social constructivist principles, its applications have promoted growth in literacy development among students (grades 1–4) identified as having mild disabilities (see Trent et al., 1998, p. 293).

Literacy programs found to be effective for children with disabilities and other special educational needs blend the principles of Whole Language with more direct instruction. In their review of the research on applications of social constructivism to literacy instruction for children with 'mild disabilities', Trent et al. (1998) point to the importance of reciprocal teaching in expanding comprehension of texts by engaging students in questioning, summarizing, clarifying and predicting with peers. Palinscar and Brown (1984) also report marked improvements in comprehension among children who engaged in these processes that were reliable, durable and generalizable.

Social constructivist approaches to science and mathematics

Although social constructivist theory supports teaching units of integrated instruction, it is also applied to discipline-based learning. Social constructivist approaches in the areas of science and math focus on developing an understanding of how basic concepts underlying their applications were first developed (Schmittau, 2003). Students are then guided toward applying these concepts in different contexts to solve authentic problems. They develop understanding through interactive learning experiences that take place in classrooms organized to support the exploration of these ideas. Students' experiences are mediated through interactions and dialogue with one another and their teachers. These approaches call on the active exploration of materials and sequenced activities designed by the teacher to mediate children's increasingly complex understanding. More in-depth discussions of social constructivist applications to teaching mathematics can be found in the work of Bauersfeld (1995), Schifter (1996) and Wood, Cobb and Yackel (1995).

Research on the application of 'Guided Inquiry Science Teaching' in inclusive classrooms has demonstrated that the deficits in reading and writing experienced by children identified as having learning disabilities need not interfere with their learning complex scientific concepts (Palinscar et al., 2000). This approach begins with a presentation of guiding questions related to a broad conceptual problem. Students then proceed through an inquiry process, guided by additional questions posed by the teacher. Working in pairs or small groups, they observe and interact with physical manifestations of the problem, reflecting on the phenomenon under study and, finally, report their findings to the teacher and other classmates in a variety of ways (for example, written and/or verbal reports, posters, illustrations, group presentations). Palinscar et al. (2000) investigated the effectiveness of this approach with students identified as having learning disabilities. They found that these students learned scientific concepts successfully when provided with additional supports by specialists and the general education teacher. The biggest barrier to the effectiveness of this approach was not its pedagogical foundation but, rather, the reluctance of some classroom teachers to differentiate their expectations for individual children (Collins, 2003; Palinscar et al., 2000).

CONCLUSION

Creating instructional approaches that enable all children's participation as active members of learning communities in ways that enrich their lives, expand their experiences, and promote their independence requires the continual problematizing of teaching and learning. The differing needs, abilities, interests and experiences found among children in heterogeneous classrooms require individualization and differentiation. Curricular and instructional adaptations need to be made in response to differences in students' temperaments, learning styles, cultures, interests and abilities, within the specific context of their classroom communities. Children's failure to be self-directed, active learners may indicate differing sociocultural expectations, developmental idiosyncrasies, and/or specific impairments. To be successful, some children may need more direct instruction than others and require external guidance from adults, while others may need more time and the space to explore on their own. Whatever the case, educators must first acknowledge that learning difficulties reflect a mismatch between the child and expectations emanating from the social context of the classroom.

At its core, social constructivism proposes that no single answer is appropriate for every student, in any given context. Rather, teachers must understand that all learning and problem-solving involves meaning-making for both themselves and their students, and that instructional decisions need to be the outcome of their reciprocal negotiations (Palinscar & Brown, 1984). This process requires an openness to interactions, devoid of negative judgments toward any child. It calls for more than a willingness to blend theories and instructional approaches but, rather, requires a deep understanding that all knowledge is inseparable from either a teacher's or student's culture, language, experience and belief (Gallagher, 2004).

Vygotsky's experiences with institutionalized children convinced him that their lack of full participation in social life was responsible for the limited development of their 'higher mental functions' (Berk & Winsler, 1995, p. 83). This understanding was particularly relevant for children with physical and sensory impairments and/or psychological problems. The sociocultural context in which he lived would not permit the inclusion of these children in general education classrooms. Instead, his theories became the foundation for the 'defectology' movement in Russia, leading to the creation of even more specialized and separate educational institutions for children with disabilities. This development can be understood in terms of the socio-historical context of the Soviet Union in the early and mid-twentieth century. The knowledge gained during the second half of the twentieth century regarding children's learning and development, combined with a growing understanding of the relationship between democracy, human rights and the creation of publicly supported schools for all children, have, however, created a different social context. Hopefully, the time has come for the realization of Vygotsky's vision of a radical transformation of educational processes.

REFERENCES

Bauersfeld, H. (1995). The structuring of the structures: Development and function of mathematizing as a social practice. In L. P. Steffe & J. Gale (Eds.), *Constructivism in education* (pp. 137–158). Hillsdale, NJ: Lawrence Erlbaum.

Berk, L., & Winsler, A. (1995). Scaffolding children's learning: Vygotsky and early childhood education. Washington, DC: NAEYC.

Berres, M., Ferguson, D., Knoblock, P., & Wood, C. (Eds.). (1996). *Creating tomorrow's schools today: Stories of inclusion, change and renewal.* New York: Teachers College Press.

Bredekamp, S., & Copple, C. (Eds.). (1987). *Developmentally appropriate practices in early childhood programs.* Washington, DC: NAEYC.

Bredekamp, S., & Copple, C. (Eds.). (1997). *Developmentally appropriate practices in early childhood programs* (revised ed.). Washington, DC: NAEYC.

Bromley, K. (2003). Finding the middle ground in literacy instruction. In B. Rainforth & J. W. Kugelmass (Eds.), *Curriculum and instruction for all learners: Blending systematic and constructivist approaches in inclusive elementary schools* (pp. 79–111). Baltimore, MD: Paul H. Brookes.

Brooks, J. G., & Brooks, M. G. (1994). *The case for the constructivist classroom.* Alexandria, VA: Association for Supervision and Curriculum Development.

Burman, S. (1994). *Deconstructing developmental psychology.* New York: Routledge.

Cambourne, B. (1999). Conditions for literacy learning. *The Reading Teacher, 53,* 126–127.

Clay, M. M. (1985). *The early detection of reading difficulties* (3rd ed.). Portsmouth, NH: Heinemann.

Clay, M. M., & Cazden, C. B. (1990). A Vygotskian interpretation of Reading Recovery. In L. Moll (Ed.), *Vygotsky and education: Instructional implications and applications of sociohistorical psychology* (pp. 206–222). Cambridge: Cambridge University Press.

Collins, K. M. (2003). *Ability profiling and school failure: One child's struggle to be seen as competent.* Mahwah, NJ: Lawrence Erlbaum Associates.

Delpit, L. D. (1995). *Other people's children: Culture conflict in the classroom.* New York: New Press.

Delpit, L. D. (1998). The silenced dialogue: Power and pedagogy in educating other people's children. *Harvard Educational Review, 58*(3), 280–298.

DeVries, R., & Zan, B. (1994) *Moral classrooms, moral children: Creating a constructivist atmosphere in early education.* New York: Teachers College Press.

Englert, C. S., Garmon, A. Marriage, T., Rozendale, M., Tarant, K. & Urba, J. (1995). The Early Literacy Project: Connecting across the literacy curriculum. *Remedial and Special Education, 18,* 253–275.

Fosnot, C. T. (1996). Constructivism: A psychological theory of learning. In C. T. Fosnot (Ed.), *Constructivism: Theory, perspectives and practices* (pp. 8–33). New York: Teachers College Press.

Fraiberg, S. (1977). *Insights from the blind: Comparative studies of blind and sighted infants.* New York: Basic Books.

Gallagher, D. J. (2004). The importance of constructivism and constructivist pedagogy for disability studies in education. *Disability Studies Quarterly, 24*(2), 1–15.

Goodman, Y. M., & Goodman, K. S. (1990). Vygotsky in a whole language perspective. In L. Moll, (Ed.). *Vygotsky and education: Instructional implications and applications of sociohistorical psychology* (pp. 223–250.) Cambridge: Cambridge University Press.

Knox, J., & Stevens, C. (1993). Vygotsky and Soviet Russian defectology: Translators' introduction. In R. W. Rieber & A. S. Carton (Eds.), *The collected works of L. S. Vygotksy* (Vol. 2, pp. 1–25). New York: Plenum.

Kugelmass, J. W. (2005). *The inclusive school: Sustaining equity and standards.* New York: Teachers College Press.

Ladson-Billings, G. (1994). *The dreamkeepers: Successful teachers of African American children.* Cambridge, MA: Harvard University Press.

Lane, H. (1976). *The wild boy of Aveyron.* Cambridge, MA: Harvard University Press.

Mallory, B., & New, R. (1996). *Diversity and developmentally appropriate practice.* New York: Teachers College Press.

Moll, L. (Ed.). (1990). *Vygotsky and education: Instructional implications and applications of sociohistorical psychology.* Cambridge: Cambridge University Press.

Montessori, M. (1964). *The Montessori method.* New York: Schocken Books.

Northeast Foundation for Children. (n. d.). *Responsive classroom.* (Accessed February 2005) http://www.responsiveclassroom.org

Palinscar, A. S., & Brown, A. L. (1984). Reciprocal teaching of comprehension- fostering and comprehension-monitoring activities. *Cognition and Instruction, 1*, 117–175.

Palinscar, A. S., Collins, K. M., Marano, N. L. & Magnusson, S. J. (2000). Investigating the engagement and learning of students with learning disabilities in guided inquiry science teaching. *Language, Speech, and Learning Services in Schools, 31*, 240–251.

Perkins, D. (1999). The many faces of constructivism. *Educational Leadership, 57*(3), 6–11.

Piaget, J. (1963). *The origins of intelligence in children.* New York: W. W. Norton & Co.

Piaget, J. & Inhelder, B. (1969). *The psychology of the child.* New York: Basic Books.

Poplin, M. S. (1988). The reductionist fallacy in learning disabilities: Replicating the past by reducing the present. *Journal of Learning Disabilities, 21*, 389–400.

Rainforth, B., & Kugelmass, J. W. (Eds.). (2003). *Curriculum and instruction for all learners: Blending systematic and constructivist approaches in inclusive elementary schools.* Baltimore, MD: Paul H. Brookes.

Rankin-Erickson, J.L. (2000). A survey of instructional practices of special education teachers nominated as effective teachers of literacy. *Learning Disabilities Research and Practice, 15*(4), 206–255.

Schifter, D. (1996). A constructivist perspective on teaching and learning mathematics. In C. T. Fosnot (Ed.), *Constructivism: Theory, perspectives and practices* (pp. 73–91). New York: Teachers College Press.

Schmittau, J. (2003). Beyond constructivism and back to basics: A cultural historical alternative to the teaching of the base ten positional system. In B. Rainforth & J.W. Kugelmass (Eds.), *Curriculum and instruction for all learners: Blending systematic and constructivist approaches in inclusive elementary schools* (pp. 113–132). Baltimore, MD: Paul H. Brookes.

Stainback, S., & Stainback, W. (Eds.). (1992). *Curriculum considerations in inclusive classrooms: Facilitating learning for all students.* Baltimore, MD: Paul Brookes.

Trent, S.C., Artiles, A.J., & Englert, C.S. (1998). From deficit thinking to social constructivism: A review of theory, research, and practice in special education. *Review of Research in Special Education, 23*, 277–307.

Van der Veer, R., & Valsiner, J. (1991). *Understanding Vygotsky: A quest for synthesis.* Cambridge, MA: Basil Blackwell.

Von Glaserfeld, E. (1995). A constructivist approach to teaching. In L. P. Steffe & J. Gale (Eds.), *Constructivism in education* (pp. 3–16). Hillsdale, NJ: Lawrence Erlbaum.

Von Glaserfeld, E. (1998). Why constructivism must be radical. In M. Larochelle, N. Bednarz, & J. Garrison (Eds.), *Constructivism and education* (pp. 23–28). Cambridge: Cambridge University Press.

Vygotsky, L.S. (1962). *Language and thought.* Cambridge, MA: MIT Press.

Vygotsky, L.S. (1978). *Mind and society.* Cambridge, MA: Harvard University Press.

Vygotsky, L.S. (1993). Introduction: The fundamentals of defectology. In R. W. Rieber & A. S. Carton (Eds.), *The collected works of L. S. Vygotksy* (Vol. 2, pp. 29–93). New York: Plenum.

Walkerdine, V. (1984). Developmental psychology and the child-centered pedagogy: the insertion of Piaget into early education. In J. Henriques, W. Hollyway, C. Urwin, C. Venn, & V. Walkerdine (Eds), *Changing the subject: Psychology, social regulation and subjectivity* (pp. 152–202). London: Methuen.

Wertsch, J. V. (Ed.). (1985a). *Culture, communication and cognition: Vygotskian perspectives.* Cambridge: Cambridge University Press.

Wertsch, J. V. (1985b). *Vygotsky and the social formation of the mind.* Cambridge, MA: Harvard University Press.

Wood, T., Cobb, P., & Yackel, E. (1995). Reflections on learning and teaching mathematics in elementary school. In L. P. Steffe & J. Gale (Eds.), *Constructivism in education* (pp. 401–422). Hillsdale, NJ: Lawrence Erlbaum.

21

Sociocultural views of learning

J. S. de Valenzuela

INTRODUCTION

Current conceptualizations of sociocultural theory draw heavily on the work of Vygotsky. However, it would be erroneous to limit understanding of this important influence in educational theory, thought, and practice to the works of one individual. This is a rich area of research and theory, which has had, and will continue to have, a significant impact on the field of special education.

Sociocultural theory attempts to provide a complex description of the dynamic contexts in which, and the processes through which, learning and development take place. Cognitive development is seen as emerging as a result of interactions within a cultural and historical context, rather than unfolding in a biologically driven sequence. In this view, learning is seen as leading, or fostering, cognitive development. Sociocultural approaches emphasize the active bi-directional interaction of individuals with their environments and with others around them and the changes in these relationships over time. Clearly, sociocultural theory is much more complex than this initial description

might suggest. The purpose of this chapter is to provide a more complex description of sociocultural theory, distinguish sociocultural approaches from other related perspectives, and to identify some of the areas within special education which sociocultural theory either currently makes or could make major contributions.

Impact on special education

Many of the innovations based on sociocultural theory are not specific to special education. Rather, they have been developed within the field of education as a whole and adapted to the diverse instructional environments where students with disabilities are educated. Sociocultural theory has been especially influential in the areas of pedagogy, language and communication, and assessment. The zone of proximal development (ZPD), is perhaps the most well-known pedagogical construct and is related to several other instructional innovations, such as scaffolding, joint productive activity, and instructional conversation. These areas will be addressed later in this chapter, following a more in-depth discussion of past and current conceptions of sociocultural theory.

HISTORY OF SOCIOCULTURAL THEORY

Sociocultural theory is generally considered to be based in the work of Vygotsky, a prominent psychologist who lived and worked in the Soviet Union in the early years of the 1900s. Vygotsky died in 1934 at the age of 38, having worked in the field of psychology for only 10 years. According to Bozhovich, one of his former students, his theory 'never achieved finished form' (1977, p. 5). Due to the political context in the Soviet Union at the time, much of Vygotsky's work was suppressed from the mid to late 1930s until the 1950s (van der Veer & Valsiner, 1994). However, development of sociocultural theory, or cultural-historical theory as it is also known, continued in the Soviet Union through the work of Vygotsky's colleagues and former students.

In the United States, Vygotsky's work was largely unknown until the abridged English translation of *Thought and Language* (Vygotsky, 1962). This was followed by an edited compilation of portions of several different works, entitled *Mind and Society* (Vygotsky, 1978). These publications sparked great interest and had a profound impact on the development of educational theory in the United States, although not without criticism of the selection, editing, and translation of these early works (Gillen, 2000; van der Veer & Valsiner, 1994). Although a good portion of Vygotsky's work was directly related to the development of individuals with disabilities, especially those with moderate learning difficulties and sensory impairments, this aspect of his theory has not had a significant impact on special education. Additionally, even though a limited number of Vygotsky's works were available in English in the form of journal articles beginning in 1934 and a number of Vygotsky's works were published in the journal *Soviet Psychology*, these works are much less frequently cited than *Thought and Language* and *Mind and Society*. In 1987, the first of six volumes[1] of collected works by Vygotsky was published (Reiber & Carton, 1987) and the educational community began to have access to a greater range of Vygotsky's work. Perhaps as more of Vygotsky's original corpus becomes better known, those aspects of sociocultural theory which pertain directly to special education will begin to have greater impact.

Key aspects of socio-historical theory

Vygotsky is perhaps best known for his general genetic[2] law of cultural development:

> We can formulate the general genetic law of cultural development as follows: every function in the cultural development of the child appears on the stage twice, in two planes, first, the social, then the psychological, first between people as an intermental category, then within the child as a [sic] intramental category. This pertains equally to voluntary attention, to logical memory, to the formation of concepts, and to the development of will. (Vygotsky, 1997, p. 106)

According to Kozulin (1990), Vygotsky's primary objective 'was to identify specifically human aspects of behavior and cognition' (p. 4) via a methodology termed *genetic analysis*. He focused on several different domains of development: human evolution (*phylogenesis*), development of human cultures (*sociocultural history*), individual development (*ontogenesis*) and development which occurs during the course of a learning session or activity or very rapid change in one psychological function (*microgenesis*) (Wertsch, 1991). While genetic analysis involves the examination of the origins and processes of development of higher mental processes within all of these domains, the most common foci of current educational research are ontogenesis and microgenesis. John-Steiner and Mahn (1996) argued that genetic analysis, with its emphasis on ever-changing social, cultural, and historical contexts of development, implies that 'there can be no universal schema that adequately represents the dynamic relation between external and internal aspects of development' (p. 194). Wertsch and Tulviste (1992) interpreted

Vygotsky's concept of the social origin of higher mental functioning as fundamentally distinct from how cognition has been traditionally viewed, as a function of the individual. They argued that 'one can speak equally appropriately of mental processes as occurring *between* people' [original emphasis] (p. 549) and that 'his [Vygotsky's] view is one in which mind is understood as "extending beyond the skin." Mind, cognition, memory, and so forth are understood not as attributes or properties of the individual, but as functions that may be carried out intermentally or intramentally' (p. 549). Vygotsky emphasized the importance of 'mediated activity' (1977, p. 71) in the development of higher psychological functions. He identified the potential of both technical/physical tools (directed externally) and psychological tools (directed internally) as mediational means (John-Steiner & Mahn, 1996). However, for Vygotsky, psychological tools, particularly language, were of primary concern.

The above is a brief summary of current Western interpretations of Vygotsky's principle thesis. Many of the aspects of Vygotsky's work described above continue to figure prominently in current conceptions of sociocultural theory. However, it must be remembered that limited access to Vygotsky's work has led to differences in interpretation (Mahn, 1999). It is also important to keep in mind that sociocultural theory has continued to develop over time. One way of understanding this process is through a sociocultural lens: as new researchers and theoreticians have joined the dialogue, they have come with their own intellectual history and have grounded their studies and theoretical formulations in different readings and interpretations of Vygotsky's work. This transactional perspective on the continuing development of sociocultural theory recognizes that it is incorrect to use 'sociocultural theory' and 'Vygotsky' synonymously.

From socio-historical theory to activity theory

Although Vygotsky is often credited with developing sociocultural theory, Radzikhov-

skii and Khomskaya (1981) emphasized the active collaboration of Leontiev and Luria in this effort. Even prior to Vygotsky's death, Leontiev, along with other researchers including Bozhovich, Zaporozhets, and P. Zinchenko, began shifting their focus toward physical or technical tools as mediators, rather than continuing Vygotsky's emphasis on psychological tools. Some, such as Kozulin (1986), see this as a major divergence between cultural-historical theory and the development of what would become known as the 'psychological theory of activity' due to its focus on action and activity. However, others such as Davydov and Zinchenko (1989) see this shift in focus as part of the ongoing development of sociocultural theory. This difference in perspective continues to play a role in ongoing theoretical debates.

Relationship to other major theoretical approaches

Sociocultural theory and constructivism are often confounded, which is problematic. There are a number of distinct theoretical positions which could be characterized under the umbrella term of constructivism. For example, psychological constructivism, historically linked with Piaget, can be differentiated from social constructivism (Cobb, 1994). While some authors position sociocultural theory within social constructivism, others do not. This conflict in terminology use, as well as identified areas of significant difference between constructivism (especially psychological constructivism) and sociocultural theory, argue for avoiding the interchangeable use of 'sociocultural theory' and 'constructivism'.

As previously discussed, a key aspect of sociocultural theory is the positioning of social, rather than individual, processes as primary in the development of higher mental functions. Cole (1996) illustrated this focus on social processes and the importance of context in the following:

> Because what we call mind works through artifacts, it cannot be unconditionally bounded by the head or even by the body, but must be seen as distributed in the artifacts which are *woven together* and

which weave together individual human actions in concert with and as a part of the permeable, changing, events of life. (pp. 136–137)

This tenet leads to several related distinctions between sociocultural theory and constructivist perspectives. While psychological constructivists attend to individual processes and socioculturalists to social processes in development, Cobb (2000) elaborated a third position, that taken by social constructivists, where 'equal significance is attributed to individual and communal processes with neither being elevated above the other' (p. 279). Differing perspectives on the relative primacy of social versus individual processes in development parallel differences in the focus of analysis. While the focus of sociocultural analyses 'typically view individuals as participating in broader sociocultural practices' (Cobb & Yackel, 1996, p. 185), constructivists typically take the individual as the unit of analysis. Cobb and Yackel proposed the *emergent* perspective,[3] which 'coordinates' (p. 188) both analytic perspectives in a reciprocal, reflexive manner. In sociocultural theory learning is said to lead development. In contrast, psychological constructivist approaches focus on developmental readiness for learning. Vygotsky's (1977) assertion that 'the first use of tools immediately repudiates the notion that development represents the unfolding of the child's organically predetermined system of activity' (p. 73) appears in direct opposition to Piaget's notion of stages of development. Clearly, genuine differences of position do exist between sociocultural theory and differing constructivist approaches.

Current conceptions of sociocultural theory

As additional works by Vygotsky and other sociocultural theorists from the former Soviet Union have become available in English, some aspects of sociocultural theory, as originally interpreted in the US and Europe, have been reconsidered. This has prompted much needed clarification of certain aspects of Vygotsky's original propositions, development

of several somewhat distinct traditions within sociocultural theory, as well as attempts to reconcile divergent perspectives, such as socio-historical and activity theory. There is a growing tendency for Western socioculturalists to incorporate perspectives from Dewey and Mead. Others suggest attempting to reconcile aspects of Piaget's theoretical work into a sociocultural perspective.

There are a number of educational theorists working within the sociocultural perspective, more recently termed by some Cultural Historical Activity Theory, or CHAT (Cole & Engeström, 1993). Each researcher or group of researchers has a unique focus, analytic framework, and theoretical perspective, as well as sharing certain fundamental similarities. Sawyer (2002a, 2002b) suggests that some of these differences stem from (a) differing perspectives on the appropriate unit of analysis and (b) hypothesized relations and interactions between individuals and the social context. The latter refers to the extent to which individuals can be separated from the sociocultural context, both in reality and for analytic purposes, as well as the directionality and mechanisms of influence. Although critically important, debate at this level of theory has not yet significantly impacted special education. The predominate impact has come from more general understandings of sociocultural theory, as defined at the beginning of this chapter. Given that the study of individuals with disabilities had a significant influence on the original development of sociocultural theory, it is reasonable to hope that the field of special education could have a reciprocal influence on further refinement of sociocultural theory.

MAJOR INTERPRETATIONS OF SOCIOCULTURAL THEORY IN SPECIAL EDUCATION

Instructional approaches

When considering instructional approaches from sociocultural perspectives, it is vital to remember that sociocultural theory addresses the development of higher psychological processes. Therefore, the focus for instructional activities under a sociocultural framework should be on development, rather than simply skill attainment. This is especially critical in special education, which has traditionally relied on reductionistic, transmission-oriented, instructional models.

Zone of proximal development

Like all other aspects of sociocultural theory, the ZPD is open to interpretation. In general, it refers to areas of developing, but still immature, cognitive functions, which can be identified through tasks which children can only accomplish with some kind of support or assistance from another, more capable, person. Chaiklin (2003) emphasized that the ZPD 'is not a property of the child … but simply an indication of the presence of certain maturing functions, which can be a target for meaningful, interventive action' (p. 43). This intervention should be focused on assisting the individual's transition to a higher level of development, not on the acquisition of specific skills. This last point differentiates instruction based on the ZPD from transmission models of instruction, which also utilize interaction with others (that is, a teacher) as a means for fostering learning. The notion of the ZPD also emphasizes another key aspect of sociocultural theory, that development occurs within sociocultural contexts that are mutually constructed by students and teachers.

Scaffolding

Another key aspect of sociocultural theory is the role of mediators (that is, psychological or technical tools) in the development of higher psychological functions. Scaffolding can provide such mediation. As a means of assisting performance, it can reveal an individual's ZPD and potentially facilitate the development of higher functions. Scaffolding can take a variety of verbal and non verbal forms, including 'gestures, eye gazes, and pauses' (Stone, 1993, p. 176). While some representations of scaffolding in the literature have painted a picture of the 'more competent other' transmitting knowledge and skills to a passive recipient, more recent descriptions emphasize the active role of the child or student in the interaction (Kinginger, 2002). Indeed, Kinginger argued that scaffolding 'implies the eventual handover of interactional control to students' (p. 254) and Stone (1998) emphasized the necessarily transitory nature of the assistance. Stone (1993) additionally suggested that scaffolding must be understood as involving 'a complex set of social and semiotic dynamics' (p. 180), including the complex interpersonal dynamics at play during the scaffolding process. Examinations of these dynamics must go beyond the typical focus on the immediate interaction of participants to 'the social or cultural factors influencing the quality and potential utility of that interaction' (Stone, 1998, p. 349).

Joint productive activity

Tharp and Gallimore (1988) discussed scaffolding as occurring during joint productive activities. Tharp (1997) identified joint productive activity, 'when experts and novices work together for a common product or goal, and during the activity have opportunities to converse about it' (p. 6), as the context in which 'learning takes place best' (p. 6). It emphasizes the importance of interaction between participants in a learning environment and the reciprocal, transactional nature of their interactions. Joint productive activity has the possibility of fostering common understandings, particularly when learners are allowed to influence the development of the learning context. This is especially crucial when students and teachers come from different cultural, socioeconomic, and experiential backgrounds.

Instructional conversation

The opportunity to engage in conversation is a critical aspect of joint productive activity. This type of dialogue, where students as well as teachers fully participate in the interaction, is termed *instructional conversation* (Goldenberg & Patthey-Chavez, 1995). Instructional conversation is often contrasted with the traditional mode of teacher–student communication, which has been variously termed recitation script or identified by its typical interaction sequence of teacher initiation, student response, and teacher evaluation (IRE) (Griffin & Mehan, 1981). Key aspects of instructional conversation include: strategic use of questions designed to deepen students' thinking about ideas, rather than 'testing' questions with a predetermined correct answer; teacher comments aimed at stimulating student reflection, rather than information transmission; and a natural evolution of the dialogue without a preset script.

Communication and language

Communication and language development
In sociocultural theory, language has a primary role in conveying sociocultural knowledge and mediating cognitive development. This perspective also focuses attention on contextual influences in language development. This has become increasingly important in recent child language research. Language socialization (Schieffelin & Ochs, 1986) views the development of sociocultural knowledge and language to be (a) mutually constituative and (b) both process and product. In terms of the latter, Ochs (1986) defined language socialization as 'both socialization through language and socialization to language' (p. 2). By examining cross-cultural variation in ways adults interact with children, this perspective has been fundamental in challenging the notion that there is one best way to promote language development in young children.

Language and culture in the classroom
Sociocultural theory fosters more culturally sensitive perspectives on language use in the classroom and reframes differences in the language use of culturally and linguistically diverse students from a deficit perspective to one which recognizes the value and importance of students' home language and culture to their learning and development. Research among diverse cultural groups in the US,

such as native Hawaiians, Native Americans, and African Americans, has demonstrated that positive student engagement with the learning context is facilitated when the language use patterns of their home communities are accommodated in the classroom. For example, Suina and Smolkin (1994) discussed the importance of group consensus and participation, learning through observation, private practice before demonstrating skill acquisition, and group rather than individual recognition, to Pueblo[4] students. When students' cultural patterns of interaction and communication are taken into account possibilities for learning are enhanced.

Dynamic assessment
Viewing development as resulting from social processes results in distinctively different approaches to assessment. *Dynamic assessment* refers to a rich and varied group of assessment techniques (Lidz & Elliot, 2000), both formal and informal, that are interactive and focus on students' learning processes (Lidz, 1995). As such, they examine the impact of the learning context of students' abilities. To accomplish this, dynamic assessments often either take a test–teach– retest format or compare the effects of different prompts, cues, or scaffolding devices with a child's unaided performance. Dynamic assessment has been used to evaluate students' learning across a wide variety of areas, ages, and abilities. Examples provided in the Lidz and Elliot volume include assessments referenced to a specific curricular focus, such as the biological classification system, or to more general developmental abilities, such as language development or problem-solving. Dynamic assessments have been used with infants and toddlers, adults, and individuals with disabilities, including both mild and severe disabilities, as well as those with more typical development. Dynamic assessment has also been suggested as a more appropriate method of assessing language ability in bilingual students (Peña, 1996). While dynamic assessment is still not commonly used during formal diagnostic eval-

uations in the US, it has been somewhat more commonly discussed within the context of classroom-based assessment. Dynamic assessment is linked to the ZPD construct, in that dynamic assessment attempts to identify areas of potential development by examining the effect of mediation on student performance.

EPISTEMOLOGICAL ISSUES

Positivism as the dominant paradigm in special education

Bogdan and Kugelmass (1984) argued that special education is based on several fundamental assumptions: '(1) disability is a condition that individuals have; (2) disability/typical distinction is a useful and objective distinction; (3) special education is a rationally conceived and co-ordinated system of services that help children labeled disabled; (4) progress in the field is made by improving diagnosis, intervention, and technology' (p. 173). These assumptions represent a positivistic epistemology, which views knowledge as 'objective, valuefree, and "scientific"' (Bennett & LeCompte, 1990, p. 25). In special education, positivism has influenced the development and application of transmission-based instructional strategies, such as direct instruction, the use of applied behavior analysis for assessment of student behavior and behavior management, the reliance on standardized, norm-referenced assessment instruments, and the positioning of experimental and quasi-experimental designs as the gold-standard for research.

Impact of dominant paradigm on acceptance of innovations grounded in sociocultural theory

Currently there is much debate in the literature about the validity of alternative paradigms, the positive or negative impact of alternative paradigms on the ability to address students' educational needs, and even whether a paradigm shift has occurred or not.

One of the obstacles to adoption of innovations grounded in sociocultural theory is the intense debate surrounding the validity of 'postmodern' paradigms. While not primarily targeted at those coming from a sociocultural perspective, too often, all non-positivistic research and theory is painted with the same brush and summarily dismissed.

A challenge for sociocultural theory will be to surmount this polarizing debate in ways which allow for thoughtful consideration of the potential contributions from a variety of perspectives. Trent, Artiles, and Englert (1998) have criticized those on both sides of 'the paradigm wars' for failure to consider methodologies associated with other camps which might be effective. For example, a sociocultural stance does not exclude strategic use of direct instruction for particular learning objectives. Similarly, the sociocultural perspective can foster the move from an emphasis on 'behavior modification', a reductionistic perspective on behavior, to 'positive behavioral supports', which locates problem behaviors in the interaction of the individual with the environment.

Progress made in the acceptance of sociocultural theory and its innovations

Paradigm wars notwithstanding, sociocultural theory has made inroads into mainstream special education. Ideas which have a basis in or are congruent with sociocultural theory, such as cooperative learning, peer-mediated instruction, and the need to evaluate students' performance within the context of the instructional setting, are all considered fairly non-controversial instructional practices today. There is widespread recognition of the need to address schooling issues related to student backgrounds, although the proposed approaches differ significantly. Additionally, the idea that context matters, in the learning, behavior, and development of individuals, is prevalent throughout the field. Nevertheless, before it can be said that special education is grounded in the sociocultural perspective, much remains to be done.

FUTURE DIRECTIONS

Sociocultural theory has the potential to provide a starting point for examining and addressing critical issues in special education. This theory is especially useful for considering dilemmas related to culturally and linguistically diverse individuals, those with extensive and pervasive needs for support, and for considering future directions in assessment. However, it may not provide sufficient direction for addressing some issues, such as systemic differences in access to power which hinder attempts to improve special education practices. Critical theory may provide a useful lens for understanding resistance to reform initiatives aimed at allowing traditionally marginalized groups a voice in the debate and power to select their own path to educational reform.

Issues of educational equity

Educational equity recognizes that equal treatment is not the same as equal opportunity to learn. This is a fundamental principle of special education – a student who is blind yet who receives the same textbook as the rest of the class is receiving the same treatment, but not the same opportunity to access the text. Yet, students who come from cultural and linguistic backgrounds different from the school culture are often not provided opportunities to access learning opportunities. Indeed, students who come from diverse backgrounds may be incorrectly identified with a disability or, even if a disability is accurately identified, their cultural and linguistic background may be assumed to be insignificant in the presence of the disability.

Bilingual multicultural special education

Calls for including diverse perspectives in special education which are sensitive to the history of minorities in the United States are not new (Baca & Lane, 1974). Bilingual multicultural special education has been established for more than 30 years and is grounded in sociocultural perspectives. A wealth of publications, instructional strategies, and training programs have been developed. Issues, such as the disproportionate representation of minority students in special education, have been brought into the national debate. However, Figueroa (1999) argued that the current theoretical base for special education prevents a coherent interface between special education and bilingual education. The incompatibility between the paradigms underlying special education and bilingual multicultural special education positions culturally and linguistically relevant, context-sensitive pedagogy within a system based on remediating deficits assumed to reside within the child. Pervasive adoption of the principles and practices of bilingual multicultural special education is predicated on wider acceptance of sociocultural perspectives within special education, and indeed education, as a whole. Until then, bilingual multicultural special education remains marginalized as a program, as much as the students it seeks to assist.

Students with extensive and pervasive needs for supports

Bilingual multicultural special education has primarily focused on the needs of students identified with learning and behavioral disabilities. However, that students with intellectual disabilities also learn and develop within a sociocultural context frequently goes unrecognized. Sociocultural perspectives emphasize the importance of psychological tools and interaction with others within learning contexts. However, too frequently, students with extensive and pervasive needs for supports are denied access to a range of psychological tools, including the use of their home language as a means of instruction, alternative and augmentative communication, and literacy instruction in print-rich environments. All too often, they are segregated from their peers, which severely restricts the possibility of interaction with more knowledgeable others across a variety of contexts. As Vygotsky (Reiber & Carton, 1993) reminded us, disabilities stem only indirectly from within child differences. Lack of opportunities to learn can have a far more debilitating impact on development than innate characteristics.

From sociocultural theory to critical theory – a needed shift for special education

Contemporary critical theory in education focuses on 'asymmetries in power and privilege' (McLaren, 2003, p. 69) and examines the role of schooling in both constructing inequality and providing possibilities for change. In many aspects, critical theory and sociocultural theory are compatible perspectives. Sociocultural theory emphasizes the importance of the social context of human development. Critical theory provides the framework to examine the ways in which special education practices both limit opportunities for individuals identified with disabilities, especially those from marginalized groups, and serve to sustain an ideology of disability which perpetuates current practices. The marriage of both approaches provides a rich foundation for examining issues of educational equity and social justice within special education.

NOTES

1   Volume 2 (Reiber & Carton, 1993) contained Vygotsky's works related to 'defectology', as the study of individuals with disabilities is translated.
2   It is important to note that in sociocultural theory the term 'genetic' is used to indicate 'origin', not a trait derived from chromosomal make-up.
3   See Sawyer (2002) for an in-depth discussion of the historical and cross-disciplinary roots of the emergentist perspective.
4   This term originates from Spanish and was used to identify the settled villages that Spanish explorers came upon during their entrance into the Southwest during the sixteenth century. The term continues to be used to refer to the people and tribes that comprise the 19 different Pueblos of New Mexico. This term distinguishes these tribes from other tribal groups in New Mexico, namely the Apache and Navajo. (C. Sims, personal communication, August 11, 2005.)

REFERENCES

Baca, L., & Lane, K. (1974). A dialogue on cultural implications for learning. *Exceptional Children, 40*(8), 552–563.

Bennett, K. P., & LeCompte, M. D. (1990). *The way schools work: A sociological analysis of education.* New York: Longman.

Bogdan, R., & Kugelmass, J. (1984). Case studies of mainstreaming: A symbolic interactionist approach to special schooling. In L. Barton & S. Tomlinson (Eds.), *Special education and social interests* (pp. 173–191). New York: Nichols.

Bozhovich, L. I. (1977). The concept of cultural-historical development of the mind and its prospects. *Soviet Psychology, 16*(1), 5–22.

Chaiklin, S. (2003). The zone of proximal development in Vygotsky's analysis of learning and instruction. In A. Kozulin, B. Gindis, V. S. Ageyev, & S. M. Miller (Eds.), *Vygotsky's educational theory in cultural context* (pp. 39–64). New York: Cambridge University Press.

Cobb, P. (1994). Where is mind? Constructivist and sociocultural perspectives on mathematical development. *Educational Researcher, 23*(7), 13–20.

Cobb, P. (2000). Constructivism. In *Encyclopedia of psychology* (Vol. 2, pp. 277–279). Washington, DC: American Psychological Association.

Cobb, P., & Yackel, E. (1996). Constructivist, emergent, and sociocultural perspectives in the context of developmental research. *Educational Psychologist, 31*(3/4), 175–190.

Cole, M. (1996). *Cultural psychology: A once and future discipline.* Cambridge, MA: The Belknap Press of Harvard University Press.

Cole, M., & Engeström, Y. (1993). A cultural-historical approach to distributed cognition. In G. Salomon (Ed.), *Distributed cognitions: Psychological and educational considerations* (pp. 1–46). New York: Cambridge University Press.

Davydov, V. D., & Zinchenko, V. P. (1989). Vygotsky's contribution to the development of psychology. *Soviet Psychology, 27*(2), 22–36.

Figueroa, R. A. (1999). Special education for Latino students in the United States: A metaphor for what is wrong. In T. V. Fletcher & C. S. Bos (Eds.), *Helping individuals with disabilities and their families: Mexican and U.S. perspectives* (pp. 147–159). Tempe, AZ: Bilingual Review/Press.

Gillen, J. (2000). Versions of Vygotsky. *British Journal of Educational Studies, 48*(2), 183–198.

Goldenberg, C., & Patthey-Chavez, G. (1995). Discourse processes in instructional conversations: Interactions between teacher and transition readers. *Discourse Processes, 19*, 57–73.

Griffin, P., & Mehan, H. (1981). Sense and ritual in classroom discourse. In F. Coulmas (Ed.), *Conversational routine: Explorations in standardized communication situations and prepatterned speech* (pp. 187–213). New York: Mouton.

John-Steiner, V., & Mahn, H. (1996). Sociocultural

approaches to learning and development: A Vygotskian framework. *Educational Psychologist, 31*(3/4), 191–206.

Kinginger, C. (2002). Defining the zone of proximal development in US foreign language education. *Applied Linguistics, 23*(2), 240–261.

Kozulin, A. (1986). Vygotsky in context. In L. S. Vygotsky, *Thought and language* (A. Kozulin, Ed. & Trans.), (pp. xi–lvi). Cambridge, MA: MIT Press.

Kozulin, A. (1990). *Vygotsky's psychology: A biography of ideas.* Cambridge, MA: Harvard University Press.

Lidz, C. S. (1995). Dynamic assessment and the legacy of L. S. Vygotsky. *School Psychology International, 16*, 143–153.

Lidz, C. S., & Elliott, J. G. (Eds.). (2000). *Dynamic assessment: Prevailing models and applications.* New York: Elsevier Science.

Mahn, H. (1999). Vygotsky's methodological contribution to sociocultural theory. *Remedial and Special Education, 20*(6), 341–350.

McLaren, P. (2003). Critical pedagogy: A look at the major concepts. In A. Darder, M. Baltodano & R. D. Torres (Eds.), *The critical pedagogy reader* (pp. 69–96). New York: Taylor & Francis.

Ochs, E. (1986). Introduction. In B. B. Schieffelin & E. Ochs (Eds.), *Language socialization across cultures* (pp. 1–13). Cambridge: Cambridge University Press.

Peña, E. D. (1996). Dynamic assessment: The model and its language applications. In K. N. Cole, P. S. Dale, & D. J. Thal (Eds.), *Assessment of communication and language* (pp. 281–307). Baltimore, MD: Paul H. Brookes.

Radzikhovskii, L. A., & Khomskaya, E. D. (1981). A. R. Luria and L. S. Vygotsky: Early years in their collaboration. *Soviet Psychology, 10*(1), 3–21.

Reiber, R. W., & Carton, A. S. (Eds.). (1987). *The collected works of L. S. Vygotsky* (Vol. 1: Problems of general psychology). New York: Plenum Press.

Reiber, R. W., & Carton, A. S. (Eds.). (1993). *The collected works of L. S. Vygotsky* (Vol. 2: The fundamentals of defectology). New York: Plenum Press.

Sawyer, R. K. (2002a). Emergence in psychology: Lessons from the history of non-reductionist science. *Human Development, 45*, 2–28.

Sawyer, R. K. (2002b). Unresolved tensions in sociocultural theory: Analogies with contemporary sociological debates. *Culture & Psychology, 8*(3), 283–305.

Schieffelin, B. B., & Ochs, E. (Eds.). (1986). *Language socialization across cultures.* Melbourne: Cambridge University Press.

Stone, C. A. (1993). What is missing in the metaphor of scaffolding? In E. A. Forman, N. Minick, & C. A. Stone (Eds.), *Contexts for learning: Sociocultural dynamics in children's development* (pp. 169–183). New York: Oxford University Press.

Stone, C. A. (1998). The metaphor of scaffolding: Its utility for the field of learning disabilities. *Journal of Learning Disabilities, 31*(4), 344–364.

Suina, J. H., & Smolkin, L. B. (1994). From natal culture to school culture to dominant society culture: Supporting transitions for Pueblo Indian students. In P. M. Greenfield & R. R. Cocking (Eds.), *Cross-cultural roots of minority child development* (pp. 115–130). Hillsdale, NJ: Lawrence Erlbaum.

Tharp, R. G. (1997). *From at-risk to excellence: Research, theory, and principles for practice* (Research Report 1). Santa Cruz, CA: Center for Research on Education, Diversity & Excellence.

Tharp, R. G., & Gallimore, R. (1988). *Rousing minds to life: Teaching, learning, and schooling in social context.* New York: Cambridge University Press.

Trent, S. C., Artiles, A. J., & Englert, C. S. (1998). From deficit thinking to social constructivism: A review of theory, research, and practice in special education. In P. D. Pearson & A. Cran-Nejad (Eds.), *Review of research in education, #23* (Vol. 23, pp. 277–307). Washington, DC: AERA.

Van der Veer, R., & Valsiner, J. (1994). Introduction. In R. van der Veer & J. Valsiner (Eds.), *The Vygotsky reader* (pp. 1–9). Cambridge, MA: Blackwell.

Vygotsky, L. (1962). *Thought and language* (E. Hanfmann & G. Vakar, Trans.). Cambridge, MA: MIT Press.

Vygotsky, L. S. (1977). The development of higher psychological functions (M. Cole, Trans.). *Soviet Psychology, 15*(3), 60–73.

Vygotsky, L. S. (1978). *Mind and society: The development of higher psychological processes* (M. Cole, V. John-Steiner, S. Scribner, & E. Souberman, Eds.). Cambridge, MA: Harvard University Press.

Vygotsky, L. S. (1997). *The collected works of L. S. Vygotsky: The history of the development of higher mental functions* (Vol. 4) (R. W. Rieber, Ed., M. J. Hall, Trans.). New York: Plenum Press.

Wertsch, J. V. (1991). *Voices of the mind: A sociocultural approach to mediated action.* Cambridge, MA: Harvard University Press.

Wertsch, J. V., & Tulviste, P. (1992). L. S. Vygotsky and contemporary developmental psychology. *Developmental Psychology, 28*(4), 548–557.

Teaching strategies and approaches

Curriculum and Assessment

22

Curriculum considerations in meeting special educational needs

Richard Rose

INTRODUCTION

Questions about the nature and purpose of curriculum – what should be taught, why it should be taught and how it should be taught – have been long debated in education. They also have been of major concern to the field of special education, where for many years, the curriculum was separate from that which was on offer in mainstream schools, as were the debates about its nature and purpose. However, in the past 20 years, two major international developments, inclusion and standards-based reform, are now forcing a reconsideration of the notion of curriculum in the field of special education.

It could be argued that this historic separation of special and mainstream curricula now presents particular challenges to the creation of more inclusive education systems, particularly as many countries have enacted education reforms that attempt to raise standards and to provide a common set of educational experiences for all children. At the heart of these challenges are questions about the extent to which a common curriculum with specified standardised content, together with high standards of achievement and a single system of assessment, can meet the needs of all learners. (For an extended discussion, see Rouse and McLaughlin, in this volume.)

But the curriculum is a contested concept and it can be defined in many ways. At its most simple it can be considered as a course of study to be followed, but such a definition ignores other vital elements of learning (Brennan, 1985). More broadly, it could be considered as being all the formal and informal opportunities for learning provided by the school. Alexander (2004, p. 16), takes a more comprehensive view when he defines the curriculum as 'the various ways of knowing, understanding, doing, creating, investigating and making sense, which it is desirable for children to encounter, and how these are most appropriately translated and structured for teaching'.

In special education, the focus of curriculum development historically entailed attempts to match content, process and outcomes of the curriculum to the cognitive, developmental, social and functional needs of the individual. Further, the special education curriculum was informed, not only by beliefs about the perceived deficits of students, but also by developments in learning theory. Thus, the influence of behavioural psychology became apparent in the widespread adoption of an objectives-based curriculum (Gagne, 1978; Ainscow & Tweddle, 1979), direct-instruction and precision teaching. But a focus on the observable outcomes of learning on one hand, and a narrow emphasis on functional skills for living on the other, lead Tomlinson (1982) to describe the special education curriculum at the time as a curriculum of 'academic non-knowledge'. The wider demands of society, such as the need for a skilled workforce, for active citizens and to ensure cultural continuity, which have so often influenced the development of the general education curriculum, were usually absent from the special education debate (Brennan, 1985) as was any philosophical discussion about a curriculum for a 'good life'. But now the current context of educational reform and inclusion provides new opportunities to review the purpose and nature of the curriculum for students described as having difficulties in learning and for a reappraisal of the extent to which all students should have a common set of educational experiences.

Philosophical debates, which have focused upon the nature and purpose of inclusion at both national and international levels over the past 20 years, have led to many countries adopting policies which are aimed at increasing inclusive educational practice (Ware, 2000; Meijer, 2003; Vislie, 2003). These policies, further buoyed by more universal statements such as the *Convention on the Rights of the Child* (United Nations, 1989) and the *Salamanca Statement and Framework for Action on Special Needs Education* (UNESCO, 1994) have begun to consider how a more equitable education system may be developed to address the needs of learners who in many instances have previously been marginalised. A growing acceptance of the need to create a more inclusive educational environment within a broader social inclusion context can be seen to have emerged, and to have influenced planning for educational provision across many countries. This movement has had a positive impact in furthering dis-cussions related to the curriculum and conditions required to create schools and other learning establishments, which meet the needs of all students.

At the forefront of developments intended to promote more inclusive practice has been a focus upon curriculum development and a renewed examination of issues surrounding the efficacy of varying approaches to teaching and learning. The debates surrounding inclusion have further enabled educators to share their experiences and to learn from each other in order to put into place policies and practices that focus on students who have too often been denied the right to learn. However, alongside this positive development has come a greater realisation of the challenges of attempting to generalise educational systems and approaches across countries, cultures and in widely varying socio-economic and political contexts. The hermeneutic process of the interpretation of concepts such as inclusion across languages and countries requires careful consideration in order that the important historical and cultural factors, which have led to the development of national characteristics within education systems is recognised and valued. Writers and re-searchers who are considering the international promotion of a more inclusive curriculum and education system, need to exercise caution when making claims regarding the transferability of education systems. A simplistic judgement of progress, or an imposition of ideas based upon the narrow standards of one country or group of countries is more likely to inhibit, rather than enhance, the overall objective of greater inclusion. As an example of this, reporting on an experience of inclusion in India, Iyanar (2000) suggests that in some instances pupils have been admitted to schools in an effort to support policies of inclusion without sufficient support provided to ensure that this is anything more than a tokenistic gesture. The curriculum, he suggests, lies at the heart of ensuring that inclusion becomes a reality rather than a series of good intentions. Where efforts have been made to impose an apparently successful curriculum structure from one country into another, this has often had the effect of alienating teachers. In some instances such action has given them cause to believe that the inclusion of pupils who have previously been segregated from their classrooms will result in changes to the detriment of those pupils with whom they have previously experienced success. Whilst it can be argued that the acceptance of pupils into school is a critical first step towards inclusion, it is essential that we recognise that it constitutes only the beginning of the process. In order to succeed it needs to be supported by a greater understanding of pupil needs and the development of curriculum and pedagogical structures, which will enable these needs to be addressed.

ESTABLISHING CURRICULUM PURPOSE

At the heart of any debate about the curriculum must be a discussion concerning its purpose and the values it purports to promote. O'Hear and White (1991) suggest as a central aim of the curriculum the preparation of students to become citizens of a liberal democratic society. A critical tenet of their argument is that the curriculum should foster an ethos of individual self-determination within a framework, which promotes respect for the rights of others. Elaborating on this idea, White (1993) challenges the notion of a curriculum which, whilst emphasising the acquisition of knowledge and understanding, fails to state why this may be important in developing autonomous individuals or in respect of creating a more democratic society. A curriculum which is perceived to be little more than a collection of subjects, and which fails to identify the ways in which learning related to these may enhance the lives of individuals or society in general, may be perceived as both weak and limited in concept.

O'Hear and White (1991) here identify an issue, which has provided a cynosure over many years. Tyler (1949) in his classic work on the curriculum emphasised the inadequacy of curriculum development that did not commence with a clear interpretation of purpose.

His views were further developed by Stenhouse (1975) who believed that the curriculum should be aspirational in facing the challenge of ensuring that the needs of both the society in which it operated and of all students being educated within that society's schools and colleges should be fully addressed. This challenge is one which has confounded policy makers and school curriculum managers for many years. In particular a concern that a curriculum should be all embracing and able to meet the needs of a diverse school population within the demands of a changing society has led to a continuous review of the curriculum, particularly in those countries which have attempted to prescribe content.

Attempting to balance the needs of individual students with those of a wider society may, at times be seen to be a source of conflict. Byers (1996) suggests that the curriculum must above all else be seen to provide effective opportunities for learning for all pupils, including those who have been labelled as having special educational needs. This may, for some pupils, require that a different or greater emphasis be placed upon certain aspects of the curriculum, in order to address individual needs, than may be the case for their peers. It may, for example, necessitate providing an additional emphasis upon the development of social independence skills for a pupil with emotional and behavioural difficulties to ensure that they can adjust to the society in which they are expected to live. Such an emphasis may force teachers into making decisions about how the extra time required for such provision may be achieved, and what other areas of the curriculum may need to be given a lesser priority. Such is the reality of curriculum delivery in most of today's classrooms. Ryndack and Weidler (1996) consider the identification of individual priorities as an essential component of the curriculum development process. However, they recognise that the personal experiences, values and expectations of the curriculum planner inevitably influence decisions made in this respect. Within the context of providing a curriculum, which supports inclusion, Ryndack and Weidler identify the need to blend the 'functional' needs of the individual student with the more general curriculum objectives provided for the whole class. Until such a process is achieved, they suggest, the route towards gaining more inclusive schools will continue to be problematic.

It is evident from the work of the authors cited above that the main purpose of a curriculum is to be all embracing in respect of the students for whom it is intended. At the same time it must foster independence and attempt to prepare students to play a role in the society in which they will live following formal schooling. An appreciation of this purpose challenges a narrow focus on subject content, but only when the curriculum is seen as a vehicle for learning rather than an end in itself (Rose, 1998). Teachers need to establish patterns of curriculum development through which they can recognise opportunities to teach what Ryndack and her colleagues view as 'functional' skills within the broader prescribed subject-based curriculum. For example, the identification of opportunities to promote social skills such as collaboration, working in groups or decision-making within subjects such as geography, history or mathematics may enable teachers to see the relevance of teaching these subjects where before they were simply perceived as irrelevant and as presenting obstacles to the learner. However, this will only be achieved when schools are given sufficient flexibility to adopt curriculum models that arise from identified pupil needs as much as from prescribed content.

These principles should inform the ways in which schools function if they are to meet the high expectations of writers such as O'Hear and White. The notion of a 'democratic liberal society' is one to which educators in most countries would subscribe. If a society aspires to such ideals, then equity must become a critical feature of the curriculum. In turn this requires that the curriculum be inclusive of all individuals who constitute the society, regardless of need or ability. If the curriculum is to shape the future of society, then the opportunities for learning the essential skills that lead to self-determination, as suggested

by Byers and by Ryndack and her colleagues, must be valued as much as an ability to recall subject focused knowledge.

A CURRICULUM WHICH PROMOTES INCLUSION

The concerns expressed by curriculum theorists such as those cited above suggests that an essential component in ensuring that pupils are effectively included within any education system is the provision of a curriculum model, which recognises and addresses a range of needs, and in so doing supports both teachers and learners in the classroom. This requires a curriculum structure, which acknowledges and values learner diversity and provides a framework, which is perceived by teachers, parents and other professional colleagues, to provide a sound basis for addressing the needs of all of the pupils in their charge. A focus upon curriculum development to promote inclusive schooling has been seen by some writers as providing an essential foundation upon which successful learning for all pupils can be built (Sebba, Byers, & Rose, 1995; Alper, 1996). This emphasis upon curriculum development to promote inclusion within the broader reform agenda can be seen in the priorities established by several national governments, including the USA and UK, where they have established structures which they anticipate will raise academic standards, particularly for under-achieving groups at the same time as promoting social and moral values. However, whilst this emphasis upon curriculum reform has been a high priority for legislators and for advocates of inclusion, this has not necessarily led to a shared agenda. Indeed, as will be discussed later in this chapter, the differing priorities of policy makers, education reformers and teachers whose primary focus is upon the needs of the pupils in their classrooms has at times brought them into ideological conflict.

The move from a segregated education system in which a small but significant number of pupils received their education separated from their peers, to one in which greater opportunities are provided for pupils, regardless of need or ability, to learn alongside each other, must acknowledge the individuality of all pupils as well as endorsing the need for whole school curriculum development. In the past, special schools may have focused upon individual needs in a way that inhibited the development of learning as a social process. Similarly, in some instances the curriculum provided in mainstream schools has been driven by a concentration upon subject content and academic outcomes, which often fails to recognise the diverse needs of learners. In order to overcome this imbalance and to create schools in which the curriculum embraces the needs of all pupils, it is essential that a balance is achieved between the recognition of individual needs and an acknowledgement of the necessity to develop a whole curriculum model, which addresses the political and socio-economic agenda within which today's schools must operate. This inevitably means that we cannot afford to divorce teaching which addresses the needs of all pupils, from the development of a curriculum which has its logical structures based upon continuity and progression of learning.

THE NEEDS OF THE INDIVIDUAL WITHIN THE CURRICULUM

The influence of the curriculum to provide appropriate learning opportunities for pupils with special educational needs was acknowledged more than 20 years ago (Brennan, 1985; Torgesen, 1986). Indeed, efforts to identify curriculum content, which would specifically address the needs of pupils who have difficulties in learning, have characterised much of the development of special education. A focus upon learning deficiencies has often resulted in the planning of curriculum content and the deployment of teaching methodologies which aimed to provide remedies for overcoming perceived difficulties and thus narrowed the learning opportunities afforded to pupils. For many years the curriculum in segregated settings, was founded upon the teaching of social

skills and the training of basic cognitive functions within a context which established low expectations of pupil performance and in some instances inhibited opportunities for pupils to demonstrate or extend their abilities. Labels, such as learning disability or emotional and behaviour difficulty, which were attached to individual pupils were interpreted in such a way as to determine that they could be legitimately provided with a limited range of curriculum experiences, in the anticipation that academic outcomes and achievements would inevitably be low. An education system, which claimed to be based upon care and the identification of individual needs, was in fact often designed to ensure that pupils received their schooling in an environment which guaranteed minimal disruption to other pupils whose learning needs and abilities fell more comfortably within 'normal' expectations. However, a change of climate, which has resulted from the promotion of inclusive education policies, has led to a reappraisal of the purpose of the curriculum. This has encouraged teachers and policy makers to examine those aspects of learning which need to be made available to all pupils and has intensified the debate about the ways in which such a curriculum may be made accessible for all learners.

It would be unwise to dismiss the efforts made by teachers in special schools to develop a curriculum focused upon the needs of pupils who were perceived as being poor learners. Teachers in segregated provision were, of necessity focused upon the development of teaching approaches, which aimed to elicit a positive response from their pupils. Some of the techniques developed for use with pupils, and in particular those who exhibited the most complex learning needs or challenging behaviours, have begun to inform changes in classroom practices within mainstream classrooms. The move towards greater inclusion has inevitably driven innovations of curriculum design and implementation. As teachers have been confronted by classes of pupils which contain a greater diversity of learning needs, they have adapted, modified and re-evaluated both what is taught in the classroom and how it is taught. In an attempt to embrace a more diverse school population, some teachers have drawn heavily upon those approaches developed in segregated educational settings. This has been done in the belief that the expertise developed over a number of years in special schools could help meet the needs of pupils who have now transferred to the mainstream of education. The expectation that teachers from special schools, as a result of years of experience and commitment to teaching pupils with a wide range of complex learning needs, may have developed teaching methods and curriculum structures from which mainstream teachers could benefit, has in fact led to the implementation of a number of innovative approaches. Structured approaches to teaching, the development of differentiated learning and the introduction of augmentative systems of communication can be observed as techniques that were commonly deployed in special schools and have since become a feature of many mainstream environments. The benefits of such approaches have been clearly articulated by a number of researchers and writers (O'Brien & Guiney, 2001; Howley & Kime, 2003; Adami, 2004). However, concern has been expressed that the transfer of teaching methods commonly used in special schools into mainstream classrooms may present some difficulties (Hart, 1992; Ainscow, 1997). Not least amongst these concerns is that when used exclusively to enable individual pupils to participate in mainstream classrooms, they may serve to emphasise the difficulties which some pupils experience, thus leading to a lowering of self-esteem and perpetuating low expectations on the part of adults. Furthermore, a worry that expectations placed upon teachers that they should adopt strategies, which are different to their previous practices, is seen as potentially alienating colleagues who already feel under pressure to achieve high academic outcomes in their classrooms.

Although there is little evidence about the practicalities of implementing techniques traditionally seen in special schools into mainstream classrooms. There is some evidence to suggest that when these become embedded as whole class approaches, rather than being aimed exclusively at individuals with special educational needs, they may have benefits for a wide range of learners and may increase curriculum access. As an example of this, we may take the use of visual schedules, which have been commonly used to support curriculum access for pupils with autistic spectrum disorders (Mesibov & Howley, 2003). Having adopted this approach to support individual pupils in mainstream classrooms, several teachers have reported that they have gone on to use visual schedules with whole classes and that this has had benefits in respect of improved behaviour and increased awareness of personal learning targets for all pupils. A similar transfer of approach from a segregated to inclusive setting has been reported by Doyle (2004). She describes the use of nurture group techniques, traditionally used with pupils who have been seen as unable to cope socially or emotionally with the stresses of a mainstream classroom, within an infant school. The social development principles, which underpin nurturing approaches, when consistently applied, were seen not only to enable the inclusion of pupils with social, emotional and behavioural difficulties, but also to create a learning ethos which fostered improved performance by others in the class.

The concerns expressed by writers such as Ainscow (1997) and Hart (1992) about the viability of transferring teaching approaches from special to mainstream classrooms need to be heeded. When these techniques remain focused upon an individual pupil they become unmanageable and can further isolate pupils from their peers. This point is further developed by Snell (1998) who described the use of parallel activities in which pupils with special educational needs, usually supported by a member of staff, were engaged on tasks which were different from those in which their peers were involved. In many instances the activity may have been related, but the work presented was distinctly different and participation with classmates was minimal. Snell suggests that whilst pupils in this situation may be located in the classroom with their peers, and may therefore be described as participating, they could not be described as 'academically active' with others in the class. The issue here is the use of teaching approaches which are based upon the needs of the individual without due consideration given to the social nature of classrooms. She suggests that one way of addressing this problem is through the greater use of classroom peer support in which 'more able' pupils are encouraged to engage in the differentiated activity with the pupil with special educational needs. In such an approach the pupil is provided with greater opportunities for direct socialisation with other pupils, and the activities in which they engage become part of the learning process for a larger group. The ideas put forward by Snell, and similarly those of Doyle, suggest that an essential part of curriculum planning must relate to the teaching approaches which teachers intend to adopt and the context in which it takes place.

The debate about teaching approaches aimed at individual pupils, which can be accommodated within a mainstream classroom and promote inclusion, remains at an early stage of development but may well be one of the most crucial issues in ensuring that schools succeed in becoming more effective for all pupils and thus achieve a more inclusive curriculum. Kame'enui and Carnine (1998) suggest that an analysis of the forms of instruction used by teachers in inclusive classrooms may be critical in enabling us to make decisions about the overall efficacy of the curriculum. They cite the ability of teachers to present learning materials in stimulating and well ordered ways that recognise individuality whilst addressing whole class needs as one of the most essential challenges facing teachers in inclusive classrooms. This view is endorsed by Florian and Rouse (2001) whose research into inclusive practice in English secondary schools revealed that teachers who had access to a wide variety of support and teaching strategies and used these in addressing the needs of a whole class, were often successful in accommodating those pupils described as having special educa-

tional needs. However, the evidence for distinctive pedagogies that address learning difficulties remains, at best, limited (Lewis & Norwich, 2001; Davis & Florian, 2004) and there is a need for much more work in this area before it will be possible to draw conclusions about those approaches which consistently enable inclusion.

Discussions about the ways in which individual needs may be addressed are essential when examining the wider issues of curriculum development. Concerns have been expressed by teachers that pupils who have discrete needs have, in some cases, been overlooked when curriculum development has been founded upon the broad issues of subject content and meeting the expectations of national initiatives. In particular, there has been a suggestion that those pupils who may have specific therapeutic needs may be marginalised in efforts to ensure that whole school, or in some instances national, priorities are addressed (Orlove & Malatchi, 1996; Crockett, 2001). There are undoubted tensions between the pressures felt by teachers about meeting national standards and the desire to address individual pupil needs. The development of curricular models and approaches, which satisfy these two apparently dichotomous factors, should exercise the minds of policy makers and school managers alike.

WHOLE SCHOOL CURRICULUM ISSUES

A driving force behind any curriculum must be to provide a framework that encourages learning and provides pupils with opportunities to gain proficiency in, and understanding of, the skills and knowledge that will enable them to function effectively as autonomous individuals within the society in which they must live. In order to achieve this it is essential that a sufficient breadth of subjects through which pupils may gain insights and an understanding of the world is provided. The curriculum must ensure a balance between subjects and their content and must be seen to be relevant to the pupils and the modern society in which they will live. In many countries such as England and Sweden, a national curriculum has been established and is regarded as an entitlement for all pupils regardless of need or ability. Within the English National Curriculum, an inclusion statement is prominently displayed within all documentation. This identifies three principles for inclusion, these being:

- setting suitable learning challenges
- responding to pupils' diverse learning needs
- overcoming potential barriers to learning and assessment for individuals and groups of pupils (Qualifications and Curriculum Authority, 1999).

Advice related to these three principles is provided and an emphasis given to the need for teachers to demonstrate high expectations of all of their pupils. Teachers are urged to provide opportunities for all pupils to achieve and to take specific action to respond to pupils' diverse needs by:

- creating effective learning environments
- securing their motivation and concentration
- providing equality of opportunity through teaching approaches
- using appropriate assessment approaches
- setting targets for learning (Qualifications and Curriculum Authority, 1999).

These actions include addressing the challenges presented not only by pupils with special educational needs, but also for those for whom English is an additional language, pupils from ethnic minority groups, refugees and asylum seekers. However, it could be argued that teachers who are able to take these actions are, in fact, likely to be addressing the needs of all pupils. The singling out of specific groups of pupils would seem quite anomalous in a document that purports to promote inclusive practice. Such lists are undoubtedly intended to ensure positive actions on the part of those who plan or teach the school curriculum, but may in fact be, to some extent, self-defeating. Here we can observe one of the major obstacles to inclusion, which is inherent in much of the curriculum documentation produced by policy makers. Whilst the intention

behind the principles for inclusion highlighted within curriculum documentation is laudable, this is often accompanied by advice written in language which suggests that the curriculum will present problems for some pupils. Teachers reading these documents are immediately given a negative message about what to expect from some of their pupils. If the curriculum documentation took full account of the needs of all pupils within an inclusive school, such advice would be superfluous. But there appears to be an expectation that some pupils will have difficulties in accessing the curriculum and for a significant minority the content may not be wholly appropriate. Where a curriculum is seen as appropriate to meeting the needs of all pupils within a nation's schools, and is indeed regarded as an entitlement, it is surely paradoxical if it is seen as being inaccessible to a significant number of pupils.

A major difficulty with any curriculum model is that it is required to provide a structure for learning for pupils of a broad spectrum of needs. In the recent past, curriculum planners often tried to provide curricula which were matched to the needs of specific individuals identified according to labels of special educational needs. Hence, many pupils with severe or complex needs were encouraged to follow a developmental curriculum, which attempted to provide learning experiences directly related to the current abilities of pupils who were grouped together for teaching purposes. Proponents of this model suggested that it was possible to assess individual needs in a way that identified the progress which they had made when measured against various developmental or psychometric scales. Whilst such an approach was clearly focused upon the individual pupil, it perpetuated deficit models by emphasising learning deficiencies and making assumptions that pupils would of necessity learn according to developmental norms, predicated by the characteristics of their categorical label. Furthermore, the focus of attention given to a curriculum model that was distinctly different from that offered to the peers of pupils with special educational needs served only to distance pupils from each other and perpetuate models of segregation. The promotion of a more inclusive education system demands a concentration upon curriculum models, which both embraces the needs of all learners and recognises the individuality of those who learn in ways, which may be different from the majority.

The anomaly within current approaches to curriculum development is centred around the polarised approaches of attempting to develop a curriculum which builds upon individual needs, or the alternative of trying to provide an all-embracing model focused upon the perceived needs of society for which all pupils must be prepared. The remedy must lie in the production of a curriculum model which, whilst having prescriptive elements, has sufficient flexibility to incorporate a broad range of learning objectives within subjects which acknowledge the wide range of needs exhibited by pupils. Such an approach is only possible where a balance is struck between recognising the individual needs of pupils with national agendas intended to raise standards and prepare pupils for post-school life in a modern society.

Williams (1993), in reviewing the factors which determine the successful inclusion of pupils with learning difficulties in mainstream schools, expressed the view that, if a child with special educational needs was able to access the same curriculum as his or her peers a major obstacle to inclusion would be overcome. His assertions about the need for an all-embracing curriculum must be central in the minds of policy makers who endeavour to create an inclusive school system. In England before the introduction of the National Curriculum many pupils were denied an opportunity to learn subjects such as science or technology, simply because they had a label of special educational needs. This was usually interpreted as meaning that they would be unable to manage the more abstract content of these subjects. The introduction of the National Curriculum in 1989 was intended to ensure that all pupils gained access to subjects seen as crucial in providing pupils with a well-balanced series of learning opportunities. Teachers in English schools, including those in special schools, became adept at analysing and modifying the content of the National Curriculum in a way which demonstrated that all pupils, including those with the most complex needs, could access these curriculum subjects where appropriate changes and teaching approaches were introduced (Byers, 1999; Carpenter, Ashdown, & Bovair, 2001). At the same time, writers from the USA (Eichinger & Downing, 1996; Scott, Vitale, & Masten, 1998) were demonstrating how changes to instructional procedures and a close analysis of intended learning outcomes could ensure greater curriculum access for pupils with complex learning difficulties in mainstream classrooms.

The indicators of curriculum accessibility, which characterise the work of researchers in this area, are all dependent upon the establishment of sufficient flexibility within curriculum models. In particular a recognition that not all pupils should be working towards the same learning outcomes, and that curriculum balance requires an acknowledgement that not all pupils require the same curriculum diet, would appear essential. Adaptations to learning goals whereby within a single lesson pupils may be working towards different outcomes is a common feature of inclusive classrooms (Udvari-Solner & Thousand, 1995; Thomas, Walker, & Webb, 1998). However, as discussed earlier in this chapter, the management of these differing learning goals needs to be carefully handled in order to ensure that the esteem of individual learners is protected. In schools where this has been achieved, recognition of progress and achievement is carefully related to the performance of individuals rather than focusing upon pre-ordained national standards. The National Curriculum in England has been driven by the definition of standards, which specify what pupils should know, understand or be able to do by certain ages. Such an approach overtly identifies those pupils who are performing well against national expectations, but also signifies those who are failing to reach this level. Critics of this approach (Booth, Ainscow, & Dyson, 1997; Rose & Howley, 2001) have suggested that government-initiated assessment policies which are so keenly centred upon arbitrary national standards mitigate against the creation of the inclusive schools which the same government claims to support. If the curriculum is to become an effective tool in the promotion of inclusion, its assessment must centre upon pupil achievement rather than attainment of national standards. Accurate development of baseline assessment which indicates the point at which a pupil can be located at the commencement of teaching will enable teachers to make informed comments about the progress which that pupil has made. It is clear that in schools where there is a concentration upon pupil progress and achievement, some pupils who are failing to reach national standards are in some instances making greater progress given their starting point than many of their seemingly more successful peers.

Just as there is a need to integrate assessment procedures which recognise individual achievement into curriculum planning, so should there be a requirement to report pupil progress in a way which provides teachers with information about teaching effectiveness and the validity of the curriculum. Within the English education system, league tables have been used to report the numbers of pupils achieving levels of national expectation in each school. This data has then been translated through comparison across schools to indicate how effectively each school is performing. Such an approach ignores the variables, which exist in respect of differing school populations. Recent efforts to use value-added measures that indicate more clearly the progress made by specific cohorts of pupils within a school, including those with special educational needs, has found favour with some teachers. However, as indicated by Florian, Rouse, Black-Hawkins and Jull (2004), the ways in which this data is compiled using a variety of psychometric measures cannot allow for viable comparison. Schools must, of course, be accountable to parents and to the local community in respect of the service, which they provide. Similarly, teachers and school managers will wish to know if the curriculum, which they are offering, is having a positive impact upon the learning and achievements of their pupils. This is less likely to be achieved through attempts to make comparisons with other schools than it will be by examining the performance of individual pupils from carefully defined baselines and against personal learning goals.

In the past, curriculum development has often concentrated upon subject content and the development of hierarchies of skills, knowledge and understanding. These components must remain at the heart of curriculum development but must not be divorced from efforts to increase our understanding of teaching and learning. A challenge for teachers to ensure that the needs of all their pupils are addressed has been intensified as a commitment to inclusion has increased. Teachers have endeavoured to adapt existing curriculum models to enable pupils with special educational needs to gain access to the mainstream school and curriculum. This has been inevitable as inclusion has progressed in a somewhat piecemeal manner and has evolved rather than being strategically managed. With a greater commitment to inclusion now being the norm, there is an opportunity to ensure that future curriculum initiatives adopt a more holistic approach to planning and implementation. Research into what works in inclusive classrooms needs to continue and to be intensified. Whilst we are learning more about the need for adaptive learning outcomes, the use of augmentative approaches and the careful structuring of classroom systems such as grouping or peer support, we still have much to learn about effective pedagogy and the motivation of pupils who have difficulties in accessing learning.

The experience of inclusion has encouraged teachers to make a more careful examination of school curricula and to begin to analyse the ways in which it facilitates or inhibits participation. In some instances national legislation has endeavoured to provide a framework that encourages teachers to recognise the individuality of pupils and accommodate diversity within the curriculum. However, if a real impact upon curriculum access is to be achieved this is likely to be through developing a greater understanding of those planning, teaching and assessment approaches which ensure pupil access and value a range of achievements. The purpose of the curriculum must be to serve the learners for whom it is designed. Progress towards this end has been made by those teachers who have demonstrated initiative and innovation in respect of modes of curriculum delivery and the development of planning and teaching formats designed to address the whole range of pupil needs. Our current level of understanding with regards to what works in the curriculum remains limited and warrants further investigation. Whilst legislation may have some impact upon promoting inclusive practice, it will be the initiatives of teachers that ultimately lead to a greater knowledge of effective classroom practice.

REFERENCES

Adami, A. F. (2004). Enhancing students' learning through differentiated approaches to teaching and learning: A Maltese perspective. *Journal of Research in Special Educational Needs, 4*(2), 91–97.

Ainscow, M. (1997). Towards inclusive schooling. *British Journal of Special Education, 24*(1), 3–6.

Ainscow, M. and Tweddle, D. (1979). *Preventing classroom failure.* London: David Fulton.

Alexander, R. (2004). Still no pedagogy? Principle, pragmatism and compliance in primary education. *Cambridge Journal of Education,* 34(1), 7–33.

Alper, S. (1996). An ecological approach to identifying curriculum content for inclusive settings. In D. L. Ryndack & S. Alper (Eds.), *Curriculum content for students with moderate and severe disabilities in inclusive settings* (pp. 19–31). Boston, MA: Allyn & Bacon.

Booth, T., Ainscow, M., & Dyson, A. (1997). Understanding inclusion and exclusion in the English competitive education system. *International Journal of Inclusive Education, 1*(4), 337–355.

Brennan, W. (1985). *Curriculum for special needs.* Buckingham: Open University Press.

Byers, R. (1996). Providing opportunities for effective learning. In R. Rose, A. Fergusson, C. Coles, R. Byers, & D. Banes (Eds.), *Implementing the whole curriculum for pupils with learning difficulties* (2nd ed.) (pp. 107–120). London: David Fulton.

Byers, R. (1999) Experience and achievement: Initiatives in curriculum development for pupils with severe and profound and multiple learning difficulties. *British Journal of Special Education, 26*(4), 184–188.

Carpenter, B., Ashdown, R., & Bovair, K. (Eds.). (2001). *Enabling access* (2nd ed.). London: David Fulton.

Crockett, J. B. (2001). Beyond inclusion: preventing disabilities from handicapping the futures of our children. In T. O'Brien (Ed.), *Enabling inclusion: Blue skies ... dark clouds?* (pp. 81–98). London: The Stationery Office.

Davis, P. and Florian, L. (2004). Teaching strategies and approaches for pupils with special educational needs: A scoping study. Research Report 516. Nottingham: Department for Education and Skills.

Doyle, R. (2004). A social development curriculum: Applying nurture group principles and practices to support socially and emotionally vulnerable children within mainstream classrooms. *British Journal of Special Education, 31*(1), 24–30.

Eichinger, J., & Downing, J.E. (1996). Instruction in the general education environment. In J. E. Downing (Ed.), *Including students with severe and multiple learning difficulties in typical classrooms* (pp. 15–34). Baltimore, MD: Paul H. Brookes.

Florian, L,. & Rouse, M. (2001). Inclusive practice in English secondary schools. *Cambridge Journal of Education, 31*(3), 399–412.

Florian, L., Rouse, M., Black-Hawkins, K., & Jull, S. (2004). What can national data sets tell us about inclusion and pupil achievement? *British Journal of Special Education, 31*(3), 115–121.

Gagne, R. M. (1978). *Principles of Instructional Design.* New York: Holt, Rhinehart and Winston.

Hart, S. (1992). Differentiation – way forward or defeat? *British Journal of Special Education, 19*(1), 10–12.

Howley, M., & Kime, S. (2003). Policies and practice for the management of individual learning needs. In C. Tilstone & R. Rose (Eds.), *Strategies to promote inclusive practice* (pp. 18–33). London: RoutledgeFalmer.

Iyanar, C. K. (2000). *Listening to different voices. How do people with disabilities experience inclusion and exclusion in education?* Paper presented at the International Special Education Congress (ISEC), Manchester, UK, 24–28 July.

Kame'enui, E. J., & Carnine, D. W. (1998). *Effective teaching strategies that accommodate diverse learners.* Upper Saddle River, NJ: Merrill.

Lewis, A., & Norwich, B. (2001). A critical review of systematic evidence concerning distinctive pedagogies for pupils with difficulties in learning. *Journal of Research in Special Educational Needs, 1*(1), 4–12.

Meijer, C. J. W. (Ed.). (2003). *Special Education across Europe in 2003*. Middelfart: European Agency for Development in Special Needs Education.

Mesibov, G., & Howley, M. (2003). *Accessing the curriculum for pupils with autistic spectrum disorders*. London: David Fulton.

O'Brien, T., & Guiney, D. (2001). *Differentiation in teaching and learning*. London: Continuum.

O'Hear, P., & White, J. (1991). *A national curriculum for all: Laying the foundation for success*. London: Institute for Public Policy Research.

Orlove, F., & Malatchi, A. (1996). Curriculum and instruction. In F. Orlove & D. Sobsey (Eds.), *Educating pupils with multiple disabilities* (pp. 377–409). Baltimore, MD: Paul Brookes.

Qualifications and Curriculum Authority. (1999). *The National Curriculum*. London: Department for Education and Employment/Qualifications and Curriculum Authority.

Rose, R. (1998). The curriculum: A vehicle for inclusion or a lever for exclusion? In C. Tilstone, L. Florian & R. Rose (Eds.), *Promoting inclusive practice* (pp. 27–38). London: Routledge.

Rose, R., & Howley, M. (2001). Entitlement or denial? The curriculum and its influences upon inclusion processes. In T. O'Brien (Ed.), *Enabling inclusion: Blue skies … dark clouds?* (pp. 65–80). London: The Stationery Office.

Ryndack, D., & Weidler, S. (1996). Application of special education curriculum areas with general education parallels. In D. L. Ryndack & S. Alper (Eds.), *Curriculum content for students with moderate and severe disabilities in inclusive settings* (pp. 177–214). Boston, MA: Allyn & Bacon.

Scott, B. J., Vitale, M. R., & Masten, W. G. (1998). Implementing instructional adaptations for students with disabilities in inclusive classrooms: A literature review. *Remedial and Special Education, 19*(2), 106–119.

Sebba, J., Byers, R., & Rose, R. (1995). *Redefining the whole curriculum for pupils with learning difficulties* (2nd ed.). London: David Fulton.

Snell, M. E. (1998). Characteristics of elementary school classrooms where children with moderate and severe disabilities are included: A compilation of findings. In S. Vitello & D. Mithaug (Eds.), *Inclusive schooling: National and international perspectives* (pp. 76–97). Mahwah, NJ: Lawrence Erlbaum.

Stenhouse, L. (1975). *An introduction to curriculum research and development*. Buckingham: Open University Press.

Thomas, G., Walker, D., & Webb, J. (1998). *The making of the inclusive school*. London: Routledge.

Tomlinson, S. (1982). *A sociology of special education*. London: Routledge.

Torgesen, J. K. (1986). Learning disabilities theory: Its current state and future prospects. *Journal of Learning Disabilities, 19*, 399–407.

Tyler, R. (1949). *Basic principles of curriculum and instruction*. Chicago, IL: University of Chicago Press.

Udvari-Solner, A., & Thousand, J. (1995). Effective organisational, instructional and curricular practices in inclusive schools and classrooms. In C. Clarke, A. Dyson, & A. Millward (Eds.), *Towards Inclusive Schools?* (pp. 147–163). London: David Fulton.

United Nations (1989). *Convention on the rights of the child*. New York: United Nations.

United Nations Educational, Scientific, and Cultural Organization (UNESCO) (1994). *The Salamanca statement and framework for action on special needs education*. Paris: UNESCO.

Vislie, L. (2003). From integration to inclusion: Focusing global trends and changes in western European societies. *European Journal of Special Needs Education, 18*(1), 17–35.

Ware, L. (2000). Sunflowers, enchantment and empires: Reflections on inclusive education in the United States. In F. Armstrong, D. Armstrong, & L. Barton. (Eds.), *Inclusive education: Policy, contexts and comparative perspectives* (pp. 42–59). London: David Fulton.

White, J. (1993). What place for values in the National Curriculum? In P. O'Hear & J. White (Eds.), *Assessing the National Curriculum* (pp. 9–14). London: Paul Chapman.

Williams, P. (1993). Integration of students with moderate learning difficulties. *European Journal of Special Needs Education, 8*(3), 303–319.

23

Curriculum-based measurement in reading and math: providing rigorous outcomes to support learning

Julie Alonzo, Leanne R. Ketterlin-Geller and Gerald Tindal

'When I use a word,' Humpty Dumpty said, in rather a scornful tone, 'it means just what I choose it to mean – neither more nor less.'

'The question is,' said Alice, 'whether you can make words mean so many different things.'

'The question is,' said Humpty Dumpty, 'which is to be master – that's all.' (Carroll, 1865/1992, p. 124)

The first use of the term curriculum-based measurement (CBM) was in 1977 with publication of *Data Based Program Modification* by Deno and Mirkin. In that document, the authors laid out the general principles for organizing an assessment system using simple tasks that could be developed, administered, and scored by classroom teachers. Since then, the field of educational measurement has 'complexified'; likewise, curriculum-based measurement also has become more complex by expanding the range of tasks within its sway, in the application to new groups of students, and in the decisions being made with the measures. In this chapter, we address the major tenets of curriculum-based measurement in three ways: first, we provide a historical overview of the principles of CBM; second, we review reading research and address a number of different decisions that can be made with CBM systems, and third, we review the latest research in mathematics, a relatively new area for this type of measurement.

Essential features of CBM include regular assessments and graphic display of performance data to enable monitoring of progress over time. This progress monitoring is not measuring for measurement's sake. Rather, it is intended to provide educators with the information they need to be reflective practitioners who base their instructional, curricular, and pedagogical decisions on technically adequate and defensible student performance data. Viewed through this lens, the measurement system we describe has as its end goal the enhancement of teachers' ability to guide their students' learning.

HISTORY OF VARIOUS CLASSROOM AND CURRICULUM ASSESSMENT SYSTEMS

A number of authors use terms so close to curriculum-based measurement that many educators are likely to be confused. Although the differences between these near definitions may appear slight, the implications are quite profound in the manner in which decisions can be made. Following are some of the more common authors, dates, and definitions:

1   Gickling and Havertape (1980) use the term curriculum-based assessment and describe it as 'assessment of students using the instructional curriculum' (p. 4). In this usage, the critical focus is on determining specific skills that students have in reading by calculating the percentage of known to unknown words (defined in terms of correct decoding). Teachers step through various passages reflecting a range of difficulties until they can find a passage of appropriate difficulty where this percentage is neither too great nor too slight.

2   Howell and Kaplan (1979), and later Howell and Nolet (1998), use the term classroom-based evaluation to reflect an approach in which two levels of assessment are applied in a sequential manner: (a) survey level measures that broadly sample a domain and allow students to be compared on the same measures to provide a skill profile, and (b) specific level measures as a follow-up for matching specific skills with individual students (for example, providing more in-depth information to target instruction).

3   Tindal and Marston (1991) use the term classroom-based assessment to address a range of measurement techniques that are quite consistent with curriculum-based measurement but are more expansive than those originally researched at the Institute for Research on Learning Disabilities (1979–1984). In their book, they use an approach that reflects the major tenets of CBM in which measurement is used to make major decisions for screening (using a norm-reference), diagnosis (using an experimental approach to instruction with a criterion reference rather than a student skill analysis of deficits), formative evaluation (using time series data to change the slope of progress with an individual reference), and summative evaluation (using any of the previous three references).

4   A variation on the theme encompasses criterion-referenced tests that are embedded within a curriculum or basal series. Most major publishers have end-of-chapter tests in which students are tested on vocabulary words, comprehension of events from the story, and other miscellaneous skills that have been targeted within the chapter or unit. These tests often appear on the surface to be viable measures of student mastery of the curriculum in that the skills taught closely match those tested. Often, a criterion of performance is established (by decree rather than by an established standard setting process) for teachers to use in determining whether or not the student should move to the next unit or be re-taught the skills in the current unit. This form of measurement, therefore, can be referred to as mastery monitoring.

5   Classroom assessment is generically defined by many different authors who reference a range of task formats for collecting information on students' performance in the classroom. Their perspectives vary considerably from a strong instructional approach (see Popham, 2002) to a strong measurement approach (see Linn & Gronlund, 2000). Most of these perspectives provide useful information on skill proficiency using single event tasks that are related to teaching by identifying a specific domain for assessment and making inferences from performance using a classical criterion-referenced approach; they differ primarily in the (definitional) breadth of the domains.

In summary, the term curriculum-based measurement can be distinguished from these other types of measures along a number of dimensions. Probably the most important defining feature of CBM is that time series data are generated to reflect improvement using frequent comparable measures. For some students (students with significant disabilities or for whom learning is difficult) more frequent measures are needed; other students may need only occasional measurement to reflect progress.

Another feature is the universality of the curriculum that each of the measurement systems is thought to reflect. In a somewhat ironic twist of terminology, CBM is not curriculum-specific like most of the other measurement systems described above (with the exception of Tindal and Marston, 1991). In CBM, the measures are considered generic representations of the general curriculum to be covered throughout the year. Teachers use CBM to sample material beyond what is being taught directly within a specific unit: material is sampled both from previous units and from units that have not yet been taught. In this sense, CBM use reflects both a pre-view and review measurement sampling plan.

Finally, CBM has all three references that reflect norms (the student's fit in groups), criteria (the student's skills and deficits), and progress (the student's improvement compared to his or her previous perfor-mance). The referents used in any given testing situation determine in large part the interpretations that can be made from student performance. The focus of this chapter is on frequent administration of measures for use in progress monitoring. This feature alone requires the measures to be (a) brief in administration and scoring, (b) inexpensive and easy to create, and (c) relevant to evaluating effects from curriculum interventions. It is important to note that *progress monitoring* involves gathering baseline data, sampling for im-provement over time, and evaluating progress in terms of an established norm or criterion. At the same time, assessments administered for monitoring progress can also yield valuable diagnostic information about student skills and enable educators to evaluate the effectiveness of specific strategies or curriculum they are using.

In the remainder of the chapter, we address the empirical literature on CBM with the important perspective that *all* measurement systems need technical adequacy. This term is used to reflect both reliability (consistency and accuracy) and validity (use in decision-making). We consider technical adequacy essential in any measurement system used to make decisions, be it large-scale testing or localized assessments used primarily by classroom teachers. Technically adequate CBMs make it possible for teachers to have information about student performance and progress that is within their span of control while at the same time predictive of perfor-mance on important large-scale tests used for accountability purposes (if the CBMs are designed to enable such predictions).

DECISION-MAKING WITH CURRICULUM-BASED MEASUREMENT (CBM) SYSTEMS

Although the use of CBM is perhaps most well established in elementary schools (for example, Fuchs & Fuchs, 1997; Swain & Allinder, 1997; Vanderheyden, Witt, Naquin, & Noell, 2001), the measures are gaining popularity both in early intervention settings (Pretti-Frontczak & Bricker, 2000; Pretti-Frontczak, Kowalski, & Brown, 2002) and in secondary school settings (Fewster & Macmillan, 2002). In addition, their inclusion as a method by which to extend state-man-dated large-scale assessment systems by mea-suring students with disabilities as part of states' alternate assessments is growing in the United States (Helwig, 2002; Hollenbeck, 2002; Yovanoff & Tindal, 2006). In these applications, measures are devised that focus on essential requisite skills in reading and math, forming a skill development continuum that reflects increasing complexity and growth over time (grades and years). Several states currently are using these curriculum-based measures as part of alternate assess-ment performances (see Oregon, Alaska, and Colorado), with more states considering their use as the federal regulations surrounding alternate assessments become adopted.

Curriculum-based measurements are used in a variety of ways in education and have an established place in the world of both special and general education. They are used as screen-ing tools, to identify students in need of acade-mic interventions. They can be used to help diagnose the nature and scope of a particular academic deficit. In addition, they are used as progress monitoring tools, to evaluate the effec-tiveness of educational programs and specific targeted interventions. In progress monitoring, especially, they serve a dual purpose: providing educators with data about the specific learning needs of their students and offering a tool by which to evaluate the effectiveness of a partic-ular approach to teaching a given student.

By providing educators with a regular influx of data about what students know and are able to do, CBM serves as a tool to enhance student learning. This statement holds true for CBM use in screening students for further assessments or for targeted interventions, for CBM use in diagnosing specific skill deficits, and for CBM use in evaluating the effectiveness of a teaching methodology, a particular curriculum, or a specific intervention. We discuss technical adequacy concerns and logistics of CBM creation and use, but the true focus of this chapter is clarifying the ability of CBM data to assist teachers in the myriad complex decisions they must make every day. Yes, CBM data can provide educators with information about skill deficits. Yes, it can help them monitor a particular student's progress and guide them in goal setting. But most importantly, CBM data can help educators evaluate their own effectiveness and improve their practice or enhance their ability to select curriculum that produces significant learning gains in students. The great utility of CBM is that it allows regular targeted assessment that educators can analyze to assess progress towards meeting these many goals.

CBM use as screening tools

The types of CBMs used as screening tools varies depending on the level of skills being assessed. For assessing emerging skills, such as those prevalent in pre-school aged children or students with significant disabilities, CBMs are typically administered orally, with a trained assessor meeting one-on-one with an individual student. For screening of early skills, care must be taken to choose a set of tasks that are not dependent upon prior skills. For example, the computations-based mathematics CBM may not be appropriate for evaluating students with emerging numeracy skills because it assumes some understanding of basic math facts.

For screening decisions, normative information provides a useful comparison when evaluating student performance to determine eligibility for special services. By comparing a student's performance with same-age peers, assessors can identify students whose skills are significantly less well developed than would be expected. With well-developed norms (see

Hasbrouck & Tindal, in press), teachers can quickly know how far from age-grade expectations students are performing. This application of CBM is generally designed to assist in resource allocations (for example, making referrals to special education, grouping students, and so on). Because such CBMs can be administered quickly – typically, each test requires no more than one to three minutes to administer and score – and easily, they are an economical means by which to screen students who might be at risk of academic failure without requiring a significant outlay of time, training, or resources (Fewster & Macmillan, 2002).

CBM use as diagnostic tools

One of the strengths of CBMs is their flexibility. While they offer efficient means by which to screen students in a very general sense, if administered carefully, CBMs also can provide diagnostic information about specific skill deficits. For instance, while administering an oral reading fluency (ORF) test, it is possible to track the specific types of errors students are making, such as dropping syllables, mispronouncing certain letters or phonemes, or skipping words. These errors can suggest possible gaps in student knowledge and provide insight into skills that need to be further developed through targeted instruction. Likewise, in mathematics, students' responses across multiple measures can be aggregated to evaluate proficiency in specific skills covered in the year's curriculum. This type of 'skills analysis' can be used to identify instructional deficits (Fuchs & Fuchs, 1990). Once such instructional deficits have been identified, educators can target instruction specifically to the needs of individual students and use follow-up assessments as a means of evaluating the effectiveness of the intervention or alternatively the need for a different pedagogical approach if the student does not show marked learning gains.

CBM use as progress monitoring tools

The process for monitoring progress toward goal attainment includes four critical steps:

collect baseline data, set goals, initiate instruction, and collect progress monitoring data (Fuchs & Fuchs, 1990). Specific CBM measures can be used to collect baseline data and monitor progress toward goal attainment within a domain or skill set. Once initial proficiency data are recorded, goals are established by multiplying the number of weeks of instruction by the expected growth rate and then adding the baseline score on a CBM measure (Fuchs & Fuchs, 1993). The targeted growth rate depends on the instructional purposes and the domain. For example, if a student is deficient in math skills and instruction is geared toward bringing this student up to grade level, an ambitious growth rate may be selected. If the observed rate of growth is exceeding the expected growth rate, the goal should be re-evaluated to provide a more challenging benchmark. On the other hand, if the observed growth rate is decreasing or falls below the target, the instructional approach should be changed to provide additional supports for the student.

It is important to note that although CBM data may well indicate the need for a different instructional approach, they do not necessarily suggest what that different approach should be. Just as a persistent high temperature might suggest to a doctor that a particular medical treatment was ineffective, but would not tell the doctor *why* the treatment was not working, a series of low scores on CBMs might suggest to a teacher the need to investigate a different educational approach, alternate curriculum, or perhaps additional instructional scaffolding. We should not expect that the CBM data would suggest what form the alternate educational intervention should take; for that, we turn to the teacher's professional judgment, just as we would look to the doctor's professional judgment to suggest a medical alternative should a fever persist. Fortunately, CBM data *do* offer sensitive gauges of educational progress.

Two features of CBMs make them particularly useful for collecting baseline data and progress monitoring: the ease with which multiple parallel forms can be created,

administered, and scored, and the emphasis on the visual display of student performance data. Because the assessments themselves come directly from the curriculum students will be covering during the year, teachers have ready access to all the materials they will need to create appropriate CBMs. As mentioned earlier, one of the basic tenets of CBM approaches is that student performance is graphed regularly, allowing for easy-to-interpret monitoring of student progress towards goals. One of most advanced applications of this use can be found in Fuchs, Hamlett, and Fuchs (1998). Educators who would like further reading on this topic are referred to this innovative software.

How CBM use can provide instructional intervention guidance

Regular and ongoing use of CBMs to monitor student progress has been shown to improve instructional planning and increase student achievement (Foegen, Espin, Allinder, & Markell, 2001). Student learning is tracked through regular administrations of CBMs, providing the teacher with sufficient information to modify curriculum and instruction as needed. If a student fails to meet a targeted learning goal or the trajectory toward the goal is not at the expected rate on three consecutive administrations of the CBM, the teacher should evaluate the problems that seem to be arising and modify instruction as needed. Teachers can administer CBMs from successively easier material to probe the magnitude of the problem and attempt to identify the instructional changes that are needed (Hintze, Christ, & Keller, 2002). For more developmentally advanced students, tracking their own progress can in itself serve a motivational role in learning. Visual displays of progress – or lack thereof – help cue both teacher and student to the possibility that a change in approach is needed. In addition, because of the way they are designed, CBM results are often easier for teachers and students to interpret.

Unlike large-scale standardized tests, CBMs are designed to have *instructional trans-*

parency: CBMs resemble the type of material students are accustomed to seeing in their classes; thus, teachers see a direct link between the CBM and the material being covered. This instructional transparency can help encourage teacher support of CBMs as well as ease student fear or discomfort that might be encountered through the use of less familiar material. This beneficial outcome of CBM use is especially significant when teachers have systematic procedures by which to interpret the CBM data (Deno & Fuchs, 1987) and the effect is even more pronounced when teachers are provided with specific suggestions for instructional interventions based on student performance (Fuchs, Fuchs, Hosp, & Hamlett; 2003). In addition, parents have used CBMs to successfully monitor their children's progress in a parental reading intervention (Fiala & Sheridan, 2003). Although scarce references to such use currently exist in the empirical literature, the feasibility of parental use of CBMs offers some promise for expansion in this area.

CBM use to aid in schoolwide accountability efforts

By linking CBMs to state content standards, some school districts are harnessing the power of CBMs to monitor progress towards meeting content and performance goals (Kame'enui, Simmons, & Coyne, 2000). Two districts currently developing such programs are the Bellevue School District in the state of Washington (http://www.bsd405.org/) and the Bethel School District in the neighboring state of Oregon (http://www.bethel.k12.or.us/). In both cases, district-supported CBM cycles occur throughout the year in both mathematics and reading, and the data from these assessments are used to assist with screening, placement, and program evaluation decisions. These CBMs are tied to district accountability efforts in that they help district and school administrators make critical decisions about which students receive additional instructional interventions, who must attend mandatory summer school, and on whom they should focus their resources, all with the goal in mind

of meeting Adequate Yearly Progress standards set by their state boards of education.

APPLICATION OF CBM IN READING AND MATHEMATICS INSTRUCTION

In this section, we will present a brief overview of the types of CBMs currently used to assess skills for the purposes described earlier in the chapter. Because more research has been conducted on the use of CBM in reading than in any other subject area, we begin each discussion with a focus on reading. When empirical support makes it possible, we will also discuss CBM use in mathematics, although this area has a much smaller research base from which to pull.

Individually administered CBMs

In early reading, virtually all CBMs are individually administered due to the age of the students (who require more careful and sustained scaffolds) and the need for production responses. The tasks generally reflect increasing complexity sequenced to reflect developmental stages in skill acquisition and include all units of reading (letters, phonemes, words, sentences, and connected text). Some of these tasks (like reading connected text in passages) continue to be used with older students because of the need for production responses on a critical datum (fluency).

Curriculum-based measurement has received considerably less attention in mathematics than in reading in the research literature over the past 25 years. As such, many of the research findings are limited to one or two forms of math CBM. However, recent work shows promise for incorporating the principles of CBM in the development of measures to identify math difficulties in young children and measure performance of students with significant cognitive disabilities. Thus, we will begin our discussion of individually administered CBMs with an overview of those used in reading and will then briefly discuss initial research in mathematics CBMs.

Letter naming

For the letter naming CBM, students are shown a list of 26 letters of the alphabet, organized randomly in five columns on one side of a single sheet of paper. They are instructed to read across each row, saying the name of each letter as they come to it. Students are given one minute to complete this task. At the end of the minute, test administrators count the number of letters correctly named to arrive at a final score. Test administrators follow along on their own copy of the test protocol, marking any letter the student names incorrectly. Teachers can later use these marked protocols to help plan instruction targeted to the letters the student has not yet mastered.

Letter sounds

The letter sounds CBM follows a similar protocol to the letter naming CBM. Students are shown a list of 26 letters of the alphabet, organized randomly in five columns on one side of a single sheet of paper. They are instructed to read across each row, saying the sound of each letter as they come to it. Test administrators follow along on their own copy of the test protocol, marking any letter the student sounds out incorrectly. To provide a running record of student mistakes that can be useful in making instructional decisions, test administrators write down any errors students make during this test. Students are given one minute to complete this task. At the end of the minute, test administrators count the number of letters correctly sounded out to arrive at a final score.

Phoneme segmentation

The phoneme segmentation CBM requires students to correctly segment words on a printed list into their phonemes. The assessors read each word aloud to the student and then ask the student to say the sounds that make up the word. When the assessor reads the word *dog*, for example, the student would respond 'd – oh – g.' Test administrators mark the phonemes as they are segmented on an individual protocol sheet. At the end of one minute, test administrators add the number of phonemes correctly segmented to arrive at a final score. The running record of student mistakes once again serves as a guide for teachers as they plan instruction.

Word reading

The word reading CBM consists of typed word lists selected from curriculum appropriate for the students' level of functioning. Words might be selected from published High Frequency Word Lists such as *The Reading Teacher's Book of Lists* (Fry, Kress, & Foun-toukidis, 2000), from basal readers, from content area texts the students are expected to encounter during the school year, or from other relevant sources. In this CBM, students are presented with a list of words typed on one side of a single sheet of paper. They are given 40 seconds to read across each row of words before moving down to the next. If students pause for longer than three seconds, they are supplied with the word and told to move on to the next word. Test administrators follow along on their own test protocol, marking any words read incorrectly or skipped. At the end of 40 seconds, test administrators count the number of words read correctly to arrive at a final score.

Unlike the previous CBMs described, teachers should avoid using the specific list of words the student missed to guide instruction, as the word lists are designed to be merely a sampling of grade-appropriate vocabulary. Poor performance on this subtest should be analyzed in terms of the specific *types* of mistakes students are making rather than the specific words they fail to read correctly. Poor performance on key sight words, for example, might suggest the need for additional practice with common grade-appropriate sight words. In contrast, if the student's mistakes center on decoding of specific phonemes, it might indicate the need for a different instructional approach.

Sentence reading

In the sentence reading CBM, students are presented with sentences (varying in length from approximately 8 to 20 words) typed on one side of a single sheet of paper and given one minute to read as many of them as possible. The sentences are constructed to reflect a number of structural characteristics of words: prefixes, suffixes, verb tense, syntactic rules relating nouns and verbs as well as conditional clauses and transitions. They are designed to sample students' ability to decode words in context. If students pause for longer than three seconds, they are supplied the word and told to move on to the next word. Test administrators follow along on their own test protocol, marking any words read incorrectly or skipped. At the end of one minute, test administrators count the number of words read correctly to arrive at a final score. As in the other measures described above, a running record of errors can serve as a useful tool for instructional decisions.

Oral reading fluency (ORF)

This measure is perhaps the most widely known and studied reading CBM. To measure a student's ORF, an assessor has the student read aloud for one minute from a 200–250 word grade-level appropriate prose passage while the assessor follows along on his/her own copy of the passage, marking any words skipped or read incorrectly. At the end of the one minute timed reading, the assessor counts the total number of words the student read and subtracts the number of words read incorrectly to calculate a score for number of words read correctly in one minute. Self-corrections and repetitions are counted as correct in determining a student's score. Oral reading fluency has consistently been shown to be an indicator of reading comprehension. Therefore, students who read at a much slower than expected rate may benefit from intensive instruction aimed at building fluency.

Emerging directions for individually administered mathematics CBM

Current research is exploring the use of mathematics CBMs for measuring young children's number sense. Number sense is characterized as the conceptual understanding of numbers and their relation to other numbers. Number sense also implies an understanding of the ability of numbers to perform work and change quantities and relations. Researchers are investigating the use of several CBMs to measure students' level of number sense. These measures include counting numbers, identifying numbers, discriminating among different quantities, and identifying numbers that may be missing from a sequence (Clarke & Shinn, 2004). Similar measures are being used to measure math proficiency for students with significant cognitive disabilities (see Oregon's Alternate Assessment).

In all cases, students are provided with items printed on a single sheet of paper and asked to perform whatever task the measure is designed to assess. For example, in the discriminating among different quantities CBM, a student might be shown a series of pictures representing different amounts of a particular item. The test administrator would ask the student to identify which picture indicates *more* of the particular item. As the student moves from item to item, the test administrator records the answers on his or her copy of the test protocol, thus developing a running record of the student's performance that can be used to select instructional goals.

Group-administered CBMs

For older students, measurements can be implemented more easily (an important criterion for CBM) with selection responses in which students can choose answers from an array of options. Therefore, group administrations become possible.

Vocabulary

Multiple-choice vocabulary CBMs can be either individually or group administered. Possible vocabulary words (drawn from texts the students are likely to encounter over the course of the year) are compiled in a database and a random sampling of 25 words is selected for inclusion on each vocabulary measure. The vocabulary measure is printed on one side of a single sheet of paper. The stem consists of a vocabulary word; below it are three possible answer choices: a correct synonym, a word that reflects a near synonym, and a word not even close to reflecting a synonym. The correct choice (in position of first, second, and third option) is randomly ordered to avoid a pattern effect.

Maze

A maze CBM is essentially a cloze test that has been turned into a selected response rather than a constructed response format. Like the cloze test, the maze requires that short reading passages be drawn from texts similar to those students are likely to encounter during the school year. Words are deleted following a pre-set deletion protocol. Articles, prepositions, conjunctions, and linking verbs are excluded from every nth word count in order to select words that will provide information about students' reading comprehension. For each deleted word, students are provided with four multiple choice answer choices: one word that correctly completes the sentence both syntactically and semantically, two words that are close but incorrect (either syntactically or semantically) in completing the sentence, and one word that is clearly incorrect. The correct choice (in position of first, second, third, or fourth option) is randomly ordered to avoid a pattern effect. Analysis of error patterns can provide teachers with insights about the types of problems students are having with comprehension. Are they consistently confused by certain types of distractors? Do they struggle more with inferential questions than they do with literal ones? As with the other CBMs described earlier, graphic display of student performance, including the types of errors students make over time, gives teachers a solid rationale for their curricular and instructional decisions.

General features of group-administered mathematics CBM

As described above, CBMs represent the year's curriculum, are easily administered, and efficiently scored. Mathematics CBMs are no exception. Content is sampled from across the skills and knowledge students are expected to learn within a specific grade level. The proportion of items measuring each sub-skill is identified and held constant across alternate forms of the CBM. A standard math CBM probe includes 25 items, printed on one side of a single sheet of paper. The items on alternate forms are displayed in random order with only the specific numerals varying from form to form, thus improving the ease with which reliable alternate forms can be created.

Typically, CBMs in math are group administered on a weekly or bi-weekly basis using standardized administration procedures. The average administration time is two minutes per probe, but the exact time may vary depending on the level of complexity of the tasks and the grade level of the students. For computation-based math CBMs, scores are calculated by counting the number of correct digits computed per minute. For conceptual problems, the number of problems answered correctly per minute is tabulated. Usually, the median of three administrations is used to evaluate student proficiency. As with the reading CBMs described earlier, running records of the mistakes students make can provide the teacher with insight into possible specific skill deficits needing remediation.

Technical adequacy of reading CBMs

Extensive research on the technical adequacy of *oral reading fluency* has appeared in the professional literature over the past three decades (see Fuchs, Deno, & Marston, 1983; Jenkins & Jewell, 1993; Marston, 1989; Tindal & Marston, 1996). When administered correctly, ORF measures have been shown to have test-retest reliability ranging from .93 to .99, inter-rater reliability ranging from .96 to .99, and criterion-concurrent validity measures ranging from .54 to .92 (Foegen et al., 2001).

Espin and Deno (1994–1995) successfully used vocabulary measures to predict content study task performance in a generalized way that was not limited to specific content areas. In an extended replication of this study, Espin and Foegen (1996) investigated vocabulary measures along with maze tasks and oral reading fluency measures and found moderately strong correlations with all three measures and other classroom measures: comprehension, daily tests, and end-of-unit post-tests. Vocabulary, however, explained most of the variance on all three of these outcomes on content tasks. Finally, Espin, Busch, Shin, and Kruschwitz (2001) systematically monitored weekly progress of seventh grade students for five months (for a total of 11 measures). They reported adequate alternate form reliability and criterion-related validity (with the Iowa Test of Basic Skills as well as content post-tests). See Busch and Espin (2003) for a summary of this research. See Parker, Hasbrouck, and Tindal (1992) for a review of the technical adequacy of the maze.

Technical adequacy of mathematics CBMs

Mathematics CBMs are designed to measure proficiency in either computation skills or application of concepts. Both types of measures follow the same procedures for creating, administering, and scoring, but notably more research has been conducted on the computation-based probes than on those that sample student knowledge of mathematics concepts and applications. For the computation probes, researchers evaluated reliability evidence to determine the consistency across raters, time, and forms. Inter-rater reliability averaged .83 (Thurber et al., 2002), test-retest reliability was calculated at .87 (Marston, 1989), and alternate form reliability was estimated at .91 (Thurber, Shinn, & Smolkowski, 2002). Generalizability studies point to the conclusion that computation-based math CBMs are dependable for norm referenced decisions ($G_{relative}$ = .95) and moderately dependable for criterion-referenced decisions ($G_{absolute}$ = .75) (Hintze et al., 2002). Evidence for concurrent-related validity for the computation-based math CBM probes suggests a moderate to strong association with other measures of computation skills, with reliability coefficients ranging from .61 to .82 (Thurber et al., 2002).

For conceptually based math CBM probes, internal consistency reliability and evidence for concurrent validity indicate a stable measure with moderate to strong association with other measures of concepts and applications. In a study with second through fourth grade students, Fuchs et al. (1994) found the internal consistency of the measure to range from .94 to .98. Concurrent-related evidence for validity suggests a moderate to strong association with known measures of math concepts and applications (r = .64 to .81). Similarly, in a study by Helwig, Anderson, and Tindal (2002), a set of 11 problems were distilled from a larger set to be maximally predictive of a statewide test. In conclusion, computation-based math CBMs appear to be technically adequate for making educational decisions, but additional research is needed on the conceptually based math CBMs before the same conclusions can be drawn.

CONCLUSIONS AND SUMMARY

We have provided a historical review and a description of technically adequate curriculum-based measurement that fits into the larger array of assessment systems. In our perspective, CBM provides essential information to assist teachers with the wide range of decisions that they need to make. The measures we described in this chapter can serve multiple functions: from screening to diagnosis to formative monitoring of progress, and finally to program evaluation and accountability. Curriculum-based measurement gives educators tools they can use to evaluate the effectiveness of their instructional interventions, to guide them in their curricular planning, and to assist with decision-making.

Furthermore, we described a measurement system that is flexible in capturing student behavior by focusing on different levels of complexity in which behavior can be quantified. For example, in reading, we presented extremely simple behaviors for very young students (letter names, letter sounds, phonemic segmentation and blending and word reading), as well as more advanced applications (sentence reading, oral reading fluency, comprehension, and maze measures) to ascertain skills in both syntax and semantics. In math, the same kind of diversity was present, although the research in this area is just beginning to emerge. Nevertheless, the measures move from simple identification and writing of numerals and counting to more advanced applications of computation and problem-solving to measure conceptual understanding.

In summary, this range of decision-making and behavior sampling provides teachers maximum flexibility in individualizing assessments for students. Properly created, administered, and interpreted, CBM is a powerful tool to assist educators with decision-making. The flexibility of CBM makes it appropriate for students with a wide range of skills: measures that sample from less complex behaviors in the target content or skill area can be used not only with younger students but also with those whose learning disabilities make modifications to the content being assessed necessary. As students' skills become more advanced, the level of complexity included in the CBMs administered can be increased to match. And, by maintaining local control over the content of the measure being administered, teachers can tailor their CBM assessments to their individual students' unique needs.

By using CBMs to assess students regularly, displaying their performance graphically, and consciously using this data to guide decisions about instruction, curriculum, and pedagogical approaches, educators can gain powerful insights into their students' learning needs. Furthermore, student-level CBM data can help educators evaluate their own performance and monitor the effectiveness of the different approaches they try with students, thereby helping them become more reflective practitioners and, in the end, better teachers.

REFERENCES

Busch, R., & Espin, C. A. (2003). Using curriculum-based measurement to prevent failure and assess learning in the content areas. *Assessment for Effective Intervention, 28*(3–4), 49–58.

Carroll, L. (1865/1992). *Alice in wonderland.* New York: Penguin Books.

Clarke, B., & Shinn, M.R. (2004). A preliminary investigation into the identification and development of early mathematics curriculum-based measurement. *School Psychology Review, 33*(2), 234–248.

Deno, S. L., & Fuchs, L. S. (1987). Developing curriculum-based measurement systems for data-based special education problem solving. *Focus on Exceptional Children, 19*(8), 1–15.

Deno, S. L., & Mirkin, P. M. (1977). *Data based program modification.* Minneapolis, MN: University of Minnesota Leadership Training Institute/Special Education.

Espin, C. A. and Deno, S. L. (1994–1995). Curriculum based measures for secondary students. Utility and task specificity of text-based reading and vocabulary measures for predicting performance on content-area tasks. *Diagnostique, 20,* 121–142.

Espin, C. A., & Foegen, A. (1996). Validity of general outcome measures for predicting secondary students' performance on content area tasks. *Exceptional Children, 62*(6), 497–514.

Espin, C. A., Busch, T. W., Shin, J., & Kruschwitz, R. (2001). Curriculum-based measurement in the content areas: Validity of vocabulary-matching as an indicator of performance in social studies. *Learning Disabilities: Research and Practice, 16*(3), 142–151.

Fewster, S., & Macmillan, P. D. (2002). School-based evidence for the validity of curriculum-based measurement of reading and writing. *Remedial & Special Education, 23*(3). Retrieved January 24, 2005 from http://b11.epnet.com

Fiala, C. L., & Sheridan, S. M. (2003). Parent involvement and reading: Using curriculum-based measurement to assess the effects of paired reading. *Psychology in the Schools, 40,* 613–626.

Foegen, A., Espin, C. A., Allinder, R. M., & Markell, M. A. (2001). Translating research into practice: Preservice teachers' beliefs about curriculum-based measurement. *Journal of Special Education, 34,* 226–236.

Fry, E., Kress, J., & Fountoukidis, D. L. (2000). *The reading teacher's book of lists.* San Francisco, CA: Jossey-Bass.

Fuchs, L.S., & Fuchs, D. (1990). The role of skills analysis in curriculum-based measurement in math. *School Psychology Review, 19*(1). Retrieved January 15, 2005 from http://search.epnet.com

Fuchs, L.S., & Fuchs, D. (1993). Formative evaluation of academic progress: How much growth can we expect? *School Psychology Review, 22*(1). Retrieved

January 15, 2005 from *http://search.epnet.com*

Fuchs, L. S., & Fuchs, D. (1997). Use of curriculum-based measurement in identifying students with disabilities. *Focus on Exceptional Children, 30*(3). Retrieved January 24, 2005 from http://b11.epnet.com

Fuchs, L. S., Deno, S. L., & Marston, D. (1983). Improving the reliability of curriculum-based measures of academic skills for psychoeducational decision-making. *Diagnostique, 8,* 135–149.

Fuchs, L.S., Fuchs, D., Hamlett, C. L., Thompson, A., Roberts, P. H., Kubek, P., & Stecker, P. M. (1994). Technical features of a mathematical concepts and applications curriculum-based measurement system. *Diagnostique, 19*(4), 23–49.

Fuchs, L. S., Fuchs, D., Hosp, M. K., & Hamlett, C. L. (2003). The potential for diagnostic analysis within curriculum-based measurement. *Assessment for Effective Intervention, 28*(3&4), 13–22.

Fuchs, L. S., Hamlett, C., & Fuchs, D. (1998). *Monitoring basic skills.* Austin, TX: ProEd.

Gickling, A., & Havertape, V. (1980). *Curriculum-based assessment.* Washington, DC: National Association of School Psychologists.

Hasbrouck, J., & Tindal, G. (In press). Oral reading fluency norms: a valuable tool for reading teachers. *The Reading Teacher.*

Helwig, R. (2002). A methodology for creating an alternate assessment system using modified measures. In G. Tindal & T. Haladyna (Eds.), *Large scale assessment programs for all students: Development, implementation, and analysis* (pp. 427–452). New York: Lawrence Erlbaum.

Helwig, B., Anderson, L., & Tindal, G. (2002). Using a concept-grounded, curriculum-based measure in mathematics to predict statewide test scores for middle school students with learning disabilities. *The Journal of Special Education, 36*(2), 102–112.

Hintze, J. M., Christ, T. J., & Keller, L. A. (2002). The generalizability of CBM survey-level mathematics assessments: Just how many samples do we need? *School Psychology Review, 31,* 514–528.

Hollenbeck, K. (2002). Determining when test alterations are valid accommodations or modifications for large-scale assessment. In G. Tindal & T. Haladyna (Eds.), *Large scale assessment programs for all students: Development, implementation, and analysis* (pp. 395–426). New York: Lawrence Erlbaum.

Howell, K., & Kaplan, J. (1979). *Curriculum based evaluation.* Columbus, OH: Charles Merrill.

Howell, K., & Nolet, V. (1998). *Curriculum-based evaluation for teachers.* Boston, MA: Allyn Bacon.

Jenkins, J. R., & Jewell, M. (1993). Examining the validity of two measures for formative teaching: Reading aloud and maze. *Exceptional Children, 59,* 421–432.

Kame'enui, E. J., Simmons, D. C., & Coyne, M. D. (2000). Intervention issues: schools as host environments: toward a schoolwide reading improvement model. *Annals of Dyslexia, 50,* 31–51.

Linn, R., & Gronlund, N. E. (2000). *Measurement and assessment in teaching.* Upper Saddle River, NJ: Prentice-Hall.

Marston, D. (1989). Technical adequacy of reading measures. In M. Shinn (Ed.), *Curriculum-based measurement* (pp. 120–154). New York: Guilford.

Parker, R., Hasbrouck, J., & Tindal, G. (1992). The maze as a classroom-based reading measure: Construction methods, reliability, and validity. *The Journal of Special Education, 26*(2), 195–218.

Popham, J. (2002). *Classroom assessment.* Boston, MA: Allyn Bacon.

Pretti-Frontczak, K., & Bricker, D. (2000). Enhancing the quality of individualized education plan (IEP) goals and objectives. *Journal of Early Intervention, 23,* 92–105.

Pretti-Frontczak, K., Kowalski, K., & Brown, R. D./(2002). Preschool teachers' use of assessments and curricula: A statewide examination. *Council for Exceptional Children, 69*(1), 109–123.

Swain, K. D., & Allinder, R. M. (1997). An exploration of the use of curriculum-based measurement by elementary special educators. *Diagnostique, 23*(2), 87–104.

Thurber, R. S., Shinn, M. R., & Smolkowski, K. (2002). What is measured in mathematics tests? Construct validity of curriculum-based mathematics measures. *School Psychology Review, 31*(4), 498–513.

Tindal, G., & Marston, D. (1991). *Classroom-based assessment.* Columbus, OH: Charles Merrill.

Tindal, G., & Marston, D. (1996). Technical adequacy of alternative reading measures as performance assessments. *Exceptionality, 6,* 201–230.

Vanderheyden, A. M., Witt, J. C., Naquin, G., & Noell, G. (2001). The reliability and validity of curriculum-based measurement readiness probes for kindergarten students. *School Psychology Review, 30,* 363–382.

Yovanoff, P., & Tindal, G. (2006). Scaling early reading alternate assessments with statewide measures. *Exceptional Children.*

24

Self-assessment as a lens for learning

Roseanna Bourke and Mandia Mentis

Assessment is arguably one of the more complex and controversial issues in an inclusive education system and generally raises heated debate around questions such as: what should be assessed? Who should assess, and be assessed? Why assess? and How to assess? As a process, assessment is most effective when used to support the learning of and about 'self' in a range of contexts, and can be a motivational force when it challenges the learner about their own learning. However, assessment can also have the opposite effect, disempowering and demotivating; something done to, rather than with the learner. These issues are explored in this chapter where we compare different models of assessment, highlight the value of self-assessment and suggest an approach whereby self-assessment as a lens for learning can contribute to the identity development and self-determination of learners with diverse learning needs.

Learners and learning are framed in different ways depending on the assessment lens through which learning is viewed. It is not only 'what' we look for when assessing learning, but also 'how' we look for it; that is, the particular aspect of learning we assess, and the tools and practices we use to assess it, which determines the picture we get of that learner.

Given the range of models that provide different perspectives on teaching and learning, the *purpose* for assessment and the related *method* of assessment becomes paramount. The 'why assess' and 'how to assess' becomes crucial given that the assessment will result in our viewing learning through different lenses.

Whether assessment is used in a summative or formative nature, both provide us with a different understanding about a student's learning – a different answer to the question why assess (Black & Wiliam, 1998). For example, summative assessment as assessment *of* learning, or end-product assessment, is often used for accountability purposes as it determines a student's level of performance on a task. On the other hand, formative assessment as assessment *for* learning, or ongoing assessment, provides feedback during learning to facilitate and understand learning and improve teaching (Black, Harrison, Lee, Marshall, & Wiliam, 2003; Black & Wiliam, 1998; Clarke, Timperley, & Hattie, 2003).

Children and young people attend school to experience new learning opportunities. In the same way that every child is a learner, so too is every child their own assessor. However, while participation in school, home and their local community provides ongoing opportunities and contexts for learning, only certain forms of learning are conventionally assessed or 'measured' in school. These are often summative and focus on the achieved end product. For children with special educational needs, these assessment systems can be demotivating and meaningless (Black & Wiliam, 1998), and can continue to reinforce a deficit theorizing of these children, and thereby hinder learning. Increasingly, it is also being recognized that there are often many cultural, social and other forms of learning that take place in school settings and beyond, that either cannot be or are not measured. Therefore, alternative forms of assessment, such as self-assessment, that actively involve the learner, will address some of the ways learners can actively participate positively towards assessing *for* their own learning. Self-assessment cannot work when 'done' to the learner. The learner needs to identify the purpose and goal for learning, measure their performance against these goals and reflect on how this contributes to their knowledge of self. This need for a clear sense of purpose when learning, along with a strong sense of self and identity, provides the best foundation for utilizing self-assessment as a tool for learning.

Through self-assessment in multiple contexts, the learner accesses a range of experiences and opportunities to understand and examine themselves, their knowledge, skills and attitudes, in order to better know themselves. It is with the true sense of self that learners are in a position to self-determine their goals, aspirations, needs and wants. Components of self-determination (that is, choice making skills, self-advocacy skills, positive perceptions of control and efficacy, self-knowledge and awareness) are critical for learners with diverse needs to participate and contribute to the contexts within which they live and learn (Thoma, Nathanson, Baker, & Tamura, 2002; Weymeyer, 1994). In all areas of education, including special education, learners need support to have control and choice over their situations, to take risks, to set goals, and be active participants in problem-solving in their own lives (Agran, Blanchard, & Wehmeyer, 2000).

But this pursuit for self-determination often goes unvalued. Assessment is usually driven by the teacher, with the student being an inactive passenger in the process, but it could be driven (or at the very least, navigated) by the learner in order to provide more experiences that utilize self-determination skills.

There are various models and practices of assessment, each of which provides us with a different perspective or different lens through which to view learning and achievement. Depending on which lenses of assessment we are looking through, a different picture of ourselves emerges and this contributes to our sense of identity. Assessment is often done *to* us, by others, and depending on the particular assessment approach used, a particular story is told about us, which shapes our sense of who we are. Self-assessment is a way to gain authorship of our own stories – to tell our own tales.

Self-assessment tells us, and others, about ourselves. It is the process of understanding more about who we are, how we interact with others and how we learn. It is a means of gathering information about our skills, values, knowledge, needs, interactions and beliefs. For all learners, and particularly those who experience difficulties in life, the use of self-assessment as a strategy to gain greater self-awareness contributes to meaningful and intrinsically motivated, rather than imposed, learning goals and associated outcomes. Self-assessment formalizes the process whereby the learner develops a sense of identity. Knowing who we are, and having a strong sense of our own identity in different contexts, are important for all learners to contribute successfully and belong to different learning communities. As Wenger (1998) says, 'the concept of identity serves as a pivot between the social and the individual, so that we can talk of one in the context of the other' (p. 145).

Self-assessment has the potential to promote learned hopefulness and empowerment. Learned hopefulness as defined by Zimmerman (1990) is 'the process of learning and utilizing problem-solving skills and the achievement of perceived or actual control' (p. 72). It is the process whereby individuals develop a sense of empowerment. Though developing intrinsic self-assessment skills within a variety of settings, learners become more knowledgeable and confident about their ability to succeed in solving tasks – and hence move towards gaining an internal locus of control, a sense of empowerment and learned hopefulness.

LOOKING AT LEARNING THROUGH DIFFERENT ASSESSMENT LENSES

Children with diverse learning needs are often required to participate in a range of assessment processes aimed at identifying their areas of strengths and difficulties so that curriculum adaptations can be made. The choice of assessment is often shaped by the teacher's or specialist's perspective of learning, and the assessment results shape the view they have about the learner. Standardized tests, for example, provide very different information about a child's learning than information from a portfolio assessment, or observations of learning in different classrooms or interviews with teachers and parents.

Standardized psychometric tests in the area of special education provide a perspective of learning that can be located within the *Psychometric Model* where often a deficit orientation is taken, and the assumption is that difficulties lie within the learner. Emphasis is placed on the diagnosis, prognosis and etiology of the problem. There is less accountability on the part of the teacher and minimal assessment of the curriculum, classroom environment or context, because the innate qualities or deficits of the learner are central to this approach. It is the learner's static knowledge and skills that are tested with the aim of determining the student's deviation from the norm. Therefore, the learner is more likely to learn what she or he cannot do, and what score has been gained in relation to others of a similar age, than any knowledge of themselves in relation to the task. Psychometric tests such as intelligence tests (for example, the WISC-IV) are still widely used in educational settings

and yet have changed very little since their first introduction almost 100 years ago. However, there are many problems inherent in the use of psychometric tests that produce static measures such as Intelligence Quotient (IQ) scores including: the lack of a theoretical framework that is supported by empirical data (Bourke & Gregory, 1996; Elliott, 2003; Flanagan & McGrew, 1997), the difficulty of translating static scores into meaningful intervention practice in the classroom (Bourke & Gregory, 1996; Feuerstein, Rand, & Hoffman, 1979), the emphasis upon static products rather than cognitive processes and potential to change (Feuerstein, Miller, & Jensen, 1981; Sternberg, 1984), and the tendency to disadvantage those from different cultural and language groups from which the tests were normed (Lopez, 1997). Irrespective of the difficulties associated with intelligence tests, the creation of expectations is one of the most limiting aspects of this form of assessment. These tests can be disempowering for the learner in that they create expectations that often unfairly further limit the learner. As Gould (1981) has stated: 'we pass through this world but once. Few tragedies can be more extensive than the stunting of life, few injustices deeper than the denial of an opportunity to strive or even hope, by a limit imposed from without, but falsely identified as lying within' (p. 28).

An alternative to the psychometric lens to viewing intelligence and learning is the *Cognitive Model*, where assessment involves identifying the concepts that learners have acquired through personal experiences and the Piagetian processes of assimilation and accommodation. According to Piaget (1979): 'knowledge is derived from action ... To know an object is to act upon it and transform it ... To know is therefore to assimilate reality into structures of transformation and these are the structures that intelligence constructs as a direct extension of our actions' (pp. 28–29). Piaget did not take account of context when exploring student learning, although he did argue that the social world has an impact on the individual's development in so far as the individual adapted to the environment (Piaget, 1929, 1979). Rogoff, Mistry, Göncü, and Mosier (1993) noted that Piaget's work examined the individual development as being general across contexts and that his primary focus 'was on the individual rather than on the aspects of the world that the child struggles to understand or on how the social world contributes to individual development' (Rogoff et al., 1993, p. 5.) Other cognitive theorists have foregrounded a more process-oriented and dynamic approach to cognitive assessment (Lidz, 1991; Sternberg, 1988), which emphasizes metacognitive aspects of learning, and focuses on the interaction between the teacher and learner with a view to maximizing learning potential. Teaching aims at assisting the learner to be aware of their cognitive strategies, to self-regulate and adapt appropriately in order to become autonomous and independent in their learning.

This links with a *Constructivist Model*, where the learner builds his or her own structure for understanding concepts. Assessment can thus examine the learner's successive understandings and meaning-making. A *co-constructivist* approach extends this to involve others in the learning process, by focusing on learning which occurs through scaffolded experiences of interacting with more experienced others. The assessment focus shifts from the learner to the interaction between the teacher and learner to show how adaptations can occur in the dynamics of the teaching–learning dyad to achieve interactions that facilitate learning. The salient feature of this form of dynamic assessment is the use of guided learning to determine a learner's potential for change (Campione, 1989; Feuerstein et al., 1979; Skuy & Mentis, 1999). Within this model, assessing the teaching and learning interaction involves such activities as prompting, asking leading questions, modeling, and collaborative problem solving, based on a test–teach–test approach.

The *Humanistic Model* shifts the assessment focus to the student's social development, self-esteem, independence and interdependence. Wanting to learn and knowing how to learn are seen to be more impor-

tant than measuring factual knowledge. Learning is seen as relating to the learner's motivation, self-direction and need for self-actualization (Maslow, 1971). Hierarchy of needs, self-expression and student-centred learning are educational goals, and the orientation of assessment is social and affective rather than scientific or biological. There is the view that within every child there is a natural desire to learn and this approach to assessment acknowledges the student's values about learning (Howie, 1999; McMillan, 2000). Assessment practices within this view of learning would include self-rating scales that generate more awareness of individual needs, values and learning preferences. Artifacts of a student's work compiled into an individual portfolio is well suited to the cognitive, constructivist and humanistic models as the artifacts provide ongoing examples of the learner's performance and progress in relation to their identified learning goals and outcomes.

Contemporary approaches within the *Behavioural Model* include the functional behavioural assessment (FBA). In this approach hypotheses are generated about potential antecedents and consequences of a specified aspect of the learner's behaviour, and then conditions are manipulated to test these hypotheses (Miller, Tansey, & Hughes, 1998). This assessment aims at identifying the communicative intent and function of the behaviour, and the purpose it serves for the individual. Because there are multiple reasons for behaviours, a variety of methods can be used to gather information about antecedents, behaviours and consequences. This involves a multimethod approach that can be indirect, such as interviews, checklists and rating scales, or direct, such as behavioural observations (Gresham, Watson, & Skinner, 2001). Within this approach to assessment the learner, and learning, are defined in terms of external observable behaviours perhaps at the expense of more internalized, less observable factors.

Linked to this is the view of learning through a *Developmental Model* which foregrounds the predetermined stages of development within the physical, cognitive and psychosocial domains of a learner's functioning. This approach places emphasis on experience and environment in terms of how learners progress through stages in a sequential, linear and definite order. The focus of this assessment approach is to determine the child's current level of functioning in relation to an assumed hierarchical structure of learning. Developmental charts and checklists provide the information required for assessment and teaching within this model. For example, the Carolina Curriculum (Johnson-Martin, Attermeier, & Hacker, 1990) outlines assessment and intervention approaches according to a developmental sequence in the five domains of cognition, communication, social adaptation, fine motor, and gross motor.

The *Ecological Model* looks at assessment through a more holistic lens and focuses on the various systems within the individual's environment. In this approach, assessment does not focus on the child in isolation, but the basic unit of analysis is the whole ecology. This model is most closely associated with the work of Bronfenbrenner (1979) who suggests that models of assessment within special education too often simply focus on students' deficits without really considering that the student with special needs is, first and foremost, a child within a family and a wider society. In Bronfenbrenner's ecological model (1979) the child is viewed as being a participant in a unique and overlapping set of ecosystems where the learner at the centre is surrounded by the home, the neighbourhood, social networks and cultural groups. Assessment involves an evaluation of the learner's environment, materials, equipment, appropriateness of teaching, goals, and strategies. More importantly within an ecological model, it is important to involve an assessment of the interactions and relationships of the child with others, within and across the different settings. Therefore, involving teachers, peers and family in the assessment is emphasized.

THE SELF-ASSESSMENT LENS FOR LEARNING

The self-assessment approach outlined in the next section identifies interconnected tiers of self-assessment focusing on the sociocultural context, and identity (see Figure 24.1). Each tier informs and is informed by the other. These consist of:

- a tier which explores the conceptions learners have about self-assessment within multiple formal and informal cultural and social contexts; and
- a tier focusing on the role and development of a sense of identity and how this can help facilitate the process of self-determination and learned hopefulness in the learner
- self-assessment, which connects the tiers as a process that legitimises the voice of the learner, and mediates the 'self' within and across multiple contexts.

Figure 24.1 The self-assessment lens for learning

SELF-ASSESSMENT WITHIN A SOCIOCULTURAL CONTEXT

As outlined above, historically within a traditional special education model, many assessment strategies have placed greater emphasis on the identification, classification and targeted interventions for children experiencing difficulty learning. The consequences of this approach to assessment have resulted in children becoming unnecessarily demotivated, and further marginalized from their own learning. To involve learners actively in their own assessment process, we must be prepared to accept differences in their goals, aspirations and routes towards achievement. Indeed, we even need to examine what we mean by achievement and what value is attributed by teachers and learners to different forms of achievement. Therefore, as teachers, we must be prepared to change the way we think about our teaching, which means changing ourselves (Black et al., 2003; Shepard, 2000). While self-assessment is used in schools, it is often teacher directed and initiated, leaving children out of the process. We are therefore not learning from children and, it seems, not prepared to change. Paley (1979, 1999) argued that educators have much to learn from children, but while there is a strong call for involving the student voice in research, students are often left out of the dialogue (Oldfather, 1995; Smith, 1996, 1998). Self-assessment and formative assessment are a means to support learners back into this dialogue. Black and Wiliam (1998) provide strong evidence from an extensive literature review to show that classroom formative assessment is a powerful means to improve student learning. They go on to claim that if formative assessment is to be productive, pupils should be trained in self-assessment so that they can understand the main purposes of their learning and thereby grasp what they need to do to achieve.

Research has shown that self-assessment can encourage pupil motivation by improving communication in the classroom, thereby counteracting to some extent the impersonality of the school (Broadfoot, 1979). The more motivated pupils are, the greater likelihood there is that their involvement, commitment and responsibility for their learning will increase (Black & Wiliam, 1998; Broadfoot,

1979; Weeden, Winter, & Broadfoot, 2002). Therefore self-assessment implicitly raises pupil status because the students' opinions are valued (Broadfoot, 1979). This in turn improves their reflective thinking skills (Kusnic & Finley, 1993) and ability to apply metacognitive strategies (Pramling, 1996) in their learning. As well as increasing student motivation for learning (Broadfoot, 1979; Ralph, 1995), self-assessment practices have been attributed to students developing a greater sense of control and ownership for their learning (Barnes, 1997; Eaton & Pougiales, 1993; van Kraayenoord & Paris, 1997).

In this relational, dynamic conception, self-assessment is not an individual, isolated or singular activity. It occurs within a context, through interactions with others and is multifaceted. Mead (1934) argued that when people adjust to different environments or communities they change themselves and, in doing so, they ultimately influence the community in which they live, which in turn changes. Assessment and learning are reciprocal processes and both are embedded within the learner's sociocultural environment.

Children and young people need the support from others to know what and how they learn. While their sense of self and self-knowledge influences how they assess their own responses and outcomes of their learning, the provision of feedback from their peers and from adults shapes their thinking, and provides a mediating influence. If we take the notion that every context is a learning context, and that every setting ultimately serves an educational purpose, then we can begin to question the relevance of external, formal assessment tools to measure learning.

The belief that all children can, and will, learn is central to creating learning opportunities for children with special educational needs. Strategies using self-assessment as a form of learning, as well as to inform learning and teaching, are something all children must be part of. Experiences in assessment have historically had learners in less than powerful circumstances. For young learners with special educational needs, both a sense of belonging and control are important. Self-assessment strategies give back some of that power by allowing the learner to identify criteria for assessment and associated measures of success, which can then contribute actively in any related Individual Educational Planning process.

Learners in both naturalistic and school settings have a range of ways of conceptualizing self-assessment. As Bourke (2000) showed, students' conceptions of self-assessment include intrinsic and extrinsic dimensions, and both involve interaction with others. Extrinsic dimensions include those aspects that require feedback by others such as seeking an opinion, getting marks and grades, performing a task modelled by others or using pre-established criteria. Intrinsic conceptions include those that relate to internal validation and purposeful learning such as setting goals for learning and evaluating learning content. Using these forms of self-assessment within appropriate sociocultural contexts results in the strengthening of the learner's sense of self-determination and self-identity. Yet children are seldom asked whether the learning content is desirable, even though they are introduced to more and more complex learning tasks, some of which appear to hold little relevance for them. Until they see the relevance, and connect meaning to these tasks, neither learning nor self-assessment is likely to take priority for the learner. At this intrinsic level of self-assessment, where evaluating the content of learning becomes the focus, students can be aided by having meaning mediated to them (Feuerstein, Rand, & Hoffman, 1979). When through interaction with teachers, parents or more experienced peers, the learner can see the value of the content and come to appreciate it as being highly desirable, necessary or interesting, the learner will actively engage in that learning. In this way, self-assessment is intrinsically linked with both the content and the learner's knowledge of him or herself in relation to that task.

Parents, teachers and more capable peers might often play the role of 'expert' in confirming that learning has occurred, but unless this learning answers the 'what do I want to learn?' goal, then it is less likely that the learner will want to persevere with this learning. If a learner gains confirmation of improvements in a writing task when the preferred communication goal is to learn to interact with peers via text messaging, then the facets of learning and assessment have shifted and need to be re-aligned so that both become meaningful. How this might be done involves listening to the learner and examining his or her ideas in a range of contexts. Self-assessment, like self-determination does not occur in isolation. As previously identified, the environments and contexts of the learner play an integral role in either facilitating or hindering the learner's ability to control their environment (Abery, Rudrud, Arndt, Schauben, & Eggebeen, 1995).

For many theorists and practitioners, learning is recognized as occurring in multiple formal and informal situations where the different relationships of the learners to others, and to the information, allows the learner to both transform their own and others' roles, thinking about and participation in the learning. As noted by Rogoff, Matusov, and White (1996) a sociocultural perspective recognizes that learners adopt different roles and responsibilities according to the group in which they are participating. Rogoff et al. take the position that all learning occurs in both cultural and social contexts, with the learner an active member of each context. The premise of a sociocultural view of learning is that cognitive change is seen as a social and interpersonal process (Granott & Gardner, 1994), and is a move away from viewing learning as beginning and ending with the individual (Lave, 1996; Lave & Wenger, 1991). The theory of the learner as an individual within a wider social context was developed by Vygotsky (1978, 1987, 1988) to emphasize the importance of the relationship between thinking and the social organization of instruction. This model of learning therefore has implications for the way we approach the assessment of, and for, learning. The centrality of the learner to the assessment process, taking different roles, is pivotal to supporting ongoing learning.

IDENTITY THROUGH SELF-ASSESSMENT

Self-assessment and identity development are inextricably linked; both occurring through lived experiences and interaction with others within multiple and different sociocultural contexts. Self-assessment and identity development are not solitary or singular activities in isolation, but occur when the learner participates in various social situations. In self-assessment and learning there is an underlying understanding that the 'self' in 'self-assessment' involves self in relation to others, that is, the 'self-in-relation' has meaning only within a complex context of relationships (Barab et al., 1999; Bateson, 1972; Wenger, 1998). Building an identity, as Wenger (1998) suggests, consists of negotiating the meanings of our experience of membership in social communities. Identity is linked to social membership but, conversely, we are also uniquely individual and we need to guard against social stereotyping. This interplay between the individual and social aspects of identity has significance for all learners – but in particular for those children with special educational needs who often, as a result of generalizations and lowered expectations about their learning needs, become excluded from certain learning contexts. This could limit their opportunities not only for further learning, but also for identity development.

If learning, self-assessment and the development of identity occur through participation, in what Brown (1997) refers to as learning communities, Rogoff (2003) describes as enculturation in cultural communities and Wenger (1998) as involvement in communities of practice, then the importance of providing inclusive learning communities for all learners becomes vital. As Leffler and Svedberg (2003) note, learners are not mere passive recipients of knowledge nor independent, solitary thinkers but rather participants in a kind of learning in which interaction with others is the most important element. In other words, children learn about themselves through others, and the messages they receive both implicitly and explicitly, help form that knowledge of self. Knowledge is transformed through meaningful interaction in a particular context, enhancing individual identity development. Through self-assessment, learners come to understand more about their identity – who they are and what they can do – and this occurs through taking on different learning roles in different sociocultural contexts.

Self-assessment then can contribute significantly to self-knowledge, which has been identified as being one of the core characteristics of self-determination (Thoma, Nathanson, Baker, & Tamura, 2002). Self-determination – the ability to make choices and decisions for oneself – is important for all learners, but in particular is widely seen as being a 'best–practice procedure in the education of students with disabilities' (Thoma et al., 2002, p. 242). As Wehmeyer and Schalock (2001) point out teaching students to become self-sufficient citizens, who can live independently and integrate within a community, should be an expected outcome of any education system. Self-assessment can play a vital role in promoting self-determination – the ability of students to know what they want and how to get it. This can be achieved through what Wehmeyer and Schalock (2001) describe as 'self-realizing' where students 'use a comprehensive, and reasonably accurate, knowledge of themselves and their strengths and limitations and act to capitalize on this knowledge' (p. 2). Algozzine, Browder, Karvonen, Test, and Wood (2001) show that, through assessment activities such as portfolios, self-determination can be *taught*, that it can be *learnt* and that it *makes a difference* in the lives of individuals with disabilities. As Malian and Nevin (2002) point out, it 'can be modeled and generalised across life and educational settings' (p. 73).

LISTENING TO THE LEARNER

The student's perspective in assessing their own learning provides another dimension for teachers to understand individual student learning; in the same way student voice has been explored in educational research to understand the phenomena of learning (Bourke, 2000; Gipps & Tunstall, 1998; Johnston & Nicholls, 1995; Lincoln, 1995; Pollard, 1996; Pramling, 1996). Through seeking, understanding and then using children's perspective, educators are better placed to facilitate improved conditions for their assessment and learning. If educators use self-assessment strategies, as an integral part of the students' learning process, it enables the use and analysis of another form of data to ensure assumptions are not made about what learners think and about how they make sense of the world and their learning. As Smith (1996) has noted 'even where people claim to be working on children's behalf there is little attempt to understand their ways of seeing the world' (p. 10).

Traditionally educators do not actively hear the voice of the child when discussing and planning their assessment and learning. Having an understanding of how children self-assess and develop self-knowledge will provide a framework for educators to listen to the learner. When children are asked about their experiences of knowing when and how they have learned, the way these learners use self-knowledge and self-assessment to evaluate their learning outcomes and set future learning goals is evident (Bourke, 2000). Many young learners require their knowledge of 'self' to be mediated by others. This extrinsic information is the first step towards learners actively shaping a sense of their self. Next, the child starts to focus on the 'amount' of learning – the 'how much' in relation to either their own learning or others. This feedback during the early years of schooling is usually in the form of verbal feedback and some identifier such as a star or stamp or sticker, and later is quantified in terms of a mark or grade. Through this process learners develop an awareness that certain learning outcomes have importance and are given priority through the school assessment system.

However, as learners become more confident in their own sense of self, their own identity, self-assessment moves to include more intrinsic elements where instead of using criteria externally set, the learner identifies internal learning goals. Through outlining their learning outcomes and goals, the student has a set direction, purpose and value in these goals, and is motivated to persevere. Often the outcomes are identified and measured differently to those specified by a teacher, simply because the learner has a greater understanding of themselves in relation to the assigned task. This conception of self-assessment relies on the learner's own sense of self-identity, or their own perceptions of their self. Therefore, what is important to them becomes the value assigned to their learning. Until learners see the relevance and connect meaning to the tasks they perform, neither learning nor self-assessment is likely to take priority for the learner. Evaluating the content of learning becomes the final stage of self-assessment and when that content is seen as highly desirable, necessary or interesting, the learner will actively engage in the learning. In this way, self-assessment is intrinsically linked with both the content and the learner's knowledge of him or herself in relation to that task. As educators we need to become cognizant of the elements of self-assessment that learners engage in so that we can support them back into the dialogue about their learning goals and aspirations.

This chapter has outlined the way different assessment approaches foreground different aspects of learning; and how self-assessment can provide a valuable lens through which to view and support further learning. Ultimately however, irrespective of the assessment approach used, it is the individual learner and their developing sense of self that needs to be the main focus. Self-assessment within a sociocultural context can facilitate the development of a sense of identity, which in turn can promote the self-determination and learned hopefulness for learners. Through knowing themselves, learners are in a stronger position to actively participate in decisions, goals, and aspirations about their own learning needs.

Self-assessment is a deliberate, intentional, and supportive process to facilitate student learning, and to acknowledge the learner as taking a key role in their own assessment and learning. It legitimizes the multiple contexts the learner experiences and challenges the notion that school-based education is the only form of learning we can measure. For learners with special educational needs, self-determination is an important outcome. A successful transition from a school context into the community, enables them to take an active part in decisions about themselves, their futures and their goals.

If we are actively supporting learners to be active participants in the learning process, they must also take an active and participatory role in their own assessment. All assessment methods can be enhanced through incorporating a self-reflective component, which creates scaffolded opportunities for learners to gain a sense of their own ability, creativity and general sense-of-self in relation to the task.

REFERENCES

Abery, B., Rudrud, L., Arndt, K., Schauben, L., & Egge-been, A. (1995). Evaluating a multicomponent program for enhancing the self-determination of youth with disabilities. *Intervention in School and Clinic, 30*(3), 170–179.

Agran, M., Blanchard, C., & Wehmeyer, M. L. (2000). Promoting transition goals and self-determination through student self-directed learning: The self-determined learning model of instruction. *Education and Training in Mental Retardation and Developmental Disabilities, 2000, 35*(4), 351–364.

Algozzine, B., Browder, D., Karvonen, M., Test, D., & Wood, W. (2001). Efffects of interventions to promote self-determination for individuals with disabilities, *Review of Educational Research, 71*(2), 219–277.

Barab, S., Cherkes-Julkowski, M., Swenson, R., Garrett, S., Shaw, R., & Young, M. (1999). Principles of self-organization: Learning as participation in autocatakinetic systems. *Journal of the Learning Sciences, 8*(3&4), 349–390.

Barnes, R. (1997). High expectations and pupil feedback. *Educational Practice and Theory, 19*(2), 5–15.

Bateson, G. (1972). *Steps to an ecology of mind.* London: Granada.

Black, P., & Wiliam, D. (1998). Inside the black box. *Phi Delta Kappan, 80*(2), 139–148.

Black, P., Harrison, C., Lee, C., Marshall, B., & Wiliam, D. (2003). *Assessment for learning. Putting it into practice.* Maidenhead: Open University Press.

Bourke, R. (2000). *Students' conceptions of learning and self-assessment in context.* Unpublished doctoral dissertation, Massey University, New Zealand.

Bourke, R., & Gregory, J. (1996). Get smart: Take intelligence out of testing. *The Psychological Bulletin, 90,* 22–30.

Broadfoot, P. (1979). Communication in the classroom: A study of the role of assessment in motivation. *Educational Review, 31*(1), 3–10.

Bronfenbrenner, U. (1979). *The ecology of human development: Experiments by nature and design.* Cambridge, MA: Harvard University Press.

Brown, A. L. (1997). Transforming schools into communities of thinking and learning about serious matters. *American Psychologist, 52*(4), 399–413.

Campione, J. (1989). Assisted assessment: A taxonomy of approaches and an outline of strengths and weaknesses. *Journal of Learning Disabilities, 22,* 151–165.

Clarke, S., Timperley, H. & Hattie, J. (2003), *Unlocking formative assessment practical strategies for enhancing students' learning in the primary and intermediate classroom.* New Zealand ed. Wellington: Hodden Moa Beckett Publishers Ltd.

Eaton, M., & Pougiales, R. (1993). Work, reflection, and community: Conditions that support writing self-evaluations. In J. MacGregor (Ed.) Student Self-evaluations: Fostering Reflective Learning. *New directions for teaching and learning, 56,* Winter, 47–63.

Elliott, J. (2003) Dynamic assessment in settings: Realising potential. *Educational Review, 55*(1) 15–32.

Feuerstein, R., Miller, R., & Jensen, M.R. (1981). Can evolving techniques better measure cognitive change? *The Journal of Special Education, 15*(2), 201–270.

Feuerstein, R., Rand, Y., & Hoffman, M. B. (1979) *The dynamic assessment of retarded performers: The learning potential assessment device, theory, instruments and techniques.* Baltimore, MD: University Park Press.

Flanagan, D. P., & McGrew, K. S. (1997). A cross-battery approach to assessing and interpreting cognitive abilities: Narrowing the gap between practice and cognitive science. In D. P. Flanagan, J. L. Genshaft & P. L. Harrison (Eds.), *Contemporary intellectual assessment: Theories, tests and issues.* New York, Guilford Press.

Gipps, C., & Tunstall, P. (1998). Effort, ability and the teacher: Young children's explanations for success and failure. *Oxford Review of Education, 24*(2), 149–165.

Gould, S. J. (1981). *The mismeasure of man.* Harmondsworth: Pelican Books.

Granott, N., & Gardner, H. (1994). When minds meet. In R. J. Sternberg & R. K. Wagner (Eds.), *Mind in con-*

text. *Interactionist perspectives on human intelligence* (pp. 171–201). Cambridge: Cambridge University Press.

Gresham, F. M., Watson, T. S., & Skinner, C. H. (2001). Functional behavioral assessment: Principles, procedures, and future directions. School Psychology Review, *30*(2), 156–172

Howie, D. (1999). Models and morals: Meanings underpinning the scientific study of special educational needs. *International Journal of Disability, Development and Education, 46*(1), 10–24.

Johnson-Martin, N., Attermeier, S., & Hacker, B. (1990). T*he Carolina curriculum for preschoolers with special needs.* Baltimore, MD: Paul H. Brookes.

Johnston, P. H., & Nicholls, J. G. (1995). Voices we want to hear and voices we don't. *Theory into Practice, 34*(2), 94–100.

Kusnic, E., & Finley, M. L. (1993). Student self-evaluation: An introduction and rationale. *New Directions for Teaching and Learning, 56,* Winter, 5–13.

Lave, J. (1996). Teaching, as learning, in practice. *Mind, Culture, and Activity: An International Journal, 3*(3), 149–164.

Lave, J., & Wenger, E. (1991). *Situated learning: Legitimate peripheral participation.* Cambridge: Cambridge University Press.

Leffler, E. and Svedberg, G. (2003). Enterprise in Swedish rural schools: Capacity building through learning networks. *Queensland Journal of Educational Research, 19*(2), 83–99.

Lidz, C. S. (1991). *Practitioner's guide to dynamic assessment.* New York: Guilford Press.

Lincoln, Y. S. (1995). In search of students' voices. *Theory into Practice, 34*(2), 88–93.

Lopez, E. C. (1997). The cognitive assessment of limited English proficient and bilingual children. In D. P. Flanagan, J. L. Genshalt & P. L. Harrison (Eds.), *Contemporary intellectual assessment: Theories, tests and issues.* New York: Guilford Press.

Malian, E., & Nevin, A (2002). A review of self-determination literature implications for practitioners. *Remedial and Special Education, 23*(2), 68–74.

Maslow, A. H. (1971). *The farther reaches of human nature.* New York: Viking Press.

McMillan, J. H. (2000). Fundamental assessment principles for teachers and school administrators. *Practical Assessment, Research & Evaluation, 7*(8). Retrieved November 12, 2005, from http://PAREonline.net/getvn.asp?v=7&n=8

Mead, G. H. (1934). *Mind, self, and society.* Chicago, IL: University of Chicago Press.

Miller, J.A., Tansey, M., & Hughes, T. L. (1998). Functional behavioral assessment. The link between problem behavior and effective intervention in schools. *Current Issues in Education* [Online], *1*(5). Available at: http://cie.asu.edu/volume1/number5/ index.html

Oldfather, P. (1995). Songs 'come back most to them': Students' experiences as researchers. *Theory into Practice, 34*(2), 131–137.

Paley, V. G. (1979). *White teacher.* Cambridge, MA: Harvard University Press.

Paley, V. G. (1999). *The kindness of children.* Cambridge, MA: Harvard University Press.

Piaget, J. (1929). *The child's conception of the world.* New York: Harcourt, Brace & World.

Piaget, J. (1979). *Science of education and the psychology of the child.* New York: Penguin. (Original work published 1969.)

Pollard, A. (with Filer, A). (1996). *The social world of children's learning.* London: Cassell.

Pramling, I. (1996). Understanding and empowering the child as learner. In D. R. Olson & N. Torrance (Eds.), *The handbook of education and human development* (pp. 565–592). Oxford: Blackwell.

Ralph, E. G. (1995). Are self-assessments accurate? Evaluating novices' teaching via triangulation. *Research in Education, 53,* 41–51.

Rogoff, B. (2003). *The cultural nature of human development.* New York: Oxford University Press.

Rogoff, B., Matusov, M., & White, C. (1996). Models of teaching and learning: Participation in a community of learners. In D. R. Olson & N. Torrance (Eds.), *The handbook of education and human development* (pp. 388–414). Oxford: Blackwell.

Rogoff, B., Mistry, J., Göncü, A., & Mosier, C. (1993). Guided participation in cultural activity by toddlers and caregivers. *Monographs of the Society for Research in Child Development, 58*(7, Serial no. 236).

Shepard, L. (2000). The role of assessment in a learning culture. *Educational Researcher, 29*(7), 4–14.

Skuy, M. and Mentis, M. (Eds. in collaboration with Rueven Feuerstein). (1999). *Bridging Learning In and Out of the Classroom.* Los Angeles, CA: SkyLight Training and Publishing Inc.

Smith, A. (1996). *Incorporating children's perspectives into research in New Zealand.* Unpublished manuscript, Children's Issues Centre, University of Otago.

Smith, A. (1998). *Understanding children's development* (4th ed.). Wellington: Bridget Williams Books.

Sternberg, R. J. (1984). What should intelligence tests test? Implications for a triarchic theory of intelligence for intelligence testing. *Educational Researcher, 13*(1), 5–15.

Sternberg, R. (1988). *The triarchic mind: A new theory of human intelligence.* New York: Viking.

Thoma, C, A., Nathanson, R., Baker, S. R., & Tamura, R. (2002). Self-determination: What do special educators know and where do they learn it? *Remedial and Special Education, 23*(4), 242–247.

Van Kraayenoord, C. E., & Paris, S. G. (1997). Australian students' self-appraisal of their work samples and academic progress. *Elementary School Journal*, *97*(5), 523–537.

Vygotsky, L. S. (1978). *Mind and society.* Cambridge, MA: Harvard University Press.

Vygotsky, L. S. (1987). *The collected works of L. S. Vygotsky.* R. W. Rieber & A. S. Carton (Eds.). New York: Plenum Press.

Vygotsky, L. S. (1988). The genesis of higher mental functions. In K. Richardson & S. Sheldon (Eds.), *Cognitive development to adolescence* (pp. 61–80). London: Lawrence Erlbaum.

Weeden, P., Winter, J., & Broadfoot, P, (2002). *Assessment: What's in it for schools?* London: Routledge.

Wehmeyer, M. (1994). Self-determination as an educational outcomes. *Impact*, *6*(4), 6–7.

Wehmeyer, M., & Schalock, R. (2001). Self-determination and quality of life: Implications for special education services and supports. *Focus on Exceptional Children*, April, 1–6.

Wenger, E. (1998). *Communities of practice: Learning, meaning, and identity.* Cambridge: Cambridge University Press.

Zimmerman, M.A. (1990). Toward a theory of learned hopefulness: A structural model analysis of participation and empowerment. *Journal of Research in Personality*, *24*, 71–86.

25

Policy, legal, and implementation issues surrounding assessment accommodations for students with disabilities

Martha L. Thurlow, Sandra J. Thompson and
Christopher J. Johnstone

Assessment has always been an important component of special education policy and practice. In the past the assessment task was largely concerned with the identification of difficulties and disabilities for the purpose of determining eligibility so that additional services could be provided. More recently, two major developments have resulted in significant changes to the ways in which assessment is conceptualized and implemented. The first of these developments is the growth of inclusive practices in schools and associated attempts to create a common curriculum for all children. Developments in inclusion have challenged traditional assumptions about disability and the purpose and nature of assessment. It has seen the rise in curriculum-based and formative assessment designed to improve teaching and learning.

The second major development is the introduction of 'standards-driven reform' policies in many school systems throughout the world. These policies are underpinned by the expectation that all children will attain common educational outcomes and they have fundamentally changed assessment policies and practice. A feature of these reforms is the central role of assessment in measuring progress toward curriculum standards as part of public accountability for the performance of all students including students with disabilities (see Rouse & McLaughlin this volume). For example, in the US, students with disabilities are expected to access the same standards, participate in the same assessments, and be included in educational accountability systems in the same manner as their nondisabled peers. These policies have led to substantial professional attention being given to how all children and young people can be included in a common system of assessment. During the past decade there has been an increase in acceptance and use of assessment 'accommodations.' This chapter uses examples from recent developments in the US to explore some of the technical and conceptual difficulties relating to the increasing use of assessment 'accommodations' *that produce valid test scores.*

The purpose of this chapter is to examine both the 'theory' of assessment accommodations and the ways in which policy, legal, and implementation issues have influenced assessment in the US. We address what is currently known about the definitions and use of accommodations, policy considerations that have pushed practice forward, research on accommodations, legal cases that have had an impact on both policy and implementation, and current implementation issues. We conclude by noting new movements in assessment practice in the US that are related to assessment accommodations.

ACCOMMODATIONS DEFINITION AND USE

Assessment accommodations are changes in the testing environment or procedures that are designed to remove irrelevant variance, thereby producing a more valid measure of students' knowledge and skills. There are many such changes that have produced lists that vary widely both qualitatively and in length. A common way of understanding accommodations is to put them into one of six groups: presentation, response, timing, scheduling, setting, and other (Thurlow, Elliott, & Ysseldyke, 2003). Sometimes these groups are combined (for example, timing/scheduling) or another one added (for example, equipment).

The extent to which accommodations are used during assessments is something that has been sparsely documented, at least in the past. Nevertheless, responses to surveys by state special education directors have indicated increased use during statewide assessments. In 2001, about half of the states in the US that kept track of the use of accommodations (n = 12) reported an increase in their use (Thompson & Thurlow, 2001). Thurlow (2001) found that there were extremely variable rates in use of accommodations from one state to the next (8 per cent to 82 per cent of students), and that there was a relationship between the level of schooling (elementary, middle, high school) and the percentage of students using accommodations (with more students using assessment accommodations in the lower levels). By 2003,

more than three-quarters of states were collecting data on the use of accommodations during state assessments (Thompson & Thurlow, 2003), and in 2005 all states were doing so (Thompson, Johnstone, Thurlow, & Altman, 2005). This dramatic change in the attention of states to the percentage of students receiving assessments with accommodations coincides with increased focus on assessment of students with disabilities. Increased participation of students with disabilities increases the likelihood of the use of accommodations, thus creating a growth of new accommodation policies, legal case activities, and implementation issues.

POLICY CONSIDERATIONS

Historically, US education assessment policy had been almost silent on the topic of accommodations, with only general references in law and in regulations. What the law had been clear about is that students with disabilities are to be included in state assessments for accountability. The Improving America's Schools Act (IASA 1994) and the Individuals with Disabilities Education Act (IDEA 1997) clarified that students with disabilities, the most likely group to be assumed to be exempted from the requirements, be included in all statewide assessments. Following this, the No Child Left Behind Act (NCLB 2002) added the force of accountability and very specifically clarified the 'all' message through its subgroup requirements (see Table 25.1). Subsequent to NCLB, IDEA was reauthorized as the Individuals with Disabilities Education Improvement Act (IDEIA 2004). The inclusion of students with disabilities in the accountability provisions of NCLB was confirmed in IDEIA's 2004 reauthorization and gave greater prominence to assessment accommodations. The law indicated that all states must have guidelines about the use of accommodations and it required that states collect data on the number of students using accommodations during each administration of a regular assessment. Clearly, accommodations are viewed as a logical part of ensuring the assessment participation of students with disabilities.

Table 25.1. No Child Left Behind: participation of all students in state accountability systems

Each state accountability system shall

(i) be based on the academic standards and academic assessments adopted … and, shall take into account the achievement of all public elementary and secondary students (Part A, Sec. 1111,2)

C. Adequate yearly progress shall be defined by the State in a manner that –

(i) applies the same high standards of academic achievement to all public elementary school and secondary school students in the State (Part A, Sec. 1111, 2, C) …

(v) includes separate measurable annual objectives for continuous and substantial improvement for each of the following

(I) the achievement of all public elementary school and secondary school students;

(II) the achievement of –

(aa) economically disadvantaged students;

(bb) students from major racial and ethnic groups;

(cc) students with disabilities, and

(dd) students with limited English proficiency … (Part a, Sec 1111,2).

(ii) not less than 95 percent of each group of students described in subparagraph (C)(v) who are enrolled in the school are required to take the assessments, consistent with paragraph (3) (C)(xi) and with accommodations, guidelines, and alternate assessments provided in the same manner as those provided under section 612(a)(17)(A) of the Individuals with Disabilities Education Act and paragraph (3) … (Part A, Sec. 1111,2).

Source: *No Child Left Behind Act, 2001*

States in the US are now setting policy and guidelines for changes in the testing situations for students with disabilities that sometimes challenge traditional measurement assumptions about standardization. Such changes raise issues about what tests are really measuring and what they *should* be measuring. Accommodations also raise concerns about assessment accessibility for all students. Recently, the US Department of Education made clear that accommodations might play a greater role in the accountability provisions of NCLB than states had suspected. For example, students who use accommodations that the state has determined produce invalid scores cannot be counted in the 95 per cent participation requirement for meeting adequate yearly progress. Given that nearly 12 per cent of students are identified as having disabilities, determining how to obtain valid scores from accommodations is of paramount importance.

Terminology

Accommodations have been defined in a number of different ways. Initially accommodations were changes that made it possible for students who might otherwise be excluded to participate in assessments. Tindal and Fuchs (1999) used the term 'leveling the playing field' to describe the role of accommodations in assessment. In other words, a student who is blind could participate in assessments when braille was allowed as an accommodation. Likewise, students who could not decode print well enough to proceed through tests of mathematics, social studies and science could participate if someone read the test questions to them.

Soon after the focus on assessment accommodations as a way to encourage participation in assessments gained momentum, a link was made to the importance of instructional accommodations. This policy perspective of linking assessment and instructional accommodations is reflected in current definitions of the term, where accommodations are defined as 'practices and procedures in the areas of presentation, response, setting, and timing/scheduling that provide equitable access during instruction and assessments for students with disabilities' (Thompson, Morse, Sharpe, & Hall, 2005, p. 14).

As accommodations policy and practice have emerged educators began to realize that accommodation was more than just participation, it was about eliminating barriers to meaningful testing. Accommodations were a way to minimize the impact of a disability on assessments by eliminating barriers that were irrelevant to the construct being assessed (Thurlow, Elliott, & Ysseldyke, 2003). Removing and minimizing barriers is a complicated process. For example, many students receive accommodations to minimize the effects of disabilities that affect language. The problem with selecting appropriate accommodations for these students is that any test that employs language is, in part, a measure of language skills (AERA, APA, NCME, 1999).

Assessments under accommodated conditions may also affect score validity. As the use of accommodations proliferates in states, questions are being asked about whether students 'can take tests under varied conditions in such a way that the scores across conditions can be seen as comparable [to non-accommodated scores]' (Kopriva, Samuelsen, Wiley, & Winter, 2003, p. 2). Accommodations research has focused on two major issues: (1) Do accommodations work to increase access, thus improving performance of students with disabilities on tests? (2) Are the test results across students who use a variety of accommodations comparable?

The acceptability of accommodations has also been addressed in state policies. All states in the US now have accommodation policies (Clapper, Morse, Lazarus, Thompson, & Thurlow, 2005), and over 80 per cent of states keep track of the use of accommodations during state assessments (Thompson, Johnstone, Thurlow, & Altman, 2005). However, there continues to be only limited consensus on what constitutes an appropriate accommodation as states grapple with decisions about how to score and report the use of accommodations that some consider 'nonstandard' or 'nonscorable.' Nonstandard accommodations are typically those that are deemed to change the construct being assessed, thus creating an invalid score.

This brief summary demonstrates that there is still a variety of terms used to describe accommodations. Researchers frequently use the terms 'valid' versus 'invalid' when describing the psychometric qualities of accommoda-

tions. States, however, use language that relates directly to the policy-level acceptability of an accommodation. Distinctions between 'appropriate' and 'questionable' accommodations (generally referred to as standard/nonstandard accommodation or accommodations/modifications in written policies) have been reflected in terminology in ways that have evolved over time. While there are many terms used in accommodations literature and policy, all terms boil down to a difference of whether an accommodation changes the essence of the constructs tested. If so, an accommodation is invalid (Thurlow & Wiener, 2000).

Purpose of accommodations

As noted, there has been a gradual shift in the purpose of accommodations, from simply enabling students with disabilities to have *access* to a test, to allowing for the *valid measurement* of students' knowledge and skills rather than obtaining a measurement that simply reflects their disabilities. This is a subtle distinction, but one that is important in discussions of test validity. According to Ryan and DeMark (2002), 'Validity is the central issue in evaluating the appropriateness of all forms of assessment and must remain the critical criterion guiding assessment development, applications, and the use of assessment results' (p. 67).

Access to general education and now the opportunity to access state assessments is a great step forward for students with disabilities in the US. Although assessment participation rates continue to vary across states (Thurlow, Moen, & Wiley, 2005), most students with disabilities can count on opportunities to participate in state assessments. Within this context, accommodations provide 'comparable opportunity, as far as possible, to demonstrate knowledge and skills they have acquired that are relevant to the purpose of the test' (Willingham & Cole, 1997, p. 10). Comparable opportunity can enhance access through the design of the assessment itself – by considering elements of universal design (see Thompson, Johnstone, & Thurlow, 2002) or through a variety of accommodations.

Enhanced access alone, however, does not ensure a valid measurement. Once a student gains access, then the need for valid measures becomes more critical. In order for an assessment to be both accessible and valid, 'examinees of equal standing with respect to the construct the test is intended to measure should on average earn the same test score, irrespective of group membership' (AERA, APA, NCME, 1999, p. 74). The *Standards for Educational and Psychological Testing* refers to this as fairness, with this definition:

> Fairness requires that all examinees be afforded appropriate testing conditions ... In some cases, aspects of the testing process that pose no particular challenge for most examinees may prevent specific groups or individuals from accurately demonstrating their standing with respect to the construct of interest. In some instances, greater comparability may sometimes be attained if standardized procedures are modified. (AERA, APA, NCME, 1999, p. 75)

If the purpose of accommodations is to preserve the validity of the test score, then accommodations would only be allowed to address factors extraneous to the test and the scores of students using accommodations would be comparable to test scores obtained under standard administration conditions. But, if the purpose of the accommodations is to 'confer a benefit on a specific subset of students' (Phillips, 2002, p. 130), it becomes important to develop policies that address what is to be done with the noncomparable scores of students who receive this benefit. Linn (2002) summarized the purpose of accommodations for assessments as 'removing disadvantages due to disabilities that are irrelevant to the construct the test is intended to measure without giving unfair advantage to those being accommodated' (p. 36).

Organization

When the National Center on Educational Outcomes (NCEO) first began analyzing assessment policies in the early 1990s, the policies were sometimes organized according to disability category (Thurlow, Ysseldike, & Silverstein, 1995). Now, almost all accommodations are organized by the categories of presentation accommodations, response accommodations, setting accommodations, and timing/scheduling accommodations. Table 25.2 lists examples of specific accommodations included in each of these categories.

Within each of the categories, regardless of the superordinate or subordinate organization, there is a long list of test changes, often with specific conditions under which they are allowed or not allowed, under which scores are aggregated or not aggregated, or under which scores are reported or not reported (Clapper, Morse, Lazarus, Thompson, & Thurlow, 2005). For students with disabilities, most of the conditions relate to the content that is being tested, an indication of the importance of clarifying the purpose of the test and the construct being tested, rather than just the goal of providing the student with access to the testing situation.

Extensiveness

In 2001, only one-quarter of the states collected information on the use of accommodations, and they did this without any prompting from the federal government (Thompson & Thurlow, 2001; Thurlow, 2001). Since that time, a few states (14 in 2002; 15 in 2003) have reported some information about the use of accommodations when they have publicly released their assessment data (Thurlow & Wiley, 2004; Wiley, Thurlow, & Klein, 2005), but the format of these reports is very different. In 2005, every state reported that it documents accommodations usage (Thompson et al., 2005a). A closer look at state practice reveals, however, that because of the different approaches to recommending and documenting accommodations that states have taken (for example, extended time may be considered an accommodation in one state but just good testing practice in another), the counts that are produced will need to be studied carefully in light of state policies. Extensiveness will be a relative concept.

Table 25.2. Examples of accommodations from each category

Category	Example of Specific Accommodation
Presentation	Large print
	Magnification device
	Braille
	Human reader
	Audiotape or compact disk
	Screen reader
	Sign language
	Audio amplification device
Response	Express response to a scribe
	Type on or speak to work processor
	Speak into tape recorder
	Use calculation device (for example, talking calculator with enlarged keys)
	Use spelling and grammar assistive devices
	Write in test booklet instead of on answer sheet
	Use augmentative device for single or multiple messages (e.g., BIG Mack, Dynovox)
Setting	Change location so student does not distract others
	Change location to increase physical access
	Change location to access special equipment
Timing and scheduling	Extended time
	Use short segment test booklets (when available)
	Allow for multiple or frequent breaks
	Schedule tests in the morning
	Cue student to begin working and stay on task
	Change testing schedule or order of subtests

RESEARCH FINDINGS

As the accommodations policies in the US grew both in number and size, there arose a desperate cry for a better research-based determination of which accommodations were 'appropriate'. For many years, researchers attempted to address appropriateness concerns by stating that an accommodation is valid if it provides a 'differential boost' to students with disabilities, that is, an increase in scores disproportionate to non-disabled students who were provided the same accommodation for research purposes (Phillips, 1994; cf. Sireci, Li, & Scarpati, 2005; Tindal & Fuchs, 1999). Many studies have been conducted on accommodations over the past 15 years primarily supported by the US Department of Education.

A summary of the research for those accommodations most frequently allowed by states – braille; computer or machine; dictated response; extended time; interpreter; large print; mark answer in booklet; read aloud; read, re-read, explain directions; test breaks – concluded that 'although there has been an increase in research on how accommodations can aid in the measurement of skills among students with disabilities, many questions remain unanswered. The degree to which accommodations may compromise the integrity of tests is not clear' (Bolt & Thurlow, 2004, p. 141). Sireci et al. (2005) summarized studies for both students with disabilities and English language learners and concluded that research conducted from 1986 to 2002 only provided firm findings about one accommodation – extended time. The 150 studies cited by Sireci et al. indicated that 'read aloud' accommodations and simplified English accommodations did not provide students with disabilities or English language learners a statistically significant boost in scores across multiple research studies. On the other hand, many studies found that accommodations improved the scores of *both* students with disabilities and non-disabled students, indicating that there may be portions of tests which are problematic for the entire test population.

Johnstone, Altman, Thurlow, and Thompson (2006) recently summarized research on the effects of accommodations in 49 empirical research studies on accommodations published between 2002 and 2004. Similar to Sireci, et al. (2005), Johnstone, et al. found great variability in the characteristics of the accommodations research. The inconclusive findings of accommodations research point to the complexities of the topic. For example, in the years 2002–2004, Burch (2002), and Pomplun, Frey, and Becker (2002) demonstrated that computer administration is an effective accommodation, but Bridgeman, Lennon, and Jackenthal (2003) found no significant effect on scores. One study found that computer administration changed item comparability (Choi & Tinker, 2002) but another found no change in comparability (Kobrin & Young, 2003).

Likewise, Helwig, Rozek-Tedesco, and Tindal (2002), Huynh, Meyer, and Gallant-Taylor, (2002), Meloy, Deville, and Frisbie (2002) and Weston (2003) found that oral presentation of a test produced positive results for students with disabilities, while Bolt and Bielinski (2002) and McKevitt and Elliott (2003) found no significant difference in results. Equally perplexing were the studies that claimed that item comparability stayed the same for tests read aloud (Barton, 2002; Huynh, Meyer, & Gallant, 2004) when others claimed that item characteristics changed under oral presentation conditions (Hall, 2002).

Bridgeman, Cline, and Hessinger (2004) and Crawford, Helwig, and Tindal (2004) found that extended time accommodations had a positive effect on scores, but, contrary to a preponderance of research findings, two studies found that extended time had no significant effect on scores (Buehler, 2002; Elliott & Marquart, 2004). One study found that extended time did not effect item comparability (Cahalan, Mandinach, & Camara, 2002), but another found that scores were not comparable under extended time conditions (Thornton, Reese, Pashley, & Dalessandro, 2002). When multiple accommodations were used, students benefited (Trammell, 2003),

but research was inconclusive as to whether items under accommodated conditions were comparable to those under standard conditions. Finally, calculator (Scheuneman, Camara, Cascallar, Wendler, & Lawrence, 2002) and dictionary use (Idstein, 2003) did not produce positive effects for students with disabilities, but technological aids (Landau, Russell, Gourgey, Erin, & Cowan, 2003) and allowances for dictated response (MacArthur & Cavalier, 2004) had positive effects on scores in one study each.

Several important observations are evident from the analysis of the 49 studies included in the Johnstone et al. (2006) report. The first is that the majority of studies examined the effects of the use of accommodations on test scores. While this purpose continues to be important, the relative lack of studies about item comparability point to the need for further research in this area and for clear definition of the constructs tested – not just for the test in general, but for each item. In addition, greater clarity in the accommodations process needs to be provided for individual students, for example, measuring whether each student who participates in an accommodation study actually needs the accommodation being studied. Once this clarity is obtained, then better studies of test score validity can be conducted.

Of course, Sireci et al. (2005) noted that accommodations research is not just complicated by the accommodation itself. In many of the 150 studies reviewed by Sireci et al., students who received accommodations were deemed a heterogeneous group. Refining the research sample for accommodations studies adds a challenge to statistical research but may be necessary to obtain consistent results for the field.

The accommodations research literature seldom explores the interaction of accommodations and students themselves. Further research that measures student factors such as experience with technology, personality traits, multiple disability characteristics requiring several accommodations, and desire for using an accommodation is needed.

In conclusion, literature reviews suggest that there is little evidence on accommodations besides extended time. Experimental studies are of naturally occuring events and are fraught with design difficulties. Understanding which students need which accommodations, the efficacy of particular combinations of accommodations, and how to administer them correctly is complex. Non-experimental research often lacks the evidence necessary to address validity claims. Both types of research appear to be limited in answering fundamental questions about the use and impact of accommodations.

Sireci et al's. 2005 review for the National Academy of Sciences, aptly outlined the future needs for accommodations research by stating:

> Our review indicates that many accommodations have positive, construct-valid effects for certain groups of students. The remaining challenge is to implement these accommodations appropriately and to identify which accommodations are best for specific students. Another challenge is developing more flexible tests that would make accommodations unnecessary. These challenges appear surmountable. (p. 68)

LEGAL CASES

Despite the challenges that are well documented in accommodations policy and research, use of accommodations continues in schools across the US. Often, because of unclear state policies, or policies that appear unfair to particular students, disputes arise. Many of these disputes are settled through mediation between state or school district department of education representatives and parents or through out-of-court settlements, but some accommodations disputes end up being challenged in courts of law. Court cases and settlements frequently address the issues of accessibility and validity.

A well-known case in Oregon was brought by parents and advocates of students with learning disabilities. In 1999, Oregon implemented a plan whereby students had to pass an assessment to earn a 'Certificate of Initial Mas-

tery'. Results from this assessment were used for graduation and scholarship decisions. After a number of students with learning disabilities failed the examination, advocates argued that the list of acceptable accommodations was too small. A 'Blue Ribbon' panel of experts was assembled and contributed to a settlement in which the state agreed to accept accommodations as valid unless shown to be otherwise. This approach is the opposite of what had been the typical approach to accommodations, in which it was the responsibility of the test taker to show that the accommodation did not change what was being measured. As a result of this case and the settlement, an accommodation panel now advises the Oregon assessment process, helping to sort through special accommodation requests before each assessment administration. This panel advises the state to ensure accommodations are made for students with disabilities (Disability Rights Advocates, 2001).

A case in Alaska (*Noon* v. *State of Alaska*) was brought because students with disabilities were failing a high school graduation examination at a disproportionate rate. In a settlement that was reached out of court, plaintiffs and the state agreed on the following provisions:

1 Students with disabilities would take the high school graduation examination in their sophomore (10th grade) year with allowable accommodations.
2 Students who failed the examination would be allowed to re-take the examination using previously disallowed accommodations (for example, test modifications like the use of a calculator).

Noon v. State of Alaska provided the State of Alaska Department of Education the opportunity to override its own policies for a student taking the examination for the second time if the help that a particular accommodation or modification gives *outweighs* the validity issues introduced by a particular change to the test. All approval of test modifications takes place on a case-by-case review process.

It is noteworthy that most of the cases that have gone to court have involved a graduation level exam or one considered equivalent to that in status for the student. The issues are not easy, and legal maneuverings are likely to have an effect on policy and practice in accommodations for some time to come.

Lawsuits have also played a role in how scores are interpreted. For example, assessment practice historically allowed students with disabilities to use a variety of accommodations, but 'flagged' such scores so that interpreters of results would know that accommodations were used. Such practice was especially problematic for persons with disabilities in competitive college entrance situations. In 2002, however, the case of *Breimhorst* v. *ETS* was settled out of court. As a result, ETS no longer flags scores of students who use accommodations on the SAT, or the Graduate Record Examination (GRE).

In short, lawsuits and out-of-court settlements have had a major impact in changing accommodations practice. Legal activity has created situations whereby both the policies (what accommodations can be used) and the interpretations of results (what inferences are derived from test scores) are influenced by advocates for students with disabilities. No discussion on accommodations is complete without understanding the powerful effects of legal action in the US. As the stakes associated with large-scale assessment continue to rise, so does the potential for legal proceedings related to test accommodations.

IMPLEMENTATION ISSUES

Consistently, the policy, research, and legal discussions surrounding accommodations quickly become discussions of implementation issues – the practice issues. Evidence above suggests that policy and legal cases have influenced accommodations practice, raising a number of important issues. Among these are:

- What happens to students who need accommodations deemed in policy to be not appropriate to participate in assessments?
- What happens to the scores of students who need accommodations deemed in policy to be

not appropriate to participate in assessments?

Each of these important questions is addressed based on research that is currently available.

What happens to students who need accommodations deemed not appropriate?

In the US, accommodation policies and practice are not always the same. Students do use accommodations that have been determined not to be appropriate for some policy reason. For example, if a student is blind, is a read-aloud accommodation inappropriate? This question was raised in the case of a student who became blind in high school. He had the skills needed to pass the high school exit test, but could no longer see to read the exam, and had not had time to learn the braille skills to be able to use the braille edition of the test. This is an accommodation that has had equivocal research evidence (Bolt & Bielinski, 2002; Helwig et al., 2002; Huynh et al., 2002; McKevitt & Elliott, 2003; Meloy et al., 2002; Weston, 2003) related to whether it produces a differential boost in test performance. If it is decided that this accommodation is appropriate for students who are blind and do not have braille reading skills, can the case also then be made for students who have significant reading disabilities and have not achieved decoding skills? The challenge is that appropriateness may change because assessments may assess constructs that are directly tied to the disability. Koretz and Barton (2003, p. 10) noted that

> For many students, the effects of disabilities on performance are at least in part related to the proficiencies the test is intended to measure – that is, they are construct-relevant. Moreover, in many cases, separating construct-relevant from construct-irrelevant impediments may be difficult. Students with learning disabilities, who constitute about half of all identified students with disabilities worldwide, are a group for whom disability-related impediments are often construct-relevant.

While some have argued that this may automatically mean that the student does not meet the standard or have the skills, others have suggested that for greater access or fairness, there may have to be rethinking of the approach that is taken to assessment – perhaps gathering additional evidence of students' knowledge and skills (for example, Thurlow & Wiener, 2000), or thinking through the importance of what we are measuring and whether there are some replacement skills that are appropriate for individuals with disabilities (see Thurlow, Johnstone, Thompson, & Case, in press).

What happens to scores from assessments taken with accommodations deemed not appropriate?

States' interpretations of accommodations differ, as do states' penalties for using nonstandard accommodations. In a recent survey of all state special education directors, Thompson, Johnstone, Thurlow, and Altman (2005) found that eight states in the US do not count these students as participants in the assessments, seven states counted them as participants, but gave them no score, 17 states counted them as participants and gave them a score of zero, and six states counted their scores as valid. As previously noted, counting students as participants or not has significant implications in the US because of the NCLB requirements that all students participate in assessments, and that if 95 per cent or more of students overall and in each subgroup do not participate, then schools do not meet NCLB requirements for Adequate Yearly Progress (AYP).

How states report the scores of students who participate in tests using nonappropriate accommodations has created difficulty. States have had the option to identify ways to obtain valid scores. Whether the solution involves gathering additional evidence, as suggested by Thurlow and Wiener (2000), or it involves specialized scoring programs, the option of simply excluding students or even just giving students zero scores will most likely fade away in the near future.

A body of literature now exists that strongly documents the difficulty of making decisions about appropriate accommodations

for students with disabilities, both for instruction and for assessment. There appears to be a tendency, except perhaps at the high school level, to over-accommodate. The work of DeStefano and Shriner, along with that of Lynn Fuchs and colleagues, has demonstrated that decisions could be improved through training (Shriner & DeStefano, 2003), a data-based decision-making system (Fuchs & Fuchs, 2001), or other new technology based data-based systems which are in development (Ketterlin-Geller & Tindal, 2005).

Despite the improvements indicated by these researchers, a recent study of state training on accommodations (Langley & Olsen, 2003) reported that nearly one-third of the sampled states provided no training on accommodations at all, and another third focused only on assessment accommodations. These findings were obtained despite the repeated connection between instructional and assessment accommodations in state policies (Clapper, Morse, Lazarus, Thompson, & Thurlow, 2005). Furthermore, nearly half of the states included only district testing coordinators and special education teachers in the training. In addition, the diversity of trainers was fairly limited; teacher trainers were not involved in any training. Training that did occur tended to focus on legal issues, definitions, and the process of selecting accommodations.

More disconcerting is that the decisions that were made by the IEP team did not get transferred to the testing itself. Fuchs and Fuchs (1999) found a lack of connection among teachers' decisions, students' needs, test accommodations, and derived benefits. They also found that 'teachers awarded accommodations to large numbers of students who benefited from the accommodation no more than students without a disability' (p. 27) and 'many educators have relatively little understanding of the purpose of test accommodations ... and have little experience in observing the actual effects of accommodations for students with and without disabilities' (p. 29). Similarly, Hollenbeck, Tindal, and Almond (1998) found inconsistent application of appropriate and allowable statewide assessment accommodations. They found that only about half of teachers could identify appropriate and inappropriate accommodations. The findings varied little between general and special educators. They also found that fewer than half of the special educators reported using accommodations for students on IEPs. According to Hollenbeck (2002) 'IEP teams are left to their own professional judgment with little clear guidance about how to proceed. They need a decision-making process grounded in accommodation and large-scale assessment research' (p. 401).

Shriner and DeStefano (2003) followed the IEPs of students whose teams had received training and found that few of the accommodations that had been selected for students were implemented on the test day, and some that had not been selected were given to students. Similar results had been obtained in a study by the Paul Sherlock Center on Disabilities (2002), which found that testing location was a more important determinant of the accommodations provided to a student than what was listed in the student's IEP (for example, if one student at a location needed the test read aloud, then all students at that location would receive the test read aloud, regardless of whether it was on their IEPs). Teachers do not necessarily know which accommodations will produce invalid scores (as defined by their states) when they are used during large-scale assessments (Lazarus, Thompson, & Thurlow, 2005). Overall, there seems to be inconsistentency in the application of accommodations.

FUTURE EFFORTS

Accommodations is an area where policy, research, and legal activity have pushed practice forward dramatically in the US, all propelled by the assessment requirements of IDEA and NCLB. Future areas for investigation include: (1) construct clarification, (2) assessment design, (3) professional development, and (4) instruction and curriculum access.

We provide just a few thoughts on each of these.

Construct clarification

According to the *Standards for Education and Psychological Testing* (AERA, APA, NCME, 1999):

> We use the term construct more broadly as the concept or characteristic that a test is designed to measure. Rarely, if ever, is there a single possible meaning that can be attached to a test score or a pattern of test responses. Thus, it is always incumbent on a testing professional to specify the construct interpretation that will be made on the basis of the score or response pattern. (p. 5)

It is important to begin the discussion about constructs – what exactly is being tested – at the item level. When this is done, it is easier to determine which accommodations affect the construct and which do not. Several states have done this in the area of mathematics by determining that a calculator cannot be used for items that assess computation, but can be used for general problem-solving. This has generally not been done in the area of reading, where most states are still at the point of setting policies related to tests that indicate that the test cannot be read to the student. In contrast, if construct clarification processes have determined that decoding of print is not being measured, then it may be able to allow for a variety of modes of print interaction, including not only visual (such as on the printed page or on a computer screen), but also tactile (feeling print, such as Braille) or auditory (such as listening to printed messages, as on the radio or television), or even multi-modal presentations (using any combination of modalities, as in assistive reading and viewing programs – digital talking news) (Thompson, Johnstone, Clapper, & Thurlow, 2004).

Construct relevance and assessment validity have been addressed by both the National Council of Teachers of English (NCTE) and the National Council of Teachers of Mathematics (NCTM), among others. According to Ryan and DeMark (2002), early on, NCTE challenged the validity of indirect measures of writing, such as tests of grammar, writing mechanics, and editing tests. NCTE insisted that the valid measurement of students' writing ability requires the assessment of samples of students' writing performance evaluated against standards or rubrics defining critical characteristics of grade-level expectations for written work. (p. 68)

This has implications for accommodations. If the writing test was a test where students were required to edit a paragraph and make corrections, then it could not be presented in a 'read-aloud' format. But, NCTE suggests that what actually constitutes a valid measure of writing must be considered first. If it is the assessment of actual student writing performance, what implications does that have for accommodations? Is spelling being assessed? If not, can students use a dictionary or a spell-check on a computer? These are the critical questions that need to be asked when accommodation policies are being set.

Assessment design

Directly connected to accommodations and the notion of construct clarification is the idea that assessment developers must look more carefully at the design and development of assessments and test items from the beginning to be sure that they can be accessed by the largest number of students. The term 'universal design' has been used to convey the notion of 'optimal standard assessment conditions.' Thompson, Johnstone, and Thurlow (2002) suggest that test developers must keep the following in mind:

- Inclusive assessment population – think about all students who will participate in the general assessment when developing items. Ideally, examinees would be afforded equal opportunity to prepare for a test.
- Precisely defined constructs – obtain or define all constructs to be tested so that irrelevant cognitive, sensory, emotional, and physical barriers can be removed.
- Accessible, non-biased items – build accessibility into items from the beginning, and use bias review to ensure that quality is retained in all

items. Bias, defined by *Standards for Education and Psychological Testing* (AERA, APA, NCME, 1999) arises 'when deficiencies in a test itself or the manner in which it is used result in different meanings for scores earned by members of different identifiable subgroups' (p. 74).
- Amenable to accommodations – test design facilitates the use of needed accommodations (for example, all items can be brailled).
- Simple, clear, and intuitive instructions and procedures – using, for example, plain language strategies and other approaches that reduce ambiguity and increase understandability.
- Maximum readability and comprehensibility – characteristics that ensure easy decipherability are applied to text, to tables, figures and illustrations, and to response formats. According to Haladyna, Downing, and Rodriguez (2002), 'Simplified language is an effective way to reduce the influence of reading ability, a source of construct-irrelevant variance when the achievement test is intended to measure something else' (p. 315).

These general universal design elements have been transformed into a set of 'considerations' that can be used by test developers and reviewers to produce better assessments for all students, particularly those with disabilities and those who are English language learners (Thompson, Johnstone, Anderson, & Miller, 2005).

Professional development

There is little preparation of teachers about accommodations, leading IEP teams to make questionable decisions (Fuchs & Fuchs, 2001; Shriner & DeStefano, 2003). No matter the sophistication of research on accommodations and the validity of scores from accommodated assessments, if educators and teams of decisions makers cannot make good decisions, then the research-based knowledge is not sufficient. Likewise, there is little research evidence at all that students are being trained to become decision-makers about their own accommodation needs. Students have informed opinions on which accommodations they are willing to use and which accommodations make a difference in their performance – yet this valuable resource is rarely tapped.

Professional development is required for those who administer the accommodations. Among these accommodations are the read-aloud accommodation, the sign language interpreter, and the scribe. The potential for variability in these accommodations is great, and the need for standardization is important. In some states in the US, tape recorders are used instead of readers. Some states are beginning to use text readers on computers. Computers have tremendous potential, but can introduce some additional challenges (Thompson, Thurlow, Quenemoen, & Lehr, 2002). Several states have written guidelines for the accommodations that involve a person (called 'access assistant'). These guidelines vary considerably in their structure and the extent to which they provide specifications about qualifications of the access assistant (Clapper, Morse, Thurlow, & Thompson, 2005).

Instruction and curriculum access

Many of the issues that arise in assessment for students with disabilities are related to issues in instruction and curriculum. Many students have not had appropriate exposure to the instructional linkages that they should have had, nor the access to the curriculum that would have given them a chance to demonstrate knowledge and skills addressed on the assessment. According to *Standards for Education and Psychological Testing* (APA, AERA, NCME, 1999):

> When some test takers have not had the opportunity to learn the subject matter covered by the test content, they are likely to get low scores. The test score may accurately reflect what the test taker knows and can do, but low scores may have resulted in part from not having had the opportunity to learn the material tested as well as from having had the opportunity and having failed to learn. (p. 76)

This is a challenge within the context of today's assessments – and a problem that cannot be solved by the assessments or by accommodations.

FINAL THOUGHTS

Accommodations have been the target of contention in assessments, and this is likely to continue. They are the avenue to access, yet they are the point of concern. A study by Bielinski, Sheinker, and Ysseldyke (2003) found that people's perceptions of how scores obtained under accommodated conditions should be treated in reporting depended on the accommodation. But it also showed that 'deep-seated beliefs lead some respondents to consider almost no accommodation as changing the construct, whereas other respondents consider almost all accommodations as influencing the construct being measured' (p. i). Years of research on accommodations has not answered all the questions. Researchers have begun to suggest that we need new ways of looking at accommodations research, such as item by item, to make accommodations decisions and to examine their effects (Tindal & Ketterlin-Geller, 2003).

The next decade of educational policy will most likely reinforce requirements that students participate in assessments. The implementation of NCLB and IDEA 2004 has had a dramatic effect on access to the curriculum in the US for students with disabilities, and the introduction of accommodations has operationalized understanding of what access really means. Indeed, accommodations issues have sharpened our definitions of access, constructs, and improved assessments in general. Future developments will enable further questions to be answered and are likely to have a positive effect on both assessment and access for students with disabilities.

REFERENCES

American Educational Research Association, American Psychological Association, & National Council on Measurement in Education (AERA, APA, NCME). (1999). *Standards for educational and psychological testing.* Washington, DC: American Educational Research Association.

Barton, K. E. (2002). Stability of constructs across groups of students with different disabilities on a reading assessment under standard and accommodated administrations (Doctoral dissertation, University of South Carolina, 2001). *Dissertation Abstracts International*, 62/12, 4136.

Bielinski, J., Sheinker, A., & Ysseldyke, J. (2003). *Varied opinions on how to report accommodated test scores: Findings based on CTB/McGraw-Hill's framework for classifying accommodations* (Synthesis Report 49). Minneapolis, MN: University of Minnesota, National Center on Educational Outcomes.

Bolt S., & Bielinski J. (2002). *The effects of the read aloud accommodation on math test items.* Paper presented at the annual meeting of the National Council on Measurement in Education, New Orleans, LA.

Bolt, S. E., & Thurlow, M. L. (2004). Five of the most frequently allowed testing accommodations in state policy. *Remedial and Special Education, 25*(3), 141–152.

Bridgeman, B., Cline, F., & Hessinger, J. (2004). Effect of extra time on verbal and quantitative GRE scores. *Applied Measurement in Education, 17*(1), 25–37.

Bridgeman, B., Lennon, M. L., & Jackenthal, A. (2003). Effects of screen size, screen resolution and display rate on computer-based test performance. *Applied Measurement in Education, 16*(3), 191–205.

Buehler, K. L. (2002). Standardized group achievement tests and the accommodation of additional time. *Dissertation Abstracts International, 63/04*, 1312.

Burch, M. (2002). Effects of computer-based test accommodations on the math problem-solving performance of students with and without disabilities (Doctoral dissertation, Vanderbilt University, 2002). *Dissertation Abstracts International*, 63/03, 902.

Cahalan, C., Mandinach, E., & Camara, W. J. (2002). *Predictive validity of SAT I: Reasoning test for test-takers with learning disabilities and extended time accommodations.* New York: The College Reporting Board.

Choi, S. W., & Tinker T. (2002). *Evaluating comparability of paper-and-pencil and computer-based assessment in a K-12 setting.* Paper presented at the annual meeting of the National Council on Measurement in Education, New Orleans, LA.

Clapper, A.T., Morse, A.B., Lazarus, S.S., Thompson, S.J., & Thurlow M.L. (2005). *2003 state policies on assessment participation and accommodations for students with disabilities* (Synthesis Report 56). Minneapolis, MN: University of Minnesota, National Center on Educational Outcomes.

Clapper, A., Morse, A., Thurlow, M., & Thompson, S. (2005). *Access assistants for state assessments: A study of state guidelines for scribes, readers, and sign language interpreters.* Minneapolis, MN: University of Minnesota, National Center on Educational Outcomes.

Crawford, L., Helwig, R., & Tindal, G. (2004). Writing performance assessments: How important is extended time? *Journal of Learning Disabilities, 37*(2), 132–142.

Disability Rights Advocates. (2001). *Do no harm – High stakes testing and students with disabilities.* Oakland, CA: Author.

Elliott, S. N., & Marquart, A. M. (2004). Extended time as a testing accommodation: Its effects and perceived consequences. *Exceptional Children, 70*(3), 349–367.

Fuchs, L. S., & Fuchs, D. (1999). Fair and unfair testing accommodations. *School Administrator, 56*(10), 24–27.

Fuchs, L. S., & Fuchs, D. (2001). Helping teachers formulate sound test accommodation decisions for students with learning disabilities. *Learning Disabilities Research and Practice, 16*(3), 174–181.

Haladyna, T.M., Downing, S. M., & Rodriguez, M. C. (2002). A review of multiple-choice item-writing guidelines for classroom assessment. *Applied Measurement in Education, 15*(3), 309–334.

Hall, S. E. H. (2002). The impact of test accommodations on the performance of students with disabilities (Doctoral dissertation, The George Washington University, 2002). *Dissertation Abstracts International*, 63/03, 902.

Helwig, R., Rozek-Tedesco, M. A., & Tindal, G. (2002). An oral versus a standard administration of a large-scale mathematics test. *The Journal of Special Education, 36*(1), 39–47.

Hollenbeck, K. (2002). Determining when test alterations are valid accommodations or modifications for large-scale assessment. In G. Tindal & M. Haladyna (Eds.), *Large-scale assessment programs for all students* (pp. 395–424). Mahwah, NJ: Lawrence Erlbaum Associates.

Hollenbeck, K., Tindal, G., & Almond, P. (1998). Teachers' knowledge of accommodations as a validity issue in high-stakes testing. *The Journal of Special Education, 32*, 175–183.

Huynh, H., Meyer, J. P., & Gallant, D. J. (2004). Comparability of student performance between regular and oral administrations for a high-stakes mathematics test. *Applied Measurement in Education, 17*(1), 39–57.

Huynh, H., Meyer, J. P., & Gallant-Taylor, D. (2002). *Comparability of scores of accommodated and non-accommodated testing for a high school exit examination of mathematics.* Paper presented at the annual meeting of the National Council on Measurement in Education, New Orleans, LA.

Idstein, B. E. (2003). Dictionary use during reading comprehension tests: An aid or a diversion? (Doctoral dissertation, Indiana University of Pennsylvania, 2003). *Dissertation Abstracts International*, 64/02, 483.

Johnstone, C. J., Altman, J. R., Thurlow, M. L., & Thompson, S.J. (2006). *A summary of research on the effects of test accommodations: 2002 through 2004.* Minneapolis, MN: University of Minnesota, National Center on Educational Outcomes.

Ketterlin-Geller, L., & Tindal, G. (2005). *Developing a new paradigm for conducting research on accommodations in mathematics testing.* Paper presented at the National Council on Measurement in Education, Montreal, Quebec, April 12–14, 2005.

Kobrin, J. L., & Young, J. W. (2003). The cognitive equivalence of reading comprehension test items via computerized and paper-and-pencil administration. *Applied Measurement in Education, 16*(2), 115–140.

Kopriva, R., Samuelsen, K., Wiley, D., & Winter, P. (2003). *Evidentiary logic in the assessment of diverse learners: An initial report of the valid assessment of English language learners project.* Paper presented at the Annual Conference of the National Council of Measurement in Education, April 2003, Chicago, IL.

Koretz, D. M., & Barton, K. (2003). *Assessing students with disabilities: Issues and evidence.* Los Angeles, CA: Center for Research on Evaluation, Standards, and Student Testing.

Landau, S., Russell, M., Gourgey, K., Erin, J. N., & Cowan, J. (2003). Use of talking tactile tablet in mathematics testing. *Journal of Visual Impairment and Blindness, 97*(2), 85–96.

Langley, J., & Olsen, K. (2003). *Training district and state personnel on accommodations: A study of state practices, challenges and resources.* Washington, DC: Council of Chief State School Officers.

Lazarus, S., Thompson, S., & Thurlow, M. (2005). *How students access accommodations in assessment and instruction: Results of a survey of special education teachers* (EPRRI Brief). College Park, MD: University of Maryland, Educational Policy Reform Research Institute.

Linn, R. L. (2002). Validation of the uses and interpretations of results of state assessment and accountability systems. In G. Tindal & M. Haladyna (Eds.), *Large-scale assessment programs for all students* (pp. 27–48). Mahwah, NJ: Lawrence Erlbaum Associates.

MacArthur, C. A., & Cavalier, A. R. (2004). Dictation and speech recognition technology as test accommodations. *Exceptional Children, 71*(1), 43–58.

McKevitt, B. C., & Elliot, S. N. (2003). Effects and perceived consequences of using read aloud and teacher-recommended testing accommodations on a reading achievement test. *The School Psychology Review, 32*(4), 583–600.

Meloy, L. L., Deville, C., & Frisbie, D. (2002). The effect of a read aloud accommodation on test scores of students with and without a learning disability in reading. *Remedial and Special Education, 23*(4), 248–255.

No Child Left Behind Act of 2001 (Public Law 107–110). (2002). Washington, DC: U.S. Government Printing Office.

Paul Sherlock Center on Disabilities. (2002). *Results from Rhode Island's assessment accommodation survey.* Providence, RI: Rhode Island Department of Education Office of Special Needs.

Phillips, S.E. (1994). High-stakes testing accommodations. Validity versus disabled rights. *Applied Measurement in Education, 7*(2), 93–120.

Phillips, S.E. (2002). Legal issues affecting special populations in large-scale testing programs. In G. Tindal & M. Haladyna (Eds.). *Large-scale assessment programs for all students* (pp. 109–148). Mahwah, NJ: Lawrence Erlbaum Associates.

Pomplun, M., Frey, S., & Becker, D. (2002). The score equivalence of paper-and-pencil and computerized versions of a speeded test of reading comprehension. *Educational and Psychological Measurement, 62*(2), 337–354.

Ryan, J. M., & DeMark, S. (2002). Variation in achievement scores related to gender, item format, and content area tested. In G. Tindal & M. Haladyna (Eds.), *Large-scale assessment programs for all students* (pp. 67–88). Mahwah, NJ: Lawrence Erlbaum Associates.

Scheuneman, J. D., Camara, W. J., Cascallar, A. S., Wendler, C., & Lawrence, I. (2002). Calculator access, use, and type in relation to performance in the SAT I: Reasoning test in mathematics. *Applied Measurement in Education, 15*(1), 95–112.

Shriner, J. G., & DeStefano, L. (2003). Participation and accommodation in state assessment: The role of individualized education programs. *Exceptional Children, 69*(2), 147–161.

Sireci, S. G., Li, S., & Scarpati, S. (2005). Test accommodations for students with disabilities: An analysis of interaction hypothesis. *Review of Educational Research, 75*(4), 457–490.

Thompson, S. J., & Thurlow, M. L. (2001). *2001 special education outcomes: A report on state activities at the beginning of a new decade.* Minneapolis, MN: University of Minnesota, National Center on Educational Outcomes.

Thompson, S. J., & Thurlow, M. L. (2003). *2003 State special education outcomes: Marching on.* Minneapolis, MN: University of Minnesota, National Center on Educational Outcomes. Available at: http://education.umn.edu/NCEO/OnlinePubs/2003 StateReport.htm./

Thompson, S. J., Johnstone, C. J., & Thurlow, M. L. (2002). *Universal design applied to large scale assessments* (Synthesis Report 44). Minneapolis, MN: University of Minnesota, National Center on Educational Outcomes.

Thompson, S. J., Johnstone, C. J., Anderson, M. E., &

Miller, N. A. (2005). *Considerations for universally designed assessments* (Technical Report 41). Minneapolis, MN: University of Minnesota, National Center on Educational Outcomes.

Thompson, S. J., Johnstone, C. J., Clapper, A. T., & Thurlow, M. L. (2004). *State literacy standards, practices, and testing: Exploring accessibility.* Minneapolis, MN: University of Minnesota, National Center on Educational Outcomes.

Thompson, S. J., Johnstone, C. J., Thurlow, M. L., & Altman, J. R. (2005). *2005a State special education outcomes: Steps forward in a decade of change.* Minneapolis, MN: University of Minnesota, National Center on Educational Outcomes.

Thompson, S. J., Morse, A. B., Sharpe, M., & Hall, S. (2005). *Accommodations manual: How to select, administer, and evaluate use of accommodations for instruction and assessment of students with disabilities.* Washington, DC: The Council of Chief State School Officers.

Thompson, S. J., Thurlow, M. L., Quenemoen, R. F., & Lehr, C. A. (2002). *Access to computer-based testing for students with disabilities* (Synthesis Report 45). Minneapolis, MN: University of Minnesota, National Center on Educational Outcomes.

Thornton, A. E., Reese, L. M., Pashley, P. J., & Dalessandro, S. P. (2002). *Predictive validity of accommodated LSAT scores.* Newtown, PA: Law School Admission Council.

Thurlow, M. (2001). *Use of accommodations in state assessments: What databases tell us about differential levels of use and how to document the use of accommodations* (Technical Report 30). Minneapolis, MN: University of Minnesota, National Center on Educational Outcomes.

Thurlow, M., & Wiener, D. (2000). *Non-approved accommodations: Recommendations for use and reporting* (Policy Directions No. 11). Minneapolis, MN: University of Minnesota, National Center on Educational Outcomes.

Thurlow, M., & Wiley, H. I. (2004). *Almost there in public reporting of assessment results for students with disabilities* (Technical Report 39). Minneapolis, MN: University of Minnesota, National Center on Educational Outcomes.

Thurlow, M., Elliott, J., & Ysseldyke, J. (2003). Testing students with disabilities: Practical strategies for complying with district and state requirements (2nd ed.). Thousand Oaks, CA: Corwin Press.

Thurlow, M., Johnstone, C., Thompson, S., & Case, B. (In press). Using universal design research and perspectives to increase the validity of scores on large-scale assessments. In R. Johnson & M. Karchmer (Eds.), *Assessing deaf students' academic achievement in an age of accountability.* Washington, DC: Gallaudet University Press.

Thurlow, M. L., Moen, R. E., & Wiley, H. I. (2005). *Annual performance reports: 2002–2003 state assessment data.* Available at website of National Center on Educational Outcomes: *http:// education.umn.edu/nceo/ OnlinePubs/APRsummary2005.pdf*

Thurlow, M. L., Ysseldyke, J. E., & Silverstein, B. (1995). Testing accommodations for students with disabilities. *Remedial and Special Education, 16*(5), 260–270.

Tindal, G., & Fuchs, L. (1999). *A summary of research on test changes: An empirical basis for defining accommodations.* Lexington, KY: University of Kentucky, Mid-South Regional Resource Center.

Tindal, G., & Ketterlin-Geller, L. (2003). *Test accommodations research: Decision-making, outcomes, and designs.* Presentation at University of Maryland, College Park, Conference: Validity and Accommodations: Psychometric and Policy Perspectives.

Trammell, J. K. (2003). The impact of academic accommodations on final grades in a postsecondary setting. *Journal of College Reading and Learning, 34*(1), 76–90.

Weston, T. J. (2003). *NAEP validity studies: The validity of oral accommodation testing.* Washington, DC: National Center for Education Statistics.

Wiley, H. I., Thurlow, M. L., & Klein, J. A. (2005). *Steady progress: State public reporting practices for students with disabilities after the first year of NCLB (2002–2003)* (Technical Report 40). Minneapolis, MN: University of Minnesota, National Center on Educational Outcomes.

Willingham, W. W., & Cole, N. S. (1997). *Gender and fair assessment.* Mahwah, NJ: Lawrence Erlbaum Associates.

Phases of Education

26

Teaching and learning in the early years

Susan A. Fowler, Michaelene M. Ostrosky, and
Tweety J. Yates

Access to childcare and education for young children from birth through to age 5, prior to formal school entry, has become a critical and nearly universal issue for families in today's world. These concerns are exacerbated further, when families have a child with a disability or developmental delay (Odom, 2000). This chapter addresses services for young children with disabilities and their families by considering first those services provided during the infancy and toddler years (birth through to age 2) and secondly through preschool years (ages 3–5) prior to entry into formal schooling. Although the age designations may appear arbitrary, they have set the stage for how services have been developed in the United States over the past 20 years for children with disabilities (Fowler, Hains, & Rosenkoetter, 1989). The chapter also addresses the need to consider the increasing range of cultural and linguistic diversity found within many Western nations, due to changes in immigration patterns resulting from political and economic unrest in many parts of the world.

Within recent years, many national organizations as well as international associations have developed basic guidelines or recommendations for the provision, funding, staffing, and access to services. Within these guidelines, they also focus on meeting the needs of young children with disabilities. The Association for Childhood Education International (ACEI), the National Association for the Education of Young Children (NAEYC), and the Division for Early Childhood of the Council for Exceptional Children (DEC), all United States based professional organizations with international memberships, have developed detailed recommendations, as well as program assessments and self-assessment tools for setting minimum standards for childcare, early childhood special education, and preschool education.

Central to the guidelines proposed by these organizations are a focus on respect, tolerance, and acceptance of all forms of diversity, whether socioeconomic, cultural, ethnic, linguistic, religious, or family composition, and a focus on continuous training or education of providers. The attention to issues of diversity has shaped services for young children with disabilities or developmental delays as well (for example, Guralnick, 2005; Lynch &

Hanson, 2004; Odom, Hanson, Blackman, & Kaul, 2003; Santos, Corso, & Fowler, 2005). The United States, Canada, and Western Europe have experienced extensive immigration, both legally sanctioned and not, over the past generation. With the increasing diversification of their populations, assumptions and beliefs based primarily on Western European culture are in many situations clashing with the assumptions and beliefs of their immigrant citizens. In the case of the United States, early childhood special education (ECSE) researchers have also focused on families whose cultural, linguistic, and ethnic/racial backgrounds have differed for multiple generations (for example, Latino/a, Native American, African American, Asian American) from European American families and the implications of those differences on access to and use of ECSE services.

In order to provide services to families with young children with disabilities, families and providers must share both a common understanding of the range of normal child development and concept of disability. Recent research clearly illustrates that cultures may vary on what constitutes the range of normal development, given culturally based child-rearing practices and beliefs, as well as what constitutes a disability (for example, Barrera & Corso, 2003; Bazna & Hatab, in press; Blackman, 2003; Fowler, Santos, & Corso, 2005; Skinner, Correa, & Rodriquez, 1999). The willingness to acknowledge the existence of a child's disability and seek help outside of the family or immediate community is yet another issue (Chen, McLean, Corso, & Bruns, 2005; Rye & Hundeide, 2005; Zhang & Bennett, 2003). The increased awareness and development of tools to determine the extent to which existing practices, programs, or curricula are culturally and linguistically responsive and respectful are critical to their successful adoption and adaptation, not only across communities within a diverse nation, but also for international consideration (Fowler et al., 2005; http://www.clas.org). Additionally, increasing emphasis on evidence-based practices has focused attention on looking more

critically to the research literature prior to the adoption of ECSE service delivery options. The Division of Early Childhood has attempted to survey the existing early childhood special education research to identify recommended practices that have an evidence base to them (Sandall, Hemmeter, Smith, & McLean, 2005).

The following section includes a discussion of the nature of early intervention services first as developed in the United States and then in the context of how services are provided internationally.

SERVICES AND MODELS FOR INFANTS AND TODDLERS

Philosophical and policy issues in early intervention

Early intervention services in the United States, as well as many other countries, have been shaped by history, legislative efforts, financial resources, and the changing role of children and families in society. The evolution of early intervention public policy in the United States progressed with the enactment of Public Law 99–457 in 1986 (cf. Hanson, 2003). This law reflected the central role of families in the early intervention process, and the recognition of the effectiveness and cost benefits of early intervention (Hanft & Place, 1997). The law called for statewide, comprehensive, coordinated, interdisciplinary, family-centered early intervention services for infants and toddlers with disabilities and their families. The key components of this federal initiative have shaped present early intervention efforts, which have in turn influenced and been influenced by international philosophies, policies, and practices (Gine, Vilaseca, Gracia, & Garcia-Die, 2004; Klein & Rye, 2004; Odom et al., 2003; Sadao & Robinson, 2002). The importance of the family is noted in the mission statement of Eurylaid, the European Association on Early Intervention, which states, 'Early intervention pertains to the child as well as to the parents, the family, and broader network' (Heinan, 1997, p. 17, as cited in Carpenter & Russell, 2005).

While the field of early intervention (EI) is still relatively young, there have been many shifts in philosophical approaches. Traditionally, services were professionally driven with the professional recognized as the 'expert'. Services are now family driven and family centered, with the family recognized as the constant in their child's life and as the most knowledgeable about their child. Families play an integral role in their child's EI services and are able to choose their preferred roles and level of involvement based on family structure, cultural and linguistic background, values and beliefs, resources, and priorities and concerns for their children (Bailey & Powell, 2005; Bruder, 2000; Dunst, 2002; Odom et al., 2003).

Being true to a family-centered philosophy has meant moving from practices that were discipline specific to an interdisciplinary, collaborative approach. Early intervention services are typically provided by a variety of professionals such as doctors, speech therapists, physical therapists, social workers, and developmental specialists. At one time, these services were fragmented, with families seeking services for each developmental and medical need of their child. Ideally, today's providers work as a team and plan together with the family to ensure a more collaborative, comprehensive approach to determining goals and creating services to best meet the complex and varied needs of young children and their families (Dunst, Trivette, Humphries, Raab, & Roper, 2001; Hanft & Pilkington, 2000). Interventions are individualized, based on the child's strengths and needs and the family's priorities and concerns. This has led to services that are more strengths based as opposed to deficit based. This approach has moved the field away from using a medical model, which is less suited to joint decision-making and team processing, to more of a collaborative medical and educational community model.

Despite this philosophical shift to a more family-centered approach to EI, there are still many challenges (Bailey & Powell, 2005; Bruder, 2000; Dunst, 2002). The ways in which EI services are provided vary widely in intensity, duration, setting, personnel, and cost. In addition, access to services is not always equitable due to funding and personnel issues. In many respects, policy has not yet caught up with and matched this philosophical framework for providing EI services. As noted by researchers involved in the US National Early Intervention Study (NEILS), 'Although best practices have been repeatedly identified, the actual realization of a comprehensive system that meets the needs of children and families remains an ambitious, but elusive goal' (Spiker, Hebbeler, & Mallik, 2005, p. 305).

Settings and contexts

Early detection of problems and delivery of appropriate interventions have been shown to improve developmental outcomes for children with disabilities as well as children at risk of learning problems (Guralnick, 1997; Shonkoff & Meisels, 2000; Shonkoff & Phillips, 2000). The question is no longer whether early experiences matter, but rather how we can deliver services and provide early experiences that influence whether children get off to a positive or a vulnerable start in life (Shonkoff & Phillips, 2001). Currently, services are delivered in a variety of settings such as children's homes, integrated childcare programs, hospital-based programs, and community playgroups. Early intervention services differ in intensity, specificity, and frequency based on the needs of children and families as well as the funding and resources available to support service delivery. The differences in the way these services are coordinated and delivered often influence the effectiveness of programs, thus affecting outcomes for young children and their families (Bruder, 2005; McWilliam, 2003). Another important component of service delivery and coordination is the successful transition of children and their families from one service or program to another (Bruder, 2005; Fowler, Donegan, Luecke, Haddon, & Phillips, 2000; Rosenkoetter,

Whaley, Hains, & Pierce, 2001). Transition procedures should ensure continuity of services, minimize disruptions, prepare children and families for the next setting and meet legal requirements (Wolery, 1989).

While there is a strong research base supporting preschool inclusion, it is only recently that EI providers have been required to provide inclusive services in natural environments (Bruder, 2001; Dunst et al., 2001; Guralnick, 2005). In the United States, natural environments are defined as 'settings that are natural or normal for the child's age peers who have no disabilities' (IDEA, Part C, 34 CFR part 303.18) and go beyond 'place' to also include families' everyday routines and activities. Providers and families work together to determine the activities within the child's or family's routines that are important and that need to be enhanced in order for the child to be successful (Walsh, Rous, & Lutzer, 2000). Similar to the issues discussed above, inclusive practices differ greatly from community to community and there is continued confusion across states as to how to define and apply the concept of natural environments (Guralnick, 2001).

Curriculum and methods

One of the primary goals of EI is to facilitate and enhance the development of infants and toddlers who are at risk or who have disabilities (Blackman, 2003; Shonkoff & Meisels, 2000; Wolery, 2005). While there is great variation among programs in how they support this goal, most are aimed at providing infants and toddlers with the best possible opportunities for optimal development. Typically, EI curricula have a developmental focus based on the notion that young children are active learners, that learning occurs during interactions with caregivers and environments, and that development of young children is highly integrated and interrelated. While most EI programs have a core curriculum based on their program's philosophy, they also recognize that one curriculum will not fit the needs of all children and families.

Thus, curricula and intervention strategies need to be individualized, developmentally and functionally appropriate, promote the needs and priorities expressed by families, and take into account the culture, values, and language of families. Materials and activities encourage active participation and engagement and use everyday routines, activities, and family and community events as opportunities to facilitate learning. These types of activities and contexts are often referred to as naturalistic interventions (Rule, Losardo, Dinnebeil, Kaiser, & Rowland, 1998) and include such practices as activity-based interventions (Pretti-Frontczak & Bricker, 2004), incidental teaching (Warren & Kaiser, 1986); milieu teaching (Kaiser, 1993; Warren, 1991), and embedded learning opportunities (Dunst, Hamby, Trivette, Raab, & Bruder, 2000).

Given that the development of the young child occurs largely in a social context and that positive relationships have a strong influence on a child's development and well-being (Erickson & Kurz-Riemer, 1999; Gowen & Nebrig, 2002; Shonkoff & Phillips, 2000), intervention strategies should facilitate the relationship between both the parent and child and the professional and parent (Gowen & Nebrig, 2002; McCollum & Yates, 1994; McCollum, Gooler, Appl, & Yates, 2001). Relationship-focused interventions not only support the competence and confidence of parents, but also strengthen their sensitivity, responsiveness, and ability to support their child's development. In Ethiopia, interventions designed to enhance the quality of parent–child interactions found a noticeable change in parents' quality of interactions and in their perceptions of their children as active partners in interactions. Six years following the intervention, Ethiopian children had better school grades and were socially and emotionally better adjusted than children in the control group (Klein & Rye, 2004).

International trends

Across countries, EI programs share a common goal – to enhance the development of young children. The African proverb that 'It takes a village to raise a child' is an appropriate motto when discussing issues around EI. Society has to see children as a priority, as everyone's responsibility (family, community, and government), and provide resources to support parents in order for children to thrive and grow (Blackman, 2003). Early intervention is still a relatively young venture in most countries and has been shaped by political, theoretical, and cultural factors. There are many issues to be addressed ranging from society's acceptance of children with disabilities, children having access to services, building a cadre of qualified personnel, finding the best avenues for serving families, to earmarking funding and resources to support these initiatives. While we still have a long way to go, there are many positive changes happening internationally. For example, attitudes towards children with disabilities have been changing in Korea, which has led to increased numbers of children receiving services as well as a better quality of services being provided (Lee, 2003). An EI program in Egypt successfully initiated partnerships with families to address the limited infrastructure to support access to EI and the scarcity of services (Khouzam, Chenouda, & Naguib, 2003). Family-centered practices are playing a major role in the implementation of services in India (Kaul, Mukherjee, Ghosh, Chattopadhyay, & Sil, 2003), Egypt (Khouzam, Chenouda, & Naguib, 2003), Australia (Johnston, 2003), the United Kingdom (Carpenter & Russell, 2005), and Portugal (Boavida & Carvalho, 2003).

Services to address development in terms of social, emotional, cognitive, and language gains tend to be indirect in many countries which lack a strong educational infrastructure. For example, Rye and Hundeide (2005) describe programs in Africa, which focus on the caregiver's perceptions of the child's abilities and disabilities, as well as the quality of the caregiver's interaction with the child. They describe a model to support and strengthen families in order to increase the family's participation within the local community. While the programs may focus primarily on daily living problems and providing basic health training to families, they conclude that a critical outcome of these interventions is increased social acceptance of the child with special needs within the community and hope by the family for the child's future.

Many of the international programs discussed above embrace the philosophy of EI and implement family-centered, relationship-based practices. It is important to share models, evidence-based practices, resources, and lessons learned across nations. The variations in practice and the ways in which communities are engaged in supporting families with very young children with disabilities provide insights that are useful in many community contexts. We know the first years of a child's life are critically important (Shonkoff & Phillips, 2000), and in order to deliver EI services that will provide all children with a positive start in life it will truly take a global village perspective.

SERVICES AND MODELS FOR PRESCHOOLERS

Philosophical and policy issues in preschool special education

In the United States, federal legislation in 1986 (PL 99–457) mandated the expansion of educational services to all children with disabilities from age 3 through to 5 and specified that services be delivered in the least restrictive environment. Previously, such services were provided by some states but not others and often were available only in segregated settings. With the provision of federal funding and an infrastructure to ensure ECSE services, the United States has moved to a systems perspective on children's development and service delivery. Given the interrelated nature of development and recognition of the extent to which early development is embedded within the family, recommended practices in early childhood special education include close collaboration among members of interdisciplinary teams and close collaboration with families in planning and delivering services (Sandall et al., 2005). The philosophy for ECSE services has developed congruently with the philosophy of EI services. Both share the belief that families know their children best and that families make a unique contribution to the family–professional partnership. Respecting family composition, cultures, parenting beliefs, and practices is emphasized in preschool special education as well as EI. Professionals work with families to access support, mobilize resources, and identify their existing strengths, concerns, and priorities toward meeting the developmental needs of the whole child. Through this strengths- and assets-based collaborative process, the competence and confidence of both families and professionals are enhanced. In other countries, such as Egypt (Khouzam et al., 2003) families and communities share the responsibility of services for young children with special needs, thus improving the quality, continuity, and cost-effectiveness of services. Increasingly early childhood special educators are called upon to collaborate across agency lines, however, national policy often does not promote integration of services at the level of the local agency, individual child, or family.

Within ECSE programs, preschool children are viewed as active participants in their own learning. Play environments that support mutually pleasurable child–child and adult–child interactions are based on developmentally, culturally, and individually appropriate principles. High-quality early childhood programs emphasize the importance of teacher–child interactions as the foundation for children's learning and development (Kontos & Wilcox-Herzog, 1997; NAEYC, 1998). Within early childhood contexts such as home, school, and the community, every moment that adults and children interact provides an opportunity to build positive adult–child relationships that are the basis for developing important skills.

During the last decade extensive attention in the United States has been focused on preparing young children to enter school ready to succeed. Federal initiatives (for example, No Child Left Behind Act, 2001), influential educational reports (Adams, 1990; Bowman, 2002; National Reading Panel, 2000; Snow, Burns, & Griffin, 1998), and research on early brain development have directed national attention to educating society's youngest members during the first five years. Likewise, the United Kingdom's Special Education Needs (SEN) Code of Practice (Department. for Education and Skills, 2001, cited in Carpenter & Russell, 2005) focuses on developing a continuum of special education services (Carpenter & Russell, 2005) to best meet the educational and developmental needs of young children with disabilities. Across all domains of learning, motivation is key, for while most young children begin school with positive attitudes and expectations for success, some children soon develop feelings of indifference (Snow et al., 1998). Early childhood educators can create environments that support or undermine early achievement-related outcomes, such as persistence, anxiety, and feelings about one's own competence (Hyson & Molinaro, 2001). Astute teachers help children sustain feelings of competence by attending to changes in motivation and by supporting the development of positive adult and peer relationships. The value of emotionally satisfying relationships and the need for adult scaffolding to support learning that challenges, yet does not frustrate, children is the foundation of quality ECSE practices.

Preschoolers within any given early childhood class develop differently from one another and in uneven ways. Individualizing instruction is important when considering children's abilities and needs. Accommodating the variability among individuals within groups of children is a major challenge for any educator. Teachers must be vigilant to recognize challenging behaviors that may arise from a child's frustration for if children are required to continually engage in tasks that are too hard, the resulting cycle of failure may be severe and rapid. Likewise, if children consistently participate in curricula tasks that are too easy, their progress may be impaired. Achieving a delicate balance of success and challenge through negotiation of support is essential for nurturing young children's self-esteem and skill development.

Settings and contexts

Preschoolers with special needs are enrolled in a variety of service delivery models including home or hospital-based, residential, school-based (for example, pre-kindergarten), and community-based (for example, childcare) sites. Quality programs require extensive collaboration among agencies. While some preschoolers are in segregated special education programs, increasingly children with disabilities and other special needs are participating in settings and activities with children without disabilities. In the United States over half of all preschool children with disabilities who are receiving educational services are in some form of inclusive setting for the majority of the day (US Department of Education, 2000). Most likely many additional children participate in other recreation, childcare, or religious activities with typically developing peers. Head Start, a compensatory early childhood program, initiated in 1964 (PL 88–452) in the United States, is mandated to reserve 10 percent of its enrollment slots for children with special needs. During the 2003–04 school year, Head Start served approximately 115,000 children with disabilities (12.7 percent of the 905,800 children served).

Despite the strong research base on preschool inclusion and the increased availability of inclusive programs and services, a number of issues still remain. Bricker (2000) notes that barriers to successful inclusion are complex and the quality of instruction, such as the provision of individualized and specialized training, often fails to adhere to recommended practices. Many of the problems related to preschool inclusion have to do with the definition of inclusion, the quality of services, the intensity and specificity of services, the creation of meaningful social experiences for children, and the infrastructure needed to ensure effective and sustainable inclusive ser-

vices (Odom, 2000). Also, changing demographics of the population of preschoolers with disabilities and the need to provide culturally appropriate and responsive services complicates the development and delivery of inclusive programs (Barrera & Corso, 2003; Lynch & Hanson, 2004).

Transition from preschool services to primary grades or formal schooling can also be a point of disjuncture for some children and families. In the United States, the use of the Individualized Education Plan (IEP) is intended to ensure continuity of services and supports for young children who leave preschool and enter primary school. However, changes in schools, staff, therapists and typically an increase in the number of peers can present challenges to successful adjustment. Practices to facilitate a smooth transition, particularly those that promote transfer of information and communication between family and school and between sending and receiving school, have been recommended widely (Kagan & Nueman, 1998; Rosenkoetter, Hains, & Fowler, 1994; Rosenkoetter et al., 2001; Wolery, 1999).

Curriculum and methods

A major purpose of preschool special education is to promote children's learning and positively influence their developmental trajectories. Typically, ECSE curricula focus on social, communicative, cognitive, adaptive, and motor development. Peer relationships become more significant during the preschool years as does self-regulation as children become more independent and begin to take more responsibility for controlling their own impulses and behavior.

Children's interactions with the social and physical environment are key to their learning and development (Horowitz & Haritos, 1998). Designing preschool environments that promote children's safety, active engagement, learning, and membership in the classroom community are important components of ECSE programs.

The field of ECSE is rich with empirical

investigations to guide practitioners' decisions around organizing and influencing young children's experiences (Guralnick, 1997; Shonkoff & Meisels, 2000). Determining what individual practices are efficacious for which children has become a primary emphasis in ECSE research. Individualization, combined with specific procedures (for example, peer-mediated interventions, behavioral momentum, prompt fading procedures) implemented in well-designed environments are key to high-quality teacher:child and peer:peer interaction. Instructional approaches described in the literature represent a continuum from those that are more naturalistic (c.f., Bricker & Cripe, 1992; Horn, Lieber, Sandall, & Schwartz, 2001; Kaiser & Delaney, 2001; Losardo & Bricker, 1994) to those that are more didactic (for example, Alig-Cybriwsky, Wolery, & Gast, 1990). Lee (2003) notes that, in the past, Korean preschool curricula focused on readiness skills for academic achievement yet practices have expanded to emphasize individual children's abilities and needs. In the United States, accountability and standards play an important role in instruction as practitioners determine how child outcomes should be measured in terms of gains and cost effectiveness. The importance of ongoing monitoring to make data-based decisions, individualize, and adapt practices to meet the ever-changing needs of young children cannot be overstated.

International trends

As Odom and Kaul note (2003) 'early intervention is creating its niche in world society'. The intersection of cultures within a society as well as the political context and demographic factors are contributing variables that impact the design of preschool special education within a country. The Division for Early Childhood's position statement (DEC, 2004) on responsiveness to family cultures, values, and languages states that:'Individualized services begin with responsiveness to differences ... this responsiveness grows from interpersonal relationships that reflect a mutual respect and appreciation for individuals' culture, values,

and languages'. The statement emphasizes that 'responsive early childhood programs and professionals honor the values and practices within the families being served as well as among the people providing the services'. While preschool special education services around the globe may look different, the emphasis on family–professional partnerships, collaboration, and individualization appear to be critical characteristics upon which there is emerging agreement.

CONCLUSION

In summary, many challenges continue to face the provision of intervention services to children and their families from the child's birth through to school entry. Key issues that have been discussed briefly, include the need for an infrastructure within nations that provides financial, legal, and cultural support for the identification of children with disabilities, as well as the provision of formal and informal supports to the family, so that the child's developmental needs can be met within the context of the family and the family's community. As noted by many authors, the services and philosophy of early intervention and early childhood special education have changed over the past 20 years and will continue to change in order to fit the cultural and political context of each nation. For many developed, industrialized nations, services have become systemic, supported by national legislation, an infrastructure of support for preparing qualified professionals, and a coordinated system of interdisciplinary services. The match between the vision of appropriate services and the delivery of services may remain uneven, based on the commitment of individual communities and the willingness or even awareness of families to access these services. Less developed nations continue to struggle to provide the most basic medical and health services, but also have developed or are developing innovative practices that often rely on increasing both family and community acceptance of children with disabilities.

The progress of developing and implementing special education services to a society's youngest members must also be considered within the context of improved rates of childhood survival. According to the World Health Organization (WHO), incredible progress has occurred during the last three decades in reducing by more than half the mortality rate for children under the age of 5 (http://www.who.int/whr/1998/media_centre/50facts/en/). The WHO currently estimates that approximately 24 million low birth weight infants are born each year; these along with the children with identified disabilities will be most in need of special education services to support optimal development throughout their childhood. The need for continued development of effective service delivery models (birth through to age 5) remains pressing for the fields of special education and health and human services.

REFERENCES

Adams, M. J. (1990). *Beginning to read: Thinking and learning about print*. Cambridge, MA: MIT.

Alig-Cybriwsky, C., Wolery, M., & Gast, D. L. (1990). Use of a constant time delay procedure in teaching preschoolers in a group format. *Journal of Early Intervention, 14*, 99–116.

Bailey, D. B., & Powell, T. (2005). Assessing the information needs of families in early intervention. In M. J. Guralnick (Ed.), *The developmental systems approach to early intervention* (pp. 151–183). Baltimore, MD: Brookes.

Barrera, I., & Corso, R. M. (2003). *Skilled dialogue: Strategies for responding to cultural diversity in early childhood*. Baltimore, MD: Brookes.

Bazna, M., & Hatab, T. (In press). Disability in the Qur'an: The Islamic alternative to defining, viewing, and relating to disability. *Journal of Religion, Disability, and Health*.

Blackman, J. (2003). Early intervention. In S. L. Odom, M. J. Hanson, J. Blackman, & S. Kaul (Eds.), *Early intervention practices around the world* (pp. 1–23). Baltimore, MD: Brookes.

Boavida, J., & Carvalho, L. (2003). A comprehensive early intervention training approach. In S. L. Odom, M. J. Hanson, J. A. Blackman, & S. Kaul (Eds.), *Early intervention practices around the world* (pp. 213–249). Baltimore, MD: Brookes.

Bowman, B. (Ed.). (2002). *Love to read: Essays in developing and enhancing early literacy skills of African American children*. Washington, DC: National Black Child Development Institute, Inc.

Bricker, D. (2000). Inclusion: How the scene has changed. *Topics in Early Childhood Special Education, 20*, 14–19.

Bricker, D., & Cripe, J. J. (1992). *An activity-based approach to early intervention*. Baltimore, MD: Brookes.

Bruder, M. B. (2000). Family-centered early intervention: Clarifying our values for the new millennium, *Topics in Early Childhood Special Education, 20*, 105–115.

Bruder, M. B. (2001). Inclusion of infants and toddlers: Outcomes and ecology. In M. J. Guralnick (Ed.), *Early childhood inclusion: Focus on change* (pp. 229–251). Baltimore, MD: Brookes.

Bruder, M. B. (2005). Service coordination and integration as a developmental systems approach to early intervention. In M. J. Guralnick (Ed.), *The developmental systems approach to early intervention* (pp. 29–58). Baltimore, MD: Brookes.

Carpenter, B., & Russell, P. (2005). Early intervention in the United Kingdom: Current policy and practice. In M. J. Guralnick (Ed.), *The developmental systems approach to early intervention* (pp. 455–480). Baltimore, MD: Brookes.

Chen, D., McLean, M., Corso, R. M., & Bruns, D. (2005). Working together in early intervention: Cultural considerations in helping relationships and service utilization. In R. M. Corso, S. A. Fowler, & R. M. Santos (Eds.), *Building healthy relationships with families* (pp. 40–58). Longmont, CO: Sopris West.

Department for Education and Skills. (2001). *The SEN (special education needs) code of practice* (revised ed.). Nottingham: DfES.

Division for Early Childhood (DEC). (2002). *DEC position on responsiveness to family cultures, values, and languages*. Denver, CO: Author.

Dunst, C. J. (2002). Family-centered practices: Birth through high school. *Journal of Special Education, 36*, 139–147.

Dunst, C. J., Hamby, D., Trivette, C., Raab, M., & Bruder, M. (2000). Everyday family and community life and children's naturally occurring learning opportunities. *Journal of Early Intervention, 23*(3), 151–164.

Dunst, C. J., Trivette, C. M., Humphries, T., Raab, M., & Roper, N. (2001). Contrasting approaches to natural learning environment interventions. *Infants and Young Children, 14*(2), 48–63.

Erickson, M. F., & Kurz-Riemer, K. (1999). *Infants, toddlers and families: A framework for support and intervention*. New York: Guilford.

Fowler, S. A., Donegan, M. M., Luecke, B., Hadden, D. S., & Phillips, B. (2000). Community collaboration in writing interagency agreements on the age 3 transition: An evaluation of the content and process.

Exceptional Children, 67, 35–50.

Fowler, S. A., Hains, A. H., & Rosenkoetter, S. E. (1989). The transition between early intervention and preschool: Administrative and policy issues. *Topics in Early Childhood Special Education, 9*, 55–65.

Fowler, S. A., Santos, R. M., & Corso, R.M. (Eds.). (2005). *Getting started: Appropriate screening , assessment and family information gathering.* Longmont, CO: Sopris West.

Gine, C., Vilaseca, R., Gracia, M., & Garcia-Die, M. T. (2004). Early intervention in Spain. Some directions for future development. *Infants and Young Children, 17*(3), 247–257.

Gowen, J. W., & Nebrig, J. B. (2002). *Enhancing early emotional development: Guiding parents of young children.* Baltimore, MD: Brookes.

Guralnick, M. J. (1997). *The effectiveness of early intervention.* Baltimore, MD: Brookes.

Guralnick. M. J. (2001). A framework for change in early childhood inclusion. In M. J. Guralnick (Ed.), *Early childhood inclusion: Focus on change* (pp. 3–35). Baltimore, MD: Brookes.

Guralnick, M. J. (Ed.). (2005). *The developmental systems approach to early intervention.* Baltimore, MD: Brookes.

Hanft, B. E., & Pilkington, K.O. (2000). Therapy in natural environments: The means or end goals for early intervention? *Infants and Young Children, 12*(4), 1–13.

Hanft, B. E., & Place, P. (1997). Early intervention public policy analysis: Issues and strategies in personnel preparation. In P. J. Winton, J. A. McCollum, & C. Catlett (Eds.), *Reforming personnel preparation in early intervention* (pp. 411–431). Baltimore, MD: Brookes.

Hanson, M. J. (2003). National legislation for early intervention: The United States. In S. L. Odom, M. J. Hanson, J. A. Blackman, & S. Kaul (Eds.), *Early intervention practices around the world* (pp. 253–279). Baltimore, MD: Brookes.

Horn, E., Lieber, J., Sandall, S., & Schwartz, I. (2001). Embedded learning opportunities as an instructional strategy for supporting children's learning in inclusive programs. In M. Ostrosky & S. Sandall (Eds.), *Teaching strategies: What to do to support young children's development* (pp. 59–70). Longmont, CO: Sopris West.

Horowitz, F. D., & Haritos, C. (1998). The organism and the environment: Implications for understanding mental retardation. In J. A. Burack, R. M. Hodapp, & E. Zigler (Eds.), *Handbook of mental retardation and development* (pp. 20–40). New York: Cambridge University Press.

Hyson, M. C., & Molinaro, J. (2001). Learning through feeling: Children's development, teachers' beliefs and relationships, and classroom practices. In S. L. Golbeck (Ed.), *Psychological perspectives on early childhood education* (pp. 107–130), Mahwah, NJ: Erlbaum.

Johnston, C. F. (2003). Formal and informal networks. In

S. L. Odom, M. J. Hanson, J. A. Blackman, & S. Kaul (Eds.), *Early intervention practices around the world* (pp. 281–299). Baltimore, MD: Brookes.

Kagan, S. L., & Nueman, M. J. (1998) Lessons from three decades of transition research. *The Elementary School Journal, 98*(4), 366–379.

Kaiser, A.P. (1993). Parent implemented language intervention: An environmental perspective. In A. P. Kaiser & D. Gray (Eds.), *Enhancing children's communication: Research foundations for intervention* (Vol. 2, pp. 63–48). Baltimore, MD: Brookes.

Kaiser, A. P., & Delaney, E. M. (2001). Responsive conversations: Creating opportunities for naturalistic language teaching. In M. Ostrosky & S. Sandall (Eds.), *Teaching strategies: What to do to support young children's development* (pp. 13–23). Longmont, CO: Sopris West.

Kaul, S., Mukherjee, S., Ghosh, A. K., Chattopadhyay, M., & Sil, U. (2003). Working with families to implement home interventions. In S. L. Odom, M. J. Hanson, J. A. Blackman, & S. Kaul (Eds.), *Early intervention practices around the world* (pp. 111–128). Baltimore, MD: Brookes.

Khouzam, N., Chenouda, E., & Naguib, G. (2003). A family partnership model of early intervention. In S. L. Odom, M. J. Hanson, J. A. Blackman, & S. Kaul (Eds.), *Early intervention practices around the world* (pp. 151–168). Baltimore, MD: Brookes.

Klein, P. S., & Rye, H. (2004). Interaction-oriented early intervention in Ethiopia: The misc approach. *Infants and Young Children, 17*(4), 340–354.

Kontos, S., & Wilcox-Herzog, A. (1997). Teachers' interactions with children: Why are they so important? *Young Children, 52*(2), 4–12.

Lee, S. H. (2003). Community-based inclusion. In S. L. Odom, M. J. Hanson, J. A. Blackman, & S. Kaul (Eds.), *Early intervention practices around the world* (pp. 49–67). Baltimore, MD: Brookes.

Losardo, A., & Bricker, D. (1994). Activity-based intervention and direct instruction: A comparison study. *American Journal on Mental Retardation, 98*, 744–765.

Lynch, E. W., & Hanson, M. J. (2004). *Developing cross-cultural competence: A guide for working with children and their families.* Baltimore, MD: Brookes.

McCollum, J. A., & Yates, T. J. (1994). Dyad as focus, triad as means: A family-centered approach to supporting parent-child interactions. *Infants and Young Children, 6*(4), 54–63.

McCollum, J. A., Gooler, F., Appl, D. A., & Yates, T. J. (2001). PIWI: Enhancing parent–child interaction as a foundation for early intervention. *Infants and Young Children, 14*(1), 34–45.

McWilliam, R. A. (2003). The primary service provider model for home and community based services. *Psicologia, 17*(1), 115–135.

National Association for the Education of Young Children (NAEYC). (1998). *Early childhood classroom observation*. Washington, DC: Author.

National Reading Panel. (2000). *Teaching children to read: An evidence-based assessment of the scientific research literature on reading and its implications for reading instruction*. Bethesda, MD: National Institute of Child Health and Human Development.

No Child Left Behind Act 2001, Pub. L. 107–110, 20 U.S. C. § 6301 et seq.

Odom, S. L. (2000). Preschool inclusion: What we know and where we go from here. *Topics in Early Childhood Special Education, 20*, 20–27.

Odom, S. L., & Kaul, S. (2003). Early intervention themes and variations from around the world. In S. L. Odom, M. J. Hanson, J. A. Blackman, & S. Kaul (Eds.), *Early intervention practices around the world* (pp. 334–346). Baltimore, MD: Brookes.

Odom, S. L., Hanson, M. J., Blackman, J. A., & Kaul, S. (Eds.). (2003). *Early intervention practices around the world*. Baltimore, MD: Brookes.

Pretti-Frantczak, K., & Bricker, D. (2004). *An activity based approach to early intervention*. Baltimore, MD: Brookes.

Rosenkoetter, S. E., Hains, A. H., & Fowler, S. A. (1994). *Bridging early services for children with special needs and their families: A practical guide for transition planning*. Baltimore, MD: Brookes.

Rosenkoetter, S. E., Whaley, K. T., Hains, A. H., & Pierce, L. (2001). The evolution of transition policy for young children with special needs and their families: Past, present and future. *Topics in Early Childhood Special Education, 21*(1), 3–14.

Rule, S., Losardo, A., Dinnebeil, L., Kaiser, A., & Rowland, C. (1998). Translating research on naturalistic instruction into practice. *Journal of Early Intervention, 21*(4), 283–293.

Rye, H., & Hundeide, K. (2005). Early intervention and children with special needs in developing countries. In M. J. Guralnick (Ed.), *The developmental systems approach to early intervention* (pp. 593–619). Baltimore, MD: Brookes.

Sadao, K., & Robinson, N. B. (2002). Interagency systems development and evaluation in the Pacific Islands: A process model for rural communities. *Infants and Young Children, 15*(1), 69–84.

Sandall, S., Hemmeter, M. L., Smith, B. J., & McLean, M. E. (2005). *DEC recommended practices: A comprehensive guide for practical application*. Longmont, CO: Sopris West.

Santos, R.M., Corso, R. M., & Fowler, S.A. (Eds.). (2005). *Working with linguistically diverse families*. Vol 3. Longmont, CO: Sopris West.

Shonkoff, J. P., & Meisels, S. J. (2000). *Handbook of early intervention* (2nd ed.). Cambridge: Cambridge University Press.

Shonkoff, J. P., & Philips, D. A. (2000). *From neurons to neighborhoods: The science of early childhood development*. Washington, DC: National Academy Press.

Shonkoff, J. P., & Phillips, D. A. (2001). From neurons to neighborhoods: The science of early childhood development – An introduction. *Zero to Three, 21*(5), 4–7.

Skinner, D., Correa, V., & Rodriquez, P. (1999). Narrating self and disability: Latino mothers' construction of identities vis-à-vis their child with special needs. *Exceptional Children, 65*(4), 481–495.

Snow, C. E., Burns, M. S., & Griffin. P. (Eds.). (1998). *Preventing reading difficulties in young children*. Washington, DC: National Academy Press.

Spiker, D., Hebbeler, K. & Mallik, S. (2005). Developing and implementing early intervention programs for children with established disabilities. In M. J. Guralnick (Ed.), *The developmental systems approach to early intervention* (pp. 305–349). Baltimore, MD: Brookes.

US Department of Education (2000). *Twenty-second annual report to Congress on the implementation of the Individuals with Disabilities Education Act*. Washington, DC: Author.

Walsh, S., Rous, B., & Lutzer, C. (2000). The federal IDEA natural environments provisions: Making it work. In S. Sandall & M. Ostrosky (Eds.), *Natural environments and inclusion* (pp. 3–16). Longmont, CO: Sopris West.

Warren, S. (1991). Enhancing communication and language development with milieu teaching procedures. In E. Cipani (Ed.), *A guide for developing language competence in preschool children with severe and moderate handicaps* (pp. 68–93). Springfield, IL: Charles C. Thomas.

Warren, S., & Kaiser, A. (1986). Incidental language teaching: A critical review. *Journal of Speech and Hearing Disorders, 51*, 291–299.

Wolery, M. (1989). Transition in early childhood special education: Issues and procedures. *Focus on Exceptional Children, 22*, 1–16.

Wolery, M. (1999). Children with disabilities in early elementary school. In R. C. Pianta & M. J. Cox (Eds.), *The transition to kindergarten* (pp. 253–280). Baltimore, MD: Brookes.

Wolery, M. (2005). DEC recommended practices: Child-focused practices. In S. Sandall, M. L. Hemmeter, B. J. Smith, & M. E. McLean (Eds.), *DEC recommended practices: A comprehensive guide for practical application* (pp. 71–106). Longmont, CO: Sopris West.

Zhang, C., & Bennett, T. (2003). Facilitating the meaningful participation of culturally and linguistically diverse families in the IFSP and IEP process. *Focus on Autism and other Developmental Disabilities, 18*(1), 51–59.

27

Teaching elementary students who experience difficulties in learning

Sharon Vaughn, Jeanne Wanzek and
Carolyn A. Denton

Adequately addressing the instructional needs of elementary students with learning disabilities (LD) is the subject of literally thousands of books and hundreds of thousands of chapters and papers (Berninger & Amtmann, 2003; Denton & Mathes, 2003; Donovan & Cross, 2002; Lyon, Fletcher, Fuchs, & Chhabra, in press; Swanson, Harris, & Graham, 2003; Vaughn & Linan-Thompson, in press). Thus, to say that this chapter can only selectively address some of the more critical current issues states the obvious. However, we have highlighted some of the current trends and issues in teaching young children with LD, including: the changing role of the teacher, response to instruction, and the features of instruction associated with improved outcomes for students with disabilities.

The past 10 years have seen large gains in our understanding of the nature of LD, particularly in reading, and of our knowledge of effective instruction for students with reading difficulties and disabilities (see Denton, Vaughn, & Fletcher, 2003). At the same time, students with disabilities have been increasingly integrated into general education, and are increasingly taught the same curriculum and held to the same standards as students without disabilities. Moreover, there is a

growing understanding that traditional methods of identifying students with LD using discrepancies between scores on tests of intelligence and achievement are not valid. These three factors have contributed to fundamental changes in the role of the special education teacher, the nature of instruction and intervention provided to students with learning difficulties, and the relationship between general and special education.

In this chapter, we have described current trends and issues in the identification and education of students with LD. Special and general educators are likely to assume new roles in school-wide systems designed to provide high-quality classroom instruction and supplemental intervention to all students who need it, regardless of identified disabilities. Response to instruction within a school-wide system is becoming a recognized part of the identification of students with LD. Both general and special educators are likely to be engaged in activities that demand new sets of knowledge and skills.

Regardless of whether instruction and intervention are provided through general education or special education, or a combination of the two, there is a growing imperative that educators in elementary schools have a deep understanding of strategies and practices that have demonstrated effectiveness for students with learning difficulties and disabilities in scientific research. This chapter has presented an overview of some of these strategies and practices, but teachers must be provided continued opportunities for high-quality professional development to implement school-wide intervention models that will ensure success for the vast majority of students in our schools.

OVERVIEW OF THE CHANGING ROLE OF THE SPECIAL EDUCATION TEACHER

Special education teachers' roles have paralleled the acceptance and accommodation of students with disabilities in our schools. Initially, most special education teachers were not considered part of regular schooling. Like their students, they were separated from general education both in terms of where they taught (often in special schools or special areas within schools), what they taught (separate and different curricula), and how they taught (specialized techniques and practices not used by general education teachers). The boundaries between special and general education teachers were as sharply drawn as the lines between general and special education students. Most general education teachers, administrators, and parents of students were satisfied that selected teachers were willing and able to 'serve' students with disabilities. Educational leaders asked few questions about the quality or type of instruction special education teachers provided and there was little concern with student progress.

A historical perspective

Historically, the role of the teacher who was previously referred to as the LD specialist (Vance, 1979) was to provide specialized, supplemental instruction in a student's area of greatest need: often reading but occasionally several other academic areas. While these supplemental programs (often referred to as resource rooms) sprung up in almost every school in the United States (Deshler, Lowrey, & Alley, 1979; Larsen, 1976; McLoughlin & Kass, 1978), there was little written about what it meant to be a resource room teacher prior to the LD Leadership Institutes in 1970 (Kass, 1970).

Perhaps one of the earliest documentations of the role of the special education resource room teacher (most often the LD specialist) was an unpublished doctoral dissertation (McLoughlin, 1973) in which the author recorded through observation the role of teachers of students with LD and students with mental retardation. Students were provided services outside of the general education classroom through a diagnostic and remediation model. In 1976, Larsen defined the three responsibilities most fundamental to the role of the LD specialist as: (a) developing and implementing procedures for accurately identifying students with LD, (b) planning and implementing effective instructional programs, and (c) establishing service delivery programs. These three issues are fundamental to the dialogue about students with LD today (Fletcher et al., 2001).

In what is considered the classic work on resource room instruction, Hammill and Wiederholt (1972) defined the ideal role for the resource room teacher as a 'decision-maker' who plans and provides instruction directly to students with LD and also provides consulting services to general education teachers who were primarily responsible for the education of students with LD. Furthermore, they identified the following competencies as essential to fulfilling the role of the LD specialist. The LD specialist should be able to provide: (a) individualized instruction, (b) educational and behavioral assessment, and (c) effective communication and consultation with parents and other professionals.

Additional responsibilities

Times have changed. Both special education teachers and their students are increasingly attending general education classes, participating in general education curricula, and using practices that integrate general and special education instruction providing most students with special education needs access to the general education curricula. Furthermore, many of the expectations that were typically held for general education students (for example, school completion, meeting state accountability standards) are also now expected of many students provided special education. The boundaries between students in special and general education programs are blurred (Sindelar, 1995), and in a parallel fashion the roles and responsibilities of teachers of students with disabilities have changed. General educators have assumed increasing responsibility for the education of students with disabilities, and special educators may now provide services to many students both with and without identified disabilities in many settings (see for case studies, Klingner & Vaughn, 2002; Zigmond & Baker, 1995).

Now that many special education teachers work with at-risk students as well as students with disabilities across multiple settings – often working with students in general education classrooms – there are new expectations for their roles and responsibilities (Klingner & Vaughn, 2002; Moody, Vaughn, Hughes, & Fischer, 2000; Vaughn, Moody, & Schumm, 1998).

The emphasis on pre-referral intervention and on using the degree of student response to instruction as a factor in determining the presence of a learning disability (described below) is likely to have far-reaching effects on the relationship between special and general education. This relationship is currently evolving, but it is clear that special educators will be involved to varying degrees in activities such as (a) screening students to identify those most at risk for learning difficulties and disabilities, (b) working with general educators to design classroom-based as well as supplemental instruction to meet the learning and behavioral needs of many students with and without identified disabilities, (c) providing intervention directly to students whose response to classroom-based intervention has

been weak, (d) administering and interpreting progress monitoring and diagnostic assessments to make instructional decisions, and (e) collaborating with colleagues in activities such as systematic problem-solving with the goal of improved outcomes for all students, those with and without identified disabilities.

Recently, special education teachers have been integrated into the reading reform movement and are providing coaching to teachers as well as interventions for students most at risk for reading difficulties or disabilities. Coaching has become a popular model in schools (Dole, 2004; Poglinco & Bach, 2004), and is seen as an important current trend in professional development ('Coaches controversy, consensus', 2004) as well as in supporting a systematic schoolwide approach to effective instruction and intervention for all students who experience reading difficulties. Hasbrouck and Denton (2005) define a reading coach as 'an experienced teacher who has a strong knowledge base in reading and experience providing effective reading instruction to students, especially struggling readers' and who 'has been trained to work effectively with peer colleagues to help them improve their students' reading outcomes … and receives support in the school for providing coaching to other teachers, instructional assistants, parents, or administrators, as needed' (p. 1). This emerging role demands expertise in areas that have not been traditionally included in the preparation of special education teachers, including (a) an understanding of reading acquisition and causes of reading difficulties and disabilities, (b) a deep understanding of research-validated effective instruction and intervention for students at risk for reading difficulties, (c) the ability to interpret student assessment data to make instructional decisions both for groups of students (that is, classrooms or grade levels) and individual students, and (d) a high level of skill in collaboration and consultation, including skills related to systematic problem-solving and providing feedback to teachers.

Defining a new role in a system

Often, the role of the reading coach is not clearly defined in schools (Poglinco & Bach, 2004), making it necessary for special educators serving in this role – as well as special educators who work with reading coaches – to clearly define the goals, processes, and activities related to new roles within the school. Researchers are just beginning to examine the role of reading coach in the context of the current reading reform movement (Dole, 2004; Morrow, 2003; Poglinco & Bach, 2004). From surveys related to coaching activities in schools we know that at times a reading coach may be called upon to do any of the following (see Hasbrouck & Denton, 2005):

- Observe reading lessons and provide feedback to teachers.
- Model effective teaching techniques and strategies for students with reading difficulties.
- Advise and support teachers to improve reading lessons.
- Administer assessments and interpret results.
- Participate in co-planning and co-teaching of lessons for students with reading difficulties.
- Engage in problem-solving within pre-referral intervention teams or with individual teachers with the goal of removing obstacles to student progress.
- Facilitate collaboration within grade-level or vertical teams of teachers.
- Conduct workshops to help introduce teachers to new strategies.

Special educators will vary in the levels of involvement in these various activities. In some cases, they will assume the primary responsibility for a school-wide program. In other schools, they will collaborate with a reading coach and general educators to implement components of an intervention program. As special educators take on new roles within the school, it is essential that they are able to clearly articulate how *they* see their roles. They must be able to describe to other teachers, parents, and administrators (a) the rationale for this new role, (b) a description of the processes they will use in coaching and/or collaboration, (c) the tasks they will be doing and services they can provide, and (d) how they will be spending their time during the school day (Hasbrouck & Denton, 2005). These considerations must be openly and purposefully discussed with administrators and colleagues so that all are working toward a shared goal of (a) providing quality instruction and intervention to enable all students to be successful and (b) identifying those students with learning disabilities who require services of the nature and duration available though special education.

RESPONSE TO INSTRUCTION

Response to instruction (RTI) is conceptualized as a pre-referral and identification procedure for the largest number of students with disabilities – those with severe academic problems in reading or math and/or with behavior problems. The fundamental conceptualization of response to instruction was designed to provide high-quality classroom instruction along with needed supplemental intervention early, before problems become intractable, and to reduce the practice of using discrepancy between IQ and achievement as the criterion for identifying students with LD. The use of IQ and achievement discrepancy has been questioned for several reasons, particularly for its failure to accurately discriminate between student with LDs in reading and other low-performing readers (Fletcher, Coulter, Reschly, & Vaughn, 2004; Fletcher, Francis, Rourke, Shaywitz, & Shaywitz, 1992; Siegel, 1992; Stuebing et al., 2002; Vellutino, Scanlon, & Lyon, 2000). Nevertheless, IQ and achievement discrepancy remains the primary procedure for identifying students with LD in most states. While concerns about implementing RTI have been raised, they largely center on issues of implementation, such as: (a) whether RTI can be appropriately used with older students, and (b) whether personnel are adequately prepared to implement such a model (Bradley, Danielson, & Hallihan, 2002; Vaughn & Fuchs, 2003). However, RTI eliminates the 'wait to fail' procedures associated with identification for special education and provides a prevention model with early identification of students at risk for academic and/or behavior problems. Thus, effective interventions can be initiated without delay (Fletcher, Coulter, Reschly, & Vaughn, 2004).

Prior to identification for special education, students at risk would be provided with intervention validated by scientific research. Based on students' response to this instruction, they would either be provided with additional interventions or referred for special education. In other words, students who respond to treatment would not be referred, and those who do not would be considered for special education. The special education teacher's role will likely include serving as a leader who assists with organizing and identifying those interventions as well as establishing criteria for RTI. In some cases, special education teachers may provide pre-referral intervention directly to students or support general education teachers who provide the intervention.

The three-tier approach to RTI

We have implemented a Three-Tier Model to assist school districts in making decisions related to RTI. The model is intended to provide a framework for meeting the instructional needs of all K–3 students in the area of reading, particularly students who do not make adequate progress in reading (Vaughn et al., in review). The focus is to identify students early; provide interventions; and then, based on students' response to these interventions, determine whether or not additional intervention is needed or whether the type or intensity of intervention needs to be adjusted. The model consists of three tiers, or levels, of instruction. Tier I includes three critical elements: (a) high-quality core reading instruction, (b) screening all students three times a year to identify those at-risk for reading difficulties, and (c) ongoing professional development for teachers. Tier II provides additional instruction in the form of a small-group intervention for students at risk for reading problems. Tier III is additional and more intensive intervention for students whose response to the Tier II intervention was less than expected (Vaughn, Wanzek,

Woodruff, & Linan-Thompson, in press).

Tier I reading instruction is designed to address the needs of the majority of a school's students. Quality Tier I instruction includes implementation of a core reading program based on scientific reading research, flexible grouping, use of assessment to drive instructional decisions, and targeted instruction to address student needs. This effective core reading instruction is sufficient to meet most students' needs. As a result, Tier I instruction enables many students to acquire necessary reading skills and be on-track for further reading development without intervention.

Classroom reading instruction is not sufficient to meet the needs of some students, and Tier II intervention is required. Tier II intervention is designed for students who need more intensive instruction to accelerate their progress. The intervention is provided in addition to the time allotted for the core reading instruction. A classroom teacher, specialized reading teacher, or another trained support person provides daily, 20-30 minute sessions of intensive, small-group reading instruction to support the reading skills addressed in the core reading program. To effectively monitor and meet individual student needs, the intervention is provided in small, homogeneous groups of four or five students.

A small percentage of students who have received Tier II intervention continue to show significant reading difficulties. These students demonstrate reading skills well below grade level as well as slow progress in the Tier II intervention. Therefore, a more intensive intervention is warranted. Tier III intervention is provided in addition to Tier I instruction and is designed to meet individual student needs. The intensity of the intervention is increased in Tier III by providing more time in intervention (50–60 minutes daily) and instruction in smaller groups (two or three students). The increased intensity in Tier III allows a specialized reading teacher, special education teacher, or external interventionist to provide specialized, explicit instruction to match student needs. Table 27.1 provides detailed information on each of the three tiers.

Table 27.1 Details of Tier I, Tier II, and Tier III

	Tier I	Tier II	Tier III
Definition	'Core' reading instruction and programs, including ongoing professional development and benchmark assessments three times per year	Instructional intervention employed to supplement, enhance, and support Tier I and takes place in groups of 4 to 5	Individualized reading instruction extended beyond the time allocated for Tier I and takes place in groups of 2 to 3
Focus	For all students in kindergarten through to 3rd grade	For students identified with reading difficulties who have not responded to Tier I efforts	For students with marked difficulties in reading or reading disabilities who have not responded adequately to Tier I and Tier II efforts
Program	Scientifically based reading instruction and curriculum emphasizing the five critical elements of beginning reading	Specialized, scientifically based reading program(s) emphasizing the five critical elements of beginning reading	Sustained, intensive, scientifically based reading program(s) emphasizing the five critical elements of beginning reading
Instruction	Sufficient opportunities to practise throughout the school day	• Additional attention, focus, support • Additional opportunities to practice embedded throughout the day • Pre-teach, review skills; frequent opportunities to practice skills	• Carefully designed and implemented, explicit, systematic instruction • Fidelity of implementation carefully maintained
Interventionist	General education teacher	Intervention provided by personnel determined by the school (classroom teacher, specialized reading teacher, other trained personnel)	Intensive intervention provided by personnel determined by the school (specialized reading teacher, special education teacher, external specialist)
Setting	General education classroom	Appropriate setting designated by the school	Appropriate setting designated by the school
Grouping	Flexible grouping	Homogeneous small-group instruction (for example, 1:4, 1:5)	Homogeneous small-group instruction (1:2, 1:3)
Time	Minimum of 90 minutes per day	Minimum of 30 minutes per day in addition to Tier I	Minimum of two 45-minute sessions per day in addition to Tier I
Assessment	Benchmark assessments at beginning, middle, and end of academic year	Progress monitoring twice a month on target skill to ensure adequate progress and learning	Progress monitoring twice a month on target skill to ensure adequate progress and learning

The Three-Tier Reading Model is designed to provide a decision-making framework to assist school districts in meeting the needs of all students and reducing the number of students with reading difficulties. Through professional development, the use of a core reading program based on scientific reading research, and integrated assessments, Tier I instruction should allow 70 to 80 per cent (or more) of students to get on track as success-ful readers. Intensive, focused intervention is provided in Tier II and Tier III for students identified as at risk for reading difficulties. The lowest 20 to 30 per cent of students may require Tier II, while 3 to 10 per cent of students may need the more intensive Tier III intervention.

The levels of the Three-Tier Model, Tier I, Tier II, and Tier III, should be dynamic, allowing students to enter and exit intervention as their instructional needs change (see Figure 27.1). When a student demonstrates response to an intervention and is able to perform at grade-level expectations on the assessments, intervention may no longer be required. Screening assessments given three times per year (fall, winter, spring) help to ensure that students in need of intervention are identified quickly and instruction in each tier can be adjusted to meet their needs. In contrast to previous interventions for reading, the Three-Tier Reading Model provides a system that is responsive to students' changing needs.

FEATURES OF INSTRUCTION FOR ELEMENTARY STUDENTS WITH DISABILITIES: GROUPING

While there are many features of instruction to consider about *how* to most effectively teach students with learning difficulties/disabilities (for example, pacing, monitoring progress), one of the critical factors to consider is grouping. Grouping for reading is a fundamental issue in education (Anderson, Hiebert, Scott, & Wilkinson, 1985; Barr, 1989) and one of the few alterable features of

instruction that 'can powerfully influence positively or negatively the levels of individual student engagement and hence academic progress' (Maheady, 1997, p. 325).

Until the 1990s, students were grouped in relatively homogeneous ability groups for instruction – for example, in reading, based on teachers' judgment, placement tests, and/or standardized test scores (Barr & Dreeben, 1991; Kulik & Kulik, 1984). Same-ability grouping occurred in several ways. Most teachers provided same-ability reading instruction within their classrooms by dividing students into three or four groups. In other cases, teachers regrouped students with those from other same-grade classrooms or cross-grade classrooms to assure that students with similar reading abilities and needs were placed into the same group.

Since 1990, there has been an increasing trend toward whole-class instruction and heterogeneous groups for reading. This has occurred for several reasons. First, research revealed that the instruction provided to students in the lowest groups was of poor quality, often focusing on isolated skills and providing minimal time for reading connected text (Allington, 1980; Hiebert, 1983).

Figure 27.1   Movement through Tiers I, II, and III

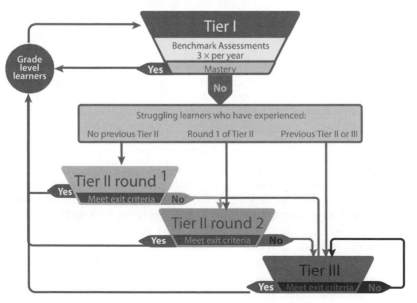

Second, same-ability groups were very stable, providing little opportunity for students to move between groups (Oakes, Gamoran, & Page, 1992). Because students' peer relations are influenced considerably by the make-up of their reading group, the stability of ability-based reading groups limited students' friendship opportunities (Hallinan & Sorenson, 1985). Finally, students' self-perceptions were also influenced by the group in which they were placed (Oakes et al., 1992), such that students who were always placed in the lowest reading groups developed negative perceptions of their reading ability and low expectations of progress.

In response to these concerns, most classroom teachers used whole-class instruction, at times complemented with small, cooperative, mixed-ability groups (Elbaum, Schumm, & Vaughn, 1997). Unfortunately, whole-class instruction cannot meet the learning needs of most students with learning difficulties/disabilities. This is particularly true for students with severe reading difficulties, including students with identified reading disabilities.

GROUPING PRACTICES AND READING OUTCOMES FOR STUDENTS WITH READING DISABILITIES

Several recent reviews have examined the effects on reading outcomes of different grouping practices: (a) within-class grouping (Lou et al., 1996), (b) ability grouping (Barr & Dreeben, 1991; Kulik & Kulik, 1982; Slavin, 1987) and (c) student pairing (Cohen, Kulik, & Kulik, 1982; Scruggs & Richter, 1985; Scruggs, Mastropieri, & Richter, 1985). Two meta-analyses (Elbaum, Vaughn, Hughes, & Moody, 1999; 2000) and a study of the effects of group size on student outcomes (Vaughn et al., 2003) have also provided valuable information about the relation between grouping practices and reading outcomes for students with reading difficulties. There is now substantial empirical evidence that supports the value of teaching reading to students in pairs and in small groups.

Student pairs

Student pairing for reading instruction is a grouping format that requires additional consideration for two important reasons: (a) when students learn to work with a partner for a specific reading activity, it can potentially 'free up' the teacher to provide instruction to other students, and (b) it may provide a means for additional directed reading time for students with reading difficulties.

A meta-analysis of several types of grouping practices (student pairs, small groups, multiple grouping formats; Elbaum et al., 1999) provided additional information on student pairing for reading instruction for students with reading disabilities. When older students served as tutors of younger children (cross-age tutoring), the tutors made significant progress, whereas the younger students did not (ES = .66 and ES = −.02, respectively). This suggests that when students are working in a cross-age tutoring model, students who need the most practice in reading should have ample opportunities to serve in the role of the tutor. The meta-analysis further revealed that when students were engaged in same-grade (peer) tutoring, the tutored students made significant progress (ES = .47); the benefits to students who served in reciprocal roles as tutors and tutees were more modest (ES = .16).

These findings suggest that pairing students for instruction can be associated with positive outcomes in reading, provided that tutors are trained, clear tutoring routines are established and followed, and teachers carefully monitor student progress to ensure that all students benefit from the activity. Student pairing is a particularly desirable grouping format for classroom teachers since it is both feasible for teachers to implement and enjoyable for students (Elbaum et al., 1997; Fuchs, Fuchs, Mathes, & Simmons, 1997; Vaughn, Hughes, Schumm, & Klingner, 1998). Furthermore, teachers report that students derive many social benefits from working in pairs (Lamport, 1982; Maheady, Harper, & Sacca, 1988; Mathes & Fuchs, 1994). See Table 27.2

for suggestions on using student pairing activities.

Small-group instruction

In a meta-analysis of the effects of within-class grouping in regular education classes, Lou et al. (1996) found that across different subject areas, group sizes of 3–4 yielded effect sizes that were twice as large as those for groups of 8–10 (ES = .22 vs. ES = .11, respectively). Moreover, low-ability students benefited more than medium- or high-ability students (ES = .37 vs. ES = .19 and ES = .26, respectively). In a study that specifically examined outcomes in reading, Taylor, Pearson, Clark, and Walpole (1999) found that first- through third-grade teachers in more effective schools spent more than twice as much time as those in less effective schools in small-group instruction for reading.

The question of how small the group needs to be for struggling readers to make adequate progress is important in that the answer influences the amount of resources needed to meet students' instructional needs and/or the amount of time that students can be instructed in smaller groups. Most educators agree that the ideal group composition for providing instruction to students with reading disabilities is one teacher with one student. However, if students make the same gains in larger group sizes, then either more students can be provided support or the support can be extended.

Vaughn and her colleagues (2003) conducted an intervention with second-grade students identified as having reading difficulties to determine whether the effect of the intervention differed across three group sizes: 1:1 (one teacher with one student), 1:3, and 1:10. The intervention included instruction in four key areas: fluent reading, phonemic awareness, comprehension of connected text, and word analysis/spelling. All groups made significant progress from pre- to post-test, but the largest gains were realized by students in the 1:1 and 1:3 groups. Of the 17 out of 77 students who made less than six months' gain

during the 14-week intervention on either word attack, word identification, or reading comprehension, only two were in the 1:1 condition, six were in the 1:3 condition, and nine were in the 1:10 condition.

The foregoing studies, as well as others (for example, Acalin, 1995; Evans, 1996; Thurlow, Ysseldyke, Wotruba, & Algozzine, 1993), underscore the positive effects of small-group instruction, particularly for students with reading difficulties. When teachers have large numbers of students who are reading below grade level, every effort should be made to provide them with at least 30 minutes of instruction daily in a smaller format such as one-to-one, pairs, or groups of 3–4. See Table 27.2 for suggestions on using student groups effectively.

OTHER FEATURES OF INSTRUCTION ASSOCIATED WITH IMPROVED OUTCOMES FOR STUDENTS WITH DISABILITIES

In addition to grouping for instruction, there are several features of instructional delivery that can positively affect student outcomes. Structured, organized lessons delivered explicitly and systematically have been shown to be beneficial to students with disabilities (Coyne, Kame'enui, & Simmons, 2001; Fuchs et al., 2003). These structured lessons should include many opportunities for student response and immediate feedback to assist students in learning new content quickly and efficiently.

Explicit instruction

Explicit instruction refers to overtly teaching all the steps needed to complete a task. Explicit instruction is planned and specified to clearly meet established goals and objectives. Use of explicit instruction including teacher modeling and step-by-step explanations or instructions for tasks and strategies is associated with improved outcomes for students with learning difficulties (Fielding-

Table 27.2 Practices for effectively using pairs and small groups

Paired instruction
- Have better readers partner with less able readers for fluency activities in which the better reader reads several paragraphs and then the less able reader rereads those paragraphs.
- Have students with reading difficulties serve as reading monitors for younger students.
- Partner students to check each other's work when they are completing activities in centers.
- Ask students to work in pairs to answer comprehension questions about a commonly read passage.
- Ask students to work in pairs using word cards. One student reads the word, the other student writes the word, and then by showing the word both students check spelling on the written word.
- Implement a peer-tutoring program in which students in the primary grades practice phonics skills that have been previously taught (see Mathes, Howard, Allen, & Fuchs, 1998; Mathes, Torgesen, & Allor, 2001).

Small group instruction
- Develop a variety of purposeful learning activities that students can engage in independently while you teach small groups of students. These activities should be based on learning objectives and planned so that students are independently practicing skills they have already been taught.
- Teach students how to use learning centers (or 'work stations') and to work cooperatively within these centers. Explicitly teach the routines, and reteach as necessary.
- Identify community volunteers or parent helpers who can guide small groups of students working in learning centers. Older students may also be able to serve in this role.
- Organize reading groups so that the students who need the most help are in the smallest group.
- Reorganize groups frequently to reflect the learning needs and progress of students within the group.
- Restructure personnel resources in the school so that Title I and other educational personnel are available to provide additional classroom support during reading instruction.
- Organize centers that engage students in projects that are related to classroom activities and require more extensive time to complete these projects. Provide specific guidelines and a sample of a completed project at the center so students know what their 'end project' should look like.
- Give specific guidelines so students can demonstrate the work they have completed. For example: (a) keeping track of many times they have reread the text, (b) timing themselves or another student in how quickly they read the text, (c) developing a 'who' and a 'what' question about the text that they read, or (d) 'reporting' the main idea of what they've read to another student who read the same text.
- Use tape recorders to listen to a story while reading along, recording reading of a story and then listening to the recording, summarizing the key ideas in a story, and/or conducting an interview with other students about what they are reading.
- Provide choices for centers with specified outcomes and flexible time so that students can complete extended work. Each center can have an 'expert' in the room (not always at the center) whose name is on the center and is available to answer questions.
- Use writing activities as a center or ongoing activity. Students can write, revise, edit, conference with each other, and engage actively in the writing process approach individually, in pairs, and in small groups.
- Have one group of students use high-quality computer software to practice skills on classroom computers.

Barnsley, 1997; Swanson, 2000; Vaughn, Gersten, & Chard, 2000).

Explicit instruction can be thought of as a continuum with the goal of effectively and efficiently building student skills toward mastery and independence. Explicit instruction along this continuum can be viewed as a scaffold that is thoughtfully planned to assist students in gaining new skills. When a skill or strategy is initially being taught, explicit instruction includes both teacher modeling and guided practice that allows students to practice with teacher assistance and feedback. They demonstrate how to complete each task

using conspicuous strategies. Table 27.3 provides an example of adjusting instruction to make a lesson more explicit for students.

Systematic instruction

Systematic instruction consists of breaking down complex skills into smaller, manageable learning units and sequencing instruction from easier to more difficult. Systematic instruction also includes the scaffolding of student learning to control the level of difficulty during initial learning and allow students to master each substep before synthesizing learning into more

Table 27.3. Explicit Instruction

Example of less explicit instruction:
Tell students the main idea of a story tells the most important part of the story. Reread Dinosaurs together and ask students to tell the main idea of the story.
Lesson adapted to be more explicit:
Tell students the main idea of a story tells the most important part of the story. Tell them the main idea names who or what the story was about and the most important thing that happened to the who or what.
Model stating the main idea for the story just read, Dinosaurs. 'Jacob is the who in the story. The most important thing about Jacob is he learned to cooperate. So, the main idea is, "Jacob learned to cooperate."'
Let me read you a short story. (Read paragraph about Sarah cooking ham.) Who or what is in this story? (Sarah) What is the most important thing about Sarah? What is the main idea of that story?
Repeat with other short paragraphs.

complex skills. Organizing instruction systematically is essential to effective outcomes for students with learning difficulties (Coyne, Kame'enui, & Simmons, 2001; Swanson, 2000; Torgesen, 2002).

Teachers who deliver lessons systematically are also able to provide instruction at a quick pace because the amount of instruction is at the appropriate level and students are more likely to be successful. Teaching complex skills in steps that allow students to be successful is likely to allow students to have confidence in their abilities, and increase the efficiency of learning. Efficiency of learning is a valued outcome allowing more time for students with learning difficulties to 'catch up' in their learning.

Similar to explicit instruction, systematic instruction can be thought of as a continuum. Some students may need a task organized into three or four steps for efficient learning, while other students may need the task organized into more manageable parts, perhaps six or seven steps, to understand and acquire proficiency in the task. When planning lessons, teachers using systematic instruction should consider how to organize the instruction according to the needs of most students in the instructional group or class. They also must consider how they will reorganize the instruction and make it more approachable for students who have difficulty learning the task. Table 27.4 provides an example of adapting a lesson for students needing more manageable steps.

Ample opportunities for student response

Opportunities for student response refers to the amount of guided practice students receive throughout a lesson. Similar to student needs for more explicit and systematic instruction, students with academic difficulties often need more practice opportunities in order to succeed. It is important that a variety of response opportunities are included throughout initial instruction so that teachers can do ongoing checks on student learning. Instruction that is low on teacher talk and high on student response or questioning is recommended (Brophy & Good, 1989). This is accomplished through concise, explicit, systematic instruction, as discussed earlier, as well as built-in questioning and practice opportunities for all students. In addition to allowing students opportunities to process the concepts being taught, this type of instruction allows teachers to continually check student understanding, provide appropriate feedback immediately (see below), and adjust the lesson as necessary to ensure student success.

When students are taught in large instructional groups, it may be difficult to design instruction so that all students in the class receive ample opportunities to respond and practice the skills or strategies being taught. However, students with academic difficulties are unlikely to learn the necessary tasks by watching or hearing other students practice. They need their own practice opportunities and may need more opportunities than students who acquire these skills more readily. Systematic organization of

Table 27.4 Systematic Instruction

Example of few manageable steps:
Telling time in 5-minute intervals
(Prerequisite: Telling time to the hour; counting by 5s)
1. Show students a clock set to 6:20. Remind students the short hand points to the hour and the long hand points to the minutes (point to each hand to demonstrate).
2. Explain that first students should tell the hour (6) that the short hand points to; then students should look at the long hand to count the minutes. Starting at 12 they should point to each number and count by 5s until they reach the long hand.
3. Demonstrate pointing and counting to 6:20. Continue modeling with several different times and have students count the minutes chorally.
4. Repeat with several different times and have students tell what time it is.

Adapted lesson with more manageable steps:
(Steps may be introduced across several days.)

Telling time in 5-minute intervals
(Prerequisite: Telling time to the hour; counting by 5s)
1. Teach students to discriminate between the short hand and long hand.
2. Teach students to identify the hour using a clock with only the hour hand present. Place the hour hand in several different positions (sometimes directly on a number and sometimes just past one of the numbers).
3. Add the long hand to the clock pointing to the 12. Practice pointing to each number on the clock and counting by fives.
4. Teach the telling time strategy: First look for the hour. Then count by fives to the minutes. Allow students to practice saying the steps.
5. Demonstrate telling time using the steps in the strategy. 'First we look for the hour. What number did it just pass? Then we count by fives to the minutes. Start at 12 and count by fives until you reach the minute hand.'
6. Repeat with several different times. Ask students for the hour; have them count by fives to determine the minutes; have students state the full time.

Table 27.5 Ample opportunities to respond

Example of few opportunities to respond:
Scientific method review
After completing the experiment, ask several students to tell one step of the method they used. Write their answers on sentence strips with magnets and place on the board. Ask a student to tell which step they used first, second, etc. Move the sentence strips in order to correspond with student responses.

Adapted lesson for increased opportunities to respond:
Scientific method review
After completing the experiment, have students pair with a different partner. Each partner tells the steps they used to complete the experiment. After sharing with their partners, invite several partners to share one step of the method. Point to each step on the board and tell all students to chorally say 'Stop' when they get to the first step in the method. Place a number 1 next to the step and move the step to first in the list. Repeat with each step of the method until the steps are in order.

instruction, as discussed previously, can assist with response opportunities as well. Complex tasks that are organized into smaller steps for instruction allow additional opportunities for practice within each of the steps.

Even during initial learning, instruction is best organized to allow for high levels of student success. If a student demonstrates a high error rate, more explicit or systematic instruction is recommended. The grouping formats discussed earlier in this chapter are also designed to increase student opportunities for response. Table 27.5 provides an example of adjusting a lesson to provide more opportunities to respond. Notice how various grouping formats are used within the lesson to provide all students with an opportunity to practice/respond.

Immediate, corrective feedback

To effectively increase student learning, corrective and positive feedback is critical, as it assists students in refining and mastering new skills (Vaughn, Gersten, & Chard, 2000). All of the features of instruction are designed to allow students to have successful learning opportunities; immediate, corrective feedback is the final step. Corrective feedback is provided to allow students to stay on the right track during practice or to remedy errors in task completion and get students back on the right track. The more immediate the feedback, the less likely it is that a student will spend time practicing incorrectly. Preventing significant amounts of inaccurate practice will allow a more efficient path to mastery. Just as important, students need precise, clear, positive feedback when they respond correctly. Teachers should make sure that their positive feedback communicates clearly what aspects of the task students perform well.

Although independent practice is a necessary part of instruction, it does not normally allow for immediate feedback. Workbook pages, worksheets, and other independent work are most effectively used after students have demonstrated mastery of a skill or concept. Independent work is intended as the last step of a scaffolding process to give practice with a skill without teacher guidance. Independent work assigned when students have not mastered a skill takes away the opportunities for immediate feedback and, thus, students may practice skills incorrectly a number of times (for example, complete much of the worksheet incorrectly) and receive correction only after the work is graded or corrected by the teacher one or more days later. Rather, independent activities should be used for additional practice and to allow students to demonstrate the final step of mastery: the ability to complete tasks or skills without teacher guidance. Teachers should continue to monitor student performance even during independent practice in order to provide additional support when it is needed.

Using progress monitoring to make instructional decisions

Progress monitoring with curriculum-based measures has emerged as a valid and reliable way of measuring students' ongoing academic growth for use in instructional decision-making (Deno, 1985; Marston, 1989). In fact, teachers who monitor the effectiveness of instruction tend to achieve significantly higher rates of student learning than teachers who rely on more traditional assessments (Conte & Hintze, 2000; Fuchs, Fuchs, Hamlett, & Allinder, 1991). Additionally, teachers using progress monitoring measures tend to be more realistic when estimating a student's rate of progress and are able to adjust instructional goals accordingly (Fuchs, Deno, & Mirkin, 1984; Fuchs, Fuchs, Hamlett, & Stecker, 1991). Progress monitoring measures are assessments that can be administered frequently and are sensitive to small changes in learning. The frequent administration of progress monitoring measures suggests the assessments should have multiple, equivalent forms that can be administered throughout the school year. Additionally, these assessments are often designed to be quickly administered, allowing for frequent administration that does not interfere with already limited instructional time.

Progress monitoring measures can serve two purposes: (a) to make instructional decisions for individual students and (b) to monitor effectiveness of instructional changes or interventions. Data from progress monitoring should allow teachers to consider in which areas students are progressing well, which instructional areas need additional attention, which students have similar needs and may benefit from targeted instruction in a small group, and whether instruction or interventions need to be altered.

Progress monitoring can allow teachers to determine skill areas students have mastered as well as areas that need additional instruction. Instruction should then be planned according to these needs – placing skill areas mastered into a review cycle and focusing instruction on the areas of need. For example, progress monitoring measures may show a student is mastering or progressing sufficiently in the area of phonological awareness but is having significant difficulties blending letter sounds into

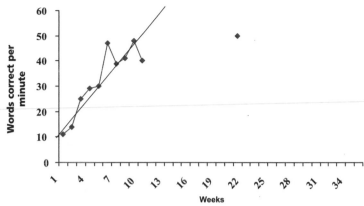

Figure 27.2   Derek's oral reading fluency

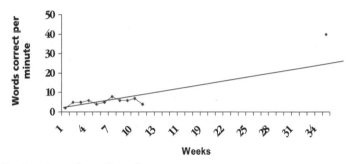

Figure 27.3   Amy's oral reading fluency

words. Closer examination of the assessments and student error patterns can be used along with day-to-day instructional observations to guide student intervention as well. Examining assessments for consistent errors can provide information about skill areas that are not yet at an independent level. Instruction should then focus on these areas. In the previous example, a look at the assessment may also illustrate specific letter sounds the student does not know. Alternatively, the assessment may show the student knows nearly all the letter sounds (there are very few errors in saying letter sounds) but cannot blend them into a word. In this instance, isolated letter sounds can be put into a review cycle and instruction should focus on using letter-sound knowledge to blend and read words. Or maybe a student can accurately do all of these things but does so very slowly. Emphasis here is on fluency of the tasks and additional practice opportunities to reach a level of automaticity with the tasks. All

of these scenarios suggest a different focus for instruction to allow the student to reach the next level.

Setting goals and examining progress monitoring on a frequent basis can also assist in determining relatively quickly whether interventions are successful or whether changes are needed in instruction. Examine Derek's data in Figure 27.2. Derek's scores are increasing, and it appears as though he is headed for the goal. For this reason, it is evident the intervention is allowing him to make sufficient progress in this area and should be continued. Alternatively, examine Amy's data in Figure 27.3. Although she is making progress, it is clear that if she continues to make the same level of progress, she will not be able to meet the goal. Therefore, the current instruction is not allowing her to make sufficient progress in this area. Instructional changes are warranted for Amy, and progress monitoring should be continued to examine whether the changes result in accelerated progress.

The inclusion of the features of instruction discussed in this chapter can be evaluated to determine possible instructional changes for Amy. Perhaps Amy needs instruction in a smaller group to help maximize her active involvement. It may be that the instruction Amy is currently receiving is not explicit or systematic enough. Perhaps Amy is not getting enough opportunities for practice, or the lessons need to be adjusted to allow for more immediate or precise positive and corrective feedback.

Whenever possible, students with learning difficulties should be monitored frequently (every week or every other week) to allow instructional decisions to be made before large amounts of time have passed. Student progress can be examined by looking at the student trend in comparison to the goal. However, several data points are needed to begin seeing a trend. If a student is monitored once each month, for example, then several months will pass before it can be determined whether the student's learning trajectory is on track, or whether the student is making insufficient progress and instructional changes are needed.

Frequent progress monitoring can allow teachers to make important instructional decisions for students with learning difficulties. Effective, efficient instruction and intervention is needed for students who are struggling. Progress monitoring data can provide substantial information for teachers to determine content changes and instructional delivery adjustments needed to accelerate the progress of students with learning difficulties and disabilities.

Our knowledge about effective instruction for students with learning disabilities has increased in the past two decades. As a result of an improved knowledge base, the role of the special education teacher has changed and the knowledge and skill required to adequately perform the job has expanded. This requires ongoing professional development so that special education teachers can provide the necessary instruction that is most beneficial to students with special needs.

REFERENCES

Acalin, T. A. (1995). *A comparison of Reading Recovery to project READ*. Unpublished doctoral dissertation, California State University, Fullerton.

Allington, R. L. (1980). Poor readers don't get to read much in reading groups. *Language Arts, 57*, 873–875.

Anderson, R. C., Hiebert, E. H., Scott, J. A., & Wilkinson, I. A. (1985). *Becoming a nation of readers: The report of the commission of reading*. Washington, DC: National Institute of Education.

Barr, R. (1989). The social organization of literacy instruction. In S. McCormick & J. Zutell (Eds.), *Cognitive and social perspectives for literacy research and instruction* (pp. 19–33). Chicago, IL: National Reading Conference.

Barr, R., & Dreeben, R. (1991). Grouping students for reading instruction. In R. Barr, M. L. Kamil, P. B. Mosenthal, & P. D. Pearson (Eds.), *Handbook of reading research: Vol. II* (pp. 885–910). New York: Longman.

Berninger, V., & Amtmann, D. (2003). Preventing written expression disabilities through early and continuing assessment and intervention for handwriting and/or spelling problems: Research into practice. In H. L. Swanson, K. R. Harris, & S. Graham (Eds.), *Handbook of learning disabilities* (pp. 345–363). New York: Guilford Press.

Bradley, R., Danielson, L., & Hallihan, D. P. (Eds.). (2002). *Identification of learning disabilities: Research to practice*. Mahwah, NJ: Lawrence Erlbaum.

Brophy, J., & Good, T. (1989). Teacher behavior and student achievement. In M. C. Wittrock (Ed.), *Handbook of research on teaching*. New York: Macmillan.

Coaches, controversy, consensus. (2004, April/May). *Reading Today, 21*(5), 1, 18.

Cohen, P., Kulik, J. A., & Kulik, C. C. (1982). Educational outcomes of tutoring: A meta-analysis of findings. *American Educational Research Journal, 19*, 237–248.

Conte, K. L., & Hintze, J. M. (2000). The effects of performance feedback and goal setting on oral reading fluency within curriculum-based measurement. *Diagnostique, 25*, 85–98.

Coyne, M. D., Kame'enui, E. J., & Simmons, D. C. (2001). Prevention and intervention in beginning reading: Two complex systems. *Learning Disabilities Research and Practice, 16*, 62–73.

Deno, S. L. (1985). Curriculum-based measurement: The emerging alternative. *Exceptional Children, 52*, 219–232.

Denton, C. A., & Mathes, P. G. (2003). Intervention for struggling readers: Possibilities and challenges. In B. R. Foorman (Ed.), *Preventing and remediating reading difficulties* (pp. 229–252). New York: York Press.

Denton, C. A., Vaughn, S., & Fletcher, J. M. (2003). Bringing research-based practice to scale. *Learning*

Disabilities Research and Practice, 18, 201–211.

Deshler, D. D., Lowrey, N., Alley, G. R. (1979). Programming alternatives for adolescents: A nationwide survey. *Academic Therapy, 14*, 389–397.

Dole, J. (2004). The changing role of the reading specialist in school reform. *The Reading Teacher, 57*, 462–471.

Donovan, M. S., & Cross, C. T. (2002). *Minority students in special and gifted education.* Washington, DC: National Academy Press.

Elbaum, B., Schumm, J. S., & Vaughn, S. (1997). Urban middle-elementary students' perceptions of grouping formats for reading instruction. *Elementary School Journal, 97*, 475–500.

Elbaum, B., Vaughn, S., Hughes, M. T., & Moody, S. W. (1999). Grouping practices and reading outcomes for students with disabilities. *Exceptional Children, 65*, 399–415.

Elbaum, B., Vaughn, S., Hughes, M. T., & Moody, S. W. (2000). How effective are one-to-one tutoring programs in reading for elementary students at risk for reading failure? *Journal of Educational Psychology, 92*, 605–619.

Evans, T. L. P. (1996). *I can read deze books: A qualitative comparison of the Reading Recovery program and a small-group reading intervention.* Unpublished doctoral dissertation, Auburn University, Auburn, Alabama.

Fielding-Barnsley, R. (1997). Explicit instruction in decoding benefits children high in phonemic awareness and alphabet knowledge. *Scientific Studies of Reading, 1*, 85–98.

Fletcher, J. M., Coulter, W. A., Reschly, D. J., & Vaughn, S. (2004). Alternative approaches to the definition and identification of learning disabilities: Some questions and answers. *Annals of Dyslexia, 54*, 304–331.

Fletcher, J. M., Francis, D. J., Rourke, B. P., Shaywitz, B., & Shaywitz, S. E. (1992). The validity of the discrepancy-based definitions of learning disabilities. *Journal of Learning Disabilities, 25*, 555–561, 573.

Fletcher, J. M., Lyon, G. R., Barnes, M., Stuebing, K. K., Francis, D. J., Olson, R. K., et al. (2001). *Classification of learning disabilities: An evidence based evaluation.* Washington, DC: U.S. Department of Education.

Fuchs, L. S., Deno, S. L., & Mirkin, P. K. (1984). Effects of frequent curriculum-based measurement and evaluation on pedagogy, student achievement, and student awareness of learning. *American Educational Research Journal, 21*, 449–460.

Fuchs, L. S., Fuchs, D., Hamlett, C. L., & Allinder, R. M. (1991). The contribution of skills analysis to curriculum-based measurement in spelling. *Exceptional Children, 57*, 443–452.

Fuchs, L. S., Fuchs, D., Hamlett, C. L., & Stecker, P. M. (1991). Effects of curriculum-based measurement and consultation on teacher planning and student

achievement in mathematics operations. *American Educational Research Journal, 28*, 617–641.

Fuchs, D., Fuchs, L. S., Mathes, P. G., & Simmons, D. C. (1997). Peer-assisted learning strategies: Making classrooms more responsive to diversity. *American Educational Research Journal, 34*, 174–206.

Fuchs, L. S., Fuchs, D., Prentice, K. Burch, M., Hamlett, C. L., Owen, R., et al. (2003). Explicitly teaching for transfer: Effects on third-grade students' mathematical problem solving. *Journal of Educational Psychology, 95*, 293–304.

Hallinan, M. T., & Sorensen, A. B. (1985). Ability grouping and student friendships. *American Educational Research Journal, 22*, 485–499.

Hammill, D. D., & Wiederholt, J. L. (1972). Review of the Frostig Visual Perception Test and the related training program. In L. Mann & D. Sabatino (Eds.), *The first review of special education: Vol. 1*. Philadelphia, PA: JSE Press.

Hasbrouck, J.E., & Denton, C.A. (2005). *The reading coach: A how-to manual for success.* Longmont, CO: Sopris West.

Hiebert, E. H. (1983). An examination of ability grouping for reading instruction. *Reading Research Quarterly, 18*, 231–255.

Kass, C. E. (Ed.). (1970). *Final report: Advanced institute for leadership personnel in learning disabilities.* Contract No. OEG-09–121013-3021–031, U.S. Office of Education, Department of Special Education of the University of Arizona. Tucson: University of Arizona.

Klingner, J. K., & Vaughn, S. (2002). Joyce: The changing roles and responsibilities of an LD specialist. *Learning Disability Quarterly, 25*, 19–32.

Kulik, C. C., & Kulik, J. A. (1982). Research synthesis on ability grouping. *Educational Leadership, 39*, 619–621.

Kulik, C. C., & Kulik, J. A. (1984). *Effects of ability grouping on elementary school pupils: A meta-analysis* (ERIC Document Reproduction Services No. ED 255 329).

Lamport, K. C. (1982). The effect of inverse tutoring on reading disabled students in public school settings. *Dissertation Abstracts International, 44*, 729. (University Microfilms N. 83–15, 707.)

Larsen, S. C. (1976). The learning disabilities specialist: Roles and responsibilities. *Journal of Learning Disabilities, 9*, 498–508.

Lou, Y., Abrami, P. C., Spence, J. C., Poulsen, C., Chambers, B., & d'Apollonia, S. (1996). Within-class grouping: A meta-analysis. *Review of Educational Research, 66*, 423–458.

Lyon, G. R., Fletcher, J. M., Fuchs, L. S., & Chhabra, V. (In press). Learning disabilities. In E. Mash & R. Barkley (Eds.), *Treatment of childhood Disorders* (2nd ed.). New York: Guilford.

Maheady, L. (1997). Preparing teachers for instructing

multiple ability groups. *Teacher Education & Special Education, 20,* 322–339.

Maheady, L., Harper, G. F., & Sacca, M. K. (1988). Peer-mediated instruction: A promising approach to meeting the diverse needs of LD adolescents. *Learning Disability Quarterly, 11,* 108–113.

Marston, D. B. (1989). A curriculum-based measurement approach to assessing academic performance: What it is and why do it. In M. R. Shinn (Ed.), *Curriculum-based measurement* (pp. 18–78). New York: Guilford.

Mathes, P. G., & Fuchs, L. S. (1994). The efficacy of peer tutoring in reading for students with mild disabilities: A best-evidence synthesis. *School Psychology Review, 23*(1), 59–80.

Mathes, P. G., Howard, J. K, Allen, S., & Fuchs, D. (1998). Peer-assisted learning strategies for first-grade readers: Making early reading instruction responsive to the needs of diverse learners. *Reading Research Quarterly, 33,* 62–94.

Mathes, P. G., Torgesen, J. K., & Allor, J. H. (2001). The effects of peer assisted learning strategies for first-grade learners with and without additional computer assisted instruction in phonological awareness. *American Educational Research Journal, 38,* 371–410.

McLoughlin, J. A. (1973). Role analysis of resource teachers of children with learning disabilities and educable mental retardation. *Dissertation Abstracts International, 34* (12-A, Pt 1), 1354A. (AAT 7412440.)

McLoughlin, J. A., & Kass, C. E. (1978). Resource teachers: Their role. *Learning Disability Quarterly, 1*(1), 56–62.

Moody, S. W., Vaughn, S., Hughes, M. T., & Fischer, M. (2000). Reading instruction in the resource room: Set up for failure. *Exceptional Children, 66,* 305–316.

Morrow, L. M. (2003). *Organizing and managing the language arts block: A professional development guide. solving problems in the teaching of literacy.* New York: Guilford.

Oakes, J., Gamoran, A., & Page, R. N. (1992). Curriculum differentiation: Opportunities, outcomes, and meanings. In P. Jackson (Ed.), *Handbook of research on curriculum* (pp. 570–608). New York: Macmillan.

Poglinco, S. M., & Bach, A. J. (2004, January). The heart of the matter: Coaching as a vehicle for professional development. *Phi Delta Kappan,* 398–400.

Scruggs, T. E., & Richter, L. (1985). Tutoring learning disabled students: A critical review. *Learning Disability Quarterly, 8,* 286–298.

Scruggs, T. E., Mastropieri, M. A., & Richter, L. (1985). Peer tutoring with behaviorally disordered students: Social and academic benefits. *Behavioral Disorders, 10,* 283–294.

Siegel, L. S. (1992). An evaluation of the discrepancy definition of dyslexia. *Journal of Learning Disabilities, 25,* 618–629.

Sindelar, P. T. (1995). Full inclusion of students with learning disabilities and its implications for teacher education. *Journal of Special Education, 29,* 234–244.

Slavin, R. E. (1987). Ability grouping and student achievement in the elementary schools: A best-evidence synthesis. *Review of Educational Research, 57,* 293–336.

Stuebing, K. K., Fletcher, J. M., LeDoux, J. M., Lyon, G. R., Shaywitz, S. E., & Shaywitz, B. A. (2002). Validity of IQ-discrepancy classifications of reading disabilities: A meta-analysis. *American Educational Research Journal, 39,* 469–518.

Swanson, H. L. (2000). What instruction works for students with learning disabilities? Summarizing the results from a meta-analysis of intervention studies. In R. M. Gersten, E. P. Schiller, & S. Vaughn (Eds.), *Contemporary special education research: Syntheses of the knowledge base on critical instructional issues* (pp. 1–30). Mahwah, NJ: Erlbaum.

Swanson, H. L., Harris, K. R., & Graham, S. (Eds.). (2003). *Handbook of learning disabilities.* New York: Guilford Press.

Taylor, B. M., Pearson, P. D., Clark, K. F., & Walpole, S. (1999). Effective schools/accomplished teachers. *The Reading Teacher, 53,* 156–159.

Thurlow, M. L., Ysseldyke, J. E., Wotruba, J. W., & Algozzine, B. (1993). Instruction in special education classrooms under varying student-teacher ratios. *Elementary School Journal, 93,* 305–320.

Torgesen, J. K. (2002). The prevention of reading difficulties. *Journal of School Psychology, 40,* 7–26.

Vance, H. R. (1979). Thoughts on the LD teacher. *Academic Therapy, 14,* 279–283.

Vaughn, S., & Fuchs, L. S. (2003). Redefining learning disabilities as inadequate response to instruction: The promise and potential problems. *Learning Disabilities Research and Practice, 18,* 137–146.

Vaughn, S., & Linan-Thompson, S. (In press). Special education for students with learning disabilities: What makes it so special? In B. G. Cook & B. R. Schirmer (Eds.), *What is special about special education.* Austin, TX: PRO-ED.

Vaughn, S., Gersten, R., & Chard, D. J. (2000). The underlying message in LD intervention research: Findings from research syntheses. *Exceptional Children, 67,* 99–114.

Vaughn, S., Hughes, M. T., Schumm, J. S., & Klingner, J. K. (1998). A collaborative effort to enhance reading and writing instruction in inclusion classrooms. *Learning Disability Quarterly, 21,* 57–74.

Vaughn, S., Linan-Thompson, S., Kouzekanani, K., Bryant, D. P., Dickson, S., & Blozis, S. A. (2003). Grouping for reading instruction for students with reading difficulties. *Remedial and Special Education, 24,* 301–315.

Vaughn, S., Linan-Thompson, S., Wanzek, J., Rodriguez, K. T., Sanderson, C., Cavanaugh, C. L., et al (In review). Effectiveness of Tier I and Tier II interventions for at-risk kindergarten students.

Vaughn, S., Moody, S., & Schumm, J. S. (1998). Broken promises: Reading instruction in the resource room. *Exceptional Children, 64,* 211–226.

Vaughn, S., Wanzek, J., Woodruff, A. L., & Linan-Thompson, S. (In press). A three-tier model for preventing reading difficulties and early identification of students with reading disabilities. In D. H. Haager, S.

Vaughn, & J. K. Klingner (Eds.), *Validated reading practices for three tiers of intervention.* Baltimore, MD: Brookes.

Vellutino, F. R., Scanlon, D. M., & Lyon, G. R. (2000). Differentiating between difficult-to-remediate and readily remediated poor readers: More evidence against the IQ-achievement discrepancy definition of reading disability. *Journal of Learning Disabilities, 33,* 223–238.

Zigmond, N., & Baker, J. M. (1995). Concluding comments: Current and future practices in inclusive schooling. *Journal of Special Education, 29,* 245–250.

28

Teaching and learning in secondary education

John McDonnell, Michael L. Hardman, and Jayne McGuire

This chapter examines effective practices in secondary education that prepare students with special educational needs to successfully make the transition into adult life. We begin with an analysis of the expected outcomes of secondary schooling and current trends in the education of these students. The chapter then addresses empirically validated instructional, curriculum, and transition planning practices that enhance access to further education, employment, and community living. We conclude with a summary of future directions in the education of students with special educational needs at the secondary level.

EXPECTED OUTCOMES OF SECONDARY EDUCATION

For most of the twentieth century, human service programs for people with disabilities were concerned with minimizing risk while protecting and caring for the individual in isolated settings. However, within the past two decades, many nations have begun to acknowledge the potential of people with disabilities to become contributors within society rather than objects of charity who merely consume resources. Public policy that

once excluded people with disabilities is being replaced with the call for an investment in their education, as evidenced by the *United Nations Salamanca Statement on the Education of All Disabled Children*. The *Salamanca Framework for Action*, supported by 92 governments, stated that 'young people with special educational needs should be helped to make an effective transition from school to adult working life' (UNESCO, 1994, p. 34). The United Nations (UN) further strengthened its position in the World Summit for Children (UNESCO, 2001), calling for schools to promote access to education for every child with a disability. To meet this intent, secondary schools are expected to provide students with the opportunity to learn and apply the skills needed for a successful transition to valued post-school outcomes.

It is important to note that although access to basic education for students with special educational needs is clearly at the heart of international policy efforts (UNESCO, 2001), some countries are moving beyond access to improved results for these children. For example, both the US and the UK have enacted reforms that hold schools accountable for the achievement of all students in a standards-driven system. As suggested by

McLaughlin and Rouse (2000), 'it is clear that higher student achievement is now a central policy goal in [the US and UK] and the needs of students who find learning difficult are now more likely to be considered in policy mandates' (p. 9). Increased academic achievement prior to exiting school is the driving force behind the No Child Left Behind Act (2001) and the reauthorization of the Individuals with Disabilities Act (IDEA, 2004) in the US, as well as the implementation of the National Curriculum in the UK.

In spite of significant shifts in public policy from exclusion to inclusion and access to results, successful post-school outcomes remain elusive for adults with disabilities. Results from follow-up studies on the transition from school to adult life indicate these individuals are not participating fully in community activities and are socially isolated in comparison to people without disabilities (National Council on Disability, 2000; National Organization on Disability/Harris, 2000; Organisation for Economic Co-operation and Development, 1996). These studies further suggest that in comparison to peers without disabilities, students with special educational needs have lower levels of academic achievement and higher dropout rates. As adults, the vast majority are unemployed or underemployed. For example, in the United States from 1982 to 2002, the unemployment rate of people with disabilities actually increased from 65 per cent to 69 per cent (Houtenville, 2005). Many other countries report similarly high and unacceptable employment rates. The International Labour Organization (1998) estimated that unemployment rates among adults with disabilities are two to three times higher than among people without disabilities. In regard to quality of life, a 2000 poll conducted in the US by the National Organization on Disability and Harris Associates found that only 33 per cent of adults with disabilities were very satisfied with life in general, compared to seven out of ten (67 per cent) of adults who were not disabled. Poor access to health care and transportation were identified as two significant barriers to life satisfaction. Nearly one in three adults with disabilities had to postpone medical treatment because they could not afford it. Similarly, 30 per cent of adults considered inadequate access to transportation a major problem in their lives.

Although international policy on education and social inclusion continues to outpace positive results for students with special educational needs, our understanding of the practices associated with successful post-school adjustment is continually increasing (Kraemer, McIntyre, & Blacher, 2003; Wagner, Newman, Cameto, Levine, & Marder, 2003). A common thread that emerges from these studies is that secondary education has a significant impact on the quality of life that students experience once they leave school. In the next section, we review evidenced-based practices in secondary schools that prepare students with special educational needs to achieve career and life aspirations.

EFFECTIVE PRACTICES

Over the last two decades, research has identified the key practices that are necessary to prepare all students with special educational needs for the various roles and responsibilities of adulthood and community life (Bouck, 2004; Flexer, Simmons, Luft, & Baer, 2001; Kohler, 1998; McDonnell, 2004; Sitlington, Clark, & Kolstoe, 2000; Wehman, 2001). Although these core practices lay the foundation for effective secondary education, curriculum and instruction must be tailored to achieve each student's personal goals and accommodate their personal preferences. For many years, the field was focused on validating practices that were designed to promote students' transition from school to employment and community living (Johnson & Halloran, 1997; Kohler, 1998). More recently, there is recognition that access to postsecondary education can significantly improve the quality of life and standard of living of many students with special educational needs (Gajar, 1998; Yelin & Katz, 1994). Consequently, a secondary program must be designed to ensure that all students who will benefit from these programs can access and successfully participate in them (Grigal, Neubert, & Moon, 2001; Sitlington, 2003). The following section will describe the (1) recommended core practices for all students in secondary programs, (2) practices correlated with the successful transition to employment and community living for students with special educational needs, and (3) practices for preparing students with special educational needs for transition to post-secondary education.

Core transition practices

Six transition practices are at the core of effective secondary programs for students with special educational needs: (1) promoting self-determination; (2) implementing person-centered planning; (3) inclusion in the general education program; (4) anchoring curriculum and instruction to the demands of adulthood; (5) providing comprehensive career awareness and preparation programs, and (6) developing social competence (Flexer et al., 2001; McDonnell, 2004; Sitlington et al., 2000; Wehman, 2001).

Self-determination

Field, Martin, Miller, Ward, & Wehmeyer (1998) define self-determination as 'a combination of skills, knowledge, and beliefs that enable a person to engage in goal-directed, self-regulated, autonomous behavior' (p. 2). Several studies suggest that the development of self-determination skills during school enhances post-school outcomes (Wehmeyer & Palmer, 2003; Wehmeyer & Schwartz, 1997; 1998). For example, Wehmeyer & Schwarz (1997) examined the relationship between levels of self-determination and post-school outcomes with 80 secondary students with mild mental retardation and learning disabilities. They found that students who had higher levels of self-determined behaviors were more likely to be employed for pay, more independent in controlling their personal finances, and more likely to have a goal

of independent living one year after exiting school.

Although the development of self-determination skills can improve post-school adjustment, there is a paucity of research on how to teach this complex set of skills, knowledge, and beliefs (Algozzine, Browder, Karvonen, Test, & Ward, 2001). In spite of this, Field and Hoffman (2002) suggest that schools can help students improve their levels of self-determination by:

- infusing knowledge, skills, attitudes for self-determination in the curriculum, in family support programs, and in staff development activities
- promoting active participation of students, parents, and staff in individualized educational decision making and planning
- providing students, families, faculty, and staff with frequent opportunities for choice
- encouraging and support students, families, faculty, and staff to take appropriate risks
- encouraging the development of supportive relationships
- providing the accommodations and supports necessary to meet individual needs
- providing students, families and staff with the opportunity to express themselves and be understood
- establishing predictable consequences for actions
- modeling self-determination behaviors throughout the school environment.

Person-centered transition planning

Several studies suggest that transition planning that is driven by the needs and preferences of the student result in better post-school student outcomes (Benz, Lindstrom, & Yovanoff, 2000; Frank & Sitlington, 2000; Merchant & Gajar, 1997) and higher levels of student and parent satisfaction with the educational program (Collet-Klingenberg, 1998; Miner & Bates, 1997). In spite of this, students and parents often do not attend planning meetings with school personnel (deFur, Getzel, & Kregel, 1994; Grigal, Test, Beattie, & Wood, 1997; Trach & Sheldon, 2000). Even when they are present, the amount of input they have in defining post-school goals and shaping the educational services necessary to achieve desired post-school outcomes is limited (Abery & Stancliffe, 1996; Collett-Klingenberg, 1998; Cooney, 2002; Johnson & Sharpe, 2000; Thoma, Rogan, & Baker, 2001). While the level of control that students and parents have over education planning is less than ideal, a number of studies suggest that if provided adequate training and support they can develop the capacity to be active participants in the process (Test et al., 2004). Given the important link between student success during transition and the educational program, secondary schools should implement procedures that encourage and support student and parental control and prepare them to be active participants in the planning process (deFur, Todd-Allen, & Getzel, 2001; Hasazi, Furney, & Destefano, 1999). Recommended strategies include training seminars on person-centered transition planning, creating pre-planning documents and procedures to encourage students and parents to weigh various post-school options, and turning control of the planning process over to the students and their parents.

Participation in general education

Research suggests that students with special educational needs benefit from being included in general education classes and from participation in the general education curriculum (Baker, Wang, & Walberg, 1994–1995; Harrower, 1999; Hunt & Goetz, 1997; Salend & Garnick-Duhaney, 1999; Wagner et al., 2003). Post-school adjustment to employment also appears to improve if students participate in general vocational education classes especially during the last two years of school (Benz et al., 2000; Phelps & Hanley-Maxwell, 1997).

There is a growing body of literature on curriculum and instructional practices that can improve educational outcomes for students in general education classes. Some of the most promising practices include (a) the use of universal design (Orkwis & McLane, 1998); (b) layered or differentiated instruc-

tion (Tomlinson, 1999); (c) strategy instruction (Deshler et al., 2001); (d) adapted instruction in which a student works on different skills within the same content area (Giangreco & Putnam, 1991); (e) peer tutoring (Mastropieri & Scruggs, 2001; McDonnell, 1998); (f) co-teaching (Mastopieri & Scruggs, 2001); and (g) embedded instruction designed to allow students receive instruction on basic skills within the ongoing activities of the general education class (McDonnell, 1998).

Anchoring curriculum and instruction to the demands of adulthood

Researchers have argued that curriculum and instruction should be linked directly to the demands of living and working in the community (Bouck, 2004; Eisenman, 2000; McDonnell, 2004; Patton, Cronin, & Jarriels, 1997; Wehman & Revell, 1997). This goal can be accomplished through a variety of strategies including the use of authentic assessment and evaluation procedures (Resnick & Wirt, 1996), the infusion of life skills instruction into all subject areas (Eisenman, 2000; Patton et al., 1997), and direct instruction in employment and community settings (McDonnell, 2004; Wehman, 2001). Secondary programs must be structured to ensure that students not only acquire knowledge and skills that promote successful transition to adulthood but are able to demonstrate they can use the knowledge and skills to meet their specific post-school goals.

Career awareness and preparation

A key role for secondary programs is to help students develop the knowledge and skills necessary to obtain a career that is personally rewarding and provides the resources necessary to support their desired lifestyle. Follow-up studies suggest that participation in general vocational education classes, especially during the last two years of school, and community-based work experience opportunities are strongly correlated with positive post-school employment outcomes for students (Benz et al., 2000; Johnson, McGrew,

Bloomberg, Bruininks, & Lin, 1997; Kraemer et al., 2003; Levine & Nourse, 1998; Sitlington, Frank, & Carson, 1992). These career preparation activities should be structured to assess students' strengths and needs; help them to develop realistic career goals; and develop the academic and work-related skills necessary for success in inclusive work environments (McDonnell, 2004; Sitlington et al., 2000; Wehman, 2001).

Develop social competence

The empirical evidence suggests that the depth and breadth of an individual's social networks has a significant impact on their perceived quality of life (Kraemer et al., 2003; National Organization on Disabilities/Harris and Associates, 2000). Friendships and other social relationships play an important role in the ability of individuals with disabilities to obtain and maintain meaningful employment (Phelps & Hanley-Maxwell, 1997), live independently (Nisbet, Clark, & Covet, 1991; Walker, 1999), and to participate in leisure and recreation activities (Bedeni, 1993; Terman, Larner, Stevenson, & Behrman, 1996). Secondary programs can address these needs by helping students develop the knowledge and skills necessary to be socially competent in employment and community settings (Chadsey & Sheldon, 1998; Kavale & Forness, 1999). This can be accomplished by teaching social skills within actual performance contexts and creating regular opportunities for students to regularly interact with peers without disabilities (Harrower, 1999; Hunt & Goetz, 1997).

Transition to employment and community living

For many students with special educational needs, the focus of secondary education is to prepare them for transition from school into employment and community living. Research suggests that students are more likely to achieve these outcomes if schools provide job placement and training services, provide community-based instruction on personal manage-

ment and leisure activities that are specific to their needs, and assist them to establish a network of natural and formal supports before leaving school (Kohler, 1998; Siegel, 1998).

Job placement and training

According to Blackorby and Warner (1996), secondary programs historically underprepare students with special educational needs to cope with employment. The types of career awareness and preparation programs described above provide an important means for exposing students to the world of work, assessing their strengths and weaknesses, and providing the opportunities for them to identify career goals. However, these approaches do not ensure that students will be able to obtain a job upon graduation. Follow-up studies have found that students who have had a paid job during school are more successful in adjusting to employment after graduation (Phelps & Hanley-Maxwell, 1997). This suggests that secondary programs must provide students, especially those with more significant needs, comprehensive job placement and training services prior to graduation. A number of models for providing these services have been described in the literature (Griffin & Targett, 2001; McDonnell, Mathot-Buckner, & Ferguson, 1996). These models share common elements, including: active job development for students; comprehensive job analysis procedures designed to identify the work and social demands of the job, matching the student's strengths and weaknesses to job demands; systematic on-the-job training; carefully fading training support; and conducting ongoing follow along.

Community-based instruction

Research suggests that students have difficulty generalizing skills learned in school to home, work, and community settings (Horner, McDonnell, & Bellamy, 1986; Rosenthal-Malek & Bloom, 1998). These studies also suggest that it is unlikely that students will successfully apply skills under natural performance conditions unless they are directly taught to do so. It seems clear that facilitating the successful transition of students from school to community life will require secondary programs to provide instruction in a variety of home, school, and community environments.

Natural and formal supports

Natural supports extend beyond the student's family, to include classmates, colleagues and neighbors (Nisbet, 1992). These individuals constitute a support network of mutual caring that promotes greater inclusion in the community, improved on-the-job support and the development of social relationships (Butterworth, Hagner, Helm, & Whelley, 2000; Walker, 1999). The concept of natural supports stresses that relying on other community members to provide support enhances the potential for inclusion more effectively than relying on specialized services and personnel.

The idea of natural supports has significant implications for how secondary programs facilitate the transition of students from school to community life (McDonnell et al., 1996; Wehman & Revell, 1997). Instead of defining post-school options based on the specialized service programs that are available in the local community, secondary programs must look first at building relationships between students and other community members that will create the opportunities for them to achieve their post-school goals. The steps for building natural supports include (a) identifying when students will need assistance or support in activities, (b) identifying individuals within the environments who are able and willing to provide support to students to complete activities, (c) providing information and training to these individuals as necessary in order for them to provide assistance or support to students, and (d) maintaining collaborative relationships with the individuals in order to address students' future needs (Hagner, Rogan, & Murphy, 1992; Hughes & Carter, 2000).

Successful secondary programs, with high-quality employment outcomes have formal agreements in place for internal and external coordination (Phelps & Hanley-Maxwell,

1997). Wehman (2001) notes that programs with documented transition outcomes for graduates are well connected to agencies and programs beyond school, as well as coordinated across different groups and departments within the school. Internal plans of support and coordination can be established between special education, guidance, school affiliated vocational programs and technology departments. External linkages should include interagency interaction between the local education and community service agencies. The purpose of establishing formal support systems is to ensure comprehensive planning and individualized service provision (Wehman, 2001). The intra- and inter-agency agreements should specify precise roles of the participating agencies in order for implementation of services and achievement of outcomes to be effective.

Transition from secondary to postsecondary education

The impact of postsecondary education on the quality of life and standard of living achieved by young adults with and without disabilities is well established (Gajar, 1998; Yelin & Katz, 1994). Unfortunately, research suggests that very few young adults with special needs access postsecondary education (Blackorby & Wagner, 1996; Henderson, 2001; Neubert, Moon, Grigal, & Redd, 2001).

Although most postsecondary programs provide a wide array of support services to students with special educational needs, these services alone do not ensure student success (Sharpe & Johnson, 2001; Stodden, Jones, & Chang, 2002; Stodden, Whelley, Chang, & Harding, 2001). Secondary programs will need to actively prepare these students for the demands of postsecondary education and provide direct support to them during the transition process (Grigal et al., 2001; Janiga & Costenbader, 2002; Sitlington, 2003). Five practices have been recommended: (1) developing the student's self-advocacy skills, (2) developing time management and study skills, (3) increasing proficiency in using technology, (4) orienting students to the campus and support services, and (5) establishing the skills necessary to cope with the demands of independent living (Brinckerhoff, McGuire, & Shaw, 2002; Gajar, 1998; Getzel, Stodden, & Briel, 2001; Sitlington, 2003; Webb, 2000).

Develop self-advocacy skills

Studies of successful adults with disabilities suggest these individuals have a clear understanding of their strengths and weaknesses, and how their disability will impact their response to the demands of adulthood (Durlak, Rose, & Bursuck, 1994; Speckman, Goldman, & Herman, 1992). Further, these individuals can develop specific plans to achieve their goals and are effective in advocating for themselves (Hitchings et al., 2001; Janiga & Costenbader, 2002; Sitlington, 2003). Secondary education needs to be designed to provide students with opportunities to develop a specific understanding of the adaptations and accommodations that will be necessary for them to succeed in college and university classes. Students must also be provided instruction on how to explain to professors the supports they will need to complete assignments and what testing modifications they will require (Durlak et al., 1994; Hitchings et al., 2001; Janiga & Costenbader, 2002).

Although the ability to identify and explain their needs is critical, students must be provided with the support necessary to develop the confidence to advocate for themselves. Many students with special educational needs have relied on their parents or special educators to meet these functions (Janiga & Costenbader, 2002). Strategies that can be used to help students become more effective in communicating their needs and developing the self-confidence necessary to approach professors and advisors include fostering their active participation in educational planning, supporting positive interactions with general educators about their needs, and providing counseling services to assist young adults to develop realistic perceptions of their strengths and weaknesses.

Develop time management and study skills

The significant differences in the organization and structure of classes in postsecondary education require that students develop a comprehensive set of time management and study skills (Brinckerhoff, 1996; Gajar, 1998). Although a sound foundation of basic academic skills is essential for success, postsecondary education also requires that students become more independent and assume more responsibility in the learning process. This means that students must: develop the ability to organize school work; be able to prioritize tasks; master study strategies that accommodate a wide range of academic tasks from memorization to synthesis and integration of knowledge; self-monitor their academic performance. In addition, students must be prepared to cope with the pressures associated with increased levels of competition between students and reduced levels of student–teacher contact. Secondary programs should attempt to replicate these demands as students move toward graduation, providing direct instruction on these unique skills (Sitlington, 2003).

Proficiency in using technology

Postsecondary education campuses are technology-dense environments. Students are increasingly being required to use technology to meet academic demands and navigate the administrative processes of postsecondary programs. Consequently, the ability of students to use computer and other assistive technologies is recognized as a critical prerequisite skill for their transition to postsecondary education (Anderson-Inman, Knox-Quinn, & Szymanski, 1999; Mull & Sitlington, 2003). Computer and other assistive technologies can be conceptualized as having two essential functions for the students. First, they may be seen as 'cognitive prosthesis' used to replace an ability that is missing or somehow limited by the student's disability (Cavalier, Ferretti, & Okolo, 1994). Second, these technologies can also be seen as a 'cognitive partner' that enhances the student's ability to successfully accomplish a task (Salomon, 1993). Improving a student's ability to use technology should be based on an assessment of the demands that will be placed on them by the postsecondary program and the current abilities of the student (Mull & Sitlington, 2003). Once appropriate options have been identified, the student must be provided direct instruction on the use of the technology that is designed to promote generalized application to a variety of tasks and activities (Anderson-Inman et al., 1999).

Orientation to the campus and student services

Several authors recommend that secondary and postsecondary programs develop collaborative orientation programs for students (Durlak et al., 1994; Gajar, 1998; Hitchings et al., 2001; Sitlington, 2003). The purpose of these programs is to help them become familiar with the campus, inform them about the programs that can provide them with academic and social supports, assist them to develop a program of study and enroll in classes, and make connections with student self-help groups. Recommended strategies for supporting these activities include formal orientation programs that are implemented by staff from the postsecondary program and other students with disabilities, and summer transition programs that are designed to allow students to acclimatize to the campus before the academic year begins.

Independent living skills

Many students in attending postsecondary programs are often living on their own for the first time in their lives. Unfortunately, it is often assumed that students who make the transition into postsecondary education do not require instruction or support in learning to cope with these demands (Patton et al., 1997; Sitlington, 2003). Secondary programs may focus the curricula on preparing students to meet the academic expectations of postsecondary education but ignore these other critical life skills. This highlights the need for comprehensive transition planning that systematically addresses all areas (Bouck, 2004; Patton, Cronin, & Veda, 1997; Sitlington, 2003).

SUMMARY

In the early years of the twenty-first century we are seeing significant changes in the lives of people with disabilities. Human services, once focused exclusively on protection and care in isolated settings, are now rejecting a facilities-driven orientation that fosters dependence on society to one that embraces person-centered planning. Secondary schools are adapting their instruction and curricula to better prepare the individual to become a productive adult and to gain access to valued post-school outcomes, including employment, community living, and further education.

As secondary schools seek to offer services and supports that will ultimately result in greater access to valued outcomes, the need to identify research-based instructional practice is self-evident. In this chapter, we have identified those practices that are at the core of effective secondary programs, including person-centered planning, curricula oriented to the demands of adult life, self-determination, access to the general curriculum, inclusive education, career awareness, employment preparation, and social competence. Together, these core practices lay the foundation for a transition planning process that becomes the vehicle in developing future goals, services and supports, and allocation of needed resources. Beyond the core, there are two primary areas of focus for students with special educational needs in secondary schools. For some, the emphasis will be on employment preparation and community living. For others, access to further education is a priority.

Students with special educational needs who leave school and seek immediate access to employment will require effective instruction in job training and placement skills. Instruction must focus on learning and applying skills under natural performance conditions within the community. Community-based instruction facilitates independence by teaching personal management and recreation skills that can be applied across multiple environments. The research suggests that secondary schools must also pay attention to natural as well as formal support networks as the individual transitions out of school. These networks of family, friends, classmates, colleagues, and neighbors are essential in identifying and providing consistent and ongoing support to adults with disabilities.

For students with special educational needs seeking access to further education, a number of effective secondary school practices have been identified as well. These include the development of self-advocacy, time management, technology, and study skills. To access programs, students must also be oriented to campus life, including expectations, activities, supports, and resources. Finally, while academic skill learning is an essential component in gaining access to postsecondary education, schools must also teach critical life skills that promote independence and autonomy.

Although much is being done to implement effective practices in secondary schools, a critical issue looms for the future. What will be the ultimate impact of standards-based reform on the education of students with special educational needs? In this era of high-stakes accountability, students with special educational needs in many countries must meet the same content and performance standards as their peers without disabilities in order to receive a secondary education diploma or certificate. Students who are unable to meet graduation requirements, including successfully passing competency exams, will find themselves at a significant disadvantage in seeking and maintaining employment. Future research is needed in two areas. First, countries must find effective ways to expand standards that will facilitate the participation of students with special educational needs in the general curriculum. Second, there is a need to identify a more effective credentialing process that communicates to employers the requisite knowledge and skills that have been learned by students who otherwise would not meet the standards for a secondary diploma or certificate.

REFERENCES

Abery, B., & Stancliffe, R. (1996). The ecology of self-determination. In D. J. Sands & M. L. Wehmeyer (Eds.), *Self-determination across the life-span: Independence and choice for people with disabilities* (pp. 111–146). Baltimore, MD: Paul H. Brookes.

Algozzine, B., Browder, D., Karvonen, M., Test, D. W., & Wood, W. M. (2001). Effects of interventions to promote self-determination for individuals with disabilities. *Review of Educational Research, 71,* 219–277.

Anderson-Inman, L., Knox-Quinn, C., & S Szymanksi, E. M. (1999). Computer supported studying: Stories of successful transition to postsecondary education. *Career Development for Exceptional Individuals, 22,* 185–212.

Baker, E. T., Wang, M. C., & Walberg, H. J. (1994–1995). The effects of inclusion on learning. *Educational Leadership, 52,* 33–35.

Bedini, L. A. (1993). Transition and integration with leisure for people with disabilities: Research Update. *Parks and Recreation, 28,* 20–24.

Benz, M. R., Lindstrom, L., & Yovanoff, P. (2000). Improving graduation and employment outcomes of students with disabilities: Predictive factors and student perspectives. *Exceptional Children, 66,* 509–529.

Blackorby, J., & Wagner, M. (1996). Longitudinal postschool outcomes of youth with disabilities: Findings from the National Longitudinal Transition Study. *Exceptional Children, 62*(5), 399–413.

Bouck, E. C. (2004). State of curriculum for secondary students with mild mental retardation. *Education and Training in Developmental Disabilities, 39,* 169–176.

Brinckerhoff, L. C. (1996). Making the transition to higher education: Opportunities for student empowerment. *Journal of Learning Disabilities, 29,* 118–136.

Brinckerhoff, L. C., McGuire, J. M., & Shaw, S. F. (2002). *Postsecondary education and transition for students with learning disabilities.* Austin, TX: PRO-ED.

Butterworth, J., Hagner, D., Helm, D. T., & Whelley, T. A. (2000). Workplace culture, social interactions, and supports for transition-age young adults. *Mental Retardation, 38,* 342–353.

Cavalier, A. R., Ferretti, R. P., & Okolo, C. M. (1994). Technology and individual differences. *Journal of Special Education Technology, 12,* 175–181.

Chadsey, J. G., & Sheldon, D. (1998). Moving toward social inclusion in employment and postsecondary settings. In F. R. Rusch & J. G. Chadsey (Eds.), *Beyond high school: Transition from school to work* (pp. 406–438). Belmont, CA: Wadsworth Publishing Company.

Collet-Klingenberg, L. L. (1998). The reality of best practices in transition: A case study. *Exceptional Children, 65,* 67–78.

Cooney, B. F. (2002). Exploring perspectives on transition of youth with disabilities: Voices of young adults, parents, and professionals. *Mental Retardation, 40*, 425–435.

DeFur, S., Getzel, E., & Kregel, J. (1994). Individual transition plans: A work in progress. *Journal of Vocational Rehabilitiation, 4*, 139–145.

DeFur, S. H., Todd-Allen, M., & Getzel, E. E. (2001). Parent participation in the transition planning process. *Career Development for Exceptional Individuals, 24*, 19–36.

Deshler, D. D., Schumaker, J. B., Lenz, B. K., Bugren, J. A., Hock. M. F., Knight, J., & Ehren, B. J. (2001). Ensuring content-area learning by secondary students with learning disabilities. *Learning Disabilities Research and Practice, 16*, 96–108.

Durlak C. M., Rose, E., & Bursuck, W. D. (1994). Preparing high school students with learning disabilities for the transition to postsecondary education: Teaching the skills of self-determination. *Journal of Learning Disabilities, 27*, 51–59.

Eisenman, L. T. (2000). Characteristics and effects of integrated academic and occupational curricula for students with disabilities: A literature review. *Career Development for Exceptional Individuals, 23*, 105–119.

Field, S., & Hoffman, A. (2002). Preparing youth to exercise self-determination: Quality indicators for school environments that promote the acquisition of knowledge, skills, and beliefs related to self-determination. *Journal of Disability Policy Studies, 13*, 113–118.

Field, S., Martin, J., Miller, R., Ward, M., & Wehmeyer, M. (1998). *A practical guide for teaching self-determination.* Reston, VA: Council for Exceptional Children.

Flexer, R. W., Simmons, T. J., Luft, P., & Baer, R. M. (2001). *Transition planning for secondary students with disabilities.* Upper Saddle River, NJ: Merrill/Prentice Hall.

Frank, A. R., & Sitlington, P. L. (2000). Young adults with mental disabilities – does transition planning make a difference? *Education and Training in Mental Retardation and Developmental Disabilities, 35*, 119–134.

Gajar, A. (1998). Postsecondary education. In F. R. Rusch and J. G. Chadsey (Eds.), *Beyond high school: Transition from school to work* (pp. 383–405). Belmont, CA: Wadsworth.

Getzel, E. E., Stodden, R. A., & Briel, R. W. (2001). Pursing postsecondary education opportunities for individuals with disabilities. In P. Wehman (Ed.), *Beyond high school: Transition strategies for young people with disabilities* (pp. 247–260). Baltimore, MD: Paul H. Brookes.

Giangreco, M. F., & Putnam, J. (1991). Supporting the education of students with severe disabilities in regular education environments. In L. H. Meyer, C. A. Peck, & L. Brown (Eds)., *Critical issues in the lives of people with severe disabilities* (pp. 245–270). Baltimore, MD: Paul H. Brookes.

Griffin, C., & Targett, P. S. (2001). Finding jobs for you people with disabilities. In P. Wehman (Ed.), *Life beyond the classroom: Transition strategies for young people with disabilities* (pp. 171–210). Baltimore, MD: Paul H. Brookes.

Grigal, M., Neubert, D. A., & Moon, S. M. (2001). Public school programs for students with significant disabilities in settings. *Education and Training in Mental Retardation and Developmental Disabilities, 36*, 244–254.

Grigal, M., Test, D. W., Beattie, J., & Wood, W. M. (1997). An evaluation of transition components of individualized education programs. *Exceptional Children, 63*, 357–372.

Hagner, D., Rogan, P., & Murphy, S. (1992). Facilitating natural supports in the workplace: Strategies for support consultants. *Journal of Rehabilitation, 58*, 29–34.

Harrower, J. (1999). Educational inclusion of children with severe disabilities. *Journal of Positive Behavioral Interventions, 1*, 215–230.

Hasazi, S. B., Furney, K. S., & Destefano, L. (1999). Implementing the IDEA transition mandates. *Exceptional Children, 65*, 555–566.

Henderson, C. (2001). *College freshman with disabilities: A biennial statistical profile.* Washington, DC: Heath Resource Center.

Hitchings, W. E., Luzzo, D. A., Ristow, R., Horvath, M., Retish, P., & Tanners, A. (2001). The career development needs of college students with learning disabilities: In their own words. *Learning Disabilities Research and Practice, 16*, 8–17.

Horner, R. H., McDonnell, J. J., & Bellamy, G. T. (1986). Teaching generalized skills: General case instruction in simulation and community settings. In R. H. Horner, L. H. Meyer, & H. D. Fredericks (Eds.), *Education of learners with severe handicaps: Exemplary service strategies* (pp. 289–214). Baltimore, MD: Paul H. Brookes.

Houtenville, A. J. (2005). *Disability statistics in the United States.* Ithaca, NY: Cornell University Rehabilitation Research and Training Center. www.disabilitystatistics.org posted May 15, 2003, accessed February 3, 2005.

Hughes, C., & Carter, E. W. (2000). *The transition handbook: Strategies high school teachers use that work!* Baltimore, MD: Paul H. Brookes.

Hunt, P., & Goetz, L. (1997). Research on inclusive educational programs, practices, and outcomes for students with severe disabilities. *The Journal of Special Education, 31*, 3–29.

International Labour Organization (1998). *Education, employment and training policies and programmes for youth with disabilities in four European countries.* Geneva: Author.

Janiga, S. J., & Costenbader, V. (2002). The transition from high school to postsecondary education for students with learning disabilities: A survey of college service coordinators. *Journal of Learning Disabilities, 35,* 462–479.

Johnson, D. R., & Halloran, W. H. (1997). The federal legislative context and goals of the state systems change initiative on transition for youth with disabilities. *Career Development for Exceptional Individuals, 20,* 109–122.

Johnson, D. R., & Sharpe, M. N. (2000). Results of a national survey on the implementation transition services requirements of IDEA of 1990. *Journal of Special Education Leadership, 13,* 5–26.

Johnson, D. R., McGrew, K. S., Bloomberg, L., Bruininks, R. H., & Lin, H. C. (1997). Results of a national follow-up study of young adults with severe disabilities. *Journal of Vocational Rehabilitation, 8,* 119–133.

Kavale, K. A., & Forness, S. R. (1999). *Efficacy of special education and related services.* Washington, DC: American Association on Mental Retardation.

Kohler, P. D. (1998). Implementing a transition perspective: A comprehensive approach to planning and delivering secondary education and transition services. In F. R. Rusch & J. G. Chadsey (Eds.), *Beyond high school: Transition from school to work.* Belmont, CA: Wadsworth Publishing.

Kraemer, B. R., McIntyre, L. L., & Blacher, J. (2003). Quality of life for young adults with mental retardation during transition. *Mental Retardation, 41,* 250–262.

Levine, P., & Nourse, S. W. (1998). What follow-up studies say about postschool life for young men and women with learning disabilities: A critical look at the literature. *Journal of Learning Disabilities, 31,* 212–233.

Mastropieri, M. A., & Scruggs, T. E. (2001). Promoting inclusion in secondary classrooms. *Learning Disability Quarterly, 24,* 265–274.

McDonnell, J. (1998). Instruction for students with severe disabilities in general education settings. *Education and Training in Mental Retardation and Developmental Disabilities, 33,* 199–215.

McDonnell, J. (2004). Secondary programs. In J. McDonnell, M. L. Hardman, & A. P. McDonnell (Eds.), *An introduction to persons with moderate and severe disabilities: Educational and social issues* (pp. 307–330). Boston, MA: Allyn & Bacon.

McDonnell, J., Mathot-Buckner, C., & Ferguson, B. (1996). *Transition programs for students with moderate/severe disabilities.* Pacific Grove, CA: Brooks/Cole Publishing Company.

McLaughlin, M.J., & Rouse, M. (2000). The struggles for reform. In M. J. McLaughlin & M. Rouse (Eds.), *Special education and school reform in the United States and Britain* (pp. 1–10). New York: Routledge.

Merchant, D. J., & Gajar, A., (1997). A review of the literature on self advocacy components in transition programs of students with learning disabilities. *Jour-*

nal of Vocational Rehabilitation, 8, 223–231.

Miner, C. A., & Bates, P. E. (1997). The effect of person centered planning activities on the IEP/Transition planning process. *Education and Training in Mental Retardation and Developmental Disabilities, 32,* 105–112.

Mull, C. A., & Sitlington, P. L. (2003). The role of technology in the transition to postsecondary education of students with learning disabilities: A review of the literature. *The Journal of Special Education, 37,* 26–32.

National Council on Disability (2000). *Transition and post-school outcomes for youth with disabilities: Closing the gaps to education and employment.* Washington, DC: Author.

National Organization on Disability/Harris & Associates (2000*). National Organization on Disability/Harris survey on Americans with disabilities.* New York: Author.

Neubert, D. A., Moon, M. S., Grigal, M., & Redd, V. (2001). Educational practices for individuals with mental retardation and other significant disabilities: A review of the literature. *Journal of Vocational Rehabilitation, 16,* 155–168.

Nisbet, J. (1992). *Natural supports in school, at work and in the community for people with severe disabilities.* Baltimore, MD: Paul H. Brookes.

Nisbet, J., Clark, M., & Covert, S. (1991). Living it up! An analysis of research on community living. In L. H. Meyer, C. A. Peck, & L. Brown (Eds.), *Critical issues in the lives of people with severe disabilities* (pp. 115–144). Baltimore, MD: Paul H. Brookes.

Organisation for Economic Co-operation and Development (1996). *Employment Outlook.* Paris: Author.

Orkwis, R., & McLane, K., (1998). *A curriculum every student can use: Design principles for student access.* ERIC/OSEP Topic Brief. Retrieved January 14, 2004, from http://www.cec.sped.org/osep/udesign.html

Patton, J. R., Cronin, M. E., Veda, J. (1997). Curricular implications of transition: Life skille instruction as an integral part of transition education.. *Remedial and Special Education, 18,* 294–306.

Phelps, L. A., & Hanley-Maxwell, C. (1997). School-to-work transitions for youth with disabilities: A review of outcomes and practices. *Review of Educational Research, 67,* 197–226.

Resnick, L. B. & Wirt, J. G. (1996). *Linking school and work: Roles for standards and assessment.* San Francisco, CA: Jossey-Bass.

Rosenthal-Malek, A., & Bloom, A. (1998). Beyond acquisition: Teaching generalization for students with developmental disabilities. In A. Hilton & R. Ringlaben (Eds.), *Best and promising practices in developmental disabilities* (pp. 139–155). Austin, TX: Pro-Ed.

Salend, S. J., & Garrick-Duhaney, L. M. (1999). The impact of inclusion on students with and without disabilities and their educators. *Remedial and Special*

Education, 20, 114–126.

Salomon. G., (1993). On the nature of pedagogic computer tools: The case for the writing partner. In S. P. Lajoie & S. J. Derry (Eds.), *Computers as cognitive tools* (pp. 179–196). Hillsdale, NJ: Erlbaum.

Sharpe, M. N., & Johnson, D. R. (2001). A 20/20 analysis of postsecondary support characteristics. *Journal of Vocational Rehabilitation, 12*, 169–177.

Siegel, S. (1998). Foundations for a school-to-work system that serves all students. In F. R. Rusch & J. G. Chadsey (Eds.), *Beyond high school: Transition from school to work* (pp. 146–178). New York: Wadsworth Publishing.

Sitlington, P. L. (2003). Postsecondary education: The other transition. *Exceptionality, 11*, 103–113.

Sitlington, P. L., Clark, G. M., & Kolstoe, O. P. (2000). *Transition education and services for adolescents with disabilities* (3rd ed.). Needham Heights, MA: Allyn & Bacon.

Sitlington, P. L., Frank, A. R., & Carson, R. (1992). Adult adjustment among high school graduates with mild disabilities. *Exceptional Children, 59*, 221–233.

Speckman, N. J., Goldberg, R. J., & Herman, H. L., (1992). Learning disabled children grow up: A search for factors related to success in young adult years. *Learning Disabilities Research Practice, 7*, 161–170.

Stodden, R. A., Jones, M. A., & Chang, K. B. T. (2002). *Services, supports, and accommodations for individuals with disabilities: An analysis across secondary education, postsecondary education and employment.* Retrieved May 25, 2004, from www.ncset.hawaii.edu /publications/pdf/services_supports.pdf

Stodden, R. A., Whelley, T., Chang, C., & Harding, T. (2001). Current status of educational support provisions to students with disabilities in postsecondary education. *Journal of Vocational Rehabilitation, 16*, 189–198.

Terman, D. L., Larner, M. B., Stevenson, C. S., & Behrman, R. E. (1996). Special education for students with disabilities: Analysis and recommendations. *Future of Children, 6*, 4–24.

Test, D. W., Mason, C., Hughes, C., Konrad, M., Neale, M., & Wood, W. M. (2004). Student involvement in individualized program meetings. *Exceptional Children, 70*, 391–412.

Thoma, C. A., Rogan, P., & Baker, S. R. (2001). Student involvement in transition planning: Unheard voices. *Education and Training in Mental Retardation and Developmental Disabilities, 36*, 16–29.

Tomlinson, C. (1999). The *differentiated classroom: Responding to the needs of all learners.* Alexandria, VA: ASCD.

Trach, J., & Sheldon, D. (2000). Meeting attendance and transition outcomes as reflected in students' individualized education programs. In D. R. Johnson & E. J. Emanuel (Eds.), *Issues influencing the future of transition program and services in the United States* (pp. 137–152). Minneapolis, MN: University of Minnesota.

United Nations Educational, Scientific, and Cultural Organization (UNESCO) (1994). *World Conference on Special Needs Education: Access and quality.* Salamanca, Spain: Author.

United Nations Educational, Scientific, and Cultural Organization (UNESCO) (2001). *We the children: Meeting the promises of the World Summit for Children.* New York: Author.

Wagner, M., Newman, L., Cameto, R., Levine, P., & Marder, C. (2003, December). *Going to school: Instructional contexts, programs, and participation of secondary school students with disabilities.* Menlo Park, CA: SRI International.

Walker, P. (1999). From community presence to sense of place: Community experiences of adults with developmental disabilities. *Journal of the Association for Persons with Severe Handicaps, 24*, 23–32.

Webb, K. W. (2000). *Transition to postsecondary education: Strategies for students with disabilities.* Austin, TX: PRO-ED.

Wehman, P. (2001). *Life beyond the classroom: Transition strategies for young people with disabilities.* Baltimore, MD: Paul H. Brookes.

Wehman, P., & Revell, W. G. (1997). Transition into supported employment for young adults with severe disabilities: Current practices and future directions. *Journal of Vocational Rehabilitation, 8*, 65–74.

Wehmeyer, M. L., & Palmer, S. B. (2003). Adult outcomes for students with cognitive disabilities three-years after high school: The impact of self-determination. *Education and Training in Developmental Disabilities, 38*, 131–144.

Wehmeyer, M. L., & Schwartz, M. (1997). Self-determination and positive adult outcomes: A follow-up study of youth with mental retardation or learning disabilities. *Exceptional Children, 63*, 245–255.

Wehmeyer, M. L., & Schwartz, M. (1998). The relationship between self-determination, quality of life, and life satisfaction for adults with mental retardation. *Education and Training in Mental Retardation and Developmental Disabilities, 33*, 3–12.

Yelin, E., & Katz, P. (1994). Labor force trends of persons with and without disabilities. *Monthly Labor Review, 117*, 36–42.

29

Postsecondary education

Stan F. Shaw

Students with disabilities have made significant strides toward fulfilling their expectation to be integrated into adult life. In fact, they have the same life objectives (that is, employment success, community participation, and economic security) as students without disabilities (Henderson, 2001). Access to the general education curriculum and transition planning for high school students with disabilities has broadened their awareness of and preparation for postsecondary education. Recent data, however, would also indicate that current graduates from secondary schools across the globe are not adequately prepared and are therefore too often unable to successfully access or complete postsecondary education (Smith-Davis, 2004; Starikova, 2004).

The graduation rates from high school for students with disabilities in the US are about 56 per cent in comparison to 90 per cent of peers without disabilities (US Department of Education, 2002a). Similarly, a study by the Canadian Council on Social Development (2001) reported that in 1998, 36.4 per cent of persons with disabilities, aged 16 to 64, had graduated from a postsecondary program, as compared to 51.4 per cent of persons without a disability. On the other hand, data from the National Center for Education Statistics

(1999) indicate that students with disabilities in the United States who do manage to graduate from college exhibit similar labor market outcomes as their counterparts without disabilities (that is, employment rates and annual salaries of the two groups do not differ significantly). Although the doors to higher education have opened for some students, policies and procedures have not been fully implemented to assure reasonable access for all. The challenge for both postsecondary students with disabilities and the professionals who provide postsecondary supports, therefore, is to assure that students really have access and opportunity. This chapter will review the development of postsecondary access for students with disabilities, describe services and supports, discuss issues and challenges and recommend areas for future research and program development.

BACKGROUND

Disability service development in the US: a historical perspective

Today's programs for postsecondary students with disabilities are the result of major societal events, legislative mandates and the persistence of advocates who recognized that students with disabilities could compete within the postsecondary arena (Madaus, 2000). Higher education was initially provided for students with disabilities who were deaf or blind (Ryan, 1993). After World War I, legislation was passed to assist injured veterans with employment and postsecondary educational programming (Scales, 1986). The primary approach toward equal access was to remove physical barriers for people with mobility and sensory impairments (Madaus, 2000). During the 1960s and 1970s educational institutions and governmental agencies began to acknowledge disability rights, thus setting the stage for dramatic change.

The 1980s saw an increase in numbers of students with hidden disabilities such as learning disabilities (Brinckerhoff, McGuire, & Shaw, 2002). Initially, the Office for Students with Disabilities (OSD), the department with responsibility for supports for students with disabilities, dealt with issues of physical access but a focus on programmatic access was now taking center stage. A surge in enrollment of students with disabilities occurred as a result of the attention brought by the passage of the Americans with Disabilities Act (ADA) in 1990. Students with learning disabilities and students diagnosed with attention deficit disorders (ADHD) were the growth areas in the 1990s, resulting in substantial development and availability of services (Steinberg, 1998; Wiener & Siegel, 1992). The most recent data indicates that the largest disability categories receiving postsecondary services are learning disabilities, ADHD and psychiatric disabilities, in that order (Harbour, 2004).

Prevalence

Students with disabilities are attending college in increasing numbers. According to the National Center for Education Statistics (1999), of those students who graduated from high school in 1992, 63 per cent of all students with disabilities enrolled in college compared to 70 per cent of students who did not have a disability. This postsecondary enrollment has resulted in the percentage of full-time college freshmen with disabilities in the United States increasing from 2.6 per cent in 1978 to 9.2 per cent in 1998 (Henderson, 2001). Canadian offices for students with disabilities reported about 7 per cent of the total enrollment were students with disabilities (Canadian Association of Disability Service Providers in Postsecondary Education, 1999). A large study conducted by the Association on Higher Education and Disability (Harbour, 2004) reported that only 6.1 per cent of the college population were students with disabilities. The lower percentage than previous studies is because the students not only self-identified but were also receiving services as documented students with disabilities. Prevalence in the United Kingdom has gone from 2.0 per cent in 1995 to 5.4 per cent in 2004. Students with dyslexia and other hidden disabilities have grown at a rate similar to that in North America and now represent 61 per cent of college students known to have disabilities (Higher Education Statistics Agency Limited, 2004).

Countries with developing support services and new laws generally have a lower prevalence rate. Only 1 per cent of the college students in Sweden are identified as students with a disability (*Higher Education Accessibility Guide*, 2004) compared to 1.1 per cent in Ireland (Higher Education Authority, 2004) and less than 0.5 per cent in Russia (Perfilyeva, 2003). Given that both transition planning for students with disabilities and access to the general education curriculum are being promoted worldwide (Brinckerhoff et al., 2002; Starikova, 2004; Tonooka, 2002), it can be anticipated that there will be continued growth in numbers of students with disabilities attending postsecondary institutions in the years to come.

Impact of legal mandates on postsecondary education

Legal mandates continue to be the primary driving force behind the growth in programs and services for students with disabilities at the postsecondary level (Dukes, 2001). Passage in the US of Section 504 of the Rehabilitation Act of 1973, for example, provided substantial opportunities for individuals with disabilities. Postsecondary institutions now had the responsibility to ensure 'reasonable accommodations'. Despite concerns about high costs and difficulty implementing these regulations (Ryan, 1993), postsecondary disability services began to gain momentum across college campuses as many institutions created programs and policies for students with disabilities (Madaus, 2000). These laws have worked to enhance the integration and participation of individuals with disabilities in all aspects of society, including the postsecondary arena and competitive employment (Brinckerhoff et al., 2002). In order to gain a better perspective on disability programs and services at the postsecondary level, it is necessary to examine essential legislation that has created these educational opportunities for students with disabilities.

United States

Section 504 of the Rehabilitation Act of 1973 was the first federal civil rights legislation designed to protect the rights of individuals with disabilities. The statute applies to people with disabilities who are viewed as 'otherwise qualified' to participate in and benefit from any program or activity that is receiving federal financial assistance. This law states that it is illegal to deny participation in activities, benefits or programs, or in any way discriminate against a person solely because of a disability (US Department of Education, 2002b). Individuals with disabilities should not only have equal access to programs and services but also auxiliary aids should be provided to individuals with impaired speaking, manual, or sensory skills. Specifically, Subpart E of the Section 504 regulations is applicable to all postsecondary educational programs and activities that receive federal funding (Madaus & Shaw, 2004). The Americans with Disabilities Act (ADA) was promulgated in 1990. Modeled after Section 504 of the Rehabilitation Act of 1973, the ADA is also a civil rights law. It pro-

hibits discrimination on the basis of disability, as long as the person is otherwise qualified. Its greatest impact in higher education was increasing awareness of people with disabilities (Ryan, 1993).

Canada

Canada also recognized the need to ensure equal access. The most notable achievement contributing to this cause was the passage of the Canadian Charter of Rights and Freedoms in 1982. This Charter guarantees Canadians with disabilities fundamental rights similar to those afforded under Section 504 (Brinckerhoff et al., 2002; Hill, 1992). In 1991, the Human Rights Act expanded the coverage of the Charter to include the private sector as well (Madaus, 1996). In Canada, provincial governments are responsible for education, therefore laws regarding students with disabilities vary from province to province (Canadian Association of Disability Service Providers in Postsecondary Education, 1999).

Western Europe

There are many countries, particularly in Western Europe, that have statutes on postsecondary disability services comparable to that of North America. The Special Educational Needs and Disability Act 2001 amended the United Kingdom's (UK) Disability and Discrimination Act of 1995 to include education. Revisions of the Act which took effect on September 1, 2005 added additional requirements to accommodate students with disabilities. It is comparable to Section 504 in its definition of disability, specification of needed reasonable adjustments, and supports for physical and learning access. Laws such as the Universities Act of 1997 in Ireland and the Equal Treatment of Students in Universities Act which took effect in Sweden in 2002 provide similar protections. The *Higher Education Accessibility Guide* (2004) supported by the European Commission describes access to higher education across countries in Europe including Austria, Belgium, Denmark, Finland, France, Germany, Italy, and Spain. Services for postsecondary students with disabilities in these countries may include disability services offices, testing modifications, scholarships or other resource allocation, distance learning, and physical and learning accommodations. It is clear that postsecondary disability policies and procedures are now undergoing rapid development in Western Europe.

Other countries

Tonooka (2002), in describing the development of supports for college students with disabilities in Japan, exemplifies the challenging worldwide effort to foster equal access to higher education for students with disabilities. Problems with college admissions, support services, lodging and social relationships resulted in the formation of the National Support Center for Students with Disabilities in 1999. The Center works to 'ban discrimination against students with disabilities such as denial of opportunities including application, entrance examinations and admission to the university' (Tonooka, 2002, p. 3). The Center provides Japanese students with a database of universities or colleges regarding applications and acceptance conditions, campus facilities, and supporting services, in spite of limited legal mandates.

While Russia has a disability law that offers access to higher education, it is discriminatory in that it lowers standards for students with disabilities. As a result, it creates a social stigma that individuals with disabilities are 'weak and helpless' (Starikova, 2004, p. 3). This problem arises from pre-university educational policy that isolates students with disabilities in special schools where they do not get an education that would allow them to be competitive in postsecondary education. Lienteva (2003) notes, disabled people seeking a college education 'typically experience fear, feelings of uncertainty, and torturous doubts, because they well know that higher education institutions are not ready to accept students with disabilities' (p. 1). Many of today's services are grounded in the legal requirements of disability law. The intent of these laws is to provide a framework that

ensures individuals with disabilities have full participation in all aspects of society, including the postsecondary setting (Brinckerhoff et al., 2002). The challenge is to both fulfill the legal mandates and provide services that actually provide reasonable access for students. Komardjaja (2002), although speaking only about Indonesia, noted the worldwide problem that laws that intend to facilitate access are often negated by weak implementation allowing for continued institutional, architectural and attitudinal barriers.

POSTSECONDARY SERVICES IN THE US FOR STUDENTS WITH DISABILITIES

Postsecondary options

A wide range of educational and vocational opportunities is now available to young adults with disabilities. The educational alternatives available after high school include four-year colleges and universities, junior and community colleges, vocational or technical schools, social development and life skills centers, thirteenth year programs, home study, and adult education (McGuire & Shaw, 1987).

Community colleges serve a larger proportion of students with disabilities than any other segment of postsecondary education (Henderson, 2001). The attraction of community colleges is greatest for students with disabilities who would like to attempt some college work while simultaneously maintaining the support of friends and the familiar routines of living at home. Since community colleges often have open admissions policies, smaller class ratios, comparatively low tuition fees, academic and personal counseling, and a wide range of vocational, remedial, and developmental courses, they are a logical and advantageous first step for many students with disabilities (Bursuck, Rose, Cowen, & Yahaya, 1989; Cocchi, 1997). As more students with disabilities are successfully included in the general education curriculum, they are increasing their participation in four-year colleges and universities and professional and graduate schools. Students with disabilities need to review their disability documentation data to help determine which postsecondary option is most appropriate and realistic for them. Most disability laws, like Section 504 and the ADA, require the student to demonstrate that they have a disability (which is particularly important for the increasing numbers of students with hidden disabilities) and provide data on the need for specific accommodations and supports (Shaw, 2005). The following section will discuss that process.

Disability documentation

The reason for documentation is that postsecondary institutions have the need to assure that only qualified individuals with significant impairments receive accommodations and supports. Furthermore, most college Offices for Students with Disabilities do not have personnel with expertise in assessment. In order to obtain information on the current impact of a student's disability, demonstrate that the student is qualified, and justify the need for accommodations, postsecondary personnel typically adhere to documentation guidelines that foster the provision of needed information. The guidelines were meant to specify frameworks that provide adequate disability documentation and assure an appropriate match between the student's needs and the accommodations and supports provided (Madaus & Madaus, 2001). An important outcome of the guidelines has been to limit appropriate accommodations and services only to students who have documented disabilities.

Students with disabilities must provide the assessment data needed to document a disability and justify supports and accommodations in postsecondary education. Secondary personnel have limited responsibility to conduct transition assessment and may be unlikely to provide the diagnostic information needed by students entering postsecondary education. This problem is further exacerbated by the different expectations for appropriate 'documentation' between sec-

ondary and postsecondary education (Shaw, 2005). Secondary schools are moving toward more functional data (for example, Summary of Performance, Response To Intervention, portfolio assessment, curriculum-based assessment) that specifies student academic progress, student learning, as well as use and effectiveness of accommodations. Postsecondary personnel, on the other hand, have increasingly required comprehensive psycho-educational evaluations as the basis for the disability determination. The recent passage of the Individuals with Disabilities Education Act of 2004 in the US, which specifies a performance summary instead of a comprehensive evaluation for students who transition from high school, will require additional policy development to bridge the differences between high school assessment and postsecondary documentation needs (Shaw, 2005).

POSTSECONDARY DISABILITY POLICIES AND PROCEDURES

As the field of postsecondary services for students with disabilities advances and issues regarding equal access to educational opportunities become more complex, postsecondary institutions need to engage in ongoing review of their disability policies and procedures (Brinckerhoff et al., 2002). Legal challenges and judicial decisions reinforce the critical need for clearly articulated written policies and procedures as a component of every postsecondary institution's compliance. Regardless of the manner by which services are provided for students with disabilities, institutions of higher education are on tenuous ground if they have not established policies and procedures that address the statutory responsibilities stipulated in the regulations. Furthermore, policy is not a static commodity. It is a roadmap that should periodically be reviewed within the context of evolving developments in the field, and emerging 'best practices' (Shaw & Dukes, 2006).

Institutional policies must assure nondiscriminatory treatment of qualified students with disabilities in their recruitment, admissions, academic programs, and nonacademic services. Academic adjustments and auxiliary aids must be available on a case-by-case basis to enable students with disabilities to compete more fairly with their peers who do not have disabilities. At the same time, colleges and universities may not be required to compromise standards, nor do they need to fundamentally alter programs or specific degrees by changing essential requirements (Brinckerhoff et al., 2002; Heyward, Lawton, & Associates, 1995).

Each institution must determine the level and scope of its policies including (a) institutional responsibility to assure equal access; (b) responsibility for the determination of accommodations; (c) confidentiality; (d) course substitutions; (e) full-time student status with less than full-time credit load; and (f) appeals of accommodation decisions. Other policy issues often included are rights and responsibilities of students and the institution; eligibility for financial aid; procedures for accessing services; and discrimination complaint procedures (Shaw & Dukes, 2006).

Program standards

The 1990s saw perhaps the greatest advances in addressing the needs of the disability profession. Guidelines were adopted and promoted by the international Association on Higher Education and Disability (AHEAD). Specifically, these guidelines include: professional standards (Shaw, McGuire, & Madaus, 1997) which identify the skills and knowledge required of service providers and define the profession as a whole; a code of ethics (Price, 1997) which frame guidelines for professional behavior; and program standards and performance indicators (Shaw & Dukes, 2001, in press) which provide researched-based guidance to Offices for Students with Disabilities.

The recently approved *AHEAD Program Standards* (Shaw & Dukes, 2006) include 90 Performance Indicators that specify 'best practices' for how the Standards can be fulfilled. There are now essential expectations for *all* postsecondary institutions in terms of minimum supports that should be available to provide equal access for students with disabilities. The Standards do not limit institutions that wish to provide supports they think are necessary for their population of students (for example, remedial coursework at a community college) or unique elements that they choose to provide (for example, summer transition program or diagnostic services). However, there is now a benchmark to review when postsecondary institutions consider availability of appropriate supports, program evaluation, staff development or program development needs. In addition, consumers now have a clear basis for reviewing the availability of supports and services (Shaw & Dukes, 2006).

Providing accommodations and supports

The National Center for Education Statistics (1999) conducted a survey of institutions in the United States to determine how they respond to students with disabilities' expectations for support services and/or accommodations. They reported that almost all (98 per cent) of the institutions that enrolled students with disabilities had provided at least one support service or accommodation to a student with disabilities. Most institutions (88 per cent) had provided alternative exam formats or additional time, and 77 per cent provided tutors to assist with ongoing coursework. Readers, classroom note-takers, or scribes were provided by 69 per cent of the institutions, and registration assistance or priority class registration was provided by 62 per cent. Institutions also frequently provided adaptive equipment or technology, such as assistive listening devices or talking computers (58 per cent), and textbooks on tape (55 per cent). Sign language interpreters/translators were provide by 45 per cent of the institutions, and course substitutions or waivers by 42 per cent.

A survey of the largely North American membership of AHEAD (Harbour, 2004) identified the following services being offered at more than two-thirds of the institutions represented:

- on-line educational services or training
- adaptive technology or computer center
- document conversion (for example, print to Braille)
- study abroad/international student exchange counseling
- transition services or orientation for new students.

According to a study completed in 1999 by the Canadian Association of Disability Service Providers in Postsecondary Education, 75 per cent of postsecondary institutions have developed formal disability and accommodation policies covering such matters as admissions, alternative academic accommodations, service accommodations, procedural considerations, and undue hardship.

Colleges in Ireland provide preferential access to computers and free photocopying in over 50 per cent of their institutions. Extra time to complete coursework, provision for copying lecture notes and permission to tape lectures are each available in more than 70 per cent of the colleges. Physical access, however, is only available in 85 per cent of new buildings and 39 per cent of refurbished buildings. On campus accommodation units are only 6 per cent accessible to wheelchair users and 27 per cent are accessible to blind or visually impaired users (Higher Education Authority, 2004). Swedish institutions of higher education each have a coordinator for students with disabilities who is responsible for putting together an individualized 'package' of support services. Services might include a campus or personal assistant, sign language interpreting, and compensatory education support. These coordinators also work with faculty and other college personnel to provide effective services and accommodations (*Higher Education Accessibility Guide*, 2004). Icelandic universities provide a standard format for accommodations information so students with disabilities know what is available at each institution. Typical services include special examination arrangements, facilities and services for those with restricted mobility, computer facilities for the blind and dyslexic and classroom assistance (*Higher*

Education Accessibility Guide, 2004). Recent research has noted the need to foster independence and self-determination when providing supports for students with disabilities (Field, Sarver, & Shaw, 2003).

Too often dependence-provoking supports such as content tutoring and course waivers and substitutions not supported by assessment data have been provided (Cullen, Shaw, & McGuire, 1996; Yost, Shaw, Cullen, & Bigaj, 1994). These practices may have helped the student receive passing grades but not necessarily learn. It is important to acknowledge, however, that supports and accommodations requested by a student that meet a documented need and which enhance student learning can be productive. On the other hand, providing instruction in note taking or role-playing various scenarios where the student self-advocates to faculty, though more time-consuming, fosters independence and, possibly, reduction in the need for support services over time. Brinckerhoff et al. (2002) suggest a guide for determining the efficacy of student supports is 'that if students who have received disability services for several semesters function in the same dependent way as they did when they entered, close examination of the program's philosophy and commitment to fostering independence is warranted' (p. 489). Field et al. (2003) emphasize that the needed supports for self-determination may vary greatly on an individual basis. Examples of individualized supports that are generally consistent with self-determination include activities such as providing students with information, listening as a student verbalizes plans, helping a student identify options, encouraging a student to make choices, and asking questions that help students reflect on and learn from the self-determination process. The ADHD coaching process has the potential to be an effective model for encouraging these behaviors (Parker, 2004). The new AHEAD Program Standards and Performance Indicators have for the first time specifically noted that Offices for Students with Disabilities need to have a mission and policies that foster self-determination (Shaw & Dukes, 2006). It is essential that postsecondary personnel have the skills and training to provide appropriate supports and accommodations.

Personnel serving students with disabilities in the US

Office for Students with Disabilities (OSD)

Data collected by Whelley (2002) confirm that disability personnel are, too often, learning on the job. Whelley goes on to assert that OSD professionals typically do not have access to a well-articulated program of study. In fact, there are only three or four programs that actually prepare postsecondary disability personnel (Brinckerhoff et al., 2002). Data have shown that disability personnel receive training from a diverse array of disciplines that typically have not been focused specifically on adult students with disabilities (Dukes & Shaw, 1999; Harbour, 2004). There is clearly a need for staff development for the many postsecondary disability professionals who do not have adequate skills to effectively do their jobs. A training program in Postsecondary Disability Services should offer courses or modules that fulfill the needs specified in the professional standards for postsecondary disability personnel (Shaw, McGuire & Madaus, 1997). The required courses could include the following: The Role and Function of Postsecondary Disability Personnel; Assessment, Documentation and Determination of Accommodations; Collaboration and Staff Development; Legal and Ethical Issues; and a Practicum in Postsecondary Disability Services (Brinckerhoff et al., 2002). It is also imperative that faculty members understand their roles and responsibilities including how to efficiently provide reasonable accommodations.

Faculty

Although personnel and services are often in place to foster access to postsecondary education for students with disabilities, unless teaching faculty are ready to provide a pro-

ductive learning experience, students with disabilities will continue to lag behind their peers without disabilities in receiving the diplomas and credentials necessary for adult success (Brinckerhoff et al., 2002). While expectations of faculty were once to merely acknowledge that accommodations must be permitted for students with disabilities (Jastram, 1979; Stewart, 1989), expectations for faculty now reflect a much broader ownership of disability issues on campus.

Faculty will continue to need information pertaining to disabilities, support services, and the law (Shaw & Scott, 2003). In addition, there is a critical need for data-based approaches and innovation in faculty development initiatives to keep pace with the ever-changing landscape in higher education. Salzberg et al. (2002) noted that disability services professionals continue to see the importance of providing faculty training in the areas of campus services, legal foundations, and characteristics of disabilities, but in keeping with evolving faculty roles, expand the list of desired topics to include considering ethical issues and designing accommodations. Topics identified by disability services professionals as on the horizon of faculty training needs include accessibility of distance education and implementation of universal design in curriculum and instruction.

FUTURE DIRECTIONS FOR RESEARCH AND PRACTICE

Challenges within the profession include assessing program effectiveness, supporting student independence and self-advocacy, and fostering access to learning. Given competition for resources at most institutions of higher education, the need for implementing evidence-based practice is critical. This section will review some of the issues facing postsecondary services for students with disabilities and propose a research agenda that will provide the data needed to advance the field.

Universal design

The primary means to assure equal access to instruction for college students with disabilities has been to provide accommodations. Although accommodations are often a necessary and appropriate means to provide access, they can foster a number of problematic dynamics, particularly for the growing number of students with hidden disabilities. Field et al. (2003) have noted that providing accommodations requires faculty to make time-consuming and difficult modifications for individual students. Most important, it forces students to disclose their disability to faculty semester after semester, to specify their disabilities and limitations and to request 'special' treatment (that is, reasonable accommodations). Although access to accommodations is guaranteed by the law, 'it is often a frustrating, embarrassing, unpleasant, stigmatizing, and unending process for students with disabilities' (Field et al., 2003, p. 346).

An approach to instruction that seeks to overcome these problems is universal design. The general concept of universal design (UD) includes a specific set of principles to systematically incorporate accessible features into a design instead of retrofitting changes or accommodations. As it is applied in the field of architecture, UD results in the creation of environments and products that are as usable, as much as possible, by a wide range of diverse individuals (McGuire, Scott, & Shaw, 2006). Legislation has fostered the application of universal design in architecture (for example, providing curb cuts, ramps, doors that open automatically, accessible bathrooms) so that all people, including those with physical disabilities, can access stores, schools and other facilities. Scott, McGuire, and Shaw (2003) developed a more inclusive paradigm for teaching by adapting the framework of UD and its principles to reflect the instructional practices that have been acknowledged as effective with students with disabilities.

Therefore, just as a student in a wheelchair needs *no* disability services in such a physically accessible environment, a student with a learning disability may not need disability services in an *instructionally accessible environment*. Universal design for instruction (UDI) anticipates the needs of diverse learners and incorporates effective strategies into curriculum and instruction to make learning more accessible (Scott et al., 2003). Such an environment will obviously foster student self-determination because options are available that allow the student to select personally productive approaches to learning (Field et al., 2003). Efforts to improve campus instruction should be given as high a priority as providing physical access was in previous decades. This approach has great appeal but requires careful study to determine and validate its efficacy (McGuire, et al., 2006).

Evidence-based practice

Although postsecondary supports for students with disabilities have been more available in recent years, little research has addressed the planning and organization of these services (Brinckerhoff et al., 2002; Shaw, McGuire, & Brinckerhoff, 1994). Service providers have, therefore, been left to develop programming for their students based on little or no empirical evidence (Gajar, 1992). Many studies have called for a more systematic approach to service provision for postsecondary students with disabilities (Hill, 1996; Shaw & Dukes, 2006). Though the growth in services for these students likely indicates a sincere desire to meet the needs of this cohort, services must be 'grounded in theory or supported by evaluation data' (McGuire, Norlander, & Shaw, 1990, p. 71) in order to be most effective.

The changing nature of postsecondary disability services has created a new and challenging environment for service providers. There are a greater number of students to serve, fewer resources, more complex accommodation needs, and most important, a greater potential for conflict and litigation (Heyward, 1998). Providing services to students with disabilities at the postsecondary level has evolved from being straightforward and student oriented with minimal programmatic influence, to being more complex and having substantial program impact (Heyward, 1998). The Office for Students with Disabilities is faced with providing quality service that is appropriate for the individual student, cost effective, and that adheres to legal mandates. Therefore, evaluating one's program in this era of accountability demonstrates a commitment to professional standards and establishes an objective foundation for supporting and, possibly, expanding services. As reform efforts lead to a loss of programming for children with disabilities when the efficacy of services cannot be supported by data, service providers in Offices for Students with Disabilities are well advised to embrace this impetus for implementing program evaluations as a routine component of professional practice (Parker, Shaw, & McGuire, 2003).

Future research

The postsecondary disability field is ever changing due to its relative youth, the disability categories (for example, psychiatric, ADHD, Asperger's syndrome) on the increase in recent years, and the non-prescriptive nature of its legal foundation that is being regularly redefined by the courts. These realities, combined with personnel who have limited postsecondary disability training and who are often relatively new to the profession, speak to the need for evidence-based interventions. Although the numbers of postsecondary 'consultants' and conferences have been increasing, there is a dearth of evidence-based training because there is little data on effective practices (Brinckerhoff et al., 2002). Postsecondary disability services are in need of field-based research that is shared with personnel serving this population. Governmental agencies need to broaden their focus beyond elementary and secondary education to invest in research efforts to identify effective interventions for students with disabilities at the postsecondary level. Opportunities already abound for researchers to implement studies with this population with whom very little empirical research has been conducted.

Basic questions that call for data based answers include:

- What accommodations are both 'reasonable' and productive?
- What assessment data is minimally necessary to document a disability and determine appropriate accommodations?
- Which instructional approaches (for example, strategic instruction, social skills training) are most effective?
- What effect will the increasing reliance on high stakes testing have on access to postsecondary education?
- Are some approaches to faculty development more productive than others?
- Is content tutoring a viable means to enhance student learning?
- What services yield better outcomes in terms of grade point average, graduation, and employment?
- To what extent do information technology, and specifically, assistive technology, impact student outcomes?
- What is the efficacy of new approaches such as coaching or universal design for instruction?

CONCLUSION

Access to postsecondary education for students with disabilities is a demonstrated successful outcome of public school law and policy that has provided a free appropriate education for students with disabilities, encouraged their placement in inclusive settings and supported access to the general education curriculum. Postsecondary disability program development, particularly over the last two decades, has provided for access to postsecondary education for students with disabilities which approaches that of students without disabilities. Now that a college degree is becoming the basis for competing in the global economy in the twenty-first century, it is critical that the efficacy of postsecondary supports and services be demonstrated. Special educators need to focus more attention and resources on research and program evaluation to assure that the promise of postsecondary education becomes a reality.

REFERENCES

Brinckerhoff, L.C., McGuire, J.M., & Shaw, S.F. (2002). *Postsecondary education and transition for college students with learning disabilities* (2nd ed.). Austin, TX: PRO-ED.

Bursuck, W.D., Rose, E., Cowen, S., & Yahaya, A. (1989). Nationwide survey of postsecondary education services for students with learning disabilities. *Exceptional Children, 56*, 236–245.

Canadian Association of Disability Service Providers in Postsecondary Education (1999). *Towards developing professional standards of service: A report on support for students with disabilities in postsecondary education in Canada.* Author. Retrieved September 8, 2004, from http://www.cadsppe.cacuss.ca/english/CADSPPE -Standards/CADSPPE-Standards.html

Canadian Council on Social Development (2001). *Disability Information Sheet Number 2.* Retrieved September 8, 2004, from http://www.ccsd.ca/drip/research/ suppl.html

Cocchi, W. (1997). The community college choice. *Postsecondary LD Report, 1*(3).

Cullen, J. P., Shaw, S. F., & McGuire, J. M. (1996). Practitioner support of self-advocacy among college students with learning disabilities: A comparison of practice and attitudes. *Journal of Postsecondary Education and Disability, 12*, 2–15.

Dukes, L. L. (2001). The process: Development of AHEAD Program Standards. *Journal of Postsecondary Education and Disability, 14*, 62–80.

Dukes, L,. & Shaw, S. F. (1999). Postsecondary disability personnel: Professional standards and staff development. *Journal of Developmental Education, 23*(1), 26–31.

Field, S., Sarver, M. & Shaw, S. (2003). Self-Determination: A key to success in postsecondary education for students with learning disabilities. *Remedial and Special Education, 24*, 339–349.

Gajar, A. (1992). Adults with learning disabilities: Current and future research priorities. *Journal of Learning Disabilities, 25*, 507–519.

Harbour, W. S. (2004). *The 2004 AHEAD survey of higher education disability service providers.* Waltham, MA: AHEAD.

Henderson, C. (Ed.). (2001). *College freshmen with disabilities: A biennial statistical profile.* Washington, DC: American Council on Education.

Heyward, Lawton, & Associates. (1995). Faculty members and service providers: The unhappy alliance. *Disability Accommodations Digest, 4*(3 & 4), 1–4.

Heyward, S. (1998). *Disability and higher education: Guidance for Section 504 and ADA compliance.* Horsham, PA: LRP Publications.

Higher Education Accessibility Guide. (2004). Belgium: European Agency for Development in Special Needs Education. Retrieved April 21, 2004, from http://www.european-agency.org/heag

Higher Education Authority. (2004). *Survey on participation rates of and provision for students with disabilities in higher education for the academic year 1998/99.* Dublin: Government Publications Sales Office.

Higher Education Statistics Agency Limited. (2004). *Disabled students in higher education.* Retrieved April 21, 2004, from http://www.hesa.ac.uk/holisdocs/pubinfo/student

Hill, J. L. (1992). Accessibility: Students with disabilities in universities in Canada. *Canadian Journal of Higher Education, 22*, 48–83.

Hill, J. (1996). Speaking out: Perceptions of students with disabilities regarding adequacy of services and willingness of faculty to make accommodations. *Journal of Postsecondary Education and Disability, 12*(1), 22–43.

Jastram, P. (1979). The faculty role: New responsibilities for program access. In M. Redden (Ed.), *New directions for higher education: Assuring access for the handicapped* (No. 25, pp. 11–22). San Francisco, CA: Jossey-Bass.

Komardjaja, I. (2002). The inclusion of people with disabilities in income generation in Indonesia. *Disability World.* Retrieved August 17, 2005, from www. disabilityworld.org/cgi-bin/db/db.cgi

Lienteva, L. (2003). Russia: Getting a college education in Yekaterinburg. *Disability World.* Retrieved August 17, 2005, from www.disabilityworld.org/06–0803/ children/russia.shtml

Madaus, J. W. (1996). *Administration of postsecondary Offices for Students with Disabilities: Perceptions of essential job functions.* Unpublished doctoral dissertation, University of Connecticut, Storrs.

Madaus, J. W. (2000). Services for college and university students with disabilities: A historical perspective. *Journal of Postsecondary Education and Disability, 14*(1), 23–38.

Madaus, J. W., & Madaus, M. R. (2001). Effective documentation practices at the postsecondary level. *Learning Disabilities: A Multidisciplinary Journal, 1*, 31–35.

Madaus, J. W., & Shaw, S. F. (2004). Section 504: The differences in the regulations regarding secondary and postsecondary education. *Intervention in School and Clinic, 40*, 81–87.

McGuire, J. M., & Shaw, S. F. (1987). A decision-making process for the college-bound student: Matching learner, institution, and support program. *Learning Disability Quarterly, 10*, 106–111.

McGuire, J. M., Norlander, K. A., & Shaw, S. F. (1990). Postsecondary education for students with learning disabilities: Forecasting challenges for the future. *Learning Disabilities Focus, 5*, 69–74.

McGuire. J. M., Scott, S. S., & Shaw, S. F. (2006). Universal design and its application in educational environments. *Remedial and Special Education, 27*(3), 166–175.

National Center for Education Statistics. (1999). *Students with disabilities in postsecondary education: A profile of preparation, participation and outcomes.* NCES 1999–187. Washington, DC: US Department of Education.

Parker, D. R. (2004). *Voices of self-determined college students with ADHD: Undergraduates' perceptions of factors that influence their academic success.* Unpublished doctoral dissertation, University of Connecticut, Storrs.

Parker, D. R., Shaw, S. F., & McGuire, J. M. (2003). Program evaluation for postsecondary disability services. *Journal of Developmental Education, 27,* 2–10.

Perfilyeva, M. (2003). *Disability World,* No. 20. Retrieved August 17, 2005, from www.disabilityworld.org/09–1003/children/russia.shtml

Price, L. A. (1997). The development and implementation of a code of ethical behavior for postsecondary personnel. *Journal of Postsecondary Education and Disability, 12*(3), 36–44.

Ryan, D. (1993). *The Federal Government and higher education for students with disabilities.* Retrieved August 22, 2005, from http://www.eric.ed.gov:80/ERICWebPortal/Home.portal?_nfpb=true&ERICExtSearch_SearchValue_0=Higher+Education+for+Students+with+Disabilities&ERICExtSearch_SearchType_0=kw&_pageLabel=RecordDetails&objectId=0900000b8013944a

Salzberg, C., Peterson, L., Debrand, C., Blair, R., Carsey, A., & Johnson, A. (2002). Opinions of disability services directors on faculty training: The need, content, issues, formats, media, and activities. *Journal of Postsecondary Education and Disability, 15,* 101–114.

Scales, W. (1986). Postsecondary education for disabled students. *AHSSPPE Bulletin, 4*(1), 20–32.

Scott, S. S., McGuire, J. M., & Shaw, S. F. (2003). Universal design for instruction: A new paradigm for adult instruction in postsecondary education. *Remedial and Special Education, 24,* 369–379.

Shaw, S. F. (2005). IDEA will change the face of postsecondary disability documentation. *Disability Compliance for Higher Education, 11*(1), 7.

Shaw, S. F., & Dukes, L. L. (2001). Program standards for disability services in higher education. *Journal of Postsecondary Education and Disability, 14*(2), 81–90.

Shaw, S. F., & Dukes, L. L. (2006). Postsecondary disability program standards and performance indicators: minimum essentials for the Office of Students with Disabilities, *Journal of Postsecondary Education and Disability, 19*(1), 14–24.

Shaw, S. F., & Scott, S. S. (2003). New directions in faculty development. *Journal of Postsecondary Education and Disability, 17*(1), 3–9.

Shaw, S. F., McGuire, J. M., & Brinckerhoff, L. C. (1994). College and university programming. In P. J. Gerber & H. B. Reiff (Eds.), *Learning disabilities in adulthood: Persisting problems and evolving issues* (pp. 141–151). Stoneham, MA: Butterworth-Heinemann.

Shaw, S. F., McGuire, J. M., & Madaus, J. W. (1997). Standards of professional practice. *Journal of Postsecondary Education and Disability, 12*(3), 26–35.

Smith-Davis, J. (2004). Transition from school to employment or college: New online information from European Countries. *Teaching Exceptional Children, 36*(5), 59.

Special Educational Needs and Disability Act 2001. Learning and Skills Council. Retrieved August 18, 2004, from www.lsc.gov.uk

Starikova, I. (2004). *Policies of inclusion of disabled students in Russia. Central European University Center for Policy Studies.* Retrieved August 17, 2005, from http://pdc.ceu.hu/archive/00001753/01/Starikova.pdf

Steinberg, H. (1998). Moving along the program continuum: From LD to AD/HD. In P. Quinn & A. McCormick (Eds.), *Re-thinking AD/HD: A guide for fostering success in students with AD/HD at the college level* (pp. 8–13). Bethesda, MD: Advantage Books.

Stewart, A. (1989). *The postsecondary LD primer: A training manual for service providers.* (USDOE, OSERS, Grant # G00830151–88.) Cullowhee, NC: Western Carolina University.

Tonooka, T. (2002). Japan: Supporting students with disabilities. *Disability World,* No. 16. Retrieved June 22, 2005, from http://www.disabilityworld.org/11-1202/il/japan.shtml

US Department of Education. (2002a). *Twenty-third Annual Report to Congress on the implementation of the Individuals with Disabilities Education Act.* Washington, DC.

US Department of Education. (2002b). *Students with disabilities preparing for postsecondary education: Know your rights and responsibilities.* Washington, DC: Office for Civil Rights.

Whelley, T. (2002, July). *Characteristics of disability support personnel in postsecondary education.* Manoa, HI: National Center for the Study of Postsecondary Educational Supports.

Wiener, J., & Siegel, L. (1992). A Canadian perspective on learning disabilities. *Journal of Learning Disabilities, 25,* 340–350, 371.

Yost, D. S., Shaw, S. F., Cullen, J., & Bigaj, S. J. (1994). Practices and attitudes of postsecondary LD services providers in North America. *Journal of Learning Disabilities, 27,* 631–640.

30

Lifelong learning and quality of life

Lesley Dee

INTRODUCTION

The rhetoric of lifelong learning has become familiar throughout the developed world – broadly speaking it describes a cradle to grave approach to learning which according to Green, 'implies the distribution of learning opportunities throughout the lifetime' (2000, p. 35). So the term is increasingly understood to encompass schooling as well as tertiary, higher and continuing education.

Why is lifelong learning important? Lifelong learning opportunities serve both economic and social purposes through enabling and supporting people to keep pace with and adapt to worldwide changes in society and the growth of the global economy. While this chapter is written from a largely UK perspective many of the central ideas reflect international concerns about the nature of lifelong learning. The Organisation for Economic Co-operation and Development (OECD, 2004, p. 1) suggests that the concept has four central features:

- Lifelong learning covers the whole life cycle and comprises all forms of formal and informal learning.
- The learner is central to the process.
- The motivation to learn is fundamental to life-

long learning and is fostered through 'learning to learn'.
- Personal goals for learning may change over time and will encompass all aspects of our lives.

The quality of people's lives may be enhanced through participating in lifelong learning. The concept of quality of life is difficult to define and can mean different things for different people in different settings and at different points in their lives. As Schalock and Alonso (2002) remind us, the concept is not new but dates back to Grecian times when philosophers debated the nature of happiness and the 'good life'. In the 1980s and 1990s, as people with learning difficulties began to leave longstay hospitals to live in the community, more attention began to be paid on how to judge the quality of their lives. There have been many attempts, mainly in the US literature, to define exactly what is meant by quality of life. Schalock and Alonso (2002) conclude that both objective and subjective measures can be used derived from the following domains: physical and material well-being; personal development and self-determination; social inclusion and interpersonal relationships; emotional well-being.

PARTICIPATION IN LIFELONG LEARNING AND QUALITY OF LIFE

The following extract from the Year 12 transition plan review of a student with learning difficulties throws up a number of fundamental questions about the nature of special provision and its relationship to quality of life and lifelong learning that forms the focus of this chapter:

Mrs Lewis	I'm not the problem, it's his Dad. He can't let him walk to school. He's worried about him. He wraps them up in cotton wool to make him feel better.
Teacher	Malcolm's probably not being stretched, this is the problem.
Deputy Head	What will happen when Malcolm's 40?
Malcolm	Yeah!

The deputy headteacher's comments belie her exasperation and concerns about Malcolm's long-term future prospects and his quality of life while Malcolm's own frustration is powerfully contained in the only word he utters, 'Yeah!' But before exploring Malcolm's situation in more depth I want to locate this particular instance in a broader discussion on quality of life and lifelong learning policy and implementation issues. In this chapter I argue that the concept of lifelong learning and its implications for the quality of life of young people and adults who experience difficulties in learning is not well understood.

Quality of life

While much of the literature on quality of life has been concerned with the measurement of the quality of the lives of adults with learning difficulties some authors such as Robertson (1998) and Holst (2000) have argued that the concept is more important as a sensitizing tool. Robertson sees the aim of education as enabling children and young people with learning difficulties to grow into adults who can make choices about their own lives without dictating what a good life might be, while

Holst argues that it is important to avoid the 'tyranny of the normal' by recognising that different people have different ideas about what constitutes the 'good life'. Quality of life can thus be conceptualised in different ways:

- as a means of measuring the quality of services
- as a way of increasing people's involvement and participation in shaping their own lives
- as a political tool to influence policy makers and service providers (Dee, Byers, Hayhoe, & Maudslay, 2002).

Research into the contribution of education to quality of life, however defined, is very limited and any writing that exists is largely limited to schooling and theoretical discussions of ideas rather than empirical enquiry (Hegarty, 1994; Schalock & Alonso, 2002). In addition writing in relation to adults and quality of life tends to focus on those with severe intellectual impairments. The needs of the wider group of adults, including those such as Malcolm who experienced difficulties in learning at school but who tend not to qualify for support from adult services, fall outside the focus of much of this literature.

However Park, Turnbull and Turnbull (2002) have drawn attention to the link between disability, poverty and the quality of life in families, a fact also noted by the UK government's recent report *Improving the Life Chances of Disabled People* (Cabinet Office, 2005). Park et al. define *family* quality of life as 'a) having their needs met, b) enjoying their life together as a family and c) having opportunities to pursue and achieve goals that are meaningful to them' (2002, p. 153). Like Park et al. the UK report concludes that poverty can lead to disability but that disability can also lead to poverty and consequently a poor quality of life. 'Poor outcomes are both a cause and a consequence of disability' (2005, p. 15). Having a low income, poor housing and a poor quality of life can lead to disadvantage and disability, while having a disability can lead to disadvantage.

In the next four sections I consider the characteristics of lifelong learning and their links to quality of life.

Learning across the life cycle

In the UK the numbers of young people remaining in education and training beyond the statutory school leaving age of 16 have risen to around 75 per cent over the last 25 years (OECD, 2004). Despite this the country has one of the lowest staying-on rates among the members of the OECD. Mirroring this trend, the numbers of young people with a range of learning difficulties participating in further education and training have also increased. The reasons for these increases are complex and must be seen in the light of seismic shifts in the labour market and the demands for a more highly skilled workforce alongside changes in how access to further and higher education is now regarded, no longer based on selection but expectation. The effects of these changes on young people with special educational needs have been particularly noticeable. For example in 1982 Walker found that employment rates among 18-year-olds with and without learning difficulties or disabilities were broadly similar (66 per cent). However, while the remainder without disabilities were in some form of education or training, those with learning difficulties or disabilities were at home or attending social services day centres. Twenty-five years on the DfES's longitudinal survey of post-school destinations for young people with special educational needs (Dewson, Aston, Bates, Ritchie, & Dyson, 2004) found that nearly half of the 17- and 18-year-olds were still at school or college while 28 per cent were in employment. Comparisons between studies of this nature are difficult because of differences in how the target groups are defined and the sampling strategies. Nevertheless what these two studies show quite clearly is the rise in the number of learners with special educational needs remaining in further education and training. Yet the worth and quality of much of this provision have been challenged. Young people participate in education and training programmes, often moving on from one to another, not as a means of progression to

employment and perhaps a better quality of life but as a means of containment and because there is nothing else for them to do. To make matters worse the majority of this provision has been criticised as having low expectations of learners (ALI, 2004; Ofsted, 2004).

Equally there has been a growth in the overall numbers of adults who return to learning although again it is difficult to arrive at exact figures. In 2002/03 just over three-quarters of adults questioned had participated in some form of learning in the previous three years, although in this case adults were defined as aged between 16 and 69 (DfES, 2005). Those least likely to participate are those aged 50 or over, those with family responsibilities and those leaving school without qualifications. Insights into the quality of life of many of this third category comes from a recent longitudinal study by Bynner and Parsons (2005 ongoing). They are more likely to be single, male, depressed and have unacknowledged low levels of numeracy and literacy. On the other hand, some adults with more severe learning difficulties may be expected to join courses and classes by their carers or service providers because there is no alternative – they are in other words 'captured customers' (Riddell, Wilson, & Baron, 1999).

The concept of lifelong learning emphasises the significance of opportunities for formal and informal learning in people's lives. While formal learning takes place in educational settings and generally leads to some form of qualification, informal learning occurs throughout our everyday lives at home, in the workplace or during leisure activities. Increasingly the boundaries between these different forms of learning are seen as blurred and permeable (Colley, Hodkinson, & Malcolm, 2004). The kind of formal learning that takes place at school or college can open up opportunities for incidental learning, for example, friends can help with learning to use a new mobile phone or how to handle the children. The skills required for informal activities such as surfing the net and getting to grips with new technology or learning to cook can be enhanced through formal courses.

Young people and adults with learning difficulties require access to both formal and informal learning opportunities. Access becomes easier where there are close relationships between formal and informal settings so that learning in one context can support and build on learning in the other. In the case of Malcolm, weekend work with his uncle delivering tables and chairs offered many such informal opportunities, and, more importantly, Malcolm knew what he needed to learn at school to make him better at his job (Dee, 2002). Here then was a perfect opportunity to build on and support his learning at work in the formal setting of school, but no one took the time to listen to what he had to say.

Perhaps more fundamentally, when young people experience work in real-life settings (informal learning) they are expected to absorb the collective ways of knowing and being integral to a particular workplace through relying on observation and imitation as well as instruction. They are expected to become members of a 'community of practice' (Lave & Wenger, 1991). Lave and Wenger suggest that learning is essentially a social and cultural activity. The knowledge that is shared in the workplace is not the property of a single individual as for example in the traditional school setting where knowledge is imparted by the teacher to the students. Instead they suggest knowledge is collectively accumulated and owned and that this collective knowledge is greater than the sum of individual knowledge. Young and Lucas (1999) suggest that experience alone is not enough, however, and that different types of learning are interdependent, for example, experience, reflection, developing new ideas, trying out ideas in practice. This means that learners will require structured, systematic support at school or college, as well as in the workplace, that enables them to reflect on and make sense of their experiences. People also become absorbed into the culture of a particular community through the relationships that

they form with their colleagues and this may in turn transform how learners see themselves. Malcolm saw himself as 'one of the lads' when he went out for a drink with his workmates after work. Yet at school he was perceived as vulnerable and at home as a dependent child. Such bonds with workmates are formed through casual exchanges, for example about the weather or discussing common interests and experiences. This sophisticated networking requires a high level of social skills , knowing when to stop as well as when to initiate an encounter, understanding the degree of detail on which to embark. So that as well as acquiring job-specific skills some people with learning difficulties will require support to develop the social skills needed to operate successfully in the workplace. Research has shown how people with learning difficulties can be taught the skills they require by engaging in casual exchanges in the workplace, which are essential to building relationships (Holmes & Fillary, 2000).

The relationship between formal and informal learning highlights the importance of the learning context and its influence on the nature of that learning. Young people with learning difficulties who attend special schools can often remain there until they are 19 or more (see Florian, Dee, Byers, & Maudslay, 2000; Florian, Maudslay, Dee, & Byers, 2000). One explanation for this delay could be special schools' mistrust of further education colleges, believing that 'we can do what they do at college better here'. However, opportunities for learning are created through and by the learning environment so the more diverse the environment and opportunities for social interaction, the richer the potential for learning. For instance, Maria who has profound and complex learning difficulties went to her local further education college each week for a music class. At first she could not tolerate the noise and bustle of the refectory so her support worker, Lynn, took her drink to her in the workshop. Over the course of several months Lynn gradually introduced new and more challenging contexts until Maria could cope with the refectory and she began to relate to some of the other students in the college. It is important to look beyond the confines of the formal learning environment, that is, the classroom or workshop (whether that is in school or college) to exploit what the community and other social settings have to offer, including the chance to widen the network of people with whom the learner has contact.

Centrality of the learner

The OECD's second dimension is the centrality of the learner in planning lifelong learning opportunities. At the heart of lifelong learning policies is the notion of a dialogue between individuals and service providers through which they explore the best route to achieving the learner's own goals and aspirations. This is sometimes described as personalised learning. This means working with the grain of people's own ideas to shape services rather than services shaping what and how individuals learn. Learners are seen as consumers of education selecting from the menu of learning opportunities on offer a programme to suit their needs. Leadbetter (2004) urges us to look beyond the consumerist model, however, to one in which the individual becomes connected to the collective, so that they are shaping and regenerating their own communities. This means enabling learners to express their aspirations, needs and preferences; providing greater choice and a 'vocabulary of experiences' on which they can base their choices; assembling solutions around the learner not around the service providers; developing closer partnerships between, for instance, schools, colleges, work-based learning providers; providing advocacy where necessary; ensuring that funding methods follow individuals not services, in other words enabling learners to shape for themselves 'a good life'. This, Leadbetter believes, will lead to individuals becoming more committed to and responsible for the quality of services and community life. At the group level similar processes are used to regenerate communities through consulting on the changes that different, often disaffected, groups would like to see in their communities and then giving them the tools to do so, for example, young single mothers living on council estates; disaffected young men living in urban areas; elderly people living in rural communities.

The concept of individualised planning and person-centred services are increasingly familiar to those working in the field of learning difficulty: individual transition plans; learning plans, health care plans, person-centred plans, direct payments, are all predicated on the idea that provision is designed to match needs and that the learner controls the agenda whether directly or through advocates (Wehmeyer, 2002). Person-centred planning has become the linchpin of service development for adults with learning difficulties in the UK (DoH, 2000) but putting the ideas into practice is beset with problems, as the example of Malcolm demonstrates. Dee (2002), Laragy (2004), Mansell and Beadle-Brown (2004), and Routledge and Gitsham (2004) all suggest that the person's voice and/or that of their families is often lost in the bureaucracy of planning processes and overridden by the taken-for-granted assumptions of professionals. Laragy argues that young people and their families are not equipped with the skills and information that they need to negotiate with services during the transition planning process, while both Mansell and Beadle-Brown as well as Routledge and Gitcham suggest that person-centred planning has become a bureaucratic hoop that has little to do with the person's own dreams and ambitions and the services and support that they receive. Producing plans in this manner has become part of the accountability culture so eloquently described by O'Neill (2002) who suggests that rather than making professionals accountable to their clients, these systems merely make them accountable to central regulators. Instead, there needs to be a shift away from measuring quality by the number of plans completed to the inherent quality of the plans and to developing the skills of staff responsible for implementing the policy.

Debates about access and participation in planning personalised learning also need to address the kind of structural barriers high-lighted by Hughes, Russell and Patterson (2005), who suggest that the concept of real choice (and in this context what to learn, how to learn, when to learn and why) that accompanies notions of personalised learning is one that remains closed to many people with learning difficulties. Barriers include practical difficulties such as transport arrangements, access to leisure and other community facilities, and communication as well as attitudinal barriers. Interestingly, they also note the importance of temporal barriers, that is, the failure of society to recognise that some people require longer to achieve certain tasks whether that is in learning to cross the road or achieving a particular qualification. To this I would add emotional or affective barriers, since the concept of choice also implies changes in people's lives. Changes to routines or relationships built up over many years can appear threatening to the person themselves and to others in their lives. In Malcolm's situation his father's failure to acknowledge Malcolm's growing autonomy and his need to separate from the family was a source of considerable stress for everyone. Negotiating plans for the future becomes an even more sensitive and difficult process for all involved.

Learning to learn

Having the motivation to learn and learning how to learn constitutes the OECD's third characteristic of lifelong learning. Attitudes to learning are formed early in a child's life. This has profound implications for schooling. Leadbetter (2004) believes that motivation and commitment in learners flow from taking responsibility for planning and shaping their own learning opportunities. But like many young men of his age Malcolm could not wait to leave school. He could not see the relationship between schooling and what he wanted to do with his life. Staff at Malcolm's school were unaware of his ambition to become a van driver's mate and his concerns about his problems in reading maps and giving directions. Had his teachers listened to him they

could have designed his school curriculum to support him in his ambitions and there is a chance that he might have begun to see the point of school and learning.

In order to prepare young people for lifelong learning, Scardamalia and Bereiter (1991) propose that schooling needs to be flexible, creative, support problem-solving, develop technological literacy and information-finding skills. Teachers and learners are both seen as learners in a joint enterprise, working together in what Daniels (2000) describes as 'knowledge building organisations'. This has implications for teaching methods and approaches, which Kershner (2000) proposes should foster communication and language development, make explicit links between learning that takes place within and outside school or college and promote choice and risk-taking. But as Byers (1998) has pointed out, much special education provision is characterised by routine and consistency and many learners are not supported in becoming active learners.

Changes across the life span

Finally, the OECD considers that lifelong learning policies should recognise the changing and multiple objectives that individuals have for learning throughout their adult lives. In practice the objectives of lifelong learning tend to vary at a national level. Purposes range from those that are largely economic where lifelong learning seeks to enhance an individual's contribution to the economy through, for example, basic education or work-based training or retraining (human capital), to those where the principle aim is individual development and enhanced quality of life such as learning to use new technologies, through to those where the main purpose is to achieve greater social equality and cohesion (social justice and social capital), for example, community-based projects. Taylor (2005) suggests that, in the UK, the rhetoric of citizenship and social cohesion has in fact masked the real economic focus of most lifelong learning initiatives. For example, the government has invested considerable sums of money in promoting adult basic skills to the exclusion of other aspects of adult education. Others argue (OECD, 2003) that it is difficult to separate out these different purposes and that enhanced employability can help to create greater social cohesion and equality, and therefore a better quality of life and greater social inclusion.

Which policies are more likely to create barriers to participation in lifelong learning which in turn can lead to social exclusion, particularly of people with learning difficulties? The answer lies in where the thrust of these policies is located and how they are interpreted. Bates and Davis (2004) are clear that policies that promote social capital which they describe as 'social networks and norms of trust and reciprocity' (p. 196), that invest in building networks and communities, and that support individual participation in those communities are more likely to be more socially inclusive of people with learning difficulties. They are optimistic about the general shift of focus and quality of mainstream opportunities, and the participation in these by people with learning difficulties. Examples include a renewed focus on volunteering, non-vocational adult classes, and supported employment schemes. Even so, Hammond (2004) in her analysis of the impact of lifelong learning opportunities on the mental health and emotional resilience of a group of 145 adults concluded that participation only makes a difference when programmes match the individual's own interests, strengths and needs.

Riddell, Baron and Wilson (2001) are more pessimistic, arguing that while mainstream lifelong learning policies in the UK are generally driven by the desire to increase human capital, much provision for adults with learning difficulties emphasises independent living and social and life skills. They argue that people with learning disabilities are excluded from mainstream lifelong learning and are bound by the social relationships that are formed within the special provision. Any work-related training that is available tends to emphasise the social benefits of the experi-

ence of training rather than the expectation that it will lead to a job. Instead, both Riddell et al. (2001) and Armstrong (2003) suggest that much post-school education and training open to people with learning difficulties acts as a subtle means of social control by containing rather than educating them. People are placed on programmes in settings to suit the convenience of services, regardless of individual interests or preferences. This is exacerbated in the UK where adults with learning difficulties can be placed on basic skills programmes to help organisations meet government targets and hence obtain funding. Whatever position is adopted it is clear that policies that foster the collective through building social capital and citizenship are more likely to be beneficial in terms of social inclusion than those policies that focus solely on the marketplace and learners as consumers of training and education for employment.

In this first section I have described some of the challenges that exist in creating a lifelong learning society that is inclusive of all learners, that enhances the quality of their lives and that recognises the diversity of society. Now we examine in more detail how Malcolm's chances of living a fulfilled and happy adult life could have been enhanced through his schooling.

WHEN MALCOLM IS 40

The long-term outlook for the quality of Malcolm's adult life was not good. Malcolm was in the upper secondary department of a special school for children with learning difficulties (Dee, 2002). He lived on a large council estate (or social housing) with his father who was agoraphobic and consequently unemployed, his mother, the mainstay of the family, and his younger brother with whom he argued constantly. Using Park et al.'s (2002) five family quality of life domains, Malcolm's family could be described as experiencing difficulties in all five: health, productivity, physical environment (they were waiting to be rehoused), emotional well-being and family interaction. But Malcolm came from a large extended family and at weekends he helped his uncle to deliver chairs and tables. Like many young people with learning difficulties, his transition to post-16 provision had been deferred and he was likely to experience what Dewson et al. refer to as 'a largely non-productive process of "churning" and stagnation' (2004, p. 144). So how could Malcolm be supported to have a better life at 40? What needs to be done?

Malcolm's experiences are examined through ideas located in two different but overlapping traditions: those of psychology and sociology. These terms are used in a general sense and in ways in which they have come to be understood within the disability movement and special education.

Ideas located within the psychological tradition are broadly interested in reasons behind human behaviour. Social psychologists have gone further by studying how external factors can influence and interact with internal processes. They have forged links with sociology. The field of special education has been strongly influenced by psychology and social psychology both in terms of the organisation of provision and in developing new strategies and ways of working with individuals.

The sociological tradition has had a profound influence, particularly on the development of the disability movement. Sociologists are interested in how deep structures in society shape and predetermine our lives, allowing some groups to be privileged over others through virtue of their gender, class, ethnicity or disability. Their ideas have influenced the social model of disability and to a lesser extent the inclusion movement in which disability is seen as socially constructed and where individuals are disabled by their environment (Oliver, 1990). More recently, and drawing on postmodernist thinking, some disability scholars have argued for an explanation that moves beyond structuralist explanations that focus on the collective experiences of disabled people to a post-structuralist perspective that takes account of personal experiences and that sees the experience of impairment as an integral part of individual identity and make-up (Allan, 1999; Shakespeare & Watson, 2001; Crow, 2003). Shakespeare and Watson (2001), while recognising the political role that structuralist models have played in arguing for changes within society, believe that postmodernist ideas are more helpful in providing a theoretical basis for the study of disability. On the whole most of these debates have centred on the experiences of people with physical and sensory impairments. Armstrong's (2003) critique of special education policy and practice using the stories of adults with learning difficulties represents one of the few attempts to engage with the experiences of those with learning difficulties

In Malcolm's case three important and interrelated issues emerge: his influence on the decision-making process; his relationship with his family; the nature of the professional support that was offered. Each of these issues is discussed from the perspective of these two traditions, although in practice ideas from both traditions have combined to assist our understanding of special education. Each has played a powerful and significant role in understanding and guiding the development of provision for young people and adults with learning difficulties and/or disabilities.

First, why was Malcolm's perspective disregarded in the planning process and how could he have been supported in playing a more proactive role in shaping the curriculum to enable him to realise his dreams and ambitions and his vision of a 'good life'? From a sociological standpoint Malcolm was disadvantaged by the special education system itself. Armstrong (2003), drawing on structuralist and post-structuralist thinkers such as Foucault and Giroux, argues that society sustains and reproduces the concept of 'otherness' and the subordination of people with learning difficulties through the systems and structures of special education, to suit its own purposes. The professionals who work within these systems sustain this otherness through failing to acknowledge the viewpoints of adults with learning difficulties, instead continuing to make assumptions about what is best and making decisions on their behalf. These systems conspire to maintain people on particular programmes and routes in an approach that Rusteimer (2000) terms 'educational and vocational positioning'.

On the other hand, many professionals act from the best of motives. Malcolm's teachers were fully aware that local opportunities were limited and that once Malcolm left school he would probably only have two years of further education college before having to find a job, which with his low levels of attainment could prove difficult. In addition, his family were poor and faced numerous financial and social problems. To maintain Malcolm in his small and protective special school and to delay his school leaving seemed the best option.

While sociologists tend to look to society for answers, those working within psychological traditions tend to focus on the individual and their interactions with their environment. So would Malcolm have been better prepared for his adult life if he had participated in a programme of self determination? Self-determination has been defined by Field, Martin, Miller, Ward, and Wehmeyer (1998) as

> a combination of skills, knowledge and beliefs that enables a person to engage in goal-directed, self-regulated, autonomous behaviour. An understanding of one's strengths and limitations together with a belief in one as capable and effective are essential to self-determination. When acting on the basis of these skills and attitudes, individuals have greater ability to take control of their lives and assume the role of successful adults in our society (p. 2).

Curriculum components said to contribute to the development of self-determination in young people with learning difficulties include self-awareness, decision and choice making, problem-solving, risk-taking and safety skills, goal-setting and self-review, self-advocacy, self-regulation and self-efficacy (Wehmeyer, Agran, & Hughes, 1998). Participation in a programme of this kind might have helped Malcolm to become more assertive, channelling his anger and frustration that were a source of considerable tension at home.

Empirical evidence on the efficacy of such approaches show mixed long-term effects on young people's ability to cope in adult life. Malian and Nevin (2002) argue for a more dynamic and time-related understanding of the development of self-determination. They reviewed the evaluations of several programmes designed to improve the self-determination skills of young people with a range of special educational needs. While concluding that young people can acquire these skills, they suggest that self-determination must be seen as fluid, developing across the life span and strongly influenced by the contexts in which the young person finds themselves.

The concept of self-determination has also been criticised for emphasising individual choice and control rather than the individual as a member of the wider community. Browder, Wood, Test, Karvonen, and Algozzine (2001) argue for a concept of self-determination that is sensitive to cultural differences and that recognises the importance of cultural and family ties. Maudslay's study of young Asian adults with learning difficulties concluded that notions of independence and self-determination have arisen out of a highly individualistic society where autonomy and individual choice are seen as ultimate goals (2003, p. 24). The ways in which young people wish to exercise their choice and control are likely to vary strongly between cultures. In any case, Robertson (2001) suggests that an overemphasis on independence and autonomy can be problematic. Degrees of dependency and interdependency are fundamental to the human condition and there will be periods throughout our lives of both giving and receiving care and depending on others.

Another important factor in Malcolm's situation was the part played by his family. The situation could be interpreted from a social capital perspective. Woolcock and Narayan, cited in Putnam and Goss (2002), define social capital at an individual level as 'a person's family, friends and associates ... one that can be called upon in a crisis, enjoyed for its own sake and leveraged for material gain' (2000, p. 226). Social networks can be important not only in providing practical and psychological support. They can also be the route to getting a job – as Putnam and Goss point out, many of us find our jobs as much as a result of who we know as what we know. Malcolm like many other people had found a part-time job through his extended family, that is, he had benefited from his social networks. He also knew what he needed to learn to take advantage of these networks.

But his father's psychological problems threatened to smother Malcolm and prevent him from capitalising on any advantages his family might have afforded him. As Riddell et al. (2001) point out, this situation is common among families of people with learning difficulties. Despite strong family ties, the family sustains them in the position of child. As adulthood approaches their position can shift from protected to abandoned child. In many ways this was beginning to happen to Malcolm. Once Malcolm dropped out of school his father became more wrapped up in his own problems and left Malcolm to his own devices. Adopting a social psychological perspective, Brannen (1996) suggests that how parents construct their children's adolescence influences their relationships with their children that in turn influences the degree of autonomy their offspring are afforded. Parents' ideas are governed by a range of cultural and gender-related factors including for these purposes the fact that their child has a learning difficulty or disability. Malcolm's father still saw Malcolm as a child in need of protection and forbade Malcolm to go to the local pub with his workmates. The nature and severity of the child's disability as well the child's gender and culture play a powerful, and in some instances, all-consuming role in constructing parental views about their child's adolescence, the autonomy they ascribe them and the quality of their future lives.

So what could have been done to improve the situation? Following the social psychological tradition, resilience has been defined as, 'the capacity for or outcome of successful adaptation despite challenging or threatening circumstance' (Masten, Best, & Garmezy,

1990, p. 425). Would these ideas have provided concrete strategies and interventions to help Malcolm and his family to cope more effectively with their situation? The concept of resilience shares many ideas with that of self-determination, emphasising the importance of developing feelings of self-efficacy, self-worth and emotional well-being in children and young people. But it also stresses the relationship between internal and environmental factors in developing the capacity to withstand everyday stresses. As Rutter (1994) points out, it is necessary to explore the accumulation of factors in an individual's life and the personal/environmental relationships. A child is not necessarily born resilient, but neither is resiliency a basic skill that can be taught – children acquire the attributes of resiliency through the experiences they have and the opportunities that are provided for them. Malcolm's decision to stop going to school cannot be seen in isolation from his father's intense anxieties and fears for his son's safety. For Malcolm this was the only means at his disposal to assert himself and get his point across. Perhaps an intervention such as family therapy might have helped them to cope better with the stress they were all experiencing, but this was not available to them.

The concepts of self-determination and resilience have led to the development of specific interventions both in the UK and the United States designed to compensate for perceived deficiencies in the individual and/or their environment. Examples include self-regulated learning programmes (Wehmeyer, 2002); shaping modelling and coaching techniques to assist in asking for help, problem-solving or working co-operatively (Frederickson & Cline, 2002); nurture groups (Cooper, Arnold, & Boyd, 2001); family literacy and numeracy programmes (Brooks, Gorman, Harman, Hutchison, & Wilkin, 2001). Many of these programmes are still in their infancy in terms of judging the long-term benefits in contributing to social inclusion and the quality of people's lives, but critics have argued that targeted programmes directed at those perceived to have special educational needs sustain social isolation and discrimination (Wedell, 2005).

So what will happen to Malcolm when he is 40? If Bynner and Parsons' (2005) research holds true then the outlook for Malcolm appears bleak despite 12 years of special education: he is likely to be unemployed, single, lonely and depressed. In this section I have drawn on a number of possible explanations for Malcolm's situation, contrasting and comparing ideas located in both psychology and sociology. The underlying reasons are complex and at times appear to contradict one another. Yet understanding Malcolm's situation is too important to locate in one tradition or another.

CONCLUSION

In this chapter I have explored the relationship between lifelong learning and quality of life and the potential contribution of education to enhancing the quality of the lives of people who experience difficulties in learning. At the level of rhetoric there are many parallels between these two key concepts. Lifelong learning emphasises that learning occurs throughout life, that it should be personalised, holistic and have meaning for individuals, recognising that personal goals may change with age. Quality of life also concerns the quality of an individual's whole life across the life span and includes their physical, material and emotional well-being, as well as their personal and social development and inclusion in the wider society. So all phases of formal education clearly have an essential contribution to make. Yet in policy, practice and research the notions of lifelong learning and quality of life and the relationship between them are characterised by fractures and discontinuities. Too often mainstream policy decisions ignore the consequences for the quality of the lives of those with learning difficulties and disabilities. In practice, schooling and special schooling in particular often neglect to look beyond the school gate and retain a focus on immediate learning outcomes, while research agendas

search for solutions in one paradigm or another. What is required is a research agenda that acknowledges and engages with the complexity of these many issues in both policy and practice, drawing on and combining explanations and, more importantly, looking beyond explanation to solutions across the life span.

ACKNOWLEDGMENT

I wish to thank Christopher Robertson for his advice and support in preparing this chapter.

REFERENCES

Adult Learning Inspectorate (ALI). (2004). *Chief Inspectors annual report.* http//:ALI.gov.uk

Allan, J. (1999). *Actively seeking inclusion: Pupils with special needs in mainstream schools.* London: Falmer Press.

Armstrong, D. (2003). *Experiences of special education. Re-evaluating policy and practice through life stories.* London: RoutledgeFalmer

Bates, P., & Davis, F. A. (2004, May). Social capital, social inclusion and services for people with learning disabilities. *Disability and Society, 19*(3), 195–207.

Brannen, J. (1996). Discourses of adolescence: Young people's independence and autonomy within families. In J. Brannen & M. O'Brien, *Children in families: Research and policy* (pp. 114–129). London: Falmer Press.

Brooks, G., Gorman, T., Harman, J., Hutchison, D., & Wilkin, A. (2001). *Family literacy works.* London: Basic Skills Agency.

Browder, D. M., Wood, W. M., Test, D. W., Karvonen, M., & Algozzine, B. (2001). Reviewing resources on self determination: A map for teachers. *Remedial and Special Education, 22*(4), 233–255.

Byers, R. (1998). Personal and social development for pupils with learning difficulties. In C. Tilstone, L. Florian, & R. Rose, *Promoting inclusive practice* (pp. 39–61). London: Routledge.

Bynner, J., & Parsons, S. (2005). *New light on literacy and numeracy.* Paper presented at the National Research and Development Centre, University of London Institute of Education, June 2005.

Cabinet Office (2005). *Improving the life chances of disabled people.* Available at http://www.strategy.gov.uk/downloads/work_areas/disability_report

Colley, H., Hodkinson, P., & Malcolm, J. (2004) *Informality and formality in learning: a report for the Learning and Skills Research Centre.* London: LSDA.

Cooper, P., Arnold, R., & Boyd, E. (2001). The effectiveness of nurture groups: Preliminary research findings. *British Journal of Special Education, 28*(4), 160–166.

Crow, L. (2003). Including all of our lives: Renewing the social model of disability. In M. Nind, J. Rix, K. Sheehy, & K. Simmons. *Inclusive education: Diverse perspectives* (pp. 135–149). London: David Fulton.

Daniels, H. (2000). *Celebrations and challenges in 2000: Diversity, inclusion and differentiation.* Unpublished paper presented to NASEN Annual Conference 2000, Robinson College, Cambridgeshire.

Dee, L. (2002). *Whose Decision? A longitudinal study of influences on the decision-making process of twelve young people with special educational needs.* Unpublished PhD thesis, University of London.

Dee, L., Byers, R., Hayhoe, H., & Maudslay, E. (2002). *Enhancing quality of life: A literature review.* London: SKILL and University of Cambridge.

Department for Education and Skills (DfES). (2005). *Trends in education and skills.* Available at http://www.dfes.gov.uk/trends/index

Department of Health (DoH). (2001). *Valuing people: A new strategy for learning disability for the 21st century.* London: HMSO.

Dewson, S., Aston, J., Bates, P., Ritchie, H., & Dyson, A. (2004). *Post 16 transitions: A longitudinal study of young people with special educational needs: Wave 2* (Research Report 582). London: DfES.

Field, S., Martin, J., Miller, R., Ward, M., & Wehmeyer, M. (1998). *A practical guide to teaching self-determination.* Reston,VA: Council for Exceptional Children.

Florian, L., Dee, L., Byers, R., & Maudslay, L. (2000). What happens after the age of 14? Mapping transitions for pupils with profound and complex learning difficulties. *British Journal of Special Education, 16*(1), 124–128.

Florian, L., Maudslay, L., Dee, L., & Byers, R. (2000, July). What happens when schooling ends? Further education opportunities for students with profound and complex learning difficulties. *Skill Journal, 76*, 16–23.

Frederickson, N., & Cline, T. (2002). *Special educational needs, inclusion and diversity.* Buckingham: Open University Press.

Green, A. (2000). Lifelong learning and the learning society: Different European models of organisation. In A. Hodgson (Ed.), *Policies, politics and the future of lifelong learning* (pp. 35–48). London: Kogan Page.

Hammond, C. (2004, December). Impacts of lifelong learning upon emotional resilience, psychological and mental health: Fieldwork evidence. *Oxford Review of Education, 30*(4), 551–568.

Hegarty, S. (1994). Quality of life at school. In D. Goode (Ed.), *Quality of life for persons with disabilities: International perspectives and issues* (pp. 240–249). Cambridge, MA: Brookline.

Holmes, J., & Fillary, R. (2000). Handling small talk at work: Challenges for workers with intellectual disabilities. *International Journal of Disability, Development and Education, 47*(3), 273–291.

Holst, J. (2000). In search of a working concept of 'Quality'. In H. Daniels (Ed.), *Special education re-formed beyond rhetoric* (pp. 31–46). London: Falmer Press.

Hughes, B. Russell, R., & Patterson K. (2005). Nothing to be had off the peg: consumption, identity and the immobilisation of young disabled people. *Disability and Society, 20*(1), 3–17.

Kershner, R. (2000). Teaching children whose progress in learning is causing concern. In D. Whitebread (Ed.) *The psychology of teaching and learning in the primary school.* (pp. 277–299). London: Routledge Falmer.

Laragy, C. (2004). Self-determination within Australian school transition programmes for students with a disability. *Disability and Society, 19*(5), 519–530.

Lave, J., & Wenger, E. (1991). *Situated learning: legitimate peripheral participation.* Cambridge: Cambridge University Press.

Leadbetter, C. (2004). *Personalisation through participation: A new script for public services.* London: Demos.

Malian, I., & Nevin, A. (2002). A review of self determination literature. *Remedial and Special Education, 23*(2), 68–74.

Mansell, J., & Beadle-Brown, J. (2004). Person-centred planning or person centred action? Policy and practice in intellectual disability services. *Journal of Applied Research in Intellectual Disabilities, 17*, 1–9.

Masten, A. S., Best, K. M., & Garmezy, N. (1990). Resilience & development: Contributions from the study of children who overcome adversity, *Development & Psychopathology, 2*, 425–444.

Maudslay, L. (2003). *Aasha: Working with young people with a learning difficulty from a South Asian background.* London: Skill.

O'Neill, O. (2002). *A question of trust.* Cambridge: Cambridge University Press.

Office for Standards in Education (Ofsted). (2004). *Why colleges fail.* Available at http//:www.ofsted.gov.uk

Oliver, M. (1990). *The politics of disablement.* Basingstoke: Macmillan.

Organisation for Economic Co-operation and Development (OECD). (2003) *Beyond rhetoric: Adult learning policies and practices.* Available at http//:www.oecd.org

Organisation for Economic Co-operation and Development (OECD). (2004). *Education at a glance – briefing note United Kingdom.* Available at http//:www.oecd.org

Park, J., Turnbull, A. P., & Turnbull, H. R., III. (2002). Impacts of poverty on quality of life in families of children with disabilities. *Exceptional Children, 68*(2), 151–170.

Putnam, R., & Goss, K. A. (2002). Introduction. In R. Putnam (Ed.), *Democracies in flux* (pp. 3–19). New York: Oxford University Press.

Riddell, S., Baron, S., & Wilson, A. (2001). *The learning society and people with learning difficulties.* Bristol: Policy Press.

Riddell, S., Wilson, A., & Baron, S. (1999). Captured customers: People with learning difficulties in the social market. *British Journal of Educational Research, 25*(4), 445–461.

Robertson, C. (1998). Quality of life as a consideration in the development of inclusive education for pupils and students with learning difficulties. In C. Tilstone, L. Florian, & R. Rose (Eds.), *Promoting inclusive practice* (pp. 264–275). London: Routledge.

Robertson, C. (2001). Autonomy and identity: the need for new dialogues in education and welfare. *Support for learning, 16*(3), 122–127.

Routledge, M., & Gitsham, N. (2004, July). Putting person centred planning in its proper place? *Tizard Learning Disability Review, 9*(3), 21–26.

Rusteimer, S. (2000). Listening for inclusion in further education. Unpublished paper presented at the International Education Congress 2000, University of Manchester, July 24–28.

Rutter, M. (1994). Stress research: accomplishments and tasks ahead. In R. J. Haggerty, L. R. Sherrod, N. Garmezy, & M. Rutter (Eds.), *Stress, risk and resilience in children and adolescents: Process, mechanisms and interventions* (pp. 354–385). New York: Cambridge University Press.

Scardamalia, M., & Bereiter, C. (1991). Higher levels of agency for children in knowledge-building: A challenge for the design of new knowledge media. *The Journal of the Learning Sciences, 1*(1), 38–68.

Schalock, R., & Alonso, M. A. V. (2002). *Handbook on quality of life for human service practitioners.* Washington, DC: American Association on Mental Retardation.

Shakespeare, T., & Watson, N. (2001). The social model of disability: an outdated ideology? In S. Barnatt & B. Altman (Eds.), *Exploring theories and expanding methodologies* (pp. 9–28). Amsterdam: JAI.

Taylor, R. (2005, March). Life long learning and the Labour governments 1997–2004. *Oxford Review of Education, 31*(1), 101–118.

Walker, A. (1982). *Unqualified and underemployed: Handicapped people and the labour market.* London: National Children's Bureau.

Wedell, K. (2005). Dilemmas in the quest for inclusion. *British Journal of Special Education, 32,* 13–11.

Wehmeyer, M. (2002). Promoting the self determination of students with severe disabilities. ERIC/OSEP.Digest E663.

Wehmeyer, M., Agran, M., & Hughes, C. (1998). *Teaching self determination to students with disabilities.* Baltimore, MD: Paul H. Brookes.

Woolcock, M., & Narayan, D. (2000). Social capital: Implications for development theory, research and policy, *The World Bank Observer, 15,* 225–249.

Young, M., & Lucas, N. (1999). Pedagogy and learning in further education: New concepts, new theories and new possibilities. In P. Mortimore (Ed.), *Understanding pedagogy and its impact on learning,* 98–114. London: Paul Chapman Publishing.

Cross-phase Issues of
Teaching and Learning

31

Collaborative teaching: critique of the scientific evidence

Jacqueline S. Thousand, Ann I. Nevin
and Richard A. Villa

INTRODUCTION AND PURPOSE

In 1994 the United Nations Educational, Scientific, and Cultural Organization (UNESCO) issued the *Salamanca Statement and Framework for Action on Special Needs Education* which supported the practice of inclusive education for students with disabilities, with the caution that 'while inclusive schools provide a favorable setting for achieving equal opportunity and full participation, their success requires a concerted effort, not only by teachers and school staff, but also by peers, parent, families, and volunteers' (p. 11). The inclusion of students with disabilities has become stated policy in more than two-thirds of the 92 signatory nations to the Salamanca Statement (Villa, 2004). International and national policy and laws combined with increasingly diverse student demographics in many nations, then, suggest that collaborative planning and teaching among school personnel can be an effective method to implement these policies for educating students in inclusive settings.

In the United States, collaborative teaching, team teaching, or co-teaching in public schools appeared in the 1960s as an example of progressive education and was advanced in the 1970s and 1980s as an educational reform in order to implement recommendations and legislative changes such as the *Education for All Handicapped Children Act 1975* (P.L. 94-142). Collaborative activities were forwarded by the 1997 reauthorization of the *Individuals with Disabilities Education Act* (IDEA) that required access to the general education curriculum in the least restrictive environment. In 2004, the *Individuals with Disabilities Education Improvement Act 2004* (IDEIA) combined with the *No Child Left Behind Act 2001* (NCLB) provided a context for collaboration between special and general educators to ensure access to highly qualified teachers (NCLB, Section 1119) and accountability for achievement of outcomes for all students (NCLB, Section 1116).

The purpose of this chapter is to report the results of a review of the collaborative teaching literature. The authors provide definitions of collaborative teaching, identify the theoretical frameworks for collaborative teaching, and describe the methodologies to study collaborative teaching. They identify issues related to collaborative teaching and gaps in the current knowledge and research bases with respect to the preparation of and administrative support for collaborative planning and teaching.

METHOD

A comprehensive search of the literature on collaborative planning and teaching and co-teaching was conducted. First, the Educational Resources Information Clearinghouse (ERIC) and PsychLit databases were searched from 1989 through to 2005. In addition, a hand search was conducted on articles cited in review articles. Finally, newsletters and newspaper articles regarding collaborative teaching were obtained. It should be noted that this yielded research that has been published primarily in the USA, although some of the journals are considered international journals (for example, *Learning Disabilities Research and Practice*, *Journal of Special Education*, and *Exceptional Children*).

Where is collaborative planning and teaching literature published?

Collaborative planning and teaching literature was reported in both research-oriented journals and practitioner-oriented journals. Researcher journals included *Teacher Education and Special Education*, *Education and Training for Developmental Disabilities*, *Journal of Special Education*, *Exceptional Children*, and *Learning Disabilities Research and Practice*. Practitioner journals included *Principal*, *Remedial and Special Education*, *Journal for Educational and Psychological Consultation*, *American Annals of the Deaf*, *Social Studies Review*, *Foxfire Journal for Teachers*, *NAASP Journal*, *Journal of Learning Disabilities*, *Teaching Exceptional Children*, *Preventing School Failure*, *Focus on Exceptional Children*, and *Academic Therapy*. Four books included empirical research on collaborative teaching or co-teaching (that is, Friend & Cook, 1992; Hourcade & Bauwens, 2002; Pugach & Johnson, 2002; Villa, Thousand, & Nevin, 2004a).

What research methodologies are featured?

Researchers and practitioners alike recommend implementing more comprehensive frameworks for evaluating collaborative teaching arrangements, as different research methods can yield different conclusions. For example, John-Steiner and colleagues (1998) recommend supplementing quantitative methods with qualitative methods, stating 'by looking for commonalities and differences across settings, tasks, working methods, goals, and values, a framework for understanding collaboration can be constructed that preserves the benefits of rich descriptive accounts' (p. 773). To reinforce this recommendation, in a synthesis of the quantitative research pertaining to co-teaching between general and special educators, Murawski and Swanson (2001) found only six out of 89 reviewed articles to have sufficient quantitative information for calculating an effect size showing the impact of co-teaching. As Table 31.1 shows, other research methods have been used to document the impact of collaborative teaching or co-teaching, including descriptive analyses, surveys, qualitative case studies, quasi-experimental studies, practitioner action research, meta-analysis, and instrument development. Each of the methods has benefits and limitations to generalization.

The mixed methods approach is a procedure for collecting and analyzing both quantitative and qualitative data in a single study or in a series of studies (Tashakkori & Teddlie, 1998, 2002). Recently mixed methods approaches have been applied in various social and behavioral science disciplines, including education, and should be uniquely useful for research designs to assess the impact of collaborative teaching arrangements. The benefits of qualitative in-depth interviews and observations of teachers and students can greatly enrich the believability and validity of the outcomes obtained through surveys and analyses of achievement data of children in co-taught classrooms. However, there is only one example of the mixed methods approach applied to collaborative teaching (Cramer & Nevin, 2005).

WHAT IS COLLABORATIVE TEACHING?

Collaborative teaching defined

Friend and Reising (1993) defined co-teaching as two or more professionals who jointly deliver substantive instruction to diverse or blended groups of students in a single space. Salend and Johansen (1997) defined co-teaching as a collaborative effort between general educators and support personnel who teach students with disabilities in general education classrooms. Walther-Thomas (1997) defined co-teaching as a way to actualize inclusion of students with disabilities in general education classrooms where the special educator co-taught at least one to two hours per day. Klingner, Vaughn, Hughes, Schumm, and Elbaum (1998) defined co-teaching as a system in which a special educator collaboratively planned lessons with a general educator for at least 30 minutes per week; instructed small groups of students; worked one-on-one with students with learning disabilities; and, along with the general educator, used literacy instruction techniques such as the writing process, strategic reading, classwide peer tutoring, and vocabulary development. Villa, Thousand, and Nevin (2004a) broadened the definition of collaborative teaching to include any number of adults and children as co-teachers. They defined co-teaching as two or more people sharing responsibility for teaching some or all of the students assigned to a classroom, and described it as a creative way for people with different ways of thinking or teaching to connect with and support one another in order to help all students learn.

Table 31.1 Collaborative teaching studies: methodologies

Descriptive	Magiera, Smith, Zigmond, & Gebauer (2005)
	Rice & Zigmond (1999)
	Welch (2000)
	Zigmond (2004)
Survey	Schwab Learning (2003)
	Liston & Thousand (2004)
Qualitative case study	Buscema (2004)
	Compton et al. (1998)
	Garrigan & Thousand (2005)
	Gerber & Popp (1999)
	Luckner (1999)
	Trent (1998)
	Salend & Johansen (1997)
	Santamaria & Thousand (2004)
	Walther-Thomas (1997)
	Weiss & Lloyd (2002)
Quasi-experimental	Klingner, Vaughn, Hughes, Schumm, & Elbaum (1998)
	Rosman (1994)
	Vaughn, Schumm, & Arguelles (1997)
	Walsh & Snyder (1993)
Practitioner	
Action research	Dieker (1998)
	Dieker & Barnett (1996)
	Kluwin, Gonsher, Silver, & Samuels (1996)
	Mahony (1997)
	Miller, Valasky, & Molloy (1998)
	Salazar & Nevin (2005)
Meta-analysis	Murawski & Swanson (2001)
Instrument development	Noonan, McCormick, & Heck (2003)
Mixed method	Cramer & Nevin (2005)

Elements of collaborative teaching

Researchers have different conceptualizations of the critical elements of collaborative teaching. For Vaughn and Schumm (1995), the elements of an effective co-teaching system include teachers choosing to participate; adequate provision of resources (for example, computers, paraprofessionals); a school-based adoption of the practice; the maintenance of a continuum of services (that is, pull-out special education remains an option); and continuous monitoring and modification of students' Individual Education Programs (IEPs). In contrast, Friend and Riesing (1993) described five elements of a collaborative relationship between general and special educators to include parity, shared responsibility, mutual accountability, trust, and planning.

Friend (1998) conceptualizes the elements of co-teaching as (a) an equal partnership in an interactive relationship, (b) both partners being involved in all aspects of planning, teaching, and assessment, and (c) the delivery of the same material jointly to one group of students using a variety of strategies. Strategies described include one teaches/one observes; one teaches/one helps students; station teaching where teachers divide the content taught and the students; each teacher repeats the content to the other group of students; alternate teaching where one teacher directs the lesson as the other teaches a small group of students based on their learning needs. In contrast, Arguelles and colleagues (2000) identify seven components of an effective co-teaching system: common planning time, flexibility, risk-taking, defined roles and responsibilities, compatibility, communication skills, and administrative support.

The Villa, Thousand, and Nevin (2004b) conceptualization of the elements of collaborative teaching is derived from social psychological theory and the work of cooperative group learning researchers (Johnson & Johnson, 1989). They identify five key elements or dimensions of behavior of effective co-teaching partners, namely, co-teachers:

1 coordinate their work to achieve at least one *common, publicly agreed-on goal*;
2 share a *belief system* that each of the co-teaching team members has unique and needed expertise;
3 demonstrate *parity*, by alternatively engaging in the dual roles of teacher and learner, expert and novice, giver and recipient of knowledge or skills;
4 use a *distributed functions theory* of leadership in which the task and relationship functions of the traditional lone teacher are distributed among all co-teaching group members; and
5 use a *cooperative process* that includes face-to-face interaction, positive interdependence, the performance as well as monitoring and processing of interpersonal skills, and individual accountability.

RATIONALE FOR COLLABORATIVE TEACHING

Collaborative teaching can be traced to some extent to epistemological or psychological frameworks. For example, Villa et al. (2004a) suggest that Glasser's Choice Theory (1999), Johnson and Johnson's Social Psychological Theory (1989), and Vygotsky's Zone of Proximal Development (1987) might provide theoretical insights. However, policy and teacher experiences are the primary sources for the examination of the rationale for and benefits of collaborative teaching. In fact, it could be argued that collaborative teaching is an example of policy leading practice that then requires more research. Both IDEA and NCLB mandates are examples of policy leading to practitioner collaboration, which then drives practitioner action research. Thus, collaborative teaching may be an example where practitioners are leading researchers. Practitioner research tends to be atheoretical. When both practice and policy are driving research, perhaps what is needed is a comprehensive flexible theoretical framework which, at this point, is absent from the literature.

Given the absence of a theoretical framework for examining collaborative teaching and a nascent research base for the practice, what are the documented benefits of collaborative teaching for teachers, students, and schools? The most comprehensive documentation comes from a study conducted by Schwab Learning (2003) where the impact of collaborative partnerships and co-teaching was studied in 16 Californian elementary, middle, and secondary schools. In these schools, teachers, administrators, and support staff creatively arranged for every student to receive instruction from teachers assigned to students at risk for school failure, reading specialists, special educators, paraprofessionals, and other support personnel in general education settings. Results included decreased referrals for intensive special education services, increased overall student achievement, fewer disruptive problems, less paperwork, increased numbers of students qualifying for gifted and talented education services, and decreased referrals for behavioral problems. In addition, teachers reported being happier and not feeling so isolated. This study reinforces the findings of Walther Thomas's (1997) evaluation of co-teaching models in 23 schools across eight school districts. Positive outcomes included improved academic and social skills of low-achieving students, improved attitudes and self-concepts reported by students with disabilities, and more positive peer relationships. The co-teachers themselves (general and special educator teaching teams) reported experiencing professional growth, personal support, and an enhanced sense of community within the general education classrooms.

Collaborative teaching has been documented to be effective for students with a variety of instructional needs in k-12 classrooms, including students with hearing impairment (Compton et al., 1998; Luckner, 1999); learning disabilities (Garrigan & Thousand, 2005; Klingner et al., 1998; Rice & Zigmond, 1999; Trent, 1998; Welch, 2000); students with cognitive delays (Buscema, 2004); high-risk students with emotional disturbance and other at-risk characteristics (Dieker, 1998); students with language delays (Miller, Valasky, & Molloy, 1998) and students with and without disabilities in secondary classrooms (Magiera,

Smith, Zigmond, & Gebauer, 2005; Mahony, 1997; Weiss & Lloyd, 2002). Welch (2000) showed that students with disabilities and their classmates *all* made academic gains in reading and spelling on curriculum-based assessments in the co-taught classrooms. Moreover, Mahony (1997) reported that 'for special education students [in co-taught classrooms], being part of the large class meant making new friends' (p. 59) in addition to meeting students' educational needs.

What could account for such results? First, co-teaching arrangements offer opportunities to capitalize upon the unique, diverse, and specialized knowledge of each instructor. Co-teaching is an instructional arrangement for bringing together people with diverse backgrounds and interests to share knowledge and skills to generate novel methods to individualize learning. Second, collaborative teaching allows students to experience and imitate the cooperative skills that teachers show when they co-teach. Third, with multiple instructors, there is a valued decrease in teacher–student ratio as well as an increased flexibility in grouping and scheduling. This makes it possible for students to experience less wait time for teacher attention and increased time on task, an important factor documented to increase achievement. Additionally, teachers who co-teach can structure their classes to use more effectively the research-proven strategies (Miller et al., 1998). Fourth, in interviews with 95 peer-collaborators and 96 others who were not collaborating, Pugach and Johnson (1995) found that teachers in the peer-collaboration group had reduced referral rates to special services, increased confidence in handling classroom problems, increased positive attitudes toward the classroom, and more tolerance toward children with cognitive deficits.

Some researchers are cautious about the claims for effectiveness of collaborative teaching methods. In a meta-analysis of the research on collaborative teaching, Murawski and Swanson (2001) found six studies published between 1989 and 1999 with sufficient quantitative data to calculate effect sizes for reading or math achievement, social interactions such as friendships, attendance and discipline, and grades. Effect sizes for the individual studies ranged from .08 (weak) to .95 (strong) with an average of .40. The authors concluded that 'co-teaching is a moderately effective procedure for influencing student outcomes' (p. 264), but caution that more research is needed to verify the impact of collaborative teaching arrangements on the academic and social progress of students with disabilities. Although the data they analyzed addressed the impact of co-teaching in both primary and secondary schools (including measures of achievement in reading and math), there was not enough data to determine if certain approaches had better outcomes for different ages, grades, disabilities, or curriculum areas. Similarly, Zigmond (2004), reporting on preliminary results of co-teaching in inclusive science classrooms at six high schools, found little difference in the amount of time students spent working on task, interacting in small groups, or interacting with the teachers.

Four approaches to collaborative teaching

Co-teaching has many faces. In a comprehensive school restructuring survey conducted in the United States, teachers who had experience meeting the needs of students in diverse classrooms reported that they used four predominant approaches to collaborative teaching: supportive, parallel, complementary, and team teaching (National Center for Educational Restructuring and Inclusion, 1995). A description of each approach follows.

Supportive teaching occurs when one teacher takes the lead instructional role and the other(s) rotates among the students to provide support. The co-teacher(s) taking the supportive role watches or listens as students work together, stepping in to provide one-to-one tutorial assistance when necessary, while the other co-teacher continues to direct the lesson (Villa et al., 2004a; Vaughn, Schumm,

& Arguelles, 1997). This approach is described by Friend and Reising (1993) as 'one teaches/one drifts'.

Parallel teaching occurs when two or more people work with different groups of students in different sections of the classroom. Co-teachers may rotate among the groups, and sometimes there may be one group of students that works without a co-teacher for at least part of the time. Parallel teaching may include cooperative group or experiment or lab monitoring as well as co-teachers facilitating student learning with each focused on a different learning style (for example, visual/spatial, bodily kinesthetic) (Villa et al., 2004a). This is described as 'station teaching' by Friend and Reising (1993).

Complementary teaching is when co-teachers do something to enhance the instruction provided by the other co-teacher(s). For example, one co-teacher might paraphrase the other's statements or model note-taking skills on a transparency. Sometimes, one of the complementary teaching partners pre-teaches the small-group social skill roles required for successful cooperative group learning and then monitors as students practice the roles during the lesson taught by the other co-teacher (Villa et al., 2004a). This is described by Friend (1998) as 'alternate teaching'.

Team teaching is when two or more people do what the traditional teacher has always done – plan, teach, assess, and assume responsibility for all of the students in the classroom. Team teachers share the leadership and the responsibilities. For example, one partner might demonstrate the steps of a science experiment, while the other models the recording and illustrating of its results (Villa et al., 2004a). Similar definitions of team teaching are provided by other researchers such as Friend (1998) who described team teaching as an interactive relationship with both involved in all aspects of planning, teaching, assessment and delivery of the same material jointly to one group of students.

ISSUES REGARDING COLLABORATIVE TEACHING

Researchers and practitioners alike face challenges to researching and analyzing the effectiveness of collaborative planning and teaching. Two major issues were identified by the authors based on the results of the literature review.

Few assessment instruments for examining co-teaching

Given expected increases in co-teaching teams, principals and other supervisory personnel may be required to use different evaluation procedures, as will university student teacher supervisors when their student teachers co-teach. Co-teachers also are interested in new ways to evaluate their roles, but few yet exist. An instrument to assess early childhood co-teachers has been systematically studied and validated by Noonan, McCormick, and Heck (2003). Systematic replications of the instrument to increase generalizability across other multicultural environments, grade levels, and subject matter expertise may be beneficial. Villa and colleagues (2004a) developed the Are We Really Co-Teachers Scale that focuses on co-teachers' actions and behaviors in the classroom.

The Noonan et al. Co-Teacher Relationship Scale focuses on the attitudes and beliefs of co-teachers and may be helpful in matching potential co-teaching team members, whereas the Villa et al. Are We Really Co-Teachers Scale emphasizes the teaching interactions and classroom behaviors of co-teachers. Thus, the Villa et al. scale may help administrators and other personnel design effective professional development activities to ensure that co-teachers have the skills to implement research-proven effective teaching practices within their co-taught classrooms.

Cramer and Nevin (2005) reported the results of a mixed methodology approach to study the relationship between general and special educators who were co-teaching using both of these assessment instruments. The sums of ratings from special educators and general elementary and secondary educators in the southwestern USA were similar to those obtained from Noonan et al.'s (2003) sample of early childhood specialists and early childhood educators co-teaching in Hawaii. Furthermore, comparisons of ratings from Noonan et al.'s scale and Villa et al.'s (2004a) survey indicated that the highest rated items on the two assessment instruments were similar in content. Interviews and observations with a subset of survey respondents corroborated the survey items. Overall, the follow-up interviews and observations corroborated and instantiated the co-teacher ratings on the survey items.

Need for agreement among researchers on definitions of impact

What do researchers and practitioners assess when studying the impact of collaborative teaching activities? Thus far, most researchers have focused upon assessing the impact on students with disabilities. A range of dependent variables have been examined. The most prevalent measure is teacher grades and student scores on standardized achievement tests for math or reading (for example, Buscema, 2004; Dieker & Barnett, 1996; Garrigan & Thousand, 2005; Klingner et al., 1998; Mahony, 1997; Miller, Valasky, & Molloy, 1998; Murawski & Swanson, 2001; Rosman, 1994; Schwab Learning, 2003; Walsh & Snyder, 1993; Welch, 2000).

Some researchers have examined the impact of collaborative teaching on the participating teachers. Dependent variables for teacher impact rely upon classroom observations and text analysis of teachers' verbatim responses to questionnaires, surveys, and/or interviews (for example, Buscema, 2004; Compton et al., 1998; Cramer & Nevin, 2005; Liston & Thousand, 2004; Luckner, 1999; Magiera et al., 2005; Salazar & Nevin, 2005; Salend & Johansen, 1997; Santamaria & Thousand, 2004; Schwab Learning, 2003; Trent, 1998; Walther-Thomas, 1997; Weiss & Lloyd, 2002; Welch, 2000).

Practitioner action research reports have relied upon anecdotal descriptions of the processes that were used to achieve the collaborative partnerships as well as case examples of how students reacted. Examples include studies by Dieker (1998), Kluwin, Gonsher, Silver, and Samuels (1996), Mahony (1997), and Miller, Valasky, and Molloy (1998).

Rarely have researchers or practitioners analyzed the impact of collaborative teaching on other variables. However in one study by Vaughn and colleagues (1997), measures were developed for friendships, self-concept, and peer acceptance. In another study (Gerber & Popp, 1999), student perceptions of impact were assessed through structured interviews of students with and without disabilities and all of their parents. Although problems were identified, students and parents alike reported positive results in student learning in co-taught classrooms that included students with disabilities. Other researchers have documented the actions taken by general and special educators as they implement co-teaching (Buscema, 2004; Garrigan & Thousand, 2005; Magiera et al., 2005).

The lack of agreement about what constitutes a dependent variable in co-teaching research may explain the apparent discrepancies in results. For example, Zigmond (2004) measured on task behavior of students with and without disabilities in co-taught high school science classes. She found no differences in on-task behavior or achievement for students with disabilities in co-taught classrooms compared to those taught in special classes with one teacher. However, no other researchers have used such a measure. Murawski and Swanson (2001) have called not only for improved definitions of what constitutes an impact measure but also for explicit measures of treatment integrity, the extent to which specific co-teaching activities are actually implemented as intended or designed. We, the authors, of this chapter further propose that research results could be improved if multiple measures were obtained for student efficacy including student achievement, social development, self-concept, and friendships. In addi-

tion, multiple measures for impact on teachers should include teacher competency and skill acquisition, confidence, and job satisfaction.

GAPS IN THE LITERATURE: A CALL FOR FURTHER RESEARCH

Through their examination of the existing research base in collaborative planning and teaching, the authors identified two major areas in which further research is needed. Although there are other potential areas for further research, these two are selected because of the overall lack of attention in the current literature.

Curriculum for preparing educators for collaborative teaching

Research confirms that there is less power in co-teaching without training in selecting and planning for implementing the various approaches to co-teaching. In the study conducted by Cramer and Nevin (2005), only one elementary general educator and one secondary special educator reported they had received training in co-teaching in their university teacher preparation programs while all co-teachers reported they had received in-service training and planning time to implement co-teaching. In contrast, Magiera et al. (2005) reported a descriptive study of 10 high school co-teachers who were observed every 5 minutes for the entire class period describing the instructional roles of the teachers. A total of 49 observations was collected; for 33 of the 49, both teachers monitored students as they completed independent assignments. For 33 of the 49 observations, the general education teacher provided the primary instruction in mathematics while the special educator monitored and tutored. For 24 of the 49 observations, the special educator assumed a supportive role. Team teaching was observed in 9 of the 49 co-taught classes – both teachers were active instructors. Interview results indicated that none of the co-teachers had training in co-teaching.

Although many universities have collaborative experiences for general educators and special educators, there are few empirical studies of preservice preparation of teachers for co-teaching. Villa, Thousand and Chapple (2000) delineated how faculty at five universities 'retooled their professional preparation programs to better ready graduates for meeting the challenges of inclusive 21st century education … to create new and innovative training initiatives that model faculty and community collaboration and depart from traditional ways of inducting educators into their profession' (p. 536). Patriarcha and Lamb (1990) reported an empirical study of implementing a co-teaching model between general and special educators at the high school level as they collaboratively planned and taught lessons together.

At the inservice preparation level, according to the research found since 1985, there is no published research regarding the preparation and coaching of incumbent teachers to engage in co-teaching arrangements. Based upon experience with school personnel who have co-taught, Villa et al. (2004a) suggest that, in addition to their unique knowledge and skills, members of co-teaching teams need to acquire a common conceptual framework, language, and set of skills that at a minimum should include training in at least the four following areas:

1 collaborative planning (Thousand & Villa, 2000; Villa, 2002);
2 approaches to co-teaching such as those discussed in this article (Bauwens & Mueller, 2000; Friend, 1998);
3 differentiation and universal design approaches to instruction (Tomlinson, 1999; Udvari-Solner, Villa, & Thousand, 2002); and
4 cooperative group learning (Johnson & Johnson, 1999), and other areas (e.g., discipline) that co-teachers self-identify as priority areas for *mutual* skill development.

Villa et al. (2004a) also identify and offer answers to frequently asked questions that implementers of co-teaching most frequently ask. These frequently asked questions are shown in Table 31.2 and should be considered in future research.

Administrative and logistical supports for collaborative teaching

Although the collaborative planning and teaching literature universally mentions administrative support, there has been no published research on the impact of the presence or absence of administrative support on the functioning or effectiveness of co-teaching endeavors. Furthermore, absent from the research literature are descriptions of administrative actions required to promote a collaborative school culture and establish co-teaching as a school-wide practice. Although there is a dearth of published research in this arena, practitioners have made suggestions in practitioner journals and books as to the logistical supports they want from administrators. For example, Villa et al. (2004a) describe five dimensions of administrative support – vision, skills, resources, incentives, action planning – requested of co-teachers. Specifically, co-teachers want administrators to (1) build a school-wide

Table 31.2 Frequently asked questions about co-teaching

- Is co-teaching a voluntary act?
- How do you schedule and most effectively use resources for co-teaching?
- Do all students eligible for special education need to be in co-taught classrooms?
- How many students eligible for special education should be in any given general education classroom?
- Will co-teaching eliminate pull-out services?
- How long should co-teaching teams stay together?
- Who can be a co-teacher?
- Should personnel who are team teaching remain together at the end of the school year, or should one of them follow the students whom they have been supporting to the next grade level, working with new teachers at that level?
- What kinds of administrative support assist in the development and evolution of co-teaching teams?
- How do you know if you are really co-teaching?

vision of collaborative planning and teaching, (2) create opportunities for teachers to develop *skills* and confidence as co-teachers, (3) provide meaningful *incentives* for people to attempt co-teaching, (4) reorganize, schedule, and expand human and other *resources* for co-teaching, and (5) systematically plan and take *action* to promote co-teaching.

When the implementation of a collaborative teaching initiative is poorly administered, treatment integrity is compromised and the assessment of the potential impact of the practice becomes problematic. To illustrate, Kirkpatrick (personal communication, September 2004) described how poor administrative leadership in Arkansas' statewide co-teaching project impeded implementation and, therefore, the assessment of the potential impact of the co-teaching project. Some of the problems included an unspecified district *vision* for co-teaching and no linkage of co-teaching to the overall school improvement plan, no staff *skill* development in co-teaching or differentiating instruction, inadequate *resources* by structuring too many co-teaching partners with inadequate planning time, and no plan for evaluating effectiveness. Clearly, each of the five dimensions of administrative and logistical support – vision, skills, resources, incentives, action planning – deserves systematic investigation.

SUMMARY AND CONCLUSIONS

In this chapter, the authors reported the results of a review of the collaborative teaching literature, identified the lack of theoretical frameworks for collaborative teaching, and described the varied definitions of collaborative teaching, and methodologies to study collaborative teaching. They identified two issues related to collaborative teaching – a lack of assessment methods to assess the quality of co-teacher actions and a lack of agreement on how to measure the impact of collaborative teaching. They also delineated two gaps in the current knowledge and research bases, namely, a well-defined cur-

riculum for preparing teachers to collaboratively teach and the necessary administrative and logistical supports to allow collaborative teaching to thrive.

Collaborative teaching requires changes in roles and responsibilities of school personnel, planning, and administrative support. Implementing and documenting the impact of collaborative teaching is intellectually challenging, particularly in an era of competing mandates, demands for accountability, and complex professional development. However, for the research promise of collaborative teaching to be realized, researchers and frontline practitioners need to join forces to simultaneously implement and research the critical requirements for success in co-teaching relationships and the impact of co-teaching on students and their families, instructors, and the culture of a school community. Co-teaching is at a point in its use where practice can inform theory and research while research and theory can inform practice. The authors suggest that the potential dual outcomes of more successful and happier children as well as more competent and confident faculty is worth the effort that effective co-teaching and rigorous documentation of the process and outcomes of collaborative teaching demands.

REFERENCES

Arguelles, M. E., Hughes, M. T., & Schumm, J. S. (2000). Co-teaching: A different approach to inclusion. *Principal, 79*(4), 48, 50–51.

Bauwens, J., & Mueller, P. (2000). Maximizing the mindware of human resources. In R. Villa & J. Thousand (Eds.), *Restructuring for caring and effective education: Piecing the puzzle together* (pp. 328–359). Baltimore, MD: Paul H. Brookes.

Buscema, E. (2004). *Collaboration of special and general educators to benefit students with cognitive disabilities in the area of social studies in an inclusive setting.* Masters thesis, California State University San Marcos, College of Education.

Compton, M., Stratton, A., Maier, A., Meyers, C., Scott, H., & Tomlinson, T. (1998). It takes two: Co-teaching for deaf and heard of hearing students in rural schools. In *Coming together: Preparing for rural special education in the 21st century.* Conference Proceedings of the American Council on Rural Special Education, Charleston, SC. (ED 417901).

Cramer, E., & Nevin, A. (2005, April). *A mixed methodology analysis of co-teacher assessments: Preliminary results.* Paper presented at American Educational Research Association, Montreal, Canada.

Dieker, L. (1998). Rationale for co-teaching. *Social Studies Review, 37*(2), 62–65.

Dieker, L., & Barnett, C. A. (1996). Effective co-teaching. *Teaching Exceptional Children, 29*(1), 5–7.

Friend, M. (1998). *The power of two: Making a difference through co-teaching* [video]. Port Chester, NY: National Professional Resources.

Friend, M., & Cook, L. (1992). *Interactions: Collaboration skills for school professionals* (4th ed.). Upper Saddle River, NJ: Allyn & Bacon.

Friend, M., & Reising, M. (1993.) Co-teaching: An overview of the past, a glimpse at the present, and considerations for the future. *Preventing School Failure, 37*(4), 5–10.

Garrigan, C. M., & Thousand, J. S. (2005). The effects of co-teaching on student achievement in the reading domain. *New Hampshire Journal of Education, 8,* summer, 56–60.

Gerber, P., & Popp, P. (1999). Consumer perspectives on the collaborative teaching model: Views of students with and without LD and their parents. *Remedial and Special Education, 20*(5), 288–296.

Glasser, W. (1999). *Choice theory: A new psychology of personal freedom.* New York: Perennial.

Hourcade, J., & Bauwens, J. (2002). *Cooperative teaching: Rebuilding and sharing the schoolhouse* (2nd ed.). Austin, TX: Pro-Ed.

Individuals with Disabilities Education Act 1990 (IDEA). 20 United States Congress 1412[a][5], Reauthorized 1997.

Individuals with Disabilities Education Improvement Act 2004 (IDEIA). Public Law No. 108-447.

John-Steiner, V., Weber, R., & Minnis, M. (1998). The challenge of studying collaboration. *American Educational Research Journal, 35*(4), 773–783.

Johnson, D. W., & Johnson, R. T. (1989). *Cooperation and competition: Theory and research.* Edina, MN: Interaction Book Company.

Johnson, D. W., & Johnson, R. (1999). *Learning together and alone: Cooperative, competitive, and individualistic learning.* Needham Heights, MA: Allyn & Bacon.

Klingner, J., Vaughn, S., Hughes, S., Schumm, J., & Elbaum, B. (1998). Outcomes for students with and without learning disabilities in inclusive classrooms. *Learning Disabilities Research & Practice, 13,* 153–161.

Kluwin, T. N., Gonsher, W., Silver, K., & Samuels, J. (1996). The E. T. class: Education together. *Teaching Exceptional Children, 29*(1), 11–15.

Liston, A., & Thousand, J. (2004, August). *Developing co-teaching skills of faculty in a secondary urban multicultural setting: Preliminary data analysis of Project Co-Teach: How can practice inform theory?* Paper presented at Association of Teacher Educators Europe, Agrigento, Sicily.

Luckner, J. (1999). An examination of two co-teaching classrooms. *American Annals of the Deaf, 144*(1), 24–34.

Magiera, K., Smith, C., Zigmond, N., & Gebauer, K. (2005). Benefits of co-teaching in secondary mathematics classes. *Teaching Exceptional Children, 37*(3), 20–24.

Mahony, M. (1997). Small victories in an inclusive classroom. *Educational Leadership, 54*(7), 59–62.

Miller, A., Valasky, W., & Molloy, P. (1998). Learning together: The evolution of an inclusive class. *Active Learner: A Foxfire Journal for Teachers, 3*(2), 14–16.

Murawski, W. A. W., & Swanson, L. (2001). A meta-analysis of the research: Where are the data? *Remedial and Special Education, 22*(5), 258–267.

National Center for Educational Restructuring and Inclusion. (1995). *National study on inclusion: Overview and summary report.* New York: City University of New York, Graduate School and University Center.

No Child Left Behind Act 2001. (NCLB). HB1. Retrieved December 2, 2003, from http://www.ed.gov/policy/elsec/leg/esea02/beginning.html#sec1

Noonan, M. J., McCormick, L., & Heck, R. H. (2003). The Co-Teacher Relationship Scale: Applications for professional development. *Education and Training in Developmental Disabilities, 38*(1), 113–120.

Patriarcha, L., & Lamb, M. (1990). Preparing secondary special education teachers to be collaborative decision makers and reflective practitioners: A promising practicum model. *Teacher Education and Special Education, 12,* 228–232.

Pugach, M., & Johnson, L. (1995). Unlocking expertise among classroom teachers through structured dialogue: Extending research on peer collaboration. *Exceptional Children, 62*(2), 101–110.

Pugach, M. C., & Johnson, L. J. (2002). *Collaborative practitioners, collaborative schools* (2nd ed.). Denver, CO: Love.

Rice, D., & Zigmond, N. (1999, December). Co-teaching in secondary schools: Teacher reports of developments in Australia and American classrooms. *Resources in Education.* (ERIC Document Reproduction Services No.ED432558.)

Rosman, N. (1994). *Effects of varying the special educator's role within an algebra class on math attitude and achievement.* Unpublished Master of Arts thesis, University of South Dakota, Curriculum and Instruction, Department of Special Education.

Salazar, L., & Nevin, A. (2005, May). Co-teaching in an urban multicultural school. *Florida Educational Leadership, 5*(2), 15–20.

Salend, S. J., & Johansen, M. (1997, January/February).

Cooperative teaching. *Remedial and Special Education*, *18*(1), 1–8.

Santamaria, L., & Thousand, J. (2004). Collaboration, co-teaching, and differentiated instruction: A process-oriented approach to whole schooling. *International Journal of Whole Schooling*, *1*(1), 13–27.

Schwab Learning. (2003). Collaboratively speaking. A study on effective ways to teach children with learning differences in the general education classroom. *The Special Edge*, *16*(3). Also available at: http://www._calstat.org/publications/pdfs/2003sumEinsert.pdf

Tashakkori, A., & Teddlie, C. (1998). *Mixed methodology: Combining qualitative and quantitative approaches*. Thousand Oaks, CA: Sage Publications.

Tashakkori, A., & Teddlie, C. (2002). *Handbook on mixed methods in social and behavioral research*. Thousand Oaks, CA: Sage Publications.

Thousand, J., & Villa, R. (2000). Collaborative teams: A powerful tool in school restructuring. In R. Villa & J. Thousand (Eds.), *Restructuring for caring and effective education: Piecing the puzzle together* (pp. 328–359). Baltimore, MD: Paul H. Brookes.

Tomlinson, C. A. (1999). *The differentiated classroom: Responding to the needs of all learners*. Alexandria, VA: The Association for Supervision and Curriculum Development.

Trent, S. (1998). False starts and other dilemmas of a secondary general education collaborative teacher: A case study. *Journal of Learning Disabilities*, *31*(5), 503–513.

Udvari-Solner, A., Villa, R., & Thousand, J. (2002). Access to the general education curriculum for all: The universal design process. In J. Thousand, R. Villa, & A. Nevin (Eds.), *Creativity and collaborative learning: The practical guide to empowering students, teachers, and families* (2nd edition) (pp. 85–103). Baltimore, MD: Paul H. Brookes.

United Nations Educational, Scientific and Cultural Organization (UNESCO). (1994). *The Salamanca statement and framework for action on special needs education*. Document 94/WS/18. Geneva, Switzerland: Author.

Vaughn, S., & Schumm, J. (1995). Responsible inclusion for students with learning disabilities. *Journal of Learning Disabilities*, *28*, 164–270.

Vaughn, S., Schumm, J., & Arguelles, M. (1997). The ABCDs of co-teaching. *Teaching Exceptional Children*, *30*(2), 116–120.

Villa, R. (2002). *Collaborative planning: Transforming theory into practice* [video]. Port Chester, NY: National Professional Resources.

Villa, R. (2004, August). *Inclusive education: Policy, research, and experience – an international perspective*. Presentation for the Vietnamese National Ministry of Education. Ha Noi, Vietnam.

Villa, R. A., Thousand, J. S., & Chapple, J. W. (2000). Preparing educators to implement inclusive practices. In R. A. Villa & J. S. Thousand, *Restructuring for caring and effective education: Piecing the puzzle together* (2nd ed.). (pp. 531–557). Baltimore, MD: Paul H. Brookes.

Villa, R., Thousand, J., & Nevin, A. (2004a). *A guide to co-teaching: Practical tips for facilitating student learning*. Thousand Oaks, CA: Corwin Press.

Villa, R., Thousand, J., & Nevin, A. (2004b, October). Co-teaching has many documented benefits: Challenges to analyzing co-teaching effectiveness. *Inclusive Education Programs*, *11*(10), 6–7.

Vygotsky, L. (1987). *The collected works of L. S. Vygotsky*. (R. W. Rieber & A. S. Carton, Trans.) New York: Plenum Press. (Original works published in 1934, 1960).

Walsh, J., & Snyder, D. (1993, April). *Cooperative teaching: An effective model for all students*. Paper presented at the annual convention of the council for Exceptional Children, San Antonio, TX. (ERIC Document Reproduction Service No. ED 361 930.)

Walther-Thomas, C. (1997). Co-teaching experiences: The benefits and problems that teachers and principals report over time. *Journal of Learning Disabilities*, *30*, 395–407.

Weiss, M., & Lloyd, J. (2002). Congruence between roles and actions of secondary special educators in co-taught and special education settings. *Journal of Special Education*, *36*(2), 58–68.

Welch, M. (2000). Descriptive analysis of team teaching in two elementary classrooms: A formative experimental approach. *Remedial and Special Education*, *21*(6), 366–376.

Zigmond, N. (2004, September) Research findings paint dark picture of co-teaching. *Inclusive Education Programs*, *11*(9), 1–3, 6.

32

Teacher assistants in inclusive schools

Michael F. Giangreco and Mary Beth Doyle

Depending on what country you live in, the personnel hired by schools to assist classroom teachers and special educators in their efforts to educate students with disabilities are known by a variety of names such as teaching assistant, learning support assistant (LSA), teacher aide, paraprofessional, paraeducator, and special needs assistant (SNA). In this chapter we purposely use the title, *teacher assistant* rather than *teaching assistant*, because in all the cases we identified around the world these individuals *assist teachers*, though not always with *teaching*.

The purpose of this chapter is to summarize selected literature regarding the utilization of teacher assistants to support the education of students with disabilities in inclusive, general education, classes. First, we will provide a brief overview of research trends and summarize what is known about teacher assistants. Second, the chapter addresses three contemporary questions:

- What are appropriate roles for teacher assistants who support the education of students with disabilities in inclusive service delivery systems?
- What is the emerging role of the classroom teacher with students who have disabilities and their teacher assistants?
- How does the assignment of teacher assistants affect the personal/social aspects of schooling for students with disabilities?

The chapter concludes with implications for practice and future research.

The chapter's content was drawn primarily from literature published between the mid-1990s and 2004. The majority of sources are from the United States and England, with a smaller set from Australia, Italy, and Sweden. Additionally, to provide a broader, international perspective, we have collected personal communications from colleagues around the world that offer a glimpse of teacher assistant practices in a wider set of countries (see Table 32.1).

Metaphorically, teacher assistant issues are like the tip of the iceberg, the part above the waterline that can be seen easily. Yet it is below the surface where the bulk of potential dangers lurk in the form of unresolved issues in general and special education practice and collaboration. It is these connections between teacher assistant issues and broader educational equity, appropriateness, and quality issues that we encourage you to consider as you proceed through this chapter.

Table 32.1 International perspectives

Country	Personal communication about teacher assistants
Canada	Education in Canada is provincially mandated; therefore the use of teacher assistants is different in each province and local school boards. A common challenge is that teachers and assistants have insufficient planning time together. This leads to the undesirable practice of assistants observing teachers' lessons and being expected to adapt and implement lessons afterwards. Effective inclusive education will necessitate that professional educators create truly differentiated plans for their mixed-ability groups. Karen Gazith, Bronfman Jewish Education Services, Montreal, Sept. 28, 2004
Finland	In 2003, 37,000 students (ages 7–15) in comprehensive schools in Finland, 6.2 per cent, received special education; two times as many as in 1995. Forty per cent of these students participated, at least partly, in regular education classes. From 1995 to 2003, the number of special teachers increased from 4,000 to 6,000. During the same time period the number of teacher assistants in special education, both in inclusive settings and special classes, increased from 2,000 to 7,000. The use of teacher assistants is a main accommodation and their use is strongly preferred, though most have no certificate. The professional nation-level association of the workers in local municipalities and the Central Union of Child Welfare have stressed that more assistants are needed and they should be used as personal helpers, not for the whole class. The teachers' professional union has been worried about the use of assistants as individual teachers. Timo Saloviita, University of Jyväskylä, December 7, 2004
Germany	Increasing numbers of paraprofessionals are working in inclusive education in Germany, most of them without any certificate. Normally, their task is to support a particular student with a disability, not the class as a whole. Some years ago the major organization of parents of persons with intellectual disabilities, the 'Lebenshilfe' ('Help for Living'), tried to find out about paraprofessional practices in the whole country. The 16 Ministries of Education in all federal states were surveyed about their regulations and practices. This turned out to be so difficult that the effort to complete the inquiry was abandoned. Ines Boban & Andreas Hinz, Martin Luther University, Halle-Wittenberg, Sept. 8, 2004
Honduras	Honduras has had a national policy of inclusion since 1992, but implementation remains slow. Teaching assistants are not used to support inclusive education in Honduras because of the poor economic situation. Suyapa Padilla, National Pedagogical University & Rich Villa, Bayridge Consortium, San Diego, CA, December 3, 2004
Hong Kong Special Administrative Region of the People's Republic of China	The Hong Kong Education and Manpower Bureau have been piloting Hong Kong inclusive education projects since 1997. While the *Progress Report on the Education Reform* (June, 2003) reports provisions to overcome the heavy burden for teachers, there is currently insufficient information to fully comprehend the extent of teacher aide deployment, the roles they assume, and their qualifications. However, a job advertisement for teacher assistants in the Hong Kong newspaper, *Ming Pao*, suggests that teacher assistants are graduates with the responsibility of teaching, conducting remedial lessons, co-curriculum duties, relief teaching, and other responsibilities required in the school. Outcomes of the employment of teacher aides have to be clarified further in terms of teacher satisfaction, actual effects on teaching quality and student success. Ming-Gon John Lian, University of Hong Kong & Kim Fong Poon-McBrayer, Hong Kong Institute of Technology, Aug. 31, 2004
Iceland	The first systematic attempt to use teaching assistants in inclusive schools in Iceland was in 1996. Teaching assistants are usually woman who have no prior training in schoolwork but are encouraged to attend special courses. Typically their role is to support pupils who need more help than the teacher can provide; they often have other duties (for example, monitor corridors, help at lunchtime, relieve teachers for short periods). Sometimes assistants are assigned to support students with the most complex challenges. Professionals often express displeasure that more skilled special education teachers are not hired for such situations. Since a teaching assistant can be hired for one-third to one-half the cost of a special education teacher, municipalities are tempted to opt for assistants, partly in response to teachers' long-standing demand for smaller student groups. This is a dilemma for schools, particularly in the advent of trade union negotiations and potential strikes by teachers. Inclusive classrooms that do not use teaching assistants may rely on team teaching (general and special education) or collaboration between teachers and developmental therapists (social pedagogues) who have 3 years of university education in working with people with disabilities, but who do not have equivalent salaries or status of teachers; they are often perceived as teaching assistants. Gretar L. Marinósson, Iceland University of Education, and Ingibjörg Haraldsdóttir, Ártúnsskóli Compulsory School, Sept. 12, 2004

Table 32.1 *continued*

Country	Personal Communication about Teacher Assistants
Ireland	The role of SNAs (Special Needs Assistants) is influenced by the English, Learning Support Assistants (LSA) model. A major difference is that the Irish SNAs are not intended to have any teaching role but, in practice, some do. According to the Department of Education and Science (2002), '... the duties of Special Needs Assistants sanctioned by this Department are of a non-teaching nature. Individual pupils with a general learning disability would typically not require the services of a Special Needs Assistant. Schools with pupils who have special care needs arising from a disability and who also require additional academic input should consider applying for additional resource teaching provision' (p. 1). Tom Daly, SOLAS Project, Boherbue Comprehensive School, Co. Cork, Sept. 14, 2004
Malta	Teaching assistants are utilized in Malta to support students with disabilities in inclusive classrooms. Though most are not trained, a part-time, two-year, diploma program at the University of Malta prepares 'facilitators' (trained assistants) to work with students with disabilities in inclusive settings. Malta does not employ 'special education teachers' as a job position, in part based on concerns that such a role would interfere with teachers' involvement. Support professionals from other fields (for example, psychologists) are available to help teachers. At times there are problems when input from support professionals is primarily shared with facilitators rather than the child's teachers. In these cases, teachers take less responsibility for the child. The roles of facilitators and other support personnel in Malta continue to evolve. Elena Tanti Burlò, University of Malta, Sept. 15, 2004
Singapore	Students with moderate disabilities may be included in the general education classrooms in Singapore. Mainstream schools have very little support for those with disabilities. Classroom teachers are solely responsible to teach these students, usually without much support. At present, the use of teacher aides is not in effect in Singapore although there has been a request to employ them by the Singapore Teachers Union. The Ministry of Education is unlikely to employ teacher aides to support students with disabilities in the mainstream setting in the near future. However, there are plans to provide specialist support in the near future as a response to the increasing demand for more support of students with disabilities. Levan Lim & Joanne Khaw, National Institute of Education, Sept. 9, 2004
South Africa	The use of assistants is primarily confined to the more affluent groups in South Africa, as it is not funded by the state. I have seen parents employ an assistant to cater to a child's physical needs in situations where the child has a severe disability. This is often seen as a way to get the school to accept the child. In my personal experience I have come across situations in mainstream schools where the teacher wanted to hand over all responsibility for teaching my child to an assistant, which we as parents did not find acceptable. I have not heard of any training specific to classroom assistants. Judy McKenzie, Educator and parent of a child with a disability, Sept. 13, 2004
Spain	Teacher assistants (known as *educadores*) are not used in regular schools in Spain to facilitate inclusion in general education classrooms. These paraprofessionals are present only in special schools to help special education teachers meet the needs of students with severe disabilities, and/or provide personal care. In Spain, it is a collaborative team (educational psychologist, speech therapist, and special education teacher) who supports general education teachers; they have the responsibility for meeting the diverse educational needs of all students. Since 1990 (LOGSE, *Ley de Ordenación General del Sistema Educativo*), special education is considered as a part of regular education programs. Consequently, special education services and resources have increased considerably in all regular schools (as an indicator of quality), but still are not enough to fulfill the principle of equal opportunities for all. Cristina M. Cardona, University of Alicante, May 25, 2005
Vietnam	Currently paraprofessionals are not used in Vietnam to facilitate inclusive education. They use consultants, trained general educators, special educators, related services providers, and typical peers to facilitate inclusion. In Vietnam it is primarily a collaborative team that supports the general education teacher. Human and fiscal resources are scarce in Vietnam; the average per pupil expenditure is $25 USD per child per year. Le Van Tac, Vietnamese National Institute on Educational Science and Curriculum & Richard Villa, Bayridge Consortium, San Diego, CA, Aug. 30, 2004

RESEARCH TRENDS

Decisions about the utilization of teacher assistants appear to be driven more by factors such as politics, local historical practices, and advocacy, than by educational research or theoretical foundations. The literature is devoid of convincing arguments that it is educationally sound to deploy the least qualified personnel to provide primary instruction to students with the most complex learning characteristics. To the contrary, it has been posited that such scenarios are illogical and reflect devaluing double standards that likely would be considered unacceptable if they were applied to students without disabilities (Giangreco, 2003). Yet the utilization of teacher assistants to provide instruction to students with disabilities not only persists, it

is increasing (Pickett & Gerlach, 2003). Stresses on the educational system such as teacher shortages, large class sizes, high special educator caseloads, and insufficient teacher preparedness for the diversity presented by students with disabilities, are among the more plausible contributors to increased reliance on teacher assistants.

Existing research offers limited guidance to policymakers and practitioners because it offers only the most basic descriptive findings (see Table 32.2), is virtually devoid of efficacy data, offers studies on disparate subtopics without a coherent line of research, and leaves too many vital topics inadequately addressed. Some of these topics include: (a) the impact of teacher assistant supports on students' academic, functional, social outcomes; (b) effective decision-making about

Table 32.2. What is known about teacher assistants?

Some main points in the professional literature	Selected sources
The vast majority of teacher assistants are women who live in the communities where they work.	(Balshaw & Farrell, 2002; Pickett & Gerlach, 2003; Riggs & Mueller, 2001)
Teacher assistants' qualifications vary widely; most are not college educated and are hired with no prior training or experience in education or special education.	(Balshaw & Farrell, 2002; Riggs & Mueller, 2001)
Teacher assistants are among the lowest paid workers in schools and have limited career ladder options.	(Bernal & Aragon, 2004; Tillery et al., 2003)
The numbers of teacher assistants utilized in schools to support students with disabilities has increased substantially over the past 20 years.	(Clayton, 1993; Pickett, Likins, & Wallace, 2003)
Teacher assistants have been specifically identified as a support to assist the participation of students with disabilities in inclusive classrooms.	(Doyle, 2002; Farrell, Balshaw, & Polat, 2000; Wolery et al., 1995; Marks, Schrader, & Levine, 1999)
Teacher assistants engage in a wide range of roles (for example, clerical tasks, supervision of students, personal care and mobility support, behavior support, instruction).	(Downing, Ryndak, & Clark, 2000; Minondo, Meyer, & Xin, 2001)
There is ongoing disagreement and confusion about what constitutes appropriate roles of teaching assistants.	(Clayton, 1993; Riggs & Mueller, 2001)
There has been a shift in the roles of teacher assistants from primarily noninstructional to increasingly instructional functions.	(Clayton, 1993; Cremin, Thomas, & Vincett, 2003; Pickett & Gerlach, 2003)
Teacher assistants tend to receive inadequate orientation, training and supervision.	(French, 2001; Giangreco, Broer, & Edelman, 2002)
Teachers have mixed reactions to using teacher assistants; some recognize them as valuable contributors, while others are concerned about having another adult in the classroom.	(Clayton, 1993; Lacey, 2001; Mcvean & Hall, 1997)
Research has documented that the utilization of teacher assistants has been associated with inadvertent, detrimental effects (for example, dependence, isolation, stigma, interference with peer interactions, interference with teacher involvement).	(Giangreco, Broer, & Edelman, 2001; Giangreco et al., 1997; Hemmingsson, Borell, & Gustavsson, 2003; Skar & Tamm, 2001)

the circumstances of their use; (c) training impact on performance; and (d) alternative support strategies (for example, peer supports; improving teacher working conditions; reducing special educator caseloads).

The majority of research about teacher assistants consists of quantitative and qualitative descriptive studies (for example, Chopra & French, 2004; Wallace, Shin, Bartholomay, & Stahl, 2001), along with a few single-subject experimental designs (for example, McDonnell, Johnson, Polychronis, & Risen, 2002; Werts, Zigmond, & Leeper, 2001). A small set of evaluation studies exists on topics such as models of teacher/teacher assistant teamwork and schoolwide planning to improve supports offered by teacher assistants (Cremin, Thomas, & Vincett, 2003; Giangreco, Edelman, & Broer, 2003).

Topically, several descriptive studies focus on employment issues, roles, training, and interactions with students (Marks, Shrader, & Levine, 1999; Minondo, Meyer, & Xin, 2001; Riggs & Mueller, 2001; Tillery, Werts, Roark, & Harris, 2003). In perspective-seeking studies about teacher assistants (for example, roles, training needs), the assistants themselves are the most common respondents, outnumbering responding professionals (for example, teachers, special educators) more than two to one. Simultaneously, students with disabilities have been minimally represented as research respondents. Only three studies were identified which sought the perspectives of students with disabilities about their direct experience of receiving supports from assistants (Broer, Doyle, & Giangreco, 2005; Hemmingsson, Borell, & Gustavsson, 2003; Skar & Tamm, 2001).

To date, no large-scale, experimental studies appear in the literature exploring the efficacy of teacher assistants to support the education of students with disabilities in inclusive classrooms. However, a large-scale study of *general education teacher assistants* offered predominantly unfavorable results about their impact on achievement (Gerber, Finn, Achilles, & Boyd-Zaharias, 2001). A small set of studies with 'at risk' learners suggests teacher assistants can have a positive impact on early literacy when they are explicitly trained to tutor students using professionally planned programs and receive consistent supervision (Miller, 2003; Vadasy, Sanders, & Peyton, 2002).

CONTEMPORARY ISSUES AND COMPLEXITIES REGARDING TEACHER ASSISTANT SUPPORTS

The following sub-sections offer responses to three interrelated questions addressing contemporary issues and complexities related to teacher assistant supports.

Question 1: What are appropriate roles for teacher assistants who support the education of students with disabilities in inclusive service delivery systems?

Forty years ago, long before students with a full range of disabilities were routinely included in general education classrooms, modest numbers of teacher assistants were primarily engaged in non-instructional roles (for example, bus duty, monitoring hallways, supervising cafeterias and playgrounds, taking attendance, preparing materials, 'housekeeping'). In response to the increasing numbers of teacher assistants, some teachers' unions and principals of that era 'expressed anxiety and opposition to them [teacher assistants] undertaking anything which gave the slightest hint of substitute or unqualified teaching which they feared might dilute the profession' (Clayton, 1993, p. 33). In fact a high-ranking English education official was quoted as saying it would be 'scandalous' if assistants were asked to teach (Clayton, 1993, p. 34). Others argued the roles of teacher assistants would inevitably include instruction,

> if kindly women are to be recruited in large numbers and sent into schools without preparation to be used as 'an extra pair of hands', a great opportunity would have been missed ... it is unrealistic to imagine that classroom assistants could be con-

fined to classroom chores and supervisory work … they would be teaching in the truest sense of the word whenever they demonstrated, encouraged, assisted and praised children. (Clayton, 1993, p. 34).

Over the past 30 years the steadily increasing number and range of students with disabilities being included in general education classes has coincided with a dramatic increase in the number of teacher assistants and a shift in their roles to become increasingly instructional in nature. Despite the literature's rhetoric that continually trumpets the politically correct message that teacher assistants should be properly trained and work under the guidance and supervision of qualified professionals, research suggests the contrary (Giangreco, Edelman, Broer, & Doyle, 2001). Too many teacher assistants continue to provide instruction and engage in other teacher-type roles without appropriate training, professionally prepared plans, or adequate supervision. In some cases, particularly for students with the most severe disabilities, teacher assistants function as their primary 'teachers' and are often left to fend for themselves. A common response to these dilemmas has been to focus on better training and supervision of teacher assistants; though desirable, it is naive to think that training and supervision of teacher assistants will be sufficient to ensure quality inclusive education.

Disagreement persists about what constitutes appropriate roles for teacher assistants. Should they be trained, supervised, and compensated to assume increasingly instructional roles? Or should their roles be more geared toward noninstructional tasks (for example, clerical, personal care, supervision of students in group settings such cafeterias and playgrounds) designed to improve working conditions for teachers and special educators so these more highly trained professionals can spend more time providing instruction to students? What is the appropriate balance of their instructional and noninstructional roles and how should this balance be determined?

In part, the lack of agreement stems from differences in cultural norms, available resources, and organized labor agreements. Regardless of these and other differences, we contend that a foundational reason for confusion about teacher assistants' roles persists because disproportionate attention continues to be focused on changes that affect teacher assistants rather than exploring potential changes in the broader system of supports. Incremental approaches to including students with disabilities in the mainstream often have led to piecemeal approaches to service delivery that lack a strong affirmative value base and clear educational logic. Attempts to clarify teacher assistant roles and improve training will remain elusive until schools are eminently clear about the expected roles of teachers and special educators in inclusive classrooms.

Question 2: What is the emerging role of the classroom teacher with students who have disabilities and their teacher assistants?

Arguably, classroom teachers hold the potential to be the single most influential individuals affecting the opportunities, instruction, and outcomes for students with disabilities who are placed in general education classrooms. The classroom teacher is the only professionally trained educator in the classroom throughout the entire day, the instructional leader, and the person who establishes the climate of the classroom community. When a teacher functions merely as a host it is unlikely that students with disabilities will be adequately included or instructed. Successful inclusion of students with disabilities in the general education classroom requires a teacher who is instructionally engaged with *all* students in the classroom.

Teachers who are instructionally engaged with students with disabilities express responsibility for educating all students in their class, regardless of characteristics or labels (for example, disability). These engaged teachers: (a) know the functioning levels and anticipated learning outcomes of all of their students, (b) instruct their students who have disabilities, (c) communicate directly with them, (d) collaborate in instructional decision-making with special educators, and (e) direct the work of teacher assistants in their classroom. They maintain an instructional dialogue with their assistants and they phase out teacher assistant support to students when they are no longer needed.

Recent research suggests that the extent of instructional engagement between teachers and students with disabilities, a critical factor affecting the success of inclusive efforts, may be influenced by the way teacher assistant services are delivered (Giangreco, Broer, & Edelman, 2001). Teachers tended to be less engaged or disengaged with their students with disabilities when those students had one-to-one support from a teacher assistant. Teachers were more engaged in situations where the teacher assistant supported the entire class under the direction of the teacher.

Other aspects of service delivery affect teachers' roles as well. In some classrooms teachers and special educators co-teach, while in others the teachers are asked to function without consistent access to special educator support and sometimes under less than favorable working conditions (for example, large class size). One of the more common service delivery models establishes the special educator as the lead professional accountable for the education of students with disabilities in general education classrooms, serving as an itinerant consultant to several classroom teachers and as a manager of teacher assistants dispersed across grades or classes. Though this model acknowledges and relies on the unique knowledge and skills of special educators, its logic has been questioned because its implementation has been associated with problems such as: (a) classroom teachers functioning primarily as hosts to students with disabilities (rather than teachers), (b) extensive utilization of unqualified teacher assistants as primary instructors, (c) isolation, stigmatization, or marginalization of students with disabilities within the classroom, and (d) overextended working conditions for special educators (Giangreco, Broer, & Edelman, 2002).

The model of special educator as itinerant consultant is not inherently problematic. Rather, its current implementation in some countries disproportionately focuses on the potential contributions of special educators, often without corresponding attention to the importance, role, and engagement of the classroom teacher; such issues could reasonably be addressed to improve this option. For example, in Italy, 'The national position is that special education and general education teachers [rather than teacher assistants] should be primarily responsible for the education of students with disabilities' (Palladino, Cornoldi, Vianello, Scruggs, & Mastropieri, 1999, p. 256). The special education support person, *insegnate di sostegno*, has a small caseload of students with disabilities (not more than four), the number of students with disabilities in a classroom generally is limited to one, and class size is not intended to exceed 20. The use of teacher assistants is far less prominent in Italy and their use is typically limited to situations where students require personal care (for example, toileting, feeding) and mobility supports.

Ultimately, in order for teachers to fulfill their important roles in the education of students with disabilities their interactions must extend beyond hosting to ongoing, substantive instruction. For some teachers, being instructionally engaged with their students who have disabilities is second nature and simply what it has always meant to be a professional educator. For others, it may mean a shift in their attitudes, expectations, or supports such as: (a) a reasonable class size and configuration, (b) opportunities to collaborate with special educators, (c) time to work their assistants, and (d) access to individually determined training (for example, differentiated curriculum and instruction to meet the needs of mixed-ability groups). In all cases it will require favorable working conditions for teachers so that the duties associated with including students with a wider range of skills and needs may be approached with the enthusiasm that will invigorate the teaching experience.

Question 3: How does the assignment of teacher assistants affect the personal/social aspects of schooling for students with disabilities?

Social relationships are a key aspect of schooling that can be assisted or hindered by the ways in which teacher assistants are deployed. Paradoxically, though teacher assistants are invariably assigned to be of help students, their presence can have unintended detrimental effects. Excessive proximity of teacher assistants can interfere with peer interactions, stigmatize students, lead to social isolation, and in some cases provoke behavior problems (Giangreco, Broer, & Edelman, 2001; Giangreco, Edelman, Luiselli, & MacFarland, 1997; Hemmingsson et al., 2003; Skar & Tamm, 2001).

Studies exploring the perspectives of students with disabilities indicate that many students perceive their assistants in varying roles as: (a) mother/father, (b) friend, (c) primary instructor, and (d) protector from bullying (Broer, Doyle, & Giangreco, 2005; Hemmingsson et al., 2003; Skar & Tamm, 2001). Even though students may perceive any of the aforementioned roles positively or negatively, they all represent areas of concern. For example, although it is positive to make a friend, what does it say about the social relationships of students with disabilities if their primary friends are their paid, adult, service providers rather than peers? Although it is always good to protect students from bullying, what does it say about a school when the well intended assignment of a teacher assistant to undertake that role may inadvertently delay attention to addressing bullying in the school?

Heightening the awareness of school personnel to these potential problems can minimize inadvertent detrimental effects of teacher assistant support. Simultaneously, recent research has demonstrated how teacher assistants may be trained to facilitate social interactions between peers with and without disabilities (Causton-Theoharis & Malmgren, 2005). Social opportunities and experiences for students with disabilities can be enhanced when school personnel proactively pursue strategies to minimize potentially detrimental service delivery practices while replacing them with those known to facilitate constructive interactions and build relationships.

IMPLICATIONS FOR FUTURE RESEARCH AND PRACTICE

As stated earlier, merely doing a better job of training and supervising teacher assistants is likely to be insufficient to ensure the appropriate education of students with disabilities in inclusive classrooms. It is our contention that students with disabilities are best served when schools: (a) provide appropriate *supports* for their existing assistants (for example, respect, role clarification, orientation, training, supervision); (b) establish logical and equitable *decision-making* practices for the assignment and utilization of assistants; and (c) select individually appropriate service delivery *alternatives to teacher assistant supports* (for example, peer supports, increasing ownership and capacity of teachers, improving working conditions for teachers and special educators) (Giangreco, Halvorsen, Doyle, & Broer, 2004). Collectively, this is designed to increase student access to instruction from qualified teachers and special educators, facilitate development of peer interactions, and promote self-determination.

Before this trio of interrelated components can be effective, schools must clearly establish access to inclusive environments, appropriate curriculum, compatible instructional approaches, and desired outcomes. Only after these foundational areas are addressed will school leaders be poised to articulate their community's vision of special and general education service delivery that best suits their context. Using this conceptualization, decisions about teacher assistant service delivery becomes one of the last pieces to fit into the service delivery puzzle, rather than one of the first.

As schools pursue contextually suitable practices, future research may assist policymakers by filling some notable data gaps.

Chief among these are the: (a) affect of teacher assistant supports on the academic/functional achievement and social relationships of students with and without disabilities; (b) interactive affects of school policies, funding provisions, and service delivery models on teacher assistant supports and student outcomes; (c) research on decision-making models designed to determine the need and appropriate utilization of teacher assistant supports, and (d) research that solicits input from consumers with disabilities and family members to increasingly promote self-determination and family-centered practices.

CONCLUSION

Teacher assistant supports to students with disabilities in inclusive classrooms are at a crossroads. At present, there is no international consensus about the extent to which teacher assistants should be utilized, circumstances that warrant their involvement, the duties they should appropriately perform, or what constitutes adequate training and supervision. Since most countries are still quite far from equitably including students with a full range of disabilities in general education classes, the opportunity is ripe for local, national, and international dialogue on this issue. It is our hope that schools in countries that are already relying heavily on the utilization of teacher assistants to include students with disabilities will closely scrutinize their practices to ensure congruence with their inclusive aims. In countries that have not yet adopted models of support that rely heavily on teacher assistants, we caution schools to remain mindful of the inadvertent problems that have been created when inclusive education efforts have been too highly dependent on teacher assistants. We encourage schools proactively to consider alternative supports that build capacity within the native, general education system in culturally contextual ways toward the benefit of all children.

ACKNOWLEDGMENTS

Partial support for the preparation of this chapter was provided by the United States Department of Education, Office of Special Education Programs, under the funding category, Model Demonstration Projects for Children and Youth with Disabilities, CFDA 84.324M (H324M020007), awarded to the Center on Disability and Community Inclusion at the University of Vermont. The contents of this chapter reflect the ideas and positions of the authors and do not necessarily reflect the ideas or positions of the US Department of Education; therefore, no official endorsement should be inferred. Thanks to the following colleagues who contributed resources or information included in this chapter: Karen Gazith (Canada), Timo Saloviita (Finland), Ines Boban and Andreas Hinz (Germany), Suyapa Padilla (Honduras), Ming-Gon John Lian and Kim Fong Poon-McBrayer (Hong Kong), Gretar Marinósson and Ingibjörg Haraldsdóttir (Iceland), Tom Daly (Ireland), Elena Tanti Burlò (Malta), Levan Lim and Joanne Khaw (Singapore), Judy McKenzie (South Africa), Cristina M. Cardona (Spain), Peter Farrell, Maggie Balshaw, and Gary Thomas (UK), Richard Villa (USA), and Le Van Tac (Vietnam).

REFERENCES

Balshaw, M. & Farrell, P. (2002). *Teacher assistants: Practical strategies for effective classroom support.* London: David Fulton.

Bernal, C., & Aragon, L. (2004). Critical factors affecting the success of paraprofessionals in the first two years of career ladder projects in Colorado. *Remedial and Special Education, 25*(4), 205–213.

Broer, S. M., Doyle, M. B., & Giangreco, M. F. (2005). Perspectives of students with intellectual disabilities about their experiences with paraprofessional supports. *Exceptional Children, 71,* 415–430.

Causton-Theoharis, J. N., & Malmgren, K. W. (2005). Increasing interactions between students with severe disabilities and their peers via paraprofessional training. *Exceptional Children, 71,* 431–444.

Chopra, R. V., & French, N. K. (2004). Paraeducator relationships with parents of students with significant disabilities. *Remedial and Special Education, 25*(4), 240–251.

Clayton, T. (1993). From domestic helper to 'assistant teacher': The changing role of the British classroom assistant. *European Journal of Special Needs Education, 8*(1), 32–44.

Cremin, H., Thomas, G., & Vincett, K. (2003). Learning zones: An evaluation of three models for improving learning through teacher/teaching assistant teamwork. *Support for Learning, 18*(4), 154–164.

Department of Education and Science (2002). *Applications for full-time or part-time special needs assistant support to address the special care needs of children with disabilities.* Retrieved September 14, 2004, from http://www.education.ie/servlet/blobservlet/spedc07_02.pdf

Downing, J., Ryndak, D., & Clark, D. (2000). Paraeducators in inclusive classrooms. *Remedial and Special Education, 21,* 171–181.

Doyle, M. B. (2002). *The paraeducators guide to the inclusive classroom: Working as a team* (2nd ed.). Baltimore, MD: Paul H. Brookes.

Farrell, P., Balshaw, M., & Polat, F. (2000). The work of learning support assistants in mainstream schools: Implications for school psychologists. *Educational and Child Psychology, 17*(2), 66–76.

French, N. K. (2001). Supervising paraprofessionals: A survey of teacher practices. *Journal of Special Education, 35,* 41–53.

Gerber, S. B., Finn, J. D., Achilles, C. M., & Boyd-Zaharias, J. (2001). Teacher aides and students' academic achievement. *Educational Evaluation and Policy Analysis, 23*(2), 123–143.

Giangreco, M. F. (2003). Working with paraprofessionals. *Educational Leadership, 61*(2), 50–53.

Giangreco, M. F., Broer, S. M., & Edelman, S. W. (2001). Teacher engagement with students with disabilities: Differences between paraprofessional service delivery models. *Journal of the Association for Persons with Severe Handicaps, 26,* 75–86.

Giangreco, M. F., Broer, S. M., & Edelman, S. W. (2002). 'That was then, this is now!' Paraprofessional supports for students with disabilities in general education classrooms. *Exceptionality, 10*(1), 47–64.

Giangreco, M. F., Edelman, S. W., & Broer, S. M. (2003). Schoolwide planning to improve paraeducator supports. *Exceptional Children, 70,* 63–79.

Giangreco, M. F., Edelman, S. W., Broer, S. M., & Doyle, M. B. (2001). Paraprofessional support of students with disabilities: Literature from the past decade. *Exceptional Children, 68,* 45–63.

Giangreco, M. F., Edelman, S., Luiselli, T. E., & MacFarland, S. Z. C. (1997). Helping or hovering? Effects of instructional assistant proximity on students with disabilities. *Exceptional Children, 64,* 7–18.

Giangreco, M. F., Halvorsen, A., Doyle, M. B., & Broer, S.

M. (2004). Alternatives to overreliance on paraprofessionals in inclusive schools. *Journal of Special Education Leadership, 17*(2), 82–90.

Hemmingsson, H., Borell, L., & Gustavsson, A. (2003). Participation in school: School assistants creating opportunities and obstacles for pupils with disabilities. *Occupational Therapy Journal of Research, 23*(3), 88–98.

Lacey, P. (2001). The role of learning support assistants in the inclusive learning of pupils with severe and profound learning difficulties. *Educational Review, 53,* 157–167.

Marks, S. U., Schrader, C., & Levine, M. (1999). Paraeducator experiences in inclusive settings: Helping, hovering, or holding their own? *Exceptional Children, 65,* 315–328.

McDonnell, J., Johnson, W., Polychronis, S., & Risen, T. (2002). Effects of embedded instruction on students with moderate disabilities enrolled in general education classes. *Education and Training in Mental Retardation and Developmental Disabilities, 37,* 363–377.

Mcvean, M. L., & Hall, L. J. (1997). The integration assistant: Benefits, challenges and recommendations. *Australian Disability Review, 2/97,* 3–9.

Miller, S. D. (2003). Partners-in-reading: Using classroom assistants to provide tutorial assistance to struggling first-grade readers. *Journal of Education for Students Placed at Risk, 8,* 333–349.

Minondo, S., Meyer, L., & Xin, J. (2001). The roles and responsibilities of teaching assistants in inclusive education: What's appropriate? *Journal of the Association for Persons with Severe Handicaps, 26,* 114–119.

Palladino, P., Cornoldi, C., Vianello, R., Scruggs, T., & Mastropieri, M. (1999). Paraprofessionals in Italy: Perspectives from an inclusive country. *Journal of the Association for Persons with Severe Handicaps, 24*(4), 253–256.

Pickett, A. L., & Gerlach, K. (2003). *Supervising paraeducators in school settings: A team approach* (2nd ed.). Austin, TX: Pro-Ed.

Pickett, A. L., Likins, M., & Wallace, T. (2003). *The employment and preparation of paraeducators.* New York: National Resource Center for Paraprofessionals. Retrieved September 28, 2004, from http://www.nrcpara.org/resources/stateoftheart/index.php

Progress Report on the Education Reform (2003, June). Retrieved August 2, 2004, from http://www.e-c.edu.hk/eng/reform/index_e.html

Riggs, C. G., & Mueller, P. H. (2001). Employment and utilization of paraeducators in inclusive settings. *Journal of Special Education, 35,* 54–62.

Skar, L., & Tamm, M. (2001). My assistant and I: Disabled children's and adolescents' roles and relationships to their assistants. *Disability and Society, 16,* 917–931.

Tillery, C. Y., Werts, M. G., Roark, R., & Harris, S. (2003). Perceptions of paraeducators on job retention. *Teacher Education and Special Education, 26*(2), 118–127.

Vadasy, P. F., Sanders, E. A., & Peyton, J. A. (2002). Timing and intensity of tutoring: A closer look at the conditions for effective early literacy tutoring. *Learning Disabilities Research & Practice, 17*, 227–241.

Wallace, T., Shin, J., Bartholomay, T., & Stahl, B. (2001). Knowledge and skills for teachers supervising the work of paraprofessionals. *Exceptional Children, 67*, 520–533.

Werts, M. G., Zigmond, N., & Leeper, D. C. (2001). Paraprofessional proximity and academic engagement: Students with disabilities in primary aged classrooms. *Education and Training in Mental Retardation and Developmental Disabilities, 36*, 424–440.

Wolery, M., Werts, M., Caldwell, N. K., Snyder, E., & Liskowski, L. (1995). Experienced teachers' perceptions of resources and supports for inclusion. *Education and Training in Mental Retardation and Developmental Disabilities, 30*, 15–26.

33

New machines and new agendas: the changing nature of special education technology research

John Woodward and Ralph Ferretti

A seemingly obvious focus of educational technology research is instruction and learning. For decades, researchers have asked questions such as, 'Can technology be used to help students master basic skills? Do computer simulations improve problem solving? Will word processors, by themselves, yield better writing?' While the learning focus certainly holds for special education research as well, it should be noted from the onset that there has also been a substantive amount of work in the administrative and assistive uses of technology. Special education laws in the United States, for example, require elaborate procedures for diagnostic procedures, criteria for qualifying students for services, and the need for ongoing reporting. The potential use of technology to address these different administrative functions is considerable. In the past, novel solutions to administrative problems have included the use of expert systems as a way of standardizing state criteria for qualifying children for special education services (see Woodward & Rieth, 1997).

Assistive technologies that enhance student mobility and create greater access to instructional materials are another significant component of special education technology research. The range of devices that have been developed is impressive, from virtual reality simulations for learning how to navigate wheelchairs, to speech synthesizers, alternative keyboards, and eye tracking devices. Research on these technologies is generally conducted with a limited number of students, and studies tend to follow a human factors methodology. That is, the usefulness of a device is validated by close observation of individual performance under conditions that simulate real world settings.

Nonetheless, the use of technology to impact student learning is unquestionably the predominant area of research in special education. Looking back over 25 years of work, the research can be captured by two broad trends. First, computer-based instruction (CBI) was an early attempt to use technology for what were traditionally labor-intensive forms of instruction (for example, one-on-one or small group drills). For that reason alone, it is not surprising that special education researchers were drawn to technology as a venue for shouldering much of this kind of instruction.

Researchers also saw that CBI programs could be designed to be more sophisticated than typical commercial drill and practice programs available at the time. In doing so, the programs could respond to individual differences by modeling new skills or by carefully tracking student responses. This framework spawned a series of influential research studies into software programs that captured student performance on a frequent basis, allowing teachers to make instructional changes that were data based. As we will note, this trend still influences the commercial software used with special education students today.

A second trend in special education technology research occurred in the early 1990s when computers and other instructional technologies acquired for schools became more powerful. This change in hardware capacity, which had been predicted by Moore's Law 20 years earlier, came at a time when technology was being embraced increasingly at home and in the workplace. A new type of research emerged which is often called information and communication technology (ICT).

Accounts of ICT and its research agenda vary, but a starting point for many educators interested in this topic has been the increased dependence on technology in industrialized societies. The widespread use of technology helps rationalize the use of web-quests, spreadsheets, graphic presentations, and the like in every special education student's learning experience. A second strand of ICT tends to focus more on the constructivist dimensions of education. In this case, technology is a tool for problem solving, data analysis, and other functions that enable students to develop critical thinking and higher order learning (Loveless & Ellis, 2001). Third, ICT researchers argue that computer technology can be harnessed to address individual differences in a sophisticated way. In the United States, much has been made of *universal design* (Rose & Meyer, 2002) as a framework for adapting technology to individual needs. At one level, this entails hardware and software adaptations such as text-to-voice output, scalable fonts, and even configurable word processors. At another level, universal design implies adapting technology to the learner's unique cognitive needs. Finally, some of the most recent writing in ICT attempts to capture the implications of student–computer interactions in a networked world. While special educators have written little about this, a number of themes that have appeared in ICT literature have direct implications for students with disabilities.

This chapter will review the work in the areas of CBI and ICT, with much greater emphasis on the latter. Space constraints do not permit a discussion of research into other uses of technology in special education mentioned at the beginning of this chapter. By focusing on CBI and ICT, the theme of increased power, range, and flexibility of technology as a driving force behind what researchers see as the best uses of technology for students with disabilities comes to light. Even though technologists over the last 25 years have varied in their theoretical orientations (for example, behavioristic, information processing, constructivist), it is equally apparent that research directions emerge as a function of new, more diverse, and more powerful technologies.

The research reviewed in this chapter is based upon a search of the Educational Resources Information Center (ERIC) Psychological Abstracts, and Dissertation Abstracts International databases from 1980 until the present. We also conducted searches of common US and European journals devoted to educational technology. Many articles, particularly in the general education literature, contained what are best described as 'idea' pieces, position papers, pilot studies, or surveys of how technologies were being used by practitioners. Generally, these articles were excluded from the first two sections of this review (that is, trends in CBI and universal design). The last section of this chapter will address future trends and the extent to which the learning needs of students with disabilities are distinguishable from what appears in the broader literature.

We should also mention that the influence of federal monies in the United States has been a major impetus for technology research in special education. Since 1986, the United States Department of Education, Office of Special Education Programs (OSEP) has provided extensive funding for much of the research described in this review. The OSEP has sponsored nearly $80 million in research and development efforts designed to advance the quality, availability, and effective use of technology. This level of support for software development and research has dramatically advanced special education research, enabling educators with the opportunity to develop as well as investigate a wide range of technologies that would have otherwise been ignored or never developed. Viewed in the context of international research, the impact of OSEP funding is striking and unique.

CBI AND THE EMERGENCE OF THE MICROCOMPUTER

A number of studies conducted throughout the 1980s attempted to determine whether CBI was a complete or 'stand alone' instructional delivery system, or if some form of explicit teacher guidance, supervision, or direct instruction was also needed. If researchers could demonstrate that CBI alone was sufficient, then two significant problems could be solved. First, CBI could become a cost-effective, labor-saving tool given the intense, individualized, and repetitive nature of special education instruction. Second, students could be tutored or drilled in content areas where human expertise was often lacking. Survey research at the time documented that many special educators did not possess detailed content knowledge in subjects like science or math. Core facts and principles from any discipline could be embedded in CBI programs, thus relieving teachers of having to develop in-depth knowledge of multiple subjects.

While many early studies attempted to compare CBI programs with some form of traditional instruction, the problem with this kind of research quickly became apparent. Clark (1983) criticized these studies because researchers tended to confound instruction

with the delivery medium (for example, the technology). This observation has proved to be an inescapable problem for technology developers and researchers. Whether the technology was drill and practice spelling programs, CD-ROM video segments that 'anchored' instruction in mathematics, or word processing that was part of communication mediated communication in threaded discussions, one could always argue that the technology was merely the delivery vehicle. How these devices are situated or what kind of pedagogy or instructional design guided the learning was the more central question.

Hofmeister (1984) voiced this concern in a trenchant critique of early software programs for special education students. Citing developers' inattention to important instructional design variables such as the selection of examples, the quantity and type of feedback, and systematic review, Hofmeister posited that specific instructional principles, many of which were gleaned from the process product research of the late 1970s, could dramatically enhance the quality of educational software. In some respects, Hofmeister's critique framed a good deal of early CBI special education research.

Thus, research from the mid-1980s through the early 1990s often examined the effects of discrete variables such as feedback, massed and distributed practice, and motivation. Computer-based instruction programs allowed researchers to explore these variables, typically under highly controlled conditions in which students in the experimental and comparison conditions used modified versions of the same CBI program. Special education technology researchers noted that in instances when the medium did vary, it was the specific instructional design principles rather than the medium (that is, not the CBI or the textbook) that contributed to any significant differences in outcomes. Many of these studies clearly attempted to address Clark's (1983) observations regarding media as a confounding variable in instructional technology research.

This focus on instructional design variables was an important phase in special education technology research. Identifying the impact of critical instructional variables had potentially significant implications because these features could be added to or subtracted from CBI programs for students with disabilities. At the very least, many at the time thought that the features could comprise important criteria for judging the overall quality of a software program and that these criteria, in turn, could influence the design of commercial software for students with disabilities. For a more thorough discussion of this phase of CBI, the reader is directed to Woodward and Rieth's (1997) historical review of special education technology research.

During this same period of time, researchers crafted an entirely different logic for tailoring the use of microcomputers to the learning needs of special education students. Rather than embedding techniques for distributing practice on skills or providing different forms of feedback into specially designed software programs, computers could simply *monitor* student progress over time. Thus, teachers or instructional aides could administer brief instructional probes and then record the results in a computer once or twice a week. Software programs could then analyze the results, graphically depict progress, and advise teachers when and how to modify instruction to meet individual needs (Fuchs, Fuchs, & Hamlett, 1993). Research on progress monitoring has been most closely associated with the curriculum-based measurement (CBM) movement in special education.

Once again, the rationale for computer-based versions of CBM was based on the issue of labor intensity. In this case, teachers were reluctant to assess student learning frequently and then analyze the results systematically. The earliest computer versions of CBM simply stored, graphed, and analyzed data that had been entered by each teacher after formative measures had been prepared, administered, and scored. Enhanced versions of these CBM systems virtually eliminated teacher administration or scoring of student performance data. Students took the tests at the computer and the program performed the analyses automatically.

Later versions of computerized CBM added detailed skills analyses and instructional recommendations for teachers. This was done largely because teachers were still unable to translate frequent assessment results into effective instructional programs (Fuchs et al., 1993). Ultimately, expert systems were used to specify *in detail* instructional remediation procedures. This technology was added because research indicated that teachers generally retaught skills using the same instructional method and were unable to present content using different methods that may be more beneficial to individual students.

The impact of the CBI phase of technology research persists. Researchers from the 1980s and 1990s have transformed elements of early research projects into commercially available software that is used in schools today. While the remainder of the chapter will review more innovative uses of technology, it should be remembered that the demand for skills development and progress monitoring in special education remains.

ICT: TOOLS FOR CRITICAL THINKING AND AS WAYS OF ADDRESSING INDIVIDUAL DIFFERENCES

By the early 1990s, it was clear that educational technologies were moving beyond stand-alone microcomputers. It was also apparent that an increasing number of adults were using technology in the workplace and more students were using computers at home. The explosive growth of the Internet in the late 1990s made it clear that experiences using technology were increasingly a part of contemporary work and, arguably, literacy. Special education researchers began to view technology as a tool in a complex learning environment rather than a means of distilling or packaging teacher-directed instruction. For example, a library of computer-based images or brief video clips could be used to enhance story comprehension or assist primary grade children in developing their own stories. Other uses of media, including rich videodisc simulations or video segments from popular movies, serve as starting points for group discussions and problem solving.

Cognitive and constructivist approaches to learning

Many researchers, particularly the Cognition and Technology Group at Vanderbilt Learning Technology Center (1997), based their instructional approaches on a constructivist orientation to learning. Thus, students are encouraged to take an active role in acquiring and analyzing data. By using 'real world' settings and ill-defined problems, these researchers have attempted to 'anchor' academic exercises in a more contextualized world, one closer to the arena where students and adults actually solve problems.

Ferretti and Okolo's (1996) work exemplified how technology could be embedded within a complex instructional environment. Teachers presented students with rich and engaging materials that often compensated for the typical reading demands found in social studies classrooms. The topics were also controversial, thus enabling students to develop different points of view in the form of persuasive essays. Multimedia tools were used as the basis for group presentations.

Technology has also been configured in elaborate ways to enhance writing. Englert, Manalo, and Zhao (2004) developed web-based tools that provide text structure supports and scaffolding for students. Their TELE-Web environment included pop-up windows with teacher prompts and explicit directions for students. Online dictionaries for spell checking and text-to-speech output were available for different phases of the composition process. Students could also post their drafts in a public space for other students to critique before submitting a final version to the teacher. Results of this study indicate that TELE-Web promoted an increase in student writing that included more genre specific characteristics as well as conventional writing skills.

Bottge, Heinrichs, Chan, Mehta, and Watson (2003) used CD-ROMs to provide a rich backdrop for specific mathematical problems such as buying pizza for a party and building an animal cage out of lumber to students with learning disabilities. Like the two previous studies, technology was just one component of the instructional environment, and in this study, students constructed cages after a series of relevant calculations and problem solving activities. This research tends to support highly anchored or authentic contexts for developing conditional knowledge in students.

All of these projects reflect ambitious attempts to change the didactic nature of instruction for students with learning difficulties. They also embed technology as a background tool rather than a primary 'delivery' mechanism. It should be little surprise, then, that factoring out the specific effects of technology on instruction – an issue that Clark (1983) raised two decades ago – has been an immense challenge for researchers.

Universal design

The concept of universal design reflects many of the broader promises and hopes reflected in the worldwide ICT movement. Mace (1998, cited in Rose & Meyer, 2002) invented the concept of universal design and established with his colleagues principles for the design of accessible physical environments. These principles include a commitment to equitable use, flexibility and simplicity of use, tolerance for error, low physical effort, and perceptibility of relevant information (Connell et al., 1997). In the recent past, the implications of universal design principles have captivated educators interested in making learning environments as widely accessible as possible. At a time of heightened performance expectation for all children and the US federal mandates to ensure the inclusion of children with disabilities in the general education curriculum (for example, *No Child Left Behind Act 2001*; US Department of Education, 2001), many educational policymakers view the universal design movement as offering a set of organizing principles for the inclusive education of students with disabilities.

However, it is important to distinguish between learning environments which create greater access to *information* and those that ostensibly afford greater access to *learning*. Much of the writing on universal design conflates these two notions, drawing on the imagery of wheelchair ramps and sidewalk curb cuts as a way of arguing for the potential of technology to make the lives of people with disabilities more on par with their non-disabled peers. The examples of universal design that signify greater access to information often amount to what are otherwise referred to in the special education technology literature as assistive technologies. These include modified keyboards, speech recognition, text to speech, scalable fonts, and so forth. Most certainly these technologies potentially enable a diverse range of students with disabilities the opportunity to communicate with teachers or technological devices as well as access media (for example, listen to text).

The argument for greater access to learning is more interesting as well as more contentious. Rose and Meyer (2000) underscore the importance of access to learning through a case of a child with dyslexia who is given computer-supported electronic text with speech synthesis to gain access to written information. The provision of this technology obviates barriers to the printed page; the child is now able to access previously inaccessible written information. However, this access to text may actually undermine important acquisitions, such as learning to decode unfamiliar words. Clearly, the principal difference between these forms of access lies in the *goals* associated with the technology's use. Universal design for access to *information* always impels the provision of maximum support for the user. Universal design for access to *learning* balances information access against the goals of the learning activity.

In a later writing, Rose and Meyer (2002) described a set of learning principles that appear to be informed by discoveries in the developmental neurosciences about the organization of brain networks. Acknowledging that these networks are extraordinarily complicated and functionally organized at multiple levels, Rose and Meyer focus on recognition, strategic, and affective networks that are thought to play an important role in learning. Recognition networks enable people to identify, understand, and attach meaning to patterns that are sensed. Strategic networks enable self-regulation of actions and skills that are essential for learning. Affective networks motivate learning because they attach emotional importance to perceived patterns.

Recent research suggests that the brain's architecture is composed of between 500 and 1,000 cell groups or nodes of brain circuitry (Bota, Dong, & Swanson, 2003) and much remains to be learned about their functional role in learning. Rose and Meyer (2002) neither explicitly articulate the theoretical or empirical basis for their proposed networks, nor contrast their functional properties with other known brain networks. Nevertheless, we suspect that the proposed networks are meant to have heuristic value, in the sense that they draw attention to design principles for accessible learning environments.

These principles, which emphasize flexible and multiple access methods, are linked with the three hypothesized brain networks: (1) Provide means and forms of representation to support recognition networks; (2) Provide methods of 'expression and apprenticeship' to support strategic networks; and (3) Provide means and methods of engagement to support affective networks (Rose & Meyer, 2002). In fact, there is considerable behavioral evidence for each of these principles (Bransford, Brown, & Cocking, 2000; Shonkoff & Phillips, 2000), and their validity does not depend on an isomorphic relationship with the hypothetical neurological networks alluded to in the universal design literature. In fact, Rose and his colleagues intimate that the theoretical and conceptual linkages among these principles and brain networks that supposedly underlie them are speculative at best.

Empirical support for the kind of universal design which affords greater access to learning is exceedingly limited. One of the earliest prototypes of universally designed educational materials for which there is some evidence is an early literacy program called *Wiggleworks* (Scholastic, 2005), which was developed collaboratively by the Center for Applied Special Technology (CAST) and the publishers Scholastic. The software, which is designed to promote early reading, writing, and communication skills in K-2 children, includes features that are designed to make it accessible to users with physical, sensory, and cognitive difficulties. Universal design principles, such as the provision of digital text coupled with speech synthesis capabilities enabling orthographic and phonological representations of the textual information, were incorporated into the software.

The validation of *Wiggleworks* is based on a single evaluation study conducted almost 10 years ago (see Schultz, 2005). While the results of the evaluation indicate that children who received the *Wiggleworks* augmented instruction generally outperformed children who received the existing literacy program on measures that tapped children's reading and writing proficiency at the end of the school year, a number of important methodological issues remain problematic. These include the failure to use statistical procedures to account for demographic differences between intervention and comparison conditions, an adequate description of the literacy programs used in the study, and perhaps more importantly, a clear articulation of those features in *Wiggleworks* that contributed to the reported differences between groups.

The concept of universal design has important practical consequences for the education of students with disabilities because it encourages planners to conceive of technologies that are generally useful for all people regardless of their individual characteristics. However, we are doubtful that empirical research will ever convincingly establish the distinctive efficacy of technologies designed in accordance with the principles of universal design for learning for two reasons. First, any assistive technology can, in principle, accomplish the same goals as technology designed in accordance with the principles of universal design as they relate to increased access to information. Therefore, the choice between assistive and universally designed technology will likely be based on criteria other than its efficacy (for example, user preferences, ease of use, customizability). Second, as we mentioned earlier, the effects of technology are often impossible to disentangle from the characteristics of effective instruction (Clark, 1983). The effectiveness of universally designed technologies that afford greater access to learning will depend upon sound principles of instructional design.

BEYOND THE RESEARCH: EMERGING THEMES IN ICT

Current conceptions of ICT reiterate a theme that has been common in technology-based education since the early 1980s. Computers present a challenge to traditional modes of classroom organization and pedagogy. Today's arguments transcend the naive belief that computers alone will transform education. There is more than enough evidence that adopting technologies, even in the most systematic fashion, rarely sustains fundamental changes in pedagogical practice. Instead, constructivist theory is often enlisted in conjunction with activities such as virtual labs, webquests, and the like to function as another avenue for challenging teacher beliefs about instruction and the centrality of the textbook in learning. We have already alluded to constructivist research in special education as well as the wider theoretical support for this work (for example, Bransford et al., 2000).

In itself, this renewed call to transform practice through technology does little to sidestep the tension between continuity and change that Cuban (1986) articulated in his seminal critique on educational technologies decades ago. More recently, Cuban (2001) has renewed his criticism of educational technologies, claiming that costly acquisitions of computing devices – ones that quickly become outdated and remain underused – have diverted valuable resources from more pressing institutional needs.

A segment of the recent ICT literature supports Cuban's observations. Brodin and Lindstrom's (2003) large-scale survey of special education teachers and administrators indicates that teachers lack sufficient professional development in order to use technology in pedagogically novel ways. Most inservices were seen as information opportunities rather than in-depth occasions for exploring innovative ways to use technology with special needs students. Many educators were also dismayed with the technical equipment and support at their schools. Finally, the effects of ICT on the special needs population, given its inherent diversity, makes generalizations about the academic benefits of ICT difficult (Pittard, Bannister, & Dunn, 2003).

Even though these logistical and professional development problems tend to dampen enthusiasm for ICT, there is no shortage of educators who are perpetually re-energized by the newest technologies. For some, there is an emerging discussion that reflects a substantive shift from a traditional perspective on the use of computers in education (that is, one student sitting in front of a stand-alone computer) to a networked world where students interact with technologies inside and *outside* of school. As we will see below, critical pedagogy supports this shift in thinking about the possible interactions between technology and students with disabilities.

The most recent ICT literature is at the forefront of technological thinking in education and, as such, is well ahead of quantitative or qualitative research. Three broad themes from this literature merit consideration as special educators look forward.

First, the increasingly complex nature of 'text' on the Internet creates the need to reassess what it means to read for information. Early special education technology research examined the impact of computing environments where students could access tools such as spell checkers, digital pads for note-taking, and vocabulary hyperlinks. Today's hypertext environments are both less controlled and more sophisticated, with the demand that the user integrate text, static and moving imagery, and hyperlinked material (Burbules & Callister, 2000). Research (for example, Nichol, Watson, & Waites, 2003) is only beginning to capture the unique contributions of hyperlinks and their effect on comprehension. It is difficult to ignore how rapidly browser environments have changed in just one decade since their inception. A careful and ongoing examination of these new literacy demands and their effects on students with disabilities would appear to be a fruitful area for new research. How good movements like universal design can be at harnessing these constantly changing features of the internet is an open question.

A second and related theme involves critical pedagogy. In a networked world where students have access to multiple perspectives on a topic, reading and evaluating the credibility of information become paramount. This is not just a matter of determining which source of information is the most factual or comprehensive. Rather, it entails cultural criticism. The reader is encouraged to evaluate the ideological dimensions of the text and, in doing so, 'read' the text to determine who is dominant and who is marginalized in the discourse (LeCourt, 2001). In this regard, ICT is much more than technical literacy where students learn new skill sets for a changing economy. Information and telecommunication technology interactions involve the development of identity. The potential for ICT as a tool for giving traditionally marginalized groups such as students with disabilities is an underexamined, if non-existent, theme in the special education technology literature. Put optimistically, computing has the potential of enabling students with disabilities to become better advocates for themselves and the unique needs of their community.

A final and somewhat opposite theme is the potential impact of new technologies on an individual student's participation in networked interactions. New forms of writing instruction enable students to post drafts of their writing and make them accessible to others for feedback and revision. Group writing projects can accelerate this process, thus moving the student beyond the 'individual' demonstration of written competence directly into group compositions. Instant messaging, chat rooms, and threaded discussions are extensions of group writing, all of which may be collectively described as part of 'computer mediated communication'.

This type of interaction, which may occur inside or outside of school, presents specific challenges for students who tend to be passive in classroom discussions and small group interactions. The first author's recent work in mathematics education involving students with disabilities suggests that these students are prone to let more competent others 'take the lead' in academic tasks because of a keen awareness of task difficulty and their comparative sense of competence (Baxter, Woodward, & Olson, 2001; Baxter, Woodward, Wong, & Voorhies, 2002). To assume that group venues such as CMC will positively foster identity may be unwarranted. Rather, it may have the opposite effect, reifying a student's position at the margins of a discourse community. It is hoped that future research in special education will move beyond the typical concern for technological literacy and entertain what it means for students with disabilities to interact *with others* in complex computing environments. To be sure, these kinds of topics are of a different order than much of the special education technology research to date. As the critical pedagogy literature intimates, the concern goes beyond the standard focus on student learning and makes central the issue of an individual's identity in a community.

REFERENCES

Baxter, J., Woodward, J., & Olson, D. (2001). Effects of reform-based mathematics instruction in five third grade classrooms. *Elementary School Journal, 101*(5), 529–548.

Baxter, J., Woodward, J., Wong, J., & Voorhies, J. (2002). We talk about it, but do they get it? *Learning Disabilities Research and Practice, 17*(3), 173–185.

Bota, M., Dong, H. W., & Swanson, L. W. (2003). From gene networks to brain networks. *Nature Neuro-science, 6*(8), 795–799.

Bottge, B., Heinrichs, M., Chan, S., Mehta, Z., & Watson, E. (2003). Effects of video-based and applied problems on the procedural math skills of average- and low-achieving adolescents. *Journal of Special Education Technology, 18*(2), 5–22.

Bransford, J. D., Brown, A. L., & Cocking, R. R. (2000). *How people learn: Brain, mind, experience, and school.* Washington, DC: National Academy Press.

Brodin, J., & Lindstrom, P. (2003). What about ICT in special education? Special educators evaluate information and communication technology as a learning tool. *European Journal of Special Needs Education, 18*(1), 71–87.

Burbules, N., & Callister, T. (2000). *Watch IT: the risks and promises of information technologies for education.* Boulder, CO: Westview Press.

Clark, R. (1983). Reconsidering research on learning from media. *Review of Educational Research, 53,* 445–459.

Cognition and Technology Group at Vanderbilt Learning Technology Center. (1997). *The Jasper project: Lessons in curriculum, instruction, assessment, and professional development.* Mahwah, NJ: Erlbaum.

Connell, B. R., Jones, M., Mace, R., Mueller, J., Mullick, A., Ostroff, E., Sanford, J., Steinfeld, E., Story, M., & Vanderheiden, G. (1997). *The principles of universal design.* Raleigh: North Carolina State University, Center for Universal Design. Retrieved January 28, 2005, from http://www.design.ncsu.edu/cud/univ_design/princ_overview.htm

Cuban, L. (1986). *Teachers and machines: The classroom use of technology since 1920.* New York: Teachers College Press.

Cuban, L. (2001). *Oversold and underused: Computers in the classroom.* Cambridge, MA: Harvard University Press.

Englert, C., Manalo, M., & Zhao, Y. (2004). I can do it better on the computer: The effects of technology-enabled scaffolding on young writers' composition. *Journal of Special Education Technology, 19*(1), 3–16.

Ferretti, R., & Okolo, C. (1996). Authenticity in learning: Multimedia design projects in the social studies for students with disabilities. *Journal of Learning Disabilities, 29*(5) 450–60.

Fuchs, L., Fuchs, D., & Hamlett, C. (1993). Technological advances linking the assessment of students' academic proficiency to instructional planning. *Journal of Special Education Technology, 12*(1), 49–62.

Hofmeister, A. (1984). Special education in the information age. *Peabody Journal of Education, 62*(1), 5–22.

LeCourt, D. (2001). Technology as critical culture: A material pedagogy of 'technical literacy.' In A. Loveless & V. Ellis (Eds.), *ICT, pedagogy, and the curriculum: Subject to change* (pp. 84–103). New York: Routledge/Falmer.

Loveless, A., & Ellis, V. (2001). *ICT, pedagogy, and the curriculum: Subject to change.* New York: Routledge/Falmer.

Mace, R. L. (1998, June). *A perspective on universal design.* Paper presented at the Designing for the 21st Century: An International Conference on Universal Design Conference, Providence, RI. Retrieved January 8, 2005, from http://www.design.ncsu.edu/cud/center/history/ronmace_ud21conf.html

Nichol, J., Watson, K., & Waites G. (2003). Rhetoric and reality: using ICT to enhance pupil learning – Harry Potter and the Warley Woods Mystery – case study 2, *British Journal of Educational Technology*, *34*(2), 201–213.

Pittard, V., Bannister, P., & Dunn, J. (2003). *The big pIC-Ture: The impact of attainment, motivation, and learning.* Sherwood Park: DfES Publications.

Rose, D., & Meyer, A. (2000). Universal design for learning: Associate Editor's column. *Journal of Special Education Technology*, *15*(1), 67–70.

Rose, D., & Meyer, A. (2002). *Teaching every student in the digital age: Universal design for learning.* Alexandria, VA: Association for Supervision and Curriculum Development.

Schultz, L. H. (2005). *A validation study of Wiggleworks, the Scholastic beginning literacy system.* Retrieved January 8, 2005, http://teacher.scholastic.com/products/wiggleworks/overview/research.htm

Scholastic (2005). *Wiggleworks.* New York: Scholastic, Inc.

Shonkoff, J.P., & Phillips, D. A. (2000). *From neurons to neighborhoods: The science of early childhood development.* Washington, DC: National Academy Press.

US Department of Education. (2001). *No Child Left Behind Act 2001.* Retrieved February 14, 2005, from http://www.ed.gov/nclb/landing.jhtml?src=pb.

Woodward, J., & Rieth, H. (1997). An historical review of technology research in special education. *Review of Educational Research*, 67(4), 503–536.

34

Peer-mediated programs to strengthen classroom instruction: cooperative learning, reciprocal teaching, classwide peer tutoring and peer-assisted learning strategies

Eric Dion, Douglas Fuchs and Lynn S. Fuchs

Academic diversity is a universal phenomenon. In every classroom – in schools rich and poor, urban and rural – some children excel while others struggle; some bide their time waiting for the rest of the class to catch up, while others never get enough instruction or practice (Greenwood, Carta, & Maheady, 1991). This is so in part because students must share the attention and efforts of one teacher. Nevertheless, it is possible to better meet the diverse needs of students by using activities such as peer-mediation, which involves students working together on structured tasks.

Teachers who use peer-mediated activities typically capitalize on classroom heterogeneity by requiring their more academically accomplished students to help their less accomplished students. Peer-mediated activities were first implemented at the turn of the nineteenth century (Topping, 1988). Their continuing relevance probably reflects the fact that classrooms have always been hetero-geneous, at least since the birth of public schools (D. Fuchs, Fuchs, Mathes, & Simmons, 1997). Worldwide demographic trends and pressure for the inclusion of students with disabilities will certainly not change this.

Originally developed by practitioners, peer-mediated activities gradually attracted researchers' attention and this latter group altered them according to their interests. Peer-mediated activity came to include elements inspired by cognitive theories (Palincsar & Brown, 1984) and by the highly structured Direct Instruction approach (Carnine, Silbert, Kame'enui, & Tarver, 2004). Dissemination of Lev Vygotsky's (1978) writings also contributed to a growing interest in peer-mediated instruction. According to the Russian developmental psychologist, mastery of complex skills and development of underlying cognitive process occur as a result of repeated interactions between novice and expert. The expert initially compensates for the novice's weaknesses by accomplishing parts of a task, but gradually pushes the novice toward more autonomous and mature performance through a series of 'scaffolded' interactions. Vygotsky recognized that the expert could be either an adult or a more accomplished peer.

In this chapter, we review the strengths and limitations of several peer-mediated programs and describe how a more recent approach, Peer-Assisted Learning Strategies (PALS), circumvents some of the limitations associated with prior work. Examples of PALS activities in reading and mathematics are described. Research on PALS indicates positive effects on the achievement of students of different ability levels. Characteristics of students who do not respond to PALS are also examined.

EARLIER PEER-MEDIATED PROGRAMS

In the late 1970s, different teams of researchers became interested in peer-mediated instruction to enhance regular classroom activities. Studying schools in high poverty areas, Delquadri, Greenwood and their colleagues were dismayed by the very low rate of student involvement during teaching activities. Delquadri and associates hypothesized that the students' low achievement was a direct consequence of their teachers' non-strategic use of time (Delquadri, Greenwood, Whorton, Carta, & Hall, 1986). Slavin, Leavey and Madden (1984) expressed skepticism about then-available programs of individualized instruction because of the programs' emphasis on individual seatwork, activities deemed not engaging for low achievers. Palincsar and Brown (1984), for their part, were convinced that the best way to help struggling students was to put them in a situation in which they (a) had to be active learners and (b) could receive appropriate guidance and frequent feedback. Palincsar and Brown argued that peers should be used to help personalize instruction to students' individual needs.

Palincsar and Brown's (1984) reciprocal teaching method is a small-group intervention designed to improve low achievers' reading comprehension. Students engage in

dialogue about text and apply various comprehension strategies. During the first several sessions, the teacher demonstrates how to formulate test-like questions about the text, summarize main ideas, clarify passages or words and formulate predictions about unread portions of the text. Gradually, students are encouraged to adopt a more active role, leading discussions and helping each other.

Research indicates that, when correctly implemented, reciprocal teaching helps low achievers gain a better understanding of what they read (see Rosenshire & Meister, 1994). Palincsar and Brown's (for example, 1986) writings have done much to popularize the notion that reading comprehension *can* and *should* be taught explicitly. However, reciprocal teaching activities are infrequently used in classrooms. Many teachers find them loosely structured and challenging to implement, notably because of what they perceive as a lack of necessary social and leadership skills among students (Hacker & Tenent, 2002). More specifically, many teachers are concerned by low achievers' inconsistent involvement in the absence of close supervision and encouragement.

Cooperative learning, according to Slavin (1994), relies on teamwork with group rewards contingent on a score reflecting all team members' achievement. The team whose members obtain the highest average on individual weekly quizzes is declared classroom 'team of week'. The idea is to encourage mutual helping among team-mates so that *all* learn. Students are grouped in heterogeneous teams with high- and low-achievers, including mainstreamed students with learning disabilities (LD), distributed evenly among teams. Two well-researched examples of cooperative learning programs are Cooperative Integrated Reading and Composition (CIRC) and Team-Assisted Initialization (TAI).

CIRC replaces all regular reading and composition activities of second- to sixth-grade elementary classrooms (Stevens, Madden, Slavin, & Farnish, 1987). It comes with its own materials, as well as detailed lesson plans for teachers. Each new text is introduced to the team during a teacher-led activity, which is followed by peer-mediated activities, including oral story reading and answering of comprehension questions. For some of these activities, students work in pairs rather than in small groups. At the end of the cycle of activities, students take individual quizzes and teams are rewarded if they meet the criterion. Text composition is also taught by the teacher and practiced by students during a cycle of drafting and editing with feedback from peers. Students accumulate points for their team by being productive writers.

TAI was developed to enhance third- to fifth-grade mathematics instruction (Slavin, Leavey, & Madden, 1984). The TAI curriculum is divided into units that are carefully sequenced in order of difficulty. Students work through the curriculum by themselves, reading explanations and completing exercises and individual quizzes. TAI teams serve only motivational and managerial purposes. In TAI, team members do not actually instruct each other. Rather, they accumulate points for their team by individually completing units. They also check each others work. Since most students work autonomously, the teacher has more time for individual or small-group instruction.

Several teams of investigators, especially those exploring the effectiveness of CIRC and TAI, have demonstrated very positive results for students with and without disabilities (Slavin, Madden, & Leavey, 1984; Stevens et al., 1987; Stevens, Slavin, & Farnish, 1991). Especially impressive are Stevens and Slavin's (1995) results. In this study, teachers mainstreamed all students with LD and, with the help of their special education colleagues, implemented CIRC for two consecutive school years. The CIRC classrooms were matched with non-CIRC classes on important dimensions. After two years, students with LD in CIRC classes outperformed students with LD in non-CIRC classrooms on reading comprehension, vocabulary and basic writing skills. Similar results were obtained when comparing non-disabled students in CIRC classes and in non-CIRC classes.

However, this tells only part of the story on cooperative learning. McMaster and Fuchs (2002) searched for published studies between 1990 and 2000, inclusive, that examined effects of cooperative learning on academic achievement for mainstreamed students (kindergarten through twelfth grade). Only studies that employed an experimental or quasi-experimental design were considered. Less than half of the studies meeting inclusion criteria reported statistically significant differences suggesting cooperative learning was a better instructional program for students with LD than control conditions. That is, in a majority of studies, cooperative learning did not promote the academic achievement of students with LD.

One explanation of these outcomes has focused on the inconsistent involvement of low achievers, including students with LD, in team activities. Low achievers are sometimes excluded from these activities by other team members who ignore their contributions or give them answers without explanations (L. S. Fuchs et al., 2000; Jenkins & O'Connor, 2003). Despite incentives for cooperation, some teams demonstrate an implicit, and probably inadvertent, policy of exclusion. One way to circumvent this exclusion is to reduce group size to two members, creating a situation in which paired students have little choice but to work together.

Two-by-two pairing of classroom students is the instructional format adopted by those who have explored peer-tutoring activities. Delquadri and his colleagues have done much to validate and generate interest in this approach, specifically by their work on Classwide Peer Tutoring (CWPT). They designed CWPT activities to facilitate rote learning (for example, word spelling) by allowing students ample practice in a fast-paced, engaging context with immediate corrective feedback (for example, Delquadri et al., 1986). At the beginning of each week, students are randomly paired with a new partner and given lists of spelling words, simple mathematical problems and reading assignments from their basal text. For a few minutes each day, partners alternate roles of tutor and tutee, asking each other questions (for example, word spelling) and reading aloud. The pair earns points for correct answers, for reading without errors and for correcting their mistakes. Each pair is assigned to one of two classroom teams and the points they accumulate go to their team. A winning team is declared each week. Teams serve only a motivational purpose. All work is done in pairs.

A majority of teachers and students seem able to conduct these activities well enough to bring about notable improvement in basic skills mastery (Greenwood, Terry, Arreaga-Mayer, & Finney, 1992). In the most ambitious study of CWPT effectiveness, Greenwood, Delquadri and Hall (1989) randomly assigned first-grade classrooms to either experimental or control conditions. Experimental students participated in CWPT activities from first to fourth grade. At the end of their fourth-grade year, they obtained much better reading, language and mathematics scores than their control counterparts on a standardized test. Furthermore, students in the CWPT condition were less likely to have been given a high-incidence disability label (for example, LD or behavioral disorders) and, when they were given this label, they were less likely to have been referred to a restrictive placement such as a self-contained classroom (Greenwood, Terry, Utley, Montagna, & Walker, 1993). The effectiveness of CWPT for mainstreamed students with disabilities has also been examined in multiple case studies, with generally positive results (for example, Sideridis et al., 1997). CWPT's main limitation seems to be its focus on basic skills (for example, word decoding). To be sure, repeated practice of these skills with immediate corrective feedback is essential for low achievers and students with disabilities (for example, Torgesen et al., 1999). Nevertheless, CWPT tends to de-emphasize higher-order skills (for example, conceptual mathematical understanding), which makes it appear a bit out of step with current curriculum reform (Gersten & Baker, 1998; Woodward, 2004).

Peer-Assisted Learning Strategies (PALS) activities, to which we now turn, were developed with the goal of combining the engaging and practical dyadic format of CWPT with the richness of content of reciprocal teaching and cooperative learning activities such as CIRC. PALS reading activities (PALS-R) have been developed and field-tested in preschool (4–5-year-olds) (D. Fuchs et al., 2004); kindergarten (5–6-year-olds) (D. Fuchs, L. S. Fuchs, A. Thompson, S. Al Otaiba, L. Yen, K. L. McMaster et al., 2001; D. Fuchs, L. S. Fuchs, A. Thompson, S. Al Otaiba, L. Yen, N. J. Yang et al., 2001; D. Fuchs et al., 2002); first grade (6–7-year-olds) (D. Fuchs, L. S. Fuchs, E. Svenson et al., 2001; D. Fuchs, L. S. Fuchs, L. Yen et al., 2001); second through six grade (7–12-year-olds) (D. Fuchs, Fuchs, Mathes, & Martinez, 2002; D. Fuchs, Fuchs, Mathes, & Simmons, 1996; D. Fuchs et al., 1997) and high school (14–17-year-olds) (L. S. Fuchs, Fuchs, & Kazdan, 1999). PALS mathematic activities (PALS-M) have been field-tested with kindergarteners (L. Fuchs, Fuchs, Yazdian, Powell, & Karns, 2001b; L. S. Fuchs, Fuchs, & Karns, 2001), first-graders (L. Fuchs, Fuchs, Yazdian, Powell, & Karns, 2001a; L. S. Fuchs, Fuchs, Yazdian, & Powell, 2002) and second- to fourth-graders (L. S. Fuchs et al., 1997; L. S. Fuchs, Fuchs, Karns, & Phillips, 1999). Following is a description of PALS-R for second grade through sixth grade (that is, ages 7–12) and PALS-M for second-, third- and fourth-graders (that is, ages 7–9).

PALS-R IN GRADES 2–6

PALS-R in grades 2–6 has a strong reading comprehension focus. It was developed to supplement and enhance regular teaching activities (D. Fuchs et al., 1996). Since PALS-R in grades 2–6 requires a modest amount of classroom time (35 minutes per session, three day per week), teachers continue to use their pedagogical approach and materials. For PALS-R, pairs of students read from material typically available in most classrooms such as basal texts or library books. Reading material is selected so that its difficulty matches the skills of the pair's weaker reader.

Students are paired and trained by their teacher so they can help each other. Pairings are based on a teacher-generated ranking of students on reading performance. The ranking list is split in half (top and bottom) and the top-ranked, second-ranked, third-ranked – and so on – students of each half are paired. Such a procedure creates relatively heterogeneous dyads similar enough to find interest and challenge in the same reading material, but also different enough so that each pair's weaker reader has a more skilled helper and model. As with CWPT, pairs earn points in a usually low-key, weekly contest between two classroom teams. Teachers train their students both in the general logistics of PALS (for example, moving their chairs) and the specifics of the three reading activities: partner reading with retell, paragraph summary and prediction relay.

Partner reading with retell is the activity most directly inspired by CPWT (see Delquadri et al., 1986). It was included because word decoding represents such a difficult endeavor for struggling readers that they are unable to follow the story unfolding or to attend to key information and arguments. Repeated practice with immediate corrective feedback has proven an effective approach to overcome this limiting factor on comprehension. During partner reading, each student reads aloud while his or her partner listens and corrects errors as they occur. The stronger reader reads first. They switch roles after five minutes. After both partners completed their turn at reading, the weaker reader takes one or two minutes to retell what has been read, permitting both students to check their understanding.

The next activity, paragraph summary, reflects reciprocal teaching content (Palincsar & Brown, 1984). Summarizing helps readers focus on the text's most important elements. It also encourages ongoing comprehension monitoring. When children demonstrate difficulty in formulating adequate summaries, this usu-

ally means that they have missed an important point. During paragraph summary, partners take turns reading aloud, pausing after each paragraph to identify its subject and main idea. The pair has a cue card with directives and questions. The student who just read the paragraph is asked 'Who or what the paragraph is about?' and has to 'Tell the most important thing about the who or what.' Students are told 'To say the main idea in 10 words or less.' The tutor reads and summarizes for five minutes, then it is the tutee's turn to read and summarize the next part of the text.

Prediction relay is the third activity. It extends paragraph summary to larger chunks of text and requires students to reflect on what has already been read and to think ahead (see Palincsar & Brown, 1984). Like paragraph summary, it also encourages ongoing comprehension monitoring. During prediction relay, the reader makes a reasonable prediction about what will be learned on the next half page, reads the half page aloud, confirms or disconfirms the prediction, summarizes the half page in 10 words or less and makes a new prediction about the next half page. The tutor prompts the tutee and checks that he or she implements all the steps correctly. Students once again switch roles after five minutes.

Effectiveness of these activities was evaluated by D. Fuchs et al. (1997) using a sample of regular second- to sixth-grade classrooms with at least one mainstreamed student with LD. These classrooms served an economically diverse sample of mostly English-speaking students. Classrooms were assigned randomly to experimental and control groups. Experimental teachers and students conducted PALS activities three times a week for four months. Average and low achievers were selected for assessment, as were mainstreamed students with LD. All three categories of students made more gains on reading comprehension in classrooms using PALS than in control classrooms. Differences were educationally significant. Sàenz, Fuchs and Fuchs (2005) have replicated these results with a sample of native-Spanish speaking English language learners. Once again, stronger gains in the comprehension of written (English) text were obtained in PALS classrooms for all categories of students, from high-achievers to those with LD.

PALS-M IN GRADES 2–4

PALS-M activities were designed to help teachers give additional support in mathematics to struggling students via peer-mediated instruction (L. S. Fuchs, Fuchs, Karns, & Phillips, 1999). As with CWPT and PALS-R programs, all students in a class work simultaneously in pairs. Low achievers are assigned tutors who have mastered the skills they have trouble with. Average achievers are paired together. Teachers can be assisted in this complex pairing task by a software that stores and manages weekly test scores reflecting individual progress in the yearly curriculum (L. S. Fuchs, Fuchs, Hamlett, Phillips, & Bentz, 1994).

Students work on individualized lists of 20 mathematical problems divided into four sections of equivalent length and difficulty. After each section, partners alternate roles of tutor and tutee. Thus, as with the PALS reading comprehension, activities are reciprocal. This arrangement has many advantages (Simmons, Fuchs, Fuchs, Hodge, & Mathes, 1994). Among other things, it offers low-achieving students the chance to share the valued role of tutor with their more proficient partner. It also encourages struggling students to carefully observe their partner while they are successfully solving mathematical problems.

PALS-M activities' objective is to foster both computational proficiency (arithmetic skills) and the conceptual understanding required to successfully apply these skills to problem-solving situations (that is, story problems). This is achieved by insuring that struggling students receive appropriate help from their partner. Most students cannot figure by themselves how to offer adequate explanations, but they can learn to do so if they are carefully trained (see L. S. Fuchs et al., 1997). This requires about four teacher-implemented

30-minute training sessions. Students are first trained to verbalize while they work. This insures that their partner is involved, that they model appropriate strategies or, in case of difficulties, that their reasoning errors become readily apparent. Students are next taught the usefulness of asking for help, offering help and receiving help. This is contrasted with strategies such as pretending to understand or simply providing answers when mistakes occur.

Students are finally trained in the use of five specific strategies for offering conceptual explanations. They are taught to (a) contextualize the problem-solving situation for their partner using an interesting real-life example; (b) draw marks or pictures that stand for the numbers, encouraging their partner to make a visual representation of the problem; (c) use manipulatives (for example, pencils) so that their partner can move and touch things that stand for the numbers; (d) discuss the meaning of the numbers (for example, money) and how this meaning relates to the way the problem is to be solved and its answer checked (for example, when you buy something, you necessarily end up with less money); (e) guide their partner through problem-solving by asking step-by-step questions using what, when, where, how and why (for example, 'What can you do next?').

L. Fuchs and her colleagues (1997) assessed the effectiveness of PALS-M activities by randomly assigning second- to fourth-grade classrooms to different conditions, notably a control condition or an experimental condition where students received all aspects of the training described above. Participating classrooms included at least one mainstreamed student with LD experiencing difficulties in mathematics. Experimental condition teachers and students implemented peer-mediated activities during two 35 minute sessions each week for four and a half months. Mathematics achievement was assessed individually. Mainstreamed students with LD, low, average and high achievers' computational skills improved more in PALS than in control classrooms. Similar positive effects were observed for conceptual understanding, except for students with LD who did not make more progress in this domain than their control counterparts. While this last group benefits from peer-mediated activities, they apparently need something that neither their peers nor their regular education teacher can offer them.

STUDENTS NON-RESPONSIVE TO PALS

No classroom program accelerates the academic achievement of all students. Some fail to make satisfactory progress even in classrooms where teachers use best-evidence instructional strategies. For example, investigators have reported that as many as 30 per cent of 5- to 7-year-old children at risk for reading difficulties (Blachman, Ball, Black, & Tangel, 1994) and 50 per cent of young children with special needs (for example, D. Fuchs et al., 2002; O'Connor, 2000), may not benefit from generally effective phonological and decoding instruction.

Furthermore, the gap between non-responding students and their better-achieving peers continues to widen across the grades, with negative consequences for their self-esteem and motivation (Stanovich, 1986). Offering an appropriate education to every student involves finding ways to better meet the needs of non-responders. Since their learning problems are probably easier to prevent than to remedy, research efforts have concentrated on kindergarteners and first-graders (for example, Torgesen et al., 1999).

First-Grade PALS-R was designed to help 6-year-old students achieve fluent word recognition, but also to help them gain a sense of what it means to read (D. Fuchs, L. S. Fuchs, E. Svenson et al., 2001). In First-Grade PALS-R, the teacher introduces new letter sounds or digraphs, models for the class how to blend sounds into words and presents students (mostly non-decodable) sight-words. Students practice these skills in pairs and take turns reading narrative text from illustrated books. A simplified version of these activities is used for Kindergarten PALS-R (D. Fuchs,

L. S. Fuchs, A. Thompson, S. Al Otaiba, L. Yen, K. L. McMaster et al., 2001). In K-PALS-R, 5-year-old children learn the sounds of all 26 letters, practice blending these sounds and read high frequency sight words and simple sentences. Teacher-led phonological awareness activities are also implemented. Kindergarten and first-grade teachers typically use these peer-mediated activities three times a week, for about 20 minutes each time (for example, D. Fuchs, L. S. Fuchs, L. Yen et al., 2001).

Characteristics of young non-responders to PALS-R activities (kindergarten or first grade) were explored by Al Otaiba and Fuchs (in press). In their longitudinal study, comparable students and teachers were randomly assigned to a condition involving the use of PALS reading activities at some point (kindergarten, first grade or both) or to a control condition (regular classroom activities only). To identify non-responders, beginning reading skills were assessed at the end of kindergarten and at the end of first grade. Only 7 per cent of students who participated in PALS-R in kindergarten, first grade, or in kindergarten and first grade were judged non-responsive. By contrast, 25 per cent of children without PALS-R experience in kindergarten or first grade classes were non-responders, suggesting the early-intervention value of PALS-R. Non-responders were distinguished from responders on the basis of their performance on rapid naming, vocabulary and sentence imitation tasks and classroom behavior.

To explore strategies to meet the needs of non-responders, McMaster, Fuchs, Fuchs and Compton (2005) monitored the reading progress of low-achieving students who participated in first-grade PALS-R activities. Students showing early signs of reading difficulty were assigned randomly to a control condition (continuation of regular PALS-R activities) or to one of two experimental conditions (that is, modified PALS-R and one-to-one tutoring by an adult). In *modified* PALS-R, students were tutored by class-mates with strong reading and social skills. In *tutoring*, students were instructed outside the classroom by a trained research assistant. Both modified PALS-R and tutoring conditions emphasized mastery of basic reading skills, with individualized pacing. These individualized activities were conducted during regular PALS-R activities. There was a continuation of the monitoring of students' reading progress. Most students who remained in the regular PALS-R program failed to make significant progress. Progress was no more apparent for students participating in modified PALS-R, possibly because of implementation problems (these activities were apparently too complicated to implement and monitor for teachers). Only the most intensive adult tutoring approach helped some (though not all) non-responders overcome their difficulties. Responding to non-responders' needs is clearly challenging, probably because of these students' attention problems and limited verbal ability (Al Otaiba & Fuchs, in press).

CONCLUSION

In studies exploring PALS effects on learning, care was taken to assess students representing a wide range of abilities and socioeconomic backgrounds. On average, students from all these strata generally benefit from PALS activities, including high achievers. In other words, use of PALS creates what appears to be a win-win situation where the diverse needs of students are better met. Practically speaking, it is also important to note that this improved response to student needs is essentially achieved as a result of the efforts of the regular classroom teacher and at a modest cost.

Two limitations of PALS activities and supporting research must nevertheless be kept in mind. First, as described, not all students benefit from PALS. Even if the vast majority of students enjoy these peer-mediated activities, including struggling students and their tutors, unsatisfactory progress is apparent among a number of at-risk low achievers and mainstreamed students with LD. Accordingly, as indicated by Fuchs et al. (1997), peer-mediated activities such as

PALS should not be considered a 'sure-fire inclusionary strategy' (p. 199), especially since PALS effects have not yet been examined for students with other disabilities like children with mental retardation. The correlation between low verbal skills and non-responsiveness to instruction (Al Otaiba & Fuchs, in press) suggests PALS may be insufficient to meet the needs of many students with mental retardation. We argue that research to make peer-mediated activities even more effective must continue (for example, D. Fuchs, L. S. Fuchs, L. Yen, et al., 2001), but also that practical supplemental teaching strategies should be explored (McMaster et al., 2005). In the same vein, social benefits of peer-mediated activities like PALS, albeit positive, are apparently not as evident or as consistent as previously thought, notably for rejected students (see Dion, Fuchs, & Fuchs, 2005).

The second limitation concerns the support PALS teachers typically receive from research staff, especially during the first several weeks when teachers train their students to implement the peer-mediated activities. We do not yet have a firm fix on the number of teachers who can implement PALS activities with fidelity with only the limited assistance that their school districts typically provide. D. Fuchs and colleagues are currently conducting a large multi-site, multi-year 'scaling-up' study funded by the Institute on Education Science in the US Department of Education to determine how much technical assistance is necessary for teachers of 5-year-olds and teachers of 9-year-olds to implement PALS with fidelity and for students to benefit academically.

Finally, it must be noted that in the hope of preventing learning problems, most recent studies on peer-tutoring have involved preschool or young elementary students. Secondary school students have been comparatively neglected. This is unfortunate since available results suggests that they respond well generally to peer-tutoring activities (for example, L. S. Fuchs, Fuchs, & Kazdan, 1999; Wong, Butler, Ficzere, & Kuperis, 1996). More research efforts need to be invested with older students, especially considering the non-trivial proportion of non-responders among younger students. At present, all learning problems cannot be prevented.

REFERENCES

Al Otaiba, S., & Fuchs, D. (In press). Who are the young children for whom best practices in reading are ineffective? An experimental and longitudinal study. *Journal of Learning Disabilities*.

Blachman, B. A., Ball, E., Black, R., & Tangel, D. (1994). Kindergarten teachers develop phoneme awareness in low-income, inner-city classrooms: Does it make a difference? *Reading and Writing: An Interdisciplinary Journal, 6*, 1–17.

Carnine, D. W., Silbert, J., Kame'enui, E. J., & Tarver, S. G. (2004). *Direct instruction reading* (4th ed.). Upper Saddle River, NJ: Merrill Prentice Hall.

Delquadri, J. C., Greenwood, C. R., Whorton, D., Carta, J. J., & Hall, R. V. (1986). Classwide peer tutoring. *Exceptional Children, 52*, 535–542.

Dion, E., Fuchs, D., & Fuchs, L. S. (2005). Differential effects of peer-assisted learning strategies on students' social preference and friendship making. *Behavioral Disorders, 30*, 419–427.

Fuchs, D., Fuchs, L. S., Eaton, S., Young, T., Mock, D., & Dion, E. (2004). *Hearing sounds in words: preschoolers helping preschoolers in a downward extension of peer-assisted learning strategies.* Paper presented at the National Disabilities Association Annual Conference, Atlanta, GA.

Fuchs, D., Fuchs, L. S., Mathes, P. G., & Martinez, E. A. (2002). Preliminary evidence on the social standing of students with learning disabilities in PALS and No-PALS classrooms. *Learning Disabilities Research & Practice, 17*, 205–215.

Fuchs, D., Fuchs, L. S., Mathes, P. G., & Simmons, D. C. (1996). *Peer-assisted learning strategies: Reading methods for grades 2–6.* Nashville, TN: Vanderbilt University.

Fuchs, D., Fuchs, L. S., Mathes, P. G., & Simmons, D. C. (1997). Peer-assisted learning strategies: Making classrooms more responsive to diversity. *American Educational Research Journal, 34*, 174–206.

Fuchs, D., Fuchs, L. S., Svenson, E., Yen, L., Thompson, A., McMaster, K. L., et al. (2001). *Peer-assisted learning strategies: First grade reading.* Nashville, TN: Vanderbilt University.

Fuchs, D., Fuchs, L. S., Thompson, A., Al Otaiba, S., Yen, L., McMaster, K. L., et al. (2001). *Peer assisted learning strategies: Kindergarten reading.* Nashville, TN: Vanderbilt University.

Fuchs, D., Fuchs, L. S., Thompson, A., Al Otaiba, S., Yen, L., Yang, N. J., et al. (2001). Is reading important in reading-readiness programs? A randomized field trial with teachers as program implementers. *Journal of Educational Psychology, 93*, 251–267.

Fuchs, D., Fuchs, L. S., Thompson, A., Al Otaiba, S., Yen, L., Yang, N. J., et al. (2002). Exploring the importance of reading programs for kindergartners with disabilities in mainstream classrooms. *Exceptional Children, 68*, 295–311.

Fuchs, D., Fuchs, L. S., Yen, L., McMaster, K. L., Svenson, E., Yang, N. J., et al. (2001). Developing first-grade reading fluency through peer mediation. *Teaching Exceptional Children, 34*, 90–93.

Fuchs, L., Fuchs, D., Yazdian, L., Powell, S., & Karns, K. (2001a). *Peer-assisted learning strategies: First grade math.* Nashville, TN: Vanderbilt University.

Fuchs, L., Fuchs, D., Yazdian, L., Powell, S., & Karns, K. (2001b). *Peer-assisted learning strategies: Kindergarten math.* Nashville, TN: Vanderbilt University.

Fuchs, L. S., Fuchs, D., & Karns, K. (2001). Enhancing kindergartners' mathematical development: effects of peer-assisted learning strategies. *Elementary School Journal, 101*, 495–510.

Fuchs, L. S., Fuchs, D., & Kazdan, S. (1999). Effects of peer-assisted learning strategies on high school students with serious reading problems. *Remedial & Special Education, 20*, 309–318.

Fuchs, L. S., Fuchs, D., Hamlett, C. L., Phillips, N., & Bentz, J. (1994). Classwide curriculum-based measurement: Helping general educators meet the challenge of students diversity. *Exceptional Children, 60*, 518–537.

Fuchs, L. S., Fuchs, D., Hamlett, C. L., Phillips, N., Karns, K., & Dutka, S. (1997). Enhancing student's helping behavior during peer-mediated instruction with conceptual mathematical explanations. *Elementary School Journal, 97*, 223–249.

Fuchs, L. S., Fuchs, D., Karns, K., & Phillips, N. (1999). *Peer-assisted learning Ssrategies: Math methods for grades 2–6.* Nashville, TN: Vanderbilt University.

Fuchs, L. S., Fuchs, D., Kazdan, S., Karns, K., Calhoon, M. B., Hamlett, C. L., et al. (2000). Effects of workgroup structure and size on student productivity during collaborative work on complex tasks. *Elementary School Journal, 100*, 183–212.

Fuchs, L. S., Fuchs, D., Yazdian, L., & Powell, S. R. (2002). Enhancing first-grade children's mathematical development with peer-assisted learning strategies. *School Psychology Review, 31*, 569–583.

Gersten, R., & Baker, S. (1998). Real world use of scientific concepts: Integrating situated cognition with explicit instruction. *Exceptional Children, 65*, 23–35.

Greenwood, C. R., Carta, J. J., & Maheady, L. (1991). Peer tutoring programs in the regular education classroom. In G. Stoner, M. R. Shinn, & H. M. Walker (Eds.), *Interventions for achievement and behavior problems* (pp.

179–200). Silver Spring, MD: National Association of School Psychologists.

Greenwood, C. R., Delquadri, J. C., & Hall, R. V. (1989). Longitudinal effects of classwide peer tutoring. *Journal of Educational Psychology, 81*, 371–383.

Greenwood, C. R., Terry, B., Arreaga-Mayer, C., & Finney, R. (1992). The classwide peer tutoring program: Implementation factors moderating students' achievement. *Journal of Applied Behavior Analysis, 25*, 101–116.

Greenwood, C. R., Terry, B., Utley, C. A., Montagna, D., & Walker, D. (1993). Achievement, placement, and services: Middle school benefits of classwide peer tutoring used at the elementary school. *School Psychology Review, 22*, 497–516.

Hacker, D. J., & Tenent, A. (2002). Implementing reciprocal teaching in the classroom: Overcoming obstacles and making modifications. *Journal of Educational Psychology, 94*, 699–718.

Jenkins, J. R., & O'Connor, R. E. (2003). Cooperative learning for students with learning disabilities: Evidence from experiments, observations, and interviews. In H. L. Swanson, K. R. Harris, & S. Graham (Eds.), *Handbook of learning disabilities* (pp. 417–430). New York: Guilford Press.

McMaster, K. N., & Fuchs, D. (2002). Effects of cooperative learning on the academic achievement of students with learning disabilities: An update of Tateyama-Sniezek's review. *Learning Disabilities Research & Practice, 17*, 107–117.

McMaster, K. N., Fuchs, D., Fuchs, L. S., & Compton, D. L. (2005). Responding to nonresponders: An experimental field trial of identification and intervention methods. *Exceptional Children, 71*, 445–463.

O'Connor, R. E. (2000). Increasing the intensity of intervention in kindergarten and first grade. *Learning Disabilities Research & Practice, 15*, 43–54.

Palincsar, A. S., & Brown, A. L. (1984). Reciprocal teaching of comprehension-fostering and comprehension-monitoring activities. *Cognition and Instruction, 1*, 117–175.

Palincsar, A. S., & Brown, A. L. (1986). Interactive teaching to promote independent learning from text. *Reading Teacher, 39*, 771–777.

Rosenshire, B., & Meister, C. (1994). Reciprocal teaching: A review of research. *Review of Educational Research, 64*, 479–530.

Sàenz, L. M., Fuchs, L. S., & Fuchs, D. (2005). Effects of peer-assisted learning strategies on English language learners with learning disabilities: A randomized controlled study. *Exceptional Children, 71*, 231–247.

Sideridis, G. D., Utley, C. A., Greenwood, C. R., Delquadri, J., Dawson, H., Palmer, P., et al. (1997). Classwide peer tutoring: Effects on the spelling performance and social interactions of students with mild disabilities and their typical peers in an integrated instructional setting. *Journal of Behavioral Education, 7*, 435–462.

Simmons, D. C., Fuchs, D., Fuchs, L. S., Hodge, J. P., & Mathes, P. G. (1994). Importance of instructional complexity and role reciprocity to classwide peer tutoring. *Learning Disabilities Research & Practice, 9*, 203–212.

Slavin, R. E. (1994). *Cooperative learning: Theory, research, & practice* (2nd ed.). Boston, MA: Allyn & Bacon.

Slavin, R. E., Leavey, M. B., & Madden, N. A. (1984). Combining learning and individualized instruction: Effects on student mathematics achievement, attitudes, and behaviors. *Elementary School Journal, 84*, 409–422.

Slavin, R. E., Madden, N. A., & Leavey, M. B. (1984). Effects of team assisted individualization on the mathematics achievement of academically handicapped and nonhandicapped students. *Journal of Educational Psychology, 76*, 813–819.

Stanovich, K. E. (1986). Matthew effect in reading: Some consequences of individual differences in the acquisition of early literacy. *Reading Research Quarterly, 21*, 360–406.

Stevens, R. J., & Slavin, R. E. (1995). Effects of a cooperative learning approach in reading and writing on academically handicapped and nonhandicapped students. *Elementary School Journal, 95*, 241–262.

Stevens, R. J., Madden, N. A., Slavin, R. E., & Farnish, A. M. (1987). Cooperative integrated reading and composition: Two field experiments. *Reading Research Quarterly, 22*, 433–454.

Stevens, R. J., Slavin, R. E., & Farnish, A. M. (1991). The effects of cooperative learning and direct instruction in reading comprehension strategies on main idea identification. *Journal of Educational Psychology, 83*, 8–16.

Topping, K. (1988). *The peer tutoring handbook: Promoting co-operative learning.* Cambridge, MA: Brookline Press.

Torgesen, J. K., Wagner, R. K., Rashotte, C. A., Lindamood, P., Rose, E., Conway, T., et al. (1999). Preventing reading failure in young children with phonological processing disabilities: Group and individual responses to instruction. *Journal of Educational Psychology, 91*, 579–593.

Vygotsky, L. S. (1978). *Mind in society. The developement of higher psychological processes.* London: Harvard University Press.

Wong, B. Y. L., Butler, D. L., Ficzere, S. A., & Kuperis, S. (1996). Teaching low achievers and students with learning disabilities to plan, write, and revise opinion essays. *Journal of Learning Disabilities, 29*, 197–212.

Woodward, J. (2004). Mathematics education in the United States: Past to present. *Journal of Learning Disabilities, 37*, 16–31.

35

The friendships and peer relationships of children and young people who experience difficulties in learning

Dawn B. Male

She's my friend – my best friend ... I'm her friend ... she's kind to me ... never horrible ... we share ... we come on the bus ... she helps me do things ... and I help her ... she sits with me ... we stay together at break time ... say secrets! No boys! (Katie, a young person with learning disabilities, describing her long-term friendship with Lizzie)

The purpose of this chapter is to offer a rationale for the importance of friendships and peer relations in the lives of children and young people with learning disabilities; to provide a summary of the literature relating to the nature of friendships among and between children and young people with and without learning disabilities; and to describe some ways of promoting friendships among and between children and young people with learning disabilities.

INTRODUCTION

It has long been recognised that friendships matter. Friendships are less like "the frosting on the cake," and more like an essential organic compound that fuels our development. (Amos, 2004, p. 4)

The benefits of friendships on psychological and physical health have been well documented. Developmental theorists (for example, Piaget, 1932) and social learning theorists (for example, Bandura, 1977) have emphasised the importance of positive child–child relations in facilitating child development. Others have emphasised the role of peer relations in the child's personal identity formation (for example, Erikson, 1968) and in the acquisition of higher level social skills (for example, Grenot-Scheyer, 2004). More specifically, the positive influence of peer acceptance has been demonstrated empirically on the socialisation of aggressive and sexual impulses (Hartup, 1978), and on cognitive (for example, Rardin & Moan, 1971), linguistic (see Bates, 1975), sex-role (for example, Fagot, 1977) and moral development (for example, Damon, 1983). Parker and Asher (1987), in a review of the literature, report general support for the hypothesis that children with poor peer adjustment are at risk for later life difficulties. Peer acceptance and social status are thus seen as vital to the well-being of the child and young person.

Various types of friendships exist at all stages of life but their cognitive, social and emotional characteristics differ with age, gender and social norms (Heiman, 2000). Friendships among pre-adolescents are described in terms of shared activities (LaGreca, 1997) whilst for adolescents friendships become more intimate and involve more intense feelings (Mussen, Conger, Kagan, & Huston, 1990; LaGreca, 1997). Whilst cross-sex relationships become increasingly common during adolescence, the majority of studies show a significant sex cleavage at all ages (Male, 2002). Friendships among girls tend to be more exclusive and less extensive, whilst friendships among boys tend to be more free-ranging, occur in larger groups, and are less exclusive (Blatchford, 1998).

THE IMPORTANCE OF FRIENDSHIPS

I made loads of friends during the summer which always makes me happy. My best friend was Robert. (Becky, 16, describing her participation in an 'inclusive' leisure programme, cited in Murray, 2002)

I am excluded from so much and I am so lonely and have few friends … (Osian, 20, describing his feelings of social exclusion, cited in Murray, 2002)

In the past the friendship needs and aspirations of people with learning disabilities have received relatively little attention in either research or policy and practice (Emerson & McVilly, 2004). However, it is increasingly acknowledged (for example, Foundation for People with Learning Disabilities, 2005) that people with learning disabilties – like their typically developing counterparts – attach great importance to friendships. In England policy has concluded that 'Helping people sustain friendships is consistently shown as being one of the greatest challenges faced by learning disability services' (Department of Health, 2001, p. 81). One of the outcome statements used by the Quality Network to assess services for people with learning disabilities is, 'I have

friendships and relationships' (Quality Network, 2005). According to Tashie and Rossetti (2004), the increasing interest in the importance of friendships among and between people with and without learning disabilities is a sign of 'true social change' (p. 35).

Parents, too, attest to the importance of friendships for their child or young person with learning disabilities: Cuckle and Wilson (2002), for example, in a study of social relationships and friendships among young people with Down's syndrome in UK secondary schools report that, 'Social development and friendships were major areas of concern expressed by parents … Most parents would have liked their children to have more friends' (p. 69). Similarly, Scottish parents, responding to a survey relating to the social inclusion of their child with visual impairments, are reported to recognise friendships and social inclusion as an important part of school life (Buultjens & Stead, with Dallas, 2002). Comparative studies conducted in Europe and the US enquiring into parents' views about special educational provision report that the development of friendships by their child with disabilities is an area of significant present and future concern (Plaute & Westling, 1996; Westling, 1996, 1997; Male, 1998). Individual accounts by parents nationally and internationally (for example, Amos, 2004; *Making friends*, 2003) provide moving accounts of the importance of friendships for their child or young person with learning disabilities.

RESEARCHING INTO FRIENDSHIPS AND PEER RELATIONS AMONG AND BETWEEN CHILDREN AND YOUNG PEOPLE WITH AND WITHOUT LEARNING DISABILITIES

A variety of research techniques have been used to study friendships among and between children and young people with and without learning disabilities. Commonly, social relationships of children and young people with learning disabilities are inferred secondarily, for example via observations (naturalistic and/or structured) and most usually in relation to their typically developing counterparts (for example, Cutts & Sigafoos, 2001). Frequently, key informants (for example, teachers, support workers, parents, peers) are surveyed (for example, Bunch & Valeo, 2004).

The self-advocacy movement affirms the right of all disabled people to enjoy the same basic human rights as their fellow citizens (Mittler, 1996). Core components of self-advocacy include being able to express thoughts and feelings with assertiveness and being able to make choices and take decisions (Further Education Unit, 1990). Accordingly, what have been termed 'inclusive research' practices (see Chappell, 2000; Walmsley, 2001, 2004) are increasingly being advocated and ways of 'hearing the voices' of children and young people with learning disabilities are being sought (see, for example, Rose, 1998; Lewis, 2002).

Enquiry techniques which seek to involve children and young people with learning disabilities in the research process include questionnaires (for example, Heiman, 2000), interviews (structured and semi-structured) (for example, Cuckle & Wilson, 2002) and sociometric measures (for example, Male, 2002).

When enquiring into friendships from the perspective of children and young people with learning disabilities an important question to ask is: does the chid/young person have a concept of what a friend is and an understanding of what friendship is all about? Notwithstanding the relative dearth of research in this area, the indications are that they do.

UNDERSTANDING 'FRIENDS' AND 'FRIENDSHIP'

What is 'friendship'? An Aristotelian conceptualisation depicts friendship as a choice to engage with goodwill towards another, goodwill reciprocated, and a shared recognition of the reciprocated goodwill by both persons (Aristotle, 1963). Katie's account of her friendship with Lizzie (above) appears to be consistent with this depiction of friendship: Katie and Lizzie provide each other with nur-

turance, support and security; they offer company and opportunities for intimacy; there is a sense of equality in the relationship.

Research more generally appears to support this 'mainstream' conceptualisation of friends and friendships held by children and young people with learning disabilities. In a study by Margalit (1994), for example, preadolescent and adolescent students with learning disabilities reported that a good friend is someone who helps them, someone with whom they can have fun, a companion, someone with whom they can journey to school, someone with whom they can play, and someone with whom they can talk on the telephone. Cuckle and Wilson (2002) report similar 'mainstream' notions of friends and friendships among children with Down's syndrome: 'a friend' is someone who is loyal and kind; who can ask and be asked for help; who likes the same things and shares activities; who 'sticks up for you' or 'is there for you'. They conclude that 'ideas among young people about what constituted friendship were very consistent. The vast majority had a strong sense of what friendship entailed' (p. 68). By way of some contrast with 'mainstream' accounts, however (but consistent with other research with children and young people with learning disabilities) Cuckle and Wilson found that the social activities engaged in by the young people with Down's syndrome tended to be organised around family, extended family activities and community activities, and frequently were strictly supervised by parents.

In a sociometric study conducted by Male (2002), reasons given by adolescents with severe learning disabilities to justify their choice of a friend indicated rational – if perhaps somewhat unsophisticated – notions of friendships:

> He's nice ... he helps me do stuff ... he plays football with me ... he helps me put them away. (Andrew, nominating Michael as his friend)
>
> I cuddle him ... he holds my hand ... I walk in with him. (Michael, nominating Andrew as his friend)
>
> He's nice and we do gardening together. (Helen, nominating Aziz as a friend)

From these and other nominations made by the

adolescents participating in the study Male concludes that 'the relationships and friendships … appeared genuine and to be of significance … choices made were stable and valid and appeared to be based on similar criteria of acceptability to "mainstream" choices'.

The work of Gleason (1989, 1994), as described by Klotz (2004), illustrates the significance of the role of the nondisabled researcher in helping us to understand the nature and 'meaningfulness' of the social relationships of those with the most profound learning disabilities. Klotz describes Gleason's work with two nonverbal multiply and developmentally disabled boys called Thomas and Daniel thus:

> Rather than correcting their behaviour and forcibly moving Thomas and Daniel away from one another as they rolled around on the floor in a seemingly meaningless and chaotic manner … Gleason allowed the boys to interact as they wished. By adopting a methodology that maintained a sense of the context within which their actions and interactions took place, Gleason discovered that Thomas and Daniel were actually engaging in meaningful and intentional behaviour. He realised that they had developed shared and learned patterns of engaging with one another … (2004, p. 100)

The conclusion that might be drawn is that Thomas and Daniel, notwithstanding their profound learning disabilities, had – like Katie and Lizzie – arrived at an Aristotelian conceptualisation of a relationship, that is, one which was engaged in through choice, which was reciprocated and which was based on goodwill.

FACTORS INVOLVED IN THE FORMATION OF RELATIONSHIPS

Numerous factors have been found to be involved in the formation of interpersonal relationships (Mussen et al., 1990). In 'mainstream' studies a factor consistently found to be associated with social acceptability is physical attractiveness: more physically attractive individuals tend to be more liked than less attractive individuals. There are some indications that this may also be the case for children

and young people with learning disabilities: in a sociometric study by Male (2002), for example, the 'star' of the group was described (admiringly) by another as 'looking like a man' whereas a rejectee was described (in a derogatory tone) as 'looking like a baby'.

Physical attractiveness (or *perceived* physical attractiveness) is a contentious issue when applied to people with disabilities. Controversial findings relating to the effects of facial plastic surgery on children and young people with Down's syndrome were presented by Reuven Feuerstein (1986) at a Down's Syndrome International Conference held in the UK. A group of 250 children in Israel were shown two sets of pictures. Both sets were of children with Down's syndrome but one group had received facial plastic surgery to 'tone down' the characteristic Down's syndrome features. The pupils were asked to assess the pupils with Down's syndrome on a scale of intelligence or stupidity, goodness or wickedness, social attractiveness or undesirability. With what is described as 'a remarkable degree of uniformity' (p. 10) the pupils gave the more positive scores to those children who had undergone facial plastic surgery, and vice versa for those who had not. In a follow-up study of 45 children with Down's syndrome who had received a variety of facial surgical procedures, teachers and parents reported improved self-confidence in class, more care in appearance and better social integration. According to Feuerstein the findings provide evidence of the way in which facial plastic surgery can help children with Down's syndrome become more socially accepted in mainstream schools.

Other factors found to be involved in the formation of interpersonal relationships are *proximity* ('nearness') and three types of similarity: *attitude similarity*; *demographic similarity* (for example, age, sex, socioeconomic status) and *similarity in personality*. According to Rubin (1973, cited in Mussen et al., 1990) similarity is important because:

- if we like those who are similar to us, there is a good chance that they will like us

- communication is easier with people who are similar
- similar others may confirm the rightness of our attitudes and beliefs
- it makes sense if we like ourselves, then we should also like others who are similar to us.

The similarity hypothesis may at least partly explain why, even in inclusive settings, children and young people with learning disabilities are more likely to form friends with other children and young people with learning disabilities than with typical peers.

In terms of rejection, differences have been found according to the status of the children and young people. Roberts and Zubrick (1992, cited in Frederickson & Furnham, 2004), in a study investigating variables associated with peer sociometric status for Australian 8–13-year-old pupils with moderate learning disabilities, reported that, for mainstream pupils, sociometric rejection was predicted by peer perceptions both of academic behaviour and of disruptive behaviour, whereas for pupils with moderate learning disabilities included in mainstream provision only peer perceptions of disruption were related to sociometric rejection. Nabuzoka and Smith (1993) also reported differences between peer-assessed sociometric status for British 8–12-year-olds and their mainstream peers. For mainstream pupils only acceptance was associated with high peer nominations for leadership and rejection was associated with low peer nominations for cooperative behaviour and high peer nominations as a victim or someone who seeks help frequently. Newcomb et al., (1993, cited in Frederickson & Furnham, 2004) note that it is consistently reported in mainstream samples that rejected children score higher than averagely accepted children on aggressive and acting-out behaviour and lower on pro-social behaviours, while popular children score higher than average on pro-social behaviours and lower on aggressive and acting-out behaviours. By contrast, however, Frederickson and Furnham (1998, cited in Frederickson & Furnham, 2004) reported that rejected pupils with moderate learning disabilities were differentiated from those of average acceptance by low scores on positive behaviours, but not high scores on negative behaviours. Popular pupils with moderate learning disabilities were characterised by lower scores on negative behaviours than children whose acceptance was average, but not by higher scores on positive behaviours.

On the basis of the finding of differences made in assessments according to the status of the individual (that is, learning disabled or nonlearning disabled) Frederickson and Furnham question the appropriateness of the generic nature of social skills programmes for promoting social inclusion of pupils with learning disabilities.

THE NATURE OF FRIENDSHIPS BETWEEN CHILDREN AND YOUNG PEOPLE WITH AND WITHOUT LEARNING DISABILITIES

International reports (for example, OECD, 1981; UNESCO, 1994) and national legislation and guidance in many countries (for example, in Great Britain, DES, 1981; DfES, 2001; in the US, IDEA Amendments of 1997 [PL 105–17]) call for the inclusion of children and young people with disabilities in 'ordinary' educational settings. A perceived benefit is increased opportunities for socialisation with 'ordinary' peers. Research interest, therefore, frequently has focused on social relations between children and young people with learning disabilities and their nondisabled peers.

Meyer et al. (cited in Grenot-Scheyer, 2004) describe six 'frames' of friendship between children and young people with and without learning disabilities. These 'frames' represent a thematic category that emerged from observing children and young people with learning disabilities and their nondisabled peers. The six 'frames' identified by Meyer et al. are

- *ghosts & guests*: this frame describes the invisible social status of children and young people with and without learning disabilities whose presence is acknowledged, but who continue to be viewed as outsiders

- *the inclusion kid/different friend*: differential treatment of either a positive or negative nature characterises this frame; children and young people with disabilities were described as, for example, 'cute' or 'weird' by their typically developing counterparts
- *I'll help:* observations within this frame included various examples of assisting
- *just another kid*: observations within this frame indicated that for some children and young people without disabilities those with disabilities were 'no big deal'
- *regular friends*: these were not 'best' friends but were friends who were part of a larger social network
- friends forever: a best friend who is unique and special (Grenot-Scheyer, 2004).

Perhaps unsurprisingly, Meyer et al. report that many observations fell within the '*I'll help*' frame; parents were reported to find this frame acceptable insofar as the indication is that their son or daughter is being cared for and looked after. The '*friends forever*' frame was described as a critical yet elusive kind of relationship between learning disabled and nondisabled children and young people that was rarely evident in the research.

The notion of 'help' also featured in a study conducted by Heiman (2000) who investigated the quality of friendships as reported by Israeli adolescents with mild learning disabilities in two different educational settings (special education and self-contained mainstream), compared with similar reports by pupils without learning disabilities. When asked to describe '*a good friend*' four categories emerged: '*one who helps*'; '*emotional support*'; '*partners for thoughts and secrets*'; '*mutual entertainment*'. Significant differences in the item of '*one who helps*' were reported, with fewer special education pupils mentioning help than pupils in self-contained mainstream settings and pupils without learning disabilities. In both groups of pupils with learning disabilities '*a good friend*' meant a person who would help with schoolwork, whereas for pupils without learning disabilities the meaning of 'help' extended into areas outside of school. The same trend was found for considering good friends as '*partners for

their thoughts and secrets'. No differences were found between groups on emotional support, nor on mutual entertainment.

Heiman also found differences in the reported *numbers* of friends according to placement, with pupils in special school tending to have fewer friends than pupils with and without learning disabilities in mainstream schools. Heiman notes that pupils with learning disabilities in special schools, 'felt lonelier than students in other groups' (2000, p. 1).

In terms of actual interactions in mainstream settings between children and young people with and without learning disabilities, the research literature (for example, Gresham, 1982; Taylor, Asher, & Williams, 1987; Nabuzoka and Smith, 1993; Gresham & MacMillan, 1997) and reviews of the literature (for example, Asher and Taylor, 1981; Madden and Slavin, 1983) conclude that, in general, children and young people with learning disabilities have lower social status than their typical peers. These children and young people are reported to be more frequently ignored (Bryan, 1976), remain socially isolated (Faught, Balleweg, Crow, & van den Pol, 1983) or are rejected (Stone & LaGreca, 1990; Vaughn, Elbaum, & Schumm, 1996) Various sociometric studies (for example, Goodman, Gottlieb, & Harrison, 1972) have consistently shown that children and young people with learning disabilities are less well accepted by their typical peers than are other typical children and young people. Other enquirers (for example, Ware, Sharman, O'Conner, & Anderson, 1992; Cuckle & Wilson, 2002) report that profitable interactions do not take place spontaneously between children and young people with and without learning disabilities: for positive social interaction to occur opportunities need to be structured to ensure that it happens. Similarly, Pijl and Scheepstra (1996) in a Dutch study of children with Downs's syndrome attending a mainstream school, reported that, whilst the nature of their interactions was similar to that of their typical classmates, the pupils with Down's syndrome took less initiative for interaction. In addition, the Down's syndrome pupils were the least likely to be engaged in small group work in the classroom. Wolfberg et al. (1999), in an American study of children attending inclusive pre-school programmes, found that, whilst the children with disabilities expressed a desire to interact with their nondisabled counterparts and experienced interactions to varying degrees, they also experienced exclusion from peer culture through neglect, social-communicative breakdown, conflict, and rejection. Farrell and Scales (1995), in a UK study of a nursery class containing eight children with severe learning disabilities and eight typical children, found that whilst children with learning disabilities were equally likely to choose to play with and sit next to typically developing children and/or their learning-disabled peers, the typical children showed a preference for other typical children.

Even when relationships are formed between children and young people with and without learning disabilities, the nature of these relationships is unlikely to be the same as that between children without learning disabilities. For example, Jenkinson (1983), in a sociometric study of pupils with moderate and severe learning disabilities, found that their sociometric status in an integrated setting suggested that acceptance of these pupils by their typical counterparts was not on an equal basis. Similarly, Lewis (1990) found that when working in cooperative pairs with children with learning disabilities, the talk of 6- to 7-year-old typically developing children was similar to the talk they would use with younger typically developing children rather than with their same-age peers.

More recent studies, however, suggest that the increasing trend in inclusion may be facilitative in terms of promoting friendships between children and young people with and without learning disabilities.

PROMOTING FRIENDSHIPS BETWEEN CHILDREN AND YOUNG PEOPLE WITH AND WITHOUT LEARNING DISABILITIES

Amado (2004) describes three myths relating to inclusion: one of these myths is that the 'social skills' of the child or young person with disabilities determines the quality of the friendships: it is assumed (wrongly, according to Amado) that if the child or young person has social 'deficits' or challenges then he or she will be less likely to establish long-lasting relationships with community members. It has been seen (above) that different behaviours and attributes might be associated with acceptance and rejection for children and young people with learning disabilities than for mainstream pupils. Frederickson and Furnham (1998, cited in Frederickson & Furnham, 2004) speculate that this difference in peer assessments might be understood by reference to social exchange theory (Thibaut & Kelley, 1959, cited in Frederickson & Furnham, 2004). According to this theory, desire for affiliation with others is held in relation to perceived costs and benefits ('What have I got to lose? What's in it for me?') set against a minimal level of expectation – the comparison level. Lower benefits and higher costs might be expected and different levels of comparison may be set for pupils with disabilities, thus resulting in differences in assessments being made; in effect, 'making allowances for', consistent with Meyer, Park, Grenot-Scheyer, Schwartz, & Harry's (1998) notion of the *'inclusion kid/different friend'*. If this is the case, then the view that the social skills deficits (or differences) of the child or young person with learning disabilities means that he or she is unlikely to enjoy meaningful friendships with mainstream peers may indeed be a myth.

Two other myths described by Amado are, 'physical presence translates into social relationships' and the belief that friendships 'should happen naturally'. According to Amado, whilst physical proximity may, indeed, cause people to 'connect naturally as friends' the reality is that, for many, relationship forming takes effort and 'significant work' – especially for people from diverse backgrounds or with different abilities. There is, however, some evidence to suggest that more 'naturalistic' contact (that is, less contrived and/or less structured) may be effective in facilitating friendships between children and young people with and without learning disabilities.

Bunch and Valeo (2004) explored the attitudes of Canadian pupils aged 6 to 18 years towards peers with disabilities in inclusive schools (that is, 'regular' classes only) and in schools with special education systems (for example, special classes). Pupils were asked general questions designed to assess their knowledge of disability and overall attitudes towards peers with disabilities and more specific questions if a pupil was placed full- or part-time outside the 'regular' classroom. From the responses, four categories emerged:

- *friendships*: whether pupils with and without disabilities were friends
- *abusive behaviour*: whether pupils without disabilities harass peers with disabilities
- *advocacy*: whether pupils without disabilities defend pupils with disabilities
- *exclusion-inclusion*: whether pupils without disabilities accept the model under which pupils with disabilities were educated in their school system.

The findings indicated the development of friendships and lower degrees of abusive behaviour in inclusive schools. Though pupils in both settings advocated for pupils with disabilities, advocacy was found to be more routine in inclusive settings. Most pupils believed the approach taken by their schools to be appropriate for the education of peers with disabilities. Bunch and Valeo (2004) conclude that the findings 'suggest support for those who argue that inclusive education compared with special education results in more positive social relationships' (p. 76).

An account by Feltham, Park, & Valler-Feltham (2004) of a joint drama project between UK primary school pupils (aged 11 years) and pupils attending a special school for children and young people with severe and profound and multiple learning disabilities appears to provide similar endorsement of the efficacy of 'naturalistic' contact in promoting friendships between children and young people with and without learning disabilities. The project (prompted by one of the mainstream primary pupils) was intended to

provide an opportunity for contact between the groups of pupils prior to a co-location of the two schools. Valler-Feltham (the mainstream class teacher) describes her pupils' initial anxiety ('the big ... guys were now on completely unfamiliar territory and the first sight of a standing frame in the corridor causes a real ripple') followed by a brief period of 'sussing out' ('being seated in a circle created a safe environment ... they could look without being told off for staring'). The development of the relationships between the pupils is described by Valler-Feltham thus:

> my pupils were hooked. When we left (the special school) for the first time it was as if they'd been to the best football match or seen their idols perform live. They relived their favourite moments and began to plan for the next visit. It was an incredibly powerful feeling ... I could not have anticipated exactly how strong the bonds between them and (the special school pupils) would grow ... (Feltham et al., 2004, pp. 12–13)

Reflecting on the experience Feltham (the special school head teacher) comments: 'What I learned ... is that the children, given the right conditions, will "sort it out" for themselves' (p. 10).

A study by Roeyers (1995), conducted among Belgian school children, also appears to endorse the efficacy of more naturally occurring, less intrusive, interactions in facilitating relationship forming between children and young people with and without learning disabilities. Using a peer-mediated proximity approach with children with autistic spectrum disorders (ASD), whereby socially competent children were placed together with children with ASD and were asked simply to play with the target children without any prior training or instruction, Roeyers found changes in the behaviour of the target children similar to those in early development, namely, increases in:

- time spent in behaviours necessary for social interaction
- time spent in peer interaction
- responsiveness
- the frequency of initiation behaviour
- longer uninterrupted interactions.

In addition, it was noted that some of the gains generalised to interactions with unfamiliar peers with and without learning disabilities.

Preparation for contact has also been found to be effective in promoting relationships between children and young people with and without learning disabilities, as illustrated by Shevlin (2003). What became known as *Fast Friends* programmes were established in mainstream schools in Ireland in response to various influential Irish government reports identifying inclusion as an educational priority (for example, Government of Ireland, 1993, 1995, 1996). Shevlin describes a particular school's link programme which was designed to facilitate interaction between mainstream pupils and those with severe and profound and multiple learning disabilities. By way of preparation mainstream pupils viewed a video programme which depicted interactions between disabled and nondisabled pupils, and reactions to the link scheme from pupils, parents and teachers. Shevlin concludes that viewing the video programme 'made a considerable impact on the perceptions and expectations of the pupils concerned' (2003, p. 95): participants reported feeling 'more confident' as a result of viewing the video; there was general agreement that they had learned significant facts about people with learning disabilities; and they reported a positive impact on their perceptions of people with learning disabilities. Viewing the friendships established between disabled and nondisabled peers was reported to make the greatest single impact on a sizable proportion of participants.

A group of children and young people who present particular challenges in terms of friendship formation are those described as having autistic spectrum disorders. One of the core diagnostic and defining features of ASD is the impairment of social interactions (Wing, 2002). Individuals with ASD have been found to have specific difficulties relating to the capacity to understand other people's minds (Baron-Cohen, 1993). Three 'sub-groups' have been identified: the aloof group (those who

avoid close proximity to others and who usually reject physical or social contact); the passive group (those who only make social approaches in order to have their needs met); the active-but-odd group (individuals whose approaches are one-sided, repetitive and considered idiosyncratic) (Wing, 2002).

An approach to promote inclusion of individuals with autism (and other learning disabilities) into mainstream schools which originated in North America and which is growing in popularity in the UK is '*circle of friends*'. It is: 'a systematic approach that recognises the power of the peer group – and thereby of pupil culture – to be a positive as well as constraining or exacerbating influence on individual behaviour' (Newton, Taylor, & Wilson, 1996, p. 42). Whitaker, Barratt, Joy, Potter, & Thomas (1998) adopted the approach with young people with autism who were being included in mainstream schools in an English local education authority. They describe the process of establishing a circle thus:

1   *Establish prerequisites*: for example, selecting a school, negotiating the necessary commitments of time and resources.
2   *Discussion with the class or tutor group*: focusing on the target child's strengths and difficulties and inviting classmates to empathise with him or her and to build on their own experience of friendships. Volunteers to form a circle are sought at the end of this meeting.
3   *Establishing a circle*: a group of six to eight volunteers meet with the target child. An approach to problem-solving is established and practical arrangements determined.
4   *Weekly meeting of the 'circle'*: children and staff meet weekly to review progress, identify difficulties and plan practical steps for resolution.

The evaluation process indicated a number of benefits: for the target child benefits included improved social integration and higher levels of peer contact, reduced anxiety and improved behaviour; for the circle members benefits included increased levels of empathy, enhanced self-esteem and improved group participation. Parents of focus children were also positive, citing changing friendship patterns and improved sociability of their child as being among the benefits. However, Whitaker et al. report that only three out of 40 circle members referred to the target child as a friend: 'to date, the focus children remain predominantly recipients of support rather than equal participants in a mutually supportive relationship' (1998, p. 64).

CONCLUDING COMMENTS

It has been noted in this chapter that friendships matter, even for those individuals with the most severe and profound disabilities. The nature of the friendships may be different for these individuals, but they are no less valuable – or valued. However, for some children and young people with learning disabilities friendships – particularly those on an equal basis – remain elusive.

Friendships cannot be 'created' or manufactured but opportunities to forge them can. In a climate of inclusion the challenge is to find ways of facilitating 'authentic' friendships between and among children and young people with and without learning disabilities, whilst protecting the genuine friendships that may already exist.

The final words on the benefits of friendship – however friendship is defined – go to Jason's mother:

I worried about letting my child 'go' – after all, he can't see, he can't walk and he can't talk … he'd been in a special school for ten years … How could I be sure that Jason would be safe and happy and would he have friends? But … we gave it a go. Before, when I pushed Jason to the store, it was as if I had an empty wheelchair – everyone ignored us. Now, it takes me twice as long because all the kids want to say 'Hi' to Jason – and this makes him smile and smile. (Cited in Male, 2000)

REFERENCES

Amado, A. (2004) Lessons learned about promoting friendships. *TASH Connections*, January/February, 8–12.

Amos, P. (2004) Supporting friendships: one parent's reflections. *TASH Connections*, January/February, 4–5.

Aristotle. (1963). *Ethics*. (J. Warrington, Ed. and Trans). London: Dent.

Asher, S. R., & Taylor, A. R. (1981) Social outcomes of mainstreaming, sociometric assessment and beyond. *Exceptional Education Quarterly*, 1, 13–30.

Bandura, A. (1977). *Social learning theory*. Englewood Cliffs, NJ: Prentice-Hall.

Baron-Cohen, S. (1993). From attention-goal psychology to belief-desire psychology: The development of a theory of mind, and its dysfunction. In S. Baron-Cohen, H. Tager-Flusberg, & D. J. Cohen (Eds.), *Understanding other minds: Perspectives from autism*. Oxford: Oxford University Press.

Bates, E. (1975). Peer relations and the acquisition of language. In M. Lewis & L. Rosenblum (Eds.), *Friendships and peer relations* (pp. 259–292). New York: Wiley.

Blatchford, P. (1998). *Social life in school*. London: Falmer Press.

Bryan, T. (1976). Peer popularity of learning disabled children: A replication. *Journal of Learning Disabilities*, 9, 307–311.

Bunch, G, & Valeo, A. (2004). Student attitudes towards peers with disabilities in inclusive and special education schools. *Disability & Society*, 19(1), 61–76.

Buultjens, M., & Stead, J., with Dallas, M. (2002). *Promoting social inclusion of pupils with visual impairment in mainstream schools in Scotland*. Retrieved February 22, 2005, from www.ssc.mhie.ac.uk

Chappell, A. L. (2000). Emergence of participatory methodology in learning difficulty research: understanding the context. *British Journal of Learning Disabilities*, 28, 38–43.

Cuckle, P., & Wilson, J. (2002). Social relationships and friendships among young people with Down's syndrome in secondary schools. *British Journal of Special Education*, 29(2), 66–71.

Cutts, S., & Sigafoos, J. (200. Social competence and peer interactions of students with intellectual disability in an inclusive school. *Journal of Intellectual & Developmental Disability*, 26(2), 127–141.

Damon, W. (1983). *Social and personality development*. New York: W.W. Norton.

Department for Education and Skills (DfES). (2001). *Code of practice on the identification and assessment of special educational needs*. Annesley, Nottinghamshire: DfES Publications.

Department of Education and Science (DES). (1981). *Education Act*. London: HMSO.

Department of Health (DoH). (2001). *Valuing people: A new strategy for learning disability for the 21st century*. London: Department of Health.

Emerson, E., & McVilly, K. (2004). Friendship activities of adults with intellectual disabilities in supported accommodation in northern England. *Journal of Applied Research in Intellectual Disabilities*, 17, 191–197.

Erikson, E. H. (1968). *Identity, youth and crisis.* New York: W. W. Norton.

Fagot, B. I. (1977). Consequences of moderate cross-gender behavior in preschool children. *Child Development, 48,* 902–907.

Farrell, P., & Scales, A. (1995). Who likes to be with whom in an integrated nursery? *British Journal of Learning Disabilities, 23*(4), 156–60.

Faught, K. K., Balleweg, B. J., Crow, R. E., & van den Pol, R. A. (1983). An analysis of social behaviours among handicapped and nonhandicapped preschool children. *Education and Training of the Mentally Retarded, 18,* 210–214.

Feltham, J., Park, K., & Valler-Feltham, M. (2004). Shakespeare goes to Harrow. *The SLD Experience, 40,* 8–13.

Feuerstein, R. (1986). A tough choice. *Special Children, 1,* 10–11.

Foundation for People with Learning Disabilities. (2005). *Friendships and relationships for people with disabilities.* Retrieved February 28, 2005, from www.learningdisabilties.org.uk.

Frederickson, N. L., & Furnham, A. F. (2004). Peer assessed behavioural characteristics and sociometric rejection: Differences between pupils who have moderate learning difficulties and their mainstream peers. *British Journal of Educational Psychology, 74,* 391–410.

Further Education Unit (1990). *Developing self advocacy skills with people with disabilities.* London: Further Education Unit.

Goodman, H., Gottlieb, J., & Harrison, R. H. (1972). Social acceptance of EMRs integrated into a non-graded elementary school. *American Journal of Mental Deficiency, 78,* 412–417.

Government of Ireland. (1993). *Report of the Special Education Review Committee.* Dublin: Stationery Office.

Government of Ireland. (1995). *Charting our education future: white paper on education.* Dublin: Stationery Office.

Government of Ireland. (1996). *A strategy for equality. Report of the Commission on the Status of People with Disabilities.* Dublin: Stationery Office.

Grenot-Scheyer, M. (2004). Friendships and other social relationships of children with and without disabilities: Considerations and strategies for families and school personnel. *TASH Connections,* January/February, 31–34.

Gresham, F. M. (1982). Misguided mainstreaming: The case for social skills training with handicapped children. *Exceptional Children, 48,* 422–433.

Gresham, F. M., & MacMillan, D. L. (1997). Social competence and affective characteristics of students with mild disabilities. *Review of Educational Research, 67,* 377–415.

Hartup, W. W. (1978). Aggression in childhood: Developmental perspectives. *American Psychologist, 29,* 336–341.

Heiman, T. (2000). Friendship quality among children in three educational settings. *Journal of Intellectual & Developmental Disability, 25*(1), 1–12.

Individuals with Disabilities Education Act (IDEA) Amendments of 1997, PL 105–17, 20 U.S.C. 1400 et seq (1997).

Jenkinson, J. C. (1983). Correlates of sociometric status among TMR children in regular classrooms. *American Journal of Mental Deficiency, 88*(3), 332–335.

Klotz, J. (2004). Sociocultural study of intellectual disability: Moving beyond labelling and social constructionist perspectives. *British Journal of Learning Disabilities, 32,* 93–104.

LaGreca, A. (1990). Children's problems with friends. *Psychotherapy in Practice, 3,* 1–21.

Lewis, A. (1990). Six- and seven-year-old 'normal' children's talk to peers with severe learning difficulty. *European Journal of Special Needs Education, 5,* 13–23.

Lewis, A. (2002). Accessing, through research interviews, the views of children with difficulties in learning. *Support for Learning, 17*(3), 110–116.

Madden, N. A., & Slavin, R. E. (1983). Effects of co-operative learning on the social acceptance of mainstreamed academically handicapped students. *Journal of Special Education, 17*(2), 171–182.

Making friends. (Anonymous.) (2003). Retrieved May 19, 2004, from www.he-special.org.uk.

Male, D. B. (1998). Parents' views about special provision for their child with severe or profound and multiple learning difficulties. *Journal of Applied Research in Intellectual Disabilities, 11*(2), 129–145.

Male, D. B. (2000). *'Making Jason Smile and Smile.' Including pupils with profound and multiple learning difficulties into mainstream educational provision.* Report to the Winston Churchill Memorial Trust.

Male, D B. (2002). Peer nominations among adolescents experiencing severe learning difficulties: An exploratory study using sociometric techniques. *Journal of Research in Special Education, 2*(3). Tamworth: National Association of Special Educational Needs. Also available at: www.nasen.org.uk

Margalit, M. (1994). Peer relations and children's friendships. In M. Margalit, *Loneliness among children with special needs* (pp. 63–89). New York: Spring Verlag.

Meyer, L. M., Park, H.-S., Grenot-Scheyer, M., Schwartz, I. S. & Harry, B. (1998). *Making friends: The influences of culture and development.* Baltimore, MD: Paul H. Brookes.

Mittler, P. (1996). Preparing for self advocacy. In B. Carpenter, R. Ashdown, & K. Bovair (Eds.), *Enabling access*. London: David Fulton.

Murray, P. (2002). *Hello! Are you listening? Disabled teenagers' experiences of access to inclusive leisure*. York: Joseph Rowntree Foundation.

Mussen, P .H., Conger, J. J., Kagan, J., & Huston, A. C. (1990). *Child development & personality* (7th edn.). New York: HarperCollins.

Nabuzoka, D.,& Smith, P. K. (1993). Sociometric status and social behaviour of children with and without learning difficulties. *Journal of Child Psychology and Psychiatry, 34*, 1435–1448.

Newton, C., Taylor, G., & Wilson, D. (1996). Circles of friends: An inclusive approach to meeting emotional and behavioural needs. *Educational Psychology in Practice, 11*(4), 41–48.

Organisation for Economic Co-operation and Development (OECD) Centre for Educational Research and Innovation. (1981). *The education of the handicapped adolescent: Integration at school*. Paris: OECD.

Parker, J. G., & Asher, S. R. (1987). Peer relations and later personal adjustment: Are low-accepted children at risk? *Psychological Bulletin, 102*(3), 357–89.

Piaget, J. (1932). *The moral judgement of the child*. New York: Free Press.

Pijl, S. J., & Scheepstra, A. J. M. (1996). Being apart or being a part of the group: The position of pupils with Down's syndrome in Dutch regular schools. *European Journal of Special Needs Education, 11*(3), 311–320.

Plaute, W., & Westling, D. L. (1996). Welche wunsche haben Eltern von entwicklungsverzgerten oder behinderten Kinder in Osterreich? *Heilpaedagogik, 39*(2), 2.23.

Quality Network. (2005). *BILD factsheets: Quality*. Retrieved February 28, 2005, from www.bild.org.uk.

Rardin, D. R., & Moan, C. E. (1971). Peer interaction and cognitive development. *Child Development, 42*, 1685–1699.

Roeyers, H. (1995). A peer-mediated proximity intervention to facilitate the social interactions of children with a pervasive developmental disorder. *British Journal of Special Education, 22*(4), 161–164.

Rose, R. (1998). Including pupils: Developing a partnership in learning. In C. Tilstone, L. Florian, & R. Rose (Eds.), *Promoting inclusive practice*. London: Routledge.

Shevlin, M. (2003). Preparing for contact between mainstream pupils and their counterparts who have severe and profound and multiple learning disabilities. *British Journal of Special Education, 30*(2), 93–99.

Stone, W., & LaGreca, A. (1990). The social status of children with learning disabilities: A re-examination. *Journal of Learning Disabilities, 23*, 32–37.

Tashie, C., & Rossetti, Z. (2004). Friendship: What's the real problem? *TASH Connections*, January/February, 35–37.

Taylor, A. R., Asher, S. R., & Williams, G. A. (1987). The social adaptation of mainstreamed mildly retarded children. *Child Development, 58*, 1321–1334.

United Nations Educational, Scientific, and Cultural Organization (UNESCO). (1994). *The Salamanca statement and framework for action on special needs education*. Paris: UNESCO.

Vaughn, S., Elbaum, B., & Schumm, J. (1996). The effects of inclusion on the social functioning of students with learning disabilities. *Journal of Learning Disabilities, 29*, 598–608.

Walmsley, J. (2001). Normalisation, emancipatory research and learning disability. *Disability Society, 16*(2), 187–205.

Walmsley, J. (2004). Inclusive learning disability research: The (nondisabled) researcher's role. *British Journal of Learning Disabilities, 32*, 65–71.

Ware, J., Sharman, M., O'Connor, S., & Anderson, M. (1992). Interactions between pupils with severe learning difficulties and their mainstream peers. *British Journal of Special Education, 19*(4), 153–158.

Westling, D. L. (1996). What do parents of children with moderate and severe learning disabilities want? *Education and Training in Mental Retardation and Developmental Disabilities, 31*, 86–114.

Westling, D. L. (1997). What parents of young children with mental disabilities want: The views of one community. *Focus on Autism and Other Developmental Disabilities, 12*(2), 67–78.

Whitaker, P., Barratt, P., Joy, H., Potter, M., & Thomas, G. (1998). Children with autism and peer support: Using 'circles of friends'. *British Journal of Special Education, 25*(2), 60–64.

Wing, L. (2002). *The autistic spectrum: A guide for parents and professionals*. London: Robinson.

Wolfberg, P. J., Zercher, C., Lieber, J., Cappell, K., Matias, S., Hanson, M., & Odom, S. L. (1999). 'Can I play with you?' Peer culture in inclusive preschool programs. *JASH, 24*(2), 69–84.

Future directions for research and practice

36

Leadership for social justice and inclusion

Katharine Shepherd and
Susan Brody Hasazi

The purpose of this chapter is to describe a social justice framework with the related values, beliefs, knowledge, and skills that are needed by educational administrators to ensure that schools are inclusive and have the capacity to support students with disabilities and their families. Our vision for social justice in schools and communities is based on a belief that social institutions must be organized and structured to value and include the experiences and perspectives of all members. We believe we can no longer afford to differentially privilege students who possess social capital commonly associated with the dominant culture. Leading for social justice and inclusion means leading for all. School leaders must recognize, understand, and promote the success of all students including those with disabilities, as well as their families, as these individuals are often devalued or marginalized.

Over the past three decades, significant strides have been made in both research and practice related to including students with disabilities in general education classrooms and schools. Recent research has identified school leadership as a key component of successful approaches to inclusion (Furney, Hasazi, Clark/Keefe, & Hartnett, 2003; Pounder, Reitzug, & Young, 2002; Thousand & Villa,

2005); however, there is a need to more clearly articulate the specific knowledge, skills and values needed by school leaders to implement best practices related to the inclusion of students with disabilities. This chapter attempts to address this need by proposing a social justice framework for operationalizing leadership approaches to (1) developing school cultures that include all students, (2) promoting effective instructional practices, (3) creating professional learning communities characterized by collaboration, reflection, and empowerment, and (4) ensuring that student, family and community perspectives are at the heart of the school. In our view, school leaders who embrace this social justice framework are more likely to ensure that all students, including those with disabilities, have access to the highest quality educational experiences leading to academic achievement and social inclusion.

A CASE FOR THE COMMITMENT TO SOCIAL JUSTICE

Emerging views of leadership

Historical conceptions of school leadership were rooted in logical, positivist approaches that equated the principal's role with management and the maintenance of a smoothly functioning system (Dantley, 2002; Giroux, 1997). The authority and power associated with school leadership were generally thought to be vested with a single individual, whose primary responsibilities included the supervision and evaluation of teachers, maintenance of the school's physical plant, compliance with bureaucratic requests, and control of student behavior. More contemporary views of leadership recognize the limitations of a managerial approach, acknowledging that issues such as growing diversity in the school population, recognition of the ways in which knowledge is socially constructed and the inherently political nature of school require a new vision for leadership and the role of the principal (Riehl, 2000). This vision, described by some as reflecting a postmodern perspective, acknowledges the need for schools and school leaders to be committed to social justice as both a means and an end to bringing about greater equity and opportunity to students and families who have been de-valued as a result of disability, race, language, poverty, gender and sexual orientation (Pounder et al., 2002).

Defining social justice

While there are differing views regarding the meaning of social justice, for the purpose of this chapter, we define it as a commitment on the part of institutions – in this case schools – to ensure that all students have access to equal opportunities and outcomes that will in turn lead to full citizenship and actualization of their full potential. We need to ensure that the socially derived characteristics of particular groups of students do not predict differences in educational outcomes. Realization of a commitment to social justice means that our schools recognize, understand, and promote the cultural contributions of everyone in the community, including those who have been de-valued, marginalized, and under-represented in society. In this regard, we believe it is the role of school leaders to value the unique aspects of all students and to organize and structure schools in ways that promote achievement and social inclusion for students with disabilities. Leaders who are committed to using a social justice framework as the basis for creating inclusive schools are those who understand the role of moral leadership (Sergiovanni, 1992; Starrat, 1999), multicultural education (McKenzie & Scheurich, 2004; Riehl, 2000), instructional leadership (Blasé & Blasé, 1999a, 1999b; Southworth, 2002), democratic discourse (Rusch, 1998), community engagement (Dryfoos & Maguire, 2002; Pounder et al., 2002), and a variety of strategies for building shared understandings of inclusive school cultures (Riehl, 2000).

Social justice and disability

Social justice is a concept that has been traditionally associated with issues such as race, socioeconomic status, and gender; however, more recent literature has begun to acknowledge disability as a social construction through which impairment is given negative social meaning, leading to inequity and limited possibilities for students with disabilities (Meekosha & Jakubowicz, 1996; Slee, 2001). Christensen and Dorn (1997) argue that earlier notions of social justice related to persons with disabilities were generally founded on individualistic assumptions in which access to education was viewed as an individual right. While individual rights are viewed as important, Christensen and Dorn maintain that a focus on individualism tends to reinforce an internal-deficit mode of disability that results in a focus on assimilating students rather than on transforming the culture of schools. In the assimilation model, 'the focus becomes the children and not the environment' (Christensen & Dorn, 1997, p. 168). In a more holistic view that places social justice at its core, schools and communities must assume responsibility for all of their members, focusing their efforts on cultural and organizational aspects that will lead to inclusive approaches and positive outcomes for all students, including those with disabilities.

Applying the social justice framework

As conceptions of school leadership begin to embrace a social justice framework in relation to students with disabilities, higher education institutions preparing school leaders need to expand their goals and perspectives to address the values, skills, and dispositions needed by principals and school leaders to ensure that schools become more equitable and just learning environments for all students. The remainder of this chapter focuses on four areas of development for leaders committed to all students: (1) developing school cultures that include all students, (2) promoting effective instructional practices, (3) creating professional learning communities characterized by collaboration, reflection, and empowerment, and (4) ensuring that student, family and community perspectives are at the heart of the school.

DEVELOPING SCHOOL CULTURES THAT INCLUDE ALL STUDENTS

This section addresses the need for school leaders to play a significant role in shaping school cultures that include students with disabilities. In this regard, we identify three critical roles of the school leader, including developing a shared vision and culture, understanding special education policies and practices, and ensuring that the structure and organization of the school reflects a commitment to inclusion.

Developing a shared vision and culture

Much of the literature on educational leadership appearing over the past 20 years has spoken to the importance of developing a shared vision or mission with stakeholders (Pounder et al., 2002; Riehl, 2000; Thousand & Villa, 2005). That being said, not all visions embrace the social justice vision that is central to developing school cultures that include all students. It is important that leaders committed to social justice take an active role in helping to articulate a belief that all children matter and can learn, and that school environments must be structured to support them in doing so (Hallinger & Leithwood, 1998). Scheurich's (1998) study of schools described as highly successful in meeting the needs of diverse students from low income backgrounds emphasized the importance of structuring schools around core beliefs, including a belief that 'the natural condition of all children is high performance ... and this high performance is not based on pushing children but on providing loving, facilitating conditions that deliver learning in a way that fits, supports, engages, and energizes the child' (p. 461).

Closely related to the notion of developing shared vision is the idea that school leaders need to set a context for democratic decision-making and participatory leadership (Pounder et al., 2002). Truly inclusive schools rarely emerge in authoritarian or hierarchically-bound structures; rather, these schools reflect democratic principles such as ongoing discourse, reflection, and community participation. In other words, inclusive schools 'prepare students *for* democracy while functioning *as* democracies' (Pounder et al., 2002, p. 269). Riehl (2000), however, cautions that the mere presence of democratic discourse does not result in a school's exploration of the degree to which its structure and practices promote social justice and equal access for children with disabilities. Thus, the school leader must assume responsibility for ensuring that, at the heart of shared leadership models and open dialogue, there is a commitment to *all* children, especially those with disabilities.

Leaders in truly inclusive schools must also ensure that members of the school community understand the varying abilities and challenges of individual students with disabilities, and the interactions of their disabilities with their cultural and linguistic backgrounds. The over-representation of students of diverse backgrounds in special education is a major concern in the United States and elsewhere; thus, it is necessary for leaders to work as change agents in addressing this complex educational issue (Harry & Anderson, 1994; McLaughlin, Artilles, & Pullin, 2001). To do so, teachers, students, administrators, and other members of the school community must be challenged to examine their personal assumptions and stereotypes and the ways in which these may influence their interactions with students with disabilities and their families. A variety of strategies may be useful to leaders in this regard, including culturally responsive teaching (Delpit, 1992; Ladson-Billings, 1997), strategies for helping teachers and administrators to understand the historical and political roots of diverse cultures as well as within-group diversity (McLaughlin et al., 2001), strategies for helping teachers to re-frame deficit views of difference (McKenzie & Scheurich, 2004), and changing the roles of principals to ensure that leadership is equated with efforts to overcome various forms of discrimination and inequity (Dillard, 1995; Riester, Pursch, Skrla, 2002). Leaders engaged in promoting social justice understand the moral dimension of leadership, in which the leader understands the obligation of public schools to be responsible for all of today's youth, including students with disabilities and those from diverse backgrounds (Wong, 1998). Leaders acting as 'moral stewards' ensure that the school's commitment to social justice is represented through a core set of values that govern day-to-day actions (Murphy, 1990, 2002). Sergiovanni (1992) advocates that leaders express their 'moral outrage' in situations where it is apparent that practices are not in keeping with the commitment to social justice and the inclusion of students with disabilities.

Understanding special education policies, inclusive practices, and their link to social justice

A second critical component of school leaders' roles in fostering inclusive cultures relates to their need to understand and apply special education policies to ensure that the intent of relevant laws is realized in local school practices. In the United States, special education was mandated through federal law in 1975, and

has, since that time, been associated with six governing principles: assurance of a free and appropriate education for students with disabilities, an appropriate education provided in the least restrictive environment, provision of an individualized education through an Individualized Education Program (IEP), the use of nondiscriminatory assessment in identifying and evaluating students, parent and student participation in the IEP process, and access to due process (Turnbull, Turnbull, Shank, & Smith, 2004). In fostering inclusive school cultures, it is imperative that school leaders understand these principles and the specific laws with which they are associated. They need to help all members of the school community see the ways in which these principles are linked to the articulation of core values and a commitment to social justice. Failure to do so may result in the implementation of separate and isolated learning conditions for students with disabilities. In contrast to a social justice perspective, 'segregated education creates a permanent underclass of students and conveys a strong message to those students that they do not measure up, fit in, or belong. Segregationist thinking assumes that the right to belong is an earned rather than an unconditional human right' (Falvey & Givner, 2005, p. 5).

As part of an understanding of special education policies, leaders need to be knowledgeable about specific disability conditions and their instructional implications. At the same time, leaders play a central role in ensuring that the school's approach to serving students with disabilities does not promote a reliance on categorical approaches. Leaders of inclusive schools need to reject a deficit view in which disability is regarded as a medical or organic condition that rests within the individual and must therefore be 'fixed' through technical approaches (Slee, 2001). Rather, school leaders must be engaged in helping to foster a broader conceptualization of disability and low achievement in which the school's goal is to create an instructional context that meets the needs of all learners within a common framework of high expectations and accountability (McLaughlin et al.,

2001). In doing so, they help to build school cultures in which diversity and disability are recognized as interrelated and socially constructed phenomena that need to be addressed through the schools' articulation of values and their focus on creating learning environments that are responsive to all students (Meekosha & Jakubowicz, 1996).

Ensuring that the structure and organization of the school reflects the underlying commitment to inclusion

Leaders who are committed to inclusion and social justice must also ensure that the moral and cultural conversations they promote in schools lead to a re-shaping of school structures and processes. As Dillard (1995) notes, 'effective leadership is transformative political work' that ultimately, must move beyond a view in which students with disabilities and those of diverse backgrounds need to assimilate to the dominant culture, to one where the very structures of school must be examined to ensure that they are in fact vehicles of social change (p. 558). McLaughlin et al. (2001) suggest that if students with disabilities and those with diverse backgrounds are to have equal access to effective education, schools need to create coherent programs in which special and general educators collaborate to ensure that school reform efforts are structured to meet all students' needs.

The resources allocated to special education and other support services need to maintain a level of flexibility in funding and structure that moves away from categorical approaches and the sorting and differentiating of students and staff (Furney et al., 2003; McLaughlin & Verstegen, 1998). More flexible staffing patterns, in which teachers and support staff work within an open system to provide support to those in need, are generally associated with inclusive approaches. They assure that students' instructional and social issues are addressed on the basis of need, rather than on the basis of availability of individual school personnel or categorically based services (Thousand & Villa,

2005). Schools generally find that an array of collaborative teams is needed to promote inclusion, including shared leadership models, school-wide student support teams, pre-referral teams that provide supports prior to identification for special education services, multidisciplinary planning teams, and team teaching models (Godek, Furney, & Riggs, 2005; Thousand & Villa, 2005).

PROMOTING EFFECTIVE INSTRUCTIONAL PRACTICES

The notion of principals as instructional leaders has been part of discussions of school leadership for well over 20 years (Blasé & Blasé, 1999a, 1999b; Sheppard, 1996). The role is one that was recognized for its potential to improve teaching and learning processes in the classroom, and over time, to enhance the performance of all students, including those with disabilities. At the same time, it has long been recognized that the reality of the role has been difficult to achieve, as principals are more often called upon to deal with a range of managerial and bureaucratic tasks (Pounder et al., 2002). In addition, more recent school reform efforts, such as the *No Child Left Behind Act 2001* in the United States, have resulted in high-stakes testing and increased accountability for schools and school leaders. As such, we propose two aspects of instructional leadership that appear critical to ensure that the concept moves from rhetoric to reality. These include the need for principals to understand effective curricula and instructional practices, and to be knowledgeable of effective assessment practices and the use of performance data in decision-making and school improvement.

Understanding effective curricula and instruction in relationship to school culture

Educational leaders who reflect principles associated with social justice and inclusion need to support teachers in building their capacity to utilize evidence-based curricula and instructional strategies that are designed to result in success for all students, including those with disabilities (Brock & Groth, 2003; Janisch & Johnson, 2003; Munoz & Dossett, 2004). In addition, effective instructional leaders serve as highly visible role models for teachers. They visit classrooms on a regular basis, praise and give feedback to teachers, discuss assessment results in relation to curriculum and instruction, and seek teachers' advice about instructional matters (Blasé & Blasé, 1999a, 1999b; Southworth, 2002). They support teachers in finding ways to increase student engagement in learning, and to implement specific strategies that have been documented to promote the inclusion of students with disabilities in general education classrooms (Quinn, 2002; Slee, 2001). The latter include strategies such as peer tutoring, cooperative learning, positive behavioral support, school-wide approaches to literacy and numeracy, and effective use of individual accommodations (Sapon-Shevin, Ayres, & Duncan, 2002; Tomlinson, 1999; Tomlinson & Allan, 2000).

Importantly, principals need to ensure that choices made about specific curricula and instructional strategies are a good match for students' needs and the culture of the school (Harthun, Drapeau, Dustman, & Marsiglia, 2002; Janisch & Johnson, 2003). Researchers have long noted the challenge of implementing educational innovations in exact accordance with their developers' intentions, in part because teachers find it frustrating and even ineffective to teach in ways that do not match their teaching styles and the needs and cultural backgrounds of their students (Elmore & Sykes, 1992; Munoz & Dossett, 2004). Pounder et al. (2002) caution that in the current era of educational reform, principals may feel pressured to adopt superficial approaches to improving students' performance such as encouraging teachers to 'teach to the test', seeking ways to exclude students who are having learning challenges from taking tests and/or failing to publicly report their scores, and offering extrinsic rewards to teachers if test scores improve. Instead, these authors argue for the implementation of

'authentic pedagogy', in which students learn in a culturally responsive environment about things that really matter to them, and experience a sense of accomplishment through the acquisition of new knowledge (Finnan, Schnepel, & Anderson, 2003).

Understanding effective assessment practices and the use of performance data in decision-making and school improvement

Closely related to the need to understand effective curricula and instructional strategies is the need for principals to have a deep understanding of the link between assessment, curricula, and instruction, and to use student performance data to improve schools. On the one hand, research on the relationship between principal instructional leadership and improved student performance as measured by standardized testing has been limited and has not uniformly demonstrated a direct link between the two (Hallinger, Bickman, & Davis, 1996; Quinn, 2002). On the other hand, the literature reports numerous case studies of principals who have demonstrated the ability to engage teachers and community members in conversations about assessment data for the purposes of improving instruction, school climate, and student outcomes (Furney et al., 2003; Janisch & Johnson, 2003). Through engaging in dialogue that focuses on individual and classroom data, principals can support teachers in identifying school-wide strengths and challenges to guide professional development, resource allocation, and over time, school-wide improvement (Brock & Groth, 2003; Morrocco, Walker, & Lewis, 2003; Reister, Pursch, & Skrla, 2002).

CREATING PROFESSIONAL LEARNING COMMUNITIES CHARACTERIZED BY COLLABORATION, REFLECTION, AND EMPOWERMENT

As indicated in the preceding discussion of effective curricula, instructional practices and assessment, the fact that a principal may be a practicing instructional leader does not in and of itself lead to school-wide change and improvement. Over the years, the research on leadership and change has suggested varied approaches to improving schools, including the implementation of strategic planning processes designed to lead to whole-school reform (Schmoker, 2004). In hindsight, it appears that strategic planning efforts were often conceived of by 'planners' who were external to schools and who proposed activities that were disconnected from the real work of teachers and the teaching and learning process (Kouzes & Posner, 1995; Schmoker, 2004). More recent advocates of school reform have instead called for approaches that build schools' capacity to function as professional learning communities in which change is viewed as a collaborative enterprise closely tied to the realities of classrooms and the core purpose of individual schools (DuFour & Eaker, 1998; Fullan, 2002, 2003; Huffman & Jacobson, 2003; Sckmoker, 2004; Senge, 1990).

The professional learning community model rejects the idea of traditional, externally developed staff development efforts, replacing them with action research models and similar opportunities for teachers to engage in dialogue and reflection on actual student work (Huffman & Jacobson, 2003). These focused efforts to engage in inquiry and reflection involve teachers in a cycle of improvement in which instruction is continuously monitored and improved as a result of analyzing the results of authentic as well as standardized student assessments (Tomlinson & Allan, 2000).

The professional learning community places teachers at the center of change efforts; however, it is clear that school leaders play an essential role in the community's establishment and continued growth. Principals in effective learning communities understand the need to create structures, time, and a general climate within their schools that enhance the ability of teachers to work together in a fashion that promotes innovation (Huffman & Jacobson, 2003; Senge, 1990; Sheppard, 1996).

Effective leaders understand the importance of collaborative teaming and action-oriented inquiry, and the ways in which these processes help to ensure the success of students with disabilities (Schmoker, 2004). Blasé and Blasé (1999a) identified specific principal behaviors in this regard, including empowering teachers through talking openly and freely with them about teaching and learning, providing time and encouraging peer connections, embracing both the benefits and challenges of professional development, and leading in ways that motivate and facilitate growth among teachers

Implementation of professional learning communities has specific implications for the goal to create inclusive schools that meet the needs of students with disabilities. School leaders need to promote an expectation within the school community that both general and special education teachers are responsible for students with disabilities (Morrocco, Walker, & Lewis, 2003; Southworth, 2002). One strategy for establishing this expectation is to create problem-solving teams with high levels of principal involvement and support that bring general and special educators together for the purpose of developing and monitoring plans to support students with disabilities as well as those at risk of educational failure (Furney et al., 2003; Furney, Hasazi, & Clark/Keefe, in press). Principals who are committed to the professional learning communities approach ensure that opportunities for teacher inquiry and reflection involve the skills and talents of both general and special educators. The dialogue that ensues provides opportunities for general and special educators to share and expand their expertise regarding teaching and learning strategies that promote success for all students. School leaders can be influential in promoting models such as co-teaching and joint professional development that enhance the capacity of general education teachers to address the needs of students with disabilities within their classrooms (Frey, Fisher, & Henry, 2005). Finally, models of distributed leadership help to ensure that both general and special educators play a vital role in designing and implementing a vision of inclusive education (Morrocco, Walker, & Lewis, 2003). These could include leadership teams that bring together general and special educators to identify professional development opportunities, planning teams consisting of general and special educators, administrators and community members that analyze student performance data, and peer coaching teams that pair general and special educators.

ENSURING THAT STUDENT, FAMILY AND COMMUNITY PERSPECTIVES ARE AT THE HEART OF THE SCHOOL

Educational leaders who believe in social justice ensure that school personnel understand, respect, and value the unique experiences, strengths and challenges of families whose children have disabilities. Key to this is the leader's role in helping teachers to examine their own assumptions about disability and diversity, and to reflect on how those assumptions positively or negatively affect their interactions with families. In a classic study of the interactions between special education professionals and Puerto-Rican families who had children with disabilities, Harry (1992) clearly articulates the ways in which school personnel failed to understand the cultural context of the families, and in turn, misinterpreted parents' actions and participation in educational planning meetings. Similarly, a case study of an African-American mother of a child with disabilities (Rao, 2000) describes the failure of school and agency personnel to understand the ways in which their language and assessment processes were tied to the use of labels with negative connotations and thus, conflicted with the parent's more positive construction of her son's challenges. In the professionals' failure to negotiate such dissonances, an opportunity was missed to create a trusting relationship that would allow for the development of a collaborative relationship (Rao, 2000).

A second key role of school leaders is to ensure that the overall culture and daily operations of the school reflect an understanding and investment in families (Lopez, Scribner, & Mahitivanichcha, 2001). That is, leaders need to ensure that their schools' classrooms, organizational structure, and climate reflect sensitivity to the needs of families of children with disabilities and those representing diverse backgrounds (Scheurich, 1998; Shapiro, Monzo, Rueda, Gomez, & Blacher, 2004). This sensitivity includes efforts on the part of the leader to ensure that all special education processes are family-centered. For example, parents need to receive information on legal and educational issues in their first language and prior to any formal meetings scheduled with school personnel. Educational planning meetings need to take into account a range of family needs, including families' preferences for meeting times, child care, and transportation issues. Moreover, they need to be conducted in a manner that demonstrates cultural sensitivity and promotes trust, open communication, and respect (Salembier & Furney, 1997).

Finally, school leaders play a vital role in ensuring that schools demonstrate a commitment to bringing families into the community and the community into the schools (Dryfoos & Maguire, 2002; Scheurich, 1998). For the parents of students with disabilities, this means ensuring that families are connected not only to appropriate supports and activities within the school, but also to supports and services available in the community. Leaders can support school personnel in ensuring that community resources and services are integrated within special education processes in a way that promotes integration of services, collaborative partnerships that place parents at the center of planning efforts, and seamless connections between the school and community (Hasazi, Furney, & DeStefano, 1999).

CONCLUSION

In the present educational context, we need to prepare school leaders who can operationalize a social justice framework for the purpose of promoting the inclusion of students with disabilities. Four approaches are suggested in this regard, including promoting a shared vision and organizational structures that lead to inclusive school cultures; utilizing effective curricula and instructional practices that reflect a sensitivity to school and community culture, and are improved over time through the analysis of student assessment results; creating professional learning communities characterized by collaboration, reflection, and empowerment; and ensuring that student, family, and community perspectives are at the heart of the educational process. Through this chapter, we have attempted to articulate the relationship between a social justice framework and the inclusion of students with disabilities. By changing the way we think about school leadership and the role of school leaders, it is our hope that the tenets of social justice will be implemented in ways that will lead to more positive outcomes for students with disabilities and their families.

REFERENCES

Blasé, J., & Blasé, J. (1999a). Effective instructional leadership: Teacher's perspectives on how principals promote teaching and learning in schools. *Journal of Educational Administration, 38*(2), 103–141.

Blasé, J., & Blasé, J. (1999b). Instructional leadership through the teachers' eyes. *The High School Magazine*, September, 17–20.

Brock, K. J., & Groth, C. (2003). 'Becoming' effective: Lessons learned from one state's reform initiative in serving low-income students. *Journal of Education for Students Placed at Risk, 8*(2), 167–190.

Christensen, C.A., & Dorn, S. (1997). Competing notions of social justice and contradictions in special education reform. *The Journal of Special Education, 31*(2), 181–198.

Dantley, M. (2002). Uprooting and replacing positivism, the melting pot, multiculturalism, and other important notions in educational leadership through an African American perspective. *Education and Urban Society, 34*(3), 334–352.

Delpit, L. D. (1992). Education in a multicultural society: Our future's greatest challenge. *Journal of Negro Education, 61*(3), 237–249.

Dillard, C. B. (1995). Leading with her life: An African American feminist (re) interpretation of leadership for an urban high school principal. *Education Administration Quarterly, 31*(4), 539–563.

Dryfoos, J. G., & McGuire, S. (2002). *Inside full service community schools.* Thousand Oaks, CA: Corwin Press.

DuFour, R., & Eaker, R. (1998). *Professional learning communities at work: Best practices for enhancing student achievement.* Bloomington, IN: National Educational Service.

Elmore, R., & Sykes, G. (1992). Curriculum policy. In P. Jackson (Ed.), *Handbook of research on curriculum* (pp. 185–215). New York: McMillan.

Falvey, M. A., & Givner, C. C. (2005). What is an inclusive school? In R.Villa & J. Thousand (Eds.), *Creating an inclusive school* (2nd ed.) (pp. 1–11). Alexandria, VA: Association for Supervision and Curriculum Development.

Finnan, C., Schnepel, K. C., & Anderson, L. W. (2003). Powerful learning environments: The critical link between school and classroom cultures. *Journal of Education for Students Placed at Risk, 8*(4), 391–418.

Frey, N., Fisher, D., & Henry, D. P. (2005). Voices of inclusion: Collaborative teaming and student support. In R. A. Villa & J. S. Thousand (Eds.), *Creating an inclusive school* (2nd ed.) (pp. 124–133). Alexandria, VA: Association for Supervision and Curriculum Development.

Fullan, M. (2002). The change leader. *Educational Leadership, 59*(8), 16–25.

Fullan, M. (2003). *Change forces with a vengeance.* New York: Routledge Falmer.

Furney, K.S., Hasazi, S., & Clark/Keefe, K. (in press). Multiple dimensions of reform: The impact of state policies on special education and supports for all students. *Journal of Disability Policy Studies.*

Furney, K., Hasazi, S., Clark/Keefe, K., & Hartnett, J. (2003). *Exceptional Children, 70*(1), 81–94.

Giroux, H. (1997). *Pedagogy and the politics of hope: Theory, culture, and schooling.* Boulder, CO: Westview.

Godek, J., Furney, K. S., & Riggs, M. L. (2005). Voices of inclusion: Changing views from the porch. In R. Villa & J. Thousand (Eds.), *Creating an inclusive school* (2nd ed.) (pp. 81–88). Alexandria, VA: Association for Supervision and Curriculum Development.

Hallinger, P., & Leithwood, K. (1998). Unseen forces: The impact of social culture on school leadership. *Peabody Journal of Education, 73*(2), 126–151.

Hallinger, P., Bickman, L., & Davis, K. (1996). School context, principal leadership, and student reading achievement. *The Elementary School Journal, 96*(5), 527–549.

Harry, B. (1992). An ethnographic study of cross-cultural communication with Puerto Rican-American families in the special education system. *American Educational Research Journal, 29*(3), 471–494.

Harry, B., & Anderson, M. G. (1994). The disproportionate placement of African American males in special education programs: A critique of the process. *Journal of Negro Education, 63*(4), 602–619.

Harthun, M. L., Drapeau, A. E., Dustman, P. A., & Marsiglia, F. F. (2002). Implementing a prevention curriculum: An effective researcher-teacher partnership. *Education and Urban Society, 34*(3), 353–364.

Hasazi, S., Furney, K. S., & DeStefano, L. (1999). Implementing the IDEA transition mandates. *Exceptional Children, 65*(4), 555–566.

Huffman, J. B., & Jacobson, A. L., (2003). Perceptions of professional learning communities. *International Journal of Leadership in Education, 6*(3), 239–250.

Janisch, C., & Johnson, M. (2003). Effective literacy practices and challenging curriculum for at-risk learners: Great expectations. *Journal of Education for Students Placed at Risk, 8*(3), 295–308.

Kouzes, J. M., & Pozner, B. (1995). *The leadership challenge.* San Francisco, CA: Jossey-Bass.

Ladson-Billings, G. (1997). *The dreamkeepers: Successful teachers of African American students.* San Francisco, CA: Jossey-Bass.

Lopez, G.R., Scribner, J.D., & Mahitivanichcha, K. (2001). Redefining parental involvement: Lessons from high-performing migrant-impacted schools. *American Educational Research Journal, 38*(2), 253–288.

McKenzie, K. B., & Scheurich, J. J. (2004). Equity traps: A useful construct for preparing principals to lead schools that are successful with racially diverse students. *Education Administration Quarterly, 40*(5), 601–632.

McLaughlin, M. J., & Verstegen, D. A. (1998). Increasing regulatory flexibility of special education programs: Problems and promising strategies. *Exceptional Children, 64*, 371–384.

McLaughlin, M. J., Artiles, A. J., & Pullin, D. (2001). Challenges for the transformation of special education in the 21st century: Rethinking culture in school reform. *Journal of Special Education Leadership, 14*(2), 51–62.

Meekosha, H., & Jakubowicz, A. (1996). Disability, participation, representation, and social justice. In C. Christensen & F. Rizvi (Eds.), *Disability and the dilemmas of education and justice* (pp. 79–85). Buckingham: Open University Press.

Morrocco, C. C., Walker, A., & Lewis, L. R. (2003). Access to a schoolwide thinking curriculum: Leadership challenges and solutions. *Journal of Special Education Leadership, 16*(1), 5–14.

Munoz, M. A., & Dossett, D. H. (2004). Educating students placed at risk: Evaluating the impact of success for all in urban settings. *Journal of Education for Students Placed at Risk, 9*(3), 261–277.

Murphy, J. (1990, April). Instructional leadership: Focus on curriculum responsibilities. *NASSP Bulletin,* 1–4.

Murphy, J. (2002). Reculturing the profession of educational leadership: New blueprints. *Education Administration Quarterly, 38*(2), 176–191.

No Child Left Behind Act 2001. 20 U.S.C. 6301. et seq. (2001).

Pounder, D., Reitzug, U., & Young, M. D. (2002). Recasting the development of school leaders. In J. Murphy (Ed.), *The educational challenge: Redefining leadership for the 21st century* (pp. 261–288). Chicago, IL: National Society for the Study of Education.

Quinn, D. (2002). The impact of principalship behaviors on instructional practice and student engagement. *Journal of Educational Administration, 40*(5), 447–467.

Rao, S. S. (2000). Perspectives of an African American mother on parent-professional relationships in special education. *Mental Retardation, 38*(6), 485–488.

Riehl, C. J. (2000). The principal's role in creating inclusive schools for diverse students: A review of normative, empirical, and critical literature on the practice of educational administration. *Review of Educational Research, 70*(1), 55–81.

Riester, A. F., Pursch, V., & Skrla, L. (2002, May). Principals for social justice: Leaders of school success for children in low-income homes. *Journal of School Leadership, 12* (2002), 281–304.

Rusch, E. A. (1998). Leadership in evolving democratic school communities. *Journal of School Leadership, 8*, 214–249.

Salembier, G., & Furney, K. S. (1997). Facilitating participation: Parents' perceptions of their involvement in the IEP/transition planning process. *Career Development of Exceptional Individuals, 22*(1), 29–42.

Sapon-Shevin, M., Ayres, B., & Duncan, J. (2002). Cooperative learning and inclusion. In J. S. Thousand & A. I. Nevin (Eds.), *Creativity and collaborative learning: The practical guide to empowering students, teachers, and families* (2nd ed.) (pp. 209–222). Baltimore, MD: Paul H. Brookes.

Schmoker, M. (2004, February). Tipping point: From feckless reform to substantive instructional improvement. *Phi Delta Kappan,* 424–432.

Schuerich, J. J. (1998). Highly successful and loving, public elementary schools populated by mainly low-SES children of color: Core beliefs and cultural characteristics. *Urban Education, 33*(4), 451–491.

Senge, P. (1990). *The fifth discipline: The art and practice of the learning organization.* London: Random House.

Sergiovanni, T. J. (1992). *Moral Leadership.* San Francisco, CA: Jossey-Bass.

Shapiro, J., Monzo, L. D., Rueda, R., Gomez, J. A., & Blacher, J. (2004). Alienated advocacy: Perspectives of Latina mothers of young adults with developmental disabilities on service systems. *Mental Retardation, 42*(1), 37–54.

Sheppard, B. (1996). Exploring the transformational nature of instructional leadership. *The Alberta Journal of Educational Research*, *42*(4), 325–344.

Slee, R. (2001). Social justice and the changing directions in educational research: The case of inclusive education. *International Journal of Leadership in Education*, *5*(2/3), 167–177.

Southworth, G. (2002). Instructional leadership in schools: Reflections and empirical evidence. *School Leadership and Management*, *22*(1), 73–91.

Starrat, R. J. (1999). Moral dimensions of leadership. In P. T. Begley & P. Leonard (Eds.), *The values of educational administration*. London: Falmer Press.

Thousand, J., & Villa, R. (2005). Organizational supports for change toward inclusive schooling. In R. Villa & J. Thousand (Eds.), *Creating an inclusive school* (2nd ed.) (pp. 57–80). Alexandria, VA: Association for Supervision and Curriculum Development.

Tomlinson, C. A. (1999). Leadership for differentiated classrooms. *The School Administrator*, *56*(9), 6–11.

Tomlinson, C. A., & Allan, S. D. (2000). *Leadership for differentiating schools and classrooms*. Alexandria, VA: Association for Supervision and Curriculum Development.

Turnbull, R., Turnbull, A., Shank, M., & Smith, S. J. (2004). *Exceptional lives: Special education in today's schools* (4th ed.). Upper Saddle River, NJ: Merrill Prentice Hall.

Wong, K. (1998). Culture and moral leadership in education. *Peabody Journal of Education*, *73*(2), 106–125.

37

What do teachers need to know about meeting special educational needs?

Ruth Kershner

This chapter focuses on the knowledge teachers use in teaching children with special educational needs (SEN), the knowledge that develops through that teaching, and the ways in which teachers' pedagogical practice may be influenced by and contribute to wider professional and public knowledge in the field. The means by which certain pupils come to be identified as having SEN and the strategies available for meeting these needs form part of the knowledge base for teachers in different national contexts. In England and other countries, current policies on inclusion call for all teachers to develop skills and confidence in teaching all pupils successfully without the assumption of specialist training, but making use of specialist services where necessary (DfES, 2004, p. 50). However the knowledge teachers require for the effective use of specialist services is both cumulative and contextualised. It builds throughout a teaching career with considerable variation in local circumstances.

It is not clear exactly how much of the knowledge about SEN can be said to be 'special' or even coherent. Special education has been critically described as 'something of an epistemic jungle ... [with] an agglomeration of bits and pieces from Piagetian, psychoanalytic, psychometric and behavioural theoretical models' (Thomas & Loxley, 2001, p. 17). Yet there is a growing body of evidence about teaching strategies for pupils identified as having SEN. Recent research reviews have suggested that certain individuals or groups of children may benefit from adaptations to general teaching approaches, but in general pupils with SEN do not need a qualitatively different pedagogy (Davis & Florian, 2004; Lewis & Norwich, 2005). The 'jungle' of theories is dealt with to some extent by establishing a more precise understanding of how teaching strategies deriving from alternative views of learning and development (such as direct instruction and experiential learning) may best be combined for particular purposes. The actual choice and combination of strategies depends on meeting the specific multiple aims in, say, teaching complex material to pupils with learning disabilities (Gersten, Baker, Pugach, Scanlon, & Chard, 2001) or improving the attentiveness and academic outcomes of pupils with attention deficit hyperactivity disorder (Cooper, 2005). The key question for teachers is how to understand the basis for making teaching decisions for particular pupils, including the degree to which such decisions depend on teachers' personal motivations, attitudes and values as well as their teaching context, and their knowledge of teaching, learning, pupils and schools. Scott, Vitale and Masten (1998) found in their literature review that the desirability, effectiveness and feasibility of making adaptations tend to be seen most positively by teachers when there are benefits to the whole class and minimal preparation is necessary, in contrast to individualised responses taking extra time to put in place. Teachers' attitudes and their ratings of self-efficacy towards inclusion were more relevant than demographic characteristics such as years of teaching experience. Although, lack of training and limited school support were seen even by teachers in favour of inclusion as barriers to accommodating the needs of pupils with disabilities.

The web of personal and social factors associated with inclusion and special educational provisions produces a knowledge base which is not neutral or value-free for individual teachers or the profession as whole. To take one example, the inseparability of values and knowledge emerges strongly when deciding whether it is relevant for teachers to understand and respond to the perspectives and aspirations of their pupils. Authors such as Diaz-Greenberg, Thousand, Cardelle-Elawar and Nevin (2000) have pointed to the need for teachers to know about the educational experiences of people with disabilities, many of whom may struggle to reach their goals of self-determination and self-regulation in adult life. An acceptance of such goals as legitimate would underpin and guide the attempts which are made to understand and meet pupils' special educational needs in school. This might lead to adaptations in the curriculum as well as the provision of particular opportunities and support for even young pupils to talk about and plan the future. In this case, the social and cultural value given to pupils' experiences would influence what is seen to be necessary, meaningful and usable knowledge for teachers, including knowledge of the strategies and materials required for helping pupils with difficulties to express

themselves (Lewis, 2004).

In this chapter, a discussion of relevant aspects of teachers' individual and collective knowledge is followed by a specific example of the incorporation of new knowledge into education – that is, the rapidly developing understandings of biological aspects of children's development, particularly in the field of genetics. This is a challenging field of knowledge for educators at the start of the twenty-first century when scientific findings in genetics and neuroscience are multiplying. Genetic research findings at the chromosomal level for individuals and groups of children have led to an array of identifiable syndromes and conditions, many of which are associated with SEN in school. We need to ask, however, about how much of this type of knowledge teachers actually need, how necessary knowledge may be acquired and used by teachers who are non-specialists in biology, and how such knowledge may best be shared between teachers and others involved with meeting pupils' SEN, including the pupils themselves and their parents.

After several years in which the medical model in special education has been rejected by many as potentially damaging to children who may be given a fixed ability label, the new genetic research presents an opportunity to look again at the question of teachers' knowledge with reference to an expanding field of scientific study which also attracts strong interest in the general public. New understandings of genetics are fertile ground for vested interests and misunderstanding between all involved in the education of pupils identified as having SEN. A need to find ways of sharing personal and professional knowledge and overcoming obstacles to communication exists. One way to move this communication forward is to build more systematically on the local knowledge which is constructed when teaching specific pupils in school, and the chapter concludes by acknowledging the importance of teachers' engagement in school-based research as a contribution to a wider knowledge base about meeting pupils' special educational needs.

WHAT ARE TEACHERS EXPECTED TO KNOW ABOUT TEACHING PUPILS WITH SEN?

> The ability to recognise and meet different needs is a significant aspect of good teaching. (TTA, 2003, p. 46)

In any educational system without a strict and centralised policy of categorisation and special schooling there will be some pupils in mainstream education whose educational needs are recognised as special compared with their peers. In these circumstances the responsibility for teaching pupils with SEN will not be seen as solely the domain of specialists and experts, although some teachers may take on particular support and advisory roles and seek further training. In England there is an expectation that all class teachers will take responsibility for teaching pupils identified as having SEN (DfES, 2001) although the government's policy on inclusion in education also incorporates routes for advanced training and specialist skill development. The Department for Education and Skills' (DfES, 2004) statement on 'Removing Barriers to Achievement' states that initial teacher training should provide a good grounding for all teachers in the 'core skills needed for teaching in today's diverse classrooms' (p. 56). The standards for the award of Qualified Teacher Status (QTS) and the requirements for the induction period in school ask teachers to understand relevant legislation, to differentiate teaching effectively for all children and, where appropriate, to plan for the deployment of additional adults to support pupils' learning (TTA, 2003).

Key aspects of knowledge are embedded in these expectations, including knowledge of how pupils' physical, intellectual, linguistic, social, cultural and emotional development may affect their learning (TTA, 2003, p. 22). However, when responding to the learning needs of all pupils, including those with SEN, one of the main requirements for trainees and newly qualified teachers is to know how to find relevant information, advice and support. This need is accompanied by an expectation

that all teachers seek further professional development on qualifying:

> With a large and growing body of knowledge and research underlying each factor affecting pupils' learning, trainee teachers cannot be expected to become experts in any one area. Their knowledge is more likely to be of a generalist nature, so that they know where to find detailed information when they need it, and to provide a sound foundation for their future training or study. (TTA, 2003, p. 22).

The implication of these expectations for trainee teachers is that teaching pupils with SEN has elements of both factual and procedural knowledge. For example, new teachers need to know about the factors which may affect pupils' learning and how best to respond to them; they need to know about the SEN support procedures and how to work effectively with other adults. New teachers also need to know when they need information and advice as well as how to gain access to what they need – including advice from specialists about less common types of SEN (DfES, 2004, p. 57).

This view of progression in teaching expertise is reflected in the earlier guidance for experienced teachers' further professional development. The National SEN Specialist Standards for experienced teachers (TTA, 1999, p. 9) specify the more detailed knowledge, understanding and skills which may be needed in certain contexts – such as knowledge about particular areas or types of SEN, including autistic spectrum disorders and sensory impairments. This knowledge goes alongside a core understanding of broader issues like stereotyping, equal opportunities, disability rights, organisational change processes, and the uses of relevant research and evaluation data. Teachers' progression towards specialist knowledge of particular special educational needs is confirmed by current policy statements where the only area mentioned specifically with reference to newly qualified teachers is behavioural, emotional and social difficulties (DfES, 2004, p. 57). Yet concerns have been expressed in recent years about the small amount of coverage in initial teacher training in knowledge about various conditions associated with SEN (for example, Mroz & Hall, 2003, on early years professionals' (lack of) knowledge about speech and language difficulties). Many introductory books for teachers are now structured in terms of areas of SEN, such as O'Regan (2005), which includes 15 short chapters on 'key terms' in SEN, in the form of specific conditions from Asperger syndrome to Williams syndrome. However, the practical imperative of having this type of information immediately to hand for any busy teacher needs to be examined in terms of how information is transformed into knowledge, and how knowledge and expertise develop over time.

THE DEVELOPMENT OF TEACHERS' KNOWLEDGE AND EXPERTISE

The TTA (1999, 2003) national standards for trainee and experienced teachers in England seem to express a view of how knowledge for teaching pupils with SEN should progress. There is a move from the general to the particular in looking at children's educational needs, and from fundamental, classroom-focused educational principles of planning, teaching and assessment towards a higher level and broader understanding of key issues in special educational provision such as multiprofessional collaboration, rights and opinions, leadership, communication and decision-making processes, and the differentiated means of responding to pupils' specific needs. This type of progression in the knowledge, skills and dispositions required for developing teachers can be compared to what is known more generally about adult learning. The extensive research on expertise in fields as wide-ranging as chess, race-track handicapping and taxi driving has been applied to teaching in order to shed light on the development of teachers' knowledge over time (Berliner, 2001). Prototypical features of expert teachers compared to novices include their:

- excellence mainly in their own domain and particular contexts

- automaticity in the repetitive operations required to reach their goals
- opportunism and flexibility in teaching
- sensitivity to task demands and social situations when solving problems
- representation of problems in qualitatively different ways
- faster and more accurate pattern recognition capabilities
- perception of more meaningful patterns in the domain in which they are experienced
- use of richer and more personal sources of information to bear on the problems that they are trying to solve (also taking more time to begin the problem-solving) (Berliner, 2001, p. 472).

Many of these features are relevant to understanding the expert knowledge base for meeting pupils' special educational needs, given the need to understand children's particular circumstances and the multiple factors which may influence their day-to-day learning in school. The idea that experts see and know a problem differently from novices, that they make more accurate inferences, anticipate outcomes and hold a more global and functional view of the situation (Berliner, 2001, p. 478) applies when responding constructively to different pupils' needs in school. Moreover the concept of expertise is dynamic and contextualised. Personal views and cultural values change in education, notably in the field of SEN. Berliner (2001) remarks that 'the cognitive competences of expert teachers must always be thought of relative to a culture, perhaps even to a decade in a culture' (p. 467). This suggests that the expectations for teachers' knowledge cannot rely on a body of factual information or a particular way of teaching. In the end, the knowledge associated with developing expertise is practical, interactive and responsive to wider social and political changes.

The crucial question for teacher training is how expertise develops. Berliner (2001) describes five typical stages of development: *novice*, *advanced beginner*, *competence*, *proficiency*, and *expert*. However it is his reference to Glaser's (1996) three interactive phases of development – *externally supported*, *transitional*, and *self-regulatory* – which gives a true sense of the combination of scaffolding, collaboration and developing agency involved in gaining the know-how of an expert teacher. This collaborative view of developing expertise does not depend on the skills of mentors in transmitting knowledge to less experienced colleagues. It is an active process in which is it important to consider each teacher's experience of learning and personal goals for professional development. Adult learning has been examined in terms of the difference between *surface* and *deep* approaches to learning. Marton and Booth (1997) identify people's alternative conce˜ ialisations of learning which reflect these different orientations to the task in hand. Surface approaches focus on the immediate task and involve acquiring, memorising, reproducing and applying knowledge. In contrast, deep approaches to learning involve understanding, seeing something in a different way and changing as a person. This latter orientation is a transformational approach to learning which is primarily to do with seeking meaning and looking beyond the immediate task to the world that is opened up.

Expertise in teaching depends on having a deep approach to learning, but this is not something that comes automatically with experience or something that is absent in novices. It is partly tied up with teachers' perceptions of professional identity. For beginning teachers, the cognitive demand of developing relevant knowledge, understanding and practical skill is accompanied by the social processes of professionalisation and the challenging emotional aspects of learning and changing social identity in adult life. Korthagen (2004) argues that the idea of knowing one's intrinsic mission in teaching, reflecting the deeply felt ideals and values each teacher holds, can provide a level of analysis and change for trainee and experienced teachers – potentially resulting in a more harmonious, holistic and positive experience of understanding and responding to pupils' difficulties in school. This change may be the basis for the wise practical reasoning and the artistry said to be involved in successful teachers' distinctive in-flight improvising, imagination and judgement (Eisner, 2002).

TEACHERS' KNOWLEDGE AND PRACTICE

Discussions about the nature of teachers' knowledge often refer back to Shulman's (1987) original categorisation of content knowledge (about the subject matter), pedagogical knowledge (about how to teach) and pedagogical content knowledge (about how to teach particular subject content in specific classroom settings). The latter is most closely connected to the practical know-how of teaching. It is, however, notoriously difficult to discover what teachers know, and attempts to do this can often reveal what may seem to be an eclectic mix of unspecific propositions (for example, MacLellan & Soden, 2003, on experienced teachers' knowledge of learning theory).

In the field of SEN, it seems obvious that the pupils themselves can provide a focus for making meaningful connections between teachers' knowledge and practice at a personal and professional level. The potential value of discussing particular pupils and situations as a way of drawing out teachers' knowledge, beliefs and attitudes has been argued with reference to the use of vignettes in research (for example, Poulou, 2003, in relation to emotional and behavioural difficulties) and more generally with reference to case analysis in teacher education (for example, Lundeberg & Scheurman, 1997). However there remains the problem in connecting a hypothetical example with actual practice. Reflection on actual experiences with particular pupils can be a powerful way of bridging the general and the particular, drawing out teachers' immediate concerns and decision-making (Shulman & Mesa-Bains, 1993). Kershner (2000) found that student teachers' accounts of their experiences of working with specific pupils who had presented them with a teaching challenge tended to concentrate on their use of strategies for developing the pupils into motivated and confident workers in the social world of the classroom rather than directly on strategies for developing the pupils' learning. These accounts do not tell us all that the student teachers actually know about promoting *learning* in the classroom, but they do suggest the point at which discussion and further training is likely to be most meaningful and effective for them, without putting things into 'expert language' too quickly (Korthagen & Lagerwerf, 1996).

One of the problems in gaining access to teachers' tacit knowledge (for the purposes of research, training or professional dialogue) lies in the doubtful validity of the idea that teachers simply apply theories developed elsewhere (Connelly, Clandinin, & He, 1997). Verloop, Van Driel and Meijer (2001) define the knowledge base of teaching as 'all profession-related insights that are potentially relevant to the teacher's activities' (p. 443) , noting that we can usefully distinguish the multidimensional professional knowledge base of teaching from the personal insights and beliefs which guide each teacher's decision-making and behaviour. They point out that we need a shared language of teaching, developed jointly with teachers, if any useful progress is to be made in research on teachers' professional knowledge (p. 451). The related conclusion of many researchers who wish to study teachers' 'personal practical knowledge' is that this knowledge is only found in actual practice, and that a collaborative, insider, interpretive approach to research is necessary to construct the narrative understanding of what teachers know and do (Connelly et al., 1997; Phillion & Connelly, 2004). From the teachers' perspective it is important to have a forum or knowledge community in which the personal stories of teaching can be shared in order for professional knowledge to develop further (Olson & Craig, 2001).

The assumption that teachers' knowledge and practice are inseparable is reflected in the sociocultural view of 'knowing as activity by specific people in specific circumstances' (Lave & Wenger, 1991, p. 52). This type of sociocultural understanding of activity and learning has raised awareness of the value of focusing on schools as sites where collective knowledge is created (Daniels, 2001). It also supports the need to examine the role of schools as institutions in defining ability and marginalising certain pupils (Olson, 2003). However this view of knowledge and practice should not be understood too simply or conservatively for a number of reasons, including the need to consider teachers' personal experiences of learning and the evident individual differences in their expertise and competence (Marton & Booth, 1997). In addition, there is a need to acknowledge the creation of new understandings and tools for learning in the course of shared practical, purposeful activity (Daniels & Cole, 2002). A typical and practical example would be the development by teachers of a new set of assessment tools and procedures for identifying pupils with SEN.

The field of SEN and inclusion can be particularly challenging for understanding the knowledge associated with teachers' individual and collective activity in schools because of the diverse set of opinions, values and skills operating in a system of limited financial and human resources. Imants (2002) uses the example of the inclusion reform in Dutch elementary schools to point out that while the associated innovations provide many theoretical opportunities for teachers' learning, the actual organisational conditions in schools may hinder the ways in which teachers' reflection can be truly evidence based and collegial. The opportunity for teachers' workplace learning in relation to wider moves towards inclusion is restricted by prevailing school organisation and culture, and by traditional interpretations rather than more critical or creative responses from teachers. In these circumstances it may be that many individual teachers find support in professional communities beyond their individual schools. These communities can be electronic networks such as the SENCo-Forum email discussion group established in England in 1995. ('SENCo' refers to the school role of 'special educational needs co-ordinator', although the discussion group is open to others as well.) An evaluation of SENCo-Forum by Lewis and Ogilvie (2003) established that many participants reported gains in personal professional knowledge in terms of broad access to up-to-date information and curriculum advice, and debate about formal developments in the SEN field. Some users of the Forum found it helpful in their studies for further qualifications in the field, reminding us that individual teachers' professional development is not entirely confined to the school setting or accredited there. Indeed, Mroz and Hall (2003) found that early years professionals' identification of their own training needs in the area of speech and language difficulties depended to some extent on the presence of pupils identified in this way. The associated danger of missing pupils in the early stages of difficulty or with relatively mild problems compared with their peers suggests the need not to limit teachers' opportunities for professional development to the immediate school setting.

INCORPORATING NEW KNOWLEDGE AND UNDERSTANDING INTO TEACHING: THE CHALLENGE OF NEW SCIENTIFIC EVIDENCE

The construction and use of knowledge within a particular community of practice are clearly not immune to new ideas from outside. It is a dynamic process in which individuals both contribute new ideas and change in turn. In schools, the balance of activity and knowledge creation is affected by the need to respond to new social concerns, research evidence or political intervention. Some notable professional and public concerns in England at the time of writing are the topics of self-esteem, multiple intelligences, learning styles, literacy teaching, boys' achievement compared to girls' achievement, classroom behaviour, and nutrition in school dinners. These may change in response to media interest as much as educational policy, practice and research findings.

In the field of special education, we need to ask about the effects of presenting strong scientific knowledge about aetiology, learning and behaviour patterns for whole groups of pupils, such as children with Down syndrome.

Individual differences soon become evident in day-to-day contact with pupils, but recent years have seen a revival of interest in identifying generic types or patterns of SEN associated with increasingly socially visible syndromes such as dyslexia, dyspraxia, autistic spectrum disorders (ASD) and attention deficit hyperactivity disorder (ADHD). All of these conditions are primarily identified in clinical or behavioural terms rather than through medical tests, but there is a great deal of research interest in causal mechanisms at biological level and in physical and medical interventions, producing a growing body of information for teachers and parents about remedies such as fatty acid supplements (Stordy, 2005). The increasingly sophisticated scientific understanding of genetics has led to some strong support for incorporating this knowledge into special education and services for adults with learning disabilities (Barr, 2002; Denckla & Cutting, 2004; Hodapp & Fidler, 1999). Attention is also given to the wide range of issues associated with genetic counselling and other uses of genetic information for people with learning difficulties and their families (Barr, 1999; Cunningham, Glenn, & Fitzpatrick, 2000; Ward, Howarth, & Rodgers, 2002). Yet researchers working in the fields of neuroscience, genetics and educational psychology mainly provide evidence about the *potential* use of research findings rather than the immediate and direct application of their work to educational practices (Hodapp & Fidler, 1999; Goswami, 2004; Plomin & Walker, 2003).

Much current research and practice in the field of SEN acknowledges the ways in which certain biological factors may interactively affect, but not determine, children's development, behaviour and learning in particular contexts. This belief connects with transactional models of child development and the combination of biological and environmental risk factors (Empson and Nabuzoka, 2004; Sameroff, 1995). A bio-psycho-social model has been applied in areas like ADHD as a framework for understanding and intervention, which avoids the 'unhelpful polarity' between biological and social explanations of learning and behavioural problems (Cooper, 2005, p. 128). Cooper proposes that teachers need to assimilate knowledge about ADHD into their practical theorising and their craft knowledge (pp. 125, 132). The outcome would be to understand ADHD as a bio-psycho-social condition in which the institutional structure and practices of school may themselves be implicated. An awareness of the intrinsic assumptions and limitations of schooling may lead some teachers to attempt to intervene at policy level. For the most part, however, Cooper argues that an understanding of the cognitive style of pupils identified as having ADHD can help teachers to build effectively on the pupils' learning characteristics and preferences in classroom activities. Yet Cooper remarks that the reduction of pupils' behavioural symptoms through medication may divert the teacher from fully adapting and innovating in classroom practice. This would seem to support the view that teachers need to understand biological factors and medical interventions at least enough to have an informed discussion about the child with professional colleagues and parents.

The assumed biological aspect of ADHD, commonly associated with medication, is not directly in a teacher's sphere of training, influence or responsibility, yet a bio-psycho-social model implies the need for an integrated view about causal mechanisms and multi-modal interventions. However it is not entirely clear exactly how the relevant biological information of different sorts can be turned into usable knowledge by teachers, particularly when the genetic or other biological origins can seem very distant from the individual pupil in class. It is possible to map the connections between biological, cognitive and behavioural aspects of development, 'revealing what you could know but don't yet know' (Morton, 2004, p. 19). Morton also suggests that the tool of causal modelling, representing possible causal links between biology, cognition and behaviour, 'enables you to establish both common ground and incompatibility with others with a degree of

precision' (p. 19). However, as Morton points out, a diagnosis of developmental disorders for the purpose of guiding medical treatment or educational intervention does not necessarily require an exact and complete understanding of original causes (pp. 137–138).

Genetic differences are particularly problematic in connecting cause, diagnosis, identification of SEN, and decisions about educational provision. One reason is the diversity of ways in which genes can be combined and expressed for individuals. In her discussion of Williams syndrome, an identifiable genetic condition, Karmiloff-Smith (2002) emphasises the developmental factor in tracing the cognitive and behavioural outcomes for particular children and adults affected in this way – that is, she argues that the mappings between genes, cognition and behaviour are indirect, and the situation at birth does not entirely predict what happens in later life. In connection with this focus on development, and on the associated child-environment transactions, neither quantitative genetic research (for example, family, twin and adoption studies) nor molecular genetic research (seeking particular gene-trait connections) gets close enough to predicting individual progress and outcomes to provide recipes for educational intervention by teachers. Although Plomin and Walker (2003, p. 10) argue that increasing knowledge about DNA risk indicators may begin to be used at least in educational psychology research and practice.

There may, however, be two main barriers to the informed use of genetic information by both educational psychologists and teachers – depending on the background and interests of the people involved. One problem is to do with the specialised field of knowledge. Introductory textbooks (for example, Ringo, 2004) explain the workings of genes and chromosomes with reference to key components like nucleic acids (DNA and RNA) and genetic mechanisms of development in terms of gene expression and changes in genome structure, with detailed accounts of the genetically regulated processes of cell proliferation, programmed cell death, differentiation, and association of functionally related cells. We have to acknowledge however that this is difficult material for many educators, calling for selection, translation and summary when particular genetic syndromes are discussed (for example, as found on the Contact a Family website, www.cafamily.org.uk).

The second barrier relates to the linguistic and social aspects of knowledge about genetics. Terminology can be important here. For example, the assumed determinism of genetic inheritance may be over-emphasised in the use of language. Richardson (1998) argues that genes do not 'express themselves', but they 'are best thought of as resources utilised by a dynamic system in a regulated manner. What we inherit from our parents is not just a set of genes, and not a genetic programme, but a whole developmental system which utilises genes as resources' (p. 58). More generally, in the public view there may be associations between different aspects of genetics which influence the ways in which genetic information is received by teachers. Durant, Hansen and Bauer (1996) found that public responses to the Human Genome Project showed dimensions of promise (for example, forensic medicine; genetic therapy) and concern (for example, eugenics; discrimination), as well as references to degrees of controllability. Durant et al. comment that ' (p)ublic understandings of science are important, not least because they are capable of exercising a powerful influence over both scientific research and clinical practice' (1996, p. 236). This supports the view that differences between teachers in their understanding, use of and demand for genetic information about pupils are likely to be influenced by wider beliefs and concerns about genetics in society as well as each teacher's immediate professional expectations and responsibilities.

EXTENDING KNOWLEDGE ABOUT MEETING PUPILS' SPECIAL EDUCATIONAL NEEDS

It has long been acknowledged that experienced teachers have wide-ranging beliefs about education, including its fundamental aims and values in society as well as what pupils should learn, how to teach and how schools work (Pajares, 1992). Teachers also know about their own skills and motivations, in the context of a broader sense of professional identity, responsibility and expectation about their role in society. Beliefs about pupils' development, their individual differences and their educational needs are of central interest and concern to many teachers, often accompanied by a commitment to social justice which reflects strong beliefs about the personal and social factors which may help or hinder pupils' educational progress. Understanding the development of teachers' knowledge about SEN must both acknowledge the importance of collaborative school-based practice and value the learning experiences and orientation of individual teachers.

In considering what teachers need to know, and how teachers' knowledge for meeting pupils' SEN might be extended, there are some points worth emphasising. These relate to understanding the nature of SEN, the personal and professional approaches to teaching pupils identified in this way, the knowledge that is shared with others involved, and the creation of new knowledge in the school context.

1   The fundamental importance of understanding child development in context, as a basis for understanding the identification of special educational needs

A complete body of expert knowledge needed by teachers or applied by specialists in school does not exist. However, there is evidence that teachers can usefully gain knowledge about certain key elements, including some characteristics of particular special needs groups, how children learn in general, curriculum and general pedagogical strategies, and self-knowledge as teachers. Lewis and Norwich (2005) argue that the first area of knowledge, about the nature of certain special needs groups, may act as a 'filter through which the other forms of knowledge are seen' (p. 212).

The visible effects on practice then depend on the degree to which the special needs group is strongly or weakly defined (for example, distinctive strategies for pupils with sensory impairments compared with more generic approaches for pupils with moderate learning difficulties). To counter any problems arising from too fixed a view of a special needs group, especially when accompanied by strong evidence of biological cause, it would seem fundamentally important for teachers to have a clear understanding of how different researchers explain children's development in the immediate and wider contexts of family, friends, school and community, and the challenges which may arise at particular points of development and life experience (Clarke & Clarke, 2000; Empson & Nabuzoka, 2004; Herbert, 2005; Hodapp, 1998). It is relevant to come to understand the critical features of particular contexts, the perceptions of opportunities afforded in the learning environment, and the dynamic interactions between the individual and the school, family and wider social circumstances.

2 The value of knowing that you do not know everything, and believing that change is possible

In a context where pupils' actual special educational needs are relative to the educational provision normally available in school, there is some benefit in not hoping to know everything about why SEN arise and how best to respond. Trainee teachers in England are required to demonstrate high expectations for all pupils and to avoid 'making assumptions about their pupils' abilities or potential based on their backgrounds' (TTA, 2003, p. 6). Croll and Moses's (2000) report of their 1981 and 1998 surveys of English primary teachers' understanding of the causes of their pupils' SEN found a greater willingness in 1998 for some teachers to say they did not know the cause of pupils' difficulties, although the teachers collectively showed high levels of attribution to 'within-child' and home causes compared with school factors at both points in time. Hart

(1996) writes persuasively about the importance of suspending judgement about children's needs and holding back from acting until more information and resources are acquired. This idea connects with a fundamental belief in the possibility of transformation in learning, requiring an imaginative understanding of how what happens in the present may affect a child's future (Hart, Dixon, Drummond, & McIntyre, 2004, p. 170). While much teaching benefits from drawing on previously accumulated knowledge and wisdom, some teaching requires a leap of imagination to break down unhelpful assumptions. For example, Clarke and Clarke (2000) helped to prompt current interests in resilience by using research to challenge the view that children's negative early experiences straightforwardly affect later life. Buckley, Bird and Byrne (1996) worked with parents to show that young children with Down syndrome can learn to read rather than being ineducable, and Feuerstein (1980) challenged the concepts of cultural deprivation and fixed intelligence with his work on dynamic assessment and mediated learning.

3 The need to communicate understanding and resolve differences between the people who have useful knowledge

Individual teachers' gaps in knowledge do not mean that useful knowledge is unavailable. One of the strengths of sociocultural beliefs about learning is the understanding that knowledge is productively situated in purposeful activity and distributed between the people involved and the tools at their disposal (Bruner, 1996). However, this is not to say that everyone involved in teaching pupils with SEN agrees with or even understands each other. There are genuine dilemmas, debates and discrepancies in the field, representing differences in knowledge, understanding, values and preferences amongst all involved. These differences can be the basis for much mutual misunderstanding. Teachers often learn to share their understanding by using the shorthand terms common in many professional communities. Yet the language of teaching, which can usefully confirm professional identities and facilitate internal communication, may also set ideas in stone and act as a barrier to outsiders.

4   The need to recognise the school as a site for the development of teaching expertise and the creation of knowledge

Given what we know about adult learning and the development of expertise, it is important to be particularly careful about how problems in teaching are represented and discussed, not only in light of the educational values and procedures found in schools and beyond, but also in relation to individual teachers' surface or deep orientations to learning discussed earlier (Marton & Booth, 1997). Too great a focus on dealing with the immediate task may prevent more fundamental understanding and transformative professional development. A particularly problematic issue in the field of SEN arises when using 'pre-packaged' definitions of the special educational needs of certain groups of pupils. Less experienced teachers need to be able to balance the security of gaining easy access to usable information about certain types of educational need with longer term aims for deep, expert understanding of the nature of individual pupils' learning and development. The disconnection between scientific and educational knowledge (for example, the educational implications of genetic syndromes discussed in this chapter) is a particular example of the need to gain further evidence from practical investigations of children's learning in school (Kershner & Chaplain, 2001). There is much current interest in teachers' involvement in research as a way of addressing the theory–practice division in education and researching for impact (Noffke & Somekh, 2005). The question of knowing how to meet pupils' SEN may best be answered in terms of the role of teachers' own school-based inquiry in contributing to personal, professional and public knowledge in the field.

In conclusion, understanding what teachers need to know about meeting special educational needs is as much to do with knowing how teaching expertise develops in particular social, cultural and historical circumstances as it is to do with knowing about particular types of learning difficulty, teaching strategy or special resource. Teachers' knowledge is cumulative, and wider expectations about provision for pupils identified with SEN may change radically in the course of any one teacher's career. As Mittler (2000) remarks in his discussion of teachers' professional development from initial training to headship and beyond, '[no] one has nothing to learn about inclusion' (p. 133). Beginning teachers often value learning about the 'real world things' of daily classroom activity (Bondy, Stafford, & Mott, 2005, p. 182), but many place similar emphasis on developing more fundamental and long-term insights into key aspects of education like child development, professional relationships and reflective practice. The development of teachers' knowledge for teaching particular pupils in particular classrooms is both informed by and contributes to the collective knowledge base about meeting special educational needs in the current context, where beliefs about inclusion and biological information about human development challenge the boundaries of the SEN concept itself.

REFERENCES

Barr, O. (1999). Genetic counselling: A consideration of the potential and key obstacles to assisting parents adapt to a child with learning disabilities. *British Journal of Learning Disabilities, 27,* 30–36.

Barr, O. (2002). Developments in genetic understanding: time to engage with the process. *Journal of Learning Disabilities, 6*(1), 5–12.

Berliner, D. C. (2001). Learning about and learning from expert teachers. *International Journal of Educational Research, 35*(5), 463–482.

Bondy, E., Stafford, L., & Mott, A. (2005). Learning from students' perspectives on courses and field experiences. In E. Bondy & D. D. Ross (Eds.), *Preparing for inclusive teaching: Meeting the challenges of teacher education reform*, pp. 179–193. Albany, NY: State

University of New York Press.

Bruner, J. (1996). *The culture of education.* Cambridge, MA: Harvard University Press.

Buckley, S., Bird, G., & Byrne, A. (1996). Reading acquisition by young children. In B. Stratford & P. Gunn (Eds.), *New approaches to Down syndrome* (pp. 268–279). London: Cassell.

Clarke, A., & Clarke, A. (2000). *Early experience and the life path.* London: Jessica Kingsley.

Connelly, F. M., Clandinin, D. J., & He, M. F. (1997). Teachers' personal practical knowledge on the professional knowledge landscape. *Teaching and Teacher Education, 13*(7), 665–674.

Cooper, P. (2005). AD/HD. In A. Lewis & B. Norwich (Eds.), *Special teaching for special children? Pedagogies for inclusion* (pp. 123–137). Maidenhead: Open University Press.

Croll, P., & Moses, D. (2000). *Special needs in the primary school: One in five?* London: Cassell.

Cunningham, C., Glenn, S., & Fitzpatrick, H. (2000). Parents telling their offspring about Down syndrome and disability. *Journal of Applied Research in Intellectual Disabilities, 13*, 47–61.

Daniels, H. (2001). Activity theory and the production of knowledge: Twin challenges for the development of schooling for pupils who experience EBD. *Emotional and Behavioural Difficulties, 6*(2), 113–124.

Daniels, H., & Cole, T. (2002). The development of provision for young people with emotional and behavioural difficulties: an activity theory analysis. *Oxford Review of Education, 28*(2/3), 311–329.

Davis, P., & Florian, L. (Eds.). (2004). *Teaching strategies and approaches for pupils with special educational needs: A scoping study* (DfES Research Report 516). London: DfES.

Denckla, M. B., & Cutting, L. E. (Eds.). (2004). Genetic disorders with a high incidence of learning disabilities [Special Issue]. *Learning Disabilities Research and Practice, 19*(3).

Department for Education and Skills DfES). (2001). *Special educational needs code of practice.* London: DfES.

Department for Education and Skills (DfES). (2004). *Removing barriers to achievement: The government's strategy for SEN.* London: DfES.

Diaz-Greenberg, R., Thousand, J., Cardelle-Elawar, M., & Nevin, A. (2000). What teachers need to know about the struggle for self-determination (conscientization) and self-regulation: Adults with disabilities speak about their education experiences. *Teaching and Teacher Education, 16*, 873–887.

Durant, J., Hansen, A., & Bauer, M. (1996). Public understanding of the new genetics. In T. Marteau & M. Richards (Eds.), *The troubled helix: Social and psychological implications of the new genetics* (pp. 235–248). Cambridge: Cambridge University Press.

Eisner, E. W. (2002). From episteme to phronesis to artistry in the study and improvement of teaching. *Teaching and Teacher Education, 18*, 375–385.

Empson, J. M., & Nabuzoka, D., with Hamilton, D. (2004). *Atypical child development in context.* Basingstoke: Palgrave Macmillan.

Feuerstein, R. (1980). *Instrumental enrichment.* Baltimore, MD: University Park Press.

Gersten, R., Baker, S., Pugach, M., Scanlon, D., & Chard, D. (2001). Contemporary research on special education teaching. In V. Richardson (Ed.), *Handbook of research on teaching* (4th ed.) (pp. 695–722). Washington, DC: AERA.

Glaser, R. (1996). Changing the agency for learning: Acquiring expert performance. In K. A. Ericsson (Ed.), *The road to excellence: The acquisition of expert performance in the arts and sciences, sports and games* (pp. 303–311). Mahwah, NJ: Lawrence Erlbaum.

Goswami, U. (2004). Neuroscience, education and special education. *British Journal of Special Education, 31*(4), 175–183.

Hart, S. (1996). *Beyond special needs: Enhancing children's learning through innovative thinking.* London: Paul Chapman Publishing.

Hart, S., Dixon, A., Drummond, M. J., & McIntyre, D. (2004). *Learning without limits.* Maidenhead: Open University Press.

Herbert, M. (2005). *Developmental problems of childhood and adolescence: Prevention, treatment and training.* Oxford: BPS Blackwell.

Hodapp, R. M. (1998). *Development and disabilities: Intellectual, sensory and motor impairments.* Cambridge: Cambridge University Press.

Hodapp, R. M., & Fidler, D. J. (1999). Special education and genetics: Connections for the 21st century. *Journal of Special Education, 33*(3), 130–137.

Imants, J. (2002). Restructuring schools as a context for teacher learning. *International Journal of Educational Research, 37*, 715–732.

Karmiloff-Smith, A. (2002). Elementary, my dear Watson, the clue is in the genes … Or is it? *The Psychologist, 15*(12), 608–611.

Kershner, R. (2000). Developing student teachers' understanding strategies for teaching SEN children. *Education Today, 50*(4), 31–39.

Kershner, R., & Chaplain, R. (2001). *Understanding special educational needs: A teacher's guide to effective school-based research.* London: David Fulton.

Korthagen, F., & Lagerwerf, B. (1996). Reframing the relationship between teacher thinking and teacher behaviour: Levels in learning about teaching. *Teachers and Teaching: Theory and Practice, 2*(2) 161–190.

Korthagen, F. A. J. (2004). In search of the essence of a good teacher: Towards a more holistic approach in teacher education. *Teaching and Teacher Education, 20*, 77–97.

Lave, J., & Wenger, E. (1991). *Situated learning: Legitimate peripheral participation.* Cambridge: Cambridge University Press.

Lewis, A. (2004). 'And when did you last see your father?' Exploring the views of children with learning difficulties/disabilities. *British Journal of Special Education, 31*(1), 3–9.

Lewis, A., & Norwich, B. (Eds.). (2005). *Special teaching for special children? Pedagogies for inclusion.* Maidenhead: Open University Press.

Lewis, A., & Ogilvie, M. (2003). Support, knowledge and identity: Reported gains from involvement in a special email group – the SENCo-Forum. *British Journal of Special Education, 30*(1), 44–50.

Lundeberg, M. A., & Scheurman, G. (1997). Looking twice means seeing more: Developing pedagogical knowledge through case analysis. *Teaching and Teacher Education, 13*(8), 783–797.

MacLellan, E., & Soden, R. (2003). Expertise, expert teaching and experienced teachers' knowledge of learning theory. *Scottish Educational Review, 35*(2), 110–120.

Marton, F., & Booth, S. (1997). *Learning and awareness.* Mahwah, NJ: Lawrence Erlbaum.

Mittler, P. (2000). *Working towards inclusive education: Social contexts.* London: David Fulton.

Morton, J. (2004). *Understanding developmental disorders: A causal modelling approach.* Oxford: Blackwell.

Mroz, M., & Hall, E. (2003). Not yet identified: The knowledge, skills, and training needs of early years professionals in relation to children's speech and language development. *Early Years, 23*(2), 117–130.

Noffke, S., & Somekh, B. (2005). Action research. In B. Somekh & C. Lewin (Eds.), *Research methods in the social sciences* (pp. 89–96). London: Sage.

O'Regan, F. J. (2005). *Surviving and succeeding in SEN.* London: Continuum.

Olson, D. R. (2003). *Psychological theory and educational reform: How school remakes mind and society.* Cambridge: Cambridge University Press.

Olson, M. R., & Craig, C. J. (2001). Opportunities and challenges in the development of teachers' knowledge: The development of narrative authority through knowledge communities. *Teaching and Teacher Education, 17*, 667–684.

Pajares, M. F. (1992). Teachers' beliefs and educational research: Cleaning up a messy construct. *Review of Educational Research, 62*(3) 307–332.

Phillion, J., & Connelly, F. M. (2004). Narrative, diversity, and teacher education. *Teaching and Teacher Education, 20*, 457–471.

Plomin, R., & Walker, S. (2003). Genetics and educational psychology. *British Journal of Educational Psychology, 73*, 3–14

Poulou, M. (2003). The role of vignettes in the research of emotional and behavioural difficulties. *Emotional and Behavioural Difficulties, 6*(1) 50–62.

Richardson, K. (1998). *The origins of human potential: Evolution, development and psychology.* London: Routledge.

Ringo, J. (2004). *Fundamental Genetics.* Cambridge: Cambridge University Press.

Sameroff, A. J. (1995). General systems theories and developmental psychopathology. In D. Cicchetti & D. J. Cohen (Eds.). *Developmental psychopathology: Vol. 1. Theory and methods* (pp. 659–695). New York: Wiley.

Scott, B. J., Vitale, M. R., & Masten, W. G. (1998). Implementing instructional adaptations for students with disabilities in inclusive classrooms. *Remedial and Special Education, 19*(2), 106–119.

Shulman, J. H., & Mesa-Bains, A. (Eds.). (1993). *Diversity in the classroom: A casebook for teachers and teacher educators.* Hillsdale, NJ: Research for Better Schools/Lawrence Erlbaum.

Shulman, L. S. (1987). Knowledge and teaching: Foundations of the new reform. *Harvard Educational Review, 57*, 1–22.

Stordy, J. (2005, Spring). Fish, fats and the facts. *Special! (Magazine of the National Association of Special Educational Needs)*, 17–19,

Teacher Training Agency (TTA). (1999). *National special educational needs specialist Standards.* London: TTA.

Teacher Training Agency (TTA). (2003). *Qualifying to teach: Handbook of guidance.* London: TTA.

Thomas, G., & Loxley, A. (2001). *Deconstructing special education and constructing inclusion.* Buckingham: Open University Press.

Verloop, N., Van Driel, J., & Meijer, P. (2001). Teacher knowledge and the knowledge base of teaching. *International Journal of Educational Research, 35*, 441–461.

Ward, L., Howarth, J., & Rodgers, J. (2002). Difference and choice: Exploring prenatal testing and the use of genetic information with people with learning difficulties. *British Journal of Learning Disabilities, 30*, 50–55.

38

Learning without limits: constructing a pedagogy free from determinist beliefs about ability

Susan Hart, Mary Jane Drummond, and Donald McIntyre

In memory of Annabelle Dixon.

Literature and research spanning many decades have drawn attention to the damaging effects of ability labelling on young people's learning and life chances. Yet determinist beliefs about ability continue to have currency in schools. Indeed, the idea that children are born with a given amount of intellectual power, which sets limits to possible future achievements, has gained renewed strength and legitimacy in recent years. Government-sponsored initiatives to raise standards and improve practice in schools have placed particular emphasis upon the need to differentiate by 'ability'. In England and Wales, school inspectors are trained to check that teaching is differentiated for 'more able', 'average' and 'less able' pupils. Teachers are expected to make explicit in their schemes of work how this differentiation is to be achieved. Government policy specifically recommends 'ability' grouping as the basis for effective teaching in secondary schools; the National Primary Strategy also firmly endorses ability-based pedagogy. Target-setting, with the constant requirement to predict future levels of achievement, is predicated on the belief that

current differences between young people, in terms of their test results, will persist in future tests and examinations. This belief, in turn, presupposes that current patterns of achievement reflect stable, underlying differences in academic potential.

Young people who are currently described as having special educational needs are particularly vulnerable to determinist beliefs about ability. The idea that what sets the limits to current and future learning is something unalterable within the child can seem all the more plausible when ceilings are thought to be associated with identifiable impairments or deficits. Educators working with such young people have for many years attempted to challenge determinist assumptions by proposing a more complex, interactive understanding of learning difficulties (for example, Ainscow and Tweddle, 1988; Booth, Potts, & Swann, 1987; Booth, Swann, Masterton, & Potts, 1992; Dyson, 1990; Norwich, 1990). Disabled activists have presented a social model of disability, arguing that people are disabled not by any impairments they may have, but by the failure of society to recognise and accommodate their needs (for example, Barton and

Oliver, 1992; Rieser and Mason, 1992). Both groups argue that there needs to be a shift in responses to learning difficulties to include changes in the educational environment and conditions in which learning takes place to enable young people to learn more successfully. None the less, provision in schools and colleges is still largely predicated on the individual-deficit view. As with ability labels, the deficits implied by special needs categories are treated as substantive, unalterable attributes of the person, with clear implications for both present needs and future potential.

The theoretical focus of this chapter reflects our conviction that one reason why these ways of thinking are so resistant to change is that they are sustained by – and sustain – the determinist beliefs about ability and potential that permeate the education system generally. Changing the ways in which difficulties are perceived and responded to will depend, we contend, upon liberating *all* students from thinking and practice shaped by determinist beliefs about ability and potential. Change in this fundamental, yet frequently taken-for-granted, aspect of general educational practice is, we argue, a precondition for the development of a more inclusive education system.

Such a radical change clearly depends, however, on the availability of credible, articulated alternatives to ability-based teaching. In this chapter, we outline one such model, derived from research carried out by a team based at the Faculty of Education, University of Cambridge. We identify the key features that distinguish it from ability-based practices and explore the relevance of these to the construction of inclusive pedagogy. It is obviously not possible, in the space of one chapter, to provide detailed evidence for, and exemplification of, the model presented here. A comprehensive account can be found in our book *Learning without Limits* (Hart, Dixon, Drummond, & McIntyre, 2004).

THEORISING ALTERNATIVES TO ABILITY-BASED TEACHING

The title of our book and the name of the project were inspired by a powerful passage in

Stephen Jay Gould's *The Mismeasure of Man* that seems to capture our central concerns: 'We pass through this world but once. Few tragedies can be more extensive than the stunting of life, few injustices deeper than the denial of an opportunity to strive or even to hope by a limit imposed from without but falsely identified as lying within' (Gould, 1981, p. 29). We saw it as a matter of profound concern that the idea of fixed ability was being perpetuated in schools, indeed positively endorsed by officially sanctioned models of good practice. Drawing on our understanding of a substantial tradition of research spanning more than 50 years, summarised in Figure 38.1, we argued that differential, fixed ability is not just a deeply flawed and unjust way of explaining differences in learning and achievement; it also exerts an active, powerful force within school and classroom processes, helping to create the very limits and disparities of achievement that it purports to explain.

It does this in subtle and unintended ways through the effects it has on teachers' thinking and practices, through the social and psychological impact it has on young people's self-perceptions, aspirations, attitudes and responses to school learning and through its narrowing effects on the curriculum and the methods of assessment used to recognise and evaluate achievement. We realised, however, that if we were to challenge the idea of fixed ability underlying the government's reform agenda, we would need to do more than simply re-open well-rehearsed debates about the impact of ability labelling on young people's education and life chances. We needed to be in a position to propose a coherent, principled and practicable alternative to ability-based pedagogy.

One possible strategy was to search the literature for alternative models and invite a group of teachers, who had themselves rejected ability labelling, to assess their practical potential. In the field of early childhood education, for instance, there has been growing interest in applying pedagogical approaches based on the work of early years professionals in Reggio Emilia, Italy, whose commitment to a particular view of children's

Effects on teachers
- Ability labelling affects teachers' attitudes and behaviour towards children and undermines belief in some children's learning capacity. Teachers vary their teaching and respond differently towards children viewed as 'bright', 'average' or 'less able' (for example, Rosenthal and Jacobson, 1968; Jackson, 1964; Keddie, 1971; Croll and Moses, 1985; Good and Brophy, 1991; Hacker, Rowe, & Evans, 1991; Suknandan and Lee, 1998).
- Fixed ability thinking reduces teachers' sense of their own power to promote learning and development through the use of their expertise and professional judgement. It therefore discourages creativity and inventiveness to overcome difficulties (for example, Bloom, 1976; Simon, 1953; Kelly, 1955; Dixon, 1989; Drummond, 2003; Hart, 1996, 2000).
- Fixed ability thinking encourages teachers to see differential performance as natural and inevitable, and so diverts attention from the part that school and classroom processes play in enabling or limiting learning for individuals and groups (for example, Jackson, 1964; Bourdieu, 1976; Bernstein, 1971; Tizard and Hughes, 1984; Rist, 1971; Coard, 1971).

Effects on young people
- Young people learn how they are perceived by teachers and respond to that perception; they tend to live up to or down to expectations (for example, Rosenthal and Jacobson, 1968; Nash, 1973; Good and Brophy, 1991, Tizard, Blatchford, Burke, Farquhar, & Plewis, 1988).
- Ability-labelling undermines many young people's dignity, their self-belief, their hopes and expectations for their own learning. It strips them of their sense of themselves as competent, creative human beings, leading them to adopt self-protective strategies that are inimical to learning (for example, Dweck, 2000; Hargreaves, 1967, 1982; Lacey, 1970, Ball, 1981; Holt, 1990; Jackson, 1968; Pearl, 1997).
- Fixed ability thinking and ability-led practices tend to disadvantage particular groups of young people. Research has repeatedly drawn attention to social class and ethnicity-based inequalities in the processes of selection, grouping and differentiation of curricula (for example, Jackson, 1964; Douglas, 1964; CACE, 1967; Ford, 1969; Heath, 1983; Taylor, 1993; Gillborn and Youdell, 2000).

Effects on curriculum
- Fixed ability thinking encourages and legitimates a narrow view of curriculum, learning and achievement (for example, Hargreaves, 1980; Alexander, 1984, 2000; Goldstein and Noss, 1990) .
- By naturalising explanations of differential achievement, fixed ability thinking perpetuates the limitations and biases built into existing curricula (for example, Gardner, 1983; West, 1991).
- Ability labelling and grouping by ability restrict the range of learning opportunities to which individual pupils are exposed (for example, Jackson, 1964; Nash, 1973; Suknandan and Lee, 1998; Hacker et al., 1991; Oakes, 1982, 1985; Boaler, 1997a, 1997b; Boaler, Wiliam, & Brown, 2000).
- Ability labelling and grouping encourage schools and teachers to privilege psychometric knowledge of young people over the knowledge acquired through day-to-day classroom interaction (for example, Kelly, 1955; Hull, 1985; Hart et al., 2004).

Figure 38.1 How fixed-ability thinking limits learning

capacity to learn is strikingly free from any concept of inherent ability (Edwards, Gandini, & Foreman, 1998). We knew as well of current work exploring the application of Howard Gardner's theory of multiple intelligences to practice in primary and secondary schools, which has aroused much interest (Chamberlain, 1996; Gardner, 1983, 1999; Jack, 1996). One member of the university team also had previous experience of working with teachers to explore the potential of applying Bloom's (1976) theory of mastery learning in Scottish secondary schools.

We decided against this approach, however, because we thought that the most pow-erful and persuasive models would be those already developed by teachers themselves. We were confident that we would find teachers who had come to their own conclusions about the damage done by ability labelling and who had already developed successful classroom practices consistent with their values and understandings. The nine teachers who joined the team worked in different contexts and phases of education and had expertise in different subject areas. Over the course of one year, we spent many hours in these teachers' classrooms, observing and interviewing both teachers and pupils. We also met to share our thinking and develop the research collaboratively. Working with the teachers, we built up individual accounts of the key constructs at the heart of each teacher's thinking, and an understanding of how these constructs worked together to create a distinctive pedagogy. Comparing the nine accounts, we found many elements of thinking and practice that the teachers had in common. Furthermore, beneath these common elements, we identified a core idea, which acts as the inspiration and driving force at the heart of these teachers' work.

THE CORE IDEA OF TRANSFORMABILITY

At the most fundamental level, it seemed that fixed ability thinking had been replaced, in these teachers' pedagogy, by an alternative mind-set: a radically different orientation towards the future, leading to an entirely different approach to the task of teaching a class of learners. Ability labels, and ability-based practices, assume a stable relation between present and future; those young people designated 'more able', 'average' and 'less able' will remain so in the future – the teacher's task is to assess ability accurately and, by matching teaching to ability, enable each individual to realise his or her given potential. In contrast, the nine teachers in our team base their work on a fundamentally different conception of the relation between the present and the future that we have come to call 'transformability': a firm and unswerving conviction that there is the potential for change in current patterns of achievement and response, that things can change and be changed for the better, sometimes dramatically, as a result of what happens in the present, in the daily interactions of teachers and students.

The accounts of the nine teachers' work provide multiple illustrations of how they conceptualise the potential for change and how they attempt to realise this in their classrooms. While the teachers shared similar concerns and used a similar range of strategies, each of them had particular emphases. For example, Julie, a

history teacher, feels passionately that young people's learning capacity is constrained by the inflexibility of the current education system. She is deeply opposed to practices of setting and streaming. She feels that these practices damage self-esteem and contribute to the negative perceptions that many young people hold about their personal capabilities; rigid ability-based groupings curtail opportunities and place preset limits on what individuals in particular circumstances can achieve. She uses her power and influence as a head of department to lift limits such as these in the way she organises groupings; in her classroom practice, she takes steps to allow young people to learn in more open and flexible ways (see also Hart, 2002).

Non, an English teacher and deputy head, believes that much of what happens in school seems, from young people's point of view, to be cut off from what happens in the world outside school and from what matters to them in their lives. Their learning is seriously limited if they cannot see the point of what they are doing and what they are expected to learn. So Non's priority in her teaching is to find ways of making connections between school learning and the students' worlds, to find ways of making learning in school meaningful, relevant and important to them.

For Alison, a primary teacher, emotional engagement is all-important. She understands that young people's capacity for learning in any given context is increased or limited proportionately to the energy and enthusiasm that they bring to their learning. A central priority for her is to fire up their interest and excitement. She wants the children to see learning as an adventure to which everybody is invited, in which everybody can take part and where everybody has an active role to play. Their capacity for learning will be enhanced, she believes, if young people 'see themselves as being part of something rather than having something done to them'.

Narinder, another primary teacher, recognises the important part that language plays in shaping thinking; she works from the premise that learning capacity can be increased by developing young people's understanding of and ability to reflect on their own thinking processes. She regularly uses key words from the domain of metacognition ('connect', 'explain', 'views' 'points', 'definitions'). Extending the idea of 'writing frames', she offers them 'speaking frames' to support their learning and the discussion of their learning.

Patrick, another English teacher, laments the passive model of learners and learning which in his view pervades national policy documents and curriculum guidelines. He believes that young people's learning capacity is ill-served by a narrow delivery model of curriculum and pedagogy that emphasizes preset objectives, and where planning leaves little or no space for learning to be shaped by young people themselves. His bedrock belief is that young people are in charge of their own learning; the teacher's task is to create conditions that will maximise their capacity for learning in any given situation by encouraging them to engage – and sustain effortful intellectual engagement – with worthwhile tasks and activities.

These examples show why these teachers are confident that there is the potential for all young people to become better learners. Their thinking is not based on judgements about individual learners but stems from a broader analysis of external influences and constraints on learning that have affected prior learning and continue to operate in the present. They know that these influences impact upon young people's states of mind – on their ability and willingness to engage with learning opportunities provided for them in school. The concept of learning capacity reflected in these teachers' work is fundamentally different in nature from the concept of fixed ability. The idea of a mysterious inner force, responsible for learning, residing in the individual, and subject to the internal limits of each individual learner, has no place or value in their thinking. They see learning capacity as a product of the interplay between external forces and internal resources and states of mind. For them, learning capacity includes social and emotional as well as cognitive-intellectual resources and states of mind;

the cognitive elements are skills and understandings that can be, and have been, learned. Learning capacity resides in the collective as well as the individual; it is contained within and constituted by how a group of young people work and operate together as a group, and by the opportunities and resources made available to them as a group.

The examples illustrate some of the external forces recognised by these teachers to have an impact upon learning capacity, including prescribed curriculum content, the language of the curriculum, management styles, modes of grouping, expectations of teachers and peers and the nature, range and distribution of learning tasks and opportunities. The teachers also consider the interplay between influences external and internal to the school. These various external influences interact with internal forces and states of mind, such as self-belief and the sense of meaningfulness and relevance of what is being learnt, which teachers know have a profound impact on capacity and willingness to engage. In addition to aspects of cognitive and intellectual functioning, the teachers also include social and emotional states; young people's feelings of confidence, competence, their sense of identity and belonging, and their commitment to the values upheld by the school.

Learning capacity is transformable because the forces that shape it, individually and collectively, internally and externally, are to an extent within teachers' control. The teachers are convinced that they have the power to strengthen and, in time, transform learning capacity by acting systematically to lift limits on learning, to expand and enhance learning opportunities and to create conditions that encourage and empower young people to use the opportunities available to them more fully. By working out practical strategies, for instance, to increase flexibility, to make learning more pertinent to the world outside school or to increase learners' control, the teachers act simultaneously in everybody's interests, to strengthen the learning capacity of everybody.

The teachers recognise, however, that if their power is to be effective, it must connect with and harness young people's power in what is necessarily a joint enterprise. As active agents in their own right, young people can – and many currently do – use their power to resist and confound teachers' best efforts to engage them and enhance their capacity for learning. However, the teachers know that how young people use their power is profoundly affected by every aspect of their school experiences. It is possible to influence young people's states of mind, their ability and willingness to invest in school learning, through the classroom conditions in which learning takes place. By understanding the connections between classroom conditions and the states of mind that affect young people's ability and willingness to invest in school learning, teachers are confident in their power to transform young people's learning capacity.

THE TEACHER'S ROLE IN TEACHING FOR TRANSFORMABILITY

In addition to the core idea of transformability, we also identified a common set of purposes that inform the teachers' work and three pedagogical principles that guide their classroom choices at a practical level, as they attempt to achieve their purposes. These are the practical tools which enable them to translate their commitment to and belief in transformability into a coherent and practicable pedagogy.

The core purposes of teaching

As the teachers talked about their work and why they chose to do what they did, it became apparent that their purposes for teaching go beyond the acquisition of particular knowledge, skills and understanding. Through the tasks and activities they provide, the contexts they create, the classroom relationships and interactions they foster, the teachers are trying to lay foundations that will enable all young people in their classes to become more powerful learners. They do this specifically by continually referencing their decision-making to the internal resources and states of mind that

they are seeking to restore, build and foster. In contrast to the differentiated objectives associated with ability-based pedagogies, these purposes – in the affective, social and cognitive domains – as summarised in Figure 38.2, provide a common framework for the planning, conduct and evaluation of teaching applicable to everybody.

Although these purposes may, at first sight, appear to be ones that most teachers would endorse, they are in fact fundamentally incompatible with ability labelling. The teachers have turned their awareness of the limits on learning imposed by ability labelling into understanding of what needs to be done – and undone – in order to free learning from those limits. The core purposes could not be achieved in a learning environment still permeated by ability-focused judgements and practices.

Three practical pedagogical principles

The process of translating these purposes into practice is guided by three practical pedagogical principles. All three words are important. These are *pedagogical* principles, in that they are concerned with the purposes of teaching. They are *practical* principles, in that they are not merely espoused ideals: these are the ideas that in practice guide the ways teachers realise their purposes. Most importantly, they are *principles*, not just instrumental ideas for achieving the teachers' purposes but also ethical ideas about the right ways in which teachers ought to engage with young people.

These principles do not function in isolation from one another. Their power to contribute to the fundamental task of progressively enhancing young people's learning capacity depends upon the use of each of them in combination with the others.

1   The principle of everybody

The principle of 'everybody' articulates teachers' fundamental responsibility and commitment to acting in the interests of everybody. It works to ensure that teachers' efforts to strengthen and transform learning

To minimise or prevent states of mind which impair young people's learning capacity, for example:	To build and strengthen the subjective states which enhance learning capacity
In the affective domain	
• Feeling insecure, or lacking in confidence • Feeling incompetent, frustrated • Feeling negative, disaffected • Negative sense of self as learner: the experience of failure • Feeling powerless to change things for the better through own effort	• Feelings of safety, growing confidence • Feelings of competence and control • Increased enjoyment and sense of purposefulness in learning • Enhanced sense of identity as learner: the experience of success • Increased hope and confidence for the future, capacity to change
In the social domain	
• Sense of being rejected, feeling a second class member of the community, with less to contribute than others • Alienation, rejection of school values, oppositional behaviour	• Increased sense of acceptance and belonging, as important and unique members of a group • Enhanced social and collaborative skills, and sense of participation in a community of learners
In the cognitive domain	
• Difficulty in accessing or engaging with activities/subject matter of curriculum • Sense of meaninglessness or irrelevance of what is to be learnt • Expectation of failure, using coping strategies to avoid risk, unwillingness to persevere with difficult tasks	• Successful access to worthwhile learning by all young people • Increased sense of relevance, capacity to see connections and find personal meaning in tasks and activities • Enhancing young people's powers of thinking, reasoning, explaining

Figure 38.2 Teachers' purposes in teaching for transformability

capacity are applied equally and fairly to everybody. It was noticeable that the nine teachers often used the term 'everybody' when talking about their teaching. This continual reference to 'everybody' expresses their determination that no one is to be left out, that the core purposes of teaching apply to *everybody* in the class, not just *some people*. Everybody can become a better learner if the subjective conditions reflected in these purposes can be achieved; and they are convinced that the purposes *can* be achieved for everybody, if conditions are right. So the teachers approach their work in a developmental way, searching for ways of enhancing subjective experiences through their own classroom choices. Since they believe that learning capacity resides in the collective as well as in the individual, they

choose strategies to enhance learning capacity that, wherever possible, construct learning as a collective experience. The strategies are carefully selected to be accessible to everybody and to enable the core purposes to be achieved, as far as possible, by everybody.

The principle of 'everybody' is not just about equality of value as expressed in the teacher's mind and actions. It is also about the value that young people place on their own and one another's contributions. Ability labels and ability-based grouping can prevent the development of community by reinforcing the idea that some people have very little to contribute to their own learning or to the learning of others. The nine teachers explicitly encourage their students to work together and value what they can contribute to one another's learning. They also invest considerable effort in developing unity and solidarity in their class-rooms. They recognise that there is immense potential, within the community of minds that constitutes the group, for enhancing and trans-forming learning capacity, if the resources of the group can be effectively harnessed and enabled to operate more purposefully and pro-ductively in support of everybody's learning. In this respect, their view of the power of the collective to enhance learning capacity has links with Perkins's (1995) notion of 'distrib-uted intelligence'. According to Perkins, the resources which support intelligent behaviour are not simply located in individual minds (the 'person-solo') but are distributed throughout the environment and social system in which we operate. They include physical resources (for example, computers), social resources (for example, human collaboration and team work) and symbolic resources (for example, sym-bolic systems, thinking oriented terms). Perkins writes, 'Intelligent behaviour is not characteristically the dance of the naked brain but an act that occurs in a somewhat support-ive physical, social and cultural context. Because of that context, the behaviour pro-ceeds with more intelligence' (1995, p. 323).

The idea of working as an integrated com-munity, with common goals, collaborative ways of working, an acceptance of mutual obligations and an appreciation of the benefits of learning from one another, is very different from the individualistic thinking associated with ability labelling. It is also very different from an approach to teaching in which the teacher takes all the responsibility. In seeking to make their classes into learning communi-ties, the teachers integrate the principle of everybody with a second key principle, *co-agency*.

2 The principle of co-agency

This second pedagogical principle follows from the awareness that the task of transform-ing learning capacity must necessarily be a joint enterprise between teachers and students. All teachers' practices are directed towards enlisting their students, both individually and collectively, as active, committed partners (*co-agents*) in the educational process. This leads them to adopt a particular approach to allowing for diversity in learning. A major consideration in the teachers' efforts to enhance learning capacity is their awareness that the emphasis on perceived differences in so-called ability, and the consequent neglect of other real differences of many kinds constitute a serious constraint on learning for many young people. The teachers recognize that one important way in which they can make a difference to future development is by organising their teaching in a way that *does* make conscious use of their knowledge about individuals that is significant for learning, but in a way that *does not* perpetuate or re-create the limiting and divisive effects associated with ability labelling. Their preferred strategy is to plan common learning opportunities for every-body in the class, ensure that tasks and activi-ties are accessible to everyone, and then offer an open invitation to everybody.

This approach reflects their understanding that allowing for diversity is not simply a task for the teacher. According to the principle of co-agency, diversity in learning is achieved by what both teachers *and* learners do and con-tribute to the learning process. The technical task of matching tasks and learners, in ability-based pedagogy, gives way to a deeper, more complex process of *connection*, a meeting of minds, purposes and actions between teachers and young people – as one teacher said 'them coming to meet you'. Tasks and outcomes are deliberately left open, or constructed in such a way as to offer alternative activities or choices of various kinds, so that young people have space to make their own connections, to make ideas meaningful in their own terms and to represent and express their thoughts, ideas and feelings in their own ways. When connection is successfully achieved, it inevitably results in different experiences and outcomes, since everyone is unique, everyone brings and con-tributes something different, making his or her own meanings through active engagement with the learning opportunities provided.

The principle of co-agency also implies active work on the part of teachers to encour-age young people to share responsibility in many ways, and in relation to many different aspects of classroom life. For example, Narinder encourages her students to organise the classroom and make rules about what is acceptable. Non helps her students reach a better understanding of the criteria by which their work will be judged, so that they can take more responsibility themselves for evaluating and improving their work. Yahi, a maths teacher, seeks to empower young people to ask questions more frequently and more freely. This sharing of responsibility – which, at its fullest, implies joint control by teacher and learners – is very important practically because it helps to make classroom teaching more manageable. It is important pedagogically because the active engagement of learners is needed for any sort of learning to happen. And it is important ethically, as noted earlier, because teachers cannot fulfil their professional responsibilities and exercise the full extent of their power unless they are able to recruit young people to work with them in what is necessarily a joint enterprise.

3   The principle of trust

The teachers also approach their task from a basic position of trust. They have an unshakeable conviction that young people are to be trusted – trusted to make meaning of what they encounter in school and out of it, trusted to find relevance and purpose in relevant and purposeful activities, trusted to contribute to one another's learning, trusted to take up the teacher's invitations to co-agency and to participate in the worthwhile activity of learning.

This basis position of trust means that, when learners choose not to engage or appear to be inhibited in their learning, teachers re-evaluate their choices and practices in order to try to understand what might be limiting their participation and learning. Trust sustains teachers' belief that young people will choose to engage if the conditions are right, and so sustains their effort to keep searching for ways to reach out and make connections that will free young people to learn more successfully. They adopt particular patterns of pedagogical thinking: continually trying to connect with their stu-

dents' consciousness as people, in order to understand their responses to learning activities and experiences from their point of view. They engage in continuous hypothesising about the states of mind lying behind young people's choices and actions, the classroom conditions that may be influencing these, and how classroom conditions might be changed to become more enabling. Aware that they are working from hypotheses and not certainties, the teachers continuously review and revise their hypotheses in the light of experience. They also engage in dialogue with young people in order to check out interpretations of behaviour. Examples of this kind of thinking permeate our accounts of the nine teachers' work, suggesting that the teachers make use of it in all areas of classroom practice – in their design and selection of tasks and topics, in their classroom interactions, in their assessment and feedback and in the evaluation and development of their teaching.

The teachers tread a fine line between, on the one hand, communicating acceptance and appreciation of young people as they currently are and, on the other, creating the conditions that will enable them to change, to find themselves able to transcend existing limits. Indeed, they are convinced that communication of interest, and willingness to listen and try to understand how the world looks through the eyes of young people, can go a long way towards making such change possible.

Making transforming choices

We have now seen how the core idea of transformability translates into a principled and practicable pedagogy (Figure 38.3). In place of a stable view of the relation between present and future, the core idea of transformability assumes that the present plays a pivotal role in determining the path of future development.. The future is in the making in the present. Absolutely everything that happens in the present will have a formative effect, for better or worse, upon future development. Either the effect will be broadly to maintain the learner's capacity as it currently manifests

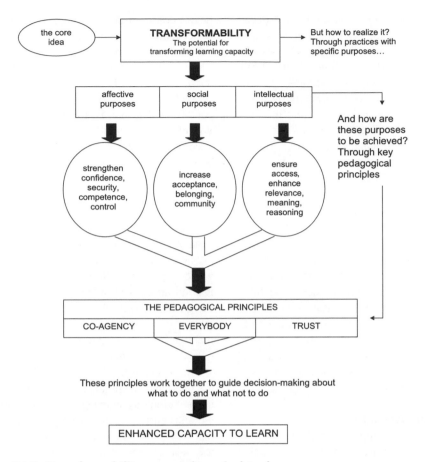

Figure 38.3 Transformability as a pedagogical tool

itself, because the balance of influences remains unchanged, or the effect will be to strengthen and progressively transform learning capacity. The teachers exercise their power to make a difference by considering the choices available to them and systematically choosing the transforming options, based on their understanding of what limits young people's capacity to learn and what will lift those limits, freeing them to become more powerful learners.

TRANSFORMABILITY: THE HEART OF INCLUSIVE PEDAGOGY?

We now move on, in this final part of the chapter, to consider the relevance of the model of pedagogy outlined so far for theory

and practice in the area of special and inclusive education. We argue that young people described as 'having special educational needs' should not be viewed as a separate group, as if the pedagogical ideas, purposes and principles outlined so far do not apply to them. Indeed, it is precisely because dominant ways of thinking mark out children described as having learning difficulties or disabilities as 'other' that it is important, in this final section, to explain our conviction that the core ideas that provide the basis for our model of pedagogy do apply to all young people without exception. We show that the core idea of transformability and the concept of learning capacity that supports it connect up with an important tradition of work in the field of special and inclusive education. This tradition challenges individual-deficit accounts of 'learning difficulties' and refocuses analysis onto the complex interactive processes that lead to the emergence of difficulties. We argue that the key ideas that form the basis of our model, together with the purposes and principles that enable them to be translated into practice, have an important contribution to make to the development of inclusive education, encompassing insights arising from that body of work in a pedagogical framework designed for all students.

We refer back to the words of Stephen Gould quoted at the start of the chapter. He speaks of the 'stunting of life' and the 'injustices' that stem from 'a limit imposed from without but falsely identified as lying within'. This, the endemic problem of fixed ability thinking, applies just as much, if not more strongly, to young people categorised as 'having learning difficulties' or disabilities. Their characteristic patterns of attainment and response that, in reality, reflect a complex interplay of influences, both external and internal, are typically attributed to inherent deficits and/or disabilities. The limits are assumed to come from within. Once the attribution is made, there is no call to look for alternative explanations. By contrast, in our model, learning capacity is not a fixed, internal property, tied to or inferred from particular inherent abilities, difficulties or impairments. It is a situated concept, the product of the interplay between internal and external influences, residing not just in the mind of the individual but also, in part, constituted by the resources of the group. It is therefore susceptible to change – in some cases, even dramatic change – if the conditions are right. The learning capacity of all young people, including those currently described as having 'moderate', 'severe' or 'profound' learning difficulties, can legitimately be understood in this way.

For example, young people designated as having 'moderate learning difficulties' are typically thought to have deficiencies in cognition, memory and language, a short attention span and social skills deficits, as well as having low overall attainment compared with their peers. These attributions take no account, however, of the multiplicity of influences, internal and external, which affect young people's capacity to attend, to think, discriminate, interact with others, recall previous learning and become absorbed in productive and meaningful activities. Adrienne Bennett, a teacher working in a school for 'moderate learning difficulties' describes what happened when she tried out some new approaches to mathematics teaching. Her students revealed qualities, characteristics and skills of which she had not previously thought them to be capable. She writes:

> I have found that the pupils designated as having moderate learning difficulties … can: concentrate for long periods of time; sustain protracted investigations; be systematic; reason logically; find patterns and relationships; make tests and predictions; generalise; record and explain their findings. I have found them working in ways I had never expected them to be able to. What they couldn't do was perform meaningless calculations and relate them to situations that were equally meaningless to them. But then, who can? (Bennett and Williams, 1992, p. 74)

If we accept current patterns of attainment and response as being reliably and unalterably tied to particular underlying deficits or impairments, our acceptance becomes part of the dynamics – the 'limit imposed from without' – that constrain both present and future development. Goldbart (1994) illustrates how deficit thinking both disempowers teachers and impacts on the development of young people described as having profound and multiple learning difficulties. She refers to a study of communication in which teachers of such students were interviewed. Out of 800 pupils discussed, 647 (80.9 per cent) were considered by their teachers to have no communication skills. This perception of students as 'non-communicators' is a matter of considerable concern, Goldbart argues, because 'it is well established in the language acquisition literature that it is by being treated as communicators that we become communicators' (Goldbart, 1994, p. 16). The implication is clear. If these students do not go on to become communicators, this may be because they have not been given appropriate opportunities to learn. Limits on their capacity to learn to communicate, while ostensibly attributable to any impairments they may have, may in fact be due to their not having experienced the kinds of interactions with teachers needed to foster the development of communication skills.

As with ability labelling, deficit thinking produces a sense of powerlessness and fatalism on the part of teachers: a sense that there is not much that can be done because the limits on learning imposed from within are unalterable. Indeed, as Mittler (2000) reminds us, not much more than 30 years ago it was widely accepted that the learning capacity of 30,000 young people was so profoundly and permanently limited that they were ineducable. These young people spent their time in long-stay hospitals with little or nothing expected of them. Mittler recalls that if, at the time, anyone had said to him that a day would come when such children would not only attend mainstream schools but succeed in passing the ordinary school leaving examinations, he would not have believed them. Nor would he have expected to meet adults who describe themselves as 'having learning difficulties' living in ordinary houses, holding down a job, having a family, lobbying Members of Parliament or addressing the United Nations. Yet, he recognizes, 'all these things, and many more, have happened to some and could have happened to many more if the opportunities had been made available and if there were enough people to turn the vision into a reality' (Mittler, 2000, p. viii).

The assumption that we can infer what the future holds for children, on the basis of present characteristics and attainments, and organise provision for them on that basis, is as erroneous today as it was 30 years ago. What we currently know about the range of attainments and patterns of development of young people with particular impairments reflects the experiences and opportunities to which they have previously been exposed. We cannot know or predict what young people might, in future, become capable of, if significantly enhanced opportunities for learning were made available to them and if externally imposed limits on their learning were to be first recognised, and then pro-

gressively lifted. The point is reiterated by Buckley (2000), Director of Research and Training at The Down Syndrome Educational Trust, who has a daughter with Down syndrome. She believes that, although young people with Down syndrome are now deemed educable, the tendency until recently to segregate them from other children means that they have still been subject to impoverished social and educational experiences.

> Until the last decade most children with Down syndrome grew up in social and educational deprivation. They were not welcome at the same clubs, play groups and social activities attended by other children of the same age. They only mixed with children with similar and more severe disabilities in segregated settings. They were denied friendships with other people of similar age who were not disabled. They were not learning and growing within the world of children in their community. Imagine how social isolation and exclusion from school would affect the development of children without a disability and then consider its probable effect on the development of children with Down syndrome. (Buckley, 2000, p. 6)

Currently available evidence of patterns of development of young people with Down syndrome inevitably reflects such limiting influences. Buckley writes 'much of the information that we have at present is based on the descriptions of the progress of children with Down syndrome who have not benefited from effective interventions or inclusive schooling' (2000, p. 20). Studies of the progress of children with Down syndrome in inclusive settings 'all indicate that the children benefit and that they achieve higher levels of literacy, numeracy and academic attainments than children in segregated settings'. The evidence also suggests that the children have 'considerably better spoken language and more mature social skills than those educated in special schools' (Buckley, 2000, p. 7). Moreover, there is no evidence to support the myth that young people with Down syndrome reach a ceiling in adolescence and do not go beyond it. Buckley writes, 'The so-called "ceiling" discussed in past literature was almost certainly the result of the lack of medical care and educational and social experience' (2000, p. 4).

From these and other examples in the literature, we can see that the concept of learning capacity in our model of pedagogy reflects many of the same concerns, and redirects attention to many of the same external influences, as proponents of social and interactive theories of 'learning difficulties' and disabilities. For example, Norwich argues for a dynamic approach to assessment in which 'learner characteristics would be assumed to interact with the context of learning and to be specific to the fields of learning' (1990, p. 107). Ainscow explains how he arrived at the conviction that 'educational difficulties have to be seen as being context bound, arising out of the interaction of individual children with a particular educational programme at a certain moment in time' (1999, p. 30). The implication of this perspective, as we have seen in the work of Mittler and Buckley, is that it is not possible to know how the learning of young people experiencing significant difficulties might develop under more favourable conditions; but since experience has unequivocally shown that their learning has been, and continues to be, subject to many externally imposed limits, including those arising from low expectations, educators can and must commit themselves to doing whatever is possible to bring about those more favourable conditions. This conclusion and the pedagogical commitments that follow from it lead to a mind-set and professional purposes entirely congruent with those that follow from the core idea of transformability. Indeed, we are confident that educators whose thinking is influenced by social or interactive perspectives on educational difficulties will recognise that they too approach their work in a spirit of transformability: refusing to accept the inevitability of certain difficulties and limitations; feeling inspired by a sense that what happens in the present can change the path of future development; using their knowledge, creativity and expertise, in partnership with students, to search for ways to enable learning to be more successful. Jones (2002) illustrates this approach in practice, in a powerful paper relating to the use of objects of reference to assist the development of communication in a college for adults with learning difficulties and physical disabilities. Describing progress with one student, Nicola, he expresses his belief that 'simply because someone apparently cannot does not mean that they will not' and 'we do not know if Nicola will make the connection but we know that if we don't try she never will' (Jones, 2002, p. 13).

The model of pedagogy that we have elaborated in this chapter places this spirit of transformability at the heart of teaching and learning for *all* students. The core idea of transformability is, we suggest, a genuinely inclusive tool because if this is how teachers are approaching their task with all students, there is no reason to single out people 'with learning difficulties' for particular mention. The task is essentially the same for everybody: teachers are trying to discover what it is possible to do to enhance the learning capacity of each and every member of the class, and intervening to create conditions in which their learning can more fully and effectively flourish. They notice where there are gaps between their purposes (as shown in Figure 38.2) and what is actually happening; they analyse the connections between internal resources and states of mind and external classroom conditions; and they work out how they can intervene in order to shift the balance of forces so that they can come closer to achieving the core purposes for each individual, and for the group as a whole. When they look to the future, then, they do not expect to see stability: the fulfillment of the expectations and predictions arising from current tests and patterns of attainment. Rather, the measure of their success is clear evidence of positive changes: evidence that the subjective, internal conditions they believe to be needed for purposeful and productive learning are being achieved, individually and collectively, by more of their students, more of the time.

The concept of learning capacity at the heart of this process is also an inclusive tool. While it has much in common with social and interactive theories of learning difficulties, it has the advantage that it does not depend on a pre-existing distinction between those 'with difficulties' and other students. It avoids the hierarchies and distinctions inherent in categories of ability and disability, and offers teachers the means to recognise and refer to everybody's learning capacity in positive terms. Perhaps most importantly, this situated concept of learning capacity helps to sustain the critical mental shift away from determinist and deficit thinking. It keeps alive and, most importantly, active in teachers' thinking and decision-making the awareness that the learning characteristics, dispositions and difficulties displayed by their students at a given point in time are not a reflection of permanent and unalterable attributes of those individuals; it insists that there is always the potential for positive change through their actions and interventions to increase and enhance learning capacity.

The core idea of transformability, and the concept of learning capacity at its heart, are also congruent with other important work on inclusive education, where inclusion is understood as involving a complex and continuing process of development in the cultures, policies and practices of schools. In *The Index for Inclusion*, educational inclusion is defined as 'the processes of increasing the participation of students in, and reducing their exclusion from, the cultures, curricula and communities of local schools' (Booth, Ainscow, Black-Hawkins, Vaughan, & Shaw, 2000, p. 12). Recognising that inclusion is concerned with all students who are vulnerable to exclusionary pressures, not just those categorised as 'having special educational needs', the task for educators is described in terms of understanding and removing, or minimising, 'barriers to learning and participation'. The *Index* provides a comprehensive analysis of possible barriers to learning, and steps that can be taken to extend and enhance school and classroom conditions, in the form of questions that teachers can use to guide development work at whole-school or individual classroom level. The distinctive contribution that our model can make to this framework is to describe in detail the practical processes

whereby the use of this powerful resource can be rooted in pedagogy – ensuring that the analysis and questioning of existing classroom conditions needed to drive the processes of inclusion are embedded in everyday classroom decision-making.

Emphasising the importance of *how we think* as well as *what we do* in the work to develop inclusive education is especially crucial in the current context. Despite official government commitment to inclusion, policy initiatives designed to raise standards and improve practice in schools have had the effect of giving new strength and legitimacy to the idea of ability 'as a fixed, generalized and measurable potential' (Gillborn and Youdell, 2000). Fixed ability and deficit thinking go hand in hand – both call for constant and concerted vigilance if their damaging effects are to be progressively eliminated from educational practice. As discussed in more detail in the first chapter of our book, *Learning without Limits* (Hart et al., 2004), we know from the experience of comprehensive reform that the attempt to remove barriers imposed by selective education was profoundly undermined by the re-emergence of fixed ability-focused thinking and practices within comprehensive schools. We need to take care that our efforts to promote inclusive education are not similarly undermined by unexamined notions of ability and disability that perpetuate deficit thinking. Mittler suggests that what is needed is a 'change of mind-set and values for schools and for society as a whole' (2000, p. 12). It is here, we suggest, that the model of pedagogy proposed in this chapter has its most crucial part to play: both offering an empirically grounded analysis of the kind of mind-set needed to break – and sustain the break – with determinism *and* showing how this alternative orientation to the future translates into everyday acts of classroom teaching. It restores to teachers and students their sense of power and purpose – their right, in Gould's words, 'to strive and to hope' – that through their work together they can transform the course of future development.

REFERENCES

Ainscow, M. (1999). *Understanding the development of inclusive schools.* London: Falmer.

Ainscow, M., & Tweddle, D. (1988). *Encouraging classroom success.* London: David Fulton.

Alexander, R. (1984). *Primary teaching.* Eastbourne: Holt, Reinhart & Winston.

Alexander, R. (2000). *Culture and pedagogy: International comparisons in primary education.* Oxford: Blackwell.

Ball, S. (1981). *Beachside comprehensive: A case study of secondary schooling.* Cambridge: Cambridge University Press.

Barton, L., & Oliver, M. (1992). Special needs: personal trouble or public issue. In M. Arnot & L. Barton (Eds.), *Voicing concerns: Sociological perspectives on contemporary educational reforms* (pp. 66–87). Wallingford: Triangle.

Bennett, A., & Williams, H. (1992). What would happen if …? An active approach to mathematics teaching. In T. Booth, P. Potts & W. Swann (Eds.), *Curricula for diversity in education* (pp. 63–75). London: Routledge.

Bernstein, B. (1971). Education cannot compensate for society. In B. Cosin, R. Dale, G. Esland, & D. Swift (Eds.), *School and society: A sociological reader* (pp. 61–66). London: Routledge & Kegan Paul.

Bloom, B. (1976). *Human characteristics and school learning.* New York: McGraw-Hill.

Boaler, J. (1997a). Setting, social class and survival of the quickest. *British Educational Research Journal, 23*(5), 575–595.

Boaler, J. (1997b). When even the winners are losers: evaluating the experiences of 'top set' students. *Journal of Curriculum Studies, 29*(2), 165–182.

Boaler, J., Wiliam, D., & Brown, M. (2000). Students' experiences of ability grouping – disaffection, polarization and the construction of failure. *British Educational Research Journal, 26*(5), 631–648.

Booth, T., Ainscow, M., Black-Hawkins, K., Vaughan, M., & Shaw, L. (2000). *The index for inclusion.* London: Centre for Studies on Inclusive Education.

Booth, T., Potts, P., & Swann, W. (1987). *Preventing difficulties in learning.* Oxford: Blackwell.

Booth, T., Swann, W., Masterton, M. & Potts, P. (1992). *Curricula for diversity in education.* London: Routledge.

Bourdieu, P. (1976). The school as a conservative force: scholastic and cultural inequalities. In R. Dale, G. Esland, & M. MacDonald (Eds.), *Schooling and capitalism* (pp. 110–117). London: Routledge & Kegan Paul.

Buckley, S. (2000). *Living with Down syndrome.* Southsea: The Down Syndrome Educational Trust.

Central Advisory Council for Education (CACE). (1967). *Children and their primary schools* (The Plowden Report). London: HMSO.

Chamberlain, V. (1996). *Starting out on the MI way. A guide to multiple intelligences in the primary school.* Bolton: Centre for the Promotion of Holistic Education.

Coard, B. (1971). *How the West Indian child is made educationally subnormal in the British school system: The scandal of the black child in schools in Britain.* London: New Caribbean Workers Association.

Croll, P., & Moses, D. (1985). *One in five: The assessment and incidence of special educational needs.* London: Routledge & Kegan Paul.

Dixon, A. (1989). Deliver us from eagles. In G. Barrett (Ed.), *Disaffection from school? The early years* (pp. 13–24). London: Routledge.

Douglas, J. (1964). *The home and the school: A study of ability and attainment in the primary school.* London: MacGibbon & Kee.

Drummond, M. J. (2003). *Assessing children's learning* (revd 2nd ed.). London: David Fulton.

Dweck, C. (2000). *Self-theories: Their role in motivation, personality and development.* Philadelphia, PA: Taylor & Francis.

Dyson, A. (1990). Special educational needs and the concept of change. *Oxford Review of Education, 16*(1), 55–56.

Edwards, C., Gandini, L., & Foreman, G. (Eds.). (1998). *The hundred languages of children: The Reggio Emilia approach – advanced reflections.* Norwood, NJ: Ablex.

Ford, J. (1969). *Social class and the comprehensive school.* London: Routledge & Kegan Paul.

Gardner, H. (1983). *Frames of mind: The theory of multiple intelligences.* New York: Basic Books.

Gardner, H. (1999). *Intelligence reframed: Multiple intelligences for the 21st century.* New York: Basic Books.

Gillborn, D., & Youdell, D. (2000). *Rationing education. Policy, practice, reform and equity.* New York: Basic Books.

Goldbart, J. (1994). Opening the communication curriculum to students with PMLDs. In J. Ware (Ed.), *Educating children with profound and multiple learning difficulties,* (pp. 15–62). London: Fulton.

Goldstein, H., & Noss, R. (1990). Against the stream. *Forum, 33*(1), 4–6.

Good, T., & Brophy, J. (1991). *Looking in Classrooms* (5th ed.). New York: HarperCollins.

Gould, S. J. (1981). *The mismeasure of man.* New York: Norton.

Hacker, R. G., Rowe, M. J., & Evans, R. D. (1991). The influences of ability groupings for secondary science lessons upon classroom processes. Part 1: Homogeneous groupings (science education notes). *School Science Review, 73*(262), 125–129.

Hargreaves, D. (1967). *Social relations in a secondary school.* London: Routledge & Kegan Paul.

Hargreaves, D. (1980). Social class, the curriculum and the low achiever. In E. Raybould, B. Roberts, & K. Wedell (Eds.), *Helping the low achiever in the secondary school* (pp. 29–39). Birmingham: University of Birmingham.

Hargreaves, D. (1982). *The challenge for the comprehensive school.* London: Routledge & Kegan Paul.

Hart, S. (1996). *Beyond special needs. Enhancing children's learning through innovative thinking.* London: Paul Chapman Publishing.

Hart, S. (2000). *Thinking through teaching.* London: David Fulton.

Hart, S. (2002). Learning without limits. In M. Nind, K. Sheehy, & K. Simmons (Eds.), *Inclusive education: Learners and learning contexts.* London: David Fulton .

Hart, S., Dixon, A., Drummond, M. J., & McIntyre, D. (2004). *Learning without limits.* Maidenhead: Open University Press.

Heath, S. B. (1983). *Ways with words: Language, life and work in communities and classrooms.* Cambridge: Cambridge University Press.

Holt, J. (1990). *How children fail* (revd ed.). London: Penguin.

Hull, R. (1985). *The language gap: How classroom dialogue fails.* London: Methuen.

Jack, B. (1996). *Moving on MI way: A guide to multiple intelligencies in the classroom.* Bolton: Centre for Promotion of Holistic Education.

Jackson, B. (1964). *Streaming: An education system in miniature.* London: Routledge & Kegan Paul.

Jackson, P. (1968). *Life in classrooms.* New York: Holt, Rinehart & Winston.

Jones, A. (2002). *Doorways: Multi-sensory referencing for people with profound and multiple learning difficulties.* Cambridge: University of Cambridge, School of Education.

Keddie, N. (1971). Classroom knowledge, in M. F. D. Young (Ed.), *Knowledge and control: New directions for the sociology of education* (pp. 133–160). London: Collier Macmillan.

Kelly, G. A. (1955). *The psychology of personal constructs.* New York: Norton.

Lacey, C. (1970). *Hightown grammar: The school as a social system.* Manchester: Manchester University Press.

Mittler, P. (2000). *Towards inclusive education: Social contexts.* London: Fulton.

Nash, R. (1973). *Classrooms observed: The teacher's perception and the pupil's performance.* London: Routledge & Kegan Paul.

Norwich, B. (1990). *Reappraising special needs education.* London: Cassell.

Oakes, J. (1982). The reproduction of inequity: The content of secondary school tracking. *The Urban Review, 14*(2), 107–120.

Oakes, J. (1985). *Keeping the track: How schools structure inequality.* New Haven, CT: Yale University Press.

Pearl, A. (1997). Democratic education as an alternative to deficit thinking. In R. Valencia (Ed.), *The evolution of deficit thinking: Educational thought and practice* (pp. 211–242). London: Falmer.

Perkins, D. (1995). *Outsmarting IQ: The emerging science of learnable intelligence.* New York: Free Press.

Rieser, R., & Mason, M. (1992). *Disability equality in the classroom: A human rights issue.* London: Disability Equality in Education.

Rist, R. (1971). Student social class and teacher expectations: The self-fulfilling prophecy in ghetto education. *Harvard Educational Review, 40*, 411–451.

Rosenthal, R., & Jacobson, J. (1968). *Pygmalion in the classroom.* New York: Holt, Rinehart & Winston.

Simon, B. (1953). Intelligence testing and the comprehensive school. In B. Simon (1978), *Intelligence, psychology and education* (revd ed.). London: Lawrence & Wishart.

Suknandan, L, & Lee, B. (1998). *Streaming, setting and grouping by ability: A review of the literature.* Slough: NFER.

Taylor, N. (1993). Ability grouping and its effect on pupil behaviour: A case study of a Midlands comprehensive school. *Education Today, 43*(2), 14–17.

Tizard, B., & Hughes, M. (1984). *Young Children Learning: Talking and thinking at home and at school.* London: Fontana.

Tizard, B., Blatchford, P., Burke, J., Farquhar, C., & Plewis, I. (1988). *Young children at school in the inner city.* London: Lawrence Erlbaum.

West, T. (1991). *In the mind's eye: Visual thinkers, gifted people with learning difficulties, computer images, and the ironies of creativity.* New York: Prometheus Books.

39

Challenging orthodoxy in special education: on longstanding debates and philosophical divides

Deborah J. Gallagher

When special education as we know it today came of age in the early to mid 1960s, it emerged as a field principally informed by the prevailing philosophical and conceptual frameworks of the era – namely, positivism, empiricism, and behaviorism. Situated squarely within the medical and scientific models of help, the special education project centered on diagnosis, prescription, assessment, and, to the extent possible, remediation of those identified as requiring our intervention. In the ensuing four decades or so, with the massive expansion of special education programs in the public schools, little has changed in either form or substance. In fact, one might make the case that now more than ever, the field of special education rests more securely on its founding assumptions. But this apparent constancy is not the product of an easy consensus among special education scholars and professionals. On the contrary, intense disagreement over methodological, practical, ethical, and social considerations has resulted in a profession deeply divided if not irrevocably polarized.

This chapter is organized around three major issues or central 'bones of contention' in the special education debates as they have unfolded over the years (see also, Gallagher,

2004a). First is the question so basic to the very idea of special education – what precisely is a disability? The question here is not one of proper identification of various disabilities, but rather a more fundamental question about the epistemological and ontological assumptions underlying opposing understandings of the very nature of disability. The second issue centers on the debates over preferred research methodology. Here, the question might even be phrased as what methodology leads to valuable and useful knowledge as opposed to that which produces useless or even dangerous knowledge. This debate mirrors the dispute over the use of empiricist/realist versus interpretivist/hermeneutical research approaches in the broader field of education. However, a strong claim could be made that because special education emerged from the medical model of disability, qualitative or interpretivist methodology has been met with far more resistance from traditional special education researchers. The third point of contention, and perhaps most discordant of all, is the conflict over 'place', or where students understood to have disabilities or 'special needs' should receive instruction. This dispute, currently referred to as the inclusion debate, in many ways subsumes the preceding ones and might be seen as the ultimate issue facing not only special education, but education in general.

In the process of examining the contours of the major issues outlined above, I will paint a picture of a history of dissent in special education that ultimately comes down to an epistemological and ontological stalemate. Beyond representing conflicts of ideologies (Brantlinger, 1997), which they surely do, the dividing lines in these debates are intensified by a conflict of philosophical and conceptual frameworks.

THE NATURE OF DISABILITY

What does it mean when we say someone has a disability? In both everyday parlance, as well as in special education professional discourse, it means that a person has an observable condition, an inability to perform physically, cognitively, or socially/emotionally in a manner considered *typical* (see Kauffman & Hallahan, 2005). While this description of disability might appear benign and uncontroversial on the face of it, how it is understood in epistemological and ontological terms, and ultimately in moral and practical ones as well, has set the stage for serious dissension.

At its core, the argument boils down to this – on the one side are those who insist that disabilities *exist*, are *real* conditions in the sense that they are intrinsic to individuals, lend themselves to quantified measurement, and are grounded in the logic of ability as normally distributed (see, for example, Hallahan & Kauffman, 1994; Kauffman & Hallahan, 2005; Kavale & Forness, 1995). The concept of disability as 'real', understood as 'existing' in an objective, neutral sense, is a direct appeal to epistemological and ontological *realism* (Skrtic, 1991, 1996). A person 'has a disability' whether we recognize it or not, acknowledge it or not, believe it or not. It is an objective fact, as distinguished from a subjective belief or personal opinion. The language of formal and legal disability definitions reify disability through the stipulation of both quantitative and descriptive criteria. Put simply, the language of definition depicts disability not as an *idea* about the nature of human difference, but rather as a *thing* – a condition detachable from ideas about it (see Kliewer & Biklen, 1996).

To most people, this depiction of disability seems to be nothing more than common sense. One can clearly see that some people cannot walk, or talk, or see, or think, and so on, the way most others obviously can. Hence disability appears, for the most part, to be a straightforward, uncontestable issue. The only difficulties associated with it might pertain to precise and accurate application of the objective criteria used to identify various disabilities. A more careful examination of the situation, however, reveals some contradictions of consequence. Those challenging this realist, orthodox version of disability have long and repeatedly pointed out:

- the changing and arbitrary nature of disability definitions (Dunn, 1968; Gallagher, 2001; Kliewer & Biklen, 1996; Poplin, 1988)
- that one's chances of being labeled with a particular disability are contingent on where she or he lives (Biklen, 1988, 1992; Lipsky & Gartner, 1996)
- the overrepresentation of minority, poor, and working-class students in special education (Dunn, 1968, Lipsky & Gartner, 1996; Patton, 1998, Tomlinson, 1981,1982,1996)
- the problem with the ongoing efforts to define and select identification criteria for various disabilities (during which time children and young people have been labeled routinely in public schools as actually having these disabilities (Carrier, 1986; Gallagher, 2001; Iano, 1986; Kliewer & Biklen, 1996; Lipsky & Gartner, 1996).

Oddly enough, these flaws and contradictions (although they do not seem to be recognized as such) have also been documented by those who continue to hold the view of disability as individual pathology (see Adelman, 1996; Kavale & Forness, 1995).

More recently, it seems that those who have long defended the *reality* of disability have found it necessary to soften their claims of objectivity. Now, it appears, disability is being framed as difference, and identification of students as having disabilities as a function of judgment. Kauffman and Hallahan (2005) describe disability as follows:

> Disability, then, is not *simply* a matter of scoring at a certain level on a test or tests. The test information or quantitative formula may *inform* judgment. In fact, subjective or 'clinical' judgment without more objective and quantitative scores is likely to be very unreliable. But in the end disability for special education purposes is a professional judgment, based on accumulated evidence that a student needs to learn something other than the general education curriculum *or* needs instruction other than that which can be provided by the regular classroom teacher *or both*. Failure to make the judgment – to draw the line, to take action that recognizes the difference – merely denies the child special services. (p. 29, italics in original)

First, it should be noted that disability is defined by the need for special education as well as by a condition that, in and of itself, requires a line be drawn so that a child is not denied special education. How do we know the child has a disability? Because he needs special education. How do we know he needs special education? Because he has a disability. Beyond this tautology, how is this rendition of disability to be understood? It seems that it attempts to cut the line between subjective versus objective, real versus constructed. It rests uneasily in a hazy space between fact and value where judgment is required but is grounded in a foundation of the '*more* objective and quantitative' (Kauffman & Hallahan, 2005, p. 29, emphasis added) test data.

In an earlier effort to draw this boundary somewhat more firmly, Hallahan and Kauffman (1994) insist 'that people with disabilities do have something inherently different about them; so social construction does not explain the whole story' (p. 503). This assertion, of course, raises the obvious question of just how much of the *story* social construction does explain. Where does one draw the line between inherent difference, understood as objective and neutral, and socially constructed, understood as interpretation or judgment? A serious engagement of this tautological reasoning and these blurred boundaries drives the concept of disability as a

neutral, inherent condition into an intellectual cul-de-sac.

This brings us to the opposing side of the issue. Stated directly, those who contend that disability is socially constructed submit that disabilities are nothing more than interpretations made of perceived differences that are inevitably values-laden and historically/culturally conditioned. Spurred on by the disabled people's movement in Britain, and the disability rights activists in the United States, British, then American scholars, in Disability Studies have made significant contributions toward advancing this perspective on disability. In the 1980s and 1990s, Disability Studies scholars developed what is now referred to as the social model of disability. In rejecting the objectivist, or what Slee (1997) refers to as the *essentialist*, view of disability, these scholars fundamentally recast disability as a cultural construction, the consequence of which is social restriction and oppression (see, for example, Barnes, 1996; Corker & Shakespeare, 2002; Finkelstein, 1980; Oliver, 1990; Thomas, 1999). American special education scholars have likewise made significant contributions to understanding disability as a social construct (see, for example, Biklen & Duchan, 1994; Bogdan & Taylor, 1994; Carrier, 1986; Danforth & Rhodes, 1997; Ferguson & Ferguson, 1995; Kliewer & Biklen, 1996; Skrtic, 1986; Sleeter, 1986; Trent, 1994).

This perspective on disability appeals to epistemological and ontological *non-realism*, which holds that there is nothing objective about human knowledge, nor is there an objective reality that can be understood as existing outside of our interpretations of it (see Gadamer, 1995; Putnam, 1981; Rorty, 1979, 1991). Instead, what we take as *factual knowledge* and *reality* are our own renditions of *the way things are*. For those who hold this conceptual framework, to say that a student has a disability is to impose one's own moral interpretation about the student's worth and adequacy. Put differently, it is to say, 'I perceive the student to have a difference that makes a difference – to me and the rest of us who consider ourselves normal, non-disabled, competent, and adequate.' Because the very act of observing a difference is to make an interpretation, there is no line to be drawn between ostensive objective versus subjective aspects of difference as a disability. Not even the seemingly objective test data provides a foundation for doing so because the normal curve, statistical procedures, and the tests themselves are not neutral. Instead, they are human creations demonstrably infused with ideological intentions and consequences (see MacKenzie, 1981, for an in-depth discussion of this point. Also see Davis, 1995, for an examination of how this relates to disability).

To think of disability as an inherent, neutral condition therefore has profound moral and practical consequences. It acts to conceal restrictive prejudices against some forms of human variation behind a highly contested mantle of objectivity (see Corbett, 1996). Davis (1997a, 1997b) makes clear the effect this objectification has had on those judged as disabled: 'People with disabilities have been isolated, incarcerated, observed, written about, operated on, instructed, implanted, regulated, treated, institutionalized, and controlled to a degree probably unequal to that experienced by any other minority group' (p. 1). No doubt most of this treatment has been justified in the name of helping.

Another serious consequence of considering someone's differences an inherent disability is that it ignores the cultural values, beliefs, and social arrangements that make a perceived difference a 'disability' in the first place. For example, Brantlinger (2004) points out the incoherence of the culturally revered concept of normal, particularly as it is formally expressed within the naturalizing logic of the normal curve. While our schools (and society) are at great pains to make all children normal, we fail to realize that the normal curve imposes a distribution, which means that it is impossible for everyone to be average or above. The seemingly well-meaning efforts to *remediate* students until they perform on grade level are no more than a Sisyphian undertaking. This is so because the normal curve forces a distribution in which a certain percentage of students must fall below average. Under the (il)logic of the normal curve, 'unless the ideal child can be cloned, human variation will have to be tolerated' (Brantlinger, 2004, p. 491).

Lurking behind this drive to normalize is a cultural consensus for creating social hierarchy. Implicit in educational and economic stratification is the valuing of competition with its requisite creation of winners and losers (see Apple, 1990; Hayman, 1998; Lewontin, 1991). Out of this enforced consensus comes the demand for the invidious comparisons disability labels invariably denote. Beyond this compulsion to sustain social hierarchy is another motivating feature Heshusius (2004a) refers to as 'exclusionary fears' on the part of ordinary people in their responses to human differences. 'The attachments to images we hold as desirable for our selves', she explains, 'create fears of others who are different in ways that do not fit these images' (p. 284). The very act of constructing the 'other' person as disabled is also the expression of a need to construct the 'self' as *not* disabled.

These days, even those who insist that disability is an inherent, objective condition concede openly that the line drawn between abled and disabled is an arbitrary one (Kauffman & Hallahan, 2005). Where and why the line is drawn says more about those drawing the line than those on the other side of it. Who gets to decide what kinds of differences makes a difference? Who is responsible for creating the conditions, criteria, and measurements under which these differences are pathologized and judged to be a problem? To acknowledge that disability is constructed (made), not discovered (found), involves a shift in metaphors, changing what appeared to be a neutral observation into a moral choice (Gallagher, 2001).

RESEARCH METHODOLOGY

The debate over quantitative versus qualitative research has occupied the educational research community over the past 20 years or so (see Denzin & Lincoln, 2000; Smith & Heshusius,

1986). As I suggested earlier, though, a case could be made that the struggle over this question has been more intensely contested in special education. As will be discussed, the special education literature certainly seems to indicate so. Two aspects of the field appear to have set the stage for this intensity. First, having emerged from the medical model of disability, special education not unexpectedly adopted empiricism as its dominant research tradition. Consequently, qualitative or interpretivist methodology has remained something of an anomaly. Second, special education centers on people who, as a group, have been historically marginalized and oppressed (Fleischer & Zames, 2001). This second point has raised serious questions about representation, voice, and so on. On the one side, empiricist special education researchers assert that the procedures of science (that is, empiricist research methodology) constitute the best hope for valid and reliable knowledge necessary for informed practices (Kauffman, 1993; Vaughn & Dammann, 2001; Walker et al., 1998). On the other side, qualitative/interpretivist researchers assert not only that empiricist claims to scientific authority/objectivity are false, but also that the dominance of empiricist methodology has had decisively undesirable consequences for the people it is intended to serve as well as for the field as a whole (Gallagher, 1998; Heshusius, 1989, 2004a; Iano, 1986; Poplin, 1987).

Let us begin by examining the case for science made by empiricist special education researchers. By numerous accounts, the field has produced a knowledge base of effective teaching interventions for students with disabilities (see Forness, Kavale, Blum, & Lloyd, 1997; Hallahan, 1998; Hallahan & Kauffman, 1997; Hockenbury, Kauffman, & Hallahan, 1999–2000; Lloyd, Forness & Kavale, 1998; Walker et al., 1998). These interventions include: behavior modification techniques, task analysis, cognitive training; medication, the commercial Direct Instruction Programs, token economies, functional assessment, and phonics-based approaches for teaching beginning reading, to name several. From their (and

those who agree with them) perspective, the procedures of science are perfectly and uniquely suited to distinguish effective teaching procedures and programs from those which are not. As Kauffman (1999) puts it, 'Special education teachers and scholars are best armed against ignorance, failure, fraud, and abuse with greater knowledge of scientific practices' (p. 266). Empiricist/positivist science, and the Enlightenment thinking that produced it, is the only thing standing between the field's credibility and its potential demise.

Beginning in the late 1980s, philosophical critiques of empiricism/positivism began to appear in prominent special education academic journals. Among the first to appear was Iano's (1986) critical appraisal of the effects of what he referred to as the 'natural science-technical model'. His main thesis was that positivist science is misapplied to the study of education in general and special education in particular. Among the pernicious effects of this misapplication are the inevitable separation of theory from practice, and the creation of a class (or caste) system in which university researchers alone assume the role of knowledge producers. He also elaborated on the deeply distorting effect of scientific, value-free objectivity on education as having stripped teaching of its moral substance and context. 'Values, norms, and interests are not merely the subjective components of education which can be attached to just any set of objective means and techniques. Rather, values, norms and interests are the very basis of the educational enterprise and educational activities are thoroughly informed by them' (Iano, 1986, p. 55). In special education, he pointed out, not only has positivist ideology made the classification system appear to be a values-free tool, thus absolving educators of the moral responsibility for making such judgments, but it has also undermined the field's credibility as confusion and controversy over disability categories continues unabated.

Rebuttals to Iano's (1986) work consisted of varying degrees of denial, reassertion, and concession (see Carnine, 1987; Lloyd, 1987; Forness & Kavale, 1987). Carnine (1987) argued that Iano's proposal for more natural-istic inquiry in special education represented, 'an equally inappropriate domination of one type of knowledge over another' (p. 42). Asserting his contention that positivist research has indeed led to significant accom-plishments, he went on to dub Iano's critique as being 'rude', 'ill-founded', and 'rather greedy' (p. 43). Lloyd (1987), while agreeing with Iano on several fronts, disagreed with 'some of the premises and with the form of argument advanced in his paper' (p. 44). Finally, both Lloyd (1987) and Forness and Kavale (1987) appeared to acknowledge Iano's concerns only to offer their assurances that these problems could be remedied by more sophisticated and ongoing applications of empiricist/positivist procedures.

Iano's article was followed by Poplin's (1987) critique of the use of the scientific method in special education research. Like Iano, she drew on the work of eminent philoso-phers of science to make the case that the exclusive use of positivist research methodol-ogy, 'has blinded us to a whole range of issues that influence the lives of the students we serve' (p. 31). Drawing on examples from spe-cial education, she elucidated the problems integral to positivist/empiricist research, prob-lems that included the decontextualizing effect of scientific reductionism and experimental separation, the moral poverty of value-free objectivity, the inevitable (yet unacknowl-edged) biases contained in hypothesis genera-tion, and the impossibility of theory-free observation. Poplin's article illustrated for her readers that the flaws in the scientific method as it is applied to educational research cannot be remedied by technical solutions. Instead, the problems are built in to the method itself. Thus, the only way to overcome these limita-tions is to open special education research to include qualitative methodology as an alterna-tive form of inquiry.

Two years later, little had changed when Heshusius (1989) added her voice to the ongo-ing exchanges over the issue of paradigm shifts in special education knowledge. Fram-ing her discussion around what she referred to

as the dominant 'Newtonian mechanistic para-digm', she employed a range of examples elu-cidating how the mechanistic reductionism of epistemological objectivity misinforms special education research and practice. Beyond that, and of particular importance, was her insight-ful discussion about the widespread confusion over the distinction between theories and para-digms. Theories exist within paradigms, while paradigms form the fundamental set of assumptions, conceptual framework, or lens, through which one sees the world. Because the Newtonian mechanistic paradigm has so dom-inated Western thinking and rationality for centuries, most of us are entirely unaware that we see the world through any particular lens at all. In the absence of paradigmatic awareness, it is virtually a foregone conclusion that theories within one's paradigm are easily mis-taken for the paradigm itself. That was, and likely is still, the reason why those who have applied non-orthodox, or non-dominant, para-digmatic thinking to the debates in special edu-cation are accused of being 'malcontents' and having 'fuzziness' in their thinking. Uncon-scious paradigmatic allegiance goes a long way toward explaining why the participants in the Iano exchange proposed solutions to the problems he raised consistent with their own paradigmatic assumptions rather than ques-tioning those very assumptions.

During the 1990s to the present, a growing number of scholars in the field began express-ing their concerns about the unidimensional focus on empiricist/positivist research in spe-cial education (see, for example, Brantlinger, 1997; Danforth, 1999; Gallagher, 1998, 2004b; Paul, 2002; Reid, Robinson, & Bunsen, 1995). Heshusius (2004b) provides a detailed account of the rocky reception encountered by these attempts to pluralize special education research. Specifically, she noted that,

> a backlash seems to have arisen in the major (US) special education journals. These journals have 'behaved' in what seems, at the surface, erratically, accepting articles from an alternative paradigmatic perspective at certain times, even making them into feature articles, while rejecting articles of the same nature at other times. But there probably is

nothing erratic about it. It can be understood in terms of the extraordinary need for mainstream special education leaders to retain the positivist and behavioral status quo in the field. (pp. 187–188)

Meanwhile, a conspicuous batch of articles defending the role of science in special education research began to surface in major journals (see, for example, Heward, 2003; Kauffman, 1993, 1999–2000; Sasso, 2001; Walker et al., 1998).

Oddly enough, some of these same researchers have expressed deep concern about how to improve the rigor of their science (Gersten, Baker, & Lloyd, 2000; Walker et al., 1998). The problems they identify in their research practices ironically affirm the philosophical critiques they have sought to discredit (Gallagher, 2004b). That notwithstanding, a special issue of the journal *Behavioral Disorders* (2001) was devoted to reasserting the empiricist framework as the only proper and responsible approach to conducting inquiry. In his opening editorial, co-editor Frederick Brigham asserted that, 'the research community should be engaged in a search for truth' (p. 5), as though the only truth that can be known is that produced by the presumably neutral and objective procedures of science.

And that is where the discussion appears to have reached an impasse. For the defenders of science (or more accurately, scientism), all that seems necessary to sustain their position is to persist in claims of epistemological objectivity. This persistence is made possible by a near total disregard for the work of some of the most eminent philosophers in the past fifty years or so (for example, Gadamer, 1995; Habermas, 1971, 1975; Hanson, 1958; Kuhn, 1962; Rorty, 1979, 1991). Rare attempts to engage this body of work reveal what can only be seen as either a selective distortion of the ideas or a bewildering failure to grasp their implications (see, for example, Carnine, 1987; Forness & Kavale, 1987; Kauffman, 2002; Sasso, 2001). Similarly, non-empiricist/positivist academics within special education are characterized as 'anything goes relativists', a facile charge based

on a straw-person version of relativism (see Heshusius, 2004b, and Danforth, 2004, for discussions of these characterizations; see Gallagher, 2004c, 2006, for a discussion of epistemological relativism in relation to special education knowledge). The standoff between those insisting on the tenents of philosophical realism versus those who oppose this framework plays a prominent role in the debate over inclusion.

INCLUSION

In any discussion of inclusive schooling, it is necessary to clear the turf of a point of contention up front. Ardent advocates of preserving the continuum of separate placements in special education maintain that they are not against inclusion per se. Rather, they are simply in favor of preserving segregated classes *for those students who need them* (Kauffman & Hallahan, 2005; Kavale & Forness, 2000). In other words, they are in favor of some inclusion, but not *full* inclusion. Much has been made of this distinction as those contesting full inclusion have accused those favoring it as having failed to define precisely what full inclusion means. Does it mean *every* child should spend *all* of his or her time in the general education classroom (MacMillan, Gresham, & Forness (1996)?

This *every* and *all* technicality has provided a convenient device to discredit calls for inclusive education. Notwithstanding, the use of the term *full inclusion* might better be understood as a means to distinguish between those who wish to maintain the status quo versus those who advocate for the end of institutionalized segregation (Gallagher, 2001). As Sapon-Shevin (1996) characterizes it, full inclusion does not mean no supports will be made available; instead, it means that supports such as occupational, speech, and physical therapy be 'provided in the most integrated way possible' (p. 39). No one is advocating, as critics imply, that students be abandoned to their fates in the general education classroom. That said, the main arguments against full inclusion fall under three categories: (a) moves toward inclusion must await empirical (empiricist) proof that it works, (b) the normal curve makes inclusion unrealistic, and (c) certain unmovable realities mitigate against inclusion.

EMPIRICAL PROOF

Reflecting their commitment to realist epistemology and ontology, defenders of the traditional continuum of placements assert that inclusion should not be implemented until scientific research proves its effectiveness (Fuchs & Fuchs, 1991; MacMillan, Gresham, & Forness, 1996). Thus they have framed the debate as a standoff between those who maintain disciplined objectivity versus those who willfully, and for self-indulgent purposes, ignore science (Kavale & Forness, 2000). Their criticism of inclusion advocates is predicated on the assumption that science can serve as the neutral arbiter, thus obviating any reason to engage inclusion as a moral issue. Inclusionists, many if not most of whom hold a non-realist or constructivist perspective, take issue with this position on a number of fronts.

First, this argument deftly shifts the burden of proof (Brantlinger, 1997). In essence, segregated education is established as the standard against which all other arrangements must be assessed. From inclusionists' perspective, if empiricist proof of effectiveness is to be required (however inappropriate), should it not be required of those who insist on assigning disability labels and segregating students from their peers? Second, efficacy studies on the effectiveness of segregated special education settings have been around for some time and have never succeeded in putting the question to rest. Interestingly, as Kavale and Forness (2000) correctly point out, studies have yielded such mixed results that they have been selectively cited as support by those on both sides in the debate. Still, the orthodox view insists that such research endeavors can put the issue to rest; and, more importantly, 'radical' and 'ideological' inclu-

sionists are obliged to await conclusive results (MacMillan, Gresham, & Forness, 1996; Kavale & Forness, 2000). For their part, most inclusionists not only reject this assertion as a red herring, but more importantly, having rejected the now discredited premises of value free objectivity, fact versus values distinction, and theory-free observation, they also reject the notion that scientific research can serve as a neutral arbiter (see, for example, Gallagher, 2001, 2004b, 2004c; Heshusius, 2004a, 2004b; Slee, 1998). The question for them is not whether inclusion can be verified by a values-free science, because, as noted above, no such thing exists. Instead, they see inclusion as a fundamentally moral issue requiring a principled commitment to make it work.

THE NORMAL CURVE

The orthodox belief that ability is normally distributed reflects yet another commitment to realist/empiricist ideology. Hallahan and Kauffman (1994) contend that because of the unmovable reality of the normal curve, improvement of education for all children will only increase the statistical variance in outcomes. Disability, and the need for segregation, will therefore always be among us. The normal curve has ordained it. More recently, Kauffman (2005) argues that, 'In education, students with disabilities are those who score low on tests *because of their disability*. Trying to close this gap is like waving to Ray Charles' (p. 520, emphasis in original).

Aside from the somewhat regrettable attempt at humor, Kauffman (2005) quite rightly critiques the ludicrous goal, as stated in the *No Child Left Behind Act 2001* in the US, that all children should perform at or above average on standardized achievement measures. What he does not appear to realize is that the normal curve enforces both disability and social inequality (Davis, 1997a, 1997b). Nor does he question why we choose to subject human beings to normative comparisons. Rather than understanding the application of the normal curve as a choice with profound moral consequences, segregationists invoke the inevitability of the normal curve as a reason to continue these arrangements. As discussed earlier, the normal curve is a human invention, reflecting the ideological and political goals that conditioned its construction. But if one starts from the idea of the normal curve as objective reality, any form of inclusion is merely a concession to political correctness and not a *scientifically* viable policy for educating children.

A related argument for segregation is that, because normative comparisons are inescapable, students with disabilities need the protection of separate settings to escape the stigma of underachievement (Kavale & Forness, 2000; MacMillan, Gresham, & Forness, 1996). Inclusionists counter that *asylum* or *protective custody* from the vicissitudes of invidious comparisons is a case of victim-blaming (Blomgren, 1993; Brantlinger, 2004). To sequester some students as a result of this choice leads others to fear and reject those who have been made pariahs. The message from adults is clear – it is dangerous not to measure up. Borrowing a term from Bourdieu (1991), segregation constitutes a form of *symbolic violence*, serving both to promote stigma and undermine the safety, security, and integrity of all students. Without an apparent sense of irony, segregationists subsequently cite research warning that negative peer attitudes threaten to undermine inclusion efforts (Kavale & Forness, 2000; MacMillan, Gresham, & Forness, 1996). Once pariahs are created, they then summon *verification* of this creation as *factual* evidence supporting continuation of the same.

THE REALITIES OF THE GENERAL EDUCATION CLASSROOM

For defenders of segregated placements, the possibility of genuinely inclusive general education is met with more than a little incredulity. For them, the exigencies of student conformity, large group instruction aimed at the aver-

age students, and teachers' preoccupation with classroom routines are fixed realities making inclusion something of a utopian pipedream (Kavale & Forness, 2000; Kauffman, 1999–2000). It is simply impractical to expect teachers to *accommodate* all students, they insist (Fuchs & Fuchs, 1995; Heward, 2003; Zigmond, 2003). And besides, many if not most students with disabilities require research-based, specialized instruction that realistically can only take place in small group settings (Kauffman, 2005).

It is not that these exigencies go unrecognized by inclusion advocates, as their critics would seem to believe. Instead, inclusionists have a very different understanding of the origins of them, reflecting once again the opposing frameworks brought to the table. Rather than seeing the *reality* of the general education classroom as neutral and fixed, they see it as one of our own making (Gallagher, 2001). More to the point, this reality is constructed to enact cultural values of technical efficiency, productivity, and competition (Blomgren, 1993; Brantlinger, 2003; Skrtic, 1996). Urging recognition and reconsideration of these values as applied to special education, Blomgren (1993) offers the following appeal:

> We must look more closely at our medical model of help and reappraise our notion of successful education as it is currently understood in terms of utility, productivity and competition. Evaluation and competition, the prized elements of today's educational practices, need to be exposed for the roles they play in establishing and maintaining the educational hierarchy that systematically excludes and dismisses vast numbers of our students and prevents them from obtaining the promised 'keys to the kingdom' as they participate in the educational obstacle course. (p. 241)

What if these values were replaced by others? What if it were more important to promote democracy, equality and human dignity as guiding values (see Edgar, Patton, & Day-Vines, 2002)? The point is, the seeming necessity to segregate and remediate (with special research-based interventions) is seen by inclusionists as a relic of unexamined knowledge and misplaced values.

It is not that schools can transform themselves single-handedly. Education takes place in a cultural context. Schools reflect and enact the dominant ideologies of their respective cultures. But this does not mean that educators are not obligated to recognize and contend with the contradictory pretenses of equality in an unequal society. To insist that the realities of the general education classroom make inclusion unrealistic is a political stance in defense of a distinct set of social and moral values, that is, those associated with the maintenance of social hierarchy. To acknowledge this means that educators can contribute to reconstructing these same classrooms in defense of the values most of us hope to enact – democracy, equality, and human dignity.

REFERENCES

Adelman, H. S. (1996). Appreciating the classification dilemma. In W. Stainback & S. Stainback (Eds.), *Controversial issues confronting special education: Divergent perspectives* (2nd ed.) (pp. 96–111). Needham Heights, MA: Allyn & Bacon.

Apple, M. W. (1990). *Ideology and curriculum* (2nd ed.). New York: Routledge.

Barnes, C. (1996). Theories of disability and the origins of the oppression of disabled people in western society. In L. Barton (Ed.), *Disability and society: Emerging issues and insights*, (pp. 43–60). London: Longman.

Behavioral Disorders. (2001). The meaning of science and empirical rigor in the social sciences. (Special issue.) *Behavioral Disorders, 27*(1).

Biklen, D. (1988). The myth of clinical judgment. *Journal of Social Issues, 44*(1), 127–140.

Biklen, D. (1992). *Schooling without labels.* Philadelphia, PA: Temple University Press.

Biklen, D., & Duchan, J. (1994). 'I am intelligent': The social construction of mental retardation. *Journal of the Association for Persons with Severe Handicaps, 19*(3), 173–184.

Blomgren, R. (1993). Special education and the quest for human dignity. In H. S. Shapiro & D. E. Purpel (Eds.), *Critical social issues in American education: Toward the 21st century* (pp. 230–245). New York: Longman.

Bogdan, R., & Taylor, S. (1994). *The social meaning of mental retardation: Two life stories.* New York: Teachers College Press.

Bourdieu, P. (1991). *Language and symbolic power.* Cambridge: Polity Press.

Brantlinger, E. (1997). Using ideology: Cases of non-recognition of the politics of research and practice in special education. *Review of Educational Research, 67*(4), 425–459.

Brantlinger, E. (2003). *Dividing classes: How the middle class negotiates and rationalizes school advantage.* New York: RoutledgeFalmer.

Brantlinger, E. (2004). Confounding the needs and confronting the norms: An extension of Reid and Valle's essay. *Journal of Learning Disabilities, 37*(6), 490–499.

Carnine, D. (1987). A response to 'false standards, a distorting and disintegrating effect on education, turning away from useful purposes, being inevitably unfulfilled, and remaining unrealistic and irrelevant'. *Remedial and Special Education, 8*(1), 42–43.

Carrier, J. G. (1986). *Learning disability: Social class and the construction of inequality in American education.* New York: Greenwood Press.

Corbett, J. (1996). *Bad-mouthing: The language of special needs.* London: Falmer Press.

Corker, M., & Shakespeare, T. (2002). Mapping the terrain. In M. Corker & T. Shakespeare (Eds.), *Disability/postmodernity: Embodying disability theory* (pp. 1–17). London: Continuum.

Danforth, S. (1999). Pragmatism and the scientific validation of professional practices in American special education. *Disability and Society, 14,* 733–752.

Danforth, S. (2004). The 'postmodern' heresy in special education: A sociological analysis. *Mental Retardation, 42*(6), 445–458.

Danforth, S., & Rhodes, W. C. (1997). Deconstructing disability: A philosophy for inclusion. *Remedial and Special Education, 18,* 357–366.

Davis, L. J. (1995). *Enforcing normalcy: Disability, deafness and the body.* London: Verso.

Davis, L. J. (1997a). Constructing normalcy: The bell curve, the novel and the invention of the disabled body in the nineteenth century. In L. J. Davis (Ed.), *The disability studies reader* (pp. 9–28). New York: New York University Press.

Davis, L. J. (1997b). Introduction. In L. J. Davis (Ed.), *The disability studies reader* (pp. 1–6). New York: Routledge.

Denzin, N. K., & Lincoln, Y. S. (2000). Introduction: The discipline and practice of qualitative research. In N. K. Denzin & Y. S. Lincoln (Eds.), *Handbook of qualitative research* (2nd ed.) (pp. 1–28). Thousand Oaks, CA: Sage.

Dunn, L. M. (1968). Special education for the mildly retarded: Is much of it justifiable? *Exceptional Children, 35*(1), 5–22.

Edgar, E., Patton, J. M., & Day-Vines, N. (2002). Democratic dispositions and cultural competency: Ingredients for school renewal. *Remedial and Special Education, 23*(4), 231–241.

Ferguson, P. M., & Ferguson, D. L. (1995). The interpretivist view of special education and disability: The value of telling stories. In T. M. Skrtic (Ed.), *Disability and democracy: Reconstructing [special] education for postmodernity* (pp. 104–121). New York: Teachers College Press.

Finkelstein, V. (1980). *Attitudes and disabled people: Issues for discussion.* New York: World Rehabilitation Fund.

Fleischer, D. Z., & Zames, F. (2001). *The disability rights movement: From charity to confrontation.* Philadelphia, PA: Temple University Press.

Forness, S. R., & Kavale, K. A. (1987). Holistic inquiry and the scientific challenge in special education: A reply to Iano. *Remedial and Special Education, 8*(1), 47–51.

Forness, S. R., Kavale, K. A., Blum, I. M., & Lloyd, J. W. (1997). Mega-analysis of meta-analysis: What works in special education and related services. *Teaching Exceptional Children, 29*(6), 4–9.

Fuchs, D., & Fuchs, L. S. (1991). Framing the REI debate: Abolitionists versus conservationists. In J. W. Lloyd, N. N. Singh, & A. C. Repp (Eds.), *The regular education initiative: Alternative perspectives on concepts, issues, and models* (pp. 241–255). Sycamore, IL: Sycamore Publishing.

Fuchs, D., & Fuchs, L. S. (1995). What's special about special education? *Phi Delta Kappan, 76*, 522–530.

Gadamer, H.-G. (1995). *Truth and method* (2nd revd ed.). (Translation revised by J. Weinsheimer & D. G. Marshall.) New York: Continuum. (Original publication 1960.)

Gallagher, D. J. (1998). The scientific knowledge base of special education: Do we know what we think we know? *Exceptional Children, 64*(4), 493–502.

Gallagher, D. J. (2001). Neutrality as a moral standpoint, conceptual confusion, and the full inclusion debate. *Disability & Society, 16*(5), 637–654.

Gallagher, D. J. (2004a). Entering the conversation: The debate behind the debates in special education. In D. J. Gallagher (Ed.), *Challenging orthodoxy in special education: Dissenting voices* (pp. 3–26). Denver, CO: Love Publishing.

Gallagher, D. J. (2004b). Educational research, philosophical orthodoxy and unfulfilled promises: The quandary of traditional research in US special education. In G. Thomas & R. Pring (Eds.), *Evidence-based practice in education* (pp. 119–130). Maidenhead: Open University Press.

Gallagher, D. J. (2004c). Moving the conversation forward: Empiricism versus relativism reconsidered. In D. J. Gallagher (Ed.), *Challenging orthodoxy in special education: Dissenting voices* (pp. 363–376). Denver, CO: Love Publishing.

Gallagher, D. J. (2006). If not absolute objectivity, then what? A reply to Kauffman and Sasso. *Exceptionality, 14*(2), 91–107.

Gersten, R., Baker, S., & Lloyd, J. W. (2000). Designing high-quality research in special education: Group experimental design. *The Journal of Special Education, 34*(1), 2–18.

Habermas, J. (1971). *Knowledge and human interests* (J. Shapiro, Trans.). Boston, MA: Beacon Press.

Habermas, J. (1975). *Legitimation crisis* (T. McCarthy, Trans.). Boston, MA: Beacon Press.

Hallahan, D. P. (1998). Sound bytes from special education reform rhetoric. *Remedial and Special Education, 19*(2), 67–69.

Hallahan, D. P., & Kauffman, J. M. (1994). Toward a culture of disability in the aftermath of Deno and Dunn. *Journal of Special Education, 27*(4), 496–508.

Hallahan, D. P., & Kauffman, J. M. (1997). *Exceptional children: Introduction to special education* (7th ed.). Needham Heights, MA: Allyn and Bacon.

Hanson, N. (1958). *Patterns of discovery.* Cambridge: Cambridge University Press.

Hayman, R. L. (1998). *The smart culture: Society, intelligence, and the law.* New York: New York University Press.

Heshusius, L. (1989). The Newtonian mechanistic paradigm, special education and contours of alternatives: An overview. *Journal of Learning Disabilities, 22*, 403–415.

Heshusius, L. (2004a). Special education knowledges: The inevitable struggle with the 'self'. In D. J. Gallagher (Ed.), *Challenging orthodoxy in special education: Dissenting voices* (pp. 283–309). Denver, CO: Love Publishing.

Heshusius, L. (2004b). From creative discontent toward epistemological freedom in special education: Reflections on a 25-year journey. In D. J. Gallagher (Ed.), *Challenging orthodoxy in special education: Dissenting voices* (pp. 169–230). Denver, CO: Love Publishing.

Heward, W. L. (2003). Ten faulty notions about teaching and learning that hinder the effectiveness of special education. *Journal of Special Education, 36*, 186–205.

Hockenbury, J. C., Kauffman, J. M., & Hallahan, D. P. (1999–2000). What is right about special education. *Exceptionality, 8*(1), 3–11.

Iano, R. P. (1986). The study and development of teaching: With implications for the advancement of special education. *Remedial and Special Education, 7*(5), 50–61.

Kauffman, J. M. (1993). How we might achieve the radical reform of special education. *Exceptional Children, 60*(1), 6–16.

Kauffman, J. M. (1999). The role of science in behavioral disorders. *Behavioral Disorders, 24*(4), 265–272.

Kauffman, J. M. (1999–2000). The special education story: Obituary, accident report, conversion experience, reincarnation, or none of the above? *Exceptionality, 8*(1), 61–71.

Kauffman, J. M. (2002). *Education deform: Bright people sometimes say stupid things about education.* Lanham, MD: Scarecrow Press.

Kauffman, J. M. (2005). Waving to Ray Charles: Missing the meaning of disabilities. *Phi Delta Kappan, 86*(7), 520–521, 524.

Kauffman, J. M., & Hallahan, D. P. (2005). *Special education: What it is and why we need it.* Boston, MA: Pearson Allyn & Bacon.

Kavale, K. A., & Forness, S. R. (1995). *The nature of learning disabilities: Critical elements of diagnosis and classification.* Mahwah, NJ: Lawrence Erlbaum.

Kavale, K. A., & Forness, S. R. (2000). History, rhetoric, and reality: Analysis of the inclusion debate. *Remedial and Special Education, 21*(5), 279–296.

Kliewer, C., & Biklen, D. (1996). Labeling: Who wants to be called retarded? In W. Stainback & S. Stainback (Eds.), *Controversial issues confronting special education: Divergent perspectives* (2nd ed.) (pp. 83–95). Needham Heights, MA: Allyn & Bacon.

Kuhn, T. (1962). *The structure of scientific revolutions.* Chicago, IL: University of Chicago Press.

Lewontin, R. C. (1991). *Biology as Ideology: The doctrine of DNA.* New York: HarperCollins.

Lipsky, D. K., & Gartner, A. (1996). Inclusive education and school restructuring. In W. Stainback & S. Stainback (Eds.), *Controversial issues confronting special education: Divergent perspectives* (2nd ed.) (pp. 3–15). Needham Heights, MA: Allyn & Bacon.

Lloyd, J. W. (1987). The art and science of research on teaching. *Remedial and Special Education, 8*(1), 44–46.

Lloyd, J. W., Forness, S. R., & Kavale, K. A. (1998). Some methods are more effective than others. *Intervention in School and Clinic, 33*(4), 195–200.

MacKenzie, D. A. (1981). *Statistics in Great Britain: 1865–1930.* Edinburgh: Edinburgh University Press.

MacMillan, D. L., Gresham, F. M., & Forness, S. R. (1996). Full inclusion: An empirical perspective. *Behavioral Disorders, 21*(2), 145–159.

No Child Left Behind Act 2001, Public Law No. 107–110.

Oliver, M. (1990). *The politics of disablement.* Basingstoke: Macmillan.

Patton, J. M. (1998). The disproportionate representation of African Americans in special education: Looking behind the curtain for understanding and solutions. *The Journal of Special Education, 32*(1), 25–31.

Paul, J. L. (2002). Perspectival and discursive discontinuities in special education research: The challenges of pluralism. *Disability, Culture and Education, 1*(2), 73–93.

Poplin, M. S. (1987). Self-imposed blindness: The scientific method in education. *Remedial and Special Education, 8*(6), 31–37.

Poplin, M. S. (1988). The reductionistic fallacy in learning disabilities: Replicating the past by reducing the present. *Journal of Learning Disabilities, 21*(7), 389–400.

Putnam, H. (1981). *Reason, truth and history.* Cambridge: Cambridge University Press.

Reid, D. K., Robinson, S. J., & Bunsen, T. D. (1995). Empiricism and beyond: Expanding the boundaries of special education. *Remedial and Special Education, 16*(3), 131–141.

Rorty, R. (1979). *Philosophy and the mirror of nature.* Princeton, NJ: Princeton University Press.

Rorty, R. (1991). *Objectivity, relativism, and truth.* Cambridge: Cambridge University Press.

Sapon-Shevin, M. (1996). Full inclusion as a disclosing tablet: Revealing the flaws in our present system. *Theory Into Practice, 35*(1), 35–41.

Sasso, G. M. (2001). The retreat from inquiry and knowledge in special education. *The Journal of Special Education, 34*(4), 178–193.

Skrtic, T. M. (1986). The crisis in special education knowledge: A perspective on perspective. *Focus on Exceptional Children, 18*(7), 1–16.

Skrtic, T. M. (1991). *Behind special education: A critical analysis of professional culture and school organization.* Denver, CO: Love Publishing.

Skrtic, T. M. (1996). The functionalist view of special education and disability: Deconstructing the conventional knowledge tradition. In T. M. Skrtic (Ed.), *Disability and democracy: Reconstructing [special] education for postmodernity* (pp. 65–103). New York: Teachers College Press.

Slee, R. (1997). Imported or important theory? Sociological interrogations of disablement and special education. *British Journal of Sociology of Education, 18*(3), 407–419.

Slee, R. (1998). High reliability organizations and liability students – the politics of recognition. In R. Slee & G. Weiner, with S. Tomlinson (Eds.), *School effectiveness for whom? Challenges to the school effectiveness and school improvement movements* (pp. 101–114). London: Falmer Press.

Sleeter, C. E. (1986). Learning disabilities: The social construction of a special education category. *Exceptional Children, 53*(1), 46–54.

Smith, J. K., & Heshusius, L. (1986). Closing down the conversation: The end of the quantitative-qualitative debate among educational enquirers. *Educational Researcher, 15*(1), 4–12.

Thomas, C. (1999). *Female forms: Experiencing and understanding disability.* Buckingham: Open University Press.

Tomlinson, S. (1981). *Educational subnormality: A study in decision making.* London: Routledge & Kegan Paul.

Tomlinson, S. (1982). *A sociology of special education.*

London: Routledge & Kegan Paul.

Tomlinson, S. (1996). The radical structuralist view of special education and disability: Unpopular perspectives on their origins and development. In T. M. Skrtic (Ed.), *Disability and democracy: Reconstructing [special] education for post-modernity* (pp. 122–134). New York: Teachers College Press.

Trent, J. W. (1994). *Inventing the feeble mind: A history of mental retardation in the United States.* Berkeley, CA: University of California Press.

Vaughn, S., & Dammann, J. E. (2001). Science and sanity in special education. *Behavioral Disorders, 27*(1), 21–29.

Walker, H. M., Forness, S. R., Kauffman, J. M., Epstein, M. H., Gresham, F. M., Nelson, C. M., & Strain, P. S. (1998). Macro-social validation: Referencing outcomes in behavioral disorders to societal issues and problems. *Behavioral Disorders, 24*(1), 7–18.

Zigmond, N. (2003). Where should students with disabilities receive special education services? Is one place better than another? *The Journal of Special Education, 37*, 193–199.

40

Special education and its contribution to the broader discourse of education

Seamus Hegarty

INTRODUCTION

Producing a handbook in any domain of education is necessarily an ambitious task, and the particular situation of special education makes the present enterprise an extremely challenging, if fruitful, one. What this handbook provides is a mapping of a changing – and contested – domain, a distillation of thinking about particular parts of it and a review of what is known about specific areas of practice. Special education is important both in its own right and as a key dimension of general education, and handbooks such as this serve a uniquely valuable function in relation to it. To the extent that it has done its work well it will continue as a valuable resource for student and scholar, for policy maker and practitioner, for some considerable time.

This volume is, however, more than a quarry or – to give it a contemporary metaphor – a database which can provide information, argument, inspiration and so on. That function is important, not least after two decades that have seen a plethora of publications in special education as authors and publishers alike have been assiduous in creating and responding to a publishing market. This proliferation of writing has enriched our field and has enhanced both policy and practice within it. By its very nature, however, such writing, addressing particular topics and serving diverse purposes and audiences, does not set out a view of the field as a whole and indeed risks purveying a fragmented view of it.

The opportunity here is to stand back and take stock of an area that has seen remarkable if uneven development over the past half century. This is not in the spirit of producing an encyclopaedic account – an unprofitable enterprise anyway given the continuing evolution within the area and the fact that strongly contested views are held about key parts of it. What it does is provide a perspective on achievements to date and some clarity as to what remains to be done. We can ill afford complacency and a resolute focus on the continuing deficiencies, whether it be of provision or policy, is fully justified, but it is good too to remember how far we have come. For all that many children and young people still receive a substandard education, the debate is no longer about whether everybody *should* receive a high-quality education but about the factors that get in the way of this and how to ensure that it does happen.

By the same token, the handbook is forward looking: by recognising and scrutinising good practice which has broad resonance, by identifying present weaknesses and knowledge gaps that need to be addressed, and, above all, by exposing the tensions in debates about how to secure the best possible education for all our children and young people, it marks out, if not the road ahead, the terrain through which we have to travel and shows the pathways through it that are most likely to be productive.

KNOWLEDGE IN EDUCATIONAL DISCOURSE

There is a more significant opportunity still – and one whereby special education challenges and illuminates the broader discourse of education. This has to do with the complex nature of knowledge in education and how agendas are set and decisions taken within it. Both policy and practice in education are shaped by multiple inputs – practical, experiential, ideological as well as the strictly epistemological. General education discourse frequently fails to distinguish clearly between these different inputs, or even to acknowledge them adequately, and it may well be that the clarity of focus within special education discourse, as provided by a handbook such as this, can be instructive more generally.

The nature of the knowledge base that underpins educational action and the relationships between the different kinds of knowledge within it are central to any understanding of educational progress. Research is a key contributor to this knowledge base but, while it is of particular interest to the academic community and has a uniquely important role, it is but one strand among several. The requisite knowledge for securing educational progress encompasses a diversity of knowledge types, each with its own epistemology, truth criteria and so on.

A comprehensive account of special education, such as contained in this handbook, provides the opportunity to ground these epistemological considerations in a concrete area of practice. The central question is: what

knowledge underpins educational action, in the sense of clarifying options, informing decisions and enabling expert action? There are, of course, many actors in the educational arena and their work entails different knowledge requirements. Policy makers and teachers are the two dominant groups and, while there is overlap between them, the knowledge drivers of intelligent action are different for the two groups. By examining these drivers in the case of special education, a more nuanced and accurate understanding of knowledge in education more generally can be derived.

INFORMING POLICY

A good deal has been written about the impact of research on policy, and writers from Weiss (1977, 1979) onward have insisted that it is not a linear process, that policy is seldom a direct response to research findings, and research, if contributing at all, must be seen in terms of its interplay with other, generally more powerful, factors. Different models of research utilisation and the policy process in education were outlined in an OPED/CERI report (CERI, 1995), and a number of writers have attempted to capture the complexity of the area. (An up-to-date, albeit selective, list of references is given in Abderrahmane, 2005. For a critique of the mainstream consensus, see Hammersley, 2005.) Despite the different emphases within the literature, there is a consensus that is shared both by those who push for a greater research engagement in policymaking and by those who question what they regard as the perversion of research to serve doctrinaire interests that the research/policy interface is problematic and that the link between research and policy must be seen within a multi-dimensional model.

Given this, it is disappointing that so much discourse on educational research and its impact on policy continues to be predicated on a linear model. Research is routinely expected to resolve difficult policy questions and, just as routinely, excoriated for not doing so. One can speculate on the reasons for this disjuncture but it is likely that one of them is the common failure to comprehend just how complex the interplay of factors impacting on policy is.

The opportunity here is to see in concrete terms how limited this linear perspective is and to draw on special education literature, specifically in relation to policy issues, in order to build a better understanding of how policy in education is formed. Consider the question that has preoccupied policymakers for close on half a century now: Where should pupils who have difficulties in learning or adjustment be educated? And the associated question: What kind of education should be offered to them? There have been major policy shifts in regard of this question, as documented throughout this handbook. In broad terms, we have moved from a situation where some young people were deemed to be ineducable, others could only attend segregated schools, often to be offered an impoverished curriculum in them, and yet others were allowed to attend regular schools but little was expected or demanded of them, to a quite different situation where all children are expected to benefit from education and where the regular school and mainstream curriculum frameworks are the options of first choice for every pupil.

Practice is, of course, uneven and the policy shift is far from complete. There can be no doubt, however, that there *has* been a policy shift, even a dramatic one, forcing the question: Why? Where has this policy shift come from? What factors have contributed to the change in thinking and, in particular, where does research fit in among them? These are important questions, and the better we answer them, the more clearly we can understand the process of policy formation. And, of course, the clearer our understanding of policy influences in the past, the better placed we are to secure beneficial policy development in the future.

Successive chapters in this handbook have considered the emergence of special education both in its own right and as a discrete area for consideration within education more generally. Thus, Winzer traces the history of special education from the Enlightenment ideas of the eighteenth century through the charitable movements of the nineteenth and early twentieth centuries, along with the institutionalisation that often accompanied them, to the many strands that shape contemporary thinking. These strands include the emergence of the common school in the USA and, rather later, the comprehensive school in some European countries; various philosophical and psychological positions; the professionalisation of special education and developments in teacher education; and reforms arising from advocacy movements and legislation.

Other contributors examine particular topics in more detail. The ferment of ideas associated with eugenics and Social Darwinism on the one hand and with the emergence of empirical psychology on the other is scrutinised by Thomas. While this history goes back over 100 years, many of the ideas have powerful resonance still, not least in the context of measured intelligence and the assessment of pupils' cognitive and academic capacities. Gallagher draws attention to the contested and shifting definitions of disability and demonstrates the profound moral and practical consequences that follow from the associated tensions.

Special education is, of course, a social construct, even if social theorists have paid little attention to it. Riddell brings a critical perspective from sociology to bear in her scrutiny of the social theories that shape contemporary understandings of special education. Rioux focuses on the legislative context and the explicit efforts to address equity issues and improve provision through legislative action. As might be expected, inclusive education is a theme that runs through the handbook: Slee, Peters, Ainscow and others are centrally concerned with inclusive education, what it means and how it can be promoted. This brings in further perspectives that have impacted strongly on views of special education. These include school improvement, pedagogical developments, the marketisation of education and Education For All.

It is worth adding that these various factors have played out differently in different countries. This can be illustrated by looking at the legislative activity of the 1970s. This was a decade when the USA and some European countries – Britain, Denmark, France, Italy, Norway, Sweden – introduced legislation to regulate special education and, generally, to move toward greater placement of pupils with special educational needs in regular schools. If we compare the USA with Italy, say, we can see major differences in the genesis, context and implementation of the respective laws. The key US legislation, the *Education for All Handicapped Children Act 1975*, grew out of prior federal legislation going back over a decade but also drew on research evidence and contemporary understandings of learning difficulties, their assessment and remediation. It attempted to be comprehensive and made numerous stipulations regarding identification, service delivery, provision, evaluation and funding. Italian legislation (initially in 1971 and later in 1975) had quite a different genesis, owing much less to research evidence on the efficacy of different ways of educating pupils with disabilities and driven essentially by an ideological conviction that children should not be segregated from their peers and, in particular, should be educated alongside them. Implementation in the US was strongly driven by judicial processes and professionals became accustomed to having to defend their actions, if necessary – and quite frequently – in courtrooms. In Italy, by contrast, implementation was driven by a public and professional consensus on de-institutionalisation and legal proceedings were not a significant feature.

The resounding message from all of this is that the development of special education has been determined by many factors – conceptual, political, juridical and practical – and its present shape in a given country is the result of a complex of interacting factors. If we take practically any aspect of special education, single-factor explanations of the current state of play are unhelpful, as well as generally being incorrect. Advocacy, legislation, new concepts of disability, school reform and better pedagogy are all important but none of

them is sufficient on its own to account for the policies that have emerged. By the same token, if we are concerned with policy going forward into the future, we must allow for the multi-dimensionality of policy formation and make our policy inputs accordingly.

This is especially an issue for research. Because of the particular nature of the knowledge that research produces with its explicit procedures, generalisability and scientific authority, many in the research community and outside it expect it to be uniquely influential on policy. The reality as demonstrated here is that research is but one source of evidence among several. In education, evidence is also drawn from inspection, from theory and from experience. Furthermore, evidence is but one influence on policy. Again in education, other influences include politics, media/lobbying, tradition and of course resources. This is a simplified, schematic picture since the different elements interact with each other, but it serves to show both how research does play a role in formulating policy and why that role can on occasion be relatively modest.

An earlier account by Hegarty (1997) provides an example of the process at work. This attempted to set out the factors that sustained the movement towards inclusive education over a 40-year period, in relation to the knowledge bases that underpinned them (Figure 40.1). While this account may need updating, given the substantial developments of the past decade, it does serve to exemplify the diversity of the knowledge base and the complex ways in which research contributes to policy in education.

IMPROVING PRACTICE

Quite different issues come into play when we turn from policy to practice. Just as in the case of policy, there is a prevailing misconception that needs to be challenged. This has to do with the link between research and teaching, and the common assumption that effective research is that which leads to direct improvement in practice. In this view the pur-

FACTORS	KNOWLEDGE BASES
Backlash against categories	Theory Research Pedagogic practice
Improved assessment	Theory R & D Pedagogic and assessment practice
Comprehensive schooling	Ideology Public debate Research Pedagogic experience
Information on practice elsewhere	Visits/descriptions Evaluations
Comparative studies	Research
Human rights debate	Public debate Campaigning

Figure 40.1 Movement toward inclusive education; motive factors and the underpinning knowledge bases

pose of research is to identify best teaching practice, dispense 'tips for teachers' and generally equip teachers with the classroom skills they need. Besides patronising teachers' professionalism *and* setting researchers an impossible task, this view of research is fundamentally misconceived. It fails to take account of the complex and subtle ways in which research and practice engage with each other, as well displayed in the National Foundation for Educational Research's (NFER's) recent study of the research-engaged school (Sharp, Eames, Sanders, & Tomlinson, 2005). This study presents vignettes from schools which sought to put research at the heart of their practice, covering topics from the role of rhyme in early language skills to promoting parental involvement, and from the use of interactive whiteboards to dealing with challenging behaviour. It demonstrates both the power of research to impact on practice but also the intricacy of the relationships between research and practice on the ground.

The ultimate purpose of special education – and justification of the very considerable expenditure on it – is to secure the best possible education for pupils who learn with difficulty. Historically, many such pupils received a raw deal from schools and had their learn-

ing difficulties compounded by a substandard educational offer, and the contemporary challenge is to address this schooling deficit through better teaching, more appropriate curricula, improved support structures and so on. All of this depends critically on securing improvement in classroom practice, and it is not surprising that there is keen interest in 'what works'. What pedagogical techniques work best with different kinds of pupils? What forms of school structures are best for including all pupils with their peers? What forms of support are most effective?

These are reasonable questions and a good deal of attention has, quite properly, gone into addressing them. Research stimulated by these questions has added greatly to our understanding of pupils who learn with difficulty or whose behaviour is challenging, and their education has been beneficially informed by the resultant research findings. A significant difficulty arises, however, when such research knowledge is given undue focus or is seen in isolation from the rest of what teachers bring to the classroom.

A key point of departure is to appreciate that teaching is a complex, knowledge-based activity. It comprises a multiplicity of cognitive, affective and interpersonal elements, and teachers draw on these elements in diverse ways in response to the different teaching/learning situations they encounter. So far as the knowledge base is concerned, this can be described in various ways. Polanyi's (1958) distinction between tacit and explicit knowledge has been widely used, most notably for our purposes by Nonaka and Takeuchi (1995) in their account of knowledge creation in business, and developed by Hargreaves (1998) to model teachers' role in knowledge creation. Gibbons et al. (1994) categorised contemporary knowledge production in terms of a shift from Mode 1 – traditional knowledge production as represented by disciplinary research and a separation between basic and applied research – to Mode 2, where knowledge production is transdisciplinary, problem-driven, with social context and values an integral part of the problem's definition, and tending to blur the distinction between fundamental and applied research. While the Mode 1/Mode 2 framework has been developed in the context of science and technology, many facets of Mode 2 knowledge seem highly pertinent to education – the focus on the context of application and problem-solving for particular purposes, transdisciplinarity, the broad range of user involvement and the importance of social accountability.

Both of these models have their roots outside education. We have to turn to pedagogy for ways of capturing the knowledge bases which are intrinsic to teaching. Schulman (1987) developed the term 'pedagogical content knowledge' as a way of pulling together the various knowledge bases which should inform teaching. This concept has provided a framework for a certain amount of research into teacher knowledge, including, for instance, a significant British study by Turner-Bisset (1999) who used it to frame an empirical account of the knowledge activities of primary teachers. Her model of the knowledge base for teaching comprises no fewer than 11 distinct sets of knowledge, covering subject knowledge, teaching knowledge, content knowledge of learners and knowledge of self.

Hegarty (2000) has drawn on these perspectives and Lonergan's (1957) philosophical analysis of common sense to put forward a model of how the diverse knowledge and skill inputs come together in the classroom. This model is focused on the 'teaching moment', where the teacher is interacting with one or more learners so as to stimulate and direct their learning. It posits the existence of a number of incomplete sets of relevant insights (and competences) which are completed in various ways in classroom practice. These sets include theoretical inputs, pedagogical skills, research findings, experience-based insights, pedagogical knowledge, subject knowledge and other knowledge. Figure 40.2 displays such a set as a penannular ring. This is an idealised structure since not all components are present in every case. Moreover, the individual components are not separate from each other within a teacher's active cognitive repertoire: subject knowledge and experience cross-fertilise each other, research findings are incorporated into pedagogical skills, and so on. Its purpose is simply to indicate the range of cognitive and skill-based components from which teachers may draw in constructing their teaching behaviour.

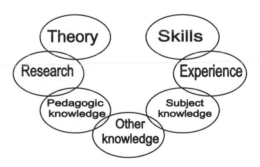

Figure 40.2 Knowledge input to teaching - incomplete ring

Figure 40.3 outlines an instance of a teaching moment or classroom intervention where the teacher has completed a ring with a fresh insight that combines the various elements into a coherent, practical response. Again, not all elements have to be present. What is essential is that the teacher relates the knowledge that is used to the particular situation, and does so by generating a new insight specific to that situation.

Figure 40.3 Insight to guide teaching moment

To exemplify the model, consider a teacher faced with a pupil who has difficulty in learning. How are the teacher's cognitive requirements and activities characterised in terms of the model? Does it help to distinguish between effective and ineffective teaching? In the first place, it highlights the multiple knowledge requirements on the teacher's part and then it suggests the necessary interactions between them. The teacher needs a general understanding of why children have difficulty in learning at school and a more focused understanding of why this particular pupil is having difficulties. These understandings will draw on a range of theories – child development, cognitive development, the relationship between teaching and learning, nature of schooling – as well, of course, as on the teacher's own experience of teaching and relating to other pupils. Subject or content knowledge is an obvious requirement. Teaching something which one has not properly mastered oneself is likely to be ineffective. There is a particular difficulty here where pupils who have difficulty in learning are concerned. Because their academic attainments are generally modest, there is a tendency to assume that the subject knowledge requirements on the part of the teacher are correspondingly modest. This may be true at one level, but from another perspective the reverse may well be the case! Teaching the basics of literacy or numeracy to children who are struggling with them is likely to require a fuller and more nuanced grasp of these basics than may be needed in the general case. In algebra, for instance, one might contrast knowledge of complex manipulations with understanding the use of unknowns in elementary equations. The former is required for teaching advanced pupils whereas the latter disappears into the taken-for-granted region. Understanding why abstract formulations are necessary can be a major stumbling block for some pupils, however, and the teacher needs a firm grasp of the rationale for them.

A significant contribution made by this handbook is its authoritative overview of the knowledge base of teachers in special education. This is far more than teaching methods, encompassing as it does theoretical underpinnings, assessment philosophies and techniques, and classroom support, as well as teaching/learning approaches. The breadth of scholarship here demonstrates the compass and complexity of the knowledge base for teaching and is a powerful argument against the reductionism that is implicit in much discussion about teaching.

A few examples will suffice here. Theoretical perspectives presented range from behavioural theories as described by Maag and sociocultural views of learning set out by de Valenzuela. Behavioural techniques have had a wide currency in special education, far more so than in general education. Their use is not simply a technical matter, however. Issues highlighted by Maag such as the social validity of behavioural interventions, the use of natural reinforcement in the classroom and the behavioural study of emotions point to a link between teachers' beliefs about behaviourism and whether and how they will use behavioural techniques. Sociocultural theory locates cognitive development within a cultural/historical context and sees individuals' learning as shaped by interactions between them and their environment. It too has led to distinctive instructional approaches in special education such as dynamic assessment, scaffolding and instructional conversation.

A very different approach is offered by Hart, Drummond and McIntyre who focus on the ubiquitous concept of ability and challenge its dominant role in educational practice. Pupils who learn with difficulty are seen as particularly vulnerable to ability-based thinking which sets fixed – and low – limits to their achievement. Their alternative proposal, based on the concept of transformability, is both a critique of current practice and a pointer to a very different kind of teaching.

Other chapters deal with pedagogy directly. Thus, Gersten and Santoro review the literature on instructional research, summarising what is known about early intervention, direct instruction, techniques for teaching cognitive skills such as procedural facilitators and cognitive strategies, and content enhancement strategies. Successive chapters, by Fowler, Ostrosky and Yates, Vaughn, Wanzek and Denton, McDonnell, Hardman and McGuire, and Shaw, deal with the specifics of teaching and learning in the different phases of education from early years to postsecondary education. In a literature review of collaborative or team teaching, Thousand, Nevin and Villa highlight the gaps in knowledge about this area of practice and indicate what needs to be done for its potential to be realised.

A particularly fecund chapter by Kershner deals explicitly with teachers' knowledge and what they need to know about special educational needs. It sets out clearly the multiple dimensions of teachers' knowledge: diverse theoretical inputs; knowledge of teaching strategies, many of them not specific to special education; knowledge of pupils and schools, both in general and in particular; understanding of support structures and how to access and use them; understanding of the web of personal and social factors associated with inclusive education; and new theoretical insights from areas such as genetics. It also includes an appreciation of the fact that some pupils' learning is complicated and the wisdom of not rushing to judgement on an individual child's learning pathways and potential. All of this is set within a framework of how adults learn and, in particular, how professionals move from novice status to expert. For teachers this takes place crucially within the learning community of the school and everyday interactions in the classroom.

What emerges here is a powerful demonstration of the richness of teachers' knowledge. Research plays an important role but it is only one strand among several, and a proper understanding of teacher knowledge and professionalism has to locate research within theoretical perspectives, experience, knowledge of pupils and so on. These considerations are not, of course, unique to special education, as there is a significant overlap between teacher knowledge in special education and in education more generally, but the specificity of this account in special education may be suggestive for the broader discourse of education.

CONCLUSION

Special education has over the years taught a great deal to general education. Its focus, for instance, on differentiation and matching teaching approach to pupil need, use of diagnostic assessment, involvement of parents in their children's learning and so on has been very instructive for education more generally. Procedures developed originally in special education have been taken up and adapted to the benefit of large numbers of pupils who do not fall within the ambit of special education.

What we have in this handbook is a further, powerful source of learning for education more generally. The detailed demonstration that both policy and practice in special education are shaped by multiple inputs should help to challenge the inadequate and often simplistic accounts purveyed in the literature. Educational policy is a construct of many factors and those who would influence policy must be aware of these factors and understand the interactions between them. Expert teaching likewise is a product of many inputs, and both teacher education and school improvement must be cognisant of that.

The hope, therefore, is that this handbook will serve a number of different purposes. It is an authoritative sourcebook on a challenging but important area of educational practice. It will be both a stimulus and a resource for developing future practice. And it can illuminate the broader discourse of education through its clarification of the nature of knowledge in education and how in practice different knowledge inputs contribute to educational policy and practice.

REFERENCES

Abderrahmane, M. (2005). *Research – policy link(age)s.* Paris: UNESCO SHS Documentation Centre. Available at: http://unesdoc.unesco.org/images/0013/001397/139757e.pdf

Centre for Educational Research and Innovation (CERI). (1995). *Educational research and development: Trends, issues and challenges.* Paris: OECD/CERI.

Gibbons, M., Limoges, C., Nowotny, H., Schwartzman, S., Scott, P., & Trow, M. (1994). *The new production of knowledge: The dynamics of science and research in contemporary society.* Stockholm: Sage Publications.

Hammersley, M. (2005). The myth of research-based practice: The critical case of educational inquiry. *International Journal of Social Research Methodology, 8*(4), 317–330.

Hargreaves, D. H. (1998). *Creative professionalism: The role of teachers in the knowledge society.* London: Demos.

Hegarty, S. (1997). Educational research in context. In S. Hegarty (Ed.), *The role of educational research in mature education systems* (pp. 1–16). Slough: NFER.

Hegarty, S. (2000). Teaching as a knowledge-based activity. *Oxford Review of Education, 26*(3&4), 451–465.

Lonergan, B. J. F. (1957). *Insight: A study of human understanding.* London: Longmans.

Nonaka, I., & Takeuchi, H. (1995). *The knowledge-creating company: How Japanese companies create the dynamics of innovation.* New York: Oxford University Press.

Polanyi, M. (1958). *Personal knowledge.* Chicago, IL: University of Chicago Press.

Schulman, L. S. (1987). Knowledge and teaching: Foundations of the new reform. *Harvard Educational Review, 51,* 1–22.

Sharp, C., Eames, A., Sanders, D., & Tomlinson, K. (2005). *Postcards from research-engaged schools.* Slough: NFER.

Turner-Bissett, R. (1999). Knowledge bases for teaching. *British Educational Research Journal, 25*(1), 39–55.

Weiss, C. (1977). *Using social research in public policy-making.* Lexington, MA: Lexington Books.

Weiss, C. (1979). The many meanings of research utilization. *Public Administration Review, 39,* 426–431.

Glossary

Cristina Devecchi

Social movements are always filled with words and word phrases that act as benchmarks and signposts … They focus discussion and debate, policy and practice. As new perspectives develop, new words are added to the list, sometimes necessarily and other times, unfortunately, usurping words that were already there.

(Pumpian, 1996, p. xiii)

With these words Ian Pumpian opened the foreword to a book on 'self-determination', undoubtedly one of the many terms that make up the field of special and inclusive education. As he claims, words are indeed powerful tools; they denote and connote, they delimit the boundaries of specific disciplines while simultaneously serving as bridges between them. With time they may become tacit and commonsensical, but they also acquire new meanings and fuel new debates and discussions. The need to have a glossary for the handbook, therefore, stemmed from an interest in what such words and phrases mean and how they have developed, but primarily to help the reader navigate this complex field where terms are contested and may mean different things in different contexts. Different disciplinary fields generate their own jargon; and words used in special and inclusive education often have a contested history. This brief introduc-

tion therefore aims to highlight how the glossary came to be and how it developed.

The first challenge was to choose which terms to include, the second was to give the glossary a practical structure, and the last, but by no means the easiest challenge, was to define the terms. While there was a desire to be comprehensive, there was also the need to provide a manageable and useful resource. The task therefore was that of producing a list of words that fit the three categories of common interest, multiple meanings, or needing further clarification, although some important terms that are explained by chapter authors are not included. Each chapter was read by two people, the editor and myself, and a first list of words was drawn. Upon discussion the list was reduced further and then broken down into three groups, that is, national and international organisations, national and international policies, and specific terminology. These lists were then combined in alphabetical order.

Once the structure had been established, the task of defining the terms was undertaken by considering that some of them did not share the same meaning in the English language literature. Personal knowledge of the field, literary and Internet searches were used to draw upon multiple perspectives and clarify meanings. Wherever possible full text links to the relevant Internet website or URL are given to provide the reader with the opportunity to access further information.

REFERENCE

Pumpian, I. (1996). Foreword. In D. J. Sands & M. L. Wehmeyer (Eds.), *Self-determination across the life span*. Baltimore, MD: Paul H. Brookes.

Activity Theory (Cultural Historical Activity Theory, or CHAT)

Assumes that goal-directed social activity is the source of human consciousness, knowledge and learning, and emphasizes the activity system as a unit of analysis. Human learning is understood to be embedded in joint activity or practice, and mediated through language, other cultural tools and artefacts. The tools of Activity Theory are often traced to the work of Russian psychologist Lev Vygotsky (1896–1934) and his students Luria and Leont'ev with more recent developments in the work of Cole, Engeström, and others.

Additional (Support) Needs (ASN) – (UK)

Term used in the *Education (Additional Support for Learning) (Scotland) Act 2004* to describe any support needed by a child whether arising from a disability or other factors such as family circumstances, ethnicity, or language. Children and young people may be said to have 'additional needs' if they need support over and above what is normally already provided for others. In its broadest sense it may be interpreted as provision designed to overcome any barrier to learning experienced by the student (see also *Education (Additional Support for Learning) (Scotland) Act 2004*).

Americans with Disabilities Act (ADA)

The Americans with Disabilities Act (Public Law 101-336) is a wide-ranging civil rights law that prohibits discrimination on the basis of disability and calls for 'reasonable accommodations' to be made so as to ensure employment and education for disabled people.
(http://www.usdoj.gov/crt/ada/pubs/ada.txt)

Assessment for learning

As stated by the UK Assessment Reform Group (2002), 'assessment for learning is the process of seeking and interpreting evidence for use by learners and their teachers to decide where the learners are in their learning, where they need to go and how best to get there'. It recognizes the role played by a shared understanding of assessment criteria that should emphasise the learner's understanding of learning, their motivation and commitment to learning, and teachers' constructive guidance and feedback on how to improve.
(http://www.aaia.org.uk/assessment.htm)

Behaviourism

A psychological theory that all behaviour is learned. It views learning as a response to external stimuli and focuses on observable behaviours rather than mental activities. Behaviourism has been influential in special education through approaches such as behaviour modification, and applied behaviour analysis and direct instruction. Major thinkers included Pavlov, Thorndike, Watson and Skinner.

Bio-psycho-social model

One of the three main models used to conceptualise disability. Unlike the medical and the social model, the bio-psycho-social model is an integrated model that does not uniquely focus on either the impairment within the individual or on environmental barriers, but acknowledges that biological, psychological, social and environmental factors contribute interactively to disability. The model, proposed by the psychiatrist George Engel in 1977, draws a distinction between the pathological processes that cause a disease or disability, and the patient's/disabled person's perception of their health or disability.

British Council of Disabled People (BCODP)
UK national organisation of the worldwide Disabled People's Movement set up in 1981 by disabled people to promote their full equality and participation in UK society.
(http://www.bcodp.org.uk/)

Canadian Association of Disability Service Providers in Postsecondary Education (CADSPPE)
Canadian association whose purpose is that of improving accessibility and enhancing the post secondary education of persons with disabilities.
(http://www.cacuss.ca/en/11cadsppe/index.lasso)

Canadian Charter of Rights and Freedoms
Enacted by the Canada Act 1982 the *Canadian Charter of Rights and Freedoms* guarantees the democratic, mobility, legal, and equal rights and the freedom of conscience and religion; of thought, belief, opinion and expression; of peaceful assembly; and of association to 'every' Canadian citizen, including those with mental or physical disability.
(http://laws.justice.gc.ca/en/charter/)

Canadian Council on Social Development (CCSD)
A non-profit social policy and research organization that focuses on issues such as poverty, social inclusion, disability, cultural diversity, child well-being, employment and housing.
(http://www.ccsd.ca/)

Centre for Studies in Inclusive Education (CSIE)
A non-profit UK independent centre working in the UK and overseas to promote inclusion.
(http://inclusion.uwe.ac.uk/csie/csiehome.htm)

Charter schools
Charter schools are publicly funded schools set up by teachers and/or parents, and permitted to operate autonomously and free from many of the regulations other US public schools must follow. This flexibility is awarded as part of a 'charter' with an authorising agency that holds the school accountable for achieving its outlined charter goals.

Choice Theory
Developed by William Glasser, choice theory views all actions as behaviour which drives us to satisfy five basic needs: survival, love and belonging, personal power, freedom and fun. In this sense individuals have choices on how to behave and they are responsible for the choices they make.

Code of Practice for the Identification of Special Educational Needs (England and Wales)
Also known as the SEN Code of Practice, the 2002 revised Code of Practice provides a framework for developing strong partnerships between parents, schools, local education authorities (LEAs) and health and social services and promotes a consistent approach to meeting children's special educational needs placing the rights of children at the heart of the process, allowing them to be heard and to take part in the decision making process whenever possible.
(http://www.teachernet.gov.uk/docbank/index.cfm?id=3724)

Committee on the Rights of the Child (CRC)
A body of independent experts that monitors implementation of the Convention on the Rights of the Child by its State parties under the auspices of the Office of the United Nations High Commissioner for Human Rights.
(http://www.ohchr.org/english/bodies/crc/index.htm)

Constructivism
A theory underpinning cognitive psychology wherein learning is seen as an active process of knowledge construction or 'meaning making'. Experience combined with reflection and social interaction allows the learner to

build on prior knowledge and create their own understanding (see also *dialectical constructivism* and *endogenous constructivism*).

Critical paradigm

A complex paradigm that draws upon techniques from both the empirical and interpretive paradigms and aims to integrate both. It deals with social values and relations of power, or hegemony as defined by Antonio Gramsci, that is a series of distortions in the way in which people behave but are unaware of the systemic influences which shape their actions and beliefs. Although such regularities in behaviour are measurable and real, they are not universal laws, but they are historical and practical products of human practice and institutions. Critical theorists study how a social system functions so as to change it. Pivotal to this task of transformation is the notion of theory viewed as the critique of common sense knowledge. Features of this paradigm are participatory research, self-determination and empowerment, community and inclusion, social justice and reflexivity.

Critical Pedagogy

Although there is no clear definition of critical pedagogy, it traditionally refers to educational theory and teaching and learning practices that are designed to raise learners' critical consciousness regarding oppressive social conditions. In particular it is concerned with reconfiguring the traditional student–teacher relationship so that the classroom is envisioned as a site for meaningful dialogue. It has its roots in the critical theory of the Frankfurt School (see *critical theory*). Main thinkers include Paulo Freire, Henry Giroux, bell hooks and Peter McLaren.

Critical Theory

In the words of Max Horkheimer, one of the founders of the Frankfurt School in 1930s, critical theory is a social theory oriented towards critiquing and changing society as a whole. Because the emancipatory aim is directed at society, critical theory integrates all major social science theories such as economics, sociology, history, political science, anthropology, psychology and more recently education (see *critical pedagogy*). Central to critical theory is the notion of ideology critique of the process by which is it possible in collaboration with others to dispel the limitations of false consciousness (see *critical paradigm*).

Dakar Framework for Action, Education for All: Meeting Our Collective Commitments

The framework adopted by 164 countries whose representatives met in Dakar, Senegal, in April 2000 for the World Education Forum, reaffirms and develops further the goal of Education for All as laid out by the World Conference on Education for All (Jomtien, Thailand, 1990) and other international conferences (see also *Salamanca Statement*). (http://www.unesco.org/education/efa/ed_for _all/framework.shtml)

Department for International Development (DFID)

A UK government department that manages Britain's aid to poor countries and works to eliminate extreme poverty. (http://www.dfid.gov.uk/)

Developmental cognitive neuroscience

A multidisciplinary area of study focused on the relationship between neural and cognitive development, for example the relationship between developmental changes in the brain and behaviour.

Developmental neuroscience

A field of study focused on the physical development of the brain and nervous system.

Dialectical constructivism

Situated within constructivism (see *constructivism* and *endogenous constructivism*), dialectical constructivism emphasises the social and interactive nature of knowledge between the learner and his/her environment (see *activity theory* and *ecological psychology*). Within this position the role of the teacher can be at times didactic and at other times can provide less obvious support.

Disability Discrimination Act (DDA)

A UK parliamentary Act of 1995, which makes it unlawful to discriminate against people in respect of their disabilities in relation to employment, the provision of goods and services, education and transport. It is a civil rights law. See Americans with Disabilities Act of 1990 for corresponding USA legislation.

(www.disability.gov.uk/dda/)

(http://www.opsi.gov.uk/acts/acts1995/1995050.htm)

Disability Rights Commission (DRC)

A UK independent body established in April 2000 by Act of Parliament to stop discrimination and promote equality of opportunity for disabled people.

(http://www.drc-gb.org/)

DSM medical classification

The Diagnostic and Statistical Manual of mental disorders (DSM), published by the American Psychiatric Association, is the handbook that provides categories and criteria for the diagnosis of mental disorders.

Ecological psychology

Studies the relationship between people and their environment and in so doing it stresses the situatedness of human behaviour and thinking (see also *activity theory*).

Education Act, 1981 (England and Wales)

The 1981 Education Act implemented some of the recommendations set down by the *Warnock Report* by abolishing the 11 categories of disability established by the 1944 Education Act and replacing these with the umbrella term of 'special educational need' (SEN). The Act defines SEN with regard to the provision, *additional to or different from provision made generally* for other children, which needs to be made to educate children with learning difficulties and/or disabilities. The Act introduced the notion of a 'statement of special educational needs' thus requiring local education authorities (LEAs) to identify and assess pupils who may require the LEA to decide on suitable provision for them (see also *Warnock Report*).

Education (Additional Support for Learning) Act 2004 (Scotland)

The Act established a new framework for supporting the education of all children and young people. It replaced existing Scottish legislation by introducing the new concept of 'additional support needs' which is based on a wider range of needs which may arise from the learning environment, family circumstances, disability or health, or the social and emotional concerns of children and young people.

(http://www.opsi.gov.uk/legislation/scotland/acts2004/20040004.htm)

(http://www.scotland.gov.uk/library5/education/shasla-00.asp for a summary of the Act's main points)

Education for All (EFA)

A global movement, supported by various UN organisations beginning with the World Conference on Education For All in Jomtein, Thailand, where participating countries pledged to provide primary education for all children and massively reduce adult illiteracy. It draws strong support from Article 26 of the *Universal Declaration of Human Rights* (1948), which recognises education as a fundamental human right. The pledge towards EFA was renewed at the World Education Framework in Dakar in 2000. Global urgency and commitment towards achieving the goals of education for all are also reflected in the Millennium Development Goals (see *Dakar Framework for Action.*)

(http://www.unesco.org/education/efa/index.shtml)

Education Reform Act 1988 (ERA)

The 1988 Education Reform Act introduced into England, Wales and Northern Ireland was one of the most significant pieces of educational reform since the 1944 Education Act. It aimed at creating an education 'market' based on school competition in order to raise academic standards and rise to the global challenge. A major area of reform was the introduction of: 'a *National Curriculum*, which made it compulsory for schools to teach subjects which were then tested through a series of standardised national curriculum assessments at the Key Stages 1 to 3 (ages 7, 11, 14 respectively) and GCSE (General Certificate of Secondary Education) at Key Stage 4 (age 16)'. (http://www.opsi.gov.uk/acts/acts1988/Ukpga_19880040_en_1.htm)

Educational triage

Triage is borrowed from the field of medicine. First used in by Gillborn and Youdell (2000) in their book *Rationing Education* to describe how marketplace reforms affect teachers' classroom practices. In education it means the division of students into three broad categories with regard to their abilities and predicted grades. Under the current UK system of marketisation, standardisation, public accountability and limited resources, teachers and schools apply a triage to direct their resources to those at risk of failing to achieve a passing grade. By so doing they can maximise both their effectiveness, that is the results they aim to achieve in terms of final grades, and their efficiency, or lowering the costs of achieving the results. It is argued that in an educational triage neither students who are most likely to succeed nor the ones with learning difficulties and/or disabilities benefit.

Enabling Education Network

A UK-based organisation committed to prioritising the needs of countries/organisations/individuals who have limited access to basic information and resources to foster the development of inclusive and sustainable education policy and practices. (www.eenet.org.uk)

Endogenous constructivism

Endogenous constructivism (see *constructivism* and *dialectical constructivism*) considers that knowledge is developed within the student. Accordingly, each student's understanding should be expected to be different in quality and to differ from the teacher's understandings. Knowledge cannot be transmitted precisely from the teacher to the student; therefore, varied understandings will be developed. Thus, according to the endogenous constructivist perspective, the appropriate role for the teacher is to facilitate learning by providing meaningfully structured experiences that provide active engagement in problem solving without overtly controlling the instructional interaction.

Functionalism

Assumes that society can be studied by an objective and value-free social science that can produce true explanatory and predictive knowledge of reality objectively by reference to empirical evidence. It attributes independence of the observer from the observed and it claims that universal standards of science determine what constitutes an adequate explanation of what is observed. The functionalist paradigm seeks to provide rational explanations of social affairs emphasising the importance of understanding order, equilibrium, and stability in society and the way in which these can be maintained.

Full inclusion (see Inclusion)

Hayekian marketplace

The term is derived from the economic theories of Friederick von Hayek. A Hayekian marketplace stands for a view of society organised around a market order in which the apparatus of state is employed solely to secure the peace necessary for a market of free individuals to function. His theories have had great impact on neo-liberal and new managerialist thinking.

Hermeneutic

Hermeneutics is the theory and practice of interpretation and understanding of a text through empirical means. The word derives from the Greek god, Hermes, whose task it was to communicate messages from the gods to the ordinary mortals. Recently, the concept of texts has been extended beyond written documents to include, for example, speech, performances, works of art, and even events. Major hermeneutic thinkers include Martin Heidegger, Hans-Georg Gadamer and Paul Ricoeur.

Highly qualified instructors (USA)
Term used in recent US legislation to designate qualified teachers as part of the drive to raise standards. The requirements for highly qualified teachers vary depending on the type of school and/or educational program in a particular school.

HM Inspectorate (**HMI**) (England and Wales)
Her Majesty's Inspectorate (HMI), a central component of the accountability system in England and Wales, is charged with inspecting the quality of education in pre-school centres, primary schools, secondary schools, special schools, community learning and development, further education colleges, initial teacher education, residential educational provision and the education functions of local authorities and services for children (see also *Office for Standards in Education*).

Human capital and social capital theories
Theories that deal differently with the notion of capital, or the existing stock of goods which are to be used in the production of other goods or services and which have themselves been produced by previous human activities. In human capital theory capital stands for the practical knowledge, acquired skills and learned abilities of an individual that make him or her potentially productive and thus equip him or her to earn income in exchange for labour. Social capital theory, on the other hand, refers to the institutions, relationships, and norms that shape the quality and quantity of a society's social interactions. Social capital consists of the stock of active connections among people: the trust, mutual understanding, and shared values and behaviours that bind the members of human networks and communities and make cooperative action possible.

Human Rights and Equal Opportunities Commission (**HREO**)
An independent statutory organisation established in 1986 by an act of the Australian Federal Parliament whose aims are to foster greater understanding and protection of human rights in Australia and to address the human rights concerns of a broad range of individuals and groups.
(http://www.hreoc.gov.au/)

Improving America's Schools Act of 1994 (**IASA**)
A reauthorisation of the Elementary and Secondary Education Act of 1965, IASA included provisions or reforms for providing extra help to disadvantaged students, including students with disabilities, and holding schools accountable for their results at the same level as other students; charter schools; safe and drug-free schools; and other programs.
(http://www.ed.gov/legislation/ESEA/toc.html)

Inclusion and **full inclusion**
'Inclusion' is a contested term that has acquired a variety of meanings depending on whether the focus is on educational placement of children with learning difficulties and/or disabilities or whether it means more generally social inclusion of all those children who are for other reasons excluded from school. For some it is defined either as a policy or as a process whereby students who are in special education programmes are placed in general education classes (also know as 'integration'). For others it is a process of identifying, understanding and breaking down barriers to participation and belonging often by addressing institutional factors and work generally on school development. Inclusion is about the quality of children's experience; how they are helped to learn, achieve and participate fully in the life of the school.

Individual Educational Plan (UK and USA)
An individual education plan (IEP) is a written plan created for students with disabilities

and/or special educational needs. It is tailored to the student's specific needs and abilities, and sets out key individual short-term targets for the pupil, the teaching strategies to be used, and any extra support that may be needed. While in the USA the IEP has legal status, it is used in the UK and elsewhere as a planning tool for teaching and accountability.

Individuals with Disabilities Education Act (IDEA)

The major piece of US legislation on special education, originally signed as the Education for All Handicapped Children Act in 1975, renamed in 1997, and most recently amended in 2004, is meant to ensure 'a free appropriate public education' for all children with disabilities from 3 through 21 years of age. The Act states that an appropriate education has to be designed around the individualised needs of the child and thus it requires children to be educated in the *least restricted environment* that is with their non-disabled peers to the greatest extent possible. It also requires schools to provide each child with an *individualised education plan* (see IEP) that details the child's special educational needs, and mandates appropriate services.
(http://www.ed.gov/policy/speced/leg/idea/idea.pdf)

Institute on Education Science (IES)

Part of the US Department of Education, IES was established by the Education Sciences Reform Act of 2002 with the aim of expanding evidence-based knowledge and providing information on the condition of education, and of practices that improve academic achievement, and the effectiveness of Federal and other education programmes.
(http://www.ed.gov/about/offices/list/ies/index.html)

International Classification of Functioning and Disability (ICF)

World Health Organization classification framework for Health and Disability intended to provide guidance for planning and decision-making. The ICF adopts a bio-psycho-social framework and focuses on functioning rather than merely impairment.
(http://www.designfor21st.org/documents/who_icf_2002.pdf)

International Standard Classification of Education (ISCED)

Adopted by UNESCO in 1997, ISCED for assembling, compiling and presenting comparable indicators and statistics of education both within individual countries and internationally.
(http://www.unesco.org/education/information/nfsunesco/doc/isced_1997.htm)

Logical positivism

Logical positivism is a philosophy of science that originated in the Vienna Circle in the 1920s and holds that philosophy should aspire to the same sort of rigour as science and consequently it should provide strict criteria for judging sentences as true, false and meaningless. Logical positivists are sceptical of theological and metaphysical propositions and exclude them from logical reasoning. The logical truth of a proposition must be ultimately grounded in its accordance with the (physical) material world. All arguments should be based on the rules of logical inference applied to propositions grounded in observable facts. Hence they support realism, materialism, philosophical naturalism, and empiricism, and favour the scientific method (see also *positivism* and *post-positivism*).

Market liberalism

As a market-emphasised descendant of classical liberalism, market liberalism advocates full freedom of markets, without obstacles for monopolies and cartels, and without consumer-protective legislation. Education policies in many countries have been influenced by such thinking over the past two decades.

Mastery learning

Mastery learning is an instructional strategy based on the principle that all students can learn a set of reasonable objectives with appropriate instruction and sufficient time to learn. Mastery learning puts the techniques of tutoring and individualised instruction into a group learning situation and brings the learning strategies of successful students to nearly all the students of a given group. In its full form it includes an integrated curriculum structure, instructional model, and student assessment procedures.

Millennium Development Goals (MDGs)

A set of eight goals agreed at the United Nations Millennium Summit in September 2000 and signed by nearly 190 countries aimed at improving the conditions of poorer countries. The Eight Millennium Development Goals are as follows: eradicating extreme poverty and hunger; achieving universal primary education; promoting gender equality and empowering women; reducing child mortality; improving maternal health; combating HIV and AIDS, malaria and other diseases; ensuring environmental sustainability; and developing a global partnership for development.

Moore's Law

The observation made in 1965 by Gordon Moore, co-founder of Intel, that the number of transistors per square inch on integrated circuits would double every year since the integrated circuit was invented. Moore predicted that this trend would continue for the foreseeable future. In subsequent years, the pace slowed down, but data density has doubled approximately every 18 months, and this is the current definition of Moore's Law.

National Center for Education Statistics (NCES)

Center within the US Department of Education whose aim is to collect, analyse and publish statistics on education and public schools in the United States and internationally. (http://nces.ed.gov/)

National Curriculum

Introduced into England, Wales and Northern Ireland, as a nationwide curriculum for primary and secondary state schools following the Education Reform Act 1988 with the aims of providing a balanced education covering 11 subjects overall, and of promoting pupils' spiritual, moral, social and cultural development and preparing all pupils for the opportunities, responsibilities and experiences of life.

National Foundation for Educational Research (NFER)

Non-profit UK organisation founded in 1946 with the aim of improving education and training, nationally and internationally, by undertaking research, development and dissemination activities and by providing information services. It is the largest independent educational research institution in Europe. (http://www.nfer.ac.uk)

National Law 118/71 (Italy)

The first law passed by the Italian Parliament concerning education for students with disabilities was in 1971, National Law 118, which established the right of compulsory education for children with disabilities in regular classes of public schools.

National Law 517/77

Law 517, passed by the Italian Parliament in 1977, reiterates the right of all children with disabilities to education in public schools as previously stated in the Law 118/71. In particular Law 517 states that all children should be assessed by a collegial team made up of the class teachers and two external examiners. Cross-curricular and extra-curricular activities should be included in the final assessment. With regard to children with disabilities, the Law states they are entitled to the examination and that schools should provide and implement a whole series of services and provision for their successful inclusion. To this extent the Law sets the number of children in a class where a disabled child is included to not more than 20, and determines that the ratio of disabled children to support teacher should not be more than 1:4.

National Plans of Action (NPAs)

National Plans aiming at the development and strengthening of already existing national

plans for the achievement of education for all as stipulated by the *Dakar Framework for Action*.
(http://www.unesco.org/education/efa/db/index_national_plans.shtml)

Naughty-teddy studies

Naughty-teddy studies were used in cognitive psychology experiments to test the Piagetian notions of conservation as applied to children in the pre-operational stage between the ages of 2 and 7 years. In conservation tasks McGarrigle and Donaldson found out that when an experimenter rearranged one of a pair of rows of counters, relatively few 6-year-old children thought that the two rows still contained the same number of counters. However, when 'naughty teddy' appeared to accidentally change the number of counters the children said that the number in the rows were still the same. Thus, McGarrigle and Donaldson showed that children's ability to show conservation can be greatly increased when the situation is more meaningful to them.

Newtonian mechanistic paradigm

A mechanistic view that explains events or parts making up a system in terms of mechanical principles of causation without reference to goals or purposive designs. Conceiving of nature as a machine, the Newtonian paradigm celebrated order and promised prediction and control. Central to this view of science was the presumption that we live in a universe governed by immutable laws.

No Child Left Behind Act (NCLB)

The 2001 Act reauthorised a number of federal programmes that strive to improve the performance of America's primary and secondary schools by increasing the standards of accountability for states, school districts, and schools, requiring all teachers to hold a state qualification, as well as providing parents more flexibility in choosing which schools their children will attend. The act requires that all children be tested several times during their school career, in reading and maths. Standardised testing is used as a measure to demonstrate that the

school has made 'adequate yearly progress' (AYP) towards proficiency in reading and maths. Schools that do not show adequate yearly progress for two consecutive years are deemed 'in need of improvement'.
(http://www.ed.gov/policy/elsec/leg/esea02/index.html)

Office for Civil Rights (OCR)

The US agency that enforces several federal civil rights laws such as section 504 of the Rehabilitation Act 1973 and the Americans with Disabilities Act 1990 that prohibit discrimination in programs or activities that receive federal financial assistance from the Department of Education.
(http://www.ed.gov/about/offices/list/ocr/index.html)

Office for Standards in Education (Ofsted)

A central element of the accountability system in England, Ofsted is a non-ministerial UK government department, established in 1993 under the Education (Schools) Act 1992 that is responsible for inspecting and reporting on the standards of schools in England. It is also required to provide independent advice to the government and Parliament on matters of policy and to publish an annual report to Parliament on the quality of educational provision in England (see also *HMI*).
(http://www.ofsted.gov.uk/)

Office of Special Education Programs (OSEP)

Part of the US Department for Education, OSEP's role is to provide leadership and financial support to assist states and local districts to improve results for infants, toddlers, children and youth with disabilities from birth through 21.
(http://www.ed.gov/about/offices/list/osers/osep/index.html)

Organisation for Economic Co-operation and Development (OECD)

International organisation made up of 30 member states whose aim is to address the economic, social and governance challenges

of globalisation.
(http://www.oecd.org)

Performativity

With regard to education, the term performativity has been used in the UK by Stephen Ball to critique the notion of performance management and the commodification and marketisation of education. In particular performativity can be seen in the ongoing cycle of target-setting, monitoring and reviewing as matters of self-surveillance.

Positivism

Positivism is an approach to the philosophy of science, deriving from Enlightenment thinkers, e.g. Auguste le Compte (1798–1857), that states the theoretical attitude maintaining that the only authentic knowledge is scientific knowledge. Positivism views social reality as objective, and thus value-free, and amenable to scientific and empirical enquiry that can determine with accuracy the relationship between cause and effect (see *logical positivism* and *post positivism*).

Postmodernism

A term applied to a wide-ranging set of developments in critical theory, philosophy, architecture, art, literature, and culture, which are generally characterised as either emerging from, in reaction to, or superseding modernism. It is concerned with questions about how knowledge is organised and questions the 'grand narratives' or 'order' of modern society because they are thought to obscure the contradictions and 'disorder' that are inherent in any social practice.

Post-positivism

As the term implies, post-positivism can be traced back to positivism. Post-positivism, like positivism, seeks to study social realities as objective and amenable to scientific methods of research. However, it also admits to the fallibility of method and therefore it emphasises the importance of multiple measures and observations, each of which may possess different types of error, and the need to use triangulation across these multiple sources. Post-positivists also believe that all observations are theory-laden albeit value-free (see also *positivism* and *logical positivism*).

Poststructuralism

A term used to describe the mostly French language scholarship that emerged in the mid to late 1960s to challenge the primacy of structuralism in the human sciences: anthropology, psychoanalysis, history, literary criticism, and philosophy. Major thinkers include Michel Foucault, Paul Bourdieu and Jacques Braudillard.

Pragmatism

Pragmatism, a school of philosophy which originated in the United States in the late 1800s, is characterised by the insistence on consequences, utility and practicality as vital components of truth. Pragmatism objects to the view that human concepts and intellect represent reality, and therefore stands in opposition to both formalist and rationalist schools of philosophy. Rather, pragmatism holds that it is only in the struggle of intelligent organisms with the surrounding environment that theories and data acquire significance. Pragmatism does not hold, however, that anything that is useful or practical, or anything that helps us to survive merely in the short term should be regarded as true, but that truth is that which most contributes to the most human good over the longest course. Major thinkers include Dewey, Peirce, Santayana, West and Rorty.

President's Commission on Excellence in Special Education (PCESE) (USA)

The PCESE was established by President George H. W. Bush in 2001 to collect information and study issues related to federal, state, and local special education programmes with the goal of recommending policies for improving the education performance of students with disabilities.
(http://www.ed.gov/inits/commissions-boards/whspecialeducation/index.html)

Primary National Strategy (PNS) (UK)

The PNS, also known as 'Excellence and Enjoyment', was launched by the UK Department for Education and Skills in 2003. It is an extension of the Literacy and Numeracy Strategies and its stated aims are to give primary schools more freedom in devising their curriculum, including planning cross-curricular activities. It also encourages primary schools to be inclusive and to forge links with other schools and external organisations as a way to achieve high standards of teaching and learning for all children. (http://publications.teachernet.gov.uk/eOrder ingDownload/dfes-0377-003PrimaryEd.pdf)

PL (Public Law) 99-457 (USA)

The 1986 amendments to the Education of the Handicapped Act established a programme to encourage states to develop services for infants and toddlers with disabilities.

Qualification and Curriculum Authority (QCA)

Established in 1997, the QCA is a non-departmental public body of the Department for Education and Skills in England and Wales whose duties are to maintain and develop the national curriculum and associated assessments, tests and examinations in England. It also accredits and monitors qualifications in colleges and at work and advises the Secretary of State for Education and Skills on these matters. The QCA oversees the work of the awarding bodies in England, to ensure that their administration, marking and awarding procedures run smoothly. (http://www.qca.org.uk/)

Salamanca Statement

As part of the wider international activities stimulated by the 1990 Jomtien Declaration on Education for All (*EFA*), the statement was signed in June 1994 by the representatives of 92 governments and 25 international organisations during the World Conference on Special Needs Education held in Salamanca, Spain. It calls upon national governments, and international organisations, to endorse the approach of inclusive schooling and to support the development of special needs education as an integral part of all education programmes. (http://unesdoc.unesco.org/images/0009/000 984/098427eo.pdf)

Section 504 of the Rehabilitation Act (USA)

Section 504 is part of the 1973 Rehabilitation Act that guaranteed certain rights to people with disabilities. The Act's Section 504 states that organisations or educational establishments in receipt of federal funding cannot discriminate on the basis of disability. In 1986 the Rehabilitation Act Amendments (PL 99-506) set out to provide supported employment programs for adults with disabilities. (http://www.blind.net/bg320001.htm)

Social constructionism

More radical than social constructivism, social constructionism is an approach to psychology that aims to account for the ways in which reality is socially constructed. Reality is thought to be created through language rather than to exist as a separate entity.

Social constructivism

Social constructivism is a school of thought interested in uncovering the ways in which individuals and groups participate in the creation of their perceived reality. Reality is seen as an ongoing, dynamic process where individual and social influences are not separable and learning is viewed as socially and contextually specific.

Social Darwinism

Social Darwinism is a social theory which holds that Darwin's theory of evolution by natural selection is not only a model for the development of biological traits in a population, but can also be applied to human social institutions. Social Darwinism is a belief, popular in the late Victorian period in England, America, and elsewhere, which states that the strongest or fittest (individuals or institutions) should survive and flourish in society, while the weak and unfit should be allowed to die. The theory was chiefly expounded by Herbert Spencer. In its most extreme forms, Social Darwinism has been used to justify eugenics programmes aimed at weeding out 'undesirable' genes from the population. Such programmes were sometimes accompanied by sterilisation laws directed against 'unfit' individuals.

Social interactionism

Theoretical school that claims that our behaviour depends on the ways we define ourselves and others. For example, labels applied to an individual have a self-fulfilling, interactive effect, and this is especially the case if labelling is carried out by formal authorities (teachers, police, and so on). Labelling, it is claimed, has harmful, discriminatory consequences which alter the individual's life chances. Main theorists include G.H. Mead, E. Durkheim and W.I. Thomas.

Social model of disability

One of the various models used to conceptualise disability (see also *bio-psycho-social model*). In its simplest form, the social model shifts the locus of disability away from the medicalised within individual model to the social barriers that turn an impairment, injury, illness, or congenital condition into a disability. It focuses on the way in which society excludes disabled people from fully participating. The social model has been promoted internationally by the disabled people's movement.

Social Psychological Theory

A set of theories which study the nature and causes of human social behaviour with an emphasis on how people understand others and how they relate to each other in social situations.

Socio-cultural theories

A combination of theoretical developments which trace their source to the Russian psychologist Lev Vygotsky (1896–1934) (see also *Activity Theory*). A core principle is the assumption that human functioning is situated and that any account of it must take account of cultural, historical and institutional contexts. Context is also thought to have a role in the creation of mental functioning.

Special Educational Needs and Disability Act (SENDA) (UK)

The 2001 Special Educational Needs and Disability Act amended the Disability and Discrimination Act (DDA) of 1995 by outlawing discrimination against disabled students in the provision of education, training and other related services. The Act ensures that disabled students are not put at a 'substantial disadvantage' and makes it unlawful to treat a disabled students less favourably due to their disability, with particular regard to admission policies and the services that are provided. Educational establishments are under the Act required to make 'reasonable adjustments' so as to avoid barriers to disabled students.
(http://www.opsi.gov.uk/acts/acts2001/20010010.htm)

Standards-Based Reform (USA)

A set of reforms aimed at the improvement of schools and basic educational outcome of children based on high standards, accountability and assessment as a measure of achievement. It is designed to raise standards in the belief that it will improve economic performance and productivity.

Structuralism

As a scientific approach structuralism claims that the way to learn about the brain and its functions is to break the mind down into its most basic elements since the whole is equal to the sum of the parts. As a linguistic approach, introduced first in the work of Ferdinand de Saussure, structuralism understands language as a system, whereby meaning is derived from the opposition of elements within that system. It has been influential in anthropology (Lévi-Strauss) and in cultural studies (Roland Barthes).

UN Convention on the Rights of the Child

An international convention, adopted by the UN General Assembly resolution in November 1989, setting out the civil, political, economic, social and cultural rights of children.
(http://www.unhchr.ch/html/menu3/b/k2crc.htm)

UN Standard Rules on the Equalisation of Opportunity for Disabled Persons

Ratified by the UN General Assembly in 1993 the document aims to equalise opportunities for disabled people and guarantee their full participation through the exercise of equal rights and responsibilities. It contains 22 non-compulsory Rules including raising awareness about the rights and needs of people with disabilities and providing appropriate medical care, support and rehabilitation services. Target areas for equal participation include accessibility, education, employment, social security, personal integrity, culture, leisure, and religion. Rule 6 on education, in particular, states that countries should recognise the principle of equal primary, secondary and tertiary educational opportunities for children, youth and adults with disabilities, in integrated settings.
(http://www.independentliving.org/standardrules/StandardRules.pdf)

Unique Pupil Number (UK)

A unique number allocated to all school pupils used to track their progress throughout their educational career, thereby providing better information for schools, local authorities and the Department for Education and Skills on pupil performance and any contextual factors affecting it.

Warnock Report (UK)

The report, which took its name from Baroness Warnock who chaired the Committee in 1978, recommended an end to the 11 categories of need used to designate children with learning difficulties and/or disabilities since the Education Act 1944, by replacing them with the umbrella term 'special educational needs' (SEN). In doing this it represented an attempt to move away from the individualised medical model of need to a more responsive or social model. It estimated that up to 20 per cent of school children might need special educational help at some stage in their school careers. This 20 per cent was generally considered to compromise 2 per cent who were thought to require special protection under the law and 18 per cent who might require additional support within the mainstream school. The report introduced the notions of continuum of SEN and integration. These found their way into the Education Act 1981 which introduced the notion of a statement of special educational need to safeguard the interests of children and their entitlement to a mainstream education (see *Education Act 1981*).

World Congress on Education for All

In 1990, delegates from 155 countries, as well as representatives from some 150 organisations, agreed at the World Conference on Education for All in Jomtien, Thailand (5–9 March 1990) to universalize primary education and massively reduce illiteracy.
(http://www.unesco.org/education/efa/ed_for _all/background/world_conference_jomtien.s html)

World Programme for Action concerning Disabled Persons

Adopted by the United Nations General Assembly in 1982, the programme aims to equalise opportunities for the full participation of people with disabilities into every aspect of social life. With regard to the education of disabled children the Programme for Action states that 'they have the same right to education as non-disabled persons and they require active intervention and specialist services'.
(http://www.independentliving.org/docs4/WPACDP.pdf)

Index